Shariʿa, Justice and Legal Order

Studies in Islamic Law and Society

VOLUME 51

The titles published in this series are listed at *brill.com/sils*

Shari'a, Justice and Legal Order

Egyptian and Islamic Law: Selected Essays

By

Rudolph Peters

TUTA SUB AEGIDE PALLAS · 1683 ·

BRILL

LEIDEN | BOSTON

Library of Congress Cataloging-in-Publication Data

Names: Peters, Rudolph, author.
Title: Shari'a law, justice and legal order : Egyptian and Islamic law : selected essays / Rudolph Peters.
Description: Leiden ; Boston : Brill, 2020. | Series: Studies in Islamic Law and Society, 1384-1130 ; volume 51 | Includes bibliographical references and index.
Identifiers: LCCN 2020012214 (print) | LCCN 2020012215 (ebook) | ISBN 9789004412514 (hardback) | ISBN 9789004420625 (ebook)
Subjects: LCSH: Law—Egypt—History. | Islamic law—History.
Classification: LCC KRM130 .P48 2020 (print) | LCC KRM130 (ebook) | DDC 349.62—dc23
LC record available at https://lccn.loc.gov/2020012214
LC ebook record available at https://lccn.loc.gov/2020012215

Typeface for the Latin, Greek, and Cyrillic scripts: "Brill". See and download: brill.com/brill-typeface.

ISSN 1384-1130
ISBN 978-90-04-41251-4 (hardback)
ISBN 978-90-04-42062-5 (e-book)

Contents

Case Studies

Legal Punishment

PART 2

Other Egyptian Periods

SECTION 2
Islamic Law in General

Foreword

A scholar's contribution to the field is usually assessed in terms of literary outputs – journal articles, book chapters and monographs are the usual genres. In this sense, the articles collected here exemplify how Ruud Peters (henceforth RP) is a giant in the field of Islamic legal studies. His publications span forty years of research and writing, covering topics from the development of early Islamic law (Chapter 27, "Murder in Khaybar") to contemporary jihadi ideology (Chapter 34, "Dutch Extremist Islamism"). There is a focus on Egypt (Parts 1 and 2), but with digressions into Sudan (Chapter 24, "Islam and the Legitimation of Power") and Nigeria (including Chapter 29, "The Reintroduction of Shariʿa Criminal Law in Nigeria"). There are studies of doctrine – RP's early work on jihad doctrine was the first major examination of the topic in English, well before the activities of the jihadi movements created such a rich seam for scholars to mine for academic research. However, reviewing RP's oeuvre overall (particularly the articles collected here), one notices an increasing use of documents and, although he has developed a keen eye for the analysis of Islamic legal practice in micro-settings, his work has major implications for the way the broader field might be envisioned. In this way, RP's work is both a contribution to, and a reflection of, the development of the field of Islamic legal studies. His research interests have both mirrored and informed the study of Islamic law over the last 40 years. How, then, might we assess the significance of the articles collected here and, hence, the importance of RP's output? I aim in what follows to place his scholarship in the context of the development of the field more broadly. RP, I think it is fair to say, has never worked as an entirely isolated scholar; his work has emerged out of a dialogue with other scholars working on Islamic law. With his affable and increasingly avuncular manner, RP has always enjoyed focused interactions with scholars in the field; he has not merely played off their scholarship – that is expected of any researcher. More than this, he has organized seminars, workshops and conferences; he edits important collections and fundamental book series; he travels the world to teach and share research with fellow scholars. For that the field must be truly grateful. Whether he recognizes this or not, RP's position in the field has grown in an organic manner, developing out of a network of scholarly contacts and nurturing research projects and agendas. It is only natural that his own scholarly endeavours be usefully understood against the backdrop of the last half century of Islamic legal studies. In this collection, RP has arranged his contributions, naturally, according to topic – but another way of assessing his influence and position in the field, is to look at his output chronologically (as I shall do here).

An account of the development of Islamic legal studies in Europe (and later in North America) in the twentieth century would most likely recognize that studies of legal doctrine dominated the 1970s and 1980s. When RP first contributed to the field, how Muslim legal actors implemented the law was considered, by and large, to be of marginal interest. What mattered for the major scholars from the 1950s onwards (perhaps even earlier than this) was how the law was laid down by jurists in their legal works – that is doctrine.[1] There was an emerging interest in the relationship of state law to Islamic law,[2] but studies of doctrine dominated the field. That practice deviated from, or conformed to, this model was considered, in the main, a matter for lawyers not academic research; Islamic law should be assessed (and by some, evaluated), primarily, as an intellectual system. Practice, it was assumed, would always be a pale imitation of the system's lofty ideals. This emphasis on understanding doctrine – the intellectual system constructed by the jurists – is, in part, the result of broader trends in academic discourse of the post-war period. The academic tendency to privilege the intellectual over the concrete has a long history, and the study of Islamic law inevitably took on such a perspective.[3] It is, though, also explained by the emergence of the study of Islam in European academic settings (and the study of Islamic law as a subset of that history). With its origins in the twin disciplines of theology and Semitic philology, the actual practice of Muslims was viewed as a less-than-serious area of research. When the social sciences were fully integrated into the Western academic curriculum, that perspective changed; for Islamicists, though, the Islamic legal texts and their contents were studied within the framework of a world of competing systems of ideas, rather than within the context of Muslim practice.[4]

1 The two classic studies are J. Schacht, *An Introduction to Islamic Law* (Oxford: Oxford University Press, 1964); and N.J. Coulson, *A History of Islamic Law* (Edinburgh: Edinburgh University Press, 1964).

2 For example, J.N.D. Anderson, *Islamic Law in the Modern World* (New York: NYU Press, 1959).

3 The principal intellectual movements of the nineteenth century in the social sciences, linked with colonialism and the study of different societies, is charted in the essays in J. Helibron, Lars Magnusson and Bjorn Wittrock (eds.), *The Rise of the Social Sciences and the Formation of Modernity* (New York: Springer, 2013).

4 The dynamics whereby Islamic studies came to be an independent academic subject (as distinct from Arabic studies, theology and Middle Eastern/Near Eastern/Oriental studies) are yet to be fully developed. Much of the intellectual history of the subject revolved around the German context in the early period of the subject's history – see Annemarie Schimmel, "Islamic Studies in Germany: An Historical Overview", *Islamic Studies* 49.3, 2010, pp. 401–10.

To an extent, RP's early work reflects this emphasis on the exposition of Islamic legal doctrine. His article with de Vries on apostasy in Islam (Chapter 21) remains a reference point for those working on Islamic legal injunctions; and his early contribution (the German language Chapter 22, "Dar al-Harb, Dar al-Islam"), dealing with the categories of jihad regulations and their position in the colonial conflict, is a foretaste of his future scholarship in jihad doctrine. It was on the latter topic that RP was to make his first monographic contribution to the field in the form of his *Islam and Colonialism: The Doctrine of Jihad in Modern History* (published in 1979).[5] It has been noted, and it is worth repeating, that RP was working on the doctrine and employment of jihad in the anti-colonial struggle long before these topics became both fashionable and matters of overwhelming security and public concern. The analysis of jihad texts and the evidence of doctrinal development, and the relationship between these and the historical context in which the texts were produced, was work in quite uncharted territory in the late 1970s. That his translations and studies are still cited in recent scholarship reflects their fundamental contribution to the field. Not for the first time, RP was ahead of the curve in his choice of research focus.

By the late 1980s, RP's interests had shifted quite decisively from doctrine to social history. Social history was not absent in his earlier output (the work in the late 1970s on colonialism and jihad was a foretaste of this), but it was to become a central focus of his research for the following decade. The articles on the Bab Zuwayla riots (Chapter 19, "Battered Dervishes"), the reception of "modern" technology (Chapter 25, "Religious Attitudes") and the application of Shariʿa in Egypt (Chapter 20, "Divine Law or Man-Made Law?") all demonstrate that he was increasingly interested in the interaction of law and social history: he now worked on how the doctrine of Islamic law was realized in a particular social context, and his focus was on Egypt, given his long association with the country. Bearing in mind that these articles would have been written some time before they were actually published, RP's shift in focus appears even more prescient. The challenge of how law related to social history was rather like the focus on the relationship of doctrine to a believer's practice – neither was seen as the purview of the Islamic law specialist. The major works in the field of the 1980s were not, generally speaking, focused on the contribution of Islamic law to history.[6]

5 R. Peters, *Islam and Colonialism: The Doctrine of Jihad in Modern History* (The Hague: Mouton, 1980).

6 See for example the many studies on the formation of Islamic doctrine in the early period, which dominated the field in the 1980s, including D. Powers, *Studies in Qur'an and Hadith* (Berkeley: University of California Press, 1986); P. Crone, *Roman Provincial and Islamic Law* (Cambridge: CUP, 1987); J. Burton, *The Sources of Islamic Law* (Edinburgh: EUP, 1990).

In terms of publications at least, RP's output level increased significantly in the 1990s; and this is reflected in the article collection here. It was during this decade that he developed a position for himself as a custodian of the field. He engaged in numerous ventures that aimed to create Islamic legal studies as a robust multidisciplinary field. He was instrumental in convening the first major international Islamic law conference (held jointly in Leiden and Amsterdam) in 1994. This was the first time experts had gathered to share research and debate the direction of the field. It created a buzz that was eventually converted into the first dedicated journal on Islamic law to be published by Brill, *Islamic Law and Society*. RP and others had managed to attract an impressive array of scholars to contribute to the establishment of the field, many in their ascendancy at the time – Wael Hallaq, Baber Johansen, David Powers, Aharon Layish, Susan Spectorsky, Norman Calder, Peri Bearman and many others debated and collaborated in equal measure. In conjunction with the new journal, RP and Bernard Weiss founded a new monograph series, also with Brill – *Studies in Islamic Law and Society*. The series aimed to provide a quality venue for emerging research priorities in the field. It immediately established itself as the principal venue for extended monographic treatments of detailed analyses of Islamic legal topics. RP was at the centre of organizing the conference, the journal and the book series, and it was on these foundations that the field was to develop in the next two decades. Turning to RP's outputs during this period, they reflect the cutting-edge areas of research during this period. The operation of laws (Chapter 1, "Murder on the Nile") and the status of fatwas (Chapter 2, "Muhammad al-ʿAbbasi al-Mahdi") became important research themes in the 1990s and after the turn of the century. The latter paper holds a special place in my own history. If I remember correctly, it was on the presentation of this paper that I first met RP – in a small conference venue in Manchester, at a workshop organized by Philip Alexander, Colin Imber and the late Norman Calder in September 1991. I was a conference helper, preparing teas and coffees and showing guests to their rooms. The organizers had managed to recruit many influential scholars in the field of Islamic legal studies, including John Burton, Wael Hallaq, Gerald Hawting and, of course, RP. For us students, embarking on our postgraduate study, this was a rather important event. His focus on fatwas, I would like to believe, demonstrated to those present the crucial importance of this neglected genre. Hallaq, Imber, and Calder all went on to make major contributions to the field of fatwa research later in the 1990s, establishing the study and analysis of fatwas as central to the study of Islamic legal literature and practice. The article was eventually published alongside Hallaq's "From Fatwas to Furuʿ" in the first issue of *Islamic Law and Society*. RP's contribution, in contrast to Hallaq's, was more forensic – RP's study was a discrete examination of a fatwa collection, providing a narrative of how it came to be and how its contents related to the social context in which it was written. It followed a model of a scholarly investigation that was much copied and re-examined in subsequent years. The expanding field of fatwa research, pioneered by RP, came to its fullest expression in the hugely influential collection of papers, jointly edited by David Powers, Brinkley Messick and M. Khalid Masood, *Islamic Legal Interpretation: Muftis and their Fatwas*. Inevitably, one of the major contributions to this collection was RP's "The Lions of Qasr al-Nil Bridge" (Chapter 8). This collection itself was the product of a conference on fatwas convened in Granada in 1990, and this collection had an immediate and important impact on the field. The collection remains one of the major pieces of scholarship to which researchers in Islamic legal studies turn – a cleverly conceived structure of broad-based theoretical studies at the start, followed by specific analyses of individual fatwas by renowned experts. The structure meant the collection had a very wide appeal. In a field still short of major publications, this collection solidified the field and created a sound base on which younger scholars might base future findings. It was to act as a model for a follow up volume jointly edited by RP (with M. Khalid Masood and David Powers) called *Dispensing Justice in Islam: Qadis and their Courts*. The nearly ten years that separated these two volumes reveal another shift in the field that RP and others led – the emergence of documentary analyses of court records as untapped and fecund sources for understanding Islamic legal practices through history.[7]

Apart from his nascent interest in fatwas, the 1990s also saw RP maintain his focus on the relationship between state law and Islamic law. The explanation for why a state enacts a particular piece of legislation will always involve a number of factors (from the purely legal to the purely political). Criminal legislation, a particular interest of RP's, is an illustrative example. Mehmet Ali, the Khedive of Egypt (1805–48) enacted criminal legislation around 1829. The reasoning the Khedive put forward includes two of the classic motives for criminal punishment in Western moral theory – deterrent and reform. RP's analysis in his important article on the topic (Chapter 4, "For His Correction and as a Deterrent") puts forward the robust thesis that, by introducing these, Mehmet Ali was departing from the Islamic rationale for punishment, and embarking on a European-style justification for legislation. This article was a detailed study of one historical episode to illuminate important changes in the operation of the law in the Muslim world in the nineteenth century, and fleshed out many

7 R. Peters, M. Khalid Masood and David Powers (eds.) *Dispensing Justice in Islam: Qadis and their Courts* (Leiden: Brill, 2005).

of RP's hypotheses in his influential 1997 article on the role of the criminal case judge (*qāḍī*) in early modern Egypt (Chapter 3, "Islamic and Secular Criminal Law"). The role of the legal profession and its training during this period was further examined in RP's 1999 article on the personnel of the courts and their operations. The relationship between the so-called "secular" and "Islamic" areas of operation were also tackled outside the Egyptian context in an important, myth-busting article on Islam and human rights, which questioned the ability of these two legal worlds ever to be in concert (Chapter 26, "Islamic Law and Human Rights"). These were articles that tackled the important questions of the field in general – can Islamic law be modernized? Did it fundamentally change (and if so, how) in the nineteenth century? How compatible might the Islamic and European systems of law be? Underpinning all these wide-ranging enquiries is RP's dedication to detailed textual evidence – the articles demonstrate that he has little time for grandiose narratives of change or modernization in Islamic law without a full presentation of the evidence.

It is RP's love of detail that led him to work on a series of case-study style expositions in the late 1990s and 2000s. In the Egyptian context, he involved himself in unearthing the micro details of cases – working with nineteenth-century court records in the Egyptian National Archives, and cooperating with Egyptian scholars such as Khaled Fahmy, Magdi Guirguis and Emad Helal. The articles from this period read like chapters in a collection of Sherlock Holmes short stories: the case of the fisherman's daughters (Chapter 10, "Petitions and Marginal Voices"), the infatuated Greek (Chapter 11), the violent schoolmaster (Chapter 12). The task RP set himself was rather like that of a detective – poring over evidence, following up on leads, picking up on clues here and there. Indeed, the more depressing aspects of the operation of Islamic law (criminals, prisons, punishment) clearly held a particular fascination for him – part of this may come from his belief that it is in the criminal law that one sees the most challenging aspects of the encounter between Islamic legal norms and supposedly "modern" legal systems. It may also be that these are among the most stereotyped and simplified elements of Islamic law as conceived by the jurists or practised by the state and its judges. RP's scholarship is not an attempt to justify these elements of the tradition or the practices that accompanied them; instead, it attempts to situate these phenomena historically and treat them not with shock and horror, but with an intellectual curiosity and a desire to understand and explain. This feature characterizes all his work, and is part of the reason for his widespread respect in the field, both among academics and legal practitioners. Understanding why Islamic criminal law – in theory and in practice – takes on its specific features is crucial before making any assessment of its place. That was the task RP set himself in his landmark monograph on the topic, *Crime and Punishment in Islamic Law*.[8]

RP's love of these micro studies, from assembling the evidence to reaching the conclusion (and delivering the verdict) is also evident. These included his "The Re-Islamization of Criminal Law in Northern Nigeria" (Chapter 32), and, personally important for myself, his analysis of documents from the Dakhla (Chapter 17, "Sharecropping in the Dakhla Oasis" and Chapter 18, "Body and Spirit of Islamic Law"). This chapter was written for a collection dedicated to our mutual friend, the much-missed Professor Bernard Weiss: RP and I were present at the conference in his honour in 2008 from which the volume emerged. His work in this chapter was, in large part, due to his involvement in the Dutch archaeological investigations in the Dakhleh oasis and the QDP (Qasr Dakhleh Project). In many ways, RP's scholarship in the twenty-first century is the result of serendipitous encounters and requests for work. The Dakhla documents were found accidentally during a Dutch archaeological mission – RP was the natural Dutch expert to become involved in analysing them, and the results of this research were published in an impressive volume.[9] RP's engagement with criminal law in Nigeria (see Chapter 29, "The Reintroduction" and Chapter 32, "The Re-Islamization of Criminal Law in Northern Nigeria") came out of a specific mission he led at the request of the European Commission, and informed his scholarship thereafter in various ways (see Chapter 29, "The Reintroduction of Shariʿa Criminal Law in Nigeria"; Chapter 30, "The Enforcement of God's Law"; Chapter 32, "The Re-Islamization of Criminal Law in Northern Nigeria"; Chapter 33, "*Shariʿa* and 'Natural Justice'"). His work on radicalized Dutch Islamism (Chapter 34, "Dutch Extremist Islamism") emerged from his analysis of materials found in the possession of Mohammed Bouyeri, the murderer of Theo van Gogh. None of these, it seems, were part of a research programme planned decades in advance. They were the result of RP's own contacts, reputation and networks in the field. The opportunity to view materials presented itself, and RP, with his catholic interests and his undoubted skills in the detailed analysis of documents, took up the challenge.

In the context of the field, RP's scholarly foci reflect not only the trend towards documentary analysis, but also the recognition that there is a wealth of

8 R. Peters, *Crime and Punishment in Islamic Law: Theory and Practice from the Sixteenth to the Twenty First Century* (Cambridge: CUP, 2005).

9 R. Peters, *Watha'iq madinat al-Qasr fi al-Wahat al-Dakhila masdaran li-tarikh Misr fi al-ʿasr al-ʿUthmani: The Documents of the Town of al-Qasr in the Dakhla Oasis as a Source for the History of Egypt in the Ottoman Period* (Cairo: Dar al-Watha'iq al-Qawmiyya (National Archive), 2011).

material for analysis available, but access is often problematic. There has been, I have noticed, an acknowledgement that conducting a comprehensive analysis of all the material on a topic is becoming less and less realistic. As archives have become available, and many resources have moved online, scholars in the field have come to know that work on Islamic law and practice has become increasingly provisional in its conclusions, and we, as researchers, can only put together building blocks for future research. When RP began his work, available materials were much more limited; not only this, but scholars were less cognizant of the overall volume of material. Ironically, with less material available, scholars felt able to write more general books on Islamic law. In the last two decades, the field has been changed by both the range of material and the field's recognition of the extent of this range. RP's trailblazing micro studies of select documents, drawing provisional conclusions about the functioning of the Islamic legal system more generally, is now, perhaps, the popular *modus operandi* of researchers. Legal anthropologists who gain access to the processes of law through embedding themselves in a community are not always carrying out a scholarly exercise that is very different from that of archival and text-based scholars. It is merely that their methods of data collection differ. In this sense, RP's *oeuvre* provides an important contextual background to the many different methodological approaches that have emerged recently in the field.

RP's collected works over four decades of scholarship have not only mirrored developments in the field more broadly, but have also had an impact on it. His contribution has enabled the field as a whole to shift from one set of source materials to another, and from one set of scholarly parameters to another. The usual trend over a scholar's career is to move from detailed to more general (one might say "popular") scholarly contributions. RP's trajectory is rather different: he started by providing comprehensive accounts of legal doctrine – particularly in jihad theory; moved on to historical analyses of time periods and state activities (particularly in the Egyptian context); and ended up editing documents and providing detailed analyses from which to refine and revise general presumptions in the field about how Islamic law functions in practice. Alongside these, he has made numerous more "state of the art" contributions, producing not only summaries of the secondary literature more generally, but adding his own views and input for the record (for example, Chapter 26, "Islamic Law and Human Rights"; Chapter 28, "From Jurists' Law to Statute Law"; Chapter 35, "(In)compatibility of Religion and Human Rights"). It is unusual for scholars to become more specialized, and to pay even more attention to detail as their careers progress, but that is what the collected works presented here (and elsewhere in RP's scholarly output) demonstrate. They reflect an impressive realization of the limitations of the field, and the potential for research work that will continue well into the future. In these respects, those of us who have learned from RP's intellectual development along the way can count ourselves extremely fortunate to have had him as a scholarly interlocutor, mentor and guide.

Robert Gleave

Preface

For this book, I have selected 35 of the articles I wrote on the history of Egyptian and Islamic law with a focus mainly on the legal order and the actual application of the law. These writings are the fruit of nearly half a century of research. After my graduation in Arabic and Turkish law, and after extensive travels in the Middle East and North Africa, I embarked on a career in academia – at the University of Amsterdam and, for five years, as the director of the Dutch (later Dutch–Flemish) Institute in Cairo, where I worked in the fields of Islamic studies, Shariʿa law and Egyptian legal history. I have written books on jihad,[1] on Islamic criminal law[2] and on legal documents found in the town of al-Qasr in the Dakhla Oasis in the west of Egypt.[3] In addition, I have written many articles for academic journals and chapters in edited books. In this book, however, the reader will find a selection of articles on the Islamic and Egyptian legal orders and on justice, that is on judicial practice, legal culture and the development and codification of the law.

When I studied it in the 1960s, I had the impression that Islamic law, with the exception of family law, was principally a theoretical discipline of doctrines, debated by religious scholars, but not actually applied by judges or political authorities. I became intrigued by the Shariʿa because the practical nuts and bolts of the law were usually missing in Western textbooks and, apparently, many fields of Shariʿa law were not enforced in practice. When, in the 1980s, I became acquainted with a voluminous collection of nineteenth-century fatwas (*Al-Fatāwā al-Mahdiyya*), I found that many of them addressed not only family

1 Rudolph Peters, *Jihad in Mediaeval and Modern Islam: The Chapter on Jihad from Averroes' Legal Handbook 'Bidayat al-Mudjtahid' and the Treatise 'Koran and Fighting' by the Late Shaykh al-Azhar, Mahmud Shaltut.* Translated, annotated and introduced by Rudolph Peters. Leiden: E.J. Brill, 1977 (Nisaba Religious Texts in Translation Series), 90 pp.; Rudolph Peters, *Islam and Colonialism: The Doctrine of Jihad in Modern History.* The Hague: Mouton, 1979, viii, 242 pp. (Religion and Society, 20); Rudolph Peters, *Jihad: A History in Documents.* 3rd updated edition of *Jihad in Classical and Modern Islam: A Reader.* Princeton NJ, 2015. (1996, 1st edn, 2005, 2nd edn) *Princeton Series on the Middle East.* Princeton NJ: Markus Wiener Publ.

2 Rudolph Peters (with the assistance of Maarten Barends), *Islamic Criminal Law in Nigeria.* Abuja: Spectrum Books, 2003, viii, 88 pp.; Rudolph Peters, *Crime and Punishment in Islamic Law: Theory and Practice from the 16th to the 21st Century.* Cambridge: Cambridge University Press, 2005. x, 219 pp. (Themes in Islamic Law, 2).

3 Rudolph Peters, *Wathāʾiq madīnat al-Qaṣr fi al-Wāḥāt al-Dākhila maṣdar*[an] *li-tārīkh Mṣsr fi al-ʿaṣr al-ʿUthmānī* (The documents of the town of al-Qasr in the Dakhla Oasis as a source for the history of Egypt in the Ottoman period). Cairo: Dār al-Wathāʾiq al-Qawmiyya (National Archive), 2011, 610 pp. (Silsilat Dirāsāt Wathāʾiqiyya, 1).

law, but also many other branches of the law, including criminal law, the law of contracts and the rules of procedure. These fatwas reflected the practice of the Shariʿa courts. While examining them, I realized that much more could be found beyond them and this encouraged me to examine the Egyptian archives. Although bureaucracy made access far from easy, the archives were rewarding. Moreover, I found that other researchers were increasingly beginning to examine these court records, not only to analyse social history but also to unearth the actual legal practice of the courts in the past. And, as you will find, many of the articles selected in this collection, are studies founded on archival court records and legal documents more than on the juridical scholarly texts.

This book is divided into two parts. Section 1 is devoted to Egypt and Part 1 deals specifically with nineteenth-century penal law (Chapters 1–15). These studies were the result of a long-term research project for which I used the court records of the Egyptian National Archive (Dār al-Wathāʾiq al-Qawmiyya) as sources. The chapter begins with the application of criminal law, both Shariʿa and state, and with the subsequent emergence of penal codes. Five more articles analyse case studies in which offenders were tried and sentenced. The records of these cases (homicide, grievous bodily harm, unlawful sexual relations and, finally, a discussion on the legitimacy of statues) provide the facts and the motivations of these sentences, with a great deal of social background. The last three articles in this chapter are on the rise of imprisonment as a penal punishment and its practice.

The focus of Part 2, Section 1 is also on Egyptian legal history, but from other periods (Chapters 16–20): it contains four titles on earlier Ottoman periods and one on the twentieth century. One study is an analysis of a dispute over whether public Sufi practices such as the *dhikr* were lawful. The opponents, a Turkish group of religious hotheads, attacked the Sufis near the Zuwayla Gate in Cairo and created a riot, to which the authorities had to restore order. In three essays set in the town of al-Qasr in the Dakhla Oasis, I discuss legal and judicial practices in the Ottoman period. The sources I was able to examine consisted of some legal documents that were fortuitously found in the remains of a dilapidated house in al-Qasr and which I edited (see footnote 3). The last article in this chapter is an account of the unsuccessful project of legal Islamization in the 1970s.

Section 2 of this book (Chapters 21–35) consists of 15 essays, though not specifically related to Egypt. In 11 articles, I again deal with the notions of legal order, justice and the actual application of Shariʿa to Islamic law. Legal order is included in studies on the practical doctrines on apostasy (Chapter 21) and in the debates on modern Islamic justice, specifically the discussion on the compatibility of Shariʿa with human rights (Chapters 26 and 35). In four essays, I discuss the method through which Shari'a is defined and adapted by fixing *madhhab* doctrines or by codification (Chapters 28, 30, 31 and 33). Two more essays deal with the codification of Shari'a penal law as implemented in Northern Nigeria immediately after 2000 (Chapters 29 and 32). These studies were the result of a European Union assignment, for which, in 2002, I visited Nigeria and collected the regional laws enforced at that time, since each state of the Nigerian federation had the autonomy to issue penal legal statutes. On the basis of these statutes, as well as interviews with several Nigerian lawyers, I could assess the impact of the recent Islamization of penal law on human rights standards. In Section 2, furthermore, I offer articles on debates on religious and political authority in nineteenth-century Mahdist Sudan and on the legal relationship between the regions of Islam and the religions of the unbelievers (Chapters 22 and 24). They both deal with justice and the legal order in its relationship between the legitimacy of the political authority and the legal culture. Finally, there are four articles not directly related to the notion of the legal order, but to Islamic law in a wider sense. One essay consists of a discussion about how modern inventions in the Ottoman Empire, such as steamships and the telegraph, must be judged according to Shari'a (Chapter 25). The subsequent articles consist of an analysis of nineteenth-century Salafi debates surrounding the notions of *taqlīd* and *ijtihād* (Chapter 23) and an investigation into the historical origins of the rules of *qasāma*, the procedure, in the case of an unknown killer, to establish financial compensation for the next of kin or the punishment of the alleged perpetrators by swearing oaths (Chapter 27). The final essay is on a topic beyond the Muslim world: it is based on a report I wrote as an expert witness for a Dutch court. The record examined the religious documents collected by the Dutch Muslims' defendants. After analysing these documents, I could chronologically expound on how this group gradually developed into a religious ideology of terrorism that could justify killing citizens. Eventually, one of them assassinated a Dutch filmmaker and journalist and was eventually sentenced to life imprisonment (Chapter 34).

This collection contains original texts that had previously been published. However, there are a few minor changes:

1. The original articles referring in footnotes to forthcoming titles have now been updated;
2. due to problems caused by the conversion of PDFs to Word texts, the transcription in many articles has been simplified, by omitting the transcription diacritics like the under dot and the macron; however, the distinction between *'ayn* and *hamza* has remained; typographic errors and misspellings have been corrected.

I could not have completed these studies without the help of many colleagues. In the individual articles you will find the acknowledgements. However, with regard to this collection, I am very much indebted to Olaf Köndgen, who suggested I publish this book and convinced Brill's staff to produce it. I am also very grateful to Khaled Fahmy, with whom I became acquainted in the Egyptian archives thirty years ago and who became a friend and colleague in studying the history of nineteenth-century Egypt. My studies on Egyptian history owe a great deal to our cooperation and discussions. Finally, I want to express my gratitude to the staff at Brill for producing this voluminous work.

SECTION 1

Legal History of Egypt

PART 1

Nineteenth Century

Penal Law: Shariʿa, Legislation, Judiciary

CHAPTER 1

Murder on the Nile

Homicide Trials in 19th-Century Egyptian Shariʿa Courts

1 Introduction*

In this paper, I intend to investigate the application of the Shariʿa in homicide cases in 19th-century Egypt, before the reception of French law codes in 1883.[1] The scope of enforcement of the Shariʿa in the Islamic world before the introduction of Western law is still a matter of controversy. On the one hand there are many Western scholars maintaining that the Shariʿa was merely a theoretical construction, hardly applied in practice except in matters of personal status and waqfs. On the other hand many Muslim authors claim nowadays that Muslim law was fully enforced until colonial rule rule imposed foreign law codes on the Muslim world.

In order to shed some light on this question I have examined the *Fatawa al-Mahdiyya fi l-Waqaʾiʿ al-Misriyya* (7 vols. Cairo: al-Matbaʿa al-Azhariyya, 1301–3; henceforth abbreviated as FM) by Muhammad al-ʿAbbasi al-Mahdi (1243/1827–1315/1897), who was for more than fifty years Hanafite mufti of Egypt (*Mufti l-Diyar al-Misriyya*).[2] Vol. 6 of his collected fatwas, with the title *Kitab al-Mahadir wa-l-Sijillat*, contains queries from the qadis which include as a rule the records of the trials. Analysing these records that span a period from 1266/1849 until 1303/1885 can give us insight in the working of Egyptian Shariʿa justice in the 19th century.

* This is a revised version of a paper read at the 14th Congress of the Union Européenne d'Arabisants et Islamisants, Budapest, 29 August–3 September 1988.

1 Baer's studies on 19th-century Ottoman and Egyptian statute law in criminal matters give us some insight into the scope and content of criminal legislation in this period. However, Baer approached the subject from a basically political angle and did hardly pay attention to the question of what laws were actually applied in the courts. Cf. G. Baer, "Tanzimat in Egypt: The Penal Code," in G. Baer, *Studies in the Social History of Modern Egypt* (Chicago, 1969), pp. 109–33, and id., "The Transition from Traditional to Western Criminal Law in Turkey and Egypt", *Studia Islamica*, 45 (1977), pp. 139–58.

2 He was *Mufti l-Diyar al-Misriyya* from 1264/1847–8 until just before his death in 1315/1897. From 1287/1870 he combined this function with that of Shaykh al-Azhar. Cf. GAL S II, 740; Jurji Zaydan, *Tarikh mashahir al-sharq fi l-qarn al-tasiʿ ʿashar* (2nd ed. 2 vols. Beirut: Dar Maktabat al-Hayat, n.d.) II, 250–5; ʿAli Mubarak, *Al-Khitat al-Tawfiqiyya al-Jadida* (20 vols. Bulaq: Al-Matbaʿa al-Misriyya, 1306) XVII, 12; Gilbert Delanoue, *Moralistes et politiques musulmans dans l'Egypte du* XIXe *siècle (1798–1882)* (Le Caire: IFAO, 1982), pp. 168–84.

 | DOI:10.1163/9789004420625_002

Shariʿa justice relies heavily on the advice of muftis. In Egypt, as elsewhere, Shariʿa courts would have a mufti attached to them who could be consulted by the qadi on the intricacies of the law. In the provincial councils (*majalis al-mudiriyya*) in Egypt the provincial mufti (*mufti l-mudiriyya*) had a seat. There were other muftis attached to administrative bodies, like the Diwan al-Awqaf and the Majlis al-Ahkam. The mufti with the highest authority was the *Mufti l-Sada al-Hanafiyya* or the *Mufti l-Diyar al-Misriyya* (henceforth referred to as the Mufti), appointed by the Viceroy (Khedive). A qadi who was in doubt with regard to some specific point of law during a process, would first consult the mufti attached to his court. If the mufti was not certain either, or if the qadi and the mufti disagreed, the point would be submitted to the *Mufti l-Diyar al-Misriyya*. Sometimes the qadi would consult the Mufti directly. The Mufti's fatwa would be read in court in the presence of the parties and regarded as binding (although officially this became only the case in 1880).[3] Occasionally the Mufti would issue special instructions to the qadis to follow certain opinions within the Hanafite school in preference to others.[4] The Mufti's function bore some resemblance to that of the courts of cassation in French or Dutch law, who are the highest authorities to expound and interpret the law and do not investigate the facts of a case.

Of the 307 fatwas included in volume VI of the FM, 137 deal with criminal matters,[5] almost exclusively homicide (129 cases).[6] In only one of these recorded homicide trials, a case of murder with robbery, the punishment was based

3 The Shariʿa Courts Ordinance (*Laʾihat al-Mahakim al-Sharʿiyya*) of 1856 laid down that "the qadi should consult the ʿulamaʾ and ask their fatwas in difficult cases and not form his opinion independently as a precaution against errors in [applying] the rules of the Shariʿa." (art. 21). Text in Filib Jallad, *Qamus al-idara wa-l-qadaʾ*. 5 vols. (Alexandria: Al-Matbaʿa al-Bukhariyya, 1890–5), vol. 4, pp. 129–31. In the Shariʿa Courts Ordinance of 1880 this became obligatory and the Mufti's fatwas became binding (art. 22), which reflected previous practice. Text in Jallad, Qamus, vol. 4, pp. 145–56. See also *Al-Fatawa al-Islamiyya min Dar al-Iftaʾ al-Misriyya*, X (Cairo: 1404/1983), pp. 3656–7. The situation was actually more complicated, due to the emergence of a hierarchical judiciary, with muftis attached to all levels. (See e.g. the decree No. 275 d.d. 5 Rab. II, 1290 that regulated the function of *iftaʾ*; text in Jallad, *Qamus*, vol. iv, pp. 136–6). Cases where capital punishment was demanded by the plaintiffs would be submitted to the mufti of the court that heard the case, the mufti of the court of appeal (*istiʾnaf*), a special committee from the Cairo High Court (Mahkamat Misr al-Kubra) or the mufti of the Majlis al-Ahkam, and, usually, the *Mufti l-Diyar al-Misriyya*.

4 Cf. FM VI, p. 95 (29 Rab. II, 1278).

5 These are the fatwas included in vol. VI. Vol. V, in the chapter on *jinayat* contains a few more fatwas issued at the request of law courts (as distinct from fatwas whose origins are not stated).

6 The eight remaining cases deal with bodily harm. No cases concerning bodily harm are reported after 1285/1868.

on *hadd*,[7] in all others the rules of *jinayat* were applied, i.e. the law with regard to homicide and bodily harm. The last of these fatwas on murder dates from Safar 1302/December 1883.

Many of the fatwas recorded in the FM offer vivid pictures of the fights and quarrels that were and sometimes still are typical of Egyptian social life in the countryside: conflicts about the distribution of water, assault and battery of peasants by Turkish officials, family quarrels, cases of revenge for injured honour, and theft of cattle are among the occasions leading to loss of life. They are worth being studied as contributions to Egyptian social history. Here, however, I will focus on the legal aspects of these trials.

We must be aware, however, that trial before the qadi was only a part – but an essential one – of the procedure in case of homicide. The Shariʿa trial was meant to deal with the private claims of the victim's heirs, whereas the state authorities would consider the crime in the light of public interest in accordance with the secular laws, i.e. the various criminal laws enacted by the viceroys and, from the early 1850s, the Qanunnameh al-Sultani,[8] which contains several articles with regard to homicide. This is not contrary to Shariʿa theory, since this authorizes the state to punish persons who commit undesirable acts on the basis of *taʿzir*.[9] The Egyptian state authorities held a firm grip on procedures in criminal matters. The following instructions were issued to the qadis with regard to homicide cases:

> The preliminary investigation and examination in cases of homicide must be carried out by the provincial administration (*mudiriyya*) of the

7 FM VI, p. 505 (19 Rab. I, 1297). The verdict was based on *hadd*, and proven by confession of the culprits, but because in *hadd* cases the culprit is at liberty to retract his confession until the moment of punishment, the Mufti explained in his fatwa.' in what way the wording of the verdict could be changed in order to obtain a basis for *qisas* punishment.

8 Text in Ahmad Fathi Zaghlul, *Al-Muhamat* (Cairo: Matbaʿat al-Maʿarif, 1900/1318), Mulhaqat, pp. 157–178; Jallad, *Qamus*, vol. ii, pp. 90–102. See for the history of this code Baer, *a.c.* There is some doubt regarding the date of introduction of the codes. Baer assumes that it was not enforced until 1855, whereas Toledano argues that the code was already applied in 1852. Cf. Ehud R. Toledano, "Law, Practice, and Social Reality: A Theft Case in Cairo, 1854," in *Studies in Islamic Society: Contributions in Memory of Gabriel Baer*. Ed. G.R. Warburg and G. Gilbar (Haifa: Haifa University Press, 1984), p. 169.

9 Before the introduction of the Qanunnameh al-Sultani, it was customary for the state to execute a murderer on the basis of *taʿzir* if it was clear that he had committed a murder, but the plaintiff could not produce sufficient legal evidence before the qadi, or if the plaintiff had pardoned him. For 17th-century practice, see Galal H. El-Nahal, *The Judicial Administration of Ottoman Egypt in the Seventeenth Century* (Minneapolis etc.: Bibliotheca Islamica, 1979), p. 34. For the early 19th century, see E.W. Lane, *Manners and Customs of the Modern Egyptians*. Repr. (London etc.: Dent, 1966), p. 108.

> province in which the case has taken place, as is the practice until now. Then the case must be examined with the most perfect scrutiny in the regional councils (*majalis al-aqalim*) in the presence of the [provincial] mufti and the members of the council. As soon as the case is clear, the Shariʿa sentence (*al-iʿlam al-sharʿi*) and the record containing the details of the procedure [i.e. the trial by the council] must be sent to the Majlis al-Ahkam al-Misriyya[10] for inspection and approval (*tasdiq*). Thereupon they must be sent to the Majlis al-Khususi[11] and from there to the Viceroy [for a decree ordering the execution of the sentence].[12]

What is clear from both this instruction and the FM is that in these councils homicide cases would be tried first, in the presence of the members of the council, by the qadi according to the Shariʿa and then, whenever the case required this, by the council itself, on the basis of secular laws. Since the councils were not bound by the strict Shariʿa rules concerning evidence, it often happened that they sentenced suspects whose guilt was not proven before the qadi, or who, if criminal intent could not be substantiated, were only condemned to pay blood money, to prison terms.[13] Illustrative is the following question submitted to the Mufti:

> When an official had sent a murderer into exile (most probably to Fayzoghli in the Sudan), after the heirs of the victim had settled for a *diya* consisting of land and an amount of money, the heirs anxiously consulted the Mufti asking whether they would lose their newly acquired

10 The Majlis al-Ahkam al-Misriyya, or Council of Justice, established in 1849, was one of the two conciliar organs of the state. It acted as a high court that checked the decisions of lower courts, and issued legislation. Cf. F.R. Hunter, *Egypt under the Khedives, 1805–1879: From Household Government to Modern Bureaucracy* (Pittsburg: University of Pittsburg Press, 1984), p. 51.

11 The Majlis al-Khususi, or Privy Council, created in 1847 was the most important conciliar body in Egypt and closest to the Khedive. It combined legislative, administrative and judicial functions. Cf. Hunter, *o.c.*, pp. 49–50.

12 Surat harakat al-afandiya hukkam al-sharʿ fi ijraʾ al-ahkam al-sharʿiyya, Art. 6. Text in Jallad, *Qamus*, vol. ii, p. 104. The Ordinance was issued as one of the appendices to the Qanunnameh al-Sultant Cf. Zaghlul, *al-Muhamat*, p. 205.

13 Contrary to Ottoman practice (cf. Johan Krcsmárik, "Beitrage zur Beleuchtung des islamischen Strafrechts, mit Rücksicht auf Theorie and Praxis in der Türkei," *Zeitschrift der Deutschen Morgenländischen Gesellschaft*, 58 (1904), p. 571), the Egyptian laws did not allow the secular courts to condemn to capital punishment a murderer who was not given a death sentence by the qadi, except in the case of officials (*maʾmur*), who had committed intentional homicide but were pardoned by the victim's heirs (Cf. the Qanunnameh al-Sultani, Ch. 1, Art. 1 and 11).

property if the culprit were to die in exile (they would know, of course, that Fayzoghli was not a very healthy place). The Mufti could reassure them: the settlement would remain valid, whatever happened to the murderer.[14]

2 Categories of Homicide and their Legal Effects

The Islamic law of homicide is essentially private law in the sense that a trial can only take place if the victim's heirs (or the state, if there are no heirs), acting as plaintiffs, want to sue the culprit. Moreover, if the murderer is sentenced by the qadi, the execution of the sentence depends on the wish of the plaintiffs. If it is legally proven during the trial that someone has caused the death of another person, there are two possible outcomes: the culprit is sentenced either to death in retaliation (*qisas*), or to payment of blood money (*diya*). In both cases the plaintiffs may pardon the defendant – in *qisas* cases the pardoning of only one heir is sufficient to prevent the execution – or settle for a sum of money which may be higher or lower than the legally fixed blood money (*sulh*). There is, however, a complicating factor if there is a minor among the heirs. With regard to the execution of a death sentence, the other heirs may act for him in pardoning the murderer, if the minor is closely related to them (that is, if he is not an *ajnabi*). Otherwise, the decision regarding the execution must be suspended until the minor has come of age. If blood money is at stake, the minor's guardian cannot remit the minor's share in it.

Capital punishment can be required if the murder is committed intentionally (*ʿamd^{an}*) and without just cause (*taʿaddiy^{an}* or *ʿudwan^{an}*). There are however two exceptions to this rule: a father cannot be sentenced to death for the murder of his son, nor the master for the murder of his slave, and a death sentence cannot be required by the heirs if there is a descendant of the murderer amongst them.

The characteristic tendency towards objectivity in the Shariʿa is also in evidence in this domain of the law: Criminal intent (*ʿamd*) is not only regarded as a subjective state of the mind but must also be apparent from the kind of weapon or object used to kill. There is some controversy on the question of what types of weapons or objects are considered to be indicative of criminal intent. Abu Hanifa has taught that the killer must have used a weapon that can sever parts of the body or an object that has been sharpened, like a sharpened rock or piece of wood, or fire. Abu Yusuf and Shaybani hold that a weapon or

14 FM V, p. 441 (19 Muh., 1269).

implement must have been used that is as a rule lethal. The Egyptian judiciary, on the strength of a decree of the Viceroy, was obliged to follow the latter opinion,[15] not surprisingly in view of the many instances in our material of homicide committed with the *nabbut*, the long wooden stick Egyptian peasants usually carry with them.

For a sentence of retaliation it is also required that the killing be without just cause. For this reason, a murderer who acted e.g. in self-defence is not liable for his acts. In general the absence of a just cause is alleged by the plaintiff, but does not need to be proven. If the defendant, however, pleads that he acted with just cause, he must substantiate his plea, as is evident from the following ruling of the Mufti:

> In a case where it was proven that the defendant had intentionally killed a Christian merchant, the defendant pleaded that he had acted with just cause because the Christian had once converted to Islam and then returned to his old belief and was therefore an apostate (*murtadd*) who must be executed and whose life is not protected by the law (*muhdar*). The Mufti ruled that if the defendant could prove his plea, he could not be sentenced to death or to payment of blood money, but would only be liable for disciplinary punishment (*taʾdib*) for not having given the apostate an opportunity to reconvert to Islam.[16]

If the murder is committed intentionally, but not all the conditions for a death sentence are satisfied, e.g. because the weapon was not a generally lethal one (for instance a bamboo cane or a foot used for kicking the victim)[17] – this is technically known as *shibh ʿamd* –, or because one of the plaintiffs is a descendant of the murderer, the defendant can be sentenced to payment of heavy blood money (*diya mughallaza*). In all other forms of a homicide, subsumed under the heading of *qatl khataʾ* (killing by error), the normal *diya* is due, regardless of whether the victim's death is due to culpable negligence or accident. But in this case the blood money is to be paid not by the defendant, but by his *ʿaqila*, his solidarity group. Examples of killing by error in our material are: death caused by someone firing his rifle during a festive occasion and accidentally hitting someone; a fatal accident when someone was felling a palm tree and, in spite of his warnings, a woman was hit by one of its branches; the

15 Cf. FM VI, p. 146 (25 Ram., 1278); FM VI, p. 147 (25 Ram., 1278).

16 However, as the defendant had not put forward his plea until the qadi had pronounced his sentence, the qadi would only be allowed to hear it after special permission from the head of state (*wali l-amr*). FM VI, p. 91 (1 Rab. II, 1278).

17 FM VI, p. 523 (18 Shaw., 1297) (bamboo cane); FM VI, p. 490 (7 Shaw., 1296) (kicking).

killing of someone with a stick, whereas the blow was aimed at someone else; a watchman (*khafir*) shooting someone at night believing that it was a robber.

There is, however, no difference between the normal and the heavy blood money, except in the unlikely case that defendant wants to pay in camels.[18] The classical works of *fiqh* lay down that the height of the *diya* of a free man, Muslim or *dhimmi*, is 100 camels of a certain specification (for the *diya mughallaza* more expensive types of camels were specified) or 1.000 dinar (gold) or 10.000 dirham (silver). For a free woman the *diya* was half this amount and for a slave his market value. In Egypt, the highest judicial authority, the *Majlis al-Ahkam* had issued a decree on 25 Rab. I, 1275 (1858) fixing the amount of blood money at 15.093,75 piasters for payment in silver[19] and on 40.762 piasters for payment in gold and laying down that the choice was the defendant's.[20] This meant, in fact, that the qadis would automatically sentence the defendant to payment of the lower amount. Although not as much as the value of 100 camels, this was by no means a small sum. In 1861 it represented the value of 15 horses or 34 donkeys or 13 buffaloes (*jamusa*),[21] or in terms of wages (taken from a budget of the two High Courts for 1279/1861–2): 200 times the monthly wage of the coffee man (*qahwaji*) (75 piasters), 20 times that of the High Court mufti (750 piasters), and 14 times that of the head clerk (*bashkatib*) (1.100 piasters).[22] Blood money is due in three annual instalments of one third of the total.

18 According to the classical authors, the *diya* could be paid in camels (100), gold (1.000 dinar) or silver (10.000 dirham). The amount of the *diya mughallaza* was only specified with regard to camels: they must be of a more expensive quality. FM VI, p. 490 (7 Shaw., 1296). This made the category of *shibh ʿamd* very theoretical. In one fatwa, where *shibh ʿamd* is mentioned, the mufti did not care to call the ensuing *diya* "*diya mughallaza*" (FM VI, p. 523 (18 Shaw., 1297)).

19 The Ottoman Shaykh al-Islam had fixed the amount of blood money at 26.666 piasters and 20 paras. (Omer Hilmi, *Miʿyar-i ʿadalet* (Istanbul: 1301), p. 71). Taking into account that the value of the Ottoman piaster was about 10 to 15% less than the Egyptian one [Cf. Roger Owen, *The Middle East in the World Economy, 1800–1914* (London etc.: Methuen, 1981), p. xiii; Charles Issawi, *The Economic History of the Middle East, 1800–1914* (Chicago: The University of Chicago Press, 1966), pp. 523–4], this amount was about 50% higher than the Egyptian blood money.

20 FM VI, p. 49 (15 Rab. I, 1277). Art. 25 of the Qanun al-Filaha, issued 1245 (1830), fixed the *diya*, in cases where death was caused by excessive beating by officials, at 3.600 piasters (Text in Zaghlul, *Al-Muhamat*, Mulhaqat, p. 105). It is not clear, however, whether this was applicable to all cases of homicide or only to the cases mentioned in the article.

21 Cf. FM VI, p. 91 (1 Rab. II, 1278), where a horse is sold for 1.000 and a donkey for 450 piasters, and FM VI, p. 134 (12 Ram., 1278), where in an inventory the price of a buffalo is 1.200 piasters.

22 Amin Sami, *Taqwim al-Nil* (Cairo: Matbaʿat al-Kutub al-Misriyya, 1928–36), vol. I, part 3, pp. 411–3; see also *ibid.* pp. 325–6 for the salaries of officials in ministries). E.R. Toledano mentions that in 1854 an unskilled labourer would earn 50 piasters monthly and a skilled labourer about twice that sum. See Toledano, *o.c.*, p. 158, n. 15.

3 Complicity

A complicating factor in this already complex system occurs when death is caused by more than one person. The law gives detailed rules for determining the liability of each of the perpetrators. The simplest case is when one person forces another to cause the death of a third person. The law lays down that if someone acts under coercion, i.e. as a result of fear for one's own life or for loss of a limb, the act is ascribed to the one who exerts the coercion, since the other is a mere instrument. It is expressly stated that an order of the sultan must be regarded as coercion, even if no specific threats are uttered.

> Ibrahim Agha, the commander of a cavalry regiment stationed in the Sudanese town of al-Ubayyid had ordered some soldiers to give fifty strokes of the cane to Baba ʿAbd Allah, a soldier who, pleading illness, had refused to carry out a command. As a result of his chastisement the soldier died the same day. His heir (in this case, since the soldier had no next of kin, the provincial governor acting as the representative of the state) demanded from the officer his due according to the law. After the plaintiff had proven his accusations, the qadi sentenced the officer to pay the *diya* to the state, as his orders, just like the Sultan's, must be regarded as constituting coercion.[23]

If the victim's death is caused by two or more persons, acting together, the plaintiff must allege and prove what precisely each of the defendants did. There is no such thing as collective liability for homicide. The plaintiff must identify the person(s) who have actually killed the victim, or his claim is not admitted.

> A man was attacked by two others, one of whom hit him with a rock on his head. When he was found, just before he died from his wounds, he told that he had been attacked by two men, whom he identified, that one of them had hit him on his head with the rock, but that he did not know which of them it had been. When his heirs brought suit against the two

23 FM VI, p. 69 (21 Raj., 1277). The Mufti in principle endorsed the qadi's decision, except that he required that the existence of coercion in the relationship between the officer and the soldiers who had carried out the caning be substantiated and not just assumed. In another case, where a civilian official ordered his servants to administer a bastinado to a merchant who did not immediately pay his taxes, whereby one of the victim's ribs were broken, as a result of which he died, the Mufti ruled without arguments, that no suit could be brought against the official. FM VI, p. 455 (30 Raj., 1295).

> men, their claim was declared inadmissible, since it did not identify the defendant, viz. the person who had caused the victim's death.[24]

For sentence to be passed against those who together caused the death of the victim, it must be clear whether the acts (blows, shots, cuts etc.) of each of them separately would have been lethal and whether they acted simultaneously or in succession. If the perpetrators have acted simultaneously and it is established that each of their acts, carried out separately, would have caused the death of the victim, they are all liable for his death. If criminal intention (*ʿamd*) is proven, they can all be sentenced to death. Otherwise they must pay the *diya* together. If all of their acts, if carried out separately, would have been lethal and if they have acted in succession, the one who first attacked the victim is liable if the victim dies within a day after the attack. Otherwise the victim's death is ascribed to the last attacker. The accomplices are then to be punished on the strength of *taʿzir*. How complicated these rules are is illustrated by the following case:

> Two men had entered the cattle pen (*dawwar*) of Muhammad Bey ʿAbd Allah at night (probably to steal cattle, although this is not mentioned in the record) and killed Ramadan Musa, who was sleeping there. The first defendant had hit him on the head with a big stone and the second one, as the victim still showed signs of life, had stabbed him in his belly with his knife. Ramadan died two days after the attack. During the trial the first defendant's guilt was established by his admission that he, together with the second defendant, had murdered Ramadan. Further it was established that both acts would have been lethal if they had been carried out separately. Against the second defendant, however, nothing was proven. Asked for his opinion, the Mufti argued that the first defendant could not be sentenced to death. Since the hitting with a stone and the stabbing with the knife had been consecutive acts and the victim had lived for more than one day after the attack, the cause of his death was to be ascribed to the second defendant, against whom nothing was proven legally, whereas the first defendant was to be punished by the state authorities on the strength of *taʿzir*.[25]

24 FM VI, p. 25 (22 Raj., 1274). In a similar case three watchmen (*khafir*) had admitted that they had shot and killed someone, thinking he was a thief. However, they added that they did not know which of them had actually hit him. The suit brought against them was not admitted, since the plaintiff could not identify the defendant.

25 FM VI, p. 480 (12 Rab. I, 1296).

4 Liability for Blood Money

One of the characteristics of the Islamic law of *jinayat* is that it is more anxious that the victim or his heirs will get their dues than that the culprit feels the consequences of his acts. A clear demonstration of this principle is the liability of the defendant, which applies in cases of unintentional homicide: unless liability is based on the defendant's confession or on an agreement with the plaintiff (*sulh*), payment of blood money, with a few exceptions, is the liability of the defendant's solidarity group, the *ʿaqila*. This liability is, however, restricted: the members of the *ʿaqila* are not obliged to pay more than four dirhams and if the total is not enough for payment of the *diya*, the *ʿaqila* has to be expanded.[26] Originally restricted to one's agnatic group, the early Hanafites had extended the notion of *ʿaqila* to other groups practising mutual assistance (*tanasur*) such as the soldiers registered in the Diwan, members of guilds, or the merchants from the same market. If the killer does not belong to such a group, the state must take over the responsibility if the defendant is a Muslim and the state finances allow this. Otherwise the killer himself must pay.[27]

In the post-classical works on *fiqh* one can already see that the institution had lost much of its practical importance.[28] To my surprise, however, the rules concerning *ʿaqila* were applied in Egypt. The existence of a *ʿaqila* was assumed if one was the member of a group that "helped each other, in the sense that if for some reason one's house was destroyed, the others would help him to restore it."[29] In those cases of *qatl khataʾ* where evidence was not based on confession of the defendant, the qadi would either decide that the *ʿaqila* pay the *diya*[30] or, what happened mostly, expressly argue that the defendant pay it since he had no *ʿaqila*.[31] In the latter cases the state was not held liable contrary to authoritative Hanafite opinion.

Another demonstration of the concern of the Shariʿa to ensure that the heirs of the victim get their due, is the institution of the *qasama*. If a body is

26 FM VI, R. 63 (24 Jum. II, 1277).

27 Cf. Ibn ʿAbidin, *Radd al-Muhtar* (Bulaq: Dar al-Tibaʿa al-Miriyya, 1299), vol. V, p. 566.

28 See e.g. Ibn ʿAbidin, *Radd al-muhtar*, V, p. 566 and the authors quoted by him.

29 FM VI, p. 4 (29 Raj., 1266).

30 FM VI, p. 63 (24 Jum. II, 1277) (liability of the *ʿaqila* of a house owner, based on a *qasama* procedure); FM VI, p. 66 (8 Raj. 1277); FM VI, p. 141 (25 Ram. 1278). In the last case the *ʿaqila* accepted its responsibility although the evidence was based on confession of the defendant. In this case, where the names of the four members of the *ʿaqila* are mentioned in the records, it is not clear what constituted its basis. Judging by the names they are not relatives. Since the defendant was a watchman, it is possible that his fellow watchmen acted as his *ʿaqila*.

31 FM VI, p. 58 (4 Jum. II, 1277); FM VI, p. 78 (22 Shaʿ., 1278); FM VI, p. 111 (15 Jum. II, 1278).

found with wounds or traces of beating or strangling and there is no evidence of the identity of the killer, the heirs can sue the owner of the house or the land where the body was found (including the state if the body was found on state land) or, if he was found on common or nobody's land, some or all of the adult males living within earshot of the place of the crime. If they cannot substantiate their claim, the owner or, in the case of collective liability, fifty free, adult, sane males to be picked by the plaintiff (if there are more than fifty people; if not, some people must repeat the oath), are made to swear fifty oaths that they have not killed the victim and do not know the murderer. This is called *qasama*, derived from *qasam*, "oath". It creates a liability to pay the *diya* for the *ʿaqila* of the owner of the house or the land, or for the *ʿaqila-s* of the inhabitants of the village. The heirs, however, forfeit their right to start the *qasama* procedure if they first sue someone else.

The records show that this procedure was still very much alive in 19th-century Egypt.[32] There are several instances where the inhabitants of a village or the owner of land (or, in some cases their *ʿaqila-s*) were held responsible for an unsolved murder. And there are quite a number of cases where it is obvious who has killed the victim, but where the plaintiffs are unable to substantiate their claims and demand payment of *diya* on the basis of *qasama*. The fifty oaths from the inhabitants of a village would be taken by an assistant of the qadi (*maʾdhun*) who would go with the plaintiff to the village to take the oaths of those whom the plaintiff would select.[33] If the owner of a house was subject to a *qasama* procedure, he was made to swear fifty times himself. Sometimes the result of the *qasama* procedure was a fortunate one, in the sense that the suspect of murder, against whom nothing could be proven, was held liable on this score:

> The mother of Fatuma, the deceased, representing the heirs, sued Fatuma's husband for her death alleging that he had taken hold of her in the presence of his other wife and his adult daughter, thrown her on the floor, stripped her and hit her about 500 times with the soft branch of a quince tree, that thereafter she stayed in bed until she died three days later. The husband, one of the shaykhs of the village, denied this and alleged that his wife had died from an illness she had caught about six

32 FM VI, p. 63 (24 Jum. II, 1277); FM VI, p. 65 (5 Raj., 1277); FM VI, p. 71 (22 Raj., 1277); FM VI, p. 76 (20 Shaʿ., 1277); FM VI, p. 77 (20 Shaʿ., 1277); FM VI, p. 78 (22 Shaʿ., 1277); FM VI, p. 80 (26 Shaʿ., 1277); FM VI, p. 98 (29 Rab. I, 1278); FM VI, p. 153 (28 Shaw., 1278); FM VI, p. 155 (8 DhQ, 1278); FM VI, p. 238 (8 Jum. II, 1284).

33 FM VI, p. 80 (26 Shaʿ., 1277).

> days before her death. The plaintiff produced two witnesses (probably the shaykhs who had washed the body before the funeral) who testified that they had seen the naked body of the deceased after her death and that there were traces of beating and wounds on it, but that they did not know who has hit her. The judge, however, did not consider this as legal evidence against the defendant, and sentenced him, after the *qasama* procedure and after having established that he had no *ʿaqila*, to pay his wife's *diya* to her heirs in his capacity of owner of the house where the deceased has been found with traces of violence on her body.[34]

In other cases, however, the plaintiffs would refuse to bring suit against the person who had obviously caused the victim's death, in order not to forfeit their right to start the *qasama* procedure. This happened in the following case. The presence in court of the actual culprit, however, indicates that he had been arrested and would not escape trial by a secular court:

> A man was found shot in a house owned by a ʿAbd al-Rahim Hasan. His heirs, represented by Hasan b. Luqman, sued ʿAbd al-Rahim for killing the deceased. ʿAbd al-Rahim admitted in court that the deceased was found shot in his house, but claimed that another person, a man named Hasan ʿAli, also present in court, had admitted to killing him. The qadi asked Hasan b. Luqman, the plaintiff, to prove his claim, which he could not. Then he allowed ʿAbd al-Rahim Hasan, the defendant, to substantiate his plea. The defendant produced six witnesses. Five of them testified that they had heard a shot of a pistol in the defendant's house, that they came to see what had happened and heard Hasan ʿAli, after his arrest, saying: "I resign to God; I couldn't do anything about it (*Amri li-Allah qahr*^{an} *ʿanni*)." The sixth witness declared that he had seen that Hasan ʿAli came out of the defendant's house with a pistol in his hand, that he had stumbled over the threshold and that then the pistol went off and the victim was hit. The qadi, arguing that legally nothing was proven against Hasan ʿAli, demanded at the plaintiff's request that the defendant swear fifty times that he had not killed the deceased and that except for Hasan ʿAli he did not know who had done so. After the defendant's oath sentence was passed against his *ʿaqila* to pay the *diya* to the heirs of the deceased.[35]

---

34 FM VI, p. 78 (27 Shaʿ., 1277).

35 FM VI, p. 63 (24 Jum. II, 1277).

5 Procedure and Evidence

That Shariʿa justice is often unsatisfactory in our eyes, in the sense that defendants who, judging by the available evidence, have clearly committed the crime, but, for formal reasons, cannot be convicted, is partly due to the complexity of the substantive law of homicide and partly to the rules of procedure and evidence. The rules of procedure lay down that a plaintiff identify the defendant in his claim and cannot bring suit against two or more defendants collectively and further that the plaintiff cannot change his claim if after its introduction it becomes clear that not the defendant but someone else has committed the murder. In both cases the plaintiff's claim is inadmissible. The main difficulty in this context, however, is connected with the very strict rules of evidence. In a large number of cases the plaintiff is unable to substantiate his claim.

The Shariʿa does not know an office of public prosecution[36] where evidence for the session can be prepared, and in theory it is the task of the plaintiff to find eyewitnesses to the crime and bring them to court or to obtain a confession of the defendant, in order to be able to prove all relevant facts during the court session. In practice, however, the state authorities would take care of this, as I mentioned before.[37] When a body was found, people would notify the local or provincial authorities (*ʿumda, shaykh al-balad, shaykh al-khufaraʾ,*

36 Cf. E. Tyan, *Histoire de l'organisation judiciaire en pays d'Islam.* 2e ed. (Leiden: E.J. Brill, 1960), p. 601.

37 The Ordinances appended to the Qanunnameh al-Sultani (introduced around 1852) contain some instructions concerning the investigation and procedure in case of homicide. Preliminary investigation is the responsibility of the local authorities (*mudir* or *hakim*). Immediately after the discovery of the body, a doctor must examine it and write a medical report. The results of the interrogations with the suspect and witnesses must be laid down in writing. Upon his arrest, the suspect and the victim's next of kin, with all the papers of the preliminary investigation, are to be sent to the nearest regional court (*majlis aqalim*) for trial. See Dhikr Wazayif Mutafarriʿa bi-l-Majlis, Arts. 9, 11 and 13 (Text in Jallad, *Qamus*, vol. II, pp. 105–6) and Bayan Khidmat wa-Harakat Mudiri l-Aqalim, Art. 13 (Text in Jallad, *Qamus*, vol. II, pp. 108–9). When local government was reorganized in 1871, the La'ihat al-Majalis al-Markaziyya of 1871 (Decree 172 of 25 Jum. I. 1288, text in Zaghlul, *Al-Muhamat*, Mulhaqat, pp. 181–206) laid down in detail the procedure to be followed in case of the detection of a heavy crime. The village council (*majlis al-balad*) had to notify immediately the district police officer. Awaiting his arrival, they and the village shaykhs were responsible for the arrest of the suspect and the investigation of the crime. The police officer had to come to the place of the crime with one or more members of the district council (*majlis al-markaz*), and, if necessary, a doctor or a deputy *qadi* (*nayib* [*sic*] *sharʿ*). They would then finish the investigation and the interrogation of witnesses together with the village council. Notes of the depositions of the witnesses and a report had to be sent to the district council, who would transfer the papers to the provincial administration (*mudiriyya*),

ma'mur, nazir, mudir). If the murderer was caught in the act, or if there were indications as to his identity, they would imprison the suspect, collect evidence, and try to extract a confession, often by beating or otherwise torturing him.[38] Such a confession, however, was in itself of little use in a Shari'a court for, if the confession was not made before the qadi during a court session, its existence had to be proven in court by an admission or by witnesses. Often a defendant would revoke his confession alleging that it had been obtained under duress. Although this is a legally valid plea,[39] no instance is recorded where the defendant succeeded in proving this. Surprisingly, in none of the cases the official who had interrogated the suspect was heard in court as a witness. Usually the existence of a confession was proven by witnesses who, judging by their professions, just happened to be present in the office (*diwan*), when the suspect was interrogated. In one case the coffee man (*qahwaji*) and an acquaintance of the official conducting the interrogation, who just entered to say hello to him, were, among others, heard as witnesses to a confession.[40] It is not difficult to imagine how imprecise their testimonies often are. That the officials in charge of the investigation were not heard in court may be due to the fact that according to the Shari'a they are not regarded as *'adl*, of good reputation. For the *shaykh al-balad* and the *'umda* this is confirmed by several fatwas stating that because they are helpers of injustice (*a'wan 'ala al-zulm*), their testimony cannot be accepted in court.[41]

---

to be sent finally to the provincial council (*majlis mahalli*) for trial. (Ch. 1, section 43; see also ch. 3, section 7 and ch. 4, section 2).

38 For cases where the defendants claimed that their confessions were obtained by beating and torture, see: FM VI, p. 291 (12 Saf., 1287); FM VI, p. 309 (5 Rab. II, 1287); FM VI, p. 401 (18 Muh., 1292); FM VI, p. 432 (11 Raj., 1294); FM VI, p. 436 (29 Sha'., 1294); FM VI, p. 447 (23 Rab. II, 1270). For a case where the suspect, his brother and his wife died in the course of the investigation, see FM VI, p. 2 (27 Muh., 1266).

39 See e.g. FM VI, p. 436 (5 Jum. II 1268).

40 FM VI, p. 519 (26 Raj., 1297). This is the only case I have seen where also a police officer was heard as a witness.

41 According to Hanafite law, the testimony of the officials (*'ummal*) of the sultan is accepted, unless they are "helpers of injustice (or oppression)". Some authors maintain that therefore the testimony of the *shaykh al-balad* and the tax collector is not accepted, unless they are known to be just. Cf. Ibn 'Abidin, *Radd al-Muhtar*, IV, p. 524; Shaykhzadeh, *Majma' al-Anhur* (Istanbul: 1309), II, pp. 158–9. Cf. FM VI, p. 259 (3 Jum. II, 1286) and p. 277 (26 DhH., 1286): Village shaykhs (*mashayikh al-balad, mashayikh al-nahiya* may not be heard as witnesses; FM VI, p. 121 and 131 (5 Raj., and 10 Ram., 1278): *khafir* (watchman) not per se unworthy of giving evidence; FM VI, p. 129 (29 Raj., 1278); FM VI, p. 466 (19 Muh., 1296): the *wakil shaykh al-khufara' al-tawwafin* (deputy chief of the watchmen) may give evidence if he belongs to the police force (*darak*) and is not a subordinate of the village shaykhs (*mashayikh al-qura*) and assists them in illegal acts and in dragging people to them.

In principle, evidence is based on either a confession (*iqrar*) of the defendant, the testimony of two male or one male and two female witnesses or oath.[42] If capital punishment is at stake, the rules of evidence are stricter and female witnesses are not allowed. Even the slightest doubt (*shubha*) prevents its application and the evidence is very carefully scrutinized by the judge and the various other authorities. This often results in the acquittal of the defendant, although on the basis of the evidence, it is entirely clear that he has committed the murder. The degree of precision in examining the testimonies is evident from the following case:

> During a session of the court in Burullus, a fight broke out between the qadi and one of the litigants. The heirs of the litigant, who had died shortly afterwards, sued the qadi alleging that he had struck the deceased twice, on his head and on his face, with a thin palm branch, that he had then chased the deceased out of the courtroom, that he had then kicked him in the belly, that this had caused his belly and breast to swell up and that he had stayed in his bed until he died eight days later as a result of this assault. The qadi stated that the deceased had been insolent during a session and admitted only of having lightly struck him twice on his turban in order to inspire respect in him. The plaintiffs produced three witnesses. The first one attested that he had seen that the deceased had attempted to prevent the qadi from sealing a deposition against him, that the qadi had struck him with his palm branch, that the deceased and the qadi had left the court room and that he had heard the deceased shouting: "You must be my witnesses!" The second witness stated that he was sitting outside the court and had suddenly seen the deceased coming out of the court room with the qadi behind him, that the qadi had kicked him once in his belly with his left foot, which had caused the deceased to fall, that the qadi had then kicked him twice with his right foot in his belly and given him two strokes with a medium sized palm branch, once on his brow and once under his ear, that the deceased had lost consciousness, was carried to the district officer (*hakim al-balad*) and had remained ill until he died as a result of the assault. The third witness declared that he was also sitting outside the court, that he had suddenly seen the deceased

42 The oath is only of secondary importance. If a plaintiff cannot substantiate his claim against a defendant, the latter is made to swear the oath of innocence. If he takes the oath, the plaintiff may not sue him anymore, unless he produces better evidence. If the defendant refuses, however, and a death sentence was requested, he is imprisoned until he swears the oath or confesses. If blood money was requested, refusal of the oath by the defendant entails the allowance of the plaintiff's claim.

> coming bareheaded out of the courtroom, shouting: "Be witness of this, folks!", that the qadi had come after him, that he had struck the deceased twice with a palm branch, once on his left ear and once on his right eye, that he had kicked him twice in his belly with his left foot, which had caused the deceased to fall down, that he was carried to the district officer and that he had remained in bed until he died as a result of the assault. After consultation of the mufti, the judge who heard this case decided that the testimony of the first witness was irrelevant as he had not seen the fatal blows and kicks and that the testimonies of the second and third witnesses were contradictory and could not serve as a basis for a sentence against the defendant.[43]

Cases like these are no exception. Legion trials with the same unsatisfactory result can be found in the material. The Shariʿa requires a standard of precision and detailedness in testimonies, that is very difficult to satisfy. A testimony with the words: "I saw the defendant here present beating a man called ʿAli" will be rejected as the victim must as a rule be identified by his *ism thulathi*, i.e. his given name and the names of his father and grandfather.

Not only the testimonies are scrutinized, but also the witnesses themselves. A witness must be Muslim and *ʿadl*, i.e. of good reputation. An indispensable part of the procedure is the *taʿdil* and *tazkiya* of the witnesses who have given evidence. As a rule, this seldom causes problems. However, in one exceptional case the testimony of two witnesses was rejected because, when interrogated by the qadi, it appeared that they were not able to recite the *Fatiha* correctly nor any other part of the Koran (which means that they cannot correctly perform the *salah*). In the same case the defendant failed in challenging another witness by trying to prove that on market days this witness used to visit bars and brothels, and, equally damaging to his reputation, used to eat in the street.[44]

There are more limitations, all stemming from a healthy tendency to preclude biased testimonies. However, in its rigid application, they often make it impossible to prove a case. Evidence against a party given by an enemy, or in favour of a party given by someone who is under his authority (an employee with regard to his employer, a peasant with regard to the landowner, the inhabitant of a village with regard to the village shaykh), is not admitted, nor is the testimony of those who live close by the place of the crime and who may be held responsible for the murder on the strength of the *qasama* procedure.

43 FM VI, p. 58 (4 Jum. II, 1277).

44 FM VI, p. 543 (18 Jum. I, 1299).

In the material there are quite a number of instances where the testimonies of the only witnesses to the crime were challenged for these reasons.

6 Conclusion

From the material in the FM it is clear that until the introduction of French law codes in 1883, the Shariʿa was fully applied in homicide cases, side by side with secular criminal justice on the strength of enacted laws. This leads to the question of why the government maintained and supported this complicated system of dual trial and why the subjects, both Muslims and Copts, continued to bring suit before the qadi in these cases. One could think of several explanations. In the first place, it seems that this system had existed already for a long time in the Ottoman Empire[45] and was therefore also followed in Egypt. In the Ottoman Empire the office of the qadi was a strong one and the Shariʿa, supplemented by secular legislation, was almost universally and carefully applied. It is noteworthy that the Egyptian authorities, by instituting several bodies and offices for the supervision of qadi justice, showed their reverence and concern for the correct application of the Shariʿa. This reverence is also apparent from the fact that the state did act as a party in homicide trials before the qadi, if the victim had no heirs.

Secondly, on the level of the litigants the Shariʿa procedure had two advantages which made them eager to submit homicide cases to the qadi. One is the fact that according to the Shariʿa the next of kin of the victim can play an active role in the proceedings, whereas, according to the secular, Western type laws, they are left out of the trial, unless summoned as witnesses. The Shariʿa procedure offers them a possibility to satisfy their feelings of revenge legally. The other reason is, I believe, of a financial nature. One must not forget that the *diya* for homicide represented a considerable sum of money. For this reason people would even sue friends and relatives who, by intervening in fights on the side of the deceased, had accidentally killed him.[46]

45 Cf. Krcmarik, *a.c.*, pp. 565 ff. This is probably due to the strong position of Shariʿa justice in the Ottoman Empire. In other periods of Islamic history, it was not customary that the qadi had jurisdiction in criminal matters, these being dealt with by other state organs like the *shurta* (police). See E. Tyan, *Histoire*, pp. 601 ff.

46 See e.g. FM VI, p. 144 (25 Ram., 1278) and FM VI, p. 156 (15 DhH., 1278).

CHAPTER 2

Muhammad al-ʿAbbasi al-Mahdi (d. 1897), Grand Mufti of Egypt, and His *al-Fatawa al-Mahdiyya*

In the second half of the nineteenth century, Egypt's administration expanded and became more and more specialized. The loyal members of Muhammad ʿAli's household, who were expected to function in any post within the military and the civil administration and stood under his personal command, were gradually replaced by a new type of bureaucrat, for whom specialized skills and a keen knowledge of the administrative regulations were as important as personal loyalty to the ruler. Increasingly, their functions and competence were formally circumscribed. Relations between the administration and the subjects, and relations between officials themselves, tended to be governed less by personal ties than by rules and regulations. This implied that the scope of freedom of the administrators was curbed by the law. As a corollary of this development, the Khedives founded secular courts, specialized councils and bodies, whose competence was governed by legislation. After the first secular laws in the fields of criminal, commercial, and administrative law were enacted during the latter part of Muhammad ʿAli's reign, legislation in these fields greatly expanded during the reigns of his successors.[1]

In this article I will examine how these changes in the organization of the state affected the administration of Shariʿa justice and, especially, the office of the Grand Mufti. After introducing my main source, the collection of fatwas issued by Muhammad al-ʿAbbasi al-Mahdi, a Grand Mufti, who held his post from 1848 until his death in 1897, and its author, I will argue that the bureaucratization of the state extended also to qadis and muftis, through the imposition of strict adherence to one of the opinions within the Hanafi school. The office of Grand Mufti played a crucial role in this connection. It developed from a relatively simple one – that of the Hanafi mufti of the Cairo Shariʿa court, who was occasionally consulted by the government – into a well remunerated post at the top of the hierarchy consisting of all those involved in the administration of Shariʿa justice, consulted by the public as well as by state agencies, and one of whose tasks it was to maintain a strict adherence to the Hanafi school

1 For a detailed survey of these developments, see F. Robert Hunter, *Egypt under the Khedives, 1805–1879: From Household Government to Modern Bureaucracy* (Pittsburgh: University of Pittsburgh Press, 1984).

within the judiciary. This prevented the Grand Mufti from introducing legal reform in the field of Islamic law.

1 Al-Fatawa al-Mahdiyya

In May 1887 (Shaʿban 1304) the publishing house associated with al-Azhar University completed the printing of a seven volume collection of fatwas issued by Muhammad al-ʿAbbasi al-Mahdi (1827–1897), who was then the Grand Mufti of Egypt, a position he had held since 1848. Entitled *al-Fatawa al-Mahdiyya fi'l-Waqa'iʿ al-Misriyya* (hereinafter FM),[2] this massive collection contains approximately 13,500 fatwas that were selected by al-ʿAbbasi from the fatwas he had issued during the period between 1848 and 1886. Beginning from 1883, al-ʿAbbasi began to prepare the fatwas for publication by arranging them into chapters reflecting the standard order of Hanafi legal texts;[3] within each chapter the fatwas are arranged in chronological order according to their date of issue.[4]

Each fatwa begins with the formula *su'ila fi* followed by a noun (a question was asked concerning). The answer is introduced by *ajaba* (he answered), sometimes followed by *naʿam* (indeed) if the wording of the question correctly anticipates the answer. A question submitted by a government agency begins with *su'ila min/min taraf … fi …* (a question was posed by … concerning …), *su'ila min/min taraf … bi-ma madmunuhu …* (a question was posed by … with the following contents …). Beginning in approximately 1860, the expressions become more bureaucratic, as, for example: *su'ila bi-l-ifada warida min … bi-tarikh … madmunuha …* (a question was posed in a missive from … dated … with the following contents …). One fatwa is written in the form of a poem in answer to a question formulated in verse.[5] All fatwas end with the formula *wa-Allah taʿala aʿlam* (and the Exalted God knows best).

The fatwas vary in length from a few lines to several pages. They do not resemble Ottoman Turkish fatwas in which the question directed to a mufti is rephrased by his clerks in such a way that "yes" or "no" (*olur, olmaz*) suffices as

2 The title page mentions 1301 AH as the year of publication, which cannot be correct as some of the fatwas included are dated as late as 1303 AH. I follow the year of publication mentioned in the colophon at the end of vol. VII.

3 For a list of the chapters, see G. Delanoue, *Moralistes et politiques musulmans dans l'Egypte du XIXe siecle (1798–1882)* (Le Caire: Institut français d'archéologie orientale, 1982), 176–78.

4 FM, I, 4–5.

5 FM, I, 299 (23 Rabiʿ I 1269).

an answer. The date on which each fatwa was issued is printed in the margin, sometimes with a note summarizing the contents of the fatwa.

Al-ʿAbbasi issued most of the fatwas included in the FM in his capacity as mufti of the Grand Shariʿa Court in Cairo, where he received requests for legal opinions from private individuals who were either involved in lawsuits or unsure about their Shariʿa rights and duties, as in the following example, dealing with a man, a woman, and a slave:

> A man sold his adult slave after becoming angry with him for entering his harem. But his wife purchased the slave from the first buyer in order to vex her husband. She wanted the slave to stay with her in her house. The husband asked the Grand Mufti [1] if he might forbid her to do so; [2] if she is allowed to unveil her face for the slave; and [3] if he is entitled to lodge her at his discretion in another residence that satisfies the requirements of the Shariʿa. The Grand Mufti answered his questions by stating that a woman's slave is in this respect like any stranger (*ajnabi*). He is allowed to see only her face and hands, and if he fears being overcome with lust, even looking at her face is forbidden. Furthermore, as a slave, the man is allowed to enter her rooms without asking permission. The expenses of a wife's slave who serves her exclusively and has no other duties are to be paid by the husband, who is not entitled to bring her another servant unless she agrees. The husband has no right to remove a servant from his wife's home, unless the slave is untrustworthy and embezzles money for shopping. In that case the husband may replace him with another who is trustworthy.[6]

The Grand Mufti did not go into the third question posed by the angry husband, limiting himself to the remark that the husband is obliged to provide a residence that satisfies the legal requirements, without specifying whether the choice of a residence is exclusively his.

Approximately seven percent of the fatwas were issued at the request of official agencies, including local Shariʿa courts.[7] A few fatwas emanated from the

6 FM, v, 291–92 (18 Rajab 1270).

7 Authorities requesting fatwas were: Shariʿa courts (33 percent) – often submitted through the provincial administration (*mudiriyya*) and from there through the Cairo Governorate (*Muhafaza*) or through the Viceregal Cabinet (*al-Maʿiyya al-Saniyya*); *Bayt al-Mal* (15 percent); Cairo Governorate (*Diwan al-Katkhuda/Muhafazat Misr*) (10 percent); the Cairo Police Department (*Dabitiyyat Misr*) (6 percent); the Waqf Administration (4 percent); The Bureau of Pensions (*al-Ruznama*) (3 percent); the *Majlis al-Al-Ahkam* (3 percent); and the Ministry of Justice (*Nazarat al-Haqqaniyya*) (3 percent).

Hijaz, India (Hind) or Turkey (al-Rum).[8] Occasionally the name of the person at whose request the fatwa was issued or whose estate was at issue is mentioned in the question. This occurs only with regard to very important personalities, such as the Khedive and members of his household.

A few fatwas were endorsed by other ulema, usually the Shaykh al-Azhar (during the period that al-ʿAbbasi did not hold this position), the secretary to the Grand Mufti (*amin al-fatwa*), and other high ranking ulema, not all of whom were Hanafis. These endorsements occurred in cases involving a controversy between groups of scholars that had to be settled at the highest level;[9] in cases that were of great political import, such as the fatwa issued against the Sudanese Mahdi;[10] and in cases in which a fatwa was requested by the Privy Council (*al-Majlis al-Khususi*), the highest conciliar body in Egypt[11] (of five such cases, four were endorsed by additional ulema).[12] It is nevertheless difficult to determine the specific circumstances in which such an endorsement was required.

The overwhelming majority of the fatwas deal with legal matters (as opposed to matters related to ritual and dietary laws). The chapter on ritual law is only ten pages long (that is, one quarter of one per cent of a total of 3,988 pages) and contains a mere twenty-one fatwas, of which eight were issued at the request of state officials. The paucity of fatwas on this subject reflects the fact that although the Egyptian law courts applied Hanafi law, the majority of the population followed the Shafiʿi or Maliki school in religious matters. It is interesting to compare the percentage of fatwas on religious topics in the FM, with that in the fatwa collection[13] of al-ʿAbbasi's contemporary,

8 See, for example, FM, III, 35 (20 Jumada II 1266), from the agent of the *waqfs* in Mekka and Medina (*wakil awqaf al-Haramayn*); FM, II, 570 (20 Jumada I 1270), from the office of *waqfs* in Mekka and Medina (*Diwan Awqaf al-Haramayn*); FM, II, 2 (4 Muharram 1283), from India (*min al-Hind*); FM, II, 27 (8 Shawwal 1296), from Turkey (*min bilad al-Rum*); FM, V, 300–09 (20 Muharram 1302), from India (*min al-Hind*).

9 FM, I, 222–26 (23 Jumada II 1283): a controversy among the ulema of Dumyat regarding the law of repudiation; FM, II, 698–700 (19 Jumada I 1283): a controversy among high ranking muftis on the permissibility of substitution of *waqf* property (*istibdal*).

10 FM, II, 28–32, 18 Dhu al-Qaʿda 1300 (*suʾila min taraf al-hukuma al-khidiwiyya*). For an analysis of this fatwa, see R. Peters, "Islam and the Legitimation of Power: The Mahdi-Revolt in the Sudan," in XXI. *Deutscher Orientalistentag (Berlin, März 1980): Ausgewählte Vorträge*. Hrsg. von F. Steppat (Wiesbaden: 1983), 409–20.

11 See J. Deny, *Sommaire des archives turques du Caire* (Le Caire: Institut français d'archéologie orientale, 1930): 120–21; Hunter, *Egypt under the Khedives*, 49–50.

12 Endorsed by additional ulema: FM, II, 730, III, 262, IV, 340, V, 523; signed only by the Grand Mufti: FM, IV, 645.

13 See Muhammad (ʿIllaysh, *Fath al-ʿAli al-Malik fi l-Fatwa ʿala madhhab al-Imam Malik* (2 vols., Cairo: Matbaʿat al-Taqaddum, 1901–02 [1319 AH]).

the Maliki mufti, Muhammad ʿIllaysh (1802–1882). Of 700 pages in ʿIllaysh's text, 181 (26 percent) deal with religious subjects.

2 The Author[14]

Muhammad al-ʿAbbasi al-Mahdi, son of Muhammad Amin al-Mahdi (d. 1831–32),[15] for some time Hanafi mufti during Muhammad ʿAli's reign, was born in the year 1827. In October 1848 al-ʿAbbasi was appointed Hanafi mufti by Ibrahim Pasha.[16] Because of his youth – he was only twenty-one years old – his professor of Hanafi fiqh, Khalil al-Rashidi, was appointed as his secretary in order to assist him in his new office.

Al-ʿAbbasi's biographers mention that he twice fell afoul of the Khedive: Once when Khedive ʿAbbas (r. 1848–1854) attempted to confiscate all properties belonging to Muhammad ʿAli's descendants and again when Khedive Ismaʿil, acting as prince-regent for Saʿid (r. 1854–1863), attempted to assimilate family waqfs (*waqf ahli*) to public waqfs (*waqf khayri*) in order to gain control over them. Due to al-ʿAbbasi's opposition nothing came of these plans. His biographers mention these incidents to emphasize not only the Grand Mufti's integrity, but also the close ties that bound him to the Khedival house, ties that, apparently, were unaffected by such incidents. The strength of his relationship with the Khedive is evidenced by the fact that in January 1871 Ismaʿil appointed him Shaykh al-Azhar, a post hitherto reserved for Shafiʿis and Malikis. Ismaʿil apparently wanted to introduce certain reforms and regarded al-ʿAbbasi as the most suitable candidate for this task. The Khedive was not disappointed,

14 Among the few sources for al-ʿAbbasi's biography, the most important are an account by his son, Muhammad ʿAbd al-Khaliq al-Hifni, included in J. Zaydan, *Tarajim mashahir al-sharq fi'l-qarn al-thalith ʿashar* (2 vols., 3rd ed., Beirut: Dar Maktabat al-Hayah, n.d.), II, 250–55, and a note in ʿAli Mubarak, *Al-Khitat al-Tawfiqiyya* (20 vols. Bulaq: Al-Matbaʿa al-Kubra al-Amiriyya, 1886–89 [1304–06 AH]), XVII, 12–13. For a complete list of sources, see A. Schölch, *Ägypten den Ägyptern: Die politische and gesellschaftliche Krise der Jahre 1878–1882 in Agypten* (Zurich: Atlantis Verlag, 1973), 332, nt. 243. Delanoue, *Moralistes et politiques* (168–74 and 136–37) summarizes the available biographical information.

15 On Muhammad Amin al-Mahdi, see E.W. Lane, Manners and Customs of the Modern Egyptians (Repr., London: Dent, 1966 [Originally publ. 1836]), 118–21.

16 His predecessor, Ahmad al-Tamimi (1801/02–1847/48) was dismissed by Ibrahim immediately after assuming power. According to al-Tamimi's son, his father was dismissed because he would not bend the law by issuing fatwas that served Ibrahim's interest. See Muhammad Efendi al-Tamimi, *Tarjamat hayat al ʿallama al-shaykh Ahmad al-Tamimi al-Dari al-Khalili mufti Misr* (Ms. Egyptian National Library, Tarikh Taymur 1096), 7. Ibrahim's appointment of a 21-year-old scholar to this important office may indicate that he wanted a submissive person who would not oppose him.

for six months later he issued a decree prepared by al-ʿAbbasi, requiring for the first time that a student pass a final examination before being admitted to the ranks of the ulema (decree of 16 Rabiʿ I 1288/15 July 1871). At the same time, the allowances and pensions of the ulema at al-Azhar were increased, no doubt as compensation for their acceptance of his reforms. In the same year, on 25 December 1871 (12 Shawwal 1288) the Khedive appointed al-ʿAbbasi a member of the Privy Council, which he was to attend two days a week in order to deal with cases that had to be decided according to the Shariʿa. His monthly salary was raised from 4,000 to 7,500 piasters.[17]

The test of al-ʿAbbasi's loyalty to the ruling house came in 1881 with the ʿUrabi Revolt, which was supported by the students and ulema of al-Azhar. Suspecting that al-ʿAbbasi was going to issue a fatwa in which he would denounce the rebels as opponents of the legitimate government and call for their execution, the Azharis campaigned for al-ʿAbbasi's dismissal as Shaykh al-Azhar, ostensibly on the ground of his outspoken support for the Khedive. Because the Hanafi school was associated with the Turco–Circassian ruling class, the Azharis put forward as their candidate the octogenarian Maliki Chief Mufti, Muhammad ʿIllaysh.[18] But as an ardent supporter of ʿUrabi, he was rejected by the government. Al-ʿAbbasi was in fact dismissed by the Khedive on 5 December 1881, and a compromise candidate, Muhammad al-Inbabi (1824–1896), a Shafiʿi, was appointed in his place.[19] Simultaneously, both al-ʿAbbasi and ʿIllaysh were made members of a council that was charged with the task of assisting the Shaykh al-Azhar. Al-ʿAbbasi remained Grand Mufti. When a number of prominent Azhar ulema issued a fatwa calling for the deposition of the Khedive Tawfiq on the ground that he had disobeyed the Ottoman Sultan and let the British take possession of the country,[20] al-ʿAbbasi refused to sign.[21]

17 Amin Sami, *Taqwim al-Nil* (3 vols., Cairo: Matbaʿat al-Kutub al-Misriyya, 1928–36), iii/3, 979. This was a high salary. In 1877 (1294 AH) members of the highest judicial bodies, the *Majlis al-Ahkam* and the Courts of Appeal (*majalis al-istiʾnaf*) received a monthly salary of 6,000 and 3,000 piasters respectively (Sami, *Taqwim al-Nil*, 111/3, 1462). When the Supreme Shariʿa Court was created on 4 June 1876 and the Privy Council no longer had to deal with Shariʿa cases, Treasury (*al-Maliyya*) inquired whether the Mufti remained entitled to his allowance of 3,500 piasters. The Khedive answered in the affirmative, arguing that the Grand Mufti's membership on the Privy Council had not been terminated (Sami, *Taqwim al-Nil*, iii/3, 1358).

18 On ʿIllaysh, see Delanoue, *Moralistes et politiques*, 129–68.

19 On Inbabi, see Delanoue, *Moralistes et politiques*, 137, nt. 80.

20 An English translation of this fatwa may be found in A.M. Broadley, *How we Defended Arabi* (Repr., Cairo: Research and Publishing Arab Centre [sic], 1980), 175–78.

21 Schölch, *Ägypten den Ägyptern*, 350, nt. 119.

The FM contains one fatwa, dated 16 Shawwal 1299 (31 August 1882), that is directly related to these events.[22] At that time, British troops had invaded Egypt and were advancing in the Delta, making their way toward Cairo. Spurred on by the religious fervour of his followers, Ahmad ʿUrabi had asked the leading ulema of the four law schools whether or not the equestrian statue of Ibrahim Pasha (the grandfather of the Khedive Tawfiq) at Azbakiyya Square and the lion statues at both ends of the Qasr al-Nil Bridge had to be demolished. Using the emotive word *sanam* (idol) to refer to these statues, ʿUrabi declared, "[O]ur country was afflicted with calamities only after idols were erected in Cairo and Alexandria." Although the Grand Mufti, who had been approached through his rival, the newly appointed Shaykh al-Azhar, had no sympathy for the ʿUrabists, he was compelled to pronounce that the removal of these statues was obligatory. In an attempt to dampen ʿUrabi's religious zeal, he had added the following supplement (*tatmim*) to his fatwa:

> The rulers of the Muslims must remove everything in their countries that is objectionable (*munkar*), such as practising usury (*riba*), the opening of places known as brothels (*karakhanat*) and bars (*khammarat*), and other offences (*mubiqat*). [They also must] prevent God's servants from suffering wrongs contrary to the Shariʿa and forbid injustice and [the application of] rules other than those revealed by God. This is more urgent [than removing these images].[23]

At the end of 1882, after the revolt had been suppressed by the English, al-ʿAbbasi was reinstated as Shaykh al-Azhar, a post that he held until 30 December 1886, when he resigned from both his functions as a result of a disagreement with the Khedive. But when his successor as Grand Mufti, Muhammad al-Bannaʾ, insisted that al-ʿAbbasi was the real Grand Mufti, he was reappointed to that office, which he occupied until his death in 1897.

To the best of my knowledge, the FM is his only independent work, although it contains at least one treatise, written in December 1858, entitled *al-Safwa al-Mahdiyya fi irsad al-aradi al-Misriyya*;[24] in this treatise, which deals with pseudo-waqfs (*irsadat*) created on state lands, al-ʿAbbasi urges the Khedive,

22 For a translation and a detailed analysis of this fatwa, see R. Peters, "The Lions of Qasr al-Nil Bridge: The Islamic Prohibition of Images as an Issue in the ʿUrabi Revolt," in M. Khalid Masud, Brinkley Messick, and David Powers (eds.) (Cambridge Ma: Harvard University Press, 1996), 214–220.

23 FM, V, 299–300 (16 Shawwal 1299). The statues were removed at the urging of the Maliki mufti, ʿIllaysh. They were placed in the Egyptian Museum and re-erected after the revolt.

24 FM, II, 645–50 (7 Jumada II 1275).

Saʿid, not to abolish the allowances deriving from them. The treatise must have been prompted by the promulgation of the Egyptian Land Law some months earlier, in August 1858.

3 The Office of Mufti in Egypt

3.1 *Muftis in General*

Due to the complexity of Islamic law, ordinary Muslims cannot be expected to be familiar with all details relating to their rights and duties. In order to know and understand the intricate rules of the Shariʿa they need the help of legal specialists, muftis, who are qualified to clarify the law relating to religious and other duties (*al-futya al-ʿamma*) and to specific lawsuits, at the request of either one of the parties or the qadi (*al-futya al-qadaʾiyya*). Until the Ottoman conquest of Egypt in 1517, there had been muftis and qadis from all four *madhhabs*; after the conquest, the Hanafi *madhhab* came to prevail in the administration of justice and only Hanafi muftis could exercise the function of *al-futya al-qadaʾiyya*, despite the fact that the overwhelming majority of the population belonged to either the Shafiʿi or the Maliki school.[25] Consequently, the task of the Shafiʿi, Maliki and Hanbali muftis (for the few Hanbalis living in Egypt) was confined to *al-futya al-ʿamma*.

During the nineteenth century, the government began to appoint Hanafi muftis to the various levels of the judiciary and the administration. These muftis were consulted by litigants, by the authorities, and by the qadis themselves. The Qadis Ordinance (*Laʾihat al-Qudah*) of 1856 established that "the qadi should consult the ulema and request fatwas from them in difficult cases, without forming his opinion independently, as a precaution against errors in [applying] the rules of the Shariʿa" (Art. 21).[26]

In 1873 the government issued a decree regulating the duties and competence of the official Hanafi muftis.[27] This decree, drafted by a body of high

25 See ʿAbd al-Rahim ʿAbd al-Rahman ʿAbd al-Rahim, "Al-qadaʾ fi Misr al-ʿUthmaniyya 1517–1798," in ʿAbd al-Rahim ʿAbd al-Rahman ʿAbd al-Rahim, *Fusul fi tarikh Misr al-iqtisadi al-ʿUthmani* (Cairo: al-Hayʾa, 1990), 319–49.

26 For the text of the ordinance, see Filib Jallad, *Qamus al-idara wa-l-qadaʾ* (5 vols., Alexandria: Al-Matbaʿa al-Bukhariyya, 1890–95), IV, 129–31.

27 Decree of 5 Rabiʿ II 1290 (for the text, see Jallad, *Qamus*, IV, 136). In 1251, Muhammad ʿAli had decreed that only the Hanafi mufti was allowed to issue fatwas in cases regarding the government and its subjects (*raʿiyya*) and that other scholars who issued fatwas would be punished (see al-Tamimi, *Tarjamat*, 4). Muhammad ʿAli's decree probably was intended to restrict the issuance of fatwas in connection with lawsuits before the Cairo Shariʿa Court and other judicial bodies in Cairo.

ranking ulema and approved by the Privy Council, mentions four categories of mufti: those assigned to the regional courts (*majalis al-aqalim*), those assigned to the provincial administrations (*mudiriyyat*), the mufti of the Waqf Administration (*Diwan al-Awqaf*), and, finally, the mufti of Cairo (that is, the Grand Mufti) and the mufti of Alexandria. The muftis of the first three categories were allowed to issue fatwas relating only to cases dealt with by the bodies to which they were assigned or whenever a government department requested one; the muftis of Cairo and of Alexandria could issue legal opinions at the behest of either the government or the general public.[28] The enumeration of muftis in the 1873 decree was not comprehensive, as the FM mentions additional categories of mufti, including those assigned to the *Majlis al-Ahkam* (one of the highest legislative and judiciary bodies), its predecessor, the Council of Justice (*Jamʿiyyat al-Haqqaniyya*), and to the Cairo Police (*al-Dabitiyya*).

The 1873 decree was based on the view that the state has a general responsibility for regulating the qualifications of muftis. In accordance with this view, al-ʿAbbasi expressed the opinion that a ruler is empowered to prohibit unqualified persons from issuing fatwas and to impose disciplinary punishment (*taʿzir*).[29] The decree of 1873 was meant not only to define the competence of the muftis mentioned in the text, but also to terminate the activities of unofficial muftis, whose knowledge of Islamic law was often defective. Although the Khedive originally had wanted to make the issuance of fatwas conditional upon previous authorisation (*maʾdhuniyya*), the ulema consulted by the Privy Council had deemed that unnecessary; they proposed that fatwas given by muftis in cases exceeding their competence should not be accepted by state agencies, and their proposal was incorporated in the final text.[30] The decree also provided redress to litigants who had lost a case because they had relied on an incorrect fatwa issued by an officially appointed mufti; such litigants might ask to have the judgment reviewed by an authority appointed by the government.

3.2 *The Grand Mufti in Egypt*

Following the Ottoman conquest of Egypt, the Hanafi mufti assigned to the Grand Shariʿa Court in Cairo (*al-mahkama al-kubra al-sharʿiyya bi-Misr*, or *mahkamat Misr al-kubra*), with the title *mufti al-sada al-hanafiyya*, came to be regarded as the highest ranking mufti in the country.[31] To emphasize his posi-

28 The Arabic text reads: *innahum munawwatan bi-ma yusʾaluna* [*sic*] *ʿanhu min al-hawadith allati ʿalayhima sawaʾan kanat min al-hukuma aw khilafiha.*

29 See FM, v, 289 (28 Dhu al-Qaʿda 1264).

30 The Arabic text reads: *law sadarat fatwa min ayy shakhs fi-ma la yakhtass bihi la yuʿawwal ʿalayha fi mahallat al-hukuma wa-la yunzar laha.*

31 See Lane, *Manners and Customs*, 118.

tion with regard to the other chief muftis, he was referred to, from the middle of the nineteenth century, as *mufti al-diyar al*-Misriyya[32] and, sometimes, simply as *bashmufti*.[33] The Grand Mufti had the following tasks:

- acting as mufti assigned to the Grand Shariʿa Court in Cairo;
- giving advice in the Khedival Council (*al-Diwan al-ʿAli*) on complicated legal questions;[34]
- issuing authoritative fatwas whenever there were controversies among ulema[35] or complaints about the misapplication of the Shariʿa by qadis;[36]
- membership, together with the chief muftis of the other *madhhabs*, the Shaykh al-Azhar, the Head of the Descendants of the Prophet (*naqib al-ashraf*) and sometimes other ulema, in the Council of Scholars (*al-majlis al-ʿilmi*) of Cairo, which was consulted by the rulers with regard to important religious matters;[37]
- issuing fatwas to both the general public and to government agencies, as prescribed in the decree of 1873.

Occasionally, the Grand Mufti was asked to issue an opinion relating to the interpretation and application of certain decrees connected with Shariʿa justice, decrees that, as a rule, were drafted by ulema. For example, we find fatwas on the question of whether a decree regulating the application of the Shariʿa becomes ineffective after the death of the ruler who enacted it;[38] on the meaning of an article in the Appendix to the Bayt al-Mal[39] Ordinance (*Dhayl Laʾihat Bayt al-Mal*);[40] and on the relationship between a Khedival decree of 1874 and

32 The title was first used in an official document in 1865. See Jad al-Haqq in *Al-Fatawa al-Islamiyya* (Cairo: Al-Majlis al-Aʿla li-l-Shuʾun al-Islamiyya, 1980-), 3655.

33 See, for example, FM, II, 699 (19 Jumada I 1283).

34 See, for example, FM, II 449 (30 Rabiʿ II 1265): "We attended the Khedival Council in Cairo and the substance of the case of … was read to us as well as the conflicting fatwas concerning the issue.… We considered their words and it appeared [to us] that the fatwa to the effect that … was the one in agreement with the stipulations of the founder of the *waqf*."

35 See, for example, FM, IV, 588 (15 Jumada I 1271): a fatwa issued at the request of the *Majlis al-Al-Ahkam* concerning a controversy among the ulema of Upper Egypt regarding the law of donation.

36 See, for example, FM, III 276–81 (10 Jumada II 1289), where the Grand Mufti is consulted by the *Majlis al-Ahkam* about incorrect judgments by the qadi of Giza.

37 Lane, *Manners and Customs*, 121–22.

38 FM, HI, 255 (17 Rabiʿ I 1280). The decree enacted by the Khedive Saʿid had authorized the local governors (*mudirun, muhafizun*) to represent the state in homicide trials if the victim had no heirs.

39 The *Bayt al-Mal* was the government agency dealing with estates without heirs or with absentee heirs, and with the estates of freedmen (*ʿutaqaʾ*) of the khedival family. For the text of the Bayt al-Mal Ordinance of 1276 and its appendices, see Jallad, *Qamus*, II, 5 ff.

40 FM, IV, 432 (21 Safar 1284).

the 1880 Shariʿa Courts Ordinance, in view of the fact that the Ordinance establishes a time period for the prescription of actions which is longer than the term of prescription for actions relating to estates and *waqfs* mentioned in the Khedival decree.[41] However, when asked to explain certain provisions of the 1858 Land Law (*Qanun al-Aradi*) relating to the mortgaging of state land (*aradi kharajiyya amiriyya*), the Grand Mufti declined to issue an opinion, since a mortgage on state lands was valid only under this Law and not under the Shariʿa. Although he did not expressly state that such a transaction was null and void, he observed that it had to be handled by the secular courts (*al-majalis al-siyasiyya*).[42]

The Grand Mufti sometimes was asked to act as an arbiter, as in a case in which the trusteeship of a *waqf*, entrusted to the leadership (*sajjada*) of a Sufi brotherhood, was disputed by the son and the daughter of the last incumbent.[43] In other instances, the Grand Mufti was asked to issue a fatwa in order to convince a defeated litigant of the correctness of a judgment.[44]

As the highest official authority on religious matters, the Grand Mufti was consulted on the permissibility of printing certain books. Between 1871 and 1884, al-ʿAbbasi issued at least twenty-three fatwas in response to queries submitted by the Cairo Police Department and the Cairo Governorate (*al-Muhafaza*) on this matter.[45] In general, the Grand Mufti opposed the printing of popular stories such as the Arabian Nights, Abu Zayd and ʿAli al-Tajir, because "they are full of lies with which one should not occupy oneself and [the reading of] which results in loss of time without benefit";[46] he also opposed books on magic because "they result in the loss of money without benefit, or in harm to God's creatures, neither of which is legally permitted."[47]

Unlike the Ottoman Shaykh al-Islam,[48] the Egyptian Grand Mufti does not appear to have issued many fatwas on political issues.[49] I have found only three such fatwas in the FM: the fatwa on the revolt of the Sudanese Mahdi, the

41 FM, III, 296 (15 Jumada I 1298).

42 FM, V, 400 (24 Dhu al-Qaʿda 1296).

43 FM, II, 739–42, especially 741 (26 Jumada II 1288).

44 See, for example, FM, V, 212 (14 Jumada II 1281); III, 295 (Rabiʿ II 1297).

45 FM, V, 292–97.

46 FM, V, 294 (7 Jumada II 1288).

47 FM, V, 293 (23 Shawwal 1285).

48 On the political fatwas of the Ottoman Shaykh al-Islam, see H. Krüger, *Fetva and Siyar: Zur internationalrechtlichen Gutachtenpraxis der osmanischen Şeyh vom 17. bis 19. Jahrhundert* (…) (Wiesbaden: Harrassowitz, 1978), 52–54.

49 It is possible – although unlikely – that al-ʿAbbasi did in fact issue significant numbers of political fatwas which, for some reason, were not included in the FM.

fatwa on the destruction of statues at the time of the ʿUrabi Revolt, and a third fatwa, issued in 1876 in response to an inquiry from the Khedive regarding a person who claimed to have knowledge of the divine secrets (*al-mughayyabat*), as a result of which people zealously occupied themselves with his words and committed actions disturbing to the public order. To this question al-ʿAbbasi responded that such a person must be punished with *taʿzir* if his words do not constitute apostasy (if they do constitute apostasy, he must be put to death).[50]

The Grand Mufti's power was augmented by the 1880 Shariʿa Courts Ordinance (*Laʾihat al-Mahakim al-Sharʿiyya*). According to this Ordinance, any complaint about the misapplication of the Shariʿa normally was handled by the Grand Shariʿa Court in Cairo. But complaints against decisions in first instance or in appeal given by this court were to be referred to the Grand Mufti, whose fatwas in this regard were binding. He had the same power regarding decisions issued in first instance by the Shariʿa Court in Alexandria (Art. 3). Another, similar, procedure, which had existed already for some time,[51] was formalized in Art. 22 of this Ordinance: Whenever a qadi was uncertain about a legal issue confronting him, he must first consult the mufti officially assigned to his court or to the district. The mufti's opinion would be binding if the qadi was in agreement; otherwise (or if the mufti himself did not know the correct answer), the matter would be presented to the Grand Mufti, whose decision would have the force of law. The same procedure applied if the Grand Shariʿa Court of Cairo was uncertain about a point of law.

The result of these statutes and ordinances was that the function of Grand Mufti came to resemble that of Courts of Cassation in French or Dutch law. The task of such courts is to ensure the correct application of the law. Therefore, they rule exclusively on the legal issues of a case without examining the facts established by the lower courts.[52] That the Grand Mufti did not deal with issues of fact is evidenced by a formula frequently found in the FM: "If the situation is as mentioned [in the question]."

50 FM, II, 27 (20 Shawwal 1293).

51 See, for example, FM, I, 222–26 (23 Jumada II 1283), where the Grand Mufti is called upon to settle a dispute between the qadi and the mufti of Dumyat.

52 For Dutch law, see Art. 398 ff. of the Code of Civil Procedure (*Wetboek van Burgerlijke Rechtsvordering*) and Art. 99 of the Law of Judicial Organization (*Wet op de Rechterlijke Organisatie*) that give the Supreme Court (*Hoge Raad*) the authority to nullify decisions of lower courts for being contrary to the law. The Supreme Court, however, must accept the facts as established by the lower court.

4 Al-ʿAbbasi's Attitude toward Innovation and Reform

Al-ʿAbbasi's career coincided with a period of rapid change in Egyptian society. In the 1870s, religious reformers such as Jamal al-Din al-Afghani and Muhammad ʿAbduh began to develop a new jurisprudential methodology in an attempt to adapt Islamic law to contemporary conditions. In a number of instances, especially in the realm of family law, the interpretations of ʿAbduh and likeminded reformers subsequently were adopted by governments and laid down in codes of personal status.[53] In Egypt, as elsewhere in the Muslim world, legal reform to a large extent was brought about by borrowing from other *madhhabs*, whose rulings on a specific issue seemed to be more in conformity with public interest or more suitable for eliminating hardships resulting from the application of the prescriptions of the prevailing *madhhab*. This method is in conformity with Hanafi legal theory. Many Hanafi scholars recognize as valid fatwas issued according to a less authoritative opinion or, in cases of "necessity" (*darura*), according to another *madhhab*. And if the mufti expressly is asked to issue a fatwa according to a *madhhab* other than his own, Hanafi doctrine allows him to do so.[54]

This flexibility enabled muftis to circumvent hardships caused by the enforcement of certain Hanafi rules. The FM contains evidence that this method had been followed prior to the introduction of state legal reform and that people used to have recourse to the law of other *madhhabs* in certain cases. As Grand Mufti, al-ʿAbbasi was asked repeatedly to comment on the legal validity of fatwas not based on authoritative Hanafi opinion. As the following examples indicate, Al-ʿAbbasi consistently rejected such fatwas as invalid and called for the *taʿzir*-punishment of the issuing mufti.

According to Hanafi doctrine, a woman whose husband is absent and does not pay her maintenance (*nafaqa*), cannot obtain a divorce or sue her absent husband for payment. In most modern legislations adopted in Hanafi countries, this position has been replaced by the Maliki (or Shafiʿi) position which holds that failure to provide maintenance contravenes the essence of marriage and therefore is a ground for dissolution by the court, and which allows proceedings upon default. In late nineteenth-century Egypt, women in these circumstances applied to Maliki muftis, demanding fatwas stating that their marriage was dissolved for non-payment of maintenance. Several such cases were submitted to the Grand Mufti, who consistently ruled that these fatwas

53 The first of these codes was the 1917 Ottoman Code of Family Rights.

54 Muhammad Amin Ibn ʿAbidin, "Sharh al-risala al-musammah bi-ʿuqud rasm al-mufti," in *Majmuʿat Rasaʾil Ibn ʿAbidin* (2 vols. Istanbul: Dar Saʿadat, 1907–08 [1325 AH]), I, 50–51.

had no effect because only Hanafi law was applicable.[55] In one case, a Maliki scholar (*ʿalim*) apparently had asked a Hanafi judge for permission to dissolve a marriage according to his own *madhhab*. The judge replied: "If you are going to do so, do it far away from me," which the Maliki interpreted as permission. The Grand Mufti, however, insisted that the Maliki should be punished, because muftis must issue fatwas according to the Hanafi school.[56]

Unlike the other *madhhabs*, the Hanafis do not allow default proceedings. But the Hanafi mufti of the *Majlis al-Ahkam*, al-Sayyid ʿAli Efendi Mahmud al-Baqli, nevertheless issued a fatwa holding that default proceedings were permitted in cases of necessity in order to prevent hardship and to protect people's rights. This fatwa may have been occasioned by the promulgation of the Law of Procedure of the *Majlis Qumisyun Misr* which permitted default proceedings.[57] In response, the Grand Mufti, acting in conjunction with a number of leading ulema,[58] reiterated the Hanafi view; he also argued that al-Baqli's position would result in false testimonies and encourage defaulters to challenge judgments based on default, thereby burdening the government.[59]

A mufti by the name of ʿAmr Abu Zayd from the village of ʿUqba (or ʿAqaba) issued a series of fatwas in which he advanced novel interpretations of the law of repudiation. Some of these, such as the invalidity of a repudiation (*talaq*) reinforcing an oath or of one pronounced against a woman during her menstrual period, and the rule that a repudiation linked to the word *three* has the force of only one repudiation, can be traced to the Zahiri *madhhab* or to the opinions of individual jurists like Ibn Taymiyya.[60] But no such support can be found for his contention that a repudiation is ineffective if pronounced by an angry man, or against a filthy woman not wearing make-up, or against a woman who

55 See, for example, FM, I, 434 (16 Muharram 1278).

56 FM, III, 132 (14 Shaʿban 1266). In other fatwas – all of them regarding phrases expressing a valid repudiation – he ruled that the adoption (*taqlid*) of another *madhhab* was under certain circumstances permitted. See FM, I, 216 (9 Rabiʿ II 1275) and 222–26 (undated). A similar case: FM, I, 219 (21 Ramadan 1281). The extent to which other *madhhabs* were officially recognized in Egypt remains to be examined.

57 Art. 9 of the *Qanun Ruʾyat al-Daʿawi fi Majlis Qumisyun Misr*, issued 29 Jumada II 1278; for the text, see Ahmad Fathi Zaghlul, *al-Muhamah* (Cairo, Matbaʿat al-Maʿarif, 1900), appendix, 85 ff.

58 Shaykh Mustafa Muhammad al-ʿArusi (Shaykh al-Azhar), Shaykh Muhammad al-Damanhuri al-Shafiʿi, Shaykh ʿAbd al-Qadir al-Rafiʿi (*Mufti al-Awqaf*), Mustafa al-Qurashi (*Amin al-Fatwa*).

59 FM, III, 262–65 (22 Jumada II 1284).

60 See Ibn Rushd, *Bidayat al-mujtahid* (2 vols., Cairo: Mustafa al-Babi al-Halabi, 1965), II, 65; J. Brugman, *De betekenis van het Mohammedaanse recht in het hedendaagse Egypte* (Ph.D. diss., University of Leiden, 1960), 97, 99.

is breastfeeding; or that a woman who has been triply divorced during pregnancy becomes lawful for her ex-husband without an intermediate marriage to another man, on the condition that she bears him a son. The Grand Mufti ruled that the government must punish this ignoramus and prevent him from issuing fatwas.[61]

From these examples it is clear that the Grand Mufti cannot be regarded as an innovator. His first concern was the uniform application of the Shariʿa in strict conformity with the most authoritative opinions of the Hanafi School. This he did with a rigour that transcended the requirements of the Hanafi doctrine regarding the mufti's profession, as we have seen above. According to Hanafi legal theory, muftis have more freedom than qadis in the selection of legal opinions as a basis for their opinions, because qadis must abide by the instructions of the rulers.[62] In Egypt, the qadis were instructed by khedival decrees to pass sentence according to the most authoritative opinions of the Hanafi *madhhab*.[63] What the Grand Mufti attempted to do was to complete the Hanafitization of Egyptian law by putting the muftis on a par with the qadis and barring them from giving fatwas according to other *madhhabs*.

5 Conclusion

During the second half of the nineteenth century the office of Grand Mufti acquired increasing authority, largely as a result of the better organization and bureaucratization of the Egyptian state, within which all agencies and

61 FM, V, 91 (28 Dhu al-Qaʿda 1265).

62 See Muhammad Amin Ibn ʿAbidin, *Radd al-Muhtar* (5 vols., Bulaq: Dar al-Tibaʿa al-Misriyya, 1881–82 [1299 AH]), I, 56.

63 According to Art. 2 of the Qadis' Ordinance of 1856, judgments must be given according to the correct opinions within the Hanafi *madhhab* (*al-aqwal al-sahiha min madhhab al-imam al-aʿzam Abu Hanifa*). Art. 10 of the 1880 Shariʿa Courts' Ordinance requires qadis to follow the most authoritative opinions (*arjah al-aqwal*) within the Hanafi *madhhab*, which by that time already was standard practice. The qadis interpreted Art. 10 as requiring them to apply only Abu Hanifa's opinions, despite the fact that "a most authoritative opinion" included one held by one of Abu Hanifa's students (*ashab*) that was accepted within the *madhhab*. For examples, see Ibn ʿAbidin, "Sharh ʿuqud rasm al-mufti," I, 35. That the Egyptian qadis felt bound to apply Abu Hanifa's opinions exclusively is clear from a criminal decree issued by the *Majlis al-Ahkam* in 1858 which establishes, exceptionally, that in cases of willful homicide the opinions of Abu Yusuf and al-Shaybani are to be applied, because they offer a wider definition of willful homicide for which retaliation may be demanded. For the text of the decree, see Sami, *Taqwim al-Nil*, III/1, 294–97 (Muharram 1275); see also R. Peters, "Murder on the Nile: Homicide Trials in 19th Century Egyptian Shariʿa Courts," *Welt des Islams* 30 (1990), 98–116.

functions acquired a distinct competence and hierarchical position. This process had three related effects on the office of the Grand Mufti. First, its competence, which previously rested largely on custom, was more precisely defined in written statutes. Second, the office of Grand Mufti was placed at the top of a hierarchy of muftis who were officially assigned to the courts of justice and to state agencies such as the Bayt al-Mal, the Waqf Administration, the *Majlis al-Ahkam*, and the Cairo Police Department; the aim of this hierarchical structure was to ensure the uniform and consistent application of the Shariʿa. The presence of official muftis in these agencies reflects the growing need for uniform administrative procedures, a need that was satisfied in part by compliance with the Shariʿa. At the same time, muftis who were not appointed by the Government were forbidden to issue fatwas on legal matters contrary to Hanafi doctrine (they might still issue fatwas on ritual matters), and sanctions were instituted to ensure compliance with this policy. Third, opinions issued by the Grand Mufti in certain circumstances were made binding and he acquired the authority to act as a court of cassation. Local qadis were encouraged to consult officially appointed muftis and, in cases of uncertainty, the Grand Mufti himself, whose opinions in such cases, as laid down in the 1880 Shariʿa Courts Ordinance, had the force of law. The same Ordinance accorded the Grand Mufti the authority to act as a court of appeal in cases of misapplication of the Shariʿa. Situated at the top of the hierarchy of the Shariʿa judiciary, charged with the task of ensuring the uniform application of the Shariʿa, and legally bound to apply the most authoritative opinion of the Hanafi *madhhab*, he was in no position to introduce legal reforms and innovative legal doctrine, even if he wished to do so.

CHAPTER 3

Islamic and Secular Criminal Law in Nineteenth-Century Egypt

The Role and Function of the Qadi

1 Introduction

The legal history of Ottoman Egypt is still very much virgin territory. There are only a few studies dealing with the topic. Based on solid archival research, the publications of Farahat[1] and El-Nahal[2] have contributed much to our understanding of the operation of the Egyptian legal system during the Ottoman period prior to the nineteenth century. For the nineteenth century, however, no such research has been undertaken yet. Studies of nineteenth-century Egyptian law[3] are based on the texts of enacted laws as found in Zaghlul's *Muhamat*,[4] Jallad's *Qamus*[5] and Amin Sami's *Taqwim al-Nil*,[6] and not on court records. The only exception is a case study by Toledano of an 1854 theft case in Cairo that provides insight into procedural matters relating to the investigation of crimes by the police. Due to the nature of his source – police records – Toledano does not pay attention to the court proceedings.[7] In this essay I want to shed light on Shariʿa justice in criminal matters in nineteenth-century Egypt by examining the qadi's role in such matters and analyzing the relationship between the religious courts and the other judicial bodies that dealt with criminal cases. I will do so relying on the texts of the various criminal codes enacted

1 Muhammad Nur Farahat, *Al-tarikh al-ijtimaʿi liʾl-qanun fi Misr al-haditha*, 2nd impr. (Cairo: Dar Suʿad al-Sabah, 1993).

2 Galal H. El-, *The Judicial Administration of Ottoman Egypt in the Seventeenth Century* (Minneapolis: Bibliotheca Islamica, 1979).

3 Gabriel Baer, "Tanzimat in Egypt: the Penal Code" in idem, *Studies in the Social History of Modern Egypt* (Chicago: University of Chicago Press., 1969), pp. 109–33; idem, "The transition from traditional to Western criminal law in Turkey and Egypt," *Studia Islamica* 45 (1977), 139–58.

4 Ahmad Fathi Zaghlul, *Al-Muhamat* (Cairo: Matbaʿat al-Maʿarif, 1900).

5 Filib Jallad, *Qamus al-idara waʾl-qadaʾ*, 5 vols. (Alexandria: al-Matbaa al-Bukhariyya, 1890–95).

6 Sami Amin, *Taqwim al-Nil*, 3 vols. (Cairo: Matbaʿat al-Kutub al-Misriyya, 1928–36).

7 E.R. Toledano, "Law, Practice, and Social Reality: A Theft Case in Cairo in 1954," in *Studies in Islamic Society: Contributions in Memory of Gabriel Baer*, ed. G.R. Warburg and G.G. Gilbar (Haifa: Haifa University Press, 1984), pp. 153–175.

 | DOI:10.1163/9789004420625_004

during the nineteenth century, on the relevant decrees, and on court records found in the Egyptian archives (*Dar al-Watha'iq al-Qawmiyya* [DWQ] and *Dar al-Mahfuzat* [DM]).[8]

What Westerners regard as criminal law is treated in the *fiqh* under three separate categories: Qur'anic crimes (*hudud*); offenses against the person (*qisas* or *jinayat*); and the discretionary power of state authorities (including the qadi) to punish sinful behavior and acts that endanger the security of the state or infringe upon public order (*ta'zir* and *siyasa*). The first two categories, which are dealt with exhaustively in the *fiqh* books, belong exclusively to the domain of the qadi. Because of the narrow definitions of these crimes, the strict rules of evidence and the importance of the notion of *shubha* (mistake, uncertainty, doubt), it is in general difficult to obtain convictions for such offenses. Therefore the third domain, which is not treated in detail in the *fiqh* books, is of considerable importance. Here the authorities – the qadi or the administrative and executive officials – have a large measure of freedom. The state often issued decrees (*qanun*) in this field, not for the sake of its subjects, but to provide guidance for qadis and other officials charged with the trying of criminals.

On the basis of their examination of pre-nineteenth-century Shari'a court records, Farahat and El Nahal have shown that in Ottoman Egypt the Shari'a was the law of the land and that it was applied by the qadi in criminal matters as well as in other areas. According to Farahat, the qadi was competent whenever there were private parties, i.e., a plaintiff and a defendant. Moreover, in cases involving *ta'zir* offenses, the qadi often acted as an examining magistrate, and he would present a report of the facts of the case to the administrative

8 The DM houses the records of the provincial shari'a courts and, from 1870, also the Cairo shari'a court of first instance (*Mahkamat Misr al-ibtida'iyya al-shar'iyya*). I have examined *sijills* from both the capital and the provinces. In the DWQ, the richest series of *sijills* from the point of view of legal history are those of the *Majlis al-Ahkam* (Sin/7). For this essay I have used mainly the series Sin/7/26 (*Sadir wa-warid qalam al-'ulama' al-shar'i*), which contains 20 *sijills* from 1274 to 1276 and from 1291 to 1305. The *Qalam al-'ulama' al-shar'i* or "The Legal Bureau of 'ulama'" was staffed by the qadi of Cairo, his deputy (*na'ib*), the Grand Mufti, and the members of the MA who were 'ulama'. They examined sentences of lower shari'a courts and referred them back to the original court if they found irregularities. A similar series that I also used is Sin/7/31 (*Qayd al-i'lamat al-shar'iyya*), which contains ten *sijills*, from 1270 to 1272 and from 1279 to 1292. Here the sentences of the lower shari'a courts were examined only by the mufti of the MA. It is not clear on what grounds shari'a sentences were sent to the MA. In view of the large proportion of sentences dealing with cases of violent death, it is plausible that all such cases were submitted for examination. Shari'a court records are in general very succinct: they identify parties by their names, occasionally mention their profession, but do not mention residence or age.

authorities, who would prosecute the suspect. Administrative and military agents such as the *wali* or governor of Egypt, the *kushshaf* or provincial governors, and police officers dealt directly with crimes relating to public order or the security of the state.[9] This was in conformity with the legal system that was in force in other parts of the Ottoman Empire.[10] In Egypt, this system changed during the nineteenth century. The punitive power of the administrative agencies was gradually delegated to specialized councils that applied criminal codes enacted by the State, and qadis ceased to act as examining judges with regard to *taʿzir* offenses. Thus, a dual judiciary – part religious and part secular – came into existence, each part with its own rules. Whereas most offenses were tried by the secular councils, some crimes, such as homicide, were dealt with under both systems and others were heard exclusively by the qadi. This situation lasted until the judicial reforms of 1883, which put an end to the qadi's competence in criminal cases.[11] In the following I define the role of the qadi in criminal matters and explain the function of his office in the Egyptian legal system prior to 1883.

2 Egyptian Nineteenth-Century Criminal Legislation

Although Egypt was part of the Ottoman Empire, its rulers had a large measure of freedom to enact legislation. During the first half of the nineteenth century, Egyptian legislation developed independently of the Ottoman metropole. The Ottoman Criminal Code of 1840 does not seem to have had any impact on early Egyptian criminal legislation.[12]

Although the Ottoman firman of 1841, issued after Mehmed ʿAli's defeat by the British and the Ottomans, established that Ottoman legislation henceforth would be applicable in Egypt, this provision remained a dead letter until 1852, when the Ottoman Criminal Code, with some additions, was enacted in Egypt.[13] However, this remained an exception, for, subsequently, Egyptian legal reform

9 See, for example, Farahat, *Tarikh*, pp. 352–54, 467–82.

10 Uriel Heyd, *Studies in Old Ottoman Criminal Law*, ed. V.L. Ménage (Oxford: Oxford University Press, 1973), pp. 254–57.

11 Not implemented in Upper Egypt until 1889.

12 Text in A. Akgündüz, *Mukayeseli Islâm ve Osmanlı hukuku külliyatı* (Diyarbakir: 1986), pp. 809–20; see further Ehud R. Toledano, "The Legislative Process in the Ottoman Empire in the Early *Tanzimat* Period: A Footnote," *International Journal of Turkish Studies* 1 (1980), pp. 99–106; and Halil Cin and Ahmet Akgündüz, *Türk Islâm hukuk tarihi*, 1. Cilt (Istanbul: Timaş Yayınları, 1990), p. 343.

13 Baer, "Tanzimat," p. 111.

continued to follow its own course, independent of the central Ottoman government.

During the nineteenth century Egyptian rulers issued the following legislation in criminal matters.[14]

1. Penal decree of 21 Rabiʿ I 1245/1829 concerning murder, highway robbery, counterfeiting, extortion by officials, theft, and embezzlement.[15]
2. *Qanun al-Filaha* or "The Code of Agriculture" (henceforth QF), issued in Shaʿban 1245 AH/1830 and numbering 55 articles that dealt mainly with crimes and offenses connected with agriculture and village life and aimed at disciplining the rural population and the officials serving in rural areas. It also provided the peasants with some protection against the arbitrary measures of their village shaykhs and district commissioners. The *Qanun al-Filaha* forms the first part of the *Qanun al-Muntakhabat*, a codification of penal laws printed in 1844 (see next item).
3. A number of other laws issued between 1830 and 1844, all included in the *Qanun al-Muntakhabat* or "Code of Selected (Enactments)" (henceforth QM). They deal with the maintenance of dams and dikes (arts. 76–80, 87–97, 199), the duties of officials (*Qanun al-Siyasatname* or "Code of Administration," also called *Qanun al-Siyasa al-Mulkiyya* or "Code of Civil Administration"), (arts. 56–75, 81–86, 98–102, 195, 200, 202, 203), and a number of general crimes (arts. 122–194, 196–197 QM). Of these, arts. 122–194 are rather clumsy translations from the French *Code Pénal* of 1810, arranged in a different order with little apparent system. The last section of the QM contains some articles dealing with the Alexandria prison and the execution of prison sentences (arts. 198, 201).[16]
4. The Pénal Code of 1265/1849 (henceforth PC49) containing 90 articles, most taken from the Qanun al-Muntakhabat.[17]
5. Al-Qanunname al-Sultani (henceforth QS), also called al-Qanunname al-Humayuni, promulgated in 1852. The introduction of this new code

14 On the character of this legislation, see Baer, "Transition," and R. Peters, "The Codification of Criminal Law in 19th Century Egypt: Tradition or Modernization?" in *Law, Society, and National Identity in Africa*, ed. J.M. Abun-Nasr, et al. (Hamburg: Buske, 1990) (Beitrage zur Afrikaforschung, 1), pp. 211–225.

15 DWQ, Sin/2/40 (*Diwan Khediwi Turki, Daftar qayd al-khulasat*), sijill 23, 21 Rabiʿ I, 1245, pp. 12–14. There is another draft in sijill 12, p. 1. The meaning of both texts is identical, but the wording is different. It appears that the text in sijill 23, which was formulated later and whose style is more polished, is the final text. The Arabic text in Zaghlul (pp. 163–64), differs on many points from the Turkish original and is spurious.

16 Text in Zaghlul, *Muhamat*, pp. 100–55 and in Jallad, *Qamas*, III, pp. 351–78.

17 *Qanun al-ʿUqubat* (Bulaq: Dar al-Tibaʿa al-ʿAmira al-Misriyya, 8 Rajab 1265 [30 May 1849]), 41 pp. Turkish text, 43 pp. Arabic text.

> was the result of negotiations between the Governor of Egypt and the Ottoman government about the application of Ottoman legislation in Egypt.[18] The first three chapters are largely identical with the Ottoman Penal Code of 1851. To these, two chapters were added containing provisions taken from previous Egyptian penal legislation.[19] In 1858 a decree of the Majlis al-Ahkam was issued to complement the code.[20]

In his publications on Egyptian criminal legislation, Gabriel Baer assumed that the penal code published in 1875 by the Ministry of Justice (*Nazarat al-Haqqaniyya*),[21] which was based on the Ottoman and French Criminal Codes, replaced *al-Qanunname al-Sultani*.[22] This code, however, was one of the codes that had been drafted by Jacques Maunoury, a French lawyer from Alexandria, for the Mixed Courts that were established in the same year.[23] The records of the *Majlis al-Ahkam* show that the judicial councils (*majalis*) continued to apply the QS.[24]

3 Development of the Judiciary

3.1 *The Secular Court System*

The councils created during the nineteenth century to enforce criminal legislation were called *majalis* or councils instead of *mahakim* or law courts in order to emphasize their position as part of the executive. These councils did not form an independent judiciary and were staffed by administrators. Before execution, sentences issued by these councils had to be approved by the Viceroy, who could change these decisions at his will.

At the beginning of Mehmed ʿAli's reign, serious offenses such as murder, high treason, or theft were tried in Cairo by *al-Diwan al-Khediwi* or, from 1240/1825–1254/1839, by *al-Majlis al-ʿAli al-Mulki* (Supreme Civil Council).

18 See Baer, "Tanzimat." Baer (p. 119) assumed that the code was not enforced until 1854. However, the court records indicate that it was already applied in 1853. See DWQ, Sin/7/47/8 (Qayd sadir al-khulasat, Turki, 7 Dhu l-Hijja 1269–21 Rajab 1270).

19 Text in Zaghul, *Muhamat*, appendix, pp. 156–78 and Jallad, *Qamus*, II, pp. 90–102.

20 Decree of the *Majlis al-Ahkam*, dated 25 Muharram 1275 (4 September 1858). Text in Sami, *Taqwim*, 3/1, pp. 294–97.

21 *Qanun al-ʿUqubat* (Cairo: Matbaʿat Bulaq, 1292/1875), 70 pp.

22 Baer, "Tanzimat," p. 118; Baer, "Transformation," passim.

23 This penal code was never put into force because the competence of the Mixed Courts in criminal matters was restricted to offenses against judges and other personnel of these courts. See J. Brugman, *De betekenis van het Mohammedaanse recht in het hedendaagse Egypte* ('s-Gravenhage: 1960), pp. 38–39.

24 See, for example, DWQ, Sin/7/10/134 (Majlis al-Ahkam, madabit sadira), 27 Ramadan–25 Shawwal 1296 [Aug.–Sept. 1879].

These were administrative councils, and the trial of crimes was only part of their duties. Less serious offenses committed in Cairo were dealt with by a police officer at the police station or by the government department in which the perpetrator was employed.[25] Outside Cairo local administrative officials tried petty criminals.

In 1258/1842 a special judicial council, called *al-Jamʿiyya al-Haqqaniyya*, was established in Cairo.[26] In addition to prosecuting serious crimes in first instance, this council also acted as a court of appeal from the decisions of lower authorities. In 1265/1849 it was replaced by the *Majlis al-Ahkam*, which exercised exactly the same functions and remained in existence – with the exception of two short intervals – until 1889.[27] These councils had to send their decisions to the Khedive for final approval. The authorities had an ambivalent attitude toward appeal in criminal matters. On the one hand, the right of appeal was regarded as a necessary remedy against miscarriage of justice by the lower instances; on the other hand, it was looked upon as an inconvenient tool in the hands of troublesome offenders. The latter attitude is reflected in art. 23 of the Penal Code of 1849:

> With the exception of the crime of murder and crimes that can be punished with forced labor or incarceration, criminal cases shall be heard by the provincial administration (*mudiriyya*) in accordance with the regulations. If someone submits a petition to the *Majlis al-Ahkam* complaining of having been unjustly treated by the provincial administration during his trial, the case shall be tried again by the *Majlis al-Ahkam*. If the sentence is found to be in order, the petitioner's punishment shall be doubled; if it is found that he was indeed treated unjustly, justice shall be done.

At the lower level, regional councils were created with the introduction of the QS in 1852–53. These councils also dealt with serious crimes. Their sentences were reviewed by the *Majlis al-Ahkam*, which then submitted them to

25 J. Deny, *Sommaire des archives turques du Caire* (Cairo: Institut francais d'archéologie orientale), 1930, p. 114.

26 The functions and duties of this council were regulated in the *La'ihat tartib al-Jamʿiyya al-Haqqaniyya*, in five articles and a concluding section. Text in *Muhamat*, appendix, pp. 27–31.

27 The duties of the *Majlis al-Ahkam* were regulated in the *La'ihat Majlis al-Ahkam al-ʿAli al-Misriyya*, issued 5 Rabiʿ II 1265, containing twelve articles. Text in Zaghlul, *Muhamat*, appendix, pp. 63–66. See also Deny, *Sommaire*, pp. 123–24. The council must have been created and named after the example of the Ottoman *Meclis-i Vala-yi Ahkam-i ʿAdliye* or "The Supreme Council of Justice", established in 1838, which also had judicial and legislative powers. Cf. Toledano, "The Legislative Process in the Ottoman Empire," pp. 99–106.

the Viceregal Cabinet (*al-Maʿiyya al-Saniyya*) for ratification and execution. In 1865, a new tier was created between the *Majlis al-Ahkam* and the regional councils by the establishment of two courts of appeal (*majlis al-istiʾnaf*), one in Cairo and one in Alexandria. Six years later, in 1871, three more courts of appeal were set up. In the same year the base of the judicial pyramid was expanded by the creation of local councils in small towns. Thus a system of four tiers came into existence with the *Majlis al-Ahkam* at the top acting as a supreme court that checked whether the lower councils correctly applied the laws. But this newly created hierarchical judiciary remained subordinate to the Khedive.

3.2 *The Shariʿa Courts*

The creation of this hierarchical secular judiciary did not displace the Shariʿa courts. Shariʿa justice developed along lines comparable to what happened to the organization of secular justice: greater bureaucratization, more precise legal circumscription of jurisdiction, and the creation of a hierarchy. This development began in 1856. Until then, the qadis were appointed by the Porte and were part of the Ottoman religious judiciary. In February 1856, Saʿid (r. 1854–1863) reached an agreement with the Porte to the effect that the appointment of Egyptian qadis, with the exception of the qadi of Cairo, was to be his prerogative.[28] In the same year the first Qadis' Ordinance was issued.[29] After the Egyptianization of Shariʿa justice, the embryonic hierarchy that had existed until then was developed further.

According to the strict rules of the Shariʿa, appeal from a qadi's decision is not possible. In practice, however, there usually was some way of remedying unjust or unfounded decisions of qadis.[30] During the first half of the century, there were two categories of judges in Egypt: qadis and deputy qadis (*naʾibs*); the latter administered the law in smaller locales. The *Qanun al-Filaha* of 1830 introduced (or confirmed) some form of appeal in art. 22: against the decisions of the *naʾibs* appeal could be lodged to the qadi, whereas the assembly of ʿulamaʾ (*al-Majlis al-ʿIlmi*), a body consisting of prominent ʿulamaʾ in the capital heard appeals against the decisions of qadis:

> If a village shaykh or a peasant goes to the qadi for the trial of a case, and if he thinks that the qadi has deviated from what is just (*al-haqq*) and acted unjustly, or if the qadi has taken more money from the people than

28 See Baer, "Tanzimat," p. 131.

29 Decree of 28 Rabiʿ II 1273 (26 December 1856). Text in Jallad, *Qamus*, IV, pp. 129–31.

30 See D.S. Powers, "On Judicial Review in Islamic Law," *Law and Society Review*, 26, 2 (1992), pp. 315–41.

> the official fee, then, if he is a *na'ib*, the case shall be brought before the qadi of the provincial capital (*al-bandar*). If, however, he [viz., the person who first heard the case] is the officially appointed qadi (*al-qadi sahib al-mansib*), then the case shall be brought before the most important 'ulama') of that region for investigation. Both the sentence of the first qadi and the sentence of the 'ulama' must be written down. The report must be submitted to the *Diwan Khediwi* in order that its clerk (*ma'mur*) can submit it to the venerable 'ulama' of the capital so that they can examine both sentences. They will be requested to provide the final verdict.

The same article was repeated in the Penal Code of 1849 (art. 56). Apparently, however, there were other remedies against incorrect judgments given by qadis. An official document from 1844 dealing with the competence of various councils mentions that parties could complain against such sentences to *al-Jam'iyya al-Haqqaniyya*.[31]

The Qadis' Ordinance of 1856 (*La'ihat al-qudat*) does not mention the possibility of appeal but recommends the consultation of muftis and 'ulama' (art. 21). In practice the sentences of qadis usually were checked by muftis appointed to the courts.[32] Important decisions were also checked by the mufti of the *Majlis al-Al-Ahkam* or by a council of 'ulama' connected with it. If the local qadi and mufti disagreed, it became customary to submit the case to the Grand Mufti, whose fatwa in those cases was authoritative. Finally, in 1880 the new Shari'a Courts Ordinance (*La'ihat al-Mahakim al-Shar'iyya*)[33] introduced a hierarchical judiciary. Through the Ministry of Justice, parties could appeal to the Cairo Shari'a Court against decisions of provincial qadis and *na'ibs*. Against sentences of the Courts of Cairo and Alexandria appeal was open to the Shaykh al-Azhar and the Grand Mufti,[34] to whom, at the discretion of the Ministry of Justice, other persons could be added (art. 3). Further, judges were to consult the muftis appointed to their courts whenever a case was not totally clear to them. If the problem was not solved, the case had to be submitted to the Grand Mufti, whose fatwa was binding on the qadi (art. 22).

31 *Bayan al-mawadd allati sayir 'anha al-isti'dhan bi'l-diwan al-khediwi ma 'ada al-dawawin* (Bulaq: 1260/1844), 22 pp. Arabic and 22 pp. Turkish text, art. 53.

32 On the role and function of muftis in nineteenth-century Egypt, see my "The Fatwas of Muhammad al-'Abbasi al-Mahdi (d. 1897), Grand Mufti of Egypt and his *al-Fatawa al-Mahdiyya*," *Islamic Law and Society* 1 (1994), pp. 66–81.

33 Text in Jallad, *Qamus*, IV, pp. 1665–76.

34 At the time of promulgation of this decree, both offices were occupied by the same person, Muhammad al-'Abbasi al-Mahdi.

All these measures indicate that until 1883, when French inspired legal codes were introduced in Egypt, there was no tendency to restrict the application of Islamic law. On the contrary, the government seems to have been keen on creating a legal system that would ensure the correct application of Hanafi law. Some Egyptian statesmen at that time, including Khedive Isma'il, opposed the rash adoption of foreign law, and there was a tendency, at least in the domain of civil law, to use the Shari'a as one or even the exclusive source of inspiration for legal reform.[35] That this might have been a viable option is demonstrated by the Ottoman *Mecelle*, enacted gradually between 1870 and 1877, which codified Hanafi civil law and was applied by secular courts. The wholesale reception of foreign law in Egypt beginning in 1883 must therefore be attributed to strong foreign pressure.

4 The Qadi's Competence in Criminal Matters

4.1 *Introduction*

The various penal codes and decrees regulating the administration of Shari'a justice mention several offenses that are to be referred specifically to the qadi. Such offenses, however, were not heard by the qadi alone. As a rule, most criminal cases for which the qadi was competent were tried first by the qadi and then by the secular authorities. With regard to homicide, this procedure is established in *al-Qanunname al-Sultani*. Ch. 1, arts. 2 and 3 state that these cases shall be tried before the regional council, in the presence of the qadi. First, the qadi deals with the Shari'a aspects of the case, applying the Shari'a rules on evidence. Then the Council tries the case according to the penal code, which allowed much more freedom in considering evidence. The following case, tried in the provincial council of Alexandria in 1860, illustrates how this system worked:

> Three girls were on their way home after having picked beans and grains. When they passed the timber yard of Khawaga Loria, they saw an ostrich walking there. One of the girls, 'Ayida, age ten, went to the ostrich and touched it to feel its feathers. At that moment a Nubian appeared and took hold of the girl. He beat her and hit her in her stomach until she fell down. Thereupon he left. One of the girls stayed with her, while the

35 Brugman, *Betekenis*, p. 39 (with regard to Nubar Pasha), p. 44 (with regard to Isma'il); Byron Cannon, *Politics of Law and the Courts in Nineteenth-Century Egypt* (Salt Lake City: University of Utah Press, 1988), p. 134 (Muhammad Qadri Pasha), p. 153 (for the Assembly during the 'Urabi Revolt).

other went to fetch her mother. The mother found the girl still alive and took her in her arms, but then the girl died. She brought the body to the police station. An officer went with the girls to the timber yard, where they found the Nubian, who denied any responsibility for the death of the girl. Nevertheless he was arrested. The post mortem examination at the hospital showed that the victim had died as a result of the blows she had received. The mother sued the Nubian before the qadi, demanding the death penalty, but she was not able to prove her claim since no adult witnesses had been present. Therefore the qadi had to dismiss the case. The case was then heard by the Diwan of the Governorate (*Muhafaza*), where the Nubian was sentenced to three years at forced labor in the Alexandrian Dockyards (*liman*) – on the strength of the testimony of the two girls, the man's admission that he was in charge of the ostrich, and the medical report.[36]

In the following I shall list the types of cases which, according to the various codes, were first dealt with by the qadi and then, as a rule, tried before the secular councils.

4.2 *Homicide (qatl)*[37]

Apart from unqualified homicide,[38] the codes refer the following homicide-related offenses to the qadi:

- death caused by an official who exceeds the fixed number of lashes or administers them at lethal spots (*maqatil*);[39]
- the killing of an official collecting taxes;[40] armed resistance against an official resulting in his death;[41]
- infanticide;[42]

---

36 DWQ, Lam/3/28/1 (*Muhafazat al-Iskandariyya, daftar qayd al-daʿawi bi-majlis al-muhafaza*) p. 211, 3 Safar, 1277. Interestingly, the Diwan mentions an incorrect art. of the QS – viz., Ch. 3, Art. 21, dealing with certain forms of complicity to murder – as a basis for the conviction. This indicates that these councils were staffed not with jurists but with administrators who possessed a limited knowledge of the law.

37 On the prosecution of homicide in nineteenth-century Egypt, see Rudolph Peters, "Murder on the Nile: Homicide Trials in 19th Century Egyptian Shariʿa Courts," *Die Welt des Islams* 30 (1990), pp. 95–115 and idem, "Who Killed (Abd Allah al-Ghazza: A Murder Trial Before a Nineteenth Century Egyptian Qadi," in *Amsterdam Middle Eastern Studies*, ed. M. Woidich (Wiesbaden: Reichert Verlag, 1990), pp. 84–98.

38 201 QM; 1/2, 1/3, 1/9, 1/11, 1/13 QS.

39 25 QF; 60 QM; 39, 46 PC49.

40 40 47 PC49; 26 QF.

41 1/16 QS.

42 50 CP49; 30 QF; 5/4 QS.

Court records indicate that all cases of violent death were brought before the qadi in order to determine whether death was the result of circumstances beyond anyone's control (*bi'l-qada' wa-qadar*) or the result of the actions of another person. In the latter case, the victim's heirs could summon the perpetrator and demand the death penalty or financial compensation. The qadi then would seek to determine whether the defendant had killed the victim with criminal intent, in which case – if all other legal requirements were satisfied – he would sentence the defendant to capital punishment as retribution (*qisas*). Such a sentence would be carried out after review by *al-Jam'iyya al-Haqqaniyya* – or, after 1849, by the *Majlis al-Ahkam* – and authorization by the Viceroy. If the qadi ruled otherwise, e.g., if he sentenced the defendant to pay blood money (which often was paid not by the offender but by his *'aqila* or solidarity group), or if he acquitted him for lack of evidence or as a result of pardon granted to the defendant by the victim's heirs, the council would try the defendant again according to the penal code and, if it found him guilty, sentence him to forced labor.

Offenses against the foetus were also regarded as falling in the first place within the competence of the qadi. In this connection, the codes refer to the following offenses:
- miscarriage as a result of a quarrel;[43]
- induced abortion.[44]

With regard to miscarriage and abortion the qadi could sentence the defendant to the payment of blood money for the foetus (*ghurra*, one twentieth of the blood money of a free man), and/or to a *ta'zir* punishment such as imprisonment or flogging. If such a sentence was pronounced, the council would not hear the case again.

4.3 *Wounding and Grievous Bodily Harm (Jarh)*

In addition to unqualified infliction of wounds and grievous bodily harm,[45] the codes refer the following specific offenses to the qadi:
- brawls in which someone is wounded and as a result is unable to work for at least twenty days;[46]
- assault and battery of an official collecting taxes;[47]

43 28 QF; 49 PC49; 5/3 QS.

44 52 PC49; 5/5 QS.

45 Art. 6 of the second *dhayl* or supplement (entitled *'an al-aqlam allati sar 'ilawatuha bi'l-majlis*) to the Qadis' Ordinance of 1856. Text in Jallad, *Qamus*, IV, p. 1654.

46 43 PC49.

47 7 QF; 53 PC49.

- assault and battery of an official or village shaykh during a rebellion of peasants.[48]

The procedure in cases of the infliction of wounds or grievous bodily harm is analogous to the one followed in homicide. The qadi must first establish whether the injuries were inflicted with criminal intent, in which case, under certain conditions, he might sentence the defendant to suffer similar injuries as retribution (*qisas*). Otherwise he could sentence the defendant to the payment of financial compensation (called *arsh* or *hukuma*). As we shall see, no *qisas*-sentences for wounding were carried out in nineteenth-century Egypt. In general, cases of wounding and bodily harm were subsequently tried by the council according to statute law.

4.4 *Offenses against a Person's Honor (Hatk ʿird)*

Offenses against a person's honor were often of a sexual nature. The codes mention [illegal] defloration (*izalat bakarat bint*)[49] as one such offense that was to be dealt with by the qadi, who could prosecute it both as a specific type of tort (viz., unlawful sexual intercourse) for which the defendant could be condemned to pay damages, in this case the proper bride wealth (*mahr al-mithl*), and as a criminal offense for which the perpetrator might suffer capital punishment, flogging or imprisonment. The general rule in Hanafi law is that in cases of unlawful intercourse, if proven, the defendant is condemned either to the *hadd* penalty or, if he pleads mistake or uncertainty (*shubha*), to the payment of the proper bride wealth. Application of *taʿzir*, however, does not exclude the liability for the proper bride wealth. In the court records, I have seen no cases in which the defendant was sentenced to the *hadd* penalty of lapidation and there is no evidence that this punishment was enforced in nineteenth-century Egypt.[50] Sometimes the criminal aspect of illegal defloration was dealt with not by the qadi but by the secular councils.

48 14 PC49.

49 16 QF; 44 PC49.

50 My sample covers the period between 1853 and 1870:

DM: Makhzan 46: ʿayn 22 (Mahkamat Misr al-ibtidaʾiyya al-sharʿiyya, dabtiyyat al-murafaʿat), sijill 1238 (1285–1287); ʿayn 159 (Mahkamat Asyut al-ibtidaʾiyya al-sharʿiyya, Madabit al-murafaʿat), sijill 141 (1273–1276), 142 (1274–1276), 147 (1282), 148 (1282–1284); ʿayn 142 (Mahkamat al-Mansura al-ibtidaʾiyya al-sharʿiyya, Madabit al-murafaʿat), sijill 281 (1273–1274), 282 (1273), 286 (1279–1280).

DWQ: Sin/7/26 (Majlis al-Ahkam, Sadir wa-warid qalam al-ʿulamaʾ al-sharʿi), sijill 1 (1273), 2 (1274), 3 (1274–1275), 4 (1275); Sin/7/31 (Majlis al-Ahkam, Qayd al-iʿlamat al-sharʿiyya), sijill 1 (1270), 3 (1279), 4 (1280), 5 (1280–81). 304/1887)).

Defamation, or, more precisely, unfounded accusation of fornication (*qadhf*),[51] was also referred to the qadi, who treated it as a *hadd* offense for which the offender could be given eighty lashes. Finally, the qadi typically dealt with quarrels involving beating (*darb, mudaraba*) or abuse (*mushatama, qawl su'*),[52] for which he would impose *ta'zir* in the form of flogging on a guilty party.

4.5 *Offenses against a Person's Property*

The qadi often dealt with theft, despite the fact that none of the codes refers such cases to him. Since the qadi was competent in matters of ownership, he heard lawsuits concerning the revindication of stolen property. Apart from passing judgment on the issue of ownership in such cases, the qadi would pronounce on the applicability of the *hadd* punishment, invariably specifying that there were no grounds for the application of the punishment of amputation; as a rule, he would impose flogging as a *ta'zir* penalty. Only in 1880 did the Ministry of Interior decree that henceforth cases of theft were to be tried not by qadis but by the councils, on the basis of statute law, and that property claims resulting from theft were to be settled before the qadi only after the state authorities had investigated the matter.[53]

The *Qanun al-Filaha* mentions one specific offense against property, viz., maltreatment of a person's animal out of spite against the owner.[54] In such cases the qadi must adjudicate damages, while the state authorities would impose a punishment of one hundred lashes.

4.6 *Offenses against Public Order*

Public drunkenness, the only offense against the public order that is referred to the qadi,[55] is punishable by the *hadd* penalty of flogging; according to *al-Qanunname al-Sultani*, this punishment may be applied only if the drunkard is noisy and picks a quarrel with people, or attacks them in the marketplace. In my sample of qadis' sentences I have seen no conviction for drunkenness and I suspect that offenses relating to drunkenness were dealt with summarily by the police.

51 48 PC49; QS 2/1.

52 16 QF; 44 PC49; 28 *Dhayl La'ihat al-qudat* (1856); 2/1 and 7 QS.

53 Decree of Ministry of Interior (*Nazarat al-Dakhiliyya*) of 20 Muharram 1297 (3 January 1880). Jallad, *Qamus*, IV, 145.

54 33 QF; 51 PC49.

55 QS 2/5.

5 The Function of Islamic Justice and the Role of the Qadi in Criminal Matters

5.1 *Adjudicating Private Claims Resulting from Offenses*

Private claims resulting from offenses are either punitive or financial. The latter, such as claims for blood money, damages or revendication of stolen property, are related to the civil law aspect of the offense and belong to the field of private rather than criminal law.

Punitive claims are based on retribution (*qisas*) for murder and wounding. I have the impression that only the qadi had the authority to pronounce a death sentence subsequent to the introduction of *al-Qanunname al-Sultani*. Retribution for bodily harm was not applied in Egypt. If a qadi felt that there were grounds for such a sentence, a higher court or mufti always found arguments to quash such a sentence, as in the following case from 1862:

> During a fight between two men, one of them took hold of the other's leg. The latter fell down and broke his forearm in such a way that it seemed to be attached to the rest of the body only by the skin. The victim was brought to the hospital where his forearm was amputated from the elbow. He then sued his adversary, who was condemned by the qadi of al-Mansura to pay blood money for the loss of an arm, half of the blood money for the life of a free man. The mufti of the *Majlis al-Ahkam*, whose task it was to check important Shariʿa sentences, noticed that, according to the facts mentioned in the sentence, *qisas* ought to be applied, since the act had been committed intentionally and without just cause. He immediately required that all papers relating to the case be sent to him. Having studied these, he concluded that the qadi's sentence was justified. There was no ground for the application of *qisas*, which, in the case of loss of limbs, is allowed only if the defendant has caused its loss from a joint. Otherwise exact retribution is impossible. The mufti further reasoned that the defendant had not caused the loss of the forearm from the elbow, as the remaining part of the forearm had been amputated by a surgeon for fear of gangrene.[56]

In one other case in which a sentence based on *qisas* might have been pronounced for loss of a limb, the plaintiff, a woman whose finger had been bitten

---

56 DWQ Sin/7/31 (Majlis al-Ahkam, Qayd al-iʿlamat al-sharʿiyya), sijill 3, no. 63, 22 Rabi' I 1279, 5 Jumada I 1279.

off by another woman during a fight, eventually pardoned the defendant.[57] In my sample of judicial records I have found no evidence that *qisas* for injuries was applied in practice.[58] I assume that in those cases in which the conditions for the application of *qisas* were present, the law was interpreted very strictly or the plaintiff was encouraged to pardon the defendant or to accept a financial settlement. It is plausible that an aversion to these mutilating penalties developed during the nineteenth century.[59]

The most important financial claims resulting from criminal offenses are claims of blood money for homicide or bodily harm. Elsewhere I have dealt extensively with the treatment of homicide by Egyptian qadis.[60] Here I present one example of a sentence of blood money for bodily harm, dating from 1863:

> A boy in a Qur'an school was first beaten by the schoolmaster with a stick and then by his blind assistant with *a falaqa* (a wooden device for holding the legs of a culprit during a bastinado). As a result the boy's forearm was fractured. After the fracture healed, the arm turned out to be paralysed. The boy's guardian, his grandmother, sued the assistant master. The latter admitted to having beaten the boy but pleaded that the master previously had hit the boy with a stick, which might have caused the fracture and that he, because of his blindness, did not know where he hit the boy. When the schoolmaster denied having caused the boy's fracture, the assistant master was asked to swear that he had not broken the boy's arm. This he refused to do. Consequently he was sentenced to pay compensation (*hukuma*) for the paralysed arm. The amount of compensation was determined by expert witnesses, in this case, slave merchants, on the basis of the reduction of the market price of a slave with a similar defect.[61]

57 DWQ, Sin/7/26 (Majlis al-Ahkam, Sadir wa-warid qalam al-ʿulama' sharʿi), sijill 4, No. 98 15 Rabiʿ I 1275.

58 This finding is corroborated by the printed collection of fatwas of the Egyptian Grand Mufti Muhammad al-ʿAbbasi al-Mahdi, who held office from 1848 until his death in 1897. This collection contains no fatwa upholding retribution for wounding. (See *al-Fatawa al-Mahdiyya fi'l-Waqa'iʿ Misriyya*, 7 vols (Cairo: 1887).

59 As evidence for such an aversion, consider that in 1835 Mehmed ʿAli reprimanded a provincial governor who reportedly had punished a person accused of having pulled out cotton plants by cutting off his nose and ears before drowning him in the Nile. Mehmed ʿAli instructed the governor that offenders were to be punished only by flogging, imprisonment or execution (Sami, *Taqwim*, II, 456, 458).

60 Peters, "Murder on the Nile," pp. 95–115.

61 DM, Makhzan 46, ʿayn 142 (Mahkamat al-Mansura al-ibtida'iyya al-Sharʿiyya, Madabit al-murafaʿat), sijill 286 (1279–1280), p. 59, 28 Rabiʿ I 1280.

Illegal defloration is regarded as a special kind of tort, compensation for which is equal to the proper bride wealth (*mahr al-mithl*), that is, the bride wealth for a girl possessing similar qualities, such as age, social status and beauty. Determination of the amount of the *mahr al-mithl* was often based on outright bargaining during the proceedings, as appears from the following example from the year 1869:

> A woman sued a man claiming that he had given her some sweets while they were in her father's house, that the sweets contained drugs, and that she fainted after eating them.[62] Then the man took her on a boat to a villa in the Gharbiyya province. There he had deflowered her with his member while she was still unconscious. The defendant admitted that he had deflowered her, but added that he had done so with his finger and not with his member.[63] The plaintiff demanded 12,500 piasters from the defendant, the value of her proper bride wealth, as an indemnity for the loss of her virginity. She claimed that her cousin had recently been married for that sum. The defendant rebutted this claim, arguing that this cousin was younger and more beautiful than the plaintiff. The parties eventually agreed on a compensation of 2,500 piasters, and the settlement was ratified by the qadi, who, in addition, sentenced the man to be flogged for his sinful behaviour. The flogging was carried out during the same session.[64]

A final property claim resulting from an offense were claims concerning stolen goods that the qadi had to adjudicate, deriving from his general competence in matters of ownership. As a standard procedure in theft cases in which the evidence was not regarded as sufficient for referral to the council, the police would send the parties to the qadi to settle the ownership dispute. Alternatively, the victim of a theft often would bring the case directly to the qadi to obtain a sentence concerning his property. As we shall see below, in such cases the qadi would also deal with the criminal aspects, since his jurisdiction was in principle unlimited.

62 In most cases of illegal defloration, the plaintiff claims to have been drugged or forced to drink an alcoholic beverage before intercourse took place.

63 This is a standard claim in admissions of illegal defloration, invoked to avert the application of the *hadd* punishment for fornication.

64 DM, Makhzan 46, ʿayn 22 (Mahkamat Misr al-ibtidaʾiyya al-sharʿiyya, dabtiyyat al-murafaʿat), sijill 1238 (Safar 1285–Rajab 1287), p. 84, 17 Rabiʿ 1286.

5.2 *Imposing Punishment on the Strength of Hadd or Taʿzir*

Apart from dealing with private financial and punitive claims arising from criminal offenses, the qadi had the power to impose *hadd* penalties for *hadd* crimes and *taʿzir* punishment for any other kind of sinful behaviour. Qadis imposed such penalties, but only infrequently. In practice the scope of penalties imposed by the qadi was restricted to flogging and short imprisonment. Mutilating penalties and death sentences by stoning or in combination with crucifixion were not carried out.[65] The following exceptional case from 1257–58 elucidates what happened when a qadi found grounds to apply the *hadd* penalty of amputation for theft:

> Two men had forced access to the storehouse of a country estate by removing the bricks closing off an opening in the wall and had stolen from it one *ardabb* (198 liters) and eight *kaylat* (132 liters) of *barsim* seed. The men were apprehended and confessed to having taken the seed from the storehouse. At the trial the qadi dealt only with the property claim. During the session the defendants returned one *ardabb* of the stolen seed to the owner and promised to hand over the rest after they returned to their village. The plaintiff agreed and the qadi gave judgment accordingly. When the sentence was submitted to the provincial mufti (*mufti al-mudiriyya*), he pointed out that no attention had been paid to the criminal aspects of the case and that the *hadd* punishment should be applied with regard to that part of the seed that had not been returned during the session. The case was referred back to the qadi, who, on the strength of this *fatwa*, sentenced the two defendants to amputation. Upon appeal, the sentence was reviewed by the Council of Appeal of the Northern Region (*Majlis Istiʾnaf Bahri*). The *ʿulamaʾ* of the Council examined the judgment and found that it could not be upheld for three reasons:
>
> 1. In the plaintiff's claim and the defendants' confessions the word "taking" (*akhadha*) was used rather than "stealing" (*saraqa*). This

65 This finding tallies with Farahat's study for seventeenth-century Egypt. (*Tarikh*, pp. 485–90). He found only two instances of the application of *hadd* penalties in the many seventeenth-century *sijills* he studied, in spite of the fact that the laws regarding *hadd* offenses were applied in practice. For the early nineteenth century, consider Lane's observation from around 1830 regarding the punishment of amputation: "In Egypt, of late years, these punishments have not been inflicted. Beating and hard labor have been substituted for the first, second, and third offence, and frequently death for the fourth." (E.W. Lane, *Manners and Customs of the Modern Egyptians* [repr., London etc., Dent, 1966] p. 110). *Al-Fatawa al-Mahdiyya* contains no fatwa upholding mutilating *hadd* punishments, which would have been expected if they had been carried out.

constitutes a well-known uncertainty (*shubha*), which prevents the application of the *hadd* penalty.

2. The judgment does not mention whether or not the remainder of the seed, which may have perished or been consumed, still exists. If the seed no longer exists, the *hadd* punishment cannot be enforced since the plaintiff cannot claim the originally stolen goods but only their replacement (*badal*).
3. The sentence does not mention whether the eight *kaylat* had been taken out of the storehouse at once or in smaller portions. This is also relevant for the application of the *hadd* penalty [as the possibility exists that none of the portions amounted to the value of the *nasib*. RP]

The Council warned the qadi and the provincial mufti that "they should be very cautious with regard to this kind of judgment and venture to pronounce it only after having reached complete certainty, for in this type of case a sentence of amputation must not be pronounced as they had done, by [only] "dipping the fingertips in the sea of Abu Hanifa's jurisprudence." In a long exposé, the qadi defended his sentence and then the papers were sent to the "*Diwan*", an undefined higher judicial authority.[66]

The only *hadd* penalty that the qadi applied to defendants was flogging, which was administered immediately during the court session. I have found a few instances of this. In one case dating from 1858, which was only summarily recorded, the defendant was sentenced to a penalty of 100 lashes for fornication.[67] In another case, the qadi sentenced a defendant to eighty lashes for an unfounded accusation of fornication (*qadhf*):

> A woman had run away from her husband and gone to live with her father. After some time her husband went to visit her father in order to settle the quarrel. His father-in-law, however, reproached him that he did not give his wife enough attention, especially now that she was pregnant. The husband became angry and retorted that he could not possibly be the father and that the child must be someone else's. The woman sued her husband for false accusation of fornication (*qadhf*) and proved her claim. The qadi sentenced him to the *hadd* punishment of eighty lashes, which was immediately carried out during the session.[68]

66 DM, Makhzan 46, 'ayn 142–143 (Mahkamat al-Mansura al-ibtida'iyya al-shar'iyya, Madabit al-murafa'at), sijill 281, p. 62, 15 Rabi' II 1274, p. 71, 14 Jumada I 1274, p. 85, 12 Jumada II 1274.

67 DWQ, Sin/7/31 (Majlis al-Ahkam, Qayd al-i'lamat al-shar'iyya), sijill 1, no. 24, 4 Safar 1270.

68 DM, Makhzan 46, 'ayn 142 (Mahkamat al-Mansura al-ibtida'iyya al-shar'iyya, Madabit al-murafa'at), sijill 281 (Shawwal 1273–Jumada I 1274), p. 19, 6 Dhu l-Hijja 1273.

The imposition of flogging as a *taʿzir* punishment occurred frequently. Sometimes it is expressly mentioned that the punishment was thirty-nine lashes, one less than the mildest *hadd* penalty (viz., forty lashes for drinking alcohol, according to the Shafiʿi school). The offenses for which this punishment was administered varied from theft to illegal sexual relations and brawls and abuse.

Sometimes the qadi imposed prison sentences, as in the following case from 1869:

> A building inspector for the Cairo Police entered a house to inform its occupants that the house was going to be demolished and that they had to leave their home. A brawl ensued during which the inspector came to blows with a woman and threw her on the floor, as a result of which she miscarried. She was two months pregnant and the foetus she lost was the size of a small lizard (*burs*) and did not yet have human characteristics (*ghayr mustabin al-khalq*) [such as nails or hair]. The woman sued the inspector and proved her claim. Since the foetus was small, she could not demand blood money for an unborn child (*ghurra*) on behalf of the heirs, but she wanted the defendant to be punished. The qadi sentenced him to three months imprisonment.[69]

In 1861 the punishment of flogging was officially abolished by the Egyptian government.[70] From that date, some qadis imposed prison sentences as a *taʿzir* punishment instead of flogging; others, however, continued to sentence defendants to flogging,[71] probably because they felt that the decree did not apply to them, being bound by the Shariʿa only and not being part of the secular judiciary created by the state.

5.3 *Reconciliation (Sulh)*

The court records frequently mention that the parties in a criminal case were reconciled before the qadi. This occurred in cases of homicide and wounding, where reconciliation as a rule meant that the plaintiffs waived their claim to demand retribution and opted for a financial settlement. Such a settlement,

---

69 DM, Makhzan 46, ʿayn 22 (Mahkamat Misr al-ibtidaʾiyya al-sharʿiyya, dabtiyyat al-murafaʿat), sijill 1238 (Safar 1285–Rajab 1287), p. 80, 22 Safar 1286.

70 *Amr ʿAli* of 26 Dhu l-Hijja 1277. *Taqwim*, 3/1, p. 375.

71 See, for example, DM, Makhzan 46, ʿayn 22 (Mahkamat Misr al-ibtidaʾiyya al-sharʿiyya, dabtiyyat al-murafaʿat), sijill 1238 (Safar 1285–Rajab 1287), p. 84, 17 Rabiʿ I 1286; DWQ, S/7/31 (Diwan Majlis al-Ahkam, Qayd al-iʿlamat al-sharʿiyya), sijill 3, no. 85, 28 Dhu ʾl-Hijja 1278, no. 253, 17 Rajab 1279.

however, did not affect the council's competence to try the case according to statute law. Reconciliation also played a role in minor cases of fighting and abuse which, as a rule, would be heard by the qadi. It seems that especially in such cases the qadi preferred to reach a reconciliation. A typical case is the following dating from 1866:

> One man sued another for having beaten him up and knocked out three teeth. The defendant claimed that the plaintiff had called him a pig (*khinzir*), a fornicator (*zani*), and an irreligious person (*qalil al-din*) and that during the ensuing fight he had lost his money. The case ended in reconciliation.[72]

6 Conclusion

Until 1883, criminal law in Egypt was the domain both of the secular councils and of the qadi. For the councils the public aspect dominated and their dealings with crime served primarily to preserve public order and security. In the qadi's involvement with criminal cases, the private aspect was most prominent. His main task was the adjudication of private claims related to offenses, as evidenced by the fact that the proceedings are always based on a claim advanced by a plaintiff against a defendant.

Private claims might be punitive or aimed at obtaining financial compensation. There were two kinds of punitive claims: the demanding of retribution in cases of homicide and wounding and the demanding of satisfaction in the form of *taʿzir* for offenses against a person's honour. In dealing with homicide, for which capital punishment could be imposed, the qadi acted as a religious judge, sanctioning the taking of the murderer's life on the strength of religious norms. The application of Islamic criminal law by the qadi was restricted by the fact that the execution of sentences (except flogging) was done by the state. The qadi's death sentences, after being duly reviewed, were carried out by the government. Retribution for wounding, however, was a different matter. Since the state apparently was reluctant to administer these sentences, the qadis took care to avoid pronouncing them. The same was true for mutilating *hadd* penalties such as amputation of the hand. The qadi also heard cases where a person's honor was offended, either through beating and abuse during a quarrel, or because of the defloration of a virgin. Upon the demand of the plaintiffs,

72 DM, Makhzan 46, ʿayn 22 (Mahkamat Misr al-ibtidaʾiyya al-sharʿiyya, dabtiyyat al-murafaʿat), sijill 1235, p. 128, 8 Rajab 1283.

he might sentence the defendant to flogging or to short terms of imprisonment, by way of *ta'zir* or, exceptionally, to the *hadd* punishment of flogging.

Most often, however, these private claims heard by the qadi were of a financial nature, such as blood money, revendication of stolen property, or compensation for illegal defloration. In these cases the qadi acted as a civil court. However, since his jurisdiction was a general one, he did not and could not close his eyes to the penal aspects of such cases, which often led to a sentence of flogging or imprisonment based on *ta'zir* or *hadd*. As in the case of retribution for wounding, the government seemed to be averse to executing *hadd* penalties such as amputation or stoning to death, and the qadis therefore did not pronounce such sentences.

Reconciliation (*sulh*) seems to have played an important part in proceedings before the qadi. Although the records do not give information on the manner in which reconciliation was reached, it is plausible that qadi played an active role in trying to bring the parties together.

There is one further question that needs to be addressed. If one studies the records of the qadi courts in nineteenth-century Egypt, one is struck by the small number of convictions. In a sample of 100 homicide cases, only five percent ended in a conviction to pay blood money (*diya*) and a mere two percent resulted in a death sentence.[73] With regard to other criminal matters, convictions also were rare. This is remarkable and one may well question the rationale underlying this system. I believe that the qadi's involvement in criminal matters was functional for two reasons. First, the qadi's main duty was the enforcement of Islamic norms and the upholding of Islam. This is a proper aim that does not require a further justification in terms of social benefit. The number of convictions is therefore irrelevant. Second, these proceedings may have offered the defendant the possibility of disculpation. If a claim was dismissed, the trial would end in an order to the plaintiff not to sue the defendant again, unless he could bring better evidence. Such a sentence might be useful in a situation in which the defendant had been publicly accused of a crime and had become an object of gossip. It is plausible that a suspect in such a position, especially if he was innocent, would challenge the accusers to sue him in court and to substantiate their charges.

73 These percentages are based on a sample of 100 homicide cases tried by the qadi of Asyut between Dhu al-Hijja 1273 and Safar 1276. DM, Makhzan 46, 'ayn 159 (Mahkamat Asyut al-ibtida'iyya al-shar'iyya, Madabit al-murafa'at), sijill 141 (Rajab 1273–Safar 1276).

CHAPTER 4

"For His Correction and as a Deterrent Example for Others"

Meḥmed ʿAlī's First Criminal Legislation (1829–1830)

The convening of the Consultative Council (*Meclis-i Meşveret, Meclis-i ʿUmūmī*[1]) in September 1829 (3 Rabīʿ I, 1245)[2] marked the beginning of Meḥmed ʿAlī's legislative activity in the fields of criminal, constitutional and commercial law. During that year (1245 H, 1829–1830 CE), two criminal codes were introduced, one dealing with crime in general and the other specifically with rural crime. The latter, commonly called *Qānūn al-Filāḥa* and enacted in Shaʿbān 1245 (January–February 1830), has been printed several times in its Arabic version and is well known.[3] The former, enacted on 21 Rabīʿ I 1245 (20 September 1829), has only been published in two rather inaccurate Arabic summaries.[4] The original text, written in Ottoman Turkish, has never been printed and is to be found in the Egyptian National Archive (Dār al-Wathāʾiq al-Qawmiyya). There are two versions of the code (henceforth called documents A and B, respectively).[5]

Document B and the first part of document A (A.1) contain a criminal code divided into ten (unnumbered) sections. Although the wording of these versions differ, their contents are identical. The text of Document B contains the

1 Since Ottoman Turkish was the only administrative language during the first half of the nineteenth century, I use the Turkish rather than the Arabic terms for administrative bodies and institutions.

2 For the Meclis-i Meşveret see Sāmī (1928–1936), 2, 349–354; Deny (1930) 110–111; Rāfiʿī (1972), 516–522.

3 The Qānūn al-Filāḥa was first printed in Shaʿbān 1245 AH (January/February 1830 AD). It consists of the penal provisions listed in an appendix to a manual on agriculture entitled *Lāyiḥat zirāʿat al-fallāḥ wa-tadbīr aḥkām al-siyāsa bi-qaṣd al-najāḥ* (Būlāq: Rajab 1245). In Shawwāl 1256 (November/December 1840) it was reprinted. A slightly modified version of this law was later included in sections 1–55 of *al-Qānūn al-Muntakhab*, printed in 1845. Text in Zaghlūl (1900), *Mulḥaq*, 100–155 and Jallād (1890–95) iii, 351–378.

4 Sāmī (1928–1936), 2, 354 (based on *al-Waqāʾiʿ al-Miṣriyya*) and Zaghlūl (1900), 163 (based on an Arabic rendering of the document to be found in the Dār al-Wathāʾiq al-Qawmiyya). Baer (1969) does not mentioned this code in his survey of early nineteenth-century penal legislation.

5 Dār al-Wathāʾiq al-Qawmiyya, Dīwān-i Hidīwī Turkī, Daftar qayd al-khulāṣāt, Sin/2/40, Sijill 23, pp. 12–17 (henceforth referred to as document A) and Sijill 12, pp. 1–2 (henceforth referred to as document B). There exists also a document containing an Arabic translation of document A, with the exception of the firman of Ibrāhīm Paşa: Maḥfaẓat al-Mīhī, doc. 8.

 | DOI:10.1163/9789004420625_005

minutes (*khulāṣat*) of the meeting of the Council that were sent to the various officials concerned. Document A is worded more like a law and in addition contains the following legislation:

- an appendix to this law, enacted on 20 Shaʿbān 1245 (14 February 1830) and consisting of one section (A.2)
- six sections, enacted on the same day and identical with some sections of the Qānūn al-Filāḥa (A.3);
- an undated firman of Ibrahim Pasha regarding gypsies (Nūrī), beggars, vagrants etc. (A.4)

In this article I will analyze this criminal code and present the transcribed Ottoman Turkish text of document A and its English translation. In analyzing the code I will also take into account, to some extent, the *Qānūn al-Filāḥa* that represents the same stage in the development of criminal legislation. Instead of focusing on the purely legal aspects of this code, I will try to read it as a social and political document that expresses the views and ideologies of the ruling class of Egyptian society in the early nineteenth century. Studied from this perspective, the document is significant for two reasons. First, it is an expression of the endeavor to centralize and rationalize government and the administration of justice; secondly, it can be read as an articulation of the social hierarchy as perceived by the ruling class.

But first a survey of the contents of these laws. The code contained in documents B and A.1 deals chiefly with misappropriation of state and private property, either by officials or private persons (sections 1–3 and 7–10). In addition it addresses counterfeiting, homicide and robbery (sections 5 and 6). Section 4 stipulates that relatives of those convicted to prison sentences may submit petitions for their release before the termination of their sentence. A.2 contains only one section (11), addressing embezzlement of state property by tax collectors and sheikhs in Upper Egypt. The four sections of A.3 deal with theft of fruits and animals (12 and 13), lying to officials (14) and the wounding of a tax collector by a peasant who refuses to pay his dues (15). These sections are identical with sections 4, 19 and 7 of the *Qānūn al-Filāḥa*.

Ibrāhīm Pasha's firman (A.4) is arranged differently from documents B and A.1: It contains four sections, each subdivided in two paragraphs. The first paragraph of each section describes the punitive measures to be taken with respect to the members of the groups defined in the second paragraph. But whereas the other laws impose penalties for committing certain acts, this decree establishes that punitive measures must be taken against certain groups of people, regardless of whether they have committed criminal acts or not. The measures are unspecified as to time: those apprehended are to be sent to forced labor in factories or drafted into the army for an unspecified period.

The provisions of the code were effective for only a relatively short period. That the code was applied appears from orders given to lower officials directing them to deal with criminal cases "ḳānūnnāme manṭūḳca", according to the enacted law code, which can only refer to the Ḳānūn al-Filāḥa or the criminal code presented here.[6] The sections on misappropriation by officials were replaced in 1837 by the *Qānūn al-Siyāsetnāme*, the penal provisions of the Organic Law establishing the new organization of government.[7] The section on theft was first amended in November 1835 by a decree of Meḥmed ʿAlī raising the penalty for theft to 7 years forced labor.[8] In August 1844, the sections on theft, forgery and homicide were replaced by provisions of a penal law consisting of translated sections of the French Code Pénal of 1810[9] and the section on highway robbery was replaced by a decree of October 1844.[10]

It has been asserted that the enactment of statute laws dealing with, e.g., homicide, theft and robbery, implied a restriction or even an abolishment of the sharīʿa in criminal matters.[11] This may have been the case in some Muslim regions. In Egypt, however, such laws were complementary to the sharīʿa. In criminal matters both the qāḍī and the administration played a role, the former applying the sharīʿa and the latter applying the enacted laws and acting on the strength of *taʿzīr* or *siyāsa*. The *qāḍī* would hear all cases involving violent death, illegal intercourse, abuse and property claims as a result of theft. He would not only consider such cases from the perspective of private law, but also from the point of view of criminal law. However, hampered as he was by the strict sharīʿa rules of evidence and procedure he often could not impose punishment. In these cases executive officials would try the offense again and examine it from the point of view of public interest. Such officials would also deal with offenses that were not heard by the qāḍī. The jurisdiction of the

6 See e.g. Sin/1/55, Qayd al-awāmir al-karīma li-l-dawāwīn wa-l-aqālīm wa-l-muḥāfaẓāt, sijill 3 (1251–1252), No. 112, 13 Jumādā II 1251. The term is also used at other places in this sijill.

7 The law was printed in Rabīʿ I, 1253. Text in Zaghlūl (1900) Mulḥaq, 4–26. On this law, see Hamed (1995).

8 Amr to Muhtār Bey, President of the *Meclis-i Mülkiye*, dated 12 Rajab 1251. Sāmī (1928–1936) II, p. 454.

9 Law enacted on 9 Shaʿbān, 1260, and included in the Qānūn al-Muntakhab, sections 122–197.

10 Decree of 29 Ramaḍān, 1260, included in the Qānūn al-Muntakhab, section 197. The wording of the passage raises questions because it implies that until then highway robbery was punished with capital punishment and that this decree introduced a punishment of forced labor for life. However, section 6 of the Penal Code of 1829 had already replaced capital punishment for highway robbery with lifelong forced labor.

11 See e.g. Baer (1969), p. 126.

administration in criminal matters was restricted in 1842, when the *Cemʿiyet-i Ḥaḳḳāniye* (*al-Jamʿiyya al-Ḥaqqāniyya*) was established. The 1829–1830 codes addressed therefore not the *qāḍī* or judicial councils but the administration. The procedures followed by officials (and later by the judicial councils) dealing with crime did not resemble those of a criminal trial as we understand it now, but were rather of a bureaucratic nature: The official or the council tried the case on the basis of police reports and without publicly hearing the witnesses and the defendant.[12]

The laws under discussion, called *qānūn*, fit in the tradition of Ottoman state legislation. Yet there are important points on which they differ from Ottoman criminal laws.[13] The most important is that these new laws (with the exception of those dealing with gypsies and vagrants) clearly specify the penalty for each offense. The Ottoman codes usually limit themselves to defining the offense and mentioning that it deserves punishment.[14] Sometimes the Ottoman codes specify the kind of punishment (e.g. flogging, detention), but hardly ever the quantity, unless the punishment is a fine. Another difference is that the new laws restrict corporal punishment to the death penalty and flogging. Under Ottoman law the range of corporal punishment was very wide and included the amputation of parts of the body (nose, ears, hands, male organ), impaling and branding.[15] During the first decades of Meḥmed ʿAlī's reign cruel corporal punishments[16] still occurred.[17] The market inspector (*muḥtasib*) of Cairo had a particularly bad reputation for his resourcefulness in this respect.[18] It would seem that this new legislation manifests Meḥmed ʿAlī's intention to put an end to such practices. In the absence of travellers' reports to the contrary, we may assume that he was generally successful in this respect.[19] Moreover,

12 Cf. Peters (1997) and Peters (1999).

13 For Ottoman criminal law in general, see Heyd (1973); for Ottoman criminal law in Egypt, see Faraḥāt (1993).

14 So in the Ḳānūnnāme-yi Miṣr of 1525. Faraḥāt (1993), 509.

15 See U. Heyd (1973) pp. 262–265. For the cruel and publicly executed modes of capital punishments during the later Mamluk period in Egypt, see Espéronnier (1997).

16 Hanging and flogging are no doubt cruel punishment. However, in the context of early nineteenth-century Egypt, I refer with the term cruel punishments to mutilation (e.g. amputation of the hand) or to punishments adding additional suffering to the death penalty.

17 For the application of the punishment of the amputation of the hand in the year 1812, see Jabartī (1297 H) IV, 144.

18 See Jabartī (1297 H) IV, pp. 277–278 (Shaʿbān, Ramaḍān, 1232), Lane, pp. 125–127. De Forbin (n.d.) 66.

19 See e.g. Lane's observation that in the 1830s theft was no longer punished with amputation (Lane (1966) 110). This was at least the policy of the central government and does not exclude the possibility that local officials treated their subjects cruelly. Travellers often recount the arbitrary behavior of officials, but do not mention punishments other than

cruel methods of execution also fell into disuse. The last instance of impaling occurred by the end of the 1830s[20] and the usual way of execution became hanging.

A final novel aspect of the new codes is the prominence given to imprisonment with forced labor as a punishment. The prisons were located either in the Alexandria Dockyards (*līmān, lūmān*) or in government building sites in the local districts.[21] The decree against vagrants and gypsies mentions in addition forced labor in factories (probably for wages)[22] and military service as punishments. The latter punishment is also included in the *Qānūn al-Filāḥa*.

The code is clear about the objectives of punishment. It mentions: correction and rehabilitation of the culprit[23] and, especially in connection with capital punishment and lifelong imprisonment, deterrence.[24] To emphasize the deterrent aspect of capital punishment the Civil Council (*Meclis-i Mülkiye*) issued instructions in November 1834 to the effect that the bodies of persons who had been hanged were to remain on the gallows for one day and that posters were to be distributed and posted all over the country informing the people of the sentence.[25]

Although notion of retribution is not explicitly referred to, the law establishes a clear correspondence between the seriousness of the offense and the resulting harm and the severity of the penalty. In the older systems of criminal law, this notion often took the form of "mirroring" punishments, i.e. punishments reflecting the act for which they are a retribution. An example can be found in classical Islamic law, where, according to some *madhhabs*, retaliation for manslaughter is to be executed after due trial by one of the heirs of the

flogging, except for the reports on the muḥtasib and one or two more or less identical stories that the authors seem to have copied from one another, which makes it difficult to judge their veracity.

20 M. Gisquet, who visited Egypt in 1844, mentions the year 1839 (Gisquet (n.d.) ii, 132), whereas V. Schoelcher, who was there in 1845, dates the event to 1837 (Schoelcher (1846) 24). See also Guémard (1936) 261.

21 The latter punishment is mentioned in section 11 the penal code (*ebniye-yi mīriyede istihdām*) and also in section 17 of the *Qānūn al-Filāḥa*: "to be employed for one year in the government building sites (*ʿimārat al-mīrī*) in the *maʾmūriyya* while being shackled."

22 This seemed to be the rule with regard to vagrants and gypsies. See e.g. *al-Waqāʾiʿ al-Miṣriyya*, 5 Jumādā II, 1247.

23 The texts use the Arabic phrases *tarbiyat^{an} lahu* or *li-ajl al-tarbiya*, "for his correction" (A9; A10; B3; B7) and also the word *taʾdīb*, "teaching a lesson" (A10; B10).

24 "*ʿIbratan li-ghayrihi, ʿibrat^{an} li-sāʾirīn*", "as a deterrent example for others" (A5; A6; A7; A8; B1; B8). See also Doc. A, section 7: "Since it is necessary to prevent embezzlements that occur, they shall in this manner be prevented."

25 Order dated 19 Rajab 1250. Dār al-Wathāʾiq al-Qawmiyya, Dīwān-i Hidīwī, Maḥāfiẓ, Mulakhaṣṣāt dafātir, no. 63, (Daftar 806, old (1250 H)), document 74.

victim with a weapon or method similar to the one used by the perpetrator.[26] In the early modern period comparable notions of punishment existed in Europe. Such punishments were meant to enhance their deterrent effect.

In the new criminal laws, however, this visible and qualitative correspondence between crime and punishments disappeared and was replaced by a quantitative one. With the exception of the death penalty, punishment was made uniform and quantifiable and consisted in imprisonment or flogging. Its primary aim was no longer deterrence, but rather retribution and rehabilitation of the culprit. In several instances the measure of retribution is precisely quantified in the new code. The section dealing with common, unqualified theft (section 3) is a case in point. It contains a table where the value of the stolen property is related to the length of imprisonment:

TABLE 4.1 Penalties for theft in the code of Meḥmed ʿAlī

Value of stolen property	Penalty (forced labor)
1–1,000 pts	1 year
1,001–5,000 pts	1½ year
5,001–10,000 pts	2 years
10,001–20,000 pts	2½ years
20,001–40,000 pts	3 years
40,001–60,000 pts	3½ years
60,001–100,000 pts	4 years

There is a slight difference in wording between document A and document B. Here I have followed the latter which seems to be more consistent.

Thus the code created a precise and objective correspondence offering unambiguous instructions for officials applying the law. In some cases these tables are quite complicated: a decree issued in February 1830 and making the violation of price regulations a punishable offense establishes that the punishment (here the number of lashes) is a function of (1) the seriousness of the offense (i.e. the difference between the price received and the prescribed price), (2) the physical constitution of the offender (in order to ensure that the measure of pain inflicted on offenders was roughly the same), and (3) the number

26 Ibn Rushd (1960), ii, 404.

of previous convictions for the same offense.[27] This precise and quantifiable relationship between crime and punishment constitutes, in my view, an important aspect of the rationality of these laws.

What were Meḥmed ʿAlī's motives in enacting these codes? There is no doubt that the code contained in document A.1 and document B was in the first place meant to curb extortion and embezzlement by officials. Five of ten sections deal with this type of offense. There was, however, another purpose, at least as important, which is also very much in evidence in the *Qānūn al-Filāḥa*. This was the centralization of power, brought about by giving officials administering criminal law precise instructions that left them little or no room for exercising their own judgment in meting out punishment. The introduction to the *Qānūn al-Filāḥa* expresses this very notion:

> There are reports that offenders who had to be punished by the officials (*ḥukkām*) were often given more lashes than what was due to them. This would sometimes result in their death. In order to eliminate this tyrannical behavior it is necessary that the punishment imposed on all [sorts of] offenders be precisely defined and that the honorable heads of the departments (*maʾmūr*), district chiefs (*nuẓẓār al-aqsām*) and subdistrict

27 The decree can be summarized in the following table, the numbers referring to the numbers of lashes:

TABLE 4.2 Punishments for violations of price regulations according to the Decree 1830

Physical constitution:	Strong	Medium	Sick or old
1 fiḍḍa	5	33	18
2 fiḍḍa	75	50	25
3 fiḍḍa	100	6	33
4 fiḍḍa	120	80	40

The seriousness of the violation expressed in its monetary value.

If the value of the offense exceeds 4 fiḍḍa, the culprit receives 20 additional lashes for every fiḍḍa. In case of second or further offense, the amount of lashes and additional penalties are determined according to the following table:

TABLE 4.3 Punishments for repeated offenses according to the Decree of 1830

2nd offense:	redoubling of number of lashes + 10 days detention
3rd offense:	a threefold increase of the number of lashes + 30 days detention
4th offense:	a fourfold increase of the number of lashes + 3 months forced labor
5th offense:	the same number of lashes as for a first offender who has received 1 fiḍḍa in excess + 6 months forced labor + prohibition to work as a shopkeeper

Sāmī (1928–1936), II, p. 360, quoting *al-Waqāʾiʿ al-Miṣriyya*, No. 108, 16 Shaʿbān 1245.

> officers (*ḥukkām al-akhṭāṭ*) be instructed that in punishing offenders they are not to exceed [the punishment] that has been defined for them.[28]

A third motive was, as appears from a slightly later document, that Meḥmed ʿAlī believed that fixed penalties instead of arbitrary punishment would contribute to the acceptance of the system of criminal law. In the preamble of an order issued by him to his cabinet (*şūrā-yi muʿāvenet*) in 1842 to establish the *Cemʿiyet-i Ḥaḳḳāniye*,[29] Meḥmed ʿAlī argued:

> If an offender is sentenced to penalties laid down [by law] without the slightest partiality and with justice and equity, then that person will have no objections anymore. It is evident that the impact of penalties laid down [by law] may be enormous. Therefore there is in Europe much attention for, and interest, in this matter. As a result, when they [the Europeans] impose punishments, they investigate and make clear the offender's fault and the punishment that he deserves to such an extent that the accused does not protest anymore and accepts it whole-heartedly.[30]

Finally, it is likely that by enacting these codes Meḥmed ʿAlī wanted to enhance his legitimacy by emphasizing his role as the patron of justice for his subjects. Meḥmed ʿAlī threatened his officials that if they disobeyed his laws and if persons died as a result of flogging or a bastinado, the officials would be sued before the qāḍī and, in addition, exposed to capital punishment or exile (probably to Abū Qīr).[31] That such directions were necessary indicates that the criminal liability for such unlawful behavior was not self-evident. By curbing the high-handed behavior of officials, these codes aimed at protecting the subjects. However, this was not done by granting the latter more rights, e.g. by creating legal remedies and judicial proceedings (with the exception of

28 Lāyiḥat zirāʿat al-fallāḥ (2nd impr. Būlāq, 1257) p. 61. The introduction to Document B contains a similar passage, this time with regard to imprisonment:

"Although during the past month of Ṣafar the blessed a debate has [already] taken place in the [General Consultative] Council, occasioned by fact that formerly it was deemed sufficient to impose forced labor in the Alexandria Harbor [without specifying a term] and that [now] it is necessary to specify appropriate penalties for some offenses that are [nowadays] current, [the outcome of] this [debate] has this time been confirmed and renewed on details by the General [Consultative] Council meeting in the *Ḳaṣr-i ʿĀlī* (...)."

29 For the Cemʿiyet-i Ḥaḳḳāniye (al-Jamʿiyya al-Haqqāniyya), see Peters (1999).

30 Zaghlūl (1900) 182–183.

31 Order of Meḥmed ʿAlī dated 28 Rabīʿ II, 1245, prompted by a report of one of the provincial officials that some persons had died as a result of the beating administered to them. Sāmī (1928–1936) ii, 356.

section 10 which gives suspects of theft some rights) to deal with wrongful acts committed by the servants of the state. Rather, these legal texts must be read as a pledge on the part of the sovereign that he would see that justice was done, once he was informed by petition of any injustice suffered by his subjects. The new laws were meant to confer greater legitimacy upon Meḥmed ʿAlī's rule, and thus enhance his power. The idea that law limits the powers of the sovereign by granting rights to subjects or citizens is totally alien to these codes, as evidenced by the fact that they were not promulgated, and that copies were only sent to officials, without any instruction to make them public.

It took Meḥmed ʿAlī several years to assert his authority, as indicated by the various instructions he gave to local officials. In 1834 he issued a decree to his provincial administrators reaffirming that sentences in criminal cases, especially death sentences, were to be submitted to him for approval, after the case had been investigated and tried locally.[32] One day later, he directed one of the governors of Upper Egypt to initiate an investigation into rumors that the district chief (*nāẓir ḳism*) of Girga had executed eighteen persons within a very short span of time.[33] When, in 1835, he learned that the governor of the Buḥayra Province had cut off the nose and ears of a peasant who had uprooted cotton plants, he censured the governor and instructed him that flogging, imprisonment and death were the only punishments that he was allowed to impose for such acts.[34] The absence of such orders after 1835 suggests that Meḥmed ʿAlī had acquired total control of criminal justice. Sentences in serious cases were henceforth submitted to him for confirmation. During the same period, travellers reported that the number of death sentences decreased.[35]

It was Meḥmed ʿAlī's ambition to impose a centralized and rational order upon his realm. The effects of this endeavor are evident in various domains of society, such as agriculture[36] and the military.[37] Criminal law, by its nature, is crucial to such a policy of disciplining, and the new laws must be regarded as a means to achieve this centralization and rationalization. The idea of centralization was very mush vested in his person. Mehmed ʿAlī wanted to be the ultimate authority in criminal justice and the new laws expressed the notion

32 Order dated 20 Rabīʿ II, 1250. Sāmī (1928–1936) ii, 426.
33 Order dated 21 Rabīʿ II, 1250. Sāmī (1928–1936) ii, 426.
34 Orders of 2 and 22 Ramaḍān, 1251. Sāmī (1928–1936) ii, 456, 458.
35 Fahmy (1997) 140, referring to Bowring, who travelled in Egypt in the late 1830s. See also Dodwell (1931) 201.
36 See for instance *Lāyiḥat zirāʿat al-fallāḥ* [2nd impr.] (Būlāq, 1257), specifying in great detail agricultural activities and the duties of peasants and officials. See Rivlin (1961) 86–99.
37 See Fahmy (1997) esp. ch. 3: "From Peasants to Soldiers: Discipline and Training".

that all punishment derived from his omnipresent authority, even if it was in fact imposed by his agents. Lawfully inflicted punishment ought to represent and symbolize the centrality of his power.

However, apart from being an expression of Meḥmed ʿAlī's aspiration to dominate the country, these new laws mark a transition from the period in which punishment was often cruel and arbitrarily imposed to a period characterized by rational punishment, consisting in controlled and precisely measured penalties; and from a period in which deterrence produced by brutal spectacles was the main objective of criminal justice to one in which punishment aimed primarily at disciplining the offender. The movement towards greater centralization and rationalization and the increased importance of disciplining the criminal rather than deterring the public resembles developments that took place in Western Europe around the turn of the nineteenth century.[38]

However, there are important differences between what happened in Egypt and in Western Europe. In Western Europe these changes were part of the process of emancipation of the bourgeoisie and the struggle for the recognition of civil rights. Codification of criminal law was a means to ensure the fundamental freedom of the citizen against the arbitrariness of the rulers. This political process was accompanied by public debate and a vast number of publications on the need for penal reform, beginning with Cesare Beccaria's *Dei delitti e delle pene*, published in 1764. There is nothing comparable in the early Egyptian criminal codification: There was no political struggle for fundamental rights. If these laws offered protection to the subjects, this stemmed from Meḥmed ʿAlī's sovereign will and was not the result of a political struggle. Moreover, there was no public debate on the matter of penal reform in Egypt. One can find only a few short remarks in the preambles of new laws. Whether the reforms were at all seriously discussed among the small ruling class cannot be established yet. If these discussions took place, they left, to the best of my knowledge, no written traces.

This leads to the question of why Egypt introduced penal reforms similar to those adopted in Western Europe in roughly the same period. A possible answer could be that this was due to European influence, mediated by European experts in Egypt and Egyptian students who had been to the West. The European example is referred to several times in laws enacted in the 1840s and, as noted, the penal law enacted in 1844 was a translation of a number of articles of the French Code Pénal of 1810. That there was some European influence already in 1829 is probable, but cannot be proved with certainty. However, the main factor, behind the reforms, I believe, was the spread of public security

38 See e.g. Weisser (1979), O'Brien (1982), and Foucault (1989).

in most of Egypt as a result of Meḥmed ʿAlī's greater control over the country, better police surveillance, and, as a result, greater efficiency in tracking and apprehending criminals.[39] As Foucault has noticed with respect to Europe, the greater the chance for a criminal to be apprehended, the less the authorities feel the need for spectacles of cruel exemplary punishments in order to discourage crime. The greater efficiency of the police and the resulting increase in public safety may well be the common factor that explains the resemblance in penal law reform in Egypt and Western Europe.

A factor of an economic nature that may have played a role in the banning of cruel corporal punishment and the decreasing occurrence of capital punishment was the shortage of manpower in Egypt. Maiming and crippling able-bodied men would affect the availability of labor and of soldiers. A similar motive obviously played a role when, in order to stop the 1824 rebellion, Meḥmed ʿAlī ordered, as a deterrent, that some of the elderly and the disabled be hanged publicly, since "they were useless and could not perform any task."[40] Forced labor as a punishment was much more profitable for the state than the destruction of human labor force and military potential. Moreover, the provisions regarding vagrants and gypsies, contained in sections 18–21 of Document A were obviously occasioned by a shortage of labor in the government factories and a shortage of soldiers for the army.

Apart from being an indication of a transition to new attitudes toward crime and punishment, these laws are significant for another reason: They can be read as documents charting the social hierarchy as perceived by the ruling class. In order to analyze them from this point of view, I will concentrate on offenses connected with misappropriation, since the protection of private and state property is clearly a central concern of these laws. Ten of seventeen sections of the first three parts of Document A deal with misappropriation, referred to as extortion (*gaṣb*), theft (*seriḳa*) or embezzlement (*ihtilās*). In addition, the punitive measures against vagrants and other urban marginals mentioned in Ibrāhīm Pasha's decree are also justified by the threat they pose to private property.[41] The sections on misappropriation can be summarized as follows:

39 See e.g. Guémard (1936) 257.

40 Fahmy (1997) 130.

41 The description of the four groups mentioned in this decree ends in each case with the words: "It has been observed that the value of the things they steal varies from five to 500 piasters and sometimes even to 1,000 piasters."

1. Extortion of private property by high officials (*muḥāfiẓ, me'mūr, nāẓir*) [Turks]: six months imprisonment in Abū Qīr (Section 2); by high ranking sheikhs (also regarded as state servants, *hademe-yi mīrīye*): six months forced labor in the Alexandria Dockyards (Section 9).[42] If state property is taken, the term of imprisonment is doubled;
2. Misappropriation by sheikhs[43] and others [Arabs]: Forced labor in the Alexandria Dockyards for one to three (or four)[44] years, the length of imprisonment to be determined by the value of the goods stolen (Section 3);
3. Misappropriation of state property by tax collectors or sheikhs in Upper Egypt: one to four months forced labor in state building sites, the length of imprisonment to be determined by the value of the misappropriated goods (100–400 piasters) (Section 11, appendix);
4. Misappropriation by Coptic tax collectors: five years forced labor in the Alexandria Dockyards if they can reimburse the value of the stolen goods; for life, if they cannot (Section 7);
5. Misappropriation by Coptic high ranking state servants: death penalty (Section 8);
6. Misappropriation by low ranking rural sheikhs: 300–500 lashes (Section 9);
7. Misappropriation by peasants: 25–300 lashes with the *ḳırbāç*, according to nature of goods stolen and the number of previous convictions; forced labor in the Alexandria Dockyards for unspecified time in case of a fourth conviction for theft of a goat or a sheep (Sections 12–13);
8. Misappropriation by urban vagrants and marginals (gypsies, beggars, run-away black slaves, fortunetellers, magicians and treasure hunters): forced labor in the ironworks (*demürhāne*), in tailor shops and in other industrial establishments; military service for young men; exile to upper Egypt for men who are unfit (Sections 18–21).

Most provisions deal with misappropriation in an official capacity and, interestingly, it would seem that this is not considered to be an aggravating circumstance (except in the case of the Coptic officials, on which see below): Theft

42 It is plausible that the stipulation about the high-ranking sheikhs was added during the debates in the Consultative Council under pressure of precisely this category of sheikhs, who were well represented in the Council. See the list of delegates published in Sāmī (1928–1936) ii, 350–352.

43 It is not entirely clear what kind of sheikhs are meant here. As in other sections the law lays down rules for high ranking sheikhs serving in the provincial administration and for village sheikhs, one may assume that the sheikhs referred to in this section are urban sheikhs, such as religious scholars, sufis, and the heads of guilds, not employed by the government.

44 Document B mentions four years.

committed by high officials (no. 1) is punished less severely than the same offense committed by ordinary subjects (no. 2). Moreover, except in the case of high officials (no. 1), the punishment for theft of state property does not differ from that for theft of private property.

In allowing a differentiation in legal treatment on the basis of social rank, these laws belong to the older legal order. In classical Islamic law, the judge who punished culprits by means of his discretionary power to punish sinful behavior (*taʿzīr*), had to take into account the social position the defendants. The underlying idea was that in order to achieve the desired result, namely deterring the culprit from repeating the offense, the punitive measures should fit his status: for high ranking offenders and *ʿulamāʾ*, the mere disclosure of their deeds or leading them to the door of the court was generally sufficient, whereas the lower classes had to be restrained by all possible means including imprisonment and beating.[45] This differentiation according to social rank was soon abolished. The *Qānūn al-Siyāsetnāme* of 1837 emphasizes in many sections the equality before the law of all officials regardless of their rank, e.g.: “Anyone who is employed in government service, regardless of his rank, …”[46]

It is my contention that the differentiation in the nature and the measure of punishment manifested in the criminal code of 1829 is largely a function of the social distance as perceived by the authors of the document. I will first examine the nature of the punishments imposed. The first distinction that catches the eye is the one between flogging and imprisonment. This distinction coincides with the division between city dwellers and peasants. As a rule city dwellers are not to be subjected to flogging, probably, because of its ignominious character.[47] Village sheikhs are put on a par with peasants and the imposition of corporal punishment is justified by the fact that agricultural work

45 See e.g. Shaykhzāde (1301 H) i, 565–566:

“Taʿzīr must be exercised according to rank: the *taʿzīr* of the most eminent notables, i.e. the *ʿulamāʾ* and the descendants of ʿAlī consists in disclosure [of their offenses], the *taʿzīr* of notables and leading personalities by disclosure and dragging them to the door of the *qāḍī*, the *taʿzīr* of the middle classes, namely the common people (*al-sūqiyya*), consists in dragging [them to the door of the *qāḍī*] and imprisoning them, and the *taʿzīr* of the lower classes (*al-arādhil*) consists in all this plus beating.”

46 “*Inna kulla man kān mustakhdam*[an] *bi-l-maṣāliḥ al-mīriyya in kān ṣaghīr*[an] *aw kabīr*[an] *wa-…*”. See sections 1, 5, 9, 10, 13, 15, and 17, with varying wordings.

47 The application of this principle was not entirely consistent. In the decree of 1830 mentioned in note 28 flogging was imposed as a punishment for the contravention of price regulations by shopkeepers. Fifteen year later a new law imposed forced labor for this offense instead of flogging (*al-Qānūn al-Muntakhab*, section 119, enacted in 1844). Interestingly, the military codes lay down that only in very rare instances soldiers may be punished with flogging. See Fahmy (1997) 138.

otherwise would come to a standstill. A further distinction is made between a specified and an unspecified period of imprisonment or forced labor. Only the groups at the base of the social hierarchy, i.e. peasants and urban marginals, could be detained for undetermined periods. These distinctions are shown in the following table:

TABLE 4.4 Punishment differentials between peasants and urban marginals

	Flogging	**Imprisonment**	
		Indefinite	**Definite period**
peasants	+	+	–
urban marginals	–	+	–
towns people	–	–	+

Finally the place of detention is indicative of social distinctions: the higher, usually Turkish-Circassian, officials were sent to Abū Qīr prison, whereas all others were imprisoned in the Alexandria Dockyards (Sections 1, 2 and 9).

Secondly, there is the matter of the severity of the punishment, especially the length of detention. Since, as I have mentioned, the illegal appropriation in the pursuit of one's official duties does not seem to be regarded as an aggravated offense, we can disregard this as an explanation for differences in punishment. My contention is that severity of punishment is related to social distance as perceived by the ruling class. This is very clear with regard to the ruling group itself. The punishment they risk for extorting their subjects (six months detention) and the punishment for misappropriation of state property (one year detention) are shorter than the punishments for the same offenses committed by other categories of persons. Arranging these categories in accordance with the severity of the punishment, taking into account only death penalty and imprisonment for specified periods, we get the following breakdown:[48]

1. Turkish-Circassian high officials and Arab high ranking sheikhs (six months to one year)

48 In this breakdown I have disregarded the tax collectors in Upper Egypt mentioned in Section 11. This section is rather enigmatic. The amounts mentioned here are comparatively small and it is not evident why petty embezzlement by tax collectors in Upper Egypt deserves to be mentioned separately.

2. Urban sheikhs and private persons (one to four years)
3. Coptic tax collectors (five years to life)
4. High ranking Coptic officials (death penalty)

This breakdown reveals two basic social distinctions: one between the ruling groups and the urban population and one between the Muslim high officials and the Coptic financial functionaries. The former distinction is self-evident, but the latter deserves some comment. Although the distinction may appear to be of a religious nature, it is actually a social and a functional one. There was a considerable social distance between the Coptic and the other officials. But there was another, perhaps more important reason for the heavy penalties to which they were subject in case of misappropriation. For centuries, the fiscal administration of the country had been a Coptic monopoly.[49] As a result, the knowledge and skills required to audit the financial records was scarce among other officials. The ample opportunities for Coptic officials to defraud explain the severity of the punishment. That the higher Coptic officials risked capital punishment for fraudulent acts can be explained by the fact that it was extremely difficult for the other officials to check their financial dealings, whereas the Coptic tax collectors at the local, village level had fewer opportunities for embezzlement, as they had to cooperate with village sheikhs and other local authorities, who, therefore, were privy to their financial dealings. Actually, this is an apt illustration of the general rule that the severity of punishment of a crime is often inversely proportional to the chances for the authorities to apprehend the offender.

In this essay I have tried to show that law codes can be read and analyzed as social and political documents, reflecting the concerns and ideas of the ruling class. The criminal laws discussed here were an essential instrument for establishing a rational disciplining order. They represent a new era in criminal practice, characterized by controlled and measured penalties, aimed at disciplining and reforming the offender, rather than at deterring the public by cruel exemplary punishment. This was made possible by more effective police methods which considerably increased the chances that an offender would be apprehended had increased considerably. Furthermore, these laws reflect the social hierarchy as viewed by the ruling class. Comparing the kinds and severity of the punishments for misappropriation (i.e. theft, embezzlement, extortion), which is the central concern of these laws, tells us something about the social relations between the ruling class and the categories of offenders.

---

49 Motzki (1979), 26ff.

Appendix 1: the Ottoman Turkish Text of the New Laws[50]

21 Rabî' I [12]45 tārīhinde ḳaṣr-i ʿālīde munʿaḳid Meclis-i ʿUmūmīde mücrimlere dāʾir tertīb olunan ḳānūn-i siyāsiyeden naḳl olunmuşdur

[1] Mīrī hidmetinde bulunan muḥāfıẓlar ve-meʾmūrlar ve-nāẓırlardan bi-gayr-i ḥaḳḳ reʿāyāya ẓulm ve-taʿaddī ile gaṣb-i māl edeni ẓuhūr eder ise cüzvī [cüzʾī] ve-küllī aldığı şeyʾ kendüsinden taḥṣīl oluna ve-altı māh müddet ile Abū Ḳīrʾe gönderile.

[2] Ve-bu muḥāfıẓ meʾmūr ve-nāẓırlardan emlāk-i mīriyeniñ seriḳat ve-ihtilāsına cerāʾet edeni olur ise emīn ve-bī-garaẓ kimseleriñ taḥrīr ve-taḥḳīḳiyle ihtilāsı baʿd al-subūt ne ise kendüsinden alına ve-bir sene müddet ile Abū Ḳīrʾe gönderile.

[3] Ve-bu seriḳat ve-ihtilās şeyhlerden ve-sāʾirinden ẓuhūr eder ise māli reʿāyā māli olsun mīrī māli olsun biñ gurūşa bāliğ ise bir sene müddet ile ve-biñ gurūşdan yuḳarı beş biñ gurūşa ḳadar olsun bir buçuḳ sene müddet ile ve-beş biñ gurūşdan on biñ gurūşa ḳadar olur ise iki sene müddet ile ve-yirmi biñ gurūşa ḳadar olur ise iki buçuḳ sene müddet ile ve-yirmi biñ gurūşdan ḳırḳ biñ gurūşa ḳadar olur ise üç sene müddet ile ve-ḳırḳ biñ gurūşdan altmış biñ gurūşa ḳadar olur ise üç sene müddet ile kezālik līmāna gönderile ve-işbu aḥkām-i siyāsiye ḳırḳ dört senesi ibtidāsinden bedʾ ile mücrimler ḥaḳḳında icrā olunacaḳ olmağla icrā oluna.

[4] İşbu meşāyihlerden ve-sāʾirlerden vech-i muḥarrar üzere līmāna gidineriñ müddeti tamām olmağsızın aḳribāları ḥāk-i ʿāli-yi hidīvī ʿarẓuḥāl verüb ʿafv-i ḥafẓ-i dāverī eylediklerinde ol mücrimleriñ iḳlīm-i ʿimāretine ve-mīrī maṣlaḥatına yarayacağı bilinür ve-tāʾib ve-mustağfir olduğı maʿlūm olur ise ve-sebīli tahliyesine irāde-yi senīye taʿalluḳ eder ise bu ṣūret zikr olunan müddet-i muḳarrare uṣūlundan müstesnā olmağla düstūrül-ʿamel tutıla ve-mūcibince ol mücrimiñ sebīli tahliye ḳılına.

[5] Ḳalpazanlıḳ fiʿli şerʿan ve-ḳānūnan memnūʿ olan efʿāldan olmağla bu fiʿl-i münkarı işlemekle her mütecāsir olunlar ele gider ise ömri tamām oluncaya değin ḳalmaḳ ve-sāʾire ʿibret olmaḳ üzere līmāna gönderilmesi lāzımeden olmağla olvecihle līmāna gönderile.

[6] Ḳātiliñ fiʿli aʿẓam-i ḳabāyıḥdan ve-bataḳcılıḳ ʿameli ekber-i fażāyıḥdan olmağla bir kimsenin üzerine ḳatl-i māddesi ve-bataḳcılıḳ cünḥası sābit olur ise ḳışāşlarına bedel ömürleri tamām oluncaya değin ḳalmaḳ ve-āhara ʿibret olmaḳ üzere kezālik līmāna gönderile.

---

50 In presenting the text I have used the transliteration system of the *International Journal of Middle Eastern Studies*.

[7] Ḳıbṭī milleti māl-i mīrī seriḳatiyle me'lūf ve-emvāl-i re'āyāyı ihtilāsı mecbūr olmalariyle ḳurā ḳubbāẓları ve-ṣarrāflarınıñ emvāl-i mīriyeden seriḳatı ve-māl-i re'āyādan ihtilāsı ẓuhūr eder ise ve-ihtilāsı ne ise ve-māli var ise ba'd al-subūt mālinden alına ve-kendüsi beş sene müddet ile līmāna gönderile māli yoğısa 'ömri tamam oluncaya değin ḳalmaḳ ve-sā'ire 'ibret olmaḳ üzere irsāl oluna ol vecihle ẓuhūr eden ihtilāsıñ def'i muḳtaẓayātdan olmağla def' oluna.

[8] Ḳıbṭī milletiniñ büyükleri hademe-yi mīriyeden olmağla işbu seriḳat-i māl-i mīrī ve-ihtilās-i emvāl-i re'āyā ef'āl-i şenī'esi anlardan ẓuhūr edüb üzerlerine sābit olur ise o maḳūlalar līmāna gönderilmiyüb 'ibretan lil-gayr i'dām oluna.

[9] Büyük şeyhler ya'nī huṭṭ şeyhleri hademeyi mīriyeden ma'dūd olmalariyle cünḥaları vuḳū'unda anlara da bāb-i evvel ve-sānīde beyān oldığı vecihle muḥāfıẓ ve-me'mūr ve-nāẓırlar misillü mu'āmele oluna ve-līmāna irsāl ile terbiyeleri icrā ḳılına ḥiṣṣe[51] şeyhleri ya'nī ḳurā şeyhleri zirā'at ve-ḥarāsetle ma'lūf olduḳlarından başḳa ḥiṣṣeleri fellāḥi kendülerinden maṭlūb idüğinden cünḥaları vuḳū'unda hidmet ve-maṣlaḥatlarına sekte gelmemin içün līmāna gönderilmeyüb cünḥasına göre üçyüzden beşyüze ḳadar ḳırbāç urıla zimmetlerinde ẓuhūr eden ihtilās ne ise taḥṣīl oluna ve-şeyhliğinden 'azl olunub sebīlī tahliye oluna.

[10] Bir kimesne seriḳat töhmetiyle methūm olsa üzerine seriḳat māddesi isbāt olunamazsa[52] ol kimesneleriñ sābiḳası varmıdır yoḳmıdır sorıla sābiḳası yoğısa te'dīb olunmiyüb beş on gün ḥabs oluna kendüye töhmet eden kimesne bu on beş gün içinde hırsızlığını isbāt edebilür ise bāb-i sālisda beyān olunan ḳānūna taṭbīḳ ile ṣūret-i iḳtiẓā ne ise icrā oluna ve-isbāt edemez ise ol methūmın kefīlī eline saliverile ve-methūmun ismi ve-kefīliniñ ismi ve-isnād olunan seriḳat huṣūṣi mufaṣṣalan dīvān defterlerine ḳayd oluna ve-bir müddet murūrunda ol methūm üzerine ol seriḳat māddesi sābit olur ise kefīli bir sene ḳalmaḳ ve-kendisi bāb-i sālisda beyān olundığı vecihle iḳāmet etmek üzere līmāna gönderile terbiye oluna ve-ol methūma kefīl olur kimesne bulunmıyub bu vecihle hırsızlığı olması mütebādir-i hāṭır[53] olur ise ol vaḳt keyfiyeti bilenlerden

51 The text has here huṭṭ şeyhleri ya'nî ḳurā şeyhleri. The word *huṭṭ* is evidently a mistake since it was used also to describe the important sheikhs at the beginning of this section. Moreover, the other version of this code uses in this connection the term *ḥiṣṣe şeyhleri*, i.e. the sheikhs of a portion of the village. The corresponding section begins with the words: Ve-kezālik ḥiṣṣe şeyhleriyle büyük şeyhlerin beyinlerinden farḳ olub ḥiṣṣe şeyhleri mīrī hademeden olmadığından ... (Since there is a similar difference between the village sheikhs (*ḥiṣṣe şeyhleri*) and the high-ranking sheikhs and since the village sheikhs do not belong to the state servants ...).

52 The text has olunhmsh (?) without the z, probably a copyist's error.

53 The text has haṭar, which is obviously a mistake.

sorıla ve-atrāfiyle taḥḳīḳ oluna ve-seriḳata dā'ir üzerine bir şey' tebeyyün eder ise bāb-i sālisda basṭ olunan uṣūl üzere iḳtiżāsı icrā oluna.

Ancaḳ me'mūrlere ve-hākimlere vācib ve-ehemmdir ki methūm olan kimesneyi methūmdur diyerek icrā-yi cezāda ta'cīl etmiyüb garaż ve-nefsāniyetden berī olan kimesne ma'rifetiyle ḥāl ve-keyfiyeti taḥḳīḳe diḳḳat ve-ihtimām edeler ve-min Allāh al-tevfīḳ.

Fī 20 Şa'bān tārīhinde Meclis-i Dāverī ḳarārgīr olub zikr olunan ḳānūn-i siyasiye zeyl olunan hulāṣeden alınmışdır.

[11] Emvāl-i mīriyeden ihtilās eden mu'allim ve-ṣarrāf ve-meşāyihin ihtilās etdiği māl yüz gurūşa bāliğ ise istirdād olunduḳdan sonra ihtilās eden Aḳālīm-i Ṣa'īdiyeden ise bir māh iki yüz gurūşa bāliğ ise iki māh ebniye-yi mīriyede istihdām oluna ve-üç yüze dört yüze nihāyet bu siyāḳ üzere olub icrāsı lāzim gelmekle icrā oluna.

Tārīh-i mezkūrda ḳaṣr-ı 'ālīde mun'aḳid 'Umūm-i Meclisinde tertīb olunan siyāset ül-hulāṣeden alınmışdır.

[12] Bir hırsız meyva ve-sebze ve-ḳavun ve-ḳarpuz ve-galle gibi şey' çalar ise ve-çaldığı şey' yiyeceği ḳadar ise huṭṭ ḥākimi ma'rifetiyle on ḳırbaç urıla satılacaḳ ḳadar ise elli ḳırbaç urıla ve-tavuḳ çalana yirmi beş ḳırbaç urıla ve-sefīneden galle çalana yüz ḳırbaç urıla.

[13] Keçi ve-ḳoyun çalar ise ve-sābiḳası yoğısa yüz ḳırbaç urıla ve-çaldığı ikinci def'a ise iki yüz ḳırbaç üçüncü def'a ise üc yüz ḳırbaç urıla dördüncü def'a ise līmāna gönderile.

[14] Bir fellāḥ veyā şeyh-i beled ḥākime gidüb āherıñ 'aleyhine bilā cerem yalan söyler ise ve-kendi ihtiyār eder ise ḳā'immaḳām ve-huṭṭ şeyhleri ma'rifetiyle tenbīh oluna tenbīh olmıyup yine ihtiyār eder ise tekdīr olunacağı tefhīm ḳılına ve-bir fellāḥ veyā şeyh-i beled ḥākim ḥużūrunda kendüden bir şey' soruldukda doğrusu söylemeyüb kezbi ẓāhir olur ise şeyh ise elli fellāḥ ise yirmi beş ḳırbaç urıla.

[15] Bir fellāḥ zimmetinde olan māli edāye muḳtadir iken vermeyüb ṭalab eden ile nizā' eder ise ve-bu nizā' göz ve-ḳulağ ve-burun ve-diş 'użvıñ ṣaḳaṭ [sic!] olmasına bā'is olur ise şer'le da'vāları görüle ve-muḳtażā-yı şer'īsi 'urf ḥākimi ma'rifetiyle icrā olur.

[16] Bir şeyh-i beled firārī celbine gidüb bulduḳda para alub salıverir ise ba'd al-taḥḳīḳ iki yüz ḳırbaç urıla.

[17] Ḳaryelerde olan cezzār veyā fellāḥ bilā ʿuzr dişi ḥayvān zebḥ eder ise ve-erkek ḥayvāndan üç yaşından aşağı olanı boğazlar ise ve-öküz ve-cāmūs gibi ḥayvānları keser ise birinci defʿada yüz ḳırbaç ikinci defʿada iki yüz ḳırbaç urıla.

[The layout of following part of the document is different from the preceding one. The paragraphs are written alternately in horizontal and vertical lines. The vertical ones (indicated with an *a*) contain the measures that are to be taken with the persons described in the following horizontal paragraph (numbered with a *b*).]

[18a] Sağlam olanları demürhaneye ve-genç olanları ʿasākire ve-ziyāde ʿācız olanları bilād-i baʿīdeye yaʿnī Esnā gibi maḥallere ibʿād ve-irsāl olsun ve-alaylara gönderilecekler cihādiyeye gönderilüb bunlarıñ hālleri bildirilsünki güzelce ẓabṭ olsun deyü irāde buyrulmuşdur.

(Written horizontally)
[18b] Maḥrūsede ve-Maḥrūse civārında kā'in baʿẓ-ı köylerde Nūrī ṭā'ifası bulunur anlarıñ ḳārılar ve-ḳızlar ve-küçük çocuḳları baʿẓan Maḥrūsede ruhṣat bulduḳları evlere ve-dükkānlere ve-gayrı maḥallere gündüzleri girerler az çoḳ ellerine geçeni alurlar yararlıḳ iḳtiẓāsiyle bunlarıñ bu hırsızlıḳ ʿādetleri olmağla işler ve-işlemeğe mecbūr olurlar bunlarıñ içinde ʿalīl ve-ihtiyārları vardır ve-ḥāmila olanı ve-baʿẓan ḳucağında ve-yanında bir veyā iki küçük çocuğı olanı da bulunur çaldığı şey' beş ḳuruşluḳdan beş yüze ḳadar ve-baʿẓan biñ guruşa ḳadar görüldiği vardır.

(Written vertically)
[19a] Bunlarıñ sağlam olanları demürhaneye ve-genç olanları ʿasākire ve-ziyade ʿacız olanları kezālik zīrde muḥarrar olan şarḥ misillü icrā olunacaḳ.

(Written horizontally)
[19b] Maḥrūse harābelerinde ve-Maḥrūse ṣūrı [sic!] hāricinde baʿẓ-ı maḥallerde baʿẓ-ı ʿācız köylü ḳarıları ve-ʿalīl ve-zelīl erkekleri ve-Maḥrūsede doğmuş ve-anasız ve-babasız ḳalmış erkek ve-dişi Mıṣr çocuḳları ve-baʿẓan dahi bir ʿillet ile maʿlūl olmuş dilencilik gezmeğe muʿtād etmiş kimesneler vardır ki anlar dahi ruhṣat bulduḳca ellerine geçeni alurlar içlerinde baʿẓı sağlamları var ise de ekserisi düşkün şaşḳın ʿalīl ve-zelīl çırılçıplaḳ kimesneler ve-çaldıḳları şey dahi Nūrī ḳarıları gibi beş guruşluḳdan beş yüze ve-biñe ḳadar görüldiği vardır

(Written vertically)
[20a] Bunlarıñ sağlam olanları daʿvāsını baʿd al-istimāʿ Cihādiyeye ilḥāḳa ve-ṣaḳaṭlarını demürhāneye kürek (or: kürük) ve-sā'ir yarayacaḳ işe istihdām ettirilsün

(Written horizontally)
[20b] Maḥrūse içinde ve-civārinde baʿẓı ḳapusuz baçasız[54] siyāh ʿabīdler vardır ki kimisine ağası izn vermiş ve-kimisi ağasına hayr etmemiş kendü başına ḳalmış ve-baʿẓının ağası fevt olub bir maḥall bulamamış ve-derbeder olmuş bunların baʿẓıları çürükdir baʿẓısı sağlamdır medār-i taʿayyüş olur bellüce birr-i uṣūlları olmadığından bunlar dahi baʿẓan ḳapma çarpma ve-öteye beri el uzatma ḥareketleri görülmüşdür

(Written vertically)
[21a] Bunların içlerinde ufaḳ çocuḳları olanları terzilere ve-Edhem Bey ṭarafına ve-faburḳalara ve-sā'ir ṣanāyiʿ olan maḥallere gönderilsün bu soyları ẓuhūr etdikce daʿvāları subūt baʿd al-subūt [sic!] hemān menvāl-i muḥarrar üzere sālif al-zikr maḥallāte gönderilsün

(Written horizontally)
[21b] Magribīlerden ve-sā'irinden baʿẓı baḳlacı ve-mendelci gibi fālcı ve-baʿẓ-ı afsūncı ve-māl çıḳarmaḳ içün yer ḳazıcı vardır ki anlar dahi birer hīle ile ʿavāmm-i nāsı dolandırmaḳdan hālī değildir erkekleri ve-dişleri vardır sağlamca olanı var ise de ʿalīl ve-zelīl bulunanları da vardır aldıḳları şey' dahi beş guruşluḳdan beş yüze biñe ḳadar görülmüşdür mendel hükmiyle āhere ẓararları irişe geldiği dahi müşāhede olunmuşdur

[22] Maḥrūsede ve-Būlāḳ ve-eski Mışırda ve-civārlarında başı boş gezen Nūrīler ve-Maḥrūse ve-ḳurā ahālīsinden ve-Ḥicāz ve-Sūdān halḳından ve-ʿabīd ve-fālcı ve-afsūncı ve-defīneci maḳūlesinden muẓirr-i nās olanların keyfiyetleri ḳaleme alınub Vālī ül-Niʿam ʿAlā-yi Himem Ibrāhīm Paşa Efendimize ʿarẓ olunduḳda yaramazlığına göre olunacaḳ muʿāmeleyi bālā-yi su'āla ṣādır olan firmān-i ʿālīleriyle beyān buyurmuş olmalariyle bu maḥalle ḳayd olundu.

Appendix 2: the English Translation of the New Laws[55]

The [following] has been copied from the penal statute (*ḳānūn-i siyāsiye*) regarding criminals drawn up in the General Council (*Meclis-i ʿUmūmī*) that was convened in the *Ḳaṣr-i ʿĀlī* on 21 Rabīʿ I [12]45 [ʿ20 September, 1829].

54 The text has erroneously pcāsz. The reading *baçasız* is based on the expression *ḳapusu baçası yoḳ*, he has no house to go to.

55 I would like to express my gratitude to Erik Jan Zürcher of Leiden for his kind help in solving some of the problems posed by the Ottoman text.

[1] If it comes to light that a provincial governor (*muḥāfiẓ*), a department head (*meʾmūr*) or a district chief (*nāẓir*),[56] who is in the service of the state, has extorted property by acting unjustly and illegally towards the subjects, the thing that he has partially or entirely taken, shall be collected from him and he shall be sent to Abū Ḳīr for a period of six months.

[2] If such a provincial governor, department head or district chief has the audacity to steal or embezzle state property, this shall be recorded and investigated by reliable and unprejudiced persons. Whatever the amount of the embezzlement proves to be, it shall be taken from him and he shall be sent to Abū Ḳīr for one year.

[3] If it comes to light that such a theft or embezzlement is committed by a sheikh or another person, regardless of whether it was state or private property, he shall be sent to the Alexandria Dockyards for one year if the value [of the stolen goods] is up to 1,000 piasters, for a year and a half if the value was between 1,000 and 5,000 piasters, for two years if the value was between 5,000 and 10,000 piasters, for two and a half years if the value was up to 20,000 piasters, for three years if the value is between 20,000 and 40,000 piasters, and also for three years if the value is between 40,000 and 60,000 piasters.[57] These penal provisions (*aḥkām-i siyāsiye*), that were to be enforced with regard to criminals beginning in the year 1244, shall henceforth be applied.

[4] The relatives of those sheikhs and other persons that have gone to the Alexandria Dockyards in the aforementioned manner may submit a petition to the Sublime Khedival Threshold (*Hāk-i ʿālī-yi hidīvī*) before the completion of their term. If [the *vali*] grants his sovereign pardon and if it is known that those criminals will be useful for the prosperity of the region and the well-being of the state and that they are repentant and penitent and if a Supreme Decree (*irāde-yi seniye*) is issued in connection with their release, then an exception shall be made from the procedure of the aforementioned fixed terms: the ruling of this document [the decree] shall be followed and the criminal in questions shall be released according to its requirements.

56 *Muḥafiẓ* is synonymous with *mudīr*, governor of a *mudīriyya*, province. A province was divided in departments (*meʾmūriyya*) headed by *meʾmūrs*. These were subdivided in districts (*ḳism*), governed by a *nāẓir*. Between the district and the village there was the subdistrict (*huṭṭ*) with the *ḥākim al-huṭṭ* or *şeyh al-huṭṭ*. The latter was represented by a *ḳāʾimmaḳām* at the village level. Hunter (1984), p. 19; Rivlin (1961), p. 88 ff.

57 The other version of this law in Document B lays down that in the last case the period of imprisonment is three and a half years and adds that if the value between 60,000 and 100,000, the period if imprisonment is four years.

[5] Counterfeiting is one of the acts that are forbidden both by divine and secular law. Therefore, if persons who have the audacity to commit this abominable deed fall into the hands [of the authorities], it is necessary that they shall be sent to the Alexandria Dockyards to remain there until the completion of their lifetime as a deterring example for others. In this manner they shall be sent to the Alexandria Dockyards.

[6] Homicide is one of the most repulsive deeds, and robbery (*baṭaḳçılıḳ*)[58] is one of the most shameful acts. Therefore, if a case of homicide or the crime of robbery is proven against a person, he shall likewise be sent to the Alexandria Dockyards to remain there until the completion of their[59] lifetime as a deterring example for others, instead of their [being sentenced to] death.[60]

[7] The community of Copts is accustomed to steal state property and is devoted to the embezzlement of the properties of the subjects. Therefore, if it comes to light that a [Coptic] village tax collector (*ḳābiż, ṣarrāf*) has stolen state property or embezzled properties of the subjects, then after the fact has been proven, it [i.e. the value of what has been stolen], regardless of what [kind of] property he has embezzled, shall be taken from his property, if he has [sufficient] property, and he shall be sent to the Alexandria Dockyards for five years. However, if he has no property, he shall be sent [to the Alexandria Dockyards] to remain there until the completion of his lifetime as a deterring example for others. Since it is necessary to prevent embezzlements that occur, they shall in this manner be prevented.

[8] The high ranking [officials] of the Coptic community are state servants (*hademe-yi mīriye*). Therefore, if it comes to light that one of them has committed infamous acts of stealing state property or of embezzling the properties of the subjects, and if it has been proven against him, he shall not be sent to the Alexandria Dockyards but be put to death as a deterring example for others.

[9] The high ranking sheikhs, that is the *huṭṭ* sheikhs, are regarded as state servants (*hademe-yi mīriye*). Therefore, if they commit crimes, they shall be treated like provincial governors, department heads or district chiefs in the manner set forth in

58 Turkish dictionaries usually translate the word *baṭaḳcı* with "fraudulent borrower" or "swindler". My translation "robber", which fits better in the context, is based on the handwritten Arabic translation, which translates *baṭaḳcılıḳ* with *al-baṭāqjiyya quṭṭāʿ al-ṭarīq*. The two Arabic summaries of the law, that have been published translate the word with "*quṭṭāʿ al-ṭarīq*". See Sāmī (1928–1936) ii, 354 and Zaghlūl (1900) 163.

59 The change from singular to plural is based on the Turkish text.

60 From later judicial practice it is clear that this section would be applied only if the *qāḍī* could not sentence the defendant to death. See Peters (1997).

Sections 1 and 2 and their correction shall take place by sending them to the Alexandria Dockyards. The village sheikhs [on the other hand] are accustomed to sowing and plowing and, moreover, the dues of the farmers of the village quarters (*ḥiṣṣe*) are collected through them. Therefore, if they commit a crime, they shall not be sent to the Alexandria Dockyards, lest their service and usefulness come to a standstill. Instead they shall receive, commensurate with the crime, 300 to 500 lashes with the *ḳırbaç* and whatever the amount of their debt resulting from the embezzlement that has come to light, it shall be collected from them. Furthermore, they shall be removed from their office and then released.

[10] If a person is accused of theft and the theft cannot be proven against him, then inquiries shall be made as to whether or not he has previous convictions. If this is not the case, he shall not be punished but put into prison for five or ten days. If the person who has accused him can prove the theft within these fifteen days, the rule set forth in Section 3 shall be applied and whatever is required shall be carried out. However, if he cannot prove it, the accused shall be released into the hands of his guarantor (*kefīl*) and the name of both the accused and his guarantor as well as the particulars of the theft that is imputed to him shall be recorded in detail in the registers of the Divan. If, after some time, that theft case can be proven against the accused, both his guarantor and he himself shall be punished and sent to the Alexandria Dockyards: his guarantor for one year and the accused for the period set forth in Section 3. If no one can be found to be a guarantor for that accused and it is therefore obvious that he was the thief, then inquiries shall be made with people who know his circumstances and he and the people around him shall be investigated. If something concerning this theft is proven against him, that what is required according to the principles expounded in Section 3 shall be carried out.

Now, on the other hand it is necessary and important for the officials (*meʾmūrlar ve-ḥākimler*) not to act too hastily in imposing punishment on the accused with the argument that he is [already accused] and they must be meticulous and careful in the investigation of his situation and circumstances through a person free from prejudice and rancor. And all success comes from God.

[The following] was decided in the Sovereign Council (*Meclis-Dâverî*) that was convened on 20 Ş[aʿbān] [1]245 [14 February, 1830], and has been copied from the minutes which have been added as a supplement to the aforementioned penal statute.

[11] If a tax collector (*muʿallim, ṣarrāf*) or sheikh who embezzles state funds is from Upper Egypt, he shall be employed, after having returned the property that he has embezzled, on the state building sites (*ebniye-yi mīriyye*), for one month if the value of the property embezzled by him amounted to 100 piasters, [and] for two months if the

value amounted to 200 piasters. Since it is necessary to apply this method [of calculating the sentence] until 300 and 400 [piasters], it shall be applied.

[The following] was taken from the minutes of (i.e. concerning a decision on, RP) a penal statute drawn up in the General Council (*Meclis-i ʿUmūmī*) that was convened in the *Ḳaṣr-i ʿĀlī* on the aforementioned date.

[12] If a thief steals things like fruits, vegetables, sugar melons, water melons and cereals and if the quantity of things stolen by him is as much as he would eat, he shall be given ten lashes with the *ḳırbaç* by the commissioner of the subdistrict (*huṭṭ ḥākimi*). However, if it is a quantity that would be sold, he shall be given fifty lashes. A person who steals a chicken shall be given twenty-five lashes and a person who steals cereals from a ship shall be given 100 lashes.

[13] If someone steals a goat or a sheep and he has no previous convictions, he shall be given 100 lashes with the *ḳırbaç*. If, however, he has previous convictions, and it is the second time he has stolen, he shall be given 200 lashes. If it is the third time, he shall be given 300 lashes. As for the fourth time, he shall be sent to the Alexandria Dockyards.[61]

[14] If a peasant or a village sheikh goes to a district commissioner (*ḥākim*) and evidently tells lies against someone else and if he does so by his own free will, he shall be given a warning by the canton lieutenant (*ḳāʾimmaḳām*) and the district sheikhs. If he does not heed this warning and does so again by his own free will, he shall be given to understand that he will be reprimanded. If a peasant or a village sheikh, upon being asked something in the presence of the commissioner, does not tell the truth in that matter and his lie is apparent, he shall be given fifty lashes of the *ḳırbaç* if he is a sheikh and twenty five if he is a peasant.[62]

[15] If a peasant who is capable of paying his debt does not pay it but starts a fight with the person who demands [payment], and if this fight results in damage to an organ such as an eye, an ear, a nose or a tooth, their case shall be dealt with according to the shariʿa, and the administrative official (*ʿurf ḥākimi*) shall execute whatever the shariʿa requires.[63]

---

61 Sections 12 and 13 are identical to section 4 of the *Qānūn al-Filāḥa* (1830).

62 This section is identical to section 19, second paragraph of the *Qānūn al-Filāḥa* (1830).

63 This section is identical to section 7 of the *Qānūn al-Filāḥa* (1830).

[16] If a village sheikh goes out to fetch fugitives and finds them but takes money [from them] and releases them, he shall be given 200 lashes of the *ḳırbāç* after the case has been investigated.[64]

[17] If a butcher in the villages or a peasant slaughters a female animal without an excuse or kills a male animal under the age of three or butchers animals like oxen or buffaloes, he shall be given 100 lashes of the *ḳırbāç* for the first offense and 200 lashes for the second one.[65]

[For the sake of clarity I (RP) have placed the concluding paragraph [22], with the details of the origin of the text, at the beginning of this section.]

[22] Here it is recorded that a report on the circumstances of the gypsies (*Nūrī*) that are wandering around unemployed in Cairo, Bulaq, Old Cairo and their surroundings, and on the circumstances of those who are harmful to the people among the inhabitants of Cairo and the villages, among the people from Hejaz and Sudan and among such slaves, fortune-tellers, magicians, and treasure-hunters, was written and submitted to the Benefactor and the Sublime Grace our Lord Ibrahim Pasha, and that, in a noble order (*firmān-i ʿālī*) issued in response to the above mentioned problem, he has explained what action must be taken against these persons in consideration of their mischief.

[18a] A decree has been issued to the effect that those [among the following] who are healthy are to be removed and sent to the ironworks,[66] those of them who are young to the troops and those of them who are very unfit to remote regions, i.e. to places like Esna. Those of them who are to be sent to the regiments shall [first] be sent to the Ministry of War (*Cihādiye*) and their circumstances must be reported [to it] so that they can be thoroughly recorded.

[18b] In Cairo and some villages on the outskirts of Cairo there are gypsies. Sometimes, [even] in broad daylight, their women, daughters and little children enter houses, shops and other places in Cairo for [the entrance of] which they have found permission and they take whatever gets into their hands, be it little or much. Since they have these thievish habits, they must be compelled to [perform] different jobs and tasks.

64 This section is identical to section 36 of the *Qānūn al-Filāḥa* (1830).

65 This section is identical to section 38 of the *Qānūn al-Filāḥa* (1830). It would seem that this penal provision intended to maintain the reproductive capacity of the existing livestock and to prevent the slaughtering of draught animals needed for farm work.

66 Probably the iron foundry in Bulaq. Cf. Fahmy (1954) 34.

Among them there are those who are disabled, old and pregnant and sometimes there are also those who have one or two small children in their arms or at their sides. It has been observed that the value of the things they steal varies from five piasters to 500 and sometimes even one thousand piasters.

[19a] Those among these [following persons] who are healthy [shall be sent] to the ironworks, those among them who are young [shall be sent] to the troops, and [with regard to] those who are very unfit also the same measures shall be taken as in the explanation mentioned below.

[19b] In the ruins of Cairo and outside the city walls of Cairo there are at certain places some poor peasant women and disabled and contemptible peasant men, and [also] city boys and girls who were born in Cairo and have become orphans, some of whom are also disabled. They have become accustomed to wandering around and begging. They, too, take what comes into their hands whenever they find permission. Although there are some healthy persons among them, most of them are destitute, confused, disabled and contemptible (*ʿalīl ve-zelīl*) and stark naked. It has been observed that the value of the things they steal, like with the Gypsy women, varies from five piasters to 500 and sometimes even 1,000 piasters.

[20a] Those among the following persons who are healthy shall be enrolled in the army after their cases have been heard. The disabled [shall be sent] to the ironworks and be employed in shovelling (or: working the bellows, *kürük*) and other jobs for which they are fit.

[20b] In Cairo and its surroundings there are at certain places some homeless black slaves. Some of those have been given leave by their masters, but others have been of no use to their masters and are now left to their own devices. Others again did not find a place after their masters had died and became beggars. Whether they are disabled or healthy, this becomes a means of livelihood for them. They are evidently devoid of honesty and it has been observed that sometimes they also commit actions like snatching and thieving.

[21a] Those among the following who have small children shall be sent to the tailors, to Edhem Bey,[67] to the factories and to the other industrial establishments. As soon as these kinds of people appear, they must immediately be sent in the aforementioned way to the places listed above, after their cases have been proven.

67 Edhem Bey was an official responsible for the arms and ammunition industry. Sāmī (1928–1936) ii, 454 (21 Rajab 1251), ii, 449 (29 Rabīʿ II, 1251); Fahmy (1954) 37.

[21b] Among the North Africans[68] and other groups there are some fortunetellers like the *baḳlacı*[69] and the *mendelci*,[70] and some magicians (*afsuncı*) and treasure hunters (lit.: people who dig in the earth in order to bring out money), none of whom is innocent of cheating the common people, each with his own tricks. Among them there are men and women. Although some of them are quite healthy, there are also [many] who are disabled and contemptible. It has been observed that the value of the things they steal also varies from five piasters to 500 and sometimes even 1,000 piasters. It has also been noticed that *mendelci* practices have come to the point that through it others have been harmed.

References

Baer, G. (1969) "Tanzimat in Egypt: The Penal Code," in: G. Baer, *Studies in the Social History of Modern Egypt* (Chicago: The University of Chicago Press), pp. 109–133.

Deny, J. (1930) *Sommaire des archives turques du Caire* (Le Caire: Institut français d'archéologie orientale).

Dodwell, H. (1931) *The Founder of Modern Egypt: A Study of Muhammad ʿAli* (Cambridge: Cambridge University Press).

Espéronnier, M. (1997) "La mort violente à l'époque mamlouke: le crime et le châtiment," *Der Islam*, 74, pp. 137–155.

Fahmy, Khaled M. (1997) *"All the Pasha's Men": Mehmed Ali, His Army and the Making of Modern Egypt* (Cambridge: Cambridge University Press).

Fahmy, Moustafa (1954) *La révolution de l'industrie en Égypte* (Leiden: Brill).

Faraḥāt, Muḥammad Nūr (1993) *Al-tārīkh al-ijtimāʿī li-l-qānūn fī Miṣr al-ḥadīth*. 2nd impr. (Kuwait: Dār Suʿād al-Ṣabāḥ).

Forbin, Count de (n.d.) *Travels in Egypt, Being a Continuation of Travels in the Holy Land, in 1817–18* (London).

Foucault, Michel (1989) *Discipline, toezicht en straf: de geboorte van de gevangenis* (Groningen: De Historische Uitgeverij).

Gisquet, M., (n.d.) *L'Égypte, les turcs et les arabes* (Paris: Amyot).

Guémard, G. (1936) *Une oeuvre française: Les réformes en Egypte, d'Al-Bey El Kébir à Méhémet-Ali*, 1760–1848 (Le Caire).

Hamed, Raouf Abbas (1995) "The *Siyasetname* and the Institutionalization of Central Administration Under Muhammad ʿAli," in Nelly Hanna (ed.), *The State and its*

68 Lane (1966) 274: "a celebrated Maghrabee magician".

69 A fortuneteller who predicts the future by throwing beans.

70 A fortuneteller who predicts the future by contemplating the surface of a reflecting liquid like ink or oil. On *ḍarb al-mandal*, see Lane (1966) 275ff.

Servants: Administration in Egypt from Ottoman Times to the Present (Cairo: The American University in Cairo Press) pp. 75–88.
Heyd, Uriel (1973) *Studies in Old Ottoman Criminal Law*. Ed. by V.L. Ménage (Oxford: Oxford University Press).
Hunter, F.R. (1984) *Egypt under the khedives: From Household Government to Modern Bureaucracy*. (Pittsburgh, Pa.: University of Pittsburg Press).
Ibn Rushd (1960) *Bidāyat al-mujtahid* (3rd impr. Cairo).
Jabartī, ʿAbd al-Raḥmān al-, (1297 H.) *ʿAjāʾib al-āthār fī al-tarājim wa-l-akhbār*, 4 vols (Būlāq).
Jallād, Fīlīb, *Qāmūs al-idāra wa-l-qaḍāʾ*. 5 vols (Alexandria: 1890–95).
Lane, Edward William (1966) *Manners and Customs of the Modern Egyptians* (Repr., London etc.: Dent) Originally publ. 1836.
Lāyiḥat zirāʿat al-fallāḥ wa-tadbīr aḥkām al-siyāsa bi-qaṣd al-najāḥ. 2nd impr. (Būlāq: 1256 H.).
Motzki, Harald (1979) *Dimma und Égalité: Die nichtmuslimischen Minderheiten Ägyptens in der zweiten Hälfte des 18. Jahrhunderts und die Expedition Bonapartes (1798–1801)* (Bonn: Selbstverlag des Orientalischen Seminars der Universität).
O'Brien, Patricia (1982) *The Promise of Punishment: Prisons in Nineteenth Century France*. (Princeton: Princeton University Press).
Peters, R. (1997) "Islamic and Secular Criminal law in 19th Century Egypt: The Role and Function of the Qadi," *Islamic law and Society*, 4, pp. 70–90.
Peters, R. (1999) "Administrators and Magistrates: The Development of a Secular Judiciary in Egypt, 1842–1871," *Die Welt des Islams*, 39, pp. 378–397.
Rāfiʿī, ʿAbd al-Raḥmān al- (1972) ʿAṣr Muḥammad ʿAlī. 4th impr. (Cairo: Dār al-Maʿārif).
Rivlin, Helen A.B. (1961) *The Agricultural Policy of Muḥammad ʿAlī in Egypt* (Cambridge, Ma.: Harvard University Press).
Sāmī, Amīn (1928–36) *Taqwīm al-Nīl*. 3 vols (Cairo: Maṭbaʿat al-Kutub al-Miṣriyya).
Schoelcher, V. (1846) *L'Égypte en 1845* (Paris: Pagnerre).
Shaykhzāde (1301 H.) *Majmaʿ al-anhur fī sharḥ multaqā al-abḥur*. 2 vols (Istanbul).
Weisser, Michael R. (1979) *Crime and Punishment in Early Modern Europe* (Hassocks, Sussex).
Zaghlūl, Ahmad Fathī (1900) *Al-Muhāmāt* (Cairo: Maṭbaʿat al-Maʿārif).

CHAPTER 5

Administrators and Magistrates

The Development of a Secular Judiciary in Egypt, 1842–1871

1 Introduction[1]

In 1812, the well-known Egyptian chronicler al-Jabarti[2] tells us, a gang of thieves were apprehended in Cairo and brought before the chief qadi. They confessed to having committed many thefts, yet the qadi could not convict them since, in their confessions, they used not the phrase "we have stolen", but the words "we have taken". Under the Shari'a, this constitutes ambiguity (*shubha*) which precludes the application of *hadd*-punishment. The qadi then wrote a report to the kethüda[3] (the first lieutenant of the *vali* and de facto governor of Cairo) and entrusted the matter to him for further disposal. The latter, after some reflection, sentenced them to amputation of their hands on the strength of his authority to impose penalties by way of *ta'zir* or *siyasa*.

This little episode illustrates some features of Egyptian criminal law enforcement in the early decades of the nineteenth century. Both the qadi and the administration were involved and both applied Islamic law. This was a continuation of the situation prevailing in the seventeenth and eighteenth centuries. During this period, the qadi would deal with criminal matters whenever there was a plaintiff and a defendant. If he could not sentence the defendant, or if there was no plaintiff, the civil or military authorities would deal with the matter.[4]

What I intend to discuss in this paper is how this simple system of law enforcement by the executive, complementing the qadi's jurisdiction, gradually evolved during the nineteenth century into a much more complex and sophisticated type of justice administered by a fully-fledged judiciary. This judiciary was finally, between 1883 and 1889, replaced by a French type court system. I will limit myself to the common courts and will not pay attention to the commercial tribunals, established in 1845, or the Council of the Qumisyun, that functioned between 1861 and 1864 to deal with civil cases between Egyptians

1 This is the revised text of a paper presented at the 2nd Joseph Schacht Conference on Theory and Practice in Islamic Law, Granada, 16–20 December 1997.

2 Jabarti (1297 H) IV, 144.

3 Since Turkish was the administrative language of Egypt until the 1850s, I will use the Turkish version of administrative terms referring to functionaries and organs existing before 1850.

4 See Farahat (1993) and El-Nahal (1979).

 | DOI:10.1163/9789004420625_006

and foreigners.[5] After sketching how this judiciary expanded from one single court of justice operating in the political centre into a five-tiered judiciary, I will discuss some essential features and characteristics of the system.

2 Law Enforcement by the Administration

Until 1842, when the *Cemʿiyet-i Hakkaniye* (see below) was created, the most important of the authorities involved in law enforcement was the *kethüda* and the council presided by him. This council, established in 1805–1806 (1220 H), was first known as *Divan-i Vali,* and later as *Divan-i Hidivi.*[6] Although its main task was administrative, it would also try serious offences. An ordinance of April 1838 defined the jurisdictions of the Divan-i Hidivi and the Police Department (Zabithane). Simple cases, such as quarrels between spouses or private persons ("Zayd wa-ʿAmr" as the Ordinance expresses it) and arguments in marketplaces were to be dealt with at the police station (located in Muski Street) by an official of the Divan-i Hidivi together with the chief of police or one of his officers. They first had to try to achieve a reconciliation between the parties. Although the decree does not make mention of it, one may assume that petty offenders were punished at the police station, usually by beating. In case the parties did not agree they were sent to the Divan-i Hidivi with the report of the police investigation. If the case had to be examined according to the Shariʿa, the parties were sent to the qadi. Petty cases could also be summarily dealt in the streets by the *muhtesib*.[7] Serious cases such as murder, theft, and indecency, were immediately brought to the attention of the Divan-i Hidivi for examination and trial.[8] If capital punishment was at stake, the case would be

5 Zaghlul (1900), 199–200, 209; appendix 85–90.

6 The Divan-i Hidivi was located in the Cairo Citadel. (Lane (1966), p. 114) For its power in criminal matters, see Deny (1930), 114. In the decree of 1837 (Rabiʿ I, 1253), creating an administration consisting of six Diwans, the existing (*ka-ma fi al-sabiq*) competence of the Divan-i Hidivi was defined as follows: (1) legal affairs of the Capital (*umur ahkam Mahrusat Misr*, (2) examination and rendering judgment in cases submitted by petitions from the regions. (Tashkil al-Dawawin wa-Qanun al-Siyasatnama, Ch. 1, Art. 1; text in Zaghlul (1900), app. 4–26). Deny observes that the Divan-i Hidivi must be distinguished from the Maʿiyet-i Seniye, also known as Sura-yi Muʿavenet, whereas Zaghlul, erroneously, regards them as identical. (Deny (1930), 92; Zaghlul (1900), 159–160).

7 The office of muhtesib was abolished some time before 1837 and the offenses that he used to deal with were now heard by the Divan-i Hidivi. (Ibid. Ch. 1, Art. 5). For the way the muhtesib functioned, cf. Lane (1966), 126; Sami (1928–1936), II, 262, 542.

8 Divan-i Hidivi Layihesi, dated 13 Muharram 1254 (8–4–1838), in 18 articles. Turkish and Arabic text in the Egyptian National Archive (Dar al-Watha'iq al-Qawmiyya, henceforth DWQ), Mahfazat al-Mihi, doc. 20.

submitted to Mehmed ʿAli himself as is evidenced by the following trial that took place in 1832.

> In a street in Cairo a man offered to take care of a donkey while its owner went shopping. However, instead of waiting for the latter's return, the man absconded with the donkey and sold it outside Cairo. Later he was caught and brought before the *Divan-i Hidivi*. It appeared that he had several previous convictions: twice to a six month term in the Alexandria Dockyards[9] and a number of times to simple detention or corporal punishment. Since evidently these measures had not deterred him from committing new crimes, his case was submitted to the Pasha himself who sentenced him to be hanged "as a punishment (*qisas*) for him and a lesson (*taʾdib*) for others".[10]

Other administrative authorities dealing with criminal matters were the provincial governors, the heads of administrative departments (for offences committed by their personnel)[11] and, finally, all persons with some type of recognised authority over the offenders. The following case, tried in 1831, evidences the authority of the *Shaykh al-Azhar* over religious functionaries.

> A woman in Cairo had a pet dog called Samara, which, she later claimed, could understand both Arabic and Turkish. After she had this dog for three years it died and she wanted to bury it in a cemetery. With two of her neighbours, both Koran reciters (*faqih*), she took the remains of the dog to a cemetery and buried it. When the guardian inquired what they were doing, they answered him that they were burying a stillbirth. Later the man decided to exhume the contents of the grave, found the dog and informed the authorities. The case was brought before the *Divan-i Hidivi*, which sentenced the woman to be sent to the House of the *Vālī* [where the women's prison was located] to stay there a few days, "since she has a weak mind and a delicate body and will not stand a beating." The guardian was released after having been given a beating, because he knew of

9 The Alexandria Dockyards (Liman Iskandariyya) was the main national penitentiary.

10 *al-Waqaʾiʿ al-Misriyya*, 1 Shaʿban, 1247.

11 The general rule was laid down in Art. 18 of the (Qanun al-Siyasatnama of 1837, dealing with offenses committed by officials. Light offenses are to be tried by the superiors of the offender. Serious offenses are to be tried by a committee, especially set up by the Vālī if the official is high ranking, and otherwise by the council of the offender's Divan. If he was not satisfied with the sentence, the offender could appeal to the council of another Divan. The offender had to be confronted with the accuser before sentence could be given. All sentences had to be approved by the Vālī.

this case [and did not inform the authorities right away]. The punishment of the two *faqih*'s was referred to His Eminence the *Shaykh al-Azhar*.[12]

3 The Beginnings of the Judiciary

The creation, in 1842, of *Cem'iyet-i Hakkaniye* marked the first step in the establishment of a secular judiciary. It was a specialised judicial council whose members had no other duties and consisted of a president and six members, two from the civil service, and two each, with the rank of general (*mirliva* or *miralay*), from the army and the navy.[13] An important objective of this new council was the enhancement of the legality of penal sentences, after the example of Europe. When the *Cem'iyet-i Hakkaniye* was about to be established, Mehmed 'Ali was leaving Cairo and had charged his Cabinet with taking care of the final steps. His ministers were then instructed to consult the *Mütercim Bey* (probably Rif'at al-Tahtawi, who, at that time was the head of the Translation Bureau) because he knew how these matters were arranged in Europe.[14] The decree itself emphasises that punishments must be imposed according to the existing laws and decrees.[15]

The *Cem'iyet-i Hakkaniye* was to deal with the following matters:[16] In first instance:

1. cases of manslaughter and theft;
2. offences committed by high officials;
3. disputes between individuals and state authorities (e.g. regarding government purchases, or *iltizams*);
4. disputes of competence between officials.
5. In review:
6. penal sentences against officers and civil servants;
7. any sentence (including those of qadis) that is appealed against by the interested party on the ground of injustice, after the Khedive has given his consent.

---

12 *al-Waqa'i' al-Misriyya*, 26 Jumada II, 1247.

13 Zaghlul (1900), 184.

14 Zaghlul (1900), 183.

15 La'ihat Tartib al-Jam'iyya al-Haqqaniyya, Ch. 3, Art. 3, 5.

16 La'ihat Tartib al-Jam'iyya al-Haqqaniyya, Ch. 2, Art. 1, 2, 3, 5. The La'iha does not list the trial of cases of manslaughter and theft and review of judgements given by qadis. This, however, is mentioned in Bayan (1260 H).

The sentences of the *Cemʿiyet-i Hakkaniye* needed the approval of the *Divan-i Hidivi* (presided by the *kethüda*) to be effective.[17] The examination of the cases was to take place on the basis of documents.[18] It is doubtful whether one can call the *Cemʿiyet-i Hakkaniye* a real court. It had clearly a hybrid character: it was a body that was part of the administrative bureaucracy and had its place in its hierarchy, but on the other hand it was specialised in legal matters, such as the investigation of the legality of sentences, settling administrative disputes and trying high officials in first instance.

After the creation of the *Cemʿiyet-i Hakkaniye* legal cases, and especially criminal cases, were to be heard at two or three levels. Serious offences were tried by the *Cemʿiyet-i Hakkaniye* acting as a court of first instance. As to other offences, they were first heard by executive authorities (in Cairo by the police, *Zabtiye*, in the provinces by the provincial government, and for official misconduct by the department of the offender) and then, by way of revision, by the *Cemʿiyet-i Hakkaniye*. The final approval for execution would be given by the *Divan-i Hidivi*.

The *Cemʿiyet-i Hakkaniye* was operational for seven years. In 1849 it was abolished and its duties were taken over by a new council, the *Majlis al-Ahkam*.[19] It consisted of a president, eight members, all high ranking officials, with title *pasha* or *bey*, and two, a Hanafite and a Shafiʿite one. Later, in 1856, when the *Majlis al-Ahkam* was re-established after its suppression in the preceding year, it had twenty members, reduced, one year later, to fifteen.[20] Its duties, according to its constitutive decree,[21] were similar to those of the *Cemʿiyet-i Hakkaniye*. It would try in first instance serious criminal cases: manslaughter and offences for which the defendant could be sentenced to forced labour (*liman*) or incarceration (*al-rabt bi-l-Qalʿa*). Less serious criminal cases were investigated, heard, and sentenced by the provincial authorities (*mudiriyya*) or

17 Ibid. Ch. 3, Art. 5.

18 Zaghlul (1900), 183; La'ihat tartib al-Jamʿiyya al-Haqqaniyya, Ch. 2, Art. 5.

19 The Majlis al-Ahkam was created on 5 Rabiʿ II, 1265 (28–2 1849). It functioned until 1889 with two interruptions, from 16 Dhu al-Hijja, 1271 (30–8 1855) until 1 Rabiʿ I, 1273 (30–10 1856) and from 24 Ramadan, 1276 (25–4 1860) until somewhere in 1277. (Deny (1930), 123–4; Sami (1928–1936), III/1, 347).

20 Zaghlul (1900), 196–197.

21 La'ihat Majlis al-Ahkam al-ʿAli al-Misriyya [sic] (5 Rabiʿ II, 1265). Text in Zaghlul (1900), appendix, 63–66. In 1856 (1 Rabiʿ I, 1273) a new decree governing the activities of the Majlis al-Ahkam was enacted, which was similar to the first one of 1849. Text in Sami (1928–1936), III/1, 194–7.

the departments (*diwan*).[22] They had to send reports to the *Majlis al-Ahkam*.[23] Persons who were convicted by the *mudiriyya* could petition the *Majlis al-Ahkam* for revision of their sentence. This, however, was a risky business, since, if the original sentence was upheld, the punishment would be doubled. There is, however, archival evidence that this harsh rule was not always applied in practice.[24] After the creation of the regional councils in 1852 the *Majlis al-Ahkam* acted only as a court of revision in criminal matters (with the exception of Cairo, where it continued to act as a court of first instance until 1855). The *Majlis al-Ahkam* would further examine difficult administrative problems that could not be solved within the departments and disputes regarding the competence of the departments. The decisions of the *Majlis al-Ahkam* were submitted to the bureau (*Divan*) of the *kethüda* for execution.[25]

4 The Regional Councils

The introduction of the Imperial Penal Code (*al-Qanun al-Sultani*)[26] in 1852–1853 brought new features to the system by creating a lower level of jurisdiction, the provincial councils (*majalis al-aqalim*). For Cairo, however, the *Majlis al-Ahkam* continued to be the court of first instance in serious criminal cases until 1855, when the Governorate of Cairo (*Muhafazat Misr* began to administer justice. In 1859 the Council of Cairo was established and took over this task.[27] In spite of the initial problems and the vicissitudes in government policy with regard to these new councils (see Appendix 1), they became an important element of the new system. Originally, they were subordinated to the local government. However, as from 1862 they fell directly under the newly established Department of Justice (*Diwan al-Haqqaniyya*) in Cairo. Although

22 Art. 23 of the Imperial Penal Code of 1265, enacted nearly simultaneously with the creation of the Majlis al-Ahkam.

23 La'ihat Majlis al-Ahkam (1265), Art. 4.

24 DWQ, Sin 1/24 (Maʿiyya Saniyya, Qayd al-khulasat al-warida min majalis daʿawi, Sijill 1 (1268–9), p. 2, 24 Jumada I, 1268: Two persons, who had been sentenced in the mudiriyya to six months forced labor in al-Qanatir al-Khayriyya for having stolen a cow and a calf, complained that their confession has been obtained by torture. The complaint was investigated by the Majlis al-Ahkam. It appeared that they did not steal the cattle themselves, but had incited others (also convicted) to steal for them. The Majlis al-Ahkam regarded the sentence of the mudiriyya as justified but did not increase the penalty.

25 La'ihat Majlis al-Ahkam al-ʿAli al-Misriyya (5 Rabiʿ II, 1265), Art. 2, 3, and 5.

26 Text in Zaghlul (1900), appendix, 156–178 and Jallad (1890–1895), II, 90–102.

27 Sami (1928–1936), III/1, 322. However, the Council was suppressed the following year (1860), to be reestablished in 1863.

their numbers varied, and there were intervals during which they were suppressed, they gained importance. By 1871 there were fifteen of them.[28] They were to hear criminal and administrative cases. After the promulgation of the Land Law of 1858, they were to take cognisance also of disputes concerning state land.[29]

The first councils consisted of a president and four or five members, all officers with the rank of major of lieutenant-colonel or middle rank civil servants (*nazir qism*, district chief). To these members two *mashayikh al-balad* were added who would attend the sessions by turns. Coptic shaykhs were also accepted and just like their Muslim colleagues, they had the right to sign or seal the sentences.[30] Finally a Hanafite and a Shafiʿite mufti were attached to each council. The councils convened daily.

The decree does not clearly circumscribe the jurisdiction of these councils.[31] The basic features of the system, as found here as well as in some articles in the Imperial Penal Code, were that criminal cases were first investigated in the offices of legal affairs (*qalam al-daʿawi*) that were part of the provincial administration (*mudiriyya*), or in the police departments (*dabtiyya*) of the main cities. Light offences such as quarrels and fights not resulting in serious injuries, petty theft (i.e. theft of objects with a value less than the *nisab*, the minimum value for the application of the *hadd* punishment), public drunkenness and gambling would be dealt with there. These offences were usually punished with flogging or beating, and, after the abolition of corporal punishment in 1861, by simple detention (*habs*) or detention on bread and water (*habs riyada*).[32] The punishment could be executed immediately, but the *Majlis al-Ahkam* would be notified of the sentence. In more serious cases, where the defendants could be punished with banishment (*nafy*) or imprisonment with or without forced labour (*al-qayd bi-l-zanjir*), trial would take place before the regional council and the sentence would be executed after approval by the *Diwan al-Katkhuda*.[33] According to Art. 4 of the Decree of 13 Rabiʿ I, 1268, these sentences were also sent to the *Majlis al-Ahkam*. The most serious crimes, homicide and offences

28 For their varying numbers and locations, see appendix 1.

29 Peters (1994), 77.

30 Wajibat maʾmuriyyat aʿdaʾ al-majlis, Art. 18. Text in Jallad, II, 104–105.

31 Decree of 13 Rabiʿ I, 1268; text in Zaghlu (1900), appendix, 70–75.

32 For the list of petty offenses that were dealt with at the police level, see Layihat tabdil al-darb bi-l-habs, an implementing order of the 1861 decree abolishing corporal punishment. Text in DWQ, Lam 1/20/8, Muhafazat Misr, p. 71, doc. 3, dated 11 Shaʿban 1278 (11–2 1862).

33 The text mentions the Diwan al-Wali. But this department must be identified with Diwan al-Katkhuda. See Art. 5 of the Decree of 13 Rabiʿ I, 1268.

against the security of the state (*al-sa'y bi-l-fasad*, as defined in Ch. 1, Arts. 5 and 6 of the Imperial Penal Code) were to be heard in first instance by the councils after which the defendants and the records would be sent to the *Majlis al-Ahkam* for revision.[34]

The following case from 1853 gives an impression of how a criminal investigation was conducted and how the regional councils gave judgement:

> On 25 Shawwal, 1269 (1 August, 1853), during the *mawlid* of Ahmad al-Badawi, a man was arrested in Tanta for having stolen a bolt of striped silk during the *mawlid* of the previous year. The owner of the silk, a merchant from Cairo, recognised him because the man was wearing a waistcoat (*sideiri*) made of that silk. The accusation was corroborated by other persons. The suspect was from Tahta in the province of Asyut and Jirja in Upper Egypt. The *mudir* of the Gharbiyya province, to which Tanta belongs, notified the *Diwan al-Katkhuda* on 3 Dhu al-Qaʿda, 1269, who on 15 Dhu al-Qaʿda requested the *mudir* of Asyut and Jirja to investigate whether the suspect had previous convictions and to dispose of the case. The authorities of the district of Tahta questioned the shaykhs of the suspect's village who testified that he had no previous convictions. On 28 Safar, 1270 the *mudir* submitted the case to the Regional Council South I (*Majlis Daʿawi Qism Awwal Qibli*). The Council examined the case and concluded that the testimonies of the witnesses and the fact that the suspect was wearing a waistcoat made of the stolen silk were sufficient proof of his guilt. However, before the Council could sentence him they needed additional information since the applicable article of the Penal Code lays down that the punishment for theft depends on the value of the stolen good and the capability of the defendant to pay compensation.[35] On 24 Rabiʿ I, 1270 the Council wrote to the *mudir* of the Gharbiyya Province to inquire about the value of the waistcoat and the suspect's ability to pay compensation. The answer, dated 7 Rabiʿ II, 1270, stated that the value could not be determined since the suspect had disposed of

34 Imperial Penal Code Ch. 3, Art. 15.

35 "If the value of the stolen goods is between 100 and 1.000 piasters, if the thief can compensate the owner of the stolen goods, and if the thief has no previous convictions, then he will be punished with forced labor in the provincial building sites or other public works without wages and only for food (*jiraya*) for a period between two months to one year, dependent on the value of the stolen goods. If the value of the stolen goods cannot be obtained from him, he will be punished in the same manner but for a period of one year and a half at the most, dependent of the value of the stolen goods." Art. 72 of the Penal Code of 1849.

> the waistcoat during his imprisonment and that he was a beggar without any properties. Thereupon, on 18 Rabiʿ II, 1270 (18 January, 1854), almost six months after his arrest, the Council decided that the man was to be released.[36]

The case is a good illustration of the bureaucratic handling of criminal affairs. The record does not indicate that the suspect has been questioned by the Council. In fact, it is not even clear where he was imprisoned during his "trial". The case was disposed of on the basis of officially obtained information and the text of the code and at no point during the proceedings before the Council did the suspect have an opportunity to defend himself.

In 1862 a new decree governing the functioning of the councils was promulgated. It is much clearer than the previous one and circumscribes the councils' jurisdiction in detail. Unless otherwise stated in specific laws, the *mudiriyyas* were competent to try

1. offences that could be punished with up to two months detention,
2. offences committed by village shaykhs or officials of the *mudiriyya* that could be punished with discharge, and
3. offences related to the recruiting of soldiers for military service.

Flogging had in the meantime been abolished as a penalty (Art. 5 of the Decree). The parties involved were entitled to complain to the regional councils if their cases were not decided in time or if they felt that they had been treated unjustly. This is a new element: previously only the *Majlis al-Ahkam* acted as an instance of appeal, and not the regional councils. In the absence of contrary statutory provisions, the councils were to take cognisance of

1. offences that could be punished with more than two months detention, forced labour (*liman* or *al-istikhdam fi al-ashghal al-sufliyya*), and banishment and
2. offences committed by officials (but not village shaykhs and officials employed by the *mudiriyyas*) that can be punished with discharge or demotion.

The cases were prepared in the *mudiriyyas* or in the police departments. The councils could also hear commercial cases, which in principle fell under the competence of the commercial courts, provided the parties agreed to submit their dispute to a council. All sentences (*madabit*) were sent for revision to the *Majlis al-Ahkam*. The *Majlis al-Ahkam* would notify the Khedival Cabinet (*al-Maʿiyya al-Saniyya*) who, after approval, would take care of the execution

36 DWQ, Sin 1/24 (al-Maʿiyya al-Saniyya, Qayd al-khulasat al-warida min majalis daʿawi al-aqalim, sijill 2, 18 Rabiʿ II, 1270, No. 13, pp. 23 and 26.

and give notice to the authorities involved.[37] In 1862, a Police Council (*Majlis al-Dabtiyya*) was established both in Cairo and Alexandria, to prepare cases before being submitted to the Cairo or Alexandria Council.[38]

In 1864 two Appellate Councils (*majlis isti'naf*) were established, one for the Northern and one for the Southern region, in order to remedy the backlog of cases for the *Majlis al-Ahkam*. The council of *'ulama'* that were operative at the Councils of Cairo and Alexandria, were not attached to the Appellate Councils in order to examine cases with a shar'ia character.[39] A year later the Councils of First Instance of Alexandria and Cairo were transformed into Appellate Councils, whereas the police councils (*majlis dabtiyya*) in these cities were henceforth to serve as Councils of First Instance (*majlis ibtida'i baladi*). Sometime before 1870 a second Appellate Council was established in the Southern region.[40] The main task of these Appellate Councils was to review all sentences of the Councils of First Instance. After revision the sentences were to be sent to the *Diwan al-Mu'awana al-Saniyya* for execution. Only criminal sentences in homicide cases or sentences of more than three years imprisonment were henceforth to be submitted to the *Majlis al-Ahkam*. If the defendant did not acquiesce in the sentence in first instance, he had to be heard before the decision in appeal. Appeal (*abillu*) could be lodged against the sentences of the Appellate Councils and was to be heard by the *Majlis al-Ahkam*.[41] It seems that many litigants would try to have unfavourable decisions of the Majlis al-Ahkam revised by submitting the case ultimately to the Majlis al-Khususi, for in February 1869 it was decreed that henceforth such cases

37 Art. 2–5, 11, Decree of 1 Muharram, 1279 [1862] regarding the establishment of regional councils in 13 articles. Text in Sami (1928–1936), III/1, 414–7; Zaghlul (1900), appendix, 94–99.

38 Zaghlul (1900), 209; Sami (1928–1936), III/2, 475, 501.

39 DWQ, Sin 7/4/33, Majlis al-Ahkam, Sadir al-Aqalim al-Qibliyya, doc. 71, pp. 184, 191–192, dated 16–8 1281. This contains the text of the Amr 'Ali of 10 Sha'ban 1281, no. 6 approving a resolution of the Majlis Khususi dated 27 Rajab 81, no. 20 concerning the establishment of new appellate councils. Art. 6.

40 DWQ, Sin 11/8 (Al-Majlis al-Khususi, al-qararat wal-lawa'ih al-sadira), sijill 8, No. 70, 3 Dhu al-Hijja, 1280, pp. 104–105; Sami (1928–1936) III/2, 550, 593; Zaghlul (1900), 209–212.

41 Khedival Decree (Amr 'Ali of 4 Dhu al-Hijja, 1280. DWQ, Sin/1/19 (Qayd al-awamir al-karima al-sadira min qalam al-majalis bi-l-Mu'awana), sijill 1 (1279–1280), No. 17, 4 Dhu al-Hijja, 1280, p. 22. The decree mentions that al-Majlis al-Khususi will issue an order regarding appeal. Text of this order containing eight articles in DWQ, Sin/7/4/33 (Majlis al-Ahkam, Sadir al-Aqalim al-Qibliyya), p. 184 (Amr 'Ali of 10 Sha'ban 1281 approving the order), pp. 191–192 (Text of the order itself dated 27 Rajab 1281), doc. 71, dated 16 Sha'ban 1281 to Majlis Isti'naf Qibli. See also DWQ, Sin/1/19 (Qayd al-awamir al-karima al-sadira min qalam al-majalis bi-l-Mu'awana), sijill 3, No. 7, 15 Sha'ban 1281, p. 9.

would not be examined anymore by the Majlis al-Khususi, with the argument that this Council was administrative and not judicial.[42]

Now, this multi-tiered organisation of judicial councils was only one part of the whole system. We have already seen that the legal bureaux of the *mudiriyyas* and police departments carried out essential judicial tasks, including sentencing. From a decree issued in 1865[43] it becomes clear that also other administrative bodies had judicial tasks. This decree circumscribes the jurisdiction of village shaykhs, district chiefs (*nazir qism*), police commissioners (*ma'mur dabtiyya*), provincial governors (*mudir, muhafiz*) and ministers (*nazir diwan 'umumi*, i.e. the heads of the departments of the central government) in civil and criminal cases. All of these had extensive judicial powers. From the preamble it can be inferred that the decree did not create something new, but rather regulated and better defined the powers these authorities already had. District chiefs and police commissioners in provincial towns (*banadir*) could sentence offenders to up to 5 days detention and try simple civil cases. To avoid overburdening the bureaucracy and, probably, for financial reasons, it was expressly stated that as a rule no records were to be kept of such cases. The legal bureaux of the *mudiriyyas* and of the police departments in Cairo and Alexandria could take cognisance of all civil cases and try offences with a maximum penalty of three months detention, provided the defendant was not a second offender, since that was an aggravating circumstance that might result in an increase of the prescribed penalty. Sentences pronounced by the *mudiriyyas* or the Cairo and Alexandria police departments could be executed by order of the governor (*mudir, muhafiz*) or the police commissioners. For more serious offences these legal bureaux would carry out the investigation and submit the results to the council of first instance for sentencing. After revision by the Appellate Council, these sentences were carried out by order of the Ministry of Interior (*Diwan al-Dakhiliyya*). However, capital sentences, sentences of more than one year imprisonment or banishment, and sentences imposing the punishment of discharge from service could only be executed by order of the Khedive (*amr 'ali*). Ministers had the power to try all offences committed by their officials for official misconduct. If they pronounced sentences of three months detention or more, these were to be sent to the Appellate Council for revision.[44]

42 DWQ, Sin 11/8/13 (Diwan al-Majlis al-Khususi, al-qararat wa-l-lawa'ih al-sadira), doc. 40, p. 52, dated 12 Dhu al-Qa'da 1285 (24–2–1869).

43 Decree of 17 Jumada II, 1282. Text in DWQ Sin 11/8 (Diwan al-Majlis al-Khususi, al-qararat wa-l-awamir al-sadira), sijill 18, No. 28, pp. 114–116.

44 Regulation of al-Majlis al-Khususi approved by the Khedive on 8 Shawwal, 1287 (Sami (1928–1936) III/2, p. 883), supplemented by regulation of al-Majlis al-Khususi issued on

5 Further Expansion of the Judiciary

About half a year later, in mid-1871, the lower end of the judicial organisation was reformed to make it conform to the principle of justice by council, rather than by a single person.[45] Judicial councils were created at the local level (*majlis daʿawi al-balad, majlis daʿawi al-bandar*, with three members) and at the district level (*majlis daʿawi al-markaz*, with 5 members)[46] to replace the judicial powers of the village shaykhs and the district chiefs. The village councils could pronounce sentences of one day detention and fines of 25 piaster, the district councils sentences of five days detention and fines of 100 piasters. The village councils would also hear civil cases. If these did not end in settlement, or if the claim exceeded 500 piasters, the initial report and the case was referred to the district councils. Civil claims of 2.500 piasters or more were the competence of the regional councils. All sentences could be enforced immediately by the shaykh of the quarter (*shaykh al-hissa*) where the person lived against whom judgement was given, respectively the district police of his residence. Decisions of the village councils could be appealed against to the district councils, whereas the judgements of the latter, if given in first instance, were subject to appeal to the regional councils. This new decree did not affect the judicial powers of the *mudiriyyas*, which could impose sentences not exceeding fifteen days detention.[47] With some slight modifications regarding the competence of the councils and the possibility of appeal,[48] this new judicial system remained in force until the French inspired judicial reform of 1883.

6 Conclusions

Within a very brief period of about thirty years, the Egyptian government created a fully developed judiciary, independent from the religious court system. These new councils, however, were not regarded as an encroachment on the Shariʿa. To some extent, Islamic rules continued to play a role in the councils, witness the fact that muftis were appointed to them and that the higher ones counted important *ʿulamaʾ* among their members. Homicide cases were tried

16 Dhu al-Hijja, 1287, approved by the Khedive on 28 Muharram, 1288 (Sami (1928–1936) III/2, 915–7).

45 Decree of 25 Jumada II, 1288. Text in Sami (1928–1936) III/2, 943–951; Zaghlul (1900), appendix, 181–206.

46 The name *qism* for district had been being replaced by *markaz*.

47 See Supplement to the Decree on the District Councils, of 6 Rabiʿ II, 1290, Art. 1.

48 See the decree mentioned in the previous note.

in one session both by a qadi and secular council.[49] And the Decree on the Village and District Councils of 1871 laid down that if an action is brought before a district council concerning succession, [the rights to] palm trees, irrigation wheels or landed property, the case will be heard in the council in the presence of the qadi of the district.

In the initial stage of the process, two principles played a role. The first principle, introduced by Mehmed ʿAli, was the notion of conciliar bodies as major building stones of the administration.[50] During his reign many administrative councils were created. Decisions were taken by the majority of the votes after due deliberation. In the beginning, the competence of these councils was not clearly defined. However, gradually the need for specialisation began to be felt. This I consider as the second operating principle in the development of the judiciary. As from the 1830 the idea spread among the ruling elite that maintenance of public order had to be regulated by statute, in the first place in order to curb the unlimited power and the arbitrariness of provincial governors, in the second place, in order to make criminal law enforcement palatable to the public.[51] In the preamble of an order of 1842 given to his cabinet (*sura-yi muʾavenet*) concerning the establishment of the *Cemʿiyet-i Hakkaniye* Mehmed ʿAli argued that:

> if an offender is sentenced to penalties laid down [by law] without the slightest partiality and with justice and equity, then that person will have no objections anymore. It is evident that the impact of penalties laid down [by law] may be enormous. Therefore there is in Europe much attention for and interest in this matter. As a result, when they (the Europeans) impose punishments, they investigate and make clear the offender's fault and the punishment that he deserves to such an extent that the accused does not protest anymore against it and accepts it whole-heartedly.[52]

Such notions led to the idea that law enforcement was a serious affair for which specialised councils had to be established. However, the next step, that of training jurists to staff these councils was never taken. So much were these councils regarded as belonging to the administration, that membership was part of the normal bureaucratic career. There are indications that these administrators may have had difficulty in functioning as impartial magistrates.

49 Cf. Peters (1994) and Peters (1997).
50 See Deny (1930), 33, quoting the Regulations of Rabiʿ II, 1233.
51 See Peters (1999).
52 Zaghlul (1900), 182–183.

Various statutes contain provisions inculcating the members of the councils that they must not be inclined to protect only [the interests] of the state (*miri*). Rather, they must take into consideration both [the interests] of the state and those of the state servants and the subjects and they must treat the latter with justice. If someone is entitled to something in a case, then his right must be protected. The members [of the council] must always proceed in such a way that they give everybody his due.[53]

As we have seen, the new judiciary evolved from the law enforcement by administrative bodies of the central government (*Katkhuda*, the *Divan-i Hidivi*, or the Khedive himself) or by the regional administration (*mudirs*) under supervision of these central bodies. The creation of specialised judicial councils such as the *Cemʿiyet-i Hakkaniye*, the *Majlis al-Ahkam*, and the regional councils did not put an end to the involvement of these central authorities. Important decisions were submitted to the central administrative bodies or the Khedive himself. In the course of time, however, increasingly fewer categories of judicial decisions had to be submitted to the central government for approval. Thus the judiciary acquired a greater degree of independence.

In the course of these thirty years the jurisdiction of the secular judiciary was extended. In the beginning the judicial councils dealt almost exclusively with criminal and administrative matters. Gradually, they also took cognisance of civil cases. This was expressly laid down in the 1871 judicial reform decree. For the lower tiers of the judiciaries, this must have been an official confirmation of the practice of informal arbitration at the village level.

During our period, the procedure before the new councils developed from a purely bureaucratic handling of cases to a procedure resembling a trial. The contrast between the procedure before the qadi and the way the newly established councils operated is striking. Trial before the qadi was in principle a public trial of an accusatory nature: Plaintiff and defendant would fight a legal battle with the qadi as a referee. The procedure before the councils was essentially inquisitory. There was no office of public prosecutor and the council would function both as prosecutor and judge, whereas the defendant was not a party in the trial, but rather the object of an investigation. Typically, there was no right to legal counsel. Only in cases of manslaughter was the defendant's presence required since such cases were tried by the council and the qadi in one and the same session, and since the rules of Shariʿa procedure require

53 Layihat Majlis al-Ahkam al-Misriyya (5 Rabiʿ II, 1265), Art. 12. Text in Zaghlul (1900), appendix, 63–66. Similar provisions in: La'ihat tartib al-Jamʿiyya al-Haqqaniyya, Ch. 2, Art. 5 (Zaghlul (1900), appendix, 27–3) and Wajibat ma'muriyyat aʿda' al-majlis (one of the implementing orders of the Imperial Penal Code), Art. 4. Text in Jallad (1890–1895), II, 104–105.

the presence of both plaintiff and defendant.[54] The councils were at liberty to interrogate the defendants, but for most of our period, this was not compulsory. If the members of a council were to question a defendant, they were admonished to interrogate him in a friendly manner and without threats or harassment.[55] It seems that this did not happen very often. The absence in the records of trials of the defendant's statements (except those taken during the preliminary investigation) can be seen as an indication that cases were usually tried on the basis of the reports of the investigation carried out by the authorities that had prepared the case. At some point, towards the end of our period, the rule was introduced that the defendant had to be heard before sentencing.[56] This must be seen as an indication of a shift from a bureaucratic and administrative handling of criminal cases, towards a judicial one.

Another indication is the development of appeal, gradually replacing automatic revision. Initially, nearly all sentences were automatically revised by higher bodies. Revision would take place irrespective of the will of the defendant, which is very much a bureaucratic procedure: an official prepares a draft and submits it to his superior for review and modification, who then, on his turn, passes it to his superior until the concept reaches the bureaucratic level authorised to take the final decision. Gradually, however, one can observe that this automatic revision of judicial decisions is restricted and that appeal becomes conditional upon the will of the defendant.[57]

---

54 Imperial Penal Code, Ch. 1, Art. 3. The required presence during the trial of the next of kin of a victim of manslaughter, of all witnesses and of the defendant caused hardship, especially if the crime was committed in a region far away from the seat of the council. In 1855 this was remedied by a new procedure according to which one council member would travel to the mudiriyya where the case had been investigated. There he would hear the case in the presence of the local qadi, the mudir and his deputy, local 'ulama' and village shaykhs. The Shari'a sentence (*i'lam shar'i*) pronounced by the qadi and the verdict (*hukm siyasi*) given by the local notables, were to be sent to the council for approval. Decree of 10 Rabi' I, 1272, Sami (1928–1936) III/1, 145.

55 Wajibat ma'muriyyat a'da' al-majlis, Art. 17. Text in Jallad (1890–1895), II, 104–105.

56 This was introduced by a decree of 1287 H (1871). The defendant in criminal cases and the litigants in civil cases had to be present and be heard before the final judgement was pronounced by the councils of first instance. After the sentence they had to state whether or not they acquiesced in it. If they did not, they had to be heard before the Appellate Council would pronounce its sentence. Regulation of al-Majlis al-Khususi approved by the Khedive on 8 Shawwal, 1287 (Sami (1928–1936) III/2, p. 883), supplemented by a regulation of al-Majlis al-Khususi issued on 16 Dhu al-Hijja, 1287, approved by the Khedive on 28 Muharram, 1288 (Sami (1928–1936) III/2, pp. 915–7).

57 In the decrees mentioned in the previous footnote, it is stipulated that after the sentence of the Appellate Council, which was a revision of the case independent of the will of the parties, they could lodge appeal with the Majlis al-Ahkam within eight days.

It is difficult to assess the justness and efficiency of this legal system. It was essentially part of the administration and, as we all know, many things can go wrong during a bureaucratic handling of a case. Bureaucrats are human too. Indeed, there are many indications that the course of justice in the period we have examined did not always flow smoothly. However, if the system operated to some extent with justice and decency, which I think it did, this was due to the institution of petitions. Petitions to the Khedive or higher judicial bodies were an important corrective against failures at a lower level. They were taken seriously and resulted in special investigations after which subjects often would get the rights that had been denied to them.[58]

Appendix 1: the Regional Councils and Councils of First Instance

	Cities	Delta	Upper Egypt
1852		Tanta	Fishn
		Samannud	Jirja
			Khartum
1854		Tanta	Fishn
			Jirja
			Khartum
1855		Tanta	Jirja
1856		Tanta	Jirja
		Zaqaziq	
1859	Cairo	Tanta	Jirja
	Alexandria	Zaqaziq	
1860:	all councils abolished		
1862		Tanta	Asyut
1863	Cairo	Tanta	Asyut
	Alexandria	Zaqaziq	Banu Suwayf
		Mansura	Isna
		Dumyat	
1864		Tanta	Asyut
		Zaqaziq	Banu Suwayf
		Mansura	Isna

58 For a typical case, see Peters (2000).

(cont.)

	Cities	Delta	Upper Egypt
1870	Cairo Alexandria	Qalyubiyya Sharqiyya Daqhaliyya Dumyat Buhayra Gharbiyya Minufiyya	Giza Banu Suwayf Fayyum Minya Asyut Jirja Qina Isna

SOURCES: SAMI (1928–1936), III/1, 97, 133, 204, 322, 341, 403, 410; 3/2, 455–7; ZAGHLUL (1900), 194, 198, 200–201, 209–212; APPENDIX, 70–75

References

Bayan (1260 H) *Bayan al-mawadd allati sayir ʿanha al-istiʾdhan bi-l-diwan al-khediwi ma ʿada al-dawawin.* (Bulaq: 1260/1844, 22 pp. Arabic text, 22 pp. Turkish text).

Deny, J. (1930) *Sommaire des archives turques du Caire* (Le Caire: Institut francais d'archéologie orientale).

El-Nahal, Galal H. (1979) *The Judicial Administration of Ottoman Egypt in the Seventeenth Century* (Minneapolis etc.: Bibliotheca Islamica).

Farahat, Muhammad Nur (1993) *Al-tarikh al-ijtimaʿi li-l-qanun fi Misr al-hadith.* 2nd impr. (Kuwait: Dar Suʿad al-Sabah).

Hunter, F.R. (1984) *Egypt under the Khedives: From Household Government to Modern Bureaucracy.* (Pittsburgh, Pa.).

Jabartī, ʿAbd al-Rahman al- (1297 H) *ʿAjaʾib al-athar fi al-tarajim wa-l-akhbar*, 4 vols. (Bulaq).

Jallad, Filib, (1890–92) *Qamus al-idara wa-l-qadaʾ*. 4 vols (Alexandria).

Layihat (1256 H.a) *Layihat ziraʿat al-fallah wa-tadbir ahkam al-siyasa bi-qasd al-najah.* 2nd impr. (Bulaq).

Peters, Rudolph (1994) "Muhammad al-ʿAbbasi al-Mahdi (d. 1897), Grand Mufti of Egypt and his *al-Fatawa al-Mahdiyya*," *Islamic Law and Society* 1, pp. 66–81.

Peters, Rudolph (1997) "Islamic and Secular Criminal law in 19th Century Egypt: The Role and Function of the *Qadi*," *Islamic Law and Society* 4, pp. 70–90.

Peters, Rudolph (1999) " 'For his Correction and as a Deterrent Example for Others': Mehmed ʿAli's First Criminal Legislation (1829–1830)," *Islamic Law and Society* 6, pp. 164–193.

Peters, Rudolph (2000) "Petitions And Marginal Voices In Nineteenth Century Egypt: The Case Of The Fisherman's Daughter," in: Robin Ostle (ed.), *Marginal Voices in Literature and Society*. Strasbourg: European Science Foundation, pp. 119–133.

Sami, Amin (1928–36) *Taqwim al-Nil*. 3 vols (Cairo: Matbaʿat al-Kutub al-Misriyya).

Zaghlul, Ahmad Fathi (1900) *Al-Muhamat* (Cairo: Matbaʿat al-Maʿarif).

CHAPTER 6

Between Paris, Istanbul, and Cairo

The Origins of Criminal Legislation in Late Ottoman Egypt (1829–58)

The introduction in 1883 of modern law codes[1] heralded a new period in the legal history of Egypt. With the exception of family law, the law of inheritance, and waqfs, all fields of the law were henceforth to be governed by these new codes, for the greater part directly translated from French codes. New national courts (*mahakim ahliyya*) that were independent from the administration were set up to apply the new laws. The introduction of the new legal system, however, did not constitute a complete rupture with the past. Before 1883 there also existed a dual judiciary consisting of state courts applying statute law and *qadi* courts applying the *Shariʿa* according to the Hanafite school of law. The state courts, it is true, were part of the administration and subordinated to the Khedive, but during the previous decades they had evolved towards greater independence. They heard various types of cases, but their most prominent task was to try criminals on the basis of enacted penal legislation. Like in the Ottoman empire, crime was dealt with by both the *qadi*, on the basis of the *Shariʿa*, and executive officials, on the basis of enacted law, *qanun*, or on the strength of their powers of *siyasa*.[2] Executive officials could impose punishment without complying with the strict *Shariʿa* rules of evidence. In criminal cases *Shariʿa* courts dealt with the claims of the victims, including capital punishment as retribution for wilful killing, and state courts tried such cases from the point of view of public security. Although not completely defined by statute, the jurisdictions of state courts and *qadi*s courts were clearly delimited. State courts heard all criminal cases but for certain offences such as homicide, wounding, fighting, verbal abuse, sexual offences, and sometimes theft, the case was also referred to the *qadi* for trial. If the *qadi* could not sentence the defendant to a punishment but only to damages (e.g. blood money), the state

1 The new laws and courts were introduced in the North of Egypt in 1883 and in the South in 1889.

2 On Ottoman *qanun* and *siyasa*, see C. Imber, *Ebu's-Suʿud: The Islamic Legal Tradition* (Edinburgh 1997), ch. 2; U. Heyd, *Studies in Old Ottoman Criminal Law* (Oxford 1973); and R. Peters, *Crime and Punishment in Islamic Law: Theory and Practice from the 16th to the 21st Century* (Cambridge 2005), ch. 3.

 | DOI:10.1163/9789004420625_007

court would do so. Egyptian court records show that criminal cases, as a rule, were examined thoroughly and tried meticulously.[3]

The successive Egyptian penal codes enacted before 1883 fitted in the Ottoman tradition of penal legislation by *qanun*. They cannot be compared with modern penal codes that are based on the principle of *nulla poena sine lege*. Initially they were not meant to be exhaustive and acts not mentioned in the laws could nevertheless be punished at the discretion of the authorities. In fact, these codes did not address the population, but rather the officials who had to apply them. However, this began to change during the second half of the nineteenth century. From the 1860s punishment was usually not imposed unless prescribed by an enacted law.

In one respect these Egyptian codes introduced innovation: whereas previously the Ottoman *qanun* applied in Egypt only defined the crimes to be punished, and sometimes the kind of punishment to be imposed,[4] the new laws began to quantify the penalties by specifying for each offence the number of lashes to be administered or the duration of imprisonment or hard labour. There were two motives behind this new legislative policy. One was the centralization of power. Mehmed ʿAli (1805–48) wanted to control his officials and to curb their powers by restricting them. By issuing criminal laws he wanted to limit the discretionary powers of his officials to impose punishments. The other motive was to make the penal system more acceptable to the population by making it less arbitrary.[5]

During the first years the penal legislation was enforced by executive officials and – at the highest level – by executive councils (like the *Diwan Khediwi*). However, the establishment in 1842 of *al-Jamʿiyya al-Haqqaniyya*, a state council with judicial as well as legislative functions, initiated the establishment of a system of judicial councils at various levels to apply the penal legislation. By 1871 this process was completed and a hierarchy of judicial councils existed, ranging from the village councils at the bottom of the pyramid to the *Majlis al-Ahkam* (the successor of *al-Jamʿiyya al-Haqqaniyya*) at the top.[6] This judiciary was not independent and was a part of the administration. It worked under the

3 For the duties and jurisdiction of *Shariʿa* courts and judicial councils in criminal cases, see R. Peters, 'Islamic and Secular Criminal Law in Nineteenth Century Egypt: The Role and Function of the *Qadi*, *Islamic Law and Society* 4 (1997), 80–90 and R. Peters, 'Administrators and Magistrates: The Development of a Secular Judiciary in Egypt, 1842–1871', *Die Welt des Islams* 39 (1999), 378–97.

4 M.N. Farahat, *Al-Tarikh al-Ijtimaʿi li-l-Qanun fi Misr al-Haditha*. 2nd ed. (Kuwait 1993), 509.

5 R. Peters, '"For His Correction and as a Deterrent Example for Others": Mehmed ʿAli's First Criminal Legislation (1829–1830)', *Islamic law and Society* 6 (1999), 164–93.

6 Peters, 'Administrators and Magistrate'.

supervision and control of the Khedive, who had to approve the execution of sentences. In important cases he would review the proceedings, whereby the sentence might be changed. The creation of this judiciary was part of a wider process of bureaucratization of the state.[7]

In this paper I will focus on the criminal legislation and discuss the penal codes enacted between 1829 and 1883, when French law codes were introduced. More specifically, I will examine them in order to ascertain their origins and to establish whether they were purely the result of Egyptian inspiration or partly or wholly imported from abroad. These Egyptian penal codes have been studied previously by Gabriel Baer.[8] However, Baer very much focused on the Egyptian-Ottoman political and diplomatic relations regarding the introduction of the Ottoman Penal Code of 1851 in Egypt. As I will point out, he failed to grasp the nature of these laws on essential points, due to the fact that, as an Israeli scholar, he did not have access to the Egyptian National Archives and could not study how these laws were applied in practice.

Between 1829 and 1858 six penal statutes were enacted and/or published (see Appendix 1). I will discuss them in chronological order.

1 The Penal Decree of 1829[9]

Egypt's first substantial penal decree written in Ottoman Turkish was introduced on 21 Rabiʿ I 1245 (20 September 1829). It was never printed and the Turkish text only survives in the Egyptian National Archives. The principal objective of this code seems to have been to limit and specify penalties for certain crimes. In its preamble we find the following statement: 'Previously it was deemed sufficient [to sentence an offender] to forced labour in the Alexandria Dockyards [without mentioning a term], whereas now the need is

7 See e.g. F.R. Hunter, *Egypt under the Khedives, 1805–1879: From Household Government to Modern Bureaucracy* (Pittsburgh 1984).

8 G. Baer, 'Tanzimat in Egypt: the Penal Code', in G. Baer, *Studies in the Social History of Modern Egypt* (Chicago 1969), 109–33 and G. Baer, 'The Transition From Traditional to Western Criminal Law in Turkey and Egypt', *Studia Islamica* 45 (1977), 139–58.

9 Text and translation in: Peters, 'For his Correction'. This criminal code was only known in two rather inaccurate printed Arabic summaries: one in Amin Sami, *Taqwim al-Nil* (Cairo 1928–1936), ii, 354 (based on the Arabic text of the official gazette, *al-Waqaʾiʿ al-Misriyya*) and Ahmad Fathi Zaghlul, *al-Muhamat* (Cairo 1900), 163 (based on an Arabic translation of the original document found in the Egyptian National Archive [*Dar al-Wathaʾiq al-Qawmiyya*]). The code is not mentioned by Baer.

felt to specify suitable punishments for certain crimes that occur [nowadays].'[10] Mehmed ʿAli believed that a penal system with fixed penalties applied without arbitrariness would further its acceptance among the population. To this end he issued a decree one week after the enactment of the code laying down that officials who did not obey the law and who caused the death of persons by flogging them excessively would be punished severely.[11]

The main part of the code consists of ten unnumbered sections. Seven of them address the misappropriation of state and private property, either by officials or private persons (arts. 1–3 and 7–10). In addition it punishes counterfeiting, homicide, and robbery (arts. 5 and 6). Finally, Article 4 lays down that the relatives of those sentenced to prison terms may submit petitions for their release before the termination of their sentence.

Three appendices were added to this law: one (dated 20 Shaʿban 1245 [14 February 1830]) about the embezzlement of state property by tax collectors and shaykhs in Upper Egypt; another one containing six articles that are identical to arts. 4, 7, 19, 36, and 38 of the *Qanun al-Filaha*; and the last one concerning the punishment of Gypsies (*Nuri*), beggars, vagrants, fortune tellers, and the like with forced labour in factories or military service for unspecified periods.

The penal system[12] underlying this code remained the basis of the penal codes enacted later. It was quite simple and consisted of the following punishments:

> **Capital punishment**, (here for one crime only: the misappropriation of state funds or private property by high ranking Coptic officials);
>
> **imprisonment at Abu Qir prison**, housed at the Abu Qir fortress on the shore of the Mediterranean, East of Alexandria. This was a special prison for officials and military officers; forced labour either in the Alexandria Dockyard (*liman Iskandariyya*),[13] for one to five years or life,

10 Egyptian National Archive (*Dar al-Watha'iq al-Qawmiyya*), Diwan Khediwi Turki, Daftar qayd al-khulasat, Sin/2/40, Sijill 12, p. 1.

11 Sami, Taqwim, ii, 356.

12 For a discussion of the development of the Egyptian penal system during the nineteenth century, see R. Peters, 'Egypt and the Age of the Triumphant Prison: Judicial Punishment in Nineteenth Century Egypt', *Annales Islamologiques* 36 (2002), 253–85 and R. Peters, 'Controlled Suffering: Mortality and Living Conditions in Nineteenth Century Egyptian Prisons', IJMES 36 (2004), 87–407.

13 In this period the work consisted in spadework, as the early references indicate: *naql al-turab, haml al-turab, toprak hizmeti* (i.e. moving or carrying earth, working with earth).

or at government building sites in the convict's region of residence for one to four months or, finally, in factories;
military service;
flogging, twenty-five to 500 lashes.

The system was clearly a response to the prevailing difficulties in providing sufficient manpower for the new industries and the army.

It is evident that this law is purely of Egyptian inspiration. Although this code fits in the general notion of Ottoman *qanun*, there is no indication of any Ottoman influence on its contents. This is not surprising, since the first Ottoman criminal legislation in the nineteenth century dates from 1840.

2 The Qanun al-Filaha (1830)

The *Qanun al-Filaha* was printed in AH Shaʿban 1245 (January/February 1830 CE). It consists of the penal provisions listed in an appendix to a manual on agriculture entitled *Layihat ziraʿat al-fallah wa-tadbir ahkam al-siyasa bi-qasd al-najah*[14] that had been printed one month earlier and that addressed the local authorities in rural areas. There are slight differences in wording and in the penalties between the text contained in the *Layiha* and the version printed separately under the title *Qanun al-Filaha*.[15] The text of this law was later included in the *Qanun Muntakhab*, printed in 1845, with some small modifications mainly of an editorial character. The text, as incorporated in articles 1–55 of the *Qanun Muntakhab*, differs for instance from the original version in that it contains references to provisions enacted after 1830.[16]

The *Qanun al-Filaha* deals with crimes and offences connected with agriculture and village life. It had two objectives: to discipline the rural population and to curb the unbridled power of state officials in the countryside:

14 Bulaq: Rajab 1245 (December 1829/January 1830 CE). The title is also given as *La'ihat al-Fallah li-Taʿlim al-Ziraʿa wa-l-Najah*, (thus in the colophon on p. 76). In Shawwal 1256 (November/December 1840 CE) it was reprinted.

15 Cf. Baer, 'Tanzimat', 110, note 2. The *Layiha* lists three crimes not mentioned in the *Qanun*: consumption of sowing-seed (200 stripes) (p. 62), misconduct of porters (p. 71), and peasants leaving their districts without written permission (*tadhkarat al-murur*) (100 stripes) (p. 74).

16 Moreover, in the version of the *Qanun al-Filaha* published in the *Qanun Muntakhab*, the punishment of forced labor in the Alexandria Dockyards is replaced in certain cases with deportation to the penal colony of Fayzoghli in the Sudan, a punishment that did not yet exist in 1830. See R. Peters, 'Egypt and the age of the triumphant prison: Legal punishment in nineteenth century Egypt,' *Annales Islamologiques*, 36 (2002), pp. 269–70.

> One often hears that criminal offenders who are punished by the district commissioners [*hukkam*] are beaten more than is their due [*qanunuhum*], which entails damage for them. In order to put an end to this injustice it is necessary that the penalties for all criminals be fixed and that it be brought to the attention of the local authorities [*ma'murin, nuzzar al-aqsam, hukkam al-akhtat*] that in punishing criminals they are not to exceed the penalties fixed for them.[17]

Local officials and village shaykhs frequently wielded the whip (*kurbaj*) and the stick (*nabbut*) to impose order and to enforce their commands. Occasionally this would result in the death of the recipient of such a beating.[18] Mehmed ʿAlī wanted to put an end to this and the code specifies that in such cases officials will be brought to justice: Article 25 lays down that any official causing death by exceeding the number of lashes prescribed for a certain offence or by administering the beating or flogging to parts of the body other than the feet or the buttocks, will be held liable according to the *Sharīʿa* and must pay blood money, which is fixed here at 3600 piasters.[19] Apart from penal provisions the code contains some rules of private law, such as the liability for certain civil wrongs, usually combined with penal sanctions.[20]

17 These are the words of Minister of War (*Nazir al-Jihadiyya*), Mahmud Bey Efendi, quoted as an introduction to the penal provisions of the *Layiha* (p. 61).

18 B. St. John, *Village Life in Egypt with Sketches From the Saïd* (2 vols, London 1852), i, 68; Sami, *Taqwim*, ii, 356. That such cases were brought to justice is evident from Muhammad al-ʿAbbasi al-Mahdi, *Al-Fatawa al-Mahdiyya* (Cairo AH 1301–03), vi, 2, 58, 455, 523.

19 Since the dominant opinion in the Hanafite school, which was the law to be applied by *Shariʿa* courts, did not consider sticks or whips to be weapons indicative of criminal intent of killing, no death sentence could be pronounced by the *qadi* against officials who had caused the death of persons by beating them. Therefore, Article 25 does not give officials a privileged position, as Baer claims (Baer, 'Tanzimat', 110, note 4).

20 Damages for unauthorized use of land (arts. 1, 2); damages and penalty (25 stripes) for the unauthorized use of another person's animals (art. 3); damages in the case of a village shaykh selling a peasant's animals (for tax arrears) against too low a price (art. 11); punitive damages for stray cattle destroying crops and harvests (arts. 14, 34); damages for cruelty to an animal inflicted out of spite against its owner (art. 33); the procedure in forcing an unwilling but solvent debtor to pay his debt by imprisoning and flogging him (art. 37); damages and penalty (200 stripes) for fraud committed by a person representing peasants in delivering their crops to the state storehouses (art. 39); damages and penalty (300 stripes) for forcing one's co-owner of the land to flee in order to usurp his share (art. 44); damages and penalty (100 stripes) for extortion by a village shaykh (art. 50); procedure for the confiscation and subsequent compensation of the owners of wood required to strengthen dams and dikes during sudden floods (art. 51); and damages and penalty (fifty stripes) for unauthorized cutting of trees by village shaykhs (art. 51).

The offences listed in the code fall under the following headings:

1. Misconduct of peasants and others vis-à-vis each other.[21]
2. Misconduct of peasants and others vis-à-vis the government. In some instances the village shaykhs are also punished, since they are held responsible for the behaviour of the peasants under their authority.[22]
3. Misconduct of officials
   a. vis-à-vis the government;[23]
   b. vis-à-vis peasants.[24]
4. Administrative and procedural regulations.[25]

21 Unauthorized use of another person's animals (art. 3); theft of crops, fowl, or cattle (art. 4), impugning another person's honor, abuse, and [illegal] defloration (art. 16); destruction of water wheels (*saqiya*) (art. 17); arson (art. 18); miscarriage as a result of a quarrel (art. 30); cruelty to another person's animals out of spite against him (art. 33); damage caused by stray cattle (art. 34); regulations concerning butchers (art. 38); fraud by the person representing the peasants in delivering the crops to the government storehouses (art. 39); harassment of one's partner in the title to the land in order to extort his share from him (art. 44); and brawls between soldiers and peasants (art. 47).

22 Neglect of agricultural work (art. 5, 35); failure to respond to a summons for *corvée* at dams and canals (art. 6); attacking tax collectors (art. 7); failure to respond to a summons of the local authorities or resistance against the *mushidd* (art. 12, 23); protection given by Bedouin to peasants who have escaped (art. 14); giving false information to the authorities (art. 19); destroying the harvest or failure to irrigate land in order to evade taxes (art. 20, 21); attacking the authorities (art. 24, 26); rebellion (art. 27); not obeying the command to till land adjacent to the village (art. 43); and unauthorized opening of dams during irrigation (art. 55).

23 Flight of a *qa'immaqam* or village shaykh with or without his peasants in order to escape tax collection (art. 8); refusal by the *qa'immaqam* or village shaykh to hand over men for military service (art. 9); fraud in the distribution of the burden of the taxes by the village shaykh to the advantage of himself, his relatives, or the peasants under his protection (art. 10); protection offered by a shaykh to a peasant with a tax debt to another shaykh (art. 13); failure of a village shaykh to appear before his superior when summoned, or his escape when his superior is to visit his village (art. 23); a village shaykh's failure to prevent his peasants from getting into a fight with the peasants of another village over the distribution of water during the flood of the Nile (art. 29); accepting money from a peasant who has escaped in order not to arrest him (art. 36); hiding and protecting bands of robbers (art. 46); inciting peasants to escape (art. 53).

24 Sale by the village shaykh (for tax arrears) of cattle for too low a price (art. 11); instructions with regard to the infliction of the punishment of beating (art. 25); abuse of power by village shaykhs with regard to women (art. 31); unauthorized use by a village shaykh of a peasant's camel or his forcing a peasant to work for him without wages (art. 40); unjust division of the fields among the peasants (art. 45); injustice in calling up men for military service (art. 49); extortion of houses and other goods (art. 50); and unlawful cutting of trees belonging to one of the peasants (art. 52).

25 Appeal against unjust decisions of *qadis* (art. 22); permission to submit petitions to the Khedive appealing against his dismissal of a previous petition (art. 42); procedures with

The following penalties are mentioned:

Death penalty by way of retribution (*qisas*), to be pronounced by the *qadi*;[26]

forced labour either in the Alexandria Dockyard (*liman Iskandariyya*)[27] for terms from six months to five years or for life or for an unspecified period,[28] or at government building sites in the convict's region of residence, for one year;

military service for the culprit and, sometimes, for his relatives as well;

flogging whereby for each crime the number of stripes, from ten to 500, is specified;[29] this is the principal punishment in this code, mentioned in thirty-one out of fifty-five articles;

confiscation of cattle;

warning (*tanbih*) and intimidation (*takhwif*).

The *Qanun al-Filaha* is a law code that addresses the situation in the Egyptian countryside at the time of Mehmed 'Ali's reign. It is very specific and was regarded so important for the government that its main provisions were copied into later penal codes.

3 The Qanun Muntakhab (1845)[30]

The *Qanun Muntakhab*, containing 203 numbered articles, is a compilation of earlier piecemeal legislation. Apart from the revised text of *Qanun al-Filaha* of 1830, which forms the first part of this code (arts. 1–55), it contains legislation enacted between 1837 and 1844. The penal decree of 1829 was not included,

regard to the detention of deserters (art. 48) or to be followed in the case of the escape of a deserter after his arrest (art. 54); and procedure for the confiscation of wood and other material required to strengthen dams and dikes in cases of unexpected floods (art. 51).

26 Arts. 24 and 26.

27 In the version of the code printed in 1845 replaced with deportation to Fayzoghli in the Sudan for some offences.

28 Art. 4 of the *Layiha* stipulates that a fourth conviction for theft entails being sent to the Alexandria dockyards for an undefined period. In the version published in the *Qanun Muntakhab*, the punishment in this case is lifelong deportation to Fayzoghli.

29 In one article (46: hiding and assisting robbers by village shaykhs) it is stipulated that the flogging – 500 stripes in this instance – be carried out on market day in the presence of a large crowd.

30 Text in Zaghlul, *al-Muhamat*, Appendix, 100–55 and Filib Jallad, *Qamus al-idara wa-l-qada'* (Alexandria 1890–5), iii, 351–78.

apparently because most of its provisions had been abolished by the more detailed penal articles of the 1837 Organic Law (*Qanun al-Siyasatname*), in which Mehmed ʿAli outlined the organization of his government and the duties of his officials. The articles of the code are not arranged according to topic, but follow the chronological order of the statutes from which they were taken.

Nearly half of the articles of the *Qanun Muntakhab*, address official crime. In addition to arts. 56–75,[31] corresponding with the penal provisions dealing with misconduct of officials listed in Chapter 3 of *Qanun al-Siyasatname*, the code lists other instances of official crime, such as embezzlement of state funds, causing damage to state property, taking bribes, and being late in answering correspondence (arts. 81–6, 98–111, 116, 117, 120, 122, 195, 200–3, enacted between 1837 and 1844).[32] Other articles deal with official crime in connection with irrigation, such as the neglect in the maintenance and repair of dams and canals (arts. 76–80, 87–97, 199, enacted between 1842 and 1844).[33] Finally, there are some regulations concerning tax farmers (*multazim*) that fall under this heading (art. 112–15).[34] All these laws are clearly of Egyptian inspiration.

The remaining articles (arts. 118, 119, 121, 123–94, 196–8, and 201), introduced during the year 1844, deal with a wide variety of offences.[35] The bulk of them (arts. 123–94), enacted on 24 August 1844, are taken from the French Penal Code of 1810 with, occasionally, some changes in the penalties. The translation from French is often clumsy and only a few of the general provisions of the Code Pénal (CP) are included. A few minor adjustments to the Egyptian legal system are included:[36] In arts. 160 and 161, which deal with abortion and unintentional homicide, the text is adapted to the provisions of the *Shariʿa* by mentioning the liability for blood money. No further references to the *Shariʿa* can be found

31 Enacted AH Rabiʿ II 1253/July–August 1837 CE.

32 Arts. 56–75 (enacted AH Shawwal 1258/November–December 1842 CE); arts. 81–6 (enacted AH Rabiʿ II 1260/April–May 1844 CE); arts. 98–106 (enacted AH Rabiʿ II 1259 (April–May 1843 CE); art. 107 (enacted AH Jumada I 1259/May–June 1843 CE); arts. 108–9 (enacted AH Dhu al-Hijja 1258 January 1843 CE); art. 110–11 (enacted AH Shawwal 1259/October–November 1843 CE); art. 116 (enacted AH Muharram 1260/January–February 1844), art. 117 (enacted AH Rabiʿ II 1260/April–May 1844 CE), art. 120 (enacted AH 9 Shaʿban 1260/24 August 1844 CE), art. 122 (enacted AH 22 Ramadan 1260/5 October 1844 CE), arts. 195, 201–03 (not dated).

33 They were part of *Layihat al-jusur* (regulations on dams) (enacted AH Rajab 1258/August–September 1842 CE), and *Qanunname ʿamaliyyat al-turaʿ wa-l-jusur* (code of operations regarding canals and dams) (enacted Dhu al-Hijja 1258/January 1843 CE).

34 Enacted in AH Shawwal 1259/October–November 1843 CE.

35 18 Muharram 1260 (8 February 1844), art. 118; Rabiʿ I 1260 (March–April 1844), art. 119; 8 Jumada II 1260 (25 June 1844), art. 121; 9 Shaʿban 1260 (24 August 1844), arts. 122–94; 30 Ramadan 1260 (13 October 1844), arts. 196–8, 201.

36 For the correspondence between the articles of both codes, see the Appendix 1.

in the law of 1844.[37] The most important crimes mentioned in this part of the code are: counterfeiting coins, fraud, forging and breaking official seals, rape, poisoning, abortion, assault and battery, theft, arson, extortion by officials, illegal detention, unintended homicide, fraudulent bankruptcy, perjury, insulting behaviour towards public servants, and obstruction of justice.

The French Code Pénal has an elaborate system of penalties distinguishing between four categories of imprisonment,[38] each with its own legal effects. The preciseness of the French terminology has not been recognized by the translator. Therefore, the translation of the penalties is sometimes defective, as it does not take into account the legal implications of certain French terms used in the Code Pénal. One of the penalties of the Code Pénal is *travaux forcés à temps*, which in art. 19 CP is explained as five to twenty years of penal servitude. Similarly, *réclusion* is defined by art. 21 as incarceration for a period of five to ten years. These definitions were not included in the *Qanun Muntakhab*, but nevertheless the translator has often rendered these terms literally: *Travaux forcés à temps* became 'to be sent to the Alexandria Dockyards (*liman*) for a specified period' or just 'incarceration' (*al-rabt bi-l-Qalʿa*) without defining the length of the detention in relation to a certain offence.[39] In addition the code includes the punishment of depriving a person from his civil rights (*al-tabriʾa min tamattuʿ al-huquq al-mulkiyya*), which does not make much sense in the Egyptian context.

Apart from the disciplinary measures for officials such as discharge, demotion, and detention at the place of employment, the code lists the following punishments:

> **Capital punishment**, mentioned only once as a penalty for hiding and assisting peasants who have fled from their villages (art. 119). Death penalty for manslaughter (*qisas*) on the strength of a sentence pronounced by the *qadi* was also applied, but is not mentioned in this code.

37 On the basis of this law Baer assumed that a change in the official attitude towards the *Shariʿa* had occurred in Egypt around 1844 (Baer, 'Tanzimat', 113). Apparently he was not aware that this law was a translation of the French Code Pénal. Court records do not support the thesis that there was a change in the attribution of jurisdiction in criminal matters between the *qadi* and the state authorities.

38 Les travaux forcés à perpétuité, les travaux forcés à temps, la réclusion, l'emprisonnement à temps dans un lieu de correction (art. 7 and 9 CP).

39 See e.g. arts. 146, 149, and 190, corresponding to arts. 141, 251, and 188 Code Pénal.

Deportation to the Sudan, i.e. to the Fayzoghli labour camps or to land reclamation regions[40] for one to five years or for life, or to land reclamation regions. This was a new form of punishment.

Forced labour either in the Alexandria Dockyards (*Liman Iskandariyya*) for three months to five years or for life, or on government building sites in the convict's region of residence.

Detention in poorhouses (*mahall al-fuqara'*), a punishment for beggars who were not able to work (art. 191–2).[41]

Incarceration (*al-rabt bi-l-Qal'a*) for six months to three years, officials were usually sent to Abu Qir, a fortress on the Mediterranean shore East of Alexandria.

Simple detention (*habs*) for eight days to two years.

Flogging, fifty to 600 stripes of the *kurbaj*.

Fining, the revenues of which were to be spent on the civilian hospitals (*al-usbitaliyya al-mulkiyya*).

4 The Penal Code of 1849[42]

The Penal Code of 1849 consists of 90 articles. It lacks an introductory article and contains essentially a list of offences and their punishments. The 1849 code is no more than a rehash and a rearrangement of the *Qanun al-Muntakhab*. Unlike the latter its articles are arranged according to subject. Its nine chapters deal with agriculture (*al-filaha*, ch. 1 and *al-zira'a*, ch. 2), the state (*al-siyasa*, ch. 3), the *Shari'a* (ch. 4), the army (*al-jihadiyya*, ch. 5), dikes (*al-jusur*, ch. 6), embezzlement (*al-ikhtilas*, ch. 7), theft (*al-sariqa*, ch. 8), forging seals etc. (*man yuqallid al-akhtam wa-ma yumathiluha*, ch. 9), and counterfeiters (*al-zaghaliyya*, ch. 10). Thirteen of the sixteen articles of the first two chapters are taken from *Qanun al-Filaha*. Interestingly, none of the provisions found in previous legislation and protecting the peasants against abuse of

40 Fayzoghli is a mountainous area in the Sennar Province of Sudan, situated on the upper Blue Nile near the Ethiopian border. Deportation of criminals to the Sudan became a punishment at some date between 1837 and 1844. On its penal settlements, see Peters, 'Triumphant prison', 269–70.

41 Poorhouses existed in Cairo and Alexandria. Here the 'deserving' poor received food, clothing, and shelter. For those arrested for begging, they also functioned as places of internment. See M. Ener, *Managing Egypt's Poor and the Politics of Benevolence, 1800–1952* (Princeton 2003), 38–42.

42 The Code was printed in a bilingual (Arabic and Turkish) edition by an official printing house (Dar al-Tiba'a al-'Amira al-Miriyya) in Bulaq on AH 8 Rajab 1265/30 May 1849 CE.

power by the shaykhs was included in the new code. Thirty-two provisions are taken from those parts of the *Qanun Muntakhab* that derive directly from the French Code Pénal.[43] The remaining articles come from the various sections of *the Qanun Muntakhab*.

The system of penalties is nearly identical to the one in the *Qanun Muntakhab*, except that fining is not mentioned anymore. In general the penalties for the same offences are more severe in the new law. The punishment of flogging, which hardly occurs in the articles of the *Qanun Muntakhab* taken from the French Code Pénal, has a more prominent position: for twenty-one out of the eighty offences mentioned in the law this punishment is prescribed – usually with a specified number of lashes (*jalda*) – ranging from ten to 500. In two articles (arts. 1 and 2) this punishment, in accordance with traditional Ottoman use, is referred to as *taʿzir* without further specification of the number of stripes.

One article deals with procedure, or rather the jurisdiction of the various courts and the possibility of appeal. It lays down that offences other than capital crimes or crimes that may entail a sentence of forced labour or incarceration (*al-rabt bi-l-Qalʿa*, incidentally a penalty otherwise not mentioned in this code) are to be tried by the provincial administrations (*al-mudiriyyat*) and that one can appeal from these sentences to the *Majlis al-Ahkam*. However, if this court finds that the sentence in the first instance was justified, the punishment imposed will be doubled (art. 23). The article does not specify where these serious crimes were to be tried, but from archival material it is clear that the *Majlis al-Ahkam* was the competent court.

5 The *Qanun Sultani* of 1852[44]

In 1851 a new penal code called *Kanun-i Cedid* was enacted in the Ottoman empire.[45] As a consequence of the Ottoman policy of strengthening its control over the autonomous parts of the empire the sultan required that this code take effect also in Egypt.[46] The outcome of the ensuing negotiations between the Khedive ʿAbbas and the Porte was that in 1852[47] the Ottoman Code was

43 Arts. 7, 24, 26, 27–9, 31–8, 41, 42, 57–9, 76–82, 86–90.

44 Text in Zaghlul, *al-Muhamat*, Appendix, 156–78 and Jallad, *Qamus*, ii, 90–102.

45 It was published on AH 15 Safar 1267/20 December 1850 CE. Text in A. Akgündüz, *Mukayeseli Islâm ve Osmanlı hukuku külliyati* (Diyarbakır 1986), 821–31.

46 For the political aspects and the negotiations, see Baer, 'Tanzimat'.

47 Baer suggests that the new code was not introduced until 1854 (Baer, 'Tanzimat', 119). However, archival material indicates that it was already applied in 1852.

introduced in Egypt under the title of *al-Qanunname al-Sultani* (The Code of the Sultan) or *al-Qanun al-Humayuni* (The Imperial Code) with some modifications and additions. The code remained in force until 1883.[48]

The most important adaptation of the Ottoman Code was that in certain cases death sentences passed in Egypt should henceforth be ratified by the Porte. Articles 2, 3, and 4 of Chapter 1 do require that capital sentences be sent to Istanbul for approval by the Şeyh ül-Islâm and the sultan. However, as a result of negotiations between the Porte and Egypt, the khedive, for a period of seven years, was granted the right to execute murderers if the victims' heirs demanded execution, but not if the victims had no heirs. For in the latter case, the death penalty could only be demanded according to the *Shari'a* proceedings by the head of state (i.e. the Ottoman sultan).[49] The Ottoman sultan, apparently, did not want to delegate this sovereign prerogative to the khedive. A note (*hashiya*) was added to Chapter 1, art. 2, stipulating that *Shari'a* death sentences for homicide in cases where the victim had no heirs, would for seven years be carried out without a decree of the sultan.[50] This was not in conformity with the agreement between the Porte and the Khedive and may be the result of a translator's error (in translating the original Turkish text into Arabic) as Baer assumes.[51] In practice, however, the terms of the agreement have remained a dead letter. Another outcome of these negotiations was that the capital crimes of the Ottoman Code, with the exception of homicide, were to be punished in Egypt with forced labour. Here a similar argument played a role: capital punishment on the strength of the powers of *siyasa* was also considered to be the exclusive right of the sultan. Finally, the Egyptian government was granted the right to add provisions with regard to specific Egyptian conditions.[52] This resulted in the addition of two chapters to the Ottoman Code.

---

48 There is some confusion about whether between 1852 and 1883 a new Penal Code was introduced. In 1863 the khedive announced that he wanted to abolish the *Qanunname Sultani* and replace it with the new Ottoman Penal Code of 1858, after a sufficient number of copies had been printed. Six weeks later he ordered that the Egyptian chapters (i.e. chs. 4 and 5) in the *Qanunname Sultani* should be added to the new Ottoman Penal Code (Sami, *Taqwim*, iii/2, 499, 513). Baer (Baer, 'Tanzimat', 128–30 and 'Transition', 141) assumes that this finally resulted in the introduction of a new Penal Code of 341 articles, which was published by the Ministry of Justice in 1875 (Nazarat al-Haqqaniyya, *Qanun al-'Uqubat* [Cairo 1292/1875]), but this is no more than a translation of the draft penal code for the mixed courts. From the records of the *Majlis al-Ahkam* it is clear that the *Qanunname Sultani* continued to be applied until the introduction of the French codes in 1883 and 1889.

49 Peters, *Crime and Punishment*, 44.

50 Jallad, *Qamus*, ii, 92.

51 Baer, 'Tanzimat', 120, note 53.

52 Baer, 'Tanzimat', 116.

The first three chapters correspond closely with the Ottoman Penal Code. They begin with general statements regarding fundamental civil rights, echoing the Ottoman Gülhane Decree of 1839, which announced that penal legislation would be enacted for the protection of life, honour, decency, and property. Accordingly the first three chapters deal respectively with homicide, offences against honour and public decency, and crime against property. The Code lays down that no one may be killed except on the basis of a sentence passed according to the *Shariʿa* (Chapter 1, art. 1), and affirms the inviolability of honour (Chapter 2, art. 1) and private property (Chapter 3, art. 1). The two chapters that were added to the Ottoman Code contain articles on rural and official crime respectively. All of these were taken from the older Egyptian codes, most of them from the Penal Code of 1849, and some directly from the *Qanun al-Filaha* or Qanun *al-Muntakhab*.[53]

From the point of view of legislative technique, the first three chapters of the new code constituted an improvement compared to the *Qanun Muntakhab* and the Penal Code of 1849. The wording is much clearer and the provisions are less casuistic than in the previous codes. Moreover, the code contains provisions regarding procedure and the jurisdiction and competence of the judicial councils and is more explicit with regard to the relationship between these councils and the *qadi* courts. Unlike the previous Egyptian statutes, it includes special rules for the criminal responsibility of slaves.

The introduction of the Ottoman code was facilitated by the similarities between Ottoman and Egyptian criminal law. In spite of Mehmed ʿAli's reforms, the foundations of both systems were identical. In both there was a division of labour and cooperation between the *qadi* and the executive officials. Moreover, both countries had begun to set up councils with judicial tasks. In the Ottoman empire the first such council was the *Meclis-i Vala-yi Ahkam-i ʿAdliye* (1838), in Egypt the *Jamʿiyya Haqqaniyya* (1843), later renamed *Majlis al-Ahkam*. Finally the penal systems of both countries were similar.

According to the Ottoman penal system, as laid down in the 1851 Code, offenders could be sentenced to capital punishment, to forced labour (*kürek*),[54] sometimes with the addition 'in chains' (*pranga*), to forced labour in lowly jobs (*süfli hizmetler*) being fettered (probably to be served in the region of

53 See Appendix 2.

54 The term *kürek*, meaning literally both 'oar' and 'shovel', is ambiguous. Originally it referred to servitude on the galleys, (U. Heyd, *Studies in Old Ottoman Criminal Law* [Oxford 1973], 304–7) but later it referred also to forced labour in general. The 1840 and 1851 Ottoman Penal Codes do not define the term. In the 1858 Penal Code *kürek* is explained as 'being employed in hard labor with the feet in iron fetters' (art. 19). It is plausible that the term had the same meaning in the two previous codes.

the convict's residence), to simple detention (*habs*), to caning, and to being reprimanded. Women were to be detained in special women's prisons (*nisaya mahsus mahbesde habs*). As we have seen all these penalties were known in Egypt as well.

There were, however, a few minor differences. A punishment in the Ottoman Code not mentioned in the Egyptian codes was banishment without detention or forced labour (*memleketinden aher mahalle ... sene durmak üzere nefy ve tağrib*). This penalty was introduced in Egypt with the *Qanunname Sultani*,[55] but it seems that in practice it was equated to deportation to the Sudan with forced labour. Another difference is that corporal punishment in the Ottoman code consisted of caning (*değenek*), whereby the number of strokes, in deference to the *Shari'a*, did not exceed seventy-nine. In this respect, there is a striking difference between Chapters 1 to 3 of the *Qanunname Sultani*, and Chapters 4 and 5, where certain offences entail a punishment of up to 250 lashes (*jalda*) administered by the whip (*kurbaj*). A final difference is that the Ottoman Code, following traditional Ottoman *qanun*, defines the length of detention of forced labour for some offences as 'until he [the offender] shows remorse and genuine repentance (*kendide nedamet ve tevbe-yi sahiha hasil oluncaya kadar*)'.[56] This occurs also in the *Qanunname Sultani*.[57] For some reason, the *Qanunname Sultani*, unlike the Ottoman Penal Code, does not mention the penalty of reprimanding.

The following penalties are mentioned in the *Qanunname Sultani*:

> **Capital punishment** (*qisas*) for wilful homicide by virtue of a sentence pronounced by a *qadi* under the *Shari'a*.
>
> **Deportation to the Sudan** (also called 'deportation to far regions' [*yunfa ila bilad ba'ida*], or just 'banishment' [*nafy wa-taghrib*]), sometimes with the addition of 'in chains' (*muqayyad*). In a few articles the period of deportation is not specified or only limited by the expression 'until he repents'. Fayzoghli is not expressly mentioned anymore as a deportation camp although it was in use until around 1865. From 1857 peasants and rural shaykhs convicted for homicide or repeated theft were deported with their families to land reclamation areas in the Khartoum Province.[58]

55 E.g. Chapter 1, art. 6: '... *yunfa ila bilad ba'ida*' ('... shall be deported to remote regions'); Chapter 3, art. 12: '*nafy wa-taghrib*' ('deportation and banishment').

56 E.g. Chapter 2, art. 5, Ottoman Penal Code.

57 See Chapter 1, art. 15, Chapter 2, art. 5, Chapter 3, art. 13.

58 Peters, 'Triumphant Prison', 269–70.

Forced labour in the Alexandria Dockyard from two months to fifteen years, or 'in degrading jobs' (*khidamat dani'a*) in the region of one's residence for two months to five years, sometimes with the specification 'in chains' (*al-wadʿ fi al-qayd, al-wadʿ bi-l-hadid*).

Detention (*habs*) in a women's prison, which in the court records is referred to as *iplikkhane* (labour prison or spinning mill), or *maghzal Bulaq*, the spinning mill in Bulaq.[59]

Simple detention (*habs*), sometimes with the specification 'in chains', from five days to five years.

Flogging (twelve to 250 lashes) and **caning** (three to 79 strokes). These corporal punishments were abolished in 1861 and replaced with detention (*habs*).[60]

6 The Decree of the *Majlis al-Ahkam* of 1858[61]

The *Majlis al-Ahkam* did not only have judicial functions; it could also draft laws and submit them to the Khedive for ratification. This happened for instance whenever the *Majlis al-Ahkam* in its judicial practice found that laws contained loopholes or were wanting in other respects. The decree of 1858 is a clear example: it was drafted because the *Majlis al-Ahkam* found existing legislation on some points inadequate. The first article rectified an inconsistency between two Khedival decrees: they both imposed deportation to the Sudan for certain offences, but in one of them the convicts' families were allowed to accompany them, whereas the other was silent on the issue. The 1858 decree extended this right also to the latter. The remaining articles were amendments to the *Qanunname Sultani*, because the *Majlis al-Ahkam* found that some of its provisions were incomplete and regarded the penalties for certain offences as too light.

The second and the third articles deal with homicide. Article 2 lays down that the *Qanunname Sultani* contains a lacuna. Chapter 1, art. 11 lays down that if wilful homicide was proven in a *Shariʿa* court, but no death penalty could be imposed, e.g. because the victim's heirs pardoned the killer, or the *Shariʿa* did

59 Although the *Qanunname Sultani* was the first to mention a special women's penitentiary, this does not mean that before that time women and men were always put in the same prisons. In the late 1840 women offenders were sent to work in the civilian hospital. See Peters, 'Triumphant prison', 270–1.

60 Peters, 'Triumphant Prison', 262.

61 Text in Sami, *Taqwim*, iii/1, 294–7; ratification by the Khedive ultimo Safar 1258 (Sami, *Taqwim*, iii/1, 301).

not allow retribution (as in cases of infanticide), state courts could sentence the killer to forced labour. The Code, however, does not treat the situation in which a person has wilfully killed and the killing could not be proven according to the high standards required by the *Shari'a*, but was established by other means. The *Majlis al-Ahkam* notices that the practice of the judicial councils was to punish the defendant with forced labour and now gives this practice a legal basis.

The third article is rooted in Ottoman tradition. Although *qadis* had to adjudicate according to the most authoritative opinion of the Hanafite school of jurisprudence, i.e. according to the opinion of Abu Hanifa if his opinion was known, the sultan could instruct *qadis* with regard to specific cases to follow other authorities if he thought their opinion more expedient.[62] Under the *Shari'a* criminal intent in homicide – a necessary condition for capital punishment – is established by the type of weapon or instrument used, according to Abu Hanifa's view, this must be a sharp object or fire. Other Hanafite authorities, like the other schools of law, are of the opinion that criminal intent is proven by the use of any instrument or method that is generally lethal. For homicide committed with a stick or by drowning no death penalty could be imposed according to Abu Hanifa's opinion. Since such murders were common in Egypt, the *Majlis al-Ahkam* instructed the *qadis* to follow the other authorities in order to make the law more deterrent. Such an Egyptian decree had previously been impossible since, until 1856, *Shari'a* justice was controlled by the Porte. A treaty concluded in 1856 brought the *Shari'a* courts (with the exception of the *qadi* of Cairo) directly under the authority of the Khedive.

The last two articles of the decree introduced a change of Chapter 2, art. 7. This article made malicious wounding with a blunt object punishable with five days to three months detention or seventy-nine strokes of the cane. The *Majlis al-Ahkam* regarded this as too light a punishment and increased it to one month to three years forced labour and payment of damages. The last article deals with slander, or, rather, malicious and unfounded accusations, for which Articles 1 and 2 of Chapter 2 of the Code imposed an unspecified *ta'zir* punishment. The *Majlis al-Ahkam* regarded this offence as very serious and made it punishable with the penalty of the offence of which the offender had falsely accused his adversary. However if this offence was homicide the punishment would be one month to five years of forced labour.

62 Imber, *Ebu's-Su'ud*, 107–9; R. Peters, 'What Does It Mean to Be an Official Madhhab: Hanafism and the Ottoman Empire', in P. Bearman, R. Peters, and F. Vogel (eds.), *The Islamic School of Law: Evolution, Devolution and Progress* (Cambridge MA 2005), 152.

7 Conclusions

Nineteenth-century Egyptian criminal legislation was influenced by both French and Ottoman law. The impact of French law, however, was superficial. Although some seventy articles from the Code Pénal found their way into the Egyptian *Qanun Muntakhab* of 1845, one can hardly speak of a reception of French law. French, and indeed Western European penal law, were characterized by elaborate classifications: classifications of the types of crimes according to their gravity and classifications of the types of punishments. These categories were legally highly relevant since they entailed legal effects not mentioned in the articles defining the specific offences or imposing punishments. These distinctions and definitions, however, were not adopted in Egyptian legislation. The same is true of most provisions of the French Code Pénal regarding general principles such as the doctrines of complicity, causality, and culpability. What was borrowed were only the definitions of a number of offences and their penalties. These could easily be adapted to the local circumstances.

The main external influence was Ottoman penal law. From the point of view of system and structure, Ottoman penal law was very similar to the system prevailing in Egypt. However, in order to adapt Ottoman law to the Egyptian practice, two 'Egyptian' chapters were added to the Ottoman Penal Code. The final result, the *Qanunname Sultani*, contains some typically Ottoman traits as we have seen, but fits on the whole very well in the tradition of Egyptian criminal legislation.

Despite some outside influences, Egyptian nineteenth-century penal legislation is Ottoman–Egyptian by origin. Some of its characteristics are the result of the complicated relationship between Egypt and the Ottoman empire. The penal codes are characterized by the following features:

1. Like in the Ottoman empire, many offences were tried both by *qadi*s and the judicial councils. The former would adjudicate on the private claims of the victims of crime, including in cases of killing, the heirs' demand to sentence the defendant to death. The councils would apply the enacted laws and deal with crime from the point of view of society and the state.
2. Between the 1850s and the British occupation in 1882, capital punishment was applied sparingly: namely only when a *qadi* would sentence a person to death, which did not happen very often. This was a result of the complicated relationship between Egypt and the Ottoman empire. The sultan regarded pronouncing *siyasa* death sentences as his personal prerogative, which he did not want to share with the Egyptian khedive. As a consequence all capital offences listed in the Ottoman code were changed into offences punishable with forced labour or deportation.

3. A typical Egyptian trait was that the codes gave a great deal of attention to rural crime and to the misconduct of officials.

Appendix 1

Penal statutes enacted between 1829 and 1858:

The penal decree of 1829.

The *Qanun al-Filaha*, printed January/February 1830.

Al-Qanun al-Muntakhab ('Selected Legislation' also referred to as *Qanun al-Muntakhabat*) of 1845.

The penal code of 1849.

Al-Qanunname al-Sultani (The Sultanic Code), also called *al-Qanun al-Sultani* and *al-Qanun al-Humayuni* (the Imperial Code), introduced around 1852.

The decree of the *Majlis al-Ahkam* of 25 Muharram 1275 (4 September 1858) amending the Imperial Code.

Appendix 2

Correspondence between the articles of *the Qanun Muntakhab* and the French Code Pénal:

123 QM = 2 CP
124 QM = 20 CP
125 QM = 22 CP
126 QM = 25 CP
127 QM = 27 CP
128 QM = 29 CP
129 QM = 30 CP
130 QM = 36 CP
131 QM = 37 CP
132 QM = 52 CP
133 QM = 66 CP
134–5 QM = 70–1 CP
136 QM = 72 CP
137 QM = 132 CP
138 QM = 133 CP
139 QM = 134 CP
140 QM = 135 CP
141 QM = 136 CP
142 QM = 138 CP
143 QM = ? CP
144 QM = 139 CP
145 QM = 140 CP
146 QM = 141 CP
147 QM = 249 CP
148 QM = 250 CP
149 QM = 251 CP
150 QM = 253 CP
151 QM = 265–7 CP
152 QM = 271 CP
153 QM = 272 CP
154 QM = 273 CP
155 QM = 290 CP

156 QM = 331 CP
157 QM = 405 CP
158 QM = 173 CP
159 QM = 301 CP
160 QM = 317 CP
161 QM = 319–20 CP
162 QM = 321–2 CP
163 QM = 324 CP
164 QM = 330 CP
165 QM = 331 CP
166 QM = 309 CP
167 QM = 318 CP
168 QM = 381 CP
169 QM = 383 CP
170 QM = 384 CP
171 QM = 385 CP
172 QM = 388 CP
173 QM = 434/437/458 CP
174 QM = 4(?) CP
175 QM = 257 CP
176 QM = 345 CP
177 QM = 174 CP
178 QM = 175 CP
179 QM = 341 CP
180 QM = 402 CP
181 QM = 238 CP
182 QM = 239 CP
183 QM = 240 CP
184 QM = 248 CP
185 QM = 361 CP
186 QM = 362 CP
187 QM = 364 CP
188 QM = 365 CP
189 QM = 373 CP
190 QM = 188 CP
191 QM = 274 CP
192 QM = 275 CP
193 QM = 277 CP

Appendix 3

Correspondence between the articles of Chapters 4 and 5 of the *Qanunname Sultani* and the previous codes:

1. Articles taken from the Penal Code of 1849:

QS 4/1 = PC 1849, 1
QS 4/2 = PC 1849, 2
QS 4/3 = PC 1849, 3
QS 4/4 = PC 1849, 4
QS 4/5 = PC 1849, 5
QS 4/6 = PC 1849, 6
QS 4/7 = PC 1849, 7
QS 4/8 = PC 1849, 8
QS 4/9 = PC 1849, 9
QS 4/10 = PC 1849, 12
QS 4/11 = PC 1849, 13
QS 4/12 = PC 1849, 11, 14
QS 4/13 = PC 1849, 15
QS 4/14 = PC 1849, 60
QS 4/15, 16 = PC 1849, 61
QS 4/17, 18 = PC 1849, 60, 62, 63
QS 5/2 = PC 1849, 32
QS 5/3 = PC 1849, 49
QS 5/4 = PC 1849, 50
QS 5/5 = PC 1849, 52
QS 5/6 = PC 1849, 78
QS 5/10 = PC 1849, 20
QS 5/11 = PC 1849, 10

2. Articles taken from the *Qanun al-Filaha*:

QS 4/19 = QF, 8
QS 4/20 = QF, 10
QS 4/21 = QF, 12
QS 4/22 = QF, 17
QS 4/23 = QF, 20
QS 4/24 = QF, 39
QS 4/25 = QF, 44
QS 4/26 = QF, 45

3. Articles taken from the *Qanun Muntakhab*:

QS 5/1 = QM 107
QS 5/7 = QM 70
QS 5/7 = QM 71
QS 5/9 = QM 115

CHAPTER 7

The Significance of Nineteenth-Century Pre-Colonial Legal Reform in Egypt

The Codification of Criminal and Land Law

1 Introduction[1]

It is generally accepted that the modernization of the Egyptian legal system was set off around 1880, with the creation of the mixed courts in 1876 and the establishment of the national courts in 1883 as the main landmarks.[2] The implicit assumption behind this periodization is that modernization could only be achieved through Western intervention. In this paper I want to challenge this standard account. Although the new courts and law codes were of foreign inspiration, they built forth on existing institutions. Before the 1876 and 1883 reforms Egypt had already an indigenous legal system with a well-structured hierarchy of courts and defined jurisdictions, operating to a large extent independently from the executive, with enacted law codes and a penal system in which corporal punishment and torture during investigation were banned. This new legal system was created between 1829 and the 1870s. I will argue that this new legal system can already be characterized as modern. I will focus on criminal law and land law. Criminal law was, in my opinion, the most important and telling area of reform. Criminal law regulates relations between the state and individuals and consequently criminal law reform reflects changing ideas about this relationship. This is eminently the field where modernizing trends, if present, can be observed. Land law, as codified in the Land Code of

1 This is an expansion of the paper "The Significance of Nineteenth-Century Pre-Colonial Legal Reform in Egypt" which I presented to the workshop "New Approaches to Egyptian Legal History: Late Ottoman Period to the Present" (Cairo, AUC, 11–14 June, 2009), whose contributions will be published presently. I owe a great debt of gratitude to the participants whose contributions to the discussions helped me shape the final version of this paper. In the original paper my argument was based only on the development of criminal law. In the present paper I will examine also land law.

2 See for a standard account e.g. Farhat J. Ziadeh, *Lawyers, the rule of law and liberalism in modern Egypt*. Stanford University, Stanford CA, 1968., ch. 1; J.N.D. Anderson, "Law reform in Egypt, 1850–1950," in P.M. Holt, ed. *Political and Social Change in Egypt: Historical Studies from the Ottoman Conquest to the United Arab Republic*. London etc.: Oxford University Press, 1968, pp. 220; Robert L. Tignor, *Modernization and British colonial rule in Egypt*. Princeton N.J., Princeton University Press, 1966, pp. 123–129, 138–9.

 DOI:10.1163/9789004420625_008

1858 is also important. Since this code regulated the law regarding state land (*arāḍī mīriyya*) and taxation, it likewise governed the relations between the state and its subjects.

The standard account of nineteenth-century Egyptian legal history is quite different from the Ottoman account. The prominent place of laicism (*lâyiklik*) and westernization in the ideology of the republic of Turkey has affected Ottoman historiography. The history of law of the Tanzimat period was seen through this ideological prism and was analysed as a struggle between two legal systems, the secular and the religious one, the former of which would in the end be victorious. The two systems were seen as separate and opposed to one another.[3] In Egyptian legal historiography, the notions of secularization and dualism did hardly play a role. Here colonialism and its ideologies have dominated legal history of the nineteenth century, with its dichotomy between pre-colonial despotism versus the colonial legal order and rule of law. British colonial administrators and travellers propagated the idea that modernization of the law did not begin before 1880s. In his *Modern Egypt*, Lord Cromer, who ruled Egypt between 1883 and 1907, wrote: "It is true that, prior to 1883, no system of justice existed in Egypt."[4] In his view, shared by many others, chaos, arbitrariness and corruption prevailed before the British occupation. One of the main justifications of the British occupation was that the British had to spread civilization in Egypt by establishing justice and the rule of law in the country. Prominent points of criticism of the pre-1883 legal system were the absence of a separation of powers between the judiciary and the executive and the frequent recourse to corporal punishment and torture. This colonialist outlook, adopted also by late nineteenth-century Egyptian lawyers such as Ahmad Zaghlūl, and in his wake, more recent historians such as Laṭīfa Sālim, has obscured the view of the pre-colonial reforms and prevented the assessment of their real import.[5]

Enid Hill[6] and Nathan Brown[7] were the first to acknowledge the importance of the pre-colonial legal reforms, which, they argued, prepared the way for the

3 Avi Rubin, *Ottoman Nizamiye courts: Law and modernity*. New York: Palgrave Macmillan, 2011.

4 Cromer, *Modern Egypt*. London: MacMillan, 1908. ii, p. 516.

5 Aḥmad Fatḥī Zaghlūl, *Al-Muḥāmāh*, Cairo: Maṭba'at al-Ma'ārif, 1900; Laṭīfa Muḥammad. Sālim, *Tarīkh Al-Qaḍā' al-Miṣrī Al-Ḥadīth*, Cairo: Al-Hay'at al-Miṣriyya al-'Āmma li-l-Kitāb, 1991.

6 Enid Hill, "Courts and the Administration of Justice in the Modern Era." In *The State and Its Servants: Administration from the Ottoman Times to the Present*. Ed. by Nelly Hanna. Cairo: The American University in Cairo Press, 1995. Pp. 98–116.

7 Nathan J. Brown, *The Rule of Law in the Arab World: Courts in Egypt and the Gulf*, Cambridge: Cambridge University Press, 1997. P. 31.

introduction of the foreign inspired legal system in 1883. Nevertheless Brown maintains that the post-1883 courts differed fundamentally from the ones they replaced, implying that real modernization was only achieved around 1880. I will discuss his views in the conclusions of this essay.

I'll begin with defining what I understand by modernization of the legal system using three criteria. The first one derives from Weber's typology of law and especially his ideal type of formal and rational law. Weber regarded a formal and rational legal system as an essential characteristic of modern capitalism. For Weber, a legal system is formal if legal judgments derive logically from general legal rules and are not pronounced arbitrarily or on extra-legal grounds, such as moral, religious, social or political considerations.[8] The latter form of justice is labelled by Weber as substantive or material justice. Rational in this context means that a judge reaches his decisions by logical reasoning and not intuitively or by relying on irrational procedures such as divination or ordeal. A modern legal system must be formal and rational. That means that there must be a set of clear and authoritative rules embodied in books of doctrine, recorded legal decisions or, preferably, law codes. The ruler should not have the power to interfere with legal decisions, because that would mean that political and not legal consideration would influence the outcome of litigation. Essential is that the court system works according to clear rules of procedure and that the various courts have well defined jurisdictions. Moreover, the law must apply equally to all persons or to all members of certain clearly defined categories of persons (e.g. women or officials). Courts must not be in a position to confer individual privileges nor to make individual exceptions to application of the law.

Weber dubbed the substantive (material) and irrational type of justice as "*Kadi-justiz*", using the image of a qadi sitting under a palm tree and deciding intuitively on an *ad hoc* basis. That this concept did not apply to sharia judges has been shown convincingly by several authors.[9] Islamic law must rather be

8 Patricia Crone contends that formal law in the Weberian sense is an impossibility since law functions in society and needs to contain extra-legal norms and concepts in order to be applicable. She forgets, however, that these may be part of formal law if the law itself admits them, e.g. by using open, flexible standards such as reasonable man or bona fides. See Crone, Patricia, "Max Weber, das islamische Recht und die Enststehung des Kapitalismus," in Schluchter, Wolfgang (ed.), *Max Webers Sicht des Islams: Interpretation und Kritik*. Frankfurt a.M.: Suhrkamp Verlag, 1987. Pp. 294–334.

9 See e.g. Crone, "Max Weber"; Schneider, Irene, "Die Merkmale Der Idealtypischen Qadi-Justiz – Kritische Anmerkungen Zu Max Webers Kategorisierung Der Islamischen Rechtsprechung." *Der Islam* 70, no. i (1993): 145–59; Powers, D.S., "Kadijustiz or Qadi-Justice? A Paternity Dispute from Fourteenth-Century Morocco." In *Law, Society, and Culture in the Maghreb, 1300–1500*, Cambridge: Cambridge University Press, 2002. Pp. 23–52; Johansen, Baber, *Contingency in a*

typified as being to a large extent formal and rational: sharia judges applied a written legal doctrine, followed clear rules of procedure and operated, at least in theory, independently from the executive. However, Weber's characterization of *Kadi-justiz* did apply to *siyāsa* justice as administered by high Ottoman executive officials and the Sultan. This was discretionary justice, with hardly any rules of procedure and evidence and often based on extra-legal, especially political considerations.

What I will argue in this essay is that in nineteenth-century Egypt (as well as in the Ottoman Empire) there was a drastic change in the administration of *siyāsa* justice, which developed from a substantive and irrational type of justice into the direction of a formal and rational type, because *siyāsa* justice became fixed by law codes and procedures. Criminal law and land law are cases in point, as I will demonstrate. Although, unlike Islamic jurisprudence, this part of the law was not based on an academic jurisprudential doctrine, its rationality derived from modern bureaucratic procedures that developed during the same time. Sharia justice in this period did also change, but less drastically. Already being to a large extent formal and rational, as we have seen, the administration of sharia justice during this period was just fine-tuned, whereby the law to be applied by the courts was better defined by instructing the courts to follow the most authoritative opinion of the Hanafi school, by introducing appeal procedures and by more precise definitions of jurisdictions.[10]

My second criterion is the relationship between the ruler and his officials on the one hand and, on the other, the law, including statutes they had enacted themselves. If subjects can appeal to these laws in order to assert their rights against the state and state officials, this is another sign of modernity of the legal system. It is a well-established principle of the sharia that the ruler is bound by the law, although this was not always enforced by the courts. With regard to *siyāsa* justice the situation was different, since here the interests of the state prevailed. This was true both in the law of land and in criminal law. The law of the land, as far as state land (*arāḍī mīriyya*) was concerned, which formed the overwhelming bulk of agricultural land, granted farmers the right to cultivate it, but limited the powers of disposal and put it under control by state officials by requiring their approval of transactions and inheritance of the land's usufruct. However, the rights of the cultivators and the powers of control of the officials were not well defined in the law. The 1858 Land Code enhanced

Sacred Law: Legal and Ethical Norms in the Muslim Fiqh. Leiden: Brill, 1999. (*Studies in Islamic Law and Society*, 7), p. 42ff.

10 See Peters, Rudolph, "Muhammad Al-'Abbasi Al-Mahdi (d. 1897), Grand Mufti of Egypt, and His Al-Fatawa Al-Mahdiyya." *Islamic Law and Society* 1, i (1994): 66–82.

legal certainty by fixing the law and better circumscribed the powers of the officials. As a result the farmers could asserts their rights against the organs of the state.

In the domain of criminal law, state officials originally had extensive powers in imposing penalties. When the Egyptian state began to enact penal statutes in the domain of *siyasa* justice in order to curb the powers of the officials, these statutes were seen as commands issued by the ruler, who was not bound by them and could change them at will. With some exceptions related to rights conferred by the sharia, criminal legislation was not viewed as rules to be invoked by subjects against the ruler and his officials. Gradually, however, they began to be regarded as law, not only binding the subjects but also conferring rights to them and binding the ruler. Justice evolved in the direction of an abstract and impersonal notion, embodied in legal rules and a judiciary, whereas previously it was a personal characteristic of the ruler, who had to be petitioned personally in order to redress injustices committed by his officials.

A final criterion, only with regard to the penal system, is in my view the abolition of torture and the replacement of corporal punishment by prison sentences as signs of modernization.[11] This happened, at least in theory, during the second half of the nineteenth century. The abolition of torture to extract confessions of crimes was brought about by the introduction of modern policing and of scientific methods of forensic investigation, whereas the banning of corporal punishment is related to more modern conceptions of judicial punishment.

2 Nineteenth-Century Legal Reform

We do not know a great deal about the Egyptian legal system during the eighteenth and first decades of the nineteenth century. Certainly, the sharia courts have left records which show that sharia justice was functioning. However, we have very little information about *siyāsa* justice.[12] During the first decades

11 This is not to say that modern states do not make use of torture or corporal penalties. However, as a rule this is not condoned by the legal system. See Rejali, Darius M., *Torture & Modernity: Self, Society, and State in Modern Iran*, Boulder: Westview Press, 1994.

12 Baldwin, James E., in his "Islamic Law in an Ottoman Context: Resolving disputes in late 17th/early 18th-century Cairo," (PhD dissertation, NYU, 2010) offers new insights into the functioning of the Cairo Dīwān. However, he focuses on its function as a judicial forum to settle civil and political conflicts and does not discuss its function as a criminal court. For the first decades of Meḥmed ʿAlī's rule, see Hilāl, Imād Aḥmad, "Irhāṣāt Lāʾiḥat Zirāʿat al-Fallāḥ: Al-tashrīʿ al-jināʾī fī Miṣr, 1805–1830," *Rūznāmeh* 4 (2006): 249–303.

of Meḥmed ʿAlī's reign, justice was administered according to the Ottoman model: Qadis and state councils like the Dīwān ʿĀlī Mulkī (The Supreme Council of Civil Affairs) and the Dīwān Khedīwī adjudicated in civil litigation according to the sharia,[13] whereas Meḥmed ʿAlī himself as well as these high councils of state administered *siyāsa* justice in criminal, fiscal and administrative matters on an *ad hoc* basis.[14] In the countryside customary law was often applied by officials in conflicts between fellahin.[15] During the first decades of the nineteenth century jurisdictions between the sharia courts, the administrative councils and the executive officials were fluid. There is no indication of French influence on the legal system. The commercial courts established by the French during the occupation, seen by some historians as the first beginnings of legal modernization, were abolished even before the French withdrawal and did not have a lasting impact.[16]

2.1 *Codification*[17]

As I have set out in the introduction, a legal system in order to be formal and rational must be based on a clearly defined written legal doctrine, preferably in the form of law codes, i.e. statutes comprehensively regulating certain branches of the law. Prior to the nineteenth century Egyptian *siyāsa* justice was certainly not formal and rational in this sense. With the exception of some ad hoc statutes,[18] *siyāsa* justice was not laid down in written laws and its administration was arbitrary and depended on political considerations. The most significant development during the nineteenth century was that *siyāsa* justice became fixed by law codes. As mentioned before, I will focus on the legislation

13 The jurisdiction of the sharia courts and these state councils overlapped and were not clearly demarcated.

14 For criminal justice in the early years of Meḥmed ʿAlī's reign, see Hilāl, "Irhāṣāt."

15 Hilal, "Irhāṣāt," p. 255.

16 See Goldberg, Jan, "On the Origins of Majalis Al-Tujjar in Mid-Nineteenth Century Egypt." *Islamic Law and Society* (1999): 193–223.

17 Regarding the penal codes, this section is mainly based on Peters, Rudolph, "Between Paris, Istanbul, and Cairo: The Origins of Criminal Legislation in Late Ottoman Egypt." In *Studies in Islamic Law: A Festschrift for Colin Imber*. Edited by A. Christmann and R. Gleave. Oxford: Oxford University Press, 2007, pp. 211–32, and my "'For His Correction and as a Deterrent Example for Others': Meḥmed ʿAlī's First Criminal Legislation (1829–1830)." *Islamic law and Society* 6 (1999): 164–93.

18 In Egypt the *Qānūnnāme-yi Miṣr* of 1525 and some ad hoc edicts issued by the governors were applied and not the Ottoman *qānūns* of the central empire. The laws did not cover complete domains of the law and did not put an end to arbitrariness. The Egyptian *qānūns* followed the same legislative technique as those enacted in the central Ottoman Empire. See, Farahat, Muḥammad Nūr, *Al-Tārīkh Al-Ijtimāʿī li-l-Qānūn fī Miṣr al-ḥadītha*. 2nd ed. Kuwait and Cairo: Dār Suʿād al-Ṣabāḥ, 1993, pp. 509–513.

concerning land law and criminal law. I will not discuss codes and statutes that more and more regulated other domains of the law such as those in the fields of the organization of the state (*Qānūn al-Siyāsetnāme*, 1837), the commercial councils (*Lāyiḥat al-Abillū*, 1857, instructing the commercial councils to apply the Ottoman code of commerce of 1850)[19] and with procedure for the Majlis Qūmisyūn Miṣr (1861), the predecessor of the Mixed Courts adjudicating civil cases between Egyptians and foreigners.

Before its codification in 1858, land law was a pluralistic mixture of the sharia, state legislation (*qānūn*), unwritten customary law and administrative practice. The impacts of these systems of law were not demarcated. At the village level, the sheikhs would act and informally settle conflicts according to established administrative practices and customary law. However, formal litigation in this field was conducted before sharia courts, which followed the sharia and Ottoman *qānūn* defining the qadis' jurisdictions[20] but did not take into account the relevant customs and administrative practices. Illustrative of the contradicting conceptions of the law is the chapter on *al-aṭyān al-amīriyya* in the *al-Fatāwā al-Mahdiyya*.[21] Time and again the mufti explains that state lands cannot be inherited, although the fatwas show that that, under customary law and according to administrative practices, usufruct of state land was inherited by the male offspring or rather that family households regarded themselves as continuously and collectively entitled to plots of land. Similarly, the mufti declared that pawning state land is invalid, although the questions indicate that the practice existed and, indeed, sharia courts regarded it as lawful.[22] However, under the sharia as expounded by the Mufti, the usufruct of state land could be "sold", i.e. ceded (*isqāṭ*) for money to another person. The principal rule of the sharia was that farmers were entitled to use the land as long as they were capable of cultivating it and to pay the taxes. If they could not, officials could assign the land to another person.[23]

The traditional view of the 1858 code is that it gave more rights to the farmers in permitting them to alienate state land and to inherit it. However, this

19 Goldberg, Jan, "On the Origins of Majalis Al-Tujjar in Mid-Nineteenth Century Egypt." *Islamic Law and Society* (1999): 193–223.

20 E.g. that the courts followed the prevailing opinion of the Hanafi madhhab, and that lawsuits could not be heard after 15 years.

21 Mahdī, Muḥammad al-ʿAbbāsī al-, *al-Fatāwā al-Mahdiyya fī al-Waqāʾiʿ al-Miṣriyya*. Cairo, Maṭbaʿat al-Azhar, 1884 (1301 H.). ii, pp. 33–244. Muḥammad al-Mahdī was the Egyptian Hanafi chief mufti between 1848 and 1897.

22 See Cuno, K.M., *The Pasha's peasants: Land, society, and economy in Lower Egypt, 1740–1858*. Cambridge, Cambridge University Press, 1991. Pp. 83.

23 Cuno, pp. 190–91.

does not agree with the facts. As is clear from the fatwas issued by Muhammad al-ʿAbbāsī al-Mahdī, the Hanafi state mufti, as well as the 1847 and 1855 laws that precede the 1858 Land Code, sale (or rather cession) of state land was lawful and binding, that state land could be inherited (although the legal foundation was unclear) and that pawning of state land was practiced (also without sanction of sharia authorities).[24] That these norms were obeyed was a result by the informal justice of the village sheikhs, who would adjudicate not by strict sharia rules, but rather by local custom and administrative practices. However, with the centralization of the state which favored the enforcement of formal law, there was an increase of cases in which customs opposed formal law and local households tried to assert their rights to land based on customs, against those who had acquired the land formally. The 1847 law[25] remedied some of the conflicts between custom and formal law. It clarified the rules of redeeming pawned land and the reclaiming of land with tax arrears by farmers who had deserted it or transferred it to others or of land reassigned by the authorities to others because the original users were not capable of cultivating them. Moreover it instructed that land transactions be officially registered. A law issued in 1855 amended and expanded the 1847 decree. It fixed shorter term for reclaiming pawned or abandoned land, it required the administrative permission of the *mudīr* (governor of a province) for certain land transactions and fixed the rules of inheritance of the usufruct of state land.

The 1858 Land Code, usually called *al-Lāʾiḥa al-Saʿīdiyya* after the Khedive who enacted it, or just *Lāʾiḥat al-Aṭyān*, was announced as comprehensive and meant to clearly and authoritatively expounding the law on state land.[26] It contained 28 articles[27] but in contrast to the penal codes, the articles of this code were very long, sometimes more than 700 words, and the complete text takes up twenty-two pages in small print. The law was effective until 1896, when the distinction between state land (*athar, aṭyān kharājiyya,* and *arāḍī mīriyya*) and fully owned land (*milk*) was legally abolished.[28] For a survey of the subjects discussed in this code, see Appendix 1. Although all subjects are related to state land, they belonged to various domains of the law: private law, such as

24 Cuno, 189.

25 Summary in Cuno, 191–92.

26 "… a code fulfilling the necessary requirements and containing the [prescriptions] that must be implemented and applied, without regard to the decrees regarding farm land issued previously, a code that will be independent and contain [all] rule that must be followed." Introduction to the 1858 Land Code.

27 Text in Mursi, M.K., *Al-milkiyya al-ʿaqāriyya fī Misr wa-taṭawwuruhā al-tarīkhiyya min ʿahd al-Firāʿina hattā al-ān*. al-Qāhira, Maṭbaʿat Turi, 1936.

28 Mursi, 94.

succession and contracts and their registration, administrative law, such as the appropriation of land by the state for public works and the granting of permits for conveyance, and fiscal law.

The principal objectives of this law were enhancing legal certainty and expanding state control of state land. The former objective was realized by proclaiming a set of unequivocal and authoritative rules, thus putting an end to the situation of legal pluralism in which formal and informal law coexisted and, often, contradicted. Secondly, the transactions regarding state land must be notarized by competent qadis or deputy qadis and, in addition, be approved and registered by administrative officials. Thirdly, the period was limited during which original users of land could reclaim from those who acquired it after a contract with the original user, or after reassignment of it by a state official. Finally rules were introduced in order to update the registration of users of the land and those taxable. The latter objective of the Code, the tendency towards greater control of administrative officials superior to the village sheikhs, is visible in the requirement that most transactions of state land must be approved or permitted by the *mudīr*. Finally the Code gives rules of appropriation by the state of used state land necessary for public works and of the uniformity of the rules concerning state law, by abolishing some types of land ownership previously instituted for the remuneration of certain offices. This meant that the categories of *ūsya*, *ibʾādiyya* and *rizaq* land was abolished. A point of reform not mentioned is the code, is that after the adoption the code litigation was to be conducted before the judicial councils and not anymore the qadis.[29]

In the domain of criminal law, too, the principle was established that *siyāsa* criminal justice was to be administered on the basis of law codes and statutes and not anymore at the discretion of officials and councils. Here, the development was more gradual. The new criminal codes were comprehensive, whereas previous *qānūn* did not replace discretionary *siyāsa* justice. This process started in 1829. Before that year, Meḥmed ʿAlī had issued legal decrees, but these were *ad hoc* decisions regarding individual persons or decrees penalizing one or two acts considered to be harmful to public order or the economy. The first more or less comprehensive law was enacted in 1829. This was a short criminal statute in ten articles defining various offences with their penalties.[30] A few

29 In the title of the chapter on state law in the *al-Fatāwā al-Mahdiyya*, it says that it includes only fatwas issued before the introduction of the Egyptian decrees and codes, indicating that sharia justice had no jurisdiction afterwards. FM, ii p. 33.

30 For the text and analysis of this code, see Peters, Rudolph, "'For His Correction and as a Deterrent Example for Others': Meḥmed ʿAlī's First Criminal Legislation (1829–1830)." *Islamic law and Society* 6 (1999): 164–93.

months later, in 1830, the much longer *Qānūn al-Filāḥa*[31] was introduced. This code, which almost exhaustively deals with punishable offences related with agriculture and life in the countryside, heralded a period of codification that continued until the British occupation. Criminal law became to be governed by comprehensive and exhaustive law codes.

The penal codes introduced in this period were *al-Qānūn al-Muntakhab* in 203 articles, which, apart from the text of the *Qānūn al-Filāḥa*, included selected statutes enacted between 1830 and 1845. In 1849 this code was replaced by a shorter one in 90 articles. The latter code was in force for only three years. After a great deal of diplomatic and political maneuvering it was decided that Egypt should adopt the Ottoman penal code of 1851. In recognition of Egypt's distinct character, it was permitted that two chapters were added containing the most important provisions from previous penal codes. The Imperial Code (*al-Qānūnnāme al-Sulṭānī*) as it was called was put into effect around 1852. In order to rectify some gaps, an additional law of five articles prepared by the Majlis al-Aḥkām was added to it in 1858. The Imperial Code and the appendix remained in force until 1883 (1889 for Upper Egypt).

The Egyptian penal codes contained general rules addressing either all subjects or special categories of subjects, such as officials or peasants, in which case they would address offences related to their offices or their living in the country side. Laws often emphasized that they applied to all and sundry regardless of their social and economic status. In the articles dealing with official crime, we often find the formulas: "If an official in the government departments, be he of high or low rank…." or "regardless who he is", emphasizing that the application of the law does not depend on rank or personal connections. An important innovation in the technique of criminal legislation was that the laws not only defined the offences, but also the quality and quantity of their penalties. This was a clear change from the criminal legislation applied previously. Traditional Ottoman penal *qānūns* defined punishable offences and laid down that offenders would be "chastised." This would mean that they would be beaten whereby the number of strokes (and thus the fine in proportion to its number) was to be determined by the qadi or an executive official. Less common was the penalty of unspecified imprisonment, which would last until the convict would repent. Only exceptionally would an offence be made punishable by death or mutilation.[32]

31 See Kato, Hirosho, "Egyptian Village Community under Muhammad Ali's Rule: An Annotation of 'Qanun Al-Filaha'." *Orient* 16 (1980).

32 See the text of the Ottoman Criminal Law. Heyd, Uriel, *Studies in Old Ottoman Criminal Law*. Oxford: Oxford University Press, 1973, pp. 95–131. For Egypt, see Faraḥāt, pp. 509–513.

During the years of reform, the function of penal laws gradually changed. Originally they were Meḥmed ʿAlī's instructions to his officials rather than laws addressing the general public. However, the *Qānūn al-Filāḥa* already contains provisions in which officials who have unlawfully caused a person's death are made liable according to the sharia. These rules made it possible that individuals sued state officials. This however was an exception based on a clear sharia norm. Acts not mentioned in the laws could be punished at the discretion of the authorities and Meḥmed ʿAlī himself, being the legislator, was above the law and could flout them at will. This situation, however, changes during the second half of the nineteenth century. Meḥmed ʿAlī's successors more and more felt that they also were under the obligation to follow the laws enacted by the state. On the other hand, the subjects became aware that they could invoke statute law to assert their rights against the government. As from the 1860s few criminal sentences were not based on legal provisions. If during trials acts were proven that deserved punishment but were not listed in any penal code, legislation was issued to remedy it. This was explicitly one of the tasks of the Majlis al-Aḥkām and the proclamation of the decree of the Majlis al-Aḥkām of 1858 served this purpose as it was intended to fill some lacunae of the Imperial Code.

2.2 *The Judicial Councils*[33]

A modern legal system requires a judiciary with clear-cut jurisdictions and transparent procedures, accessible to all and operating independently from political power. In the domain of *siyāsa* justice, such a judiciary did not exist before the 1870s. During the first decades of Meḥmed ʿAlī's reign *siyāsa* justice was administered by himself, by state councils, by provincial governors and the police departments in the large towns. It was, therefore, essentially substantive or material justice, since non-legal considerations, especially political ones played an important role.

Moreover, the jurisdictions of these authorities and the procedure followed by them were not clearly demarcated. There must have been some rules based on bureaucratic practice, but if they were put in writing, they have not been preserved. However, during the last years of Meḥmed ʿAlī's reign, this began to change. An ordinance of April 1838 defined the jurisdictions of the Dīwān

33 This section is mainly based on Peters, Rudolph, "Administrators and Magistrates: The Development of a Secular Judiciary in Egypt, 1842–1871." *Die Welt des Islams* 39 (1999): 378–97 and Peters, Rudolph, "Islamic and Secular Criminal Law in 19th Century Egypt: The Role and Function of the Qadi." *Islamic law and Society* 4 (1997): 70–90.

Khedīwī and the Cairo Police Department (Ḍābiṭkhāne). Criminal cases that were reported to the police were summarily investigated and then either dealt with by the police, or, if they were serious, submitted to the Dīwān Khedīwī, which would further investigate the matter and punish the culprits, or, if the matter fell under the jurisdiction of the sharia, sent to the qadi. Capital cases were submitted to the Pasha for sentencing. In other cities comparable practices must have existed. In the following decades more legislation was enacted defining and demarcating jurisdictions whenever new courts were established. Moreover the jurisdictions of these councils were extended. Litigation regarding the issues of the 1858 Land Law was also assigned to the councils, whereas before litigation concerning state law was adjudicated by sharia courts and, informally, by the village sheikhs.

Departing from the situation wherein crime was tried by administrative bodies and executive officials, Egypt developed, in the course of thirty years, a full-fledged specialized *siyāsa* judiciary, parallel to the sharia courts. As of 1871 all crime was tried by judicial councils and not anymore by executive officials. Judicial reform began in 1842 with the creation of the Jamʿiyyat Haqqāniyya and ended in 1871 when the establishment of judicial councils at the village level completed the construction of a four-tiered judiciary. The Jamʿiyyat Haqqāniyya would hear in first instance cases of serious crime, like theft and manslaughter and, in addition, offences committed by high officials. It would also act as a court of review or appeal. In 1849 it was replaced by the newly created Majlis al-Aḥkām, which remained operative until 1883 (1889 for Upper Egypt).

In 1852 regional councils were established as courts of first instance. By 1871 there were fifteen of them. Criminal cases were first investigated in the offices of legal affairs (*qalam al-daʿāwī*) that were part of the provincial administration (*mudīriyya*), or in the police departments (*Ḍabṭiyya*) of the main cities. Light offences would be dealt with there, usually with flogging, and, after the abolition of corporal punishment in 1861, by detention. The punishment could be executed immediately. In more serious cases, trial would take place before the regional council and the sentence would be executed after approval by the Dīwān al-Katkhuda, or, in very serious cases, after revision by the Majlis al-Aḥkām. The latter would be notified of all criminal sentences.

In 1864 two Appellate Councils (*majlis istiʾnāf*) were established to remedy the backlog of cases for the Majlis al-Aḥkām. The main task of these Appellate Councils was to review all sentences of the Councils of First Instance. After revision the sentences were to be sent to the *Dīwān al-Muʿāwana al-Saniyya* for execution. Only criminal sentences in homicide cases or sentences of more than three years imprisonment were henceforth to be submitted to the

Majlis al-Aḥkām. Appeal (*abillū*) could be lodged against the sentences of the Appellate Councils and was to be heard by the Majlis al-Aḥkām.

Besides the judicial councils, some executive bodies and officials had judicial tasks, mainly in trying and sentencing petty offenders. Their involvement came to an end in 1871, when judicial councils were created at the local level (*majlis daʿāwī al-balad, majlis daʿāwī al-bandar*, with three members) to replace the adjudication of minor cases – both civil and criminal – by single officials (village sheikhs and the district chiefs). Henceforth, adjudication and sentencing was exclusively the task of specialized judicial councils. With some slight modifications regarding the jurisdiction of the councils and the possibility of appeal, this new judicial system remained in force until the judicial reform of 1883 (1889 in Upper Egypt).

Judicial councils grew out of administrative bodies and their judgments were seen as administrative decisions, subject to review by higher authorities, and often, if they were of importance, by the Khedive. They had a hybrid character: although rooted in the administration and staffed by administrators, they had specialized judicial tasks. The members of these councils were instructed to take into account not only the interests of the state but also those of the subjects. Various statutes contain provisions inculcating the members of the councils that

> they must not be inclined to protect only [the interests] of the state (*mīrī*). Rather, they must take into consideration both [the interests] of the state and those of the state servants and the subjects and they must treat the latter with justice. If someone is entitled to something in a case, then his right must be protected. The members [of the council] must always proceed in such a way that they give everybody his due.[34]

As from the 1860s the judicial character became more prominent and the councils began to resemble more and more "real" courts operating independently form the executive.

There were no comprehensive codes regulating procedure. The decrees establishing judicial councils and the penal codes contain procedural rules, but, especially in the early decades, these were fragmentary and do not offer

34 *Lāyiḥat Majlis al-Aḥkām al-Miṣriyya* (5 Rabīʿ II, 1265/ 9 March 1849), Art. 12. Text in Zaghlūl, *al-Muḥāmāh*, appendix, 63–66. Similar provisions in: *Lāyiḥat tartīb al-Jamʿiyya al-Ḥaqqāniyya*, Ch. 2, Art. 5 (Zaghlūl, *al-Muḥāmāh*, appendix, 27–3) and *Wājibāt maʾmūriyyat aʿḍāʾ al-majlis* (one of the implementing orders of the Imperial Penal Code), Art. 4. Text in Fīlīb Jallād, *Qāmūs al-Idāra wa-l-Qaḍāʾ*. 4 vols, Alexandria, 1890–1892, ii, pp. 104–105.

a comprehensive picture of the procedural law observed by the tribunals. Judging by the evidence provided by the records of the Majlis al-Aḥkām, strict procedure was followed in trying criminal cases. The criminal procedure before the councils was essentially inquisitorial. There was no office of public prosecutor and the councils would sentence the accused on the basis of a report of the investigation prepared by the police or, in the countryside, by the provincial authorities. The accused was not a party in the trial, but rather the object of an investigation. Typically, he had no right to be heard or to be assisted by legal counsel. The accused would be questioned by the police or by provincial officials and the report of the interrogation would be part of the dossier submitted to the council. The accused would only be heard if the council found that the report was not clear and that the accused could clarify the facts. This was changed in 1871 when the councils were instructed to hear the accused before sentencing and to give him the opportunity to defend himself against the charges. In most cases review of judgments took place regardless of the will of the person convicted or the parties involved. However, this also changed and in 1871, revision, at least in criminal cases, was replaced by a system of appeal at the request of the accused, which, therefore, gave the accused some influence on the proceedings

In certain types of criminal cases both the sharia courts and the state councils had jurisdiction. This was standard procedure in cases of killing and wounding, sexual offences and defamation. But there was a grey area. A victims of theft could go to the police, who would then start a criminal investigation that could result in the trial of the thief before a judicial council. But he also could go directly to a sharia court in order to reclaim his stolen property. In that case the sharia judge would investigate whether the defendant ought to be punished according to the sharia. The state courts looked at the case from the point of view of public order and security, whereas the sharia courts investigated the claims of the victim or his heirs. This would mostly result in financial liabilities, but could also entail punishment. The jurisdictional uncertainty was settled in 1880 by a decree of the Minister of Interior to the effect that property claims resulting from theft could only be heard by sharia courts after the criminal investigation by the proper authorities had been completed.[35]

2.3 *Judicial Punishment*

The third domain where significant reform took place is the legal system of penalties. This evolved from a system characterized by capital punishment – often

35 Decree of the Naẓārat al-Dākhiliyya, 20 Muḥarram 1297 (3 January 1880), Jallād, *Qāmūs*, iv, p. 145.

carried out in a cruel way such as impaling –, and corporal punishment, i.e. flogging, to a system in which imprisonment was the main penalty.

During the first decades of Meḥmed ʿAlī's reign, capital punishment was frequently applied. The deterrent effect of executions was regarded as an essential aspect of the punishment and those brought to death were left hanging from the gallows for one day with placards stating the culprit's name and his crime. Public executions had a highly symbolic function as expressions of state power. As soon as he had established, in the early 1830s, full control over all regions of the country, Meḥmed ʿAlī enforced the rule that executions needed his approval. During the first half of the 1830s execution by impaling or "by other barbarous means" was abolished ("excepting in extreme cases").[36] Travellers report that the number of executions decreased during Meḥmed ʿAlī's reign. This trend continued until the British occupation. Executions had become relatively rare by the middle of the century. The only death sentences were those for manslaughter after a sharia sentence pronounced by the qadi. Other incapacitating punishments, such as lifelong banishment to Ethiopia and transportation to the Sudan, both introduced in the 1840s took the place of capital punishment.

As from the 1830s Meḥmed ʿAlī followed a policy of putting an end to mutilating corporal punishments. Until then, flogging, imprisonment and death were the only punishments that were allowed. There is no evidence that mutilating or cruel sharia punishment such as stoning to death or amputation were applied. In the rare cases that lower sharia courts pronounced such sentences (for instance in cases of theft or wounding), they were invariably commuted by higher authorities.[37] The only forms of corporal punishment mentioned in the laws issued in Meḥmed ʿAlī's time were flogging with the *kurbaj* on the buttocks or the bastinado on the soles of the feet.[38] This became the preferred penalty to punish cultivators, since imprisonment would result in a decline in productivity.[39] In 1861, however, flogging and caning were abolished as judicial punishments and replaced by detention.

36 Scott, C. Rochfort, *Rambles in Egypt and Candia: with details of the military power and resources of those countries, and observations on the government, policy, and commercial system of Mohammed Ali.* 2 vols. London: Colburn, 1837, ii p. 115.

37 Peters, Rudolph, "Islamic and secular criminal law in 19th century Egypt: the role and function of the qadi." *Islamic Law and Society*, 4 (1997): 84, 86.

38 *Qānūn al-Filāḥa* Art. 25 lays down that an official who causes the death of a person by hitting him on spots other than the buttocks or the soles of the feet is liable according to the sharia.

39 This is mentioned explicitly in various penal laws. See Penal Code 1829, Art. 9; Imperial Code, Ch. 3, Art. 19.

Until the early 1850s, torture during investigation was standard procedure, sanctioned by state law[40] although not by the Shariʿa.[41] As a rule, it consisted in flogging and the bastinado, but other methods were used too. When the Imperial Code was introduced in the early 1850s, one of the organic decrees issued in connection with it banned the use of physical pressure during criminal investigation. The prohibition was repeated in 1858 and in 1861, when, in the decree abolishing flogging as a penalty (see below), instructions were issued regarding the extent of pressure to be applied on suspects during the investigation. It prohibited torture but permitted beating during investigation in exceptional situations as a means to induce a suspect to confess if there was already some evidence for his guilt. It is of course not clear to what extent these instructions were obeyed in practice.

2.4 *The Political and Economic Context of Legal Reform*

Until roughly mid-century legal reform was a by-product of the efforts of Meḥmed ʿAlī and his successors to centralize the state and to create an efficient bureaucracy. Regulating and fixing *siyāsa* justice was one of Meḥmed ʿAlī's tools to these ends. It served three aims. The most important was the control of state officials. The second one, closely related to the first, was to create an orderly administration. Lastly, Meḥmed ʿAlī wanted his government to be accepted by the population through eliminating arbitrariness in the administration of justice. Let us have a closer look at each of these objectives.

3 Penal Law

During the first decades of his rule, Meḥmed ʿAlī had to wage a hard struggle to gain control over the country. In the end he succeeded and in order to consolidate his power he appointed trustworthy relatives and close associates to the most important offices. However, because of their relationship to him, they

40 *Qānūn al-Filāḥa*, Art. 26; *Dīvān-i Hidīvī Lāyiḥesi* (Regulations of the Khedival Bureau), issued 13 Muḥarram 1254 [8–4 1838], art. 13. Text in Maḥfaẓat al-Mīhī, doc. 20. See also Lane, E.W., *Manners and Customs of the Modern Egyptians*. repr. ed, London, 1966., p. 114.

41 During the investigation of a case of manslaughter the suspects had been beaten severely and finally confessed considering that being sent to the Alexandria jail was better than continuously being whipped. The Grand Mufti stated: "The defendants cannot be convicted for manslaughter because their confessions have been obtained by what according to the shariʿa is regarded as coercion (*ikrāh sharʿī*)." Fatwa, 5 Jumādā II 1268 [27–3 1852], Muḥammad al-ʿAbbāsī al-Mahdī,. *Al-Fatāwā al-Mahdiyya* v, pp. 435–6.

were prone to acting independently and, whenever they saw fit, to inflicting, without due process, harsh punishments, including death. Legislation was an important instrument to curb these practices. The *Qānūn al-Filāḥa* (1830), the penal code of 1829 and the *Qānūn al-Siyāsetnāme* of 1837 were enacted by Meḥmed ʿAlī mainly to circumscribe the powers of the officials and to penalize abuse of power. These laws dealt for a considerable part with official crimes. The Penal code of 1829 is a case in point: Of the eight articles defining offences, five address offences committed by officials. However, provisions addressing offences committed by private persons were also instruments to restrict the powers of the officials since these provisions limited the discretion of the officials in inflicting punishment. They would themselves be punished if they did not heed these laws. In the early 1830s Meḥmed ʿAlī issued a decree that *siyāsa* capital punishment could not be carried out without his approval. This was also part of the struggle over the symbols of sovereignty. A modern centralized state has the monopoly of violence and the right to sentence persons to death and execute them is one of the foremost symbols of sovereign authority.

Curbing and limiting the powers of his officials meant circumscribing them. The powers of an official were not anymore in the first place defined by his personal relationship with Meḥmed ʿAlī – although, naturally, that still was important – but rather by the office he held. Meḥmed ʿAlī enacted organic laws – such as the *Qānūn al-Siyāsetnāme* (1837) – that laid down how the state was organized, which offices there were and what were the tasks and duties of their incumbents, irrespective of the persons who held the office. Hunter has dubbed this process *From Household Government to Modern Bureaucracy* and showed that at the time of Meḥmed ʿAlī's death, this process was set in motion but by no means completed.[42] A modern bureaucracy requires general laws and regulations, in order to make its workings uniform and independent of personal relationships. The laws that Meḥmed ʿAlī enacted in this domain laid the groundwork on which a modern bureaucracy could be built.

It is tempting to see Meḥmed ʿAlī's penal legislation as an expression of Enlightenment views on criminal law based on the principle of legality, i.e. that criminal (as well as other) laws address and are known to all citizens and that they define punishable acts in the understanding that all behaviour not falling under the definitions of penal laws is allowed and will not entail punishment. However, that would not be a correct appreciation of the character of these laws. The criminal codes were not in the first place meant for the public, but addressed the state officials. The laws were not officially proclaimed and

42 Hunter, F. Robert. *Egypt under the Khedives, 1805–1879: From Household Government to Modern Bureaucracy*. Pittsburgh: Pittsburgh University Press, 1984.

their texts were distributed only among the state agencies. The preliminary paragraphs of the *Qānūn al-Filāḥa* illustrate this point:

> One often hears that criminal offenders who are punished by the district commissioners [*ḥukkām*] are beaten more than is their due [*qānūnuhum*], which entails damage for them. In order to put an end to this injustice it is necessary that the penalties for all criminals be fixed and that it be brought to the attention of the local authorities [*maʾmūrīn, nuẓẓār al-aqsām, ḥukkām al-akhṭāṭ*] that in punishing criminals they are not to exceed the penalties fixed for them.[43]

For Meḥmed ʿAlī, one of the motives for enacting penal laws and specifying the penalties for each offence was to make his government palatable for his subjects by attempting to ban arbitrariness. In the preamble of an order of 1842 concerning the establishment of the *al-Jamʿiyya al-Haqqāniyya* Meḥmed ʿAlī argued that:

> If an offender is sentenced to penalties laid down [by law] without the slightest partiality and with justice and equity, then that person will have no objections anymore. It is evident that the impact of penalties laid down [by law] may be enormous. Therefore there is in Europe much attention for and interest in this matter. As a result, when they (the Europeans) impose punishments, they investigate and make clear the offender's fault and the punishment that he deserves to such an extent that the accused does not protest anymore against it and accepts it wholeheartedly.[44]

For Meḥmed ʿAlī this was a practical matter of furthering the smooth running of his government and not one of granting fundamental rights to his subjects. It is unlikely that he intended that they could legally demand to be treated according to statute law. However, if they felt that they were treated unjustly, people would petition the ruler and appeal to his justice.

To be treated according to enacted laws, however, was increasingly felt as a right. During Meḥmed ʿAlī's reign enacted laws were his commands and instructions to his officials and his subjects. He himself was not bound by them and the penal statutes were not meant to be exhaustive: Although officials

43 These are the words of Minister of War (*Nāẓir al-Jihādiyya*), Maḥmūd Bey Efendi, quoted as an introduction to the penal provisions of the *Lāyiḥat zirāʿat al-fallāḥ wa-tadbīr aḥkām al-Falāḥ*. 2nd ed. ed. Bulaq: 1840–1841. P. 61.

44 Zaghlūl, *al-Muḥāmāh*, pp. 182–183.

were bound by the statutes and could not punish subjects except by virtue of a statutory provision, the ruler himself and the high judicial councils could impose punishment for acts that were deemed to be injurious to the state or society regardless of whether there was a provision in the law (sharia or *qānūn*) defining them as punishable offences. Moreover, his subjects could not found rights on the enacted laws. If subjects had suffered injustices, the way to have them redressed was by petitioning the ruler and appealing to his sense of justice. Since part of the legitimation of the power of the Ottoman sultan and the Egyptian khedives was that they were "just princes," their subjects could always inform them of unjust treatment by officials and the ruler was expected to investigate the matter and address the injustice. Such petitions often resulted in thorough investigations and punishments of officials who had violated instructions.[45] This, however, was not an enforceable right but depended on the ruler's benevolence.[46]

Gradually, knowledge about these enacted laws spread. People became familiar with them and began to regard them, after the example of sharia norms, as addressing not only the state apparatus, but the subjects as well. They began to appeal to them and to sue officials if they felt that they had violated such laws and, as a consequence, the right of the subjects. At the same time the attitude of the government and high officials towards legal reform began to change. Instead of a by-product of the centralization and bureaucratization of the state, law became a domain of reform in its own right. Legal reform was deemed to be an inseparable part of modernization and was a topic of debate. At the same time we can observe that the legality principle in penal law wins ground: sentences not based on legal provisions become rare. One of the important responsibilities of the Majlis al-Aḥkām was to provide for cases in which individuals had committed acts that were regarded as harmful for society or the state but were not defined in a penal provision. The 1871 law regarding the judicial councils is another case in point. Its reforms were not anymore just a function of centralization and bureaucratization but, as we have seen, rather a step toward a greater independence of the judiciary and a better procedural position of the accused. Here we see the contours of a legal

45 See for example Peters, Rudolph, "Petitions And Marginal Voices In Nineteenth Century Egypt: The Case Of The Fisherman's Daughter," in: Robin Ostle (ed.), *Marginal Voices in Literature and Society*. Strasbourg: European Science Foundation, 2000. Pp. 119–133.

46 Justice as a personal quality of the Sultan is defined in two ways: as the protecting of his subjects against oppression by officials and those who disturb law and order and, secondly, as upholding and enforcing the injunctions of the sharia. See Boğaç A. Ergene, "On Ottoman Justice: Interpretations in Conflict (1600–1800)," *Islamic Law and Society* 8 (2001): 52–87. In this context, the first conception of justice is meant.

system based on the rule of law slowly taking shape and the concept of just governance slowly evolving from the personalized notion of the "just prince" towards the idea of an abstract legal system that conferred rights to individuals that could be asserted against the government and the ruler. In the 1870s the Khedive and state organs were bound by the law and the law could be invoked against them. Enacted *siyāsa* laws evolved from being tools of power and control for the rulers, to institutions that, in addition, could ensure legal certainty and justice by banning arbitrariness and conferring rights to the population.

One of the achievements of our period is the reform of the penal system, from one characterized by a high incidence of the death penalty and of corporal punishment, notably flogging, into one whose main punishment was imprisonment. Death sentences had become rare after the 1850s and corporal punishment was banned in 1861. The decrease in death sentences was the result of several factors. The first is the improvement of police methods in tracing and arresting suspects.[47] As the chances for offenders of being caught increased, the need for deterrent spectacles of harsh justice decreased. The second point was a legal one: during diplomatic negotiations on the introduction of the Imperial Code, Egypt, and the Porte, had agreed that death sentences, other than those pronounced by a sharia court, had to be approved by the Sultan. As the records of the Majlis al-Aḥkām after the 1850s only include death sentences by virtue of a sharia decision, it would seem that the Egyptian authorities were loath to do so and rather issued sentences of hard labour or deportation instead of submitting capital sentences to the Porte for approval.

That torture and corporal punishment were banned before 1882 contradicts the commonly held colonialist inspired view. According to Lord Cromer,[48] torture and corporal punishment (the use of the *kurbaj*) were not abolished until after the British occupation. Although Cromer concedes that there may have been previous orders to that effect,[49] he claims that these were not enforced. As we have seen, torture and corporal punishment were abolished in 1861. Archival sources confirm that people were not anymore sentenced to be flogged but, instead, sentenced to detention. Whether torture during the investigation really stopped, is difficult to tell, especially since the text of the 1861 decree allowed its use in exceptional circumstances. However, what is of interest for us here is why in 1861 such a decree was issued.

47 On the police in this period, see Fahmy, Khaled, "The Police and the People in Nineteenth Century Egypt." *Die Welt des Islams* 39, no. 3 (1999): 340–77.

48 Cromer, *Modern Egypt*, ii, p. 298 ff.

49 Cromer, *Modern Egypt*, ii, p. 400.

The abolition of flogging and caning in Egypt in 1861 was part of a deliberate policy to reduce official violence, which had become feasible due to certain social and economic transformations of the country. An important factor, although one for which we do not have direct documentary evidence, was the presence, among the Egyptian ruling elite, of reformers, who began to consider corporal punishment as backward and uncivilized and argued that it had to be replaced in order to modernize the country. It is my contention that they influenced penal policy, especially with regard to the abolition of torture and corporal punishment. They must have followed the example of the Ottoman Empire, where corporal punishment had been abolished with the introduction of the Penal Code of 1858.[50]

In order to explain why they could successfully implement their program, we first have to consider the function and meaning of official violence in nineteenth-century Egypt. Official violence was a mode of repression practised in three contexts: (1) generic official violence, i.e. violence as a means of coercion, to make people obey official orders (often in connection with tax collection, or drafting men for military service or *corvee*); (2) torture, i.e. violence as a means to obtain confessions during criminal investigations, and, finally, (3) violence as a form of judicial punishment. During Meḥmed ʿAlī's reign the Turkish elite ruled by means of violence. Public flogging and beating were used to symbolize the power relations between the Turkish rulers and the Egyptians, especially the fellahin. It was one of the means to emphasize the ethnic divide between rulers and ruled. But its use was also conditioned by economic factors. The crops, the taxes and the manpower requisitioned by the state were often excessive and endangered the subsistence of the population. Therefore, they could only be collected by using brutal force. Moreover, corporal punishment was, especially in the countryside, economically more efficient than imposing prison sentences, because after a period of recovery, the peasant could go back to work. That the use of torture was regarded as normal and as a useful and helpful method in investigating crime, stemmed from the fact that the techniques of investigating crimes were still very primitive: investigation, usually conducted by administrative officials, focused on extracting a confession from one or more suspects. For all these reasons, the flogging of peasants by Turkish officials was common and widespread.

Meḥmed ʿAlī's measures to restrict to some extent the use of violence were inspired by two factors: First, it had to be made clear that wielding the *kurbaj* as a symbol of power was ultimately controlled by the central government. Since

50 Unlike the Ottoman previous criminal codes, the 1858 one does not include corporal punishment such as flogging and caning in the detailed list of penalties (arts. 16–39).

the execution of capital punishment was the Khedive's prerogative, an official who killed a subject by an excess of beating or flogging, would intrude on the Khedive's rights. This rule was indeed enforced and officials who killed subjects were brought to justice. A second point was that official violence should not damage the productive capacity of his subjects by killing or incapacitating the subjects. Within these restrictions, flogging continued to be practised as a way of repression and enforcing obedience.

The first substantial legal steps in restricting official violence were taken in connection with criminal investigation. These steps were made possible by the extension and growing efficiency of the state apparatus. By the 1850s a fully-grown, specialised police force had come into existence as well as an extensive public health administration which was also involved in police work.[51] The increased professionalism of those involved in criminal investigations and the use of scientific methods, showed that there were better ways of finding the truth than trying to obtain a confession. This led to the realisation that torture was not a very effective instrument of finding the truth and made it possible for reformers as from the early 1850s to enforce measures to restrict and finally, in 1861, banning it.

It is not entirely clear what immediately prompted the abolition of flogging as a punishment in 1861.[52] The decree itself is silent on its considerations. At the political level, the reformers could point at the example of the Ottoman Empire where corporal punishment had been abolished in 1858. But that this ban could be effectively introduced was because the need of official violence in the countryside had decreased due to economic developments. Before 1842, Egypt was a command economy, dominated by Meḥmed ʿAlī's monopoly. Peasants produced for the Pasha, who therefore had a direct interest in their productive capacity. Corporal punishment was therefore economically more advantageous than imprisonment. This changed after the state monopoly was abrogated and the state's extraction of the rural surplus became limited to tax collection. Meḥmed ʿAlī's successors had therefore a more abstract and remote

51 See Fahmy, Khaled, "The Anatomy of Justice: Forensic Medicine and Criminal Law in Nineteenth-Century Egypt." *Islamic Law and Society* 6, (1999): 224–71.

52 Fahmy forcefully argues that the abolishment of torture must not be seen as a westernizing, civilizing reform, but mainly as a practical measure to control state officials and stemming from a growing awareness that torture during investigation had become ineffective as a means to find the truth. See Fahmy, Khaled, "Justice, Law and Pain in Khedival Egypt." In *Standing Trial: Law and the Person in the Modern Middle East.* Edited by Baudouin Dupret. London: I.B. Tauris, 2004. Pp. 85–116. I agree, but think, as will be clear from my text, that there were more social and economic factors that made official violence less necessary.

interest in the productive capacity of peasants. They were not any more concerned about the imprisonment of peasants. Connected with this development is the fact that during Meḥmed ʿAlī's reign demands on the rural population in produce, *corvée* labour and men for conscription often jeopardised its existence and could only be collected by force. With the reduction of the army in the 1840s and the easing of *corvée* in the 1850s,[53] the need for violent coercion diminished. A final but crucial factor was that the dearth of rural labour in the countryside had come to an end. If peasants fled from their villages during Meḥmed ʿAlī's time, they were forcibly returned, because their labour was needed. This changed during the 1850s with the rise of large estates and the dispossession of many smallholders. Peasants became expendable and there was no need any more to exempt them from imprisonment if they committed an offence. If sentenced to hard labour, they could be profitably employed in the agricultural projects in the Sudan.

By the 1860s imprisonment had prevailed in the Egyptian penal system as the main punishment. Prison conditions had improved and mortality among the inmates had dropped drastically.[54] This meant that imprisonment did not anymore entail the risks of gratuitous and unintended suffering and death due to pernicious prison conditions. Imprisonment, therefore, became a penalty that could be better quantified and become a substitute of flogging that could also be quantified precisely, except that its impact, i.e. the actual suffering, depended on a person's constitution and build and therefore differed from person to person.

4 Land Law

As we have seen before, no important legislation concerning land law was issued before the last years of Mehmet ʿAlī's reign. Land law legislation, therefore, does not illustrate, as criminal legislation does, the way the law developed in tandem with the centralization of the state and the emergence of a rational bureaucracy. During the first decades of Meḥmed ʿAlī's rule, the life of the farmers, or rather the relationship between the state and the farmers was characterized by oppression and the use by officials of force, rather than the law. The main producers, the small farmers, were exploited on several scores: They

53 Toledano, Ehud R. *State and Society in Mid-Nineteenth Century Egypt*, Cambridge: Cambridge University Press, 1990. (*Cambridge Middle East Library*, 22) pp. 181, 188.

54 See Peters, Rudolph. "Controlled Suffering: Mortality and Living Conditions in Nineteenth Century Egyptian Prisons." *International Journal of Middle Eastern Studies* 36 (2004): 387–407.

suffered not only from the low prices the state offered for their harvests and from the heavy tax burden, but also by the military draft and *corvée* duties. The large landowners, members of the Turkish ruling elite and of families of village sheikhs, enjoyed fiscal privileges and, having full or partial control of the selection of recruits for the drafts and the corvee labour for public works, were not exposed to the extortions of the state.

After 1840, the abolition of the state monopoly and the decrease of the army and consequently the lighter burden of the military draft, the situation in the countryside changed. The centralization of the state, the greater security and the improved infrastructure for irrigation resulted in higher yields. Moreover, the abolition of the monopoly permitted trade of agricultural produce between the countryside and the towns. These urban traders began to invest their profits in land, buying land often from indebted farmers. These factors, i.e. the disappearance of the monopoly of agriculture and the acquisition of land by traders form the towns, seem to have resulted in the legislation of land law between 1847 and 1858. After the monopoly of agriculture and the farmers' access to the markets, the state wanted to continue to have control over the countryside, where most taxes were collected. However, the characteristic of control was changing: from control based on the direct oppression and force, to a form of control based on law. This was made possible by the abolition of monopoly. But a perhaps more important factor was the emergence of urban landholding traders. They differed from the ruling landholding Turkish elite and the landholding families of village sheikhs, who had fiscal privileges, and, in addition, could resolve their problems either through their contacts with the dynasty and high officials or because the power they had enjoyed in their villages. The new landholding traders did not have these advantages and needed law to deal with both the farmers and the state.

Thus, like was the case in criminal law, fixing the law through legislation and codification had two functions. On the one hand it expanded the ruler's control over his population and officials not by force or family ties, but by creating a more rational and impersonal bureaucracy. But on the other hand the laws conferred rights to the subjects who could be asserted in the courts of law. The introduction of the 1858 Land Code represented a further step of the modernization of the Egyptian legal system.

5 Conclusions: the Significance of Pre-Colonial Legal Reform

Before assessing the significance of the pre-colonial reform, I will discuss critically Brown's views on this point. Brown agrees that the pre-colonial law reforms had brought a structured and hierarchical court system, but argues that

> [t]he judicial reforms adopted in the 1870s and 1880s entailed fundamental changes in the administration of justice in Egypt.... What separated the new court system from their predecessors was therefore not their hierarchy and structure (where they simply accentuated previous trends) but three other features – their separation from administration, their use of comprehensive codes, and their abandonment of Islamic and Ottoman for European models.[55]

My reading of this quotation is that in Brown's view there had been changes in the pre-colonial Egyptian legal system, but they were not sufficiently fundamental to be qualified as modernization. It is of course a matter of appreciation whether the features mentioned by him were real innovations. I do not think that the use of 1883 comprehensive codes was a fundamental change because such codes did already exist: The Imperial Code of 1852 (whose first three chapters were identical to the Ottoman Penal Code of 1851) with the appendix of 1858, the 1857 *Lāyiḥat al-Abillū*, instructing the commercial tribunals to apply the Ottoman Code of Commerce of 1850, and the Land Law of 1858. The use of comprehensive codes, therefore, was not a fundamental innovation. The only thing is that they did not exist in the realm of civil law, where the sharia applied, and that of adjective law, which was governed by various *ad hoc* laws and unwritten bureaucratic practice.

In regard to the separation from the administration, Brown has a point. The organization of the state was in no way informed by the notion of the separation of powers. The executive also made laws and administered justice. In the course of our period specialized bodies were created, but even these sometimes combined both legislative, judicial and executive duties. Thus the Majlis al-Aḥkām, the highest judicial body, was also assigned to prepare legislation. Moreover the decision of the judicial councils had to be approved by the executive. Only sharia justice had some extent of independence. The British did not seem to have objected to the fusion of duties of judicial and legislative duties in the Majlis al-Aḥkām, probably because the common law system with its doctrine of stare decisis also allows the judiciary to enact laws. But what they decried in the pre-1883 Egyptian legal system was the absence of a formal separation between the judiciary and the executive. They were of the opinion that without independence of the judiciary, justice could not be administered and they constantly harped on the issue, describing the pre-1883 legal system as despotic, arbitrary and oppressive. Indeed, as we have seen, the councils before 1883 were part of the administration and staffed by administrators.

55 Brown, *Rule of law*, p. 31.

However, as I argued, they became increasingly independent and individuals could sue state officials before these councils. On the other hand, the separation between the judiciary and the administration that was introduced after 1883 did not protect the Egyptian population from infringement of their fundamental rights guaranteed in the new code of criminal procedure. The British thought that the new penal code was culturally inappropriate for Egypt. They supported the Commissions of Brigandage, which operated between 1884 and 1889 and were directly subordinated to the provincial governors.[56] These commissions summarily tried rural crimes, applied torture when interrogating the accused and deprived the national courts to a large extent of their criminal jurisdiction. Moreover, in 1886, special military tribunals were created with extraordinary powers to deal with offences committed by Egyptians against British military personnel. So, yes, on the ideological level there was a separation between the judiciary and the administration after 1883, but in practice it was often disregarded if law and order and British interests were at risk.

Finally the issue of the models. Brown regards the abandonment of the Ottoman and Islamic models for the French one as fundamental. Here I disagree too. By the 1880s the Ottoman legal system was quite modern and included many laws entirely or partially of European inspiration. Replacing the Ottoman with the French model was not a big step. Abandonment of the Islamic model does look fundamental but even this point must be qualified. Yes, important parts of civil law were now governed by the French Code Civil instead of sharia law. But sharia law still occupied a very important position as it regulated family law, the law of persons, of succession and of *waqf*s. Indeed, change there was, but no drastic and fundamental change.

The establishment and development of a *siyāsa* judiciary with its hierarchy of judicial councils was a great achievement, considering that they were created out of nothing. As we have seen, *siyāsa* justice in Meḥmed ʿAlī's time, before 1842 when the *Jamʿiyya al-Haqqāniyya* was established, was administered by executive officials and administrative councils and there were no specialized judicial bodies to do so. By 1871, Egypt had, in addition to the sharia and the commercial courts, a well-structured, hierarchical judiciary with courts having clear-cut jurisdictions vis-à-vis one another and a penal system based on legality and without corporal punishment. These councils were practically independent from the executive. They heard criminal cases, cases related to state land and, especially in the later decades of our period, civil cases. With regard to the latter field, there does not seem to have been a clear cut demarcation with the jurisdiction of sharia courts. Of course, family law and succession

56 Brown, *Rule of law*, pp. 36–37.

were the uncontested domains of the sharia courts and continued to be so after 1883. Financial claims, however, appear to have been adjudicated by both sharia and *siyāsa* courts. This point, I would suggest, deserves further research.

By 1871 *siyāsa* justice had become to a large extent formal and rational by fixing it by legislation and applying it through specialized and institutionalized judicial bodies. The councils applied law codes or, in civil matters, the sharia. Extra-legal considerations did not play a role. The councils had, by then, clear-cut jurisdictions and followed fixed procedures. The rulers and high officials were not above the law. That was not only true of the sharia, but also of enacted laws. Criminal sentences were based on legal provisions and individuals could invoke them against the state. The legal system was moving in the direction of a system based on the rule of law. Finally, corporal punishment had been entirely abolished and torture during investigation to some extent. According to the criteria that I mentioned in the introduction, the Egyptian legal system had taken great strides on its way to becoming modern. Taking these points into consideration, we must conclude that legal modernization in Egypt had for the greater part been achieved before 1883 and that the 1883 reform of the system was important but not as fundamental as the gradual reforms prior to that year.

Appendix 1: Summary of the 1858 Land Code

Succession: the application of the sharia rules of inheritance to state lands (including female heirs) and the distribution (for payment of registration fees to the state) by the state of land fallen to the state for lack of heirs (arts. 1–4, 27)

Contracts: the permission and regulation of private contracts like conveyance of the right of use (*isqāṭ*), lease (*ījār*) for maximum three years, sharecropping (*mushāraka*), pawn of land (*rahn*) and their requirement of registration, consequences of taxation and the ownership of buildings, saqiyas and trees constructed or planted by the tenant or pawnholder, (arts. 8–12, 19–20);

Distribution of land by the state: Redistributed of the land of farmers who leave the village or who cannot work the land and/or cannot pay the taxes, and whose land is therefore forfeited to the state. Demobilized soldiers returning to their villages are entitled to a share if they are not artisans (*arbāb al-kārāt*) or are entitled to an undivided estate. (Arts. 7, 21, 22, 27)

Appropriation of state land for the public good: Decrease of the shares of the farmers in the village and their tax burden if state land is required for public works and assignment of land to farmers whose land has been appropriated if they need land for their sustenance. (Arts. 11, 16)

Correction and updating the registration of state land: If the area if the farm land is increased after the flood, or through the accretion by the river, the increased must be auctioned. Regulations the administrative subordination and the taxation regarding newly emerged islands in the Nile. The rewarding of those who inform the authorities of irregularities of land registration. (arts. 15, 16, 18, 23, 26, 28)

Abolition of *abʿādiyya, ūsiya* and *rizqa* land (Arts. 13, 14, 24, 25)

Statute of limitation: The original users of farm land who had sold it (*isqāṭ*) or whose land was forfeited by the state cannot contest it after five years. (Arts. 5, 7, 17)

Transitionary provisions: (Art. 6)

Case Studies

CHAPTER 8

The Lions of Qasr al-Nil Bridge

The Islamic Prohibition of Images as an Issue in the ʿUrabi Revolt

Al-Fatawa al-Mahdiyya fi l-Waqaʾiʿ al-Misriyya, a collection of some 13,500 fatwas issued by Grand Mufti Muhammad al-ʿAbbasi al-Mahdi of Egypt (d. 1897), contains only three fatwas whose political implications are more or less evident.[1] Here I will present one of them. Although the fatwa seems to deal with a purely religious question – namely, the obligation to remove images of human beings and animals – the underlying issue was highly political. The fatwa was given on August 31, 1881, at the request of the ʿUrabi government, during the last turbulent weeks after the attempted deposition of the Khedive and before the government's surrender to the British.

The author of this text, Muhammad al-ʿAbbasi al-Mahdi,[2] was born in the year 1827, a son of Muhammad Amin al-Mahdi (d. 1830–1831),[3] for some time the Hanafi mufti during Mehmed ʿAli's reign. In October 1848 his son, Ibrahim Pasha, appointed al-ʿAbbasi the Hanafi chief mufti (*mufti 'l-sada al-Hanafiyya*), an office he was to hold for almost half a century, until his death in 1897. Because he was only twenty-one years old at the time of his nomination, his professor of Hanafi law, Khalil al-Rashidi, was appointed head of the fatwa department (*amin al-fatwa*) to assist him in his new office.

From the time of the Ottoman conquest of Egypt (1517), Hanafi law was applied exclusively in the law courts, and the Hanafi chief mufti was the highest ranking mufti in the country. During al-ʿAbbasi's tenure in office, this Hanafi supremacy over the other chief muftis was emphasized by the use of the new title, *mufti al-diyar al-Misriyya* (mufti of the Egyptian lands), or simply

1 A fatwa against the Sudanese Mahdi issued at the request of the Khedival government (al-Mahdi 1304/1887, 2:28–32; 18 Dhu al-Qaʿda 1300 [September 20, 1883]). For an analysis of this fatwa, see Peters 1983. Of another one issued in 1876, we do not know the precise political context. The Khedive asked about a person claiming to have knowledge of the divine secrets (*al-mughayyabat*), as a result of which people were busying themselves zealously with his words and committing actions that disturb public order. The grand mufti responded that such a person must be punished with *taʿzir*, if his words do not amount to apostasy. (al-Mahdi 1304/1887, 2:7, 20 Shawwal, 1293 [November 8, 1876]).

2 Of the small number of sources on al-ʿAbbasi's life, the most important are an account by his son, Muhammad ʿAbd al-Khaliq al-Hifni, in Zaydan (n.d., 2:250–255), and that in ʿAli Mubarak (1304–1306/1886–1889, 17:12–13). For a complete list of sources, see Schölch (1973:332, n. 243). Delanoue (1982:168–174 and 136–137) summarizes the available biographical information.

3 On Muhammad Amin al-Mahdi, see Lane (1966: 118–121).

 | DOI:10.1163/9789004420625_009

headmufti (*bashmufti*). The primary task of the Hanafi chief mufti was to serve as a mufti at the Grand Shariʿa Court in Cairo (Mahkamat al-Qahira al-Kubra), but in the nineteenth century he also had other functions. *Al-Fatawa al-Mahdiyya* indicates that one of the grand mufti's tasks was to attend the Khedival Council (*al-Diwan al-ʿAli*) in order to give advice on complicated legal questions.[4] Together with the chief muftis of the other law schools (*madhhab*s), the rector of the Azhar University (*Shaykh al-Azhar*), the dean of the descendants of the Prophet (*naqib al-ashraf*), and occasionally other ʿulamaʾ, the grand mufti was part of the Council of Scholars (al-Majlis al-ʿIlmi) of Cairo, which was consulted by the rulers in important religious matters (Lane 1966:121–122.).

Occasionally he would be asked for an authoritative fatwa to settle controversies among jurists[5] or to deal with complaints about the misapplication of the Shariʿa by qadis.[6] A decree of 1873 regulating the duties and competence of the official (and therefore Hanafi) muftis gave the grand mufti and the Alexandrian mufti unrestricted authority to issue fatwas to both the general public and government agencies, unlike other appointed muftis, who were allowed to give fatwas only in connection with the agency or court to which they were appointed.[7]

The grand mufti's power was greatly increased by the Shariʿa Courts Ordinance (*Laʾihat al-Mahakim al-Sharʿiyya*) of 1880 (text in Jallad 1890–1895, 4:145–156), which granted him the authority under certain circumstances to give binding decisions. If there was a complaint about the misapplication of the Shariʿa, the matter would be investigated and decided by the Grand Shariʿa Court in Cairo. However, if there were misgivings or complaints about the decision in appeal, the case would be submitted to the grand mufti, whose fatwa would be binding. The grand mufti could also give binding fatwas in appeal

4 See, for example, al-Mahdi 1304/1887, 2:449 (30 Rabiʿ II 1265 [March 25, 1849]): "We attended the Khedival Council in Cairo and the substance of the case of … was read to us as well as the conflicting fatwas concerning the issue … We considered their words and it appeared to us] that the fatwa to the effect that … was the one in agreement with the stipulations of the founder of the waqf." The sources do not allow us to establish whether the grand mufti attended these council meetings on a regular basis, or only when his legal advice was required.

5 See, for example, al-Mahdi 1304/1887, 4:588 (4 Jumada I 1271 [February 3, 1855]); The Majlis al-Ahkam (one of the higher legislative and judicial councils) wants a fatwa concerning a controversy among the ʿulamaʾ) of Upper Egypt regarding the law of gift.

6 See, for example, al-Mahdi 1304/1887, 3:276–281 (10 Jumada II 1289 [August 15, 1872]), where the grand mufti is consulted by the Majlis al-Ahkam about incorrect judgments of the qadi of Giza.

7 Decree of 5 Rabiʿ II 1290 (July 2, 1873); text in Jallad (1890–1895, 4:136).

from judgments of the Grand Shariʿa Court in Cairo or the Shariʿa Court in Alexandria, acting as courts of first instance (Art. 3).

Another similar procedure, which apparently had already existed for some time,[8] was formalized in Art. 22 of this ordinance: whenever a qadi was in doubt about a legal issue of a case brought before him, he first had to consult the mufti officially appointed to his court or to the district. If the qadi and the mufti could not agree on the issue, or if the mufti himself did not know the correct answer, the matter would be laid before the grand mufti, whose decision would be binding. This would also be the case if the Grand Shariʿa Court of Cairo was uncertain about a point of law in a lawsuit and consulted the grand mufti.

The result of these provisions and practices was that the function of grand mufti began to bear resemblance to the Courts of Cassation known, for example, in French or Dutch law, whose task it is to ensure the correct application of the law and who, just like the grand mufti, decide the purely legal issues and do not examine the facts as established by the lower courts. That the grand mufti did not deal with issues of fact is clear from the formula frequently to be found in his fatwas: "If the situation is as mentioned [in the question]."

Al-ʿAbbasi's biographers mention that he twice fell foul of the Khedive: once when ʿAbbas wanted to confiscate all properties of the descendants of Mehmed ʿAli (r. 1805–1848), and another time when Ismaʿil (r. 1863–1879), acting as prince-regent for Saʿid (r. 1854–1863), wanted to assimilate the family endowments (*waqf ahli*) to public endowments (*waqf khayri*), to gain control over them. Due to al-ʿAbbasi's opposition, nothing came of these plans. However, these must have been exceptional incidents, for his relationship with the ruling house was generally very close. This is borne out by the fact that in January 1871 Ismaʿil appointed him Shaykh al-Azhar, a post usually occupied by a Shafiʿi. The reason seems to have been that Ismaʿil wanted to introduce reforms and regarded al-ʿAbbasi as the most suitable person for carrying out this task. He was not disappointed: six months later (16 Rabiʿ I 1288 [July 15, 1871]) he issued a decree, prepared by al-ʿAbbasi, introducing, among other things, the requirement that students must pass a final examination before being admitted to the ranks of the ʿulamaʾ. At the same time, al-ʿAbbasi succeeded in improving the allowances and pensions of the ʿulamaʾ at al-Azhar, no doubt in exchange for the acceptance of his reforms.

8 See, for example, al-Mahdi 1304/1887, 1:222–226 (23 Jumada II 1283 [November 2, 1866]), where the grand mufti is called on to settle a dispute between the qadi and the mufti of Dumyat.

The test of al-ʿAbbasi's loyalty to the ruling house came with the ʿUrabi revolt in 1881, when he was attacked by ʿulamaʾ and Azhar students who supported the ʿUrabi movement. These people suspected him of preparing a fatwa advising that the ʿUrabi revolt was a rebellion against a legitimate government and that the rebels deserved to be put to death. The students and ʿulamaʾ of al-Azhar campaigned for his dismissal as shaykh al-Azhar, primarily on the ground that he was too outspoken in his support for the Khedive. They also wanted a candidate who was not a Hanafi, the madhhab of the ruling Turco-Circassian class against whom the ʿUrabi revolt was directed, whereas the majority of Egyptians belonged to either the Shafiʿi or the Maliki madhhab. The candidate put forward by the opposition, the Maliki chief mufti Muhammad ʿIllaysh (1802–1882),[9] was unacceptable to the government. Eighty years old, he was nevertheless an ardent and militant follower of ʿUrabi. As a compromise, the Shafiʿi scholar Muhammad al-Inbabi (1824–1896) was appointed to the office after al-ʿAbbasi's dismissal on December 5, 1881. But to attain a certain equilibrium, a council consisting of both al-ʿAbbasi and ʿIllaysh was created to assist the Shaykh al-Azhar. Al-ʿAbbasi remained grand mufti (Schölch 1973:170–171; Delanoue 1982:136–137) and loyal to the Khedive. When a number of prominent Azhar ʿulamaʾ issued a fatwa advising that Tawfiq had to be deposed for disobeying the Ottoman sultan and allowing the British to take possession of the country (Engl. trans. in Broadley 1980: 175–178), al-ʿAbbasi refused to sign (Schölch 1973:350, n. 119).

The fatwa presented here is situated in the context of the ʿUrabi revolt. It is dated 16 Shawwal 1299 (August 31, 1882), two weeks before ʿUrabi's final defeat. British troops had already invaded Egypt and were advancing through the Delta, but had not yet taken Cairo. Because his supporters were motivated by Islamic religious fervor (Peters 1979:75–84), ʿUrabi apparently wanted to make a public gesture showing his Islamic zeal. This gesture took the form of an attack on some statues that had been placed in Cairo about a decade earlier. It was a cleverly chosen move. The erection of the statue of Ibrahim Pasha in 1872 had created popular disaffection (Ebeling 1878, as quoted in Beyer 1983:262). The demolition of this and other statues was a symbolic act that carried both religious and political implications. To show that the destruction of these statues was warranted and even required by the Shariʿa, and that the different madhhabs were in agreement about this issue, ʿUrabi, through the mediation of the shaykh al-Azhar, asked for fatwas based on the four madhhabs. Following is the fatwa given by the grand mufti according to Hanafi law.

9 On ʿIllaysh, see Delanoue (1982:129–168). On the uncertain vocalization of his name, see ibid., p. 129, n. 69.

Question sent to our part in a missive from the Reverend Shaykh Muhammad al-Inbabi[10] holder of the Rectorat of the Azhar University [*mashyakhat al-Jamiʿ al-Azhar*], with the following text:

> We have received a missive from His Excellency the Undersecretary of State for the Army [*Saʿadat Wakil al-Jihadiyya*][11] to the effect that His Excellency the Secretary of State for the Army and the Navy [*Saʿadat al-Basha Nazir al-Jihadiyya wa'l-Bahriyya*] (Ahmad ʿUrabi) has ordered in a telegram, which the Undersecretary of State received from him, to deal with the question of destroying and burning the idol erected in al-Azbakiyya near the minaret of the Azbakiyya Mosque,[12] as well as the question of cutting the heads of the images situated at both ends of the Qasr al-Nil Bridge,[13] and to give His Excellency the required notification that the aforementioned idol will be annihilated, so that he may be assured that the religious duties protecting the order and the hearts of the community [*umma*] are observed, for the religion of Islam forbids us to erect idols such as the ones that the Companions of the Prophet destroyed when they entered Mecca the Honorable, so as to comply with the obligations of the Religion. In the same telegram it is emphasized that no misfortunes befell our country until after the erecting of idols in Cairo and Alexandria, and it is requested that clear information be given about what the texts of the sublime Shariʿa require in this matter, so that measures can be taken accordingly, etc. Because His Excellency is to be informed about the legal rules in this matter according to all law schools, it is necessary to write this missive to Your Worship [*siyadatuka*] so that you may give information on the

10 Muhammad al-Inbabi, 1240–1313/1824–1896; Shaykh al-Azhar from 1881 to 1882 and from 1886 to 1896. See Delanoue (1982:137, n. 80).

11 This was Yaʿqub Sami (d. 1304/1882–1883), a professional soldier in the Egyptian Army, descended from a Greek family in Istanbul. During the ʿUrabi revolt he chose the side of the ʿUrabis and acted as undersecretary of state for war and president of the emergency government (*al-majlis al-ʿurfi*). See Schölch (1973:336, n. 337).

12 This was the equestrian statue of Ibrahim Pasha, the son of Mehmed ʿAli, who ruled Egypt for about nine months in 1848. It was created by Charles Cordier in 1872 and placed at al-ʿAtaba al-Khadra' Square, opposite the ruins of the Azbakiyya Mosque, which had been partially demolished in 1869 to create a large square, part of the new layout of Cairo. The statue currently is situated at Opera Square. See Baedeker (1929:54); Behrens-Abouseif (1985:92, 111, and plate xxii, a photograph of the statue in front of the remains of the Azbakiyya Mosque).

13 These are the four bronze lion statues that can still be seen at both ends of the bridge, which was built in 1871. See Baedeker (1929:86).

pertinent rules according to the madhhab of the Greatest Imam [viz., Abu Hanifa].

We hope that you can give this information promptly, because at the same date we also received a request to expedite the matter.

Answer: God be praised. Our scholars have clearly stated that the acquisition of a large image of a being with a soul, which is visible to a spectator without having to look attentively, and which is in possession of all parts of the body that are indispensable for it to live, is reprehensible to the degree that it is almost forbidden [*makruh tahrim*^{an}],[14] Therefore, it is legally obligatory to remove such images. The *Radd al-Muhtar ʿala al-Durr* [*al-Mukhtar*][15] says: "In the Supercommentary [*Hashiya*] by Abu al-Suʿud[16] it is related on the authority of the *Khulasa*[17] that [its author] held it permissible to remove [such] an image for whomever sees it in somebody else's house. [In fact,] it ought to be his obligation. If one hires a person who produces [such] images, the latter is not entitled to wages, since his work is sinful. This has been related on the authority of Muhammad [al-Shaybani].[18] If someone destroys a house that contains [such] pictures, he is liable for the value of the house but not for the value of the pictures." From this one learns the rule regarding the removal of the aforementioned idol and the decapitation of the images [*suwar*] located at both ends of the Qasr al-Nil Bridge. The Exalted God knows best.

Supplement to the Aforementioned Answer: The rulers of the Muslims must remove everything in their countries that is objectionable [*munkar*], such as practicing usury [*riba*], the opening of places known as brothels [*karakhanat*] and bars [*khammarat*], and other offences

14 "*Makruh tahrim*" is an intermediate category between *makruh* (reprehensible) and *haram* (forbidden).

15 This is the supercommentary by Muhammad Amin Ibn ʿAbidin (d. 1836) on *al-Durr al-Mukhtar* by al-Haskafi (d. 1677), itself a commentary on the *Tanwir al-Absar* by al-Timirtashi (d. 1595). See Brockelmann (suppl., 2:427–428). The *Radd al-Muhtar* was an authoritative and widely used Hanafi text in nineteenth-century Egypt.

16 Probably *Fath al-Mubin*, the supercommentary by a certain Muhammad Abu al-Suʿud al-Misri on Muʿin al-Din Muhammad al-Harawi's commentary on the *Kanz al-Daqaʾiq* of al-Nasafi (d. 1310). See Aghnides (1961:181). But Brockelmann (suppl., 2:267) identifies the author as Abu al-Masʿud and his work as a commentary, not as a supercommentary.

17 Probably the *Khulasat al-Fatawa* by Tahir al-Bukhari (d. 1147). See Brockelmann (suppl., 1:641).

18 Muhammad al-Shaybani (d. 805), a "companion" of Abu Hanifa, was one of the founders of the Hanafi madhhab.

> [*mubiqat*]. [They also must] prevent God's servants from suffering wrongs contrary to the Shari'a and forbid injustice and [the application of] rules other than those revealed by God. This is more urgent.[19]

In 'Urabi's formulation of the question, he underlines the religious aspect by referring to the equestrian statue as an idol (*sanam*), a term associated with the Jahiliyya period, and by mentioning the removal of idols by Muhammad's Companions after the conquest of Mecca in 630. Further, he attributes the "misfortunes" that had befallen Egypt to the erection of these statues. Although he does not specify these misfortunes, he was in all likelihood referring to the increasing foreign control over Egypt's government and finance, especially after Egypt's bankruptcy and the institution of the Anglo-French dual control in 1876. He seems to imply that this state of affairs should be regarded as God's punishment for religious neglect in tolerating these statues (and other manifestations of Western behavior).

The classical law books give two grounds for the prohibition of images: that their makers try to copy God's creation (*Mudahat al-khalq*) and that they thereby imitate the unbelievers (*al-tashabbuh bi'l-kuffar*) (Snouck Hurgronje 1923, 2:453). The latter ground, which provides the link between religion and politics, is highly relevant in the present context, because the erection of these statues had been part of Cairo's Western-inspired modernization.

The attack on the statues also had political implications, perhaps less obvious, but nonetheless present. The call for demolition of the statues was a political stance, first and foremost against European influence in Egypt, and, second, against the ruling house, which, among other things, was responsible for the increasing foreign presence in, and control over, Egypt. It is no coincidence that the statues in question were located in the "European" parts of Cairo: the equestrian statue in the Azbakiyya quarter, which, during the second half of the nineteenth century, was the location of consulates, foreign commercial establishments, hotels, and bars; and the lions of the Qasr al-Nil Bridge at the fringe of Isma'iliyya, a Western-style quarter designed and partly constructed by Isma'il on the model of Haussmann's Paris.[20] Because these statues were erected by Isma'il, 'Urabi's action also implied criticism of the Khedival dynasty. This was obvious, because one of the statues under attack

---

19 Al-Mahdi 1304/1887, 5:299–300 (16 Shawwal 1299 [August 31, 1882]). The episode is discussed in Schölch (1973:244) and Delanoue (1982:140). The statues were removed at the instigation of the Maliki mufti 'Illaysh in early September. They were preserved in the Egyptian Museum and re-erected after the revolt.

20 For the development of Cairo under Isma'il, see Abu-Lughod (1971:103–113).

represented Ibrahim Pasha, the son of the founder of the dynasty, Mehmed ʿAli, and the father and grandfather, respectively, of ʿUrabi's adversaries, the Khedives Ismaʿil and Tawfiq (r. 1879–1892).

The grand mufti's response to the question is rather brief. It consists of the general rule with regard to images, a quotation from the *Radd al-Muhtar* by Ibn ʿAbidin, a standard nineteenth-century Hanafi text, and a final sentence, connecting the first part of the answer to the actual issue. Although the wording of the fatwa is clear, the last sentence is not a very articulate and forceful statement, leaving the reader to draw his own conclusions. This suggests that the grand mufti have been reluctant to issue this fatwa. He must have been in a quandary. From the legal point of view, he could not but endorse the actions envisaged in ʿUrabi's question, but politically he was loyal to the Khedive and ʿUrabi's adversary. Therefore, he did not want to lend him any ideological support.

It is significant that the fatwa is signed only by the grand mufti. In the *Fatawa Mahdiyya*, we find several fatwas endorsed by other religious scholars: apart from the grand mufti, usually the Shaykh al-Azhar (during the period that al-ʿAbbasi did not hold this position), the head of the fatwa department (*amin al-fatwa*), and other high ranking ʿulamaʾ), not necessarily all Hanafis. These fatwas usually deal with such important matters as controversies between religious scholars or political issues, as in the aforementioned fatwa against the Sudanese Mahdi. Some were issued at the request of the highest conciliar body of state, al-Majlis al-Khususi. The topic of the fatwa under discussion here, the provenance of the question, and the circumstances under which the fatwa was requested, would certainly call for such special treatment. That the grand mufti chose to issue this fatwa separately is, I believe, indicative of his isolated political position. At the same time, it gave him the opportunity to add the supplement, which makes the fatwa unique. As a rule, a fatwa deals only with the issue expounded in the question addressed to the mufti, without digressions to other related topics. None of the fatwas contained in the *Fatawa Mahdiyya* is followed by such a supplement. In this case, however, the grand mufti must have felt that he could not confine himself to the legal aspects of the issue and that he had to make it known where he stood politically. The grand mufti did not want ʿUrabi to increase his legitimacy by posing as a Muslim ruler faithfully carrying out the commands of Islam. He therefore pointed to a number of political and social phenomena connected with the foreign presence in Egypt that were contrary to the prescriptions of Islam, implying that ʿUrabi had in fact been slack in enforcing the religious commands and did not deserve to be regarded as a defender of Islam, his attack on the statues notwithstanding.

References

Abu-Lughod, Janet L. 1971. *Cairo: 1001 years of the city victorious*. Princeton: Princeton University Press.

Aghnides, Nicholas P. 1961. *Mohammedan Theories of Finance with an Introduction to Mohammedan Law and a Bibliography*. Repr. Lahore. The Premier Book House.

Baedeker, Karl. 1929. *Egypt and the Sudan: Handbook for Travellers*. 8th rev. ed. Leipzig: Baedeker.

Behrens-Abouseif, Doris. 1985. *Azbakiyya and its environs: from Azbak to Isma'il, 1476–1879, Supplément aux Annales Islamologiques, Cahier no. 6*. Cairo: IFAO.

Beyer, Ursula. 1983. *Kairo: die Mutter aller Städte*. Frankfurt a.M.: Insel Verlag. Brockelmann GAL.

Delanoue, Gilbert. 1982. *Moralistes et politiques dans l'Égypte du XIXe siècle (1798–1882)*. Cairo: IFAO.

Jallad, Filib. 1890–1895. *Qamus al-idara wa-l-qada'*. 5 vols. Alexandrie: Al-Matba'a al-Bukhariyya.

Lane, E.W. 1966. *Manners and Customs of the Modern Egyptians*. repr. ed. London.

al-Mahdi, Muḥammad al-'Abbasi. 1304/1887. *al-Fatawa al-Mahdiyya fi'l-Waqa'i' al-Miṣriyya*. 7 vols. Cairo: al-Maṭba'a al-Azhariyya.

Mubarak, 'Ali. 1304–1306/1886–1889. *Al-Khitat al-Tawfiqiyya al-jadida li-Misr al-Qahira*. 20 parts in 4 vols. Cairo.

Peters, Rudolph. 1979. *Islam and Colonialism: The Doctrine of Jihad in Modern History*. Den Haag: Mouton.

Peters, Rudolph. 1983. "Islam and the Legitimation of Power: The Mahdi-Revolt in the Sudan," in: *XXI. Deutscher Orientalistentag (Berlin, März 1980): Ausgewählte Vorträge*. Hrsg. von F. Steppat. Wiesbaden: 1983; pp. 409–20. (ZDMG, Supplemente, V).

Schölch, Alexander. 1973. *Ägypten den Ägyptern! Die politiche und gesellschaftlichen Krise der Jahre 1878–1882*. Zürich: Atlantis Verlag.

Snouck Hurgronje, C. 1923. *Verspreide Geschriften*. 2 vols. Bonn and Leipzig, K. Schroeder.

Zaydan, J. n.d. *Tarajim mashahir al-Sharq fi'l-qarn al-thalith 'ashar*. 3rd ed. 2 vols. Beirut: Dar Maktabat al-Hayah.

CHAPTER 9

An Administrator's Nightmare

Feuding Families in Nineteenth-Century Bahariyya Oasis

In this paper I will present a legal case that was heard before Egyptian courts in the early 1860s.[1] My aim is to identify the different sets of norms that were at stake in this case, to clarify their relationship, and finally to draw some conclusions about the relevance and usefulness of the theory of legal pluralism for understanding the legal history of Egypt.

The case is set in the village of al-Bawiti, the administrative center of the Bahariyya Oasis situated in the Western desert of Egypt. It was just one episode of an ongoing conflict between two groups, to which henceforth I will refer as group A and group B. Because of the complexity of the case I shall first introduce the *dramatis personae*:

Group A consisted of the following persons:
- A1. Khalaf Allah Salim (brother of A2 and A3)
- A2. Husayn Salim (brother of A1 and A3)
- A3. Tantawi Salim (brother of A1 and A2)
- A4. ʿUthman Tantawi (son of A3)
- A5. Shaʿban (full cousin of A1, A2 and A3)

To this group belonged also a number of further unidentified village sheikhs (*mashayikh*).

Group B consisted of three subgroups, which, according to the record, belonged to one family:
- B1. Kaʿban Ahmad Kaʿban (brother of B2 and B3)
- B2. Muwaymin Ahmad Kaʿban (brother of B1 and B3)
- B3. Husayn Ahmad Kaʿban (brother of B1 and B2)
- B4. Nujaym Muwaymin Ahmad (son of B2)
- B5. Yusuf Hallam (brother of B6)
- B6. Abu Zayd Hallam (brother of B5)
- B7. ʿAmmar Abu Zayd Hallam (son of B6)
- B8. ʿAli Ramadan

The two families had been at loggerheads for more than fourteen years. Both families laid claim to the functions of *shaykh al-nahiya* (head village sheik, also

1 Egyptian National Archives (Dar al-Watha'iq al-Misriyya), S/7/10/19, (Majlis al-Ahkam, Al-madabit al-sadira), pp. 92–4, 9 Shaʿban 1280, no. 417.

 | DOI:10.1163/9789004420625_010

called *'umda*) and *mashayikh* (*al-hissa*, i.e. the sheiks of the districts of the village). Originally the office of *shaykh al-nahiya* was in the hands of family A. However, after members of this family had killed Abu Zayd Hallam (B6) of family B, the then *shaykh al-nahiya* was dismissed and the office passed to Muwaymin (B2) of family B. The latter was killed two years later by the district sheikhs, acting jointly. Apparently these offices were still occupied by members of family A. Muwaymin was then succeeded by his son Nujaym (B4).

Somewhere during Ramadan 1277 (March–April 1861), a new confrontation takes place. Khalaf Allah (A1) accuses 'Ali Ramadan (B8) of having burgled his house together with Khalaf Allah's slave 'Isa and of stealing about 1700 piasters from a box. The accusation is corroborated by a written document, certified by the qadi of Asyut, with the names of people who are willing to testify that the slave had been with 'Ali Ramadan and that the latter had wanted to sell him. 'Ali Ramadan was arrested by the police inspector (*mulahiz*) and put into prison.

Thereupon, the head sheikh, Nujaym Muwaymin (B4), together with Ka'ban Ahmad Ka'ban (B1) visited the police inspector and requested that he set 'Ali Ramadan free. Upon his refusal they went to the prison and released 'Ali Ramadan forcefully. Then they fetched Yusuf Hallam (B5) and the three of them threatened the accuser and four of his relatives: his brother Husayn Salim (A2), his nephew 'Uthman Tantawi (A4), and his cousin Sha'ban (A5). During the ensuing scuffle, which took place just after sunset, Ka'ban Ahmad (B1) shot 'Uthman Tantawi (B4), as a result of which he died. The perpetrator and his relatives then barricaded themselves in their houses, so that the police inspector could not arrest them. Later, the police inspector would complain that he could not do anything about it, because he was there alone (i.e. the only representative of the central government).

On 27 Ramadan 1277 (8 April 1861) six members of group B (Ka'ban Ahmad, Nujaym Muwaymin, Husayn Ahmad Ka'ban, 'Ali Ramadan, Yusuf Hallam and 'Ammar Abu Zayd) were arrested. Two guns were impounded. During the investigation, Tantawi (A2), the victim's father, produced three eyewitnesses testifying that Ka'ban Ahmad (B1) had shot 'Uthman Tantawi (A4). One of them affirmed in addition that Khalaf Allah's brother Husayn (A3) and Yusuf Hallam (B5) had been fighting one another with sticks (*nabbut*). The victim's father and the district sheikhs (group A) later denied that anybody had been fighting with sticks. The district sheikhs confirmed that 'Uthman had been shot by Ka'ban. Further they stated that on the side of the accused also his brother Husayn and 'Ammar Abu Zayd (B7) had taken part in the siege and fired shots, without, however, hitting anybody. The accused claimed that all these testimonies were prompted by enmity against them.

Thereupon the suspected murderer and his helpers were transferred to the *mudiriyya* of al-Fayyum for further investigation and their trial.[2] Kaʿban Ahmad persisted in his denial. He contended that the district sheikhs had been put under pressure by the police inspector to testify against him and claimed that he had found two fellow prisoners in the local prison (*hasil*) willing to testify that they had overheard a conversation between some of the district sheikhs and Kaʿban during which they had said words to this effect. However, none of the other prisoners was willing to confirm this. Furthermore Kaʿban Ahmad maintained that he could produce four witnesses who would testify that the three witnesses against him had been bribed by the victim's father. Finally he alleged that one of these three witnesses had not been present in al-Bawiti during the events and that another had been the servant of the district sheikhs who had killed his uncle Muwaymin. The four witnesses were brought to the *mudiriyya* and affirmed that the victim's father, Tantawi Salim, and his two brothers had hired two of the witnesses against Kaʿban Ahmad for 600 piasters. Confronted with the testimony, Tantawi Salim and the district sheikhs answered that they could not accept these testimonies, as the four witnesses were relatives of the suspects. In the meantime, Khalaf Allah had submitted a petition to the *mudiriyya*, requesting that the burglary of his house and the theft be dealt with. The case was then referred to the qadi of al-Fayyum, who had to dismiss the case for lack of sufficient evidence.

In prison, Yusuf Hallam and Kaʿban Ahmad fell ill and died on 7 and 17 Rajab 1278 (8 and 18 January, 1862). The remaining suspects were released on 4 Shaʿban 1278 (4 February, 1862). Less than a year later, one of them, ʿAmmar Abu Zayd, was killed and the first victim's father, Tantawi, was accused of having committed this murder. Later the record mentions that Khalaf Allah was convicted for that murder. On 11 Jumada I 1279 (4 November, 1862) the qadi of al-Fayyum heard the case of ʿUthman's killing. However, since the main suspect, Kaʿban had died in the meantime, he could not convict anybody for lack of a defendant. Another suspect, Nujaym Muwaymin died on 5 Jumada 1279 (28 October 1862) in a hospital. The two remaining suspects were arrested again on 20 Ramadan 1279 (11 March 1863), and imprisoned, this time in the *Mudiriyya* of Bani Suwayf instead of al-Fayyum, since the case was referred to the Majlis of Bani Suwayf, that had been established two months earlier.[3]

---

2 Between the abolition of the regional judicial councils in 1860, and their re-establishment in 1863, the provincial administration (*mudiriyya, muhafaza*) dealt with all criminal cases. Sami, 1928–1936: 3/1, 347. In this case the *Mudiriyya* of a-Fayyum would be competent.

3 Decree of 27 Rajab 1279 (18 January 1863). Zaghlul, 1900: 207; Sami, 1928–1936: 3/1, 355–8. At the time of the offense, the judicial body to deal with it was the *Mudiriyya* of Fayyum. After the re-establishment of the judicial councils of first instance (*majalis*) the council of Bani

For all clarity I shall here give a survey of the clashes between group A and group B:

1. A → B: unidentified members of group A kill Abu Zayd Hallam (B5). As a result the head village sheikh (from group A) is dismissed and Muwaymin (B2) is appointed;
2. A → B: district sheikhs belonging to group A kill Muwaymin (B2). His son Nujaym is then appointed head village sheikh. Members of group B start provoking group A (especially Khalaf Allah);
3. B → A: Nujaym (B4) allegedly beats up Khalaf Allah (A1);
4. B → A: 'Ali Ramadan (B8) steals from Khalaf Allah (A1) and misappropriates his slave. Members of group B release 'Ali Ramadan (B8) from prison by force;
5. B → A: Ka'ban Ahmad (B1) kills 'Uthman Tantawi (A5) during the ensuing scuffle;
6. A → B: Khalaf Allah (A1) kills 'Ammar Abu Zayd (B7)

The Council decided as follows:

Regarding the murder of 'Uthman, it contented itself with the qadi's sentence, since his suspected murderer had died.

With regard to Husayn Ahmad Ka'ban and 'Ali Ramadan, the Council was of the opinion that their presence during the fight has been established by the testimonies of the district sheikhs and other witnesses in spite of Husayn's denial. Therefore they have committed the offence of riotous assembly (*ta'assub*) as defined in Section 12 of Ch. 4 of the Law.[4] Since Husayn had been imprisoned for 19 months during the investigation, the council sentenced him to 19 months imprisonment with deduction of the period of his detention awaiting trial.

With regard to 'Ali Ramadan, the Council viewed that there were aggravating circumstances and other offenses:

1. The circumstance that his forceful release from prison was the cause of the quarrel.

Suwayf was to take cognizance of the case, which had then to be prepared by the *Mudiriyya* of Bani Suwayf.

4 This section reads: "If a village sheikh assembles with the peasants, or a peasant with other peasants rioting against the village chief (*nazir al-balad*) or the [head] sheikh, and attack him with sticks or other weapons, and if they only beat him and do not shoot at him with firearms, then it is necessary for reasons of public order that the sheikh or the peasant who is the leader of the gang receives two hundred lashes and the peasants who were with him, one hundred lashes. However, if they have shot with firearms, then they shall receive the punishment specified for their likes." The last sentence probably means that they will be prosecuted for manslaughter or malicious wounding.

2. The accusation of having burgled a house and misappropriated a slave. Although the qadi in al-Fayyum could not sentence him on the basis of the available evidence, there existed a strong suspicion against him founded on the testimonies the witnesses who had seen him with the slave and had testified that he wanted to sell the slave and share the price [the record does not indicate with whom].[5]
3. The circumstance that he was not able to reimburse the stolen money and to indemnify the owner of the slave.

On these grounds, the Council sentenced ʿAli Ramadan to three years of forced labor in lowly jobs (*ashghal daniʾa*) in the *mudiriyya* for theft as defined in Section 11, Ch. 3 of the Law.[6]

The Council's sentence was reviewed by the highest court in Egypt, the Majlis al-Ahkam on 9 Shaʿban 1280 (19 January 1864). In the meantime, on 21 Jumada II, 1280 (3 December 1863) one of the two remaining convicts, ʿAli Ramadan had died of a stroke.

The Majlis al-Ahkam held that the remaining convict Husayn Ahmad Kaʿban had been given too light a sentence, since the Council did not take in consideration the circumstance that he was among the gang who caused ʿUthman Tantawi's death. Therefore the Majlis al-Ahkam sentenced him to five years deportation to Fayzoghli Camp in the Sudan,[7] on the strength of Section 12, Ch. 4 (riotous assembly) and Section 11, Ch. 1 (manslaughter).

1 Analysis

The record shows clearly that at least two sets of rules were at play in this case: state enacted criminal law and the Shariʿa. At several stages of the proceedings, certain aspects of the case were referred to the qadi. First some words on the relationship between statute law and the Shariʿa in criminal matters.[8] Until 1883, when French law was introduced, the Shariʿa was the law of the land. This law was applied by the qadi, a single judge. In criminal and commercial matters

5 A possible scenario may have been that ʿAli Ramadan shared the slave's price with the slave himself, who was planning to run away after the sale. At any rate, the slave had disappeared and was not brought to justice.

6 This section makes theft punishable with forced labor in lowly jobs being chained, from 3 months to 3 years according to the value of the stolen property.

7 This penitentiary had been in use since the 1830s and was closed in 1863. (Hill, 1959: 163) This sentence must have been pronounced just before its closure.

8 For a detailed analysis of the qadi's authority in criminal matters in this period, see Peters, 1995 and Peters, 1997.

other jurisdictions existed, the judicial councils, *majalis*, which were part of the executive power and applied statute law, in our case the Imperial Code (*al-Qanunname al-Sultani*) of 1852.[9] These councils were staffed not by religious scholars, *'ulama'*, – although a religious legal advisor, *mufti*, was attached to them – but by administrators without a formal legal training. In criminal matters this state of affairs fits in the framework of the theory of Islamic jurisprudence, *fiqh*, according to which state authorities have the discretionary power to punish sinful or undesirable behaviour. This power is called *ta'zir*. Statute law in criminal matters, such as the codes enacted in nineteenth-century Egypt, must be regarded as instructions of the head of state to his officials restricting their discretionary powers and ordering them to apply *ta'zir* according to certain rules.

As a rule in criminal cases, and especially in cases of violent death, the qadi would first hear the case. In the qadi's involvement with criminal cases, the private aspect was most prominent. His main task was the adjudication of private claims related to offenses, as evidenced by the fact that the proceedings are always based on a claim advanced by a plaintiff against a defendant.

These private claims could be either punitive or aimed at obtaining financial compensation. There were three kinds of punitive claims: the demanding of retribution in cases of homicide and wounding, the demanding of the application of *hadd* penalties (i.e. the fixed penalties for offenses named in the Koran), and the demanding of satisfaction in the form of *ta'zir*, discretionary punishment for sinful behavior. In dealing with homicide, which could entail capital punishment, the qadi acted as a religious judge, sanctioning the taking of the murderer's life on the strength of religious norms. The qadi also heard complaints of persons whose honor was injured, usually because of beating and abuse during a quarrel or because of the unlawful defloration of a girl, and further complaints involving *hadd* crimes. Upon demand of the plaintiffs, he could sentence the defendant to flogging, based on of *ta'zir* or, exceptionally, *hadd* punishment, or, to short terms of imprisonment on the strength of *ta'zir*. The application of Islamic criminal law by the qadi was curbed by the fact that his sentences (except flogging, which was administered in court immediately after the verdict) were carried out by the executive. The qadi's death sentences did not pose a problem: after due revision, they would be executed by the government. Retribution for wounding, however, was a different matter. Since the government was apparently reluctant to administer such sentences,

9 Text in Zaghlul, 1900: *Mulhaq*, 156–178 and Jallad, 1890–95: II, 90–102. For further details regarding this code, see Baer, 1969, Peters, 1991 and Peters, 1997.

the qadis carefully avoided pronouncing them.[10] Most often, however, these private claims heard by the qadi were of a financial nature, such as demanding blood money, revendication of stolen property, or compensation for illegal defloration. In these cases the qadi acted as a civil court. However, since his jurisdiction was a general one, he did not and could not close his eyes to the penal aspects of such cases, which often led to a sentence of flogging or imprisonment based on *taʿzir* or *hadd*. As in the case of retribution for wounding, the government seemed to be averse to executing *hadd* penalties such as amputation or stoning to death, and the qadis therefore did not pronounce such sentences.

In our case the first involvement of the qadi was when the burglary and theft was referred to him by the *mudiriyya* of al-Fayyum. My impression from other material is that in the 19th century a victim of theft could follow two courses: he could bring the case before the qadi or he could report it to the police. The qadi would deal, according to the Shariʿa, with the revendication of the stolen property and with the criminal aspects of the case. However, since the qadi was dependent of the government for the execution of his sentences and since he would be aware of the fact that the government would not carry out the *hadd* penalty of amputation, he would always find grounds for not sentencing the defendant to this punishment. Only in 1880 did the Ministry of Interior expressly prohibit that cases of theft be immediately submitted to the *qadi*s, instructing them that they were to hear such cases only after they had been dealt with by the police.[11] The latter procedure had been the more usual procedure. A victim of a theft would go to the police, who would investigate the matter and, if there was sufficient evidence, submit the case to the Council. During the same procedure the property claim would be dealt with. Only if the complaint did not result in criminal proceedings would the case be referred to the qadi to look into the property claim. This is what happened in our case. There was no proof of ʿAli Ramadan having burgled Khalaf Allah. Therefore the case was brought before the qadi to settle the property claim. As we have seen, the plaintiff's claim could be awarded.

The second instance of the qadi's involvement was when he was asked to try the killing of ʿUthman Tantawi. As a rule all cases of violent death would be investigated by the qadi in order to establish whether the heirs could sue anybody. For manslaughter, the procedure was laid down in the Imperial Code

10 For a discussion of this reluctance, see Peters 1997.

11 Decree of Ministry of Interior (*Nazarat al-Dakhiliyya*) of 20 Muharram 1297 (3 January 1880). Jallad, 1890–1895: IV, 145.

of 1852. Chapter 1, section 3 stipulates that outside Cairo these cases be tried both by the qadi and by the Council in one session. If the qadi would not find grounds for capital punishment, the council would try the case and could impose a sentence of maximum fifteen years of forced labor. In our case, the qadi could not pronounce a judgment as the defendant had died in the meantime.

Whereas the Shariʿa courts primarily dealt with private claims, the councils were more concerned with the public aspect and in trying criminal cases their primary aim was to preserve public order and security. The procedural rules were less strict than those of the Shariʿa courts and very much resembled an administrative investigation. From the records it is not clear to what extent the defendants were entitled to defend themselves during the trial. They certainly had no right to legal counsel. One gets the impression that they were only present, not to defend themselves, but rather to be there in case one of the members of the council wanted to interrogate them. Moreover, the requirements for evidence were not as strict as those in the Shariʿa courts. Therefore it was easier for these councils to sentence defendants. It was not even required that an offense was proven beyond reasonable doubt: strong suspicion was enough and as a rule the punishment was more severe as the suspicion, corroborated by evidence, was stronger.[12]

The result of these arrangements was that in criminal matters statute law and the Shariʿa were mostly complementary. The two systems overlapped only occasionally, e.g. in theft related cases. This dual legal system was subordinate to the state for two reasons. First because the state had the power to define the relative competence of the courts (the attribution), either on the strength of legislation or because the police, to whom criminal cases first would be reported, decided on further steps to be taken. Secondly because the Shariʿa courts (with the exception of sentences of flogging) depended on the state for the execution of their sentences. However, although both systems were subordinate to the state, they differed regarding the source of the rules to be enforced and the authority to interpret them: for the Shariʿa this authority belonged to the ʿulamaʾ, whereas statute law was by its nature a matter of the state. So, the two sets of norms were different from each other in the following aspects:

12 See e.g. a decree from 1275 complementing the Imperial Code, which in section 2 imposes a prison sentence of five years or less for certain instances of manslaughter, whereby the length of the sentence was to be determined "in accordance with the measure of weakness or force of the evidence produced against the accused". Sami, 1928–1936: III/1, 295.

	Origin of the rule	Enforcement by	Decision on attribution
Shariʿa	ʿulama	qadi	state
statute law	state	councils	state

Although not explicitly mentioned in the record, it is clear that another set of rules played a role in this case. We must be careful here, because the record of the case does not reveal the whole story of the relationship between the two groups involved. But a closer look at the course of the events mentioned in the record may clarify a few more aspects.

It is not clear what the origins were of this lasting conflict between the two families. We do not know what prompted the first murder. However, the overall picture is evident: it is a matter of vendetta (*thaʾr*), retaliation for murder and aggression. Part of the conflict was a struggle between both groups for the office of head village sheikh. Feuding, a social phenomenon usually found in tribal societies, can provide a certain measure of public security in societies where there is no state or the state cannot impose its authority. However, feuding tends to persist even when the state becomes more powerful and can assert itself, e.g. by enforcing criminal laws. When this is the case, two competing and conflicting normative systems exist. However, as appears from this case, adherence to the customary rules of vendetta does not totally exclude any recognition of state authority. This is evidenced by the fact that both groups had village sheikhs among them and that the office of head sheikh was one of the stakes of the conflict. As is the case, these sheikhs are state appointed officials with important functions in enforcing state laws. However, with regard to vendetta, it would seem that customary practice was to keep state authorities out of it. This would explain the vehement reaction of group B, when group A had recourse to state justice after the burglary of Khalaf Allah's house (group A) by ʿAli Ramadan (group B) and his subsequent arrest. One cannot help feeling that group B regarded the reporting of the case to the police as improper.

Thus, in addition to statute law and Shariʿa, there were customary norms involved in the case. There is no dispute about labeling the first two sets of norms as law. But is it helpful to apply the term law to the rules of vendetta in the context of the case? One of the beneficial effects of the theory of legal pluralism is that is has made us aware of the existence of competing norm systems in society. And as I have said the introduction, advocates of legal pluralism tend to call these systems law in order to emphasize their equivalence. Now, I have certain reservations in this respect. In my view, an essential element of the notion of law is that it gives procedures and institutions for settling conflicts and I am inclined to regard this as the foremost criterion for establishing whether or not a given set of norms must be regarded as law. In the present case, the record does not give any information on whether the vendetta was just a concrete pattern of social ordering based on notions of individual and collective honor or that it involved procedures or institutions of mediation and arbitration aimed at settling the conflict. Present-day evidence from Egypt indicates that vendetta is still an accepted and wide-spread custom, especially in rural areas. (Botiveau, 1987–1988, Ben-Nafisa, in this publication; for the Sinai, see al-Hilw and Darwish, 1989) Studies of the phenomenon show that the norms governing vendetta include the possibility of setting up courts of customary arbitration (*mahkama 'urfiyya ahliyya*) in order to put an end to the conflict and provide certain procedural rules to be followed by these courts. Therefore, there are strong reasons to assume that such norms also existed when our case took place. In this light, I do not hesitate to apply the term law to these norms of feuding.

References

Baer, G., 1969, "Tanzimat in Egypt: the Penal Code," in: G. Baer, *Studies in the Social History of Modern Egypt*. Chicago: University of Chicago Press, 109–33.

Botiveau, B., 1987–1988, "Faits de vengeance et concurrence de systèmes de droit," *Peuples Méditerranéens* (41/42), 153–166.

Griffiths, J., 1986, "What is legal pluralism?" *Journal of Legal Pluralism*.

Hill, R., 1959, *Egypt in the Sudan, 1820–1881*. Oxford.

al-Hilw, K.A. and S.M. Darwish, 1989, *Customary Law in Northern Sinai*. Cairo.

Jallad, F., 1890–5, *Qamus al-idara wa-l-qada'*. 5 vols, Alexandria, Al-Matba'a al-Bukhariyya.

Peters, R., 1991, "The Codification of Criminal Law in 19th Century Egypt: Tradition or Modernization?" in: *Law, Society, and National Identity in Africa*. Ed. J.M. Abun-Nasr a.o. Hamburg: Buske, 211–225.

Peters, R., 1995, "Sharia and the State: Criminal Law in nineteenth century Egypt," in: *State and Islam*. Ed. C. van Dijk and A.H. de Groot. Leiden: CNWS, 152–177.

Peters, R., 1997, "Islamic and secular criminal law in 19th century Egypt: the role and function of the qadi," *Islamic Law and Society*, 70–90.

Sami, A., 1928–36, *Taqwim al-Nil*. 3 vols, Cairo, Matba'at al-Kutub al-Misriyya.

Tamanaha, B., 1993, "The folly of the 'social scientific' concept of legal pluralism", *Journal of Law and Society*, 192–217.

Zaghlul, A.F., 1900, *Al-Muhamat*. Cairo, Matba'at al-Ma'arif.

CHAPTER 10

Petitions and Marginal Voices in Nineteenth-Century Egypt

The Case of the Fisherman's Daughter

1 Introduction

The right to submit petitions to those in power was an important institution in pre-modern states. If the rulers responded sensibly to petitions, the institution would result in greater legitimacy of the political and legal system and its acceptance by the subjects. For it would instil into the minds of the ruled the feeling that law and the state did not only exist for the ruling groups, but for everybody, and that by means of it they could complain and remedy injustice, especially injustice committed by the political elite. This was linked to the assumption that the sovereign would offer the ultimate refuge for the oppressed and that he was ignorant of the injustices committed by his servants. But this assumption could only persist if he showed that he took these petitions seriously and that they often led to serious action on the part of the authorities.

Petitions are therefore an important instrument for marginal groups (marginal in the sense of being remote from the centres of power). By studying such petitions we can hear the voices of these marginal groups, perhaps not literally since those who submitted them, being more often than not illiterate, depended on the services of professional letter writers or scribes, but to the extent that the petitions expressed the authentic concerns and worries of these groups. Petitions then are an important source for social and cultural history of pre-modern societies.

In nineteenth-century Egypt petitions were frequently submitted. In the judicial records they are often referred to. However, to the best of my knowledge, petitions have not been studied systematically and comprehensively from the perspective of social and cultural history. In this essay I cannot pretend that I will do so. However, by presenting one case I will show how petitions could be effective in redressing oppression and how they could express the voices of marginal groups. My essay is based on events that took place in the summer

 | DOI:10.1163/9789004420625_011

of 1862 and were tried in last instance by the Majlis al-Ahkam,[1] Egypt's highest judicial council at that time.

The leading character in the case is a fisherman living in a small village in the Nile Delta. He took a stand against the village head (*ʿumda*), who had tried to cover up his criminal acts resulting in the death of the fisherman's daughter. As a result of her father's persistence in submitting petitions, the *ʿumda*, along with his accomplices, did not escape the punishment that they deserved.

2 The Events of the Case

On 16 June 1862 (16 Dhu 'l-Hijja 1278), Yusuf al-Hadidi, the *ʿumda* of the village of Tahla[2] in the Qalyubiyya province, sent his watchman (*ghafir*) Muhammad Sahlul to summon a number of girls for *corvée*, because the walls of his house needed to be plastered with mud (*dihaka*). One of the girls, fourteen year old Gimêʿa, daughter of the fisherman Mitwalli al-Sayyad, refused to go, but Muhammad carried her off by force. In the afternoon the watchman sent Gimêʿa to the other house of the *ʿumda* to fetch straw which was to be mixed with the mud for the plastering. When she arrived at the other house, she found that the *ʿumda* was drunk. He grabbed her, took her to a room on the second floor of the house (*maqʿad*) and raped her. When he tried to assault a second time, she ran away from him, out of the room. Somehow, she fell off the gallery (*hadir*) and hit the ground of the courtyard. One of the *ʿumda*'s hands, Musa ʿId, tried to bring her round by throwing cold water in her face. But this was to no avail and she died. Apart from the *ʿumda* and Musa, there were two other persons present: the *ʿumda*'s son Ahmad and his storekeeper, Muhammad al-Dib. Musa ʿId took her body to a barn and buried her under the straw that was stored there.

After the body had been hidden, two of the *ʿumda*'s brothers, Muhammad (the section head, *shaykh al-nahiya*, of the part of village where Mitwalli lived) and Musa, and two of his men (Musa ʿId and Dasuqi Abu Subul) went to the girls who had been there that day, and threatened them that they would be thrown in prison if they would tell anybody that Gimêʿa had been with them that day. Thus, when Gimêʿa's father and mother went around the village to

1 *Dar al-Wathaʾiq al-Qawmiyya* (Egyptian National Archive), *Diwan Majlis al-Ahkam, al-Madabit al-Sadira*, sin 7/10, sijill 18, p. 112, case no. 428, dated 11 Shaʿban 1280. For jurisdiction and function of the *Majlis al-Ahkam*, see R. Peters, 1999.

2 A village in the district of Benha, located at the eastern shore of the Rosetta branch of the Nile. Mubarak, *Khitat*, xiii, p. 31.

inquire after the whereabouts of their child, they met with a wall of silence. But there must have been rumours about the girl's fate. When Mitwalli approached the *ʿumda*, and apparently told him what he had heard, the *ʿumda* and his son Ahmad beat him up thereby knocking out one of his teeth and put him in prison for four days. They tried to frighten him from complaining to the authorities, i.e. the provincial government in Qalyub.

Meanwhile, in the night after the event, Muhammad the watchman and Musa ʿId, who had been instructed by the *ʿumda* to stay in his house, put the girl's body in a large sack, partially filled with beans. Then the *ʿumda*, together with his brother Salim and his son Ahmad, loaded the sack on a horse, went to the neighbouring village Minyat al-ʿAttar, situated 3,5 km north of Tahla, and dropped the body into the Nile. Perhaps they were caught in the act by the watchmen of Minyat al-ʿAttar, or maybe they acted out of precaution, but during the trial it was established that they had approached the head of these watchmen and bought their silence for thirty *bintu*,[3] five *bintu* for each man. The height of the amount, probably several times their monthly wages,[4] suggests that these watchmen knew what the *ʿumda* and his companions were doing. They returned to their village through the fields in order to escape further attention. Interestingly, one of the watchmen later handed over his share to Mitwalli. The records do not mention his motives for doing so. What is remorse when he learnt about the girl's death? During the investigation, Mitwalli had handed the money over to the *mudīriyya*, the Provincial Administration (no doubt against a receipt).

3 The Investigation

So much for the events of the case. As for to the investigation, in the absence of the office of prosecutor, the provincial governor (*mudir*) was the competent authority for the investigation of crimes committed in the countryside.[5] As a rule he would act upon information passed to him by local authorities such as the *ʿumda*s or the shaykhs of the watchmen. For obvious reasons this did not happen.

---

3 Napoléon, a gold piece of 20 French francs; at that time worth about 80 Egyptian piasters. C. Issawi, 523.

4 In 1860, the wages of an unskilled worker were about 75 pts.

5 See for example articles 3 and 4 of the Decree of 12 Muharram 1279. Text in Zaghlul, 1900, App. 94–99, and the decrees supplementing the QS in Jallad, 1890–1895, ii, 102–111.

If the *ʿumda* had hoped to be able to cover up the case, his hopes were shattered by Mitwalli's persistence in trying to bring the matter to trial. He was not frightened by the *ʿumda*'s conduct and threats. After his release from the village prison he went to the government physician and had himself examined in order to have official proof of the injuries he had suffered as a result of the beating. Further he wrote (or had written) a petition to the provincial administration (*mudiriyya*) of Qalyubiyya.[6] In it, he requested an investigation of the disappearance of his daughter, who, he claimed, had been raped and killed by the *ʿumda*, and into the beating he had suffered when he confronted the *ʿumda* with the rumours about his daughter. When, after a reminder, the *mudiriyya* did not react, he submitted a petition to the Vice-Regal Household (*al-Muʿawana al-Saniyya*). Furthermore, he went to the government physician and had himself examined in order to have official proof of the injuries that he had suffered as a result of the beating. This, it seems, was too late: the medical report was inconclusive. The examining doctor stated that he did not find signs of beating and that he could not establish whether Mitwalli's missing tooth had been lost due to blows or to other causes. The Khedive then ordered the *mudiriyya* to examine the case thoroughly and get to the bottom of it.

This investigation, however, did not yield any results: the *ʿumda* denied that he had sent the watchman to fetch the girl and that his walls had recently been plastered. All the others involved corroborated his statement. The section heads (*mashayikh al-nahiya*) and the chief of the watchmen (*shaykh al-ghafara*) launched a counterattack by dragging Mitwalli's name through the mire. They testified that, some time ago, Mitwalli had opened a brothel and some bars and that therefore he was expelled from the village. He had gone to live in Shibin al-Qanatir and had returned only recently. Further they declared that, according to the census, his daughter was only six years old and not fourteen. If she had disappeared, that was most probably because she had fallen overboard and drowned, or because he had sent her away to some relatives. After these interrogations the *Mudiriyya* did not proceed in the matter.

When Mitwalli understood that no further steps were being undertaken, he wrote a new petition to the Vice-Regal Household. In it he complained about the *Mudiriyya*'s inactivity, which he attributed to a collusion between the *ʿumda* and one of the clerks at the *Mudiriyya*, a man called Ilyas, and requested that the matter be investigated by the Judicial Council in Tanta, which had recently been re-established.[7] This request was granted: The Council in Tanta

6 *Mudir* of al-Qalyubiyya and al-Sharqiyya was from 16 Muharram 1275–17 Shaʿban 1279, Fayd Allah Nuri Bey. Sami, 1928–1936, iii, 1, 290.

7 By Vice-Regal decree of 22 Dhu 'l-Qaʿda, 1278: Sami, 1928–1936, iii, 1, 403.

instructed the *Mudiriyya* to hand over the dossier of the case. Having examined it, the Council ordered the arrest of the *ʿumda* and the watchman.

The first efforts of the Council focused on establishing that the girl had really existed and that she was indeed fourteen years old at the time of her disappearance. For this they used three approaches. Firstly, the *ʿumda* was released for a period of forty days to enable him to find the girl. Of course, this attempt at rehabilitation failed for obvious reasons and he was arrested again. Secondly, the registers and censuses were consulted. It was found that the 1264 (1847–8) census did not mention the girl, whereas in 1278 (1861–2) the girl was listed, but as being only six years old. The registers of births and deaths were examined until the end of Shawwal 1273 (May–June 1857), but there was no entry referring to the girl. Thirdly, the complainant was requested to produce evidence for her existence and age. To this end, he gave the names of several people who had known her. First her husband. It appeared that the girl was given into marriage in Shaʿban 1278 (February 1862). The marriage, however, had not yet been consummated and she still lived with her parents. Secondly, the *faqih* and the witnesses who had been present when the marriage contract was concluded. And finally, a former fiancé who had broken off the betrothal because he found her too young, the shaykh of the guild of the fishermen and some others. Without exception they testified that the girl at the time of the marriage was fourteen years old. This evidence was accepted and the section heads were summoned to account for the faultiness of the registers for which they were responsible.

The second step for the Council was to establish exactly what had happened. Mitwalli, however, could not prove beyond doubt that Muhammad, the watchman, had collected the girl. The persons who, according to his statement, should have been present at the time, all denied having been there and declared that they had only heard rumours that the girl had been taken away by the watchman. The Council, however, regarded the evidence produced so far sufficient ground for further investigation. The *Mudiriyya* was ordered to proceed with the examination of the case.

The *ʿumda*'s imprisonment proved to be a master move: it had a wholesome effect on the memories of some of the witnesses. The first one to be interrogated was the *ʿumda*'s brother, Muhammad al-Hadidi. Once more he claimed that on the day in question he had been away in al-Qanatir with the other section heads. This time, however, his colleagues did not corroborate his statement and declared that he had been present in the village on that very day. The next one summoned for questioning was the watchman, Muhammad Sahlul. His testimony provided the break-through needed to overcome the impasse in the investigation. He retracted his former statements and confirmed the allegations made by the girl's father. He added that the day after events, when he met the *ʿumda* and his brother Salim in the former's guesthouse (*dawwar*), they had told him that they had thrown the girl's body in the Nile. His statement was then confirmed by Musa ʿId. This was a sufficient ground for the Governor to instruct the district chief (*nazir qism*) of Benha to dismiss the *ʿumda* and his brother Muhammad. However, neither of them admitted guilt. But now the evidence against them was accumulating. When the girls who had been plastering the *ʿumda*'s house were questioned again, they told that Gimêʿa had been with them that day. She had been ordered, they said, to go to the *ʿumda*'s other house and had not come back at the time they returned to their homes. They added that during the first interrogation they had not dared to tell the truth as two of the *ʿumda*'s brothers, Muhammad and Musa al-Hadidi, and two of his men, Musa ʿId and Dasuqi Abu Subul, had told them that they would be arrested if they were to say anything about the girl.

The *ʿumda*, however, had not yet lost all allies. When his storekeeper, Muhammad al-Dib, was questioned, he tried to disculpate the *ʿumda* by giving a totally different version of the events, a version which was backed up by the *ʿumda*'s son Ahmad. According to the storekeeper the girl had accidentally been buried under a falling bale of straw in the straw shed and had died as a result. He had discovered her after a few days because of the bad odour in the shed. After he had informed the *ʿumda*, the body of the girl was put on a horse and carried away. Ahmad added that he, his father, and his uncle Salim had taken the body to Minyat al-ʿAttar, where they had dumped it into the Nile. The *ʿumda* confirmed this version of the events.

Finally the watchmen of Minyat al-ʿAttar were questioned concerning the complainant's accusation that they have accepted money for not reporting that the *ʿumda* and his helpers had transported the body over the fields of their village. This they admitted.

At this point the *Mudiriyya* decided that the preliminary investigation was completed. The statements of all persons questioned had been recorded in a report (*mantiqname*) in the presence of the *qadi* of Tanta. The papers, the accused and all those who were involved – from the final sentence it appears that these were all remanded into custody at some point during the investigation – were sent to the Council in Tanta.

4 Courts and Procedure

Trial in cases of homicide was a double trial: first before the *qadi* according to Islamic law, then before the secular council (*Majlis*) according to the penal code, in this case the Qanunname al-Sultani,[8] that had been enacted in 1852 and was based on the Ottoman Penal Code of 1850.[9] It had been established practice that all cases of violent death were examined by the *qadi*. The function of these proceedings was first to establish whether such a death was an act of God (*bi-'l-qada' wa-'l-qadar*), i.e. an accident for which no one was to blame or the result of human acts. In the latter case the plaintiffs had to establish, under Islamic law, whether there were grounds for death penalty by way of retribution (*qisas*), or, alternatively, they were entitled to a financial compensation (blood money.[10] The secular council would not pronounce death penalties or rule on cases of blood money. Homicide trials by the *qadi* took place immediately before the trial by the secular council, and in the presence of the provincial mufti and the members of the council.

These councils were a recent institution.[11] Before their creation, the executive authorities – the local governors and his subordinates in the countryside, the heads of departments (*dawawin*), the Khedival Council and the police in the cities – dealt with criminal justice. The first councils were established in Alexandria and Dumyat in 1830–1832 AD (1246 and 1247 AH respectively). In 1852, nearly simultaneously with the introduction of the Ottoman Penal Code (*al-Qanunname al-Sultani*), five more councils were created.

The number and precise competence of these councils varied, but, at the time of the case studied here, these councils were courts of first instance for serious offences for which penalties of more than two months' imprisonment, forced labour or deportation could be imposed. They would act after the investigation by the local authorities had been completed. Petty crime was to be dealt with by the administrative authorities, viz. the provincial governors (*mudir* or *muhafiz*), or, in the cities, by the police with the possibility of appeal to the Council. All sentences pronounced by the Council had to be reviewed by the *Majlis al-Ahkam* in Cairo, the highest judicial body. The sentence of the *Majlis al-Ahkam* was to be sent to the Vice-Regal Household (*al-Ma'iyya al-Saniyya* or *al-Mu'awana al-Saniyya*) for an authorization of its execution.

Trial before the Councils differed considerably in character from the trial before the *qadi*. In the first place, the Councils would not apply Islamic law, but statute law, in our case *al-Qanunname al-Sultani*. But there were more dissimilarities. Whereas the proceedings under Islamic law dealt with the private claims of the heirs, claims resulting in either revenge in the form of a death

8 Text in Zaghlul, 1900, pp. 156–178.
9 Peters 1997.
10 For the trial of homicide according to Islamic law in the nineteenth century: Peters, 1990.
11 For the development of the judiciary in nineteenth century Egypt: Peters 1999.

sentence, or in a financial compensation, the trial before the Majlis dealt with the public aspect of crime. The aim of punishment by the Council was not retribution, but reform of the offender and protection of society. Words to this effect were often added as a comprehensive motivation of the penalty imposed.[12]

Another difference is related to the judge's function. Under Islamic law, the trial is accusatorial and the *qadi*'s role is to a great extent a passive one. He acts as an arbiter in a contest between two equal parties and during the trial he only rules on matters of procedure. He takes no active steps in finding the truth and finally decides on the strength of the evidence produced by the plaintiff and the defendant. The councils on the other hand, functioned differently. There was no prosecutor and the Council's task was both the investigation – finding the truth – and the pronouncement of the judgement. The trial, therefore, had an inquisitorial character. The Council would act on the dossier prepared by the local authorities and interrogate the suspect(s) only if matters were not clear. The rules of evidence were less strict and formal than the rules of the Shariʿa. The defendant had no right to be heard during[13] the trial nor was he entitled to legal counsel. In fact, legal counsel did not exist at all.

These secular courts were called in Arabic *majlis*, council, and not *mahkama*, court. The use of this term is significant. It meant that these councils were viewed as having an administrative rather than a judicial character. This can be illustrated by three aspects.

The first regards the staff. The councillors were members of the administrative and military personnel of the state. They did not form a special group of judicial officials but were regularly transferred between all branches of the civilian and military apparatus. Due to the absence of formal legal training in secular law their justice skills were limited. This is evident from their decisions. As shall be seen, the application of the criminal codes was rather rudimentary and unrefined. One does not find sophisticated argumentations about whether a certain act falls under the legal definition of a certain crime or not. Often the articles that were applied were not even mentioned in the verdict.

The second aspect concerns the way that these councils handled criminal cases. When they dealt with crime, they dealt with a coherent dossier consisting of a number of related offences rather than with individual offenders.

12 For instance: *nadamat*^{an} *lahu* (to make him repent), *tarbiyat*^{an} *lahu* (for his education), *adab*^{an} *lahu, ta'dib*^{an} *lahu* (to teach him a lesson), *wiqayat*^{an} *min sharrihi* (in order to protect [society] from his evil.

13 Only in 1871 was the right of the defendant to be heard recognised in an Vice-Regal Decree to *Majlis al-Ahkam*, dated 8 Shawwal 1287 regarding criminal procedure (Sami, 1928–1938, iii, 2, 883), supplemented by a Decree of al-Majlis al-Khususi of 16 Dhu 'l-Hijja 1287, approved by *Amr ʿAli* of 28 Muharram 1288 (Sami, 1928–1936, iii, 2, pp. 915–7).

Not only the perpetrator of the main offence and his accomplices were on trial, but also all officials who had failed to prevent the crime because of negligence or lack in vigilance. In serious cases of murder and robbery, one finds as a rule that village and section heads and watchmen were also tried. They often received stiff prison sentences, but from prison records, one has the impression that they were usually released before the end of their term.[14]

Third aspects relates to the hierarchy in which these councils were placed. All their decision had to be ratified by the *Majlis al-Ahkam*, the highest judicial body, and then finally, before execution of the sentence, by the Khedive. Review by the *Majlis al-Ahkam* cannot be regarded as appeal, as it was automatic, and not dependent on the will of the defendant. Rather it was similar to the regular administrative procedure whereby a superior official checks the work of his subordinates. Although the records are not totally clear, it seems that, unless the *Majlis al-Ahkam* saw reasons to question the defendant, review of the case was carried out on the basis of the dossier and in the absence of the defendant, who, as a rule would already have been sent to a prison. At the top of the pyramid there was the Khedive, who controlled the whole judicial apparatus and could change sentences as he pleased.

5 The Sentences

Eleven months after the events, on 15 May 1863 (26 Dhu 'l-Qa'da 1279), the plaintiffs, Mitwalli and his wife, formally accused the *'umda* and Muhammad Sahlul, before the *qadi* of having caused the death of their daughter and demanded either the death of the plaintiffs or financial compensation for their daughter's death (*diya*) which would amount to about 7.500 piastres.[15] The *qadi* however, dismissed the claim since the plaintiffs could not specify the exact role of each of the defendants nor the instrument with which the girl had been killed. The first element is essential for establishing the responsibility

14 See for instance: DWQ, *Diwan al-tarsana*, M 19/2, *qayd asma' al-madhnubin bi-liman tarsana Iskandariyya* [This is the title as given on the first leave of the sijill.] On the cover, as in the index, this series is called: *Qayd asma' al-madyuniyya bayan tarsana Iskandariyya*. Further, the series is marked on the label as Mim 14, whereas it should be Mim 19, Sijill 1, 29 Safar 1263–14 Dhu 'l-Hijja 1268–Sijill 3, 1281–1283.] Of 135 persons admitted to the Liman in Alexandria between 5 Dhu 'l-Qa'da and 7 Dhu 'l-Hijja, 16 were guardsmen convicted for negligence of duty.

15 This is half the *diya* of a man. It was a considerable sum. In 1861, it represented the value of 7.5 horses or 17 donkeys or 6.5 buffaloes (*jamus*), or in terms of wages 100 times the monthly wage of a coffee man in an office (*qahwaji*) (75 piastres), 10 times that of the High Court *mufti* (750 piastres), and 7 times that of the head clerk (*bashkatib*) (1,100 piastres). See Peters, 1990.

of each of the defendants separately since Islamic law does not recognise collective criminal responsibility. The second element is of importance for two reasons. First, a causality must be established between the acts of the defendant and the victim's death which is necessary for determining the defendant's criminal and civil (financial) liability. Secondly, the details of the killing are of consequence in order to establish whether the killing was wilful or not. Only in cases of wilful killing can the defendant be sentenced to death. Criminal intent is assumed to exist if the instrument used for the killing is one that would normally cause death. The result of these proceedings in this case were that the two defendants were not sentenced to death and the plaintiffs' claim for financial compensation for their daughter's death was denied by the *qadi*.

It may be assumed that the trial by the Council of Tanta took place the same day. These criminal proceedings were, in the first instance, directed against the *ʿumda*, Yusuf al-Hadidi, his brother Salim, his son Ahmad, his hired hands Muhammad al-Dib and Musa ʿId, Dasuqi Abu Subul, and, finally, against the watchman Muhammad Sahlul. The council first investigated whether they had previous convictions. This was an important element for determining the severity of the sentence. Repeated offenders would get considerably longer prison terms. At the absence of a nationwide criminal documentation system, such an investigation meant, if the defendant lived in the countryside, that trustworthy persons from his village, as a rule his village or section heads, would be consulted. If they declared that the defendant had previous convictions, this would be checked in the registers of the council or authority before whom the trial had taken place.[16] In the cities the police spies, *bassasin*, would be consulted, as it was one of their to keep track of convicted criminals. The result of this investigation was that they had not been convicted before. Then the record lists the sentences with their grounds.

Yusuf al-Hadidi is convicted to five years forced labour in the Alexandria Dockyards (*liman*), the main penal institution in Egypt in the nineteenth century. From this period time spent in custody is to be deducted. This is done on the strength of Art. 2 of the Ordinance of the *Majlis al-Ahkam* (promulgated in 1858 (Muharram 1275 H)).[17] This Ordinance, consisting of five Articles, was a supplement to the Qanunname al-Sultani. Art. 2 makes punishable wilful manslaughter for which the evidence points to the guilt of the accused, but does not meet the requirements of the Shariʿa. It further stipulates that the severity of the punishment inflicted should also be determined by the strength

16 See for instance art. 13, *Qarar al-Majlis al-Khususi*, 17 Jumada II, 1282. DWQ Sin/11/8/18, *Diwan Majlis al-Khususi, al-qararat wa-'l-awamir al-sadira*, p. 112. This must already have been established practice.

17 Text in Sami, 1928–1936, iii, 1, 294–7.

of the evidence produced. This would mean that a defendant who was merely suspected of having committed a murder, would nevertheless be punished, but receive a lighter sentence than one whose guilt was established beyond reasonable doubt. In this case the court considers that the girl has died as a result of a situation for which the *ʿumda* was responsible. It regards the fact that he did not immediately confess, but only after evidence had been produced against him, as an aggravating circumstance.

Against the watchman Muhammad Sahlul and Musa ʿId, one of the *ʿumda*'s hands, a sentence of two years forced labour in the Alexandria Dockyards is pronounced on the ground of the Ordinance. Here no article and no further argumentation is specified. One cannot but assume that as accomplices after the fact, they are also held responsible for the manslaughter, but this is not explicitly argued. For them, too, their lateness in confessing to the facts was considered an aggravating circumstance.

The storekeeper Muhammad al-Dib and the *ʿumda*'s relatives Salim, Ahmad and Musa, and Dasuqi Abu Subul get the same sentence. Here no article is mentioned and for the punishment the following grounds are given: they have not confessed immediately, they have put witnesses under pressure and some of them were involved in dumping the body in the Nile.

The girls who had initially given false evidence were not punished.

The Council also addressed the question of whether officials had been guilty of negligence in connection with the case. The council argued that the section heads of the village (among whom was Muhammad al-Hadidi) had given false evidence in the case to the benefit of Yusuf al-Hadidi, that they had not registered all births in their districts, that they had not informed their superiors about what was going on in the village sections, and that they had entered an incorrect age in the census. For all this the council ruled that they were to be discharged forever from government service and had to serve one year in the Alexandria Dockyards.

The village's watchmen were not punished. They were accused of negligence, since they had not apprehended the *ʿumda* and his relatives when they disposed of the body. Their defence that they were not expected to see everything at night, especially not of people walked through the fields, was accepted.

The Council's sentence is then sent to the *Majlis al-Ahkam* for approval. The *Majlis al-Ahkam* discusses the case on 21 January 1864 (11 Shaʿban 1280). Its members take a tougher stand. For most defendants the penalties are increased. The *ʿumda* is sentenced to 10 years deportation to the penal colony of Fayzoghli in the Sudan,[18] without deduction of the time spent in custody.

18 The Fayzoghli penal colony continued to be operative until 1863: Hill, 1959, 83, 87.

Here the *Majlis al-Ahkam* mentioned Art. 11, Chapter 1 of the *Qanunnama al-Sultani* (which deals with manslaughter and murder), and its own Ordinance (to which it incorrectly gives 1273, instead of 1275 as date of promulgation). As aggravating circumstances the *Majlis al-Ahkam* added to the ones already enumerated by the Council, the rape, the drunkenness, and the fact that the *ʿumda* had exerted pressure on the witnesses.

Muhammad Sahlul sentence is reduced to one year forced labour, not in the Alexandria Dockyards, but elsewhere (this is called *ʿamaliyyat wa-waburat*, which probably means that they had to work in factories). His punishment is reduced in recognition of the fact that his statements were crucial in bringing the case into the open. Yet he deserves punishment because he was the one who fetched the girls from her house, because he was late in confessing and because he was involved in the dumping of the body into the Nile.

The punishment of Muhammad al-Dib, Dasuqi Abu Subul, and Salim, Musa and Ahmad al-Hadidi is increased to three years, to be spent in the military punishment battalion (*al-firqa al-islahiyya*). This was a penalty that had been introduced in 1862–3 (1279) for civilians who had been sentenced to three years of more in the Alexandria Dockyards. Apparently it was no success because already after two years it was abolished and the inmates were sent to the Alexandra Dockyards to complete their sentences.[19] After their sentence they were to be drafted into the army. No motivations for the increase in punishment is given except the fact that they had distorted the truth in their statements.

The sentence against the section heads was increased to two years of forced labour in factories (*ʿamaliyat wa-waburat*). However, after four months, they were transferred to the Alexandria Dockyards from where they were released on 12 December 1865, having served approximately one year and a half.[20] A letter was written to the *mudiriyya*, ordering that they were to be replaced and that the new heads may not be the sons of the former ones. The acquittal of the watchmen was also upheld. Only their shaykh was discharged and sentenced to six months of forced labour. The *mudiriyya* was instructed to replace him. The same sentence was pronounced against the shaykh of the watchmen of Minyat al-ʿAttar for having accepted bribes. A person who had mediated in this bribery affair was also sentenced to six months. All these persons served their six-month sentence completely.[21] Finally, the *Majlis al-Ahkam* ruled that the

19 Decree of 26 Ramadan 1281. DWQ, *Maʿiyya Saniyya ʿArabi, Qayd al-Awamir al-Karima al-sadira min Qalam Majalis bi-'l-Muʿawana*, Sin 1.19/3, p. 9.

20 DWQ, *Diwan al-tarsana*, M 19/2, *Qayd asmaʾ al-madhnubin tarsana Iskandariyya, sijill* 2, 10 Rabiʿ 1, 1281.

21 Ibid.

five *bintu* that Mitwalli had received from one of the watchmen that had been handed over to the *mudiriyya* were not to be put into the *Bayt al-Mal*, but to be handed over to Mitwalli.

At the end of the sentence, the Council of Tanta is instructed to conduct an investigation in the *Mudiriyya* of Qalyubiyya to find out why the petitions had disappeared, what the role of the clerk Ilyas was, why the investigation, when it finally was initiated, was faulty and why the investigators had not been tougher on the accused. In the minutes of 12 Safar 1281 (17 July 1864)[22] the results of this investigation are discussed. The Council of Tanta proposed that the former *mudir* was to be given a warning (*iqaz*) for having been too slack in investigating the case.

Thus Justice was done.

6 Conclusions

What can be learned about the personality and circumstances of Mitwalli the Fisherman? Unfortunately, the records of the *Majlis al-Ahkam* do not include the *verbatim* texts of the relevant documents. They are possibly included in the records of the lower judicial councils (in this case, the Tanta Council) that are as yet not classified and officially not accessible. Therefore, the original text of the petition is not available. One cannot, therefore, establish whether Mitwalli wrote the petitions himself or had them written. Moreover, it is possible that some significant details were left out in the summarised records of the *Majlis al-Ahkam*. His person, therefore, remains rather hazy. We do not know his age nor his complete name apart from Mitwalli. There is no patronymic mentioned in the records and al-Sayyad (hunter, fisher) obviously refers to his occupation. He was a member of the guild of the fishermen and the shaykh of the guild was one of those who testified about the age of the girl. About his family, it is not known whether he was still married or that his wife was alive. He had at least one son and one daughter. But, through the record, one can hear his voice loud and clear, a voice of grief calling for justice with an amazing tenacity. Others might have been scared away by the *'umda*'s physical intimidation or by the repeated silence and inactivity after the submission of his petitions to the *mudiriyya*. All in all, he presented five petitions, three to the *mudiriyya* and two to the Vice-Regal household. Not a bad score for a probably illiterate fisherman.

22 DWQ, *Majlis al-Ahkam, al-Madabit al-Sadira*, S 7/10, *sijill* 241, case no. 1062.

In the Egyptian legal system of the nineteenth century, petitions were of crucial importance. They provided a remedy against oppression and injustice or whenever bureaucratic obstacles obstructed the course of justice. The case of the fisherman's daughter demonstrates that petitions could produce the intended effects. At the top level, they were taken seriously and resulted in instructions to lower authorities to investigate the complaints. But, at that lower level the investigation was often stranded due to sabotage of the officials against whom the complaint was directed. The case clearly illustrates this: at the administrative level of the *mudiriyya*, the investigation was thwarted, probably as a result of a combination of sabotage by officials who were in too close a contact with the village heads as well as the lack of diligence on the part of the governor for which he was later reprimanded. Only when the Khedive assigned the investigation to the judicial council of Tanta which was recently established and staffed, it would seem, with councillors who did not have close links with either the *mudiriyya* or the village head, could the impasse in the investigation be overcome by putting the *ʿumda* behind bars and thus depriving him of his power to exert pressure on the witnesses. And, from that moment, with the ball rolling, truth came to light to the extent that, in the end, even the provincial governor was reprimanded for his negligence. So petitions did work, but often only for those who had the strong motivation and stamina to oppose the authorities who had caused oppression or injustice and to persist in complaining.

References

Hill, R., *Egypt in the Sudan, 1820–1881*, Oxford, Oxford University Press, 1959.

Issawi, C., *The Economic History of the Middle East, 1800–1914, A Book of Readings*, Chicago, Chicago University Press, 1966.

Jallad, Filib, *Qamus al-idara wa 'l-qada'*, 5 vols, Alexandria, al-Matbaʿa al-Bukhariyya, 1890–1895.

Mubarak, ʿAli, *al-Khitat al-Tawfiqiyya*, Cairo, Bulaq, 1306 A.H.

Peters, R., "Murder on the Nile: Homicide Trials in 19th Century Egyptian Shariʿa Courts", *Die Welt des Islams*, 30, 1990, 95–115.

Ibid., "Islamic and secular criminal law in 19th century Egypt: the role and function of the qadi", *Islamic Law and Society*, 4, 1997, 70–90.

Ibid., "Administrators and Magistrates: The Development of a Secular Judiciary in Egypt, 1842–1871", *Die Welt des Islams*, 39, 1999, 378–397.

Sami, Amin, *Taqwim al-Nil*, 3 vols, Cairo, Matbaʿat al-Kutub al-Misriyya, 1928–1936.

Zaghlul, Ahmad Fathi, *al-Muhamat*, Cairo, Matbaʿat al-Maʿarif, 1900.

CHAPTER 11

The Infatuated Greek

Social and Legal Boundaries in Nineteenth-Century Egypt

Society is made up of a multitude of social groups sharing common characteristics such as level of wealth, origin, age and gender. Some of these groups may have a special legal status, assigning to their members special rights and obligations. In this case the law gives a precise definition of the group and draws a clear-cut boundary between this and the other groups. Nowadays, under the influence of the doctrine of equality before the law, the number of groups that have a legal position distinct from other categories has decreased. What remains is, for instance, the distinction between nationals and aliens. In pre-modern societies, however, there were more categories and some of these existed until quite recently, e.g. the difference in legal status between men and women. Belonging to such a legally relevant group implied that one had special privileges, but also that one had to behave in a certain manner. The law would also regulate to what extent and how it was allowed to cross such boundaries by abandoning one group and entering another. Infringement of the rules connected with one's status would entail legal sanctions.

The case presented here is one where the *dramatis personae* broke the rules connected with their status. It was a criminal case tried in Egypt in the 1860s. Through it I intend to show how the Egyptian legal system, as it existed in the period before the British occupation, enforced the rules connected with the legal status of certain groups in society.

1 The Legal and Judicial Setting of the Case

The case was tried by Egyptian state courts (as distinguished from the Islamic court of the *qâdî*) that were part of a judiciary which had evolved since the time of Mehmed ʿAlî. It consisted of councils that were part of the executive and specialized in the trial of criminal cases and in dealing with administrative conflicts. These councils were staffed not by professional jurists, but by officials serving for some time in these councils as a normal part of their administrative career. The sentences of these councils, just like administrative decisions, were the result of examination and review of the case in several instances, the last one being the decision of the *majlis al-ahkâm*, the highest judicial and legislative council. However, in capital or other important cases the sentence of

 | DOI:10.1163/9789004420625_012

the *majlis al-ahkâm* had to be approved by the Khedive. The present case was first heard and prepared by the Police Council (*majlis al-dabtiyya*). Then it was looked into by the Cairo Council, whose decision was subsequently reviewed by the *majlis al-ahkâm*. The proceedings before these councils were juridically not very sophisticated. The defendant had no right to legal assistance and appeared during the session only if it was necessary for the investigation, for example, when one of the councilors wanted to interrogate him.

The criminal code applied in this case was the Imperial Code (*al-qânûnnâme al-sultânî or al-qânûn al-humâyûnî*) introduced in 1852.[1] This was essentially the Ottoman Penal Code of 1851. As a consequence of the Ottoman policy of strengthening its control over the autonomous parts of the Empire, the Sultan had required that this code take effect also in Egypt.[2] The outcome of the ensuing negotiations between the Khedive ʿAbbâs and the Porte was that in 1852[3] this code was introduced in Egypt with some modifications and additions. The Ottoman Penal Code consisted of three chapters. To these, two others were added, containing provisions from previous Egyptian codes. Criminal legislation did not abolish the application of the *sharîʿa* in criminal matters. The *qâdî* also heard such cases, but dealt with them from a different angle, namely as an adjudication of private claims, generally financial (i.e. damages), but sometimes also punitive (e.g. retribution in cases of wilful killing or wounding). In fact, these codes fit in the framework of Islamic law, as they must be regarded as codified *taʿzîr*, which was also the basis of Ottoman *qânûn*. Two sections (Chapter 2, Sections 1 and 2) of the Imperial Code referred to in the record clearly evidence this state of affairs since they are entirely in harmony with the prescriptions of the *sharîʿa*. Section 1 lays down that, in cases in which a person's honor is injured (*hitk al-ʿird*), the appropriate *sharîʿa* punishments must be imposed, whereas Section 2 stipulates that such acts, if they are not punishable under the strict prescriptions of the *sharîʿa* can be punished on the strength of *taʿzîr*, the general power of the authorities to punish sinful behavior.

1 Text in Ahmad Fathî Zaghlûl (1900, appendix: 156–178) and Fîlîb Jallâd (1890–95, II: 90–102).
2 For the political aspects and the negotiations, see Gabriel Baer (1969: 109–33).
3 Baer suggests that the new code was not introduced until 1854 (Baer, 1969: 119). However, archival material indicates that it was already applied in 1852.

2 Legal Personality in Classical Islamic Law

In nineteenth-century Egypt, there was no legal doctrine or branch of jurisprudence based on enacted law and separate from Islamic jurisprudence. The application of statute laws was informed by the *sharīʿa*. Since these laws as a rule did not define general legal concepts, such as criminal responsibility, causality and so forth, they were adopted from Islamic jurisprudence. The investigation will now discuss the concept of legal capacity in classical Islamic law in order to clarify the legal boundaries that existed between different categories of legal persons. Legal personality in Islamic law is defined by three dichotomies, creating legal boundaries between dominant and non-dominant groups: Muslims versus non-Muslims; men versus women; free persons versus slaves.

Every person's legal capacity is a function of these three dichotomies and therefore there are eight categories of persons. The differences in legal capacity extend to most spheres of the law. The fullest legal capacity is that of a Muslim free male. All others have fewer rights. The clearest illustration of the existence of these categories is the differentiation in blood money which must be paid if a person is killed. The highest amount must be paid for a free Muslim male, whereas no blood money is due if a non-Muslim from outside the Abode of Islam (*harbī*) is killed. The latter category of persons lack almost any form of legal personality. Their lives (except the lives of women and children), like their properties, are not protected by the law. Non-Muslims living legitimately on Islamic territory do enjoy protection of life, property and freedom. However, their legal capacity is restricted by the fact that they are incapable of performing legal acts or entering into legal relationships implying some form of authority over Muslims. Therefore, they cannot hold public offices, be guardians over Muslim minors or possess Muslim slaves. Moreover, non-Muslim men may not marry Muslim women, whereas there is no legal impediment for Muslim men to marry Christian and Jewish women. In view of the notion of marriage in Islamic law, with the husband having matrimonial authority over his wife, this is a logical rule. In order to emphasize the divide between Muslims and non-Muslims, the law lays down that protected non-Muslims must distinguish themselves in their attire from the Muslims and imposes certain restrictions on their social life aimed at making manifest their subject position. These restrictions affected, for example, their ways of transport – they were not allowed to mount horses – and their houses, which had to be lower than neighboring houses in which Muslims lived.

The distinction between free persons and slaves is of a different nature. Slaves are both property and persons. Their lives are protected, but they lack the capacity to fully own property or to have legal authority over free persons.

The limitations of their legal capacity are a function of their owners' property rights over them. And like non-Muslims, they are not allowed to have legal authority over free persons.

Finally, the distinction based on gender will not be elaborated here as the legal status of women in Islamic law is well-known. Although in financial matters women have the same rights as men, this is not the case in other fields of the law such as family law, succession, procedure and public law, where women are considered to have a status inferior to men. Furthermore, there is a body of rules governing the relations, social and otherwise, between the sexes.

The nature of these legal boundaries is very different. The gender boundary is related to a person's innate physical characteristics. As a rule, these are evident. In exceptional cases, however, the physical signs are ambiguous and most classical legal textbooks include a chapter on the hermaphrodite in which the jurists go to great lengths to find criteria for classifying them in either category. The legal significance of this boundary is emphasized by the strong sanctions attached to forms of conduct ignoring or obscuring gender categories such as homosexuality and transvestism (*takhnîth*). Recently, Islamic jurists in Egypt had to address the question of sex change operations. Although the Mufti of the Republic, Sayyid Tantâwî, held that such an operation is permissible, being a form of treatment meant to make manifest the gender which a person "really" possesses, the case was widely debated and the *fatwâ* gave rise to fierce opposition from persons who regarded it as an unlawful and arbitrary blurring of gender boundaries.[4]

The other boundaries are related to a person's belief and to a specific form of power exercised by one person over another. Here the crossing of the boundaries is thinkable. Islamic law permits it only in two cases: a non-Muslim may convert to Islam and a slave may be freed. Crossing them in the opposite direction is legally impossible. A Muslim abjuring his religion does not acquire the status of a protected non-Muslim, but loses his legal capacity and is put to death or (in the case of the female apostate under Hanafite and Shiʿite law) excluded from society by perpetual imprisonment. Similarly a free person, Muslim or protected non-Muslim, may not be enslaved.

The following case deals with the position of non-Muslims in Muslim society. The main characters of the drama transgressed the rules concerning the divide between Muslims and Christians.

---

4 For the *fatwâ* and the ensuing discussion, see Skovgaard-Petersen (1997: 319–335).

3 The Case

On 9 August,[5] 1863 (4 *rabîʿ* I, 1280), a certain Sulaymân Shahâta from Alexandria notified the Cairo police that his sister, a girl named Sitêta, had been seduced by a *dhimmî*, an Ottoman subject of Greek ethnicity, named Filibû Wânîs (Filippo Yoannis?), who used to live in the tenement house where their father worked as doorman, and that on 3 June, 1863 (15 *dhû al-hijja*, 1279), she had fled to Cairo, to where the Greek had moved earlier. He requested that the police trace her and her seducer. The police immediately began to work on the case and on the same day they found the couple living in an apartment belonging to a certain Shîmî al-Hallâq, located in the hâra of the Darb al-Jadîd in Muskî. They were then taken to the police station and interrogated. They did not deny the essentials of the complaint. The girl (and probably the man as well, although there is no specific mention of it) were taken into custody, where they were detained awaiting trial.

The girl's version of the events included some elements meant to alleviate her guilt: a Greek couple, Mikhali Aglanios and his wife Fanîl (?), a washerwoman, had incited her to leave her home and stay with them. She had stayed with them for three days before they put her on a train to Cairo. Filippo had met her at the station and taken her to his home. There he had plied her with liquor and slept with her. When she woke up, she found that she had lost her virginity. In Filippo's statement, it is the girl who took the initiative. She had written a letter complaining about her hardship and suggesting that she come to him, but he had not sent an answer. On 28 May (*yawm al-waqfa*, i.e. *dhû al-hijja* 9), he had gone to Alexandria on business and stayed there two nights. Eight days later, Mikhali visited him and gave him the letter from the girl. In it she informed him that she had left her parents seven days earlier and could not return to them. She asked him to let her come to Cairo or else she would drown herself in the sea. Thereupon, he told Mikhali to put her on the train to Cairo, which he did upon his return to Alexandria. Filippo picked her up at the station, and took her home, pretending that she worked for him. When he slept with her, she did not bleed, although she had claimed to be a virgin. His only motive to let her come to Cairo was his fear that she would commit suicide. He finally declared that he had become a Muslim and was willing to marry the girl.

When the police tried to interrogate Mikhali and his wife, it turned out that they had Greek nationality. The police, in turn, applied to the Greek consulate

---

5 The presentation of the case is based on the sentence of the *majlis al-ahkâm*, to be found in the Egyptian National Archives (*dâr al-wathâʾiq al-qawmiyya*): *sîn*/7/10 (*majlis al-ahkâm, al-madâbit al-sâdira, sijill* 24 (14 *dhû al-hijja* 1280/4 *rabîʿ* I 1281), p. 53, no. 986, 7 *muharram* 1281.

requesting to question Mikhali and his wife. The answer from the consulate did not arrive until nearly eight months later (4 May, 1864/27 *dhû al-qa'da*, 1280), after the intervention of the Ministry of Foreign Affairs. They were then questioned by the Alexandria Police, but the result was disappointing: Mikhali and his wife acknowledged that they knew the girl, as she had occasionally delivered laundry to them, but they said they knew nothing of the case. Later, both Filippo and Sitêta admitted that they had made up the story of the Greek couple's incitement and assistance by way of mitigation.

After the interrogation of the couple, police investigations focused on two issues: Filippo's antecedents and the circumstances under which he had rented the apartment in Cairo. Concerning Filippo's background, they found out that he was a tobacco merchant (*dakhâkhinî*), who had nearly gone bankrupt. His debts amounted to some 64 000 piasters. However, he had paid off about 58 000 piasters and his creditors had accepted bonds for the remaining debts. The interest of the police in his financial affairs ended here and they stopped the investigations in this direction. In order to get information on how Filippo rented his apartment, they summoned the *shaykh al-hâra* (head of the district) a man called 'Îsa al-Habbâk. His questioning focused on why he had not demanded a guarantor (*daman*) from Filippo when he came to live in the *hâra*. The *shaykh* stated that Filippo had told him he was married but that his wife was still in Alexandria and would join him later. Furthermore, he declared that he had asked Filippo several times to bring a guarantor, and that he always promised to bring one. When Filippo had reached an agreement with the landlord, he let him have the keys even though Filippo had not yet brought a guarantor, because he knew that Filippo was a well-known merchant. Two witnesses confirmed that the *shaykh* had repeatedly reminded Filippo to bring a guarantor. The *shaykh*'s antecedents were examined and turned out to be not entirely unblemished. Some five years earlier (in *safar* 1275, September/October 1858), he had been dismissed from his office after complaints that he had evicted shopkeepers and tenants in order to line his purse. However, after witnesses had testified that he was an honest man, he had been reinstated some months later, in March 1859.

After the investigation, the case was submitted to the Police Council (*majlis al-dabtiyya*) for trial in the first instance. The council considered that there was sufficient circumstantial evidence indicating that Filippo had incited the girl to leave her parents and come to him and that, according to his own confession, he had violated her honor by deflowering her. As to his conversion, the council held that it did not absolve him from his punishment. The council asked why his conversion took place at this particular moment, since if it had been prompted by sincere belief, he could have "obtained this honor" at any time before. Considering further that inciting a girl to leave her parents and violating her honor are very serious offenses, the council proposed to sentence Filippo to one year light forced labor ("lowly jobs in factories or other activities") on the strength of Chapter 2, Sections 2 and 6 of the Penal Code. (For the texts of these Sections, see the Appendix). The offenses listed in these sections are the injuring of a person's honor and abduction of a girl. Since the girl willingly participated in these acts and therefore injured the honor of her family, the sentence proposed for her was eight months in the women's prison (*iplikkhâne*, the spinning mill in Bûlâq) on the strength of Chapter 2, Section 2, with deduction of the time spent in custody awaiting trial. With regard to the Greek couple, who allegedly helped the girl to leave her parents, the council could not give a verdict since they had not yet been questioned. Finally the council looked into the matter of whether the *shaykh al-hâra* deserved to be punished. Considering that he allowed Filippo to live in the *hâra* without having brought a guarantor, and knowing that Filippo was staying there alone, this factor facilitating the subsequent events, the council, on the strength of Chapter 5 Section 7, sentenced ʿÎsâ al-Habbâk to be permanently removed from the office of *shaykh al-hâra*, taking into account the fact that he had been dismissed previously.

By the end of March or early April 1864[6] the Cairo Council dealt with the case. The Council first looked into the *sharîʿa* aspects of the case.[7] Sitêta was asked whether she wanted to sue Filippo before the *sharîʿa* court for damages resulting from her defloration. She declared that she had no claim against him. The council's mufti concluded that in view of the girl's statement, Filippo was not liable to Sitêta for damages. Having dealt with the civil aspects, the Council proceeded with the trial. Like the Police Council, they considered the circumstantial evidence sufficient to establish Filippo's guilt in making the girl leave her family with the aim of violating her honor. However, taking into account that Filippo was not from Egypt, the Council, on the strength of Chapter 2, Sections 1 and 2, sentenced him to be deported to his country of origin. The sentences of the other defendants were found to be appropriate. When, in early May of that year, a letter arrived from the Alexandria Police with a report about the questioning of the Greek couple, who had allegedly helped the girl in leaving her family, the Council decided that they were innocent.

Finally, on 12 June, 1864 (7 *muharram*, 1281) the case was examined by the *majlis al-ahkâm*. The *majlis* considered that in view of the seriousness of

6 The sentence of the Cairo Council was sent to the *majlis al-ahkâm* on 27 *shawwâl* 1280/5 April 1864. This means that the case was tried by the Council a few days before.

7 For the role of the *qâdî* in criminal justice, see Peters (1997).

the offenses, the punishments imposed by the Cairo Council were too light and sentenced Filippo to one year of hard labor in the Alexandria Dockyards, and Sitêta to one year in the women's prison, both with deduction of the time spent in custody. The *shaykh al-hâra* was sentenced to two months light labor, in addition to his dismissal.

4 Analysis

The case concerns an illicit love affair between a young girl, Sitêta, and a Greek merchant, Filippo, who knew each other because he lived in the tenement house in Alexandria where her father was the *bawwâb*, or doorman. Now, under Islamic law, sexual intercourse is permitted only within two legal relationships: marriage and concubinage, i.e. a man's right of ownership over a slave woman. Otherwise, sexual intercourse is unlawful and may entail either the application of the *hadd* penalty for *zinâ* (punishment limitatively acknowledged by the *sharîʿa* for fornication) for both partners, or a liability of the man for damages, resulting from illegal intercourse, to be paid to the woman. The damages amount to her proper bride-price, i.e. her "market value on the marriage market," in other words the bride-price a woman of her age, social status, beauty and so forth, would normally receive when she marries. In addition, the man or both parties may be punished by *taʿzîr*, the general power of the *qâdî* or the executive to punish persons for sinful behavior. At the time of this case, Islamic law was still the law of the land in Egypt. The Penal Code enforced at that time, must be regarded as codified *taʿzir*. As is clear from the proceedings, Islamic law was not superseded by the Criminal Code, but existed alongside with it. During the trial by the Cairo Council, Sitêta was asked whether she had any financial claim against Filippo, which refers to a claim for damages according to the *sharîʿa*.

The record does not mention the ages of the defendants, but it is plausible that the girl, being unmarried and lower class, was in her late teens. Filippo, who seems to have been a well-established merchant in view of the amount of his debts and what he had discharged, may have been in his thirties or forties. Interestingly, the record does not mention whether or not Filippo was married. If he was, this might explain his reluctance in bringing a guarantor after he had rented the apartment in Cairo. It is not plausible that a merchant with his background, a member of the large Greek community, could not have found a person in Cairo willing to vouch for him. His reluctance must have been the result of his apprehension that Cairo acquaintances would discover what he was up to. The court did not mention his marital status, although it is likely that he was married, because from a Muslim viewpoint, this was irrelevant. The affair was scandalous in Muslim eyes not because Filippo may have been married, but first and foremost because these sexual relations were unlawful, as they took place outside wedlock or legal concubinage.

There are some indications that the affair was more than casual. Filippo had gone out of his way to provide an opportunity to consummate their love. From the case, it is clear that renting an apartment was not a simple affair for a single man and that it was difficult to do so anonymously. This was evidently true even for quarters inhabited mainly by foreigners, such as the Muskî area, where Filippo found his lodging. He must have known this but was still prepared to run a great risk. On the part of the girl, there was first the willingness to leave her family for her lover and secondly her refusal to sue Filippo for damages, although there must have been pressure on her to do so from relatives.

This leads to the question of why they could or would not regularize their status by conversion and marriage. Was there a possibility to cross the boundaries of their respective religions? Only during the police investigation did Filippo express his wish to become a Muslim and marry Sitêta. One cannot get away from the impression that he did so only under the pressure of the circumstances, hoping for leniency on the part of the councilors. Why had he not done this earlier? A person's religion was, in nineteenth-century Egypt, as in many other times and periods, more than a matter of personal conviction and belief. Having a religion had legal consequences and also social effects. For Filippo, the social consequences must have weighed heavily. By conversion to Islam he would have been expelled from his community. It is plausible that his business network was mainly located within his own community. Therefore, conversion to Islam, while enabling him to marry Sitêta and at the same time solving the problem of his being married – if he was –, would also have entailed the ruin of his business. Therefore, it is not difficult to imagine his hesitance to do so. For Sitêta, a change of religion would have been out of the question as it would not have solved the problem. A Muslim who renounces his faith loses his or her legal capacity and enters a state of what may be compared to *mort civile* (legal, but not physical dead). That means that even if she had expressly adopted Christianity, she would not have been able to contract a marriage with Filippo in Egypt. In addition, there is the aspect of criminal law. I have no information on the question of how apostasy was punished in this period in Egypt, but it is not unlikely that Sitêta would have faced imprisonment. However, at least as serious are the social consequences: the apostate as a rule is repudiated by his family and his social environment.

The charges brought against Filippo were that he had incited the girl to leave her family and injured her honor by having deflowered her. The Police Council quoted Sections 2 (injuring a person's honor) and 6 (abduction of a girl) of Chapter 2 of the Imperial Code. The latter Section, however, was not mentioned by the Cairo Council and the *majlis al-ahkâm*, no doubt because the councilors felt that inciting a girl to leave her parents cannot be put on a par with abduction, especially since the girl came to Cairo of her own accord. The Cairo Council and the *majlis al-ahkâm* added Section 1 of Chapter 2 as extra grounds for the sentence. It is not immediately clear why they should have done so, since the Section deals with the same offense as Section 2. The only plausible reason is that Section 1, although it only mentions punishment according to the *sharîʿa*, to some extent specifies the notion of injuring a person's honor to which Section 2 refers with the words "a case of this nature." However, in neither Section are unlawful sexual relations expressly mentioned. The wording of these Sections shows that the level of the legislative technique used in drafting the law was not very advanced. Actually, Section 2 does not even specify the punishment. It simply repeats provisions from Islamic law textbooks with regard to *taʿzîr* punishment. The low level of juridical sophistication is also apparent in the way the law was applied. The councilors had not been trained as lawyers and this is often evident in the way they handled the laws. The reason for this absence of juridical skills is that no law schools existed, apart from the religious institutions where Islamic jurisprudence was taught.

It is striking that the difference of religion is not explicitly referred to in the records of the trial. In introducing the characters, the religious status of Filippo is mentioned. He is called a *dhimmî* which, under Islamic law, defined his legal status, being a *rûmî* (Greek Orthodox) and a subject of the Ottoman Empire. However, when the councils specified the offenses committed by the couple, this aspect remains in the background. It was discussed only indirectly when the Police Council considered his conversion and decided that it came too late and therefore could not prevent his conviction (*hukm siyâsî*). This implies that the difference in religion certainly played a role as an aggravating circumstance. However, this is difficult to prove without further systematic archival research in order to examine the sentences for these offenses. The sentences for illegal sexual relations that I have seen vary between caning and six months of detention for the man, whereas no mention is made of the woman's punishment. The sentences of one year hard labor for Filippo and one year in the women's prison for Sitêta seem quite harsh in this light. This can only be explained by the circumstance that Filippo was a Christian and Sitêta a Muslim.

5 Conclusion

In this essay, I presented a criminal case tried in Egypt in the early 1860s. I attempted firstly to make the case understandable by situating it in its legal, social and historical context and secondly to examine how the state authorities at that time dealt with persons from juridically defined non-dominant groups who transgressed the rules that reinforced their marginality. The case selected here centered around sexual relations that were doubly forbidden: first, because they took place outside of a lawful marriage and second, because they could not simply be regularized, due to the existence of a religious obstacle. From the trial it became clear that the presence of this religious obstacle did not constitute an offense in itself – rather, the unlawful sexual relations and the circumstance that the girl had left her family were the central grounds for the sentence. However, there are strong indications that the religious impediment, in spite of the man's conversion to Islam during the police investigation, was regarded as an aggravating circumstance.

Appendix: the Text of the Pertinent Sections of the Imperial Code

Chapter 2

(Section 1) Whereas all subjects of the Ottoman Empire have acquired lawful rights consisting of safety of life and property and protection of one's honor and good name, and whereas consequently they can claim their rights, regardless of their status, in accordance with freedom as circumscribed by the law, and not in accordance with absolute freedom, and whereas a person's honor and good name is as dear and respected to him as his own soul, and whereas the safeguarding and protecting of honor is required by virtue and humanity, and whereas slander (*al-qadhf bi-l-kalâm*)violates a person's respect and prestige and beating or abusing him without good reason is regarded as an injury to one's honor and an assault on his respect, it is therefore necessary that anyone against whom it has been proven, according to the *sharîʿa*, that he has had the audacity to injure a person's honor in a manner that makes the application of the *hadd* punishment obligatory, shall be punished with the *hadd* punishment according to the *sharîʿa*.

(Section 2) If a case of this nature [injuring a person's honor, mentioned in the previous section] is committed in Cairo and if it must be punished only with *taʿzîr*, then the defendant's situation and social position must be examined since the ways and manners of *taʿzîr* vary according to these factors. If the person to be punished by *taʿzîr* is an important religious dignitary (*min al-ʿulamâʾ al-fikhâm wa-l-sâdât al-kirâm*), a prominent personality, or a high-ranking official, he shall be summoned to the *majlis al-ahkam* and receive a proper punishment. If he belongs to the middle classes (*awsât al-nâs*) or common people (*al-sûqa*) and their likes, he shall be brought before the

Council and be punished with imprisonment or banishment, according to the circumstances. If he belongs to the lowest classes (*âhâd al-nâs*), he shall be disciplined by imprisonment, banishment or a beating consisting of three to seventy-nine strokes according to the *sharî'a*. Outside Cairo, these cases shall be dealt with in the same way by the provincial governor (*mudîr al-mahall*). People shall not be convicted for these offenses on the strength of complaints only and there must take place careful examination to find evidence and if the complainant is proven to have lied, he shall be punished with five to forty-five days detention.

(Section 6) If someone has the audacity to commit unacceptable acts such as abducting Muslim or non-Muslim girls to another region or another country claiming that he has married her without her relatives knowing it, then he must be arrested and his case must be investigated by the governor of the region. Then he and the dossier of his case shall be sent to the Regional Council for trial. If his offense is proven, he shall be punished according to what the Council sees legally fit, with six months [detention] to chastise him. (…)

Chapter 5

(Section 7) If an official in government service, regardless of whether he is of high or low rank, does not obey the contents of the enacted laws, or an order of the *wâli* or one of his superiors, his case must be investigated. If it appears that his disobedience did not result in damage to the service, he shall be punished by detention in the bureau of the directorate [of his department] for a period of ten days to one month in accordance with his circumstances. If it has resulted in damage to the service, he shall be detained in the same place for a period of one to six months in accordance with the extent of the damage. If this occurs a second time and results in damage, he shall be removed from the service and not be employed again in any government position until he regrets it and shows sincere repentance.

References

Baer, G., 1969, "Tanzimat in Egypt: the Penal Code," in: G. Baer, *Studies in the Social History of Modern Egypt*, Chicago: University of Chicago Press.

Jallâd, F., 1890–95, *Qâmûs al-idâra wa-l-qadâ'*, 5 vols, Alexandria: al-Matba'a al-Bukhâriyya.

Peters, R., 1997, Islamic and Secular Criminal Law in 19th-century Egypt: the Role and Function of the *Qâdî*, *Islamic Law and Society* 4/4:70–90.

Skovgaard-Petersen, J., 1997, *Defining Islam for the Egyptian State: Muftis and Fatwas of the Dâr al-Iftâ'*, Leiden: Brill.

Zaghlûl, A.R., 1900, *al-Muhâmât*, Cairo: Matba'at al-Ma'ârif.

CHAPTER 12

The Violent Schoolmaster

The "Normalisation" of the Dossier of a Nineteenth-Century Egyptian Legal Case

1 Introduction

On nine Safar 128 [26 July 1863] ʿAli Ghunaym, a seven-year-old pupil of the Koran school of the village of Dimas, Daqhaliyya province, was beaten by the head master and the assistant teacher of the school, as a result of which his arm was fractured. His grandmother reported the case to the village head (*ʿumda*), who sent the boy with one of his men to Mit Ghamr, the centre of the administrative district. The following day he was examined by the government doctor, who, in his turn, sent him to the provincial hospital in al-Mansura for treatment. When the boy came out of the hospital, the fracture had healed but the arm was paralysed.

We know of the incident because it gave rise to legal proceedings that left written traces. The first time I came across the case was while working in the Shariʿa archives located in the *Dar al-Mahfuzat* in Cairo. There I found the records of a Shariʿa sentence (*iʿlam sharʿi*) passed on 28 Rabiʿ al-Awwal 1280 [12 September 1863] by the qadi court of al-Mansura and awarding financial compensation for the boy's injury.[1] Some years later I came across the minutes of a session of the highest judicial council at the time, the *Majlis al-Ahkam*, dated 15 Shawwal 1280 [24 March 1864], in which it was decided to punish the offenders in the same incident.[2]

In the following, I will first discuss the two documents and point out the differences in their textual structure and relating them to the different functions of both courts. My main aim, however, is to compare and analyse the narratives found in them. I will show how the narrative was constructed during the court proceedings and went through a process of "normalisation" during the investigation and the trial. Those who took the statements of the complainants, the witnesses and the experts and finally compiled the dossier to be used by the courts, wanted to produce a "clean" account of the facts. That is to say that

1 Mahkamat al-Mansura al-ibtidaʾiyya al-sharʿiyya; Madabit al-murafaʿat, makhzan 46, ʿayn 142, sijill 286, p. 59, 28 Rabiʿ I 1280.

2 Madbata of the *Majlis al-Ahkam*, 15 Shawwal 1280, no. 626. Dar al-Wathaʾiq al-Qawmiyya (Egyptian National Archives), Sin 7/10/21, pp. 16–19.

 | DOI:10.1163/9789004420625_013

the dossier must show that the relevant procedural rules had been followed and that the facts are presented in a such a way that the substantive legal categories to be applied are clear. In order to do so, legally irrelevant facts were omitted and certain versions of the events were implicitly rejected in favour of others that presented the facts in ways that were more plausible in the eyes of the investigators and clerks.[3] The text of the record in its "raw" form, therefore, is a construct and does not necessarily reflect what "really happened".

2 The Qadi's Sentence

The proceedings before the qadi were adversarial and the record tells us what happened during the public session and contains, apart from the judgement, only the statements of the parties and the witnesses made during this session. We are left in the dark about the investigation before the trial, since the record is constructed on the assumption that the proceedings are civil litigation, between two essentially equal private parties. The sentence settles the dispute between the them. The document is formulaic and includes only legally relevant information. Moreover, it is a public document since authenticated copies are handed over to the parties so that they could enforce the sentence or defend themselves in case a plaintiff who had lost the suit would again sue the defendant for the same issue. As a rule, these sentences have the following basic structure:

Introduction and identification of the parties
The plaintiff's claim
The defendant's reply
The plaintiff's rejoinder
Evidence
The sentence

In the first part, the plaintiff and the defendant are introduced with their own and their father's name and their places of residence. Their identity and, in

3 For the process of the moulding of the facts of a case into legal form, ready for handling by courts and judges, see Baudouin Dupret, "The practice of judging: The Egyptian judiciary at work in a personal status case," in *Dispensing justice in Islamic courts: qadis, procedures and evidence*, ed. M. Khalid Masud, R. Peters, and D.S. Powers (Leiden: Brill, 2005).

cases of representation at law (e.g. if parties act as agents or guardians for others), the ground of their authority to act as such are established by the testimonies of witnesses. In this case the plaintiff was ʿAyusha, the boy's grandmother, who had become his testamentary guardian (*wasiyya*) when his father died shortly after the incident. The defendant was ʿUmar Hassan, the blind assistant teacher.

After the identities of the parties had been established, ʿAyusha introduced the following claim:

> My grandson, who was a pupil in the Koran school of Mustafa al-Aswad in the village of Dimas, was slapped in his face by this Mustafa, and was then handed over to the aforementioned ʿUmar [the defendant] in order to recite the Koran. ʿUmar, then, hit him on his right arm with the *falaqa*[4] that was there to be put on the legs of the children for chastising them, as a result of which the [boy's] ulna (*ʿazam al-mirfaq*) was fractured. After treatment in the hospital, the arm remained paralysed and could not be used anymore. Therefore I demand my due according to the Shariʿa.

In reply, defendant said at first:

> Mustafa first hit the boy with a stick and subsequently handed him over to him, having given permission to chastise him further. Then I struck the boy with a stick, aiming at his back, but without knowing where I hit him, due to my blindness. However, I did not break the boy's arm.

Later, however, he admitted that the boy's injury was the result of either his or Mustafa's beatings.

It was uncontested that both the assistant teacher and the headmaster had beaten the boy. The grandmother claimed that the assistant had caused the fracture, whereas the assistant maintained that it could have been the result of either beating. In her rejoinder, however, the plaintiff blamed only the assistant and exonerated the headmaster. Although the rules of procedure did not require so, since the plaintiff had not introduced a formal claim against him, the headmaster, who apparently was also present during the session, declared that he denied all responsibility for the fracture. The qadi regarded the assistant teacher's reply as a denial of the plaintiff's allegation and requested that the latter produce proof, which she could not. When the qadi exacted the

4 A piece of hard wood with a rope looped though its ends used to secure the feet of those undergoing a bastinado.

oath of denial from the defendant, as prescribed whenever a plaintiff is unable to substantiate his claim, he refused to swear it. As a consequence, the judge found for the plaintiff. In order to determine the amount of damages to be paid, he had recourse to experts, who stated that the price of a slave with a similar defect would be one third less than that of a sound slave. The qadi then fixed the compensation for the loss of the use of boy's arm at one third of the full blood price (*diya*). The assistant teacher was ordered to pay the amount of 5.031 piasters and 10 *fidda* within one year.[5] This must have been a heavy financial burden for him, since it represented the value of five horses, or 11 donkeys or seven months' salary of a high court mufti.[6] The record mentions that the defendant paid the sum of 810 piasters and 3 *fidda* to the grandmother.

3 The Decisions of the Regional *Majlis* and the *Majlis al-Ahkam*

3.1 *Structure of the Text of the Minutes of the Majlis al-Ahkam*

The minutes of the session of the *Majlis al-Ahkam*[7] (*madbata*) where the case was discussed are more complicated than the qadi's sentence. They contain a summary of the dossier and the verbatim text of the final decision. The document consists of the following elements:

1. Introduction
2. The reporting of the case to the authorities
3. The medical examination of the victim
4. The investigation
    - 4.1. Statement of the accused
    - 4.2. Statement of the boy's grandmother
    - 4.3. Interrogation of witnesses proposed by the grandmother
    - 4.4. Second interrogation of the accused
5. Medical report on the healing of the injury
6. Trial before the qadi
    - 6.1. Claim
    - 6.2. Reply
    - 6.3. Evidence

5 The full *diya* had been fixed at 15.093,75 piasters by a decree of the *Majlis al-Ahkam* issued on 25 Rab. I, 1275 (1858). Rudolph Peters, "Murder on the Nile: Homicide Trials in 19th Century Egyptian Shari'a Courts," *Die Welt des Islams* 30 (1990).

6 Ibid.

7 For the competence and jurisdiction of the *Majlis al-Ahkam*, see: Rudolph Peters, "Administrators and magistrates: The development of a secular judiciary in Egypt, 1842–1871," *Die Welt des Islams* 39 (1999).

6.4. Qadi's sentence
6.5. Payment
6.6. Recording the sentence
7. Investigation of the handling of the case by the officials concerned
7.1. The *ʿumda*
7.2. The deputy chief of the district
8. Inquiry into previous convictions
9. Approval of the qadi's sentence by the mufti of the council
10. Decision of the regional council of al-Mansura
10.1. Regarding the assistant teacher
10.2. Regarding the schoolmaster
10.3. Regarding the *ʿumda*
10.4. regarding the deputy head of the district and the district's clerk
11. Approval of the qadi's sentence by the mufti of the *Majlis al-Ahkam*
12. Decision of the *Majlis al-Ahkam*
12.1. Regarding the sentence of the council of al-Mansura
12.2. Instructions for the future
12.3. Conclusion

The recorded minutes of the *Majlis al-Ahkam*, like the qadi's sentence, contain a legal decision and the grounds which have led to it. However, as a result of the difference in functions of the two courts and the procedures followed by them, the documents have different structures. The minutes of the *Majlis al-Ahkam* do not register what happened during a public trial, but give a chronological narrative spanning, in our case, a period of about eight months. It tells the story of the investigation of the case by the various administrative authorities in all its ramifications, beginning with the notification of the local authorities, and records the statements of all persons involved in the case, both the suspects and the witnesses. The minutes also include the judicial decisions taken at the various levels. They end with the text of the judgement passed by the *Majlis al-Ahkam*, endorsed by the stamps of the members' signets. This final decision is not taken after a public trial, but entirely on the basis of the documents, although the councils were entitled to interrogate suspects and witnesses in order to clarify certain points.

From the minutes it is clear that the proceedings before the qadi were incorporated in the procedure of the state courts (see no. 6 in the schedule above). In cases of homicide, wounding, sexual offences and verbal abuse, a trial in a qadi court, initiated by a claim of the victim(s), was required in order to establish whether he (they) were entitled to financial compensation or, as private prosecutors, could demand punishment, such as retaliation for homicide or injuries. These Shariʿa proceedings took place during the session of the local council where the case was tried. At the level of the *Majlis al-Ahkam*, the qadi's sentence was checked by a high ranking mufti.[8]

Unlike the proceedings in the Shariʿa courts that were adversarial and public, those followed by the regional councils and the *Majlis al-Ahkam* were inquisitorial and took place in camera. There was no public trial and parties and witnesses were questioned and heard not in order to present their cases, but only to establish the facts and create a dossier, containing all information necessary for the final decision. The minutes we find in the *sijills* of the *Majlis al-Ahkam* were meant for internal use and not for the parties. They contain a summary of the dossier that was submitted to the *Majlis al-Ahkam* and the *verbatim* text of the decision. The complete dossier with all relevant documents and the decision would be sent to the Khedive's Household (*Maʿiyya*) for an *exequatur*. In the margin of the *sijill* the scribe would record the number and date of the covering letter with which the dossier was forwarded and the date of the Khedive's decision.

The principal elements of the record of our case, which is typical for all cases involving injuries, are the following:

- the investigation of the complaint, consisting of the statements of the plaintiff, the accused and witnesses and medical reports on the victim's injuries and their healing (1–5) (the numbers between brackets refer to the numbered outline of the document above)
- the decision of the qadi regarding the plaintiff's claims under the sharia; this decision is embedded in the proceedings before the state court and must be approved by the mufti of the council (6, 9)
- the examination of the handling of the case by the executive officials (7)
- the decision of the regional council concerning the punishment of the offender and the officials that handled the case or were otherwise involved in it and instructions to officials for the future if the case gave reason to do so (10)
- the review of that decision by the *Majlis al-Ahkam* (11)

Its scope, evidently, is much wider than that of the litigation before the qadi. In criminal cases Shariʿa courts dealt with the victim's private rights to damages and to demand retaliation for death of injuries or punitive satisfaction for insults and brawls. In our case the damages for the boy's injury were at stake. The regional councils and the *Majlis al-Ahkam*, on the other hand, examined the matter from the point of view of the administration and the public interest.

8 For the jurisdiction and competence of the qadi in criminal cases, see Rudolph Peters, "Islamic and secular criminal law in 19th century Egypt: The role and function of the qadi," *Islamic law and Society* 4 (1997): 70–90.

That means that they would look into the question of whether the behaviour of all persons concerned, including those charged with the investigation, deserved correction. The *Majlis al-Ahkam*, therefore, not only acted as a supreme court of criminal law, but also as a watchdog overseeing the proper functioning of the administration, meting out punishment to negligent officials and issuing instructions for the future wherever deemed necessary. In addition, the mufti of the *Majlis al-Ahkam* would check whether or not the qadi's sentence was correct. In the following I will concentrate on the issue of the grievous bodily harm inflicted in the boy and not discuss the way the *Majlis al-Ahkam* dealt with the officials who investigated the case.

3.2 *The Investigation*

The case started when the boy's father brought the incident to the notice of the district chief of Mit Ghamr:

> A man called Mahfuz Khunda, a resident of Dimas, Daqhaliyya Province, informed the district chief (*nazir qism*) of Mit Ghamr that he has a seven year old son called ʿAli Ghunaym, who was being taught the Koran in the school of the schoolmaster (*muʾaddib al-atfal*) in that village, called Mustafa al-Aswad, who for his teaching received one piaster weekly. When the boy came to the school on 9 Safar 1280 [26 July 1863], the aforementioned shaykh Mustafa asked him for the tuition, since it had not been paid for three weeks due to his [the father's] absence. His son then asked that teacher (*faqih*) for respite until he [the father] would return from the place of his absence at that time, but then the teacher slapped him with his hand on his face with the result that the signet ring left a mark on it. Thereupon he handed him over to shaykh ʿUmar Hassan, the assistant teacher (*ʿarif*) of the school, to let him recite and to beat him. The latter then also beat him, wielding a stick made of acacia wood [*sant*, acacia nilotica], which was used as *falaqa*, and hit the boy's right arm, which was fractured. Therefore he requested that what he had mentioned be investigated.

This is the first written report of the case we find in the minutes. However, from the dossier it is clear, as we shall see, that this was not the actual beginning of the investigation. The first one to report the incident was the boy's grandmother (who remained nameless in the minutes of the *Majlis al-Ahkam* but whose name we know from the Shariʿa sentence as she was a party in the trial before the qadi). Immediately after she learnt of the incident she went to the local *ʿumda*. Upon hearing her complaint he summoned both teachers for questioning. However, he did not make an official report, but sent the boy with one of his men to the district centre, in order that the boy be examined by the government doctor there. The boy's father accompanied the boy and notified the deputy district head, who made a report and ordered that the boy be medically examined. Since the doctor had urgent business elsewhere, the boy was not examined until the next day. He then was sent to the hospital in al-Mansura for treatment and further investigations were carried out by the provincial administration (*mudiriyya*) in that town.

There, the father was asked to confirm the statement he had made earlier at the district centre, which he did. However, shortly thereafter he died. Then the boy's grandmother, with whom he was apparently living and who had been appointed as his guardian, was called in for questioning. She confirmed what the boy's father had said before and added:

> On the day the boy had been wounded, some children of the school came to her house to inform her of what had happened. She immediately went to the school to find out the facts of the matter and met the boy on her way to the school, clutching his arm. When she asked him what had happened, he told her as stated above. She then took him with her to Abu al-Majd ʿAbd al-Rahman, the *ʿumda* of the village. When she informed him of the matter, there were with him a number a people, some of whose names she specified. The *ʿumda* then summoned the schoolmaster, who admitted to him that after he had beaten the boy, he had handed him over to the assistant teacher and had ordered him to beat him because he had difficulties in memorising [the Koran] and that the assistant schoolmaster had administered a beating to him with a stick made of the wood of Indian cotton. (4.2)

When the accused were first called in for questioning at the *mudiriyya*, they denied everything. The headmaster even had claimed that he had not been at school on that particular day, having assisted at a funeral. This was confirmed by the assistant teacher (4.1). Thereupon those who had been present in the *ʿumda*'s office were questioned and they corroborated the woman's statements. Confronted with these testimonies the headmaster admitted before the provincial authorities that he had beaten the boy with a stick made of the wood of the cotton plant because the boy had problems in memorising the Koran and that he then had handed the boy over to his assistant. The assistant admitted that he also had beaten the boy with that stick and that that had been the cause of the boy's fracture. This, however, had happened inadvertently, because he was blind. (4.4)

3.3 *Sentencing*

When the boy's fracture had healed, the chief physician of the state hospital sent a medical report, in which he explained that although the bone had knit together, the boy could not move his forearm since the joint had got locked. Further he notified the administration that the hospital had spent 138 piasters and 26 *fidda* on the boy's drugs and food. Now the case was ready for being heard by the qadi of al-Mansura. The trial, which took place on 28 Rabiʿ I 1280 [12 September 1863], about six weeks after the incident, has been discussed above. The minutes of the decision of the *Majlis al-Ahkam* contain a summarised report of the trial. The sentence was then approved by the mufti of the regional council.

Before the council could give a decision, an investigation took place on whether the defendants had been convicted previously. The result was negative.

The Council regarded the following facts as being proven:

> During the investigation of the matter shaykh Mustafa al-Aswad has finally admitted that after he had beaten that boy on his feet with a stick of Indian cotton wood, as usual in schools, because it was difficult for him to memorise, he had handed him over to the assistant teacher, named ʿUmar Hassan, in order to let him recite. The aforementioned assistant teacher admitted that the master had given him not only permission as stated before [i.e. to let the boy recite], but also to beat him. He then had beaten the boy in that situation with the aforementioned wooden stick, with the result that his arm broke. However, that had happened accidentally and not wilfully, because he is blind.

Concerning the assistant teacher, the Council decided not to impose any punishment in view of the Shariʿa sentence ordering him to pay damages for the injury, "considering the fact that he is blind and has no previous convictions," and only to condemn him, in addition to the obligation imposed by the qadi, to pay to the *mudiriyya* the sum of 138 piasters and 26 *fidda*, being the costs of the victim's medical treatment. In addition, the Council ruled that "he and his likes are instructed to abstain in the future entirely from beating."

The headmaster was sentenced to imprisonment "in the provincial prison for the period of one month, to teach him a lesson and as an example for others, (…) taking into account that he neither has previous convictions." The ground for his punishment was not related to the beating, but the fact that he had made a false statement during the investigation. The Council examined the question of whether the headmaster had ordered or permitted the assistant teacher to beat the boy, but decided that this permission could not be a ground for punishment, arguing:

> that the aforementioned shaykh Mustafa has not admitted that he has given permission to the assistant teacher to beat the boy; that his denial is not taken into account since it has been established by the testimony of witnesses that he has acknowledged in their presence that this [permission] was given because he [the boy] had difficulties in memorising; that, however, it cannot be inferred from this permission that he had the intention that the beating would be administered as it actually occurred, but only that he intended it to be administered in the way that is usual in Koran schools.

After the Mufti of the *Majlis al-Ahkam* had endorsed the sentence of the qadi of al-Mansura, the *Majlis al-Ahkam* confirmed the sentence of the Regional Council. The *Majlis al-Ahkam* only objected against the instruction forbidding schoolmasters to beat their pupils,

> since in schools as a rule it is sometimes unavoidable to chastise the children because good education depends on it. Therefore a prohibition of chastisement cannot be approved. But it is neither permitted that a chastisement is of such a nature as to cause damage, since what has happened [in this case] was excessive.

Therefore, the *Majlis al-Ahkam* ordered that the Chief Mufti and other religious dignitaries draft an instruction concerning the methods and limits of how schoolmasters were allowed to chastise their pupils.

4 The Various Accounts of the Events

We may assume that the statements of the parties, recorded during the investigation and the trial were subjected to a process of selection and logical arrangement. This, however, is impossible to prove. What we can establish is that the clerks, confronted with several contradictory versions of the facts, tried to create a "clean" dossier by presenting only those accounts that at first sight appeared logical and plausible and by leaving out "abnormal" or legally irrelevant details. This dossier, which constituted the basis for the decision of the regional council and the *Majlis al-Ahkam*, must have contained the reports of the plaintiffs, the reports of the questioning of the accused and of the witnesses, the medical reports and, in this case, the sentence of the qadi. Unfortunately, these full dossiers are not available anymore (although they may be reconstructed by going through the *sijills* of the police, the provincial administrations and the regional courts). What we find in the records of the *Majlis al-Ahkam* is a summary of these dossiers, drafted by the clerks of the *Majlis al-Ahkam* after the session where the decision was taken. Details that were irrelevant to the final decision were sometimes left out. It even occurred that the summarising was too drastic and details were omitted that later appear in the text of the final decision. An example in our case is that the verdict of the Council mentions that the headmaster struck the boy on the soles of his feet, whereas this is not recorded in the summarised report of his questioning. This detail must have been included in the full dossier, or else the Council's decision would not have mentioned it.

Concerning the qadi's sentence, we still do not know very much about how the statements made during the court session were drafted. My impression is that the authorities charged with investigating the case (the provincial administration (*mudiriyya*) in the regions and the police (*dabtiyya*) in the cities) would assist the plaintiffs and the witnesses in formulating their claims and testimonies and that the court clerks, who would record their statements, would edit or reformulate them to clarify their legal implications. Most legally irrelevant details, i.e. details that would not in any way affect the liability under the Shariʿa (such as the fact the beating may have been prompted by the arrears in the payment of the tuition) are left out.

In the narratives of the events, we find the following differences regarding the presentation of the facts.

The motive for the beating. When the father reported the incident, he suggested that the beating of the boy was motivated by the fact that the father was in arrears with the payment of the tuition. Both the accused, on the other hand, emphasised that the boy was beaten because he had difficulties in memorising the Koran.

The headmaster's instructions to his assistant. Both the father and the grandmother in their initial statements, as well as the assistant teacher in his reply before the Shariʿa court, reported that the headmaster had ordered or given permission to the assistant master to chastise the boy. Although the headmaster had confirmed this during the first questioning by the *ʿumda*, he later denied it.

The nature of the chastisement. The father and the grandmother claimed that the headmaster had slapped the boy in his face and did not hit him with a stick. On the other hand, the headmaster admitted having beaten the boy with a stick on the soles of his feet.[9] The assistant teacher claimed in his reply before the Shariʿa court, that the headmaster had also hit the boy on his arm and that the fracture could have been caused by either of them. As to the assistant's teacher's chastisement, the boy's father reported that he had struck the boy with a *falaqa* made of wood of the acacia tree (*sant*), whereas the assistant master maintained that he used a stick made of the wood of the Indian cotton plant.

In the following I will analyse these differences and show that in the course of the proceedings the clerks and judges, often without further argumentation, accepted the version that conformed to their idea of normalcy. This was essentially the headmaster's version. His – successful – strategy to exonerate himself was based on the following assertions that were all accepted by the court:

- that the reason for punishing the boy was pedagogical;
- that he himself had first punished the boy with an ordinary bastinado on the soles of his feet, administered with a light stick;
- that he had nothing to do with the way the assistant master punished the boy.

The first point is the motive of the beating: did the boy incur the punishment for not memorising the Koran, or was it an act of revenge on the boy for his father's default in paying his tuition? The boy's father and grandmother claimed that the boy was beaten for the latter reason. The schoolmaster, however, realised that it would create a bad impression of him if it was accepted that he had chastised the boy for something of which he was innocent. Therefore, he maintained that the chastisement was prompted by the boy's difficulties in memorising the Koran, presenting the punishment as a routine matter, a pedagogical correction that, inadvertently and regrettably, had resulted in a serious injury due to the blindness of his assistant. This latter version of the events was accepted by the Regional Council and the *Majlis al-Ahkam*.

The investigators and the Council focused on the assistant master as the one whose beating had caused the boy's fracture. However, neither his motive for the beating nor the circumstances surrounding it played a role in the proceedings and the final outcome. In the trial before the qadi, they were not mentioned since the only question that matters for establishing a financial liability under the Shariʿa in cases of homicide and wounding is that of who caused the death or the injury. The liability does not require that the person who killed or wounded acted at fault, e.g. on the ground of criminal intent or neglect. Nor does the motive of the person who caused the damage affect in

9 The fact that the beating was administered on the soles of the boy's feet was only mentioned in decision of the Council and not in the report of the questioning of the accused.

any way the liability. Therefore, the trial before the qadi of al-Mansura had only one issue: the question of whose beating caused the boy's injury. As we have seen, the qadi held the assistant master liable. Since the Council regarded the payment of damages as an adequate penalty, it did not consider the possibility of imposing additional punitive measures for the determination of which the motive might have been important. The Council's decision was confirmed by the *Majlis al-Ahkam*.

Although the qadi did not hold the headmaster liable for the fracture of the boy's arm, the Council could have examined whether he had committed an offence punishable under statute law and sentenced the headmaster if his beating was regarded as exceeding the limits of what was normal. The headmaster, however, successfully presented his role in the incident as an ordinary and acceptable form of disciplining: Without further argumentation, the investigators and the Council, in spite of the statements of the boy's father and grandmother that the boy had been maltreated because his father had not paid the school fees, accepted his explanation that the beating was a punishment for the boy's bad scholastic performance.

According to the accepted custom in Koran schools, the teachers were entitled to discipline their pupils with a light bastinado. This is exactly how the headmaster presented his beating of the boy. There were, however, two other accounts, that were implicitly rejected by the Council. The boy's father and grandmother maintained that he has slapped the boy in his face, whereby his signet ring left an imprint on his face (*aththar fihi*). This might indicate that the act was prompted by sudden anger because the boy had not brought the money for the school fees. This would be inconsistent with the headmaster's version that he disciplined the boy for pedagogical reasons. The assistant teacher claimed that the headmaster had beaten the boy with a stick before him and shared in the responsibility for the boy's injury. However, being blind, he cannot be regarded as a reliable eyewitness. In the Shariʿa court, however, the beating administered by the headmaster was no issue, since the plaintiff did not sue him. The Council, holding as proven that the headmaster had beaten the boy on the soles of his feet with a stick of cottonwood, regarded this implicitly as a normal form of chastisement in schools and did not regard this as a ground for punishing the headmaster.

Although he had originally admitted it, the headmaster during later interrogations denied that he had instructed his assistant to beat the boy. The other parties, however, insisted that the assistant teacher had acted by order or by express permission of the headmaster. It is clear that the headmaster wanted to exonerate himself by denying any responsibility for the way his assistant chastised the boy. In view of his earlier admissions and the evidence against him, the Council held as proven that the assistant teacher has acted under orders. However, the Council argued that these instructions must be understood as an order to beat the boy in a way that is usual in schools and not as a command to punish the boy in the way the assistant master actually used. Therefore the Council exonerated the headmaster from any responsibility for the boy's injury. nevertheless the headmaster was sentenced to one month imprisonment. The ground for this punishment was the fact that he had made false statements by denying that he had given instructions to his assistant.

5 Conclusions

The documents that I have analysed here show that during the investigation and the hearing of the incident, its account was streamlined and made to conform to what the clerks and judges regarded as an ordinary and routine event in a Koran school. Some details were not further investigated because they were immaterial for the application of legal categories. There are two main versions of the story. According to his relatives, the boy, when he told the headmaster that he had not brought the tuition money, was slapped by the latter, whereby the headmaster's signet ring left a mark on his face. Subsequently, the headmaster instructed his assistant to give the boy a thrashing, for which the assistant use the heavy wooden *falaqa*. Due to his blindness, the assistant struck him on his arm with the result that it became fractured. The account, however, that was finally accepted by the Council, was essentially the headmaster's version, except that the Council regarded as proven that the headmaster had given instructions to his assistant to chastise the boy. According to this account the headmaster first gave the boy a bastinado with a light stick on the soles of his feet, because the boy had been negligent in memorising the Koran. Thereupon, he ordered his assistant to punish him, which the latter did, also using a light stick. How the arm then was broken remains unexplained. Since the type of instrument was irrelevant for establishing the assistant's liability, the matter was not further examined by the Council, although it is highly improbable that he would have broken the boy's arm with the chalk of a cotton plant, as mentioned in the documents.

Legal documents never present the exact words of statements of the parties. This is true of documents like contracts, especially those recorded by public writers or notaries. But also the statements taken from parties and witnesses during civil or criminal proceedings do not reflect the exact words, but are edited in order to construct a logical case, including the elements recognisable by and relevant for those who must work with these documents. In this paper

I have shown that during the course of the investigation of a criminal case and in the process of sentencing, the different versions of the facts are transformed into an authoritative account containing almost exclusively the legally relevant elements and presenting a logical and plausible narrative. The richness of often contradictory details found in the statements of the parties and witnesses makes way for a coherent account shorn of its irrelevant or troublesome details. This happens at various stages. First, in recording the statements of those involved in the case. This, however, is difficult to prove. But secondly in the compilation of the dossier by the investigators and its summarising by the court clerks after sentencing. Historians who want to use these documents as sources for social history ought to be aware of the distortions they contain.

References

Dupret, Baudouin (2005) "The practice of judging: The Egyptian judiciary at work in a personal status case" in M. Khalid Masud, R. Peters and D.S. Powers (eds.) *Dispensing justice in Islamic courts: qadis, procedures and evidence* Leiden: Brill: 143–168.

Peters, Rudolph (1999) "Administrators and magistrates: The development of a secular judiciary in Egypt, 1842–1871" *Die Welt des Islams* 39: 378–97.

Peters, Rudolph (1997) "Islamic and secular criminal law in 19th century Egypt: The role and function of the qadi" *Islamic law and Society* 4: 70–90.

Peters, Rudolph (1990) "Murder on the Nile: Homicide Trials in 19th Century Egyptian Shariʿa Courts" *Die Welt des Islams* 30: 95–115.

Legal Punishment

CHAPTER 13

Prisons and Marginalisation in Nineteenth-Century Egypt

Al-sijn li'l-jadʿan

['Prisons are for real men']
Egyptian saying

One of society's most forceful instruments of exclusion and marginalisation is its penal system.* Punishment of offenders may result in definitive removal from society, either by physical elimination, as in the case of death penalty or by permanent incarceration, as in the case of life long imprisonment or deportation. Punishment may also consist in temporary removal from society. But this may have a more lasting effect: Stigmatisation attached to having served a prison sentence may lead to the social or moral exclusion or marginalisation of released inmates. Corporal punishment, at least if it does not leave permanent visible traces as in the case of amputation of parts of the body, does not have such an impact. The victim remains in his social environment and unless the offence for which the victim was punished was considered a particularly heinous one by his community, the penalty will not have an enduring effect on his position in society.

In this paper I will try to examine the impact, in terms of stigmatisation, social exclusion and marginalisation, of the Egyptian prison system on its inmates during the nineteenth century, before the British occupation of 1882. I will argue that prison sentences had no strong stigmatising effect and that released prisoners were not marginalised socially. It is my assumption that the degree of marginalisation or social exclusion of ex-convicts is related to at least

* I want to express my thanks to the staff of the Egyptian National Archives for their assistance in making available the relevant documents for this study. I owe a great debt of gratitude to Khaled Fahmy, who generously shared his extensive knowledge of these archives and helped me in many other ways during my research.

 | DOI:10.1163/9789004420625_014

five factors: The knowledge in the local community of the ex-convict's background; the attitude of the population at large towards the offences for which the inmates had been convicted; the homogeneity of the prison population; the relationship between the actual duration of imprisonment and the seriousness of the offence for which the inmate was convicted; and the degree of isolation to which the inmates were subjected.

The first factor is of course a necessary condition for stigmatisation and exclusion. If a released prisoner could keep his past secret, there would be no social exclusion at all. Furthermore, it is obvious that stigmatisation depends on the attitude of the ex-convict's social environment towards the legal system. If many people were in prison for offences that were regarded as criminal by the state and the ruling elite but not by the majority of the population, prison sentences would lose their stigmatising effect. Another factor with an impact on marginalisation of ex-convicts is the homogeneity of the prison population. If it were public knowledge that among prison inmates there were not only convicted offenders, but also political prisoners or those detained for their debts, the social stigmatisation of released prisoners would be less severe. The same applied to convicts who served their sentences not in penitentiaries, but in institutions such as the army or factories not primarily intended for punishment and imprisonment. Another mitigating factor on stigmatisation is the presence in prison of members of the middle or higher classes. Stigmatisation would probably have been greater had all prisoners belonged to the lower classes and less had there been a considerable number of prisoners from other social strata as well. In addition, I would argue that arbitrariness in the penal system would also have worked against the stigmatisation of ex-convicts. If the length of imprisonment was not proportionate to the seriousness of the offence, but more or less arbitrary, the lengths of prison terms would not be a reliable measure for the gravity of the crime. Of course this might also work the other way, in that persons who had served short sentences might also have been suspected of committing serious crimes. However, in combination with the other factors, I am convinced that the mitigating effect was stronger. A final but important factor is the degree of isolation in which the inmates were kept. If inmates had the possibility of remaining in contact with their families and relatives or others outside the prison system, it is plausible that, after their release, it proved easier for them to be re-integrated into society.

Little is known about the Egyptian system of judicial punishment before the British occupation.[1] To the best of my knowledge, Egypt lacks the richness of

1 For the administration of criminal justice, see Rudolph Peters, 'Islamic and Secular Criminal Law in 19th Century Egypt: The Role and Function of the Qadi,' *Islamic Law and Society* 4

sources on the subject found in most Western European countries, including official and press reports, diaries, and literary texts that add liveliness and detail to institutional history. This is particularly true of sources reflecting the attitude of society towards released prisoners. In the absence of such first-hand information my conclusions are by necessity inferential and to some extent speculative.

The main sources for this article are official documents, located in the Egyptian National Archives (*Dar al-Watha'iq al-Qawmiyya*, henceforth DWQ). They consist in the first place of criminal codes and related decrees and documents. I have also made use of the records of criminal cases, especially the records of trials of prison guards for neglect of duty, and of five registers (the only ones that could be traced) listing the inmates of the Alexandria Prison for the years 1847–1852 and 1861–1869. I also went through some years of the official journal, *al-Waqa'iʿ al-Misriyya*, which summarily recorded the trials in the Khedival or Viceregal Council [*Divan-i Hidivi*]. All this is supplemented by the scarce information that can be culled from the publications of contemporary Western observers.

1 Imprisonment in Nineteenth-Century Egypt

In 1855, a certain Muhammad ʿAli was arrested on a charge of theft. Goods were impounded from his home that he was accused of having stolen. The victim, Muhammad Rifʿat *Efendi*, living in the Cairo Bab al-Khalq quarter, accused him of having stolen money and goods from his home with a total value of about 18,000 piasters. Muhammad ʿAli declared that the victim's wife, with whom he claimed to have spent a day and a night, had given him a sum of money of her own free will, part of which he had spent on the goods that were impounded in his quarters. The price of the goods was recovered from the seller and was returned to Muhammad Rifʿat *Efendi*, together with the rest of the money that in the meantime had been found in Muhammad ʿAli's lodgings. At this point the suspect admitted that he had in fact stolen the money. When his criminal record was examined, it appeared that he had been arrested twice before, once for theft of a camel – for which he later was proven innocent – and once for pretending to be a police spy (*bassas*). Both times he had managed to escape from custody. Taking this into consideration, he was sentenced to lifelong forced labour in the fortifications of *al-Qanatir al-Khayriyya* (also called

(1997) 70–90; and Peters, 'Administrators and Magistrates: The Development of a Secular Judiciary in Egypt, 1842–1871,' *Die Welt des Islams* 39 (1999) 378–97.

al-Qalʿa al-Saʿidiyya). Later, he was transferred to the Alexandria Dockyards Prison (*Liman* or *Tarsanat Iskandariyya*). In 1858, he was drafted into the army to serve the remainder of his sentence as a soldier. However, while serving in the military, he committed another theft and was sent back to the Alexandria Dockyards Prison. When the amnesty of March 1861 was announced, he was released from the Alexandria prison. However, being regarded as incorrigible (*shaqi*) he was not set free but transferred to the Department of Industry (*Diwan al-Waburat wa-l-ʿAmaliyyat*, also referred to as *Diwan al-Fabriqat wa-l-ʿAmaliyyat*) as forced labour. From there he escaped again. Upon being discovered by a police spy, he threatened the latter with a knife and wounded a person who came to the policeman's rescue. But he could not save his skin and was apprehended. On 16 September 1861, the Cairo Police Department sent him to the Alexandria Dockyards Prison in order to complete his life sentence. However, when Khedive Ismaʿil succeeded Saʿid, he reversed this decision and instructed the *Majlis al-Ahkam* to review the cases of inmates of the Alexandria Dockyards Prison with life sentences or unspecified terms. On 19 November 1866, his sentence was commuted to five years forced labour in the Alexandria Prison. However, since he was classified as belonging to the 'group of evildoers' (*zumrat al-ashrar*) mentioned in the *Qanun al-Sultani*, the penal code of 1852–53, he was not to be released after this period unless it had become clear that he had become honest and of good behaviour and he could find a relative willing to be his guarantor (*damin*).[2]

My first reaction upon reading this account was regret that this jailbird did not write his memoirs. He was familiar with most of the larger prisons in Egypt and the story of his life behind bars would be invaluable for the penal history of Egypt. The account as we have it is representative of the type of sources we have at our disposal. They are factual and written from an official point of view. Their value lies in the information they impart regarding the functioning of the penal institutions, but they do not give information about the experiences of the inmates.

2 Egyptian National Archives [*Dar al-Wathaʾiq al-Qawmiyya*, hereafter DWQ; note that the Arabic letters *sin* and *lam* used in the classing of documents have been rendered S and L, respectively], S 7/10/29, *Majlis al-Ahkam, al-Madabit al-Sadira*, pp. 135–136, *madbata* 133, dated 11 *Rajab* 1282/30 November 1865; order issued to the Ministry of the Navy (under whose jurisdiction the Alexandria Dockyards Prison came) dated 21 *Rajab* 1281/20 December 1864, DWQ, S 1/1/30, *Maʿiyya Saniyya, al-Awamir al-Sadira*, p. 90 and 121; DWQ, L 2/2/5 (old 530), *Dabtiyyat Misr, Sadir al-Aqalim*, p. 24, no. 7, letter to *Muhafazat Iskandariyya*, dated 12 Rabiʿ I 1278/17 September 1861 (this is the letter with which Muhammad ʿAli was sent to the Alexandria Dockyards Prison).

As illustrated by Muhammad 'Ali's story, imprisonment was the principal form of punishment in nineteenth-century Egypt. The Egyptian penal system, like all nineteenth-century systems, rested on three pillars: capital punishment, corporal punishment (flogging or caning) and imprisonment, usually combined with hard labour and sometimes with deportation. Capital punishment had become rare in the second half of the nineteenth century. Travellers report that the number of executions decreased during Mehmed 'Ali's reign because of greater public security brought about by a more efficient police force.[3] This trend continued until the British occupation.[4] The number of capital offences was small. With very few exceptions,[5] capital punishment was only enforced on the strength of a *Shari'a* sentence of retribution (*qisas*) for homicide, pronounced by the *qadi* and approved by the Khedive. Corporal punishment meant flogging (with a maximum of 600 stripes[6]), which was a frequently applied form of punishment for petty crime, especially in the countryside. In 1861 it was abolished and replaced with detention (*habs*).[7] By then, imprisonment had practically become the only form of punishment.

The story of Muhammad 'Ali is informative on several characteristic traits of the Egyptian prison system in the nineteenth century. In the first place the account shows that the term specified in a sentence could be subject to all kinds of changes. The period one actually spent in prison was often shorter than the time specified in the sentence, mainly as a consequence of general amnesties, but also as a result of escapes. Prison security was not very tight and escapes were frequent in spite of the severe punishments to which guards were sentenced if they let prisoners escape. Usually they had to serve the remaining part of the escaped inmate's term. Secondly, it becomes evident from the account that there were a variety of penal institutions and that, in addition, convicts were sometimes sent to the army instead of completing their sentences in penal institutions. Finally it demonstrates that attempts were made, although

3 John Bowring, 'Report on Egypt and Candia,' *Great Britain Parliamentary Papers vol. 21* (1840), p. 123; James August St. John, *Egypt and Mohammed Ali, or Travels in the Valley of the Nile*, vol. 2 (London, 1834) p. 474; see also G. Guémard, *Une Oeuvre française: Les Réformes en Egypte, d'Ali-Bey El Kébir à Méhémet-Ali, 1760–1848* (Cairo, 1936) p. 257.

4 H. Couvidou, *Étude sur l'Égypte contemporaine* (Cairo, 1873) p. 307.

5 I have seen only one such sentence pronounced against a soldier charged with having willingly allowed a prisoner to escape; order to the *Muhafiz* of the *Qal'a Sa'idiyya*, dated 3 *Rabi'* II 1272/13 December 1855, DWQ, S 1/1/5, *Sadir al-Awamir al-'Aliyya*, p. 144, doc. 15.

6 *Al-Qanun al-Muntakhab* (1844), Art. 111.

7 *Amr 'Ali* of 26 *Dhu al-Hijja* 1277/6 July 1861; Amin Sami, *Taqwim al-Nil* (Cairo, 1928–1936) vol. 3/1, p. 375. The interdiction to flogging was repeated one year later, in an instruction to newly-founded regional courts; *Irada Saniyya* of 22 *Dhu al-Qa'da* 1278; Sami, *Taqwim*, 3/1, p. 403.

not very consistently, to single out habitual offenders and keep them permanently imprisoned. In what follows I will discuss these and other aspects of the Egyptian prison system as it evolved between 1830 and 1882. I will restrict myself to imprisonment served in Egyptian jails. Deportation and imprisonment in the Sudan was also part of the penal system and applied as a punishment for serious offences. However, due to the limited availability of the archival sources we know very little about the conditions of the Sudanese labour prisons.[8]

2 Attitude of the Public towards the Penal System

The attitude of the Egyptians towards the penal system was ambivalent. On the one hand they expected the state to provide a minimum level of security and law and order by means of the penal system, and appealed to it themselves as one of the available means to secure their rights. On the other hand, their attitude must have been influenced by the widespread mistrust of the government. The relationship between the state and its rural subjects had come to be reduced to the collection of men for military service and *corvée* and of taxes. The idea that the state ought to protect the interests of the entire population was not common in nineteenth-century Egypt. Most Egyptians saw clearly that the state mainly served the interests of the Turkish elite. This awareness affected the way they looked at criminal justice.

Of course, people would accept it when 'ordinary' criminals like thieves and murderers were punished. However, many of the offences listed in the penal codes and punished by the state were based on norms not shared by ordinary Egyptians. Some of these, they realised, only served the interests of the state and the ruling group; others patently conflicted with their established customs, such as those connected with honour or feuding. Violations of such norms were not looked upon as moral transgressions, and their punishment was regarded as a tool of oppression or exploitation by the state. Those sentenced for tax evasion, draft-dodging, desertion, sheltering deserters, escaping *corvée*, and official negligence, were certainly not seen as criminals, but rather as victims of the arbitrariness and oppression of the state. The same would be true for those who had killed in the context of a feud or in order to vindicate the honour of one's family or tribe.

Inmates held for 'official' or 'state' offences (as opposed to offences rooted in norms shared by the entire population) often formed a considerable segment of

8 To the best of my knowledge, the registers of the Sudan provinces in the Egyptian National Archive have not yet been catalogued.

the prison population. The register of admissions of the Alexandria Dockyards Prison for 1861 is a case in point. Of the 401 persons who entered the prison between 30 March and 21 May 1861 and between 1 August and 3 September 1861, 170 were imprisoned for desertion and another 26 for military offences such as absence without leave, malingering and insubordination, and 10 for offences related to the draft.

3 Modes of Imprisonment

From the texts of the successive penal codes it is not possible to reconstruct the penal system that was operative in nineteenth-century Egypt. The terminology used in these laws was copied from the foreign models that had inspired these codes and did not necessarily apply to the Egyptian system.[9] This is especially true for articles 123 to 194 of the *Qanun al-Muntakhab* (henceforth QM) of 1844, that were translated from the French Penal Code of 1810 and of the first three chapters of the *Qanun al-Sultani* (henceforth QS) of 1852–1853 that corresponded to the Ottoman Penal Code of 1850. Moreover, the terminology was not uniform: sometimes the same term is used for different modalities of imprisonment, whereas in other instances the same category is referred to by various terms. In order to reconstruct the prison system, we have to rely in the first place on the earliest Egyptian legislation, that was not inspired by foreign examples (i.e. the Penal Code of 1829, the *Qanun al-Filaha* of 1830, and parts of the QM) and on court records. The essential traits of the system hardly changed during our period. A first point we have to realise is that convicted offenders, if they were fit for military service, were often sent to the army by way of punishment, instead of serving a sentence of hard labour in prison.[10]

Imprisonment consisted of simple detention (*habs*), which could be made more severe by putting the prisoner on bread and water or in solitary confinement (both for a period not exceeding three weeks),[11] forced labour in regional

9 See Rudolph Peters, 'The Origins of Nineteenth Century Egyptian Criminal Legislation Enacted Before 1883,' in *Law, Society, and National Identity in Africa*, edited by J.M. Abun-Nasr a.o. (Hamburg, 1991) pp. 211–225.

10 Army service was mentioned as a form of punishment in the *Qanun al-Filaha* of 1245 (arts. 15 and 17) and the Penal Code of 1265 (arts. 8, 11, 32). Although not listed in the QS as a separate form of punishment, young offenders who were fit for military service were often sent to the army. See, for example, DWQ, L 1/20/1 *Muhafazat Misr, al-qararat al-sadira bi-majlis Muhafazat Misr*, p. 19, no. 22, dated 18 *Rabi*ʿ II 1272/28 December 1855; and, p. 33, no. 29, 12 *Jumada* I 1272/20 January 1856.

11 *Amr ʿAli* of 26 *Dhu al-Hijja* 1277/6 July 1861; Sami, *Taqwim*, 3/1, p. 375.

or national prisons, or forced labour with deportation to the Sudan. In the archival material, I have not found other categories, although the names and localities would sometimes change. Women would not be deported to the Sudan and were held in special women prisons.

Simple detention meant that convicts were imprisoned in the police prisons in the big cities, the prison in the Cairo Citadel, and prisons in the various provincial capitals. Convicts sentenced to forced labour in their own region were also sent to the provincial prisons.[12] At the national level there was the Alexandria Dockyards Prison that continued to function throughout our period and fell under the authority of the Department of the Navy (*Diwan al-Bahriyya*). From about 1853 until the early 1860s there was another national labour prison near the fortifications at al-Qanatir al-Khayriyya (called *al-Qalʿa al-Saʿidiyya*), which in 1857 was transferred from the Ministry of War (*Diwan al-Jihadiyya*) to the Department of Industry.[13] In the early 1850s various industrial establishments (*tarsana*), such as the one in Bulaq,[14] employed convicts. From the mid-1850s until late 1864, the judicial councils sentenced offenders to be put at the disposal of the Department of Industry. They must have formed a labour pool for work in various state factories.[15] Prisons fell under the authority of various departments, such as the local police forces, the governorates (*mudiriyya, muhafaza*), the Ministry of War, the Department of the Navy and the Department of Industry. The administrative organisation of the prison system was therefore diverse. A small measure of uniformity was introduced by the appointment of a special inspector of prisons in February 1865,

12 The QM (art. 17) speaks of 'employment in government building sites in the district of [the convict's] origin' (*istikhdam fi l-abniya al-miriyya al-mawjuda fi al-ma'muriyya al-lati huwa minha*). The QS refers to this punishment as 'employment in lowly jobs' (*al-tashghil/al-istikhdam fi khidamat dani'a/ashghal sufliyya*).

13 Order of 16 *Dhu al-Hijja* 1273/7 August 1857, DWQ, Card index s.v. *sijn*, Box 14 *Turki*, leaf 132, doc. 398. By the end of 1862 the *Qalʿa Saʿidiyya* was still in use as a prison; see order of 27 *Jumada* II 1279/20 December 1862, DWQ, *Maʿiyya Saniyya, daftar* 1905, p. 36, doc. 23 (Based on DWQ card index s.v. *sijn*).

14 Reference is made to prisoners in a large factory in Bulaq in an order dated 29 *Ramadan* 1252/7 January 1837. DWQ, *Mulkiyya Turki*, 5 (old), p. 174, doc. 174. (based on DWQ Card index s.v. *sijn*). See also DWQ, *Majlis al-Ahkam*, Box 2, doc. 2/63, dated 16 *Dhu al-Hijja* 1266/23 October 1850, and doc. 2/82, dated 24 *Dhu al-Hijja* 1266/31 October 1850.

15 Letter dated 24 *Jumada* I 1281/25 October 1864 to *Majlis Isti'naf Qibli*, on the abolition of the department of works (*al-Waburat wa-l-ʿAmaliyyat*); DWQ, S 7/4/33, *Majlis al-Ahkam, Sadir al-aqalim al-qibliyya*, p. 83, doc. 21. Order to *Hukumdar al-Sudan* no. 5, dated 21 *Safar* 1272/2 November 1855, mentioning that a person was sentenced to life imprisonment in the *tarsanat al-Khartum*; DWQ, S 1/1/5, *al-Maʿiyya al-Saniyya, Sadir al-Awamir al-ʿAliyya*, p. 79.

with the task of checking the conditions of the prisons and the punctual release of the prisoners.[16]

The local prisons were relatively small and held a few dozen prisoners. In 1856 the two principal Cairo jails – the police jail and the jail of the governorate – held 81 and 32 prisoners, respectively.[17] The provincial prisons contained comparable numbers of prisoners. The large prisons were the Alexandria Dockyards Prison and, between 1853 and the early 1860s, the *Qalʿa al-Saʿidiyya*. On the basis of the prison registers and other records it is possible to make a rough calculation of the number of their inmates. In 1845, a French traveller estimated the total number of prisoners in Cairo and Alexandria together at 300 inmates.[18] The Alexandria Dockyards Prison housed in the late 1840 ca. 450 and in the early 1860s between 250 and 650 convicts.[19] The *Qalʿa al-Saʿidiyya* was a larger penitentiary. In October–November 1855, it housed some 1,100 to 1,200 prisoners, half of them Bedouin, and the wardens complained repeatedly that they did not have sufficient personnel for guard duties.[20] In August 1859, about 100 prisoners were detained the Cairo police jail, among them those held for debt.[21]

4 Prison Population

Not all prison inmates were convicted criminals. Most prisons also held suspects whose cases were still under investigation. That was standard procedure

16 Appointment of Salim Pasha al-Jazaʾirli, 9 *Ramadan* 1281/5 February 1865. Sami, *Taqwim*, 3/2, p. 597.

17 DWQ, S 1/8/42, *Sadir al-Maʿiyya al-Saniyya li-l-Dawawin wa-l-Aqalim wa-l-Muhafazat*, p. 593, doc. 261, dated 18 *Rajab* 1272/25 March 1856 to *Muhafazat Misr*.

18 Victor Schoelcher, *L'Égypte en 1845* (Paris, 1846), p. 30.

19 The figures over time were as follows: 1847: 450 inmates; 1860: 600 inmates; 1865: 400 inmates; 1866: 650 inmates; 1868: 250 inmates. I have found these figures with the help of the five *sijills* concerning the Alexandria Prison, by counting the number of prisoners that entered in a given year and multiplying it with the average period spent in the prison. Another source states that on 4 December 1862 the number of inmates was 443. See DWQ, S /7/10/23, *Majlis al-Ahkam, al-Madabit al-Sadira*, no. 893, dated 28 *Dhu al-Qaʿda* 1280, p. 132. The variation in these figures can be explained by the frequent amnesties. On the basis of the admittedly limited material, it would seem that amnesties were granted to ease overcrowding of the prisons.

20 Letter dated 29 *Safar* 1272 from the *Qalʿa Saʿidiyya* to the *Khazin Diwan Khidiwi* DWQ, *Maʿiyya Turki*, Box 8, leaf 11, doc. 58; letter dated 3 *Safar* 1272 from the *Qalʿa Saʿidiyya* to the *Katib al-Diwan al-Khidiwi*; and, leaf 12, doc. 474. There were 609 bedouins in the *Qalʿa Saʿidiyya* in 1855; see letter from *Wakil Nazir al-Jihadiyya* to *al-Maʿiyya al-Saniyya*, dated 8 *Muharram* 1272/20 September 1855 in DWQ, *Maʿiyya Turki*, Box 8, doc. 58.

21 Letter from *al-Maʿiyya al-Saniyya* to *Dabtiyyat Misr*, dated 4 *Muharram* 1276, DWQ, S 7/33/1, *Majlis al-Ahkam, Daftar Majmuʿ umur idara wa-ijraʾat*, p. 233.

in the local prisons, but occasionally, in complicated cases involving many persons, all suspects, witnesses and persons otherwise involved would be sent to the Alexandria Prison. Of the 78 persons imprisoned for homicide during the periods mentioned above, 67 were detained in connection with the killing by villagers of an unknown person from outside the village. Of these, 41 persons were released within 5 months for lack of evidence.[22] Another category of inmates were persons imprisoned for debt. As in Dickensian England, imprisonment for debt was common. Under Islamic law it is the only means a creditor has to enforce payment by his debtor.[23] It seems that it was not too difficult to have a person imprisoned on these grounds, until in February 1869 a decree was issued stipulating that a person could only be detained for debt if his debt was proven and the creditor was willing and capable of paying for the prisoner's maintenance.[24] The last category was political prisoners. These were mainly Bedouin.[25] It is sometimes difficult to distinguish between Bedouin who were imprisoned for robbery and those who had been taken hostage as a guarantee for the good behaviour of their tribes. I regularly came across Khedival orders issued to prison commanders instructing them to submit lists of the Bedouin inmates and to specify whether they had been imprisoned for a certain term or without a term.[26] During certain periods, e.g. in the 1860s, the Alexandria Dockyards Prison also served as a place of imprisonment for foreigners who had been sentenced to imprisonment by their consular courts. As a rule, they served short sentences of only a few weeks.[27] From the 1850s attempts were

22 Register of criminal inmates in the Alexandria Prison, DWQ, *Diwan al-tarsana*, 954 (old), *Qayd asma' al-madhnubin bi-liman tarsanat Iskandariyya*. There were no military prisons at that time. Soldiers would be sent to regular prisons.

23 See I. Schneider, 'Imprisonment in Pre-Classical and Classical Islamic Law,' *Islamic Law and Society* 2 (1995) 157–74.

24 Order of the *Majlis Khususi* no. 32, dated 5 *Dhu al-Qa'da* 1285/17 February 1869. DWQ, S 11/8/13, *Majlis al-Khususi, al-qararat wa-l-lawa'ih al-sadira*, no. 32.

25 See e.g. 8 *Muharram* 1272, *Wakil Nazir al-Jihadiyya* to *Ma'iyya*, Box 8 *Ma'iyya Turki, waraqa* 11, doc. 58: mentions that apart from the ordinary prisoners there were 609 bedouins in the *Qal'a Sa'idiyya*; Khedival order to *Diwan 'Umum Bahriyya Iskandariyya* dated 23 *Jumada* II 1272, DWQ, *Ma'iyya Saniyya, awamir, Daftar* 1884, p. 49, doc. 28: release of 71 Bedouin from the *liman* at the request of their *shaykh*; information taken from DWQ card index, s.v. *sijn*.

26 Order to send a list of all imprisoned Bedouins addressed to the commander of the *Qal'a Sa'idiyya* no. 20, dated 5 *Jumada* II 1272/12 February 1856. DWQ, S 1/1/5, *Ma'iyya Saniyya, Sadir al-Awamir al-'Aliyya*, p. 144; same order to the Alexandria Prison, dated 25 *Jumada* II 1272; and p. 70, doc. 29. *Diwan al-tarsana, sijill* 954, p. 131, 19 *Rajab* 1279/10 January 1863, entry of 82 Bedouins from Upper Egypt, referred to as *'urban ashqiya'*, aged between 10 and 70, without specification of crime or prison term.

27 See e.g. DWQ, *Diwan al-tarsana*, 956 (old), p. 14.

made to separate the various categories of prisoners.[28] It is not clear how successful these attempts were.

One of the characteristics of the Egyptian administration of justice was that the trials of criminal cases did not focus on individual defendants, but rather on the case itself. All those who were involved in a given case, however remotely, were objects of investigation in order to establish whether they had been negligent in preventing the offence. In connection with serious crimes such as murder or robbery, village sheikhs and village guards would be on trial too for neglect of duty and were often given sentences of several months or even years of hard labour. This was already usual during Mehmed ʿAli Pasha's reign.[29]

5 The Isolation of the Inmates from Society

In August 1848 a certain Umm Shahata from Suez informed the Cairo police that two *bintu* (a gold coin) and some gold and silver rings had been stolen from her. She had come from Suez to visit her brother and her sister's husband who were held in the police prison and to give them bread and money. She had wrapped the money and the rings, which she intended to sell, in a handkerchief and put them in a basket. While sitting together with other women near the gate of the police prison and distributing bread to her relatives and to other prisoners, she was robbed of her valuables.[30]

Prisoners, especially those in local prisons, could receive frequents visits. The main aims of imprisonment were basic – control of the prisoner's movements and, in case of forced labour, harnessing his capacity for work. The restrictions put on prisoners did not go beyond these two direct aims. I have not found indications of the existence of an explicit philosophy of punishment – other than the general notions of retribution and deterrence – that resulted in a specific penal policy. Prisons were located in normal houses, bought or rented for the purpose, in wards e.g. in the Cairo Citadel, and in sheds or barracks

28 See e.g. *Dhikr wazaʾif mutafarriʿa bi-l-majlis*, art. 5, in Filib Jallad, *Qamus al-idara wa-l-qadaʾ*, vol. 2 (Alexandria, 1890–1892) pp. 105–106, laying down that those held in custody and those held for debt at the local prisons had to be separated from the convicts, who in turn had to be separated according to the seriousness of their crimes.

29 Letter to the *Muhafiz of Alexandria* dated 5 *Safar* 1246/26 July 1830, informing him that 112 Turkish and Arab officials from Upper Egypt were on transport to Alexandria to serve a term of six months in the Alexandria Prison. DWQ, *Diwan Khediwi Turki, daftar* 757 (old), p. 35, doc. 117 (Information from the DWQ Card index, s.v. *sijn*).

30 DWQ, L /2/6/2, *Dabtiyyat Misr, Sadir*, no. 99, pp. 1–3, dated 24 *Ramadan* 1264/24 August 1848.

(*hasil*). Prisoners spent the night in large communal rooms and there were no individual cells until 1861 when, as mentioned above, solitary confinement was introduced in the police jails as an exceptional punitive measure. There was no special prison architecture based on precise ideas about the treatment of prisoners and aimed at maximum security against escapes. Prison buildings as a rule allowed the inmates to communicate with the outside world through the windows or thin walls and were hardly protected against escapes, which took place frequently. Such security as existed was realised by guards and by chaining prisoners.

Prison conditions were not aimed at isolating prisoners from society and prisoners were in close contact with the outside world. This was facilitated by two factors: inmates depended on their relatives for food, particularly in local prisons; and those sentenced to forced labour would often work together with free labourers.

From the story of poor Umm Shahata it becomes clear that the inmates, usually through their relatives, were in first instance responsible for their own food. It was customary for relatives and friends to hand food and money to the prisoners. Only when there were no relatives was food provided at the expense of the local government for men or by the *Bayt al-Mal* (state fund for social affairs) for women.[31] Since 1836 prisoners who were unable to support themselves were entitled to a standard ration of some 900 grams of coarse bread (*khubz jiraya*) per day.[32] The inmates of the Alexandria Prison and the *Qalʿa al-Saʿidiyya*, who due to the distance could not be visited by their relatives frequently, were entitled to more varied rations, including lentils, rice, clarified butter and even a small amount of meat per month, apart from 28 kilograms of coarse bread. As from 1863 these rations were also provided in the other local prisons.[33] They were not very different from the food schoolboys in state boarding schools received during the same period.[34] Since most prisoners had

31 QS Ch. 3, arts. 15 and 17.

32 DWQ, S 7/33/1, *Majlis al-Ahkam, Daftar Majmuʿ umur idara wa-ijraʾat*. This *sijill* contains some decrees regarding prisons. P. 234: *Khulasa min Majlis Mulkiyya* (*tarjama*) from 1252 (1836–1837), decree stating that all indigent prisoners, wherever they are kept, are entitled to three loaves of coarse bread (*jirayat*) of 309 grams (100 *dirham*) each; p. 233: Decree of the *Majlis Al-Ahkam*, dated 19 *Ramadan* 1266/29 July 1850, with the same contents.

33 A Khedival order dated 11 *Dhu al-Hijja* 1279/30 May 1863, sent to all *mudiriyya*s and other relevant authorities, instructing them to distribute the rations already in use in the Alexandria Prison and *al-Qanatir al-Khayriyya*; DWQ, S 1/1/22, *al-Maʿiyya al-Saniyya, Sadir al-awamir al-ʿAliyya ila al-majalis wa-l-dawawin-wal-aqalim wa-l-muhafazat*, p. 24, doc. 2.

34 These pupils received monthly rations consisting of: 23.2 kg of bread, 3.7 kg of lentils, 1.9 kg of *ful* beans, 0.9 kg of clarified butter, 1 kg of rice and 2.2 kg of meat. Sami, *Taqwim*, 3/2, p. 554, 1 *Muharram* 1281/6 February 1864.

to work, the supply of sufficient quantities of food was seen as necessary for the prisoners' productivity and perhaps even as a form of wages.

All prisoners had to work except those held in simple detention. The nature of the work varied. Those detained in the regional prisons and sentence to 'lowly jobs' were employed in simple chores like cleaning, sweeping and activities connected with construction, such as making mud bricks. Forced labour in factories was regarded as more tiresome than the "lowly jobs". Often prisoners would work together with free labourers, as illustrated by the following account, which also gives an impression of the circumstances under which the convicts were put to work.

In 1849 a certain Ahmad al-Sa'idi, a convict sentenced to five years of hard labour working in the bakery of the Alexandria Dockyard Prison, managed to escape. The bakery foreman, Muhammad al-Farran, was tried for al-Sa'idi's escape, and his trial shed light on the circumstances of this escape. The prisoners worked in the bakery together with other workers. Usually prisoners were chained together in pairs. However, they were disconnected from one another in the bakery since each prisoner independently operated a bellows. During the afternoon break, when the prisoners were left in the workshop and the other workers sat outside, Ahmad managed to escape through one of the chimneys. Later his shackles were found on the roof of the bakery. As only the foreman was present with the prisoners in the bakery – it appeared that he usually ate together with them – he was accused of connivance with the escaped prisoner, and, on the strength of the relevant provisions, sentenced to a prison term equal to the time that the escaped convict still had to serve.[35]

With regard to the Alexandria Prison, the sources, especially the records of trials of negligent guards, allow us to form an impression of the working conditions of the inmates. Prisoners were detained in the Navy Arsenal, which was located in the Western shore of the peninsula. They represented only a small fraction of all people employed here. In the late 1830s there were about 200 prisoners out of a total workforce of several thousands.[36] As the prison represented such a small part of the Arsenal workforce, the gatekeepers were not especially instructed to keep an eye on the prisoners. When some prisoners escaped the Nubian gatekeepers were questioned about the affair. They

35 DWQ, S 6/9/6, *al-Jam'iyya al-Haqqaniyya*, *Daftar Qayd al-Khulasat*, p. 3, no. 2, dated 8 *Shawwal* 1263/19 September 1849.

36 Bowring, 'Report,' p. 59, mentions 200 prisoners and over 5,000 employees; for other estimates of the number of employees in the Alexandria Arsenal (4,000 to 8,000), see Robert Ilbert, *Alexandrie, 1830–1930* (Cairo, 1996) vol. 1, p. 18 and Michael Reimer, *Colonial Bridgehead: Government and Society in Alexandria, 1807–1882* (Boulder and Cairo, 1997) p. 56.

answered that it was their duty was to protect government property and not to guard prisoners. The gatekeepers noted that there were specially appointed military units to guard prisoners, and that their only obligation was to prevent prisoners from leaving without a guard.[37]

The inmates were originally employed in digging and carrying earth, activities connected with the construction of the harbour and the docks. Later their work consisted in chores like loading and unloading ships and carts or in activities connected with numerous workshops of the arsenal. Every morning the prisoners were distributed over the various activities and workshops. The foreman of a workshop would sign a receipt upon the arrival of the prisoners, who would work side by side with the ordinary workers, but were not allowed to leave the workshop during the breaks (*faydus, fadus*). Two of the ordinary labourers would be placed near the doors of the workshop in order to prevent the prisoners from leaving and to accompany prisoners to the latrines. Prisoners would also work outside the Arsenal, in which case each pair (*qatr* or *habl*, lit. 'rope') of prisoners, would be accompanied by one guard.[38]

6 Duration of Imprisonment

As a rule, sentences of imprisonment were pronounced for a specified period. This had been one of the objectives of Mehmed 'Ali Pasha's penal law reforms.[39] However, both the QM and the QS contained articles imposing unspecified prison terms.[40] Where it occurred in the QS, it was a continuation of traditional Ottoman practice and at the same time an attempt to single out habitual

37 DWQ, *Majlis al-Ahkam, al-Madabit al-Sadira*, DWQ, S 7/10/23, p. 132, doc. 893, dated 28 *Dhu al-Qa'da* 1280/5 May 1864.

38 Unless otherwise indicated, the data on the organisation of the Alexandria Arsenal are culled from the following trials of guards for negligence in guarding prisoners: DWQ, *al-Jam'iyya al-Haqqaniyya, Daftar Qayd al-Khulasat*, S 6/9/6, p. 3, no. 2, 8 *Shawwal* 1263/19 September 1847; DWQ, *Diwan al-Tarsane, Sijill* 1037, *Qayd al-qararat* p. 22, no. 12, dated ult. *Rabi'* I 1275/December 1858; DWQ, *Majlis al-Ahkam, al-Madabit al-sadira*, DWQ, S 7/10/18, p. 35, no. 336, dated 13 *Jumada* II 1280/25 November 1863; DWQ, *Majlis al-Ahkam, al-Madabit al-sadira*, DWQ, S /7/19/23, pp. 132–135, doc. 893, dated 28 *Dhu al-Qa'da*, 1280/5 May 1864.

39 See Rudolph Peters, 'For His Correction and as a Deterrent Example for Others: Mehmed 'Ali's First Criminal Legislation (1829–1830),' *Islamic Law and Society* 6 (1999) 164–93.

40 See e.g. QS, Ch. 1 Art. 15: female accomplices to homicide must be imprisoned in a women's prison 'until her attitude is suitable and her repentance is good.' Ch. 3 art. 13: evildoers (*ashrar*), or in modern terminology, habitual offenders, were only released from prison after the completion of their term, only if it had become clear that he had become honest and of good behavior and could find a relative willing to be his guarantor (*damin*).

offenders and keep them in prison regardless of their sentences.[41] However, from the prison records it is clear that most convicts were sentenced to specific terms.[42] These terms were taken seriously by the administration, although there are examples of a certain sloppiness on the part of the prison officials in releasing the inmates on time. Complaints on this account, however, were carefully investigated at the highest level.[43]

When prisoners were released they had to provide a guarantor (*damin*) to vouch for their good behaviour. These guarantors were often the village *shaykhs*, which meant that the fact that someone had served a prison sentence was well known, especially in the countryside. It seems that they were sent to their village or town of origin and had to report to the authorities there.

A prison term was not immutable and every offender had a good chance of early release before the completion of his sentence. There were frequent: between 1829 and 1869 I have found eleven instances.[44] They were probably used to ease the overcrowding of prisons. As a result there often was no obvious relationship between the time actually served and the seriousness of the crime.

41 Uriel Heyd, *Studies in Old Ottoman Critical Law*, ed. V.L. Ménage (Oxford, 1973).

42 There are rare exceptions: see e.g. letter from *Muhafiz al-Qalʿa al-Saʿidiyya* to *Khazin Khidiwi*, dated 19 *Shawwal* 1272, DWQ, *Maʿiyya Turki*, box 12, leaf 24, doc. 254. Military offenders were, at least in 1861, usually sentenced without a term (*bidun mudda*). As a rule, deserters were released after six months. DWQ, *Diwan al-Tarsana*, *sijill* 954 (old), *Qayd asmaʾ al-mudhnibin bi-liman tarsanat Iskandariyya* (1277–1281).

43 E.g. petition of a prisoner under the authority of the Department of Industry (*al-waburat wa-l-ʿamaliyyat*) dated 17 *Rabiʿ* II 1275/24 November 1858, in which he complained that he was not released in time, since the period of pre-trial detention had not been deducted from his prison term as stipulated in his sentence; DWQ, S 7/9/5, *Majlis al-Ahkam*, *Qayd al-ʿarduhalat al-sadira*, p. 105, no. 1.

44 The list of general amnesties: 10 *Muharram* 1244 (1828) amnesty for all prisoners in Abu Qir; 6 *Muharram* 1248 (1832), amnesty for all prisoners except murderers and robbers in celebration of the capture of ʿAkka; 24 *Jumada* I 1265 (1849), general amnesty for all prisoners except murderers and robbers; 19 *Shawwal* 1272 (1856), amnesty for all prisoners except murderers and robbers; 6 *Ramadan* 1277 (1861), amnesty for murderers and robbers in the Alexandria dockyards on occasion of circumcision of the khedive's son; 12 *Muharram* 1279 (1862), amnesty for all prisoners on occasion of circumcision of the khedive's son; 12 *Shaʿban* 1279 (1863), general amnesty for all prisoners except murderers and robbers; 15 *Ramadan* 1281 (1865), amnesty for those in 'work companies' who had completed their term in the 'reformatory unit'; 21 *Rajab* 1282 (1865), amnesty for all prisoners with less than ten months remaining of their sentences; 5 *Rabiʿ* I 1283 (1866), amnesty for all prisoners with less than 3 ½ year-sentences except murderers, robbers and debtors; 1 *Rabiʿ* I 1285 (1868), amnesty for prisoners with less than three months remaining of their sentences; 28 *Shaʿban* 1286 (1869), amnesty for 200 inmates of the Alexandria Dockyards on occasion of the visit of the Austro–Hungarian emperor.

7 Conclusions

This essay sought to question the extent to which the prison system, as it existed in nineteenth-century Egypt, led to stigmatisation and social exclusion or marginalisation of released prisoners. As there are no sources giving information about personal experiences of ex-convicts and of the people who had contact with them, or contemporary official reports on the reintegration of ex-prisoners in society, I cannot give an unequivocal and unassailable answer. The only way to find an answer is by inference. I will examine whether or not the system would be conducive to social exclusion or marginalisation by establishing the absence or presence of the factors listed in the introduction.

The first point to notice is that the necessary condition for stigmatisation was fulfilled: as a result of the system of guarantors after the release of prisoners, the local community would know of a prison sentence of one of its members. Yet, my conclusion is that the prison system was not very conducive to social exclusion. I have several arguments to support this conclusion.

The stigmatisation of ex-convicts would be strongest in legal systems where all prison inmates are convicted of crimes that are widely recognised as moral crimes. In such a system, serving a prison term would point unequivocally to a criminal background. This was obviously not the case in Egypt.

Having served a prison term did not necessarily testify to a criminal past, nor did it automatically mean that one was a morally evil person deserving to be shunned by his community. Many people were in prison for having violated a legal order alien to the norms and values of large segments of the population or for other reasons than having committed criminal offences, as in the case of debtors and political prisoners. In addition, village and neighbourhood *shaykh*s and rural guards were often sentenced to prison terms for negligence in connection with crimes committed in the areas under their authority. They and their communities must have regarded this as a professional hazard and not as something for which they were morally to blame. To make matters more confusing, some criminal convicts were not released from prison but demobilised from the army. Young offenders were often sent to the army as an alternative for imprisonment. It is plausible that a prison term was in many cases regarded as a calamity inflicted by the state and of the same order as military service or *corvée*. Such a view must have been reinforced by the frequent inconsistencies between the seriousness of the crime and the time actually spent in prison due to the frequent amnesties.

My second argument would be that prisoners were not isolated from society. They could be visited by their relatives and worked side by side with other workers in factories and workshops. This was important for their reintegration in society, since the time spent in prison would not totally alienate them from society outside the prison walls and, even more important, would prevent the spread in society of a demonised image of convicts. This may have been different for those deported to the Sudan, but that falls outside the scope of this paper.

Observations by European contemporaries seem to corroborate this conclusion. Clot *Bey*, the French director of the Egyptian Health Service, wrote in his *Aperçu*:

> Those guilty of certain crimes are sentenced for greater or lesser periods of forced labour; but the Egyptian convict is not stigmatised: after having served his punishment he returns to society and holds the same rank as before his stay in prison; should he wish to marry, no family of his station would consider itself sullied by the alliance.[45]

The French traveller Victor Schoelcher, who visited Egypt in 1845 and had a chance to enter several prisons, repeatedly emphasised that Egyptians did not regard imprisonment as shameful.[46] And in 1897 an English official remarked: 'The great difficulty in Egypt is to make imprisonment a real punishment. The disgrace of being put in prison – a factor of considerable efficacy in more advanced countries – is scarcely felt by the mass of the population here.'[47]

Naturally, one has to be cautious in accepting such observations by Western visitors because of their cultural bias. However, in combination with the arguments I mentioned above, I believe that the conclusion is justified that imprisonment in general was not seen as a shameful event and that released convicts were not socially excluded from society or marginalised.

---

45 A.-B. Clot Bey, *Aperçu général sur l'Égypte, vol. 1* (Paris, 1840) p. 105.

46 Schoelcher, *L'Égypte en 1845*, p. 27 and 30.

47 'Report on the Administration, Finances, and Conditions of Egypt and the Progress of Reforms,' *Parliamentary Papers*, 1898, CVII, 621, pp. 25–26, as quoted by Judith Tucker, *Women in nineteenth-century Egypt* (Cambridge, 1985), p. 159.

CHAPTER 14

Egypt and the Age of the Triumphant Prison

Legal Punishment in Nineteenth-Century Egypt

1 Introduction

In the nineteenth century a legal system emerged in Egypt, that complemented the Shariʿa. It was enforced by administrators and not by Shariʿa courts. Criminal law was a prominent part of this system. As from 1829 criminal codes were enacted[1] and from 1842 judicial councils were created to enforce them. An important element in this system was the notion of legality: the judicial authorities could only impose penalties by virtue of enacted criminal laws defining the offences and their punishments. Moreover, sentences should exactly specify the amount of punishment, which must be commensurate with the gravity of the crime. Thus a well-ordered and regulated system of legal punishment came into being, with capital penalty, corporal punishment and imprisonment with forced labour as its most important elements.[2]

One of the most striking developments of the Egyptian penal system in the nineteenth century is the shift towards imprisonment as the main form of punishment at the expense of corporal and capital punishment. This is very similar to what happened in Western Europe and other regions during roughly the same period, which for that reason has been named "the age of the triumphant prison".[3] In the following I will study the emergence and development of the Egyptian system of judicial punishments between 1829, when the first penal code was enacted, and 1882, the year the British occupied Egypt. I will compare these developments with those in the West and examine whether the theories advanced to explain the changes in the European penal system can help us understand what happened in Egypt.

In his study *Surveiller et punir: naissance de la prison*[4] Foucault argues that around 1800 there was a marked change in the character of punishment. Corporal and capital punishment, i.e. punishment directed at the culprit's

---

1 For a succinct survey of the criminal codes enacted between 1829 and the British occupation, see appendix 2.

2 For nineteenth-century Egyptian criminal law, see Peters (1990), Peters (1991), Peters (1997), Peters (1999a) and Peters (1999b).

3 The term was coined by Perrot (1975), p. 81, who characterises the period between 1815 and 1848 in France as *"l'ère de la prison triomphante."*

4 Foucault (1975).

 | DOI:10.1163/9789004420625_015

body, executed as a spectacle on the scaffold, was replaced by punishment directed at the culprit's mind and hidden from the public eye. The cruel spectacles of suffering were meant to serve as strong deterrents in an age when, owing to the lack of well-ordered police forces, the chances that criminals were caught were rather slim. Around 1800 this began to change: public punishment was gradually replaced by imprisonment. According to Foucault, this change was the result of the emergence of a centralised state, capable of ensuring law and order by an efficient police apparatus, and attempting to discipline its subjects. The near certainty of being caught replaced the deterrence instilled by spectacles of cruel executions and torture. The new form of punishment was aimed at disciplining the offender by subjecting him to a rigorous regime, to which end a centralised and hierarchical system of prisons was created.

In his study *The Spectacle of Suffering*,[5] Spierenburg criticises Foucault's ideas. He concurs with Foucault in that the nineteenth century saw the emergence of imprisonment as the ordinary mode of punishment and the decrease of capital and corporal punishment and that punishment ceased to be a public spectacle. However, his main objection to Foucault's study is that the changes described by Foucault as having occurred in a rather short period of time, were in fact part of a process that lasted for more than a century. Other points of critique are that Foucault focused exclusively on France and that some of his examples used to show the prevalence of brutal public punishment, such as the execution of the French regicide Damiens in 1757, were exceptional and cannot be regarded as ordinary forms of punishing criminal offenders.

Spierenburg asserts that torture, corporal punishment and public executions disappear in Western Europe between 1770 and 1870. Until that period the standard punishment consisted in the infliction of pain, administered in public. This included the sufferings of the "*chaînes*", the transport of galley convicts on their way to Marseilles and, after the abolition of the galleys, to the naval arsenals (*bagnes*).[6] An important function of publicly administered punishment, according to Spierenburg, was to emphasise the authority and power of the state. For the changes in the modes of punishment that occurred during the late eighteenth and most of the nineteenth centuries Spierenburg offers two explanations: Elias' "civilising process" (*der Prozess der Zivilisation*) and the strengthening and better integration of the Western European states. As a result of the "civilising process", the sensibilities to officially inflicted pain increase. In the first phase, a growing aversion to the sight of physical suffering prompted groups among the elite to become advocates of penal reform.

5 Spierenburg (1984).
6 Spierenburg (1991), p. 278; Zysberg (1984), pp. 86–91. For Spain, see Pike (1983), 76–79.

These endeavours were successful and mutilating penalties, the exposure of bodies after capital punishment and torture were abolished in most Western European countries during the second half of the eighteenth century. During the second phase, roughly the first half of the nineteenth century, the various social groups became better integrated in the nation state and began to identify with one another. The sensibilities to spectacles of suffering began to extend to the sufferings of other classes. This resulted in new attempts to reform the system of legal punishment. These attempts could succeed since states had become better integrated and therefore more stable. Therefore, the political authorities were not anymore in need of the deterrence produced by public executions and could respond to the new sensibilities by concealing punishment from the public eye. Imprisonment became the common penalty, capital sentences were increasingly executed behind prison walls and corporal punishments such as flogging and branding decreased in importance and were finally abolished in most countries. In order to explain why these changes in the penal systems of the various Western European countries occurred roughly in the same time and order, whereas centralised nation states did not emerge simultaneously, Spierenburg has recourse to the notion of a "European network of states". In other words, he regards these developments not as related to the formation of separate states, but as a common European process.

The common element in these explanations is the emergence of a centralised nation state. However, whereas Foucault sees the changes in the penal system as a direct consequence of the rise of a centralised, intrusive, and disciplining state, Spierenburg argues that these changes were mediated by changes in the mentalities of the elites, changes that were part of Elias' process of civilisation and related to the emergence of centralised nation states. In this essay I will argue, following Foucault, that the changes in the Egyptian penal system were in first instance a direct result of the centralisation of state power and the establishment over the country of an efficient apparatus of control, of which the police[7] was a part. This had an effect on the number and the modes of executions. Contrary to Western Europe, the Egyptian prisons were not transformed into instruments of discipline. Imprisonment, like corporal punishment, was a mode of repression of the population aimed at its subjection. Disciplining activities of the state, especially during the first half of the nineteenth century, were directed at the state servants, both civil and military,[8] and not at the population at large. The abolition of corporal punishment in 1861, however, cannot be explained by the availability of more effective disciplinary

7 For the nineteenth-century police, see Fahmy (1999b).
8 For the disciplining of the military, see Fahmy (1997).

expedients, nor by the growing sensibilities among the elite. Decisive were, in my view, the wish to modernise among important segments of the elite in combination with economic factors.

These aspects of nineteenth-century Egyptian history, have hardly been the subject of scholarly research.[9] This is partly due to the fact that the history of marginal groups in Egypt is still in its infancy, but also and perhaps more importantly, to the nature of the available sources, which imposes serious limitations on the research of the penal system. To the best of my knowledge Egypt, unfortunately, lacks the richness of sources on the subject found in most Western European countries and consisting in official and press reports, diaries, and literary texts that may add liveliness and detail to institutional history. Therefore, I have to rely on official documents, that give information on the institutional aspects, but only rarely on the experience of those who suffered punishment. These sources, regrettably, do not allow us "to construct the history of prisons from the inside out," as a number of Western historians have done.[10]

My main sources apart from published law codes and statutes, are official documents located in the Egyptian National Archives (Dār al-Wathā'iq al-Qawmiyya, DWQ). They consist in the first place of unpublished decrees and Khedival orders, of correspondence between the various state authorities, and of sentences of the various judicial councils. Since at this moment only a very small part of all documents in the DWQ is accessible, it is likely that in the future better sources will be found that will help in completing our knowledge of the penal system. In addition I went through some years *of al-Waqā'i' al-Miṣriyya*, which summarily recorded the trials in the Dīvān-i Hidīvī. All this is supplemented by the scarce information that can be culled from the publications of contemporary Western travellers.

To the best of my knowledge there was no public debate in nineteenth-century Egypt about penal policies, nor have I found express official statements laying down e.g. a philosophy of legal punishment or the principles of penal reform. What the rulers regarded as the objectives of and grounds for punishment can only be inferred from the preambles and texts of penal codes and decrees and from the wording of criminal sentences. Here we find brief references to some aims and justifications. The two mentioned most frequently are rehabilitation and deterrence. In the 1861 decree abolishing corporal punishment (see below) this is formulated as follows: "The aim of punishment is to teach manners (*ta'dīb*) to those who have committed crimes, to prevent them

9 The only studies known to me are Fahmy's article on the medical conditions in nineteenth-century Egyptian prisons Fahmy (2000) and Peters (2002).

10 See e.g. O'Brien (1982), who used the phrase "history from the inside out". (p. 9).

from returning to criminal behaviour and to deter others." In most sentences we find formulas like: "for his correction/for making him repent and as a deterrent example to others" (*adab^{an} lahu/nadāmat^{an} lahu wa-ʿibrat^{an} li-ghayrihi*). That by "teaching manners" to the offender or "making him repent" some form of rehabilitation of the convict is meant, is corroborated by some articles in the penal codes that lay down that in certain cases repentance and improvement of conduct (*ḥattā taṣluḥ ḥāluhu/ḥāluhā*) are conditions for releasing a prisoner.[11] The causal relationship between serving a prison sentence and repentance or improvement of conduct is somehow assumed and not made explicit. The same is true for deterrence. I have not seen any theoretical reflections on the matter. Protection of society is rarely mentioned, and then only as a justification for incapacitating penalties i.e. physical elimination or exclusion of the criminal through capital and life sentences. That retribution, although not explicitly mentioned, was also important is shown by the simple fact that the law codes lay down that more serious offences entail more severe penalties. That it is not referred to could indicate that it was so self-evident that nobody thought of mentioning it.

We are not well informed about the penal system before and during the early years of Meḥmed ʿAli's reign. There are reports that in the eighteenth century there were private prisons, due to the existence of various centres of power connected with Mamluk households. It is not clear, however, whether these can be regarded as part of a system of law enforcement or rather as tools in the struggle for power between these households. There were also state prisons, run by prison wardens as concessions.[12] We do know, however, that by 1829, a penal system was functioning based on death penalty, corporal punishment (essentially flogging and caning) and imprisonment, usually with hard labour. In the same year a central prison was created for convicts from all over Egypt. This was the notorious *līmān Iskandariyya*, named after the Turkish word for harbour (*liman* from Greek *limèn*). It was part of the Alexandria Arsenal (*tarsāna*) and its establishment was prompted by the large scale construction works connected with the Alexandria harbour that had begun in the same year.[13] It resembled very much the kind of hard labour prisons connected with naval arsenals existing in other Mediterranean ports, e.g. in France (*bagnes*) and Spain, that came into existence during the eighteenth century to replace

11 See e.g. Art. 4 PC 1830 and Ch. 1, Art. 15 and Ch. 2, Art. 5, Ch. 3, Art. 13 QS.
12 Hanna (1995), pp. 12–13.
13 Mubarak (1306 H), vii, p. 51.

galley service for convicts.[14] During the 1840s transportation to the Sudan was introduced as a penalty for serious offenders.

In this essay I will focus on the three main elements of the penal system: capital and corporal punishment and imprisonment. I will not go into the function of the poorhouses, such as the Takiyyat Ṭūlūn in Cairo, although these sometimes served as places of detention as mentioned in the Penal Code of 1845 (Qānūn Muntakhab, henceforth QM).[15] Their punitive function, however, was only marginal.[16] There were also other penalties of minor importance, some of them expressly meant as supplementary punishment. I will mention them here for completeness' sake, but not elaborate. The QM introduced fining, the revenues of which were to be spent on the Civil Hospital (*al-isbitāliyya al-mulkiyya*).[17] Later codes, however, do not mention this punishment. The QM also introduced supplementary penalties adopted from French criminal law: those sentenced to long terms of forced labour had to be paraded in their regions carrying sign with the offences for which they had been convicted.[18] Moreover, criminal sentences for serious crimes had to be publicised by posting placards in the main centres of the province.[19] Other supplementary punishments were conscription after the completion of the prison term and, for non-Egyptians, expulsion to one's country of origin. The latter measure was routinely applied, also in the case of non-Egyptian Ottoman subjects.[20] Finally, some forms of punishment were reserved for officials: discharge and demotion, and detention in the office, with or without wages.

14 See e.g. Pike (1983); Zysberg (1984).

15 Art. 191 QM.

16 Ener (2002).

17 QM Art. 178.

18 QM Art. 124, 125, (corresponding with articles 22 and 25 of the French Code Pénal of 1811). Although the wording of the French code was adopted in the QM, the practice itself was already common in Egypt. Offenders were paraded about public places on donkeys with their faces turned to the tail and a crier precede them shouting: "Beware, o good people, of imitating their offences." See (St. John 1852), ii, 72–3.

19 QM art. 130.

20 It is mentioned in a few articles in the CP 1849 (art. 30, 86–88, 90), but not in the QS. The sentences of the Majlis al-Aḥkām show that it was standard practice that foreigners (also Ottoman subjects from other regions than Egypt) were deported to their countries of origin after completion of their prison term. See also Majlis al-Aḥkām, Qayd al-qarārāt, Sīn 7/2/1 (1273–1276), p. 11.

2 Capital and Corporal Punishment

2.1 *Capital Punishment*

During the first decades of Meḥmed ʿAlī's reign capital punishment was frequently applied, not only for murder and robbery, but also for rebellion, official negligence[21] and recidivism.[22] It was usually carried out by hanging (*ṣalb*) or, in case of military personnel, by the firing-squad.[23] Those of high rank were beheaded or strangled with a bowstring.[24] Women who deserved capital punishment for apostasy was strangled[25] drowned in the Nile.[26] During the first half of the 1830s execution by impaling or "by other barbarous means" were abolished ("excepting in extreme cases").[27] The deterrent effect of executions was regarded as an essential aspect of the punishment. A decree issued by the Dīwān-i Hidīwī in November 1834 laid down that those brought to death were to be left one day hanging from the gallows and that posters stating the name and the crime of the culprit had to be shown at the place of execution and all over the country in places frequented by people.[28] Executions did not draw large crowds as they did in Western Europe. Even if they were carried out in market places, which was customary, those present there would continue with their business of selling and buying without paying attention to the spectacle.[29]

Public executions were not only meant for deterrence, but also had a highly symbolic function as expressions of state power. As soon as he had established full control over all regions of the country, Meḥmed ʿAlī wanted to leave no doubt that state authority and the monopoly of violence were vested in his person. Therefore, Meḥmed ʿAlī enforced the rule in the early 1830s that executions needed his approval, barring emergencies such as open rebellion.[30]

---

21 Maʿiyya Saniyya to Aḥmad Pasha Yegen, 12 Ṣafar 1248 [11 July 1832] and referring to Meḥmed ʿAlī's orders to the maʾmūr of Tanta to execute sheikhs who had not delivered the harvest to the storehouses. Maʿiyya Saniyya Turkī, 44 (old), doc. 91.

22 *al-Waqāʾiʿ al-Miṣriyya*, 1 Shaʿbān, 1247 [5–1 1832].

23 See e.g. Khedival order, 3 Rabīʿ II 1272 [13–12 1855] issued to the governor of the Qalʿa Saʿīdiyya to execute a soldier by shooting him. Maʿiyya Saniyya, Ṣādir al-Awāmir al-ʿĀliya, Sīn 1/1/5, p. 144, doc. 15.

24 Bowring (1840), p. 123.

25 Lane (1966), p. 111.

26 See e.g. Sāmī (1928–1936) ā, ii, p. 365, 13 Dhū al-Qaʿda 1245 [6–5 1830].

27 Scott (1837), ii, 115. The last instances of impaled offenders were recorded in 1837 or 1839. See Gisquet (n.d.) ii, p. 132; Schoelcher (1846), p. 24; Gémard (1936), p. 261.

28 Dīwān Khidīwī, Mulakhkhaṣat dafātir, Maḥfaẓa 63, No. 5 (Daftar 806 old), doc. 74, 19 Rajab 1250 [21–11 1834]; Majlis al-Aḥkām, maḍbaṭa 19 Dhū al-Qaʿda 1266 [26–9–1850], Majlis al-Aḥkām, Maḥfaẓa 2, doc. 2/31.

29 Clot Bey (1940), ii, 107.

30 Scott (1837), ii, 115.

Previously, the local governors could execute criminals on their own accord. Travellers report that the number of executions decreased during Meḥmed ʿAlī's reign because of greater public security brought about by a more efficient police force.[31] This trend continued until the British occupation. Executions became relatively rare.[32] The number of capital offences was small: the QM, enacted between 1837 and 1844, mentioned only three capital offences: certain types of aggravated theft, arson resulting in loss of life and hiding runaway peasants. Manslaughter (*qatl ʿamd*) would only be punished with death if the qāḍī pronounced a sentence of retribution (*qiṣāṣ*). Robbery ceased to be a capital offence in 1844.[33] After the introduction of the Penal Code of 1849, which does not mention capital punishment at all and the Imperil Penal Code (*al-Qānūnnāme al-Sulṭānī*, henceforth QS) around 1853, death sentences other than for manslaughter were extremely rare.[34] Other incapacitating punishments, such as lifelong banishment to Ethiopia and transportation to the Sudan, both introduced in the 1840s took the place of capital punishment.

An additional factor that may have kept the number of executions low was the conflict between the Khedive and the Sultan about the right to sanction capital sentences, that arose during the negotiations about the introduction of the Ottoman Penal Code of 1850. The Sultan insisted that this was his prerogative, inextricably bound up with his sovereignty, whereas the Khedive wanted to retain a right that he and his predecessors had always been exercising.[35] Although there is no documentary evidence, it is possible that the Khedive, in order not to give new fuel to the conflict, has instructed the judicial councils that he would not sanction capital sentences except those sanctioned by qadis.

2.2 *Corporal Punishment*

During the early years of Meḥmed ʿAlī's reign, various types of corporal punishments were applied, of which flogging was the most common. Other forms existed too but were unusual. From the early years of Meḥmed ʿAlī's reign we have two pertinent reports by the contemporary chronicler al-Jabartī. That he included these reports in his history is an indication of the exceptional character of the penalties mentioned in them. The first report is that in 1812 the

31 Bowring (1840) p. 123; ii, p. 474; s St. John (1834); see also Guémard (1936), p. 257. On the Egyptian police, see Fahmy (1999b).

32 Couvidou (1873), p. 307.

33 Art. 197 QM.

34 After 1850 I have come across only one capital sentence. It was pronounced against a soldier who was convicted for having wilfully let escape a prisoner. See the document referred to in note 32.

35 See Baer (1969).

governor of Cairo sentenced three robbers to the punishment of amputation of their right hands.[36] This must have been an unusual penalty as is corroborated by al-Jabartī's remark that the executioner was not proficient in this operation, as a result of which one of the robbers died. The executioner's lack of proficiency was no doubt a consequence of the infrequent occurrence of this type of punishment. The second report is about a market inspector (*muḥtasib*), a certain Muṣṭafā Kāshif Kurd, who went around and punished those violating the market regulations by nailing them to the doors of their shops, piercing their noses and hanging pieces of meat from them, clipping their ears, sitting them on hot baking trays and so forth.[37] These stories are often quoted as an indication of the cruelty and arbitrariness of justice in Meḥmed ʿAlī's time. In my view, however, thus *muḥtasib*'s rather brutal way of dealing with offenders must have been an exception. Al-Jabartī mentions that Meḥmed ʿAlī appointed him for his ruthlessness after he had heard that the lower orders of Cairo could not be made to obey ʿUthmān Aghā, Muṣṭafā's predecessor.

As from the 1830 it is clear that Meḥmed ʿAlī followed a policy of putting an end to mutilating corporal punishments. When, in 1835, he learned that the governor of the Buḥayra Province had cut off the nose and ears of a peasant who had uprooted cotton plants, he censured the latter and instructed him that flogging, imprisonment and death were the only punishments that he was allowed to impose for such acts, which was in accordance with the Penal Code of 1829.[38] There is no evidence that mutilating *ḥadd* penalties or *qiṣāṣ* punishment for wounding were enforced. In the rare cases that lower courts pronounced such sentences, they were invariably commuted by higher authorities.[39]

The only forms of corporal punishment mentioned in the laws issued in Meḥmed ʿAlī's time were flogging with the *kurbāj* (with a maximum of 600 stripes[40]) on the buttocks or the bastinado on the soles of the feet.[41] Most penal provisions specify the number of lashes. Only in a few articles, the older

36 Jabartī (1879–1880), iv, 144.

37 Jabartī (1879–1880), iv, p. 278 (Ramaḍān, 1232 [July, 1817]); see also Lane (1966), pp. 126, 127; Sāmī (1928–1936) ii, pp. 262, 542.

38 Orders of 2 and 22 Ramaḍān, 1251. Sāmī, (1928–1936), ii, pp. 456, 458.

39 See Peters (1997).

40 QM art. 111 mentions this number as a punishment for officials committing for the third time the offence of returning late from an official journey.

41 QF art. 25 stipulates the liability according to the shariʿa of an official who causes the death of a person by hitting him on spots other than the buttocks or the soles of the feet. The technical term *falaqa* for bastinado, however, is not mentioned in the penal codes.

Ottoman practice is followed: they just prescribe a fitting corporal penalty.[42] Beating with a wooden stick (*nabbūt*), although not listed in the codes, was also practised.[43] Flogging was frequent in the countryside and the Agriculture Code (*Qānūn al-Filāḥa*, henceforth QF) of 1830 mentions it as a punishment in 31 out of its 55 articles. It was the preferred form to punish cultivators since imprisonment would result in a decline in productivity.[44] In a few articles the number of stripes is not indicated. They a continuation of the older system of Ottoman criminal law, in which, as a rule, only the kind of punishment was prescribed for specific offences, but not the quantity. With regard to some offences, the application of the punishment of flogging depended on the social class of the offender: those belonging to the lower classes were to be flogged, whereas those of the higher classes were to be punished with imprisonment.[45] This must reflect an explicit penal policy. The relevant provisions are part of a group of articles that are direct borrowings from the French Code Pénal of 1810, which does not list flogging as a punishment.

Under the influence of Ottoman criminal law, caning was introduced by the QS. The first three chapters of this Code, for the greater part identical with the Ottoman Criminal Code of 1850, meticulously followed the Shariʿa provisions for *taʿzir*, in that the maximum number of strokes was not to exceed 79, one less than the minimum *ḥadd* punishment. However, in the chapters summarising previous Egyptian legislation (chapters 4 and 5), the traditional Egyptian system was maintained, except that the term *kurbāj* (whip) was now replaced by *jalda* (lash), a term used in the standard works of Islamic jurisprudence. The maximum number of stripes mentioned in the code was 250. Flogging or caning by way of *taʿzir* or as a *ḥadd* punishment could also be administered in a qadi's court. From the archival material it is clear that if the qadi imposed such punishment, it was immediately carried out during the session.

Flogging and caning as judicial punishments were abolished in 1861. In order to put this in its proper perspective, it is necessary to discuss it in the context of official violence. During the nineteenth century acts of violence committed by officials against the population were frequent and common. We can distinguish the following forms:

---

42 See e.g. Peters (1999b). In a few articles the numbers is not specified, probably due to editorial oversight. See PC 1849, Art. 1: "an appropriate (corporal) punishment" (*al-taʿzīr bi-mā yalīq*).

43 See e.g. Khedival order of 16 Muḥarram 1252 [3–5 1836]; Sāmī (1928–1936), ii, p. 466.

44 This is mentioned explicitly in various penal laws. See PC 1829, Art. 9; QS, Ch. 3, Art. 19.

45 Art. 164 and 166 QM, corresponding with arts. 330 and 309 of the French Code Pénal of 1811.

- generic official violence in situations where officials needed to assert their authority and force persons to carry out their orders (army, civil servants supervising *corvee*, collecting taxes etc.);
- physical pressure during criminal investigations;
- judicial corporal punishment based on sentences pronounced by qadis, councils, or officials with judicial powers.

From the middle of the nineteenth century the Egyptian government made attempts at controlling and limiting generic official violence. The motives behind these measures were diverse and I will discuss them in the conclusions. The first steps in limiting official violence were taken by Meḥmed ʿAlī who enacted legislation making officials financially and criminally responsible for excessive violence resulting in loss of life[46] and for unlawful detention.[47] This was part of his policy of curbing the arbitrary behaviour of his administrators and soldiers and to inculcate discipline into them. However, these measures were not intended to put an end to generic official violence and it remained a common phenomenon: tax collection in the countryside was usually accompanied by the whipping of those unwilling or unable to pay until at least the end of the 1870s.[48]

Until the early 1850s, torture (*al-taḍyīq ʿalā al-mathūm*) during investigation was standard procedure, sanctioned by state law[49] but not by the Shariʿa.[50] It consisted generally in flogging and beating, often on the soles of their feet. Other forms of torture were forcing people to stand for 48 hours until their feet were swollen, depriving people from food, drink and sleep, confinement in too small a cell, hanging a person from his fingers or his toes and the use of

46 For liability of officials for death caused by flogging, see Khedival order, 28 Rabīʿ II 1245 [27–9 1845], i.e. before the enactment of Meḥmed ʿAlī's first criminal code to the effect that officials who would cause the death of persons by beating would be liable according to the Shariʿa and also face banishment; the order was occasioned by a report that a *maʾmūr* in the Gharbiyya province had beaten to death some persons. Sāmī (1928–1936), ii, p. 356; see further: QF Art. 25; QM At. 60; PC 1849 Art. 46. QS Ch. 1, art. 1.

47 Officials who unlawfully imprison persons must pay a compensation of 5 to 10 piaster per day: QM Art. 179; PC 1849, Art. 34. The provisions were not adopted by the QS.

48 Cole (1993), p. 87.

49 QF, art. 26; Dīvān-i Hidīvī Lāyiḥesi (Regulations of the Khedival Bureau), issued 13 Muḥarram 1254 [8–4 1838], art. 13. Text in Maḥfaẓat al-Mīhī, doc. 20. See also (Lane 1966), p. 114.

50 During the investigation of case of manslaughter, the suspects had been beaten severely and finally confessed considering that being sent to the Alexandria gaol was better than continuously being whipped. The Grand Mufti stated: "The defendants cannot be convicted for manslaughter because their confessions have been obtained by what according to the shariʿa is regarded as coercion (*ikrāh sharʿī*)." Fatwa, 5 Jumādā II 1268 [27–3 1852]. Al-Mahdi (1301 H) v, 435–6.

shackles.[51] When the QS was introduced in the early 1850s, one of the organic decrees issued in connection with the QS banned the use of physical force during criminal investigation. The prohibition was repeated in 1858[52] and in 1861, when, in the decree abolishing flogging as a penalty (see below), instructions were issued regarding the extent of pressure to be applied on suspects during the investigation. It prohibited certain methods of torture and further stipulated that the *mudīr* or *maʾmūr* of the department where the investigation was carried out was to supervise the interrogation.[53] Beating during investigation was henceforth allowed only in exceptional situations to induce a suspect to confess if there was evidence for his crime and it proved to be impossible after some days to make him confess by means of verbal abuse (*zajr*), frightening and threatening him (*tahdīd, takhwīf*), and by showing instruments of beating.[54] It is of course not clear to what extent these instructions were obeyed in practice. But complaints of suspects who claimed that their confessions were obtained under physical pressure were taken seriously and resulted in official investigations.[55]

Whereas the banning, or rather, the restricting of violence during investigation was a gradual process that lasted nearly ten years, the abolition of flogging as a punishment was brought about at once, although previously certain measures were taken to restrict excesses. In 1858 it was decreed that if a punishment

51 Some of these forms of torture were routinely mentioned in official correspondence about criminal investigations. See e.g. Mudīriyya Minūfiyya to wakīl Qism Samādūn, 6 Dhū al-Qaʿda 1260. Mudīriyyat Minūfiyya, Ṣādir, Lām 6/1/1, p. 209. Mudīriyyat Minūfiyya to al-Jamʿiyya al-Haqqāniyya, 5, Dhū al-Qaʿda 1260, ibid. 254. Others are listed in the 1861 decree abolishing corporal punishment and torture (see below).

52 See art. 14 Dhikr waẓāʾif mutafarriʿa bi-l-majlis (List of further duties of the regional councils), an organic decree enacted when the QS was introduced, forbidding torture (*taʿdhīb*), suffering (*adhiyya*) and physical pressure (*taḍyīq*) during investigations [Jallād, 1890–1892 #22], ii, pp. 105–106; Irāda Saniyya, 9 Ramaḍān 1274 (24–4 1858). Majlis al-Aḥkām, Daftar Majmūʿ Umūr Jināʾiyya, p. 90.

53 Irāda Saniyya, 19 Jumādā II 1278, and summarised in Lām 1/20/8, Muḥāfaẓat Miṣr, p. 71, doc. 3, 11 Shaʿbān 1278. Precise details of the commuting of sentences of flogging to sentences of detention are given in the Lāyiḥat tabdīl al-ḍarb bi-l-ḥabs (Ordinance regarding the replacement of beating by detention), an order issued by Muḥāfaẓat Miṣr on 11 Shaʿbān 1278 [11–2 1862], implementing the Khedival decree of 26 Dhū al-Ḥijja 1277 [5–7 1861] no. 120 replacing the penalty of beating by detention. Muḥāfaẓat Miṣr, Qayd al-qarārāt al-ṣādira bi-Majlis Muḥāfaẓat Miṣr, Lām 1/20/8, p. 71, doc. 3.

54 See arts. 8 and 10 of the order implementing order issued by Muḥāfaẓat Miṣr mentioned in note 56.

55 See e.g. decision of the Maʿiyya Saniyya, 24 Jumādā I 1268 [16–3 1852]. Maʿiyya Saniyya, Qayd al-khulāṣāt al-wārida min majālis daʿāwī al-aqālīm, Sīn 1/24 sijill 1, p. 2. Investigation by the Majlis al-Aḥkām at the request of two persons who had been convicted for theft of cattle and claimed that their confessions had been obtained by whipping them.

of more than two hundred lashes was to be carried out, the victim should first undergo a medical examination.[56] The penalty of flogging or caning was finally abolished on 9 July 1861. The decree is silent on the considerations for this step. Flogging was henceforth replaced by detention (*ḥabs*), which could be made more severe, for serious offenders, by providing only water and bread for food (*ḥabs al-riyāḍa*), by putting them in shackles, or by isolating them from the other inmates and denying them the right to receive visitors.[57] The decree was enforced by the courts, although in the years immediately following the decree, I have seen a few sentences imposing flogging, most of them pronounced by Shariʿa courts by way of *taʿzir*.[58]

3 Imprisonment

> In 1855 a certain Muḥammad ʿAlī was arrested on a charge of theft. In his home goods were impounded that he was accused of having stolen. The victim, Muḥammad Rifʿat Efendi, living in the Cairo Bāb al-Khalq quarter, accused him of having stolen money and goods from his home with a total value of about 18.000 piasters. Muḥammad ʿAlī declared that the victim's wife, with whom, he claimed, he had spent a day and a night, had given him out of her own free will a sum of money, part of which he had spent on the goods that were impounded in his quarters. The price of the goods was retrieved from the seller and was returned to Muḥammad Rifʿat Efendi, together with the rest of the money that in the meantime had been found in Muḥammad ʿAlī's lodgings. At this point the suspect had admitted that he had stolen the money. When his criminal record were examined, it appeared that he had been arrested twice before, once for theft of a camel – of which he later was proven innocent –, and once for pretending to be a police spy (*baṣṣāṣ*). Both times he had managed to

56 Irāda Saniyya, 9 Ramaḍān 1274 [24–4 1858]. Majlis al-Aḥkām, Daftar Majmūʿ Umūr Jināʾiyya, p. 90.

57 Amr ʿĀlī of 26 Dhū al-Ḥijja 1277 [6–7 1861]. Majlis al-Aḥkām, Daftar Majmūʿ Umūr Jināʾiyya, p. 155; [Sāmī, 1928–1936 #21] iii, 1, p. 375. A year later, in an instruction to newly founded regional courts, the interdiction of flogging was repeated. Irāda Saniyya of 22 Dhū Qaʿda 1278 [21–5 1862]. [Sāmī, 1928–1936 #21], 3/1 p. 403.

58 See e.g. Majlis al-Aḥkām, al-Maḍābiṭ al-Ṣādira, Sīn/7/10/23, p. 183, doc. 945, 8 Dhū al-Ḥijja, 1280, commuting a sentence of flogging pronounced by Majlis al-Manṣūra into imprisonment; for examples of Shariʿa sentences see sentence of Cairo Shariʿa Court of First Instance, 17 Rabīʿ I 1286 [17–7 1869], Dār al-Maḥfūẓāt, Maḥkamat Miṣr al-ibtidāʾiyya al-sharʿiyya, Ḍabṭiyyat al-murāfaʿāt, Makhzan 46, ʿayn 22, sijill 1238, p. 84; Dīwān Majlis al-Aḥkām, Qayd al-iʿlamāt al-sharʿiyya, Sīn 7/31/3, no. 85, 28 Dhū al-Ḥijja, 1278, no. 253, 17 Rajab 1279 [3–1 1863].

> escape from custody. Taking this into consideration, he was sentenced to life long forced labour in the fortifications of al-Qanāṭir al-Khayriyya (also called al-Qalʿa al-Saʿīdiyya). Later he was transferred to the Alexandria Dockyards Prison (*Līmān Iskandariyya*). In 1858 he was selected for the army. However, while serving in the military he committed another theft and was sent back to the Alexandria Dockyards Prison. When the amnesty of March 1861 was announced, he was released from the Alexandria prison. However, being regarded as incorrigible (*shaqī*) he was not set free but transferred to the Department of Industry (Dīwān al-Wābūrāt wa-l-ʿAmaliyyāt) for forced labour. From there he escaped again. Upon being found out by a police spy, he threatened the latter with a knife and wounded a person who came to the policeman's rescue. But he could not save his skin and was apprehended. On 16 September 1861, the Cairo Police Department sent him to the Alexandria Dockyards Prison in order to complete his life sentence. However, when Khedive Ismāʿīl succeeded Saʿīd, he reversed this decision and instructed the Majlis al-Aḥkām to review the cases of inmates of the Alexandria Dockyards Prison with life sentences or unspecified terms. On 19 November 1866 his sentence was commuted to five years forced labour in the Alexandria Prison. However, since he was classified as belonging to the "group of evildoers" (*zumrat al-ashrār*) mentioned in Ch. 3, art. 13 of the QS, he was not to be released after this period unless it had become clear that he had become honest and of good behaviour and he could find a relative willing to be his guarantor (*ḍāmin*).[59]

My first reaction upon reading this account was one of regret that this gaolbird did not write his memoirs. He was familiar with most large prisons in Egypt and the story of his life behind bars would be invaluable for the penal history of Egypt. The account as we have it is representative of the type of available sources. They are factual and written from an official point of view. Their value lies in the information they impart regarding the functioning of the penal institutions, and they tell us little about the experiences of the inmates.[60]

---

59 Sīn 7/10/29, Majlis al-Aḥkām, al-Maḍābiṭ al-Ṣādira, pp. 135–136, maḍbaṭa 133, 11 Rajab 1282 [30–11 1865]; Khedival order to the Ministry of the Navy (under whose jurisdiction the Alexandria Arsenal came), 21 Rajab 1281 [20–12 1864], Sīn 1/1/30, Maʿiyya Saniyya, al-Awāmir al-Ṣādira, p. 90 and 121; Cairo Police to Muḥāfaẓat Iskandariyya, 12 Rabīʿ I 1278 [17–9 1861], letter by which Muḥammad ʿAlī was sent to the Alexandria Dockyards Prison), Ḍabṭiyyat Miṣr, Ṣādir al-Aqālīm, Lām 2/2/5 (old 530), p. 24, no. 7.

60 For a description of prison conditions in nineteenth-century Egypt, see (Peters 2004).

The story of Muḥammad ʿAlī illustrates several characteristic traits of the Egyptian prison system in the nineteenth century. In the first place it is evident from the account that there were a variety of penitentiary institutions and that, in addition, convicts were sometimes sent to the army instead of completing their sentences in prison. Secondly, the account shows that the term specified in a sentence could be subject to all kinds of changes. The period one actually spent in prison was often shorter than the term of the sentence, usually as a consequence of general amnesties, but also as a result of escapes. Prison security was not very tight and escapes were frequent in spite of the severe punishments to which guards were sentenced if they let prisoners escape. Finally, it demonstrates that attempts were made, although not very consistently, to single out habitual offenders and keep them permanently imprisoned. In the following I will discuss these and other aspects of the Egyptian prison system.[61]

3.1 *The Function of Prisons*

Prisons had various functions: In the first place they served as places of confinement for those sentenced to prison terms. In addition, the police prisons and in the prisons of the provincial capitals held arrested suspects in custody pending the investigation of their cases. In exceptional cases, this might take a long time. I found a petition from a murder suspect, who had been in custody for over seven years, because the victim's heirs could not be traced so that the Shariʿa proceedings could not be initiated.[62] As prescribed in Islamic law,[63] most prisons also served as debt prisons. Debtors unable to pay their debts were normally held in the local prisons.[64] If they proved to be unable to pay their debts, they were sometimes sent to the Alexandria Arsenal Prison.[65] In Cairo and possibly in other big cities there was a special debt prison. It seems that it was not too difficult to have a person imprisoned on this ground, for in February 1869 a decree was issued to remedy the frivolous arrest of debtors. It stipulated that persons could only be imprisoned for debts if these were duly substantiated and the creditor was willing and capable of paying for the prisoner's maintenance.[66]

---

61 For a discussion of prison conditions, see (Peters 2004).

62 Petition, 11 Jumādā II 1291. Dākhiliyya ʿArabī, Maḥfaẓa 14 (1291), doc. 656. For the relationship between shariʿa and secular justice in homicide cases, see (Peters 1997).

63 In classical Islam, this was the most important function of prisons. See Schneider (1995).

64 Sīn 2/29/2, Dīwān Khidīwī, Ṣādir al-aqālīm, p. 43, doc. 14, 21 DQ 1243.

65 Khedival order, 21 Dhū al-Qaʿda 1243 [4–6–1828], Dīwān Khidīwī, Ṣādir al-aqālīm, Sīn 2/29/2, p. 43, doc. 14; Khedival order, 28 Dhū al-Ḥijja 1258 [30–1 1843], Shūrā Muʿāwana Turkī 158 (old), p. 219, doc. 1053.

66 Order, 5 Dhū al-Qaʿda 1285 [17–2 1869], Majlis al-Khuṣūṣī, al-Qarārāt wa-l-Lawāʾiḥ al-Ṣādira, Sīn 11/8/13, no. 32.

Other groups of non-criminal inmates were persons, often Bedouin, held in hostage by the government so as to force their relatives or tribe into obedience and persons punished vicariously for acts committed by their relatives.[67] This latter form of pressure upon crime suspects seems the have disappeared after the 1850s. With regard to the imprisoned Bedouin,[68] it is sometimes difficult to distinguish between those who were imprisoned for robbery and those who had been taken hostage as a guarantee for the good behaviour of their tribes. I regularly came across Khedival orders to prison commanders instructing them to submit lists of the Bedouin inmates, specifying whether they had been imprisoned for a certain term or without a term.[69] During certain periods, e.g. in the 1860s, the Alexandria Arsenal also served as a place of imprisonment for foreigners who had been sentenced to imprisonment by their consular courts. They as a rule served short sentences, of a few weeks only.[70]

Almost all prisoners had to work. Many of them were attached to factories or quarries to supplement the numbers of the "free" workers, many of whom could hardly be distinguished from the convicts, having been brought by force to the industrial establishments. Moreover, as becomes clear from the aforementioned account of Muḥammad Alī, young convicts who were physically fit, often served their terms as soldiers in the army, or were drafted immediately after the termination of their terms.[71] Prison labour had essentially an

67 Majlis Mulkī to the Ma'mūrū al-Dawāwīn, 26 Rabīʿ II 1246 [14–9 1830], ordering that local officials must take the sons of peasants who are unable to pay their taxes and send them to the army if they are strong, or to the Alexandria Arsenal or the Ṭurʿat al-Maʿṣara in order to carry earth if they are weak. Dīwān Khidīwī Turkī, 759 (old), p. 102, doc. no. 209. Khedive to Aḥmad Pasha al-Yegen, 12 Ṣafar 1248, Maʿiyya Saniyya Turkī 44 (old), doc. 91.

68 See e.g. missive from Wakīl Nāẓir al-Jihādiyya to Maʿiyya, 8 Muḥarram 1272 [20–9 1855] mentioning that apart from the ordinary prisoners, there were 609 Bedouin in the Qalʿa Saʿīdiyya, Maʿiyya Turkī, Maḥfaẓa 8, waraqa 11, doc. 58 (from DWQ card index, s.v. sujūn); Khedival order to the Dīwān ʿUmūm Baḥriyya Iskandariyya, 3 Jumādā II, 1272, ordering the release of 71 Bedouin from the Alexandria Arsenal at the request of their sheikh, Maʿiyya Saniyya, Awāmir, Daftar 1884 (old), p. 49, doc. 28 (from DWQ card index, s.v. sujūn); Entry to Alexandra Prison on 19 Rajab 1279 [3–1 1863] of 82 Bedouins from Upper Egypt, called *ʿurbān ashqiyā'* (criminal Bedouin), aged between 10 and 70, without specification of prison term, Dīwān al-tarsāna, sijill 954 (register of prisoners in the Alexandria Arsenal), p. 131.

69 See e.g. Khedival order to the commander of the Qalʿa Saʿīdiyya, 5 Jumādā II 1272 [12–2 1856], Maʿiyya Saniyya, Ṣādir al-awāmir al-ʿāliya, Sīn 1/1/5, p. 144, no. 20; same order to Alexandria Arsenal, 25 Jumādā II 1272 [3–3 1856], Maʿiyya Saniyya, Ṣādir al-Awāmir al-ʿĀliya, Sīn 1/1/5, p. 70, no. 29.

70 See e.g. Dīwān al-Tarsāna, 956 (old) (Register of prisoners of the Alexandria Arsenal), p. 14.

71 That offenders could be sent to the army as a punishment is mentioned in the oldest criminal legislation: e.g. PC 1829 Arts. 18–20, QF arts. 15, 7 and 27, PC 1849, arts. 8 and 11. Although it is no mentioned in the QS, the practice of sending convicts to the army continued.

economic function as a means to provide manpower for necessary but arduous, dirty or unhealthy work. Since especially in the early half of the nineteenth century there was a chronic shortage of factory workers and soldiers, prisoners were matter-of-factly sent to industrial establishments and the military. I have found no indications that prison labour was seen as a means to rehabilitate the inmates, which occupied such a prominent place in nineteenth-century Western European debates on crime and punishment. Within the framework of penal policy, hard labour was regarded as a form of retribution. In addition it functioned as a deterrent since the inmates were not isolated from the public space and could be seen in shackles during transport or when carrying out work outside the prison.

3.2 *Types of Prisons*

In order to get an insight in the type of gaols that were operative in Egypt during our period, we have to rely on archival sources and on the earliest Egyptian legislation, that was not inspired by foreign examples (i.e. the Penal Code of 1829, the Code of Agriculture of 1830, and parts of the Penal Code of 1845). The texts of the other penal codes are often misleading since their terminology was copied from the foreign models that had inspired these codes[72] and did not necessarily reflect the Egyptian system. This is especially true with regard to arts. 123 to 194 of the QM, that were translated from the French Penal Code of 1810 and of the first three chapters of the QS that corresponded with the Ottoman Penal Code of 1850. Moreover, the terminology was not uniform: sometimes the same term is used for different modalities of imprisonment, whereas in other instances the same modality is referred to by different terms.

Although the names and locations varied, the essential traits of the system hardly changed during our period. Serious offenders were sent to national labour prisons or, as of the early 1840s, deported to labour prisons in Sudan. For those whose offences were not as serious, there was the possibility to serve prison terms at forced labour locally in factories, on building sites or in menial jobs in government offices. Since the convicts were closer to their homes, this was considered to be a lesser degree of punishment. Those sentenced to short terms were held locally, in police gaols in the big cities or in gaols in the provincial capitals.

At the national level there were at various times three prisons. The one that remained operative during our entire period was the one connected with the Alexandria Arsenal (*Tarsānat Iskandariyya*),[73] called *līmān* (or *lūmān*)

72 See Peters (1991), p. 216.

73 For a map of the Alexandria Arsenal as it existed in 1829, see Ilbert (1996), ii, 766.

Iskandariyya, where the convicts were originally employed in digging and moving soil and later also in the workshops.[74] It seems that in the 1830s convicts were paid wages for their labour.[75] This prison fell under the jurisdiction of the Department of the Navy (Dīwān al-Donanma or Dīwān al-Baḥriyya). The overall responsibility, according to art. 197 QM, was with the Inspector of the Navy (*mufattish al-Donanma*) and the Director of the Arsenal (*Nāẓir al-Tarsāna*). For its daily functioning, the prison warden (*maʾmūr al-mudhnibīn*) was responsible. The number of the inmates of the Alexandria prison fluctuated between 200 and 650. In the early 1830s Bowring counts about 200 prisoners (among several thousands of non-convict workers) in the Alexandria Arsenal. This number must have been practically constant until 1845, when a French traveller estimated the total number of prisoners in Cairo and Alexandria together at 300 inmates.[76] A few years later, however, in 1847, there were already about 450 prisoners in Alexandria. In the early 1860s the number of inmates varied between 250 and 650 convicts.[77] The fluctuations can be explained by changes in penitentiary policies, i.e. variations in the categories of prisoners that were sent to Alexandria and by general pardons, ordered especially when the prisons became overcrowded.

Apart from the Alexandria gaol there was a forced labour prison near the fortification at al-Qanāṭir al-Khayriyya (called al-Qalʿa al-Saʿīdiyya or al-Istiḥkāmāt al-Saʿīdiyya) that was operative from about 1853 until at least 1865.[78] Its inmates worked in constructing the fortifications. As a prison it

74 In the sentences pronounced during the first half of the nineteenth century, the following words are used: *naql al-turāb* (transporting earth), *ḥaml al-turāb* (carrying earth), *toprak hizmeti* (earth works). Later they also worked in the workshops. See e.g. Bowring (1840) and Pückler-Muskau (1985), p. 69.

75 Al-Waqāʾiʿ al-Miṣriyya, 5 Jumādā II 1247 [11–11 1831]: A Gypsy (Niwari) is sent to the Dīwān al-Abniya to work there against wages (*ujra*). In the 1247 issues of the Waqāʾiʿ al-Miṣriyya one often finds the formula "He was sent to the Dīwān al-Abniya to work there for wages but under detention (*maḥbūs*) to punish him. Bowring, writing about the late 1830s, reports that the "galley slaves employed in the different works" [of the Alexandria Arsenal] are paid 4 piasters a day, including provisions and clothing, which is only one piaster less than the other workers received. Bowring (1840), p. 59.

76 Schoelcher (1836), p. 30.

77 This breaks down as follows: 1847: 450 inmates; 1860: 600 inmates; 1865: 400 inmates; 1866: 650 inmates; 1868: 250 inmates. I have found these figures with the help of the five sijills concerning the Alexandria Arsenal (see appendix 3), by counting the number of prisoners that entered in a given year and multiplying it with the average period spent in the prison. These figures are confirmed by a source stating that on 4 December 1862 the number of inmates was 443. See Majlis al-Aḥkām, al-Maḍābiṭ al-Ṣādira Sīn 7/10/23, no. 893, 28 Dhū al-Qaʿda 1280, p. 132.

78 See note 71.

was much bigger than the Alexandria Arsenal. In October–November 1855, it housed some 1,100 to 1,200 prisoners, half of them Bedouin, and the wardens repeatedly complained that they did not have sufficient personnel at their disposal for guard duties.[79] Initially it fell under the authority of the War Office (*Jihādiyya*), but in 1857 it was transferred to the Department of Industry.[80] Finally there seems to have been a national prison in Sudan (apart from the deportation camps). In the beginning it held only Sudanese convicts until, in 1857, it was decided that, in order to make the punishment more deterrent, serious offenders from the Sudan would serve their terms in Alexandria, whereas those from Egypt would be sent to the Sudan.[81]

The provincial prisons and various industrial establishments held less serious offenders sentenced to hard labour. Hard labour in factories and on construction sites goes back to the late 1820s, when convicts were sent to the iron foundry (Turkish: *demürkhane*) in Bulaq or to building sites in Alexandria (Turkish: *Iskenderiye ebniyesi*). Apparently there was at that time no differentiation in the various forms of hard labour. In the 1830s and 1840s prisoners were either put at the disposal of the Department of Construction (*Dīwān al-Abniya*) or sent to the Alexandria Arsenal. Later the Alexandria Arsenal became the prison for the more serious criminals. In the early 1850s convicts were sent to various industrial establishments (*tarsāna*), such as the ones in Bulaq[82] and Khartoum, (until the latter, as we have seen, became a national prison in 1857).[83] Finally, from the mid-1850s until late 1864, convicts were put at the disposal of the Department of Industry (Dīwān al-Wābūrāt wa-l-ʿAmaliyyāt, also

79 Qalʿa Saʿīdiyya to the Kātib al-Dīwān al-Khidīwī, 3 Ṣafar 1272, Maʿiyya Turkī Maḥfaẓa 8, leaf 11, doc. 58; Qalʿa Saʿīdiyya to the Khāzin al-Dīwān al-Khidīwī, 29 Ṣafar 1272, ibid., leaf 12, doc. 474; in 1855 there 609 Bedouins in the Qalʿa Saʿīdiyya, Wakīl Nāẓir al-Jihādiyya to al-Maʿiyya al-Saniyya, 8 Muḥarram 1272 [20–9 1855], Maʿiyya Turkī, Maḥfaẓa 8, doc. 58.

80 Order of 16 Dhū al-Ḥijja 1273 [7–8 1857], DWQ Card index s.v. *sujūn*, Maḥfaẓa 14 Turkī, leaf 132, doc. 398; by the end of 1862 the Qalʿa Saʿīdiyya was still in use as a prison, see order of 27 Jumādā II 1279 [20–12 1862], DWQ, Card index s.v. *sujūn*, Maʿiyya Saniyya, daftar 1905, p. 36, doc. 23.

81 Amr ʿĀlī to Mudīr Tākā, 29 Jumādā I 1273 [24–2 1857]. Majlis al-Aḥkām, Daftar Majmūʿ Umūr Jināʾiyya, p. 133.

82 Khedival order, 29 Ramaḍan 1252 [7–1 1837], DWQ, Card index s.v. *sujūn*, Mulkiyya Turkī 5 (old), p. 174, doc. 174: Reference to prisoners in big factory in Bulaq. See also e.g. Majlis al-Aḥkām, Maḥfaẓa 2, doc. 2/63, 16 Dhū al-Ḥijja 1266 [23–10 1850] and doc. 2/82, 24 Dhū al-Ḥijja 1266 [31–10 1850].

83 Khedival order to Ḥukumdār al-Sūdān, 21 Ṣafar 1272 [2–11–1855] mentioning that a person was sentenced to life imprisonment in the *tarsānat* al-Kharṭūm, Maʿiyya Saniyya, Ṣādir al-awāmir al-ʿāliya, Sīn 1/1/5, p. 79, no. 5.

called Dīwān al-Fābrīqāt wa-l-ʿAmaliyyāt) to be used as a labour pool for work in factories and quarries.[84]

Hard labour in provincial gaols existed already in 1830. It is defined in the Law of Agriculture enacted in that year, as "to be employed, with his feet in chains, on the government building site (*al-abniya al-mīriyya*) in the district (*maʾmūriyya*) where he comes from" (art. 17). The Penal Code of 1845 mentions expressly that these building sites are located both in Cairo and in the provincial centres (Art. 192). Since this type of hard labour was served not too far from home, it was considered to be lighter than terms served in the national prisons. The QS referred to it with the term "lowly jobs" (*khidamāt danīʾa* or *ashghāl sufliyya*). Convicts serving time in the provincial prisons were employed in sweeping, cleaning and light construction labour. This type of punishment was less strenuous than hard labour in factories.[85]

Places for simple detention (*ḥabs*) were the police prisons in the big cities, the prison in the Cairo Citadel, and prisons in the various provincial capitals. These prisons fell under the authority of the local police departments or the provincial administrations (*mudīriyyāt, muḥāfaẓāt*). They were relatively small. In August 1859, about 100 prisoners were detained in the Cairo police gaol, among them those held for debt.[86] The provincial prison of the Mudīriyya Beni Suweif and Fayoum housed 74 inmates in 1854.[87] For higher officials and military officers[88] there was detention in the fortress of Abū Qīr, which was in use until at least 1855.[89] I have not been able to establish whether or not the detainees were forced to work. For some time after 1849 it was replaced by imprisonment in Aswan, with a reduction of half of the prison term because of the heat.[90]

84 Majlis al-Aḥkām to Majlis Istiʾnāf Qiblī, 24 Jumādā I 1281 [25–10 1864], informing this council that al-Wābūrāt wa-l-ʿAmaliyyāt had been abolished, Majlis al-Aḥkām, Ṣādir al-aqālīm al-qibliyya, Sīn 7/4/33, p. 83, doc. 21.

85 Majlis al-Aḥkām to al-Muʿāwana, 6 Ramaḍān 1280: Transfer of a sick seventy-year-old convict, with bad eyesight to the lowly jobs in the *mudīriyya* because the work in the factory was too strenuous form him. Majlis al-Aḥkām, Ṣādir al-Dawāwīn, Lām 7/3/46, p. 5.

86 Maʿiyya Saniyya to Ḍabṭiyyat Miṣr, 4 Muḥarram 1276 [3–8 1859], Majlis al-Aḥkām, Daftar Majmūʿ umūr idāra wa-ijrāʾat, Sīn 7/33/1, p. 233.

87 Khedival Order to Mudīr Banī Suwayf and Fayūm, 9 Dhū al-Qaʿda 1270 [3–8 1854]. Maʿiyya Saniyya 1879 (old), awāmir, p. 4, doc. 4 (from DWQ card index).

88 Art. 62 of the Penal Code of 1849 lays down that here officials with the rank of *qāʾimmaqām* (lieutenant-colonel in the army and a government official at the village level in the civil ranks) or higher were held.

89 Khedival order to the Muḥāfaẓa of Cairo, 23 Ṣafar 1272 [4–11 1855] to send a certain village sheikh to the Abū Qīr prison. Sīn 1/1/5, p. 74. The QS does not mention Abū Qīr anymore.

90 Decree of the Majlis al-Aḥkām, 8 Rajab 1265 [30–5 1849]. Majlis al-Aḥkām, Daftar Majmūʿ Umūr Jināʾiyya, p. 133.

As we have seen, prisons fell under various departments: Ministry of War, of the Navy, and of Construction, the various police departments (*ḍabṭiyya*) under the authority of the city administrations (*muḥāfaẓāt*) and the provincial administrations (*mudīriyyāt*). Therefore, the organisation of the prison system was diverse. A small measure of uniformity was introduced by the appointment of a special inspector of prisons in February 1865, with the task of checking the conditions of the prisons and the punctual release of the prisoners.[91]

3.3 *Transportation*

Transportation to the Sudan was regarded as the most serious form of imprisonment. We do not have any details of prison life there, but the climate, the distance from home and the working conditions must have made life very hard for the inmates. Transportation was introduced as a means of incapacitation of serious criminals by means of total exclusion from society, and thus as an alternative for capital punishment. Economic considerations played a role in its introduction. Prisoners had to work in those areas where free workers were not available: in the gold mines and quarries in Eastern Sudan and, later, in the reclamation projects in Central Sudan. In the end, however, the authorities realised that prison inmates were not very efficient and productive workers. By then it was decreed that those deported to the Sudan could work in agriculture as free labourers and had to support themselves by their own labour. The only restriction to which they were subjected was that they were forbidden to return to Egypt.

During Meḥmed ʿAlī's reign, there were three modalities of transportation. The first one was perpetual banishment from Egyptian territory. This was introduced in 1846, for those with life sentences. They were to be sent via the Sudan to Ethiopia, out of reach of the Egyptian government (*jihat al-Ḥabash allatī hiya khārija ʿan ṣūrat al-ḥukūma bi-ṭarīqat al-Sūdān*).[92] This order, which was indeed enforced,[93] was revoked in March 1852, when the Majlis al-Aḥkām decreed that henceforth convicts with life sentences were to be sent to Jabal Qīsān.[94] The other modalities were deportation with forced labour in mines and quarries, and deportation to reclamation areas.

91 Appointment of Salīm Pasha al-Jazāʾirlī, 9 Ram 1281 [5–2 1865]. (Sāmī 1928–1936) 3/2, p. 597.

92 See note 98.

93 Majlis al-Aḥkām, Maḥfaẓat 2, doc. 2/70, Maḍbaṭa 21 Dhū al-Ḥijja 1266 [28–10 1850]; doc. 2–2/42, Maḍbaṭa 1 Dhū al-Ḥijja 1266; doc. 2/37, 23 Dhū al-Qaʿda 1266.

94 Decree of the Majlis al-Aḥkām, 26 Jumādā I 1268 [18 March 1852], Daftar Majmūʿ Umūr Jināʾiyya, p. 133.

When deportation was first introduced as a punishment, the convicts were sent to a mountainous area in the Sennār Province on the upper Blue Nile near the Ethiopian border, where they had to work in gold mines and stone quarries. The most notorious labour camp was located in Fayzoghli, but there were other camps as well, notably in Jabal Qīsān and, more to the East, Jabal Dūl, which was located on Ethiopian territory. Fayzoghli is mentioned for the first time in the version of the QM printed in 1845[95] By then it had become the normal destination for those convicted for embezzlement, theft, manslaughter, robbery, false testimony and forgery, even for relatively short terms of six months.[96] Before that time it was already in use as a place of exile for political opponents.[97] On 9 February 1846 (12 Ṣafar 1262) Meḥmed ʿAlī decreed that those sentenced to two years or more of hard labour, were to be deported to the gold mines (i.e. Fayzoghli and environment).[98] This order was not consistently enforced until 1848, when, at the instigation of the *Jamʿiyya Ḥaqqāniyya* (the highest judicial council and predecessor of the Majlis al-Aḥkām), serious offenders were indeed sent to the Jabal Dūl and Jabal Qīsān labour camps.[99] Between 1863 and 1865 Fayzoghli and the other labour prisons on the Blue Nile were closed.[100] As from 1865 prisoners with sentences longer than ten years were to be deported to the White Nile area in the Sudan.[101]

The third modality of deportation to the Sudan was hard labour in agriculture. This was introduced in 1844 as a special punishment for officials guilty of

95 The QM incorporated previous legislation such as the Qānūn al-Filaha of 1830 and the Qānūn al-Siyāsatnāma of 1837. Several articles of these laws as included in the QM impose deportation to Fayzoghli as a punishment, whereas the original versions of these laws do not mention it. Therefore, deportation to Fayzoghli must have been introduced between 1837 and 1845.

96 QM Art. 201.

97 Shuqayr (1972), pp. 113–114.

98 Hand-written note in the printed copy of the Penal Code of 1849, found in the Egyptian National Archive. The order was given orally as appears from a later document containing a resolution of the Majlis al-Aḥkām, 27 Jumādā I 1268 (17 April 1852), stipulating that convicts with life sentences were to be sent to Jabal Qīsān. Maḥfaẓat al-Mihi, doc. 103. That this order was enforced appears from the sijill listing the names of the convicts in the Alexandria Arsenal prison for the years 1263–1268.

Diwān al-Tarsāne, sijill 953, where there are frequent entries saying the prisoner was transported to the Sudan.

99 For the order of the Jamʿiyya Haqqāniyya, see al-Waqāʾiʿ al-Miṣriyya, 24 Rajab 1264 [26–6 1848]; for deportations to Jabal Dūl and Jabal Qīsān, see al-Waqāʾiʿ al-Miṣriyya, 1848, passim, and Hill (1959), pp. 83, 87.

100 Hill (1959), p. 163.

101 Majlis al-Aḥkām, Ṣādir al-aqālīm al-qibliyya, Sīn 7/4/33, p. 134, doc. 48, 9 Shaʿbān 1281 [7–1–1865]. The order was repeated later that year on 4 Jumādā I, 1282, Sāmī (1928–1936), iii, 2, p. 625.

embezzlement.[102] As from 1857, peasants and rural sheikhs sentenced to five years or more for manslaughter were deported to land reclamation areas in the Khartoum Province and could be accompanied, on a voluntary basis, by their families.[103] They were not to be detained, but had to work as free labourers. One year later, this was extended to persons convicted for theft for the fourth time.[104] When these convicts and their families began to arrive in 1858, the Sudanese officials were at a loss. To be on the safe side, they imprisoned everybody and wrote to the Ministry of Interior for instructions. The query was referred to the Majlis al-Aḥkām, who had originally drafted the decree. The Majlis al-Aḥkām explained that those sentenced to banishment according to this decree were free to go anywhere in the Sudan and seek their livelihood in whatever way they wanted and that their families had accompanied them voluntarily. Therefore, they all had to be released and the government was not obliged to support them.[105]

3.4 *Differentiation*

3.4.1 As to Gender and Age

Male and female inmates were housed in separate prisons.[106] In Meḥmed ʿAlī's time, women in Cairo were held in a special prison called Bayt al-Wālī and in a women's prison connected with the Shariʿa court in the capital.[107] Around the same time, in the early 1830s, a women's prison was created in Alexandria. Before that time, women in Alexandria were not imprisoned but were given corporal punishment instead.[108] Local police prisons also had sections for women. The one in Cairo was moved to a newly rented house in 1860, because it was too close to the men's prison.[109] Where women were detained in the

102 QM Art. 196.

103 Decree of 3 Dhū al-Ḥijja, 1273. Sāmī (1928–1936), iii/1, p. 230.

104 Art. 1, decree of the Majlis al-Aḥkām, 25 Muḥarram 1275 [4–9 1858]; text in Sāmī (1928–1936).

105 Majlis al-Aḥkām, al-Maḍābiṭ al-Ṣādira, Sīn 7/10/3, p. 115, maḍbaṭa no. 412, 6 Jumādā I 1275 [1–12 1858].

106 I have found no evidence for Tucker's assertion that women were kept in the same prison as men as a form of additional punishment special to women. See Tucker (1986).

107 Dīwān Khidīwī, Daftar qayd al-khulāṣāt (Turkī), S/2/40, sijill 18 (1246), p. 180, doc. 329, 15 Shawwāl 1246 [29–3 1832].

108 Khedival order of to the Naẓir Majlis Iskandariyya, 11 Jumādā I 1249 [6–10 1832], instructing him to find a place where women can be imprisonment in the same way as in Cairo and to provide for their maintenance. Sīn 1/55/2 (1248–1249), p. 108. doc. 496.

109 Khedival order to the Muḥāfaẓat Miṣr, 23 Shawwāl 1277 [4–5 1861] to rent a house for 50–75 piasters to serve as a women's prison and appoint a guard with a monthly wage of 150 piasters, because the existing women's prison in the Police Department (Ḍabṭiyya) is

provincial centres is not clear. In view of the strict separation between men and women elsewhere, there is no doubt that they were confined in different localities.

Women were also sentenced to forced labour under the supervision of the Department of Construction (*dīwān al-abniya*).[110] Here the conditions left much to be desired. In 1850 it was discovered that at some places men and women not only worked together, but also had to spend the night in the same wards. When this became known, the authorities immediately ordered this to be remedied.[111] In special cases, for instance if they had to take care of small children or were pregnant, women were not sent to factories or building sites, but were allowed to serve their sentences in the civil hospital.[112] Women convicts were never sent to the Alexandria Arsenal or the Sudanese labour camps. In 1856, a national prison for women sentenced to forced labour was established in a spinning mill (Turkish: *iplikhāne*, Arabic: *maghzal*) in Bulaq.[113] This must have been the result of the introduction of the QS, which, following the Ottoman Penal Code of 1850, lays down that women are to be detained in a women's prison (Ch. 2, art. 22).

There is no evidence that there were special reformatories for juvenile delinquents. This in spite of art. 133 QM (corresponding with art. 66 of the French Penal Code of 1811), laying down that boys of twelve years and older, not possessed of discretion (*ghayr mumayyiz*), shall not be punished as adults, but be detained in a reformatory (*maḥall al-tarbiya*) for a period to be determined by the government or be handed over to his parents. Most prisoners in the Alexandria Arsenal were at least seventeen years old, but I came across some

too close to the men's prison. Maʿiyya Saniyya, daftar 1894 (old), Awāmir, p. 125, doc. 65 (from DWQ card index s.v. sujūn).

110 See e.g. al-Waqāʾiʿ al-Miṣriyya, 24 Rajab 1264: woman is sentenced to forced labour in the Dīwān al-Abniya.

111 Order of Majlis al-Aḥkām, 1 Rabīʿ I 1266 [26–1 1850]. Majlis al-Aḥkām, Daftar Majmūʿ Umūr Jināʾiyya, p. 89.

112 al-Jamʿiyya al-Ḥaqqāniyya, Qayd al-khulāṣāt al-Ṣādira ilā al-aqālīm wa-l-dawāwīn, Sīn 6/11/9, 4 Jumādā II 1264 [8–5 1848], p. 189: woman is sentenced to serve two years in the civil hospital (*isbitāliyya mulkiyya*) assisting the sick, because she is pregnant and has a baby that she is still breastfeeding. Majlis Miṣr, 3 Ṣafar 1272 [15–10 1855], Muḥāfaẓat Miṣr, Lām 1/20/1, p. 2, no. 5: Woman condemned to serve in the civil hospital.

113 See e.g. (all taken from DWQ card index s.v. sujūn): Khedival order of 8 Muḥarram 1272 [20–9 1855], to Mudīriyya Minūfiyya, Maʿiyya Saniyya, Daftar 1883 (old), Awāmir, p. 12, doc. 2: a woman is sentenced to six years hard labour to be spent in a certain prison until the *iplikhane* is opened; Khedival order of 23 Shaʿbān 1272 [29–4 1856], to Muḥāfaẓat Miṣr, Maʿiyya Saniyya, Daftar 1884 (old), Awāmir, p. 129, doc. 122: approval of a life sentence iplikhane for theft.

instances of younger boys,[114] even younger than twelve years, the statutory minimum age for criminal responsibility.[115] Such boys were usually put under the care of one of the foremen of a workshop for learning a trade, and special arrangements were made for their lodgings.[116] Occasionally I have found petitions of parents requesting the release of their minor children.[117]

Arts. 134 and 135 of the QM, also following French law, lay down that persons of seventy years and older shall not be sentenced to a term of hard labour or to deportation for life and that the punishment of persons who reach that age while serving a sentence of forced labour shall be commuted to incarceration (*al-rabṭ bi-l-Qalʿa*) with the possibility of a reduction of the term. The QS is silent on this point. That there were inmates of seventy years and older is confirmed by the records.[118]

114 Dīwān al-tarsāna, sijill 954, p. 127, fourteen-year-old pickpocket with five previous offences, in first instance sentenced to life, but after revision to three years. Sijill 955 (1281–1283): Inmates younger than 17 years are exceptional. Among the 135 convicts that entered the līmān between 5 Dhū al-Qaʿda 1281 and 7 Dhū al-Ḥijja 1281, I found one boy of 12 (theft) and one of 14 (desertion) years old.

115 As fixed in the Ordonnance concerning the prohibition for children and toddlers to roam in the streets (Lāyiḥa fī manʿ murūr al-awlād wa-l-aṭfāl fī al-ṭuruq) 28 Dhū al-Ḥijja 1261 [28–12 1845]; text in Majlis al-Aḥkām, Daftar Majmūʿ umūr idāra wa-ijrāʾāt, Sīn 7/33/1, p. 177.

116 Dīwān al-Tarsāna, 954 (old), p. 131 and 956 (old) p. 7: Eleven-year-old Sayyid Aḥmad Buḥayrī was sent to the Alexandria Arsenal on 15 Shawwāl 1281 [13–3 1865] for petty theft. He is entrusted to the regimental tailor and is allowed to spend the night at the ship al-Zarkh. Ibid. sijill 954 (old), p. 132: Three days later, on 18 Shawwāl 1281, 10 years old Nūr al-Dīn Ibrāhīm Muḥammad enters the Alexandria Arsenal. Because his father is willing to vouch for him, he is allowed to spend the night outside the prison, but had to work in the forge during the day.

117 Maʿiyya Saniyya to the Qalʿa Saʿīdiyya, 16 Rabīʿ II 1272 [26–12 1855], Sīn 1/8/40, Maʿiyya Saniyya, Ṣādir al-Maʿiyya ilā al-Dawāwīn wa-l-Aqālīm wa-l-Muḥāfaẓāt, p. 132, doc. 17, ordering the release of a minor boy in response to a petition submitted by his mother.

118 Majlis al-Aḥkām to al-Muʿāwana, 6 Ramaḍān 1280, ordering the transfer of a sick and nearly blind prisoner more than 70 years of age from forced labour in factories (*al-wābūrāt wa-l-ʿamaliyyāt*) to forced labour in the region of residence (*al-ashghāl al-danīʾa bi-l-Mudīriyya*, Sīn 7/3/46, Majlis al-Aḥkām, Ṣādir al-Dawāwīn, p. 5; Mudīr ʿumūm Asyuṭ wa-Jirjā to the kātib al-Dīwān al-Khidīwī, 18 Ṣafar 1272 [22–10 1855], requesting the release of an 80 year old man who had been sentenced to one year of forced labour by the Majlis Qiblī, without having seen him, Maʿiyya Turkī, Maḥfaẓa 8, leaf 20, doc. 376; Majlis al-Aḥkām to Majlis Istiʾnāf Qiblī, 1 Jumādā II 1281[1–11 1864], informing this Majlis of a Khedival order to transfer the former tax collector ʿAbd Allāh Ṣāliḥ from the Firqa Iṣlāḥiyya (see below) to the Alexandria Arsenal, on the ground that he is about 80 years old and cannot be corrected by the Firqa Iṣlāḥiyya, Majlis al-Aḥkām, Ṣādir al-aqālīm al-qibliyya, Sīn 7/4/33, p. 86, doc. 25; see also correspondence regarding the release from al-Wābūrāt wa-l-ʿAmaliyyāt of four prisoners of whom three are over 70 and one nearly blind, al-Maʿiyya al-Saniyya, al-awāmir al-ʿāliya, Sīn 1/1/27, pp. 17, doc. 4, 17 Jumādā I 1281

3.4.2 As to the Type of Offender

The Egyptian prison system was not based on the idea that different types of offenders needed different "treatment", but rather on the principle of retribution requiring that serious or repeated offenders be punished more severely. The prison system was organised according to harshness, which was conceptualised as a function of living and work conditions, distance from home and length of the period of imprisonment. Those convicted for serious crimes were usually either transported to Sudan or sent to the Alexandria Arsenal. The dividing lines between both shifted continuously. (See Appendix 1) Short terms were served either in the police gaols (simple detention) or in the provincial prisons (simple detention, lowly jobs), or in industrial establishments (hard labour). The boundaries between these forms of confinement were not always clear.

From the early 1850s the separation of the different types of inmates became a special concern for the authorities. They proposed that separate wards or prisons be used for those held for debts, those kept in custody pending investigation and those convicted for light and for serious offences.[119] The sources do not give information on whether this differentiation was ever implemented. In 1863 a general instruction was issued to the effect that gaols (i.e. police gaols and the gaols in the provincial centres) were to keep apart the following three categories of inmates: serious criminals like murderers and thieves, light offenders together with drunks, and debtors.[120]

The first, and to the best of my knowledge only, time that the authorities showed interest in the rehabilitation of prisoners was in 1863, when a special program was initiated for convicts with sentences of three years or less, and for vagrants. The program was prompted by a concern about soaring crime rates, especially theft of cattle and cotton. Since the authorities believed that imprisonment had lost its deterrence, they ordered that the offenders be trained in crafts so that they could support themselves after their release. For the duration of their prison term they were enlisted in a special military unit, called

and p. 25 doc. 7, 24 Jumādā I 1281; Al-Fābriqāt wa-l-ʿamaliyyāt wa-l-wābūrāt, Maḥfaẓat 311, doc. 112, 10 Jumādā II 1274 [25–1 1858].

119 See e.g. Dhikr waẓāʾif mutafarriʿa bi-l-majlis (List of further duties of the regional councils), enacted in the early 1850s, art. 5, Jallad (1890–1892) II, pp. 105–106, laying down that those held in custody and those held for debt had to be separated from the convicts, and that these had to be separated according to the seriousness of their crimes.

120 Al-Maʿiyya a-Saniyya, Qayd al-Awāmir al-karīma al-ṣādira min qalam al-majālis bi-l-muʿāwana, Sīn 1/19/2, p. 1, doc. 1, order to the Majlis al-Aḥkām, 28 Rabīʿ I 1280 [12–9 1863]. For a similar order instructing that serious offenders should henceforth be detained in the Citadel rather than in the Cairo police prison, see Khedival order of 8 Dhū al-Ḥijja 1281 [4–5 1865] (summary in card index s.v. *sujūn*).

al-firqa al-iṣlāḥiyya, reformatory unit, (also known as *firqat al*-mudhnibīn, unit of delinquents, and *orta al-mudhnibīn*, battalion of delinquents). After the completion of their terms they would be trained in special trades and crafts companies (*bulūkāt al-ṣanāyi'*).[121] I have not found any information about the setup of this unit. For reasons that are not clear, this unit was operative for only a short time. Early 1865 it was disbanded and the prisoners who had not completed their sentences were sent to the Alexandria Arsenal. Those serving in the trades and crafts companies, having completed their prison sentences, were released.[122]

3.5 *Release*

During the early years of Meḥmed ʿAlī's reign, offenders were as a rule sentenced to imprisonment of unspecified duration and would not be released until they had repented and mended their ways. This was customary in the Ottoman Empire and Tunis before the nineteenth century.[123] In practice this meant that after some time they or their relatives would send petitions requesting their release and that the Meḥmed ʿAlī would decide whether or not the term they had already served, had been sufficient.[124] The system came to an end around 1830. The main purpose of the criminal legislation of 1829–1830 was to introduce a system in which law enforcers would pronounce specified sentences on the strength of legal provisions. This was successful. As from 1830, we can observe that criminal sentences began to define the term of imprisonment, as required in the criminal legislation of 1829–1830, and the previous practice of unspecified sentences began to be abandoned.[125]

121 Khedival order, 12 Jumādā II 1280 [24–11 1863], al-Maʿiyya al-Saniyya, Qayd al-Awāmir al-karīma al-Ṣādira min qalam majālis bi-l-muʿāwana, Sīn 1/19/2.

122 Text of the order, 26 Ramaḍān 1281 [22–2 1865] in Majlis al-Aḥkām to Majlis Istiʾnāf Qiblī, 11 Shawwāl 1281, Majlis al-Aḥkām, Ṣādir al-aqālīm al-qibliyya, Sīn 7/4/34, p. 6, doc. 83. See also Sāmī (1928–1936), iii/2, p. 599.

123 See Heyd (1973), pp. 302, 306; Henia (1983).

124 See e.g. Khedive to al-Ḥajj Aḥmad Agha, Naẓir al-Mabānī (Alexandria), 16 Shawwāl 1243 [1–5 1828], Sīn/2/29/2, Dīwān Khidīwī Turkī, Ṣādir al-Aqālīm.

125 See e.g. Majlis ʿĀlī Mulkī to the maʾmūr of the Dīwān Khidīwī, 16 Rajab 1246, instructing him to direct the local officials to specify terms of imprisonment according to the seriousness of the offence when sentencing offenders, and to inform the Dīwān Khidīwī of these sentences. Majlis ʿĀlī Mulkī, Daftar 759 Turkī (old), p. 144, doc. 283 (From DWQ card index s.v. sujūn). Unspecified sentences, however, continued to be pronounced, but only in exceptional cases. see e.g. Governor of al-Qalʿa al-Saʿīdiyya to the Khāzin Khidīwī, 19 Shawwāl 1272 [12–6 1857], Maʿiyya Turkī, Maḥfaẓa 12, leaf 24, doc. 254. Military offenders were, at least in 1861, usually sentenced without a term "*bidūn mudda*". As a rule, deserters were released after six months. Dīwān al-Tarsāna, 954 (old).

In the early years of Meḥmed ʿAlī's reign, the local administrators would send the convicts after sentencing directly to the prisons and labour camps. From the late 1820s, we find continuous missives to these local officials directing them to send lists of these prisoners to the Civil Council (Majlis Mulkī), so that the situation of these prisoners could be monitored at the national level.[126] Even after the central government, during the 1830s, finally established its control over criminal justice, numerous missives were sent, until well into the 1860s, to prison authorities to instruct them to send lists of the inmates and their cases, so that the central government could check whether convicts were released after the completion of their term. Complaints on this account submitted by prisoners were seriously investigated at the highest instance.[127] From time to time, especially in the 1860s, the Majlis al-Aḥkām would be instructed to review the cases of those whose terms for some reason were not specified, or who had been given life sentences.[128]

Completion of the prison term did not always imply freedom: young convicts were usually sent to the army after their release.[129] On the other hand, however, convicts would often be released without having fully served their sentences due to the frequent general amnesties: between 1829 and 1869 I have found eleven instances.[130] They were probably used to ease the overcrowding of prisons. When prisoners were released, they had to find a guarantor (*ḍāmin*), who would be personally responsible to produce him if the authorities requested his presence. If he failed to do so, he himself would be detained.

4 Conclusions

In the introduction I briefly summarised the theories of Foucault and Spierenburg explaining the development of the penal systems in Western

126 See e.g. Khedival order to Wakīl Nāẓir al-Majlis, 17 Ramaḍān 1243 [2–4 1828], Dīwān Khidīwī Turkī, daftar 744 (old), p. 31, doc. 69; Khedival order, 4 Shaʿbān 1252 [14–11 1836], Maʿiyya Saniyya Turkī, 81 (old), doc. 80 (both taken from DWQ card index, s.v. sujūn).

127 See e.g. Majlis al-Aḥkām, qayd al-ʿarḍuḥālāt al-Ṣādira, Sīn 7/9/5, p. 105, no. 1, 17 Rabīʿ II 1275: a complaint of an inmate of the wābūrāt wa-ʿamaliyyāt (see below) that the period in which he was detained before the sentence was not deducted from the time of his imprisonment as was indicated in the sentence.

128 See e.g. Bāshmuʿāwin Janāb Khidīwī to Majlis al-Aḥkām, 29 Dhū al-Ḥijja 1279 [16–6–1863]. Majlis al-Aḥkām, Sīn 7/10/18, 29 Rajab 1280, no. 400, pp. 93–95.

129 See e.g. Majlis al-Aḥkam, Qayd al-qaḍāyā al-wārida, Sīn 7/32/4, case, 2 Shawwāl 1280, p. 30; ibid. case, 8 Shaʿbān 1280, p. 42. The practice was based on a decree of the Majlis al-Aḥkām which I have not been able to trace.

130 See appendix 4 for a detailed list.

Europe. Both of them relate the emergence of prisons as the main form of punishment to the rise of strong, centralised states. Foucault emphasises that France emerged as a centralised and strong state, with an efficient police force that could catch and bring to justice many more criminals than under the *ancien régime*. Therefore, deterrence by gruesome spectacles of suffering was not necessary anymore. It was replaced by deterrence based on the great risk for criminal offenders of being apprehended. Instead of publicly executed corporal punishment, imprisonment became the main form of judicial punishment. Prisons became disciplining institutions aimed at creating obedient subjects of the state. For Spierenburg the relationship with the rise of strong centralised states is more complicated. He situates the abolition of publicly executed corporal punishment in Elias's *civilising process*. This process resulted in an aversion, among the elite, to the sight of corporal punishment and torture and the restraint of aggressive impulses. First this was restricted to the members of the elite groups, but as the nation state became better integrated the aversion extended towards all classes of society. Political action motivated by these sensibilities could be successful because the newly emerging centralised nation states were more stable and did not need anymore the spectacles of public executions and torture to enhance their authority.

As for Egypt, the link between the changes in the penal system and the process of political centralisation initiated by Meḥmed ʿAlī is obvious. The history of criminal law during his reign shows, on the one hand, how he succeeded in bringing his officials under his control and, on the other, that enacted criminal law was one of his instruments of centralisation. Officials were made to realise that they could only administer it according to Meḥmed ʿAlī's instructions and under his supervision. When once he reprimanded an official for having tortured and mutilated a peasant who had committed an offence, before finally killing him,[131] what was at stake were not humanitarian considerations but rather an assertion of Meḥmed ʿAlī's authority, since the official had violated his instructions. Once he had disciplined his officials, his policy of centralisation could succeed. From then on punishment could only be imposed by virtue of enacted criminal laws. *Prima facie* this resembles the rule of law and the principle of *nulla poena sine lege* in Western European law. On closer inspection, however, both notions of legality were quite different. In Western Europe its first and foremost function was to restrict the power of the state and to protect the citizen against its encroachments. In Meḥmed ʿAlī's realm, on the other hand, it was a tool of state control and centralisation. Meḥmed ʿAlī's criminal laws aimed at tightening his grip on the corps of officials by forbidding them

131 See note 45.

to commit certain acts and penalising them, and ordering them to behave in certain ways, i.e. imposing specific punishments when trying offences committed by their subjects. The criminal laws addressed the officials rather than the subjects. It is illustrative that these penal laws were not officially publicised. If they were printed, then this was only for official use. The penal provisions must be read, not as guarantees for the citizens, but as instructions to officials on how to proceed when dealing with certain offences. The principal difference between the Egyptian and the Western European ideal of legality, is that according to the latter, the ruler had to obey the law, whereas the Pasha, regarding legislation as his personal commands, did not feel bound by it. His legal system can better be labelled as an instance of "rule by law", as we find in many contemporary dictatorial states, than as a form of "rule of law".[132]

By the end of his reign Meḥmed ʿAlī had established tight control over both his officials and over the population. Instruments for the control of his subjects were a network of village, neighbourhood and guild sheikhs, monitoring the doings and dealings of those under their authority, and an efficient police force, using classical methods such as police spies as well as modern, scientific ones such as forensic medicine and chemical analysis.[133] As a result of his greater grip on the country, public security increased and, as noted by contemporary European travellers, the number of executions decreased. Spectacles of brutal suffering such as death by impaling were not staged anymore after the 1830s. Banishment or deportation to the Sudan became a substitute for capital punishment. The public character of punishment, however, did not change. The execution of death sentences still took place in public and the bodies of the executed were left hanging on the gallows. And those sentenced to imprisonment and hard labour were not totally locked away behind prison walls but remained to some extent part of public life. They were transported in chains like the columns of prisoners (*chaînes*) in eighteenth and early nineteenth-century France and Spain and those sentenced to hard labour often worked side by side with other workers, in industrial establishments as well as on construction sites. Moreover, public floggings were usual. This persistence of the public character of punishment is not exceptional. Spierenburg and others have criticised Foucault for presenting the change in penal policy as a sudden and abrupt one, and shown that it was a more gradual process. In France, for example, public executions (in some cases preceded by the amputation of the right hand) and other forms of public penalties such as the pillory and public

132 See on this distinction Brown (1997), pp. 241–2.

133 On the development of the police, see Fahmy (1999b).

branding were practised until the 1830s,[134] although less frequently than before. In other Western European countries public executions and floggings continued until the second half of the nineteenth century.

The abolition of flogging and caning in Egypt in 1861 deserves separate discussion. It was part of a deliberate policy to reduce official violence, which had become feasible due to certain social and economic transformations of the country. An important factor, although one for which we do not have direct documentary evidence, was the presence, among the Egyptian ruling elite, of reformers, who began to consider corporal punishment as backward and uncivilised and argued that it had to be replaced in order to modernise the country. The importance of groups of Westernising reformers for the nineteenth-century developments of penal systems has been documented for non-western countries like Russia,[135] early colonial India (where the reformers, of course, were British and not Indian),[136] and Peru.[137] In Egypt, there were reformers in the nineteenth century, but they have left no documents regarding their ideas on legal punishment. Nevertheless, it is my contention that they influenced penal policy, especially with regard to the abolition of torture and corporal punishment. They must have followed the example of the Ottoman Empire, where corporal punishment had been abolished with the introduction of the Penal Code of 1858. It is doubtful, however, whether the Egyptian reformers were motivated by growing sensibilities against public punishment. The persistence of official violence outside the judicial sphere is evidence to the contrary. The ethnic gap between the Turkish speaking elite and the native Egyptian peasants must have been an effective barrier to empathy.

In order to explain why they could successfully implement their program, we first have to consider the function and meaning of official violence in nineteenth-century Egypt. As I outlined in the section on corporal punishment (section 2.2), official violence was a mode of repression practised in three contexts: (1) as a means of coercion, to make people obey official orders (often in connection with tax collection, or drafting men for military service or *corvée*); (2) as a means to obtain confessions during criminal investigations, and, finally, (3) as a form of judicial punishment. During Meḥmed ʿAlī's reign the Turkish elite ruled by means of violence. As the crops, money and the manpower demanded by the state from the population were often excessive and endangered its subsistence, they could only be collected by using brutal force. Moreover,

134 Léonard (1980), p. 12.
135 See Adams (1996).
136 See Singha (1998).
137 See Aguirre (1996).

corporal punishment was, especially in the countryside, economically more efficient than imposing prison sentences, because after a period of recovery, the peasant could go back to work. That the use of torture was regarded as normal and as a useful and helpful method in investigating crime, stemmed from the fact that the techniques of investigating crimes were still very primitive: investigation, usually conducted by administrative officials, focused on extracting a confession from one or more suspects. In addition, the use of violence, and especially the wielding of the *kurbāj*, symbolised authority, in the same manner as public executions did. For all these reasons, the flogging of peasants by Turkish was common and widespread.

Meḥmed ʿAlī's measures to restrict to some extent the use of violence were inspired by two factors: First, it had to be made clear that wielding the *kurbāj* as a symbol of power was ultimately controlled by the central government. Since the execution of capital punishment was the Khedive's prerogative, an official who killed a subject by an excess of beating or flogging, would intrude on the Khedive's rights. This rule was indeed enforced and officials who killed subjects were brought to justice. A second point was that violence should not damage the productive capacity of his subjects by killing or incapacitating the subjects. Within these restrictions, flogging continued to be practised as a way of repression and enforcing obedience.

The first substantial steps in restricting official violence were taken in connection with criminal investigation. These steps were made possible by the extension and growing efficiency of the state apparatus. By the 1850s a fully-grown, specialised police force had come into existence as well as an extensive public health administration which was also involved in police work. The increased professionalism of those involved in criminal investigations and the use of scientific methods,[138] showed that there were better ways of finding the truth than trying to obtain a confession. This led to the realisation that torture was not a very effective instrument of finding the truth[139] and made it possible for reformers as from the early 1850s to enforce measures to restrict and finally, in 1861, banning it.

It is not entirely clear what immediately prompted the abolition of flogging as a punishment in 1861, because the decree itself is silent on its considerations. At the political level, the reformers could point at the example of the Ottoman Empire where corporal punishment had been abolished in 1858. But that this

138 See Fahmy (1999a).

139 For the relationship between effective police methods and the abolition of torture in Europe, see Asad (1996), p. 1089, referring to John Langbein, *Torture and the Law of Proof* (1977).

reform could be effectively introduced was because the need of official violence in the countryside had decreased due to economic developments. Before 1842, Egypt was a command economy, dominated by Meḥmed ʿAlī's monopoly. Peasants produced for the Pasha, who therefore had a direct interest in their productive capacity. Corporal punishment was therefore economically more advantageous than imprisonment. This changed after the state monopoly was abrogated and the state's extraction of the rural surplus became limited to tax collection. Meḥmed ʿAlī's successors had therefore a more abstract and remote interest in the productive capacity of peasants. They were not too much concerned about the imprisonment of peasants. Connected with this development is that fact that during Meḥmed ʿAlī's reign demands on the rural population in produce, *corvée* labour and men for conscription often jeopardised their existence and could only be collected by force. With the reduction of the army in the 1840s and the easing of *corvée* in the 1850s,[140] the need for violent coercion diminished. A final but crucial factor was that the dearth of rural labour in the countryside had come to an end. If peasants fled from their villages during Meḥmed ʿAlī's time, they were forcibly returned, because their labour was needed. This changed during the 1850s with the rise of large estates and the dispossession of many small holders. Peasants became expendable and there was no need any more to except them from imprisonment if they committed an offence. If sentenced to hard labour, they could be profitably employed in the agricultural projects in the Sudan, as was decreed in 1857 (see Appendix 1).

By the 1860s imprisonment had prevailed in the Egyptian penal system as the main punishment. By that time prison conditions had improved and mortality among the inmates had dropped drastically. This meant that imprisonment did not anymore entail the risks of gratuitous and unintended suffering and death due to with pernicious prison conditions.[141] Imprisonment, therefore, became a penalty that could be better quantified and become a substitute of flogging, that could also be quantified precisely. Now, was this development linked to a change in penal policy? Did the rulers begin to regard imprisonment as a means of reform and rehabilitation of the prisoner? And did they introduce changes in the prison system to this end? There is little evidence that this was the case. There have been no attempts to set up penitentiaries and introduce prison regimes that were intended to morally improve and rehabilitate the prisoners. The only exception is the short-lived experiment of the military trade and craft units, established in 1863 because of a concern about the rise in rural crime. However, these units were dissolved a year and a half

140 Toledano (1990), 181, 188.
141 See Peters (2002).

later. It is not clear how they functioned, but the fact that the experiment was not continued shows, I believe, that there was no sufficient support for the idea. Rehabilitation of offenders seemed not to have been on the agenda of the ruling elite. The reforming zeal had stopped at the banning of corporal punishment. The main punitive functions of imprisonment were not the imposition of discipline but rather deterrence and retribution. In other words, imprisonment was an instrument of repression aimed at the subjection of the population, not at the disciplining or reforming of the offender.

Appendix 1: Distribution of Categories of Prisoners over the Penal Institutions

The articles of the various penal codes specify the type and duration of imprisonment to be imposed on the perpetrator of the offence defined in the article. However, from time to time decrees were issued modifying this and laying down that certain types of offenders or persons sentenced to a certain prison term, were to be transported to Sudan or serve their time in specific prisons. Hereunder I will give a survey of such decrees in order to make clear the hierarchy and relations between the different penitentiaries.

Banishment from Egyptian Territory

1846–1852: convicts with a life sentence were to be sent via the Sudan to Ethiopia.[142]

Sudan

1844: Officials guilty of embezzlement shall be sent to the Sudan to work in agriculture (art. 196 QM)

1846: prisoners with sentences of two years and more to be deported to the gold mines.[143]

1848: serious criminals to be deported to Jabal Dūl.[144]

1852, convicts with life sentences were to be deported to Jabal Qīsān.[145]

1857: peasants and rural sheikhs sentenced to five years or more of forced labour for manslaughter to be deported to land reclamation areas in the Khartoum Province (could be accompanied, on a voluntary basis, by their families).[146]

142 See note 107.

143 Ibid.

144 al-Waqāʾiʿ al-Miṣriyya, 24 Rajab 1264 [26–6 1848]; Hill (1959), p. 83.

145 Decree of the Majlis al-Aḥkām, 26 Jumādā I 1268 [18 March 1852], Daftar Majmūʾ Umūr Jināʾiyya, p. 133.

146 Decree of 3 Dhū al-Ḥijja, 1273. Sāmī (1928–1936), iii/1, p. 230.

1858: measure extended to persons convicted for theft for the fourth time.[147]
1863: convicts with sentences longer that five years to be deported to Fayzoghli.[148]
1865: convicts with sentences of over ten years were to be sent to the White Nile.[149]

Alexandria Prison

1860: convicts with sentences of one year or more were to be sent to The Alexandria Arsenal.
1862: convicts with life sentences, murderers and repeated offenders had to serve their time in Alexandria.[150]
1865: convicts with terms under ten years to Alexandria Prison.[151]
1866: convicts with sentences up till three years in the Alexandria arsenal, as appears from the registers of the Alexandria Arsenal.[152]

Appendix 2: The Nineteenth-Century Egyptian Criminal Laws

Penal Code of 1829 (PC 1829)
Turkish text and translation in (Peters 1999b).

Qānūn al-Filāḥa of 1830 (QF)
Text published as an appendix to Lāyiḥa (1840–1841) and in 1845 included in the QM (art. 1–55).

Al-Qānūn al-Muntakhab of 1845 (QM)
Text in Zaghlūl (1900), app. 100–155 and Jallād (1890–1892), iii, 351–78.

Penal Code of 1849 (PC 1849)
Printed in a bilingual (Arabic and Turkish) edition by Dār al-Ṭibāʿa al-ʿĀmira al-Mīriyya in Bulaq on 8 Rajab 1265.

147 Art. 1, decree of the Majlis al-Aḥkām, 25 Muḥarram 1275 (4 September 1858); text in (Sami/Sāmī 1928–1936), iii/1, pp. 294–297; ratification by the Khedive ultimo Ṣafar 1258, ibid., p. 301.
148 Decree, 28 Rabīʿ I 1280 [12–9 1863], Maʿiyya Saniyya, Ṣādir al-Awāmir al-karīma, Sīn 1/1/25, p. 5, doc. 4.
149 Khedival order to the Majlis al-Aḥkām, 4 Jumādā II 1282 [25–10 1865], (Sami/Sāmī 1928–1936), iii/2, p. 625.
150 Missive from the Maʿiyya Saniyya 29 DH 1276 [18–7 1860]. Majlis al-Aḥkām, Daftar Majmūʿ Umūr Jināʾiyya, p. p. 133. Missive from Ḥāfiẓ Pasha, commander of the Navy, 12 Rabīʿ I 1278 [7–9 1862], ibid.
151 Khedival order, 4 Jumādā II 1282 [25–10 1865], Majlis al-Aḥkām, maḥfaẓa 9, doc. 323/3.
152 Dīwān al-tarsāna, 955 (old).

Qānūnnāme al-Sulṭānī (QS)
Text in Zaghlūl, (1900), app., 156–178; Jallād (1890–1892), II, 90–102. Jallād also gives the administrative regulations (*Ḥarakāt*) issued together with the Code (pp. 102–111).
The Supplement of 5 articles to the QS drafted by the Majlis al-Aḥkām in 1275 [1858]. Text in Sāmī (1928–1936), iii/1, pp. 294–7.

Appendix 3: A Description of the Five Sijills regarding the Alexandria Prison

DWQ, Dīwān al-tarsāna, 953–957 (old), Qayd asmā' al-madhnūbīn bi-līmān tarsāna Iskandariyya [This is the title as given on the first leave of the sijill]. On the cover, as in the index, this series is erroneously referred to as: Qayd asmā' al-madyūniyya bayān tarsānat Iskandariyya.]

Sijills:

954: 13 Rajab 1277 till 5 Dhū al-Qaʿda 1281
955: 5 Dhū al-Qaʿda 1281 till 24 Rabīʿ I 1283
956: 24 Muḥarram 1278 till 26 Rabīʿ I 1285
957: 26 Rabīʿ I 12 85 till 10 Ṣafar 1286

There is a gap between no. 1 (29 Ṣafar 1263 to 4 Dhū al-Ḥijja 1268) and no. 2 that begins in 13 Rajab 1277. The nos. 2 to 5 are consecutive. No. 4 seems to be an exception as no. 3 ends on 24 Rabīʿ I 1283 and the first entries are dated 24 Muḥarram 1278. The reason is that the first 20 pages of no. 4 are a recapitulation of the previous sijills, listing all by their date of entry, all prisoners present on 1 Jumādā I 1283, that is all prisoners convicted for homicide who had not benefited from the amnesty of 5 Rabīʿ I 1283.

The sijills give the following information:

- name
- beginning of detention spent before arrival
- description and estimated age (is lacking in sijill 953)
- short description of offence
- length of sentence
- date of arrival
- number and date of covering letter
- date of the end of the sentence
- date of release or decease with date and number of pertinent correspondence

These sijills offer suitable material for statistical analysis that could deepen our knowledge about nineteenth-century Egyptian criminality and the judicial system.

Sources

Archival Sources

Almost all of the archival material that I used is located in the Egyptian National Archive (Dār al-Wathā'iq al-Qawmiyya, DWQ). If the location is not mentioned in the note, the document belongs to the collection of the DWQ.

Dār al-Wathā'iq al-Qawmiyya

Series
Maʿiyya Saniyya, Sīn 1
Maʿiyya Turkī, maḥāfiẓ
Diwān Khidīwī, Sīn 2
Diwān Khidīwī, maḥāfiẓ
al-Jamʿiyya al-Ḥaqqāniyya, Sīn 6
Majlis al-Aḥkām, Sīn 7
Majlis al-Aḥkām, maḥāfiẓ
al-Majlis al-khuṣūṣī, Sīn 11
Muḥāfaẓat Miṣr, Lām 1
Ḍabṭiyyat Miṣr, Lām 2
Mudīriyyat Minūfiyya, Lām 6
Mahfaẓat al-Mīhī
Dīwān al-Tarsāna
al-Fābrīqāt wa-l-ʿamaliyyāt wa-l-wābūrāt, maḥāfiẓ
al-Waqā'iʿ al-Miṣriyya (xeroxed)

Dār al-Maḥfūẓāt

Maḥkamat Miṣr al-ibtidā'iyya al-sharʿiyya, makhzan 46, ʿayn 22

References

Adams, Bruce F. *The politics of punishment: Prison reform in Russia 1863–1917*. DeKalb: Northern Illinois University Press, 1996. viii, 237 pp.

Aguirre, Carlos. "The Lima Penitentiary and the modernization of criminal justice in nineteenth-century Peru." In *The birth of the penitentiary in Latin America: Essays on criminology, prison reform, and social control, 1830–1940*, ed. Ricardo D. Salvatore and Carlos Aguirre, 44–77. Austin: The University of Texas Press, 1996.

al-Mahdī, Muḥammad al-ʿAbbāsī. *al-Fatāwā al-Mahdiyya fī 'l-Waqā'iʿ al-Miṣriyya*. 7 vols. Cairo: al-Maṭbaʿa al-Azhariyya, 1301 H.

Asad, Talal. "On torture, or cruel, inhuman, and degrading treatment." *Social Research* 63, no. 4 (1996): 1081–1109.

Baer, Gabriel. "Tanzimat in Egypt: The penal code." In *Studies in the social history of modern Egypt*, ed. Gabriel Baer, 109–133. Chicago: The University of Chicago Press, 1969.

Bowring, John. *Report on Egypt and Candia addressed to the Right Hon. Lord Viscount Palmerstone*. London: Command Paper, 1840.

Brown, Nathan J. *The Rule of Law in the Arab World: Courts in Egypt and the Gulf*. Cambridge: Cambridge University Press, 1997.

Clot Bey, A.-B. *Aperçu général sur l'Égypte*. 2 vols. Paris: Fortin, Masson et Cie, 1840.

Cole, Juan R.I. *Colonialism and revolution in the Middle East: Social and cultural origins of Egypt's 'Urabi movement*. Princeton NJ: Princeton University Press, 1993. xiii, 342 pp.

Couvidou, H. *Étude sur l'Égypte contemporaine*. Cairo, 1873.

Ener, Mine. "Getting into the shelter of Takiyat Tulun." In *Outside in: On the margins of the modern Middle East*, edited by Eugene Rogan, 53–76. London: I.B. Tauris, 2002.

Fahmy, Khaled. *All the Pasha's men: Mehmed Ali, his army and the making of modern Egypt*. Cambridge: Cambridge University Press, 1997. xviii, 334 pp. (Cambridge Middle East Studies, 8.

Fahmy, Khaled. "The anatomy of justice: Forensic medicine and criminal law in nineteenth-century Egypt." *Islamic Law and Society* 6, no. 2 (1999a): 224–271.

Fahmy, Khaled. "The police and the people in nineteenth century Egypt." *Die Welt des Islams* 39, no. 3 (1999b): 340–377.

Fahmy, Khaled. "Medical conditions in Egyptian prisons in the nineteenth century." In *Marginal voices in literature and society*, ed. Robin Ostle, 135–155. Strasbourg: European Science Foundation/Maison Méditerranéenne des Sciences de l'Homme d'Aix-en-Provence, 2000.

Foucault, M. *Surveiller et punir: naissance de la prison*. Paris: Gallimard, 1975.

Gisquet, M. *L'Égypte, les turcs et les arabes*. 2 vols. Paris Amyot, n.d.

Guémard, G. *Une oeuvre française: les réformes en Egypte, d'Al-Bey El Kébir à Méhémet-Ali, 1760–1848*. Cairo, 1936.

Hanna, Nelly. "Administration in Egypt From Ottoman times to the present: An introduction." In *The State and its servants: administration from the Ottoman times to the present*, ed. Nelly Hanna, 1–16. Cairo: The American University in Cairo Press, 1995.

Henia, A. "Prisons et prisonniers à Tunis vers 1762: système répressif et inégalités sociales." *Revue d'Histoire Maghrebine* 10, no. 31–32 (1983): 223–252.

Heyd, Uriel, and V.L. Ménage (ed.). *Studies in old Ottoman criminal law*. Oxford: Oxford University Press, 1973. xxxii, 340 pp.

Ilbert, R. *Alexandrie, 1830–1930*. 2 vols. Cairo: IFAO, 1996.

Jabartī, ʿAbd al-Raḥmān al-. *ʿAjāʾib al-āthār fī al-tarājim wa-l-akhbār*. 4 vols. Bulaq, 1879–1880.

Jallād, Fīlīb. *Qāmūs al-idāra wa-l-qaḍāʾ*. 4 vols. Alexandria, 1890–1892.

Lāyiḥa. *Lāyiḥat zirāʿat al-fallāḥ wa-tadbīr aḥkām al-falāḥ*. 2nd ed. Bulaq, 1840–1841.

Lane, E.W. *Manners and customs of the modern Egyptians*. Repr. ed. London, 1966.

Léonard, Jacques. "L'historien et le philosophe: A propos de Surveiller et punir: naissance de la prison." In *L'impossible prison*, ed. Michelle Perrot, 9–29. Paris: Eds du Seuil, 1980.

Mubārak, ʿAlī. *Al-Khiṭaṭ al-Tawfīqiyya al-jadīda li-Miṣr al-Qāhira*. 16 parts in 4 vols. Cairo, 1306 H.

O'Brien, Patricia. *The promise of punishment: Prisons in nineteenth century France*. Princeton, NJ: Princeton University Press, 1982. xiii, 330 pp.

Perrot, Michelle. "Délinquance et système pénitentiaire en France au 19e siècle." *Annales ESC* 30 (1975): 67–91.

Peters, Rudolph. "Murder on the Nile: Homicide Trials in 19th Century Egyptian Shariʿa Courts." *Die Welt des Islams* 30 (1990): 95–115.

Peters, Rudolph. "The codification of criminal law in 19th century Egypt: tradition or modernization?" In *Law, society, and national identity in Africa*, ed. J.M. Abun-Nasr a.o., 211–225. Hamburg: Buske, 1991.

Peters, Rudolph. "Islamic and secular criminal law in 19th century Egypt: The role and function of the qadi." *Islamic Law and Society* 4 (1997): 70–90.

Peters, Rudolph. "Administrators and magistrates: The development of a secular judiciary in Egypt, 1842–1871." *Die Welt des Islams* 39 (1999a): 378–397.

Peters, Rudolph. "'For his correction and as a deterrent example for others': Meḥmed ʿAlī's first criminal legislation (1829–1830)." *Islamic Law and Society* 6 (1999b): 164–193.

Peters, Rudolph. "Prisons and marginalisation in nineteenth century Egypt." In Eugene Rogan (ed.), *Outside in: On the margins of the modern Middle East*. London: I.B. Tauris, 2002, pp. 31–53.

Peters, Rudolph. "Controlled suffering: mortality and living conditions in nineteenth-century Egyptian prisons." *International Journal of Middle Eastern Studies*, 36 (2004), pp. 387–407.

Pike, Ruth. *Penal servitude in early modern Spain*. Madison, WI: The University of Wisconsin Press, 1983. xiii, 204 pp.

Sāmī, Amīn. *Taqwīm al-Nīl*. 3 vols. Cairo: Maṭbaʿat al-Kutub al-Misriyya, 1928–1936.

Schneider, Irene. "Imprisonment in pre-classical and classical Islamic law." *ILS* 2, no. 2 (1995): 157–174.

Schoelcher, Victor. *L'Égypte en 1845*. Paris: Pagnerre, 1846.

Scott, C. Rochfort. *Rambles in Egypt and Candia: With details of the military power and resources of those countries, and observations on the government, policy, and commercial system of Mohammed Ali*. 2 vols. London: Colburn, 1837.

Shuqayr, Naʿūm. *Jughrāfiyyat wa-tārīkh al-Sūdān*. Repr. ed. Beirut, 1972.

Singha, Radhika. *A despotism of law: Crime and justice in early colonial India*. Delhi etc.: Oxford University Press, 1998. xxix, 342 pp.

Spierenburg, Pieter. *The spectacle of suffering: Executions and the evolution of repression: from a preindustrial metropolis to the European experience*. Cambridge: Cambridge University Press, 1984. xiii, 274 pp.

Spierenburg, Pieter. *The prison experience: Disciplinary institutions and their inmates in early modern Europe*. New Brunswick: Rutgers University Press, 1991. x, 339 pp.

St. John, Bayle. *Village life in Egypt*. 2 vols. London: Chapman and Hall, 1852.

St. John, James August. *Egypt, and Mohammed Ali, or travels in the valley of the Nile*. 2 vols. London: Longman, 1834.

Toledano, Ehud, *State and society in mid-nineteenth century Egypt*. Cambridge: Cambridge University Press, 1990. xiv, 320 pp.

Tucker, Judith. *Women in nineteenth century Egypt*. Cairo: The American University in Cairo Press, 1986. xii, 251 pp.

Zaghlūl, Aḥmad Fatḥī. *al-Muḥāmāh*. Cairo: Maṭbaʿat al-Maʿārif, 1900. 434 + 211 (app.) + 8 pp.

Zysberg, André. "Galley and hard labor convicts in France (1550–1850): From the galleys to hard labor camps: essay on a long lasting penal institution." In *The emergence of carceral institutions: Prisons, galleys and lunatic asylums, 1550–1900*, ed. Pieter Spierenburg, 78–124. Rotterdam: Centrum voor Maatschappijgeschiedenis, Erasmus Universiteit Rotterdam, 1984.

CHAPTER 15

Controlled Suffering

Mortality and Living Conditions in 19th-Century Egyptian Prisons

> Whereas it is required by equity and justice that, in accordance with the principles of hygiene, the gaols in the governorate and the district capitals be clean and have access to so much fresh air that a person's health is not impaired, and whereas it has been noticed that some of these prisons do not satisfy these conditions, therefore the governors are instructed to conduct personally an examination and inspection of the prisons in their governorate, together with the chief engineer and the regional health officer.
>
> Order of the *Majlis al-Alkam*, issued in 1849[1]

∵

Between 1829 and the 1870s, the administration of criminal justice in Egypt was rationalized and bureaucratized. The most prominent features of this reform were the emergence of a hierarchical judiciary consisting of judicial councils and Shariʿa courts with clearly circumscribed jurisdictions; the introduction and enforcement of penal codes with well-defined offenses and penalties; and, finally, the development of a system of punishment in which imprisonment had become the main penalty, corporal punishment had been abolished, and the death penalty had become rare.[2] As a result of these reforms, Egyptian criminal law during the second half of the 19th century was – at least, before the British occupation – not as cruel and arbitrary as European travelers and British colonial servants made it out to be. During this period of penal reform, prison conditions improved drastically, which resulted in a noticeable drop in prison mortality between the late 1840s and the early 1860s. In this essay

1 *Majlis al-Ahkam*, Mahfaza 1, doc. 1/89, 16 Shaʿban 1265/13 June 1849, no. 451.

2 For the development of criminal law in 19th-century Egypt, see Rudolph Peters, "Islamic and Secular Criminal Law in 19th Century Egypt: The Role and Function of the Qadi," *Islamic Law and Society* 4 (1997): 70–90; idem, "Administrators and Magistrates: The Development of a Secular Judiciary in Egypt, 1842–1871," *Die Welt des Islams* 39 (1999): 378–97; idem, " 'For His Correction and as a Deterrent Example for Others': Mehmed ʿAli's First Criminal Legislation (1829–1830)," *Islamic Law and Society* 6 (1999): 164–93.

 | DOI:10.1163/9789004420625_016

I will argue that this improvement was the result not of a conscious policy of Westernizing reform introduced by Khedive Isma'il but of a number of more general processes that had begun by the 1830s.

The first factor was the emergence of a public health service[3] and the growing concern of health officers with prison conditions.[4] A second development that contributed to the improvement of prison conditions was the better organization of the state, which resulted in a greater capability and efficiency of state services. Finally, it was a consequence of the ideas behind the penal reform – namely, the notion that judicial punishment must not be arbitrary but based on laws and that criminal sentences must specify and quantify the punishment that they impose so that a just quantity of suffering could be administered to individual offenders. The implementation of such an idea required control of prison conditions to provide minimum living standards for all prisoners and to obviate serious health risks that might result in unintended and gratuitous aggravation of suffering.

My main sources for reconstructing prison conditions are official documents, which give information on the institutional aspects but rarely on the experience of those who suffered punishment. By necessity, this study cannot offer more than a view from the outside. In addition to the printed texts of penal codes that I used (for a list of the relevant codes, see Appendix 1), these documents are located in the Egyptian National Archive (*Dar al-Watha'iq al-Qawmiyya*), in Cairo. They consist of unpublished decrees and khedival orders,[5] correspondence among the various state authorities, and the sentences of the various judicial councils. Finding relevant material was complicated by the fact that prisons were administered by various departments, some of whose documents are not yet accessible. A rich source of information proved to be the few records of trials of prison guards for negligence, which I had the good fortune to come across. They often contain detailed reports on prison organization and the daily life of the inmates.

---

3 On the 19th-century public-health service, see Khaled Fahmy, "Medicine and Power: Towards a Social History of Medicine in Nineteenth-Century Egypt," *Cairo Papers in Social Science* 23 (2000); Laverne Kuhnke, *Lives at Risk: Public Health in Nineteenth Century Egypt* (Cairo: American University in Cairo Press, 1992).

4 Khaled Fahmy, "Medical Conditions in Prisons in the Nineteenth Century" in *Marginal Voices in Literature and Society*, ed. R. Ostle (Strasbourg: European Science Foundation/Maison Méditerranéenne des Sciences de l'Homme d'Aix-en-Provence, 2000), 135–55.

5 Although the title "khedive" (*khidiw*) did not become official until 1867, when the Ottoman sultan conferred it to Isma'il Pasha, it was used by his predecessors. During Mehmed 'Ali's reign, the department of the interior was called (in Turkish) *Divan-i Hidivi*.

All this is supplemented by the scarce information that can be culled from the publications of contemporary Western observers. These sources, however, must be used with extreme caution. Most of these travelers did not know the local language and therefore had difficulty in interpreting what they saw. Moreover, they had preconceived notions of Oriental justice as being arbitrary and cruel, which demonstrably tainted their observations. To substantiate these notions, they had a tendency to present as eyewitness reports the cock-and-bull stories that they had heard or read.

1 The Prison System

During the 19th century, imprisonment emerged as the main form of judicial punishment in Egypt.[6] The penal reforms that brought this about were, at first glance, very similar to those introduced in Western Europe during the same period: the abolition of corporal punishment, with its concomitant spectacles of suffering, and its replacement by imprisonment. Michel Foucault analyzed this development in his study *Surveiller et punir* and argued that around 1800 – at least, in France – the object of punishment shifted from the body to the soul as a result of the emergence of a centralized, powerful state with an effective police force for tracing criminals and enforcing the law.[7] Punishment through publicly administered suffering was functional when the state was weak and there were no effective means to trace and apprehend offenders. In such a situation, deterrence was needed to restrain people from committing crimes. However, when the police became efficient and most criminals were caught, the aim of punishment became disciplining the offender instead of deterring the public. The state needed obedient and disciplined subjects, and the prison became – alongside the school, the conscript army, and the psychiatric hospital – a disciplining institution.

Elsewhere I have discussed in detail the extent to which Foucault's theories are relevant for explaining the Egyptian developments.[8] Briefly, my conclusions are that the emergence of imprisonment as the main form of judicial punishment and the decrease in the number of executions in Egypt were

6 For a detailed description of the development of the prison system, see Rudolph Peters, "Egypt and the Age of the Triumphant Prison: Legal Punishment in Nineteenth Century Egypt," *Annales Islamologiques* 36 (2002): 253–285.

7 Michel Foucault, *Surveiller et punir. La naissance de la prison* (Paris, 1975).

8 Peters, "Egypt and the Age of the Triumphant Prison."

indeed the result of the emergence of a strong, centralized state with a well-functioning police force.[9] However, apart from a very short-lived experiment in the early 1860s, I have not found any signs of a conscious and deliberate policy of disciplining and rehabilitating prison inmates. Regarding the abolition of the judicial penalty of flogging in 1862, this was caused by factors other than those mentioned in Foucault's analysis. The most important cause, in my view, was that social and economic changes in the countryside had reduced the need for official violence, especially in the domains of product extraction and the collecting of men for the military, whereas there was a growing awareness among parts of the administrative elite that corporal punishment was a sign of "backwardness," especially after its abolition in the Ottoman Empire in 1858. An additional factor was that the need for torture during the interrogation of suspects had decreased due to the adoption of scientific methods of forensic investigation.[10] The result was that the role of violence diminished in legal proceedings. In the direct interaction between administrators and subjects, however, physical pressure was never totally abandoned.

The Egyptian prison system, as far as its punitive functions are concerned, was based on retribution, deterrence, and rehabilitation.[11] These objectives are usually briefly mentioned in laws and sentences but not elaborated into a detailed and coherent philosophy of punishment. Deterrence and rehabilitation were regarded as self-evident. Only the notion of retribution left a clear mark on the prison system. Its underlying principle was that punishment must be commensurate with the seriousness of the offense. The amount of suffering was conceptualized as a combination of the length of the prison term and the harshness of the prison regime. The latter depended primarily on the prison's distance from the prisoner's home and the type of labor that had to be performed. These factors structured the prison system and determined the relative severity of the various types of imprisonment, ranging from simple detention in one's district of residence, without work, to deportation with hard labor in Sudan. Not until the early 1860s do we see attempts to calibrate or fine-tune the amount of suffering by increasing it through the withholding of food

9 On the Egyptian police, see Khaled Fahmy, "The Police and the People in Nineteenth Century Egypt," *Die Welt des Islams* 39 (1999): 340–77.

10 See idem, "The Anatomy of Justice: Forensic Medicine and Criminal Law in Nineteenth-Century Egypt," *Islamic Law and Society* 6 (1999): 224–71.

11 Egyptian prisons served not only as penitentiaries. Many prisons, especially the local ones, also held suspects in custody during police investigation, debtors, and political prisoners.

or isolation for limited periods to inflict "a just measure of pain." This was done to enhance the effect of short terms of simple detention when flogging was abolished as a legal punishment and replaced by imprisonment.

Egyptian prisons were part of a four-tier hierarchy consisting of (1) labor camps in Sudan for those sentenced to hard labor with transportation, (2) national labor prisons in Egypt, (3) local labor prisons and factories at the provincial level, and (4) gaols for simple detention. Transportation to Sudan was introduced as a punishment in the early 1840s. We do not have any details of prison life there, but the distance from home and the working conditions must have made life very hard for the inmates. The introduction of transportation was motivated by two factors. First, it enabled the total exclusion of serious criminals from society, which could serve as a substitute for capital punishment. And second, there were economic considerations. Prisoners had to work in those areas where free labor was not available or not sufficiently available – in the gold mines and quarries in eastern Sudan and, later, in the reclamation projects in central Sudan. Because of the lack of information on the Sudanese labor prisons, I will not discuss them in this essay.

At the national level there were, at various times, three prisons for men. In addition, there was the spinning factory (*iplikkhane, maghzal*) in Bulaq, established in 1856 as a national prison for women. The national prison that remained operative during the entire period under study was the one connected with the Alexandria arsenal, where convicts were originally employed in digging and moving earth in connection with the construction of a new harbor and later also in the arsenal's workshops. The prison accommodated 200–650 inmates. This prison fell under the jurisdiction of the Department of the Navy (*Diwan al-Donanma* or *Diwan al-Bahriyya*). The second national prison, located near the fortifications at al-Qanatir al-Khayriyya (called *al-Qalʿa al-Saʿidiyya* or *al-Istihkamat al-Saʿidiyya*), was operative from about 1853 until at least 1865.[12] Its inmates worked on the construction of the fortress. As a prison it was much bigger than the Alexandria arsenal. At some time, it housed up to 1,200 prisoners. Initially, it fell under the authority of the War Office (*Jihadiyya*), but in 1857 it was transferred to the Department of Industry (*Diwan al-Waburat wa-l-ʿAmaliyyat*, also called *Diwan al-Fabriqat wa-l-ʿAmaliyyat*).[13] Finally, there was, apart from the deportation camps, a national prison in Sudan, at that time under Egyptian rule. It held only Sudanese convicts until it was decided in 1857

12 See khedival order sending people to the Qanatir, 7 Safar 1282/22 July 1865, Amin Sami, *Taqwim al-Nil*, 3 vols. (Cairo: Matbaʿat al-Kutub al-Misriyya, 1928–36), iii/2:615.

13 Khedival order of 16 Dhu al-Hijja 1273/7 August 1857, Maʿiyya Saniyya Turki, Mahfaza 14, leaf 132, doc. 398, Egyptian National Archive card index, s.v. "*sujun*."

that, to make the punishment more of a deterrent, serious offenders from Sudan would serve their terms in Alexandria, and those from Egypt would be sent to Sudan.[14]

The provincial prisons and various industrial establishments held less serious offenders sentenced to hard labor. Hard labor in factories and on construction sites goes back to the late 1820s, when convicts were sent to the iron foundry (*demürhane* in Turkish) in Bulaq or to building sites in Alexandria (*Iskenderiye ebniyesi* in Turkish). Prisoners were put at the disposal of the Department of Industry. Hard labor in provincial gaols existed also at that time. It is defined in the Law of Agriculture (*Qanun al-Filaha*),[15] enacted in 1830, as "to be employed, with his feet in chains, on the government building site (*al-abniya al-ma'muriyya*) in the district (*ma'muriyya*) where he comes from" (Article 17). The Penal Code of 1845 (*Qanun al-Muntakhab*) mentions expressly that these building sites are located both in Cairo and in the provincial centers (Article 192). Since this type of hard labor was served not too far from home, it was considered to be lighter than terms served in the national prisons. The Imperial Penal Code (*Qanunname Sultani*, introduced in Egypt around 1853) referred to it using the term "lowly jobs" (*khidamat dani'a* or *ashghal sufliyya*). Convicts serving time in the provincial prisons were employed in sweeping, cleaning, and light construction labor.

Places for simple detention (*habs*) without hard labor were the police prisons in the big cities, the prison in the Cairo Citadel, and prisons in the various provincial capitals. These prisons fell under the authority of the local police departments (*dabtiyya*) or the provincial administrations (*mudiriyyat, muhafazat*). These provincial prisons also held inmates sentenced to hard labor. The police and provincial gaols were relatively small. In August 1859, about 100 prisoners were detained in the Cairo police gaol, among them those held for debt.[16] The provincial prison of the Mudiriyya Bani Suwayf and Fayum housed seventy-four inmates in 1854.[17] In Cairo, there were, in addition to the police gaols, prisons for debtors and gaols connected with the Shari'a court and the judicial councils.

14 Khedival order to *Mudir* of Taka, 29 Jumada I 1273/24 February 1857, Majlis al-Ahkam, Daftar majmuʿ umur jina'iyya, 133.

15 For a short survey of the 19th-century Egyptian criminal codes, see app. 1.

16 Maʿiyya Saniyya to Dabtiyyat Misr, 4 Muharram 1276/3 August 1859, Majlis al-Ahkam, Daftar majmuʿ umur idara wa-ijra'at, Sin 7/33/1, 233.

17 Khedival order to *Mudir* Bani Suwayf and Fayum, 9 Dhu al-Qaʿda 1270/3 August 1854, Maʿiyya Saniyya 1879 (old), *awamir*, doc. 4,4 (from Egyptian National Archive card index, s.v. "*sujun*").

For higher officials and military officers there was detention in the fortress of Abu Qir on the Mediterranean shore not far from Alexandria.[18] This prison was in use until at least 1855.[19] I have not been able to establish whether the detainees were forced to work. For some time after 1849 it was replaced by imprisonment in Aswan, with a reduction of half of the prison term because of the heat.[20]

Prisons fell under various departments: the Ministry of War, the Ministry of Navy, and the Ministry of Construction; the various police departments; and city and provincial administrations. The organization of the prison system was therefore diverse. A small measure of uniformity was introduced by the appointment of a special inspector of prisons in February 1865, with the task of checking the conditions of the prisons and the punctual release of the prisoners.[21]

2 Mortality

Among the catalogued holdings of the Egyptian National Archives are five unique registers listing the entries of prisoners in Egypt's principal national prison of the 19th century, the one housed in the Alexandria Arsenal (*tarsanat Iskandariyya*) and usually called *liman* (or *luman*) *Iskandariyya*.[22] It is possible – and, indeed, likely – that comparable registers for other prisons exist among the uncatalogued holdings of the archive. However, these have not yet been found. The Alexandria registers cover two periods: 16 February 1847 to 19 September 1852 and 25 January 1861 to 22 May 1869. They list the date of release or of death of the inmates and are thus a major source of information on the composition of the prison population and on prison conditions.

---

18 Article 62 of the Penal Code of 1849 lays down that this is where officials with the rank of *qa'immaqam* (lieutenant-colonel in the army and a government official at the village level in the civil ranks) or higher were held.

19 Khedival order to the Muhafazat Misr, 23 Safar 1272/4 November 1855, to send a certain village shaykh to the Abu Qir prison: Sin 1/1/5, 74. The *Qanunname Sultani* (hereafter QS) does not mention Abu Qir anymore.

20 Decree of the Majlis al-Ahkam, 8 Rajab 1265/30 May 1849, Majlis al-Ahkam, Daftar majmuʿ umur jina'iyya, 133.

21 Appointment of Salim Pasha al-Jaza'irli, 9 Ramadan 1281/5 February 1865, Amin, *Taqwim*, iii/2:597.

22 For a detailed description of these registers, see app. 2.

With the help of these registers I have calculated the mortality of the inmates in the Alexandria prison. For the late 1840s, I have followed eighty-six convicts with sentences of five years or more who entered the prison between 18 March 1847 and 27 September 1847. For the early 1860s I followed 108 prisoners who entered the Alexandria arsenal between 26 August 1863 and 6 September 1866; were sentenced to three years or more; and were not released during the first year. An exact comparison with the 1847 numbers was not possible: in the 1860s, the Alexandria arsenal was no longer used as a prison for convicts with long sentences, and most of them during that period were deported to Sudan. Prisoners who spent more than one year in the Alexandria prison were rare in this period.

As Table 15.1 shows, the average mortality rate during the first period was higher than 15 percent per year. Calculating the mortality of this group without taking into account the twenty-six inmates who were released before their term results in an even more dramatic mortality rate of 20 percent – that is, after five years, only one-third of the inmates were still alive (Table 15.2). The exceptionally high mortality rate of 25 percent in the second year of their imprisonment (see Table 15.1) must reflect the toll taken by the cholera epidemic that raged in Egypt during the summer of 1848.[23] But even if one disregards the second year, the average mortality rate is still over 13 percent. A comparison with the mortality rate in 19th-century European prisons puts these figures in perspective. In the most insalubrious bagne (hard-labor prison) in France, that of Rochefort, the mortality rate between 1816 and 1827 was 9 percent per annum, which was higher than that of all other French *bagnes*.[24] In 19th-century Dutch prisons, one finds such high numbers (up to 30 percent in some prisons) only in exceptional circumstances, such as during the years 1846–48, when prisons became overcrowded as a result of a rise in criminality due to bad harvests and famine. In ordinary years the mortality rate fluctuated between 3.5 and 6 percent.[25] The 13 percent mortality rate in Egyptian prisons in the late 1840s was very high in comparison and must reflect pernicious prison conditions.

23 Kuhnke, *Lives at Risk*, 57.

24 Andre Zysberg, "Politiques du bagne 1820–1850," in *L'impossible prison: recherches sur le système pénitentiaire au XIXe siècle*, ed. Michelle Perrot (Paris: Eds du Seuil, 1980), 191.

25 Herman Franke, *The Emancipation of Prisoners: A Socio-historical Analysis of the Dutch Prison Experience* (Edinburgh: Edinburgh University Press, 1995), 39–40.

TABLE 15.1 Prison mortality (1847): Mortality and releases of eighty-six inmates sentenced to five years or more

Year after entry into prison	Number of deaths in prison that year	Accumulated number of deaths	Number of those released in that year	Accumulated number of releases	Number of prisoners remaining at the end of the year	Mortality*
1	9	9	12	12	65	10%
2	16	25	3	15	46	25%
3	7	32	5	20	34	15%
4	6	38	0	20	28	17%
5	3	41	3	23	22	11%

* Number of deaths during a year as a percentage of the number of prisoners present at the beginning of that year

Sixteen years later, the conditions in the Alexandria Arsenal must have improved a great deal, for the mortality rate had decreased to an average of 4.5 percent in the years 1863–1866 (Table 15.3), becoming roughly the same as the mortality rate in French and Dutch prisons (which varied from 2 to 9 percent for the French and from 3.5 to 6 percent for the Dutch prisons).[26] Although 4.5 percent is exactly as high as the overall death rate of the entire Cairo population between 1868 and 1871, that comparison is misleading.[27] The prison population under consideration consisted of men with an average age of thirty-five years at the time of entrance. They were not affected by infant or old-age mortality or by perinatal mortality, which together made up a large part of the mortality of the overall population. Prison mortality was therefore still much higher than the overall death rate for the comparable age and sex group. As can be expected, those who died in the Alexandria prison were older than the others: their mean age was forty years old when they entered the prison, five years older than the mean age of the whole prison population at the date of entry.[28] Moreover, the time they had spent in prison before entering the Alexandria prison may have played a role. The average inmate had spent 370 days in custody, whereas those who died had been imprisoned for an average of 595 days.

26 Ibid., 39, 94; Zysberg, "Politiques du bagne," 191.

27 Daniel Panzac, "Endémies, épidemies et population en Égypte au XIXe siècle," in *L'Égypte au* XIXe *siècle. Aix-en-Provence, 4–7 juin 1979* (Paris: Éditions du CNRS, 1982), 88.

28 This could only be established for the 1860s, since the register covering the late 1840s does not record the age of the inmates: see app. 2.

TABLE 15.2 Prison mortality (1847): Mortality of sixty prisoners sentenced to five years or more and not released before the end of their term

Year after entry into prison	Number of deaths in that year	Mortality*	Accumulated number of deaths	Number of remaining prisoners	Number of prisoners as a percentage of the original group
1	9	15%	9	51	85%
2	16	31%	25	35	58%
3	7	20%	32	28	45%
4	6	21%	38	22	37%
5	3	14%	41	19	32%

* Number of deaths during a year as a percentage of the number of prisoners present at the beginning of that year

TABLE 15.3 Prison mortality (1863–66): Mortality of 112 prisoners with sentences of three years or more, who were not released during the first year

Year after entry into prison	Number of deaths in that year	Accumulated number of deaths	Number of those released in that year	Accumulated number of releases	Number of prisoners remaining at the end of the year	Mortality*
1	10	10	0	0	98	8%
2	2	12	23	23	73	2%
3	2	14	38	61	33	2%
4	2	16	19	80	12	6%
5	10	10	0	0	98	8%

Since no data exist for the other prisons, it cannot be excluded that this drop in mortality was restricted to Alexandria. The Alexandria prison might have received special attention from the government to create a model prison to impress European visitors, for most of whom Alexandria was the port of entry. However, this is not very likely, and there are several factors that make it plausible that these figures reflect a general trend. First, the Alexandra prison was not a separate institution but part of the arsenal, where, as I will show, the prisoners represented only a small part of the entire workforce. That its prison function was not very conspicuous is demonstrated by the fact that two very detailed recent studies of 19th-century Alexandria do not mention it.[29] Second, the attempts to show that Egypt was really part of Europe are associated with Khedive Ismaʿil (r. 1863–79). Because the reduction in mortality had already set by 1863, the change of policy of which it was a result must have taken place before that year and thus cannot be ascribed to measures taken by Ismaʿil. Finally, as I will show, there were general changes in the administration and government of Egypt that can explain the improvement of prison conditions and would apply to all prisons, not just the one in Alexandria.

3 Prison Conditions

In this section I will try to give an impression of what Egyptian prisons were like in the 19th century. Unfortunately, the source material is scarce and fragmentary, and many questions must remain unanswered. I will especially highlight those changes in prison conditions that may have had an effect on prison mortality.

3.1 *Accommodation*

By the end of 1850, officials of the State Health Inspection (*Taftish al-Sihha*) had examined the state of the Cairo prisons. Their findings were devastating. They observed that gaols were in an abominable state and so detrimental to the inmates' health that their lives were in jeopardy. The prisons were in need of drastic reconstruction, or even demolition and rebuilding, to satisfy health standards. However, since they realized that the budgets were limited, the health officials proposed only the most urgent alterations: one prison lacked latrines, which should be built, and in all others the accumulated excrement and urine needed to be removed. Some prisons lacked light holes, which should be remedied immediately. Certain wards were so small that the prisoners were piled on top of one another. Finally, the officials discovered that in some gaols the inmates slept on damp floors because there were no stone or wooden platforms (*mastaba*) to sleep on. Therefore, they recommended that the wooden benches stored in the Hospital of the Sultan Qalawun Mosque should be transferred to these prisons.[30]

29 See R. Ilbert, *Alexandrie, 1830–1930*, 2 vols. (Cairo: IFAO, 1996); and Michael J. Reimer, *Colonial Bridgehead: Government and Society in Alexandria, 1807–1882* (Cairo: American University in Cairo Press, 1997).

30 Taftish Sihhat Misr to Diwan Khediwi, 19 Muharram 1267/24 November 1850 and 4 Jumada I 1267/7 March 1851, Mim 5/1 (old 163), Taftish Sihhat Misr, Sadir Taftish, doc. 47, 21; doc. 128, 62.

This report gives some impression of the state of prisons in the first half of the 19th century. It is not difficult to imagine the stifling atmosphere, the stench of unwashed bodies, the vermin and dirt in a ward without sanitary facilities and with a limited supply of water – all of which had to be brought in by water carriers – where many men were confined and one had to call for a guard to be taken to the latrines. There was little concern about prison buildings. Prisons were not specially constructed as prisons but established in ordinary houses that were bought or rented for the purpose;[31] in wards such as those existing in the Cairo Citadel; in storehouses (*hasil*); and, in one instance, in a disused stable.[32] They were often located on large guarded government compounds accommodating, apart from the prisons, administrative offices (*diwan*) and police guardrooms.[33] Prisons were often ramshackle, which caused security problems. At one prison, the wooden walls were so dilapidated that prisoners managed to escape through them.[34] In 1856, all pertinent authorities were instructed to reinforce the prisons to prevent such escapes.[35]

The prison inmates were locked up together in wards, not in separate cells. They slept on the floor or on wooden or stone platforms. Bedding seems not to have been provided.[36] Sometimes inmates were put in chains for the night. The idea of solitary confinement was not introduced until 1862 (when flogging was abolished as a legal penalty), and then only in special cases as a way to aggravate the punishment of simple detention (*habs*) for certain types of offenders. It could not be imposed for a period of more than three weeks. Such

31 Khedival order to *Mudir* al-Rawda, 2 Jumada II 1272/9 February 1856: *Mudir* must find a solid building that can serve as a prison instead of the houses now used for the purpose (Maʿiyya Saniyya, Sadir al-Maʿiyya, 1616 [old], doc. 3, 446); khedival order to Muhafazat Iskandariyya, 7 Dhu al-Hijja 1272/9 February 1856: order to pay a rent of 37 piasters per month for a house used as a women's prison in Alexandria (Maʿiyya Saniyya, *awamir*, 1884 [old], doc. 144, 46); khedival order to the Muhafazat Misr, 23 Shawwal 1277/4 May 1861: to rent a house for 50–75 piasters to serve as a women's prison and appoint a guard with a monthly wages of 150 piasters, because the existing women's prison in the Police Department (*Dabtiyya*) is too close to the men's prison (Maʿiyya Saniyya, *awamir*, 1894 [old], doc. 65, 125 [from Egyptian National Archive card index, s.v. "*sujun*"]).

32 On the disused stable, see Fahmy, "Medical Conditions," 142.

33 For a precise description of the location of the provincial prison of Dumyat, see Majlis al-Ahkam, al-madabit al-sadira, Sin 7/10/15, 10 Rabiʿ I 1280/25 August 1863, no. 784, 51–55.

34 See, for example, *Majlis al-Ahkam* to Mudiriyyat Bani Suwayf and Fayum, 11 Jumada II 1267/13 April 1851, *Majlis al-Ahkam*, Mahfaza 4, doc. 3.

35 Khedival order, 4 Jumada II 1272, Maʿiyya Saniyya, Sadir al-Maʿiyya, Daftar 1616 (old) (from Egyptian National Archive card index, s.v. "*sujun*").

36 Coles Pasha mentions that during his time as an inspector of the Egyptian prison administration (1897–1913) this was not the case: C.E. Coles Pasha, *Recollections and Reflections* (London: Saint Catherine Press, 1919), 100.

prisoners were not allowed to have contact with relatives and friends.[37] I have not seen indications that the introduction of a system of solitary confinement with the objective of stimulating the inmates to repent or to enhance prison security was ever considered.

For rich prisoners the harshness of prison life could be mitigated. In 1845, a traveler observed, there were glaring differences between the conditions of rich and poor inmates. In Alexandria, the rich prisoners had their own furnished rooms and even servants or slaves and did not have to work, unless Mehmed ʿAli had expressly ordered so. In the Cairo prison they had their own café and could have food brought in from outside, whereas the poor were detained in a dark ward without daylight and given only two round loaves of bread per day. At night they were chained to one another.[38] These observations have a ring of truth. Unfortunately, the author does not give a clue about the type of prisoners who enjoyed these privileges. It may well be the case that the possibility of acquiring better treatment was reserved for those held for debts or for the political hostages and not for those convicted for crime.

The 1849 order of the *Majlis al-Ahkam* directing the regional authorities to examine the prisons together with health officers[39] heralds the beginning of official concern for the health conditions in the prisons – essentially, their cleanliness and access to fresh air and daylight. The report summarized at the beginning of this section is one of the examples of this new policy. I do not know the extent to which the recommendations of the health officials were implemented. Improvement of prison conditions must have been a slow but steady process. After his accession to the throne, the Khedive Ismaʿil gave this policy a new boost. A khedival order of 1863 instructed the prison authorities that all circumstances that were injurious to the inmates' health were to be eliminated; that all prisons had to be cleaned and repaired; and that inmates needed to have access to fresh air.[40] The prison authorities responded that rebuilding the prisons to bring them into agreement with these health standards would entail considerable expense, and it is not clear whether the necessary funds were allotted.[41] However, one of the results of Ismaʿil's new policy was

37 *Layihat tabdil al-darb bi-l-habs* (11 Shaʿban 1278/11 February 1862), art. 11. This was an implementing order of the 1861 decree banning corporal punishment: text in Muhafazat Misr, *Lam* 1/20/8, doc. 3, 71.

38 Victor Schoelcher, *L'Égypte en 1845* (Paris: Pagnerre, 1846), 27–29.

39 *Majlis al-Ahkam*, Mahfaza 1, doc. 1/88, 16–8–65 (7 July 1849).

40 Khedival order to *Majlis al-Ahkam*, 28 Rabiʿ I 1280/12 September 1863, Maʿiyya Saniyya, Qayd al-awamir al-karima al-Sadira min qalam majalis bi-l-muʿawana, Sin 1/19/2, doc. 1, 1.

41 Fahmy, "Medical Conditions," 145.

that, in 1864, the Cairo Police Department received permission to renovate the police gaol because the stench and the filth were unsupportable.[42]

3.2 *Food*

In principle, the inmates or their relatives had to provide their food.[43] This applied of course especially to the inmates of local and provincial prisons, whose relatives could regularly visit them. If prisoners could not support themselves, food for the men was provided by the local government and for the women by the Treasury (*Bayt al-Mal*).[44] During the 1830s, prisoners in the national prisons and those working for the Department of Construction received wages with which they could buy their food.[45] It is not clear when this was abolished and the inmates became dependent on government rations. In 1830, the standard daily ration for indigent prisoners was fixed at about 900 grams of coarse bread (*khubz jiraya*).[46] This was approximately the same quantity of bread that the inmates of the French *bagnes* were entitled to (917 grams), a quantity that

42 Khedival order to Muhafazat Misr, 23 Ramadan 1280/2 March 1864, Maʿiyya Saniyya, Sadir al-awamir al-ʿaliyya ila al-majalis wa-l-dawawin-wal-aqalim wa-l-muhafazat, Sin 1/1/24, doc. 23, 106.

43 See, for example, Dabtiyyat Misr, Sadir, *Lam* 2/6/2, 1–3, no. 99, 24 Ramadan 1264/ 24 August 1848: case of a women from Suez who was robbed of money and jewelry while sitting in front of the Cairo police gaol waiting to hand over bread and the valuables to her relatives in prison.

44 In 1834, the Pasha ordered to distribute meat twice monthly to the inmates of the Alexandria Arsenal and Abu Qir and to provide them with cloaks (*ʿabaʾat*) and hats (*tawaqi*): khedival order of 5 Shawwal 1249/15 February 1834, Maʿiyya Saniyya, sin 1/56/1 (1248–50), doc. 715. In 1836, the pasha approved the distribution of food rations to indigent prisoners: khedival order to the wakil al-Majlis al-Mulki, 9 Ramadan 1252/18 December 1836; text also in sin 7/33/1, Majlis al-Ahkam, Daftar Majmuʿ umur idara wa-ijraʾat, 233. For the period after 1855, see QS chap. 3, arts. 15, 17.

45 In the 1247/1831–32, issues of *al-Waqaʾiʿ al-Misriyya*, one often finds the formula "He was sent to the Diwan al-Abniya to work there for wages but under detention (*mahbus*) to punish him." Bowring, writing about the late 1830s, reports that the "galley slaves employed in the different works" of the Alexandria Arsenal were paid four piasters a day, including provisions and clothing, which is only one piaster less than the other workers received: John Bowring, *Report on Egypt and Candia Addressed to the Right Hon. Lord Viscount Palmerstone* (London: Command Paper, 1840), 59.

In the 19th-century French *bagnes*, the *forçats* were also paid: see Jacques Valette, "Le bagne de Rochefort 1815–1852," in *L'impossible prison*, 206–35.

46 This was a standard ration during most of the 19th century. It is mentioned in the *Qanun al-Filaha* (1830), art. 48, laying down that local authorities must provide this ration to prisoners who are left with them by the army. See, further, Resolution of the Majlis Mulki of 1252/1836–37, Sin 7/33/1, *Majlis al-Ahkam*, Daftar majmuʿ umur idara wa-ijracat, 233. The ration is described as charity (*sadaqa*) from the khedive: decree of the Majlis al-Ahkam, 19 Ramadan 1266/29 July 1850, ibid., 234. The latter decree also mentions that

had been constant since the 18th century.[47] Although this could point at some form of influence, a more obvious explanation is that it was a matter of experience that the hard physical work that the inmates had to perform would require such a quantity of calories. Occasionally, the inmates received an additional ration of meat.[48] A khedival decree of 1856 stipulates that hardtack was to be distributed to indigent prisoners sentenced to transportation to serve as provisions during the journey.[49] It is not clear how one should read this order. Perhaps the deportees previously received ordinary bread rations that went bad during the journey, whereas hardtack was supposed to keep well. But it is not unthinkable that, prior to this order, the deportees who could not provide for themselves did not receive anything and were left to beg.

In the early 1860s a marked improvement can be observed in the quality of food distributed to the prisoners. A khedival order of April 1863 states that the following monthly rations were already standard in the national labor prisons and lays down that these were henceforth to be distributed to all inmates of local and police prisons who could not support themselves:

- 28 kilograms of coarse bread (which amounts to the ration of about 900 grams per diem mentioned earlier)
- 3.7 kilograms of lentils
- 1.8 kilograms of rice
- 0.37 kilograms of clarified butter
- 0.88 kilograms of beef[50]

This was a somewhat one-sided diet but adequate as far as caloric value is concerned. It is not very different from the rations provided to students in the state boarding schools during the same period.[51] The French *bagnes* provided a

the governors must inspect the gaols under their authority every two weeks and check whether the prisoners are getting their rations.

47 Valette, "Bagne de Rochefort," 209; Zysberg, "Politiques du bagne," 189. Spanish convicts received about 700 grams of hardtack in the late 18th century: Ruth Pike, *Penal Servitude in Early Modern Spain* (Madison: University of Wisconsin Press, 1983), 81. In the French *bagnes*, this amount of hardtack was regarded as equivalent to 900 grams of bread: Zysberg, "Politiques du bagne," 189.

48 Khedive to Burhan Bey, 5 Shawwal 1249/15 February 1834, ordering the distribution of meat twice a month to the inmates of the Tarsana, the Liman, and Abu Qir: Sin 1/56/1, doc. 715.

49 Maʿiyya Saniyya to Muhafazat Misr, 27 Jumada II 1272/5 March 1856, Maʿiyya Saniyya, Daftar 1616 (old) (from Egyptian National Archive card index, s.v. "*sujun*").

50 Khedival order, 11 Dhu al-Hijja 1279/30 May 1863, Maʿiyya Saniyya, Sadir al-awamir al-ʿaliyya ila al-majalis wa-l-dawawin-wa-l-aqalim wa-l-muhafazat, sin 1/1/23, 47, doc. 27.

51 Monthly rations consisting of 23.2 kilograms of bread, 3.7 kilograms of lentils, 1.9 kilograms of ful, 0.9 kilograms of clarified butter, 1 kilogram of rice, and 2.2 kilograms of meat: Sami, *Taqwim*, iii/2:554, 1 Muharram 1281/6 February 1864.

similar diet.[52] We have no way to tell whether these rations ultimately reached the inmates. It is possible that part of it was appropriated by guards or other officials. The 1863 decree stipulates that storekeepers (*makhzanji*) were to be appointed to supervise the distribution of food, implying that this task could not be entrusted to the guards.

From the early 1860s, all prisoners were entitled to adequate standard rations. For those held in simple detention, who did not have to work, rationing could then be used to increase the measure of suffering. This was indeed introduced by the 1862 ordinance abolishing corporal punishment, which stipulated that detention could be aggravated for some categories of offenders by putting them on "bread and water" (*habs al-riyada*). Until that time, this form of punishment was applied only to military and state officials. The idea behind it was that simple detention would not be a sufficient deterrent. The ordinance specified that such offenders would get about 450 grams of bread daily – that is, half the normal bread ration – and a jug with 1.2 liters of water. With regard to the latter, the instructions mention that, especially during summer, prisoners would get more water if they asked for it.[53]

3.3 *Work*

Sometime in the early 1860s, Fadil Pasha, the governor of al-Minufiyya province, noticed that not all inmates in the provincial prison who were sentenced to "lowly jobs in the *mudiriyya*" were working. They should be employed in manufacturing mud bricks for the repair of the buildings of the provincial administration. When he pointed this out to the prison warden (*ma'mur al-sijn*), the latter replied that he was short of staff. Apart from the common guards, there was only one sergeant-major (*bashjawish*), who could not guard all prisoners that had to work outside the prison. Fadil Pasha then suggested that the warden himself could also take a batch of prisoners to their work, while the prisoners who did not have to work could be left in the prison with a few soldiers. There was no reason, he said, why the warden would sit idly in his office. The warden angrily rejected the suggestion, saying that he was a warden and not a common guard (*qawwas*). The warden must have been a stubborn man, because the case was finally brought before the *Majlis al-Ahkam*, who decided

52 27.5 kilograms of bread (or 21 kilograms of hardtack) and 3.6 kilograms of dry beans: Zysberg, "Politiques du bagne," 189. In late-18th-century Spain, prisoners received 20 kilograms of hardtack, 9 kilograms of dry beans, and 2.5 kilograms of rice: Pike, *Penal Servitude*, 81.

53 *Layihat tabdil al-darb bi-l-habs*, art. 11.

that the warden should be reprimanded and instructed him to do as the governor had told him.[54]

Apart from showing the arrogance of some petty officials, this story makes clear that the separation between those prisoners who had to work and those who did not was strictly maintained and that this work was carried out outside the prison. The work assigned to them, manufacturing mud bricks (*darb al-tub*) by filling molds and letting them dry in the sun, cannot have been very strenuous. Moreover, being outside the prison probably gave the inmates a chance to converse with friends and acquaintances and receive food. "Lowly jobs" in the provincial gaols was obviously much lighter than hard labor in Alexandria.

In Alexandria, prisoners were detained in the Navy arsenal, which was located on the western shore of the peninsula. They made up only a small fraction of all people employed there. In the late 1830s, there were about 200 prisoners in a total workforce of several thousand.[55] The prison was therefore only a small element in the whole establishment, to the extent that the gatekeepers were not especially instructed to guard the prisoners. When prisoners escaped and the Nubian gatekeepers were questioned, they answered that their first duty was to protect government property and not to guard prisoners. For the latter task, they said, there were specially appointed military guards; the gatekeepers' only duty was not to allow prisoners to leave without someone to guard them.[56]

The inmates were originally employed in spadework and carrying earth, activities connected with the construction of the new harbor and the docks. Later they were also employed in the various workshops of the arsenal, such as those for rope making, saddle making, sail making, painting, carpeting, and smithing, and in other activities such as loading and unloading ships and carts.[57] The available sources do not give information about how these jobs were assigned. It is plausible that the inmates could progress from strenuous and dirty jobs to more comfortable ones in the workshops. Every morning the prisoners were

54 Majlis al-Ahkam, al-Madabit al-Sadira, Sin 7/10/17, no. 11, 3, 2 Rabiʿ II 1280/16 September 1863.

55 Bowring mentions 200 prisoners and more than 5,000 employees: Bowring, *Report*, 59. For other estimates of the number of employees in the Alexandria Arsenal (4,000–8,000), see Ilbert, *Alexandrie*, i:18; Reimer, *Colonial Bridgehead*, 56.

56 Majlis al-Ahkam, al-Madabit al-Sadira, Sin 7/10/23, doc. 893, 132, 28 Dhu al-Qaʿda 1280/5 May 1864.

57 In the sentences pronounced during the first half of the 19th century, the following words are used: *naql al-turab* (transporting earth), *haml al-turab* (carrying earth), *toprak hizmeti* (spade work). Later, they also worked in the workshops: see, for example, Bowring, *Report*; H. von Pückler-Muskau, *Aus Mehemed Alis Reich: Ägypten and der Sudan um 1840*, repr. ed. (Zürich: Manesse Verlag, 1985), 69. For a map of the Alexandria Arsenal as it existed in 1829, see Ilbert, *Alexandrie*, ii:766.

distributed over the various activities and workshops. The foreman of a workshop signed a receipt when the prisoners arrived, and the prisoners worked together with the ordinary workers but were not allowed to leave the workshop during the breaks (*faydus, fadus*). Two of the ordinary laborers were placed near the doors of the workshop to prevent the prisoners from leaving and to accompany prisoners to the latrines. Prisoners also worked outside the arsenal, in which case each guard accompanied two prisoners chained together.[58]

I have not been able to establish whether there was any change in the working conditions of the prisoners in the 1850s and early 1860s.

3.4 *Medical Care*

In the 1850s, the public-health administration became involved in the sanitary conditions of prisons. Khaled Fahmy attributes this to two factors: the growing prison population as a result of the decrease of capital sentences and sentences of flogging and as a result of the growing crime rate; and the close connection between law and medicine that had already been firmly established.[59] Overcrowding in prisons apparently became a problem, and from 1850 on we see health personnel beginning to play an active role in improving the living conditions of prisoners, as was shown in the section on housing. This concern was primarily informed not by humanitarian but, rather, by practical considerations: the unhealthy conditions in prisons were regarded as a possible source of epidemics and therefore as a health risk for the population as a whole. The involvement of the official health administration manifested itself in the attachment of medical doctors and orderlies to the various prisons and industrial establishments where prisoners worked.[60] They not only treated sick inmates; they were also expected to carry out daily medical inspections and to report the conditions of the prisoners, as laid down in the 1862 ordinance implementing the decree abolishing corporal punishment.[61]

Prisoners held in simple detention (*mahbusun*) were entitled to a suspension of their punishment if they fell seriously ill. They were allowed to go home

58 Unless otherwise indicated, the data on the organization of the Alexandria Arsenal are culled from the following trials of guards for negligence in guarding prisoners: sentence of al-Jamʿiyya al-haqqaniyya, Sin 6/9/6, 8 Shawwal 1263, no. 2, 3; Sentence of Diwan al-Tarsane, Diwan al-Tarsane 1037 (old), 22 (30 Rabiʿ I 1275); sentences of Majlis al-Ahkam, Sin 7/10/15, 10 Rabiʿ I 1280, no. 784, 51–55; sin 7/10/21, 10 Dhu al-Qaʿda 1280, no. 750, 157; Sin 7/10/18, 13 Jumada II 1280, no. 336, 35; Sin 7/10/23, 28 Dhu al-Qaʿda 1280, 133–36; Sin 7/4/33, 43.

59 Fahmy, "Medical Conditions."

60 Khedival order, 28 Rabiʿ I 1280/12 September 1863, Maʿiyya Saniyya, Sadir al-awamir al-ʿAliyya ila al-majalis wa-l-dawawm wa-l-aqalim wa-l-muhafazat, Sin 1/1/24, doc. 2, 8.

61 *Layihat tabdil al-darb bi-l-habs*, art. 9.

for medication on the condition that they could produce a guarantor (*damana qawiyya*). They would be visited every other week by an official of the civil administration (*ma'mur al-umur al-mulkiyya*) to ascertain that they were still sick.[62] If convicts sentenced to hard labor became ill, they were treated in hospitals. Prison wardens appear to have been quick to send inmates to the hospitals even for light complaints such as scabies, ulcers, and sores. In 1865, the administration of the Civil Hospital in Cairo informed the War Department that there were 130 convicts of the Tura Prison among its patients, most of whom were not seriously ill, and suggested that they be sent back to be treated by the medical staff of the prison.[63] This behavior on the part of the prison wardens may be explained by an eagerness to get rid of the responsibility for unproductive prisoners who also might die. In addition, inadequate medical facilities in the prisons may have played a role.

3.5 *Guards and Security*

The buildings where the prisons were housed did not offer much security. Preventing the inmates from escaping was achieved by the presence of gaolers (*sajjan*) or soldiers and by chaining the inmates. The police prisons in the cities and the provincial capitals were under the command of a gaoler or prison warden (*ma'mur al-sijn*), who typically had at his disposal a number of ordinary soldiers for guard duty. Female prisons also had a male gaoler.[64] In the Alexandria prison there was a company of prison guards (*buluk ghafar al-mudhnibin*) staffed by regular soldiers.[65]

Nevertheless, escapes were frequent. Inmates and their relatives used various means to get out of prison, including bribery, as in the following case:

> A certain ʿAbd Allah Jad al-Nabi, whose brother Ahmad was held in custody in the Khartum gaol, feared that the latter would die in gaol. He, therefore, had bribed a certain Musa Ibrahim, a clerk in the provincial administration and given a sum of over 4,000 piasters so that the clerk would arrange the prisoner's release. When the prisoner was indeed set free, it turned out that this was because there was not sufficient proof against him and that the clerk had nothing to do with it. The brother

62 QS, chap. 3, art. 16.

63 Muhafazat Misr to Diwan Jihadiyya, 28 Dhu al-Hijja 1281/24 May 1865, Muhafazat Misr, Sadir, Lam 1/4/3, doc. 48, 102.

64 See n. 31.

65 Maʿiyya Saniyya, Sadir al-awamir al-ʿaliya ila al-majalis wa-l-dawawin wa-l-aqalim wa-l-muhafazat, Sin 1/1/30, doc. 14, 125, 3–8–82, correspondence regarding reinforcement of the detachment of soldiers in the arsenal for guard duties.

> protested with the clerk and demanded that he return the money that he had paid him. The clerk offered a deal: he would give him a Sudanese slave girl, worth 2,500 piasters, and would repay the rest later. This he accepted. However, soon it became clear that trade in Sudanese slaves was not permitted anymore and that the sale, therefore, was null and void. ʿAbd Allah sued the clerk before the Shariʿa court and won his case: he returned the girl and received the amount he had paid the clerk. When the case was examined by the *Majlis al-Ahkam* and reviewed by the khedive, the clerk was sentenced to two years hard labor on the White Nile and fired from his office, and the money that was returned to ʿAbd Allah was confiscated for the benefit of the *Bayt al-Mal*.[66]

When prisoners fled, guards were often implicated.[67] If this could be proved, the guard faced capital punishment.[68] Otherwise, the guards were charged with negligence and had to complete the sentence that the fugitive was serving. This rule was actually enforced, although in some cases this entailed legal problems. For instance, when a murder suspect managed to escape due to the negligence of a guard, the guard first got a life sentence. Later it appeared that the fugitive was innocent and that the alleged victim had committed suicide. The charges against the accused were dropped, and, as a consequence, the sentence against the guard was commuted to five years at hard labor.[69]

The guards were ordinary conscript soldiers without special training. Sometimes they do not seem to have been up to their duties, as in the following case:

> On 15 Rabiʿ I 1275 [23 October 1858], Ahmad Hasan and ʿAmr Hasan and two inmates of the Alexandria Prison were working outside the prison near the Abu Shahba Fort, close to the sea. They were loading stones onto a cart. When Muhammad Salim, the soldier who guarded them, told them that he wanted to relieve himself in the sea and that they should come with him, they replied that they could be trusted and would wait

66 Maʿiyya Saniyya to hukumdar Sudan, 2 Jumada I 1282/23 September 1865, Maʿiyya Saniyya, Sin 1/1/31, 37, no. 8.

67 See, for example, Maʿiyya Saniyya to Mudiriyyat Asyut, 3 Dhu al-Qaʿda 1281, Sadir al-awamir al-ʿaliya ila al-majalis wa-l-dawawin wa-l-aqalim wa-l-muhafazat, Sin 1/1/28, doc. 5, 18.

68 See, for example, khedival order, 3 Rabiʿ II 1272/13 December 1855, issued to the governor of the Qalʿa Saʿidiyya to execute a soldier by shooting him. Maʿiyya Saniyya, Sadir al-awamir al-caliya, Sin 1/1/5, doc. 15, 144.

69 Majlis al-Ahkam, sin 7/10/15, al-Madabit al-sadira, 10 Rabiʿ I 1280, no. 784, 51–55.

> for him. When he returned, Ahmad and ʿAmr had escaped. Muhammad Salim had failed to ask the soldier working close by to keep an eye on the prisoners. The latter had left the spot and gone to the fort's storehouse (*jabkhana*) because his prisoners had finished loading the cart and wanted a drink. Since the escaped prisoners were serving life sentences, the guard was sentenced to the same penalty, with the provision that, if the fugitives were found, his punishment would be reconsidered.[70]

This story gives some insight into the relationship between the guards and the prisoners that were entrusted to them. They were often of the same class background, and their daily contact seems to have been characterized by a certain geniality. The soldier who let these inmates escape was probably extremely naive, but the example of the other, who at the request of his men went to the fort so they could have a drink, shows that gaolers and inmates were usually on good terms. The situation was no doubt different with regard to the officers commanding the guard units.

I have not found any documents concerning cases of violence committed by prison officials against the prisoners. The absence of evidence might point to the absence of excessive violence – that is, the absence of a level of violence higher than what was usual outside prison in the relations between officials and subjects. However, it might be the consequence of the prisoners' lack of rights and the impossibility for them to submit complaints. The latter assumption can easily be shown to be false, though, because the holdings of the Egyptian National Archive include petitions and complaints submitted by prisoners. Therefore, however tricky and deceptive an argument *e silentio* may be, I am inclined to accept the first explanation.

In addition to the presence of guards, security was achieved by shackling and chaining the prisoners. This was standard practice during transportation, when the prisoners were chained to one another by foot irons (*hadid, qayd*) or by iron neckbands (*tawq* or *al-hadid bi-l-halq*). Both the foot irons and the neckbands could be attached to long chains (*zinjir*). Sometimes the prisoners' hands were attached to a wooden plank (*khashab*).[71] The usual method of transportation of prisoners was by ship. Prisoners held in simple detention as a rule were not chained or were chained only at night.[72] When they were al-

70 Diwan al-Tarsane, sijill 1037, Qayd al-qararat, 22, no. 12, 30 Rabi I 1275/7 November 1858.

71 See, for example, Dabtiyyat Misr, Sadir, Lam 2/5/6 (old 23), doc. 13, 21, 27–1262/18 October 1846, Majlis al-Ahkam, Sadir al-aqalim al-Qibliyya, Sin/7/4/33, doc. 1, 43, 7 Jumada I 1281/8 October 1864, to hukumdariyya al-Sudan.

72 Schoelcher, *L'Égypte*, 27–29.

lowed out to relieve themselves, to assist in bringing in and distributing food, or to be interrogated, they were accompanied by one guard and not chained. As many prisoners used this situation to escape, a khedival order of 1864 stipulated that in such situations a prisoner had to be accompanied by two guards and to be shackled.[73]

Chaining could also be used as a means to increase punishment. The order of 1862 implementing the decree that replaced beating by detention laid down in Article 7 that the hands and feet of those held in simple detention could be shackled to make the punishment more severe.[74] For those sentenced to hard labor, being chained was part of their punishment. Article 198 of the Penal Code of 1845, enacted in 1844, expressly mentions that the practice of using foot shackles with metal balls attached to them was adopted after the European example. There are many articles in the successive penal codes enjoining that hard labor sentences be served in chains (*muqayyad, muqayyad bi-l-hadid, muqayyad bi-l-zinjir*). This was taken very seriously. Even when prisoners were transferred to a hospital the chains were not removed. When Clot Bey, the head of the health service, protested in 1857 that this could hinder medical treatment, the *Majlis al-Ahkam* permitted the shackles to be removed at the request of the hospital's chief physician (*hakimbashi*) in serious medical cases.[75] In prison, the inmates were shackled two by two (called a *habl* or *qatr*). If the nature of the work required it, they could be unlinked. This was done, for example, in the bakery of the Alexandria Arsenal, where each prisoner operated one bellows.[76] I have no idea how the chains were attached to the prisoners' feet. That they were forged or riveted around the ankles seems unlikely in view of the many cases I have come across where prisoners, during their escape, could get rid of them in a very short time.

A final security measure was the tattooing of the letter *lam* (for *liman*) on the right shoulder of convicts serving life sentences. This was borrowed from the French Code Pénal, which actually prescribed branding.[77] That this measure was indeed applied – at least, between 1847 and 1852 – is clear from the entry

73 Khedival order to Mudiriyyat Minufiyya, 4 Jumada II 1281/4 November 1864, Maʿiyya Saniyya, Sadir al-awamir al-ʿaliyya ila al-majalis wa-l-dawawin wa-l-aqalim wa-l-muhafazat, doc. 7, 49.

74 *Layihat tabdil al-darb bi-l-habs, art.* 11.

75 Diwan al-Jihadiyya, Sadir mashwarat al-tibb, 444 (old), doc. 43, 8, 8 Rajab 1273/4 March 1857; ibid., doc. 125, 24, 15 Dhu al-Qaʿda 1273/7 July 1857. See also Fahmy, "Medical Conditions."

76 Jamʿiyya Haqqaniyya, Daftar Qayd al-Khulasa, Sin 6/9/6, 3, no. 2, 8 Shawwal 1263/ 19 September 1847.

77 124 QM, art. 124, corresponding with French Code Pénal, art. 20.

register of the Alexandria prison in which it was recorded whenever a prisoner was tattooed.[78] I have not been able to ascertain whether the prisoners wore special clothes, which, as in Western Europe and the United States also served as a security measure by marking prisoners.[79]

4 Conclusion

How can we explain this improvement of prison conditions between roughly 1850 and 1865? In my view, three factors played a role: the growing involvement of the public-health service with prisons; the increased capabilities of the Egyptian administration; and, finally, a change in thinking about crime and punishment. The improvement was not the result of a specific policy of the khedives, except that Isma'il actively supported the process during the first years of his reign. It was, rather, the achievement of a new class of Egyptian administrators who staffed the emerging rational bureaucracy. There is an interesting parallel here with the first wave of prison reforms in England in the 18th century. As Roy Porter has shown, these were not the result of a conscious policy from above; rather, they were the result of the efforts of those directly involved in prison administration:

> Not from philosophies, prison reform arose from practicalities, and it was generated from below, in the localities.... It arose out of local crisis, it proceeded piecemeal. Traditionally, as everyone knows, criminals were hanged, transported, whipped, fined or accorded mercy. Few had ended up long gaol sentences. Most of those in gaol had been debtors or those awaiting trial. Therefore gaols had been small and ramshackle and their makeshift nature had not mattered much. In the second half of the [18th] century, things changed. Population rose, crime rose; the prison population grew, especially when transportation of felons was drastically interrupted by American Independence.... And the upshot of overcrowding was typhus.[80]

78 The tattooing of prisoners was indeed practiced: see, for examples, Diwan al-Tarsane, 953, 7.

79 I have seen only one reference to the distribution of clothes, ordered in 1834. It is not clear whether these were conspicuous prison clothes: see n. 49.

80 Roy Porter, "Howard's Beginning: Prisons, Disease, Hygiene," in *The Health of Prisoners: Historical Essays*, ed. Richard Creese, W.F. Bynum, and J. Bearn (Amsterdam: Rodopi, 1995), 15–16.

In general, these conclusions apply also to Egypt. When Isma'il became interested in prison conditions and issued orders to raise the living standards, the process of prison reform had already been under its way for more than a decade due to the efforts of lower-rank officials and administrators.

Of these, the health officials were the most important. In the late 1820s, a health service was established that worked not only in the field of curative medicine but also in public health and was intimately linked with the organs of law enforcement. From the 1850s on, health officials increasingly became involved in the conditions of prisons and were the motor behind the improvement of the conditions of the prisoners during the 1850s and early 1860s. They were prompted by official concern about the public-health risks of prisons.[81] Diseases due to the overcrowding of prisons must have been common in Egypt, too. Although there are no statistical data, it is plausible that the number of inmates rose from the late 1840s due to the rise of crime connected with urbanization and the gradual replacement of corporal punishment by imprisonment.[82] By the end of the 1840s, the health situation in the Alexandria prison was critical, and this must have been true of most other prisons. As Khaled Fahmy has shown, this led to a growing involvement of the health authorities in prison conditions and, as a consequence, to their improvement.

That they could realize these improvements was a consequence of the increased capabilities of the state. Until 1840, Egypt was organized as a command economy. Production, marketing, and the allocation of labor to the industrial establishments were carried out by order of the Pasha. However, the administrative apparatus was small and in general lacked the skills of running such large-scale operations. Often, things went wrong, as becomes clear from the Pasha's frequent orders addressing with violent abuse officials who had committed mistakes or been negligent. This may well have affected the provisioning of the prisons, which was not a high political priority for Mehmed 'Ali in any case. The situation of prisons in the late 1820s is illustrated by the following incident:

> When, somewhere during 1829, Khalil Bey, one of Mehmed 'Ali's aides (*mu'awin*), was returning from an official assignment, he came upon a prison ward (*hasil*) with twenty starved, suffocating, and moribund prisoners and the bodies of three unfortunate prisoners who had already died. They had not been fed for some time, and the atmosphere in the shed was stifling. It seems that they had been forgotten by the official in

81 See Fahmy, "Medical Conditions."

82 See Peters, "Egypt and the Age of the Triumphant Prison."

> charge. Khalil Bey reported the incident to Mehmed ʿAli, who then did not punish or reprimand the responsible official but just instructed him to show more compassion for the fate of these poor people.[83]

Mehmed ʿAli's lukewarm reaction – so different from his usual rebuking of negligent officials, which was riddled with invectives – shows that the matter did not unduly worry him. With the growth of the administration and the appointment of officials not only on the basis of trust and loyalty, but also on the basis of training and skills,[84] the capabilities of the state increased, and the provisioning of prisons could be more efficiently carried out. This constituted a necessary condition for the introduction of the reforms proposed by the health officials. A final factor that made the improvements possible is the increase in state revenues due to the cotton boom that started in 1861.[85]

Reforms to improve the living conditions in prisons were supported by the administration as a result of the spread of new ideas about crime and punishment that informed the penal system that emerged in Egypt after 1829. One of its characteristics was the notion of quantification of penalties to avoid arbitrariness in criminal justice.[86] After 1829, penal codes listed the punishment for each offense, and criminal sentences specified the penalties imposed. However, such a system can work only if prison conditions do not expose the inmates to serious health risks. In that case, imprisonment might result in excessive and gratuitous suffering or death, which would be in conflict with the idea of precisely quantified penalties. Control of suffering was therefore necessary so that a "just measure of pain" would be inflicted on every convict: convicts sentenced to the same type of imprisonment must be imprisoned under the same conditions. This required that prisons provide health standards, accommodations, and a subsistence-level diet that met, but did not exceed, that to which the lowest strata of society (the prisoner's "honest neighbor," as Jeremy Bentham has expressed it) was accustomed. For in that case, imprisonment would lose its deterrent effect. These notions, although never explicitly formulated, must have been a strong justification for the improvement of prison conditions around the middle of the 19th century.

83 Maʿiyya Saniyya to Ma'mur qism al-Jaʿfariyya, 20 Dhu al-Hijja 1244/23 July 1829, Sin 1/47/13, Maʿiyya Saniyya, Sadir ifadat wa-awamir wa-mukatabat ila jihat mutafarriqa (1243–45), doc. 390.

84 See F.R. Hunter, *Egypt under the Khedives, 1805–1879: From Household Government to Modern Bureaucracy* (Pittsburgh: University of Pittsburgh Press, 1984), 80–85.

85 See E.J.R. Owen, *Cotton and the Egyptian Economy, 1820–1914: A Study in Trade and Development* (Oxford: Oxford University Press, 1969), chap. 4.

86 See Peters, "For His Correction."

Author's Note

I thank the staff of the Egyptian National Archives for their assistance in making available the relevant documents for this study. All of the archival materials used for this study are in that archive. I owe a great debt of gratitude to Khaled Fahmy, who generously shared his extensive knowledge of these archives and helped me in many other ways during my research. Finally, I thank the anonymous *IJMES* readers for their comments.

Appendix 1: The 19th-Century Egyptian Criminal Laws

Penal Code of 1829 (PC 1829)

Turkish text and translation in R. Peters, "'For His Correction and as a Deterrent Example for Others': Mehmed 'Ali's First Criminal Legislation (1829–1830)," *Islamic Law and Society* 6 (1999): 164–93.

Qanun al-Filaha (Code of Agriculture) of 1830 (QF)

Text published as an appendix to *Layihat zira'at al-fallah wa-tadbir ahkam al-falah* (Bulaq, 1840–41). In 1845, it was included in the QM (Article 1–55).

Al-Qanun al-Muntakhab (Code with Selected Penal Provisions) of 1845 (QM)

Text in Ahmad Zaghlul, *al-Muhamah* (Cairo: Matba'at al-Ma'arif, 1900), app. 100–55; also in Filib Jallad, *Qamus al-idara* wa-l-qada' (Alexandria, 1890–92), iii, 351–78.

Penal Code of 1849 (PC 1849)

Printed in a bilingual (Arabic and Turkish) edition by Dar al-Tiba'a al-'Amira al-Misriyya in Bulaq on 8 Rajab 1265/30 May 1849.

Al-Qanunname al-Sultani (QS)

Text in Zaghlul, *al-Muhamah*, app., 156–78; Jallad, *Qamus*, ii, 90–102. Jallad also gives the administrative regulations (*harakat*) issued together with the code (pp. 102–11).

Supplement of Five Articles to the QS Drafted by the Majlis al-Ahkam in 1858

Text in Amin Sami, *Taqwim al-Nil* (Cairo: Matba'at al-Kutub al-Misriyya, 1928–36), iii/1:294–97.

Appendix 2: A Description of the Five *Sijills* regarding the Alexandria Prison

Diwan al-tarsana, 953–57 (old), *Qayd asma' al-madhnubin bi-liman tarsanat Iskandariyya*. This is the title as given on the first leaf of the *sijill*. On the cover, as in the index, this series is erroneously referred to as *Qayd asma' al-madyuniyya bayan tarsanat Iskandariyya*.

Sijills

953: 29 Safar 1263/16 February 1847 to 4 Dhu al-Hijja 1268/19 September 1852
954: 13 Rajab 1277/25 January 1861 to 5 Dhu al-Qaʿda 1281/1 April 1865
955: 5 Dhu al-Qaʿda 1281/1 April 1865 to 24 Rabiʿ I 1283/8 August 1866
956: 24 Muharram 1278/1 August 1861 to 26 Rabiʿ I 1285/17 July 1868
957: 26 Rabiʿ I 1285/17 July 1868 to 10 Safar 1286/22 May 1869

There is a gap between the first *sijill* (ending on 4 Dhu al-Hijja 1268/19 September 1852) and the second *sijill* (beginning 13 Rajab 1277/25 January 1861). The second through fifth *sijills* are consecutive. The fourth *sijill* seems to be an exception, as the third *sijill* ends on 24 Rabiʿ I 1283/8 August 1866, and the first entries of the fourth one are dated 24 Muharram 1278/1 August 1861. The reason is that the first twenty pages of the fourth *sijill* are a recapitulation of the previous *sijills*, listing by their date of entry, all prisoners present on 1 Jumada I 1283/11 September 1866, that is, all prisoners convicted for homicide who had not benefited from the amnesty of 5 Rabiʿ I 1283/18 July 1866.

The *sijills* give the following information:

- Name
- Beginning of detention spent before arrival
- Personal characteristics and estimated age (this is lacking in the first *sijill*)
- Short description of offense
- Length of sentence
- Date of arrival
- Number and date of covering letter
- Date of the end of the sentence
- Date of release or decease, with date and number of pertinent correspondence

PART 2

Other Egyptian Periods

CHAPTER 16

New Sources for the History of the Dakhla Oasis in the Ottoman Period

In 2003 workers restoring an eighteenth-century mud-brick house in the town of al-Qaṣr in the Dakhla Oasis, discovered pieces of paper in the rubble of an adjacent house that had collapsed. Apart from scraps and small fragments of documents, the finds included many complete or nearly complete legible documents. The restoration of the mud brick house was carried out by the Qasr Dakhleh Project (QDP) under the aegis of the Dakhleh Oasis Project (DOP), a mainly but not exclusively archaeological international project dealing with the history of the Dakhla Oasis from prehistoric times to the present.[1] During the subsequent campaigns of 2004, 2005 and 2007 more written pieces of paper were found in the remains of the ruined house, which, according to local informants, was known as *Bayt al-Qurashī* and had been abandoned before 1940, probably due to its sudden collapse. This information tallies with the fact that the most recent document in the collection dates from 1937. The finds include religious texts, personal letters, magical texts, amulets and about 200 undamaged or nearly undamaged legal and financial documents written in the period between 1579 (987 H) and 1937. A preliminary examination showed that they are the remains of a family archive of a branch of the local Qurashī family. All pieces of paper have been rehydrated, put between glass plates for conservation and numbered, and are now stored in Mūṭ, in the storerooms of the Egyptian Antiquities Organization, Inspectorate of Dakhla. My colleague Dr Fred Leemhuis of the University of Groningen, the Netherlands, who is in charge of the Qaṣr Dakhleh Project, asked me to examine and eventually publish the legal and financial material. He himself will edit the personal letters and the religious texts and Dr Alexander Fodor of the University of Budapest will study the magical texts and amulets. The purpose of this paper is to give a global description of the legal and financial documents and an impression of their value as sources for historical research by presenting an analysis of two related documents.

1 For information on and the annual reports of the DOP and QDP, see http://arts.monash.edu.au/archaeology/excavations/dakhleh/index.php. The documents mentioned in this article have been published in R. Peters, *Watha'iq madinat al-Qasr fi al-Wahat al-Dakhila masdaran li-tarikh Misr fi al-'asr al-'Uthmani* (Cairo: Dar al-Watha'iq al-Qawmiyya (National Archive), 2011).

 | DOI:10.1163/9789004420625_017

The town of al-Qaṣr is situated in the middle of the Western Desert, about 800 km SSE of Cairo and 350 km W. of Luxor, halfway between the Nile and the present-day Libyan border. It goes back to Roman times as evidenced by the remains of a Roman wall that were recently discovered and dated. Having been the main town of the Dakhla Oasis for centuries, its functions as an administrative centre have now been taken over by the town of Mūṭ. According to the 1848 (1264 H) and 1867 (1284 H) censuses, the number of its inhabitants was around 3.500, most of them engaged in agriculture, made possible by the abundance of springs and wells in its vicinity. In the arid desert environment, these wells were economically just as important as land. They were owned collectively, often by tens of persons for one single well and there existed complicated legal arrangements for sharing their water for the irrigation of the orchards and fields. A substantial part of the documents deals with titles to the use of water from these wells.

Little is known about the history of al-Qaṣr. There are rumours that there exists a privately held manuscript chronicle of the town but as yet it has not been discovered. The holdings of the Egyptian state archives (Dār al-Wathā'iq al-Qawmiyya) contain documents relative to al-Qaṣr in the Shari'a court *sijills* but only after 1849.[2] The censuses of 1848 and 1867 give detailed information about its inhabitants and their occupations.[3] 'Alī Mubārak devotes only a few lines to al-Qaṣr in his *al-Khiṭaṭ al-Tawfīqiyya*.[4] A little bit more may culled from the travelogues of nineteenth-century Western travellers, but in general the available sources do not yield very much. In view of this dearth of information, the present collection is valuable, especially for the social and economic history of the town.

I have summarily catalogued all complete or nearly complete legal and financial documents found so far, in total 207 pieces. These documents consist mainly of contracts, often notarized in court, of receipts of payment of taxes, IOUs, appointment of attorneys and notes or lists regarding debts or

2 The series with the oldest documents is Mudīriyyat Asyūṭ/al-Wāḥāt al-Dākhila/Sijill al-ishhādāt, 26 registers from 1265 till 1307 H. With regard to the neighbouring Kharga Oasis, the DWQ holdings include the remains of a family archive, a collection of about one hundred microfilmed documents, dating from the 9th to the 13th centuries H. and related to the al-Anṣārī family, a family of local sheikhs. DWQ, Wathā'iq al-Wāḥāt, Ḥujja # 392, Film #9. The collection has been catalogued and partly edited by Salwā Mīlād. See Salwā 'Alī Mîlād, *Wathā'iq Al-Wāḥāt Al-Miṣriyya. Dirāsa Wa-Nashr Wa-Taḥqīq*. Rev. ed, Cairo: Dār al-Kutub wa-Wathā'iq al-Qawmiyya, 2003.

3 DWQ, Sijill 4959 (*qadīm*), Rabī' I 1264, Ti'dād al-nufūs bi-mudīririyat Asyūṭ, Nawāḥī al- Wāḥāt al-Dākhila; DWQ, Sijill 5486 (*qadīm*), Ramaḍān, 1284, Ti'dād al-nufūs fī nāḥiyat al-Qaṣr bi-l-Wāḥāt al-Dākhila.

4 'Alī Mubārak, *Al-khiṭaṭ al-tawfīqiyya al-jadīda li-Miṣr al-qāhira*. 16 parts in 4 vols. Cairo, 1306 H, xvii, pp. 30–1.

expenses. In addition, I have found a few *waqfiyyas*, judicial sentences and fatwas. A substantial part of the documents are related to agricultural activities: lease or sale of land or of water rights, sharecropping or the payment of taxes on land or springs and wells. (See Table 16.2) Moreover, there are some documents regarding the maintenance of a springs and lists made by individual farmers recording those from whom they leased water rights. I have found no documents indicating that the family were engaged in cattle breeding, trade or artisanal production.

The oldest document of the collection is a *waqfiyya* with a length of more than one meter and dated 987 H. Unfortunately the first lines are missing. The most recent document is a tax receipt from 1937. The following table shows the distribution of the documents over the Hijri centuries:

TABLE 16.1 Chronological distribution of the legal and financial documents

10th century	02	1(1%)
11th century	28	(13%)
12th century	44	(21%)
13th century	78	(38%)
14th century	24	(12%)
Undated or not datable	31	(15%)

Al-Qaṣr had its own court of law. Forty-three documents in the collection were issued and sealed by this court and seven more by Cairo courts. The inhabitants of al-Qaṣr followed the Shafiʿite school of jurisprudence and nearly all of the deeds registered in court of al-Qaṣr bear the name and the seal of Shafiʿite *qāḍīs* from local families. Nearly all of these deeds record contracts and depositions and only three are sentences ending litigation. From the titles the local *qāḍīs* used to refer to themselves it is clear that they regarded themselves as belonging to the Ottoman-Egyptian judiciary: they call themselves deputies (*nāʾib, khalīfa*) of the (Ottoman) *qāḍī* of the Western Oases (*qāḍī al-Wāḥāt*, or *al-nāẓir fī al-aḥkām al-sharʿiyya fī kāmil aqālīm al-Wāḥāt*).[5] This is consistent with the legal practice in Ottoman Egypt before the nineteenth century. The Hanafite *qāḍīs* in Egypt would have deputies belonging to the other schools, adjudicating disputes and registering documents according to their own

5 The *qāḍī* of the Oases (Alwāḥ) belonged to the first (lowest) rank of the six ranks of the Egyptian Ottoman judicial hierarchy. Galal H. El-Nahal, *The Judicial Administration of Ottoman Egypt in the Seventeenth Century*, Minneapolis etc.: Bibliotheca Islamica, 1979. *Studies in Middle Eastern History*, 4. Appendix B.

school but under the supervision of the Hanafite *qāḍī*. At least three documents were issued by *qāḍīs* from other *madhhabs*. I found a sentence in a lawsuit about water rights, pronounced in 1055 by a Hanafi *qāḍī* in al-Qaṣr, calling himself the *khalīfa* of the *qāḍī* of the Oases[6] and a deed of appointment of a guardian over a deaf-mute person, issued in 1090 by the court of al-Qaṣr but with the Hanafi *qāḍī* of the Oases (*al-qāḍī bi-l-wāḥāt*) presiding.[7] The third one contains a sentence dated 1116 pronouncing a divorce for unjustified absence of the husband issued by a Maliki *qāḍī* with the express authorization of the local Shafiʿite *qāḍī*. The reason for calling in the Maliki *qāḍī* is that Shafiʿite law does not recognize unjustified absence of the husband as a ground for divorce.

As said before, only a part of the documents are contracts and sentences notarized by *qāḍīs*. The following table gives an impression of the types of documents.

TABLE 16.2 Categories of documents

Transactions regarding land, water and buildings:		66 (32%)
Sale of land, buildings or trees	22	
Sale of water rights	17	
Sale of both land and water rights	5	
Lease of land and/or buildings	14	
Sharecropping (*jaʿāla*)	8	
Other transactions:		33 (15%)
Acknowledgement of debts	12	
Appointment of agents	4	
Financial arrangements (*taṣāduq*)	6	
Related to family matters (marriage, succession, waqfs, guardianship)	11	
Receipts:		42 (20%)
For taxes	23	
Other	19	
Accounts and lists:		37 (18%)
Accounts	26	
Lists (creditors, expenses)	11	
Miscellaneous		29 (14%)
Total number of legal and financial documents:		207

6 D.05.002.
7 D.05.024.

The significance of these documents is great. In the first place this is due to their coherence. They form the, admittedly incomplete, remains of a family archive, which allows us to pursue the social and economic history of one family over more than three centuries. Although in the state archives similar documents are kept, they are catalogued in such a way that, unless they are completely digitalized and searchable, research on one particular family would be difficult to carry out. The Qurashī family seem to have belonged to the notables of the town: Among them there were several local judges and administrative sheikhs. Unfortunately, no documents were found related to their public offices. That this family was involved in agriculture adds to the significance of the collection, since documents written by agriculturalists are scarce. But there is another point that makes this collection extremely interesting: it includes types of documents such as personal letters, receipts, IOUs, contracts of minor importance, lists of debtors and financial accounts, documents that are usually not found in state or public archives. These documents, not written by official scribes, allow us to study the culture of writing in a remote desert town like al- important source for the legal history as it informs us on the application of the Shari‘a and the prevailing legal culture.[8]

The documents can be used as sources for studying various aspects of al-Qaṣr's history. They shed light on the social and economic history of the Qurashī family, one of the prominent families of the town, on landholding practices, social and economic and gender relations, and on the relationship between al-Qaṣr and the rest of Egypt, and especially Cairo. Moreover, by comparing different documents and analysing the data, biographical details can be collected. In the following I will analyse two documents in order to illustrate the potential of the collection. They drew my attention because they contain contracts in the field of family law, a type of document that is rare in this collection. My curiosity was roused by the fact that they were issued by Cairo courts and record contracts that were concluded in Cairo, whereas the few other documents issued by Cairo courts contain sales and leases of land and water rights in al-Qaṣr.

I will have a closer look at the following texts:

- (1) A document[9] issued by the Hanafi deputy *qāḍī* of the court of Qanāṭir al-Sibāʿ recording a marriage concluded on 19 Rajab 1111 (10 January 1700) between a certain Ṣāliḥ b. Ḥusayn b. Muḥammad b. Majīd al-Qurashī

8 See e.g. on shareholding practices in al-Qaṣr: R. Peters, "Sharecropping in the Dakhla Oasis: Sharia and customary law in Ottoman Egypt," in: *The Law Applied: Contextualizing the Islamic Shari‘a: A Volume in Honor of Frank E. Vogel*. Ed. P. Bearman, a.o., London: I.B. Taurus, 2008.

9 D.04.205. See Appendix 1 for the edited text.

al-Wāḥī al-Qaṣrī and a white (*bayḍā*) woman called ʿĀyisha Khātūn bt. ʿAbd Allāh, the manumitted slave (*maʿtūqa*) of the late Ḥasan Agha. The bride was represented by a certain Ḥasan b. Makkī al-Jāwīsh in the corps of retired soldiers (*silk al-mutaqāʿid*).[10] The stipulated bride price was fifteen piasters (450 *niṣf fiḍḍa*), of which ten piasters were paid immediately. In addition, Ṣāliḥ promised to pay the rent of the apartment in the Suwayqat al-Lālā neighbourhood[11] where she lived and to support her minor daughter Fāṭima. In exchange, she allowed him to live with her.

– (2) A document[12] issued by the Maliki deputy *qāḍī* of the court of Qūṣūn recording an agreement (*taṣāduq*) dated 17 Muḥarram 1116 (21 May 1704) in which a certain Muṣṭafā b. Murtaḍā Agha, formerly of the Mutafarriqa regiment,[13] acting as an attorney for both *al-Sharīfa* Fāṭima bt. al-Sayyid Aḥmad, the widow of his uncle Sulaymān, and for ʿĀyisha b. ʿAbd Allāh,[14] the manumitted slave of his uncle and the wife of Ṣāliḥ b. Ḥusayn, declares that Fāṭima will pay for the sustenance of ʿĀyisha and her daughter Ruqayya whenever Ṣāliḥ leaves Cairo. This is done as a gift and Fāṭima nor ʿĀyisha will have the right to recover from Ṣāliḥ the amounts paid to him. The latter, present in court, accepts this arrangement.

The person linking these documents with al-Qaṣr is Ṣāliḥ b. Ḥusayn al-Qurashī, a party to both contracts. He appears in at least fifteen other documents in our collection, all issued by the court of al-Qaṣr between 1113 and 1143. Most of them are related to transactions regarding water rights, landed property and buildings.[15] From these documents it is clear that he lived in a house on the

10 The *silk* or *jamāʿat al-mutaqāʿidīn* consisted of retired soldiers, supported by the Porte. See Shaw, Stanford. *The Financial and Administrative Organization and Development of Ottoman Egypt* (1517–1798), Princeton: Princeton University Press, 1962. pp. 189, 201.

11 On al-Lālā Market (Suwayqat al-Lālā), see Mubārak, *Khiṭaṭ*, vol. iii, 93–96.

12 D.04.270. See Appendix 2 for the edited text.

13 By the end of the seventeenth century, the Mutafarriqa regiments was the richest and the most powerful of the army corps. Among its duties was the garrisoning of provincial fortresses. It was the main military base of support for the governors (*vālī's*). Shaw. *The Financial and Administrative Organization*, pp. 193–4.

14 Although the name of former owner of ʿĀyisha is different in the two documents (Ḥasan Agha or Sulaymān Agha) I assume that ʿĀyisha bt. ʿAbdallah refers to the same woman.

15 D.05.006 (1113, purchase of water rights); D.05.041r (Purchase of land and water rights, 1116); D.04.273 (sale of land, 1117); D.04.290r (lease of land, 1119); D.04.236 (lease of a storehouse in al-Qaṣr, 1119); D.05.078 (sale of water rights, 1119); D.05.080 (purchase of water rights, 1122); D.04.290v (lease of land, 1122); D.04.281r (purchase of water rights, 1123); D.05.003 (sentence about water rights, 1125); D.04.289v (purchase of water rights, 1129); D.04.289r (purchase of water rights, 1129); D.05.081 (lease of land, 1131); D.05.014,(the inventory of his estate, 1143).

Shāriʿ al-Quḍāt in al-Qaṣr,[16] most probably the house in whose ruins the documents were found. He died in 1143 (1730), leaving a wife called ʿĀyisha Muṣṭafā Majīd al-Qurashī (a first or second cousin) and three children: Ruqayya, Fāṭima and Muḥammad.[17] From an undated document about the payment of the deferred bride price it is clear that he had married before in al-Qaṣr and that this marriage had ended in a divorce. His first wife, Sayyidat al-Banāt bt. Abū al-ʿIzz al-ʿImādī, belonged to another family of notables in al-Qaṣr.[18] It is likely that he divorced her because she did not bear him any offspring: among the three children mentioned in the inventory of his estate there are none borne by this wife. We do not know what Ṣāliḥ's business was in Cairo. What we do know is that his brother had lived there too or was, perhaps, still living there when Ṣāliḥ married. In at least three document issued by Cairo courts in 1101 and 1106, he appears as a party. Curiously, the contracts registered in Cairo deal with land and water in al-Qaṣr and the other parties and some of the witnesses are from al-Qaṣr.[19] This suggests that there was a small and probably fluid community of Qaṣrians in Cairo. It is plausible that Ṣāliḥ intended to stay for some time in Cairo, interrupted by visits to his hometown, as shown by a document issued in 1113 by the court of al-Qaṣr in which he is mentioned as the purchaser of water rights.

The other leading character in the two documents is ʿĀyisha bt. ʿAbd Allāh. ʿĀyisha's background is clear from the two documents. She was a white woman, who had been brought as a slave to Egypt. As her patronymic (*nasab*) "bint ʿAbd Allāh" indicates, she was a convert to Islam. She must have been an imported slave, probably of Circassian origin. In the first document she has the honorific *khātūn*, which would mean that she originally belonged to a family of a certain standing, in this case military rank. Her former owner was a soldier (there is confusion between both documents and is called Ḥasan Agha or Sulaymān Agha), her proxies in the two contracts are retired soldiers: Ḥasan b. Makkī, *al-jāwīsh* in the corps of retired soldiers (*silk al-mutaqāʿid*) and Muṣṭafā b. Murtaḍā (a nephew of her former owner), one-time officer (*agha*) in the corps of the Mutafarriqa. Another indication of the standing of the family of her former owner is that his wife bears the title of *sharīfa*. That they were rich is clear from the fact that they could afford a white slave woman. That the second document was issued by the court of Qūṣūn could also be a sign of wealth,

16 D.04.236, dd. 1119, lease by Ṣāliḥ of part of a storehouse in al-Qaṣr adjacent to Ṣāliḥ's house.

17 D.05.014, the probate inventory of his estate.

18 D.04.289 recto–1 (or D.04.238); last line with dating missing, but judging by the name of the *qāḍī*, must have been issued between 1110 and 1130.

19 D.05.004r (sale of land, 1101); D. 05.012r (sale of land and water rights, 1106); D.05.012v (*isqāṭ* of water rights, 1106).

since Qūṣūn quarter was a rich residential neighbourhood whereas people would do their business in courts close to their homes or businesses.

Ṣāliḥ probably came into contact with her via a marriage broker. The bride price Ṣāliḥ paid, fifteen piasters (450 *niṣf fiḍḍa*), ten of which paid immediately as the prompt bride price, contrasts starkly with the bride price of 4.000 *niṣf fiḍḍa* he paid to his first wife in al-Qaṣr. The difference is certainly due to the fact that ʿĀyisha was not a virgin anymore: She had an infant daughter, Fāṭima, to take care of, most probably a child of her former master Sulaymān Agha. Before his death he must have manumitted ʿĀyisha, or recognized Fāṭima as his child, thus making ʿĀyisha an *umm walad*, who would be free upon her master's death. She cannot have been totally destitute: The *Suwayqat al-Lālā* neighbourhood (*khaṭṭ*), where she lived, is located in the Ḥanafī quarter, a middle class area at the southwest end of the city, close to the Sayyida Zaynab Mosque on the other bank of the Khalīj Canal.[20] When she died sometime before 1143, her daughter inherited 5.000 *niṣf fiḍḍa* from her.[21] Assuming that Ruqayya had one sister (Fāṭima) or was alone (if Fāṭima had died), ʿĀyisha's fortune must have been 15.000 *niṣf fiḍḍa*.[22] Finally, the fact that in the marriage contract she waived her right to demand that Ṣāliḥ pay the rent of her apartment, can be construed as an indication that she did have some means.

The documents give rise to two questions. The first one is what were Ṣāliḥ's and ʿĀyisha's motives in marrying one another and the second is why would the wife of ʿĀyisha's former owner take it upon her to pay for her food whenever Ṣāliḥ was absent. The first question is not too difficult to answer, although there remain white spots in the overall picture. As we have seen, Ṣāliḥ wanted to stay in Cairo for some time. His marriage with ʿĀyisha must have been a convenient arrangement for him, providing him, whenever he was in Cairo, with a home for free and a wife to take care of his practical needs. Maybe there was also another motive: ʿĀyisha might bring him into contact with members of the military elite. Some other men of the Qurashī family used the titles *shūrbajī* and *oḍabāshī*, which suggests that they were somehow connected with one of the Egyptian Ottoman military corps (*ojaq*) and probably received revenues from them. Perhaps Ṣāliḥ also wanted to be incorporated in such a corps.

---

20 André Raymond, *Le Caire*, Paris: Fayard, 1993. pp. 219, 263. The marriage was registered at the court of Qanāṭir al-Sibāʾ which is located very close to where ʿĀyisha was living.

21 The probate inventory of Ṣāliḥ's estate (D.05.014) lists a debt of 5.000 *niṣf fiḍḍa* to Ruqayya for money inherited from her mother.

22 According to the rules of the Shariʿa, one or two daughters without any brothers inherit third each as Koranic heirs, whereas, in the case of ʿĀyisha, the remainder of the state would go to the agnatic heirs of her former master.

He was willing to pay the bride price of ten piasters and to support not only his wife but also his stepdaughter.[23] As to ʿĀyisha, it would seem that her motives were also practical. My guess is that after her master's decease and upon becoming a free person, she and her daughter Fāṭima had to leave the household where she used to live. Was it because of the widow's jealousy? In order to gain respectability she needed a husband, but at the same time she wanted a certain independence. That must have been the reason for including the clause that Ṣāliḥ was allowed to live in her home and did not have to pay rent. Such a stipulation suggests that the wife controls the conjugal home and that the husband's authority is restricted.[24] A match with Ṣāliḥ was not a bad opportunity. Although he was a peasant hailing from a remote place in the desert, with a culture very different from the Turkish Circassian military one in which she had been brought up, and probably speaking a heavy regional dialect, he was also a man of some means. We don't know how long the marriage lasted, although it is clear from the dates of the documents in which his name appears (see note 15) that after 1116 he lived permanently or most of the time in al-Qaṣr. ʿĀyisha bore him a daughter, Ruqayya, who eventually followed her father to al-Qaṣr, where we meet her in two documents: the inventory of her father's estate (1143) and an agreement with her brother Muḥammad after a financial dispute (1162).[25] These documents make no mention of a husband and she must have remained unmarried.

The transaction mentioned in the second document poses more problems of interpretation. Its wording is clear but we are left in the dark as to the motives of the parties concerned. Why should the widow of ʿĀyisha's former master suddenly be so generous as to offer financial support to her and her daughter Ruqayya whenever Ṣāliḥ would leave Cairo? In the absence of more documentary evidence, my explanation is speculative but plausible. I think a clue is the absence of any reference to ʿĀyisha's daughter Ruqayya in the second document. In the marriage contract Ṣāliḥ takes the responsibility for the child's maintenance. In the second text only the younger daughter Ruqayya is mentioned and not Fāṭima. In the marriage document (dated 19 Rajab 1111/10 January 1700) the latter is described as having been weaned (*faṭīma*), i.e. two

23 Such a clause seems to have been common when women with children from a previous husband or master remarried. A.-R. Abdel-Rehim, "The Family and Gender Laws in Egypt During the Ottoman Period." In *Women, the Family, and Divorce Laws in Islamic History*, edited by A.E. Sonbol. Syracuse: Syracuse University Press, 1996, p. 100.

24 See Hanna, Nelly. "Marriage among Merchant Families in Seventeenth-Century Cairo." In *Women, the Family, and Divorce Laws in Islamic History*, edited by A.E. Sonbol. Syracuse, N.Y.: Syracuse University Press, 1996. Pp. 147–8.

25 D.05.005.

or three years old. At the time of the second document (dated 17 Muḥarram 1116/21 May 1704) her age must have been six or seven. Assuming that she had not died, which is of course a possibility in societies with a high child mortality, my explanation for the fact that the second document is silent on her is that her father's family had claimed her and that, in order to placate the mother, the father's widow offered some financial compensation. Since the documents show that Ṣāliḥ stayed more and more in al-Qaṣr, the support must have been most welcome.

The reading and understanding of these documents is not easy. Familiarity with the cultural contexts is indispensable to give social and cultural meaning to these purely legal transactions, recorded in a terse and formulaic style. However, by combining data from different documents with historical background information one can bring these documents to life, as I have tried to show using these two contracts as examples. After editing all available documents, we will try to use them to deepen our knowledge of the history of al-Qaṣr and the Dakhla oasis.

Appendix 1

Paper, 26,3 by 14,4 cm.
Writing clearly legible.
Orthography: *Hamza*'s omitted; dots sometimes omitted, but two dots consistently placed underneath the *alif maqṣūra*.
Marriage contract, dated 19 Rajab 1111.

1. الامر كما ذكر فيه نمقه الفقير اليه سبحانه
2. مصطفى المولى خلافة بمحكمة قناطر السباع
3. غفر له
4. (ختم)
5. بالمحكمة الشرعية المطهرة المرضية بقناطر السباع بمصر المحروسة بين يدي متوليها سيدنا ومولانا
6. فخر قضاة الاسلام الحاكم الشرعي الحنفي الموقع خطه الكريم اعلاه
7. اصدق فخر امثاله الاجل المكرم الزيني صالح بن حسين الواحي
8. القرشي مخطوبته المصونة عايشة خاتون بنت عبد الله البيضا معتوقة
9. المرحوم حسن اغا على الكتاب والسنة الشريفة المحمدية صداقا

10. قدره من القروش الفضة التي عبرة كل قرش منها ثلاثون نصفا فضه
11. خمسة عشر قرشا الحال لها عليه من ذلك عشرة قروش مقبوضة
12. منه لها بمناولة وكيلها فخر اقرانه الزيني حسن بن مكي
13. الجاويش بسلك المتقاعد الثابت توكيله عنها في ذلك وفيما يذكر فيه
14. لدى مولانا الحاكم المشار اليه بشهادة الحاج عودة بن سفيان
15. الصيرفي والاستى علي بن عبد الحافظ الخياط ثبوتا شرعيا
16. قبضا شرعيا بتمام ذلك وكماله بالمجلس والباقي بعد الحال
17. المرقوم وقدره خمسة قروش تحل لها عليه بموت او فراق زوجها
18. له بذلك وكيلها المشار اليه بما له من التوكيل المزوج عنها بايجابه
19. تزويجا شرعيا وقبله الزوج المرقوم منه لنفسه على ذلك قبولا شرعيا
20. والله سبحانه مع المتقين ورحمته قريبا من المحسنين ثم اباح الوكيل
21. بما له من التوكيل عن موكلته المذكورة[26] للزوج المرقوم السكنى بمحل
22. سكنها الكاين بخط سويقة اللالا انه ما دام ساكنا بها فيه لا تطلبه[27] (؟)
23. باجرة نظير ذلك اباحة شرعية مقبولة وتصادقا على ذلك ورضي
24. الزوج المذكور بابنتها فاطمة الفطيمة بانها تاكل من اكله وتشرب
25. من شربه وتنام في فراشه التصادق الشرعي وثبت الاشهاد بذلك
26. لدى سيدنا الحاكم المشار اليه بشهادة شهوده ثبوتا شرعيا وحكم بموجب ذلك حكما
27. شرعيا مسيولا في ذلك وبه شهد وحرر في تاسع عشر شهر رجب سنة احد عشر
ومائة والف

[4 شهود]

Appendix 2

Paper, 14 by 15,5 cm.
Upper part with the authentication of the *qāḍī* and a small part of his seal missing.
Writing clearly readable.

---

26 المذكور.

27 The writing is unclear and looks more like تطابه. However, my reading is based on the fact that according to Abdel-Rahim stipulations that the husband would not pay rent were sometimes included in marriage contracts. Abdel-Rahim, "Family and gender laws," p. 100.

Orthography: *Hamza*'s omitted; dots sometimes omitted, but two dots consistently placed underneath the *alif maqṣūra*.

Agreement about the payment of maintenance of a woman and her child by a third party whenever her husband leaves Cairo, dated 17 Muḥarram 1116.

1. [الامر كما ذكر فيه نمقه الفقير اليه سبحانه]
2. [...المالكي المولى بمحكمة قوصون خلافة]
3. [غفر له]
4. (ختم)
5. بمحكمة قوصون بمصر المحروسة لدى متوليها سيدنا ومولانا الحاكم الشرعي المالكي الموقع خطه الكريم اعلاه
6. اشهد علي فخر الاقران الزيني مصطفى بن المرحوم مرتضى اغا من المتفرقة كان بوكالته الشرعية عن
7. زوجة عمه المرحوم سليمان اغا هي الشريفة فاطمة بنت السيد احمد وعن معتوقة عمه المذكور هي الحرمة عايشة
8. بنت عبد االه زوجة المحترم صالح بن حسين مجيد القرشي الواحي القصري الحاضر بالمجلس الثابت معرفتهما
9. وتوكيله عنهما في ذلك وفيما يذكر فيه لدى مولانا الحاكم المشار اليه بشهادة الاستا(...؟) ابن
10. محمد والاستا حسن بن المحترم عبد الله الحايك كل منهما بخط سويقة السباعين[28] ثبوتا شرعيا بشهودة الاشهاد
11. الشرعي ان الشريفة فاطمة المذكورة التزمت في ذمتها ومالها ان متى سافر المحترم صالح زوج عايشة المذكورة
12. من مصر وضواحيها فيكون عليها القيام بمونة عايشة المذكورة وبنتها رقية من اكل وشرب الى
13. حين حضوره الى مصر بالغا ما بلغ التزاما شرعيا على وجه الصلة والمعروف من غير رجوع للشريفة
14. فاطمة والحرمة عايشة الموكلتين المذكورتين على المحترم صالح المذكور بشي من ذلك باعتراف الزيني

28 See ʿAlī Mubārak, *Khitat*, iii, 90.

15. مصطفى الوكيل المذكور بما له من التوكيل المعين اعلاه بذلك جميعه بشهوده الاعتراف الشرعي وقبل ذلك
16. منه لنفسه المحترم صالح المذكور قبولا شرعيا وتصادقا على ذلك كله وشمل ذلك ثبوتا وحكما شرعيين من
17. قبل مولانا الحاكم المشار اليه بشهادة شهوده وبه شهد في سابع عشر محرم الحرام سنة ستة عشر ومائة والف توكلنا على الله ونعم الوكيل

(8 شهود)

CHAPTER 17

Sharecropping in the Dakhla Oasis

Shari'a and Customary Law in Ottoman Egypt

In this essay[1] I will present and analyse two documents from a family archive found in the town of al-Qaṣr (henceforth, al-Qasr) in the Dakhla Oasis. They contain arrangements regarding a sharecropping contract and I will show that these must be regarded as attempts to reconcile legal doctrine with customary practice. The documents were found during clearance activities in connection with the restoration of an early eighteenth-century mud brick house, carried out by the Qasr Dakhleh Project (QDP) under the aegis of the Dakhleh Oasis Project. In the rubble of the ruined house a considerable number of objects and written pieces of paper were found.[2] According to local informants, the house was already abandoned before 1940, probably due to its sudden collapse. The pieces of paper are the remains of a family archive belonging to a branch of the Qurashi family. Their study may shed light on the pre-modern history of this little Islamic town. Although much of the paper material consists of scraps or small fragments of documents, there are also many complete or nearly complete documents. These include religious texts, personal letters, magical texts, amulets, and about 170 legal documents or documents regarding financial transactions, dating from 1579 (987 AH) to 1929. The documents have been numbered and placed between glass plates for conservation, and are now stored in the storerooms of the Egyptian Antiquities Organization Inspectorate of Dakhla. My colleague Fred Leemhuis of the University of Groningen, who is in charge of the QDP, asked me to examine and eventually publish the legal material.

Family archives are important for historical research. Their special value is that they give a great deal of information on a specific family and are, therefore, a rich source for social history. Such information cannot easily be culled from public archives, unless these are completely digitized and searchable. But even then, family archives have an added value because they usually contain many documents of minor importance (receipts, IOUs, lists of creditors,

1 This is a revised version of a paper presented at the Customary Law in the Middle East Workshop, Dept. of Near Eastern Studies, Princeton University (May 13–14, 2006) with the title "Shari'a and Customary Law in al-Qasr (Dakhla Oasis, Egypt) in the Eighteenth Century".

2 For more information on the project, see http://weekly.ahram.org.eg/2006/787/heritage.htm. The documents mentioned in this article have been published in R. Peters, *Watha'iq madinat al-Qasr fi al-Wahat al-Dakhila masdaran li-tarikh Misr fi al-'asr al-'Uthmani* (Cairo: Dar al-Watha'iq al-Qawmiyya, 2011).

 | DOI:10.1163/9789004420625_018

etc.) not found in the state archives. The documents found in al-Qasr are for these reasons of great significance. In fact, they are unique, since very little is known of the Ottoman history (nor of any other period) of the town. There are rumours that there exists a privately held manuscript chronicle of the town. However, I have not seen it and cannot judge its value as a source. The holdings of the Egyptian state archives must undoubtedly contain documents relative to al-Qasr. However, since in the main archive, Dar al-Watha'iq al-Qawmiyya (DWQ), only about 10% of the material has been catalogued, it will be difficult to conduct a specific search. Moreover, the main holdings of this archive, i.e., the documents of the Egyptian government, do not go back further than 1822, when a fire destroyed the then existing records. Shariʿa court records exist from earlier periods. Those of the provincial courts are now available either in the DWQ (where they were housed in recent times) or in the Dar al-Mahfuzat, an archive belonging to the Ministry of Finance. These archives may offer better prospects, but at the moment it is still unclear whether or not the records of the al-Qasr court are preserved, and if so, where they are located.

The legal documents found in al-Qasr consist mainly of contracts, often notarized in court, of receipts of payment of taxes, appointment of proxies, and notes regarding debts or expenses. In addition I have found a few charitable endowment deeds (*waqfiyya*), judicial sentences, and fatwas. The documents that I have studied so far clearly point to the fact that the Qurashi family, or at least that part of it that lived in this house, was mainly involved in agriculture. More than half of the documents are related to agricultural activities: lease or sale of land or of water rights, sharecropping, or the payment of taxes on land or springs and wells. In addition there are some documents regarding the maintenance of a spring and lists made by individual farmers of those from whom they leased water rights. I have found no documents indicating that the family was engaged in cattle breeding, trade, or artisanal production, nor documents related to the sale of the date harvest. The family seems to have belonged to the notables of the town: Among them, there were several judges and administrative sheikhs.

Al-Qasr used to be the main town of the Dakhla Oasis. It is situated about 350 km west of Luxor, halfway between the Nile and the present-day Libyan border. Nowadays the town of Mut has taken over its function as administrative centre. The town of al-Qasr goes back to Roman times, as evidenced by the remains of a Roman wall that was recently discovered and dated. An important source of livelihood was agriculture, made possible by the abundance of springs and wells, located mainly to the south and east of the town. These wells were in private hands, often owned collectively by tens of persons. A substantial part of the documents deals with titles to water, evidently just as important as titles to land.

The inhabitants of al-Qasr followed the Shafiʿi school of jurisprudence and the Shariʿa court of the town was also Shafiʿi. Nearly all of the deeds that were registered in court bear the name of a Shafiʿi qadi, whose main task, like that of other qadis, was notarizing contracts and depositions. From the titles used in the documents it is clear that the local qadis felt themselves to be part of the Ottoman judiciary. They referred to themselves as the deputies (*naʾib, khalifa*) of the Ottoman qadi of the Western Oases (*qadi l-Wahat*, or *al-naʾib fi l-ahkam al-sharʿiyya fi kamil aqalim al-Wahat*). This is consistent with the legal practice in Ottoman Egypt before the nineteenth century. The Hanafi qadis appointed to various cities in Egypt would have deputies belonging to the other schools, adjudicating disputes and registering documents according to their own school, but under the supervision of the Hanafi qadi.

The two documents presented here were written with an interval of sixteen years, each on one side of an undamaged piece of paper measuring 15 by 39 cm.[3] The first document is an unofficial copy of a notarized contract. The last sentences mention that it has been notarized (*talab al-hukm bihi*) by a qadi. Since there is no heading with the name and the seal of the judge, as we find in other documents, I assume it was an unofficial copy of the original one. It is signed by four witnesses. The second document, written overleaf, is not notarized and is signed by two witnesses. One of the parties is Salih Muhammad Salih al-Qurashi, whose papers are part of the al-Qurashi collection. He was a farmer and appears between 1771 and 1801 in eight documents of the collection, all of them contracts with regard to land, palm trees, or water rights, and without exception concluded with relatives. According to these documents, he cultivated plots south and west of the town.

The documents are not only of interest for social history, they are also relevant for legal history, or rather for the history of the application of the Shariʿa. They show how local jurists tried to reconcile customary practices with the legal doctrines of Islamic jurisprudence. In Islamic law, according to most schools of jurisprudence, there is no general theory of contract because the law regards as valid and binding only those contracts that are expressly mentioned and permitted in the law. If parties conclude contracts not recognized by the law, such contracts are void and cannot be enforced in a court of law. Thus, classifying customary agreements in accordance with the Shariʿa is important. Since the community of al-Qasr was in the habit of concluding certain sharecropping contracts that were not regarded as valid under Shafiʿi law, the jurists sought creative solutions by characterizing these contracts differently.

3 Document D.04.291 recto and verso. Published in R. Peters, *Wathaʾiq madinat al-Qasr fi al-Wahat al-Dakhila masdaran li-tarikh Misr fi al-ʿasr al-ʿUthmani* (Cairo: Dar al-Wathaʾiq al-Qawmiyya, 2011), doc. 55, pp. 344–48.

However, these new classifications posed new legal problems. Realizing this, the jurists of al-Qasr also invoked the authority of custom, in the event the binding character of the contract would not be recognized.

The first document runs as follows:

> Glory to God alone.
>
> This is a *ja'ala*[4] regarding cultivation (*islah*) and a written document regarding customary practice (*istilah*), whose purport will be specified and whose implications will be explained, [namely], that the honourable Shaykh al-ʿArab Muhammad Abu Khalifa al-Muhaji (?)[5] al-ʿAmrani (?) has requested that his following statement be witnessed (*ishhad*). He has offered a *ja'ala* undertaking and has agreed with both al-Zayni Salih, son of the late Muhammad Salih al-Qurashi, and Muhassib, son of the late Rida, with regard to a parcel (*qit'a*) of land on which there are here and there some old palm trees, in the region of the al-Najabin spring, south of the town of al-Qasr, and known as the Farmers' Patch (*buq'at al-fallahin*), confined by four boundaries: to the south on the western side [a plot] owned by the heirs of ʿAli ʿAtiyya and on the eastern side [a plot] owned by ʿUbayd ʿAbd al-Ghafur (?), to the north the road (*al-tariq*), to the east [a plot] owned by his aunt Fatima, and to the west the pond, as well as with regard to a piece (*khatt*) of land near the aforementioned spring close to the alleyway (*zuqaq*), confined by four boundaries: to the south the road, to the north [a plot] owned by the heirs of Abu Khatir, to the east [a plot owned by] Sulayman Majid, and to the west the rest of the piece of land owned by Muhammad ʿAli and his co-owners, exactly as here delimited, inherited by the aforementioned Muhammad from his mother Umbaraka, daughter of the late Muhammad Fayid al-Muhaji, to the effect that the aforementioned persons al-Zayni Salih and Muhassib, plant that part of the land that is fallow with various kinds of crops in accordance with their ability and desire and look after the land by guarding, inundating, and fertilizing it [with manure] and by trimming [the plants], and that in consideration of what they have planted, they will be entitled to one third, eight *qirat*,[6] to be divided among them in three parts, one third for the aforementioned Salih, one third for the

4 *Ja'ala* (also pronounced *ji'ala* and *ju'ala*) is a legal arrangement whereby one person undertakes to pay a remuneration to another person after the latter has completed a task. See below for the legal discussion concerning this contract.

5 The question marks indicate that the original Arabic text was not entirely clear.

6 *Qirat* in this context is not a square measure, but is used for a share of 1/24.

aforementioned Muhassib, and one third for Muhammad, the landlord (*al-muja'il*), on account of the [already existing] plants, and moreover, Muhammad will also be entitled to two thirds, sixteen *qirat*, on account of the land and the irrigation (*al-rida'*). Whatever God – Who is to be praised and Who is exalted – causes to grow, regardless of whether or not it has been planted, will be divided along the lines of the aforementioned *ja'ala* in accordance with the fact that they have agreed upon it (*tawafaqu*) and consented (*radu*) to it in conformity with the Shari'a. Now, consent has legal effect (*al-rida hukm*). [Moreover], this is the custom (*'urf*) of the people of the region and the practice (*istilah*) of the people of the oasis. It has been enjoined that custom must be followed, at least to the extent that it is regarded as valid. That is the case according to the honourable scholars (*al-sada al-'ulama'*) on the basis of any of the four legal schools because of the words of God – Who is exalted – in his clear Book, addressing the Lord of Messengers: "Keep to forgiveness (o Muhammad), and enjoin kindness (*'urf*) and turn away from the ignorant." [Q 7:199] [The *ja'ala* has been concluded] in a valid and legal manner, in a pleasant spirit and a joyful mind (*'an tib qalb wa-sharh sadr*), and was provided with an authorization regarding its being witnessed (*thubutuhu*), with the request for a legal ruling (*talab al-hukm bihi*) and with a behest for the witnessing of the latter. It was [then] witnessed and that took place and was recorded on the blessed Friday, the last day of excellent month of Safar in the year 1206, twelve hundred and six [28 October, 1791].

Witnesses
'Abd al-Latif Yusuf al-Muhaji
Ibrahim 'Abd Allah Mustafa
Muhammad 'Uthman
Mas'ud Muhammad al-Muhaji

The other document reads as follows:

Glory to God alone
A division and an agreement took place between Muhammad Khalifa, mentioned overleaf, Salih Muhammad, mentioned overleaf, and Muhassib Rida, mentioned overleaf, as to all of the shares mentioned overleaf with regard to the third of the plants mentioned overleaf, since one third of the plants were to be divided among those mentioned overleaf in three thirds. Now [add] to which Salih, mentioned overleaf, is entitled is two

young Saʿidi palm trees (*wudaya*),[7] a palm sapling (*ʿuzb*) in the middle of the field, and also a pomegranate tree with wood at the south end [of the plot]. [The division took place] in a valid and legal way as the aforementioned persons divided the aforementioned plants before they began to bear fruit. Then Muhammad Khalifa undertook to irrigate the aforementioned palm trees (*wudy*) until they bear fruit, [from which moment] every one, pursuant to the stipulations of the *jaʿala*, shall irrigate in proportion to his share. He [Muhammad Khalifa] requested that this accordingly be witnessed (*ishhad*). That took place and was recorded in the month of Rabiʿal-akhar, one of the months of the year 1222, twelve hundred twenty two [i.e., between 8 June and 7 July 1807].

As witness thereof
Ibrahim Mustafa
As witness thereof
Al-Qurashi ʿAbd al-Ghafur Husayn [?]

In the first document, the owner of two plots of land, on one of which some palm trees were already growing, promises two other men, on condition that they plant and cultivate trees, a share of 2/9 each in what they have planted on the fallow parts of the plots. The landowner takes 7/9 of the trees, i.e., his customary share of two thirds increased with one ninth, apparently in consideration of the fact that one plot had already some palm trees on it belonging to him. Part of the arrangement was a stipulation that the landlord will irrigate the plants until the moment they start to bear fruit and that after that moment all parties to the contract shall water the plants in proportion to their shares. Almost all other *jaʿala* documents in the collection include this clause, which was apparently part of the customary law governing this arrangement. That this clause was omitted here must be due to an oversight of the scribe and cannot have been deliberate since in the second document it is referred to as part of the contract.

In the second document, dated sixteen years later, Salih's share is defined and transferred to him. It consists of two young palm trees, one sapling, and a pomegranate tree. The division took place at a time when the palm trees Salih had planted had not yet borne fruit, since, in accordance with customary law, Muhammad undertakes to continue to water them until that moment. Salih

7 I am grateful to several inhabitants of al-Qasr for explaining to me the agricultural terms in the documents during my stay there in February and March 2006.

had this contract written on the back of his copy of the original contract. If Muhassib also had a specific share assigned to him, it must have been recorded on the back of his own copy.

I found eight *jaʿala* documents in the collection. One of them, written in 1866 CE,[8] is a contract in which more than fifty persons, who together own a spring, contract two persons to repair the spring for a share in the property rights. A judge's note in the margin, dated about a year and a half after the contract was concluded, indicates that there were some problems with its implementation: it states that the remuneration is only due after the completion of the tasks and that the person who undertook the task can only claim it from the other parties if he can prove that they are owners of the well. The other *jaʿala* documents,[9] dated between 1773 and 1823 CE, deal with sharecropping of planted trees and are practically identical to the first document presented here, except that most of them include the stipulation about the irrigation.

According to the terms mentioned in the document, it is a typical *mugharasa* contract, that is, a sharecropping contract whereby a landowner agrees with a person (the sharecropper) that the latter plants trees on his land and cultivates them in exchange for a share in them (or, in addition, a share in the land), to be transferred to him after they bear fruit.[10] The question then arises why this contract is called *jaʿala* and not *mugharasa*. In order to answer this we must consider what the different legal schools say about these contracts.

Let us first consider the position of the schools on sharecropping (*muzaraʿa, musaqat, mugharasa*).[11] It is a contract that can be construed as either hire of labour or lease of land, both called *ijara* in the works of jurisprudence. The crucial problem, however, is that it is a contract in which one of the performances, i.e., the wages or the rent, is uncertain, because it involves the future transfer of ownership of objects that do not exist at the time of the contract and whose quantity and value are not precisely determined. This constitutes a form of risk (*gharar*) which vitiates the contract. Therefore, it cannot be a valid lease of land or hire of labour. The Malikis construe it as a form of partnership

8 D.05.063 from 1283 H.

9 D.05.045 recto, dated 1217; D.05.045 verso, dated 1217; D.05.049 recto, dated 1198; D.04.166, dated 1187; D.04.277, dated 1239; D.04.228r, dated 1220.

10 *Mugharasa* is one instance of a group of sharecropping contracts, to which also belong *musaqah* and *muzaraʿa*, i.e., agreements whereby a person undertakes to cultivate another person's land for one or more years in exchange for a share in the crop.

11 Unless otherwise indicated, this part relies on Ibn Rushd, *Bidayat al-mujtahid*, 2 vols. (Cairo: Mustafa al-Babi al-Halabi, 1960) 2:244–51 (*kitab al-musaqa*), and William J. Donaldson, *Sharecropping in the Yemen: A Study in Islamic Theory, Custom and Pragmatism* (Leiden: Brill, 2000), chs. 3 and 4.

(*sharika*), but this also brings about legal constraints. However, there exists a Prophetic tradition (*hadith*) that is regarded by most schools as legitimizing an exception to the principle that the performances in a contract must be precisely specified. The *hadith* relates that, after the conquest of Khaybar, the Prophet Muhammad concluded a contract with the Jews who were living there, stipulating that they could remain on the land and cultivate the palm orchards, but had to pay one half of the crop to the Prophet.[12] The law schools, however, differ on the legal implications of this *hadith*. Most schools allow on the strength of the *hadith* some form of lease of land against a part of the crop. Only Abu Hanifa maintained that such contracts were forbidden. His argument was that the *hadith* is unclear on a number of legal points, and therefore may not be regarded as introducing an exception to a general principle of the law of contracts. For instance, the Jews might have been slaves (who cannot have ownership rights) or the obligation to pay half of the date harvest may have been imposed on them not by contract but by the state as taxation for non-Muslims (*kharaj*). However, Abu Hanifa's students Abu Yusuf and al-Shaybani regarded the contract as valid and their opinion became the prevailing one in their school because it was customary practice.[13]

The Hanbalis allow sharecropping contracts (both *muzaraʿa* and *musaqat*) with hardly any restrictions. The Malikis make a distinction between *muzaraʿa* and *musaqat*. The former is valid, according to them, but only under certain conditions and by virtue of a rather complicated legal construction. They view it as a composition of three separate contracts: lease, rent, and partnership. The parties must agree on a fixed rent of the land and fixed wages of the labour in order to circumvent the problem of uncertainty of the wages or rent. The rent and wages may be balanced so that neither party is in debt to the other. On that basis they conclude a contract of partnership and share the profit (the harvest, which can be of all types: fruits, cereals, cotton) in equal proportions. On the other hand, a *musaqat* contract is held to be valid by them without fixing the rent and the wages and for unequal shares between landowner and labourer. However, such a contract may only be concluded with regard to fruit trees.[14] The Shafiʿis do not allow *muzaraʿa* at all, but like the Malikis, regard *musaqat* contracts as valid, but only with regard to grapes and dates. Al-Shafiʿi's argument is that the legitimacy of *musaqat* is a permission by way of exception

12 al-ʿAsqalani, *Bulugh al-maram fi adillat al-ahkam* (Cairo: Dar al-Kitab al-ʿArabi, n.d.), no. 765, where the variants are also listed.

13 Shaykhzade, *Majmaʿ al-anhur fi sharh Multaqa al-abhur*, 2 vols. (Istanbul, 1301 H), 2:393–94.

14 Abd al-Rahman al-Jaziri, *Kitab al-Fiqh ʿala al-madhahib al-arbaʿa*, vol. 3: *al-Muʿamalat* (5th impr., Cairo: al-Maktabat al-Tijariyya al-Kubra, n.d.), 4, 21–5.

(*rukhsa*) based on the *hadith* (there is also a similar one regarding grapes) and that exceptions to rules may not be extended by analogy. Another controversy is the remuneration of the person who contributes his labour: should that only be a share in the crop (as in the contracts of *muzaraʿa* and *musaqat*) or the labourer allowed to receive part of the trees that he has planted (as in the *mugharasa* contract)? Malikis and Hanbalis regard the latter contract as valid; the Shafiʿis and the Hanafis do not allow it.

The jurists of al-Qasr were obviously well aware of this position of the Shafiʿi school. They therefore tried to cast the contract in another mould, that of *jaʿala*. The idea of constructing this form of sharecropping in this way must have come from jurists familiar with Maliki jurisprudence. For Maliki jurists point out that the *mugharasa* contract, which they regard as valid, is like *jaʿala:*

> As to *mugharasa*, that is a contract whereby a man hands over his land to another who will plant trees on it. There are three modes of it: (1) hire (*ijara*), whereby a person plants for the owner for fixed wages; (2) *juʿl* (a synonym of *jaʿala*, RP), whereby a person plants trees for the owner on condition that he acquire a share of what grows out of it [the saplings]; (3) something between hire and *juʿl*, whereby a person plants for the owner on condition that he acquire both a share of that [planting] and of the land.[15]

It is doubtful, however, that such a legal construction is valid according to the Shafiʿi doctrine.[16] The Shafiʿi jurists define *jaʿala* as "the undertaking to give a specific remuneration (*juʿl*) for work, regardless of whether it[s amount] is defined and known or unknown and difficult to define precisely" (*iltizam ʿawad maʿlum ʿala ʿamal maʿlum aw majhul yaʿsur dabtuhu*). *Jaʿala* is therefore a legal act that can be used to contract labour for producing a result if the amount of labour required for it cannot be determined. This result may be to restore something, such as the finding and returning of stray cattle or lost objects, or to produce something new, such as the digging of a well until the water appears, or teaching a skill to someone. It differs from hiring labour (*ijara*) in that for *ijara* to be valid and binding the amount of work must be specified. The *jaʿala* contract, therefore, is an exception to the strict rule that in synallagmatic contracts the performances must be known and well defined. The textual basis for the exception is Q 12:72: "They said: We have lost the king's cup, and he

15 Ibn Juzayy, *al-Qawanin al-fiqhiyya* (N.p.: n.d.), 212 (kitab 4, bab 3: Fi al-muzaraʿa wa-l-mugharasa).

16 See al-Ramli, *Nihayat al-muhtaj fi sharh al-Minhaj* (Cairo: Dar al-Fikr, 1969), 5:465–81.

who bringeth it shall have a camel-load, and I (said Joseph) am answerable for it."[17] In addition there is a tradition according to which the Prophet approved of an arrangement whereby a person who was bitten by a snake undertook to pay thirty sheep to a person who would recite the Qur'an in order to heal him, in the event he succeeded.[18] The remuneration is only due if and when the desired result has been produced. Jurists stress that *ja'ala* is not a contract but a unilateral legal act of the person who promises the remuneration. He is entitled to revoke his promise at any time until the result has been achieved and the reward is due. However, in order to prevent unfair advantage, he must pay standard wages (*ujrat al-mithl*) if the labour accomplished until that moment is beneficial to him, for instance if the object of the *ja'ala* is the digging of a well until it reaches the water table and the *ja'ala* is revoked before water is reached. According to the Shafi'i doctrine, it is essential for the *ja'ala* that the remuneration is well defined; otherwise, the conditions are the same as for the rent or wages in a contract of lease or employment. And here, I think, lies the crux in the application of the *ja'ala* contract to sharecropping, for the remuneration does not exist at the time of the *ja'ala* and is not well defined.

The document shows that the person who drafted it was familiar with the unilateral character of the *ja'ala*. In conformity with standard practice, the documents in our collection record synallagmatic contracts as declarations of both parties, such as: A has bought from B and B has sold to A. In this document we find only that the landlord requests that witnesses hear that he undertakes (*ja'ala*) to pay a remuneration on certain conditions. Only at the end of the document is it mentioned that the other parties agreed to the arrangement. Moreover, I believe that the lawyer who wrote the document was well aware of the problematic character of the way the sharecropping contract was framed. For this reason he also invoked custom (*'urf*) as a ground for regarding the contract as valid and binding. At the end of the first document there is the following statement about the validity of customary law (also found in some other *ja'ala* documents):[19]

> Now, consent has legal effects (*al-rida hukm*) and that is the custom of the people of this region and the customary practice (*istilah*) of the people of the oasis. It has been ordered that custom must be followed,

17 It is an episode from the Yusuf story. After he had hidden his precious cup in Binyamin's luggage and the brothers were leaving the town, it was announced that this cup was missing and that the person who found it, would get a camel load of goods as a reward.

18 al-Bukhari, *Sahih* (*kitab al-tibb*).

19 See, e.g., D.04.166 and D.05.045 verso.

> at least to the extent that it is regarded as valid. That is the case according to the honourable scholars (*al-sada al-ʿulamaʾ*) on the basis of any of the four legal schools because of the words of God – Who is exalted – in his clear Book, addressing the Lord of Messengers: "Keep to forgiveness (o Muhammad), and enjoin kindness (*ʿurf*)[20] and turn away from the ignorant." [Q 7:199]

It seems as if the lawyer who drafted the document is saying here: "Yes, I know that the way this contract is constructed is not entirely in conformity with Shafiʿi doctrine. However, this is the way we always do it here in the oasis; moreover, it is the will of the parties and therefore it must be regarded as valid and binding." But even this argument would not pass the scrutiny of strict Shafiʿi jurists. Under Shafiʿi law, custom cannot override provisions of the Shariʿa. Shafiʿi doctrine is rigorous in this respect, as illustrated, for instance, by the fact that, unlike the other schools, it regards the contract of *istisnaʾ* (a contract whereby a person pays another to manufacture something for him, which is a transaction about objects that do not exist at the time of the contract) as not valid despite the fact that it is a customary transaction.[21] We do not know whether the validity of the contracts recorded in these documents were ever tested in a court of law However, it seems that this did not bother the inhabitants of al-Qasr very much.

The documents examined in this essay, as well as most others found in al-Qasr, show that its inhabitants were committed to their Shafiʿi *madhhab*. Otherwise, they could have had recourse to the Maliki school. *Madhhab* shopping was common practice in Ottoman Egypt. In most major towns, there were, in addition to the Hanafi supreme qadi appointed by the Porte, deputy qadis of the three other schools of jurisprudence. As shown by the court records from that period, people would go to the qadi who could formulate contracts or draft endowment deeds as they wanted it. People knew that in order to found a religious endowment (*waqf*) with certain specific clauses you had to go to the Hanbali qadi, for instance, or to another for a specific type

20 Most Qurʾan exegetes explain the word *ʿurf* in this context as fear of God and observance of His commands, or as *maʿruf*, i.e., fair and equitable, and not as custom. However, some jurists, especially the Malikis, regard this text as a command to take custom into account. See Mohammad Hashim Kamali, *Principles of Islamic Jurisprudence* (Cambridge: Islamic Texts Society, 1991), 284, 292.

21 See, e.g., Jalal al-Din ʿAbd al-Rahman al-Suyuti, *al-Ashbah wa l-nazaʾir fi qawaʿid wa-furuʿ fiqh al-shafiʿiyya* (Beirut: Dar al-Kutub al-ʿIlmiyya, 1990), 99.

of lease.[22] There are no indications at all that this practice was considered to be blameworthy. Therefore, it is striking that the inhabitants of al-Qasr stuck to the Shafiʿi doctrine, although sharecropping in the form they practised it was valid under Maliki and not under Shafiʿi law. It is not clear why they did not ask a Maliki qadi (and there are one or two documents signed by a Maliki qadi in al-Qasr)[23] to draw up a *mugharasa* contract. Instead the drafter of the document invoked two general principles as a justification of the binding force of the contract: the fact that it was sanctioned by custom and the fact that is was based on mutual agreement. However, neither would have carried any weight in a Shafiʿi court of law.

22 R. Peters, "What Does It Mean to Be an Official Madhhab? Hanafism and the Ottoman Empire," in *The Islamic School of Law: Evolution, Devolution, and Progress*, ed. P. Bearman, R. Peters, and F. Vogel (Cambridge, Mass.: ILSP/Harvard University Press, 2005), 147–58.

23 E.g., a divorce on grounds of abandonment (which is a ground for divorce under Maliki but not under Shafiʿi law) pronounced by a Maliki qadi, authorized by the regular Shafiʿi qadi. D.05.050, dated 1116 H.

CHAPTER 18

Body and Spirit of Islamic Law

Madhhab Diversity in Ottoman Documents from the Dakhla Oasis, Egypt

In chapter 6 of *The spirit of Islamic law* Bernard Weiss discusses juristic authority and the diversity of schools. One of the topics of this chapter is that *mujtahids* often derive different opinions from the same source texts. The jurists accepted this diversity as they were fully aware of the fact that *fiqh* was human understanding of the divine Sharia and that scholar could differ in their interpretations of Koran and hadith. This resulted, already early in Islamic history, in the emergence of the *madhhabs*, which, as it were, institutionalized difference of opinion. Doctrinal diversity, I would argue, is part of the spirit of Islamic law. Now Weiss' focus in chapter 6 of his book is the role of the *mujtahids* in finding the law and the criteria which would help laymen in finding which *mujtahids* are the most learned and trustworthy and, thus, in selecting the correct opinions from the enormous diversity of legal views. This diversity of Islamic law is the central theme of my paper. However, I will look at it from a different angle: I want to examine legal diversity not with a top-down approach, as Weiss did, but from a bottom-up perspective. My concern will be how legal practice dealt with this diversity on the ground. If Weiss applied the term "spirit of Islamic law" to the theory of the law and especially the process of finding the law, I would like to use the term body as a metaphor for legal practices and the documents recording them: contracts, judgements and fatwas. The corpus I will use is a family archive from the Ottoman period found in the Egyptian town of al-Qasr in the Dakhla Oasis. I will begin with a brief description of the collection.

In 2003 workers restoring an eighteenth-century mud-brick house in al-Qasr discovered pieces of paper in the rubble of an adjacent house that had collapsed. Apart from scraps and small fragments of documents, the finds included many complete or nearly complete legible documents. The restoration of the mud brick house was carried out by the Qasr Dakhleh Project (QDP) under the aegis of the Dakhleh Oasis Project (DOP), an international project aiming to study the history of the Dakhla Oasis from prehistoric times to the present.[1] During the subsequent campaigns of 2004, 2005 and 2007 more written pieces of paper were found in the remains of the ruined house, which, according to

1 For information on and the annual reports of the DOP and QDP, see http://arts.monash.edu.au/archaeology/excavations/dakhleh/index.php.

 | DOI:10.1163/9789004420625_019

local informants, was known as *Bayt al-Qurashī* and had been abandoned before 1940, probably due to its sudden collapse. The finds include religious texts, personal letters, magical texts, amulets and 216 undamaged or nearly undamaged legal and financial documents written in the period between 1579 and 1937. A preliminary examination showed that they are the remains of a family archive of a branch of the local Qurashī family. All pieces of paper have been rehydrated, put between glass plates for conservation, numbered and photographed, and are now stored in the storerooms of the Dakhla Inspectorate of the Supreme Council of Antiquities. I have edited all complete and nearly complete legal and financial documents found so far and published them in 2011 in *Wathā'iq madīnat al-Qaṣr fī al-Wāhāt al-Dākhila maṣdar^{an} li-tārīkh Miṣr fī al-ʿaṣr al-ʿUthmānī.* (Cairo: Dar al-Wathā'iq al-Qawmiyya (National Archive), 2011, 610 pp. (Silsilat Dirāsāt Wathā'iqiyya, 1))

Two-thirds of these documents are legal: contracts, often notarized in court, receipts of payment of taxes, IOUs and appointment of attorneys. The remainder are mainly accounts or lists regarding debts or expenses. In addition I have found a few *waqfiyyas* (4), judgements (2) and fatwas (3). A substantial part of the documents are related to agricultural activities: lease or sale of land or of water rights, sharecropping or the payment of taxes on palm trees or springs and wells. In addition there is a document regarding a contract for the maintenance of a spring and some lists made by individual farmers recording those from whom they leased water rights. Table 18.1 gives an impression of the types of documents. Table 18.2 shows the distribution of the documents over the Hijri centuries. The oldest document of the collection is a *waqfiyya* with a length of more than one meter and dated 987/1579. Unfortunately the first lines with the name of the founder of the *waqf* are missing. The most recent document is a tax receipt from 1937.

Many documents were issued and sealed by a court: forty-seven by the al-Qasr court and seven more by Cairo courts. The oldest one dates from 997/1589 and the most recent one from 1264/1848. Only two of these are judgements, ending litigation; all others are notarized contracts. Except for the two documents issued by the al-Qasr court in the 19th century,[2] the *qāḍīs* mention their *madhhab* affiliation. Nearly all (41) of the deeds registered in the court of al-Qasr bear the name and the seal of Shafiʿi *qāḍīs*, belonging to local families.

2 This was probably a result of the 1802 decree that *qāḍīs* had to follow Hanafi law. See Rudolph Peters, "What Does It Mean to Be an Official *Madhhab*?: Hanafism and the Ottoman Empire." In *The Islamic School of Law: Evolution, Devolution, and Progress.* Edited by P. Bearman, R. Peters and F. Vogel. Cambridge MA: Harvard University Press, 2005. P. 157 (based on Jabarti).

The population of al-Qasr and, indeed all of the Dakhla and Kharga Oases followed the Shafiʿi *madhhab*. In this paper I will first examine to what extent the *qāḍī*s of al-Qasr were incorporated in the Ottoman, Hanafi, judiciary and, secondly, why *qāḍī*s of other *madhhab*s than the Shafiʿi one, issued documents in the al-Qasr court.

The Ottoman judiciary was hierarchically organized. The *qāḍī*s in the principal cities were appointed by the chief *qāḍī*s in Istanbul. Those regional *qāḍī*s could appoint deputies (*nāʾib*), both to their own court and to the smaller courts within their districts. *Qāḍī*s did receive salaries but mainly lived off the fees the people had to pay for getting judgements and for having contracts notarized. The deputies had to hand over part of their fees to the *qāḍī* who had appointed them. The Hanafi *madhhab* was the official one in the empire and until the beginning of the sixteenth century, Ottoman judges belonged exclusively to that *madhhab*. However, after the conquest of the Arab regions of the Middle East, the situation became complicated since here the population belonged to other *madhhab*s and, moreover, a judicial system had developed in the Mamluk period whereby courts in the main cities would be staffed by *qāḍī*s from different *madhhab*s. After the Ottoman conquest, this system was continued, except that the supremacy of Hanafi law was institutionalized by appointing a Hanafi chief *qāḍī* in each court, whereas the *qāḍī*s belonging to the other *madhhab*s held office as his deputies. In Egypt the *qāḍī*s of the regions (*quḍāt al-aqālīm*) resided in main cities and were usually Hanafi Turks, appointed by the *qāḍī ʿaskar* of Anatolia in Istanbul.[3] Later, however, only a few of the most important regional *qāḍī*s were appointed in Istanbul and the rest by the chief judge (*qāḍī ʿaskar*) of Egypt.[4] The regional *qāḍī* would appoint local ulema from different *madhhab*s as deputies in his courts and in the other towns of his district.[5] These deputies would adjudicate disputes and notarize documents according to their own school but under the supervision of the Hanafi *qāḍī*.[6] The *qāḍī* of the Oases (*qāḍī al-Wāḥāt* or *al-nāẓir fī al-aḥkām al-sharʿiyya fī kāmil aqālīm al-Wāḥāt*), who probably resided in Girga or Asyut in the Nile valley, was one of these regional Hanafi Turkish *qāḍī*s.[7] However,

3 ʿAbd al-Rāziq Ibrāhīm ʿĪsā, *Tārīkh al-Qaḍāʾ fī Miṣr al-ʿUthmāniyya* (1517–1798), Cairo: Al-Hayʾa al-Miṣriyya al-ʿĀmma li-l-Kitāb, 1998. (*Tārīkh Al-Miṣriyyīn, 117*). P. 96.

4 Muḥammad Nūr Faraḥāt, *Al-Qaḍāʾ al-Sharʿī fī Miṣr fī al-ʿAṣr al-ʿUthmānī*, Cairo: Al-Hayʾa al-Miṣriyya al-ʿĀmma li-l-Kitāb, 1988. (*Tārīkh al-Miṣriyyīn, 17*). P. 381.

5 ʿĪsā, *Tārīkh*, p. 97.

6 Peters, "What Does It Mean?" Pp. 147–58; ʿĪsā, *Tārīkh*, p. 97.

7 The *qāḍī* of the Oases (Alwāḥ) belonged to the first (lowest) rank of the six ranks of the Egyptian Ottoman judicial hierarchy. Galal H. El-Nahal, *The Judicial Administration of Ottoman Egypt in the Seventeenth Century*, Minneapolis etc.: Bibliotheca Islamica, 1979. *Studies in Middle Eastern History, 4*. Appendix B.

from the early eighteenth century we find that there were local Shafiʿi *qāḍīs* of the Oases (e.g. in 1702 and 1704)[8] and Hanafi deputies (e.g. in 1722).[9] It would seem that from about 1700 the office of the qadi of the Oases was held by Egyptian, local scholars.

The *qāḍī* of the Oases would appoint the deputy *qāḍīs* of al-Qasr. In a collection of documents from the Kharga Oasis also dating from the Ottoman period, there are several letters of appointment in which the *qāḍī* of the Oases appoints deputies in towns comparable to al-Qasr. The oldest ones, dated 1050/1640[10] and 1058/1648,[11] show that these deputies had extensive jurisdiction: it was defined as hearing claims and testimonies, adjudicating disputes, writing official documents, court records and marriage contracts, making inventories of estates, [recording] payments of IOUs, and dealing with all legal cases arising in the Kharga Oasis, an accordance with the doctrine of the Shafiʿi *madhhab*. Excepted were matters coming from or going to the Diwan[12] and the investigation of homicide. The deputy was entitled, in case of necessity, to appoint deputies from the four *madhhab*s.[13] We may safely assume that the deputies in al-Qasr had a similar jurisdiction. In a letter of appointment, dated 1167/1754, we find that the deputy had full jurisdiction, without any exceptions, but that the term of his appointment was restricted to one year. These remained the normal clauses until the nineteenth century.

From the formulas used in these documents by the *qāḍīs* of al-Qasr to refer to their office it is clear that they regarded themselves as part of the Ottoman-Egyptian judiciary, being deputies of the *qāḍī* of the Oases. Throughout the seventeenth century, they call themselves "the pride of the deputies and the head of the court clerks" (*fakhr al-nuwwāb wa-raʾs al-kuttāb*), whereas the full *qāḍīs* used the title "the most proficient of the *qāḍīs* of Islam and the most excellent of the governors of men" (*aqḍā quḍāt al-Islām wa-awlā wulāt al-anām*). And when these deputies describe their official position, they call themselves, until the early eighteenth century, sharia judge by virtue of substitution (*al-ḥākim al-sharʿī khilāfat*[an]).

8 "ʿUbayd Allāh b. Mūsā al-Dīnārī, *al-nāẓir fī al-aḥkām al-sharʿiyya fī kāmil aqālīl al-wāḥāt.*" D.04.189, dated 1114, D.05.041recto, dated 1116.

9 "Ḥusayn ʿAlī al-Ḥanafī, *al-muwallā bi-Alwāḥ khilāfat*[an]." D.04.167 dated 1133.

10 Dār al-Wathāʾiq al-Qawmiyya (Egyptain National Archive), Wathāʾiq al-Wāḥāt, Microfilm 9, No. 20. The documents of this collection have been catalogued and partially edited by Salwā ʿAlī Mīlād (*Wathaʾiq al-Wāḥāt al-Miṣriyya. Dirāsa wa-Nashr wa-Taḥqīq*. Rev. Ed., Cairo: Dār al-Kutub wa-l-Wathāʾiq al-Qawmiyya, 2003).

11 Mīlād, *Wathāʾiq al-Wāḥāt* p. 135.

12 The phrase probably refers to serious matters that had to be dealt with by the Council of the Governor in Cairo.

13 Mīlad, *Wathāʾiq al-Wāḥāt*, Doc. 23, p.135. The 1050 appointment is found in Dār al-Wathāʾiq al-Qawmiyya, Wathāʾiq al-Wāḥāt, Microfilm No. 9, doc. 20.

Although, as we have seen, the lower echelons of Egyptian judiciary, as from the eighteenth century, became increasingly Egyptianized and the Hanafi school had to concede ground to the local ones as far as the appointment of judges was concerned, the overall legal system, headed by chief *qāḍī* in Cairo, appointed by Istanbul, remained Hanafi and Ottoman with a limited recognition of the other legal schools. The question of which *qāḍī* would hear a case if there were several *qāḍīs* with jurisdiction was moot in Hanafi law. Abū Yūsuf's opinion was that in such a situation, the choice was the plaintiff's, because the lawsuit was his. Muḥammad al-Shaybānī, however, asserted that the choice is the defendant's, on the ground that he is defending himself against the plaintiff's claim. The latter opinion was regarded as the authoritative one. Later Hanafi scholars, however, pointed out that this rule only applied if the *qāḍīs*' jurisdictions did not overlap, e.g. in situations that each of them had exclusive jurisdiction over one region or neighbourhood, or one over soldiers and the other over civilians. In such a situation, these jurists asserted, the choice of the court is the defendant's and he cannot be summoned to a court in another neighbourhood or to a military court if he is a civilian. However, if there are several *qāḍīs* in a city, each of them with general jurisdiction, the jurists disagree on which party may select the court. Al-Tīmūrṭāshī (d. 1004 /1595) held that the plaintiff is entitled to choose the *qāḍī*, provided there is no obvious advantage for either party as a result of this selection, whereas Ibn Nujaym (d. 970/1569) claimed that the choice was the defendant's. The issue was resolved in the Ottoman empire by a sultanic edict, issued on the basis of a fatwa given by the *Shaykh al-Islām* Abū al-Su'ūd, instructing *qāḍīs* not to adjudicate contrary to the defendant's *madhhab*:

> *Question*: If Zayd, who is a Hanafi, dies while being away [from his hometown], and his Shafi'i creditors produce evidence of their claims [against the estate] in the absence of the heirs, and if the Shafi'i *qāḍī* finds for them and the Hanafi *qāḍī* thereafter issues execution on the judgement, is this legally acceptable?
> *Answer*: No. The *qāḍīs* in the Well-Protected Dominions (i.e. the Ottoman empire. RP) have been forbidden to give judgement contrary to the defendant's *madhhab* and the Hanafi *qāḍī*'s order of execution is therefore null and void. Abū al-Su'ūd. Muḥammad [al-Shaybānī] held that the defendant's choice of *qāḍī* is decisive. This is the ruling according to which fatwas must be issued. Qāḍīkhān and *Majma' al-Fatāwā*.[14]

14 P. Horster, *Zur Anwendung des islamischen Rechts im 16. Jahrhundert*. Stuttgart: Kohlhammer, 1935. P. 48.

The second question that was discussed among Ottoman Hanafi jurists was the status of the sentences and documents issued by the non-Hanafi *qāḍīs*. After the Ottoman conquest, the Hanafi *qāḍī* in the Arab regions was given precedence over the other *qāḍīs* who were henceforth regarded as deputy *qāḍīs*.[15] However, as appears from the fatwa quoted above, they could still adjudicate, at least if the defendant wanted it. For the enforcement of such a judgements a warrant of execution issued by the Hanafi supreme *qāḍī* was required. In principle, all decisions and documents of other *qāḍīs* would be endorsed. The basic rule here is that sentences based on *ijtihād* cannot be reversed by other *qāḍīs*. Its rationale is to prevent endless litigation. Yet there were certain limits. Hanafi doctrine in this respect was very much like the modern law of conflict of many states with Western legal systems, according to which national courts, under certain conditions, may apply foreign law, but only if this does not violate the *ordre public* (public policy), i.e. essential values of the legal system. For the Hanafi jurists, these essential values consisted in unequivocal texts of the Koran and hadith or the *ijmāʿ*. The Hanafi *qāḍī* would issue warrants of execution for the judgements of the other *qāḍīs*, unless they violated such texts, as interpreted by Hanafi doctrine.[16] Hanafi textbooks list a number of issues that are legal according to other *madhhabs*, but cannot be endorsed by Hanafis *qāḍīs*. Among these issues we find the following:

- Capital sentences based on the *qasāma* procedure, i.e. fifty oaths sworn by the victim's next of kin, a possibility recognized in Maliki law;
- Sentences based on the testimony of one witness and an oath sworn by the plaintiff, recognized by all *madhhabs* except the Hanafis;
- Sentences upholding the validity of a temporary marriage (*mutʿa*), recognized in Imami Shiʿi doctrine;
- Capital sentences pronounced in spite of the fact that one of the victim's female heirs has waived her right to demand retribution, valid under Maliki law;
- Sentences regarding a triple repudiation pronounced in one session as a single one, as is held by some Hanbalis.[17]

---

15 Galal H. El-Nahal, *The Judicial Administration of Ottoman Egypt in the Seventeenth Century*, Minneapolis etc.: Bibliotheca Islamica, 1979. (*Studies in Middle Eastern History*, 4). Pp. 14–17.

16 Ibn Nujaym and al-Ḥamawī, *Ghamz ʿuyūn al-baṣāʾir sharḥ al-ashbāh wa-l-naẓāʾir li-Ibn Nujaym*. Istanbul: Dār al-Ṭibāʿa al-ʿĀmira, 1873 (1290 H) Vol. i, pp. 340–2.

17 Ibn Nujaym, *Al-Baḥr al-Rāʾiq, Sharḥ Kanz al-Daqāʾiq li-l-Nasafī*. Beirut: Dār al-Kitāb al-Islāmī, n.d. Vol. vii, pp. 11–12; Ibn ʿĀbidīn, *Radd al-Muḥtār ḥāshiyat al-Durr al-Mukhtār sharḥ Tanwīr al-Abṣār li-l-Tīmūrtāshī*. Bulaq: Dār al-Ṭibāʿa al-Amīriyya, 1882 (1299 H) Vol. iv, p. 451.

Through the application of this law of conflict, the Ottomans could both uphold Hanafi supremacy and meet the practical demands of the local population. However, we must not exaggerate the practical importance of this system. It functioned only in a few large cities.

Having sketched the institutional framework, I will now examine the documents issued in the al-Qasr court by non-Shafiʿi *qāḍīs* in order to try and find out why the case or the notarization was not handled by a Shafiʿi judge. I found the following documents:

Documents Issued by a Non-Shafiʿi Deputy of al-Qasr:

- A judgement ending litigation about water rights, pronounced by a Hanafi deputy *qāḍī*, dated 1055/1645;[18]
- Notarization of a contract recorded overleaf, by a Maliki deputy *qāḍī*, dated 1056/1646;[19]
- Annulment of a marriage on account of the husband's lasting absence, by a Maliki deputy *qāḍī*, dated 1116/1705.[20]

Documents Issued by a (Deputy) *Qāḍī* of the Oases:

- Appointment of a legal guardian for a deaf-mute person, by the Hanafi *qāḍī* of the Oases, dated 1090/1679;[21]
- Sale of land and water rights, issued by the Shafiʿi *qāḍī* of the Oases, dated 1114/1702;[22]
- Sale of land and palm trees, issued by the Shafiʿi *qāḍī* of the Oases, dated 1116/1704;[23]
- Settlement (*sulḥ*) about the payment of a bride price (*ṣadāq*), issued by the deputy Hanafi *qāḍī* of the Oases, dated ca. 1133/1722;[24]
- Sharecropping contract (*jaʿāla*) issued by the deputy Hanafi *qāḍī* of the Oases, dated 1133/1722;[25]
- Lease of land issued by the Maliki deputy *qāḍī* of the Oases, dated 1234/1817.[26]

18 D.05.002.

19 D.05.079v.

20 D.05.050.

21 D.05.024.

22 D.04.189.

23 D.05.041recto.

24 D.04.225. The last part of the document with its date is missing. Since it was issued by the same Hanafi deputy *qāḍī* of the Oases as D.04.167 from 1133 H, I assume that it must have been issued around the same year.

25 D.04.167.

26 D.05.065recto.

Let us first give a closer look at the documents issued by local deputies in al-Qasr. The first one is a judgement pronounced in the court of al-Qasr by a certain Abū Hafṣ Sirāj al-Dīn ʿUmar al-Ḥanafī, the Hanafi deputy *qāḍī* (*Khalīfat al-ḥukm al-ʿazīz bihā* (i.e. in the court of al-Qasr) *niyābat*[an]) of a certain Jamāl al-Dīn Yūsuf Efendi al-Ḥanafī, the *qāḍī* of the Oases. The case was simple: a person sued a second cousin claiming that the latter had unlawfully taken possession of certain water rights. The defendant denied the claim and the plaintiff could not substantiate it. The *qāḍī* offered the oath of denial to the defendant. After the latter had sworn it, the *qāḍī* found for the defendant and debarred the plaintiff from suing the defendant for the same issue. In our collection, judgements are rare: there are only two of them. The other one was pronounced by a Shafiʿi deputy[27] and here the issue was also a dispute about water rights. It is difficult to explain why in our document the claim was heard by a Hanafi, instead of the Shafiʿi *qāḍī*. Under Ottoman Hanafi law, the choice of the *madhhab* in litigation was the defendant's. In this case the defendant might have opted for adjudication under Hanafi law because he knew that the plaintiff had one witness, but not two. According to the doctrine of all *madhhab*s but the Hanafi, the *qāḍī* will find for a plaintiff whose claim is corroborated by one witness and his own oath. However, even if the plaintiff's claim would have been awarded by the Shafiʿi deputy, the defendant had nothing to fear because an Ottoman *qāḍī* would never grant the required *exequatur* since judgements based on the testimony of one witness corroborated by the plaintiff's oath were regarded as being against Hanafi *ordre public*. Therefore, *madhhab* shopping cannot explain the choice for a Hanafi deputy.

I think we must look in a different, more practical direction. It is remarkable that the next document, dating from about a year later (1056), is also issued by a non-Shafiʿi deputy *qāḍī*, this time a Maliki. It is an ordinary notarization of a contract concluded a year previously and written on the backside of the document. Our collection includes several notarizations by Shafiʿi deputies and their wording is almost identical with the one issued by the Maliki deputy. Therefore, we may assume that the handling of this particular document by a Maliki deputy was not prompted by differences between *madhhab* doctrines. A plausible explanation might be that in 1055 and 1056 H the Shafiʿi deputyship was vacant and that his duties were performed by a Hanafi and a Maliki deputy. We don't know exactly how long the position was vacant, but by 1061 H there was a Shafiʿi deputy in office.

Only in the third document did the *madhhab* doctrine play a role in the choice for a deputy. It contains a decision by a Maliki deputy *qāḍī* authorizing

---

27 D.05.003, dated 1125 H/1713.

a woman to rescind her marriage on the ground that her husband has left her more than seven years ago without providing maintenance. It is expressly mentioned that the Maliki deputy in this case acts with the permission of the Shafiʿi deputy *qāḍī*. The reason for the woman to approach the Maliki deputy is obvious: the differences between Shafiʿi and Maliki doctrines. Shafiʿi doctrine does not offer relief for a woman who has been abandoned by her husband. She may demand dissolution (*faskh*) of her marriage for non-payment of maintenance, but only if she can prove that the husband is indigent, and not if he refuses to support although he has the wherewithal for it. If he disappears and leaves his wife without maintenance, she is not entitled to an annulment if the husband had sufficient means at the time of his disappearance.[28] Maliki doctrine is more favourable to women in this respect. A woman may obtain a divorce for absence of her husband – opinions on the minimum duration vary between one and three years – if she fears that she will commit immoral acts due to her husband's absence. Her statement to this effect suffices and need not be corroborated by witnesses. If the husband's whereabouts are known, a letter must be sent to him to summon him to rejoin his wife either by returning to her or by sending for her. If he refuses to do so or fails to answer, the *qāḍī* may pronounce the divorce. If it is impossible to get in touch with him, the *qāḍī* may do so immediately. It is irrelevant whether or not the husband has made arrangements for her maintenance.[29] Another course open under Maliki law to a woman in such a situation is that she petitions for divorce on the ground that her husband does not provide maintenance. In this case the woman appears to use both options: She produces witnesses testifying to her husband's absence for over seven years, to the fact that he has left her without maintenance and to her fear that she may commit immoral acts. The *qāḍī*, after making her swear an oath to corroborate these facts, gives her permission to rescind her marriage.

Six documents were issued in the al-Qasr court but by *qāḍī*s of the Oases or their deputies. To leave no doubt, these were not exequaturs of Hanafi *qāḍī*s, sanctioning the execution of judgements or documents issued by judges of other madhhabs, but rather documents originally issued by a (deputy) *qāḍī* of

28 Al-Ramlī, *Nihāyat Al-Muḥtāj ilā sharḥ al-Minhāj li-l-Nawawī*, Beirut: Dār al-Fikr, 1984. Vol. vii, pp. 212–3. It seems, however, that the practice of Shafiʿi judges in Ottoman Palestine was to grant wives in these circumstances an annulment. See Tucker, J.E. *In the House of the Law: Gender and Islamic Law in Ottoman Syria and Palestine*, Berkeley: University of California Press, 1998. pp. 83–85.

29 Al-Dasūqī, *Ḥāshiya ʿalā al-Sharḥ al-Kabīr li-l-Dardīr*, al-Qahirah: ʿĪsā al-Bābī al-Ḥalabī, n.d. Vol. ii, p. 431; al-Jazīrī, *Kitāb al-fiqh ʿalā al-madhāhib al-arbaʿa*. Cairo: Dār al-Irshād, n.d. Vol. ii, pp. 581–4.

the Oases. The first one is issued by the Hanafi *qāḍī* of the Oasis and records the appointment of a person as a legal representative (*mutaḥaddith sharʿī*) for his deaf-mute nephew whose father had died. The uncle is authorized to take possession of his nephew's share in the inheritance and will support him from it. The subject-matter of the documents gives no clue as to the reason why a Hanafi *qāḍī* should issue it and not a Shafiʿi deputy. According to the letters of appointment these deputies were competent in such matters and the collection contains several documents in which Shafiʿi deputies appoint legal representatives for orphans. The following two documents (1114/1702 and 1116/1704) bear the seal of a Shafiʿi *qāḍī* of the Oases, ʿUbayd Allāh b. Mūsā al-Dīnārī, a scion of a family of ulema from al-Qasr, who between 1099/1688 and 1129/1718 was one of the Shafiʿi deputies in the al-Qasr court. Two further documents, recording a *ṣulḥ* agreement and a contract of sharecropping and dating from around 1133/1722 were issued by a Hanafi deputy. This probably means that at that time the *qāḍī* of the Oases was not a Hanafi and supports the notion that at the lower levels of the judicial hierarchy in Egypt the Hanafi *madhhab* had lost terrain by the eighteenth century. Neither document gives an indication why the Hanafi doctrine should have been chosen for handling the transaction. In fact, the sharecropping contract (*jaʿāla*) which would have been null and void under Hanafi law.[30]

The last document is a run-of-the-mill contract of lease of land, literally identical to many others issued by Shafiʿi judges, bearing the seal of the Maliki deputy of the Oases. None of these documents contains a clue as to why a *qāḍī* from a certain *madhhab* should have dealt with them. There are no doctrinal issues that could explain the choice of a specific *madhhab* and, at least in one case, a transaction was notarized that was not recognized in *qāḍī*'s own *madhhab*. The impression one gets is that the (deputy) *qāḍī*s of the Oases from time to time visited the smaller courts falling under their jurisdiction for practical reasons, such as the collection of their due of the court fees or the appointment or annual reappointment of local deputies[31] and at the occasion would sign and seal legal documents and adjudicate. However, it these documents and judgements had been prepared by the local court clerks

30 Ibn Rushd, *Bidāyat al-mujtahid*. Cairo: Muṣṭafā al-Bābī al-Ḥalabī, 1960. Vol. ii, p. 235; For the legal discussion about the use of the *jaʿāla* contract for sharecropping, see Rudolph Peters, "Sharecropping in the Dakhla Oasis: Sharia and Customary Law in Ottoman Egypt." In *The Law Applied: Contextualizing the Islamic Shariʿa. A Volume in Honor of Frank Vogel*. Edited by P. Bearman, W. Heinrichs and B. Weiss. London: I.B. Tauris, 2008. Pp. 79–89.

31 Documents 23 and 39 in the Kharga collection show that the local deputies were appointed by the (deputy) *qāḍī* of the Oases in the local courts. Milād, *Wathāʾiq al-Wāḥāt*, pp. 135 and 149.

in accordance with the local practices and the visiting *qāḍīs* just put their signs and seals on them.

What may we conclude from this admittedly small sample of documents? The conclusions are not world shattering, but they confirm and complement our knowledge of the Ottoman Egyptian legal system and specifically the hierarchically lower end of the judiciary. In the first place the collection as a whole testifies to the fact that the inhabitants of al-Qasr, being Shafiʿis, were allowed to regulate their legal affairs to a large extent according to the Shafiʿi school. This tallies with what we know of legal practice elsewhere in Ottoman Egypt. The second point is that in those cases handled by non-Shafiʿi *qāḍīs* (7 out of 47) *madhhab* doctrine hardly played a role in the choice of the *qāḍī*. Only in one document does the choice of the judge appear to have been occasioned by *madhhab* doctrine. The other documents contain contracts whose wordings were identical or nearly identical with those issued by Shafiʿi *qāḍīs*. That they were issued by judges from other *madhhabs* can only be explained by practical considerations. I have suggested that the fact that in 1055 and 1056 non-Shafiʿi *qāḍīs* issued documents in the al-Qasr court may have been contingent on the Shafiʿi deputyship being vacant. But lacking sources to corroborate this, this explanation remains speculative. As to the *qāḍīs* of the Oases and their deputies, they would visit the al-Qasr courts – as well as other courts in the Kharga and Dakhla Oases – not for administering justice, but for practical reasons, such as the collection of court fees or appointing deputies. However, while being there, they would rubberstamp documents that had been drafted by the local court clerks.

Tables

TABLE 18.1 Distribution of the documents according to subject

Sale and lease of land, water and palm trees	70	32%
Sale and lease of urban property (houses)	09	04%
Other legal transactions (debts, attorney, family business)	39	18%
Receipts (taxes and other debts)	41	19%
Accounts and lists	37	18%
Miscellaneous (fatwas, waqfiyyas, sulḥ, judgements)	20	09%
TOTAL	216	100%

TABLE 18.2 Chronological distribution of the legal and financial documents

10th C. (1494–1591)	02	01%
11th C. (1591–1688)	29	13%
12th C. (1688–1785)	49	23%
13th C. (1785–1882)	80	37%
14th C. (1882–1979)	25	12%
Undated or not dateable	31	14%
TOTAL	**216**	**100%**

TABLE 18.3 Documents issued by Sharia courts according to *Qāḍī*'s rank and *madhhab*

Issued in a Cairo court				7
Issued in the al-Qasr court				47
	By a (deputy) *qāḍī* of the Oases		6	
	Hanafi	3		
	Shafiʿi	2		
	Maliki	1		
	By a deputy *qāḍī* of a-Qasr		41	
	Shafiʿi	38		
	Maliki	2		
	Hanafi	1		

CHAPTER 19

The Battered Dervishes of Bab Zuwayla

A Religious Riot in Eighteenth-Century Cairo

One of the most important motivating forces behind eighteenth-century Islamic renewal and reform is undoubtedly Islamic fundamentalism. By its nature, fundamentalism is activist and militant and tends therefore to produce movements and organizations aimed at implementing the Islamic ideals. The best known of these movements are those that succeeded in creating states or state like organizations and were politically significant. Other movements, however, failed or were suppressed before they could ever reach that stage. These are, of course, usually less well known. In this chapter, I shall deal with a short-lived fundamentalist movement of the latter category – a movement among Turkish soldiers in Egypt, led by a Turkish student of religion. Fundamentalist fervor made them attack dervishes performing Sufi rituals and brought them into open conflict with the Egyptian *'ulama'*. After a few days of unrest, the military authorities suppressed the movement by force and restored order. Although little is known about the leader of the movement – even his name remains a mystery – the events are well documented. Since both al-Djabarti[1] and von Hammer-Purgstall[2] have reported the episode, it has drawn the attention of several authors.[3] However, apart from Barbara Flemming's informative article,[4] which is an assessment of a Turkish chronicle as a source for the incident as compared with al-Djabarti's account, the events have not been dealt with in a more detailed study.

In the first part of this chapter I shall give an account of the occurrences. This is essentially a translation of the richest source available, Ahmad Shalabi's chronicle *Awdah al-isharat fi-man tawalla Misr min al-wuzara' wa-l-bashat*, complemented with two other contemporary sources, Yusuf al-Mallawani's *Tuhfat al-ahbab bi-man malak Misr min al-muluk wa-l-nuwwab* and Muhammad

1 'Abd al-Rahman el-Djabarti, *'Adja'ib al-Athar fi Taradjim al-Akhbar* 4 vols. (Bulaq: 1297 H), I, 48–50.

2 Joseph V. Hammer-Purgstall, *Geschichte des Osmanischen Reiches* 10 vols. (Graz: Akademische Druck- u. Verlagsanstalt, 1963; photogr. repr. of ed. Pest, 1831), VII, 168–69.

3 For a survey, see Barbara Flemming, "Die Vorwahhabitische Fitna im osmanischen Kairo 1711," in *Ismail Hakki Uzunçarşılı Armağani* (Ankara: Türk Tarih Kurumu Basımevi, 1975), 55–65.

4 See Flemming, "Die Vorwahhabitische."

 | DOI:10.1163/9789004420625_020

b. Yusuf al-Hallaq's *Tarih-i Misr*.[5] Passages from these other sources are printed in italics, the source being identified in the footnotes. In the second part the behavior and motives of the different actors will be analyzed against the background of the existing religious trends and traditional roles, with the aim of giving some insight into the conflict between fundamentalism and the established religious and political order.

> *In the beginning of Ramadan 1123 (October 1711) a Turkish (Rumi) student of religion* (softa, sukhte) *with a group of companions took up lodgings in cells* (khalwa) *belonging to the Mu'ayyad Mosque in Cairo. The following day they sat together to study a treatise by Birgili.*[6] On the 10th of Ramadan the student started to preach in one of the galleries of the mosque. He gave his sermons on several consecutive days and, as more and more people flocked in to hear him, he moved to the main hall of the mosque and ascended the pulpit there. His audience filled up the mosque; they were not only sitting in the main hall, but also stood in the galleries and took up half of the central court. His sermons dealt with the following issues:
>
> 1. Miracles of saints cease after death and accounts of miracles performed by them after their death are therefore false.
> 2. What al-Sha'rani[7] reports in his *al-Tabaqat*, namely that some saints can see the Well-Preserved Tablet (*al-Lawh al-Mahfuz*) is untrue and groundless, and he who holds this opinion is an unbeliever. For the Well-Preserved Tablet cannot be seen by prophets, so how would it be possible for saints? He even denied that the Prophet – may God bless him and grant him salvation – has ever seen the Well-Preserved Tablet.

---

5 Ahmad Shalabi b. 'Abd al-Ghani, *Awdah al-Isharat fi man Tawalla Misr al-Qahira min al-Wuzara' wa-l-Bashat*. Introduced and edited by 'Abd al-Rahim 'Abd al-Rahman 'Abd al-Rahim (Cairo: Maktabat al-Khandji, 1978) 251–55; Yusuf al-Mallawani, *Tuhfat al-Ahbab bi-man Malak Misr min al-Muluk wa-l-Nuwwab* (Ms Sohag 28 *tarikh;* microfilm: Ma'had al-Makhtutat al-tabi' li-Djami'at al-Duwal al-'Arabiyya, Cairo: *Tarikh* 136), 295–300. Muhammad b. Yusuf al-Hallaq, *Tarih-i Misr*. Ms Istanbul Üniversitesi Kütüphanesi, TY 628, ff. 296r–301r.

6 This beginning of the episode is only mentioned by Ibn al-Hallaq. Birgili Mehmed or Muhammad Birgewi (928/1522–981/1573), Turkish fundamentalist scholar and author of many books on religious subjects. Fought against what he considered as *bid'as*. Became famous for his polemic with *Shaykh al-Islam* Abu l-Su'ud Efendi about the unlawfulness of the *waqf* in cash and movable property. Cf.: E/, I, 1235 (Birgewi); GAL, II, 440–42; Katib Celebi, *Mizan al-Haqq*. Translated by G.L. Lewis (*The Balance of Truth*) (London: Allen and Unwin, 1957), 128–32.

7 'Abd al-Wahhab b. Ahmad al-Sha'rani (899/1493–973/1565), Egyptian mystic and religious scholar. Cf.: Michael Winter, *Society and Religion in Early Ottoman Egypt: Studies in the Writings of 'Abd al-Wahhab al-Sha'rani*. (New Brunswick & London: Transaction Books, 1982); GAL, II, 335–38.

3. It is not allowed to burn candles and oil lamps at the tombs of saints and it is to be feared that those who kiss their thresh-holds and tombs are unbelievers. Muslims and their authorities must strive to put an end to this.
4. It is obligatory for Muslims to destroy the cupolas built over graves (*tekkes*), like the Gülşeni and the Mevlevi *tekke*, and over the tombs of saints.
5. *The* tekkes *that have been constructed for a crowd of dervishes, like the Gülşeni, the Mevlevi, the Bektaşi and similar* tekkes *must be abolished, the dervishes living there must be ejected, their places be taken over by students of religion, and the* tekkes *thereafter be converted into* madrasas.[8]
6. *It is forbidden to visit in groups Imam Shafiʿi and other tombs during the nights before Saturday in order to perform public* dhikrs.[9]
7. *It is forbidden and an act of polytheism* (shirk) *that a band of ignoramuses among the groups that during the nights of Ramadan are to be found near Bab Zuwayla* (Demür kapu), *shout and jump until midnight on the pretense of performing a* dhikr. *It is incumbent upon the* qadi *and others to stop them, for a person who fails to forbid what is abominable* (al-nahy ʿan al-munkar) *will be punished in the Hereafter.*[10]

Spurred on by these words, his followers (*hizbuh*) lay in ambush until after evening prayer. Then they attacked with swords and cudgels those who were holding a *dhikr* there and beat them up[11] Upset, the crowd took to their heels. The attackers then began to beat the door with their cudgels and to tear off the balls[12] *and the pieces of red*[13] *cloth that were hanging from the door*, saying, "Where are the saints?" Then a Turk, called Yusuf, a retainer of Faruh Katkhoda, went to the niche behind one of the

8 This point is only mentioned by Ibn al-Hallaq.

9 This point is only mentioned by Ibn al-Hallaq.

10 Ibn al-Hallaq. The other sources only mention that the preacher incited his audience against the dervishes holding *dhikrs* near Bab Zuwayla.

11 According to al-Mallawani they only frightened them.

12 These must be the iron cannon balls that are still visible on the outside of the wall. These balls were probably regarded as amulets to protect the gate against attacks. The practice seems to have existed also in other Ottoman towns. Cf.: F.W. Hasluck, *Christianity and Islam under the Sultans*, edited by M.M. Hasluck, 2 vols. (Oxford: at the Clarendon Press, 1929), I, 203; Peter W. Schienerl, "Eisen als Kampfmittel gegen Dämonen: Manifestationen des Glaubens an seine magische Kraft im Islamischen Amulettwesen," *Anthropos* 75 (1980): 504. I am grateful to Dr. Schienerl for explaining to me the significance of these balls and drawing my attention to the aforementioned references.

13 Only in al-Mallawani.

door leaves and pissed in it. But God afflicted him then with jaundice until he died.

Some people went to Shaykh Ahmad al-Nafrawi and informed him of what the student had said. Thereupon a *fatwa* was written and signed by the Malikite Ahmad al-Nafrawi, the Hanafite al-Sayyid ʿAli and the Shafiʿites Ahmad al-Khalifi and ʿAbduh al-Diwi. Its contents were as follows:

1. The wonders of saints are a reality and they are possible both during their life and after their death. Whosoever denies this is a Muʿtazilite.
2. Denying that the Prophet – may God bless him and grant him salvation – can see the Well-Preserved Tablet is a statement that one is not allowed to make. If someone says so, he must be rebuked by the ruler and [if he does not come to reason] be killed.
3. *It is not allowed to change the nature of* tekkes *and to convert them into* madrasas, *for the founder's* (waqif) *stipulations are like clear provisions of the Divine Law and cannot be changed.*[14]

Some people took the *fatwa* to the al-Muʾayyad Mosque, waited for the preacher to climb the pulpit, and handed it to him. When he saw it, he became furious and said: "O you men! Your *ʿulamaʾ*, those Arabs (*awlad al-ʿArab*), have issued a *fatwa* contrary to what I have mentioned to you, saying that it is allowed to kill me. I want a disputation with them in the presence of the *qadi ʿaskar*.[15] Are there among you people who want to help me in upholding and supporting the Truth and in suppressing the power of these heretical unbelievers (*al-kafara al-zanadiqa*) who have issued an unfounded *fatwa?*" Then the group who supported him rose and said: "Lead us to any place you want. We are with you in anything you intend to do." He descended from the pulpit and about a thousand of those present gathered around him, all of them [illiterate] Turks, who could not distinguish between a written *mim* and *nun*. Thereupon he led them through the centre of Cairo to the house of the *qadi*. All this took place on Monday 19 Ramadan (30 October), just before the afternoon prayer.

When the *qadi* saw them, he was annoyed and said: "What do they want?" They answered: "We want you to summon for us Shaykh Ahmad al-Nafrawi, Shaykh Ahmad al-Khalifi and al-Sayyid ʿAli, who have signed

14 This point is only mentioned by Ibn al-Hallaq.

15 Al-Mallawani. Ahmad Shalabi calls him *Shaykh al Islam*, but from the rest of the story it is clear that he meant the *qadi ʿaskar*. Contrary to the Ottoman capital, where the title was reserved for the grand *mufti*, the honorific *shaykh al-Islam* could be given in Egypt to any religious scholar of great importance. Cf.: Ahmad Shalabi, 310, where both the *qadi ʿaskar* and the *shaykh al-Azhar* are given this title.

this *fatwa*." They showed the *fatwa* to the *qadi* and when he had read it he said to them: "Send those crowds away; we will summon them for you and hear your case." Then they said to him: "What do you think of this *fatwa*?" He answered: "It is unfounded, *since they do not adduce evidence for it*."[16] And so they asked for a document to this effect. But he replied that there was not much time left, that the clerks (*shuhud*) had already gone home and that they should be patient until the next day. Thereupon the interpreter (*tardjuman*) of the *qadi* went outside to submit the matter to them. They, however, did not listen to his words but attacked him and gave him a good hiding. Then the *qadi* got up and entered his private rooms (*harim*). All those present in court fled.... As for the deputy-qadi (*na'ib*), he had no choice but to write a document as they required.

Next day they assembled as usual at noon to listen to the preacher, but he did not show up. *They sent someone to look for him in his room, but they did not find him. Then they asked the other religious students but they replied that they did not know where he was.*[17] They began to wonder what had prevented him from coming. Then one of them said: "I think the *qadi* has prevented him from preaching." Thereupon another man said: "O you men! Whosoever wants the truth and wishes to support it, let he come with me to where I intend to go." About a thousand people followed him as he led them to the *qadi*. *The crowd became larger as they took along not only those who were present in the assembly, but also those whom they happened to meet in the markets and the bazars.*[18] When the *qadi* and those present in court saw them, they lost their minds from fear and panic. All the clerks and bailiffs (*rusul*) fled and only the *qadi* remained. Having entered they said: "Your Honor, where is our shaykh?" When he answered that he did not know they said to him: "Get up and ride with us to the *Diwan* so that we can ask the Pasha about him and request him to summon for us our adversaries who have issued a *fatwa* to the effect that our shaykh is to be killed. We shall hold a disputation with them and if they can prove their case, they will be safe, but if they cannot, we shall kill them." Then they forced the *qadi* to ride to the *Diwan*, while they were walking behind him. There the Pasha asked him about the reason for all the commotion and why he had appeared at such an unusual time. He answered: "Look at those who are filling the courtyard of the *Diwan*. They came to me and forced me to ride to here." And he informed

16 The last phrase is from Ibn al-Hallaq.

17 Ibn al-Hallaq.

18 Ibn al-Hallaq.

him of what had happened the day before and the same day; they had beaten up the interpreter and had taken a document from him stating what they wanted. "And now they have forced me to ride [and I had to yield] for fear that they would take my life." Thereupon the Pasha sent for the lieutenant-commanders (*katkhoda*) of the Janissaries (*Mustahfizan*) and the *ʿAzaban* and said: "Ask them what they want." They answered: "We want al-Sayyid ʿAli, al-Nafrawi and al-Khalifi so that they can have a disputation with our shaykh about their *fatwa.* If they fail to show up, we shall attack their houses." The Pasha gave them a written order (*firman, buyuruldi*)[19] in accordance with their wishes and said: "Come tomorrow, then your case will be dealt with." Thereupon they descended in a large crowd and entered the Mu'ayyad Mosque. They sent people to bring the shaykh front his cell, told him what the situation was, and showed him the buyuruldi that they had obtained. In the afternoon the same crowd sent for him to [ascend] the pulpit.[20] He then started to exhort them to come to the Mu'ayyad Mosque the following day. And all the time they were as deluded as ever in their obedience to this Muʿtazilite and their deep attachment to him. I (Ahmad Shalabi) once sat in the company of our teacher, Shaykh ʿAli al-Tayluni, talking about the fanaticism of this errant band and their affection for this Muʿtazilite. Then the shaykh said: "The person who has said: The first people to obey the *Dadjdjal* are the inhabitants of Egypt has certainly spoken the truth." The preacher continued exhorting them to come the following day, to assemble in the Mu'ayyad Mosque, and to go *en masse* to the *qadi.* "Anyone who failed to turn up would be a sinner," he said. He went on: "Help the truth, then God will help you [cf. K. 47:71. How can you be silent when someone says that saints can perform miracles after their death?" They answered him that they were with him in everything he wanted and then they dispersed.

As for the Pasha, after he had given the order to them, he sent another order to Ibrahim Abu Shanab and Ghitaz Bey [the two Mameluke commanders] to inform them of what had happened. *He mentioned that these people, by committing these impertinent acts, meant to cause another civil war* (fitna), *that the case of the preacher was only a pretence, that their*

19 Al-Mallawani and Ibn al-Hallaq both have *buyuruldi*, which is the more correct term. However, it has become customary to use the term *firman*, officially reserved for decrees with the *tuğra* of the sultan and for decrees of the government of Egypt. Cf.: Huseyn Efendi, *Ottoman Egypt in the Age of the French Revolution*. Trans. from the original Arabic by Stanford J. Shaw. (Cambridge, Mass.: Center for Middle Eastern Studies/Harvard University Press, 1964), 115.

20 Ibn al-Hallaq.

> *flocking to the court, their humiliation of the judge, their beating of his men, their disrespect in making him ride and come to him at an untimely hour and their attack on the imperial Diwan were not their own deeds and that there was someone who had incited them. Finally he declared that if they [the army commanders] intended to foment another civil war* (fitna)*, he and the qadi would go to Istanbul before the Sultan's and his honour could be injured.*[21] When they [the two Mameluke commanders] had read the order, they were upset and summoned the other *sandjaqs* [Mameluke beys] and army commanders (*aghawat*) to the house of the Chief Treasurer (*defterdar*). They submitted the matter to them and agreed to investigate which regiments the gang fitna following the preacher belonged to, to discharge them [once this was known], and to send the preacher into exile. They ordered the commander of the Janissaries to ride out, to arrest those of them whom he might see, to enter the mosque, *to eject the students living in the cells* (*khalawi*),[22] to interrogate them and finally to intimidate them and those heretics. Having reached a decision on these measures, they broke up. The next day ʿAli Agha (the commander of the Janissaries) rode out to the Mu'ayyad Mosque and sent the *çavuşan* in. They entered and inspected the place but did not find anybody. *The preacher had gone into hiding in the house of one of his followers* (murid)*, whereas the others had taken off the shawls* (taylasan) *they were wearing on their heads* [*over their turbans*].[23] All of them had fled and evacuated their cells. He then had their cells nailed up and arrested those who sat and waited for the preacher to come in order to benefit from his sermons. They were all sent to their regiments and then some of them were beaten and others were sent into exile. Then the sedition (*fitna*) came to an end. *As for the preacher, news arrived that he had escaped from the place where he had been hiding, that he had secretly boarded a ship in Bulaq, that he had reached the Syrian coast via Damietta, and that he had gone to Jerusalem.*[24]

So much for the events. What I shall do now is to explain what has happened by successively concentrating on the various actors and trying to discover the motives that prompted them to act as they did, the roles they assumed, and the religious trends and traditions they were part of. But before going into this, I will describe the stage where the main scenes of the narrative were enacted.

21 Ibn al-Hallaq.
22 Al-Mallawani and Ibn al-Hallaq.
23 Ibn al-Hallaq.
24 Ibn al-Hallaq.

The story begins and ends in the Mu'ayyad Mosque, one of the biggest and grandest mosques in Cairo, constructed in 818 H/1415 CE by sultan al-Malik al-Mu'ayyad Shaykh al-Mahmudi. It was meant to serve both as a Sufi center and as a *madrasa* and in the *waqf* deed the founder had made provisions for the salaries of Sufi shaykhs and teachers of the religious sciences and for scholarships to students. In the seventeenth century it had fallen into disrepair, but was restored in 1690 by the governor Ahmad Pasha.[25] Immediately adjacent to it is Bab Zuwayla, known among the Turks as Demür Kapu, the Iron Gate, on the southern end of the Qasaba, the main thoroughfare of Fatimid Cairo. The present gate was built in 485 H/1092 CE. It is also known as Bab al-Mitwalli since popular belief has it that a niche behind one of the leaves is inhabited by a very important saint (*mitwalli, qutb*), who is invisible. People asking the intercession of the saint would tie a piece of cloth to the door or drive a nail in it. On the walls of the gate some large stone balls are suspended, probably as protective amulets.[26]

In the Mu'ayyad Mosque we meet the first actor, the instigator of the ensuing events: a Turkish *softa* or student of religious sciences, who, with a group of companions, had taken residence in the cells adjoining to the mosque. They distinguished themselves from their Egyptian colleagues by donning the *taylasan*, a shawl worn over the turban, characteristic of the Turkish *'ulama'*. We have no way of ascertaining why our *softa* and his friends had come to Egypt. What we do know, however, is that the situation for religious students in Turkey was not very bright. The upper strata of the judicial and educational hierarchy was impenetrable for those who did not belong to the right families or had not enough money to bribe their way into them.[27] The ranks of students and lower *'ulama'* were swollen with youngsters from rural areas who had fled the misery

---

25 'Ali Mubarak, *Al-Khitat al-Tawfiqiyya al-Djadida li-Misr al-Qahira wa-Muduniha wa-Biladiha l-Qadima wa-l-Shahira*, 20 vols. (Bulaq: 1307 H), II, 31, V, 124–32; Ahmad Shalabi, 189.

26 'Ali Mubarak, III, 50; for the popular religious practices and beliefs connected with Bab Zuwayla, see E.W. Lane, *Manners and Customs of the Modern Egyptians* (London and New York: Everyman's Library, 1966), 237; H.H. Harrison, "The Bab it Metawalli," MW 8 (1918): 141–44. See also note 12.

27 Cf. H.A.R. Gibb and Harold Bowen, *Islamic Society and the West.* Vol. I, *Islamic Society in the Eighteenth Century*, 2 parts. (London etc.: Royal Institute of International Affairs/ Oxford University Press, 1957), II, ch. IX; Richard Repp, "Some observations on the Development of the Ottoman Learned Hierarchy," in *Scholars, Saints and Sufis: Muslim Religious Institutions since 1500*, edited by Nikki R. Keddie (Berkeley: University of California Press, 1972), 17–33; R.C. Repp, "The Altered Nature and Role of the 'ulama'," in *Studies in Eighteenth Century Islamic History*, edited by Thomas Naff and Roger Owen (London/Carbondale: Feffer & Simons/Southern Illinois University Press, 1977), 277–88.

of the countryside and were in first instance attracted by the austere but secure life of *softa* with its free daily food rations. However, gradually realizing that they had no social prospects, they became radicalized and often participated in political or religious upheavals.[28]

The situation of the Egyptian students of religion was very different. Except for some positions in the Ottoman religious hierarchy to which usually Turks were appointed by the central government, all religious functions were in principle open to all graduates of the religious schools. For bright boys of simple descent the *'ulama'* profession was the only path to social mobility and it is indicative that most of the *shuyukh al-Azhar* were of peasant stock.[29] These prospects, or rather the fear of spoiling them, kept many an Egyptian student out of mischief. They were certainly much less radical than their Turkish counterparts, and when they participated in demonstrations or revolts they did so together with their teachers, often on behalf of the population in protest against certain measures taken by the ruling groups.

That our Turkish *softa* was a radical is beyond dispute. His radicalism was of a religious kind and appears in his fierce stance vis-à-vis certain popular Sufi rituals and saint veneration. It is significant that he and his friends had been studying a treatise by Birgili, a popular author well known for strict views on these matters.[30] These attitudes are typical of fundamentalist Islam, by which I mean those trends in Islam that emphasize the transcendence of God versus His imminence, the authenticity of religious experience as based on the revelation (direct and indirect, i.e. Quran and *hadith*), unity of religious experience, and, finally, the basic equality of all believers in the face of God. As a rule, fundamentalism is action-oriented; it wants to change the world by subjecting it to fundamentalist ideals. Central to fundamentalist thought is the claim that the gate of *idjtihad* is not entirely closed and the condemnation of saint veneration.

28 Cf. Stanford Shaw, *History of the Ottoman Empire and Modern Turkey, Vol. I, Empire of the Gazis: the Rise and Decline of the Ottoman Empire, 1280–1808* (Cambridge: Cambridge University Press, 1976), 174, 186, 227–28, for the seventeenth and beginning of the eighteenth century.

29 Afaf Lutfi al-Sayyid Marsot, "The 'ulama' of Cairo in the Eighteenth and Nineteenth Centuries," *in Scholars, Saints, and Sufis*, 157.

30 Cf. Muhammad al-Birgewi, "Risalah fi Ziyarat al-Qubur," in *Al-Madjmuʿ al-Mushtamil 'ala l-Durar al-ʿAtiya* (Cairo: Matbaʿat Kurdistan al-ʿIlmiyya, 1329 H), 531–56; Id., *Al-Tariqa al-Muhammadiyya*. 2nd pr. (Cairo: Mustafa al-Babi al-Halabi, 1379/1960), 139–41 (singing and music during *dhikrs*), 183–84 (dancing during *dhikrs*).

Since I have done so elsewhere[31] I shall not go into the relationships between these issues and the trends just mentioned, except for their relationship with equality, as this is pertinent to our argument.

The link between the rejection of saint veneration and the idea of equality between all believers is not difficult to see. Worshiping holy men not only infringes upon the right of God to be worshiped alone – in fact the most important reason for fundamentalists to be against it – but also gives some people a much higher status than ordinary believers. They are placed, in eternity, between man and God and are believed to possess supernatural powers to which other men can appeal. Now this is in patent conflict with the notion that all believers are equal to God. Although fundamentalists accept the common doctrine that God, as a token of respect to the very pious, may grant them the faculty of miracle working, they usually maintain that this faculty ceases after death and normal order is restored. The relation between the doctrine that the gate of *idjtihad* is still open and the idea of the equality of believers is more complicated. Orthodox doctrine holds that after the fourth century H., the gate of *idjtihad* was closed and that, in order to know the *Shariʿa*, one must follow the opinions of the great founders of the *madhhabs* and those who have elaborated the doctrine within the *madhhabs* after them. This is known as *taqlid*. The claim that any Muslim with a minimum amount of knowledge has the right to consult the Quran and the *Sunna* in order to find the prescriptions of the *Shariʿa* on any specific point, undermines the monopoly of the *ʿulamaʾ* and saps the carefully formulated chronological hierarchy of absolute *mudjtahids*, *madhhabs* and *fatwa mudjtahids* and what other ranks you have.

This basic notion of equality was highly relevant for the situation the *softa* found himself in. It enabled him to regard himself as the peer of all those established *ʿulamaʾ* that blocked his entry into the ranks of professors and judges. In our particular case it gave him the audacity to summon the leading Azhar shaykhs for a discussion on an equal footing.

Despite the fundamentalists' insistence on *idjtihad*, the number of practical rules on which they differ with established opinion is usually very small. This is also apparent from the issues the *softa* dealt with in his sermons. Two of them contain nothing new or controversial and are to be found in most books on *fiqh*

---

31 See my "*Idjtihad* and *Taqlid* in 18th and 19th Century Islam," WI 20 (1980): 131–46; "Erneuerungsbewegungen im Islam vom 18. bis 20. Jahrhundert und die Rolle des Islams in der neueren Geschichte: Anti-kolonialismus und Nationalismus," in *Der Islam in der Gegenwart*, Hrsg. von W. Ende und U Steinbach. (Munich: C.H. Beck, 1984), 91–131; "Islamischer Fundamentalismus: Glauben, Handeln, Führung," in: *Max Webers Sicht des Islams: Interpretation und Kritik*. Hrsg. von Wolfgang Schluchter. (Frankfurt a.m.: Suhrkamp Verlag, 1987) 217–42.

of whatever *madhhab* – the prohibition of building cupolas over graves[32] and the prohibition of burning candles and lamps in tombs and of kissing the floor of the thresholds of these shrines.[33] Controversial are his opinion that saints cannot perform miracles after their death,[34] his claim that neither prophets nor saints can see the Well-Preserved Tablet in Heaven,[35] his view that dhikr-sessions with dancing are forbidden (although it seems that a great number of legal authorities are with him here),[36] and finally, his assertion that all *tekkes* must be converted into *madrasas*.

The Arabic sources mention that the protagonist of our episode was a Turkish student of religion. It is evident, therefore, that we must place his ideas in a Turkish-Ottoman intellectual context. This is corroborated by the names of the *tekkes* he mentions – those of the Gülşeniye (a branch of the Khalwatiyya order, singled out here because of its popularity with the Turkish

32 See e.g.: ʿAbd al-Rahman al-Djaziri, *Kitab al-Fiqh ʿala l-Madhahib al-Arbaʿa*. Vol. I, *Al-Ibadat* (2nd impr. Cairo: al-Maktaba al-Tidjariyya al-Kubra, n.d.), 535–36; Muhammad ʿArafa al-Dasuqi, *Hashiyat al-Dasuqi ʿala l-Sharh al Kabir li-( )Ahmad al-Dardir ʿala Mukhtasar (…) Khalil b. Ishaq*, 4 vols. (Cairo: Dar Ihya' al-Kutub al-Arabiyya, n.d.), 424–25; Ibrahim al-Badjuri, *Hashiya ʿala l-Qawl al-Mukhtar fi Sharh Ghayat al-Ikhtisar li-Abi Shudjaʿ (…)*, 2 vols. (Cairo: ʿIsa l-Babi al-Halabi, n.d.), I, 257; ʿAbd al-Rahman Shaykhzade, *Madjmaʿ al-Anhur fi Sharh Multaqa l-Abhur li-Ibrahim (…) al-Halabi*, 2 vols. (Istanbul: Dar al-Tibaʿa al-Amira, 1301 H), I, 181.

33 See e.g.: Djaziri, I, 540; Dasuqi, II, 171; Muhammad ʿIllaysh, *Fath al-ʿAli al-Malik fi l-Fatawa ʿala Madhhab al-Imam Malik*, 2 vols. (Cairo: Matbaʿat al-Taqaddum al-ʿIlmiyya, 1319 H), I, 173; Khayr al-Din al-Faruqi al-Ramli, *al-Fatawa l-Khayriyya*. Printed in the margin of: Muhammad Amin b. ʿAbidin, *al-ʿUqud al-Durriyya fi Tanqih al-Fatawa l-Hamidiyya* (n.p., n.d.), I, 31.

34 See e.g.: Ahmad b. Taymiyya, "Risalat Ziyarat al-Qubur wa-l-Istindjad bi-lmaqbur," in *Madjmuʿat Rasa'il li-Ahmad b. Taymiyya*. (Cairo: Matbaʿat al-Manar, 1340 H), 163; Muhammad al-Birgewi, "Risala fi Ziyarat al-Qubur," in *Al-Madjmuʿ al-Mushtamil ʿala l-Durar al-ʿAtiya*. (Cairo: Matbaʿat Kurdistan al-ʿIlmiyya, 1329 H), 538.

35 Opinion prevails that prophets can see the Well-Preserved Tablet. On the question of whether saints are capable of it, opinion is divided according to whether one classifies al-Khadir (al-Khidr) as a saint or a prophet. Cf. Ibn al-Hadjar al-Haytami, *al-Fatawa l-Hadithiyya* (Cairo: Matbaʿat al-Taqaddum al-ʿIlmiyya, 1347 H), 222; Muhammad Amin b. ʿAbidin, "Sa'il al-Husam al-Hindi fi Nusrat Mawlana Khalid al-Naqshabandi," in *Madjmuʿat Rasa'il Ibn ʿAbidin*, 2 vols. (Istanbul: Der Saadet, 1325 H), II, 312.

36 Cf. Abu Hamid al-Ghazali, *Ihya' ʿUlum al-Din* (Cairo: ʿIsa l-Babi al-Halabi, n.d.), II, 266–302 (Kitab Adab al-Samaʿ wa-l-Wadjd); Ahmad Ibn Hadjar al-Haytami, *Kaff al-Ruʿaʿ an Muharramat al-Lahw wa-l-Samaʿ*. Printed in the same volume as his *Al-Zawadjir ʿan Iqtiraf al-Kaba'ir*. 2nd pr. (Cairo: Mustafa l-Babi al-Halabi, 1398/1978), 267–421; Abu Saʿid al-Khadimi, *Al-Bariqa al-Mahmudiyya fi sharh al-Tariqa al-Muhammadiyya li-Muhammad al-Birgawi* and Radjab b. Ahmad *Al-Wasila al-Ahmadiyya wa-l-Dhariʿa al-Sarmadiyya fi sharh al-Tariqa al-Muhammadiyya;* printed together (Cairo: Mustafa l-Babi al-Halabi, 1348) IV, 133–39; Georges Vajda, "Un libelle contre la dance des soufis," SI 51 (1980), 163–77.

soldiers and the vicinity of its *tekke* to Bab Zuwayla), the Mevleviye, and the Bektaşiye. These *tariqahs* were the most popular ones in the Central Ottoman Empire, but not very prominent in Egypt, where their followers were in the main found among the Turks residing there.[37]

Flemming has already drawn attention to the similarities between our *softa's* ideas and the movement of the Qadizadililer (also called *Faqiler*, from Ar. *faqih*) in seventeenth-century Istanbul, a movement also inspired by the works of Birgili. It is named after Qadizade Mehmed Efendi (d. 1045/1635–36), a student of Birgili's son and a preacher notorious for his polemical stance in doctrinal matters and his fierce attacks on *bid'as*, especially those connected with Sufism. Among other things he condemned saint veneration, *dhikrs* with music and dancing, a number of collective festive prayers not warranted by the *Sunna*, and expressions of humble respect before notables (like kissing their hands or feet and bowing before them).[38] Apparently these controversial issues occupied the minds of many of his contemporaries and in 1632 a public disputation was held between him and Sivasi Efendi (d. 1049/1639), another renowned preacher and deputy shaykh of the Khalwati order.[39] After Qadizade's death his followers began putting his ideas into practice by disturbing Sufi gatherings, closing down or destroying *tekkes* and attempting to prevent musical recitals of laudatory poems on the Prophet. The movement raged for twenty years and was only suppressed in 1656 by the newly appointed grand vizier Mehmed Köprülü.[40] Their program was very similar to our *softa's*, with one notable exception. They had wanted to demolish the Sufi *tekkes* where musical *dhikrs* and dancing had taken place, as in their opinion such buildings had become impure. This point carried such weight with them that in order to cleanse the place, they regarded it necessary to remove all the building materials as well as several inches of the surface soil.[41] This view is probably an exaggerated version of a Hanafite opinion that the mats on which Sufis have

37 ʿAli Mubarak, III, 50; VI, 54, 56–57; Gibb and Bowen, II, 191–96, 198; B.G. Martin, "A Short History of the Khalwati Order of Dervishes," in *Scholars, Saints, and Sufis*, 296; Huseyn Efendi/Shaw, 100–102; Lane, *Modern Egyptians*, 248–9.

38 Katib Celebi, *Balance*, 133; Mustafa Naʿima, *Tarikh Rawdat al-Husayn fi Khulasat Akhbar al-Khafiqayn* (Istanbul: Matbaʿa-yi ʿAmira 1281–83/1864–66), VI, 229–30 (where a list of Qadizade's controversial opinions is given, which is identical to the table of contents of Katib Celebi's *Mizan al-Haqq*), 232.

39 Naʿima, III, 172–3; H.J. Kissling, "Aus der Geschichte des Chalvetijje Ordens," ZDMG 103 (1953), 277.

40 Naʿima, VI, 227–41 (for an account of the movement; Abdulbaki Golpinarlı, *100 Soruda Turkiyede Mezhepler ve Tarikatler* (Istanbul: Gercek Yayınevi, 1969), 87–89; Kissling, *Chalvetijje*, 277–80.

41 Naʿima, VI, p. 235.

danced must be ritually purified before they can be used for prayer again.[42] For our *softa* this point did not seem to be of great consequence. For practical reasons, as Flemming has also noted, he proposed the conversion of these *tekkes* into schools, so that *softas* could more easily finish their studies and find lodgings. This, too, emphasizes his Ottoman background and that he was a foreigner in Egypt, since, as we have seen, there was no "*softa* problem" in Egypt. Interestingly, the Arab contemporary sources do not mention this proposal, probably because they could not make sense of it.

As important as ideology is action in fundamentalist Islam. As I mentioned before, fundamentalists want to change the world and to subject it to their ideals. This aspect is very clear in the *softa's* preaching. He mentioned a number of practices and customs that have to come to an end and be checked by either the authorities – as representatives of the community of Muslims – or the believers themselves, and appealed to the duty of "commanding what is reputable and forbidding what is disreputable" (*al-amr bi-l-maʿruf wa-l-nahy ʿan al-munkar*, cf. K. 3:110), which is a collective duty (*fard al-kifaya*) for all Muslims. After several days of haranguing his appeals began to have effect; the crowds that had gathered around him came under his control and assaulted the dervishes holding a *dhikr* at Bab Zuwayla.

The texts tell us that these followers were mostly illiterate Turkish soldiers. There were seven regiments (*ocak*) then stationed in Egypt: Janissaries, *ʿAzaban, Çavuşan, Mutefarrika*, and three cavalry (*Ispahiye*) regiments, but probably only the first two of them were involved. The *Mutefarrika* and the cavalry regiments served mainly in the provinces and that the *Çavuşan* had nothing to do with it may be deduced from the fact that although the Janissaries and the ʿAzaban were the normal police troops,[43] the Janissary commander took *Çavuş* soldiers to restore order in the Mu'ayyad Mosque, evidently because he did not want to use Janissaries and *ʿAzaban* against their regimental comrades.

The sources mention that the band of followers totalled around one thousand men. Of course, one has to take such round numbers with a grain of salt, but even if there were, say, seven hundreds of them, this would be at least 10 percent of the troops garrisoned in Cairo, and probably more.[44] If we take into

42 Al-Khadimi, *al-Bariqa al-Mahmudiyya*, IV, p. 137.

43 Huseyn Efendi/Shaw, pp. 82–94.

44 According to Dr. Layla ʿAbd al-Latif Ahmad (as quoted by Daniel Crecelius, *The Roots of Modern Egypt: A study of the Regimes of Ali Bey al-Kabir and Muhammad Bey Abu Dhahab, 1760–1775* [Minneapolis etc.: Bibliotheca Islamica, 1981], 21) the total strength of the Janissaries and Azaban in Egypt numbered 8,500 in 1710. Part of these served in the provincial towns and further we have to take into consideration the heavy toll of lives that the revolt of 1711 – which ended only four months earlier – had taken. It is improbable that the

account that these soldiers were not known for their orthodox leanings and that Sufism was very popular amongst them,[45] this is a considerable proportion that needs explanation.

In order to understand this sudden outbreak of religious zeal, we have to link it to the internecine struggle between different military factions earlier that year. Certainly, violent quarrels and even large scale fighting were then endemic among the military establishment in Egypt. The Mameluke emirs were divided between hostile factions, the Qasimites and the Fiqarites. Among the Ottoman soldiers, there was a traditional rivalry between the largest regiments, the Janissaries and the Azaban, over the control of financial resources, such as the lucrative rights to protect certain groups of merchants. In the civil war of 1711, however, the lines of division had shifted and split the existing factions and regiments; Janissaries fought Janissaries, *ʿAzaban* fought *ʿAzaban*, *Çavuşan* fought *Çavuşan* and the officers of the cavalry regiments stood against their own men. The struggle was fiercer than ever before and the three months of fighting took a heavy toll in human lives, estimated by some at about 4,000 people.[46] For soldiers brought up in the ethos of regimental solidarity, the events must have been unsettling, as they seemed to flout some of their basic values. In these troubled times the soldiers must have been responsive to religious calls implying a break with the past and offering a clear and simple way of salvation.

During the fighting the people of Cairo had attributed the calamity that had befallen them to their own impiety and sinfulness,[47] and these soldiers may have had similar feelings. So, when a preacher showed them a new way of being pious – a departure from their habitual, mystical religiosity or indifference to religion – which, because of its active and practical character appealed to their soldierly temperament, many must have felt attracted to it. And more than attracted; they identified with the movement to the extent that they were willing to risk their lives for it.

As for the dervishes who were chased from Bab Zuwayla, we must be brief. The sources represent them only as the passive objects of the soldiers' punitive

---

regiments had already been brought to their original strength. Taking these factors into account, my estimate is that their numbers in Cairo cannot have been more than 7,000 and were probably much less.

45 ʿAli Mubarak, VI, 55; Gibb and Bowen, II, 198; J. Spencer Trimingham, *The Sufi Orders in Islam* (London: Oxford University Press, 1971), 76.

46 Andre Raymond, "Une 'révolution' au Caire sous les Mamelouks: la crise de 1123/1711," *Annales Islamologiques*, 66 (1965): 95–119.

47 ʿAli al-Shadhili, "Dhikr ma waqaʿ bayn ʿaskar al-Mahrusa bi-l-Qahira," edited by ʿAbd al-Qadir Ahmad al-Tulaymat, *Al-Madjalla al-Tarikhiyya al-Misriyya*, 14 (1968): 333.

action. Frightened away, they did not play a role of their own. The scuffle, however, brought another party on the stage, the Egyptian *'ulama'*, who became the *softa's* intellectual opponents.

As I have mentioned before, there were two groups of *'ulama'* in Egypt: a small number of judges who formed part of the Ottoman clerical hierarchy, and the Egyptian *'ulama'*, who worked as teachers and occupied the lower positions in the judiciary. As a rule, the first group consisted of Turks who came for a very short term of service to Egypt. Unfamiliar with the vernacular, they depended on the services of interpreters and on their Egyptian deputies who generally did most of the work. There were often severe and prolonged disputes and contentions between these Ottoman dignitaries and the Egyptian *'ulama'*.[48] The latter, constituting an indigenous elite, often acted as intermediaries between the population and the alien rulers, or even as the leaders of popular protest movements. If the people had grievances, they would first go to the Egyptian *'ulama'* at the Azhar Mosque, the centre of higher learning in Cairo. The *'ulama'*, however, were no radicals. They had their stake in the existing political system and did not want to overthrow it. By fulfilling the role as intercessors for the people with the Turkish rulers, they actually strengthened the established order and protected it from disintegration. Since this order was essentially legitimized by religion, the *'ulama'* corroborated it by showing that Islam was an ideological system that had something to offer to all classes in society and not only to the ruling groups.

So when Turkish soldiers assaulted Egyptian dervishes, it was only natural for the bystanders to go to the Azhar of a *fatwa* signed by the most important of them at that time: Ahmad al-Nafrawi, who was then probably the *Shaykh al-Azhar*;[49] Ahmad al-Khalifi, a prominent Shafi'ite scholar,[50] 'Abduh al-Diwi,

48 Huseyn Efendi/Shaw, pp. 95–100.

49 Ahmad b. Ghunaym b. Salim b. Muhanna al-Nafrawi was born in Nafra around 1631. He was the author of several commentaries on religious topics and became the chief of the Malikites at al-Azhar. In 1709 he was involved in a skirmish with Shaykh al-Qalini over the *mashyakhat al-Azhar*. Firearms were used and ten victims remained dead in the court of al-Azhar. The Pasha punished him with house arrest and it seems that al-Qalini became Shaykh al-Azhar, although the sources do not mention it. Al-Qalini died on 18 Radjab 1123 (1 September 1711) and Nafrawi probably succeeded him then, since Ahmad Shalabi mentions that when Nafrawi died in 1125 he was succeeded as *Shaykh al-Azhar* by Muhammad Shanan. Ahmad Shalabi, pp. 220, 261; Djabarti, I, pp. 35, 73, 208–209; Shadhili, p. 397.

50 Shihab al-Din Abu al-'Abbas Ahmad b. Muhammad b. 'Atiyya al-Sharqawi *al-shahir* bi-l-Khalifi, Shafi'ite scholar born in Minyat Musa, about 1649. He was one of the most prominent teachers at al-Azhar, and during the 1711 revolt he tried to mediate between the different parties in order to prevent further bloodshed. He was given this task probably

the chief of the Shafiʿites,[51] and al-Sayyid Ali, a Hanafite shaykh.[52] The first three persons were among the most eminent and popular scholars of their time and their names are frequently mentioned as teachers in the biographies of the *ʿulamaʾ* of the next generation. The *fatwa* is a short one and deals only with three issues of which the second is the most crucial.

The first point is a reply to the *softa's* contention that the faculty of saints to perform miracles ceases after their death, a typically fundamentalist issue. Interestingly, the matter is not touched upon in the more mainstream works of dogmatism, but this does not prevent the authors of the *fatwa* to pronounce firmly that this power is not affected by a holy man's death. Had they ruled differently, they would have sapped the theoretical foundations of the cult of saints, which was obviously something they did not want. They condemned the preacher's view as being Muʿtazilite, which is not very precise, since the Muʿtazilites denied the possibility of saints performing miracles categorically, both during their lifetime and after their deaths.

The third point is an answer to the *softa's* claim that all *tekkes* ought to be converted into *madrasas* and argues that this is impossible since it would involve changing the stipulations of the founder of the *waqf*, which is illegal. This argument, however, passes over the real issue raised by the *softa:* that these *tekkes* – with their domes built over graves and their Sufi gatherings with music and dance – ought to be demolished or converted into something else because they were illegal and a means toward forbidden actions (the *dhikrs*).

The second point is the most vital one because it provided the authorities with a legal weapon to take action against him and, were he to persevere in his opinions, to execute him. Although they do not expressly mention so, they

since al-Qalini must have already been ill – he would die a few months later. Khalifi died in 1127/1715. Ahmad Shalabi, p. 234; Djabarti, I, pp. 40, 73.

51 ʿAbd Rabbih b. Ahmad al-Diwi al-Darir was head of the Shafiʿites at al-Azhar. He was one of the Azhar shaykhs to be sent in exile for having supported during the 1711 revolt the defeated party with their *fatwas*. His signing of the *fatwa* against the *softa* could mean that his exile had been only of short duration. However, it is curious that he is mentioned by one author only, and then not more than once, whereas the other *ʿulamaʾ* are mentioned several times. Perhaps this was a slip of Ahmad Shalabi and al-Diwi was still in exile. According to his *laqab* he was blind. He died in 1126/1714. Ahmad Shalabi, p. 264; Shadhili, pp. 297–98; Djabarti, I, p. 72.

52 Al-Sayyid ʿAli b. al-Sayyid ʿAli al-Husayni al-Shahir bi-Iskandar al-Hanafi al-Siwasi al-Darir. Hanafite scholar and descendant of the prophet, born around 1661. Had travelled and taught in Turkey. Was one of those who considered the use of coffee as *haram*. It is obscure whether he was blind; al-Djabarti calls him *al-Darir*, whereas Ahmad Shalabi gives him the *laqab al-Basir*. He died in 1146/1734.

probably charged him with having insulted the Prophet by denying that he could see the Well-Preserved Tablet. Actually, this was not essential to his main argument that saints lacked this ability. It would seem that in the fire of his argument he had overstated his case by lumping holy men and prophets together in this respect without sound scriptural argument. Thus he provided his adversaries with a weak spot through which they could attack him without having to deal with the principal issue.

It is clear that the interest of the *fatwa* lies not so much in its contents, but rather in what it remains silent on: the central issue of the *softa's* preaching – the unlawfulness of saint veneration and ecstatic Sufi practices. This must have been deliberate, and the question then arises: why did they fail to deal with these issues? There are three answers to this question. The first is that prevailing opinion was on the side of the *softa* in these matters. Assuming that the *ʿulama'* wanted to draft a *fatwa* against him, they would find it hard to disprove his views firmly embedded in orthodox doctrine as most of these were. However, jurists are resourceful and it is not impossible that they could have come up with some refutation, although that would have meant walking on thin ice.

There has to be a second, more cogent answer to this question. I believe it is to be found in the fact that the *ʿulama'* were of two minds about these phenomena. In spite – or perhaps even because – of their dominantly rural background, many of them must have felt an aversion to these popular, and in their eyes vulgar, religious practices of the lower classes. The contemporary Azhar scholar and poet Hasan al-Badr al-Hidjazi (d. 1131/1719) expressed these feelings in two poems berating saint veneration and the practices of certain Sufi shaykhs.[53] Most *ʿulama'* must have felt some sympathy for the *softa's* opinions, although probably not for all their radical consequences. But on the other hand, many of them had their links with Sufism and were members of a *tariqa*. The fact that Abduh al-Diwi, mentioned as one of the signatories of the *fatwa*, was a member is expressly mentioned in Djabarti's brief biographical note about him. However, this does not imply that the others were not. These bonds with Sufism may have made many of the *ʿulama'* more tolerant toward these popular practices. Thus, being divided among themselves, they considered it prudent to remain silent on the matter.

In addition to all this, there was a third consideration why they should pass over the issue. This revolves upon the relationship between the *ʿulama'* and

53 Djabarti I, 75, 78–79; partial translation of the poems in Gamal el-Din el-Shayyal, "Some Aspects of Intellectual and Social Life in Eighteenth-century Egypt," in *Political and Social Change in Modern Egypt*, edited by P.M. Holt (London: Oxford University Press, 1968), 131.

the population. As I have argued, the *ʿulamaʾ* were bent on maintaining the all-embracing character of Islam, even if this might to some extent compromise doctrinal purity. Now, any explicit stand in matters of popular religion would involve an outright condemnation of certain customs, and this is exactly what the *ʿulamaʾ* wanted to avoid so as not to alienate the lower classes. Their position in Egyptian society and their authority vis-à-vis the rulers was in part based on the idea that they represented the indigenous population and on the support in the form of popular movements they could muster to sustain this role. Therefore they wanted to maintain a form of symbiosis that was also reflected in a common religious ideology.

The preacher's reaction upon reading the *fatwa* was vehement. He inveighed against the *ʿulamaʾ*, calling them heretical unbelievers. This actually implies that they were to be killed for apostasy. He then urged the assembled crowds to follow him to the *qadi ʿaskar*, a man called Rasulzade. He wanted him to summon the signatories of the *fatwa* to his court in order to hold a public disputation. Convinced of the soundness of his case, he was certain that he would be victorious and that the *qadi* would take measures against the *ʿulamaʾ*.

The idea of having recourse to the *qadi ʿaskar* was logical from his point of view, since this official was the highest religious and judicial authority in Egypt and had the power to force the *ʿulamaʾ* to come to his court. But there was also another consideration that played a role: the fact that the chief judge was a fellow Ottoman-Turk. For in the background of the events there lay an element of ethnic friction which came to the surface when the *softa* emphasized the ethnic origin of the *ʿulamaʾ* by calling them deprecatorily "those Arabs (*awlad al-ʿArab*)." Since the Egyptians had gone to their *ʿulamaʾ*, he resorted to the Ottoman religious officials.

Initially the *qadi*, despite his annoyance, seemed well disposed toward the delegation of fellow Turks that suddenly entered his court. He agreed to summon the *ʿulamaʾ* and to hear the case and pronounced the *fatwa* to be unfounded. This had more to do with the animosity existing between the Ottoman and the local *ʿulamaʾ* than with intimidation. Only gradually did he realize that the crowds outside the court could be dangerous. If he had not expected that they would obey and disperse, he would not have sent his interpreter without any protection to tell them to come back next day. When they gave the interpreter a sound thrashing, the *qadi*, understanding that events had got out of control, fled into his private apartment.

The following day the preacher, fearing the repercussions of the incident at the *qadi's* court, kept a low profile. His supporters, however, suspected that the *qadi* had a hand in his absence and marched again to the court. When they then coerced him to ride to the Pasha, matters became really serious. The religious issue was overshadowed by considerations of public order. The troops' unruly behaviour and their assault on one of the highest ranking Ottoman officials demanded disciplinary measures to be taken by the military leadership. I shall not elaborate on how and by whom order was restored. Those events would belong to the field of military or institutional history and fall therefore outside the scope of this study that centred on the religious aspects of the events.

In order to understand the significance of the movement we have just dealt with it is essential to realize that, although Cairo provided the scenes of the action and the decors, the movement itself was embedded in Ottoman-Turkish traditions. The preacher's ideas and actions were rooted in both Turkish *softa* radicalism and a brand of Turkish fundamentalism that went back, via Birgili Mehmed, to Ibn Taymiyya and Ibn Qayyim al-Djawziyya. So far little is known about this tradition and it certainly deserves a closer study in order to find out how the essentially Hanbalite ideas of Ibn Taymiyya and Ibn Qayyim al-Djawziyya could survive in Hanafite Ottoman religious culture.

Had the *softa* preached in Istanbul, his audience certainly would have consisted mainly of his fellow students. In Egypt this was different. The only larger audience that, for reasons of language, did present itself were the Turkish soldiers serving in Cairo. That many of them responded to his call was due, I believe, to a state of mind on their part that was receptive to radical religious messages linked to practical action and had been brought about by the bloody and psychologically unsettling civil war that had ended only a few months earlier. As the movement developed they began dominating the form of action, and the religious controversy that had triggered off the events was more and more overshadowed by the riotous and mutinous behaviour that Ottoman soldiers so often displayed toward civil authorities.

As is becoming in a basically Ottoman-Turkish episode, the Egyptian *ʿulamaʾ* played their part behind the scenes and did not appear on the stage. Their *fatwa*, however, whose contents and omissions are indicative of the *ʿulamaʾ*'s position in Egyptian society, had its impact on the course of events in the sense that the signatories replaced the dervishes as objects of the movement's hostility. Yet, fortunately for them, a confrontation between them and the *softa's* supporters did not take place. In the end it was the Ottoman judge and his court personnel that had to bear the brunt of the soldiers' aggression.

The trend that I have labelled fundamentalism – and that for equally good reasons may be called revivalism – has its roots deep in Islamic history. Over the centuries, fundamentalist opinions have been expressed by Islamic scholars. Time and again, fundamentalist movements of protest arose arguing that religion had become corrupted and that they wanted to purify it by going back to the revealed sources and ridding it of unwarranted accretions. These movements often had a militant and activist character because they wished to change the world and subject it to the values of a pure and unadulterated Islam based on *tawhid*, the recognition of God's unity and uniqueness, and the *sunna*, the ideal standard of behaviour set by the Prophet Mohammed.

Because of their militancy and their opposition to the existing order, rife, in their view, with *shirk*, polytheism, and *bid'as*, customs contrary to or not authenticated by the Prophet's example, these movements could serve as powerful vehicles of protest, especially in times of social and political crises. Fundamentalist idiom would provide grounds to castigate and assail the religious and political establishments and open vistas of communal salvation in this world once a truly Islamic society had been founded. Fundamentalist movements have emerged all over the Islamic world in various types of societies. Their social carriers also were diverse; in fact, almost any social class or coalition of classes that had cause to oppose the established order could rally behind the banners of fundamentalism.

During the eighteenth and first half of the nineteenth century, there was an upsurge of fundamentalism and numerous fundamentalist movements arose in different regions of the Islamic world. Since, on a world scale, this coincides with an acceleration of European economic, political, and military expansion, it is tempting to hypothesize a causal relationship between the latter and the former phenomena. Wherever fundamentalist movements organized resistance against Western military invasions, this relationship is obvious, although closer inspection reveals that sometimes these movements already existed and flourished before the foreign occupation. In many instances the causal relationship is much more complicated. This is true, for example, for al-Hajj Umar Tal's *jihad* in West Africa which gained momentum by organizing resistance to slave raids by indigenous coastal states for the sake of Western slave trade, and for the Padri Movement in Central Sumatra, which was connected with the growth of indigenous trade as a result of Western commercial expansion and for which the fundamentalist program was meaningful since an increased Islamization of society would create better conditions for traders. Often, however, like in the cases of the Wahhabi movement or the Fulani *jihad*, it is difficult if not impossible to establish a relationship with Western expansion.

It will be evident that the episode analyzed in this chapter belongs to the last category. It is true that Egypt had, to some extent, been affected by the shift in trade routes due to the rise of Western commercial capitalism. Yet, it is impossible to relate the events I have mentioned to these economic changes. It would appear that our movement – which began as a form of protest of a very small group of Turkish religious students and then became the expression of the unsettled psychological mood of Turkish soldiers in Egypt – is unique with regard to its setting (few, if any, fundamentalist movements arose in big cities) and its social carriers. It is linked only to apparently similar movements because of the employment of the same fundamentalist idiom. This chapter shows once more that behind the uniform ideological facade of Islamic fundamentalism, very disparate social and political movements are hidden.

CHAPTER 20

Divine Law or Man-Made Law?

Egypt and the Application of the Shariʿa

1 Introduction*

The application of the Shariʿa has been a central issue in Egyptian politics since the beginning of the seventies. Originally advocated only by Islamic opposition groups, it gained such popularity as a political slogan that the government could not remain passive. As of 1976 there was feverish and largely government-promoted legislative activity with the aim of codifying and, subsequently, applying the Shariʿa. During the first years of the eighties this activity came to a sudden stand-still, again at the instigation of the government. This paper will focus on the various legislative proposals to codify parts of the Shariʿa and on the public debate surrounding its attempted introduction. Special attention will be given to the government's policy in this domain in order to shed some light on the importance of Islam for the legitimacy of the state. In an Appendix a survey will be given of the draft codes of Islamic penal law.

By the end of the last century the Egyptian legal system was largely secularized by the introduction of codes based on French law. Only in the fields of personal status, inheritance, and religious endowments did the Shariʿa remain in force. Before the introduction of French law codes there were some suggestions to base at least the civil code on the Shariʿa as Turkey had done in 1876, when it enacted the *Mecelle*, a codification of Islamic civil law. However, once the choice of French law had been made, opposition against it ceased.

This opposition reappeared, however, in the thirties with the emergence of Islamic political groups and, especially, the Society of Muslim Brethren. Promoting the creation of a truly Islamic state and an Islamic order whose main characteristic would be the application of the Shariʿa, their principal slogan was: "The Koran is our constitution." How they wanted to apply the Shariʿa, however, was not very clear. They were unanimous in their opinion that this did not mean the application of the rules of one single *madhhab* as laid down in the classical books on *fiqh*. But beyond that there was little consensus. When they spoke of creating new legislation, derived through interpretation (*ijtihad*) on the basis of the public interest (*maslaha*) from the general principles of the

* I am indebted to Dr. Enid Hill of the American University in Cairo for valuable criticism and editorial advice.

 | DOI:10.1163/9789004420625_021

Shari'a, they never specified what actually these general principles were. Were they, for example, general legal maxims, ethical principles, or any legal rule to be found in the paramount source of the Shari'a, the Koran?

In spite of the Muslim Brethren's vagueness concerning the general application of the Shari'a, they proposed a number of specific legal reforms to adjust the existing legal order to Islamic ideals. In the field of civil law they advocated the nullification of statutory and contractual interest and of speculative contracts such as insurance. Further, they advocated the prohibition of the sale and consumption of alcoholic beverages and stricter morality laws.

With regard to the enforcement of Islamic penal law, and especially the Koranic injunctions in this domain (the so-called prescribed penalties (*hudud*, sing. *hadd*), they were of different minds. Some of them, extolling the example of Saudi Arabia where Islamic penal law had already been applied for some time, advocated their immediate application, claiming that this would result in greater security and a decrease in crime. Others, however, were of the opinion that the Koranic punishments for theft and robbery ought not to be introduced before the justice and eliminated poverty.[1]

After the revolution of the Free Officers in 1952 and Nasser's ascent to power, the Society of Muslim Brethren was outlawed. A number of them, who had been involved in a plot to assassinate Nasser were condemned to death or to long term imprisonment. Many others fled the country. As a result of the suppression of the Muslim Brethren the issue of the introduction of the Shari'a assumed less prominence. While it is true that immediately after the July Revolution some members of the religious establishment had suggested measures in this direction, these aspirations were nipped in the bud when the revolutionary government announced that it did not advocate any drastic changes in the legal system.[2]

In the seventies Islam re-emerged in Egyptian politics. Egypt's defeat in the June War of 1967 was by many regarded as a demonstration of the failure of secular and socialist nationalism, the leading ideology of the Nasser era. They turned to religion for a solution and, as a result, Islamic opposition groups began to mushroom. These groups argued that the cause of the defeat was the fact that Egyptian society had abandoned Islam as a political ideology and as a guiding principle for its organization. During the Sadat era some of these groups received discreet government support in order to form a counterforce

1 See Richard Mitchell, *The Society of the Muslim Brothers* (London: Oxford University Press, 1969) pp. 240–241, and Jan Brugman, *De betekenis van het Mohammedaanse recht in het hedendaagse Egypte* (Leiden: 1960; printed Ph.D. diss.) p. 150.

2 Brugman, *op. cit.*, p. 135.

to Leftist and Nasserist organizations, especially at the universities. As a result of the government's more favourable attitude towards political Islam, many Muslim Brethren were released from the prison-camps and many others were allowed to return from exile. At the same time the government began using more Islamic symbols and gave Islam more room in politics. For example, Article 2 of the Constitution of 1971 not only laid down that Islam is the religion of the State – a provision also to be found in previous constitutions – but that the principles of the Shariʿa are a principal source of legislation.[3]

In this period the issue of the application of the Shariʿa gained in political importance. With regard to this issue, several tendencies can be distinguished in Egyptian politics. On the one hand there are Islamic political groups varying as to their degree of radicalism. Enforcement of the Shariʿa is a crucial element of their program. The establishment of a political, economic, and social order based on the Shariʿa is in their view the solution to all problems with which Egyptian society has to cope. Therefore they advocate that the Shariʿa be put into practice forthwith since this is the only means of bringing society closer to the Islamic ideals. The most radical Islamic groups regard the existing legislation as null and void, considering it to be in conflict with the Shariʿa and the politicians responsible for its continuance to be unbelievers. Therefore it is permissible, in their view, to use violence against these politicians.[4] More moderate Islamic trends, such as the group of Muslim Brethren organized around the monthly publication *al-Daʿwa*, respect the political and legal system to the extent that they want to change it by legal means. They had – and still have – members and sympathizers in Parliament (*Majlis al-Shaʿb*) who initiated Islamic legislation.

On the other side of the political spectrum we find the adversaries of the application of the Shariʿa, secularized Muslim intellectuals and Copts. Their influence declined during the seventies as a consequence of the increased Islamic impact on politics.

As usual the position taken by the political establishment was between the two extremes. Working within a largely secularized political system which they wanted to maintain, they did indicate nevertheless that they appreciated the importance of Islam as an expression of Egypt's cultural identity and as an instrument which was useful for enhancing the regime's legitimacy. When it

---

3 For the discussion preceding the adoption of this provision, see Joseph P. Kane, "Islam in the New Egyptian Constitution: Some Discussions in Al-Ahram," *Middle East Journal* 26 (1972) pp. 137–149.

4 See e.g. ʿAbd al-Salam Faraj, "al-Farida al-gha'iba," in *al-Fatawa l-Islamiyya min Dar al-Iftaʾ al-Misriyya*, vol. 10 (Cairo: al-Majlis al-aʿla li-l-shu'un al-Islamiyya, 1983), pp. 3765–6.

was feared that the propaganda of the Islamic opposition might endanger this legitimacy, the government was forced to come forward with its own program of enacting legislation according to the Shari'a.

The position of the official religious establishment was very near to that of the government. When it became clear that the political leadership was no longer opposed to the application of the Shari'a, leaders of al-Azhar and its specialists in the Shari'a began enthusiastically to prepare legislative proposals. Their enthusiasm was without doubt prompted by religious zeal, but perhaps also by the prospect of "more jobs for the boys," that is, the graduates of the religious faculties.

2 Legislative Proposals to Enforce the Shari'a

Since 1972 a number of private bills concerning the enforcement of the Shari'a have been introduced in Parliament by members sympathizing with the Muslim Brethren. Only one of these was actually passed. The Speaker and the parliamentary committees provide the government with sufficient possibilities of thwarting any bill it does not want enacted. The most important of these is based on Article 61 of the Standing Orders (*al-La'iha al-dakhiliyya*) of the Parliament. This article stipulates that the Speaker shall refer private bills to the Committee for Private Bills and Complaints (*Lajnat al-iqtirahat wa-l-shakawa*) which must examine whether the bill is in a form to be referred to the appropriate committee.[5] Via this road many bills that displeased the government disappeared into stuffy drawers never to reappear in spite of repeated insistence by those who introduced them. Another expedient used by the government has been to introduce its own proposal on the same issue, thereby blocking the debate on the other bill.[6]

The first private bill, in the field of Islamic penal law, proposed that the amputation of the right hand as a punishment for theft be introduced.[7] A year later, in 1973, a bill was brought before Parliament to make it unlawful for ladies' hairdressing shops to employ male hairdressers since, according to those who introduced the bill, Islam forbids men to touch women who are not their wives or close relatives.[8] It should be noted also that in some strata of popular

5 Mustafa Abu Zayd Fahmi, *al-Nizam al-dusturi al-Misri* (Alexandria: Munsha'at al-ma'arif, 1984) p. 359.

6 I. Altman, "Islamic Legislation in Egypt in the 1970s," *African and Asian Studies*, 13 (1979), pp. 212–13.

7 *al-Da'wa*, vol. 25, n°2 (Aug. 1976).

8 *Ibid.*

consciousness in Egypt ladies' hairdressing shops have a bad reputation and are thought to be places where married women can make contacts for adulterous affairs. Also in 1973 a private bill was introduced to prohibit the consumption, production, and sale of alcoholic beverages. It made an exception, however, for the consumption of alcohol by foreigners in tourist establishments, paid for in hard currency. This bill was finally passed, but in a version so heavily amended that little remained of the intentions of those who introduced it. The law, which came into force on 1 August 1976, forbade the consumption of alcohol only in public places and excepted tourist establishments. It did not distinguish between Egyptians and foreigners.[9] The effect produced by this law is minimal as anyone who has recently visited Egypt will have noticed. In Cairo, even in the small local bars where no tourist usually ventures to go, liquor is served freely.

In the beginning of 1976 two private bills providing for the prohibition of interest were introduced into Parliament. According to the Shariʿa interest on loans is unlawful, but this prohibition was usually circumvented by ingenious legal constructions. As a result of the development of banks and postal saving accounts the discussion on the permissibility of interest was reopened around the turn of the century. The well-known Egyptian reformer Muhammad ʿAbduh issued a *fatwa* to the effect that, according to the Shariʿa, interest on saving accounts was legal. In a series of lectures given in 1912 on the occasion of the intended launching of plans to found a national bank with Egyptian capital, a number of religious scholars argued that the Shariʿa did permit moderate interest, either because such interest would fall outside the scope of the Koranic prohibition of usury (*riba*), or because in contemporary times it had become a necessity. And according to the Shariʿa necessity may make lawful what is forbidden.[10] These notions, however, were not shared by the Muslim Brethren who, since the 1930s, have striven for the outlawing of all interest. The first bill, introduced by *Shaykh* Salah Abu Ismaʿil, a member of Parliament in sympathy with the Muslim Brethren, was in this spirit.[11] It proposed amendment of the Civil Code to make interest illegal and stipulations to the contrary null and void. However, in order not to cut off the supply of capital to banks and business enterprises, the proposal permitted "investment loans" (*qard istithmari*), i.e. risk bearing loans, where the creditor is regarded as a sleeping partner in a commenda partnership (*mudaraba*). This is exactly the legal basis of the Islamic investment companies that are mushrooming in Egypt nowadays.

---

9 Altman, *op. cit.*, pp. 209–212; *al-Ahram* 2–12 1975.

10 Brugman, *op. cit.*, pp. 75, 146.

11 Proposal publ. in *al-Muhamah*, 58 (1978), vol. 3–4, p. 154.

In Abu Isma'il's proposal bank deposits and bank loans are also regarded as "investment loans". Adoption of this proposal would have had drastic consequences for the organization of the Egyptian economy and put a check on foreign investments stimulated by the government within the framework of the Open Door Policy. In order to block this bill, the chairman of the Committee of Constitutional and Legislative Affairs, Gamal el-Oteifi (Jamal al-'Utayfi), at the instigation of the government, laid a counter-proposal before Parliament.[12] At first sight the counter-proposal looked more severe than the proposal itself, making the stipulation of interest not only null and void, but also a criminal offence. On the other hand, however, the sting had been taken out, since the prohibition applied only to loans between private persons. Financial transactions with banks, companies, government institutions and the like would fall outside its scope. By the introduction of this bill, the discussion of the first one was blocked, but el-Oteifi's bill was also not passed. Although it was approved by his committee, it was never discussed in the full Parliament.[13]

The stream of proposals aiming at the enforcement of Islamic legislation have included the following bills:

1. Proposal introduced on 7 January 1976 by Isma'il 'Ali Ma'tuq (Delegate for Qena in Upper Egypt and professor at the Faculty of Arts, Cairo University) to amend some articles in the Penal Code to bring it in line with Islamic penal law.[14] (For a discussion of this proposal, see the Appendix) On 7 March 1976 the bill was referred to the Committee for Constitutional and Legislative Affairs but dropped on the strength of the Standing Orders on 13 July 1977 as a consequence of the introducer's decease.[15]
2. Proposal to collect *zakah*, the Islamic tax. This proposal was referred to the Committee for Economic Affairs on 24 September 1977.
3. Proposal to make it a criminal offence to break the fast in public during Ramadan, introduced in September 1977 by *Shaykh* Salah Abu Isma'il.
4. Proposal of a law "to protect women and society against temptation and perversion". Its aim was to enforce Islamic morality, especially with regard

12 Publ. *ibid.*, pp. 153–4. See also Altman, *op. cit.*, p. 212.

13 Altman, *op. cit.*, p. 213.

14 Published in *Majallat al-Azhar*, vol. 42, n° 2 (Feb. 1976), pp. 128–38; see also *al-Ahram* 8–3 1976 and 11–6 1976 (interview with Ma'tuq). Until his death, he was, with Salah Abu Isma'il who had assisted him in preparing this bill, among those members of Parliament that most energetically devoted themselves to the cause of the enforcement of the Shari'a. See e.g. *al-Ahram* 14–11 1976 and 27–3 1977.

15 Muhammad Salim al-'Awwa, *Fi usul al-nizam al-jina'i al-Islami*. 2nd ed. (Cairo: Dar al-Ma'arif, 1983), p. 32, n. 35.

> to the relations between the sexes in public. Among other things, it laid down that in public transport there ought to be separate compartments for men and women, that a similar separation should exist in University lecture halls, that female students must wear Islamic clothes, that women would not be admitted in certain professions like private secretary or air hostess, that ladies' hairdressing shops where male hairdressers were employed were to be closed, and, finally, that sensual advertising must be removed from the streets.[16]

None of these private bills were ever discussed in the full Parliament.

In the meantime, government policy with regard to enforcing the Shari'a had changed under the pressure of the Islamic opposition.[17] On 20 November 1975 the Minister of Justice inaugurated a committee chaired by the president of the Court of Cassation (*Mahkamat al-Naqd*), and entrusted to it the task of preparing legislation in accordance with the Shari'a. Between 1976 and 1978 this committee produced a number of proposals in the field of penal law.[18] (For a discussion of these proposals, see the Appendix). At the same time an amendment of Article 2 of the Constitution was prepared, laying down that the principles of the Shari'a were "*the* principal source of legislation" and not just "*a* principal source" as in the wording of the original article. This amendment

16 For all these proposals, see *al-Da'wa*, vol. 26, n° 18 (Nov. 1977).

17 Unless otherwise stated in the notes, my source for the preparation of the codification of the Shari'a by the state was the Reports of the Proceedings of Parliament (*Madbatat Majlis al-Sha'b*), Session 61, 20 June 1982, p. 5.

18 These proposals were:
1. *Mashru' qanun hadd al-shurb* of 17–6 1976 in 27 arts;
2. *Mashru' qanun hadd al-qadhf* of 17–6 1976 in 22 arts.;
3. *Mashru' qanun hadd al-hiraba* of 21–6 1976 in 25 arts.;
4. *Mashru' qanun hadd al-sariqa* of 17–2 1977 in 24 arts.;
5. *Mashru' qanun hadd al-zina* of 13–4 1977 in 20 arts.;
6. *Mashru' qanun hadd al-ridda* of 7–5 1977 in 21 arts.;
7. *Mashru' qanun fi sha'n al-jinaya 'ala al-nafs* of 8–6 1977 in 45 arts.;
8. *Mashru' qanun fi sha'n jara'im al-i'tida' 'ala ma dun al-nafs* of 4–5 1978 in 65 arts.
They have been publ. in *Mashru'at qawanin al-qisas wa-l-diya wa-l-hudud al-shar'iyya*. [Taqdim] Muhammad 'Atiyya Khamis (Cairo: Dar al-I'tisam, n.d. [ca 1979]); in Nabil 'Abd al-Fattah, *al-Mushaf wa-l-sayf: sira' al-din wa-l-dawla fi Misr* (Cairo: Maktabat Madbuli, 1984), pp. 141–74 (only the bills n° 1 to 6; it is mentioned here erroneously that these were proposals prepared by al-Azhar); and further in *al-Muhamah*, vol. 60, n° 1–2 (Jan.–Feb. 1980), pp. 212–27 (bill n° 8), *ibid.*, vol. 60, n° 5–6 (May–June 1980), pp. 166–92 (bill n° 1), *ibid.*, vol. 60, n° 9–10 (Nov.–Dec. 1980), pp. 108–46 (bill n° 2), *ibid.*, vol. 60, n° 3–4 (March–Apr. 1980), pp. 164–80 (bill n° 3), *ibid.*, vol. 62, n° 1–2 (Jan.–Feb. 1982), pp. 166–75 (bill n° 7).

was adopted by referendum on 22 May 1980.[19] The government wanted thereby to express a sympathetic concern for making the laws of the state Islamic. However, the practical legal effects of this amendment were not very clear. According to most specialists it was no more than an instruction to the legislative power. Others, however, argued that the new wording of Article 2 implied the nullity of all existing legal enactments conflicting with the Shariʿa.[20]

On 18 December 1978 the Committee established by the Minister of Justice and entrusted with the task of preparing Islamic codes was replaced by a special parliamentary committee. It was expressly instructed to consult the University of al-Azhar, the various faculties of law, and the judiciary. After three and a half years the Committee had drafted six codes[21] which were presented to Parliament on 1 July 1982. These proposals were based on the following principles:

1. In preparing these codes the Committee had not limited itself to the rules and principles of one single *madhhab*; by selecting the opinions of the different *madhhab*s, the Committee could adopt those rules that were most suitable to the requirements of the present time.
2. Every article mentions the rule or the principle from the Shariʿa from which it derives.
3. With regard to modern social relations and financial transactions that are not dealt with in the *fiqh* the Committee has formulated its own rules

19 A proposal to amend the Constitution was introduced by more than one third of the members of Parliament on 17 July 1979. It was debated the first time on 19 and 20 July and then referred to the Committee for Constitutional and Legislative Affairs. It was finally passed by the Parliament on 30 April 1980 and sanctioned by a referendum on 22 May of that year.

20 See e.g. the words of Dr. Muhammad ʿAli Mahjub, Chairman of the Parliamentary Committee for Religious Affairs. He argued that the citizens could invoke the nullity of legal provisions contrary to the Shariʿa and, consequently, to Article 2 of the Constitution (*al-Ahram* 25–5 1980). In the same sense: Jamal al-Din Mahmud, "Qabl an yatimm al-taqnin: kayf yansarif al-qadi wafqan li-l-Shariʿa al-Islamiyya," *Mayu*, 17–8 1981. A contrary opinion, however, was held by Mustafa Kamal Wasfi, Vice-President of the Council of State (*Majlis al-Dawla*). He maintained that the new Article 2 of the Constitution did not have retroactive effect and that an amendment of the Law regarding the Supreme Constitutional Court would be required in order to give citizens the right to invoke the nullity of laws contrary to the Shariʿa (*al-Ahram 30–5 '82*).

21 The Committee had also prepared drafts concerning the *zakah* (the Islamic tax), the banking system, and social insurance. These drafts, however, were not presented to Parliament, since the University of al-Azhar did not want or was not able to give a unanimous advice on the Islamic fiscal and financial system (*al-Ahram* 22–4 1979, 12–3 1982 and 24–6 1982).

in accordance with the necessities of the present, taking care that such rules do not run counter to the provisions and the spirit of the Shariʿa.

4. In order to ensure the continuity of the Egyptian legal system and jurisprudence the Committee has used the established legal terminology.[22]

The six draft codes that the Committee had prepared were the following:[23]

1. A Civil Code (*Mashruʿ qanun al-muʿamalat al-madaniyya*) in 1044 articles. The proposal had adopted many provisions from the Civil Code currently in force, but differed from it in the following ways:
   a. Stipulation of interest is null and void. The *commenda* partnership (*mudaraba*) ensures remuneration for the investment of capital.
   b. Speculative contracts, i.e. contracts whereby, at the time of the agreement, there is uncertainty as to the counter values to be exchanged are null and void. For insurance, which clearly falls under this category, but is also considered a socially and economically necessary institution, a special legal form has been developed, based also on a *commenda* partnership. The purpose of this partnership is to indemnify the partners in case of calamities. The insured are regarded as sleeping partners who participate in this partnership by paying their premiums and, consequently, share in the profits. Thus the contract of insurance is transformed from a speculative contract into a contract of cooperation based on mutual solidarity which is commendable in the Shariʿa.
   c. A number of provisions have been added with regard to abuse of rights, i.e. exercising one's right in a way contrary to the social purpose for which this right has been instituted.
   d. Some provisions have been included to protect weaker parties, e.g. parties that bind themselves by signing printed contract forms.
   e. Rights do not extinguish by negative prescription, but, after fifteen years of acquiescence by the plaintiff, they cannot be enforced anymore since courts are forbidden to hear claims based on these rights.

22 *Madbatat Majlis al-Shaʿb*, Session 70, 1–7 1982, pp. 33–4.

23 These draft codes have been publ. as appendices to Records of the Proceedings of Parliament (*Madbatat Majlis al-Shaʿb*), Session 70, 1 July 1982. They are, however, not included in the normal edition of these Records. I have not been able to obtain permission to consult them in the Library of the Parliament. The information given here is based on the records of the session and, concerning the Civil Code, on the following publications: Sami Mitwalli, "al-Qanun al-jadid li-l-muʿamalat al-madaniyya wafqan li-l-Shariʿa al-Islamiyya," *al-Ahram* 12–7 1982; ʿAbd al-Munʿim Nimr in *al-Ahram* 15–11 and 24–11 1982; and ʿAbd al-Munʿim Faraj, "al-Tanzim al-qanuni li-ʿaqd al-taʾmin fi Mashruʿ al-taqnin al-madani li-ahkam al-Shariʿa al-Islamiyya," *al-Ahram* 6–12 1982.

2. With regard to the law of procedure, two separate codes had been prepared: a Code of Procedure (*Mashruʿ qanun ijraʾat al-taqadi*) in 513 articles, dealing with the law of procedure *sensu stricto* and a Code of Evidence (*Mashruʿ qanun al-ithbat*) in 181 articles.
3. A Penal Code (*Mashruʿ qanun al-ʿuqubat*) in 635 articles, arranged in three chapters: an introductory part, a part dealing with the *hadd* punishments and retaliation for manslaughter and injuries based on the proposals prepared between 1976 and 1978, and a part containing *taʿzir* punishments. This last chapter is largely identical to the Penal Code currently in force.
4. A Code of Maritime Commerce (*Mashruʿ qanun al-tijara al-bahriyya*) in 443 articles.
5. A Code of Commerce (*Mashruʿ qanun al-tijara*) in 776 articles. Since the Shariʿa is silent on many of the topics dealt with in these commercial codes and the existing Egyptian codes were already about a century old, the Committee had sought inspiration from comparable codes recently enacted in other Arab states.

When, in 1975, the government had decided to begin codifying the Shariʿa, the University of al-Azhar did not wish to lag behind. In 1976 the *Shaykh al-Azhar*, ʿAbd al-Halim Mahmud, inaugurated the "High Committee for Amending the Existing Laws in Accordance with the Shariʿa" (*al-Lajna al-ʿulya li-taʿdil al-qawanin al-wadʿiyya bi-ma yutabiq al-Shariʿa al-Islamiyya*). This Committee resolved to start with those laws that were most flagrantly in contradiction with the Shariʿa and, on 28 March 1977, presented a proposal dealing with *hadd* punishments to the Prime Minister, the Minister of Justice and the Parliament.[24] (For a discussion of this proposal, see the Appendix). The Committee found it unnecessary to draw up a totally new Penal Code, since most of the provisions of the Code in force could be regarded as *taʿzir* punishment. The Committee's next project was to purge the Civil and Commercial Codes from provisions contrary to the Shariʿa, such as those on interest and insurance. This project, however, was shelved when the Azhar's advice was sought on the more drastic proposals prepared by the Parliamentary Committee mentioned above. On 15 January 1981 the Azhar informed Parliament that it had approved these proposals. This was the end of the Azhar's independent activities in this field.[25]

---

24 The only text of this proposal I could find is the not entirely reliable translation in Ghali Shoukri, *Egypt: Portrait of a President, 1971–1981* (London: ZED Press, 1981), pp. 443–7. To some extent I could check this translation as al-ʿAwwa, *Fi usul al-nizam al-jinaʾi al-Islami* discusses this draft and quotes a number of its articles.

25 al-Sayyid ʿAbd al-ʿAziz Hindi, "Juhud al-Azhar fi taqnin al-Shariʿa al-Islamiyya al-gharraʾ," *Majallat al-Azhar*, 54 (1981–2), pp. 548–55 and id., "al-Azhar wa-taqnin al-Shariʿa al-Islamiyya," *Majallat al-Azhar*, 55 (1983–4), pp. 866–78.

The six draft codes, presented to Parliament on 1 July 1981, were, on the same day, referred to the Committee for Constitutional and Legislative Affairs in order that it might prepare them for discussion in Parliament. On that occasion, the Speaker, Dr. Sufi Abu Talib, who during the previous years, had put forward much effort for the sake of the application of the Shariʿa, spoke these memorable words:

> Hereby [with the referring of the proposals to the Committee], this venerable House has fulfilled its pledge in record time. In forty months this venerable House has carried out this work, which, God willing, will be everlasting.[26]

One is tempted to conclude that these draft codes did not have God's approval, since eternal life was not granted to them. On the contrary, they were aborted before they were given life. The government had changed its policy with regard to the enforcement of the Shariʿa and was no longer willing to promote the enactment of these proposals. Three factors had contributed to this political *volte-face*. In the first place the government's stand towards the Islamic opposition had hardened. After 1979 the government began to abandon its attempts to render a large part of the Islamic opposition harmless and obtain its support by following policies designed to give greater prominence to Islamic ideals. Particularly after President Sadat's assassination on 6 October 1981, it had sought confrontation. Therefore, there was no longer a need for conciliatory gestures, such as the policy of codifying the Shariʿa. Another factor was fear of sectarian clashes. The publications of the first proposals concerning Islamic penal law had been one of the causes of the confessional disturbances of 1977 and 1978. Sticking to the policy of enforcing the Shariʿa could only increase the tension between Muslims and Copts. Finally there was some apprehension in government circles as to possible repercussions in the sphere of foreign, especially economic, relations.[27] It was to be expected that the American

26 *Madbatat Majlis al-Shaʿb*, Session 70, 1–7 '82, p. 44.

27 During the Parliamentary debate on the issue of enforcing the Shariʿa held in May 1985, both the government and the Islamic opposition brought this issue forward. The government pointed out the importance for Egypt of its economic relations with other countries and the possible adverse effects of the enforcement of the Shariʿa. The Islamic opposition countered this with an historical example from the first years of Islam. One of their representatives, ʿAtiyya Saqr, said:

"When God had barred the pagans from the *Masjid al-Haram* (the Holy Mosque in Mecca), the believers feared that they would suffer heavy losses, which would affect their economic situation. But then God revealed the following verse: "O believers, the idolators

administration would not be sympathetic – to say the least – with the policy of enforcing the Shariʿa which might destroy Egypt's relatively positive image in the United States and affect American domestic support for the enormous amounts that the U.S. government annually pumps into the Egyptian economy as military and civil aid.

As a result of this change of government policy the draft codes were not discussed in Parliament. After many protests by the opposition the Parliament passed a resolution stipulating that it would debate the matter on 4 May 1985, on the occasion of the discussion of the annual report of the Committee for Religious and Social Affairs and Religious Endowments. This report[28] contained a section on the purification of existing laws from provisions contrary to the Shariʿa, but did not mention at all the draft codes that had been prepared. The Committee's recommendation – which no doubt reflected the government's point of view – was that the existing laws must be "gradually and scientifically" (these words are to be found four times in this section) cleared from all provisions conflicting with the Shariʿa. According to the Committee this operation would not entail drastic revisions, since many laws, like the Civil Code of 1949, already contained a great number of provisions deriving from the Shariʿa. The Committee deemed it necessary that the process of purifying the existing laws be coupled with measures designed to create a suitable climate. "It is inevitable," said the report,

> that society be raised gradually to the level of sufficiency and justice and that an end be put to [sensual] stimulation and temptation in their various forms, before we can impose severe and heavy punishments.[29]

In brief, the government, speaking here through the mouth of the Committee, wanted to relegate the operation of making the law Islamic to the background. During the debate, the opposition insisted vigorously that Parliament discuss the draft codes. The Speaker, however, refused this on formal grounds, arguing that these proposals had lapsed since they had not been renewed at the end of the previous session:

---

are indeed unclean; so let them not come near the Holy Mosque after this year of theirs. If you fear poverty, God shall surely enrich you of His Bounty, if He will." (Koran 9:28)." *Madbatat Majlis al-Shaʿb*, Session 74, 4–5 1985, pp. 35 and 16.

28 *Ibid.*, pp. 5–14.

29 *Ibid.*, p. 14.

> I declare emphatically again that there are no bills or proposals of bills [concerning the enforcement of the Shari'a] in charge of this House. Even if something of the sort had been introduced, it would have lapsed upon the expiry of the [previous] session.[30]

3 The Judiciary and the Application of the Shari'a

On the very day of the debate in Parliament the Supreme Constitutional Court (*al-Mahkama al-dusturiyya al-'ulya*) pronounced a judgement on the interpretation of the amended Article 2 of the Constitution, which was perfectly in line with the new government policy with regard the application of the Shari'a. In this case, a debtor, the University of al-Azhar, had asked for a fundamental decision on the constitutionality of interest. The University had been condemned by a lower court to pay a debt it had incurred together, on the strength of Article 226 of the Civil Code, with interest on the amount of the debt at the rate of 4%, starting from the date of the legal action to collect that debt. The debtor refused payment of the interest and appealed to the Supreme Constitutional Court arguing that Article 226 of the Civil Code, which provides for a fixed interest to be paid in case of delay in the fulfilment of an obligation to pay a debt of money, was null and void as it conflicts with the principles of the Shari'a which are, by virtue of Article 2 of the Constitution, the principal source of legislation. The Court rejected the appeal ruling that:

> the limitation provided in Article 2 as amended – to the effect that the Legislator is bound in his choice of sources by the principles of Islamic Law – cannot be made applicable to former legal enactments which were already in force before it was adopted.

However, the Court also denied that:

> the Legislator is freed from all responsibility concerning past legislative enactments, despite their being contrary to the principles of Islamic Law. On the contrary, [Article 2, as amended] imposes on the Legislator, from a political point of view, the duty of purifying the texts of such past legislation and clearing them from any trespass against the said principles.[31]

30 *Ibid.*, p. 35.

31 The Supreme Constitutional Court (which decided on the constitutionally of legal enactments and can void them for unconstitutionality) argued as follows:

In ruling against the automatic application of Article 2 to previous legislation by the judiciary but passing to the Legislator the responsibility of conforming the laws, the Court indicated a position significantly different from that found in a case decided in 1976. In April of that year the Supreme Constitutional Court had ruled that Article 2 of the Constitution implied that conformity with the principles of the Shari'a *was* a criterion for the constitutionality of legislation, *even if this legislation had been enacted before the promulgation of the Constitution*.[32] This was, moreover, *before* the amendment of

---

"(...).

And Whereas it follows the above that only the legal enactments issued after the coming into effect of the obligation to conform to Islamic law are affected, so that, should any such legal enactments be in conflict with the principles of Islamic law, such legal enactments alone would fall in the domain of constitutional illegality;

And Whereas legal enactments which antedated the Amendment are not affected by the obligation to conform; ...

And Whereas His Eminence the Claimant argues that the Amendment of Article 2 of the Constitution necessarily implies that the principles of Islamic law have become legal rules of positive legislation immediately applicable to all former legislation which preceded such Amendment. This in turn implies cancellation of all such positive legislation as may contradict the principles of Islamic law;

And Whereas this view is unacceptable in the light of the Court's ruling indicated above on the true purpose of the said Amendment; ...

And Whereas, to the reasoning set forth above, should be added the argument that if the Founders of the Constitution had specifically meant to incorporate the principles of Islamic law into the Constitution, or if they had meant these principles to be enforced by the Courts which apply the law – without the necessity of formulating such principles in the shape of clearly defined legislative texts which follow the procedures set forth in the Constitution – then they would not have lacked the power to provide so clearly and unambiguously;

And Whereas the plea of His Eminence the Claimant to the effect that the principles of the Shari'a should be directly enforced by the Courts leads to the conclusion that all past legislation which contradicts these principles should be scrapped, despite the fact that such past legislation organizes the various domains of civil and criminal law and governs the social and economic life of the community;

And Whereas such plea also implies the necessity for the Courts to investigate the unformulated rules which have to be applied to the disputes submitted to them in lieu of the cancelled rules;

And Whereas this would lead to contradictions and confusion in the judicial process in a manner which would threaten stability; ...

For the above reasons the Court rejects the Complaint ..."

Publ. in *al-Jarida al-rasmiyya*, vol. 28, n° 20 (16–5 1985); Engl. tr. (from which I have quoted) in *Arab Law Quarterly* (1985), pp. 100–107; commentary by Saba Habachy in ALQ (1986), pp. 239–41.

32 The Supreme Constitutional Court then ruled that the provision in the Shari'a Courts' Ordinance (*La'ihat al-mahakim al-shar'iyya*) which made it possible for the husband who

Article 2 when the Constitution still contained the "weaker" wording which made the principle of the Shariʿa *a* principal source of legislation rather than *the* source. The 1985 decision is rather in line with a judgement given by the Court of Cassation (*Mahkamat al-Naqd*) three years earlier. A lower court had condemned two police officers for assault of a suspect during interrogation. Since the only evidence in this case was the testimony of the victim, the officers appealed against this sentence arguing that it was in conflict with Article 2 of the Constitution because the Shariʿa does not admit the testimony of a victim as evidence in a criminal case. The Court of Cassation dismissed the plaintiffs' appeal on the ground that the principles of the Shariʿa cannot be applied by the judiciary until they have been formulated in precise legal enactments by the Legislator.[33]

The decisions of 1982 and 1985 put an end to the uncertainty as to the current interpretation of Article 2 of the Constitution. Since 1980 there had been courts that, invoking this article, refused to apply provisions in laws which were contradictory to the Shariʿa and advocated its immediate application.[34]

---

refuses to pay his wife's maintenance in spite of being able to do so, to be imprisoned for debt, was constitutional, since this provision was in agreement with the Shariʿa which, the Court expressly stated, is a criterion for the constitutionality of legal enactments. *al-Ahram* 4–4 '76.

33 The Court of Cassation (which, as in French, law, supervises the correct application of legal enactments by the lower courts) stated, among other things, the following:

"And Whereas the provision of Article 2 of the Constitution to the effect that the principles of the Shariʿa are the principal source of legislation has no legal force in and of itself, but is only an instruction to the legislator to take the Shariʿa as a principal source of the laws he enacts;

And Whereas, consequently, the Shariʿa can only be applied after the Legislator has obeyed this instruction and has formulated its exalted principles in well-defined and precise enactments according to which the judiciary must pass judgement as from the date fixed by the Legislative Authority for their coming into force;

And Whereas the opposite view would lead to a blending of, on the one hand, the obligation of the judiciary to enforce the existing legal enactments and, on the other hand, the enactment of legal principles that are incompatible with a precise definition of its jurisdiction, not to mention the fact that the application of the Shariʿa requires that it should be determined which exactly of the manifold conflicting views of the founders of the law schools (*a'immat al-madhahib*), existing with regard to one single case, must be used as a basis for judgements; ..."

al-Ahram 7–4 1982.

34 See in this connection the article by the Chief Prosecutor (*Ra'is al-Niyaba al-ʿAmma*), Mustafa Faraghli [al-Shuqayri], himself a supporter of immediate application of the Shariʿa, entitled "al-Qada' al-Misri wa-qadiyyat tatbiq al-Shariʿa al-Islamiyya," *al-Jumhuriyya* 3–9 1983; and an article on the same issue by Faraj Fawda in *al-Ahram* 3–10 1985.

Usually they would refer the case to the Supreme Constitutional Court to obtain a ruling with regard to the constitutionality of the provisions concerned. In nearly half of the cases I have been able to trace the issue at stake was the lawfulness of interest.[35] Illustrative are the following words, taken from an opinion given by the District Court of Mit Ghamr:

> The Court feels too embarrassed in front of God – be He praised and exalted – to give judgement for the plaintiffs … or even to consider their claim, since this is in reality claiming usury which, in all its forms, is made unlawful in the Shariʿa. This is pointed out by God's words: "O believers, devour not usury, doubled and redoubled." (Koran 3:130)[36]

Most other cases were in the field of penal law. When in certain cases all material and formal requirements for the application of *hadd* punishments, e.g. for theft or drunkenness, were satisfied, some courts ruled that there was a contradiction between the articles concerned in the Penal Code and the Shariʿa, and referred these cases to the Supreme Constitutional Court.[37] Other courts would in such cases state that, in the absence of legal means to enforce the Islamic punishments, they had no choice but to apply the provisions of the existing Penal Code, while urging the Legislator to enforce the Shariʿa without delay.[38]

The application of Islamic penal law as proposed by some courts did not put the defendants in all cases in a worse position. After a serious accident whereby a train had collided with a bus full of passengers resulting in the death of thirteen persons and many more being injured, the driver of the bus and the level-crossing keeper were prosecuted for having caused death and injuries through criminal negligence. During the criminal procedures the victims or their heirs

---

35 *al-Ahram* 20–9 1980 (District Court Giza); *al-Ahram* 25–1 1982 (District Court ʿAbidin, Cairo); Mustafa Faraghli al-Shuqayri, *Fi wajh al-muʾamara ʿala tatbiq al-Shariʿa al-Islamiyya* (Cairo: Dar al-Wafa, 1986), pp. 120–21 (Court of Appeals (*Mahkamat al-istiʾnaf al-ʿali*) Cairo, 13–12 1984); *al-Jumhuriyya* 5–2 1986 (District Court Mit Ghamr); District Court Ismaʿiliyya 25–2 1986 (sentence quashed in appeal; see Court of Appeals, Ismaʿiliyya 5–1 1987; I am grateful to Mr. H. Botje of Cairo who kindly supplied me with a copy of this sentence).

36 The defendant in this case was a former official after whose dismissal a deficit was found in the cash entrusted to him. The service where he was employed and the Ministry under whose authority the service came, claimed the amount of the deficit in addition to the legal interest. *al-Jumhuriyya* 5–2 1986.

37 *al-Ahram* 10–1 '81 (District Court Badrishayn); *al-Ahram* 25–1 1981 (District Court Badrishayn); *al-Ahram* 25–1 1982 (District Court Bani Suwayf); *al-Ahrar* 8–2 1982 (District Court al-Baladiyya), also cited in Shuqayri, *op. cit.*, pp. 134–5.

38 *al-Ahram* 10–1 1981 (District Court Bani Suwayf); Shuqayri, *op. cit.*, pp. 121–29 (District Court al-ʿAyyat, criminal sentence 115/1981); *al-Wafd* 17–2 1985 (District Court al-Fayum), also cited in Shuqayri, *op. cit.*, pp. 135–36.

brought an action for damages. Referring to Article 2 of the Constitution the District Court of Badrishayn ruled that in this case the provisions of the Shariʿa were applicable. Quoting from the bills on Islamic penal law prepared by the government committee, the Court contemplated condemning the defendants to pay blood money (*diya*) to the victims or their heirs, a legal concept which combines punishment and damages. The Court held that in this case these provisions of the Shariʿa were more just than those of the Penal Code and the Code of Penal Procedure, prescribing both imprisonment and damages. In its opinion the Court commented further that, in general, the rules governing payment of blood money are more in harmony with the principle of human equality since the amount is the same for anybody regardless of his descent and status. Nevertheless, the Court did not condemn the defendants, but referred the case to the Supreme Constitutional Court.[39]

Another instance whereby the application of the Shariʿa was advantageous for the defendant can be found in a sentence by the District Court of Suez. The Court ruled that the law which made it possible for repeated offenders and habitual criminals to be given additional punishments such as confinement to a labour camp or restriction of residence, was inapplicable since the Shariʿa does not admit of additional punishments concurrently with the main punishment for the offence perpetrated.[40]

Interestingly, these kind of sentences still occur, even after the decision of the Supreme Constitutional Court of 1985. This means that a small group of judges are prepared, out of religious zeal, to hand down demonstrative sentences which they know will be quashed in appeal,[41] but through which they are able to demonstrate how the Shariʿa can be applied. In doing so these judges certainly have one eye on the legislative power in whose hands the conforming of past legislation to Shariʿa principles now rests.

4 The Public Debate

In this last section I want to focus on recent discussions of the enforcement of the Shariʿa and the arguments used both for and against. My sources are some recently published books written by both advocates and opponents,[42]

39 *al-Ahram* 10–1 1981.

40 District Court Suez, 11–5 1981, sentence publ. in Shuqayri, *op. cit.*, pp. 137–59.

41 I have not been able to ascertain what happened to these judgements on appeal.

42 Advocates: Shuqayri, *op. cit.*; Tawfiq al-Shawi, *Siyadat al-Shariʿa al-Islamiyya fi Misr* (Cairo: al-Zahraʾ li-l-iʿlam al-ʿarabi, 1987); ʿAbd al-ʿAzim Fawda, *al-Hukm bi-ma anzal Allah* (Cairo: Dar al-buhuth al-ʿilmiyya, 1987; in 1980 defended as a Ph.D. dissertation, Kulliyyat Dar al-ʿUlum, University of Cairo, under the title *Salah al-mujtamaʿ fi tatbiq al-Shariʿa*

the records of the Parliamentary debates on the issue, and the articles dealing with the topic that have been published in *al-Ahram* during summer and autumn 1985.

Why must the Shariʿa be enforced? For most faithful Muslims this question is not difficult to answer. Because the supreme sovereignty belongs to God, man must submit to His will, as revealed in the Koran and through the example of the Prophet. The Koran contains many verses urging the believers to administer justice and to govern according to God's revelation. Since the Shariʿa is of divine origin, it is naturally superior to any human law. The principles of the Shariʿa are immutable and cannot, for that reason, become tools in the hands of despotic and tyrannical rulers. For they, like all other Muslims, have to follow the Shariʿa and cannot amend it at their pleasure as rulers can when there is only man-made law. Since the Shariʿa is superior to any other law, it offers solutions to many of the problems with which Egyptian society has to cope, problems which have in large measure been caused by the fact that Egyptian Muslims have turned away from Islam. One of the properties that testifies to the superiority of the Shariʿa is the fact that it is a law suitable to any time and any place. For whereas the principles are fixed and well-established the details can always be adjusted to the needs of a specific society.

Opponents of the application of the Shariʿa point out that the assertion that divine legislation and divine government are necessarily better that human legislation and human government, is not as self-evident as it appears at first sight. The Shariʿa, according to the advocates of its application, consists mainly of very general principles. Deriving concrete and detailed provisions from these principles requires human effort which will become more important as society develops and becomes more complex. As a consequence, one and the same general principle can be elaborated in totally different ways. Take as an example the principle of social justice, which most Muslim thinkers claim is an essential part of Islam. According to some this principle means no more than that *zakah* tax must be collected, part of which to be used to alleviate the needs of the poor, that the ban on interest must be enforced to protect weak debtors, and that the rich must be exhorted to part with some of their riches in favour of the poor and needy. Other Muslim thinkers, however, claim that this principle can only be made operative if the means of production and capital are nationalized so that Islamic state can impose a just distribution

---

al-Islamiyya). Opponents: Faraj Fawda, *Qabl al-Suqut* (Cairo: no. publ., 1985); Fu'ad Zakariyya, *al-Haqiqa wa-l-wahm fi l-haraka al-Islamiyya al-muʿasira* (Cairo: Dar al-fikr, 1986).

of wealth. Such widely divergent interpretations can also be found with regard to the principle of consultation (*shura*) in government. Blue-prints proposed by Muslim reformers to implement this principle range from a rather authoritarian system of government whereby the head of state must consult his subjects or their representatives, but takes the decisions himself, to a system that is all but identical with parliamentary democracy. The various elaborations of these two principles testify to the great impact of non-Islamic ideas upon the interpretation of the general principles of the Shariʿa. Therefore, the opponents of the enforcement of the Shariʿa conclude, the claim that application of the Shariʿa is tantamount to the application of a purely divine law, is unfounded, in view of the great role played by human – and therefore fallible – reasoning.

The Shariʿa's religious foundation is another argument often put forward to prove its excellence. Because Muslims know that they fulfil a religious duty if they observe the rules of the Shariʿa and commit a sin if they act against it, it is claimed that voluntary obedience to the law is much greater in societies where the Shariʿa is enforced than in societies ruled by human laws. The high crime rates in the West are often cited to prove this point, since they are supposedly caused by the fact that in the West offending against the law is not regarded as a sin. In addition to this, defenders of the Shariʿa, in order to underscore its superiority over other systems, often mention the fact that the Shariʿa, as a system of law based on religion, not only coerces people into behaving in certain ways, but also offers guidance in this respect.

Of a different order is the argumentation that the introduction of the Shariʿa is an expression of national independence and the completion of the process of decolonization. This viewpoint considers the prevailing laws to be nearly entirely of European origin and as such not to reflect the notions current in Egyptian society. As evidence, the provisions on sexual morality in the Penal Code of 1937 are quoted. These do not make relations between unmarried adults a criminal offence, which, it is asserted, runs counter to the views on these matters prevailing in Egypt and, moreover, also shows that such Western laws do not pay attention to morality and purity.

Egypt is a country with a substantial non-Muslim minority, the Copts. Those opposed to the application of the Shariʿa often point out that its enforcement will result in an Islamic, religious government instead of a national government and, consequently, in the oppression of the Copts. This will disturb the carefully cherished national unity between Muslims and Copts. Against this, the advocates of its enforcement argue that the Shariʿa guarantees freedom of religion to non-Muslim subjects of the Islamic state and gives them the same rights and obligations as Muslims (thereby, obviously, glossing over the numerous discriminatory provisions to be found in the Shariʿa[43]). They claim, therefore, that the Copts have no justification for being opposed to the introduction of the Shariʿa. The following words of the former *Shaykh al-Azhar*, Muhammad al-Tayyib Najjar, are typical:

> Applying the Shariʿa is applying Islam, the religion of humaneness.... Therefore, the application of the Shariʿa cannot exacerbate those who advocate what is good. In Egypt, we, Muslims and Christians, have been living side by side for a long time, while everyone has enjoyed complete justice and equity since the first period of the Islamic conquest. Therefore, the application of the Shariʿa should not disquiet anyone of our Coptic brethren in our Egyptian society, for all religions proclaim the application of justice in its various forms.[44]

In spite of this and comparable unctuous reassuring statements, the plans to enforce the Shariʿa created alarm in the Coptic community. When the first proposals in the field of penal law (whereby conversion of Muslims to Christianity was made a capital crime) were made public, the Coptic Church organized a conference which was held in Alexandria on 17 January 1977. This conference passed a resolution to the effect that it was unacceptable for the Copts to be governed by the prescriptions of the Koran and Sunna and that this would be contrary to the teaching of Islam itself, in particular the Koranic verse: "There is no compulsion in religion" (Koran 2:256) and also contrary to the fundamental right of freedom as guaranteed by the Constitution.[45]

Opponents of the enforcement of the Shariʿa often insist that its principal element is the application of the *hadd* punishments, and that these are cruel and not in accordance with contemporary notions of penal law. The argument is not entirely unfounded in view of the fact that the Government Committee and the Committee of al-Azhar charged with codifying the Shariʿa both began their activities with preparing an Islamic penal code. Those in favour of applying the Shariʿa parry this attack in two ways. Some maintain that these modern notions of penal law all come from the West and are therefore of no concern to the Muslims. Moreover, they say, these notions are based on excessive concern for the criminal and do not take into account the protection of the victims and

43 For the prescriptions concerning distinctive clothes, the prohibition to mount horses, the ban on building churches and the like, see e.g. Muhammad Amin Ibn ʿAbidin (d. 1836), *Radd al-muhtar ʿala l-durr al-mukhtar* (Bulaq, 1299 H), vol. 3, p. 374 ff.

44 *al-Ahram*, 2–8 1985.

45 For the text of the resolution, see Nabil ʿAbd al-Fattah, *al-Mushaf wa-l-sayf*, pp. 225–27.

society as a whole. Enforcing the *hadd* punishments will act as a deterrent to crime. Others, however, emphasize that the Shariʿa includes more than just *hadd* punishments, and that their enforcement only makes sense if seen as a part of the total package of conforming the legal system with the Shariʿa. Application of the Shariʿa will entail social justice and guarantee for everybody the satisfaction of basic needs. Once this is accomplished, it will be justifiable to impose severe punishments for crimes against property. The introduction of heavy punishments for illicit sexual relations must be preceded by legislation banning from public life all sexual stimuli and temptations, such as certain movies and television programs, and the wearing by women of provocative clothing. When such legislation has taken effect, those who commit sexual offences can no longer be excused.

The standpoint of the political establishment fluctuates between the views of both groups. For reasons explained above, the government has not been prepared, since the beginning of the eighties, to promote the enforcement of the Shariʿa. However, were it to come out clearly against this issue, its credibility and legitimacy with large groups of the population would be openly in question. During the public debate it had to exorcize the ghosts that it had let escape from the bottle during the seventies. The Parliamentary debate of 4 May 1985 made it clear that the proposals for the codification of the Shariʿa had been shelved and the government did not intend to expedite the project of purging existing laws of provisions contrary to the Shariʿa. Since many Egyptians had had high expectations of the plans to revise the legal system in the light of the Shariʿa principles, the government, in order not to alienate large sections of the population, obviously felt the need to mount a public relations campaign and to create understanding for its new stand. During several months many specialists in legal and religious affairs were mobilized to explain the government's new policy in the press. In order to give the campaign the appearance of a serious discussion, some opponents were invited to participate too. During the campaign, it appeared that the leading scholars of al-Azhar, who only a few years previously had enthusiastically embarked on their own project of codifying the Shariʿa, now supported the policy of procrastination that the government had chosen.

The government's first tactical objective was, apparently, to persuade the public that those in favour of immediate enforcement of the Shariʿa were extremists who did not shrink from the use of violence. This was facilitated when a number of persons headed by a certain Hafiz Salama, the imam-preacher of the Nur Mosque in Cairo, announced their plans to hold a "Green March" in June 1985 to emphasize their demand that the Shariʿa be applied forthwith. The authorities refused permission for this demonstration and, when the organizers nonetheless went ahead with their preparations, security troops were brought in to prevent the march. At the same time students at some universities in Cairo demonstrated for the same cause.[46] These events were later strongly exaggerated in the media and represented as extremist disturbances. The words of *Shaykh al-Azhar* Jad al-Haqq ʿAli Jad al-Haqq are typical in this respect:

> There is a group that calls for the immediate application of the Shariʿa with violence, marches, and demonstrations, and there is a group that asks that this be done with patience, without haste, and without violence. Islam has nothing to do with demonstrations and marches.[47]

Keywords in the declarations of the government and its supporters were "gradualness", "carefulness", "preparation of society", and "the scientific approach". Several specialists pointed out that the Prophet Mohammed in his time had also worked gradually, e.g. that the final prohibition of wine had been prepared by revelations of mounting severity upon it, and that his first efforts had been concentrated on creating Islamic Man, then Islamic Society, and, finally, the Islamic State. Before Islamic legislation can be successfully applied, they wrote, the spirit of Islam must permeate Egyptian society through education at home and at school and through the mass-media, so that Egyptian society can develop in an Islamic direction. The old argument, put forward in the 1930s by the Muslim Brethren, is also frequently used, that Islamic penal law must not be enforced until social justice prevails. In this connection one often finds the example mentioned of the Caliph ʿUmar (AD 634–644), who did not apply the *hadd* punishment for theft during a famine. Also recommended is that the government take measures to solve the housing problem so that youths can marry at an earlier age. Only then the enforcement of the *hadd* punishment for illicit sexual relations is justified.

Much research, it is pointed out, is still needed before the Shariʿa can be applied, and it is noted that the Committee which prepared the codification of the Shariʿa did not always come up with "satisfactory results". In the Committee's proposal, for instance, there was a provision requiring a debtor who fails to pay his debt to indemnify the creditor for losses the latter has incurred by not being able to invest his money elsewhere. The present legislation provides that the interest in this case is 4 or 5% in civil or commercial cases respectively. If the

46 *Le Monde* 29–5 1985; for interviews with Hafiz Salama, see *al-Musawwar* 26–6 1985 and *al-Liwa' al-Islami* 24–7 1985.

47 Interview in *al-Akhbar* 13–7 1985.

legislation according to the Shariʿa would be applied, it was pointed out, the position of the debtor might be much worse that it is now. Several specialists made mention of the mistakes that occurred due to the hasty introduction of the Shariʿa in a neighbouring country (they meant the Sudan, of course). Another argument put forward against precipitous action is reflected in the claim that already 94% of the provisions of the prevailing legislation are in harmony with the Shariʿa, with the implication that there should not be undue concern about the remaining 6 %. The formula, however, which lay at the basis of this calculation was never made public.

The discussion on the application of the Shariʿa still continues. Until this moment books and articles pro and contra are being published. However, with the government's change of approach in the beginning of the eighties there is little chance that legislation based on the Shariʿa will be enacted in Egypt in the near future. Nevertheless, in order to ward off the ideological attacks of the Islamic opposition the government will need to use its skills of persuasion if it is to steer a middle course successfully between the Scylla of wide-spread sentiments favouring the application of the Shariʿa and the Charybdis of the undesirable effects that would accompany its enforcement.

Appendix

A Survey of the Legislative Proposals to Enforce the Hadd Punishments[48]

One of the most spectacular parts of the Shariʿa – spectacular by virtue of being most remote from our present-day notions of criminal law – is the parts that deals with *hadd* punishments. For many Muslims, enforcement of these punishments is the symbol and hallmark *par excellence* of a truly Islamic state. This is not only because these provisions are directly rooted in the Koran, but also because their enforcement is regarded as an expression of independence from the West. It is a striking fact that the committees charged with the codification of the Shariʿa started with this part of the law. Three proposals have been published between 1976 and 1978: the private bill introduced by Ismaʿil ʿAli Maʿtuq, the draft code prepared by the Committee of al-Azhar, and the eight draft laws drawn up by the Committee created by the Ministry of Justice and later adopted by the Parliamentary Committee. It is of interest to take a closer look at these proposals in order to see to what extent they conform to the classical doctrine and at what points they differ from one another.

48 For the places where the texts of these proposals have been published, see notes 14, 18, and 23.

The Maʿtuq bill and the government proposals deal not only with *hadd* punishments, but also with *qisas*, retaliation for homicide and injuries. All proposals contain penal provisions based on *taʿzir* (i.e. the right of the ruler and, by virtue of delegation, also the judge to impose punishment for committing undesirable acts) for offences connected with *hadd* crimes and for those cases where a *hadd* crime is indeed proven, but not in a way satisfying the strict requirements of the Shariʿa, viz. confession or the testimony of two – in cases of illicit sexual relations four – male Muslim eyewitnesses of good reputation. In the following I shall set out in detail the way the different *hadd* crimes are treated in the three proposals.

Theft (Sariqa)

The definition of theft is in the Shariʿa is much narrower than in Western systems of law. In the *fiqh* the following elements are mentioned: the taking away by stealth of a movable object with a value higher than a certain minimum (*nisab*), in which the perpetrator has no right of ownership, out of custody (*hirz*, i.e. a properly secured or guarded place). This definition excludes e.g. open robbery (because the stolen good is not taken away by stealth) and embezzlement (because the stolen good is not in a properly secured place). The punishment for theft is the amputation of the right hand and, in case of a second offence, the left foot.

The three proposals follow the classical rules faithfully, with the exception of the Maʿtuq bill which contains an interesting novelty: the first offender is to be punished with 20 to 50 lashes and the caution that the next time his right hand will be cut off (Art. 311). Maʿtuq grounds this on a rather far-fetched interpretation of the Koranic verse: “And the thief, male and female: cut off the hands of both, as a recompense for what they have earned, and a punishment examplary from God.” (Koran 5:38) To be called a thief, Maʿtuq argues, stealing once does not suffice, no more than lying once makes one a liar.[49] The variety of opinions in the classical *fiqh* as to the minimum value of the stolen good is reflected in the proposals: this value is fixed respectively on LE 55 (Government proposal, Art. 1), 2 grams of pure gold (Maʿtuq proposal, Art. 311) and 4,45 grams of pure gold (Azhar proposal, Art. 14). The Maʿtuq proposal mentions apart from theft, some other offences against property, such as embezzlement and wrongful appropriation and makes them, on the basis of *taʿzir*, punishable by flogging instead of imprisonment as provided in the Penal Code (Arts. 314 and 315). Only the Government proposal contains provisions for the execution of the punishment: the hand must be amputated from the wrist by a surgeon in a hospital (Art. 19). It further includes a number of macabre details regarding the manner of punishment if the author is already disabled. In case he has lost his right hand otherwise than as a result of a previous

49 The interpretation was first put forward by Muhammad Abu Zahra, the Egyptian specialist of *fiqh*, recently deceased. See al-ʿAwwa, *op. cit.*, p. 178.

conviction the alternative punishment is five to ten years imprisonment. If the right hand is paralyzed or is missing one or more fingers amputation is still to be carried out (Art. 20). If one of the other limbs is paralyzed or mutilated the thief shall not be condemned to amputation but to five to ten years imprisonment (Art. 20).

Highway Robbery (Hiraba or Qatʿ al-Tariq)

Highway robbery in the Shariʿa comprises a number of related offences, each with its own specific penalty, having in common the element of going out to a public road with the intention of holding up traffic and/or robbing and/or attacking travellers. The penalties mentioned in the Koran (5:33, 34), viz. capital punishment, crucifixion, amputation of hand and foot, and banishment, are applied according to the occurrence of other accompanying acts. If the hold-up only results in the frightening of the passers-by the punishment is banishment or, according to some authorities, imprisonment. In case of robbery without homicide, the perpetrator's right hand and left foot are cut off. If the hold-up ends in homicide, without any property being taken, the culprit will be executed by the sword. If, finally, there is loss of both life and property, the robber will be both "crucified" and "put to death". There is some controversy as to how to combine these two penalties. Some hold that the condemned must first be crucified and then, after some time, put to death. Others argue that crucifixion here means exhibiting the body of the robber after his execution. If the author repents before he is apprehended, the punishment for highway robbery lapses, but not those for other crimes he has committed during the event, such as theft, homicide, or inflicting injuries.

With the exception of some minor details, the proposals follow the classical doctrine. In controversial issues each proposal chose one of the established opinions. With regard to the combined punishment of crucifixion and execution, the Government proposal opted for the interpretation that the robber's body must be exhibited for three days at the most after he has been put to death (Art. 2), whereas the Maʿtuq bill stipulates that the condemned is to be crucified for three days before his execution (Art. 318). The Azhar proposal does not mention crucifixion. The Maʿtuq bill provides that that in case of rape (*hatk al-ʿird*) and indecent assault (*hatk al-ʿird dun al-zina*) during an act of highway robbery the punishment is the same as for robbery with homicide and robbery with the taking of property respectively (Art. 318, pars. 2 and 3). Concerning the amputation, the Maʿtuq bill lays down that the whole arm from the shoulder and the whole leg from the hip must be cut off and that, if one of these is already absent, the left arm and the right foot are to be amputated. This is also the punishment for the second offence (Art. 13 bis), after which the criminal has few opportunities left for deviating from the straight path. The Government proposal is less extreme. Here we find the provision, as in the section on theft, that hand and foot must be amputated by a surgeon in a hospital and that the punishment will be three to fifteen years imprisonment if one of the other limbs is absent or defect.

Illicit Sexual Intercourse (Zina)

The Shariʿa makes unlawful and punishable all sexual intercourse between man and woman, not legalized by marriage or ownership, i.e. the relationship between master and slave girl. If the perpetrator has never had lawful intercourse before, he or she is punished with a hundred lashes and, for the male, banishment or imprisonment. If the culprit has had lawful intercourse before, he or she is then called *muhsan*(*a*), and the punishment is death by stoning. For a conviction in case of unlawful intercourse, the Shariʿa requires stricter proof than for the other *hadd* crimes: the act must be proven by confession (according to some to be repeated four times) or the testimony of four male Muslim eye witnesses of good reputation.

These provisions are essentially adopted in the three proposals. There are, however, some differences on minor points. Article 4 of the Government proposal stipulates that the requirement for applying the heavier punishment, *ihsan* (i.e. being a *muhsan*), is that the person be married, whereas in the classical theory it suffices to have had lawful intercourse, regardless of whether the bond legalizing intercourse still exists or not. The Maʿtuq bill does not define the notion of *ihsan*, but the new interpretation, which was first put forward by the reformer Muhammad ʿAbduh, is mentioned in the memorandum attached to it.[50] In the traditional *fiqh* there is controversy on the question of whether homosexual intercourse and anal intercourse between man and woman (*liwata* for both notions) must be regarded as falling under the *hadd* crime, or are to be punished as separate crimes on the basis of *taʿzir*. The Azhar proposal opts for the first view (Art. 2, Sec. b), whereas the other proposals regard sodomy as a distinct crime to be punished, on the basis of *taʿzir*, with forty to ninety lashes and, in case of second offence, death (Maʿtuq bill, Art. 270), or forty lashes combined with three to seven years imprisonment (Government proposal, Art. 16). The classical rules of evidence have been adopted in the three proposals. For the sake of completeness the Maʿtuq bill adds two modes of proof, both also known in classical *fiqh*: pregnancy of an unmarried woman (controversial in classical theory since, according to most authorities, her statement that intercourse had happened against her will must be accepted without further evidence) and the wife's failure to swear a fivefold counter-oath after her husband has sworn four times that she has committed adultery, a procedure known as *liʿan* (Art. 272). The Azhar proposal provides that in case of necessity the testimony of female witnesses can be admitted whereby it takes the testimony of two women to replace that of one man (Art. 21, Sec. 2 in conjunction with Art. 3). Both the Maʿtuq bill and the Government proposal contain a number of new sexual crimes or impose more severe punishments on crimes already mentioned in the Penal Code. Maʿtuq specially seems to have been a staunch supporter of flogging.

---

50 *Ibid.*, p. 226.

False Accusation of Illicit Intercourse (Qadhf)

If someone accuses another of having had illicit sexual relations without being able to furnish the evidence required for a conviction, he is liable to be punished with eighty lashes and, in addition, with the loss of the right to bear testimony in court. There is some difference of opinion among the classical authorities as to the question of whether the crime can be prosecuted directly or only after the victim has lodged a complaint. The classical provisions are adopted in the three proposals, whereby both the Government and the Azhar proposal stipulate that prosecution is conditional upon the victim's complaint. Maʿtuq has included in his bill also a number of offences connected with defamation, to be punished with flogging.

Drinking Wine (Shurb al-Khamr)

The Koran forbids Muslims to drink wine. Tradition (*hadith*) has fixed its punishment at forty or eighty lashes. Opinions vary with regard to other alcoholic beverages and drugs. Some authorities hold that these must be equated to wine, whereas others maintain that their consumption can only be made punishable on the basis of *taʿzir*, unless drunkenness results, in which case the *hadd* punishment applies. Some argue that the consumption of alcoholic beverages other than wine is allowed in quantities that do not produce inebriation.

This variety of opinions is reflected in the three proposals. Following the classical doctrine, Maʿtuq has made wine-drinking a punishable act for Muslims only, unlike the other proposals that tend to apply this prohibition to non-Muslims also. In the memorandum accompanying the Government proposal, the Bible is quoted extensively in order to prove that in Judaism and Christianity wine-drinking is actually also unlawful. The Maʿtuq bill makes a distinction between wine and other alcoholic drinks and regards as equivalent to the latter all drugs mentioned in the Unified International Convention of New York regarding drugs (Art. 323). The drinking of wine in any quantity whatsoever and drunkenness or intoxication caused by other alcoholic beverages or drugs are to be punished as a *hadd* crime with eighty lashes (Art. 324). On the basis of *taʿzir*, then, the consumption of these other alcoholic drinks or drugs in quantities that do not produce intoxication, is punishable with fifty lashes (Art. 325). Muslims attending a drinking bout without drinking themselves are liable to be punished with ten to twenty lashes (Art. 326). Neither the Azhar nor the Government proposal distinguishes between wine and other alcoholic beverages. The consumption of any alcoholic drink in any quantity, however small, is considered a *hadd* crime to be punished with forty lashes (Azhar proposal, Art. 23; Government proposal, Art. 2). Apart from making the consumption of alcoholic drinks unlawful, all proposals contain provisions against their production and sale. The Government proposal, finally, stipulates that additional penalties can be imposed such as suspension or withdrawal of the offender's driving licence or his confinement to a clinic for alcoholics (Art. 21).

Apostasy (Ridda)

According to the Shariʿa a Muslim who, by unequivocal words or acts, renounces his religion, must be put to death unless he repents and returns to Islam. He is given respite in order to consider the matter. Some authorities hold that female apostates are not to be put to death but imprisoned for life, unless they repent. All proposals make apostasy a capital crime following the classical doctrine. The Maʿtuq bill has opted for the opinion that women are to be excepted from capital punishment and lays down that female apostates are to be banished (Art. 160). The respite given to the apostate to consider repentance and return to Islam is sixty days in the Azhar proposal (Art. 33), thirty days in the Government proposal (Art. 1), and three days in the Maʿtuq bill (Art. 160).

From the foregoing it is clear that the three legislative proposals follow the classical rules of the Shariʿa very closely. The issues on which the three proposals differ from one another are in general also controversial in the traditional doctrine. Only on some minor points do they bring forward new interpretations, but it would not seem that any of these were meant as steps towards the modernization of Islamic penal law. In fact, the reverse is the case. Especially the Maʿtuq bill and the Government proposal testify to a tendency on the part of the authors to expand the application of corporal punishment outside the sphere of the *hadd* crimes.

SECTION 2

Islamic Law in General

CHAPTER 21

Apostasy in Islam

with G.J.J. de Vries

In the first centuries of Islam, the Islamic legal scholars elaborated a complex set of rules pertaining to the legal status of those Moslems, who gave up their religion, the apostates. These rules belong to the sphere of penal as well as civil law.[1] This doctrine remained valid until, in the latter half of the 19th century, punishment for apostasy fell into desuetude, though it was almost nowhere expressly abolished. At the same time the principle of freedom of religion was gaining ground in the Moslem world. These two factors compelled Moslem thinkers to reconsider the doctrine of apostasy (or to reinterpret the principle of freedom of religion). However, in the sphere of civil law, the rules concerning the apostate are still being applied and seldom is the problem raised whether these rules are compatible with the constitutionally guaranteed freedom of religion. The first part of this article is an *expose* of the classical prescriptions pertaining to apostasy, according to the four orthodox schools (*madhahib*) and

1 For general literature on apostasy see: Muhammad Abu Zahrah, al-*ʿUqubah*. al-Qahirah: Dar al-Fikr al-ʿArabi, n.d., 695 p.; pp. 192–208. ʿAbd al-Qadir ʿAwdah, *al-Tashriʿ al-djinaʾi muqaran^{an} bi-al-qanun al-wadʿi*. Bayrut: Dar al-Kitab al-ʿArabi, n.d., 2 vols.; vol. 1 pp. 534–8, vol. 2 pp. 706–30. Ahmad Fathi Bahnassi, *La responsabilité criminelle dans la doctrine et la jurisprudence musulmanes*. Tr. par Mohammed A. Ambar. Rev. par Ahmad Ahmad Moukhtar. [Caire] Le Conseil Supérieur des Affaires Islamiques, 1969, 332 p.; pp. 104–37. Omer Nasuhi Bilmen, *Hukuk-i Islamiyye ve Istilahatı Fıkhiyye Kamusu*. Istanbul: Istanbul Universitesi Hukuk Fakultesi, 1949–52, 6 vols.; vol. 3 pp. 474–502. W. Heffening, *Murtadd*. In: EI[1], vol. 3 pp. 795–7; SEI, pp. 413–4. *Mawsuʿat Djamal ʿAbd al-Nasir fi al-fiqh al-Islami*. al-Qahirah: al-Madjlis al-Aʿla li-al-Shuʾun Islamiyyah, 1382: vol. 4 (1389) pp. 252–73. S.A. Rahman, *Punishment of Apostasy in Islam*. Lahore: Institute of Islamic Culture, 1972, 144 p. F.H. Ruxton, *The Convert's Status in Maliki Law. Moslem World* 3 (1913) pp. 37–40. Eduard Sachau, *Muhammedanisches Recht nach Schafiitischer Lehre*. Stuttgart & Berlin: W. Spemann, 1897, 879 + 27 p.; *passim*, see index. Nuʿman ʿAbd al-Raziq al-Samarraʾi, *Ahkam al-murtadd fi al-Shariʿah al-Islamiyyah*. Bayrut: Dar al-ʿArabiyyah, 1968, 291 p. David Santillana, *Istituzioni di diritto musulmano malechita con riguardo anche al sistema sciafiita*. Roma: Istituto per l'Oriente, [1926, 1939], 2 vols.; vol. 1 pp. 167–71. Samuel M. Zwemer, *The Law of Apostasy. Moslem World* 14 (1924), pp. 373–91. Id., *The Law of Apostasy in Islam*. London: Marshall Bros., 1924, 164 p. In India and Pakistan a few books dealing with the question of capital punishment for apostasy appeared in Urdu. These, however, we could not consult. Cf. Rahman, *Punishment*, pp. 143–4.

 | DOI:10.1163/9789004420625_022

the Shi'ites. From this description we have excluded those subjects that touch upon the ritual (*'ibadah*) or that are nowadays of small importance, in practice as well as in theory, like for instance the legal status of the apostate's slaves and his penal and civil responsibility for crimes and torts. In the second part we shall examine the situation of the apostate in modern Islam, both from the practical as from the theoretical point of view. This part contains sections on the definition of apostasy, the present-day legal status of the apostate, modern opinions on this topic and finally how the complex relationship between the doctrine of apostasy and the principle of freedom of religion is perceived in contemporary Islam.

1 The Classical Doctrine

1.1 *The Legal Definitions of Apostasy and the Apostate*[2]

Riddah or apostasy is defined as "turning away from Islam" (*al-rudju' 'an din al-islam*) or "severing the ties with Islam" (*qat' al-islam*). By the *murtadd* or apostate is understood the Moslem by birth or by conversion, who renounces his religion, irrespective of whether or not he subsequently embraces another faith.[3] Apostasy is materialized by "expressions of unbelief", specified as words

2 Ibrahim al-Badjuri, *Hashiyah 'ala sharh* Ibn Qasim al-Ghazzi. al-Qahirah: 'Isa al-Babi al-Halabi, 1340 H, 2 vols.; vol. 2 pp. 263–5. Muhammad Ibn 'Arafah al-Dasuqi, *Hashiyah 'ala al-sharh al-kabir.* al-Qahirah: 'Isa al-Babi al-Halabi, n.d., 4 vols.; vol. 4 pp. 301–3. Ahmad Ibn Mahmud al-Hamawi, *Ghamz 'uyun al-basa'ir sharh al-ashbah wa-al-naza'ir* li-Ibn Nudjaym. Istanbul: Dar al-Tiba'ah al-'Amirah, 1290 H, 2 vols.; vol. 1 pp. 288–90. Abu 'Ali Muhammad Ibn Muhammad al-Hattab, *Mawahib al-Djalil li-sharh mukhtasar* Khalil. Tarabulus (Libiya): Maktabat al-Nadjah, n.d., 6 vols. (repr. of the 1329 H. Cairo ed.); vol. 6 pp. 279–80. Nadjm al-Din Dja'far Ibn Muhammad al-Hilli, *Shara'i' al-Islam fi masa'il al-halal wa-al-haram. Tahqiq Muhammad Taqi al-Hakim.* al-Nadjaf: Matba'at al-Adab, 1389/ 1969. 4 vols.; vol. 4 p. 183. Muhammad Amin Ibn 'Abidin, *Radd al-muhtar 'ala al-durr al-mukhtar.* Bulaq: Dar al-Tiba'ah al-Amiriyyah, 1299 H, 6 vols.; vol. 3 pp. 391–4. Id., *Madjmu'at al-rasa'il.* Istanbul: Der Sa'adet, 1325 H, 2 vols.; vol. 2 p. 284. Muwaffaq al-Din 'Abd Allah Ibn Ahmad Ibn Qudamah, *al-Muqni'*. 2nd impr. al-Qahirah: al-Matba'ah al-Salafiyyah, 1382 H, 3 vols.; vol. 3 pp. 514–6. Abu 'Ali Muhammad Ibn Yusuf al-Mawwaq, *al-Tadj wa-al-iklil li-mukhtasar* Khalil. Printed in the margin of al-Hattab's commentary; vol. 6 pp. 279–80. Muhyi al-Din Abu Zakariya' Yahya Ibn Sharaf al-Nawawi, *Minhadj al-talibin.* Ed. & tr. by L.W.C. van den Berg. Batavia: Imprimerie du Gouvernement, 1882–3, 3 vols.; vol. 3 p. 205. 'Abd al-Rahman Ibn Muhammad Shaykhzadeh, *Madjma' al-anhur sharh multaqa al-abhur.* Istanbul: Dar al-Tiba'ah al-'Amirah, 1302 H, 2 vols.; vol. 1 pp. 626, 629–37.

3 Malikite doctrine attaches particular importance to the *murtadd's* profession of Islam prior to his apostasy. They define *riddah* as *kufr ba'd Islam taqarrar:* "unbelief (of the Moslem whose) Islam has been established beyond doubt". It is equally stated, that this Islam needs to be evident in both *qawl* and *'amal*; a person who embraced the faith by merely pronouncing the

implying unbelief, deeds implying unbelief or, according to Shafiʿite doctrine, the mere intention of unbelief. The apostatical words can be either explicit, *viz.* solemnly abjuring Islam, or implicit, *viz.* utterances incompatible with the theological consensus (*idjmaʿ*) or with the axiomatic articles of faith (*ma ʿulima min al-din darurat^an^*).[4] General rules providing criteria for the practical admissibility of these expressions have not been constructed, but examples of sayings and acts considered to imply unbelief and, therefore, constituting *riddah* are abundant.[5] An extensive collection is given by the Hanafite scholar Shaykhzadeh in his book "*Madjmaʿ al-anhur*" (I, pp. 629–37). His classification is quoted below; the examples listed there are more an anthology.

(*a*) *Relating to Allah:* to deny Allah's divinity; to conceive of Allah as a woman or a child; to attribute partners to Allah; to hold Jesus for the son of Allah or to conceive of Allah as part of a trinity; to deny Allah's unity or one of his divine qualities. (*b*) *Relating to prophets and angels*: to deny the prophethood of Muhammad; to assert that prophets are free of error; to consider oneself a prophet; to assert that all animal species have their specific prophets; to declare that the Angel of Death Azraʾil does not always correctly fulfil his task and occasionally picks the wrong people. (*c*) *Relating to the Koran, pious formulas* (*adhkar*) *and ritual prayer* (*salah*): to repudiate some of the Scriptures; to add or to omit koranic verses; to assert the createdness of the Koran; to translate the Koran into for instance, the Persian language; to utter the "*bismillah*"-formula while raising the wineglass or throwing the dice at backgammon. (*d*) *Relating to science* (*ʿilm*): to ridicule scholars; to address scholars in a derisive manner as by the diminutive *ʿuwaylim*; to reject the validity of the *Shariʿah-courts*; to prefer an ignorant ascetic (*zahid djahil*) to a sinful scholar (*ʿalim fasiq*). The more miscellaneous expressions of unbelief may be illustrated by the following examples: to pay respect to a non-moslem; to celebrate *Nawruz* (the Iranian New Year); to assert one's belief in transmigration or in the uncreatedness of the world.[6] A detailed discussion within the *madhahib* on the question whether

---

shahadah without conforming to religious orthopraxy (such as the daily *salah's*) would not be considered qualified to perform a legally valid act of apostasy. Cf. Mawwaq in the margin of Hattab: *Mawahib al-djalil.* VI, pp. 279–80.

4 Not all legal matters covered by *idjmaʿ* are considered "axiomatic articles of faith". Agreement may exist on, for instance, subordinate questions of the law of inheritance, while rules of such limited scope are not thought to belong to the unquestionable axioms of religion.

5 There exist several treatises exclusively dealing with words and acts constituting unbelief. For an enumeration of those works, see al-Samarraʾi, *op. cit.*, p. 116.

6 Certain expressions may carry an ambivalent meaning. If their contents admit several interpretations, Hanafite theory acknowledges only that one, which does not constitute *riddah.* Cf. Shaykhzadeh: I, p. 626.

the practice of magic arts constitutes apostasy has not resulted in a *communis opinio*. The Moslem who states his intention to apostatize at a later point in time, is an apostate at the very moment of his announcement. Sayings not considered to reflect the speaker's inner conviction, such as words spoken in jest, may equally entail *riddah* (as stated in the Koran.[7]

Not only the act of apostasy is subject to certain conditions in order to be legally valid, but also with regard to the perpetrator (*murtadd*) specific qualifications have been laid down. He can perform a legally effective act of *riddah* only out of free will (*ikhtiyar*), at an adult age (*baligh*), being *compos mentis* (*ʿaqil*), and, as emphasized by the Malikite school, after his unambiguous and explicit adoption of Islam (cf. note 3).

1.2 *The Legal Consequences of Apostasy*

1.2.1 Penal Law[8]

The punishment laid down for apostasy is the death penalty.[9] The opinion that this punishment constitutes a *hadd* or "restrictive ordinance" (the fixed punishment for crimes against religion which have been forbidden or sanctioned by punishment in the Koran) is contested by Hanafite and Shafiʿite lawyers. Hanafite theory excludes some categories from capital punishment; although qualified to perform a valid act of *riddah* they will not face its ultimate consequence: (*a*) *Women* are "kept in hostage" instead. They shall be beaten every three days in order to effect their return to Islam. To justify this exception Hanafite scholars adduce a tradition according to which the prophet disapproved of the killing of females.[10] It was also argued, that because of her

7 Cf. K 9:65–6 (…) *Qul a-bi-Allah wa-ayatih wa-rasulih kuntum tastahziʾun.* (66) *La taʿtadhiru qad kafartum baʿd imanikum* (…).

8 Burhan al-Din ʿAli Ibn Abi Bakr al-Marghinani, *Al-hidaya sharh bidayat al-mubtadiʾ*. al-Qahirah: Mustafa al-Babi al-Halabi, n.d., 4 vols.; vol. 2 p. 165.
Badjuri: 2, pp. 265–6. Dasuqi: 4, pp. 304–6. Ibn Qudamah: 3, p. 516; 519–21. Shaykhzadah: 1, p. 263. Ibn ʿAbidin: *Radd al-muhtar* 3, p. 394ff.; 403; 412–3; 420. Id.: *Madjmuʿah* 1, p. 315 and 2, p. 284. Hilli 3, p. 183ff. Hattab 6, p. 281. Mawwaq 6, pp. 281–2. Hamawi 2, p. 289. Nawawi 3, p. 208.

9 The sentence is to be executed by the sword of the *Imam* or his lieutenant. Other ways of putting the apostate to death (such as burning, drowning, flaying, impaling or breaking the bones) are not admitted. The Mamluk sultan Baybars is reputed to have introduced these disapprovable varieties; cf. Badjuri, *l.c.* Beating the apostate to death with clubs is recommended by the Shafiʿite scholar Ibn Suraydj: this prolonged manner of execution would leave the apostate more opportunity to revoke his *riddah*. Cf. al-Mawardi, *al-Sultaniyyah wa-al-wilayat al-diniyyah.* 2nd impr. al-Qahirah: Mustafa al-Babi al-Halabi, 1386/1966, 264 p.; p. 56.

10 When Rabah ibn Rabiʿah once rode out with the Messenger of Allah, he and the companions of the Messenger of Allah passed by a woman who had been killed. The Messenger

physical disposition the female apostate could hardly be expected to pose a threat to the Islamic state (the *ratio*, according to the Hanafite school, for the execution of *murtadds*). Finally, a woman's submissiveness to her husband was considered to exclude a fully independent judgement on her part, and to render her thus not fully responsible. Shiʿite law equally forbids the execution of female apostates and imposes solitary confinement instead during which they shall be beaten at the hours of the *salah*. (*b*) *Hermaphrodites*. (*c*) "*Discriminating minors*", i.e. minors capable of exercising responsible judgement. Although entailing no death sentence, their acts of *riddah* are deemed legally valid by the Hanafites; according to the remaining schools, no minor is qualified to produce an acceptable apostasy, whether he be "discriminating" or not. (*d*) *Converts to Islam* when substantial doubts exist regarding the validity of their conversion (like those having adopted Islam under force,[11] in a state of drunkenness, as an infant independent of the parents, or when the conversion was testified by unreliable witnesses).

The Malikite school equally recognizes the requirement of *husn al-islam:* prior to his apostasy the *murtadd* needs to have been "a good Moslem" (cf. note 3). The other schools, however, make no such distinctions. They advance another tradition ("If someone changes his religion, then kill him"[12] which they interpret as leaving no room for penal differentiation.[13] The legal validity

of Allah stopped and said: 'She was not capable of fighting'. Then he looked at the face of the men and said to one of them: 'Catch up with Khalid ibn al-Walid [and tell him] that he should not kill children, serfs and women.'" Cf. Abu Dawud: *djihad*, 111; Ibn Madjah: *djihad*, 30; *Musnad* Ibn Hanbal II, 110; III, 488; IV, 178.

11 Goldziher relates the case of Maymuni (Maimonides) who during his residence in Spain was compelled to adopt the Islamic faith. When he afterwards assumed leadership of the Jewish community in Egypt, the zealous Moslem Abu al-ʿArab accused him of *riddah*. His adoption of Islam, however, was considered involuntary and Abu al-ʿArab's charge was consequently invalidated. Goldziher also quotes the legal opinion delivered by the Mufti of Constantinople, acquitting the Maronite emir Yunus of a similar charge on similar grounds. Cf. I. Goldziher. *Vorlesungen über den Islam*. Darmstadt: 1963, p. 310.

12 *Man baddal dinahu fa-'qtuluhu*. Cf. Bukhari: *djihad*, 2; Muslim: *hudud*, 1; Tirmidhi: *huhud*, 25; Nasaʾi: *tahrim*, 14; Ibn Madjah: *hudud*, 2; *Musnad* Ibn Hanbal: I, 2, 7, 282, 283, 323 and V, 231. The following hadith is equally invoked: *La yahill dam imriʾ muslim illa bi-ihda thalath: kufr baʿd iman wa-zina baʿd ihsan wa-qatl nafs bi-ghayr nafs*. Cf. Bukhari: *diyat*, 6; Muslim: *qasamah*, 25, 26; Abu Dawud *hudud*, *1*; Tirmidhi: *hudud*, 15; Nasal: *tahrim*, *5*, *11*, 14; Darimi: *siyar*, 11; *Musnad* Ibn Hanbal: I, 61, 63, 65, 70, 123, 382, 428, 444, 465 and VI, 181**, 214. Finally, reference is made to the koranic *ayah* 9:5 (*fa-'qtulu al-mushrikin*) and all other verses in which the killing of unbelievers is declared to be imperative.

13 In order to protect the *foetus*, however, certain precautions are made regarding female apostates. Malikite theory prescribes an adjournment of the execution to determine

of *riddah* thus having been established, the sentence is not passed on the apostate immediately. He is invited to repent (*istitabah*) and reembrace his former faith. The orthodox schools acknowledge the possibility of revocation and repentance (*tawbah*). The Shiʿites only do so with regard to an apostate, born an unbeliever. With the exception of the Hanafites, all scholars even agree, that it is obligatory to exhort the apostate to repent during a certain period or a specific number of times.[14] At the same time, some categories, like magicians (*suhhar*), treacherous heretics (*zanadiq*) and recidivists are excluded from *istitabah.* The sincerity of their return to the faith cannot be established with reasonable certainty and their apostasy is considered legally irrevocable.

1.2.2 Civil Law[15]

The apostate remains legally entitled to his property. His rights to dispose of it, however, are in abeyance (*mawquf*), pending his repentance. Upon returning to Islam he is fully reestablished in his rights. The legal effects of the apostate's acts are also suspended. If he fails to repent and dies as an unbeliever, his acts are legally void;[16] if he readopts the faith, they are considered to have been legally valid from the beginning and without interruption. According to the Hanafites, the female apostate remains legally capable and in full possession of

---

whether the *murtaddah* is pregnant. If so, she will be put to death only after delivery. Cf. Dasuqi, 4, p. 304.

14 Reference is made to K 16:125 (*Udʿu ila rabbika*).

15 Ibn ʿAbidin: *Radd al-muhtar:* II, 539–40 and III, 414–5, 417, 420. Mawwaq: VI, 282, 284; Nawawi: II, 209–10, 243, 349–50 and III, 209; Ibn Qudamah: II, 450 and III, 68.522; Marghinani: II, 165–6; Hilli: II, 294, 297–8 and IV, 11–2, 183–4; Dasuqi: II, 270 and IV, 486; Hattab: VI, 282; Badjuri: II, 127–8, Secondary literature not mentioned in note 1:

ʿUmar ʿAbdallah, *Ahkam al-mawarith fi al-Shariʿah al-Islamiyyah.* 4th enl. and rev. impr. al-Qahirah: Dar al-Maʿarif, 1385/1966, 408 p.; pp. 91–9. Muhammad Abu Zahrah, *al-Ahwal al-Shakhsiyyah.* al-Qahirah: Matbaʿat Mukhaymar, n.d. [ca. 1957], 543 p.; pp. 296–7. K.N. Ahmed, *The Muslim Law of Divorce.* Islamabad: The Islamic Research Institute, 1972, 1107 p.; pp. 793–813. Neil B.E. Baillie, *A Digest of Moohummudan Law.* 4th impr. Lahore: Premier Book House, 1965, 2 vols.; *passim,* consult indices to both vols. ʿAbd al-Rahman al-Djaziri, *Kitab al-fiqh ʿala al-madhahib al-arbaʿah.* 5th impr. al-Qahirah: al-Maktabah al-Tidjariyyah al-Kubra, n.d., 4 vols.; vol. 4, pp. 223–37. Ahmad al-Husari, *al-Nikah wa-al-qadaya al-mutaʿalliqah biha.* al-Qahirah: Maktabat al-Kulliyyah al-Azhariyyah, 1387/1967, 538 p.; pp. 455–64. [Qadri Pasha], *al-Ahkam al-sharʿiyyah fi al-ahwal al-shakhsiyyah ʿala madhhab al-imam Abi Hanifah al-Nuʿman.* al-Qahirah: Matbaʿat al-Saʿadah, 1327 H, 110 p.; arts. 303–9, 587. Muhammad Mustafa Shalabi, *Ahkam al-mawarith bayn al-fiqh wa-al-qanun.* al-Iskandariyyah: al-Maktab al-Misri al-hadith, 1967, 443 p.; pp. 92–9. ʿAbd al-Rahman al-Sabuni, *Mada hurriyyat al-zawdjayn fi al-talaq.* 2nd enl, and rev. ed. [Bayrut:] Dar al-Fikr, 1968, 2 vols.; vol. 2 pp. 967–74.

16 Cf. K 2:217: *Wa-man yartadid minkum ʿan dinih fa-yamut wa-huwa kafir fa-ulaʾika habitat faʿmaluhum fi al-dunya wa-al-akhirah.*

her rights to dispose of her property, this in accordance with their view that she is not to be put to death. Within the Hanafite school Muhammad al-Shaybani (d. 805) and Abu Yusuf (d. 798) hold that this rule applies to the male apostate as well. They compare him with a criminal awaiting his execution, who does not lose his legal capacity either. The other schools compare him with a *harbi* or enemy alien (a non-Moslem not belonging to one of the "tolerated" religions and not protected by treaty of armistice), who cannot legally hold property.

The apostate lacks the capacity to inherit, even from those whose co-religionist he has become. This demonstrates that the apostate's exclusion from the right to inherit goes beyond the rule that difference of religion forms a bar to inheritance. His own estate falls upon his death to the *Bayt al-Mal* or Public Treasury as it has become *fay'* (enemy property "returning" to the Islamic Treasury without warfare as distinct from *ghanimah* or booty taken from the enemy after a military victory). Hanafite legal theory regards the apostate's flight to the *Dar al-Harb* (enemy territory) legally as his death and distinguishes, with regard to the male apostate, between property acquired before the act of apostasy and property acquired after it. The first part of his estate passes to his Moslem heirs, for the Hanafites regard as crucial for the application of the rules of inheritance not the actual moment of his decease, but the moment of the act that necessitated his execution. At that moment, the moment of the act of apostasy, he was technically still a Moslem. The other part becomes *fay'* and falls to the Public Treasury.[17] The estate of the female apostate passes, according to Hanafite law, entirely to her Moslem heirs. The Shi'ites and the Hanafite scholars al-Shaybani and Abu Yusuf hold that all the apostate's property goes upon his death to his Moslem heirs according to the normal rules of succession.

Upon apostasy of one or both partners the marriage contract expires immediately and without need for judicial intervention. This dissolution is considered *faskh* or nullification, rather than *talaq* or repudiation. If the apostate repents, a new marriage is to be contracted. However, Shafiʿite and Shiʿite legal theory consider the marriage contract in some cases to be in abeyance during the wife's waiting period (*ʿiddah*), so that, if the apostate repents during this period, the marriage remains valid. The Shafiʿites do so if the apostasy takes place after the consummation (*dukhul*) of the marriage, the Shiʿites if the

17 Hanafite doctrine makes an exception for the widow of the apostate. If he is executed during her waiting-period (*ʿiddah*), she remains an heir to his property. Hanafite lawyers claim a legal analogy between this situation and the repudiation pronounced by the husband on his deathbed, which is not considered to affect the wife's inheritance claims. A similar rule applies to the succession of the estate of a female Moslem who apostatizes on the deathbed. Cf. Ibn ʿAbidin, *Radd al-muhtar:* III, 414–15.

apostate was born an unbeliever. Only the Malikite and the Hanafite schools give provisions for the case of a woman apostatizing in order to free herself from the bonds of matrimony, a legal trick still resorted to in countries where there is hardly any social *stigma* and no penal consequence attached to apostasy, as e.g. in the former Dutch East Indies and British India.[18] The Malikites hold that in this case marriage is not dissolved.

Actually, one can hardly see a point in her doing this, as she will be executed anyway. On the other hand, provisions of this kind do make sense in Hanafite legal theory, according to which the female apostate is not to be killed. The prevalent Hanafite opinion, first put forward by the scholars of Bukhara, is that the former husband, upon repentance of the wife, can claim that the judge conclude a new marriage between them for a dower (*mahr*) of trifling value, the wife's consent not being required. Besides this prevailing view, there are, within the Hanafite school, two other opinions: the scholars of Balkh held that apostasy of the wife never dissolves marriage: the other opinion is that upon apostasy women become slaves. In present times one can hear voices advocating that the rule of the Balkh scholars should be applied in court.[19] In former British India this rule has been introduced by statute, *viz.* section 4 of the Dissolution of Muslim Marriages Act, 1939.[20]

2 Apostasy in Modern Islam

2.1 *Who Is an Apostate?*

As we shall see below, the question whether one is an apostate or not still has very important legal effects. In most cases there is no problem: a Moslem who formally embraces another religion or who explicitly renounces Islam is an apostate. In cases where this is not so obvious, the scholars still apply the criterion mentioned in 1.1: one becomes an unbeliever by denying those religious tenets and prescriptions that one must necessarily know, or by committing acts of contempt for Allah, the Koran or Mohammed.[21] It was the emergence

18 G.F. Pijper, *Echtscheiding en Apostasie.* In: G.F. Pijper, *Fragmenta Islamica. Studiën over het Islamisme en Nederlandsch-Indië*, Leiden: Brill, 1934, 195 p.; pp. 79–94, A.A.A. Fyzee, *Outlines of Muhammadan Law.* 3rd ed. London: Oxford University Press, 1964, 509 p.; p. 171.

19 Djaziri, *op. cit.* IV, p. 224.

20 Fyzee, *op. cit.*, p. 171; Mulla, *Principles of Mahomedan Law.* 16th ed. by M. Hidayatullah and R.K.P. Shankardass, Bombay: Tripathi Private Ltd, 1968, lxii + 392 p.; p. 344.

21 Cf. Muhammad ʿAbduh wa-Muhammad Rashid Rida, *Tafsir al-Manar*, vols. 1–8, 3rd impr.; vols. 9–11, 2nd impr.; vol. 12, 1st impr. al-Qahirah: Dar al-Manar, 1367–72 H, 12 vols.; vol. 1

of new sects like the *Ahmadiyyah* and the *Baha'iyyah*, who considered themselves as Islamic or, at least, as an offspring of Islam, that gave rise to problems. At the same time the spreading political of ideologies like socialism and communism raised the question whether adherents of these ideologies could still be considered as Moslems.

The *Ahmadis* of the Qadiyani-branch, who regard the founder of their sect, Mirza Ghulam Ahmad, as a prophet, are generally considered as unbelievers.[22] Nevertheless in former British India a court decided in 1922 that a Moslem who became an *Ahmadi* was not to be considered an apostate.[23] Apparently this decision was prompted by a general principle of Anglo-Mohammedan law, *viz.* the elimination of religious discrimination where possible. When Pakistan came into being as an independent Islamic state, the position of the *Ahmadis* became a very serious political issue. The government was put under heavy political pressure to place the *Ahmadiyyah* outside the boundaries of Islam.

---

p. 140. Muhammad Rashid Rida, *Takfir muslim bi-ma la yasihh 'indah min masa'il al-din. Madjallat al-Manar*, 19 (1916) p. 279 (also publ. in: Id., *Fatawa. Djama'aha wa-haqqaqaha Salah al-Din al-Munadjdjid wa-Yusuf Q. Khuri.* Bayrut: Dar al-Kitab al-Djadid, 1390/1970, 4 vols.; vol. 4 p. 1309. Mahmud Shaltut, *'Aqidah wa-Shari'ah.* al-Qahirah: Dar al-Qalam, n.d., 574 p.; p. 292.

When 'Abd al-Hamid Bakhit, a history professor at al-Azhar-University who, in 1955, published a sensational article on dispensation for fasting during Ramadan, was summoned to the disciplinary council of al-Azhar, the text of the summons alluded to this classical formula where it said: "... on the ground of the article which he published in the newspaper al-Akhbar ... under the title "Permissibility of breaking the fast during Ramadan and its conditions", and which contained opinions obviously contrary to those rules of fasting that almost necessarily must be known as belonging to the Islamic religion (... *al-mukhalafat al-sarihah li-ahkam al-sawm allati takad takun ma'lumah min al-din al-Islami bi-al-darurah*). Cf. *Madjallat al-Azhar* 1374 H, p. 1135. For the Bakhit-case see: J. Jomier & J. Corbon, *Le Ramadan au Caire, en 1956. Mélanges de l'Institut Dominicain des Études Orientates*, 3 (1956), pp. 1–71; especially pp. 46–48.

On January 7th 1970, after the appearance of Sadiq Djalal al-'Azm's book "*Naqd al-fikr al-dini*" (Bayrut: Dar al-Tali'ah, 1969, 230 p.), the Lebanese *Dar al-Fatwa* issued a *fatwa* declaring al-'Azm a *murtadd*, on the ground that he questioned uncontestably established Islamic doctrines (*musallamat qat'iyyah li-al-thubut fi al-Islam*). For the German translation of this *fatwa*, see: Stefan Wild, *Gott and Mensch in Libanon. Der Islam*, 48 (1972), pp. 230–1.

22 Cf.: Hasanayn Muhammad Makhluf, *Fatawa shar'iyyah wa-buhuth al-Shari'ah Islamiyyah.* 2nd impr. al-Qahirah: Mustafa al-Babi al-Halabi. 1385–1965, 2 vols.; vol. 1 pp. 86–96. This *fatwa* was issued in 1953 on the request of a group of Pakistanis and also published in Urdu.

F.M. Pareja a.o., *Islamologie.* Beyrouth: Imprimerie Catholique. 1957–63, 1148 p.; p. 670.

23 Asaf A.A. Fyzee, *Cases in the Mohammadan Law of India and Pakistan.* Oxford: Clarendon Press, 1965, xxxvi + 573 p.; pp. 57–67.

However, the government did not yield to this pressure and finally this movement failed.[24]

As for the *Baha'i* faith, there is not the slightest doubt that this sect cannot be regarded as Islamic, as its founders are venerated as prophets and as their prescriptions concerning *e.g.* praying and fasting are totally different from those of the *Shari'ah.* Many authoritative legal opinions (*fatwas*) confirm that Moslems, turning *Baha'i*, are apostates.[25] In Egypt, the highest administrative court (*Madjlis al-Dawlah*) decided accordingly, when a *Baha'i* employee of the Egyptian State Railroad Company applied for a marriage allowance.[26]

Several Moslem scholars regard communists as unbelievers, as the tenets of Marxism are incompatible with Islam.[27] The *Fatwa* Committee of al-Azhar took a similar stand when asked for a *fatwa* by a man whose daughter was betrothed to a young man from a Moslem family, who was a known communist. The *Fatwa* Committee stated that a marriage concluded with him would be null and void, as he must be considered an apostate.[28]

It is a moot point whether those who refuse to judge, or to be judged, according to the *Shari'ah* are apostates. The Koran reads: "Those who do not judge according to what Allah has sent down, they are the unbelievers" (K 5:44). Nevertheless Muhammad Rashid Rida and Mahmud Shaltut do not take this verse literally. In their opinion a judge or a lawgiver only becomes an apostate if, within the territory of Islam, he judges according to laws or enacts laws, that are contrary to an immutable (*qat'i* and not *idjtihadi*) rule of the *Shari'ah*, and if he does so because he thinks the non-Islamic rule is better and more just than the Islamic rule.[29] A stricter doctrine is advocated by 'Abd al-Qadir 'Awdah, one of the leaders of the Society of Moslem Brethren.[30] The question

---

24 Leonard Binder, *Religion and Politics in Pakistan.* Berkeley/Los Angeles: Univ. of California Press, 1961, 440 p.; pp. 259–97 *et passim.*

25 Cf. Muhammad Rashid Rida, *Du'at al-Baha'iyyah wa-Madjallat al-Bayan al-Misri. Madjallat al-Manar* 17 (1914), pp. 178–80 (also published in his *Fatawa*, vol. 4, pp. 1245–7).
Makhluf, *Fatawa*, vol. 1, pp. 84–5.
al-Baha'iyyun malahidah murtadd[an]. *Fatwa. Madjallat al-Azhar*, 1373 H, p. 1102.
Hal yadjuz zawadj al-muslimah bi-al-Baha'i. Fatwa. Madjallat al-Azhar, 1373 H, p. 1193.

26 *Mahkamat al-qada' al-idari bi-Madjlis al-Dawlah, al-Da'irah al-rabi'ah*, 11–6 1952. Integrally published in: 'Ali 'Ali Mansur, *al-Baha'iyyah bayn al-Shari'ah wa-al-qanun.* 2nd impr. Bayrut: al-Maktab al-Islami, 1391 H, 54 p.

27 Cf. Makhluf, *Fatawa*, vol. 1, pp. 81–3. Samarra'i, *Ahkam*, pp. 83–90.

28 *al-Ahram*, 9–8 '65, p. 1. According to Samarra'i, Ahkam, p. 84, Iraqi 'ulama' had previously issued a similar *fatwa.*

29 Mahmud Shaltut, *al-Fatawa, dirasah li-mushkilat al-Muslim al-mu'asir fi hayatih al-yawmiyyah wa-al-'ammah*, al-Qahirah: Dar al-Shuruq, 1969, 403 p.; pp. 37–9.
'Abduh & Rida, Tafsir al-Manar, vol. 6, p. 405ff.

30 'Awdah, *op. cit.*, vol. 2, pp. 708–11.

whether those who refuse to be judged according to the *Shari'ah* should be regarded as apostates became a serious political issue in Tunisia. In 1923 the French had made it possible for Tunisians to obtain French nationality. This implied that the *naturalisé* would be judged by the French courts in Tunisia, according to French law. The nationalist movement in Tunisia launched a campaign against this naturalisation law in 1932 declaring that the *naturalisé* should be considered an apostate. In December 1932 the *mufti* of Bizerta issued a fatwa declaring that a *naturalisé*, being an apostate, could not be buried in a Moslem cemetery. However, this view was not shared by the leading Tunisian *muftis*. The Hanafite *mufti* issued a *fatwa* stating that naturalisation did not imply apostasy; the Malikite mufti, al-Tahir Ibn 'Ashur, emphasized the possibility of repentance before a Moslem judge. Broadly speaking one can say that the *'ulama'* did not use their religious authority to condone this nationalisation law. Yet there was much unrest among the people and finally the authorities had to yield by opening special cemeteries for *naturalisés*. Though not as outspoken as in Tunisia, also in Algeria there was opposition against naturalisation on the same ground.[31]

2.2 *The Penalty for Apostasy*

There is no evidence that apostates are still being put to death in Islamic countries. Though in Saudi Arabia the *Shari'ah* is officially still in force,[32] no contemporary cases of executions of apostates have been reported, which may be due to the fact that apostasy does not occur. In the Ottoman Empire and Egypt, the last cases of capital punishment for apostasy date from the first half of the last century. Edward William Lane, who lived in Egypt, with intermissions, from 1825 to 1835, relates how a female apostate was strangled and then cast into the Nile.[33] In 1843 an Armenian youth, who had once accepted Islam, but later returned to his former belief, was beheaded in Istanbul. The Western powers, led by Great Britain, seized the opportunity to launch a campaign against the Ottoman Empire in order to obtain complete freedom

31 Cf. Charles A. Micaud a.o., *Tunisia, the Politics of Modernization*, London: Pall Mall Press, 1964, 205 p.; pp. 60–2. *Oriente Moderno*, 13 (1933), pp. 381–6.
'Allal al-Fasi, *al-Harakah al-istiqlaliyyah fi al-Maghrib al-'Arabi*. Al-Qahirah: Ladjnat. al-thaqafah al-wataniyyah li-Hizb al-Istiqlal, 1368/1948, 560 p.; p. 73.
Ali Merad, *Le réformisme musulman en Algérie de 1925–1940*. Paris/La Haye: Mouton, 1967, 472 p.; pp. 406–8.

32 Subhi Mahmasani, *al-Awda' al-tashri'iyyah fi al-duwal 'Arabiyyah*. 2nd enl. rev. ed. Bayrut: Dar al-'Ilm li-al-Malayin, 1962, 541 p.; pp. 364–5.

33 Edward W. Lane, *Manners and Customs of the Modern Egyptians*. London: Alexander Gardner, 1895, 595 p.; p. 122.

for Christian missionaries to work amongst the Moslems. This was successful and on March 21st 1844 Sultan Abdulmecid gave the British Envoy Stratford Canning (later Stratford de Redcliffe) a written pledge as follows: "The Sublime Porte engages to take effectual measures to prevent henceforward the persecution and putting to death of a Christian who is an apostate".[34]

In this century some isolated instances have been recorded in Afghanistan. In 1903 and 1925, Moslems converted to *Ahmadiyyah* were condemned to be stoned to death.[35] Recently a curious trial was held in Morocco. On December 14th 1962 the criminal court of Nador condemned some school-teachers who had been converted to *Baha'iyyah*, to death on the accusation of rebellion, formation of criminal bands and disturbance of religious practices. Fortunately on December 13th 1963, this verdict was quashed by the Court of Appeal in Rabat with the argument that none of the charges brought against them was conclusively proven so that it appeared that the only reason for their condemnation was their apostasy.[36]

Though apostasy no longer falls under criminal law, the question whether the apostate should be put to death is still debated in Islamic circles. Modernists[37] hold that the apostate cannot be put to death on the mere ground

34 Stanley Lane-Poole, *The Life of the Rt. Hon. Stratford Canning*. London: Green & Co, 1888, 2 vols.; vol. 2, pp. 89–98.

35 *Oriente Moderno* 5 (1925), p. 128. Pareja a.o., *Islamologie*, p. 670. Rahman, *Punishment*, p. 6, relates that this incident occasioned a discussion between two Indian vernacular daily newspaper about the question whether the apostate should be killed or not.

36 *Journal de Droit International* 93 (1966), p. 383.

37 'Abduh & Rida, *Tafsir al-Manar, vol.* 5, p. 327. Muhammad Rashid Rida, *al-Djawah 'an mas'alat hurriyyat al-din wa-qatl al-murtadd. Madjallat al-Manar* 23 (1922), pp. 187–91 (also publ. in *Fatawa*, vol. 4, pp. 1539–43).

Id., *al-Idjtihad fi al-din wa-qatl al-murtadd. Madjallat al-Manar* 10 (1907), p. 288 (also publ. in *Fatawa*, vol. 2, pp. 576–7). Shaltut, *al-Islam 'aqidah wa-shari'ah*, pp. 292–3. Rahman, *Punishment, passim*. The *Ahmadiyyah* hold similar views. Cf. Muhammad Ali, *The Holy Qur'an. Arabic Text, Translation and Commentary.* 4th ed. Lahore: Ahmadiyyah Anjuman Isha'at Islam, 1951, 1254p.; pp. 91–2. Id., *De Religie van den Islam.* Tr. fr. engl. by Soedewo. Batavia: Ahmadijah Beweging Indonesia, 1938, 582 p.; pp. 421–7.

'Uthman Safi in his book "*Ala hamish naqd al-fikr al-dini*" (Bayrut, Dar al-Tali'ah, 1970, 102 p.), the publication of which was occasioned by the appearance of Sadiq Djalal al-'Azm's book "*Naqd al-fikr al-dini*", concludes that in present-day society the apostate should not be punished. His arguments, however, do not touch on the Islamic doctrine of apostasy itself, but are derived from his views, revolutionary for Islamic circles, on the relationship between Islamic and secular laws. He beliefs in the supremacy of man-made law, *i.e.* law made by a constitutional legislator. As there is no Islamic country at the present time in which laws exist that regard apostasy as a penal offence, apostates cannot be punished. Even if there were such laws, Safi continues, many apostates could not be punished as the required criminal intention is often lacking. – Cf. Safi, *op. cit.*, pp. 87–93.

of his apostasy. This should only be done if he is also a danger to the Islamic state. They adduce the following arguments: No verse in the Koran prescribes capital punishment for the apostate *qua* apostate; on the contrary, verses like K 2:218 and K 3:86–97 clearly envisage a natural death for the apostate. Moreover, K 4:89 and 90 (Bell's translation: If then they withdraw from you, and do not fight against you, but offer you peace, Allah hath not opened for you a way against them.... If they do not withdraw from you, and offer you peace, and restrain their hands, take them and kill them wherever ye come upon them), verses that have not been abrogated by any other verse, offer proof that only the dangerous, aggressive apostate may be killed. A further argument is that capital punishment for apostasy is founded on two Traditions (see note 12) that are contrary to the explicit Koranic rulings of K 4:89 and 90. There exist a much debated controversy on the question whether a Tradition can abrogate a Koranic rule. Whether in this case these Traditions can abrogate the Koranic ruling is even more doubtful, as they belong to the category of Traditions relying on only one authority (*khabar al-ahad*) and were not widely known amongst the Companions of the Prophet. So, even if one accepts the authenticity of these Traditions, they cannot contradict the Koran. Therefore, they must be interpreted as referring only to the inimical and fighting apostates. If one rejects however the above mentioned Traditions as spurious, the fact that apostates were killed in the first period of Islam van be explained as a relic of the *Djahiliyyah* when everybody who was not formally protected, could be killed, or as the application of martial law (*siyasah ʿurfiyyah ʿaskariyyah*), necessitated by rebellion and disturbances. Finally the argument is put forward that killing the apostate must be considered as compulsion in religion, which has been forbidden in K 2:256 (There is no compulsion in religion), though this verse was traditionally interpreted in a different way.[38]

A very detailed plea against capital punishment of the apostate was put forward by ʿAbd al-Mutaʿali al-Saʿidi in his book entitled "*al-Hurriyyah al-diniyyah fi al-Islam*" (Religious freedom in Islam).[39] In addition to the aforementioned arguments,[40] al-Saʿidi refers to an isolated opinion of Ibrahim al-Nakhaʿi

38 According to some classical scholars this verse had been abrogated by later verses. Others held this rule only to be valid with regard to those from whom *djizyah* can be accepted. The current interpretation of this verse, however, was that it forbids compulsion to things that are wrong but not compulsion to accept the truth. Cf. Abu Bakr Muhammad Ibn ʿAbd Allah Ibn al-ʿArabi, *Ahkam al-Qurʾan. Tahqiq Muhammad al-Badjawi.* 2nd impr. al-Qahirah: ʿIsa al-Babi al-Halabi, 1387–8/1967–8, 4 vols.; vol. 1 p. 233.

39 ʿAbd al-Mutaʿali al-Saʿidi, *al-Hurriyyah al-diniyyah fi al-Islam.* 2nd impr. al-Qahirah: Dar al-Fikr al-ʿArabi, n.d. (probably second half of the fifties), 179 p.

40 Saʿidi, *op. cit.*, pp. 72, 149, 170–1.

(d. 95 or 96 H) that the apostate should forever be asked to repent (*an yustatab abad*[an]), from which it can be inferred that he may not be killed.[41] However, this should not mean, as some scholars say, that the apostate should be kept in jail until he repents.[42] According to al-Saʿidi there should not be any difference between an apostate and a born unbeliever (*kafir asli*). The Moslems have the obligation of inviting them to be converted. That is as far as they can go with regard to the apostate. For if the repentance of the apostate is caused by the fear of death or lifelong imprisonment, it is a form of compulsion, which is explicitly forbidden in the Koran.[43] Though al-Saʿidi goes a long way in offering scriptural evidence for his opinions, he states very clearly that his motives are upholding the principle of freedom of religion in Islam and reconciliation of Islam with the actual situation of the Moslems.[44] In order to attain these goals he claims the right to free interpretation of the sources (*idjtihad*) which in some cases may result in adopting a weak and isolated opinion, if this opinion is better suited to modern circumstances.[45]

Contrary to these modernist ideas, there are still many Moslem scholars who adhere to the classical doctrine. However, *vis-a-vis* these views, these scholars were more or less compelled to defend their position and clarify their concepts. Only the very traditionalistic authors refused to do so, as – according to them – the *Shariʿah* is beyond defence or justification.[46] The commonest argument in support of the death penalty for the apostate is based on the principle that Islam is not only a religion, but also a social and political order. A person who disagrees with the basis of organized society has only two alternatives open to him: he may either go out of the boundaries of the society's operation

41 Saʿidi, *op. cit.*, pp. 72, 148, 156. This opinion can be found in: Abu Muhammad ʿAli Ibn Ahmad Ibn Saʿid Ibn Hazm, *al-Muhalla*. Tahqiq Ahmad Shakir. Bayrut: al-Maktab al-Tidjari li-al-Tibaʿah wa-al-Nashr wa-al-Tawziʿ, n.d., 11 parts in 8 vols.; part 11 pp. 189 and 191; and also in: ʿAbd Allah Ibn Ahmad Ibn Muhammad Ibn Qudamah, *al-Mughni sharh mukhtasar* al-Khiraqi. Tahqiq Taha Muhammad al-Zayni, Mahmud al-Wahhab Fayid wa-ʿAbd al-Qadir Ahmad. al-Qahirah: Maktabat al-Qahirah, 1389/1969, 9 vols.; vol. 9 p. 6. Saʿidi's conclusion that the apostate's life should be spared is, however, not consistent with al-Nakhaʿi's opinion that the female apostate should be killed, mentioned in: Ibn Qudamah, *al-Mughni*, vol. 9 pp. 3–4.

42 Saʿidi, *op. cit.*, pp. 167–9.

43 Saʿidi, *op. cit.*, pp. 158–60.

44 Saʿidi, *op. cit.*, pp. 73, 156, 160.

45 Saʿidi, *op. cit.*, pp. 88, 156.

46 Cf.: ʿIsa Manun, *Hurriyyat al-raʾy wa-hududuha fi al-maqtuʿ bih min al-Shariʿah. Madjallat al-Azhar* 1374 H, pp. 1143–7. Id., *Hukm al-murtadd fi al-Shariʿah al-Islamiyyah. Madjallat al-Azhar* 1375 H, pp. 884–92. Both articles were also published in full in Saidi, *op. cit.*, pp. 56–64 and 74–88, however, with the exclusion of the introduction to the first article. In this introduction the author stated that this article was prompted by the Bakhit-case.

or submit to deprivation of all rights as a citizen. As the latter state would he worse than death, it is better to kill him.[47]

Generally the danger the apostate constitutes for Islamic society is emphasized. By abandoning Islam one rebels against the Islamic state and society. Therefore, it is highly probable that the apostate will attempt to destroy the structure of Islamic society and to change the contents of the Islamic religion. Moreover having lost his loyalty to Islam, he is prone to support foreign nations against the Islamic state.[48] Muhammad Muhiy al-Din al-Masiri puts it as follows:

> Apostasy (constitutes) an offense against the social order of Moslem society, for the social order of every Moslem society is Islam. Apostasy means treason to Islam and rebellion against its principles. It causes scepticism as to its truth. No society can function properly if its social order is made an object of scepticism and defamation, for that may lead in the end, to the destruction of this order.[49]

So the apostate must be put to death for the protection of the Islamic society. At the same time, these authors argue, this severe punishment will have a preventive effect by deterring others from committing such a serious error. Moreover, elimination of political dissenters, is a generally accepted principle, they say. In a communist state, a person becoming fascist or democrat will be punished just as in a democratic state a person turning communist or fascist will be punished, the reason being that they form a danger to the social order.[50]

Comparing these fundamentalist opinions with those of Muhammad Rashid Rida and Mahmud Shaltut, one will notice that the main difference is to be found in the fact that according to the former opinions the apostate is automatically considered to be a dangerous enemy of the Islamic state, whereas the latter state that enmity is not implied in the mere condition of being an apostate, and must be proven separately. This can be illustrated by the words

47 Abu al-Aʿla Mawdudi, *Murtadd ki saza islami qanun men.* 4th ed. Lahore: Islamic publications, 1963: pp. 45–8. Quoted from Rahman, *Punishment*, pp. 120–1.

48 Cf. ʿAwdah, *op. cit.*, p. 536; Bilmen, *op. cit.*, vol. 3 pp. 483–5. Shawqi Abu Khalil, *al-Islam fi qafas al-ittiham.* [Bayrut] Matbaʿat al-Insha', 1971, 387 p.; pp. 165–8. Muhammad Muhiy al-Din al-Masiri, *al-Nuzum allati yuqam ʿalayha kiyan al-mudjtamaʿ al-Islami. Madjallat al-Azhar*, 1374, pp. 859–68. Muhammad al-Ghazali, *Huquq al-insan bayn taʿalim al-Islam wa-iʿlan al-Umam al-Muttahidah.* al-Qahirah: al-Maktabah al-Tidjariyyah, 1383/1963, 272 p.; pp. 101–2.

49 Masiri, *op. cit.*, p. 861.

50 See note 48.

of Muhammad al-Ghazali, who can be regarded as a representative of the fundamentalist school of thought:

> Apostasy seldom is a matter that only concerns one's inner self alone. If that would be the case, nobody would notice it. In most instances apostasy is a psychological pretext for rebellion against worship, traditions and laws, even against the foundations of the state itself and against its stand towards its external enemies. Therefore apostasy is often synonymous with the crime of high treason.[51]

Now that the state no longer punishes the apostate anymore, there are some Moslems who hold the view that the killing of an apostate has become a duty of individual Moslems. ʿAbd al-Qadir ʿAwdah even argued that a Moslem who kills an apostate can, according to Egyptian law, plead impunity, for art. 60 of the Egyptian Penal Code states that acts that are committed in good faith on the basis of a right laid down in the *Shariʿah* will not be punished and art. 9 of the same Code says that the Egyptian Penal Code does not infringe on any right recognized by the *Shariʿah*.[52]

2.3 *The Legal Position of the Apostate*

In section 1.3 we gave an *expose* of the legal position of the apostate according to the civil law of Islam. In this chapter we shall examine to what extent these rules are still being applied, taking Egypt as a typical example of an Islamic country where the *Shariʿah* and Western law coexist.[53] Only in those countries that were under direct colonial rule as India, Pakistan and Algeria is the situation different.[54]

51 Ghazali, *op. cit.*, p. 102.

52 ʿAwdah, *op. cit.*, vol. I pp. 535–8.

53 For the situation in Tunisia, see: Maurice Borrmans, *Religion et succession en Tunisie. Oriente Moderno*, 49 (1969), pp. 204–12.

54 In India and Pakistan the situation is as follows: According to section 4 of the Dissolution of Muslim Marriages Act of 1939, apostasy of the husband immediately dissolves the bond of marriage. Apostasy of the wife does not, unless she was not born a Moslem and returned to her former faith. The clause is probably meant to be a prevention of fraudulent apostasy on the part of the wife with the sole aim of obtaining a divorce. Therefore this principle is not operative if the wife was not born a Moslem in which case her sound intention is supposed. As for inheritance, by virtue of Act XXI of 1850 (Removal of Caste Disabilities Act) apostasy does not operate as a legal bar. Cf. Mulla, *op. cit.*, pp. 55, 297–8 and Fyzee, *op. cit.*, pp. 170–1, 387.

During colonial rule, the situation in Algeria was rather complicated (cf. André Bonnichon, *La conversion au Christianisme de l'indigène Musulman Algérien et ses Effets*

In Egypt the *Shari'ah is* applied in matters of personal statue. The non-Moslem communities, as far as family law *stricto sensu* is concerned, are governed by their own statute. Up till January 1st 1956, Islamic law was applied in the *Shari'ah* Courts (*mahakim shar'iyyah*), the law of the other creeds in the denominational assemblies (*madjalis milliyyah*). After that date only the secular national courts became competent. An important fact is that, Egypt being an Islamic state, the *Shari'ah* occupies a higher order than the other religious laws. In cases where the litigants differ in religion, it is the *Shari'ah* that will be applied. Some parts of the *Shari'ah* are even regarded as affecting public order to the extent that they are also applied to non-Moslems. The rules relating to the apostate fall into this category, which explains why he is subject to Islamic law. Most cases of apostasy in Egypt concern non-Moslems who were converted to Islam for some practical reason (marriage or *fraus legis*) and later returned to their former belief.[55] Actually the frequency of these cases is sometimes put forward as an argument for reintroduction of the punishment of the apostate.[56]

As early as 1929 the Egyptian government promised to introduce separate legislation regarding the legal position of the apostate. No such legislation has, however, yet appeared.[57] Therefore, in matters of personal statute, the classical rules of apostasy, according to the Hanafite school, are still being applied. Thus, in Egypt, the legal consequences of apostasy pertain to family law and

---

Juridiques. Thèse-Paris: Recueil Sirey, 1931, 152 p.; and G.H. Bousquet, *Précis de Droit Musulman, principalement Malékite et Algérien.* Alger: La Maison des Livres, 1950, 371 p.). Generally apostasy did not raise any legal problem as the majority of the apostates were naturalized and subject only to French law. As for the apostates who were not naturalized, the *Cour de Cassation* (30–6–1919, *Journal de Robe*, 1921, p. 39; quoted by Bonnichon, *op. cit.*, pp. 126–8; cf. also Bousquet, *op. cit.*, p. 277) decided that, colonial public order forbade the exclusion of an unbeliever from the inheritance of a Moslem *propositus*. Practice with regard to the celebration of marriages of this category of apostates varied. Generally the simple procedure of option of French law (*option de législation*) was followed (Bonnichon, *op. cit.*, pp. 21–2). The question whether apostasy would affect the validity of a marriage concluded *more islamico*, has never been brought before an Algerian court. Bousquet (*op. cit.*, p. 131) holds that in that case the marriage would remain valid, as a contrary decision would be in conflict with colonial public order. Now, after the independence there is a general tendency towards a stricter application of the *Shari'ah* (cf. Maurice Borrmans, *Perspectives algériennes en matière de droit familial. Studia Islamica*, 37 (1973), pp. 129–53). This may entail the application of the classical rules concerning apostasy in matters of personal statute.

55 Jan Brugman, *De betekenis van het Mohammedaanse recht in het hedendaagse Egypte.* Den Haag: Ned. Bock- en Steendrukkerij v/h H.L. Smits, 1960, 215 p.; p. 185.

56 Abu Zahrah, pp. 205–8; Ghazali, *op. cit.*, p. 101; Sabuni, vol. 2, p. 990.

57 J.N.D. Anderson, *Recent Developments in Shari'ah Law. Moslem World* 42 (1952), p. 125; 'Abd Allah, *op. cit.*, p. 97; Brugman, *op. cit.*, p. 184; Shalabi, *op. cit.*, p. 99.

the law of inheritance. The act of apostasy dissolves marriage. Even if both spouses apostatize at the same time, and are converted to *e.g.* Christianity, or if the wife alone is converted to Christianity, the bond of matrimony is dissolved. In fact, unless he repents, the apostate can never marry again.[58] The apostate lacks the capacity to inherit, even from a coreligionist. If he himself dies, or leaves Islamic territory, the property acquired before his apostasy will be inherited by his Moslem heirs, whereas the property acquired thereafter, will fall to the Public Treasury.[59] That this may lead to strange consequences is demonstrated by a decision of the High Shariʿah Court (14–6 1943): The Ministry of Finance claimed the estate of a deceased Copt, pleading that he was an apostate. They alleged that he was the issue of a Coptic father and a Moslem mother, so that, in accordance with the rule that the child follows the "best of his parents", he was born a Moslem. As he lived as a Copt, he could only be an apostate. The verdict put the plaintiff in the right.[60] The Egyptian draft Law of Personal Statute, which has not yet been enforced, devotes one article to the position of the apostate as far as the law of inheritance is concerned. Art. 414 runs as follows:

1. The apostate lacks the capacity to inherit from whomsoever.
2. The apostate's property, be it acquired before or after his apostasy, falls upon his death to his Moslem heirs. If there are no Moslem heirs, his property falls to the Public Treasury.
3. If the apostate obtains the nationality of a non-Islamic state, he is considered as being dead. His property falls to his Moslem heirs.
4. If the apostate, after having obtained the nationality of a non-Islamic state, returns to Islam, he will have that part of his property that can still be found in the possession of his heirs or of the Public Treasury.[61]

It is noteworthy that section 2) does not conform to the prevailing Hanafite opinion followed in the Egyptian courts, but to the opinion of Abu Hanifah's pupils Muhammad al-Shaybani and Abu Yusuf. Section 4) represent the classical doctrine with one difference: according to the classical doctrine the judge had to decide on the question whether the apostate had really fled to the non-Islamic territory (*Dar al-Harb*) or not, whereas now the criterion lies in naturalisation.

58 Brugman, *op. cit.*, pp. 185, 187: Sabuni, *op. cit.*, pp. 991–2.
59 Anderson, *op. cit.*, pp. 130–1; Brugman, *op. cit.*, pp. 109, 185–6.
60 Brugman, *op. cit.*, pp. 186–7.
61 ʿAbd Allah, *op. cit.*, p. 87.

2.4 *Apostasy and the Principle of Freedom of Religion*

One of the values recently adopted in the Islamic world is the principle of freedom of religion. According to Art. 18 of the Universal Declaration of Human Rights, this freedom contains three elements: freedom to practice one's religion, freedom to express one's religious feelings and freedom to change one's religion. Modern Moslem authors emphasize the fact that religious liberty is already recognized in the Koran, *viz.* K 2:256: "There is no compulsion in religion".[62] As one will readily notice, this principle is incompatible with the classical Islamic doctrine of apostasy, according to which a Moslem is not free to change his religion. Most Moslem authors are aware of this contradiction or, at least, conscious of the fact that in the West the doctrine of apostasy is generally considered to be opposed to the principle of religious liberty. Therefore they try to eliminate this contradiction. This can be done in two ways. One can limit the scope of the principle of freedom of religion, or one can change the legal theory of apostasy. The first method is used by those who are of the opinion that freedom of religion, as guaranteed by Islam, is embodied in the right of unbelievers to practice their religion freely without being forced to give it up or change it, excluding thereby, sometimes implicitly, the freedom for Moslems to change their religion.[63] Muhammad Rashid Rida excludes freedom to apostatize *expressis verbis* with the argument that apostasy infringes on the freedom of others and on the respect due to the religion of the State.[64] Muhammad al-Ghazali does the same, using the *reductio ad absurdum* as an argument:

> Must Islam allow rebellion against itself? No religion of a similar nature will readily answer in the affirmative. (...) Take for instance a man who wants to be an unbeliever and a communist. Communism means: there is no God, life is only matter. Besides this it has a special theory concerning the social foundations of the State. Can one demand from Islam that it stupidly recognizes the freedom to apostatize in this manner? Or take a man who wants to be an unbeliever and an existentialist. Existentialism is a philosophy that sets human behaviour free from any restriction and rejects what we call worship, virtue and tradition. It turns the world into

62 See note 38.

63 Cf. Ali Abdel Wahid Wafi, *Human rights in Islam. Islamic Quarterly* 11 (1967), pp. 64–75; pp. 64–5. Sayyid Qutb, *Fi zilal al-Qur'an.* 5th enl. & rev. impr. Bayrut: Dar Ihya' al-Turath al-ʿArabi, 1386/1967, 30 parts in 8 vols.; vol. 1 part 3 pp. 34–6. This opinion was already common in the Ottoman Empire in the latter half of the 19th century. Cf. Zwemer, *The law of apostasy in Islam*, p. 45.

64 ʿAbduh & Rida, *Tafsir al-Manar*, vol. 11 pp. 139–40.

> an unbridled anarchy. Can one demand from a religion, whose message is a creed and a law, that it allows these evils in the name of freedom?

He then continues to demonstrate that conversion to Christianity or Judaism can neither be tolerated, as these religions have, since Mohammed's life-time, always harboured inimical feelings towards Islam.[65] 'Abd al-Muta'ali al-Sa'idi and S.A. Rahman, whom we met before, follow the other method of escaping from the contradiction. They state unequivocally that capital punishment for the apostate is not compatible with freedom of religion and conclude that this rule must therefore be abolished.[66] However, they are white crows amongst the *'ulama'*. Most authors evade the problem by declaring that the reason why an apostate is to be punished, is not the abandonment of his religion, but his rebelliousness against Islamic social and political order. Modernists like Muhammad Rashid Rida and Mahmud Shaltut hold, as we have seen, that an apostate should be killed only if he constitutes a danger to the Islamic society, whereas fundamentalists are of the opinion that an apostate is *per se* a danger to the Islamic community.

It is noteworthy that the discussion about freedom of religion and the doctrine of apostasy concentrates on the question whether the apostate deserves the death penalty, though in practice this is no longer being applied. However, nowadays there is still a conflict between the legal situation of the apostate in the sphere of civil law and the principle of freedom of religion.[67] This problem has as far as we know not been dealt with by contemporary *'ulama'*, but by practical lawyers, since most constitutions in the Islamic world guarantee freedom of religion. Taking again Egypt as an example, we see that this problem was first raised in 1943 during the preparation of the Law of Inheritance (*Qanun al-Mawarith*). Article 6 section 2 of the draft law excluded, in accordance with the rules of the *Shari'ah*, the apostate from the right to inherit. In the final text this article had been left out as many members of the Legislative Committee considered it to run counter to the principle of freedom of religion as recognized in the Article 12 of the Egyptian Constitution of 1923, which read: "Freedom of conviction is absolute". However, as the Egyptian *Shari'ah* courts must apply the rules of the *Shari'ah* according to the prevailing Hanafite opinion in cases where there is no statute law, in fact nothing changed.[68] The interpretation put forward by those members of the Legislative Committee

---

65 Ghazali, *op. cit.*, pp. 99–101.

66 Sa'idi, *op. cit.*, pp. 73, 156, 160. Rahman, *Punishment*, pp. 136–7.

67 Brugman, *op. cit.*, p. 187.

68 'Abd Allah, *op. cit.*, pp. 97–8; Shalabi, *op. cit.*, p. 99.

has never found general acceptance. On several occasions it has even officially been rejected. On an international scale this occurred during United Nations debates concerning freedom of religion. The Egyptian delegates repeatedly expressed their country's opposition to the principle of freedom to change one's religion, as this would promote the machinations of Christian missionaries.[69] Professing this view, they implied that according to the official interpretation, Art. 12 of the Egyptian Constitution does not guarantee the freedom to change one's religion. In 1952 this exegesis of Art. 12 was "canonized" by the highest Egyptian administrative court, the *Madjlis al-Dawlah*, when it gave a decision in the afore-mentioned case of the *Baha'i*, employed by the Egyptian State Railway Company, who after his marriage (contracted outside Egypt, according to *Baha'i* formalities) claimed his marriage allowance, which had always been refused till then on the ground that, as an apostate, he could not legally be married. One of the arguments put forward by the claimant was that the rule that apostates could not legally be married had been invalidated by Art. 12 of the Constitution. The court rejected this plea. In the first place, they argued, the claimant's plea cannot find any support in the history of the drafting of this article. The first draft of this article, as originally prepared by the British Foreign Secretary, Lord Curzon, reads: "Freedom of religious conviction is absolute" (*Hurriyyat al-i'tiqad al-dini mutlaqah*). During the debates in the Legislative Committee it appeared that many members thought this formulation too wide, especially as it would protect apostates. Therefore it was decided to delete the word "religious" (*dini*). The difference between "conviction" (*i'tiqad*) and "religion" (*din*), was characterized by one of the committee-members as follows:

> Moslem are divided in 73 sects, each of which has its own conviction. Nevertheless they share one religion.

From these events the court inferred that:

> The text of Article 12 protects the Moslem who changes his *madhhab*, e.g. from *Shafi'i* to *Hanafi*, or the Moslem who leaves the *Shari'ah* to become a *Sunni*, or a *Kharidji*, or a *Mu'tazili*. Equally the text protects the Christian who leaves Catholicism to become a Protestant. However, it does not relieve a Moslem who apostatizes, of the responsibility for his apostasy, be it in the sphere of civil law, or outside it.

69 Brugman, *op. cit.*, pp. 183–4.

A second refutation of the claimant's plea, the court argued, can be found in Article 149 of the Constitution, which establishes that Islam is the official State religion. This implies, according to the interpretation of the court, that Islamic law has complete supremacy in Egypt, abrogating all that runs counter to it as being unconstitutional.[70] As the wording of this Article has not been changed in later Constitutions,[71] it appears that this interpretation still holds.

3 Conclusions

The rules concerning apostasy originated in a society that was entirely dominated by one religion. Its political structure and laws were, at least in theory, exclusively based on the Koran and Tradition. In this ambiance it was natural that giving up one's religion also meant being disloyal to the state and the society. Therefore the apostate was considered to be a danger that should be eliminated. The increasing political and economic impact of the Western Powers on the Islamic world put an end to this. It was the outcome of two different processes. In the first place, the death penalty for apostasy was abolished in those Islamic countries that were under colonial rule or where Western Powers could exert enough pressure to attain this, as in the Ottoman Empire. The motives for this attitude may be found partly in a certain amount of idealism, partly in the then widespread opinion that converted natives were easier to rule. Yet the Western Powers were generally careful enough to put the Christian mission under certain restrictive measures so as not to stir up religious feelings. As for the Ottoman Empire, the Western Powers were recognized as the protectors of the Christian minorities. A growth of the Christian population, it was thought, would lead to greater influence of the Western Powers on the Ottoman Empire. The second process was the gradual adoption of liberal values by the growing Moslem bourgeoisie. Of these values the principle of freedom of religion and that of separation of Church and State were important in this connection.

However, the second principle has not been enforced in its entirety in any Islamic country, with the exception of Turkey. The Islamic character of those states did not disappear completely. Officially the supremacy of the Islamic

70 Mansur, *op. cit.*, pp. 45–50.

71 Art. 4 of the Constitutional Proclamation of Feb. 10th 1953; Art. 43 of the Constitution of Jan. 10th 1956; Art. 34 of the Constitution of March 25th 1964. The texts of these constitutions were published in: J.E. Godchot, *Les constitutions du Proche et du Moyen Orient*. Paris: Sirey, 1957, 442 p. (pp. 50 and 77); and in: *Oriente Moderno*, 1964, pp. 685–95.

law was never challenged and parts of it remained in force. Therefore many still regarded apostasy as having political implications.

As capital punishment for apostasy fell into desuetude by the introduction of Western inspired penal codes and by the spreading of the principle of freedom of religion, among the upper *strata* of Moslem society, Moslem thinkers were induced to reconsider the doctrine of apostasy. Some of them concluded that Islam does not require the execution of the apostate. However, a large majority of the Moslem, still regard the apostate as a traitor, who should be killed, or, in the best case, be treated as a social outcast. Conversions of Moslems to *e.g.* Christianity still cause a great deal of commotion.[72] These views, expressed by fundamentalist authors, are still very strong. This may explain why the legal discrimination of the apostate, which some authors expressly consider as a form of punishment,[73] has been maintained in most countries.

72 Cf.: Brugman, *op. cit.*, p. 185.

73 Cf.: Abu Zahrah, *Al-ʿUquba*. P. 197 (*la taqtasir ʿuqubat al-murtadd ʿala qatlih faqat*; ʿAwdah, *op. cit.*, vol. 2 p. 728 where he calls this legal discrimination *ʿuqubah tabaʿiyyah*.

CHAPTER 22

Dar al-Harb, Dar al-Islam und der Kolonialismus

Das Vordringen des europäischen Kolonialismus in die islamische Welt im 19. Jahrhundert hatte für die Bevölkerung der kolonisierten Gebiete tiefgreifende Folgen, die sich auf vielerlei Ebenen manifestierten. Es verursachte radikale wirtschaftliche und gesellschaftliche Umbrüche und demzufolge auch ideologische und religiöse Veränderungen. Im Laufe der islamischen Geschichte wird immer wieder deutlich, daß sich sozio-politische Strömungen in ein religiöses Gewand kleiden, und daß die gesellschaftlichen und politischen Auseinandersetzungen im religiösen Bereich ihren Ausdruck finden. Dieses Phänomen läßt sich in der islamischen Welt auch beim Widerstand gegen den Kolonialismus nachweisen: der Kampf gegen die kolonialen Unterdrücker wurde religiös begründet und als *djihad* verstanden, nämlich als der vom Islam sanktionierte Krieg gegen die Ungläubigen. Bei dieser Begründung tauchte immer wieder die Frage auf, ob das unter Kolonialverwaltung stehende Gebiet zum *Dar al-Islam* oder zum *Dar al-Harb* gerechnet werden müsse und die damit eng verknüpfte Frage, ob die Muslime verpflichtet seien, das von den Ungläubigen besetzte Land zu verlassen. In diesem Vortrag soll untersucht werden, welche Rolle die klassischen Theorien zur Frage, welche Gebiete zum *Dar al-Islam* und welche zum *Dar al-Harb* gehören und unter welchen Bedingungen sich der Status eines bestimmten Gebietes wandeln kann[1] und die Theorien zur Auswanderung (*hidjrah*) im frühen antikolonialen Kampf in Vorderindien und Algerien gespielt haben.

Das erste Problem wird in den klassischen *Fiqh*-werken nicht sehr ausführlich behandelt. In der Praxis war der Unterschied doch klar, man hatte keine theoretische Begründung nötig. *Dar al-Islam* war das Gebiet, das unter islamischer Herrschaft stand und wo die *Shari'ah* angewandt wurde, *Dar al-Harb* alle

---

1 Sekundarliteratur zu den Theorien über *Dar al-Islam* und *Dar al-Harb:* A. Abel. *Dar al-Harb.* In: E.I.², II, S. 126, Ders. *Dar al-Islam.* In: E.I.², II, S. 127; Ö.N. Bilmen. *Hukuk-ı islamiyye ve ıstılahatı fikhiyye kamusu.* 6 Bde. Istanbul: Istanbul Üniversitesi Hukuk Fakültesi: 1949–52, III, S. 394–6; H. Inalcık. *Dar al-'Ahd.* E.I.², II, S. 116. Majid Khadduri. *War and Peace in the Law of Islam.* Baltimore: The John Hopkins Press, 1955, S. 155–7; Hans Kruse. *Islamische Völkerrechtslehre. Der Staats-vertrag bei den Hanafiten des 5./6. Jahrhunderts d.H.* (*11. /12. Jh.n.* Chr.). Diss., Göttingen: 1953, *S.* 58–63; F. Lökkegaard. *Islamic Taxation in the Classic Period.* Copenhagen: Branner og Korch, 1950, *S.* 81–3; D.S. Macdonnald & A. Abel. *Dar al-Sulh.* In: E.I.², II, S. 131. Wahbah al-Zuhayli. *Athar al-harb fi al-fiqh al-Islami. Dirasah muqarinah.* Beirut: *Dar al-Fikr al-'Arabi,* 1965, *S.* 166–94.

 | DOI:10.1163/9789004420625_023

übrigen Gebiete. Die Shafiʿitischen Gelehrten erwähnen allerdings noch eine dritte Kategorie, *Dar al-ʿAhd* oder *Dar al-Sulh*. Dies sind Gebiete, in denen die Muslime mit den Ungläubigen Einwohnern einen Waffenstillstand geschlossen haben, mit der Bedingung, daß die Ungläubigen die Eigentumsrechte über ihren Grund behalten, dafür aber eine von diesem Grund erhobene Steuer bezahlen müssen. Diese Steuer heißt *kharadj*, gleicht aber mehr der *djizyah*, da die Zahlungspflicht mit der Bekehrung erlischt.[2] Die anderen Schulen, die nur eine Dichotomie anerkennen, sind aber der Meinung, daß das von den Shafiʿiten *Dar al-Sulh* genannte Gebiet zum *Dar al-Islam* gehöre, weil die Einwohner unter islamischer Herrschaft stehen; für sie ist entscheidend ob die Muslime eine Schutzherrschaft (Suzeränität) ausüben oder nicht. Die islamische Schutzherrschaft zeigt sich in der Anwendung der *Shariʿah* (*idjraʾ ahkam al-Shariʿah*), aber über die Frage, in welchem Maß die *Shariʿah* angewandt werden muß, besteht keine einheitliche Meinung. Einige sind der Ansicht, daß es genüge, wenn die Muslime in diesen Gebieten sicher seien, und wenn einige Vorschriften der *Shariʿah* wie das Freitagsgebet und die Feier islamischer Festtage beachtet würden. Andere sind der Meinung, daß es zumindest einen islamischen *Qadi* geben müsse. Eine Theorie über die Umwandlung von zum *Dar al-Islam* gehörende Gebiete in *Dar al-Harb* und umgekehrt ist nur von den Hanafiten entwickelt worden. Abu Hanifah (gest. 767), nennt für den Übergang von *Dar Islam* in *Dar Harb* drei Voraussetzungen: a) die Gesetze der Ungläubigen müssen angewandt werden; b) das Gebiet muß an das *Dar al-Harb* grenzen; c) die primäre Sicherheit (*al-aman al-awwal*) für Leben und Gut der Muslime und deren Schutzbefohlene (*Dhimmis*) muß fehlen, unabhängig davon, ob der neue Herrscher eine Sicherheitsgarantie gibt oder nicht. Spätere Autoren sind der Ansicht, daß ein von Ungläubigen erobertes Gebiet so lange *Dar Islam* bleibt wie die Muslime und deren Schutzbefohlene sicher sind und die neue Gewalthaber einen islamischen Qadi ernennen, der nach der *Shariʿah* Recht sprechen kann. Die Lehre Abu Hanifah's war jedoch innerhalb der hanafitischen Schule nicht unumstritten. Seine Schüler Abu Yusuf (gest. 798) und Muhammad al-Shaybani (gest. 805) akzeptieren nur seine erste Voraussetzung, nämlich die Anwendung der Gesetze der Ungläubigen. Damit schließen sie sich der Meinung der anderen Schulen an. Die Lehre Abu Hanifah's hat sich aber innerhalb seiner Schule durchgesetzt.[3] Schließlich

2 Muhammad ibn Idris al-Shafiʿi. *Kitab al-Umm*. 7 Teile. Kairo: Kitab al-Shaʿb, 1377 d.H./1968 n.Chr., IV, S. 103–4. Abu al-Hasan ibn Muhammad al-Mawardi. *al-Ahkam al-Sultaniyyah wa-al-Wilayat al-Diniyyah*. 2. Dr. Kairo: Mustafa al-Babi al-Halabi, 1386 d. H.11966 n.Chr., S. 138.

3 Muhammad ibn Ahmad al-Sarakhsi. *Sharh Kitab al-Siyar al-Kabir Muhammad ibn al-Hasan al-Shaybani*. 5 Bde. Ed. Salah al-Din al-Munadjdjid. Kairo: Maʿhad al-Maktutat bi-Djamiʿat al-Duwal al-ʿArabiyyah, V, S. 1856–7, 2165; ʿAbd al-Rahman ibn Muhammad Shaykhzadeh.

haben einige Shafiʿitische Juristen die Meinung vertreten, daß *Dar Islam* niemals *Dar Harb* werden könne. Wenn Ungläubige islamisches Gebiet erobern, bleibt es *de jure* (*hukm^{an}*) *Dar Islam* und kann nur *de facto* (*surat^{an}*) *Dar Harb* genannt werden.[4] Sie begründen diese Ansicht mit dem Hadith "Der Islam ist überlegen und wird nicht übertroffen".[5]

Das zweite Problem, das sich im Zusammenhang mit dem antikolonialen Kampf stellt, ist die Frage der Emigration (*hidjrah*). Die Theorie lehrt, daß Muslime unter bestimmten Voraussetzungen aus dem *Dar al-Harb* ins *Dar al-Islam* emigrieren müssen. Diese Vorschrift wird begründet mit K 4:97–100 und einigen Hadithen wie z.B.: "Ich habe nichts zu tun mit Muslimen die sich unter den Heiden aufhalten".[6] Emigrieren muß, wer dazu im Stande ist und wer seinen religiösen Pflichten nicht öffentlich nachkommen kann. Aber auch wenn Muslime ihre Religion öffentlich ausüben können, bleibt die Emigration empfehlenswert; dadurch wird der islamische Staat gestärkt und der Umgang mit den Heiden unterbunden. Die Malikiten vertreten sogar die Meinung, daß Auswanderung aus dem *Dar al-Harb* unter allen Umständen erfolgen müsse, während dagegen die Hanafiten der Ansicht sind, daß Emigration nicht unbedingt nötig sei. Letztere begründen ihre Meinung mit dem Hadith "Keine Emigration nach der Eroberung (von Mekka), aber Krieg und Entschlossenheit".[7] Sie erkennen diesem Hadith Universalgültikeit zu, während die anderen Schulen meinen, daß er nur für die Muslime galt, die in und um Mekka wohnten, und die nach der Eroberung nicht mehr zur Emigration verpflichtet waren.[8] Ursprünglich bezog sich diese Forderung nur auf neubekehrte Muslime,

---

Madjmaʿ al-anhur sharh multaqa al-abhur. 2 Bde. Istanbul: Dar al-ʿAmirah li-al-Tibaʿah, 1301, I, S. 609; Muhammad Amin Ibn ʿAbidin. *Radd al-Muhtar ʿala al-Durr al-Mukhtar sharh Tanwir al-Absar.* 5 Bde. Bulaq: Dar al-Tibaʿah al-ʿAmiriyyah, 1299 d.H., III, S. 349–50; Abu Bakr ibn Masʿud al-Kasani. *Badaʾiʿ al-sanaʾiʿ fi tartib al-sharaʾiʿ.* 10 Bde. Kairo: Zakariyaʾ ʿAli Yusuf, o.J. (um 1970), IX, S. 4374–5; Muhammad Aʿla ibn ʿAli al-Tahanawi. *Kitab kashshaf istilahat al-funun.* Ed. Muhammad Wadjih, ʿAbd al-Haqq und Ghulam Qadir. 2 Bde. Calcutta: 1862 (Neudruck, Teheran: 1968), I, 466.

4 ʿAbd al-Hamid al-Shirwani. *Hashiyah ʿala Tuhfat al-Muhtadj* (li-Ibn Hadjar al-Haythami) *sharh al-Minhadj li-Abi Zakariyaʾ Yahya al-Nawawi.* 8 Bde. Mekka: al-Matbaʿah al-Miriyyah, 1304–5 d.H. (1886–8 n.Chr.), VIII, S. 62.

5 Bukhari: *djanaʾiz* 79.

6 Abu Dawud: *djihad* 95; Nasaʾi: *qasamah* 27.

7 Bukhari: *djihad* 1, 27, iman 41, *sayd* 10, *maghazi* 35; Muslim: *imarah* 85, 86; Abu Dawud: *djihad* 2; Tirmidhi: *siyar* 32; Nasaʾi: *bayʿah* 15.

8 Abu Bakr ibn ʿAli al-Razi al-Djassas. *Ahkam al-Qurʾan.* Ed. Muhammad al-Sadiq Qamhawi. 2. Dr. 5. Bde. Kairo: Dar al-Mushaf, o.J. IV, S. 262; Abu Bakr Muhammad Ibn ʿAbd Allah Ibn al-ʿArabi. *Ahkam al-Qurʾan.* Ed. °Ali Muhammad al-Badjawi. 4 Bde. Kairo: ʿIsa al-Babi al-Halabi 1387 d.H. /1967 n.Chr., II, S. 876; Abu al-Walid Muhammad Ibn Rushd (der Großvater). *Kitab al-Muqaddamat.* 2 Bde. Kairo: Matbaʿat al-Saʿadah, 1325 d.H./1907 n.Chr., II, S. 285; al-Shirwani,

die außerhalb des *Dar al-Islam* lebten und dort zum Islam übergetreten waren. Später wurde diese Interpretation aber auch auf Muslime angewandt, die in den von Ungläubigen eroberten Gebieten wohnten.

Die britische *East India Company* breitete in Vorderindien von 1750 an allmählich ihren Machtbereich durch Protektionsverträge, Annexierung und Eroberung aus. 1765 übertrug der Mogulkaiser Shah ʿAlam II den Briten die Rechte auf die Einnahmen Bengalens, das vornehmlich von Muslimen bewohnt war. Durch das von den Briten entwickelte Steuersystem (the *Permanent Settlement*) wurde die Klasse der muslimischen Feudalherren (*zamindars*) ruiniert, gleichzeitig verloren viele muslimische Bauern ihr Land und wurden in die Lage landloser Lohnarbeiter versetzt. Da die *East India Company* ohne Rücksicht auf die Folgen den Anbau der für die gewinnbringenden Produkte stark förderte, wurde die Landwirtschaft in Bengalen weitgehend zerstört. Auch die einheimische Handwerksindustrie kämpfte mit großen Schwierigkeiten wegen der Einfuhr billiger industrieller Produkte. In anderen Teilen Indiens waren die Folgen der britischen Machtausbreitung vielleicht weniger katastrophal, aber fast überall verkümmerte die Klasse muslimischer Feudalherren und erlitten die Händler in den Großstädten schwere Verluste durch die Konkurrenz europäischer Händler. Dazu kam noch, daß die Muslime sich den Hindus unterlegen fühlten, da diese den fremden Einflüssen aufgeschlossener gegenüber standen, eher geneigt waren, englisch zu lernen und deshalb in der Verwaltung und im Militär stärker vertreten waren.

Dies alles verstärkte die spezifisch islamische Prägung des anti-britischen Widerstandes, der von den indischen Muslimen angeführt wurde. In der ersten Hälfte des 19. Jahrhunderts äußerte sich dieser Kampf gegen die britische Kolonialherrschaft in puritanischen, vom Wahhabitentum beeinflußten[9] politischen Strömungen. Die wichtigsten Gruppierungen waren die *Faraʾizi* Bewegung in Bengalen und die *Tariqa-i Muhammadiyya*-Bewegung, deren Anhänger von den Briten "*Wahabites*" genannt wurden, obwohl sie keine organisatorische Verbindung mit den Wahhabiten Zentralarabiens hatten. Die religiöse Triebfeder ihres Kampfes war die Überzeugung daß Indien durch

---

o.c. VIII, S. 62–3; Abu Muhammad ʿAbd Allah ibn Ahmad Ibn Qudamah. *al-Mughni sharh Mukhtasar al-Khiraqi*. Ed. Taha Muhammad al-Zayni. 10. Bde. Kairo: Maktabat al-Qahirah, 1388–9 d.H./1968–9 n.Chr., IX, S. 293–5.

9 Die Führer der antibritischen Bewegungen haben fast alle einige Zeit in Arabien zugebracht, wo sie mit dem Wahhabismus in Kontakt kamen. Der wahhabitische Einfluß zeigt sich auch deutlich in den von ihnen erteilten *Fatwas*, die darlegen, daß das Freitagsgebet in dem von ihnen als *Dar al-Harb* angesehenen Indien ungültig sei. Diese Meinung stimmt nicht überein mit der in Vorderindien verbreiteten hanafitischen Schule. Cf. Ibn ʿAbidin, o.c. I, S. 589, 594.

die britische Fremdherrschaft *Dar Harb* geworden sei und für den Islam zurückerobert werden müsse. Bereits 1803 hatte der Gelehrte Shah ʿAbd al-ʿAziz (1746–1824), Sohn des berühmten Theologen Shah Wali Allah in einer *Fatwa* dargelegt, daß Indien *Dar Harb* sei, da die Ungläubigen die faktische Herrschaft besäßen und die Verwaltung, die Steuererhebung und die Bestrafung von Verbrechen gemäß den Gesetzen der Ungläubigen ausgeübt würden.[10] Daß Shah ʿAbd al-ʿAziz bezüglich der Herrschaft der Marathas, der hinduistischen Fürsten, denen der Mogulkaiser früher unterstand, nicht dieselbe Ansicht vertreten hat, kann nicht theologisch begründet werden[11] und beweist deutlich seine anti-britische politische Gesinnung. Ähnliche *Fatwas* wurden von Hadjdji Shariʿat Allah (1781–1840) erteilt, dem Führer der Fara'izi-Bewegung[12] und von Shah Ismaʿil Shahid (gest. 1831) und Shah ʿAbd al-Hayy (gest. 1828) der eine Schwiegersohn und der andere Neffe von Shah ʿAbd al-ʿAziz, zwei Gelehrte die sich der *Tariqa-i Muhammadiyya* angeschlossen hatten.[13] Sayyid Ahmad Barelvi (1786–1831), der Führer der *Tariqa-i Muhammadiyya* zog daraus den Schluß, daß die Briten zwar bekämpft werden müßten, daß dieser Kampf jedoch von einem sicheren, außerhalb der britischen Einfluß sphäre liegenden Gebiet ausgeführt werden sollte. Deshalb riefer zur Emigration aus dem *Dar al-Harb* auf und begründete sein strategisches Konzept mit der klassischen islamischen Lehre von der Emigration (*hidjrah*) als religiöser Pflicht.[14]

Nach dem von den Briten niedergeschlagenen Aufstand des Jahres 1857, sahen die Muslime der oberen Schichten ein, daß nur durch die Zusammenarbeit mit den Briten ihre eigenen Interessen gesichert werden konnten. Diese Muslime, die in Sayyid Ahmad Khan (1817–1898) ihren ideologischen Anführer fanden, wollten ihre Loyalität gegenüber der Kolonialmacht beweisen. Dabei kam ihnen die Zweideutigkeit der klassischen juristischen Texte zu Hilfe.

Viele *Fatwas* aus dieser Zeit betonen, daß die Briten die Religionsfreiheit schützten und die Anwendung der *Shariʿah* zuließen, sodaß Indien folglich als

10 M. Mujeeb. *The Indian Muslims*. 2. Dr. London: Allen & Unwin, 1969, S. 390–1. Muhammad Abdul Bari, *The politics of Sayyid Ahmed Barelvi*. Isl. Cult. XXXI (1957) S. 156–64.

11 P.M. Holt, Ann K.S. Lambton & Bernard Lewis. *The Cambridge History of Islam*. 2 Bde. Cambridge: Cambridge University Press, 1970, II, S. 73. Auch der Inder al-Tahanawi meint, daß in jener Zeit Indien als *Dar Islam* angesehen werden müsse. Er schrieb um 1745: "Vorsichtshalber wird dieses Land als *Dar al-Islam wa-al-Muslimin* betrachtet, obwohl es den Verfluchten gehört und diese Teufel offenbar die Herrschaft ausüben". (al-Tahanawi, o.c., I, S. 466). Cf. W.W. Hunter. *The Indian Musalmans: Are they Bound in Conscience to Rebel against the Queen?* London: Trübner & Cy. 1871, S. 133–4.

12 Mujeeb, o.c. 391; Qeyamuddin Ahmad. *The Wahabi Movement in India*. Calcutta: Mukhopadhyay, 1966, S. 88.

13 Hunter, o.c. S. 140.

14 Ahmad, o.c. S. 217, 325, 340; Hunter, o.c. S. 70.

Dar Islam angesehen werden müsse. Die Briten sollten daher nicht bekämpft werden; sie seien außerdem durch Verträge legitimierte Gewalthaber. Selbst wenn diese Argumentation nicht akzeptiert würde, widerspräche doch jeder Widerstand den Gesetzen der *Shari'ah*, da die britische Macht weit überlegen sei und ein solcher Kampf keine Aussicht auf Erfolg haben könne. Mit derartigen *Fatwas* und Abhandlungen[15] versuchte diese Gruppe von Muslimen den Briten zu beweisen, daß der Islam die britische Fremdherrschaft nicht grundsätzlich ablehne und daß die Muslime treue und loyale Untertanen des britischen Imperiums sein könnten. In dieser Zeit wurden auch die *Muftis* in Mekka um ihr Urteil über die Lage Vorderindiens gefragt. Ihnen wurde die Sache leichter gemacht, indem die Frage eingeschränkt formuliert wurde: ob der, Indien unter der britischen Herrschaft *Dar Harb* oder *Dar Islam* sei. Auf diese Frage konnten sie ohne mit den Texten der Fiqh-Bücher in Konflikt zu kommen, antworten daß Indien zum *Dar al-Islam* gerechnet werden müsse. Wären sie aber gefragt worden, ob die indischen Muslime zum Kampf gegen die Briten verpflichtet seien, hätten die Antworten ihnen sicher mehr Schwierigkeiten gemacht. Die durch die *Shari'ah* festgelegte Antwort ist klar und eindeutig: jeder Angriff von Ungläubigen auf islamisches Gebiet muß abgewehrt werden, gleichgültig ob das eroberte Gebiet *Dar Harb* wird oder nicht. Mit einer irenischen Auslegung des Gesetzes hätten sich in diesem Fall die mekkanischen *Muftis* den Zorn der Orthodoxie zugezogen; mit einer Antwort die zum Widerstand gegen die Briten aufgerufen hätte, wären sie mit den osmanischen Behörden in Konflikt gekommen, da zu dieser Zeit die Beziehungen zwischen Großbritannien und der Pforte ziemlich gut waren.[16] Jedenfalls war die Ansicht, daß Indien *Dar Islam* sei und daß die Briten nicht bekämpft werden sollten die herrschende Meinung der muslimischen Bourgeoisie bis zu den Balkankriegen (1912–14). Dann erst kamen neue fundamentalistische und nationalistische Strömungen auf, die das Verhältnis zu den Briten in neuem Licht sahen.[17]

Die französische Eroberung Algeriens trug einen grunsätzlich anderen Charakter als die britische Kolonisation Indiens. Während die Briten ihre Gewalt allmählich und nur in Ausnahmefällen mit militärischen Mitteln

---

15 Mujeeb, o.c. S. 399; Hunter, o.c. S. 112, 121 ff. 214–5; Syed Ahmad Khan Bahadur. *Review on Dr. Hunter's Indian Musulmans.* Benares: Medical Hall Press, 1872, *passim;* Abdur Rahim. *The Principles of Muhammadan Jurisprudence.* 2. Dr. Lahore: All Pakistan Legal Decisions, 1963. S. 395–7.

16 Die Texte dieser *Fatwas*, bei Hunter, o.c. 213–4; Ahmad Khan, *Review*, S. I, II; weiter noch: C. Snouck Hurgronje. *De Atjehers.* 2. Bde. Batavia/ Leiden: Landsdrukkerij/E.J. Brill, 1894, II, S. 387–8.

17 Mujeeb, o.c. S. 400.

ausbreiteten, war die Eroberung Algeriens ein ausschließlich militärisches Unternehmen. 1830 besiegte die französische Armee den türkischen Herrscher und besetzte die Küstenstädte Algeriens. In diesen Städten ertrug man gelassen die französische Besetzung, Widerstand wurde nur von den Stämmen des Hinterlandes geleistet, die sich auch vorher schon öfters der türkischen Herrschaft entzogen hatten. Der Widerstand organisierte sich hauptsächlich in religiösen Orden (*Turuq*), unter denen der *Qadiriyyah-Orden* vom Anfang an eine bedeutende Rolle spielte.[18] 1832 riefen die westalgerischen Stämme ʿAbd al-Qadir ibn Muhiyy al-Din (1808–1883) zum Emir der Stammeskonföderation aus, der den Kampf gegen die Franzosen anführen sollte. ʿAbd al-Qadir gehörte zum *Qadiriyyah-Orden*. Zusammen mit seinem Vater hatte er einige Jahre zuvor (zwischen 1827 und 1829) die *Hadjdj* vollbracht und war während der Reise in Kontakt mit dem Wahhabismus gekommen und von dieser Lehre stark beeindruckt worden. Im Kampf gegen die Franzosen verstand er es, in gewisser Weise den Partikularismus der algerischen Stämme zu überwinden. Das verbindende Element war für ihn der Islam; seine Anziehungskraft wurde noch verstärkt durch die islamfeindliche Politik der Franzosen in den besetzten Gebieten, die sich in der Umwandlung von Moscheen in Kirchen und der Zerstörung islamischer Friedhöfe manifestierte. ʿAbd al-Qadir war immer bestrebt, sein politisches und militärisches Tun in Übereinstimmung mit der *Shariʿah* zu bringen. Davon zeugen seine Briefe, in denen er ausländische Religionsgelehrte um Gutachten bittet, in denen ihm ausgelegt wird, was der Islam in Bezug auf bestimmte Aspekte des von ihm geführten Krieges und seines Verhältnisses zu den ihm feindlich gesinnten Stämmen vorschreibt.[19]

18 Cf. Ahmed Nadir. *Les ordres religieuses et la conquete francaise* (1830–1851). *Rev. Alg. des Sc. pol.* IX No. 4 (Dez. 1972) S. 819–73.

19 Mir sind die folgenden Briefe und Antworten bekannt:
(1) Ein Brief aus dem Jahre 1837 an den marokkanischen Sultan mit der Bitte, von seinen Gelehrten eine *Fatwa* erteilen zu lassen hinsichtlich einiger spezifischer Fragen. Die *Fatwa* wurde verfaßt vom *Shaykh al*-Islam al-Hasan ibn ʿAbd al-Salam al-Tasuli. Text des Briefes und der *Fatwa* in: Muhammad ibn ʿAbd al-Qadir *Tuhfat al-zaʾir fi taʾrikh al-Djazaʾir wa-al-amir ʿAbd al-Qadir.* 2. Dr. Kmt. und Anm. v. Mamduh Haqqi. Beirut: Dar al-Yaqazah al-ʿArabiyyah, 1964, S. 316–29. Franz. übers.: E. Michaux-Bellaire. *Traduction de la Fetoua du Faqih Sidi ʿAli Et Tsouli contenant le "Soual" du Hadj Abdelqader ben Mahi Ed Din et la response. Archives Marocaines* 11 (1907), S. 116–28, 395–454; 15 (1909), S, 158–84.
(2) Im selben Jahre ergeht die Bitte um eine Fatwa an ägyptische Gelehrte Cf. *Tuhfat al-zaʾir*, S. 329. Der Verfasser der Tuhfah, der Sohn ʿAbd al-Qadirs, behauptet, die Antwort nicht gesehen zu haben. Diese ist jedoch in der Fatwa-Sammlung des ägyptischen malikitischen Gelehrten Muhammad ʿIllaysh (1802–1881) erhalten. Cf. Muhammad ʿIllaysh. *Fath al-ʿali al-malik fi al-fatwa ʿala madhhab al-imam Malik.* 2 Bde. Kairo: Matbaʿat al-Taqaddum al-ʿIlmiyyah, 1319 d.H., I, S. 313–28.

Die Frage, ob der von den Franzosen besetzte Teil Algeriens *Dar Harb* oder *Dar Islam* sei, spielte dabei kaum eine Rolle. Die Lage war allerdings auch viel eindeutiger als in Indien, wo die muslimischen Fürsten großenteils ihren Thron behalten hatten und die Machtausbreitung der Briten eher durch Protektionsverträge als durch direkte Eroberung verwirklicht wurde. Außerdem gab es in der in Indien vorherrschenden hanafitischen Schule verschiedene Theorien, während die in Algerien vertretene malikitische Lehre eindeutig war. Die von ʿAbd al-Qadir angefragten *Fatwas* setzen alle voraus, daß das von den Franzosen besetzte Gebiet *Dar Harb* sei und dass die Franzosen bekämpft werden müßten. In der Politik ʿAbd al-Qadirs spielt die Theorie der Emigration eine viel wichtigere Rolle, da durch massives Überlaufen der von den Franzosen unterworfenen Stämme seine Macht gestärkt wurde. Mit Ausnahme einer einzigen *Fatwa*, behandeln alle die Frage, ob unter nichtislamischer Verwaltung stehende Muslime zur Emigration verpflichtet seien. ʿAbd al-Qadir selbst verfasste im Jahre 1843 eine Abhandlung zu diesem Thema.[20] Über diese Frage hat es heftige Auseinandersetzungen gegeben zwischen den Gelehrten, die unter französischer Verwaltung geblieben waren und die die Meinung vertraten, daß die Emigration keine religiöse Pflicht sei und den Gelehrten, die entgegengesetzter Ansicht waren.[21] Da die malikitische Schule nur eine Meinung kannte, kann man annehmen, daß die erste Gruppe von Gelehrten zur hanafitischen Schule gehörte, die bezeichnender Weise die Schule der türkischen Herrscherklasse war. In seiner Abhandlung greift ʿAbd al-Qadir in heftig polemisierendem Ton in die Diskussion ein, wofür das folgende Zitat als Beispiel gelten soll:

> Ich habe gehört, daß jene Dummköpfe, die ohne Wissenschaft zu besitzen, *Fatwas* erteilen und deshalb irren und irreführen, und auf die die Worte des Propheten: ʻEs wird für den Menschen eine Zeit kommen, in der ihre Gelehrten mehr stinken als das Aas eines Esels' anwendbar ist, daß diejenigen für ihre Meinung, daß Emigration keine religiöse Pflicht sei als

(3) Ein Brief aus dem Jahr 1840, an den *Qadi* von Fes, mit der Bitte um eine *Fatwa* über den Krieg und die gesetzliche Lage der mit den Franzosen kollaborierenden Stämme. Text in: *Tuhfat al-zaʾir*, S. 384–93.

(4) Ein Brief, geschrieben um 1846 an den ägyptischen Gelehrten ʿIllaysh mit der Bitte um eine *Fatwa* über den Verrat des marokkanischen Sultans. Text in: *Tuhfat al-zaʾir*, S. 471–80; Illaysh, Fath, I. 328–34.

20 Text in: *Tuhfat al-zaʾir*, S. 411–23.

21 ʿIllaysh, *Fath*, I, S. 313; M.B. Vincent. *Études sur la loi musulmane (rite de Malik) Legislation criminelle.* Paris: Joubert, 1842, S. 123–4.

> Argument anführen den Hadith: 'Keine Emigration nach der Eroberung (von Mekka)'. Dieser Hadith kann aber nicht als Beweis gelten.[22]

Die *Fatwas* und 'Abd al-Qadirs Abhandlung betonen alle oft unter Anführung von Präzedenzfällen aus der Zeit des islamischen Rückzuges aus Spanien, daß die Emigration aus dem Gebiet der Ungläubigen für die Muslime eine bindende Pflicht sei von der man nur in Fällen absoluter Unmöglichkeit, z.B. wenn man blind ist und keinen Begleiter finden kann oder so krank ist, daß man nicht mehr reisen kann, entbunden werden kann. Viele folgten dem Aufruf zur Emigration.[23] Es gab sogar im Lager von 'Abd al-Qadir eine große Gruppe, die wieder auswandern wollte, weil sie sich an das schlichte, karge Leben nicht gewöhnen konnte.[24]

Auch nach den Sieg des französischen Heeres über 'Abd al-Qadir und seiner erzwungenen Übergabe blieb der Geist des Widerstandes und des *djihad* noch unter den Algeriern lebendig. Hungersnot, Epidemien und der von den Franzosen begangene Landraub brachten das Volk noch verschiedentlich in Aufstand gegen die Unterdrücker. Erst 1871, nach der Unterdrückung der Rebellion in der Kabylei, hatte Frankreich Algerien fest in seiner Gewalt. Die algerischen Muslime waren gezwungen in einem Lande zu leben, in dem die politischen Strukturen nur dem Interesse der *colons* dienten und in dem das Erziehungswesen bewußt die arabisch-islamische Identität unterdrückte. Die militärische Überlegenheit der Franzosen machte jeglichen weiteren Widerstand unmöglich. Wirtschaftliche Krisen und die Überzeugung daß es Muslimen verboten sei, unter der Verwaltung der Ungläubigen zu leben, brachten viele dazu sich dem islamischen Gebot der Emigration zu unterwerfen und aus zu wandern, vor allem nach Marokko, Tunesien und Syrien, wo 'Abd al-Qadir sich nach seiner Freilassung aus französischer Gefangenschaft niedergelassen hatte. 1893, nach einer Hungersnot im Gebiet um Constantine, nahm der Auszug algerischer Muslimen nach Syrien für die Franzosen beunruhigende Ausmaße an. Die Kolonialverwaltung, die hier hauptsächlich die Wirkung der panislamischen Propaganda des osmanischen Sultans sah, wollte der Emigration gebieten.[25] Um ihre Maßnahme auch religiös unterbauen zu können, wandte sich der Generalgouverneur, Jules Cambon, an die mekkanischen Muftis mit der Bitte um *Fatwas* in dieser Angelegenheit. Wie vor zwanzig

22 *Tuhfat al-za'ir*, S. 316.

23 Charles-Robert Ageron. Les Algériens Musulmans et la France (1871–1919) 2 Bde. Paris: Presses Universitaires de France, 1968, II, S. 1080.

24 'Illaysh, Fath, I, 320.

25 Ageron, o.c., II, S. 1080–2.

Jahren, als sie über die Lage in Indien befragt wurden, gaben die mekkanischen Muftis auch jetzt keine eindeutige, auf die Lage in Algerien bezogene Antwort. Sie gaben sich damit zufrieden, die diesbezüglichen Texte der älteren Juristen zu zitieren. Einig waren sie sich darüber, daß Muslime zur Emigration verpflichtet sind wenn sie ihre religiösen Pflichten nicht öffentlich erfüllen können. Sie enthielten sich jedoch jeglicher Beurteilung der Lage in Algerien.[26] Die *Fatwas* wurden in Algerien verbreitet und die Zahl der Auswanderer nahm ab; da sich aber zur gleichen Zeit die wirtschaftliche Lage besserte,[27] ist es unmöglich zu sagen, ob die *Fatwas* allein den Rückgang der Abwanderung bewirkt haben.

Am Beispiel Indiens und Algeriens habe ich zu erläutern versucht, welche Rolle der Islam im frühen Widerstand gegen die Kolonialmächte gespielt hat. Primäre Ursachen des Widerstandes waren wirtschaftliche und gesellschaftliche Faktoren: große Teile der einheimischen Bevölkerung wurden in ihrer Existenz bedroht. Daß der Kampf jedoch stark religiös geprägt war, lag daran, daß in einer Zeit, in der die Begriffe Nation und Nationalismus noch nicht existierten, der Islam das einzige Element war, das die Bevölkerung verband und aktivierte und außerdem die Opposition gegen die christliche, koloniale Macht motivieren konnte. Es ist auffällig, daß die wichtigsten Widerstandsbewegungen stark vom Wahhabismus beeinflußt waren. Wahrscheinlich konnte gerade diese puritanische Richtung, die den Islam rein erhalten wollte, sich gegen alle Erneuerungen sträubte und dementsprechend scharf gegen die Ungläubigkeit reagierte, in dieser Periode am besten das ideologische Konzept für den anti-kolonialen Kampf liefern.

---

26 Octave Depont & Xavier Coppolani. *Les Confréries Religieuses Musulmanes.* Alger: Adolphe Jourdan, 1897, S. 33–7.

27 Ageron, o.c., II, S. 1082.

CHAPTER 23

Idjtihad and *Taqlid* in 18th- and 19th-Century Islam

Islamic reformism as it came into existence by the end of the 19th century was a response to the challenge of the increasing Western impact in the Islamic world.* The way this reformism expressed itself was, however, to a large extent conditioned by tradition. All kinds of issues that became particularly associated with it had already been part and parcel of the Islamic heritage and subject of fierce debates. One of these issues – a crucial one in present-day reformism – is the *idjtihad* versus *taqlid* discussion.[1] Reformers claimed the right to interpret the Koran and the *Sunnah* independently from the prevailing opinions of the lawyers of the four *madhhabs*. Their claims were opposed by the followers of these *madhhabs*, who held that since long nobody was qualified anymore to interpret the sources on his own, and that all Moslems were nowadays bound to abide by the decisions of the scholars of the *madhhabs*.

This discussion is not a novel one. Throughout Islamic history there have been scholars to attack the prevailing notion that *taqlid* is obligatory. In general they belonged to the fundamentalist tradition in Islam. This is no coincidence as the concept of *idjtihad* is structurally related to fundamentalism. John Voll has applied the term fundamentalism to such tendencies in Islamic thought as stress the transcendence of God as opposed to his immanence, unity as opposed to diversity and authenticity as opposed to openness.[2] In my opinion a further characteristic ought to be added: the emphasis on the essential equality of all believers.

The link between *idjtihad* and authenticity is quite obvious. For the fundamentalists, *idjtihad* means to approach the sources of Islam directly in order to ascertain as positively as possible Allah's commands, as revealed by Him to His prophet Mohammed. Obligatory adherence to the opinion of a *madhhab* introduces the element of human reasoning, which is liable to err. Therefore it forms an obstacle for the believer in his quest of the authentic prescriptions, the knowledge of which can only be obtained from the prophet. Moreover,

* Paper read at the 10th Congres de l'Union Européenne des Arabisants et Islamisants (Edinburgh, September 1980).

1 This discussion is still going on. For a recent example, cf: S. Wild, "Muslim und Madhab. Ein Brief von Tokio nach Mekka und seine Folgen in Damaskus", in: *Die islamische Welt zwischen Mittelalter und Neuzeit. Festschrift fur H.R. Roemer zum 65. Geburtstag.* (Beirut, 1979), pp. 674–89.

2 John Voll, "The Sudanese Mahdi, frontier fundamentalist", IJMES 10 (1979), pp. 147–8.

 | DOI:10.1163/9789004420625_024

these *madhhabs* did not come into existence until the third century of Islam and do therefore not belong to the pure Islam of the Companions and the Followers. In addition, these *madhhabs* have been one of the causes of disunity amongst the Moslems by compelling them to follow different opinions.

The relation, finally, between the fundamentalists' emphasis on the transcendence of Allah and *idjtihad* is more complicated. Transcendence in this connection means that Allah is completely independent and separate from His creation. Man cannot know Allah's commands except through His revelation to the Prophets. Prophecy therefore forms the sole line of communication between the Creator and His creation. Only by following and obeying Mohammed can a Moslem be a true believer. In accordance with this notion of separation between Allah and mankind, the fundamentalists consider it impossible that men, other than prophets, can communicate with Allah, for example by mystical illumination. Consequently, they strongly condemn the view that the founders of the *madhhabs*, being saints, had direct access to divine knowledge and were therefore infallible (*ma'sum*), a notion to be found for instance in the works of the 16th-century scholar al-Sha'rani.[3] For the champions of *taqlid* this was one of the principal justifications for their position. This last point is also intimately connected with the fundamentalists' emphasis on the essential equality of all believers. The only hierarchy they acknowledge is one based on piety and learning, qualities that one can acquire by one's own efforts. The most radical fundamentalists claim therefore that, through assiduous study, any Moslem can obtain the rank of *mudjtahid*.

In this paper I shall analyse the views on *idjtihad* and *taqlid* of four fundamentalist authors who lived in the 18th and 19th centuries.[4] They are the well-known Indian scholar Shah Wali Allah al-Dihlawi (1703–62),[5] the Wahhabite

3 'Abd al-Wahhab al-Sha'rani, *al-Mizan* (Cairo, Matba'at al-Azhar, 1351/1932), vol. 1, pp. 40 ff.

4 In this article I shall not deal with the ideas of the Sudanese *Mahdi* on *idjtihad* and *taqlid*. Although they certainly fit within the wider framework of fundamentalist thought, they depart radically from the established doctrine. The *Mahdi* rejected *taqlid* and abolished the existing *madhhabs*. Just as the other fundamentalists, he wanted to found his rulings exclusively on the Koran and the *Sunnah*. However, claiming to be in direct contact with the prophet Mohammed, his notion of *idjtihad* was different from the accepted notion. In his view, his decisions derived immediately from the source of the *shari'ah*, the prophet, and were therefore superior to decisions arrived at by normal *idjtihad*. Consequently, he could refute the argument of his opponents that he was not qualified to practise *idjtihad*, by pointing out that the prophet himself communicated with him. Cf. al-Hasan b. Sa'd al-'Abbadi, *al-Anwar al-saniyyah li-zalam al-munkirin 'ala l-hadrah al-Mahdiyyah* (Omdurman, 1305 [1888]), pp. 230–41.

5 For general information on Shah Wali Allah, see Saiyid Athar Abbas Rizvi, *Shah Wali-Allah and his times* (Canberra, Ma'rifat Publishing House, 1980). He wrote two treatises on the

scholar and judge Hamd b. Nasir b. Mu'ammar (d. 1810),[6] who was a pupil of Muhammad b. 'Abd al-Wahhab and a faithful servant of the first Sa'udi state and can therefore be regarded, in the absence of any substantial treatise on the subject by the founder of the movement,[7] as representative of Wahhabite thought; the Yemenite scholar Muhammad b. 'Ali al-Shawkani (1760–1832)[8]

---

subject: *'Iqd al-djid ahkam al-idjtihad wa-l-taqlid* (Cairo, al-Maktabah al-Salafiyyah, 1398 [1978], 56 pp.) (henceforth: SHWA-Iqd) and *al-Insaf fi bay' sabab ikhtilaf fi l-ahkam al-fiqhiyyah* (Cairo, al-Maktabah al-Salafiyyah, 1385 [1965], 48 pp.). The first treatise has been partially translated by M.D. Rahbar in MW 45 (1955), pp. 346–58.

6 Hamd b. Nasir b. 'Uthman b. Mu'ammar al-Nadjdi al-Tamimi was born in 'Uyaynah. He studied in Dir'iyyah under Muhammad b. 'Abd al-Wahhab, his brother Sulayman b. 'Abd al-Wahhab and under Ibn Ghannam. Then he became a teacher himself. In 1211 (1796–7) the Wahhabite ruler 'Abd al-'Aziz sent him to Mecca in order to defend the Wahhabite doctrine in a debating contest with Meccan scholars, which was held at the instigation of the *sharif* of Mecca, Ghalib b. Musa'id. His defence of Wahhabism was later published in *Al-Hadiyyah al-Sunniyyah wa-l-tuhfah al-Wahhabiyyah al-Nadjdiyyah* (Collected by Sulayman b. Sahman, ed. by Muhammad Rashid Rida, 2nd impr. Cairo, Matba'at al-Manar, 1344 [1925–6]), pp. 52–88. After the Wahhabite conquest of the Hejaz, he was appointed as inspector of the administration of justice in Mecca (*mushrif 'ala ahkam qudat Makkah al-mukarramah*). He died in 1225/1811. See: 'Abd al-Rahman b. 'Abd al-Latif Al al-Shaykh, *Mashahir 'ulama' Nadjd wa-ghayrihim* (2nd impr. Riyad, Dar al-Yamamah, 1394 [1974]), pp. 202–6, and 'Abd Allah b. 'Abd al-Rahman b. Salih al-Bassam, *'Ulama' Nadjd khilal sittat qurun* (Mecca, Maktabat al-Nahdah al-Hadithah, 1397 [1978]), vol. I, pp. 239–43. His treatise "*Risalat al-idjtihad wa-l-taqlid*" (henceforth: HIM-Ris) has been published in *Madjmu'at al-rasa'il al-Nadjdiyyah* (Cairo, Matba'at al-Manar, 1346–9 [1928–31]), vol. II, pt. 3, pp. 2–30.

7 The only statement on the problem of *idjtihad* and *taqlid* that I could trace in the works of Muhammad b. 'Abd al-Wahhab, is a rather lapidary passage in his "Sittat usul 'azimah mufidah djalilah" (publ. in *Madjmu'at al-Tawhid al-Nadjdiyyah*, Cairo, Matba'at al-Manar, 1345 [1926], p. 140). It runs as follows:

"The sixth principle: Rejecting the practice, established by Satan, with regard to abandoning the Koran and the *Sunnah* and following various divergent opinions and tendencies. This, i.e. the practice established by Satan, is [based on the opinion] that the Koran and the *Sunnah* can only be known by an absolute *mudjtahid* and that an absolute *mudjtahid* is a person with so many qualifications that they are maybe not even to he found completely in Abu Bakr and 'Umar. If someone is not like this, he must [according to this opinion] keep away from them [i.e. Koran and *Sunnah*, as [if bound by] a positive and unequivocal obligation, and if he [nevertheless] seeks guidance in them, he is either a heretic or a fool because of their difficulty".

This brief passage contains by implication a number of basic elements to he found in most fundamentalist writings on the subject: the fact that the obligation of *taqlid* keeps the believer away from Allah's revelation and leads to disunity amongst the Moslems, and that *idjtihad* can still be practised and is not as difficult as the adherents of *taqlid* pretend.

8 Muhammad b. 'Ali al-Shawkani (1760–1832) studied, taught and issued *fatwas* in San'a', Yemen. Originally he belonged to the Zaydite *madhhab*, but before he reached his thirtiest year, he realized that *taqlid* was to be rejected. Therefore, he began practising *idjtihad* independently of the existing *madhhabs*. In 1795 the *Imam* of Yemen, al-Mansur billah,

and finally the North African founder of the Sanusiyyah tariqah, Muhammad b. ʿAli al-Sanusi (1787–1859).[9] They all wrote treatises on the subject. On the other hand I shall pay some attention to the writings of their opponents.[10]

---

appointed him supreme judge, an office he occupied until his death. He often acted as the *Imam's* secretary and in that capacity he corresponded between 1807 and 1813 with the leaders of the first Saʿudi state. See: his autobiography in *al-Badr al-taliʿ bi-mahasin man baʿd al-qarn al-sabiʿ* (Cairo, Matbaʿat al-Saʿadah, 1348 [19301), vol. II, pp. 214–25 and further vol. II, pp. 6–8 and vol. I, p. 464; Muhammad b. Muhammad b. Yahya Zabarah, *Nayl al-watar min taradjim ridjal al-Yaman fi l-qarn al-thalith ʿashar* (Cairo, al-Matbaʿah al-Salafiyyah, 1350 [1931–2]), vol. [1, pp. 297–302; another biography is to be found in the introduction to his *Nayl al-awtar sharh muntaqa l-akhbar min ahadith sayyid al-akhyar* (Cairo, Mustafa l-Babi l-Halabi, n.d.), vol. I, pp. 3–8. For his ideas on *idjtihad* and *taqlid* I have consulted the following works: *al-Qawl al-mufid fi adillat al-idjtihad* (ed. Muhammad Munir, 2nd impr., Cairo, Idarat al-Tibaʿah al-Muniriyyah, n.d. [ca. 1925], 48 pp.) (henceforth: SHAW-Qawl) and *Irshad al fuhul ila tahqiq al-haqq min ʿilm al-usul* (Cairo, Idarat al-Tibacah al-Muniriyyah, 1348 [1929], 252 pp.) (henceforth: SHAW-Irshad), esp. pp. 220–40.1 have not been able to see the following works, which, according to their titles, deal with the subject: *Tashkik ʿala l-tafkik*, summarized by Muhammad Siddiq Khan under the title *al-Iqlid li-adillat al-idjtihad wa-l-taqlid* (Istanbul, 1295), *Djawab al-muwahhidin fi dafʿ al-shubah ʿan al-mudjtahidin*, ms. (both listed in GAL, S II, pp. 818–9) and *Risalat bughyat al-mustafid fi l-radd ʿala man ankar al-idjtihad min ahl al-taqlid* (listed in the biographical introduction to *Nayl al-awtar*, p. 8).

9 For general information on al-Sanusi, see: Ahmad Sidqi al-Dadjdjani, *al-Harakah al-Sanusiyyah. Nash'atuha wa-numuwuha fi l-qarn al-tasiʿ ʿashar* (Beirut, Dar Lubnan, 1967), Helmut Klopfer, *Aspekte der Bewegung des Muhammad b. ʿAli al-Sanusi* (Wiesbaden/Cairo [1967]) and Nicola A. Ziadeh, *Sanusiyah. A study of a revivalist movement in Islam* (Leiden, E.J. Brill, 1958). For this article I have used the following works by al-Sanusi, *Iqaz al-wasnan fi l-ʿamal bi-l-hadith wa-l-Qur'an* (Beirut, Dar al-Kitab al-Lubnani, 1388–1968, 143 pp.) (henceforth: SAN-Iqaz) and *Kitab al-masa'il al-ʿashar al-musamma Bughyat al-maqasid fi khulasat al-marasid* (Beirut, Dar al-Kitab al-Lubnani, 1388–1968, 297 pp.) (henceforth: SAN-Bughyah). Brockelmann and Dadjdjani mention other titles on the same subject, viz. *Bughyat al-sul fi l-idjtihad wa-l-ʿamal bi-hadith al-rasul* (GAL, S II, p. 883: Dadjdjani, *op. cit.*, p. 136), *Tawaʿin al-asinnah fi taʿani al-sunnah, Risalah shamilah fi mas'alatay al-qabd wa-l-taqlid, Izahat al-akinnah fi l-ʿamal wa-l-Kitab wa-l-Sunnah, Fahm al-akbad fi mawadd al-idjtihad* and *al-Usuliyyah fi l-ʿamal bi-l-Kitab wa-l-Sunnah* (Dadjdjani, *op. cit.*, pp. 135–6). These works have not been printed and as yet I have not been able to locate their mss.

10 I have made use of the following material: a) *Fatwas* against the Sanusiyyah, issued by two Egyptian Malikite *muftis*, Mustafa l-Bulaqi (1800–47) and Muhammad ʿIllaysh (1802–83), published in Muhammad Illaysh, *Fath al-ʿAli al-Malik fi l-Fatwa ʿala madhhab al-imam Malik* (Cairo, Matbaʿat al-Taqaddum al-ʿIlmiyyah, 1321 [1903], I, pp. 51–98; b) Da'ud b. Sulayman al-Baghdadi al-Naqshabandi al-Khalidi (1816–1882), *Ashadd al-djihad fi ibtal daʿwa l-idjtihad* (Istanbul, al-Maktabat Ishiq [sic], 1978, 44 pp.; which is a photographical reprint of the ed. Bombay, 1305 [1887]). This treatise, composed in 1876, was written as a refutation of the views of some Indian Moslems who claimed that they were *mudjtahids* and not bound to follow one of the *madhhabs*. Probably the *Ahl-i Hadith* are meant, spiritual heirs of Ibn ʿAbd al-Wahhab and Shawkani. c) Ibrahim al-Samannudi al-Mansuri,

The classical meaning of *idjtihad*, as found with some minor variations in the technical dictionaries and handbooks on legal methodology, is "exerting one's effort in order to derive from the bases of the law (*adillah*) an opinion concerning a legal rule".[11] Its complement is *taqlid*, by which term is understood "accepting an opinion concerning a legal rule without knowledge of its bases".[12] From about the 10th century AD the opinion came to prevail that independent *idjtihad* was not admitted anymore and that all Moslems, laymen as well as scholars, had to accept the opinions of the founders of the *madhhabs*. This view was substantiated by a number of Traditions to the effect that in the course of time real knowledge will disappear. One of these, often cited in the discussion on *idjtihad* and *taqlid*, says: "Allah will not take knowledge away by removing it from the people. He will rather take it away by seizing the scholars. Then, when there is no [true] scholar left, people will take ignorant leaders and these will give *fatwas* without knowledge. Thus they err and lead people astray".[13] At some point of time, scholars, looking back, began to describe the process of "closing the door of *idjtihad*" (*insidad bab al-idjtihad*) as a historical process characterized by a gradual narrowing down of the scope for *idjtihad*. As a result they distinguished different degrees of *idjtihad*. The founders of the *madhhabs* were absolute *mudjtahids* (*mudjtahid mutlaq*). After them came the *madhhab-mudjtahids* (*mudjtahid fi l-madhhab*), followed by the *fatwa-mudjtahids* (*mudjtahid fi l-fatwa*) and finally the pure *muqallids*. There is some variation in the terminology and the number of degrees, but the general idea is clear.[14]

Saʿadat al-darayn fi l-radd ʿala l-firqatayn al-Wahhabiyyah wa-muqallidat al-Zahiriyyah (2 vols., Cairo, Matbaʿat Djaridat al-Islam, 1319 [1901–2]). This voluminous work, completed in 1895, is a refutation of Wahhabite and Sanusite views. The problem of *idjtihad* and *taqlid* is dealt with in vol. II, pp. 206–309. In this part the author draws extensively on Da'ud b. Sulayman's book *Ashadd al-djihad* and the *fatwas* by al-Bulaqi and ʿIllaysh. More remarkable, however, is the fact that he gives many quotations from SHWA-Iqd and SHWA-Insaf (which he summarizes on pp. 238–49), in support of his own view. Of course, he does not cite the crucial passages where Shah Wali Allah deviates from the traditional theory.

11 See e.g. ʿAli b. Muhammad al-Djurdjani, *Kitab al-taʿrifat* (Cairo, al-Matbaʿat al-Hamidiyyah al-Misriyyah, 1321 [1903]), p. 5; Muhammad Aʿla b. ʿAli al-Tahanawi, *Kitab kashshaf istilahat al-funun* (ed. Muhammad Wadjih e.a., Calcutta, The Asiatic Society of Bengal, 1862), vol. I, pp. 198–9.

12 See e.g. Djurdjani, *op. cit.*, p. 44; Tahanawi, *op. cit.*, vol. II, p. 1178.

13 Wensinck, *Concordance*, vol. IV, p. 320.

14 *EI*[2], vol. III, pp. 1026 ff., s.v. *Idjtihad;* Nicolas P. Aghnides, *Mohammedan theories of finance, with an introduction to Mohammedan law and a bibliography* ([2]Lahore, Premier Book House, 1961), pp. 116–7; Abdul Rahim, *The principles of Muhammadan jurisprudence according to the Hanfi* [sic], *Maliki, Shafiʿi, and Hanbali schools* (Lahore, Indus Publishers,

The obligation of *taqlid*, however, was never universally accepted. It was opposed by Ibn Hazm (994–1064), but also by scholars belonging to the existing *madhhabs*, such as Abu ʿUmar Yusuf b. ʿAbd al-Barr (978–1070), Sind b. ʿInan al-Azdi (d. 1146) and ʿIzz al-Din b. ʿAbd al-Salam (1181–1262). Up to the 16th century there have been scholars who claimed the rank of *idjtihad* themselves, or were recognized as such by other scholars.[15] There existed also the doctrine, held by the Hanbalites and a number of Shafiʿites that no period would ever be devoid of a *mudjtahid*, generally understood as absolute *mudjtahid*.[16] In the 13th century some kind of compromise was worked out in the Shafiʿite *madhhab* by al-Nawawi (1233–77) and others. They did so by making a distinction between the independent absolute *mudjtahid* (*mudjtahid mutlaq mustaqill*) and the affiliated absolute mudjtahid (*mudjtahid mutlaq muntasib*). Whereas the *mudjtahids* of the former category, that of the founders of the *madhhabs*, had complete freedom in deriving the rules from the bases of the law, those of the latter category were in some general way bound to adhere to the principles laid down by their *imams*, the founders of the *madhhabs*. On specific points decisions would often concur with those of the *imams*. This, however, cannot be regarded as *taqlid*, since the affiliated *mudjtahid* accepts his *imam's* ruling with complete understanding of its bases and arguments. Those who claimed to be absolute *mudjtahids*, after the establishment of the *madhhabs* were, according to this theory, absolute *mudjtahids* of the second category since the first category had ceased to exist after the 10th century AD.

n.d.), pp. 182–3; Muhammad Abu Zahrah, *Tarikh al-madhahib al-Islamiyyah* (Cairo, Dar al-Fikr al-ʿArabi, n.d.), vol. II, pp. 112–22; Id., *Usul al-fiqh* (Cairo, Matbaʿat Mukhaymir, n.d.), pp. 374–85.

15 For lists of those who claimed to be *mudjtahids* up to the 16th century, see SHAW-Irshad, p. 224, SHWA-Insaf, pp. 31–2 and SAN-lqaz, p. 72. Al-Sanusi quotes Ahmad Baba (d. 1672), *Kifayat al-muhtadj li-maʿrifat man laysa fi l-Dibadj* (GAL II, 467, S II, 716) and Abu Bakr al-ʿArabi al-Hadrami, *Nihayat al-sul* (not listed in GAL).

16 ʿAbd Allah b. ʿAbd al-Muhsin al-Turki, *Usul madhhab Ahmad b. Hanbal, Dirasah usuliyyah muqtarinah* (Cairo, Matbaʿat Djamiʿat ʿAyn Shams, 1394 [1974]), pp. 635–7; Muhammad Abu Zahrah, *Ahmad b. Hanbal, hayatuh wa-ʿasruh, araʾuh wa-fiqhuh* (Cairo, Dar al-Fikr al-ʿArabi, n.d.), p. 369; W. Montgomery Watt, "The closing of the door of *igtihad*", in: *Orientalia Hispanica*, I (ed. J.M. Barral, Leiden, E.J., Brill, 1974), pp. 675–8. Watt's article is based on SHAW-Irshad, p. 223, where the words of the Shafiʿite al-Zarkashi (d. 1392) are cited. A similar text is to be found in SAN-Iqaz, pp. 81–3, where the Shafiʿites al-Birmawi (d. 1427) and al-Suyuti (d. 1505) are quoted. The latter appears to have written a separate treatise on the subject, entitled *al-Radd ʿala man akhlad ila l-ard wa-djahil ann al-idjtihad fard* (not listed in GAL).

Thus this theory recognized the possibility that there were still absolute *mudjtahids*, without however compromising the superiority of the founders of the *madhhabs*.[17]

Returning to our fundamentalist authors, we find that two of them, Shah Wali Allah and al-Sanusi, have adopted the above-mentioned theory lock, stock and barrel. With obvious approval they quote these Shafiʿite authors and declare emphatically that the rank of affiliated absolute *mudjtahid* can still be attained. Implicitly, they seem to claim this rank for themselves.[18] Ibn Muʿammar, who relies mainly on Hanbalite authorities, differs in terminology. He distinguishes between the absolute or independent *mudjtahid* on the one hand, and the *mudjtahid* who is bound to adhere to the opinions of the *imams* (*al-mudjtahid al-muqayyad bi-madhahib al-aʾimmah*) on the other. The latter one's *idjtihad*, he says, is mixed with *taqlid*. Given the decisions of the different *imams*, he must look for the best-founded opinions. This form of *idjtihad*, Ibn Muʿammar claims, can still be exercised.[19] All three authors complain about the fact that most people seem not to be aware of this distinction and that they erroneously think that, in the absence of an independent absolute *mudjtahid*, there can be only *taqlid*. Al-Shawkani is the most radical of the four. He rejects the theory that there are different degrees of *idjtihad*. In his view there is but one form of *idjtihad*, which can be practised by anybody possessing sufficient knowledge. Those who maintain that the door of *idjtihad* has been closed and that only the four *imams* have truly understood the Koran and the Sunnah:

> tell lies. about Allah and accuse Him of being not capable of creating people that understand what is His law for them and how they must worship Him. They make it appear as if what he has enacted for them through His Book and His Messenger, is not an absolute but a temporary law, restricted to the period before the rise of the *madhhabs*. After their appearance, there was no Book and no *Sunnah* anymore [if these people are to be believed], but there emerged persons that enacted a new law and invented another religion for this community and replaced the Book and the *Sunnah*, that were there before them, by their personal opinions and sentiments.[20]

17 SHWA-Iqd, pp. 7–8, 26–8; SHWA-Insaf, pp. 31–2; SAN-Iqaz, pp. 62–3; SAN-Bughyah, pp. 83–6.
18 *Ibid.*
19 HIM-Ris, pp. 5, 26–7.
20 SHAW-Qawl, p. 27; SHAW-Irshad, p. 224.

One of the arguments of the traditional scholars for the obligation of *taqlid* is the complexity and difficulty of deriving rules from the Koran and the *Sunnah.* Only people of eminence, such as the four *imams* could handle this, because they belonged to the best generations, the generations among whom the pure knowledge still prevailed, knowledge obtained immediately or almost immediately from the Prophet. Moreover, these *imams* were aided by supernatural talents. Since then, however, times have only deteriorated and people with the skills and knowledge of the *imams* no longer exist.[21] The fundamentalists' main argument, that they rely solely on the Koran and the *Sunnah,* whereas traditional scholars base their opinions only on the words of their *imams,* is false according to their adversaries. When traditional scholars relate the words of their *imams,* they do so since they consider these opinions as founded on the Koran and the *Sunnah,* as interpreted by these *imams* with their superior knowledge. When the fundamentalist assert that they rely exclusively on the Koran and the *Sunnah,* they nevertheless make use of interpretation. But being of a later generation, their understanding of the rules of interpretation is far below the standard of the *imams.* Therefore, their argument is based on a false contrast and does not hold good.[22] Against this, fundamentalist authors argue that *idjtihad* has in fact become easier. Whereas the people of the first generations travelled for months in order to collect Traditions, now everything has been compiled in books that are easily accessible. Consequently, it is no longer difficult to acquire the tools needed for *idjtihad.* Al-Shawkani goes as far as to assert that it suffices for a *mudjtahid* to have studied one compendium (*mukhtasar*) in each of the five disciplines required for *idjtihad.*[23]

The cornerstone of traditional doctrine is that *taqlid* is lawful, and that it became obligatory in the course of time, due to the absence of *mudjtahids.* About this last point, the traditional scholars maintain, there is consensus. In fact, they contend, it ought to be regarded as an article of faith that one must necessarily know (*maʿlum min al-din daruratan*).[24] They hereby implicitly accused their opponents of apostasy. For the lawfulness of *taqlid* they produce the following Koranic texts: "*Question the people of the Remembrance, if ye do not know.*" (K. 16:43; 21:7) and "*O believers, obey Allah, and obey the Messenger and those in authority amongst you.*" (K. 4:59). Moreover, they quote the following Traditions: "*My companions are like the stars: no matter whom of them you*

21 ʿIllaysh, *op. cit.*, pp. 80–7; Baghdadi, *op. cit.*, *passim;* Samannudi, *op. cit.*, *passim*, esp. II, pp. 282–93. They all quote long passages from al-Shaʿrani's *Mizan* (*cf.* note 3).

22 ʿIllaysh, *op. cit.*, p. 88; Samannudi, *op. cit.*, II, pp. 302–3, quoting ʿIllaysh.

23 HIM-Ris, pp. 10, 23; SHAW-Qawl, p. 29; SAN-Iqaz, p. 68; SAN-Bughyah, pp. 89–90, 92.

24 ʿIllaysh, *op. cit.*, p. 79.

follow, you are on the right path." and "*If one does not know what to do, the only remedy is to inquire.*"[25]

The views of al-Shawkani and al-Sanusi are diametrically opposed to this doctrine.[26] Following Ibn Hazm, they hold that *taqlid* is *bid'ah* and forbidden. They reject the assertion that there is consensus on this issue. Although, al-Shawkani adds, it would nowadays appear that almost all scholars are agreed upon this point, this of no relevance, since for a valid consensus, having force of law, only the opinions of *mudjtahids* count, whereas the scholars of these days consider themselves as mere *muqallids*. Now, by putting a ban upon *taqlid*, these authors did not imply that everybody was qualified to be a *mudjtahid*. The majority of the Moslems are laymen that have no sufficient knowledge to consult the sources. They must, therefore, have recourse to specialists. However, they must not blindly accept their opinions, but ask to be told the bases of their decisions. Or at least they must make sure of the fact that these decisions are in conformity with the Koraṇ and the *Sunnah*, by querying whether the answer contains Allah's decree or only human opinion. If the latter is the case, they must consult another specialist. This procedure then is called *ittiba'*, following or obeying, viz. the Koran and the Sunnah.[27] The Koranic arguments adduced in support of the lawfulness of *taqlid*, are not conclusive according to al-Shawkani and al-Sanusi. The verse: "*Question the people of the Remembrance, if ye do not know*", contains no general command, but has, as appears from the context, only a limited purport. It is addressed to the polytheist Meccans and exhorts them to question the Jews and the l in order to get a confirmation of Mohammed's message. However, were it to embody a general command, then it means no more than that those who do not know, must approach specialists in order to be informed of Allah's decrees. This, then, is

25 The complete text of this Tradition runs as follows: "Djabir has said: 'Once we went on a journey. Then one of our men was hit by a stone which fractured his skull. Afterwards he had a seminal emission and asked his companions whether they thought that he was allowed to perform *tayammum*. They answered that they did not think so since he had water at his disposal. He then did his ablutions and died. When they came to the messenger of Allah, they told him what had happened. Then he said: They have killed him. May Allah kill them. Why didn't they inquire, when they were at a loss [what to do], for if one does not know what to do, the only remedy is to inquire (*innama shifa' al-'iyy al-su'al*)'," *Cf.* Wensinck, *Concordance*, vol. IV, p. 457.

26 SHAW-Qawl, 2–12, 14, 17, 34–5, 38; SHAW-Irshad, 236; SAN-Iqaz, 94–5, 99, 102, 105, 118–20; SAN-Bughyah, 95–103. Many of their arguments are, sometimes even verbatim, taken from Ibn Qayyim al-Djawziyyah (*I'lam al-muwaqqi'in 'an Rabb al-'alamin*, Cairo, Idarat al-Tiba'ah al-Muniriyyah, n.d., esp. vol. II, pp. 128–208).

27 This distinction between *taqlid* and *ittiba'* is not a new one. The term *ittiba'* had already been used by Ahmad b. Hanbal and Ibn 'Abd al-Barr (*cf.* Ibn Qayyim al-Djawziyyah, *op. cit.*, vol. II, pp. 131, 137, 139). Ibn Daqiq al-'Id (d. 1302–3) had called it "the layman's *idjtihad*" (*cf.* SAN-Naz, p. 94).

ittibaʿ and not *taqlid*. As for K. 4:59, that orders the believers to obey "those in authority", i.e. the lawyers, they reply that this duty of obedience is not absolute. Only when their commands are in agreement with Allah's decrees as laid down in the Koran and the *Sunnah*, are these commands to be followed. This, then, also amounts to *ittibaʿ* and not to *taqlid*. The same holds for the Tradition "*If one does not know what to do, the only remedy is to inquire*". Finally they consider the Tradition "*My Companions are like the stars*" to be weak. For the interdiction of *taqlid* they quote the second part of the verse about obeying "those in authority" (K. 4:59): "*If you should quarrel on something refer it to Allah and the messenger*". Since the *imams* have quarreled, problems must be referred to Allah and the messenger, i.e. the Koran and the *Sunnah*, and *taqlid* is therefore forbidden. Shah Wali Allah, who expressly refutes Ibn Hazm's view that *taqlid* is forbidden, and Ibn Muʿammar have a more differentiated approach to the matter.[28] *Taqlid*, they say, is lawful for laymen (*ʿammi*) and scholars without sufficient knowledge, but not for those who can comprehend and appreciate the bases of the law. Neither is *taqlid* lawful for those who are bent on following the rulings of only one specific lawyer in everything he says, even if this be against the Koran and the *Sunnah*, because they are convinced that he is infallible (*maʿsum*).

In fact the whole discussion boils down to the question what is to be preferred: a clear text of the Koran and the *Sunnah* or the rulings of one *madhhab*. The point our authors have in common is that they all reject the strict adherence to one *madhhab*, as if its founder were infallible and like a prophet.[29] They denounce *madhhab* fanaticism (*taʿassub al-madhhab*) as an innovation (*bidʿah*), since there were no *madhhabs* in the period of the *Sahabah*, and as one of the major causes of the division and enmity amongst Moslems.[30] They further criticize the practice of the *madhhab-people*, of only citing such traditions as are in agreement with the opinions of their *imam*. When confronted with other traditions, they go to great length in order to prove that this special tradition is not authentic or has been abrogated by another tradition. If they are at their wits' end, they retort: "Do you think that you are better versed in the science of tradition than our *imam?* No doubt, he was aware of this tradition, but he must have seen some reason for not following it".[31] Against this form of fanatical *taqlid*, the fundamentalists argue, the Koran warns in several places,

---

28 SHWA-Iqd, pp. 24–5, 42–3; HIM-Ris, pp. 6–7.

29 HIM-Ris, p.23; SHWA-Iqd, pp. 18, 24; SAN-Iqaz, pp. 55, 58, 116; SAN-Bughyah, pp. 62, 123. Both al-Sanusi and Shah Wali Allah cite the Shafiʿite scholar ʿIzz al-Din b. ʿAbd al-Salam (d. 1262) in this connexion.

30 HIM-Ris, p.23; SHAW-Qawl, pp. 14, 17; SAN-Iqaz, p. 106; SAN-Bughyah, p. 73; (*cf.* Ibn Qayyim al-Djawziyyah, *op. cit.*, vol. II, pp. 162–3, 204).

31 HIM-Ris, p.23; SHWA-Iqd, pp. 18–24; SAN-Iqaz, pp. 43, 55, 58, 106, 112–3; SAN-Bughyah, 73.

e.g. in K. 9:31 ("*They have taken their rabbis* and their monks as lords apart from Allah and the Messiah, Mary's son."), K. 43:23 ("We indeed found our fathers upon a community, and we are following upon their traces."), and K. 33:67 ("They shall say. 'Our Lord, we obeyed our chiefs and great ones, and they led us astray from the way'.").[32] Moreover, they quote sayings of the four imams to the effect that their opinions should be disregarded if they are at variance with an authentic traditions.[33] Finally, they mention a number of logical refutations of blind taqlid that had already been developed by al-Muzani (d. 877–8) and Ibn 'Abd al-Barr.[34]

However, beyond their common condemnation of blind *madhhab* fanaticism, our authors' opinions vary. Again, the most radical position is taken by al-Shawkani and al-Sanusi. Their view is unambiguous: Under all circumstances Moslems must follow the Koran and the *Sunnah*, even in the case of texts that no *imam* has ever followed. Having cited a number of authorities to this effect, al-Shawkani remarks that he is ashamed of having to record all these opinions and asks rhetorically why Moslems are in need of the authority of any scholar in order to be convinced that the words of Allah and His prophet must be preferred to the opinions of scholars.[35] Traditional doctrine cautions against immediately following a tradition. Only when it has been established beyond doubt that there is no counterargument (*muʿarid*), e.g. another tradition that abrogates it, is it allowed to follow it. Al-Sanusi's reply to this objection is that abrogation seldom occurs with regard to the *hadith* and that there are at the most ten traditions with abrogating force. Immediately following a tradition entails therefore less risk of falling into error, than relying on the opinions of fallible scholars.[36] In theory at least, al-Shawkani's and al-Sanusi's views amount to a total rejection of the *madhhabs*. The opinions of the four *imams*, al-Sanusi says, should only be used to come to a better understanding of the bases of the law.[37] Shah Wali Allah and Ibn Muʿammar do not go that far. They accept the four *madhhabs* and hold that Moslems are bound to follow

32 SHWA-Iqd, p. 25; SHAW-Qawl, p. 29; SAN-Iqaz, p. 92. Al-Shawkani and al-Sanusi quote Ibn 'Abd al-Barr, as cited by Ibn Qayyim al-Djawziyyah (*op. cit.*, vol. II, p. 134).

33 HIM-Ris, pp. 3, 27; SHWA-Iqd, p. 48; SHAW-Qawl, p.21; SHAW-Irshad, p. 236; SAN-Iqaz, pp. 23–6, 118, 121 (*Cf.* Ibn Qayyim al-Djawziyyah, *op. cit.*, vol. II, pp. 139–40).

34 HIM-Ris, pp. 28–9; SHWA-Iqd, p. 24; SHAW-Qawl, pp. 15, 24; SHAW-Irshad, p. 237; SAN-Iqaz, pp. 122–3. (*Cf.* Ibn Qayyim al-Djawziyyah, *op. cit.*, vol. II, pp. 136–8).

35 SHAW-Qawl, p. 23.

36 SAN-Bughyah, pp. 124–5, quoting Ibn Qayyim al-Djawziyyah; SAN-Iqaz, pp. 116–7, quoting Salih al-Fullani (d. 1803; v. GAL S II, 523) and Muhammad Hayah al-Sindi (d. 1750; *v.* GAL S II, 522). Fullani's book *Iqaz al-himam* is one of Sanusi's major sources. Pp. 98–128 of SAN-Iqaz consist almost exclusively of quotations from Fullani's book, which, in its turn, draws heavily upon Ibn Qayyim al-Djawziyyah's *Iʿlam al-muwaqqiʿin.*

37 SAN-Iqaz, p. 120, quoting Fullani.

them, since beyond them there is no truth.[38] Shah Wali Allah argues that in their existence there is great benefit. In jurisprudence, just as in all other sciences and trades, it is helpful to make use of the experience of your predecessors. Moreover, the Prophet has summoned the believers to follow the majority (*al-sawad al-aʿzam*). For Shah Wali Allah, it seems, all *madhhabs* are of equal value. Ibn Muʿammar, however, in accordance with the official Wahhabite doctrine, shows some predilection for the Hanbalite School, since, he remarks, Ahmad b. Hanbal was the *imam* that, more than any other one, clung to the bases of the law.[39] A follower of a *madhhab*, however, provided that he has a certain knowledge of jurisprudence, may follow a tradition against the opinion of his own *madhhab*, if an *imam* of another *madhhab* has also done so. In general they hold it advisable to follow those opinions upon which the majority of the *imams* are agreed. If there is no majority, one should follow the opinion with the strongest arguments.

From the foregoing it will be clear that the views of our four fundamentalist authors with regard to the *idjtihad-taqlid* issue are not identical. Remotest from traditional doctrine are al-Shawkani's ideas since he does not differentiate between the various ranks of *idjtihad*, claims that anybody with a minimal knowledge of jurisprudence can be a *mudjtahid* and considers *taqlid* absolutely forbidden. Second comes al-Sanusi, who adopts the distinction between the independent and the affiliated *mudjtahid* and thereby acknowledges the superiority of the four *imams*, although he reserves the right to go beyond the pale set by them if a tradition is to be preferred. He is followed by Shah Wali Allah, who holds that Moslems are bound to accept the rulings of the four *imams*, but shows no bias towards any of the Schools. Finally comes Ibn Muʿammar, whose ideas are similar to those of Shah Wali Allah, except that he has strong affinity with the Hanbalite *madhhab*. The point they have in common, is that they criticize the strict adherence to one *madhhab*, for better and for worse.

The study of these fundamentalists texts on *idjtihad* and *taqlid* is not yet completed. Further research may yield interesting results. The texts contain a wealth of quotations reproducing fragments of earlier discussions on this issue. Therefore, they are mines of information, that can give us some insight in the historical process of "the closing of the door of *idjtihad*", a process of which we still know very little, and provide us with a solid starting-point for further investigations.

Systematical exploration of the quotations to be found in these texts may also shed light on another problem: the continuity of the fundamentalist tradition. It would appear that there was an upsurge of fundamentalism in the 18th

38 SHWA-Iqd. pp. 23, 36; HIM-Ris, pp. 21, 26–7.
39 HIM-Ris, p. 22.

and 19th centuries. In my view, this is only partly true. What we actually do observe is an upsurge of politico-religious movements with an ideology based on fundamentalist ideas. Since these ideas criticize prevailing beliefs and institutions and are therefore orientated towards change, they can provide a suitable ideology for activist movements. These ideas, however, did exist long before these movements appeared. It is a well-known fact that many of these ideas can be traced back to Ibn Taymiyyah (1263–1328) and his student Ibn Qayyim al-Djawziyyah (1292–1350). This is also borne out by the fact that, except Shah Wali Allah, all of our authors quote these scholars frequently. There are, however, a number of identical passages by other, sometimes quite obscure, authors to be found in these texts. This may well be evidence of a common tradition on which our authors have drawn. This impression is corroborated when one studies their "intellectual family-trees". John Voll has pointed out the relationship between Muhammad b. ʿAbd al-Wahhab and Shah Wali Allah on the one hand and a group of Medinese scholars with Muhammad Hayah al-Sindi (d. 1750) as a focal point on the other.[40] They were all connected with Ibrahim b. Hasan al-Kurani al-Kurdi (d. 1690)[41] and Abu l-Baqaʾ al-Hasan b. ʿAli al-ʿUdjaymi (or al-ʿAdjami) (d. 1702).[42] Now, it can be established that al-Sanusi is also linked with these scholars, not only through his intellectual "grandfather" Muhammad Hayah al-Sindi, but also via independent chains of teachers.[43] Al-Shawkani is connected with Ibrahim al-Kurani through one chain of teachers.[44] In my view, these relationships deserve more study. Systematical examination of the body of quotations, in combination with the use of the available biographical and autobiographical material (e.g. the *fahrasahs* and *idjazahs*) can give us more insight into the continuity of the fundamentalist tradition.

40 John Voll, "Muhammad Hayya al-Sindi and Muhammad ibn ʿAbd al-Wahhab: an analysis of an intellectual group in eighteenth-century Madina", BSOAS 38 (1975), pp. 32–9.

41 GAL, II, p. 385, S II, p. 520.

42 GAL, II, p. 392, S II, p. 536.

43 One of al-Sanusi's teachers, al-Badr b. ʿAmir al-Miʿdani was a student of al-Sindi's, which links him with both al-Kurani and al-Hasan b. ʿAli al-ʿUdjaymi. Further he is connected with them through his teacher, the Meccan *mufti* and *qadi* ʿAbd Sulayman ʿAbd al-Hafiz b. Muhammad al-ʿUdjaymi via the Meccan muftis ʿAbd al-Malik and ʿAbd al-Qadir b. Abi Bakr. The latter was a student of both al-Kurani and al-Hasan al-ʿUdjaymi. Finally he is connected with them through his teacher ibn Sharif. These "intellectual pedigrees" are to be found in: Muhammad b. ʿAli al-Sanusi, *al-Manhal al-rawi al-raʾiq fi asanid al-ʿulum wa-usul al-taraʾiq* (Beirut, Dar al-Kitab al-Lubnani, 1388–1968), pp. 13–5.

44 Al-Shawkani is connected with al-Kurani through his teacher Yusuf b. Muhammad b. ʿAlaʾ al-Din, whose grandfather was a student of al-Kurani's. See: Muhammad b. ʿAli al-Shawkani, *al-Badr al-Taliʿ*, vol. 1, pp. 11–2.

CHAPTER 24

Islam and the Legitimation of Power

The Mahdi-Revolt in the Sudan

The authority of any state is, in the last instance, founded on physical force. Force alone, however, is not sufficient.* A viable administration presupposes a general conviction that the existence and the maintenance of the state is necessary for the public weal and is in everybody's interest. When this conviction is absent, which may be the case e.g. in newly conquered and occupied territories, a government is compelled to fall back on the use of brutal force. This, however, is an anomalous situation. In general, the use of force is minimised because of the existence of a common ideology, shared by the majority of the people, which justifies the existence and functioning of the state. Now, such an ideology contains a basic contradiction. On the one hand, it must legitimatise the state and the way it is governed by its rulers. On the other hand, it must, in order to be universally accepted, pay some attention to the needs and problems of its subjects, e.g. by setting standards for just and equitable government. However, more often than not, rulers do not live up to these standards. In order to fulfil its stabilising role, such an ideology must deal with this problem in such a way as to give a certain satisfaction to the ruled, without endangering the position of the government and the rulers.

The topic of this article will be how Sunnite Islamic political theory has come to grips with this problem and how it was affected by it. I shall do so by analysing a discussion in connection with a particular event, a revolt of Moslems against Moslems, during which both parties brought forward arguments taken almost exclusively from Islamic political theory. This polemic, one of the last of its kind,[1] was part of the ideological struggle between the followers of the Sudanese *Mahdi* and the supporters of the Turco-Egyptian government in the Sudan. It remained totally within the framework of Islam and was unaffected by Western political ideas and concepts.

* Thanks are due to the staff of the Oriental Section of Durham University Library, where the Durham Sudan Archive is kept, for their kind assistance in providing me with the material for this article.

1 At the XXI. Deutscher Orientalistentag (Berlin, 23–29 March 1980) Dr. Hans Kruse read a paper entitled: "*Takfir und Gihad bei den Zaiditen des Jemens*" in which he discussed a very similar polemic that took place around 1890 between representatives of the Ottoman government and the Zaydite Imam.

 | DOI:10.1163/9789004420625_025

Basically a *Herrschaftsideologie*, the pivot of Islamic political theory, as found in the works on *kalam* and *fiqh*, is the duty of obedience to the ruler. Besides K. 4:59 ("*O ye who have believed, obey God and obey the messenger and those of you who have the command.*") there are legion Traditions to the same effect. To mention but a few: "*Obedience is obligatory on you, even if an Abyssinian slave with a head like a raisin* (or: *with his nose cut off*) *be put in command over you*", and: "*You are obliged to hear and to obey in prosperity and adversity, willingly or unwillingly, and even when you are treated unjustly.*" This duty, however, is not unrestricted. Its limits are to be found in the Tradition: "*Obedience is a duty as long as one is not ordered to do what is sinful* (bi-l-maʿsiyyah) *and if one is ordered to do what is sinful, then there is no obedience.*" Some authors, however, have clung to the old Murdjiʾite position that obedience is due as long as the ruler remains nominally a Moslem. As a consequence of his right to be obeyed, the ruler may fight those that resist his orders and rise against him.

Islamic constitutional theory lays down a number of qualifications for the ruler, the caliph. He must be just (*ʿadl*, in its technical legal sense), capable of interpreting the sacred texts, competent in administration and warfare, able-bodied and of Qurashite descent. His main task is to uphold religion and to rule according to the *Shariʿah*. He must be appointed either by an oath of allegiance (*bayʿah*) on the part of people of influence (*ahl al-hall wa-l-ʿaqd*) or by designation on the part of his predecessor. The legitimacy of succession by usurpation, however, was already recognized in an early period. Only the Shafiʿites maintained that a ruler forfeited his right to rule for immorality, injustice or heterodoxy, but they shrank from its consequences: armed rebellion.[2] The other schools held that a caliph could not lose his right to rule. The subjects, then, had to console themselves with the thought that an unjust and tyrannical ruler would surely be punished in the Hereafter. As one Tradition has it: "*Do not abuse* [*people of*] *authority, for if they act rightly, they will receive recompense and you must be grateful. However, if they act wrongly, the responsibility is theirs and you must patiently endure it. They are a punishment that God inflicts upon*

2 See e.g. the words of the Shafiʿite theologian al-Amidi (d. 631/1233–4): "They [the Moslems] have the right to depose him (…), when there is on his part something that leads to disturbance in the affairs of the religion and the situation of the Moslems or in that for the sake of which an *Imam* is appointed. If they are not able to depose him and to install another because of his superior power and enormous equipment and if that [his deposition] would lead to corruption of the world and to the loss of lives and if its evil consequences are more certain than the evil consequences of obeying him, then it is possible to commit the less evil of the two acts in order to avoid the greater." Sayf al-Din al-Amidi, *Ghayat al-maram fi ʿilm al-kalam*, ed. by Hasan Mahmud ʿAbd al-Latif, Cairo: Al-Madjlis al-Aʿla li-l-Shuʾun al-Islamiyya/Ladjnat Ihyaʾ al-Turath al-Islami 1391/1971, 385–6.

whomsoever He will. Meet, therefore, God's punishment not with furious rage, but with humble submission." Some authors deal with the problem whether Moslems are bound to assist their ruler in fighting rebels. They hold that this duty exists only when the ruler is just, not when he is unjust. This does not mean, however, that in the latter case they are allowed to help the rebels.[3]

After the Mongol conquest of Bagdad, which put an end to the Abbasid Caliphate, scholars had to accommodate their theory to the existing political situation. The actual exercise of power became for them the main criterion for the legitimacy of authority. Ibn Djamaʿah (d. 1333) asserts that Moslems must render obedience to a ruler who has come to power by sheer force, even if he does not possess the necessary qualifications, "in order that the unity of Moslems may be preserved".[4] Simultaneously the Hanafite-Maturidite doctrine, which restricted the caliphate in the true sense of the word to the four Rightly Guided Caliphs (*al-khulafaʾ al-rashidun*), gained wide acceptance. It was founded on the Tradition: "*The caliphate will last thirty years, then, afterwards, there will be kingship* (*mulk*)." But caliph or not, the ruler had to be obeyed for fear of civil strife (*fitnah*) and anarchy. The social and political order was to be maintained at any price, since, as the Prophet has said: "*Sixty years of tyranny are better than one hour of civil strife.*"

When the actual rulers could not claim anymore to be caliphs, religious sanction to authority had to be sought elsewhere. It was found in the theory that all power was of divine origin, a theory that can be traced back to pre-Islamic, Sassanid times. Already under the early Abbasids this theory had a certain influence, as can be seen from their titles. Instead of *khalifat rasul Allah* they began to call themselves *khalifat Allah* and *zill Allah fi l-ard.* In the handbooks for rulers, the Mirrors for Princes, a literary genre that became popular after the disintegration of the empire, this theory of the God-founded power of the ruler played a fundamental role. Political authority was regarded as the sole means to maintain social order in view of man's natural inclination to greed and violence. Therefore it was seen as a divine institution. Consequently, the religious character of obedience to the ruler was emphasized. On the other

3 For some Hanafite opinions, see Fritz Steppat, Kalifat, *Dar al Islam* and die Loyalität der Araber zum osmanischen Reich bei hanafitischen Juristen des 19. Jahrhunderts, in *Actes du Ve Congres International d'Arabisants et d'Islamisants* (Bruxelles, 31 aout–6 septembre 1970), Brussels 1971, 453–4; for Malikite opinions, see: Abu ʿAbd Allah Muhammad ibn Yusuf al-Mawwaq, *al-Tadj wa-l-iklil li-Mukhtasar Khalil*, Tripoli, Maktabat al-Nadjah, n.d., VI, 277; Muhammad ibn ʿArafah al-Dasuqi, *Hashiyah ʿala l-Sharh al-Kabir*, Cairo, Dar Ihyaʾ al-Kutub al-ʿArabiyyah, n.d., IV, 299.

4 Badr al-Din ibn Djamaʿah, *Tahrir al-Ahkam fi tadbir ahl al-Islam*, ed. H. Kofler. *Islamica* 6 (1934), 357.

hand the ruler was exhorted to be just towards his subjects and to act according to the *Shari'ah*. But apart from these general exhortations the prevailing theories contained little to satisfy the needs of the subjects.

No religion, however, is a monolithic and homogeneous body of ideas. This is also true for Islam. Besides the official, scriptural Islam of the ruling classes, there exists popular religion, more adapted to the needs of the common people, with characteristic features such as saint-worship, magic and millenarian expectations. These expectations, embodied in the belief in the coming of the *Mahdi*, are important in this connection. According to this belief, the *Mahdi* would rise towards the End of Time and conquer the whole earth in order to establish Islamic rule. He would put an end to injustice and tyranny and fill the earth with equity and justice.

His advent would inaugurate a period of prosperity and righteousness, lasting till Doomsday. Obviously, such a belief is attractive in times of social and political crises. On the one hand it can give people comfort and hope that their misery will not last forever. In that case it may lead to resignation and quietism. On the other hand it can serve as a revolutionary ideology whenever a leader arises, claiming to be the expected *Mahdi* and revolting against the existing political order. Islamic history has known many movements of this kind.

One of the last of these movements was the one led by Muhammad Ahmad Ibn 'Abd Allah (1834–85) in the Sudan. In 1881 he proclaimed that he was the expected *Mahdi*, sent by God. He claimed that he had seen the Prophet in a vision, while being free from legal impediments such as sleep, ecstasy, drunkenness or insanity. The Prophet then sat him on his throne, girded him with his sword, purified his heart and filled it with faith, wisdom and knowledge and finally declared that God had bestowed upon Muhammad Ahmad the Supreme Caliphate (*al-khilafah al-kubra*) and the mahdiship. Furthermore he informed him that he would conquer the world for Islam in order to restore the *Sunnah* of the Prophet.

Before long he had gathered followers and rose in rebellion against the Turco-Egyptian government of the Sudan. Muhammad Ahmad's principal argument for opposing the government was that God had installed him as the Supreme Caliph and that, consequently, all other rulers had to recognise him as the *Mahdi* and submit to him. If they would not do so, they were to be regarded as "unbelievers who had to be fought, since they acted against the commands of the messenger to follow us [Muhammad Ahmad] and were bent on extinguishing God's Light (cf. K. 9:32), through which He wants to make His justice visible.[5] Moreover, the Turco-Egyptian rulers – the Turks, as Muhammad

5 *Manshurat al-Imam al-Mahdi*, Omdurman 1304 (1886–7), I, 20; Na'um Shuqayr, *Tarikh al-Sudan al-qadim wa-l-hadith wa-djughrafiyyatuh*, Cairo, Matba'at al-Ma'arif, 1903, III, 134.

Ahmad used to call them – had deviated from the true religion and did not rule according to God's commands. They acted unjustly and tyrannically towards the Sudanese population and had taken "unbelievers as patrons to the exclusion of God", asking "their assistance in shedding the blood of the Community of Mohammad".[6]

About a year after the outbreak of the Mahdist revolt, the governor of the Sudan, 'Abd al-Qadir Hilmi Pasha, having suffered several serious defeats, asked the leading, pro governmental *'ulama'* to compose treatises against the *Mahdi* to incite the Sudanese to remain loyal to the existing government. A number of these treatises were published in the summer of 1882.[7] More than a year later, on 21 September 1883 (18 *Dhu l-Qa'dah* 1300), the *'ulama'* of al-Azhar issued a *fatwa* to the same effect at the request of the Egyptian government.[8]

6 *Manshurat,* II, 277; Shuqayr, III, 349. It is worthy of note that all *madhhabs* agree that in fighting Moslem rebels, unlike in fighting unbelievers, the help of non-Moslems may not be sought. The Hanafites hold that this is only allowed in case of necessity.

7 *Al-nasihah al-'ammah li-ahl al-Islam 'an mukhalafat al-hukkam wa-l-khurudj 'an ta'at al-imam* (General advice to the people of Islam not to oppose the rulers and not to shirk [the duty of] obedience to the imam), by Ahmad al-Azhari ibn Isma'il, *shaykh al-Islam* of Western Sudan; text publ. in Shuqayr, III, 383–91 and in 'Abd Allah 'Ali Ibrahim, *Al-sira' bayn al-Mahdi wa-l-'ulama'*, Khartum, Shu'bat Abhath Djami'at al-Khartum, 1968, 49–57; this treatise was finished in *Sha'ban* 1299 (June/July 1882).

Risalah fi butlan da'wa Muhammad Ahmad al-mutamahdi (Treatise on the invalidity of the claim of Muhammad Ahmad, the self-styled *Mahdi*), written by Shakir al-Ghazzi, *mufti* at the Court of Appeal in Khartum; text publ. in Shuqayr, III, 375–82.

Hady al-mustahdi fi bayan al-Mahdi wa-l-mutamahdi (Guidance for him who seeks it, to the explanation of [the difference between] the true and the false *Mahdi*), written by Muhammad al-Amin al-Darir, *shaykh al-Islam* of the Eastern Sudan; according to Ibrahim Fawzi (*Kitab al-Sudan bayn yaday Gordon wa-Kitchener*, Cairo, Matba'at al-Adab wa-l-Mu'ayyad, 1319 (1901), I, 247) it was the first pamphlet to be composed against the *Mahdi*; Shuqayr (III, 374) mentions it, but does not give the text, which seems to be lost (cf. Muhammad Ibrahim Abu Salim, *Manshurat al-Mahdiyyah*, Beirut, Dar al-Djil, 1979, 333, n. 1, where the text of Muhammad Ahmad's reply dated 28 *Sha'ban* 1299 (15 July 1882) is published). Finally Shuqayr (III, 374) lists a poem (*ra'iyyah*) by Muhammad Sharif, of which he publishes some lines. Apparently more treatises in refutation of Muhammad Ahmad's claims have been written, since in a letter dated 26 *Shawwal* 1299 (10 September 1882), addressed to the people of Ubayyad, Muhammad Ahmad mentions letters (*khutub*) "written to criticise and to refute us" by Ahmad ibn Isma'il al-Wali [=Ahmad al-Azhari], Husayn Madjdi, al-mufti Shakir [al-Ghazzi], Muhammad [al-Khudjali] walad Hatik, Walad al-Dalil a.o. During the siege of Khartum, on 23 *Dhu l-Qa'dah* 1301 (14 September 1884), the leading 'ulama' of Khartum wrote an *anti-Mahdi* letter on the instigation of Gordon, addressed to two followers of the *Mahdi, 'Abd* al-Qadir Ibrahim and Wad Nudjumi. It was signed by Musa Muhammad, Muhammad Amin al-Darir, Shakir al-Ghazzi, Husayn Madjdi and Muhammad al-Khudjali; Engl. transl. in *The Journals of Major General C.G. Gordon, C.B. at Kartoum*, ed. by A.E. Hake (London, Kegan Paul and Trench, 1885), 410–20.

8 Text publ. in Muhammad al-'Abbasi al-Mahdi, *Al-Fatawa al-Mahdiyyah fi l-Waqa'i' al-Misriyyah* (Cairo, al-Matba'ah al-Azhariyyah, 1301), II, 28–32.

A major part of these tracts was devoted to the refutation of Muhammad Ahmad's claims to be the expected *Mahdi*. With this aspect I shall not deal here. Of more interest within the framework of this article, are the arguments in support of the legitimacy of Turco-Egyptian rule. They fall in with 19th-century official Ottoman policy, that tended to emphasis the religious character of Ottoman rule and to revive the idea of the caliphate. Lawful authority, the Sudanese *'ulama'* asserted, was in the hands of the caliph in Istanbul and his lieutenant (*na'ib*), the khedive of Egypt. Obedience is due to them as a religious obligation, since their power derives from God. Shakir al-Ghazzi, *mufti* of the Western Sudan, opens his treatise with the following words:

> In the name of God, the Merciful, the Compassionate. Praise belongs to God, who has made authority a divine mystery and a religious and legal ordinance, and who has made obedience to it a binding obligation and an undisputable command. (…) Know, o Brethren (…) that religion and authority are inseparable brothers, for religion is the foundation whereas authority protects it and keeps it erect. Now, that which is not protected will perish and lack support. Therefore, religion can only exist through authority (*sultan*). The sultan then is really the one that protects the Religion and guards the lands of the Moslems. He is the shadow of God on His earth. Through him can the recommended and obligatory religious practices be carried out. He is God's deputy (*khalifah*) over His creation and the trusted guardian of what is due to Him. He has elected him from among His creatures and He has ordered them to obey him.[9]

Then he quotes the relevant Koranic verses and Traditions with regard to obedience, and concludes the chapter by summoning the Sudanese "to return to harmony and agreement", since "the consequence of dissension, strife and enmity is destruction and ruin."

In another treatise, composed by the *mufti* at the Court of Appeal in Khartum, Ahmad al-Azhari (d. 1882), a similar line of argumentation is used. The author also invokes the classical theory with regard to the caliphate without, however, mentioning the condition of Qurashite descent:

> They [the *'ulama'*] have also laid down that his [the caliph's] *bay'ah* cannot be withdrawn and that his designation (*'ahd*) cannot be revoked, unless he orders someone to become an unbeliever, or becomes an unbeliever himself. If he does not become an unbeliever, he cannot be

9 Shuqayr, III, 375.

> deposed (…), not even when he loses his justice (*ʿadalah*) and is to be described as a sinner (*fasiq*).[10]

Further he writes:

> In short, the *Imam*, who is the successor (*khalifah*) of the messenger of God, is alive today and his state is functioning in good order, supported by his ministers. All the people of Islam pronounce the *khutbah* from the pulpits in his name and pray for his victory and success. As a result of his presence and the functioning of his state, life and property of all the inhabitants if the state are protected. Disobedience to him, despite the fact that the qualities on the strength of which the people of authority have sworn allegiance to him do still exist, is forbidden for every Moslem.[11]

In the *fatwa* issued by the *ʿulamaʾ* of al-Azhar authorities are quoted to the effect that, after his death, communications by the Prophet to men, whether they receive these in their sleep or being awake, cannot alter the established rules of the *Shariʿah.* One of these rules is that a caliph can only be installed either by an oath of allegiance (*bayʿah*) on the part of the people of influence or by designation on the part of his predecessor. Muhammad Ahmad's visions have not abrogated this and therefore the present caliph in Istanbul is to be regarded as the legitimate ruler. Muhammad Ahmad's argument that the people of his region have sworn allegiance to him cannot be accepted since there are numerous Traditions declaring that when there is a caliph, a *bayʿah* to another person is null and void and has no effect whatsoever. The *fatwa* is of political interest, since it totally ignores the British occupation of Egypt and emphasises the legitimate rule of the Ottoman sultan.[12]

Muhammad Ahmad hardly responded to these treatises. When he did, he only dealt with the arguments refuting his claims to be the expected *Mahdi.* In one instance, in an undated letter (probably written in the first half of 1885, after the conquest of Khartum) to the *ʿulamaʾ* of Egypt, he gives his opinion on the Ottoman sultanate:

> You also know that the caliphate has since long passed away since its conditions have ceased to exist. What has remained are only lofty ceremonies and momentous formalities that have nothing to do with supporting

10 Ibid., 385.
11 Ibid., 391.
12 Steppat, 446–7,449 nt. 28.

> the Religion. They [the rulers] have turned themselves, their religion and their subjects over to the unbelievers, who began to act towards them as if they owned them.[13]

In this letter he further refers to "the rulers who are (or: must be) deposed because they have killed the religion of God and have given the unbelievers a strong position, with the result that they [the rulers] have begun administering justice amongst Moslems on the basis of secular laws (*qawanin*) and have turned away from the law of the Lord of the messengers." He then exhorts the *ʿulamaʾ* to refrain from obeying the Turks in accordance with the Tradition: "*No obedience is due to a creature [if this leads] to disobeying the Greater.*" Apparently, Muhammad Ahmad did not attach much importance to these constitutional questions. He believed that his Mahdiship, which God had bestowed upon him, entitled him to an authority higher than any ruler in the world. If his adversaries would not recognize his Mahdiship, they were unbelievers and could be fought. That they were bad rulers who did not pay heed to God's commandments, was not essential, but only additional evidence for his mission.

For propagandistic reasons, however, demonstrating that the Ottoman sultan and the Khedive could not be regarded as legitimate rulers, was a useful thing to do. The subject was taken up, independently from each other, by two authors, who both wrote their treatises in 1884. During the reign of Muhammad Ahmad's successor, the *khalifah* ʿAbd Allah al-Taʿayishi, both works were lithographed in Omdurman in the year 1305 H (1887–8). Ahmad al-ʿAwwam[14] (d. 1884), an Egyptian who had been exiled to the Sudan for his participation in the ʿUrabi revolt, composed his treatise[15] in Khartum during

13 Letter not included in the *Manshurat*, copy in Durham Sudan Archive, 98/2/3.

14 A resident of Alexandria, Ahmad al-ʿAwwam worked as an orator and propagandist for ʿUrabi's cause. After the British occupation of Egypt he was arrested and sentenced to banishment in the Sudan by the military court in Alexandria. In Khartum he began to sympathise with the *Mahdi* When he expressed his sympathies openly, Gordon had him arrested. Sometime later, however, he was released and given a post as a clerk in the administration. In 1884 he was executed after it had been discovered that he had a hand in the attempted burning of an ammunition plant. Cf. Richard Hill, *A bibliographical dictionary of the Sudan*, London, Frank Cass, 1967, 30, 397; Ibrahim Shahatah Hasan, *Misr wa-l-Sudan wa-wadjh al-thawrah fi Nasihat al-ʿAwwam. Dirasah muqarinah fi l-usul al-tarikhiyyah l-l-thawratayn al-ʿUrabiyyah wa-l-Mahdiyyah wa-ttidjahat al-fikr al-thawri fi ʿahdihima*, Alexandria, Muʾassasat al-Thaqafah al-Djamiʿiyyah, 1971, 10–2; Shuqayr, III, 265; Fawzi, I, 358–61.

15 *Nasihat al-ʿAwwam li-l-khass wa-l-ʿamm min ikhwanih ahl al-iman wa-l-Islam fi wudjub ittihadihim wa-ʾtilaf qulubihim bi-ttibaʿ Sayyidina Imam al-Zaman Muhammad al-Mahdi*

the siege. The other author, al-Hasan ibn Sa'd al-'Abbadi[16] (1844–1907) wrote a book[17] in which he refuted the arguments of the *Mahdi's* adversaries, devoting one chapter to the question whether obedience was due to the Ottoman sultan or the Egyptian khedive.

'Awwam's central themes, as can be expected from a former propagandist of the 'Urabi movement, are the division of the Moslem world, the corruption of the Turkish rulers of the Ottoman Empire and Egypt and the increasing European influence. Had the rulers acted in conformity with the prescriptions of Koran and *Sunnah*, he writes, the Moslems would still have been united and the Islamic world would not have become a prey to the Western powers. The rulers have furthered this development by taking unbelievers as patrons, despite clear Koranic interdictions (cf. K. 3:28; 4:144; 5:51) and allowing them to extend their influence and power. The khedive has even handed over the Sudan to the British. The result is that the *Shari'ah* is not applied anymore and that moral corruption is rampant: the rulers tolerate prostitution, bars and gambling, even in the vicinity of mosques. In such a situation the Moslems need someone, a *Mahdi* or a pious believer, to renovate their religion, to reunite the community and to arrange its affairs properly.

Islam forbids that Moslims fight each other. Should this happen, the *Imam* must mediate between the parties, as prescribed in K. 49:4 (*"If two parties of the believers fight, set things right between them, and if one of the parties oppress the*

al-muntazar 'alayh al-salam, ('Awwam's advice to all his brethren, the people of faith and Islam, concerning their duty to become united and of one mind in following our Lord, the Imam of the Time, Muhammad the expected *Mahdi*, peace be upon him), Omdurman, 1305 H (1887–8), 98. Cf. Muhammad Ibrahim Abu Salim, *Al-Harakah al-fikriyyah al-Mahdiyyah* (Khartum, Djami'at al-Khartum, Qism wa-l-Ta'lil wal-Nashr, 1970, 199–201). The text has also been published as an appendix to Hasan, *Misr wa-l-Sudan*, 228–53. According to the colophon, the author finished his treatise on 20 *Ramadan* 1301 (14 July 1884). After the fall of Khartum the manuscript fell in the hands of the Mahdists. The *taqriz*, written by 'Abd al-Ghani al-Salawi, relates that 'Awwam's treatise was read before the *Mahdi* and that he approved of it. During the reign of the *khalifah* 'Abd Allah, it was lithographed together with a commentary (*ta'liq*) by Muhammad Ibn Ibrahim Zahra (d. 1894), a Mahdist religious notable with an Azhar training.

16 al-Hasan Ibn Sa'd al-'Abbadi was born at Berber in 1884. After his training as a religious scholar, he joined the Mahdist forces in an early stage of the revolt. He then served as a provincial governor. The *khalifah* 'Abd Allah transferred him to Omdurman, where he was made a religious notable. On the Anglo-Egyptian occupation he was appointed an Islamic judge. He died in the Hejaz while making the pilgrimage. Cf. Hill, 159, 401.

17 *Al-anwar al-saniyyah li-zalam al-munkirin 'ala l-hadrat al-Mahdiyyah*, (The brilliant light beams for the darkness of those who deny the presence of the *Mahdi*), Omdurman, 5 *Dhu l-Qa'dah* 1305 H (14 July 1888), 268. The author finished his book on 5 *Ramadan* 1301 (29 June 1884). Cf. Abu Salim, *Harakah*, 197–9.

other, fight the one which is oppressive until it returns to the affair of God.") In the case of the Sudan war, the sultan or the khedive ought to have inquired into the arguments of the *Mahdi* through a committee of qualified *'ulama'*. Since they have not done so, they are worse than Pharao, who at least had asked Moses to produce evidence for his mission. The fact that the khedive has asked the scholars of al-Azhar for a *fatwa* in this matter cannot be considered as acting upon the above-mentioned Koranic order, since this was not done until two years and four months after the outbreak of hostilities, when the Egyptian army had been defeated and the Sudan had been handed over to the British.

The only instance of war between Moslems that is allowed, the author continues, is war against rebels (*bughah, khawaridj*) and bandits (*qat' al-tariq*). However, the group that rose against the government in the Sudan, and which consists of the entire Sudanese nation (*ummah sudaniyyah*), cannot be regarded as such, since their leader says that the prophet has announced to him that he is the *Mahdi* and that the Turks – i.e. the people of the Turkish government and their subjects that are like them in deeds and intention, not the whole nation – are the worst unbelievers of all people since they try to extinguish God's light. According to the *Shari'ah* their unbelief is established by the following facts: they have ceased to act in conformity with God's Book and the *Sunnah* of His messenger and follow their own inclinations (*ahwal*) instead; they neglect their Islamic subjects; they do not administer Islamic penal law but follow the European (*Ifrandji*) errors and falsehoods nowadays known as political laws (*qawanin siyasiyyah*). As a consequence immorality, wickedness and whoredom have spread in all Islamic countries under their sway.

In this situation rebellion against the Turkish government is not only allowed, but obligatory for all Moslems, in order to replace it by a just government that acts upon God's commands and prohibitions and upon the *Sunnah* of the prophet. Shirking this duty amounts to approval of unbelief, which is as bad as unbelief itself. The argument that the Ottoman sultan is the caliph in the legal sense, to whom obedience is due and who can only be dethroned for apostasy, is not valid, since the Ottoman sultans have never fulfilled the requirements for the caliphate. As for the Egyptian khedive, whose government is based on delegation by the Ottoman sultan, his rule is invalid, too, on the strength of the principle that what is based on something invalid, is itself invalid.

Whereas 'Awwam's treatment of the problem is rather unsystematic and lacks a clear line of argumentation, 'Abbadi deals with the problem in a very consistent and perspicuous way. Due to his thorough religious training he could defend his case with arguments taken from the traditional and orthodox texts. He approaches the constitutional problems of the *Mahdi* revolt in the chapter entitled: "Concerning their sixth objection, that disobedience to the sultan is only allowed if he becomes an unbeliever, that the Moslems owe allegiance to a Moslem sultan in Constantinople, that this *Mahdi* and his followers have rebelled against him and that their refusal to obey him is not permitted".[18] He logically discusses the case from different angles. In the first place he deals with the topic on the supposition that Muhammad Ahmad is really the expected *Mahdi.* In that case every ruler, regardless whether he be just or not, is obliged to follow him, since the Prophet has declared that he holds the Supreme Caliphate (*al-khilafah al-kubra*). Those who resist him are unjust tyrants on the strength of the Tradition: "*He* (*the Mahdi*) *will fill the earth with justice and equity, as it was filled with injustice and tyranny.*" If they do not recognise the *Mahdi;* they are unbelievers who must be fought according to the Tradition: "*Whosoever repudiates the Mahdi, is an unbeliever*".[19]

However, since Muhammad Ahmad's claims were based on subjective experience and thus an easy target for his sceptical adversaries, ʿAbbadi then proceeds to argue his case on the assumption that Muhammad Ahmad is not the expected *Mahdi.* To justify the rebellion against the government, he quotes several Malikite authors who hold that if a just man revolts against an unjust *Imam*, the believers are allowed to help the rebel, and even obliged to do so if the object of the rebellion is to render God's religion victorious. As for Muhammad Ahmad, no one who had known him before or after the beginning of his mission, calls his justice in question, whereas the "Turkish kings" are unbelievers, or, at any rate not far from it. Obeying them is not allowed on the strength of K. 18:28 ("... *and obey not anyone whose heart We have made neglectful of Our remembrance, but who follows his own desire, and whose behaviour is profligate.*") and K. 11:113 ("*Lean ye not upon those who have done wrong lest the Fire touch you.*"). He dwells at length on the impiety and evil deeds of the "Turks", and especially on the fact that they admire the unbelievers and have appointed them as military commanders and administrators. Moreover, the "Turks" imitate thein in dress, by wearing trousers (*mantalun*) and hats, and in their customs. They even learn their languages and praise these more than Arabic, the language of the Koran and the *Sunnah.* They call this civilisation (*tamaddun*). In the field of taxation they have neglected the Islamic prescriptions and imposed excessive taxes which they ruthlessly collect with the result that many people have fled from their homes. Finally they do not take action against those scandalous deeds that are forbidden on the strength of *idjma*ʿ, such as the production and sale of alcoholic beverages by women in the markets, the establishment of wine shops for the unbelievers, prostitution

18 ʿAbbadi, *al-Anwar al-saniyyah*, 161–81.

19 This Tradition cannot be found in any of the authoritative collections.

and overt homosexual practices. "O you Turks," the author exclaims, "if you are not identical with the people of Lot, then the people of Lot are not far away from your!" In fact they are apostates because they deny religious prescriptions that one must necessarily know. They justify the fact that they do not observe the *Shari'ah* with the word freedom (*hurriyyah*), which is a word taken from the language of the European unbelievers. They have requested the "Turks" to apply this freedom in their Islamic state and this request was granted. This means that they do not feel themselves bound by God's ordinances. As a consequence, women that ought to be secluded walk about in the markets, showing their charms and committing fornication with unbelievers. When their husbands or guardians try to prevent this, they retort: "Life is free" (*al-dunya hurriyyah*). In addition the "Turks" deride people who behave as Moslems by performing the *salah* and wearing a turban. Thus the "Turks" change God's ordinances and abolish the prescription of the Religion.

Suppose, however, the author continues, that not only the ruler but also the rebel is unjust. The problem has been dealt with by some Malikite authorities, who held that in this case Moslems must refrain from helping either party, since God will punish one tyrant by means of the other and then deal with the one that has been left. It is not allowed to fight the rebels because of the possibility that their revolt is provoked by the ruler's impiety (*fisq*) or injustice (*djawr*). In the Sudanese situation this means that Moslems may not help the Turks against the *Mahdi*, since they are unanimously regarded as unjust tyrants. Shaykh Muhammad 'Illaysh, one of the important Azhar scholars, has issued a *fatwa* to the effect that fighting the Turks is permissible under the leadership of any Moslem and obligatory if the revolt is led by a just man.[20]

Only when the ruler is just is rebellion against him forbidden. In that case it is incumbent upon the Moslems to assist the ruler, regardless whether the leader of the rebels is just or unjust. When, however, a Moslem rises against unbelievers, all Moslems must aid him. This applies to the present situation, since the English unbelievers are now the real masters in Egypt. Its governor (*wali*) has become a mere figurehead, whom they use as a means to attain their aims and to accustom the Moslems to their satanic laws. The Turks have handed over the Sudan to the English, who have sent Gordon as governor. The adversaries

20 Muhammad 'Illaysh (1802–1882) was since 1854 the Malikite *mufti* of Egypt. In spite of his old age he took an active part in the 'Urabi revolt. After the British occupation he was tried as a rebel. He died in prison. During the revolt he signed a *fatwa*, together with seven (or ten) other Azhar 'ulama', to the effect that the khedive Tawfiq was unworthy of ruling Egypt because of his cooperation with the unbelievers. Cf. Alexander Schölch, *Ägypten den Ägyptern. Die politische und gesellschaftliche Krise der Jahre 1878–1882 in Ägypten*, Zürich/Freiburg i. Br., Atlantic Verl., n.d., 216, 350. Engl. tr. of the *fatwa* in A.M. Broadley, *How we defended Arabi and his friends*, London, Chapman and Hall, 1884, 175–7.

of the *Mahdi* have chosen the side of the unbelievers, have placed themselves under their protection and fight with them against the Islamic community, in spite of Koranic verses like: "... *and God will not open for the unbelievers against the believers a way,*" (K. 4:141) and "*O ye who have believed, do not take the unbelievers as friends rather than the believers.*" (*K.* 4:144). Therefore, their argument that they owe allegiance to a Moslem sultan in Istanbul has lost its validity.

Summarising the arguments of both parties, we find that the *ʿulamaʾ* that supported the Turco-Egyptian government in the Sudan, built their case upon the following elements: the divine institution of authority; the fact that the Ottoman sultan was a caliph in the true sense of the word (which ran counter to the generally accepted doctrine in the 19th century);[21] that the Moslems owe allegiance to the caliph unless he becomes an unbeliever or orders someone to do so; and that civil strife is pernicious and ruinous and ought to be staved off at any price. In as far as they were written after September 1882, they were, for obvious reasons, silent about the British occupation of Egypt. The arguments of the defenders of the Mahdist revolt centred upon the following points: that the Ottoman sultan in not a caliph; that allegiance to the ruler is only due when he is just and acts in conformity with the *Shariʿah*; that the sultan and the khedive, because of their neglect of the *Shariʿah*, their corruption, their misrule and their cooperation with the unbelievers had virtually become unbelievers; and that the Sudan was in fact ruled by the British unbelievers.

From the foregoing it will have become clear, I hope, that Islamic political theory is not a homogeneous and rigid body of doctrine. In general it functioned as a *Herrschaftsideologie*. But in order to serve as such, it had to proclaim ideals and deal with problems that had relevance to the subjects and could offer them comfort. Political theoreticians, therefore, had to steer between the Scylla of the Islamic ideals of just government ruling according to the prescriptions of the *Shariʿah* and the Charybdis of sanctioning the existing political order. The course they followed varied and depended to a large extent upon the political situation in their times and upon their personal loyalities. This tension between ideal and practical considerations is evident from the various ways they circumscribed the obligation of obedience to an unjust ruler – especially in assisting him in fighting Moslem rebels – and the permissibility of deposing him. Some of them allowed some scope for the Islamic ideals to be implemented in case there was a flagrant discrepancy between these ideals and actual conditions. For others, however, the commitment to these ideals amounted to no more than lip service. Nevertheless, these ideals remained alive and could be used as ideological levers by political-religious movements in order to justify opposition and revolt against the existing political order.

21 Cf. Steppat, 447–50.

CHAPTER 25

Religious Attitudes towards Modernization in the Ottoman Empire

A Nineteenth-Century Pious Text on Steamships, Factories and the Telegraph

1 Introduction

The historiography of the Ottoman Empire in the nineteenth century is mainly concerned with the process of modernization and change. There is an abundance of studies on the measures of reform that were introduced in the fields of warfare, education, law administration and communication, and on the men and ideas behind them. But information on the forces of opposition and their leaders and ideologies is difficult to find. This, of course, is a result of the outcome of the historical process. Since the forces of modernization have been victorious, they have determined the vision of history. And in this vision there is little room for the losers.

What we know of the oppositional forces is that their main centre was among the ulema. During the "Auspicious Events" (*Waqaʾiʿ-i Khayriyya*) of 1826 Sultan Mahmud II had crushed the power of the main opponents to reform, the Janissaries, and thus opened the road for further innovative steps. Thereafter protests against modernization came from the ulema. Their interests were at stake, for the principal reforms affected law and education, the very fields where the ulema had a monopoly. Moreover, Mahmud II founded a Ministry of *Awqaf* in order to get some control over these religious foundations. This meant that the ulema's financial independence was gradually undermined.

The ulema did not, however, react as a body. The interests of those who belonged to the official religious hierarchy, and especially to its higher echelons, were closely linked to those of the state. Some of them even entered the ranks of the reformers. The official ulema, therefore, hardly ever voiced protest against the policy of reform. This was left to the lower clergy: preachers in small mosques, *sufi* sheikhs and, of course, the *softas*, the students of the religious schools, who sometimes came out into the streets to demonstrate against certain policies.

Although the reforms were introduced by the Ottoman sultans and their governments, it was clear to most that they were not only inspired by the West, but also were often introduced under heavy pressure of the Western powers. Thus protest against these reforms was usually coupled with an anti-Western stand. This association was strengthened, when after the Crimean

 | DOI:10.1163/9789004420625_026

War (1853–1856) the foreign impact in the Ottoman Empire became increasingly visible. Western dress – not only worn by foreigners but also by a growing number of Turks from the upper classes–, Western architecture, and modern means of transport became more prominent and began to leave their imprint on the general appearance of the major cities.

The text here translated must be seen in this context. It is one of the few known statements of religious protest against Western inspired reform and technical innovation. There must have been more of these. But printed on cheap paper and often published anonymously, many of them have been lost and the remainder is difficult to retrieve. Therefore, our text is to a certain extent unique. Moreover, its contents are original. The author has not limited himself to the ancient authorities. In this case he could not, because of the relative novelty of the problem. Therefore, he had to have recourse to his own creative intelligence. The result is an interesting example of independent reasoning.

2 The Text

The text whose translation is offered here, forms part of a small booklet which I found in Istanbul in December 1978. It is a lithograph, measuring 23,8 by 15,5 cm and containing 56 pages. It is divided into two sections of 32 and 24 pages respectively, each with its own pagination. In neither section are the first two pages numbered.

Page [1] of section one lists its contents:

a. *Risala fi bayan waza'if al-insan fi l-shari'a*, p. 1 [actually this treatise begins on p. [2]]
b. *Risala-yi nasihatname*, p. 13
c. *Risala-yi fi bayan khulasa-yi Shari'a*, p. 17
d. Risala-yi irshadiyya fi bayan al-fabur wa-l-faburqa wa-tilighraf [sic!], p. 22.

The rest of the first page is taken up by a small treatise beginning with the words: "*Bismillah al-hamd wa-l-salam 'ala rasul Allah fa-hadhih bayan waza'if wa'ziyya*". Section two contains a large treatise entitled *Risala-yi tuhfat al-ikhwan fi haqq al-dukhan* (p. [2] to 24). Page [1] comprises a short tract with the *incipit: Bismillah al-rahman al-rahim fa-hadhih bayan manafi' wa-fawa'id man tab min shurb al-dukhan wa-l-narkila wa-l-anfiyya.* The first pages of both sections are written by the same hand, which is different from the one that has copied the rest of the treatises. All these texts consist of two or three layers. That is, within a rectangular framework containing usually 23 lines, we find the basic text or the basic text with a running commentary. In the latter case the basic text is overlined. Sometimes small explanatory notes have been scribbled between the lines. Outside the framework there are marginal glosses written in oblique lines. The booklet has no imprint and none of the texts mentions the name of the author or commentator.

٢٢

رسالهٔ ارشادیه

بسم الله الرحمن الرحيم

الحمد لله الذى خلق الخلق بقدرته وشرح صدور بعض عباده بحكمته والصلوة والسلام على من خلق الموجودات بحرمته وعلى اله واصحابه وجميع ذرياته وعترته وبعد فيقول الضعيف الحقير الفقير الذليل عصمه ولوالديه ولجميع اخوانه خصوصا استاذيه * الله القدير هذه تعليقات علية على الرسالة الارشادية لى اردت بها ايضاح بعض عباراتها خشية الاستصعاب لطالبها ولسهولة اخذ مسائلها فالمسؤل من الناظرين ان لا ينسا محوافي دعائى الى رب العالمين وحسن عاقبتى فاكون من الفائزين فانى بمثل ذا لهم مشغول قال عصمه الله اعلموا اخوانى اى فى الاسلام ان بعض الاخوان اى من المؤمنين قد سئلنى اى ارشادا فيما ظهر من الكفرة من السفن جمع السفينة النارية والفابور مطلقا اى بريا او بحريا والارحى بفتح الهمزة وكسر الحاء جمع رحى على وزن عصا وهى مؤنثة ومعناها بالتركى دكيرمن كذلك اى آلنا رية والفابرقه والتلغراف المحدثات بعد المأتين والاربعين بعد الالف فلم اجب اى عقيبه قبل التفكر فتفكرت زمانا فوجدت اى بالهام المولى تعالى فى نفسى اى فى قلبى بعناية الله تعا جوابا شافيا اى مقنيا لنفسى اى لذاتى ولمن سئلنى اى من الاخوان فقلت اى بسبب السؤال من الله تعا التوفيق لا الغير الى السبيل السديد اعلموا انى ابين ما ظهر اى خطر فى قلبى بعناية ربى اى بلطفه فى رسالة مرتبة على بابين موسومة بارشادية * الباب الاول فى احوالها * والباب الثانى فى ثمراتها اعلموا ان الله تعالى خلق على ظهر الارض بحرا وخلق فيها فوائد كثيره واوجد فيها السفن والزوارق من زمن نوح عليه السلام لمنافع العباد وخلق رياحا مختلفة من كل جانب اى من القدام والخلف واليمين والشمال تجرى اى السفن بها اى الرياح التى تهب من كل جانب انعاما للبعض واستدراجا للاخر اى احسانا للمؤمنين واستدراجا للكافرين واستمر الامر على ذا من تلك المدة الى السنة الرابعة والاربعين بعد المائتين والالف من هجرة من له العز والشرف والاثار المترتبة

عمى

FIGURE 25.1 The first page of the treatise

Although the list of contents on p. [1], section one is written in Ottoman Turkish or Persian, as appears from the use of the *idafa* sign over the *ta' marbuta*, the texts themselves are in Arabic. They teem with mistakes, many of which are due to the interference of Turkish. In the text translated here we find the following types of mistakes:

يقتضي ان يكون الكفار هذا الزمان كلهم مساويا في سببية المذكورات وليس كذلك
بل بعض الكفار لا يسمع مثل هذه السفن وغيرها فكيف يستقيم هذا البيان قلت نعم ولكن
عذاب الكفار في العقبى كذلك اى ليس مساويا بل عذاب البعض اكبر واشد كما قال الله تعالى
وسيق الذين كفروا الى جهنم زمرا فلا يجوز النظر اليهم بالرغبة والمحبة مع الطمع الى حطام الدنيا
نعوذ بالله من هذا النظر واما اضلال المؤمنين الضعيفين في الايمان من الكبراء والامراء
والفقراء بمحبتهم الى الدنيا ثم نظرهم الى اهلها وهم الكفرة بالرغبة والمحبة مع الطمع الى
حطامها وجرهم ذلك النظر الى الاختلاط باهل الدنيا وتوغلوا الى الامور الكفرة اصلا وفرعا حتى تزينوا
بزينتهم الخبيثة وصورتهم الشنيعة مع المحبة وحتى اعتقدوا ان عاداتهم انفع للعباد وتمسكوا
بعباداتهم تاركين بقانون الالهية واتخذوا الكفرة مرشدا واستاذا ليتوصلون الى تعمير الدنيا مترو[كين]
تعمير الدين اعني طريق الاخرة والعبادة والتوكل على الله لانهم اعتمدوا على صنايع الكفرة وتدبير
امورهم معتقدين بالسلامة في مجرد افكار الكفرة وايجادهم وعاداتهم حتى وضعوا وعينوا
محلات مختلفة لتعلم انواع العلوم والقواعد العرفية الكفرة وتركوا تعلم احكام القرآن وآداب الاسلام
فضلوا واضلوا مثل ضلالتهم وهم يحسبون انهم يحسنون صنعا حاشا ثم حاشا بل قد هلكوا ابلا[ث]
اذ لا حسن في الصنايع سوى صنع الاسلام والقرآن فمن اعتقد ان الحسن والسلامة والشفاء في غير
القرآن فهو من اهل الرزالة والحقارة والخسران الابدي ان النبي عليه الصلاة والسلام والخلفاء وائمة المسلمين
لم يفعلوا شيئا منهم وهم غلبوا مع قلتهم وقلة اموالهم واسلحتهم على جميع الكفرة وغلبتهم انما بالتمسك الى حكم الله
والاسلام والقرآن واما في هذا الزمان ففعلوا اما فعلوا من الامور الكفرة مطلقا اى سواء صورة او سيرة او عملا
فلا يفيد شيئا سوى الرزالة والحقارة واتلاف المال الجسيم والمشقة بين العباد بالظلم والتجاوز خدود الاسلام
وغرابت ديار الاسلام فيا خسارة الدين المتين كيف الحال ليوم حضور مالك يوم الدين فتب الى الله تعالى واتخذ
القرآن مرشدا ومنها القرآن كذلك ولا تغتر بكلام المداهنين لما سبق بان ظاهرهم وكلامهم مزيف ولكن
سيرتهم وباطنهم خبيث محروف عن الحق بل هم اشد من الخنزير لموافقتهم الدنسهم عين السم القاتل لانهم
من الزنادقة وهذا هو الحق للقبول لمن له ادنى ادراك وشعور * الحمد لله على التوفيق الى المقاصد
خصوصا هذا التأليف واستغفر الله من كل التقصير من القصور في امر الدين الذي يوجب العتاب والعقاب
او التفرقة من المحبة اليه تعالى * والصلوة والسلام على سيد الخلائق الكبير والصغير وآله واصحابه اجمعين
صلاة دائمة ابد الآبدين آمين يا رب العالمين

FIGURE 25.2 The last page of the treatise

- incorrect application of *hamza*-rules (15 times), which in some cases goes back to common Ottoman orthography: e.g. رايحة for رائحة and صنايع for صنائع.
- orthographical mistakes due to the incapability of distinguishing between certain Arabic phonemes (6 times): e.g. رذالة for رزالة,
  تغمسوا for تغمصوا
  مقنعا for مقنيا
- confusion between ta' and *ta' marbuta* (5 times): e.g.
  تكثرت for تكثرة
  زالت for زالة
  تسبة for نسبت
  خدمت خدمة
- incorrect use of prepositions (22 times): e.g.
  رغبة الى, للقتال بالكفار, لا يخفى لمن
- incongruity in gender and number (28 times): e.g.
  وهذا الغفلة, كثير منهم تكثروا رغبتهم الى الدنيا, فلم تغن ذلك عنهم, وهذا الاحوال مقرر
- mistakes in the use of the article (8 times): e.g.
  الكفار هذا الزمان, امور الدنيوي
- other forms of faulty syntax (46 times): e.g.
  ليتوصلون, خمس عشر سنين, كان ذلك مفض الى
- semantic interference of Turkish, i.e. the use of Arabic words in meanings they usually only have in Turkish: e.g. *madar*, help, livelihood; *lawazimat*, equipment.

In addition to these faults, we find mistakes, like the omission of words and letters, that are obviously scribal slips.

An important question is whether these errors are the author's or the scribe's. Fortunately, the main text of section two contains a lengthy quotation from a treatise on tobacco by Abu Sa'id Muhammad al-Khadimi, of which there exists a printed edition.[1] Comparison between this quotation and the printed text shows that the quotation is accurate. Apart from some scribal errors, there are a few spelling mistakes that are due to the interference of Turkish, like confusion between *dhal* and *za'*, *kha'* and *ha'*, and *ta'* and *ta' marbuta*. We find, however, none of the other errors that are so abundant in our text and may therefore assume that the author is responsible for these.

1 Abu Sa'id Muhammad al-Khadimi, *al-Madjmu'a al-sharifa al-Qudsiyya li-l-mawla l-'allama al-qutb al-rabbani wa-li-ba'd al-'ulama' al-a'lam wa-l-mashayikh al kiram.* (Istanbul: Matba'a-yi 'Amira, 1302), pp. 234–5.

The purpose of the text is to give an answer to two basic questions related to the introduction into the Ottoman Empire of some Western technical inventions, viz. steamships (*sufun nariyya*), steam-driven means of transport in general (*fabur*, derived from Italian *vapore*, an ambiguous word defined by the author as: "something which traverses a long distance in a short time with little effort, in general, i.e. both on land and on sea"), steam mills (*arha nariyya*), factories (*faburqa*, a word evidently derived from Italian *fabbrica*, but in popular consciousness associated with the word *fabur*, steam) and the telegraph (*tilighraf*). One problem the text deals with is the question of why God has created these things only now and has let them come from the hands of unbelievers. The other question is what the Muslims' attitude ought to be vis-a-vis these inventions.

The absence of an imprint and any express reference to the date of composition make it difficult to date the text with precision. We have to rely on internal evidence and, fortunately, the text gives some clues. The first one, of course, is the mention of a number of technical innovations, for the text must have been written after their introduction into the Ottoman Empire. Steamships began to carry out regular runs between Ottoman and other ports from 1825.[2] The first factories with steam engines were probably established in about the same period.[3] The first telegraph lines were opened in 1854,[4] and the first railway connections started to function in 1860.[5] So the text must have been written after that year. There is, however, one clue in the text that enables us to assign a later *terminus post quem* to it: it mentions the establishment of "places for teaching (…) the secular laws of the unbelievers (*al-qawa'id al-ʿurfiyya al-kafara* [sic!])". This cannot refer to anything but the opening of the Imperial Law School (*Maktab-i Huquq-i Shahane*) in 1880.[6] This then means that the text dates from after that year.

The dating of the composition of the marginal glosses offers more problems. The only indication we have is in note 4 where the commentator says that the pollution of the air by the smoke of "these things" has, during the last 25 years, affected plants, animals and people. Now, since we have established that the main text dates from after 1880, it is impossible that the commentator

2 Stanford J. Shaw and Ezel Kural Shaw, *History of the Ottoman Empire and Modern Turkey*, vol. II. (Cambridge etc.: Cambridge University Press, 1977), p. 120.

3 I have not been able to verify the exact date.

4 Shaw & Shaw, ibid. The text itself mentions the year 1265 (1848–9).

5 This was the Chernavoda – Constanza line and part of the Izmir – Aydin line. Cf. C. Issawi, *The Economic History of Turkey, 1800–1914*. (Chicago: The University of Chicago Press, 1980), pp. 148, 183.

6 Shaw & Shaw, vol. II, p. 494.

had steamships and factories in his mind as sources of the pollution, since these were introduced early in the century and thus much longer than 25 years before. This leaves the railways as the malefactor, which is also more logical, as trains spread their smoke over the countryside Since the foundations of the Ottoman railway network were laid in the period between 1860 and 1874,[7] we can tentatively assume that the marginal commentary was written between 1885 and 1900. Thus the main text was probably composed between 1880 and 1900.

3 The Author

As said before, none of these texts contains a direct indication as to the identity of the authors or commentators.[8] Neither can any of the titles be traced in GAL or in *Muʿdjam al-matbuʿat al-ʿArabiyya wa-l-Muʿarraba* by Y.A. Sarkis. At the present I have no access to Ottoman bibliographical material, where clues with regard to the authorship of these treatises might be found. Therefore, I can do no more than establishing some kind of a profile of the author. In doing so, I assume that the basic texts of these tracts were written by the same author, with the exception of *Risala fi bayan waza'if al-insan fi l-shariʿa*.[9] There are three arguments for this assumption. The first is that the style is very similar. One finds the same expressions and combination of words and the same mistakes. Secondly, the same small number of authorities are quoted in all texts, with the exception of the text translated here (this is probably due to the originality of the topic which had not been dealt with by previous writers). Finally we find that in *Risala-yi fi bayan khulasat-i shariʿa* (p. 21), the author writes: "… which I have explained in *Risalat tuhfat al-ikhwan*", referring to the major treatise of section two. Thus, making use of the information to be found in these tracts,

7 In this period the following lines were completed: Chernavoda – Constanza, 93 km (1860), Izmir – Aydin, 73 km (1866), Izmir – Kasaba, 159 km (1866), Istanbul – Izmit (1873), Mudanya – Bursa (1873) and Istanbul – Edirne – Sofia (562 km), with a branch from Edirne to Dedeağac (1874). Cf. Shaw & Shaw, vol. II. p. 121, and Issawi, pp. 148, 183, 188.

8 It is, however, possible to identify the marginal commentator of *Risala-yi nasihat name* with a certain amount of certainty. In his commentary he mentions by name three Turkish tracts which he has written for the common people. Two of these, viz. *Hifz-i iman* and *Nasayih-i ikhwan* are listed in M. Seyfettin Özege, *Eski harflerle basılmis Türkce eserler kataloğu*, vol. 2 (Istanbul: 1973), p. 553, No. 7402 and vol. 3 (Istanbul: 1975), p. 1299, Nos. 15149(?) and 15150, and ascribed to a certain Mehmed Emin bin Hasan. I am grateful to Prof. Dr. Werner Ende of Freiburg i.B. for drawing my attention to this reference.

9 According to internal evidence the basic text was written around 1300 CE and the commentary just before 1800.

the following elements of the author's profile can be listed: The author was an Ottoman Turk. This is evident from the fact that the setting of the text is obviously the Ottoman Empire and that Turkish words are sometimes used to explain the Arabic. That the author was not an Arab appears also from the frequency of serious grammatical mistakes. The use of Arabic by Ottoman Turks in this period was not very common.[10] However, the author probably saw himself as part of an Ottoman fundamentalist tradition, associated with scholars like Muhammad al-Birgewi (1522–73) and Abu Saʿid Muhammad al-Khadimi (1710–62, *vide infra*) that used Arabic as their main vehicle of thought. Moreover, the author consciously wrote for the educated elite who had learned Arabic. This is endorsed by a remark in the marginal commentary to *Risala-yi nasihat name* (p. 16) which reads: "And those who belong to the common people (*al-ʿawamm*) must read my translated treatises called *Risala-yi Iman, Hifz-i Iman* and *Nasayih-i ikhwan*". From the titles and the word "translated" it is clear that we have to do with Turkish texts for non-educated people.

There is reason to believe that the author did not live in Istanbul, but rather in a provincial town. The text mentions that especially "the people of Constantinople" associate with the unbelievers. This smacks somewhat of the cliché-like denunciation of the capital by a provincial. Admittedly, this argument is not very strong, but on the other hand, the tenor of the tract fits in well with the picture of a provincial religious scholar who was disquieted about the increasing centralization of the Ottoman State, embodied in novel means of communication like steamships, trains and the telegraph.

The treatise could not have been written by someone without a formal religious training. It is, however, unlikely that the author belonged to the hierarchy of official ulema. His attitude towards them is one of unequivocal disapproval. They are accused of flattering the unbelievers and being inimical to the believers. The latter phrase may be an indication that the author was involved in a conflict with leading ulema. Moreover he censures them for not being able to distinguish between what is true and what is false "since they argue about the truth with false [reasonings] in order to flatter the people of corruption and insolence, more than that they argue with the evil-doers among the official rulers". In the other treatise the ulema, sometime called by him the evil ulema (*ʿulamaʾ al-suʾ*) are blamed for introducing unwarranted novelties (*bidaʿ*) smoking tobacco and accepting money for performing religious functions like Koran reciting. He advises his hearers "to frequent the learned gatherings of the scholars of the hereafter and to avoid the gatherings of the heedless and hypocrite scholars who by their scholarship try to reach worldly

10 Cf. GAL, S II, p. 866.

aims." (section I, p. 15). It would appear, then, that our author was one of a group of pious religious scholars, who were opposed to the official ulema for having taken on scholarship as a career.

Finally it is possible to say something about the intellectual tradition of which the author was part. Owing to the novelty of the topic the author could not find much support with the older authorities and we therefore find but one quotation in the text translated here. However, in the other texts more authorities are cited or referred to. Al-Ghazali is mentioned a number of times, but the authors who are quoted most often are Muhammad ibn Pir ʿAli al-Birgewi (Birgili)[11] and a commentator of one of his main works, Abu Saʿid Muhammad al-Khadimi.[12] About the latter not much is known, but al-Birgewi was quite famous. That his works were very popular, is evidenced by the number of commentaries and printed editions. Having studied in Istanbul, he gave up his career as an official scholar and withdrew to the small provincial town of Birge, where he taught at a local *madrasa*. He insisted on strict adherence to the *Shariʿa* and condemned everything he considered *bidʿa*, thus becoming involved in violent polemics with high ranking scholars, whose economic position his opinions threatened. For al-Birgewi maintained that a *waqf* of money or other movable property was invalid and that it was forbidden for a scholar to accept payment for teaching the Koran or performing acts of worship. Because of his fundamentalist views and his consistent stand, which brought him into conflict with the religious establishment, he can be compared with someone like Ibn Taymiyya. From the number of quotations and the similarities between their ideas, it is clear that our author considered himself a follower of al-Birgewi. And the number of printed editions of the latter's works shows that he was not the only one.

Summing up, the following portrait can be sketched: the author of this treatise was an Ottoman Turk, a religious scholar, who flourished in the last quarter of the nineteenth century and probably lived in the provinces. He had strict fundamentalist ideas and considered himself a follower of al-Birgewi. Like him, he voluntarily stood outside the religious establishment of official ulema and sufi shaykhs.

---

11 On al-Birgewi, see *EI*², *vol.* I, p. 1235 and GAL *vol.* II, pp. 440–2 and vol. S II, pp. 654–8.

12 On al-Khadimi, see GAL, S II, pp. 663–4.

4 The Translation

The translation follows the original as close by as possible. This means, among other things, that the translation of the basic text (in the original overlined, here set in **bold type**), just as the original, can be read independently from the commentary (set in normal type). The marginal notes are marked by letters and placed between the lines of text. The interlinear notes from the original are in the translation placed between double parentheses. The translator's annotations are to be found in the numbered footnotes. Wherever in the translation, for greater clarity, the original Arabic words are added, they are placed between parentheses. Square brackets have been used whenever words or phrases that are not to be found in the original, were added to the translation by way of explanation.

DIDACTIC TREATISE

(p. 22) **In the name of God the Merciful, the Compassionate.** Praise be to God Who has created the creatures through His omnipotence and has expanded the breasts[1] of some of His servants through His wisdom. Blessing and peace be upon him in veneration of whom the universe has been created, on his family, his companions and all his descendants and relations. Here, then, the weak, insignificant, poor, and humble [author] – may the powerful God protect him, his parents, all his brethren and especially both his teachers – says: These are causal (? *ʿilliyya*) explanatory notes to my "Didactic Treatise",[a] by means of which I would like to explicate some of its expressions, because I fear that it will be found difficult by those who study it, and in order to facilitate the understanding of its issues. What is requested from those who examine it, is to pray unremittingly to the Lord of all Being for me and for a good outcome for me in order that I shall be amongst the triumphant [in the Hereafter], for I am busy doing the same for them. Now he [the author] – may God protect him – says: **Know, Brethren,** viz. in Islam **that some Brethren,** viz. amongst the Believers, **have asked me,** viz. for guidance **with regard to the steamships (*sufun nariyyah*)** plural of ship (*safina*), of

a In it there are various inventions and small, delicate and wondrous [mechanical] parts. [*ʿunwan* is certainly erroneous. I propose to read *adjza'* because of the similarity of this phrase with one used in note u. R.P.].

1 Cf. K 6:125, 20:25. 39:22 and 94:1.

the unbelievers, **steam engines (*fabur*) in general,** viz. at land or at sea, **mills,** (*arhi*) with a fatha on the *hamza* and a *kasra* on the *ha'*, the plural of mill (*raha*) of the same pattern as *ʿasa*; it is feminine and its meaning in Turkish is *değirmen* [mill], of **the same kind,** viz. steam-driven, **the factory (*faburqah*)**[b] **and the telegraph,** things which first appeared from the unbelievers after [the year] 1240 [= 1824–5]. **However, I did not answer,** viz. immediately without reflection **but reflected for some time. Then I found,** viz. through the inspiration or the Lord, Who is exalted, **in myself,** viz. in my heart, through the grace of God, Who is exalted, **an answer satisfactory,** viz. convincing, **to myself,** to my person, **and to those who have asked me,** viz. amongst the Brethren. **Then I said,** viz. because of the question, : **Success in finding the correct path comes from God, Who is exalted,** and from no one else. **Know that I shall expound what has come,** viz. occurred, **to my mind through the grace of my Lord,** viz. through his kindness, in a treatise divided in two chapters and named "Didactic [Treatise]". **The first chapter is about their conditions and the second about their fruits.**

[Chapter One]

Know that God has created seas on the surface of the earth and has created in them many useful things. He has put ships and boats in them from the time of Noah – peace be upon him – for the benefit of [His] servants. He has created different winds [coming] from every direction, viz. from before and behind, from the right and the left, **by means of which,** viz. the winds that blow, **they,** viz. the ships, **can sail in every direction as [divine] favour for some and as deceitful assistance**[2] **for others,** viz. as [divine] benevolence for the believers and as deceitful assistance for the unbelievers. **This state of affairs has lasted thus from that period until the year 1244 [1828–9] of the Hidjrah of him who is entitled to honour and respect, as have also the effects deriving** (p. 23) **from their conditions. Then the things which,** viz. the explanation of

b That is *bawruqa* in Turkish.

2 That God sometimes bestows favours upon sinners and unbelievers in order that they persist in their sins and unbelief and do not ask forgiveness, with the result that their punishment in the hereafter is more severe, is called *istidradj*. Cf. al-Djurdjani, *Kitab al-Taʿrifat* (Cairo, 1321), pp. 11–12; A.J. Wensinck, *The Muslim Creed: Its Genesis and Historical Development* ([2]New Delhi, 1979), pp. 226 ff.; R. Brunschvig, "De la fallacieuse prospérité – *Makr Allah* et *istidradj*," *Studia Islamica* 58 (1983), pp. 5–33.

whose circumstances, **are the topic of the first chapter,** the article is [used here] because it is [already] known; now, take note of this, **were produced, namely the steam engine (*fabur*, i.e. steamship and steam train), and the like,** an expression for that which traverses a long distance in a short time with little hardship. **Know then that all these things exist through the omnipotence of the almighty God, Who is exalted,** viz. through His omnipotence and His will and He has recorded it in the Essence of the Book (*Umm al-Kitab*)[3] **and not through the power of the** scandalous **unbelievers as a favour,** explanation of the circumstance that it is a favour, **on the one hand and a punishment on the other,** viz. hand. **As for the first** viz. the explanation of their being a favour, **that is because one can attain one's destination easily,** viz. without full effort and without fear and apprehension, **both** (?) **are a mercy to the believers.**[4] **As for the second,** viz. the explanation of their being a punishment, i.e. a chastisement in the present world of in the hereafter, **that is because one can attain what one wants without effort, for,** the word 'for' is [used here] for introducing a detailed statement, **the present world is vile and short-lived,** viz. without any doubt because of [its] inconstancy and its being before (*sabaqiyyah*).[5] **God, Who is exalted, has created it only as arable land of the hereafter,** viz. for His servants. He means that this is an expedient[6] in spite of the fact that it is vile and that it will soon disappear and be destroyed. **He,** the Lord, Who is sublime and exalted, **has created it only**[c] in order that it is a place of cultivation for them and that they sow therein the seed of obedience to Him, Who is exalted and then reap harvest in the beloved hereafter, which, in spite of its being exalted and sublimely adorned, is eternal and everlasting. Thus they will reach the highest triumph. God has made us triumphant by [our] venerating the trustworthy prophet – may God bless him and grant him salvation – amen, amen, amen! **[as a field of the hereafter] whereas the cultivation in it,** viz. in this world, **is worship,** devoted only to Him, with [all] its

---

c He wants the sentence to be a recommencement for clarification. The supervisor.

---

3 The Essence of the Book (*Umm al-Kitab*) is the book in which God has recorded everything that exists and will happen. Cf. K 13:39.

4 The text has *wa-huma rahmatān li-l-muʾminin.* It is, however, not clear to what the dual refers.

5 The author probably means that, because life in the present world by necessity antecedes the hereafter, it must cease to exist.

6 The text reads *wa-yaʿni inna hadha l-maʿuna*, which I have translated as if it read *wa-yaʿni inna hadhih hiya l-maʿuna*, since mistakes like these are very common in this treatise. On the other hand, it is also possible that *hadha l-maʿuna* (for *hadhih al-maʿuna*) is the subject of the sentence and that the predicate has been omitted.

conditions and essential elements. **Of this,** viz. worship, **there are two kinds: corporeal and financial. Its,** viz. of worship, of which there are two kinds, **instrument is the body and its strength,** viz. of the body, **derives only from eating, drinking and sleeping,** and clothing and shelter. **All this,** viz. eating, drinking etc., **is obligatory,** viz. since it is a means to attain its strength, **because the means to obligatory worship is definitely [also] obligatory,** based on the fact that means have the same legal qualifications (*hukm*) as [their] ends. **These beginnings and means are therefore obligatory, and who sets out doing them,** the things that have been mentioned, with a good intention **will be acting in accordance with it,** viz. the obligation and is therefore entitled to recompense (*yasta'djir*) from God, Who is exalted. **Now the increase of effort therein,** viz. in attaining all this, **is an affliction. [Mohammed] – blessing and peace be upon him – has said: "Everything that troubles the believer is an affliction".**[d] [The reason of] quoting this Tradition is to endorse his statement that effort is affliction. **Affliction in general,** viz. be it small or great, **is a mercy if they patiently endure it and say: "Surely we belong to God, and to Him we return".** He, Who is powerful and sublime, has said: ["Yet give thou good tidings to the patient] who, when they are visited by an affliction, say: 'Surely we belong to God, and to Him we return'; [upon those rest blessings and mercy from their Lord, and those – they are the truly guided." K 2.156] **Therefore, it,** viz. effort, **is approved and accepted therein,** viz. in attaining all this, because it is obedience to our Lord, **since the most excellent of deeds,** this is the explanation of the fact that effort in acts of obedience is accepted, (p. 24) **are [also] the most painful and the most troublesome**[7] **to people. Facilitating the affairs of believers is therefore a cause for the mercy of affliction disappearing. In that case it is a punishment,** this then is the aspect of it being a punishment for the believers, **because of the diminution of their recompense,** in the hereafter. **For if the affairs of the believers are made easy for them, this will be a cause for the benefit of patience disappearing and an inducement to negligence,** for many people with but few exceptions, **whereas negligence causes universal corruption,** viz. in religion and in the present

d This tradition has been transmitted by Ibn al-Shanni on the authority of Abu Idris, with an incomplete chain of authorities. [It cannot be found in any of the authoritative collections, R.P.].

7 The words *afdal al-a'mal ahmazuha* are a saying of the prophet transmitted by Ibn 'Abbas. Cf. Lane, *Dictionary*, vol. 2, p. 643. This Tradition, however, cannot be found in any of the authoritative collections.

world. **This has indeed happened in our epoch,** as those who are on our side know very well. **We shall expound this later. The most important [form] of it,** viz. of this corruption that is generated by it, **is the hardness of hearts and the prevalence of rust,** viz. darkness, **therein,** viz. in the hearts, **which engenders lack of understanding (*fiqh*),** viz. of discernment and knowledge with regard to religion, **for one does not [anymore] distinguish between what is true and what is false** and one does not understand [anymore] the intentions and purposes of the Lord, Who is exalted, His prophets, and His books. He, Who is exalted, has said: "No indeed; but what they were earning has rusted upon their hearts". [K 83:14] **as we shall explain in detail if God, Who is exalted, will.**

Their qualification (*hukm*), viz. of the mentioned things that have recently appeared, **according to Divine Law is permission.**[e] **We have said according to Divine Law, because we are people of it, [Divine Law], not people of secular law (*ʿadah*).**

If you ask: "Why did these mentioned things not appear before they [actually] came into existence?" I answer with God's help: God, Who is exalted, has decreed everything in past eternity (*azal*) and has attached [everything] to a certain time. Therefore, [events] will, definitely, not appear before it [= the time set for them], for you have just learned before this that everything of these things occur through the decree and omnipotence of God, Who is exalted. **Thus the time of their appearance,** viz. according to God, **is the moment of their appearance. If you ask: "What is the reason of delaying their time [of appearance],** viz. in past eternity until it appears?" **My answer is: God is the wisest and knows best** His true intention. **However, the wisdom [in it] is perhaps the following: Prophets – peace be upon them – were sent to summon to Him Who is to be worshipped,** the only One, and to His worship and

e Their qualification according to the law is permission. Therefore there is no harm in employing them. However, in their smoke and smell, there is much harm and damage according to the rule of the physicians that smoke and repulsive smells are absolutely harmful to the body. In the aforementioned things there is much harm because of the diffusion of their smoke and their profuse smell. Therefore, the air, which is crucial to everything, has changed because of them. Now, if it changes for the worse, the conditions of everything change in the same direction and then it is the cause of deterioration in the sprouting and growth [of plants], in fruits and their tastes,[8] in livelihood and life, as has happened during the past twenty five years to fruit, grapes, animals and people. Everything comes from God, Who is exalted, but their [of those phenomena] cause – God knows best and is the wisest – is the aforementioned things.

8 Reading لذاتها instead of للذائها.

most of them [have done so] with the sword in the face of people who stubbornly resisted, as was the case with our prophet – peace be upon him – .

For he and the believers were ordered to [use] the sword for fighting the unbelievers, the Hypocrites, and the idolaters, as [you can find in] the words of Him Who is exalted: "O Prophet, struggle with the unbelievers and Hypocrites and be thou harsh with them." [K. 9:73 and 66:9] and in His words: "O believers, fight the unbelievers who are near to you, and let them find in you a harshness; and know that God is with the god-fearing". [K. 9:123][f] **His victory was due to harshness and the sword, but only since he,** viz. our prophet, **was supported and assisted by God, Who is exalted.** Thus he was victorious over the unbelievers and the stubborn through God's grace despite the fact that he was alone in the beginning and had few [followers] in the middle of his [career]. In the beginning the unbelievers made light of him, but in the end they were dismayed by his sword, blows, courage and force – may God's blessing and peace be upon him –.They were unable to counter him and to fight against him, in spite of the fact that [his] weapons were few[g] and that his soldiers were a small group without strongholds or a fortress ((*kal'e* in Turkish)), whereas their ((the unbelievers')) weapons were perfect, their armies extensive, their equipment complete, their strongholds and fortress firm, and their food abundant. But this was of no avail to them because the prophet – peace be upon him – (p. 25) relied on Him Who is to be worhipped, the

f This victory on the part upon whom be peace [Mohammed] is a proof of his truthfulness and of the height of his position with God, Who is exalted, because, in spite of miserable weapons and of the fewness of his soldiers, he – peace be upon him – was victorious over the idolaters, who displayed arrogance on the surface of the earth. They exceeded the proper bounds towards despotism (? *sultaniyya*) and vainglory. Then God, Who is exalted, left them helpless by means of the sword of His beloved one [Mohammed]. Look, my brethren, how the situation of the haughty and stubborn [unbelievers] was, in conformity with the words of him, upon who be peace [Mohammed]: "Who is haughty, will be brought down by God and who brings himself down, will be raised up by God."[9] That is, He has raised up His messenger with the believers and God has brought down the unbelievers and put them in a helpless position. Those who followed His messenger, were raised up by Him and those who were haughty and acted in accordance with their inclinations, were put by Him in a helpless position. Let this be taken into consideration!

g His swords with his army in the Badr campaign were six, as is related in the commentary of *Amantu bi-Llah* (?).

9 The text has *Man takabbar wada'ah Allah wa-man tawada' rafa'ah Allah,* which is an abridged version of a Tradition to be found in Ibn Hanbal's *Musnad* (iii, 76): *Man takabbar 'ala Allah daradja wada'ah Allah wa-man tawada' daradja rafa'ah Allah daradja.*

Almighty Creator, Who helps and assists, whereas the unbelievers relied on their strongholds, their power, their force, their outrageous strength, the magnitude of their army and on their idols. Therefore God has made them helpless. **The prophet – peace be upon him – has summoned to worship God and to reflect on His greatness and magnificence. The believers have chosen to love God, Who is exalted, passionately. The goal of the first generations and of God's friends (awliya'),** and the object of their passionate love, **was God, Who is exalted,** and none else. **The scholars of the first generations were likewise and the ordinary people of the first generations were like the scholars of the later generations,** in occupying themselves with the affairs of the hereafter and in preparing themselves for death, nay they were better than them. **God has taught them that,** in past eternity, **and then He has decreed it** ((viz. love)) **for them,** because knowledge follows that what is known. Therefore they did not desire or value [the things of] the present world nor its people, but only God, Who is exalted, and the approval of His messenger. **Therefore they did not consider it [the things of the present world] with desire but rather with scorn** and contempt. **For this reason it,** [viz] the adornment of the present world[10] and the other worldly things that have appeared amongst them, **has not appeared.** Therefore take heed, you who have eyes! [K 59:2] This position will presently be explained, if God, Who is exalted, wills.

Now, if you say: "This answer is correct and acceptable, but what do you think of the unbelievers that existed in the past until just before the appearance [of these inventions]? Why has God not decreed for them what has appeared [now] and why did it not appear amongst them, although they [also] loved and desired [the things of] the present world?" My answer is: Certainly, but that time was the time of the Mission and the Summons, and this requires that heart and body are occupied [by it], and totally immersed in it,[11] **and [also a time] of worship, of the Magnificent Light [Mohammed], of reflection about the hereafter, and of fear,** viz. time of fear. As a consequence of this the unbelievers could not think of anything, let alone things like those that have [recently] been invented, **either of God,** viz. fear either of God's punishment and His Magnificence, like the prophets, God's friends (*al-awliya'*), the scholars, and the believers had, **or of human beings,**

10 Cf. K 18:28 and 46.

11 The text reads *wa-hadha yudjib mashghuliyyat al-qalb wa-stighraqah iyyahuma*. The meaning of the last two words is obscure.

like the unbelievers had, who were afraid of the prophets, the caliphs, the scholars and the believers and of their ((the believers')) lording it over them ((over the unbelievers)) and taking of their houses, their goods, their women and their children. **The unbelievers that lived in that time,** viz. the time of the Mission, Worship, Light, Reflection and Fighting, **were overcome by the things just mentioned and therefore curtailed in their insolence (*tughyan*)** and defective in their preoccupation with the objects of [their] desires and [their] falsehoods. **Thus they could not obtain precision in reflecting,** about the affairs of the present world, **because of [their] fear of the** manifold **perils and the great fame**[h] of the prophets and the believers. **Therefore their wish for things like those which have [recently] appeared could not be realized. This is why it** [viz.] what has [recently] appeared **has come later.** [But] God knows best. **However, when [these things] did appear, all that has been mentioned had gone,** I mean the Mission, Summons, Worship,[i] the Light of Worship, Fighting, and the Fame and Dignity of Islam, which caused the intimidation of the unbelievers. **Thus the unbelievers became safe** (p. 26) **and got engrossed in their false intentions and determined to reflect with precision about the affairs of the present world, in accordance with God's – He is exalted – knowledge and with the fact that He has attached** in past eternity **His will to their [the unbelievers'] disgusting nature and inclinations. Thus have they brought to light what they have brought to light,** viz. the astonishing inventions.

Now, if you ask: "What is your opinion about the telegraph which the unbelievers have brought to light, after [the year] 1265 [1848–9], **and which can transmit messages from a far distance in a very short time to the extent that if one reflects about it, one is at a loss,** because neither reason nor tradition can accept it?" I **answer with the help of God, Who is exalted: Certainly, but this also comes from God, Who is exalted. It belongs to the [category of] miracles,** of which deceitful assistance (*istidradj*) is one of the varieties, **which God has brought to light through sinners and unbelievers and which is called that what fulfils a want,** as the Greatest Imam [= Abu Hanifah] has explained in *al-Fiqh al-Akbar*,[12]

h Viz. religious fame and the dignity of the Islamic religion.

i If you object, saying: "Worship still existed at the time of their appearance and even in the present time and therefore what you say is not correct", my answer is: Certainly, but these acts of worship are in reality routine, because they are sham and feigned. This will become clear through reflection.

12 The relevant passage of the *Fiqh al-Akbar*, commonly but erroneously ascribed to Abu Hanifa, runs as follows: "The signs of the Prophets and the miracles of saints are a

or magic by making use of its science. **[However] through whichever of those two it exists, it is there by God's creation and by His decree,** by His knowledge and He has written it on the Tablet.[13] **Its qualification according to Divine Law is like that of correspondence,** viz. like that of a letter. **It can only furnish presumption** and not certainty **and it cannot serve as evidence for a legal verdict. If you ask: "Why did it not appear before [the time of] its appearance?" My answer is the same as that with regard to the ships.**

If you ask: "What is the wisdom of its delay?" My answer is: God knows best and is the wisest, but perhaps the wisdom is that recently many people have gone astray, because they are engrossed in and love the present world and look with desire and love at its [= worldly] people, whereas the worldly people are the unbelievers. **God, Who is exalted, has created this kind of thing through the hands of the unbelievers in order to lead astray,** and deceive, **the sinners,** and the shameless. **For this reason you have seen that most people** ((belonging to the sinners and the heedless)) **have [now] turned** completely **to the unbelievers and have left the direction of the morning sun,** I mean the Light of the Chosen One [Mohammed], may God bless him and keep him in peace. **First they began to prefer the riches of the present world to those of the next. Then, secondly, there originated from it an engrossment in [their] causes. Thus they found that the most important and most useful of them** ((of the riches of the present world)) **were in the hands of the unbelievers. This view and this sentiment** ((on the part of the sinners)) **stemmed from impotence** and stupidity. They began to support it [? the riches of the present world] because of their greedy appetite and the temptation of the devil and have forgotten the Provider, the Powerful, the Compassionate. Apart from the desire and the love [for the things of the unbelievers] **they** ((viz. the sinners)) **have turned their lives towards that what has appeared on the part of the unbelievers, who are [our] enemies in all respects, so much so that their outward appearance,** and their behaviour, **are identical with them and that the**

---

reality. {As to those which were performed by His enemies, such as Iblis, Fir'aun, and the Anti-Christ, and which, according to historical tradition, have taken place or will take place, we do not call them signs or miracles, but we call them the fulfilling of their wants. Allah fulfils the wants of His enemies, eluding them in this world and punishing them in the next. So they are betrayed and increase in error and unbelief." Engl. tr. from A.J.} Wensinck, *Muslim Creed*, p. 193. For the Ar. text and commentaries, cf. al-Maghnisawi, *Sharh al-Fiqh al-Akbar* (Hayderabad: Da'irat al-Ma'arif, 1312), p. 31 and 'Ali al-Qari, *Sharh al-Fiqh al-Akbar* ([2]Cairo: Mustafa l-Babi al-Halabi, 1375/1955), pp. 80 ff.

13 I.e. the Essence of the Book (v. note 3).

unbelievers are the ones they believe and obey, or rather their leaders [*imam*], and the ones they emulate, **whereas the believers are the ones they avoid,** and detest. **Their scholars**[j] **are like them,** nay even more inimical than them to the believers who say the truth. **If their situation is like this, they have gone very far astray. Therefore, if they see something like the aforesaid telegraph, they will flee away [from Islam].** Then they will accept neither treatment nor guidance. On the contrary, they are convinced that the unbelievers are people of merit and vision. Consequently, they will extol them and then embrace unbelief – may God, Who is exalted, save us from that – as is the case at the present time with most people. This explanation (p. 27) is sufficient for people of skill. Therefore, take heed and be informed, o brethren. Disaster and insolence have increasingly come over you because you hold fast to the rules of the Koran and the commands of the prophet of the end of time.

Chapter Two

Concerning the fruits of the ships, the mills, the factory and the telegraph
[This chapter] contains four paragraphs. The first one is about [their] main fruit, viz. the fruit itself, **which is obtaining what one wants easily** without effort **in a short time and arriving at destinations in order to see what is desired,** by means of all of them in the same way[14] ((viz. easily)).

The second one is about the consequences of their fruits and yields. It has six aspects. First, **the fact that one forgets God's help and assistance,** His protection, His omnipotence and His mercy. Second, **the fact that one's soul becomes conceited, that one relies upon created beings** and ceases to put one's trust anymore in the Powerful, the Creator, **and that one ignores Him, Who must be worshipped, the Only One.** Third, **the fact that one's recompense is diminished,** because one attains one's goal easily without effort. Fourth, **the fact that one's soul becomes insolent,** because the soul is inclined to wicked deeds and most evil deeds are generally [committed] for money and valuables; and now, if someone wishes to commit a sin in a far city, he can reach it quickly and do what he wishes. Fifth, **the fact that one's desire for [the things of] the present**

j The meaning of "their scholars" is those who flatter them for worldly gain.

14 The text has الوصلة الى المقاصد رأية المطلوب من كل منها كذلك and is not totally clear.

world increases and that one forgets death, and that one does not prepare oneself for death. Sixth, **the fact that one's heart dies,** because committing that what has been mentioned entails that. **There is nothing more disgusting than that,** because the heart dominates the body. For if the heart is heedless, the body is [also] heedless and if the heart is alert, the body and [its] members are [also] alert. **The symptom of that,** viz. death, **is that one's eyes do not become moist and, what is worse, that one does not act according to the Koran,** that one does not even discriminate between what is true and what is false, that one does not accept the truth, **and that one even becomes an enemy of the truth,** and even of those who tell the truth. May God save us from sins and conceit.

The third ((viz. of the four paragraphs)) **is about what results from these fruits,** namely that it leads to wicked deeds and sins and even, by persevering in them, generally to unbelief on the strength of the words of him upon whom be peace [Mohammed]: "There is no small sin with perseverance and no great sin with asking forgiveness", for sins draw [men] to other, worse things(?).[15] **These states exist [now] with regard to many people, because many of them have forgotten God,** viz. His worship and what is due to Him **and have become engrossed in serving that what has been created [man] in any respect**[k] **together with flattering,**[l] and humiliating themselves,[m] **whereby they rely upon him,** as if he were their creator, the one they must worship and their provider, **and believe that if they were to leave him, they would die** of hunger

k In manufacture, commerce or agriculture, by land, animals or people.

l Viz. towards someone with wealth. That is not allowed, nay it is forbidden on the strength of the words of him upon whom be peace [Mohammed]: "Who stands up [out of respect] for a rich man, loses two thirds of his faith."[16] What then, o heedless one, is your opinion with regard to someone who stands up [out of respect] for an unbeliever because of his worldly goods and his riches. Reflect [upon that], you who adorn yourselves with the attire of scholarship, for scholars are taken as models. If they are pious, the people are [also] pious and if they are corrupt, the people are without doubt [also] corrupt.

m Viz. in manufacture, handicraft and the like.

15 The text reads لا صغيرة مع الاصرار ولا كبيرة مع الاستغفار لأن المعاصي يجر الاخره الاكبر.

Allegedly a saying of the prophet, it cannot be traced to one of the authoritative collections. The wording of the last part is rather obscure. I have tentatively reconstructed its meaning on the basis of a parallel text in one of the other treatises (part II, p. 7, l. 15ff): *wa-li-hadha waqaʿu ma waqaʿu hatta shaʿ anwaʿ al-maʿsiyya wa-l-kabir bi-hayth tadjurruhum al-israriyya ʿala mithl al-dukhan wa-l-tawaghghul ilayh mithlih ila l-akbar min al-dukhan.*

16 This Tradition cannot be found in any of the authoritative collections.

and would not arrive at [their] goal. **From this**[n] **there arose reverence and aggrandizement for him and reflecting about him to the extent that, if [only] a tenth of a tenth of a ninth of it would be [directed] towards God, Who must be worshipped, the Almighty, they would be friends of God, Who is exalted (*awliya'*). Many of them**[o] **have become conceited because of the workings of their souls, since they [the souls] understand the strange and wondrous things and since they [the souls] arrange the affairs of livelihood** and its means. **They have become overbearing towards those who do not understand [it] and proud of the fact that they respect heedless** and insolent **people.** (p. 28) **As a consequence they do not worship God [anymore] because they do not expect any favour from Him**[p] **for which they must thank Him by enhancing worship. Many of them have become insolent** and have overstepped the boundaries of Divine Law **for the sake of wealth by means of them,** viz, the aforementioned things, either immediately or by means [of them] or as a result [of them]. **In many of them the desire of [the things of] the present world has increased because an abundance of [worldly] ephemeral goods and riches makes that** generally **inevitable. Its result is that one forgets death,** which leads to the fact that one stops preparing oneself for it. **From it arose greed**[q] **for more**

---

n From this, viz. from that belief. Reverence is like bowing and prostrating for someone of wealth and falsely mentioning words indicating aggrandizement and excessive praise. May God curse the liars, especially in the case of someone who is known as an evildoer and then is praised in his presence. This is because of the words of Him who is exalted: "And lean not on the evildoers, so that the Fire touches you." [K 11:113] Al-Fahi (?) has said: Dot not in the least incline to them for leaning is inclining, but to a smaller extent, like arraying themselves with their adornment and mentioning them with aggrandizement. If the condition of those who lean on evildoers is such, what then do you think of those who are known as evildoers. Therefore take heed, you who have eyes! [Cf. K 59:2].

o These words are not clear. He has only mentioned them because they are suitable to clarify the condition of most people in the present time. [Nor are these words very clear. R.P.].

p Viz. from God, for they believed that livelihood comes from what has been created [man] by manufacture, commerce, or agriculture or from people of wealth. The evidence for this belief of theirs is their eagerness for and their pursuit and aggrandizement of the aforementioned things and even of the unbelievers [themselves]. Thus they have become unbelievers along with them, because aggrandizement of the unbelievers is unbelief, thereby ceasing to aggrandize the Provider, Who must be worshipped, the Almighty. These conditions are firmly established in many people. Oh! How strange are those who think or imagine that these people can be any good or of any use in this present world or in the text!

q As in the present time, in that, when riches and property increase, greed for more increases [too], so that a man with [already] a large fortune is hardly satisfied with tenfold the [riches of the] world. This is a sign of disgusting things and distress. May God save us from that.

of them and death of the heart. Now, if the heart is sound, the body is sound [too] and if the heart becomes corrupted and dies, the body becomes corrupted [too][17] **as [it is said] in the noble Tradition: "Verily, in the body is a small part. If it is sound, the whole body is sound and if it is corrupted, the whole body is corrupted. Verily, this is the heart.**[18] Death of the heart [therefore] is death of the body. **If the aforementioned death occurs for some reason or another, this leads** to sins and insolence. **Therefore you see that most people are worse than the dead, indeed, greater ones for leading astray than Iblis, for Iblis only insinuates, whereas the afore mentioned heedless ones can easily lead astray, either by words,** or behaviour, **or by guiding [others] to certain activities. They do not know that God gives sinners,** and unbelievers, **much abundant favour in order to beguile [them] into,** and punish [them] for, **their increased insolence** and disobedience, **so that they will suffer the worst chastisement** on the Day of Resurrection. **Therefore it is not allowed to regard with favour the ways of worldly people as a precaution against becoming dependent [upon them], since many** people **have been overcome by a total attachment for them [the things of the present world] because of having regarded with favour things like the mentioned ones as well as the people associated with them,** and have become engrossed in forbidden and reprehensible things(?)[19] like cultivating this present vanishing world,[r] that will soon cease to exist. For they have gone crazy and their religion has passed away from them, because of their satisfaction with and love for this cadaverous world. **Most of those who oppose the truth and remain unbelievers [do so] for the sake of this,** viz. love for, dependence upon, and satisfaction with [the things of] the present world. May God save us from the cursed Satan.

The fourth paragraph is about what is incumbent upon the believer with regard to what has been mentioned before, viz. the ships that have been mentioned before. **What is incumbent upon the believer is that he believe and know that all these things come from God, Who is exalted,**

r My opinion is that, were it not for fools, the present world would have gone to ruin. The number of fools has increased in the present time. Constantinople and the other cities of the Muslims, have been embellished as much as they could. This is evidence of their foolishness and immorality.

17 Reading *wa-mawt al-qalb alladhi idha salah salah al-djasad wa-idha fasad wa-mat fasad al-djasad* for ... *wa-idha fasad wa-mat al-djasad wa-fasad*, which is certainly corrupt.

18 Al-Bukhari, *Sahih*, II, 39.

19 Reading توغلوا الى المنهيات والمكروهات for الهنزينات (او: الهزينات) والدرهات which is certainly corrupt.

through His creation and doing and not from someone else. **Therefore, if one obtains what one wants through them,** viz. by means of them, **one must know that it comes from God, Who is exalted,** viz. through His creation **as a benefit from Him, Who is exalted, and not from someone else besides Him, and then one must thank and praise God, Who is exalted, and remember Him often. One must not forget God, Who is exalted, because of not having experienced** any **trouble**[s] and hardship, nay one must remember Him with one's heart and one's tongue **lest what one has found be a punishment, as has been mentioned** before. **One must often ask forgiveness** (p. 29) **with repentance for the sins one has already committed, for man is not free from them nor protected against them,** and our prophet in spite of his being protected against great and small sins, used to ask forgiveness a hundred times daily. **If worldly affairs are difficult for a believer, he will atone for them [his sins], but if the affairs are easy for him, the sins remain. Therefore the continuous asking for forgiveness is incumbent** upon people of equity. **Someone** from the people of insight **has said: If a believer receives a favour** from God, **he must reflect,** viz. upon himself: **If he finds a sin in himself he knows that that** ((viz. the favour)) **is a punishment and not a favour,** viz. a device **in order that on the strength of it he confirms to himself that they [the sins] were something good** and acceptable **to God. Then he will not ask for forgiveness or he will commit others so that they,** the sins, **will become rust upon his heart [cf. K. 83:14]. Then he will not discriminate [anymore]** between what is true and what is false **and the punishment for them,** viz. the sins, **will remain in the end. In this respect it [the favour] is a punishment, but many** people **do not know this state of affairs,** viz. the fact that it can be a punishment. **Thus one will think,** viz. know, **that everything that one receives is a favour and one will be glad about it. Thereupon one will be overcome by heedlessness** and rust **and will not see what is true** as true **and what is false** as false. **On the contrary, one will see it in reverse,** viz. one will see what is false as true and what is true as false. **This is more repulsive** and worse **than the first [state, viz. that**

s For, if hardship and trouble come his way, man prays to God, humiliates himself before Him, asks God to protect him and remembers Him with sincerity, submission and humility, as happens to many, especially at sea. However, when nothing befalls to him and he attains his goal easily without effort, then he is happy and usually forgets God. This is not proper for a believer. On the contrary, he must thank Him, remember Him and ask forgiveness for his sins, because hardship [suffered by] a believer is the atonement for his sins. Let people think this over.

one ceases asking forgiveness and commits more sins] and it is also the state of most people in the present time, **especially of the scholars of the present time since they argue about the truth with false [reasonings] in order to flatter the people of corruption** and insolence, **more than they argue with the evil-doers** among the official rulers, **out of fear lest their disgusting flattery of the evil-doers become manifest. The evildoers make this disgusting flattery incumbent upon them. They have no discernment** at all **because their hearts have died** and their discrimination has ceased to exist. **Therefore they have remained in** a state of **illiteracy.**[t] Wake up, you heedless ones, by considering the sign of Him, Who is exalted. Equity is obligatory. **May God save us from this heedlessness and this reversal.**

[It is also incumbent upon a believer] that he be positive, as much as he can, **with respect to everything he sees, hears, tastes and smells, that his creator and maker is God,** and no one else. **He is powerful over everything and He is aware of and sees the circumstances of His servants, especially the things that have been mentioned,** viz. the ships and other things that we are explaining.

[It is also incumbent upon a believer] that he know that in everything that He has created there is wisdom and usefulness. **With regard to some of it, it [its wisdom] can be known quickly, with regard to other things [only] by contemplation,**[u] **and with yet others it is secret,**

---

t Like it has been said: A scholar may descend to the rank of an ignoramus for not behaving in accordance with his knowledge.

u My opinion is that someone who sees those ships, those steam engines and the like, as well as the tools, the craftsmanship and the small and delicate parts that they contain and by means of which these [specially] equipped (? *ma'murah*) ships run, needs an admonition, a warning and a lesson to the following effect: All of [God's] servants are incapable and can only do something through God's omnipotence. The use of tools, that have been created [by Him], belongs to Him and [also] the [mechanical] parts that have been created [by Him]. [Secondly,] God is almighty and ruling. He is unique, one, the everlasting refuge and in Himself sufficient, for the heavens, the sun, the moon, and the stars all move without a tool or [mechanical] parts through the omnipotence of God, Who is exalted, despite their large bodies and volumes, without supports or connexions and without help from someone else. So do not become confused, you unfortunate one, by what you have seen in what the unbelievers have produced and invented and which you thought wondrous and strange. What do you think of what I have reminded you of concerning the craftsmanship and the omnipotence of Him, Who is exalted. Look and take example by your body and the joints, the bones, the veins, and the various strange and wondrous organs contained therein without [mechanical] parts or a tool. Does it resemble what they have fabricated? May God, Who is exalted, forsake them, viz. the unbelievers. Therefore take heed, you who have eyes! [K 59:2].

concealed, or hidden for human beings **in His** knowledge **of the Unseen. Furthermore, with regard to some of it, it [the wisdom] is related to the present world and with other things, to the hereafter. Perhaps the wisdom with regard to the things that have been mentioned, is to make clear the privilege of some [of God's] servants. That means that God has made clear the privilege of the Magians**[20] **in cultivating and embellishing this unclean** and accursed **corpse,** viz. this present world, **because the unclean** (p. 30) **have a privilege with regard to that what is unclean, for the idolaters,** the Magians, and the unbelievers **are all unclean.** and they all form one community, on the strength the words of Him, Who is exalted: "… the idolaters are indeed unclean, so let them not come near the Holy Mosque …" [K 9:28] **Therefore they are entitled,**[v] on the strength of their own will, **to the present world,** which is **inferior to an** unclean **corpse. [This is just] like the fact that some worms,** and some insects, **are entitled to disgusting** and unclean **things, and other animals to good things, like bees that are entitled to beautiful deeds,** I mean [collecting] honey. **Thus they are used for it, whereas others are used for unclean** and disgusting **things. Now, some [of God's] servants are entitled to good things like the words of the profession of the unity of God and belief** and obedience and charity **on the strength of their own will, like God, Who is exalted, has said: "… and [God] fastened to them [the believers] the word of god-fearing to which they have better right and are worthy of; and God has knowledge of everything." [K 48:27] God has taught the believers to be good. He has made manifest among them good things like the words of the profession of the unity of God, belief, and obedience and he has taken away from them the desire for disgusting,** unclean, and cadaverous **things. He has**

v If you object saying: "On this ground it would be necessary that all unbelievers, from their ancestors to this time, have busied themselves in the past with what has appeared in this time; but they were not like that and therefore the view which you have expounded is not correct". Then my answer is: Certainly, but the answer to this has been given before in the beginning of the first chapter, namely that they lived in the time of the Mission, the Summons and Fighting and therefore did not find a possibility for this. But this time, they have found a possibility and, what is more, they found on the side of Islam prestige, help and love for them. Therefore they took pains to cultivate and embellish it. Some foolish Muslims admired what they arranged, made the choice they have made and fell into the state of helplessness and insolence in which they still are. They have absolutely no discernment.

20 It seems unlikely that the word Magian (*Madjus*) here specifically refers to Zoroastrians. Probably the author uses the word here loosely as a synonym of unbeliever (*kafir*).

made them pure outside and inside. [On the other hand] He has taught the unbelievers and the idolaters **to be unclean** and disgusting. **He has made manifest among them abomination** and uncleanliness **like idolatry, unbelief,** insolence, and disobedience, **and a desire for unclean and disgusting things.** I mean like cultivating the present world, which is the most enormous disgusting thing and the vilest mean thing. **Now, if this has been established, it is not allowed for a believer** and a Muslim **to look upon these disgusting people with desire** and love, **because of what has been said before, nor [may he do so] with the belief that the unbelievers** and idolaters **are people of perception** and craftsmanship. **Similarly, someone who sees a worm carrying** or turning around **the filth of a camel** or a cow, **will not look upon it with desire, but abhor from looking at it. In the same way someone who sees dogs eating** a corpse and filth **will abhor from looking at it. Similarly a believer will abhor from unbelievers who sit down at something filthy and eat from it and who are** from top to toe **immerged in materially, legally, and morally disgusting things. Now, if you object, saying: "You have explained that believers abhor from the conditions of the unbelievers because they are such and such, whereas I claim: 'I am a believer who does not abhor from their conditions and therefore [your] reasoning is not correct.'" Then my answer is: Certainly, but if a dog sees his like eating a corpse and defiling himself, he will not abhor from him, but have a desire for his situation. Now, our discourse was only about the fact that the relationship of man to dog is one of abhorrence, while the relationship of a dog to a dog**[w] **is not like that. Therefore, the reasoning is perfect and unambiguous. Rather it is becoming** ((obligatory)) **for a believer to look upon them for admonition by the fact that it is their affair** and condition to **cultivate these disgusting,** unclean **things,** and the accursed corpse, I **mean the present world,** because the present world is an accursed corpse, and the same goes (p. 31) for those who pursue it by cultivating, embellishing, and paying respect. **Only those who belong to it,** who are like it, **cultivate it and they are the unbelievers** and idolaters, **because to cultivate it is their duty,** as you have learned before. **As for the believers, they are good people and someone who is good has only a desire for things that are good. The most important of good things is belief** and obedience. **This can only be obtained** and acquired **in the present world,** for they [live] on it and not somewhere else. **Now, if one looks with love at the wondrous and strange things that they [the**

w The worst dogs are the unbelievers.

unbelievers] have produced and made manifest, **this draws one towards them,** to their company, **and to associating with them. It is well known that if someone mixes with something, he will certainly be afflicted by it. For that reason**[x] **God has forbidden His believing servants to associate with evildoers** and unbelievers **with His words: "... do not sit, after the reminding, with the people of the evildoers." [K 6:68] In the present time many people,** especially the people of Constantinople, **are associating with the unbelievers** out of their desire for them for numerous reasons. **Therefore they have been afflicted by their conditions,** their outward appearance, and their behaviour, **and their forms of address,** so that they have become identical with them. **Thus they go astray** and lead [others] astray **and thus they perish** and cause the perdition [of others] **in the present world** and in the hereafter. **They have** absolutely **no discernment. On the contrary, it is their belief that they are in the right** and they think that they act well. "Away, away with that you are promised! [There is nothing but our present life; we die and we live, and we shall not be raised up. "] [K 23:36].[22] **Similarly the unbelievers have no discernment** with regard to their unbelief and their perdition. **Day after day they become more engrossed in false things and they grow in insolence** and evildoing, **yes even in unbelief. May God save us from such things.**

From these things then, viz. the ships et cetera, **there results a leading astray,** viz. of God's creatures through His justice and His abandonment, **in every respect,** viz. both with regard to the unbelievers and with regard to the believers, **because of their becoming engrossed in the** mean **[things of the] present world,** with complete love, **and in the abundance of its ephemeral goods, for [the] acquisition [of these goods], without exception,** viz. be it rightfully or wrongfully, **takes place**

x Viz. and in order that the believers will not be afflicted by the moral uncleanliness of unbelief and evil which exist in the unbelievers and evildoers, for [their] company[21] is, with God's permission, a cause of being afflicted. This is a temptation and a great trial, like what has certainly happened in the present time, where tyrannical evildoers have been afflicted by the unbelief of the unbelievers and the scholars have been afflicted by the evil of the evildoers, because of mixing [with one another] and avidity. May God save us from that.

21 Reading: مجالسة for مجادة which does not make sense here.

22 The quotation is part of a Koranic passage that contains a discussion between one of the earlier prophets and the people to whom he was sent and who refused to believe his message. The implication here is that those who have associated themselves with the unbelievers are like the opponents of earlier prophets (and Mohammed himself, of course), in that they believed that there is no afterlife and that only the present life counts.

in the present world. The present world looks outwardly beautiful to the people except to those whom God, Who is exalted, has protected. **Now, love for the [things of the] present world is the beginning of every sin** and the pinnacle of [all-] sins is unbelief. For that reason it has been established that the most important foundation of unbelief is love for [the things of] the present world and for fame, which is one of the things connected with the present world. **If this has been made plain, then the leading astray of the unbelievers consists, apart from [their] unbelief, in the acquiescence to unbelief along with comfort for the body and the large quantity of money available in it** (?),[23] as well as in their insolence. **These conditions are firmly established among them in the present time more than among their ancestors. Perhaps the wisdom of this situation is that some of their ancestors were unbelievers for nine hundred years. Others [were so for an even] longer [period] and again others less than that, even sixty year or less. Their unbelief and insolence then increased each year in quantity. The insolence of the unbelievers of the present time,** however, **is little in duration and quantity, but all of them [both the unbelievers from the past and those of the present] are made to remain in the Fire for ever and ever. Now God, Who is exalted, has created this helplessness [on the part of the believers]** and insolence [on the part of the unbelievers] **in order that their qualitative insolence become in a short time greater and viler than their [their ancestors'] disgusting behaviour was quantitatively** over a long time, so that their [the present unbelievers'] chastisement will be like their [their ancestor's] chastisement in the end.[24] Now, if you object, saying: "This, viz. the insolence of the unbelievers of the present time caused by them ((the ships)), (p. 32) implies that the unbelievers of the present time are all equal in the causing of the mentioned things ((the ships etc.)). However, this is not so. On the contrary, some unbelievers have never heard of things like these ships etc. So how can this explanation stand up?". My answer is: Certainly, but the chastisement of the unbelievers in the end is like that, viz. is not equal. Rather the chastisement of some is greater and worse, like God, Who is exalted, has said: "Then the

23 The text reads *fa-idlal al-kuffar ba'd al-kufr al-itmi'nan 'ala l-kufr ma'a stirahat al-badan wa-kuthr al-mal ma'dudan fiha.* The meaning of the last words is not clear.

24 The sense of the reasoning seems to be that, since all unbelievers are condemned to remain in the Fire forever, the amount of their sinfulness must be approximately equal. However, since the average age of the earlier generations was much higher than nowadays, they had a longer time to accumulate sins and evil. In order to make up for this, the sinfulness, of the present generations must be worse and graver in quality.

unbelievers shall be driven in companies into Gehenna ..." [K 39:71]. **So it is not allowed to look upon them with desire** and love **together with greed for the ephemeral goods of the present world,** may God save us from this [way of] looking.

Now, the leading astray of the believers who are weak in belief among the notables, the rulers and the poor people, is due to their love for [the things of] the present world and, subsequently, to their looking upon worldly people, that is the unbelievers, with desire and love, together with greed for its ephemeral goods. This [way of] looking draws them towards associating with worldly people. **They became root and branch engrossed in the affairs of the unbelievers, to the extent that they began to array themselves with their** disgusting **adornment** and their infamous outward appearance, **together with love** [for these things], until they began to believe that their [the unbelievers'] customs were more useful to [God's] servants. **They became attached to worshipping them [the unbelievers] abandoning the code of Divinity (?).**[25] **They have taken the unbelievers as guide** and teacher **in order to gain access to the cultivation of the present world, thereby abandoning the cultivation of the religion,** I meant the road to the hereafter and to worship, **and [their] trust in God, relying upon the crafts of the unbelievers,** and upon their [way of] managing affairs, **believing that well-being can only be found in the ideas and inventions of the unbelievers,** and in their customs. **They have even set up and designated various places for teaching**[26] **the different sciences and the secular laws of the unbelievers (*al-qawaʿid al-ʿurfiyya al-kafara* [sic]) and they have abandoned teaching the Koranic rules** and Islamic manners. **Thus they have gone astray and have led [others] astray** in the same way. **They, however, think that they act well – God** forbid, verily, God forbid –, **but in fact they have,** without doubt, **already perished since there is no good in works except in the works of Islam and the Koran. Thus, whoever believes that there is goodness,** well-being and remedy **in something other than the Koran, belongs to those who are scandalous,** contemptible, **and depraved. Doesn't he see that the prophet – blessing and peace be upon him –, the Caliphs, and the Imams of the Moslims did nothing like them and yet, in spite of their small number,** and paucity of financial means and weapons, **they were victorious over all unbelievers.**

---

25 Reading تاركين بقانون لا لهية for تاركين قانون الالهية which is certainly corrupt.

26 Reading *taʿlim* for *taʿallum*, since the verbal nouns of the second and the fifth form are several times confused in this text and my reading makes better sense.

Their victory was only due to the fact that they clung to the rules of God, Islam and the Koran. As for the present time, they have begun acting like unbelievers in every respect, both in outward appearance, in behaviour, and in conduct. **This, however, is of no use [to them] except [that it leads to] scandalousness, contemptibleness, enormous waste of money, and hardship amongst [God's] servants,** because of evildoing, overstepping the boundaries of Islam, and because of the outlandishness of the countries of Islam. **What a pity for [this] strong religion. How will the situation be at the day of the advent of the Master of the Day of Doom [cf. K 1:4]. Repent to God, Who is exalted, and take the Koran as a guide and [do] the same with the people of the Koran. Do not lose zeal because of the words of the flatterers, because** of what has been said before, namely that **their exterior** and their words **are elegant, but their behaviour** and their interior **is disgusting** and deviating from the truth. **In fact they are worse than swine,** because they agree in appetite. **They are the same lethal poison,** because they belong to the freethinkers (*zanadiqah*). **This is the truth,** acceptable **to those who have [even] the slightest perception** and discernment.

Praise be to God for success, viz. [the arriving] at [one's] aims, especially [of] this writing. **I ask God's forgiveness for all inadequacy,** deriving from neglecting the affairs of the religion, which requires censure, chastisement, and separation from the love for Him, Who is exalted. Blessing and peace be upon the Lord of all creatures, big and small [Mohammed], upon his family and all his companions for ever and ever. Amen, O Lord of all Being.

CHAPTER 26

Islamic Law and Human Rights

A Contribution to an Ongoing Debate

1 Introduction[1]

During recent decades a host of publications have seen the light with titles like: 'Islam and X' or 'X in Islam', where X is typically a concept with a positive connotation, such as democracy, peace, social justice, or women's rights. Titles like 'Islam and Human Rights' and 'Human Rights in Islam' have been particularly popular. Publications with such titles are as a rule partisan and indicative of one of two attitudes: they are either incriminating or they are apologetic.

In the first case the authors attempt to prove that Islam does not foster these concepts at all but, on the contrary, propagates doctrines totally contradictory to these notions. In the latter case the authors' purpose is to demonstrate that Islam promotes or enjoins these positively valued concepts to the same extent or even more than 'Western culture' or Christianity and that it has done so for a much longer period. Therefore, whenever I see such a title, I become cautious, and will peruse the book or article with an attitude that is more critical than usual. These topics are fluid, and dealing with them requires special methodological care in order to avoid the traps by which they are surrounded.

In this paper I will start with a critique of the methodological flaws in much of the existing literature and then suggest ways in which the topic may be approached. My intention is to contribute to the debate on Islam and human rights, not to offer ready-made solutions.

2 A Critique of the Partisan Approaches

No one can expect that Islamic law as laid down in the classical texts of the various law schools (*madhahib*) should protect human rights as recognized in present-day international instruments. Islamic law was formulated some thousand years ago, and although it has been subject to some development and

1 I would like to thank Joost Hiltermann, Ann Mayer and Chibli Mallat for having read the draft of this article and for their constructive comments and criticisms that helped me shape this version.

elaboration through the ages, there were no drastic changes until the nineteenth century.

The concept of human or fundamental rights, on the other hand, is relatively recent. It was first developed in Western European intellectual circles during the eighteenth century. With the American and French revolutions the legal bases were laid for the enforcement of fundamental rights and they were given a place in the new constitutions in order to underline their special nature. However, we should not forget that these fundamental rights were still in an embryonic stage and applied essentially only to white free men, and not to women and black people, and that slavery was still lawful.

Judging and criticizing these eighteenth-century texts and their contemporary authoritative interpretations by the criteria of a present-day understanding of human rights is meaningless, since this understanding is the result of two centuries of intellectual and juridical development after the proclamation of these cardinal declarations. The same, of course, is true if one compares classical *fiqh* with modern international human rights instruments in order to establish whether or not Islamic law is in conformity with modern human rights standards. Depending on the author's intentions, it leads either to an anachronistic approach, or to an approach whereby the classical heritage of *fiqh* is totally spirited away and replaced by inconsistent and haphazard quotations from Qur'an and Hadith serving to prove that Islam has always protected fundamental human rights as they are known and recognized nowadays.

Before discussing the approaches that in my view are sound, I will first pay some attention to main currents in the existing literature on the subject.

2.1 *The Incriminating Publications*

There are Western publications arguing that Islam is incompatible with democracy and with the idea of human rights. Their authors' main argument is that the provisions of the Shariʿa are in conflict with these concepts and that these provisions continue to control the minds of Muslims. Now, it is obvious that classical Islamic law, whose foundations were laid by Muslim jurists living between the eighth and eleventh centuries, does not contain much in the way of modern human rights principles. Islamic law is therefore an easy target for criticism: its classical legal doctrine is not founded on universality, nor on equality of persons, religions or beliefs before the law. However, such an approach is anachronistic. It resembles judging Roman law with the yardstick of modern international public law, and at the same time fails to recognize the variety within Islam and the potential for change and development.

Nevertheless, one may object that Islamic law is in many countries still being enforced, especially in the domains of family law and the law of succession, and, in some countries, also in the field of criminal law. This is undoubtedly true. However, in these countries, law, including laws based on the Shariʿa, is now enacted by the state, on the basis of legislation and codification. If these sovereign states choose to introduce codes based on Islamic law that are in conflict with the principles of human rights as recognized in international law, then the legislative authorities of these states are to be criticized and not Islamic law. In many countries Islamic family law has been codified and reformed in order to change certain rules that were regarded as socially undesirable. There is no reason why this cannot be done in order to reconcile Islamic law with international human rights standards, without abandoning the principle that the resulting laws are essentially governed by the Shariʿa.

The same can be said with regard to states that have made the choice to Islamize their entire legal system. For this does not necessarily entail the enforcement of all rules to be found in the classical textbooks. For over a hundred years, Muslim scholars have argued that Islamic law can and must be revised and reinterpreted in order to adapt it to present-day needs. Islam and an adherence to Islamic law does not in itself have to be an obstacle to the enforcement of human rights principles.

2.2 *The Apologetic Publications*

Authors of apologetic publications[2] attempt to prove that Islam has always recognized and proclaimed human rights even before they were known in the West. This is then substantiated by quoting qur'anic verses and sayings of the Prophet Muhammad, usually with total disregard of the classical exegetical tradition and the classical body of Islamic jurisprudence. The classical tradition is not even criticized or attacked but for the most part ignored. A typical example is the following from a book by the famous Indian Islamist thinker al-Mawdudi (d. 1979):

> *The right to equality*
> The Qur'an puts strong emphasis on the principle of the equality of the entire human kind, and says that if one person has precedence over another, then this relates only to his character or his faith: 'O mankind! Lo! We have created you male and female, and have made you nations and tribes that ye may know one another. Lo! the noblest of you, in the sight of Allah, is the best in conduct. Lo! Allah is Knower, Aware' (Q. 49:13). The

2 For an analysis of the main themes discussed in these publications, see V. Rispler-Chaim, 'Human rights in Islam: the literary genre,' in: BRISMES *Proceedings of the 1991 International Conference on Middle Eastern Studies, London 10–12 July 1991* (Exeter, 1991), 478–490.

> first point mentioned in this verse is that the origin of all humanity is one and the same and that the difference of races, colours and languages is in reality no reasonable ground for dividing mankind and differentiating between them. The second point is that God has created these differences between peoples only so that they may know one another. Or in other words, no family, tribe or people has a precedence that gives it better rights, increases its importance and diminishes the value of others. (…) The Messenger – may God bless him and preserve him – clarified these notions in different ways. He said in his address after the conquest of Mecca: 'An Arab has no precedence over a non-Arab nor a non-Arab over an Arab, nor a red skinned person over a black skinned person nor a black skinned person over a red skinned person, except in piety. And there is no precedence based on descent.' This means that there is only precedence on the basis of religion and piety, for it is not true that some men are created from silver and others from stone or mud. No, all human beings are equal.[3]

As will be clear from this quotation, the concept is given a meaning that is slightly different from the one it has in human rights discourse. Equality in Mawdudi's reasoning refers to equality between ethnic groups, but not to equality between religions or the sexes. Comparable changes of meaning can be observed when the notions of other fundamental rights are discussed by Muslim authors. Freedom of religion is usually interpreted as the right to practice freely one of the tolerated religions and the right to be converted to Islam, but certainly does not include the freedom for a Muslim to embrace another religion.

What the treatment of human rights by Muslim apologetic authors boils down to is that, on the one hand, they claim that Islam has always recognized these human rights, whereas, on the other hand, they subtly change the contents of these rights. In their argumentation classical *fiqh* does not play a role. It is totally disregarded and the arguments put forward for their claims are as a rule isolated qur'anic verses and Prophetic traditions, quoted out of context and without reference to the classical exegetical tradition. Such an approach, in my view, evidences intellectual poverty and can never be the point of departure for successful attempts to embed present-day concepts of human rights in Islamic law.

3 Abu A'la al-Mawduli, *Al-hukuma al-islamiyya*, 2nd impression (Cairo, n.d.), 263–4.

3 Islamic Law and Human Rights: Other Approaches

In my view there are two methodologically sound approaches for studying the relationship between Islam and human rights: one dealing with the present, the other with the past. As to the study of the present situation, my position is that it should focus on the analysis of documents issued by Islamic authorities and the actions and declarations of governments in the Muslim world insofar as they claim that their words and deeds are prompted by Islamic principles or motives. Such an analysis will help us determine the role of Islamic notions in the human rights policies pursued by these governments. The studies of Professor Mayer are an eminent example of such research.[4] Whereas her studies address the present, I will focus on another dimension, namely human rights and classical Islamic law.

Now what is the sense of discussing Islam and human rights with regard to the past? In the beginning I said that such an approach is by its very nature anachronistic.[5] That is true, if one judges classical *fiqh* by the standards of modern human rights discourse. My intention, however, is different. In my view it might be useful to examine and analyse classical *fiqh* texts in order to find out what are the elementary values and inalienable rights of individuals recognized and protected by Islamic law. These are certainly not identical with or as numerous as the human rights that are now internationally recognized. But this analysis may serve as a basis for an Islamic human rights discourse, which is better founded and intellectually stronger than much of the discourse nowadays current in the Muslim world.

I will discuss two points:

1. Universality and equality before the law;
2. Elementary rights protected by Islamic law.

3.1 *Universality and Equality before the Law*

As we all know, the operation of Islamic law is not meant to be universal. It is restricted to the 'Abode of Islam' (*dar al-islam*) and according to most legal schools, Muslims entering the 'Abode of War' (*dar al-harb*) are no longer subject to the Shari'a, in the sense that if they commit crimes there, they cannot be tried for them after their return. *A fortiori*, the same rule applies to non-Muslims residing in enemy territory (*harbis*). Being enemy persons and not

4 Ann Mayer, *Islam and Human Rights: tradition and politics*, 2nd ed. (Boulder, CO 1995).

5 For a similar critique of anachronistic approaches, see Chihli Mallat, 'Introduction – On Islam and Democracy,' in Chibli Mallat (Ed.), *Islam and Public Law: classical and contemporary studies* (London, Graham & Trotman, 1993), 1–18.

falling under the protection of the Islamic state, their legal capacity is suppressed to the extent that it is virtually non-existent and their lives, property and freedom are not safeguarded. It is true that certain categories of persons may not be killed, but this protection is rather academic, since a violation of this protection, according to the majority of scholars, does not entail an action for retribution or blood money.[6] The extremely weak legal personality manifests itself only insofar as *harbis* may be party to certain binding agreements. In addition, as soon as they lawfully enter Islamic territory,[7] they acquire a legal capacity which is almost equal to that of a free Muslim.

Within the Islamic territory, all lawful residents are protected by the law. That is, their lives and bodies are protected and this protection may result in legal action in the case of its being violated. Furthermore, if they are free, their freedom and property are safeguarded by the law. This last statement, however, shows that not all persons have the same legal capacity or legal personality. Like all pre-modern legal systems, Islamic law does not recognize the notion of the natural equality of all persons before the law. There are several categories of person and their legal capacities are different from each other. Legal personality in Islamic law is defined by three dichotomies, creating legal boundaries between dominant and non-dominant groups:

Muslims *vis-a-vis* non-Muslims
Men *vis-a-vis* women
Free persons *vis-a-vis* slaves.

Every person's legal capacity is a function of these three dichotomies and therefore there are eight categories of persons. The differences in legal capacity have effect in most spheres of the law. The fullest legal capacity is that of a free Muslim male. All others have fewer rights. The clearest illustration of the existence of these categories is the differentiation in bloodmoney, the amount of money to be paid if a person is killed. The highest amount must be paid for a free Muslim male, whereas no bloodmoney is due if a *harbi* is killed. Non-Muslim lawful residents in the Abode of Islam do enjoy protection of life, property and freedom. However, their legal capacity is restricted by the fact that they are incapable of performing legal acts implying any form of authority over Muslims or of entering into such legal relationships. Therefore, they

6 Only the Shiʿites hold that the killing of *a harbi* woman or minor entails liability for bloodmoney. See e.g. Ibn Qudama, *Al-Mughni* (Beirut, Dar al-Turath al-ʿArabi, n.d.) Vol. 7, 796–797.

7 These can be permanent residents or *dhimmis*, who must pay a special tax, the *jizya*, or temporary residents, who by virtue of a safe-conduct, may reside one year in Islamic territory.

cannot hold public office, be guardians over Muslim minors or possess Muslim slaves. Moreover, non-Muslim men may not marry Muslim women, whereas there is no legal impediment for Muslim men to marry Christian and Jewish women. This is a logical rule in view of the notion of marriage in Islamic law, which confers on the husband matrimonial authority over his wife. In order to emphasize the divide between Muslims and non-Muslims, the law lays down that protected non-Muslims must distinguish themselves in their attire from the Muslims and imposes certain restrictions on their social life aimed at making manifest their subject position. These restrictions affect e.g. their ways of transport – they are not allowed to ride horses – and their houses, which have to be lower than neighbouring houses in which Muslims live.

The distinction between free persons and slaves is of a different nature. Slaves are both property and persons. Their lives are protected, but they lack the capacity fully to own property or to have legal authority over free persons. The limitations on their legal capacity are a function of their owners' property rights over them and of their lower status, which prevents them from having legal authority over free persons.

Finally there is the distinction based on gender. I will not elaborate here, as the legal status of women in Islamic law is well-known. Although in financial matters women have the same rights as men, this is not the *case* in other fields of the law such as family law, succession procedure and public law. As in the case of non-Muslims and slaves, the inferior status of women precludes legal authority over free men.

This has been a brief survey of some aspects of the classical Islamic law of persons. It is clear that its purview is not universal but restricted to Islamic territory and that the Shariʿa does not, at first sight, recognize the principle of the natural legal equality of persons. However, in spite if this, there are important notions of universality and equality to be found in the Shariʿa. For these we have to turn to legal theory, the *usul al-fiqh*, and here we find some basic principles that can be regarded as an expression of the idea of the universality of the law and some elementary equality of all human beings. The most important of these is that all are endowed with legal personality and thus are proper subjects of law. This is a requirement for legal capacity. The following passage from a fourteenth-century Hanafite work on legal theory may demonstrate this point:

> The capacity of a human being (…) in legal usage means his ability to have lawful rights and obligations [in other words, his legal capacity. RP]. This is a trust that is borne by every man as God – Who is powerful and exalted – has informed [us]: '[Lo! We offered the trust unto the heavens

> and the earth and the hills, but they shrank from bearing it and were afraid of it.] And man assumed it' (Q. 33:72). (...) Legal capacity (*ahliyyat al-wujub*) is based on the existence of legal personality (*dhimma*) (...) since this legal personality is the centre of obligations and rights. Because of it, only human beings can have obligations and not the living beings that do not have legal personality. As soon as a human being is born, he has a legal personality capable of having rights and obligations. (...) This is based on the promise [made by God] in the past. Thus it is certain that man possesses legal personality, i.e., in legal usage, the quality by means of which a person becomes capable of binding himself and others. This certainty is the result of the promise in the past that took place between the servants and the Lord, as God has informed us in His words: 'And (remember) when thy Lord brought forth from the Children of Adam, from their reins, their seed, and made them testify of themselves, (saying): Am I not your Lord? They said: Yea, verily. We testify. (That was) lest ye should say at the Day of Resurrection: Lo! of this we were unaware' (Q. 7:172).[8]

It appears from this text that Islamic law is founded on the notion that God has endowed every human being equally with legal personality. This innate and universal legal personality cannot be eliminated but may be affected by accidental attributes, such as unbelief or slavery, which then results in a diminished legal capacity.

Another indication of the universal character of Islamic law is the view held by the Shafi'ites and many Hanafites that the precepts of the Shari'a address all mankind. As to the secular provisions of Islamic law (*ahkam al-dunya*), they are binding in Islamic territory for Muslims and non-Muslims alike. With regard to religious rules there is an authoritative view that these are universal and address all mankind, regardless of a person's status, gender or religion. This means that non-Muslims will be punished in the Hereafter not only for their failure to convert to Islam, but also for not having heeded the commands of the Shari'a.[9]

8 'Abd al-'Aziz b. Ahmad al-Bukhari, *Kashf al-asrar: sharh kanz al-wusul ila ma'rifat al-usul li-Muhammad b. al-Husayn al-Pazdawi* (Istanbul: 1308 H), Vol. 4, 237–238. A similar text is to be found in al-Ghazali, *Al-mustasfa fi 'ilm al-usul* (Beirut, Dar al-Kutub al-'Ilmiyya, 1993), 67. The latter argues that all beings endowed with reason are capable of understanding God's commands and, therefore, have legal capacity.

9 Some scholars object to this view, arguing that a person cannot be required to perform something of which he is incapable, since complying with the religious commands of Islam is conditional upon being a Muslim. This argument is parried with the following analogical reasoning: since the command to perform *salat* addresses also Muslims who are in a state

Although this universality does not extend to other fields of the Shariʿa and there are, for all practical purposes, legal differences between various categories of persons, there is this deep fundamental level at which the Shariʿa can be regarded as universal, addressing all humankind and based on an essential equality of human beings.

3.2 *Elementary Rights Protected by Islamic Law*

In order to establish what elementary rights or legal values classical Islamic law protects, I want to examine unequal legal relationships in which one party has nearly total control over the other and is entitled to be obeyed. The limits set by the law to the powers of the party in control may tell us something about the elementary rights and legal values protected by classical Islamic law. The first domain of the law where one would look is, of course, constitutional law. Here the individual is confronted with the all-powerful state and in this context the doctrine of the inalienable rights of the citizen vis-a-vis the state was first formulated in Western Europe and America. In Islam, however, constitutional law is not well developed. The standard text books of *fiqh* do not have special chapters on the subject, and the first treatise on the subject was not composed until 1050 when al-Mawardi wrote his *Al-ahkam al-sultaniyya* (The Rules of Statecraft). This work and the few that were written after it discuss the organization of government and the duties of the ruler rather than the rights of individuals vis-a-vis the ruler. Most authors assert that the ruler is bound by the Shariʿa and must enforce it and that the duty of a subject to obey and assist the ruler ceases whenever carrying out the ruler's orders implies committing a sin. However, these principles are not elaborated into something resembling a Bill of Rights of the subjects. They remain very global and, consequently, the topic does not yield very much for our purposes. Therefore I will not pursue it, and leave the field of constitutional law.

Instead, I have selected two other legal relationships, belonging to the domain of civil law and entailing the wielding of power of one party over the other, namely marriage and slavery. I intend to examine the basic and inalienable rights of wives in relation to their husbands and those of slaves in relation to their masters. Of course, these relationships differ a great deal from the relationship between the state and its subjects, which forms the framework of the Western doctrines of human rights. The greatest difference, in my view, is

of religious impurity and therefore cannot comply with the command immediately without first taking ablutions, one must assume that it is possible that commands address people who cannot obey immediately but only after complying with a condition if this is in their power. See al-Bukhari, *Kashf al-asrar*, Vol. 4, 234, 243–244; al-Ghazali, *Al-mustasfa*, 73–74.

that the relationship between the state and its subject is an anonymous and impersonal one, whereas both the other relationships are eminently personal, not least because of affection and physical proximity. Therefore, much of the interaction within these relationships remains outside the sphere of the law, at least law in the Western sense. Yet, the classical jurists of Islam discuss these relationships from the point of view of the law, and define the limits of lawful behaviour both for the husband with regard to his wife and for the master with regard to his slave. It is these limits that I want to examine here in order to establish which inalienable rights are guaranteed by the Shariʿa.

Marriage – I shall first consider the relationship between husband and wife. One of the legal effects of the marriage contract is that the husband is under obligation to provide his wife with maintenance. Another is that, if certain conditions are satisfied, he is entitled to marital control over his wife. After the conclusion of the marriage contract and the payment of the brideprice, the husband may demand that his wife 'deliver herself' (*taslim nafsiha*) to him, or 'put herself at her disposal' (*tamkin nafsiha*), provided she is capable of sexual intercourse or longs for it and provided he can offer to her adequate housing. Putting herself at his disposal means first that she goes to live in the conjugal home, secondly, that she enters his control, which is sometimes referred to as detention or custody (*ihtibas*), and thirdly, that she is available for sexual intercourse. If after the conclusion of the marriage contract the wife does not put herself at her husband's disposal without good cause, she forfeits her right to maintenance. The same happens if she withdraws from his control without good reason, usually by leaving the conjugal home without his consent or by failing to comply with his demands. She is then considered to be rebellious or disobedient, *nashiz*. In this connection the *fiqh* books discuss two questions. First the question of when she can lawfully refuse to put herself under his control or leave his control and, secondly, the question of whether or not she is still entitled to maintenance, even if she acted lawfully in refusing to put herself under her husband's control or leaving his control. Finally, the jurists explain the lawful measures that the husband has at his disposal in order to force his wife to compliance, if she is disobedient but has not left the conjugal home.

From the texts on these topics[10] it appears that a wife has the following elementary rights that her husband may not infringe.

10 With regard to marriage, I have mostly relied on Hanafite texts, especially Muhammad Qadri Pasha, *Al-ahkam al-sharʿiyya fi ahwal al-shakhsiyya* (Cairo, 1327 H). This contains a reliable survey of Hanafite family law, focusing on the legal rules and omitting the religious aspects.

1. The right not to be subjected to acts that may impair her health.[11] I have deliberately not used the term 'right to physical integrity' since a married woman (like a slave girl) is not entitled to refuse intercourse, unless there is a lawful excuse, such as illness or physical or psychological incapability of having intercourse.[12]
2. The right to perform her religious duties. The test case here, of course, is the obligation of *hajj*. The jurists agree that a wife, if the *hajj* is religiously obligatory for her, is entitled to perform the *hajj*, even without her husband's consent, provided she travels in the company of a close relative, though he is not then obliged to pay for her maintenance.[13] And if she is fasting during Ramadan, her husband may not demand intercourse during daytime. This right to perform religious duties also extends to non-Muslim wives.[14]
3. The right to own and administer her own property.
4. The right to have relations with her parents and relatives:[15]
5. The right to lawful social intercourse within her home. Although the husband is entitled to confine his wife to the conjugal home, she has the right not to be alone. If there are no children or servants, the wife is entitled to a female companion.[16]

---

11 This is a generalization. The classical texts mention a number of specific rights: e.g. the right, in case of illness, to refuse to enter her husband's custody and to refuse intercourse. Moreover the husband's right to chastise her when she is disobedient, does not extend beyond light heating. If he beats her excessively, he can be punished by the judge on the basis of *taʿzir*. See Qadri Pasha, articles 163, 167, 211.

12 Such a case is discussed in a nineteenth-century Malikite *fatwa*. A married woman had left her husband and had gone to live with her father. She then claimed maintenance from her husband, arguing that she was entitled to do so since she was incapable of sexual intercourse and lived in constant fear that her husband would force her to it. The only way to get rid of her fear was by leaving her husband's house. The mufti decided that under these circumstances she had acted lawfully and was still entitled to maintenance. See Muhammad ʿIllaysh, *Fath al-ʿali al-malik fi fatwa ʿala madhhab al-imam Malik* (Cairo, 1319 H) Vol. 2, 69.

13 Qadri Pasha, article 168.

14 A. Fattal, *Le statut légal des non-musulmans en pays d'islam.* (Beirut, Imprimérie Catholique, 1958), 131–132.

15 She has the right to visit her parents once a week and her other relatives once a year, but she is not allowed to spend the night there. Although the husband may refuse access to his wife's relatives, he may not prevent her from seeing them and talking to them. A wife may lawfully refuse to follow her husband if he intends to live at a distance of more than three days walk (*masafat al-qasr* in Hanafite law) from the place where the marriage has been concluded. The husband may not withhold his consent if his wife goes to live with her parents in the case of her presence being indispensable for nursing her sick father. See Qadri Pasha, articles 162, 215, 216.

16 Qadri Pasha, article 187.

Slavery – *The* nature of the legal relationship between a slave and his master is totally different from matrimony. Marriage is a synallagmatic contract between two legal persons who by virtue of this contract acquire rights and obligations towards each other. The relationship of slavery is not based on a contract between the owner and his slave. On the contrary, in this relationship the slave is first and foremost property. His master is entitled to the fruits of his labour. As to female slaves, their masters can have lawful sexual intercourse with them. However, since the slave is endowed with legal personality and has not totally lost his or her legal capacity he or she has certain rights, which can be enforced against the owner. The discussion of these rights in the *fiqh* books is rather terse, but it is possible to identify certain elementary rights.

1. The right to life. The existence of this right *vis-à-vis* third parties is obvious. Like all other lawful residents of Islamic territory, a slave's life is protected by his *ʿisma* and if someone violates this protection, the owner of the slave can sue him and, under Hanafite law, even demand the killer's life, if the killing was wilful and unlawful. If the killing was accidental, the owner can demand bloodmoney, which for a slave is equivalent to his market value. Since the slave's owner is the 'avenger' (*wali al-dam*), there is a procedural problem if the owner himself has killed the slave. Most jurists assert that, although he cannot be sued for retribution or for payment of the blood price, the state can punish him on the strength of *taʿzir*.[17] 'The right to life further includes the right to be kept alive. The slave has an enforceable claim against his owner for maintenance (including the expenses of medical treatment), which is not dependent on whether or not the slave has worked. He may take what he needs from the owner's property if the owner is absent or refuses to give it to him. Unlike a wife's right to maintenance, a slave's right is not lost in the case of his disobedience. If the owner cannot support him and the slave cannot be sold or hired out, the slave has a claim against the Treasury (*bayt al-mal*) for maintenance.[18]
2. The right not to be subjected to acts that may impair his health.[19] As in marriage, this right does not include the right of a female slave to refuse intercourse without a lawful excuse.

---

17 Bukhari, *Kashf al-asrar*, Vol. 4, 288.

18 *Ibid.*; Shaykhzade, *Majmaʿ al-anhur fi sharh multaqa al-abhur* (Istanbul, 1301 H), Vol. 1, 469–470; Al-Bajuri, *Hashiya ʿala al-qawl al-mukhtar fi sharh ghayat al-ikhtisar* (Cairo, n.d.), Vol. 2. 188.

19 This is manifest from the following rules:
   a. Slaves may not be overburdened with work and are entitled to adequate periods of rest.
   b. If an owner maltreats his slave, the judge, under Malikite law, can force him to sell the slave. See EI², s.v. ʿAbd, Vol. 1, 27.

3. The right to perform religious duties such as prayer and fasting during Ramadan. This does not include the right to perform *hajj*, since the *hajj* is not obligatory for a slave, having no financial means and being deprived of the free disposal of his body. Further, male slaves cannot participate in *jihad* without their master's consent, because of the risk of losing his property.[20]
4. Male slaves are, according to some law schools, entitled to lawful sexual intercourse. Upon the slave's demand, his master must provide him with a wife.[21]
5. Slave women have the right to take care of their young children. During this period transfer of her ownership without that of the child is, according to most schools, null and void.[22]

4 Conclusions

The exercise I have followed, i.e. the analysis of classical *fiqh* in a search for certain elementary values and inalienable rights related to the modern concept of human rights, was not meant to be judgmental. In my introduction I emphasized that it is meaningless to judge classical Islamic law by present-day values and standards. My aim, therefore, was not to demonstrate that Islamic law has always protected human rights, nor that Islamic law is essentially incompatible with the notion of human rights. What I wanted to show is that Islamic law recognizes certain basic values and inalienable rights. The contents of these values and rights must be seen against the historical background of the period when Islamic law was created and developed. But the fact that they are there, can be the starting-point for a debate on a new interpretation of Islamic law that recognizes and protects human rights as they are now internationally accepted. This debate, however, is one that must in the first place be conducted by Muslims.

20 Bukhari, *Kashf al-asrar*, Vol. 4, 287; EI^{2,} Vol. 1, 26.
21 Ibn Qudama, *Al-mughni* (Beirut, n.d.), Vol. 7, 631–632.
22 EI^{2}, Vol. 1, 26.

CHAPTER 27

Murder in Khaybar

Some Thoughts on the Origins of the Qasama Procedure in Islamic Law

The institution of *qasāma* has intrigued both Muslim jurists and western scholars.* The first were puzzled by its violation of essential legal principles, the latter by its apparent pre-Islamic origins. Because of its archaic and irrational character, western scholars assume that the institution was not applied in practice: "[I]t does not appear that this institution functioned much, even in the past, when the penal law of Islam had a certain practical application."[1] However, material from fatwa collections shows that the *qasāma* was indeed enforced by courts as late as the nineteenth century[2] and the rules connected with it have now found their way into some modern Islamic criminal codes.[3] The *qasāma*, it appears, was a living institution in Islamic law and not just theory. In this essay I will try to shed some light on the origins of this institution and its reception into Islamic law. I will attempt to chart the earliest developments of Islamic jurisprudence by analyzing the available hadith material and the statements of the first generation of jurists. In my conclusions I will suggest that my analysis of the material on *qasāma* corroborates Motzki's[4] and Powers'[5] revision of the chronology of the development of Islamic jurisprudence first put forward by Joseph Schacht in *The Origins of Muḥammadan Jurisprudence* (1950).

* I thank Harald Motzki and Gautier Juynboll for introducing me to the unfamiliar field of *isnād* analysis and for their critical remarks on earlier versions of this essay, from which I have greatly benefited. Needless to say that the conclusions expressed here are mine alone.

1 *EI*², s.v. qasam.

2 For a case from 12th-century al-Andalus, see Aḥmad b. Yaḥyā al-Wansharīsī, *al-Miʿyār al-muʿrib wa-'l-jāmiʿ al-mughrib ʿan fatāwā ʿulamāʾ Ifrīqiyya wa-'l-Maghrib*, ed. Muḥammad Ḥajji a.o. (Beirut: Dār al-Gharb al-Islāmī, 1981): vol. 2, 308–310; for 15th-century Ottoman law, see Paul Horster. *Zur Anwendung des islamischen Rechts im 16. Jahrhundert: Die "juristische Darlegungen" (maʿrūẓat) des Schejch ul-Islam Ebu Suʿud (gest. 1574)*. (Stuttgart: Kohlhammer, 1935): 58–59; for a case from 19th-century Egypt, see Muḥammad al-ʿAbbāsī al-Mahdī, *al-Fatāwā al-Mahdiyya fī 'l-Waqāʾiʿ al-Miṣriyya*. 7 vols. (Cairo: al-Maṭbaʿa al-Azhariyya, 1301–3): vol. 6, 78 (27 Shaʿbān, 1277). These fatwas are based on real court cases.

3 Arts. 239–256 of the Iranian Criminal Code of 1991; arts. 81–90 of the Yemeni Criminal Code of 1994.

4 Harald Motzki, *Die Anfänge der islamischen Jurisprudenz: Ihre Entwicklung in Mekka bis zur Mitte des 2./8. Jahrhunderts*. (Stuttgart: Franz Steiner Verlag, 1991).

5 David S. Powers, *Studies in Qur'an and Hadith: The Formation of the Islamic Law of Inheritance*. (Berkeley etc.: University of California Press, 1986).

 | DOI:10.1163/9789004420625_028

1 The Classical Doctrines

The *qasāma* institution seeks to determine who is liable for a murder if the perpetrator is unknown or the legal evidence against him or her is inadequate. There are two different interpretations of *qasāma*: the Maliki and the Hanafi doctrine. I will discuss first the Maliki rules, shared by most schools of law, and then the Hanafi doctrine, also held by the Zaydis.

According to the Malikis, *qasāma* is a procedure that the next of kin of a murdered person can invoke if there is only a strong suspicion against a person based on incriminating indications (*lawth*), but no legal evidence. Under these circumstances, the victim's agnatic male relatives may swear fifty oaths in order to corroborate the suspicion. In the oath they must indicate whether the murder was committed willfully or by mistake. If they swear that the murder was willful, they may demand either retaliation (*qiṣāṣ*), or payment of the blood price (*diya*). Otherwise, they are entitled only to blood price, to be paid by the defendant's solidarity group (*ʿāqila*). The incriminating indications (*lawth*) required for initiating the *qasāma* procedure may be circumstantial, e.g. the fact that a body is found in a hostile village or among a hostile tribe, the fact that a dead person was found lying on the ground shortly after a group of people had left that spot, or the fact that a person was found with blood on his clothes or carrying a blood-stained knife in the vicinity of a place where someone had been stabbed to death. The suspicion also may be based on legally incomplete evidence, e.g. the fact that before he expired the victim named his attacker, the testimony of a single witness to the killing, or the testimony of one or two witnesses who did not observe the actual killing, but saw that the victim had been attacked or beaten by a person prior to his death. The circumstances on which the suspicion is based must be proven by the plaintiff(s).

The Hanafi doctrine is substantially different.[6] If a body manifesting traces of violence is found in a city quarter, in a village or its vicinity (within shouting distance), in a house or on a person's land, and if the killer is unknown, the victim's heirs can bring an action against one or several persons from among the inhabitants of the quarter or village or against the owner of the house or the land. If the defendant denies the accusation, the heirs can initiate the *qasāma* procedure by exacting fifty oaths to the effect that the inhabitants or owner did not kill the victim and do not know who did. These oaths must be sworn

6 For a detailed survey of the Hanafi doctrine, see Baber Johansen, "Eigentum, Familie und Obrigkeit im hanafitischen Strafrecht: Das Verhältnis der privaten Rechte zu den Forderungen der Allgemeinheit in hanafitischen Rechtskommentare," in *Contingency in a Sacred Law: Legal and Ethical Norms in the Muslim Fiqh* (Leiden: Brill, 1999): 367–372.

by fifty inhabitants of the quarter or village – chosen by the plaintiffs – or by the owner of the house or the land. If anyone refuses to take the oath, he is imprisoned by the court until he confesses to the killing or swears the *qasāma* oath. The swearing, however, does not remove the responsibility of the defendants. As a result of the *qasāma* procedure they or their *ʿāqila*s are liable for the victim's blood price.

2 Anomaly of the *Qasāma* Procedure

The Maliki jurist, philosopher and systematic thinker Ibn Rushd (d. 595/1198)[7] mentions that a number of early jurists had objected to the *qasāma* procedure in its accusatory, Maliki form. These objections, he explains, were rooted in the lack of convincing textual support and in the conflict between the Maliki doctrine of *qasāma* and the following general legal principles:

1. The doctrine violates the principle that one may swear an oath only with regard to something one knows or has observed.
2. It conflicts with the rule that the plaintiff must prove his claim and that only if he is unable to do so must the defendant swear an oath. This is one of the basic principles of the law of procedure.
3. It violates the general rule that retaliation must be based on full and complete evidence, i.e. a confession or the concurring testimonies of two legally qualified male eyewitnesses.

With regard to the textual basis of the Maliki doctrine, the Khaybar murder hadith (see below) is most often quoted to prove the lawfulness of retaliation based on *qasāma*. This hadith, Ibn Rushd comments, is not conclusive, since the plaintiffs refused to take the oaths on the ground that they had not witnessed the killing, and the Prophet did not pronounce a judgment. Some opponents of *qasāma* in the Maliki form even suggested that the Prophet's words in this hadith were not meant to be taken seriously. The Prophet, they claim, was joking in order to show that this Jahili institution was not binding and question to the Anṣār was rhetorical. ("You don't want to swear, do you?"). Finally Ibn Rushd mentions a story reported by al-Bukhārī, according to which ʿUmar b. ʿAbd al-ʿAzīz did not accept retaliation based on the *qasāma* procedure.[8]

---

7 Ibn Rushd, *Bidāyat al-mujtahid wa-nihāyat al-muqtaṣid*. 2 vols. (Cairo: Muṣṭafā al-Bābī al-Ḥalabī, 1960): vol. 2, 427ff.

8 Bukhari, 6390 (Diyat, 22). The hadith material from the standard compilations is taken from the Sakhr hadith CD-ROM, GISCO (Global Islamic Software Company), *Mawsūʿat al-ḥadīth al-sharīf* (Version 2.0), 1997. I refer to a hadith by the name of the compiler followed by the number given in the ʿĀlimiyya Program (*tarqīm al-ʿālimiyya*) of this CD-ROM, and, in

Ibn Rushd concludes that it is preferable not to punish on the basis of *qasāma*. To be fair, he also lists the arguments of supporters of *qasāma* – especially Mālik – according to whom (1) the hadith establishes a special *sunna* that constitutes an exception to a general principle and (2) *qasāma* promotes the protection of society because murderers usually commit their crimes out of the sight of potential witnesses.

3 The Textual Basis of *Qasāma*

The *qasāma* is mentioned in two Prophetic reports. The text of the first one reads (with minor and insignificant variations):

> The *qasāma* existed in the Jahiliyya. Then the Prophet confirmed it as it was practiced in the Jahiliyya and pronounced a judgment on the strength of it among some people of the Anṣār ("Helpers", i.e. the Medinese Muslims) regarding a person who they claimed had been murdered by the Jews.[9]

Henceforth I will refer to this narrative as the *confirmation hadith*. The second hadith, transmitted in many variants, gives the details of the event referred to in the confirmation hadith. There are numerous versions of this hadith, all of which have the following narrative elements in common:

> Two Anṣār, named ʿAbd Allāh b. Sahl and Muḥayyiṣa b. Maḥmūd of the Banū Ḥāritha tribe, went to Khaybar. When they reached the oasis, they parted company and each took care of his own business. Later Muḥayyiṣa found ʿAbd Allāh murdered. He buried him and returned to Medina where, accompanied by his brother Ḥuwayyiṣa and the victim's brother ʿAbd al-Raḥmān b. Sahl, he went to see the Prophet. When ʿAbd al-Raḥmān began to speak, the Prophet said: "Give due respect for age", for ʿAbd al-Raḥmān was the youngest of them. He stopped talking and the other two related the story of ʿAbd Allāh's killing. The Prophet asked: "Are you willing to swear fifty oaths and demand [the blood] of

parenthesis, the identification according to Wensinck's *Concordance et Indices de la Tradition Musulmane*.

9 Muslim, 3161 (Qasāma, 8). Ahmad b. Hanbal, 16003 (vol. 4, 62), 22103 (v, 375), 22557 (v, 432). Nasa'i, 4628 (Qasāma, 2), 4629 (Qasāma, 2), 4630 (Qasāma, 2). ʿAbdal-Razzāq al-Sanʿānī, *al-Muṣannaf*, ed. Ḥabīb al-Raḥmān al-Aʿẓamī. 11 vols. (Simlak, Dabhel/Beirut, 1983): 18252, 18254. Ibn Abī Shayba, *al-Muṣannaf*, 8 vols. (Beirut, Dār al-Fikr, n.d.): vol. 6, 409.

> your companion or your killer (*ṣāḥiba/ikum aw qātila/ikum*)?" They answered: "How can we swear if we have not witnessed the event?" The Prophet said: "In that case the Jews may establish their innocence to you (*fa-tubri'ukum Yahūd*) by swearing fifty oaths." The three men objected, saying: "How can we accept the oaths of unbelievers?" Thereupon the Prophet paid the blood price himself.[10]

I will refer to this hadith as the *Khaybar murder hadith*. The numerous variants add picturesque but inconsequential details such as the exact spot at which the companions parted company, the purpose of their visit, the location where the body was found, an exchange of letters between the Prophet and the Jews before the *qasāma* procedure was initiated, and the fact that the first transmitter, Sahl b. Abī Ḥathma, was kicked sometime after the event by one of the camels paid as blood price. Most of these can be understood as later additions meant to give more liveliness to the narrative. In a few variants the name of the victim is not mentioned, or the names of his companions are different. One variant situates the murder in Medina, where one of the Anṣār was killed upon leaving the Prophet's house and the Jews were accused of the murder.[11] In some variants the Prophet begins by asking the plaintiffs whether they have proof of their allegation. When they admit that they have no evidence, the Prophet proposes that the Jews swear fifty oaths of purgation as defendants.[12]

As already noticed by Ibn Rushd, the wording of the Khaybar murder hadith is ambiguous from a juridical point of view. In most versions, the victim's next of kin refuse to take the oath because they did not witness the event. They also refuse to accept purgatory oaths sworn by Jews. The hadith, therefore, describes

10 Bukhari: 2937 (Djizya, 12), 5677 (Adab, 89), 6389 (Diyāt, 22), 6655 (Aḥkām, 38); Muslim: 3157 (Qasāma, 1), 3158 (Qasāma, 2), 3159 (Qasāma, 3), 3160 (Qasāma, 6); Tirmidhi: 1342 (Qasāma, 22); Abu Dawud: 3917 (Diyāt, 8), 3918 (Diyāt, 8), 3920 (Diyāt, 9), 3921 (Diyāt, 9); Ibn Maja: 2667 (Diyāt, 28), 2668 (Diyāt, 28); Aḥmad: 15509 (vol. 4, 2), 15515 (vol. 4, 4), 15515, 16639 (vol. 4, 142); Nasa'i: 4631 (Qasāma, 3), 4632 (Qasāma, 3), 4633 (Qasāma, 4), 4634 (Qasāma, 4), 4635 (Qasāma, 4), 4636 (Qasāma, 4), 4637 (Qasāma, 4), 4638 (Qasāma, 4), 4639 (Qasāma, 5), 4640 (Qasāma, 5), 4641 (Qasāma, 5); Malik: 1372 (Qasāma, 1), 1373 (Qasāma, 2); Dārimi: 2247 (Diyāt, 2). 'Abd al-Razzāq al-Ṣan'ānī, al-Muṣannaf, 18252, 18254, 18255, 18257, 18259, 18260. The Imami Shi'ites have the same story, but with anonymous personalities and a totally Shi'ite isnād. See Abū Ja'far Muḥammad b. 'Alī Ibn Babawayh, *Man lā yaḥduruhu al-faqīh*, ed. 'Alī al-Akhondī. 4 vols. (Tehran: Dār al-Kutub al-Islāmiyya, 1390 H): vol.4, 72–3.

11 Bukhari, 6390 (Diyāt, 22).

12 Bukhari, 6389 (Diyāt, 22); Nasa'i, 4640 (Qasāma, 5); Abu Dawud, 3920 (Diyāt, 9), 3921 (Diyāt, 9), 3922 (Diyāt, 9); 'Abd al-Razzāq al-Ṣan'ānī, *al-Muṣannaf*, 18252, 18255. Ibn Hishām, *al-Sīra al-nabawiyya*, ed. Muṣṭafā al-Saqqā a.o., 2nd ed. (Cairo: Muṣṭafā al-Bābī al-Ḥalabī, 1955): vol. 2, 355–6.

a stalemate caused by the plaintiffs' refusal to initiate the *qasāma* procedure, with the result that the Prophet pays the blood price himself. However, the fact that the Prophet proposed the application of the *qasāma* procedure has led all the law schools to adopt this hadith as the legal basis of *qasāma*.

4 Origins of the *Qasāma*

The received wisdom among Muslim and Western scholars alike is that *qasāma* was a pre-Islamic Arabian tribal institution. Western scholars identify this institution with the accusatory *qasāma* of Maliki doctrine. They hold that the Maliki version points to the archaic, tribal character of Medinese society; and that the Hanafi doctrine, which is based on the notion of territorial liability, is a subsequent development, more in agreement with the conditions of sedentary society in post-conquest Iraq.[13]

Fundamental objections to the received wisdom were raised by Crone,[14] who argues that the Hanafi form of *qasāma* was the older one and that it shares only its name with the pre-Islamic *qasāma*. In conformity with her revisionist approach to the origins of Islam,[15] Crone regards the Hanafi doctrine as having been adopted from Jewish law. She asserts that many Islamic legal institutions that are allegedly of Jahili origin have been shown to be borrowings from foreign legal systems and that, therefore, "[t]here is in fact nothing in the present state of the evidence to prevent one from turning the generally accepted theory upside down. Islamic law, so it may be argued, is overwhelmingly of foreign origin, one of the most important sources being Jewish, not Jahili law."[16] In her view, *qasāma*, in its Hanafi form, derives from a Pentateuchal ritual that involves purifying a region in which an unsolved murder has taken place by killing a red heifer, mentioned in Deuteronomy 21:1–9.[17] This ritual points at

13 See e.g. Robert Brunschvig, "Considérations sociologiques sur le droit musulman ancien," *Studia Islamica* 3 (1955): 69–70.

14 Patricia Crone, "Jahili and Jewish law: the qasāma," *Jerusalem Studies in Arabic and Islam* 4 (1984): 153–201.

15 See Patricia Crone and Michael Cook, *Hagarism: The making of the Islamic world* (Cambridge: Cambridge University Press, 1977).

16 Crone, "Jahili and Jewish law," 155.

17 (1) If anyone is found slain, lying in the field in the land which the LORD your God is giving you to possess, and it is not known who killed him, (2) then your elders and your judges shall go out and measure the distance from the slain man to the surrounding cities. (3) And it shall be that the elders of the city nearest to the slain man will take a heifer which has not been worked and which has not pulled with a yoke (4) The elders of that city shall bring the heifer down to a valley with flowing water, which is neither ploughed

the notion of territorial liability for murder, as found in Hanafi doctrine.[18] The Hanafi requirement that the inhabitants of the region swear an oath of compurgation can be viewed as a ritual of purification similar to the one described in Deuteronomy.[19] The Maliki doctrine, according to Crone, was introduced later and also owes its existence to Jewish law, to wit, the Rabbinical rule according to which judges must offer the oath to the party who has the presumption in his favor. It is highly unlikely, she argues, that the Maliki doctrine was of pre-Islamic, tribal origin, because tribal law, as a rule, is committed to the status quo, which plaintiffs try to change. Using contemporary Bedouin customary law as an example, Crone asserts that tribal law is biased in favor of defendants and that it is not plausible that arbiters will find for a plaintiff who has not formally proven his claim. Moreover, if the accusatory *qasāma* was in fact an ancient survival in Maliki law, one would have expected the later schools to have dropped it. But they did not.[20] Crone also argues that the Khaybar murder hadith, with its clear Maliki position on *qasāma*, is long and elaborate and must therefore be regarded as a later variant of the confirmation hadith. The latter, she argues, was circulated after what she calls the Pentateuchal period of Islamic history, in order to give the Jewish institution of the *qasāma* an Arabic pedigree. The Khaybar murder hadith was adopted only after the Maliki view gained adherents at the expense of the acceptance of the Hanafi doctrine.[21] That the notion of the *qasāma* as compurgation was also held by scholars outside Iraq is for Crone additional evidence for its being the original doctrine.[22]

Pace Crone, I will argue that *qasāma* is an indigenous, Arabian tribal institution and that it is plausible that the Prophet introduced it into Islam. Although we do not have sources for the first century, I will use the hadith material and the statements of early jurists to demonstrate that in the second half of the

---

nor sown, and they shall break the heifer's neck there in the valley (5) Then the priests, the sons of Levi, shall come near, for the LORD your God has chosen them to minister to Him and to bless in the name of the LORD; by their word every controversy and every assault shall be settled. (6) And all the elders of that city nearest to the slain man shall wash their hands over the heifer whose neck was broken in the valley (7) Then they shall answer and say, "Our hands have not shed this blood, nor have our eyes seen it (8) Provide atonement, O LORD, for Your people Israel, whom You have redeemed, and do not lay innocent blood to the charge of Your people Israel.' And atonement shall be provided on their behalf for the blood. (9) So you shall put away the guilt of innocent blood from among you when you do what is right in the sight of the LORD. (New King James Version).

18 Crone, "Jahili and Jewish Law," 162–3.

19 Ibid., 166–73.

20 Ibid., 182–95.

21 Ibid., 195.

22 Ibid., 162–3.

first century there were two separate doctrines regarding the *qasāma* procedure, one associated with Hijazi centers of learning and one espoused by Iraqi scholars. The first doctrine, a continuation of pre-Islamic practice, was adopted by the Malikis. The second doctrine, originally an administrative measure to secure law and order in the garrison towns of the Iraq, survived as the Hanafi doctrine of *qasāma*.

That there was a legal institution called *qasāma* in pre-Islamic Arabia is beyond dispute.[23] It is not clear, however, whether there was a clear body of rules connected with it. Gräf has already observed that there was considerable confusion in early Islam regarding the details of the procedure.[24] We have little information on its application in pre-Islamic Arabia. Reports allegedly dating from the Jahiliyya or the early decades of Islam indicate that the *qasāma* was practiced to establish paternity[25] and the name of a well.[26] But there was usually a connection with bloodshed. Incidental reports suggest that the *qasāma* served to determine whether a person had been outlawed by his tribe so as to ascertain whether or not the tribe bore a responsibility for manslaughter committed by that person, to establish whether a person who had entered a house and was killed there had entered by invitation or as a burglar,[27] and to substantiate or avert an accusation of murder.[28] Reviewing the available material and taking into account the common versions of the Khaybar murder hadith (see below), it is my impression that the main function of the *qasāma* in pre-Islamic Arabia was to establish disputed facts and liability, usually, but not always in connection with bloodshed.

5 A Story in Search of Authorities: an Analysis of the *Isnāds*

In order to sketch the early doctrinal development of the *qasāma*, it is necessary to establish a relative dating of the two main hadiths. This can be done

23 See Julius Wellhausen, *Reste arabischen Heidentums*. 2nd ed. (Berlin: 1927): 187–8; J. Pedersen, *Der Eid bei den Semiten in seinem Verhaeltniss zu verwandten Erscheinungen sowie die Stellung des Eides im Islam* (Strassburg: Karl J. Truebner, 1914): 180–81, 183. Crone, "Jahili and Jewish Law." 157.

24 E. Gräf, "Eine wichtige Rechtsdirektive 'Uthmans aus dem jahre 30," *Oriens* (1963): 130–131.

25 Crone, "Jahili and Jewish Law." 159, referring to 'Abd al-Razzāq al-Ṣan'ānī, al-Muṣannaf, *al-Muṣannaf*, 5800.

26 Al-Mas'ūdī, *Kitāb murūj al-dhahab*, ed. and tr. A.C. Barbier de Meynard and A.J.-B. Pavet de Courtelle (Paris: 1861–77): vol. 4, 304 ff. As quoted by Pedersen. *Der Eid*: 180, note 2.

27 'Abd al-Razzāq al-Ṣan'ānī, *al-Muṣannaf*, 18281.

28 Pedersen, *Eid*: 181 and Wellhausen, *Reste*: 187, both referring to a story in the *Kitāb al-Aghānī*; Bukhari, 3557 (Manāqib al-Anṣār, 27); Nasa'i, 4627 (Qasāma, 1).

by analyzing both the texts and the *isnāds*, using the method for dating hadith developed by Juynboll[29] and Motzki.[30] I will show that the wording of the common version of the Khaybar murder hadith dates from the first half of the second century, but that versions of the story were circulating in Medina in the second half of the first century. This is because the confirmation hadith and some variants of the Khaybar murder hadith can be shown to date from the turn of the first century and must be understood as a reaction against the original version of the Khaybar murder hadith, in which the oath is first offered to the plaintiffs. I present the *isnād* bundles of the Khaybar murder hadith in Figures 27.1 and 27.2, and those of the Confirmation hadith in Figure 27.3.

Let us first look at the *isnād* structure of the Khaybar murder hadith (see Figures 27.1 and 27.2). I will start with Figure 27.2 and will argue that the common link (cl) is Yaḥyā b. Saʿīd b. Qays (d. 144/761–2), a Medinese Follower, and that neither Bushayr b. Yasār (a Medinese of the Followers' generation, date of death unknown), nor Sahl (Companion, d. in the early 40s/660s)[31] can be regarded as such. I will show that Sahl was later added to the *isnād* and that the Mālik – Abū Laylā – Sahl *isnād*, the Saʿīd b. ʿUbayd – Bushayr – Sahl *isnād* as well as the Ibn Isḥāq – Bushayr b. Yasār/al-Zuhrī – Sahl *isnāds* are almost certainly spurious. That means that the wording of the common version of the Khaybar murder hadith goes back to Yaḥyā b. Saʿīd and dates from the first half of the second century.

As shown in Figure 27.2, Yaḥyā b. Saʿīd (d. 144/761–2) was evidently a central figure in the transmission of this hadith. His numerous students report the hadith with three different *isnāds*: Yaḥyā b. Saʿīd – Bushayr – the Prophet (the bold line in Figure 27.2), Yaḥyā b. Saʿīd – Bushayr – Sahl b. Abī Ḥathma – the Prophet (the thin, uninterrupted line in Figure 27.2), and Yaḥyā

29 G.H.A. Juynboll, "Some *isnâd* analytical methods illustrated on the basis of several woman-demeaning sayings from hadîth literature", *al-Qantara* 10 (1989): 343–84; Idem, "Early Islamic society as reflected in its use of isnâds", *Le Muséon* 107 (1994): 151–94; Idem, *Muslim tradition: Studies in chronology, provenance and authorship of early hadith* (Cambridge: Cambridge University Press, 1983).

30 Harald Motzki, "Quo vadis *Ḥadīth*-Forschung? Eine kritische Untersuchung von G.H.A. Juynboll: 'Nāfiʿ the *mawlā* of Ibn ʿUmar, and his position in Muslim *Ḥadīth* Literature'," *Der Islam* 73 (1996): 40–80; 193–231; Idem, "The Prophet and the Cat. On dating Mâlik's *Muwatta*ʾ and Legal Traditions." *Jerusalem Studies in Arabic and Islam* 22 (1998): 18–83; Motzki (1991).

31 Sahl b. Abī Ḥathma is said to have died at the beginning of Muʿāwiya's reign. According to most reports he was eight years old when the Prophet died; thus he was probably born around 3/624. ʿIzz al-Din Ibn al-Athīr, *Usd al-ghāba fī maʿrifat al-ṣaḥāba*, ed. Muḥammad Ibrāhīm Bannā a.o. (Cairo: Dār al- Shaʿb, 1970): vol. 2, 468; Ibn Ḥajar al-ʿAsqalānī, *al-Iṣāba fī tamyīz al-ṣaḥāba* (Cairo: 1969–1977): vol. 4, 272, no. 3516.

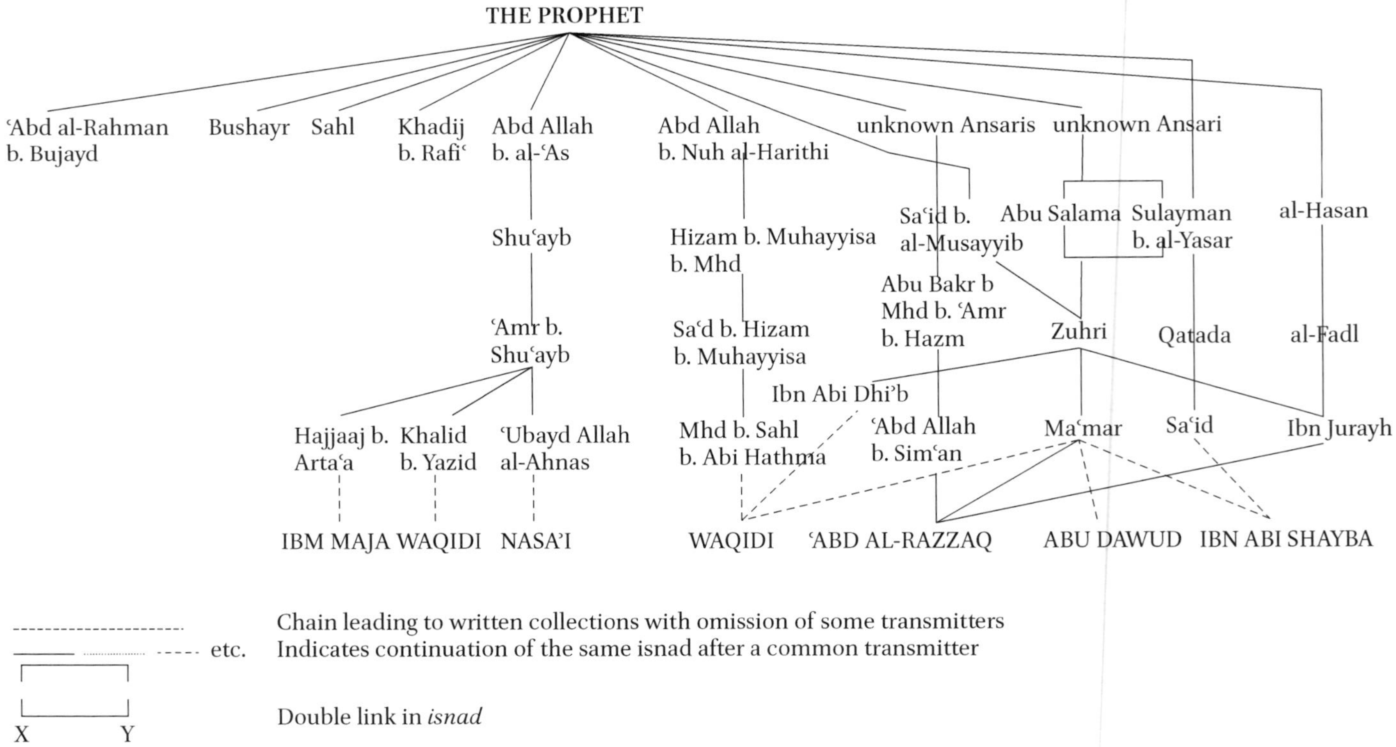

FIGURE 27.1 Khaybar murder *isnād*s 1
SOURCES: IBN MAJA, 2668 (DIYAT, 28); NASA'I, (QASAMA, 5); ABU DAWUD, 3923; SANʿANI, 18252, 18254, 18255, 18260; IBN ABI SHAYBA, VI, 409; WAQIDI, II, 713, 715

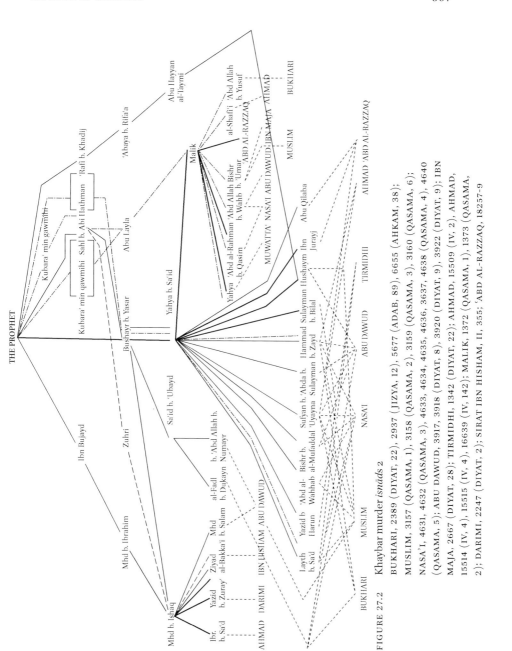

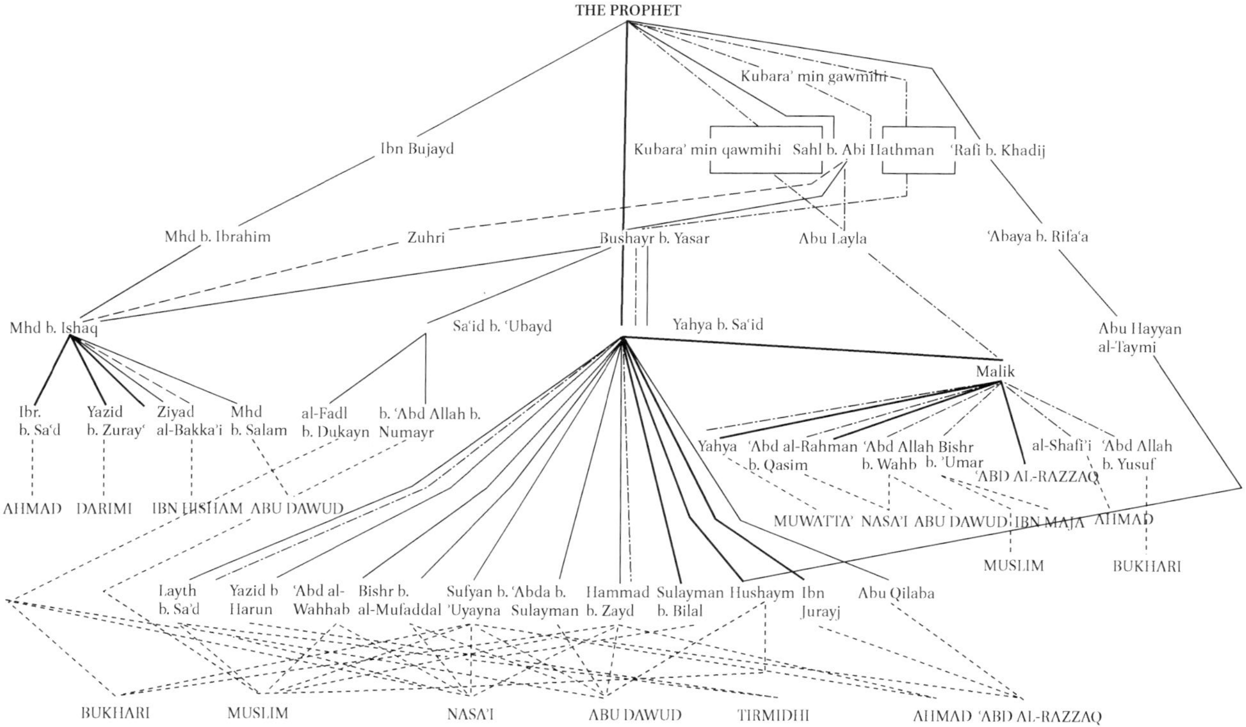

FIGURE 27.2 Khaybar murder *isnāds* 2

BUKHARI, 2389 (DIYAT, 22), 2937 (JIZYA, 12), 5677 (ADAB, 89), 6655 (AHKAM, 38); MUSLIM, 3157 (QASAMA, 1), 3158 (QASAMA, 2), 3159 (QASAMA, 3), 3160 (QASAMA, 6); NASA'I, 4631, 4632 (QASAMA, 3), 4633, 4634, 4635, 4636, 3637, 4638 (QASAMA, 4), 4640 (QASAMA, 5); ABU DAWUD, 3917, 3918 (DIYAT, 8), 3920 (DIYAT, 9), 3922 (DIYAT, 9); IBN MAJA, 2667 (DIYAT, 28); TIRMIDHI, 1342 (DIYAT, 22); AHMAD, 15509 (IV, 2), AHMAD, 15514 (IV, 4), 15515 (IV, 4), 16639 (IV, 142); MALIK, 1372 (QASAMA, 1), 1373 (QASAMA, 2); DARIMI, 2247 (DIYAT, 2); SIRAT IBN HISHAM, II, 355; 'ABD AL-RAZZAQ, 18257-9

b. Saʿīd – Bushayr – Sahl b. Abī Ḥathma and Rāfiʿ b. Khadīj – the Prophet (the dot-stroke line in Figure 27.2). Since *isnād*s tend to improve over time, it is plausible that Yaḥyā b. Saʿīd initially transmitted the hadith on the authority of Bushayr – the Prophet.[32] Now, this is not a very good *isnād*, since Bushayr b. Yasār was not a Companion and cannot have been an eyewitness to the events described in the hadith. Yaḥyā transmitted the story with this *isnād* to four of his students: Hushaym, Ibn Jurayj, Abū Qilāba and Mālik. At a later stage, Yaḥyā or one of his students completed the *isnād* by inserting Sahl's name. Although Sahl was a Companion and a member of the victim's tribe, he does not seem to have been the best choice: born in 3 H, Sahl was only a child at the time of the Prophet's decease and he died young in the early 40s/660s. That would explain the inclusion of Rāfiʿ b. Khadīj (d. 73/ 692–3)[33] as a parallel authority to Sahl in some *isnād*s and the addition of some further anonymous "old men of his tribe" (*rijāl kubarāʾ min qawmihim*) in the Mālik – Abū Laylā – Sahl *isnād*s.

Those of Yaḥyā's students who related the Khaybar murder hadith with the *isnād* Yaḥyā – Bushayr – the Prophet apparently were not satisfied with it. Indeed, three of them also transmitted the narrative with entirely new *isnād*s that by-passed both Yaḥyā and Bushayr.[34] One of the three is Mālik, who by-passed Yaḥyā and Bushayr by creating an independent *isnād*: Mālik – Abū Laylā – Sahl. This *isnād* is highly suspect, since Abū Laylā, allegedly the grandson of Sahl, does not appear in any *isnād* except this one, and Sahl cannot be regarded as an authority for this hadith. Moreover, the text of the hadith transmitted by Mālik with the Abū Laylā – Sahl *isnād* is clearly an elaboration of the text transmitted by him with the Yaḥyā – Bushayr – the Prophet *isnād*

32 Muslim 3159 (Qasāma 3); Muwatta', 1373 (Qasāma 2); Nasa'i, 4639 (Qasāma 5); ʿAbd al-Razzāq al-Ṣanʿānī, *al-Muṣannaf*, 18257, 18258. Interestingly, Bushayr's authority is questioned ("*zaʿama Bushayr*" i.e. Bushayr alleged) with regard to some parts of the story: the part about the Anṣār being allowed to swear first (Muslim, 3159, Sulaymān b. Bilāl from Yaḥyā) and the part about the Prophet paying the blood price himself (ibid., and Nasa'i, 4639; Malik, 1373: Mālik from Yaḥyā b. Saʿīd). Precisely at these points alternative versions circulated in transmission by al-Zuhrī. The later insertion of Sahl b. Abū Ḥathma into the *isnād* is already anticipated in the variant transmitted by Hushaym from Yaḥyā b. Saʿīd – Bushayr – the Prophet (Muslim, 3159). Here Sahl is introduced at the end of the story as someone who was kicked by one of the camels paid as blood price, a detail also found in the versions transmitted by Ḥammād – Yaḥyā b. Saʿīd – Bushayr – Sahl.

33 When Rāfiʿ b. Khadīj is mentioned, he is listed as the second authority after Sahl. Only in one *isnād* does he appear as the sole authority (see next footnote).

34 Hushaym relates a variant of the story with the *isnād* Hushaym – Abū Ḥayyān al-Taymī (nearly a namesake of our cl Yaḥyā; his full name was Yaḥyā b. Saʿīd b. Ḥayyān al-Taymī) – ʿAbāya b. Rifāʿa – Rāfiʿ b. Khadīj – the Prophet (Abu Dawud, 3921); Ibn Jurayj does so with the *isnād* Ibn Jurayj – al-Faḍl – al-Ḥasan – the Prophet (see Figure 27.1) (ʿAbd al-Razzāq al-Ṣanʿānī, *al-Muṣannaf*, 18255).

and must be regarded as later. Although it is not entirely impossible that Mālik, through Abū Laylā has tapped a vein of family stories of the Banū Ḥāritha, that is highly unlikely. In view of the similarities between the two texts, it is more likely that Mālik fabricated this family *isnād*. The conclusion must be that Mālik cannot be regarded as an independent cl apart from Yaḥyā b. Saʿīd.

Another apparent cl is Muḥammad b. Isḥāq (d. 150/767), who transmits two different versions of the story to four students with three *isnāds*: One version with the *isnāds* Bushayr – Sahl – the Prophet and al-Zuhrī – Sahl – the Prophet, and another, different variant on the authority Muḥammad b. Ibrāhīm – 'Abd al-Raḥmān b. Bujayd – the Prophet. The story attached to the first two *isnāds* is very similar to the narratives transmitted by Yaḥyā b. Saʿīd. Since I have established above that Sahl was not a real transmitter, it is plausible that Ibn Isḥāq heard the story from Yaḥyā b. Saʿīd himself and appropriated his *isnād*. The other *isnād* (al-Zuhrī – Sahl – the Prophet) is certainly spurious. In none of the canonical collections do we find al-Zuhrī relating a report on Sahl's authority. What may have happened is that Ibn Isḥāq knew that al-Zuhrī also transmitted some version of the Khaybar murder hadith and included him in the *isnād*. However, he must have done so without having checked the versions passed on by al-Zuhrī, for, as we shall see, these were in many respects different from the Yaḥyā b. Saʿīd variants. The story attached to the Ibn Bujayd *isnād* is presented as a correction of the common version:

> Muḥammad b. Ibrāhīm [Medina, d. 120] said: "I swear by God, Sahl was not more knowledgeable than he [Ibn Bujayd], but he was older." He [Ibn Bujayd] said to him [Muḥammad b. Ibrāhīm]: By God, the case was not like that: Sahl has made up the words of the Messenger of God (pbuh) "Swear to what you do not have any knowledge about." [The true versions is that] the Messenger of God (pbuh), wrote to the Jews of Khaybar after the Anṣār had spoken to him: "Someone has been found murdered amidst your houses, so pay his blood price." They then wrote that they would swear that they did not kill him and did not know who had done so'. Then the Messenger of God (pbuh) paid the blood price from his own property.[35]

Muḥammad b. Isḥāq must have been familiar with the alternative version of the Khaybar murder hadith (in which the oath was first offered to the Jews as defendants) and invented the narrative in which Ibn Bujayd corrected Sahl, his fellow tribesman. The change in the contents of the story reflects a legal

35 Ibn Hishām, al-*Sīra*, vol 2, 355–6. A shorter variant in Abu Dawud, 3922 (Diyāt, 9).

dispute that had emerged in Medina by the end of the first century and to which I will return.

Finally we have to consider the Saʿīd b. ʿUbayd (Kufa, date of death unknown) strands (see Figure 27.2) within the complicated *isnād* cluster. The two versions transmitted by him have identical beginnings and endings ('Some people from his [Sahl's] tribe set out for Khaybar and there they parted and they found the body of one of them, having been killed ... Then the Prophet did not want to leave his blood without compensation (*kariha an yubṭila damahu*) and therefore paid as his blood price 100 camels from the *zakah*") but have different middle parts. The hadiths transmitted by al-Faḍl b. Dukayn (Kufa, d. 218)[36] indicate that after the Anṣār had told him that they had accused the Jews and that the Jews had denied the charge, the Prophet said to the Anṣār: "Can you bring evidence against those who have killed him?" They answered: "We have no evidence." Then he said: "In that case they shall swear." The other version was transmitted from Saʿīd b. ʿUbayd by Muḥammad b. ʿAbd Allāh b. Numayr (Kufa, d. 199).[37] Muslim includes the hadith immediately after a common Yaḥyā b. Saʿīd variant, but quotes only the first and last part of it. He gives the first line of the Saʿīd b. ʿUbayd version, continues with the words "and then he cited the [previous] hadith [i.e. the one transmitted by Yaḥyā]" and then concludes with the last part of the Saʿīd b. ʿUbayd version. Muslim, it seems, deliberately attempted to normalize the hadith and to adapt it to the most common version as transmitted by Yaḥyā b. Saʿīd and Mālik. Therefore, we may regard Saʿīd b. ʿUbayd as the transmitter who put these variants into circulation. It must date, then, from the second half of the second century. Saʿīd's date of death is not known, but taking into account that his students al-Faḍl b. Dukayn and ʿAbd Allāh b. Numayr died in 218 and 199 respectively, he cannot have transmitted them before the middle of the second century. As Saʿīd and his students were Kufans, this version represents an Iraqi attempt to come to grips with the Khaybar murder hadith and bring it into conformity with the Iraqi doctrine of *qasāma*. By the middle of the second century the Khaybar murder hadith apparently had become generally known in Iraq.

Finally we have to examine the single strand *isnād*s (see figure 27.1). Among these I also count the three hadiths in which ʿAmr b. Shuʿayb (d. 118/736–7) seems to be the cl. The three *matn*s of this bundle differ so much[38] that they

36 Bukhari, 6389 (Diyāt, 22); Nasa'i, 4640 (Qasāma, 5); Abu Dawud, 3920 (Diyāt, 9).

37 Muslim, 3159 (Qasāma, 3).

38 The main differences are the following (A = Nasa'i, 4641 (Qasāma, 5); B = Ibn Maja, 2668 (Diyāt, 28); C = Wāqidī, *Kitāb al-Maghāzī*, ii, 715: A and C are silent about the names of the Helpers who went to Khaybar, whereas B mentions four of them: the three usual ones

must be regarded as three separate hadiths with single strand *isnāds*. Although Motzki argued that hadiths with the ʿAmr b. Shuʿayb family *isnād* are often authentic,[39] these three hadiths almost certainly represent later attempts to provide Khaybar murder stories with respectable *isnāds*. The ʿAmr b. Shuʿayb *isnād* would be attractive to use, since it was a family *isnād* and many other hadiths relating to penal law were transmitted on his authority.

Some of these single strand hadiths are very close to the common version transmitted by Yaḥyā b. Saʿīd. One of these, given by ʿAbd al-Razzāq with an *isnād* that includes transmitters not listed in the standard biographical dictionaries (ʿAbd Allāh b. Simʿān – Abū Bakr b. Muḥammad b. ʿAmr b. Ḥazm – unknown Anṣāris)[40] is identical to the version reported by Mālik on the authority of Yaḥyā b. Saʿīd. Also close to the common version is one of the reports with the ʿAmr b. Shuʿayb *isnād*.[41] A special case is a hadith given by al-Wāqidī.[42] It contains a very elaborate and detailed version of the Khaybar murder hadith and has an *isnād* (ʿAbd Allāh b. Nūḥ al-Ḥārithī – Muḥammad b. Sahl b. Abī Ḥathma – Saʿd b. Ḥizām b. Muḥayyiṣa – his father) which seems too good to be true. This *isnād* includes the descendants of two of the story's protagonists. The fact that the *matn* provides a wealth of details not to be found in any of the other versions indicates that Wāqidī collected and put together all the information on the episode that was available to him and provided it with an *isnād* of his own making including persons figured who were relatives of some of the protagonists, but were otherwise unknown as transmitters of hadith. In all these cases the *isnāds* must have been fabricated to create better authority for stories heard from other sources.

Other single strand hadiths seem to be independent attempts – their texts do not seem to be related – to provide support for the view that the *qasāma*

---

with the addition of ʿAbd al-Raḥmān, the victim's brother. In A the victim is identified as the youngest son of Muḥayyiṣa, in B as ʿAbd Allāh b. Sahl, and in C not at all. In A and C the Prophet imposes blood price on the Jews and pays part of it himself; in B the Prophet pays all of it and there is no mention of its first having been imposed on the Jews; C relates only the last part of the episode, starting with "The Messenger of God, pbuh, imposed his (?) blood price on the Jews", leaving out the story of the killing and the discussion on the procedure. That it refers to the Khaybar murder is clear from the words: "This was the first time that the *qasāma* was applied (*fa-hiya awwal ma kānat al-qasāma*)", meaning of course the first time in Islam.

39 Motzki, *Anfänge*, 190–1. Juynboll regards the *isnāds* of ʿAmr b. Shuʿayb going back to his great-grandfather as suspect (Juynboll, "Early Islamic Society," 172–4).

40 ʿAbd al-Razzāq al-Ṣanʿānī, *al-Muṣannaf*, 18260.

41 Ibn Maja, 2668 (Diyāt, 28).

42 Wāqidī, *Kitab al-Maghāzī*, vol. 2, 713.

oaths are first imposed on the side of the defendant.[43] Most of these can be shown to have been introduced by Kufan scholars during the second century. Two hadiths with the ʿAmr b. Shuʿayb *isnād*, they must have been put into circulation after his death in 118/736–7 by the Kufan scholars, since the Kufans Ḥajjāj b. Arṭa'a (d. 145) and ʿUbayd Allāh b. al-Aḥnas (date of death unknown) are reported to have heard it from ʿAmr. Another hadith has an *isnād* going back, via his son, to Rāfiʿ b. Khadīj, who we have met before in the company of Sahl b. Abī Ḥathma in the Yaḥyā b. Saʿīd *isnāds*.[44] If we accept that this family *isnād* was fabricated, the first person who could have put it into circulation would have been Yaḥyā b. Saʿīd b. Ḥayyān (not to be confused with Yaḥyā b. Saʿīd b. Qays, the common link of the common version), who died in d. Kufa in 145. A second group consists of four very similar versions of the hadith, transmitted by al-Zuhrī from Saʿīd b. al-Musayyib, Abū Salama ʿAbd Allāh and Sulaymān b. Yasār.[45] They must be regarded as supplements to the confirmation hadith and will be discussed in the next section.

The *isnād* pattern of the Confirmation hadith (see Figure 27.3) is much simpler than that of the Khaybar murder hadith. It clearly shows that the wording was attributed to the Medinese jurist Ibn Shihāb al-Zuhrī (d. 124/741–2). Although the *isnād* pattern is problematic – al-Zuhrī's words were transmitted only by single strand *isnād*s – and cannot be regarded as convincing proof for al-Zuhrī's authorship, I do accept it on the strength of other evidence, to be discussed below. The confirmation hadith contains a strong doctrinal statement based on a specific event. Whereas the doctrinal statement must have been formulated by al-Zuhrī or his teachers (Saʿīd b. Al-Musayyib (d. 93/711–2), Sulaymān b. Yasār (d. 110/728–9) and Abū Salama b. ʿAbd al-Raḥmān (d. 94/712–3)), the historical information – the Khaybar murder story – goes back to older material. It is my contention that in the older versions of the narrative, only referred to in the Confirmation hadith, the oath was first offered to the Anṣār as plaintiffs and that they, therefore, correspond with the later common version transmitted by Yaḥyā b. Saʿīd. If we examine the above-mentioned versions of the Khaybar murder hadith transmitted by al-Zuhrī and his teachers as a supplement to the confirmation hadith, it is evident that they are a polemical reaction to a version in which the oath is first offered to the Anṣār. Two hadiths say: "The Prophet (pbuh) said to the Jews, *and he began with them*

43 Nasa'i, 4641 (Qasāma, 5); Abu Dawud, 3923 (Diyāt, 9); Abu Dawud, 3921 (Diyāt, 9); Wāqidī, ii, 715; ʿAbd al-Razzāq al-Ṣanʿānī, *al-Muṣannaf*, 18252, 18255.

44 Abu Dawud, 3921 (Diyāt, 9).

45 Abu Dawud, 3923 (Diyāt, 9); ʿAbd al-Razzāq al-Ṣanʿānī, *al-Muṣannaf*, 18252; Wāqidī, *Kitab al-Maghāzī*, ii, 715; Ibn Abī Shayba, *al-Muṣannaf*, vol. 8, 409.

(emphasis mine, RP): 'Are fifty of your men willing to swear?'" Another one reads: "Thereupon the Messenger of God (pbuh) *began with the Jews* (emphasis mine, RP) and imposed fifty *qasāma* oaths upon them." The hadiths are distinctive in that the blood price is imposed on the Jews and not paid by the Prophet, as in the standard version. If this version was formulated by al-Zuhrī or his teachers as a reaction to the common version, then the common version must be older and go back at least to the second half of the first century. Indeed, some evidence suggests that the story is historical and goes back to the Prophet.[46]

As for the confirmation hadith itself, its wording is apodictic and sounds almost polemical. It has all the characteristics of a summarized plea in a debate about the legitimacy of the *qasāma* procedure. If we understand it as an answer to the question: "What is your opinion on the *qasāma*?" it makes perfect sense: "[I consider it as lawful, since] the *qasāma* existed in the Jahiliyya period, was adopted by the Prophet in its original form, and was applied by him when a Medinese was murdered in Khaybar and the Jews were accused of having killed him." Evidently, its goal is not to give a detailed report on the Khaybar murder case, but to establish the legitimacy of the *qasāma* procedure.

This debate can be traced and dated. Around the turn of the first century the *qasāma* had come under attack by Hijazi jurists because it contradicted general principles of the shari'a and because the Khaybar murder hadith is legally inconclusive.[47] According to several reports the Umayyad Caliph 'Umar b. 'Abd al-'Azīz (r. 99/717–101/720) was confused about the *qasāma*. One day he asked several notables gathered around his throne whether a sentence of retribution (*qawad*) could be pronounced on the strength of the *qasāma* procedure.[48] They responded that such sentences were lawful and that

46 Since the Khaybar *qasāma* is mentioned in the *awā'il* literature (reports about who introduced certain practices in Islam) and Juynboll has shown that many of the *awā'il* reports are historical. See Ibn Qutayba, *Kitāb al-Ma'ārif*, ed. Tharwat 'Ukāsha. 2nd impr. (Cairo: 1969) p. 551; Wāqidī, *Kitāb al-Maghāzī*, vol. 2, 715; G.H.A. Juynboll, *Muslim tradition: Studies in chronology, provenance and authorship of early hadith* (Cambridge: Cambridge University Press, 1983) Ch. 1.

47 The jurists who reportedly rejected the legitimacy of the *qasāma*, i.e. the legitimacy of sentences of retaliation on the strength of the accusatory *qasāma*, included the Medinese Salīm b. 'Abd Allāh b.'Umar (d. 106/724–5) and Sulaymān b. Yasār (d. 110/728–9). Of course, criticism was also voiced by the Iraqis, such as the Basrans Abū Qilāba (d. 104/722–3) and Qatāda b. Di'āma b. Qatāda (d. 117/735–6), and the Kufan al-Ḥakam b. 'Utayba (d. 113/731–2). See Ibn Rushd, *Bidāya*, vol. 2, 427ff.; Muḥammad b. 'Alī al-Shawkānī, *Nayl al-awtār*, (Cairo: Dār al-Ḥadīth, n.d.) vol. 7, 46.

48 Bukhari, 6390 (Diyāt, 22), 3872 (Maghāzī, 37); Muslim, 3163 (Qasāma, 12); 'Abd al-Razzāq al-Ṣan'ānī, *al-Muṣannaf*,18278; Ibn Abī Shayba, *al-Muṣannaf*, vol. 6, 409.

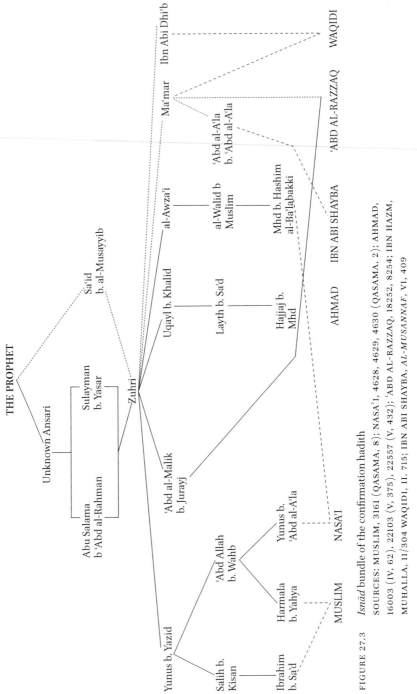

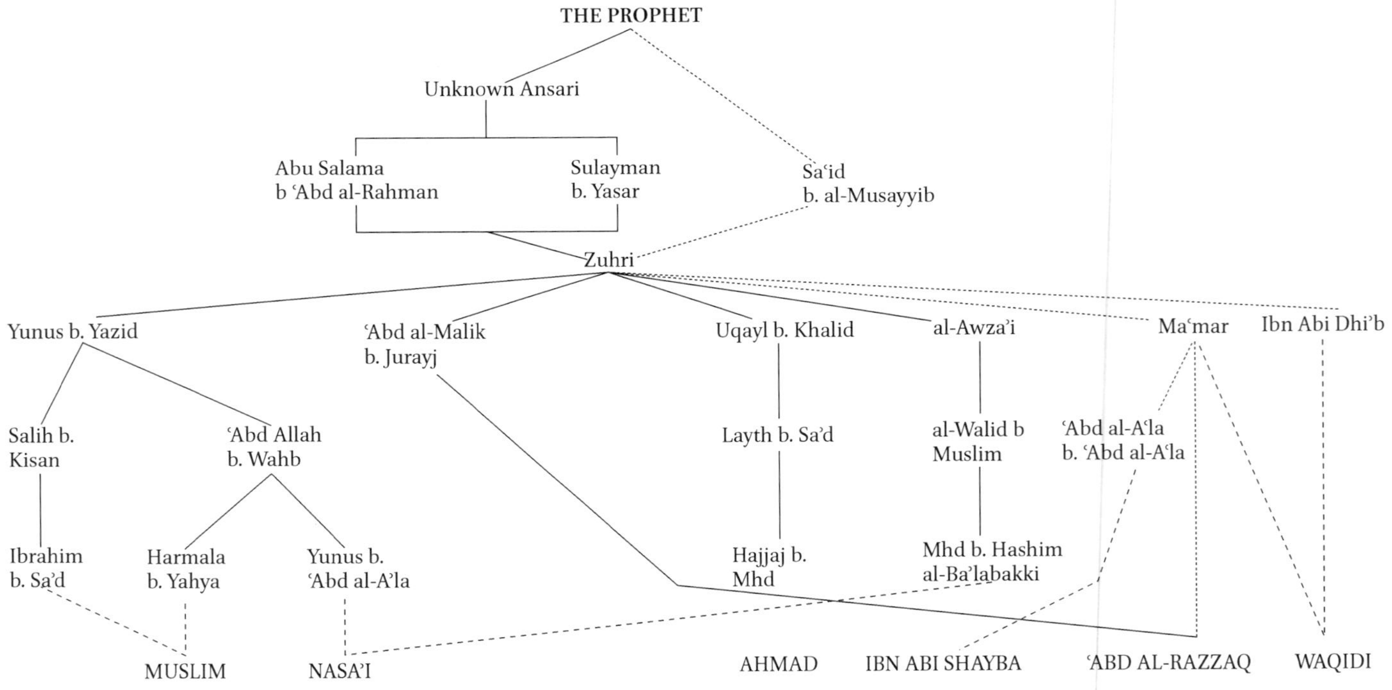

FIGURE 27.3 *Isnād* bundle of the confirmation hadith
SOURCES: MUSLIM, 3161 (QASAMA, 8); NASAʾI, 4628, 4629, 4630 (QASAMA, 2); AHMAD, 16003 (IV, 62), 22103 (V, 375), 22557 (V, 432); ʿABD AL-RAZZAQ, 18252, 8254; IBN HAZM, MUHALLA, 11/304 WAQIDI, II. 715; IBN ABI SHAYBA, *AL-MUSANNAF*, VI, 409

previous Caliphs had pronounced them. Only the chief qadi, the Basran jurist Abū Qilāba (d. 104/722–3), objected on the ground that penal sentences may not be pronounced on the basis of the statements of persons who had not witnessed the crime. It is not clear whether al-Zuhrī and his teacher, Sulaymān b. Yasār, were present at this meeting. But the Caliph ʿUmar b. ʿAbd al-ʿAzīz reportedly asked their opinion on the same issue and they answered, like most of those who attended the meeting, that *qasāma* is lawful and that the Prophet and the Caliphs after him had pronounced sentences on the strength of it. Al-Zuhrī also argued that the *qasāma* procedure prevented people from being killed with impunity and he asserted, alluding to Koran 2:179,[49] that there is life for people in the *qasāma*.[50] Even if the reports about the debate in the presence of ʿUmar ʿAbd al-ʿAzīz are not historical, there must have been a discussion of the *qasāma* around the turn of the first century. The confirmation hadith must be understood in the context of this debate.

What can we conclude from the analysis of the *isnād* patterns and the *matn*s? First, the text of the standard variant of the Khaybar murder hadith, in which the oath was first offered to the Anṣār, dates from the first half of the second century, i.e. prior to Yaḥyā b. Saʿīd's death in 144/761–2, but goes back to a story that was known in Medina already in the second half of the first century and possibly even before that time. As a reaction to it, al-Zuhrī or his teachers circulated a version of the hadith in which the Prophet wanted the Jews to swear first around the turn of the first century. A second cluster of versions of the hadith in which the defendants were first offered the oath date from about the middle of the second century and reflect attempts of Kufan scholars to provide the Iraqi doctrine with a more solid textual base.

I will now examine three issues about which the Iraqi and the Hijazi schools were in disagreement: the lawfulness of sentences of retaliation on the strength of the *qasāma* procedure; the question of who is allowed to swear first; and finally the notion that the *qasāma* procedure is based on territorial liability. My aim is to demonstrate that the doctrines of the two schools had different origins and developed independently.

6 Retaliation on the Strength of *Qasāma*

One of the most prominent features of the Hijazi doctrine is that it allows sentences of retribution to be pronounced on the strength of the *qasāma*

49 "And there is life for you in retaliation (*qiṣāṣ*)."

50 ʿAbd al-Razzāq, *al-Muṣannaf*, 18279; Ibn Abī Shayba, *al-Muṣannaf*, vol. 6, 409.

procedure. Among the Hijazis this view was not challenged until al-Shafiʿi changed his mind because he regarded the variants of the Khaybar murder hadith in which only the liability of blood price is mentioned as more authentic than the other versions.[51] Even al-Zuhrī subscribed to the common Hijazi view. However, since he and his circle were of the opinion that *qasāma* was an oath of compurgation, they allowed a sentence of retaliation after a *qasāma* procedure only if the defendants refused to swear and the oath was shifted to the plaintiffs.[52] Al-Zuhrī's view, however, did not prevail in the Hijaz. The Iraqis disagreed with the Hijazis and held that the *qasāma* procedure could only entail a liability for blood price.[53] The Hijazi position is based on the standard version of the Khaybar murder hadith that presents the *qasāma* as an accusatory oath. The Prophet is reported to have said: "You may demand (the blood of) your companion or your killer [i.e. the person who killed one of your people] (*ṣāḥibakum* (or: *dam ṣāḥibikum*) *aw qātila/ikum*)",[54] or "Then they shall hand him over to you."[55] or "He will be turned over to you entirely."[56] These versions explicitly support the lawfulness of sentences of retaliation as a result of *qasāma*. Another report expressly states that the Prophet pronounced a sentence of retaliation after a *qasāma* procedure. This, however, must have been a fabrication.[57] As I have shown before, this standard version of the Khaybar

51 Ibn Daqīq al-ʿĪd, *Iḥkām al-aḥkām sharḥ ʿumdat al-aḥkām*. 4 vols. (Beirut: Dār al-Kutub al-ʿIlmiyya, n.d.) vol. 4, 91.

52 ʿAbd al-Razzāq al-Ṣanʿānī, *al-Muṣannaf*, 18254, 18263. As we have seen, al-Zuhrī allowed the plaintiffs to swear first in exceptional cases. In these cases the *qasāma* might also entail capital punishment.

53 E.g. al-Ḥasan al-Baṣrī (d. 110/728–9), Ibrāhīm al-Nakhaʿī (d. 95 or 96/713–5), Qatāda b. Diʿāma (d. 117/735–6), Abū Qilāba. Ibn Ḥazm, ʿAlī, *al-Muḥallā bi-'l-āthār*. 12 vols. (Beirut: Dār al-Fikr, n.d.): vol. 11, 295–7.

54 Nearly all versions transmitted by Yaḥyā b. Saʿīd include these words. Of the many versions of the hadith transmitted by him, only three do not mention the consequences (Ahmad 15509; Nasa'i 4634 and 4638) and two (Bukhari, 5677; Ahmad, 16639) read: "and demand your companion or your victim (*qatīlakum*)." The last word could easily be a copyist's error for 'your murderer' (*qātilakum*) as in the other variants. Those versions transmitted by Mālik – Abu Laylā have *dam ṣāḥibikum* and leave out *qātila/ikum*. The hadiths of the latter group are confusing on this issue since they first have the Prophet write or say the following words to the Jews: "Either they pay your man's blood price (*yadū ṣāḥibakum*) or war will be declared on them."

55 Thus in all versions transmitted from Ibn Isḥāq – Bushayr – Sahl (Ahmad b. Hanbal, 15515 (vol. 4, 4); Dārimi, 2247 (Diyāt, 2); Ibn Hishām, *Sīra*, vol. 2, 355).

56 Muslim, 3158 (Qasāma, 2); Abu Dawud, 3917 (Diyāt, 8). This must be a late interpolation as it is only found in the variants transmited by ʿUbayd Allāh b. ʿUmar al-Qawārīrī from Ḥammād from Yaḥyā, and not in the other versions transmitted by Hammad.

57 There is one report to the effect that the Prophet pronounced a death sentence on the strength of *qasāma*. Abu Dawud, 3919 (Diyāt, 8). This hadith, however, does not play any

murder hadith must have existed already in the second half of the first century and is probably older. In my view it reflects a continuous Medinese practice.

As a result of the differences between the Iraqi and the Hijazi doctrine, there was no consistent state policy. Reports on how *qasāma* was applied during the first half of the first century, although maybe not all of them historical, show that there was no clear policy. We are told that ʿUthmān,[58] ʿAbd Allāh b. Al-Zubayr,[59] and ʿAbd Al-Mālik b. Marwān[60] issued sentences of retribution on the basis of *qasāma*, whereas Abū Bakr[61] and ʿUmar b. Al-Khaṭṭāb[62] did not. Muʿāwiya[63] and ʿUmar b. ʿAbd al-ʿAzīz reportedly espoused both views.[64] ʿUmar, we are told, had scruples about capital sentences based on *qasāma*, precisely the issue of the above-mentioned debate. All of the notables and army commanders present during the debate regarded such sentences as lawful. Only the Iraqi Abū Qilāba (d. 104/722–3), who was drawn into the debate because of his position as chief qadi, objected to this view and eloquently exposed its inconsistency by asking the Caliph whether he would be prepared to stone a person to death for fornication or cut off somebody's hand for theft on the strength of the testimony of fifty of his notables in Damascus who had not witnessed the crime.[65] Evidence, of course, is the crux of the issue. Capital punishment was regarded as a serious matter and, evidently, there were those who were reluctant to take a life, in the absence of sufficient evidence, on the strength of an oath.

---

role in the later discussions and is almost certainly a fabrication. The *isnād* does not reach the Prophet (is *mursal*) and ends with ʿAmr b. Shuʿayb (d. 118/736). The cl is al-Walīd b. Muslim (d. 195/810–1). The incompleteness of the *isnād* may be an argument for its authenticity. However, considering that there is only one version of it and that its contents are connected with a controversial issue, I regard it as a fabrication by al-Walīd. On the other hand, Mālik reportedly admitted that the Prophet never pronounced a sentence of retribution on the strength of *qasāma*, and justified his view that such sentences were valid with the argument that if the Prophet had been confronted with such a case, he would have pronounced such a sentence. ʿAbd al-Razzāq al-Ṣanʿānī, *al-Muṣannaf*, 18276.

58 Ibn Ḥazm, al-*Muhalla*, vol. 11, 295.

59 Ibid., vol. 11, 291.

60 ʿAbd al-Razzāq al-Ṣanʿānī, *al-Muṣannaf*, 18275; Bukhari, 6390 (Diyāt, 22).

61 Ibn Ḥazm, *al-Muḥallā*, vol. 11, 289; ʿAbd al-Razzāq al-Ṣanʿānī, *al-Muṣannaf*, 18276.

62 Ibn Abī Shayba, *al-Muṣannaf*, vi, 410, 415;. ʿAbd al-Razzāq al-Ṣanʿānī, *al-Muṣannaf*, 18276, 18286, 18287.

63 As an opponent: Ibn Ḥazm, *al-Muḥallā*, vol. 11, 291; as an advocate: Muḥammad b. Abī Sahl al-Sarakhsī, al-*Mabsūṭ*. 30 vols. (Cairo: Dār al-Maʿrifa, n.d.): vol. 26, 109.

64 As an opponent: Ibn Ḥazm, *al-Muḥallā*, vol. 11, 297; as an advocate: ʿAbd al-Razzāq al-Ṣanʿānī, *al-Muṣannaf*, 18276; Ibn Ḥazm, al-*Muḥallā*, vol. 11, 297.

65 Bukhari, 6390; ʿAbd al-Razzāq al-Ṣanʿānī, *al-Muṣannaf*, *al-Muṣannaf*, 18278.

7 Who Swears First?

Hijazi doctrine holds that the *qasāma* oaths are sworn by the plaintiffs. As I have demonstrated, the oldest versions of the Khaybar murder story that circulated in Medina during the second half of the first century must have presented the *qasāma* as an accusatory oath. This doctrine, however, was not without opposition in Medina. By the end of the first century a group of Medinese scholars emerged around al-Zuhrī, who argued, like the Iraqis, that *qasāma* was an oath of compurgation. Their main argument, it seems, was that the prevailing doctrine conflicted with the general rules of procedure, according to which an oath is sworn only by a defendant when the plaintiff has failed to produce evidence for his claim. Evidently, al-Zuhrī[66] tried to ward off criticism of the lawfulness of the *qasāma* by showing that it followed the normal rules of procedure and was offered to the defendants when the plaintiffs could not prove their allegation. That al-Zuhrī's doctrine was independent and was not adopted from the Iraqis is clear from the differences between al-Zuhrī and the Iraqi view: according to al-Zuhrī, the *qasāma* oath, following the normal rules of procedure, shifts to the plaintiff when the defendants refuse to swear, whereas according to the Iraqi doctrine, the defendants, represented by persons selected by the plaintiffs, are compelled to swear and imprisoned if they refuse to do so. The opinion of al-Zuhrī and his circle did not prevail in the Hijaz. Later scholars, however, were aware of the procedural irregularity and tried to give the *qasāma* an exceptional status, by putting into circulation a report to the effect that the Prophet had said that the plaintiff must produce evidence and the defendant must swear, except in the *qasāma* procedure.[67]

In Iraq, the *qasāma* was generally regarded as an oath of compurgation, i.e. to be sworn by those on the side of the defendant(s). This view is ascribed to leading Iraqi scholars such as Shurayḥ (d. ca. 80/700), Ibrāhīm al-Nakhaʿī

66 al-Zuhrī is reported to have put forward the following two views on this issue: (1) the *sunna* of the Prophet was to offer the *qasāma* to the defendant and his agnatic male relatives whenever the plaintiff(s) did not produce sufficient evidence (ʿAbd al-Razzāq al-Ṣanʿānī, *al-Muṣannaf*, 18254); (2) this was the practice of ʿUmar b. al-Khaṭṭāb, except in cases in which the victim had accused someone before he died (Ibn Ḥazm, *al-Muḥallā*, vol. 11, 290, par. 2152). It is true that al-Zuhrī held that under certain circumstances the plaintiffs are entitled to swear first, as in the case in which three persons confess to having murdered someone, when only one of them could have killed him; or the case in which a person is found murdered in a house, the inhabitants of which claim that he had entered it to steal, whereas his next of kin assert that he had been invited to enter (ʿAbd al-Razzāq al-Ṣanʿānī, *al-Muṣannaf*, 18280 and 18281). However, such cases were exceptions to his general rule that the defendants are the first to swear the *qasāma* oaths.

67 Bayhaqī, al-*Sunan al-Kubrā*, vol. 8, 123; Dāraqutni, al-*Sunan*, vol. 3, 110, 111.

(d. 95–96/713–5), Abū Qilāba (d. 104/722–3), al-Shaʿbī (d. 110/728–9) and al-Ḥasan al-Baṣrī (d. 110/728–9).[68] This must have been the prevailing view in Iraq during the second half of the first century. As I will argue below, this type of *qasāma* probably originated in a practical administrative measure that was based on common sense. The reports in which the Iraqi doctrine is attributed to the Caliph ʿUmar (see below) may well possess a core of historical truth.[69] It would seem that the Khaybar murder hadith, which was transmitted almost exclusively by Medinese scholars, was originally unknown in Iraq. There is no indications that the Iraqis were concerned about its doctrinal implications until the middle of the second century. Only then did they try to come to grips with it by circulating versions in which the Jews, as defendants, were first offered the oath, and by inventing interpretations of the common version in order to bring its meaning into conformity with their doctrine. Of the latter, the most common is that the Prophet's words, when he offered the oath to the Anṣār, implied disapproval. ("How can you swear and demand the blood of your companion!")[70]

8 *Qasāma* and Territorial Liability

A distinctive feature of the Hanafi doctrine is the notion of territorial liability: the very fact of a body being found on a person's private land or in his house or in a village or quarter, in combination with a formal accusation of the victim's heirs against the owner or one or more of the inhabitants, suffices for initiating the *qasāma* procedure and results in an obligation to pay the blood price after fifty oaths of purgation have been sworn.[71] The owner of the house or land or

68 ʿAbd al-Razzāq al-Ṣanʿānī, *al-Muṣannaf*, 18255 (al-Ḥasan al-Baṣrī), 18256 (ʿUbayd Allāh b. ʿUmar); 18270 (Ibn Sīrīn – Shurayḥ); 18271 (Ibn Sīrīn – Shurayḥ); 18284 (Ibrāhīm al-Nakhaʿī); Ibn Ḥazm, *al-Muḥallā*, vol. 11, 292, par. 2152 (al-Ḥasan al-Baṣrī); Ibn Qudāma, al-*Mughnī*. 11 vols. (Beirut: Dār Ihyā' al-Turāth al-ʿArabī, n.d.): vol. 8, 76 (al-Shaʿbī and al-Nakhaʿī); Bukhari, 6390 (Diyāt, 22) (Abū Qilāba).

69 ʿUmar ordered that the *qasāma* was to be sworn by the defendants (Ibn Abī Shayba, *al-Muṣannaf*, vol. 6, 410; ʿAbd al-Razzāq al-Ṣanʿānī, *al-Muṣannaf*, 18287) and that the *qasāma* procedure could not result in capital punishment (Ibn Abī Shayba, *al-Muṣannaf*, vol. 6, 414; ʿAbd al-Razzāq al-Ṣanʿānī, *al-Muṣannaf*, 18286). For his decision on territorial liability, see the references in Figure 27.4.

70 Sarakhsī, *al-Mabsūṭ*, vol. 26, 109.

71 Although al-Zuhrī held a similar doctrine, there are important differences, e.g. the rule, mentioned in the previous section, that the defendants are not compelled to swear, as in Hanafi law. Also al-Zuhrī's doctrine is not based entirely on territorial liability, but also on the procedural rule that the defendant swears first in litigation.

the inhabitants selected by the plaintiff for swearing the *qasāma* have no real choice: if they refuse to swear that they did not kill the victim and do not know anything about it, they will be imprisoned until they either swear or confess. The only function of the swearing is to put pressure on the killer to confess, if he is among those inhabitants selected to swear.

Although the Hanafi doctrine is closer to the rules of procedure and evidence than the Hijazi one, it is still anomalous. According to these rules, if an accusation is unsubstantiated and the defendant swears a purgatory oath, the plaintiff's claim is denied. This was precisely the view of ʿUthmān al-Battī (Basra, d. 143/760),[72] an Iraqi scholar who obviously attached great importance to the general rules of procedure. According to the prevailing view, however, in spite of their collective purgatory oaths, the defendants are still liable for the blood price. The anomaly is noticed in a report in which ʿUmar b. al-Khaṭṭāb explains the Hanafi doctrine to the inhabitants of a place in which a body had been found. Realizing the inconsistency, one of them protested: "O Commander of the Believers, our oaths did not protect our properties, nor did our properties protect us against [the obligation of swearing] oaths."[73] In other words: by swearing the *qasāma* we incurred a liability instead of being absolved from the plaintiff's claim, and if we had been willing to pay, we still were obliged to swear.

This liability can only be explained as territorial liability, i.e. a liability resulting from the duty of the inhabitants of a quarter or village or of the owner of land to guarantee the security of their territory. This is exactly what later Hanafi jurists mentioned as the main justification for the procedure: the inhabitants or owners of landed property, they say, are in the best position to guarantee the security of a place and therefore they are held responsible for any blood shed on their territory. In this way the perpetrator, if he were among the inhabitants, might be exposed, since most people take oaths seriously and would not swear a *qasāma* oath if they knew anything about the killing. Therefore the Hanafi jurists argued that the obligation to pay the blood price originated in the legal ties – right of ownership or usufruct –connecting people with the location in which the body is found. Other arguments to be found in Hanafi literature are not very convincing. The most common one is that the claim of retaliation is averted by the *qasāma*, and that the liability for the blood price remains. This, however, is an unlikely explanation as there are no grounds whatsoever for demanding capital punishment.

72 Ibn Ḥazm, *al-Muḥallā*, vol. 11, 300; Shawkānī. *Nayl al-Awṭār*, vol. 7, 49. A similar view has been reported from al-Awzāʿī. Ibid.

73 ʿAbd al-Razzāq al-Ṣanʿānī, *al-Muṣannaf*, 18266, 18267.

Little is known about the origin of the Iraqi *qasāma*. There is no evidence that it emerged as a reaction against an older doctrine. It is plausible, therefore, that the Iraqis followed this doctrine from a very early period. The doctrine of territorial liability is attributed to the Caliph ʿUmar. He is reported to have ordered that, when a murder victim is found in the area between the territories of two tribes, the distances between the body and these territories are to be measured and the *qasāma* is to be imposed on the tribe whose territory is closest to the body. This report is widely known and was first circulated by the Iraqi jurist al-Shaʿbī (d. 103 or 110/721–2 or 728–9), as the *isnād* bundle shows (see Figure 27.4).[74] We may, therefore, assume that the doctrine existed in the second half of the first century. However, it is possible that territorial liability is even older and was introduced even earlier, immediately after the conquest of Iraq, as a measure to insure law and order in the newly founded garrison cities. This possibility finds support in the position, according to Hanafi doctrine, of the *aṣḥāb al-khiṭṭa*, the members of the Arab tribes or clans to whom certain plots of land in these cities were allotted. Early Hanafi scholars were of the opinion that the *aṣḥāb al-khiṭṭa* were the persons to swear the *qasāma* oaths and to pay the blood price:

> If a victim of murder is found among a tribe in Kufa, and there are [also] inhabitants [not belonging to the tribe] and persons who have bought their houses [from the *aṣḥāb al-khiṭṭa*], then the *qasāma* and blood price is imposed on the *ahl al-khiṭṭa* and not on the inhabitants and buyers. The following issues are connected with this point. One: As long as one of the *aṣḥāb al-khiṭṭa* remains in the place, then, according to Abū Ḥanīfa and Muḥammad [al-Shaybānī], the buyers are not liable in this matter. According to Abū Yusūf, however, the buyers in this respect are in the same position as the *aṣḥāb al-khiṭṭa*.... Abū Ḥanīfa and Muḥammad argued that the *aṣḥāb al-khiṭṭa* have a greater right to manage the affairs of the quarter than the buyers.[75]

74 Ibn Abī Shayba, *al-Muṣannaf*, vol. 6, 411, 413, 417; ʿAbd al-Razzāq al-Ṣanʿānī, *al-Muṣannaf*, 18266–7–8; Ibn Ḥazm, *al-Muḥallā*, vol. 11, 290; Bayhaqī, *al-Sunan al-Kubrā*, vol. 8, 134–5; Shawkānī, *Nayl al-Awṭār*, vol. 7, 46–7. It is evident that al-Shaʿbī first reported the story directly on the authority of ʿUmar, whom he cannot have met, and that later transmitters added intervening links or invented totally new *isnāds* that by-passed al-Shaʿbī. In order to give it even higher authority, later scholars attributed the story to the Prophet and to ʿAlī, in both cases with single strand *isnāds*. Ahmad b. Hanbal, 10913 (vol. 3, 39), 11416 (vol. 3, 89); Ibn Ḥazm, *al-Muḥallā*, vol. 11, 291.

75 Sarakhsī, al-*Mabsūṭ*, vol. 26, 111–12.

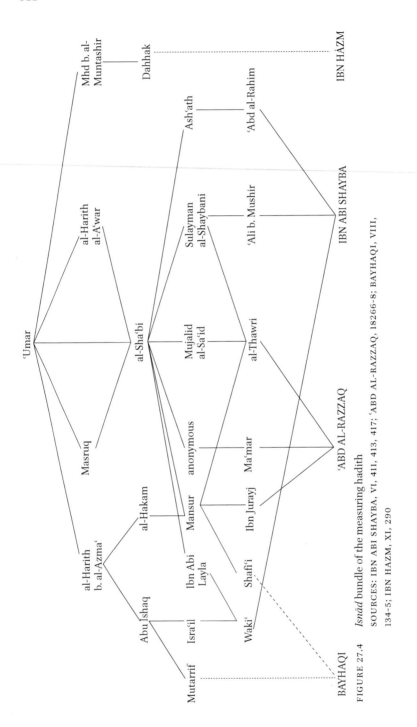

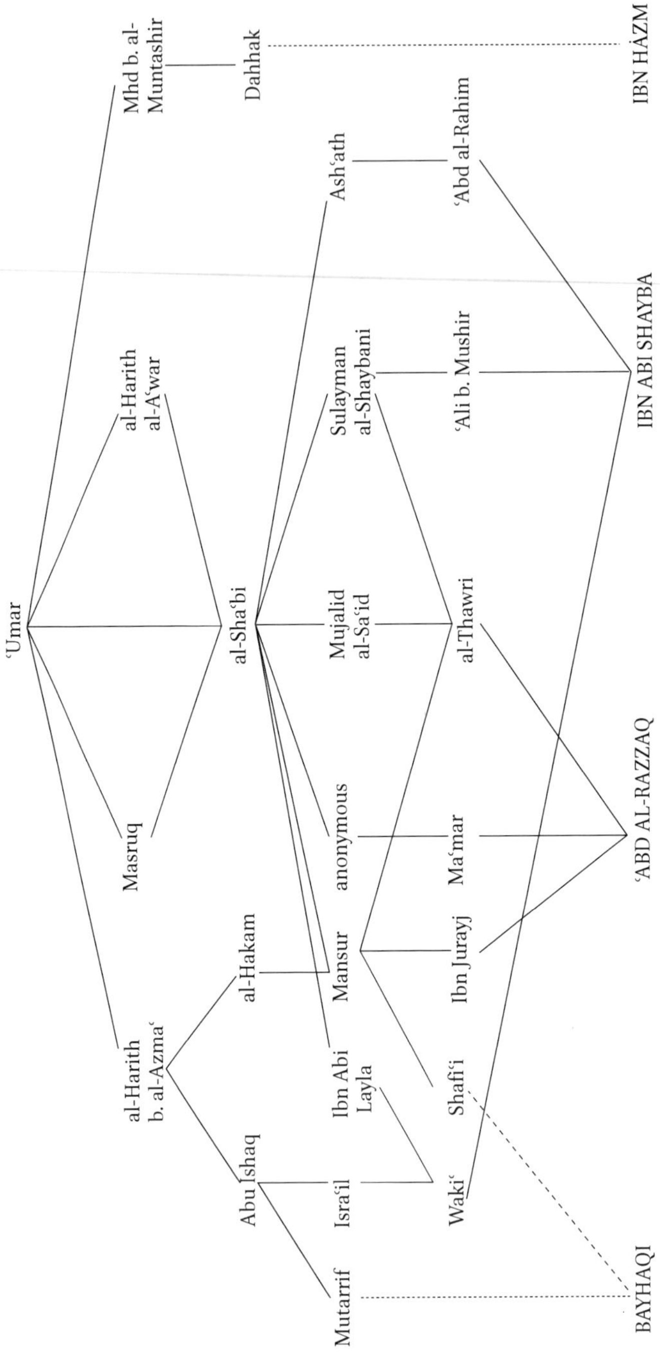

FIGURE 27.4 *Isnād* bundle of the measuring hadith
SOURCES: IBN ABI SHAYBA, VI, 411, 413, 417; 'ABD AL-RAZZAQ, 18266–8; BAYHAQI, VIII, 134–5; IBN HAZM, XI, 290

The special status of the *aṣḥāb al-khiṭṭa* indicates that the doctrine was introduced in a period before the *khiṭaṭ* as administrative units had become obsolete, i.e. before the last decades of the first century.[76] Although the evidence is indirect, it is likely that the responsibility of the inhabitants of quarters and villages for unsolved murders committed in their neighborhoods was introduced as a practical measure to ensure law and order in the newly founded garrison towns shortly after the conquest of Iraq. Such an arrangement is characteristic of a military environment, where collective penalties are often used to ensure discipline. As we have seen, the distinctive elements of Iraqi doctrine were ascribed to ʿUmar b. al-Khaṭṭāb. If, as I maintain, the doctrine originated in Iraq not long after its conquest, it is tenable that these reports are historical.

9 Conclusion

I have examined here the earliest developments of the *qasāma* doctrines in Islamic jurisprudence. By analyzing the relevant hadiths, taking into account both their *isnād*s and their *matn*s, and by studying the statements of the earliest jurists, I arrived at the conclusion that by the middle of the first century, and probably even before that time, there were two distinct doctrines of *qasāma*, one espoused by the Iraqi community of scholars, the other by the Medinese; and that these doctrines had separate and independent origins. These findings contradict the standard wisdom regarding the origins of the *qasāma*, i.e. that in the early days of Islam there was only one type of *qasāma* (either the Hijazi type according to the standard view or the Iraqi type according to Crone) and that one type developed out of the other.

That the Iraqi type of *qasāma* had its origin in governmental measures to ensure law and order in the new military garrisons of Iraq is suggested by the original Hanafi doctrine that only the *aṣḥāb al-khiṭṭa* are liable for the blood price of persons killed in the quarter by unknown persons. The Iraqi *qasāma* is based on two elements: the rule that the *qasāma* as an oath of compurgation is imposed on the defendants and the rule of the exclusive territorial liability that is unaffected by the swearing of the oath. The first rule has been attributed to a number of Iraqi jurists from the second half of the first century. The second rule reportedly was introduced by the Caliph ʿUmar b. al-Khaṭṭāb. The best known of these reports, which requires that the distance between a dead body and neighboring villages be measured, was put into circulation by

76 *EI*², s.v. *khiṭṭa* (P. Crone): "the erosion of the tribal ties in the Marwanid period rendered the system obsolete; … the *khiṭaṭ* survived only as place-names."

al-Shaʿbī (d. 103 or 110/721–2 or 728–9). Now, Schacht was very skeptical about opinions ascribed to representatives of the "ancient" Iraqi school. In general he regarded such opinions as having originated at a much later date.[77] However, in the case of *qasāma*, I find his skepticism unwarranted. Because of the rule that as long as t *aṣḥāb al-khiṭṭa* are present, they, and not the actual inhabitants are liable, the doctrine must have been introduced in a period in which the *khiṭaṭ* were functioning as administrative units, i.e. before the last decades of the first century. Indeed, the doctrine, may have been introduced shortly after the conquest of Iraq and the reports ascribing it to ʿUmar may have a kernel of historical truth. Iraqi scholars did not attempt to provide more authoritative textual support for the doctrine by means of Prophetic hadiths, until the middle of the second century, when versions of the Khaybar murder hadith were put into circulation in which the defendants were first offered the oath after the plaintiffs had admitted that they did not have sufficient evidence.

The Khaybar murder hadith plays a central role in the Medinese doctrine. The wording of the hadith as we have it now goes back to Yaḥyā b. Saʿīd (d. 144/761–2). The doctrine of *qasāma* as an accusatory oath, however, must be much older. That it existed already by the end of the first century is shown by the Confirmation hadith and the variants of the Khaybar murder hadith, put into circulation by al-Zuhrī (d. 124/741–2) or his teachers, in which the Jews were allowed to swear first. These variants were prompted by a controversy regarding the legitimacy of the accusatory *qasāma* that was held around the turn of the first century. Several independent reports indicate that the Caliph ʿUmar ʿAbd al-ʿAzīz and a number of contemporary Medinese jurists had misgivings about sentences of retaliation pronounced on the strength of the accusatory *qasāma*. These misgivings were inspired by the anomalous character of the Medinese doctrine of *qasāma*: it violated the normal rules of procedure and the rule that sentences of retaliation required high standards of proof. This discussion apparently prompted al-Zuhrī (or his teachers) to deviate from the Hijazi doctrine and to argue that in the case of *qasāma* the oath is offered to the defendants. Since these views were a reaction to the prevailing Hijazi doctrine, the accusatory *qasāma* must have existed in the second half of the first century. I would suggest, with due caution, that the Medinese doctrine was a continuation of the pre-Islamic practice, which is the generally accepted view.

My findings contradict Crone's theory on the origins of the *qasāma*. She maintains (1) that the Hanafi doctrine is the older one and has its origins in Jewish, Pentateuchal law and (2) that the Maliki notion goes back to Jewish,

77 Schacht, *Origins*, 228–37.

Rabbinical law and was later made to look like a Jahili institution. The validity of her theory is undermined by her failure to situate the developments she describes on a time scale, which makes it difficult to refute her position. I will discuss her main arguments:

1. *The commitment of tribal law to the status quo and its bias in favor of the defendant suggest that it is highly unlikely that the Maliki doctrine was originally a tribal institution.*

   This argument is circumstantial and not very solid. Crone founds it on present-day Bedouin customary law. The underlying assumption is that Bedouin societies and Bedouin laws have not changed over the course of thirteen or fourteen centuries. Since Bedouin communities cannot exist independently and live in symbiosis with settled communities, it is unlikely that the social and economic changes that these settled communities underwent, did not affect the lifestyle of the Bedouin. Present-day Bedouin customs, therefore, do not necessarily reflect those of early Islam.
2. *The fact that the confirmation hadith is shorter than the Khaybar murder hadith suggests that it is older.*

   As I have shown above, this conclusion is not supported by our examination of the *matn*s and the *isnād* clusters of these reports. The version of the Khaybar murder story in which the plaintiffs are offered the oath first must be older than the confirmation hadith.
3. *That there was a discussion among the early jurists about the lawfulness of death sentences on the strength of the qasāma procedure, and that there were scholars in the Medina who regarded the qasāma as an oath of compurgation is for Crone additional evidence that the Maliki doctrine was later and had to overcome strong resistance.*

   This argument is not convincing. The existence of a discussion about retaliation on the strength of *qasāma* does not constitute proof that one view preceded the other. If both views originated at roughly the same time, as I argue, a similar debate can be expected. Moreover, the existence of Medinese scholars holding that *qasāma* is compurgation can be explained as a reaction against the older, opposite view, and does not have to be understood as a remnant of the older, Hanafi view.

Crone's main argument, however, are the similarities between the Hanafi doctrine and the Pentateuchal ritual described in Deuteronomy in cases of unsolved murder. The Deuteronomic law clearly combines two ideas: the collective responsibility of the inhabitants of a region for murders committed therein, and the pollution of the land by an unpunished murder, which necessitates the expiation of the blood-taint by ritual purification.[78] Both elements, according to Crone, exist in the Hanafi doctrine. In her view this doctrine makes sense only if we regard the *qasāma* sworn by the inhabitants as a ritual of expiation. On the basis of these similarities, she concludes that the Hanafi *qasāma* is derived from Jewish law.

The conclusion that one legal system borrowed from another on the strength of similarities in institutions and doctrines is often unwarranted. Before raising the issue of influence, one should investigate whether the emergence of a certain doctrine or institution can be explained from within a legal system. As I have shown, such an explanation is possible, indeed highly plausible. The Iraqi doctrine can be explained as the introduction of a practical measure, that was equated by those who introduced it with the Jahili *qasāma* to give it legitimacy. Of course, we may speculate about whether or not they invented it themselves by bending a vaguely known Jahili institution to their purposes, or followed other models. There are indeed interesting parallels in ancient Middle Eastern law. One of these is the ancient Hebrew ritual of Deuteronomy 21:1–9, mentioned by Crone and described above. Although ancient Jewish law does not recognize an actionable liability in such cases, the ritual is implicitly based on the notion that the inhabitants of a region are in some way responsible for serious crimes committed in their area and must perform rituals to cleanse the area. Another parallel is the legal notion of territorial liability found in paragraphs 23 and 24 of Hammurabi's Code, which stipulate that the inhabitants of a region must provide compensation for damage resulting from theft and robbery if the perpetrator is not apprehended. Moreover, the Hittite laws contain a provision establishing that the owner of the land on which a person is found murdered, or the inhabitants of neighboring villages, are liable for his blood price.[79] Now, similarities in legal institutions do not necessarily imply borrowing.[80] Different groups may find similar solutions for similar problems. In view of the gaps in our knowledge of the legal history of the Middle East immediately before the rise of Islam, theories on the influence of older

78 Henry McKeating, "The development of the law of homicide in ancient Israel," *Vetus Testamentum* 25 (1975): 46–68, 62–3.

79 See H.A. Hoffner, "On Homicide in Hittite Law," in *Crossing Boundaries and Linking Horizons: Studies in Honour of Michael Astour on His 80th Birthday*, ed. G.D. Young a.o. (Bethesda, Maryland: CDL Press, 1997): 293ff.

80 On the problems of tracing the influence of other legal systems in Islamic law, see Ulrike Mitter, "Das frühislamische Patronat: Eine Untersuchung zur Rolle von fremden Elementen bei der Entwicklung des islamischen Rechts." (Doctoral dissertation, Katholieke Universiteit Nijmegen, 1999): 14–8.

Middle Eastern legal systems on the development of Islamic law are perforce speculative.

Fifty years ago, Schacht argued that Islamic jurisprudence did not begin until the second century and that hadiths going back to the Prophet were first put into circulation in the first half of the second century. With regard to the circulation of prophetic hadiths, I have found no solid evidence to challenge his conclusion. I have argued that both the Khaybar murder and the confirmation hadiths with its *isnād* going back to the Prophet, were in existence before 144/761–2. The underlying story, however, circulated already in the second half of the first century, either without an *isnād* or with an incomplete *isnād* (e.g. Bushayr – the Prophet; Ibn al-Musayyib – the Prophet). In my opinion it is plausible, although difficult to prove that the hadith refers to an historical incident which was remembered and informed Medinese practice.

As for the origins of Islamic jurisprudence, my findings regarding the *qasāma* support Motzki's conclusions[81] as well as those of Powers with regard to the law of succession[82] and suggest that the religious specialists, as Schacht calls them, of the late first century were not only interested in religious and ethical issues, but also in technical aspects of the law. Even if the report about ʿUmar b. ʿAbd al-ʿAzīz's misgivings about the *qasāma* and his questioning of scholars about it does not refer to an actual debate held in his presence, there is ample evidence to suggest that purely legal questions in connection with the *qasāma* were being discussed by Medinese jurists around the turn of the first century. From the reactions of al-Zuhrī and the members of his circle we can infer that there was a Medinese doctrine of *qasāma* as an accusatory oath in the second half of the first century. It is inconceivable that such a doctrine and its implications were not discussed by the scholars of the period. A similar conclusion can be drawn regarding contemporary Iraqi scholars. Schacht assumed that the attribution of opinions to Iraqi scholars of the second half of the first century is not historical. This view can be challenged. From the *isnād* bundle of the report in which ʿUmar orders agents to measure the distance between two villages before deciding which village would be subjected to the *qasāma* procedure, it is clear that al-Shaʿbī played a pivotal role in the discussion (see figure 27.4). If that is true, it is likely that the other jurists of his generation participated in the discussion. This is corroborated by the fact that the Iraqi doctrine is based on the short-lived institution of the *khiṭṭa* and must have been introduced before the institution became obsolete. It is highly unlikely

81 Motzki (1991).

82 Powers (1986).

that the consequences of this development were not discussed by the religious specialists.

References

Bayhaqī, Aḥmad al-, al-*Sunan al-Kubrā*. 10 vols. Haydarabad: 1344–1355/1925–1934.

Brunschvig, Robert, "Considérations sociologiques sur le droit musulman ancien," *Studia Islamica* 3 (1955): 61–73.

Crone, Patricia, "Jahili and Jewish law: the qasāma," *Jerusalem Studies in Arabic and Islam* 4 (1984): 153–201.

Crone, Patricia, and Michael Cook, *Hagarism: The making of the Islamic world*. Cambridge: Cambridge University Press, 1977.

Dāraquṭnī, ʿAlī b. ʿUmar, *Sunan*. 4th impr. Beirut: ʿĀlam al-Kutub, 1986. 4 vols.

GISCO, (Global Islamic Software Company). *Mawsūʿat al-ḥadīth al-sharīf* (Version 2.0) [CD-ROM]. Sakhr/Global Islamic Software Compere, 1997.

Gräf, E., "Eine wichtige Rechtsdirektive ʿUthmans aus dem Jahre 30," *Oriens* (1963): 122–33.

Hoffner, H.A., "On Homicide in Hittite Law," in *Crossing Boundaries and Linking Horizons: Studies in Honour of Michael Astour on his 80th Birthday*, ed. G.D. Young a.o., Bethesda, Maryland: CDL Press, 1997: 293ff.

Horster, Paul, *Zur Anwendung des islamischen Rechts im 16. Jahrhundert: Die "juristische Dārlegungen" (maʿruzat) des Schejch ul-Islam Ebu Suʿud (gest. 1574)*. Stuttgart: Kohlhammer, 1935. 109 pp. (Bonner Orientalistsiche Studien, 10).

Ibn Abī Shayba, *al-Muṣannaf*. 8 vols. Beirut, Dār al-Fikr, n.d.

Ibn al-Athīr, ʿIzz al-Dīn, *Usd al-ghāba fī maʿrifat al-ṣaḥāba*, ed. Muḥammad Ibrāhīm Bannā a.o. 7 vols. Cairo: Dār al-Shaʿb, 1970.

Ibn Bābawayh, Abū Jaʿfar Muḥammad b. ʿAlī, *Man lā yaḥḍuruhu al-faqīh*, ed. ʿAlī al-Akhondī. 4 vols. Tehran: Dār al-Kutub al-Islamiyya, 1390 H.

Ibn Daqīq al-ʿId, *Iḥkām al-aḥkām sharḥ ʿumdat al-aḥkām*. 4 vols. Beirut: Dār al-Kutub al-ʿIlmiyya, n.d.

Ibn Ḥajar al-ʿAsqalānī, *al-Iṣāba fī tamyīz al-ṣaḥāba*, ed. Ṭāhā Muḥammad al-Zaynī a.o. 13 vols. Cairo: Maktabat al-Kulliyyāt al-Azhariyya, 1969–1977.

Ibn Ḥazm, ʿAlī, *al-Muḥallā bi-'l-āthār*. 12 vols: Dār al-Fikr, n.d.

Ibn Hishām, *al-Sīra al-nabawiyya*, ed. Muṣṭafā al-Saqqā a.o. 2nd ed. 2 vols. Cairo: Muṣṭafā al-Bābī al-Ḥalabī, 1955.

Ibn Qudāma, Abū ʿAbd Allāh Muḥammad, *al-Mughnī*. 11 vols. Beirut: Dār Ihyāʾ al-Turāth al-ʿArabī, n.d.

Ibn Qutayba, *Kitāb al-maʿārif*, ed. Tharwat ʿUkāsha. 2nd impr. Cairo: 1969.

Ibn Rushd, Abū al-Walīd Muḥammad, *Bidāyat al-mujtahid wa-nihāyat al-muqtaṣid*. 2 vols. Cairo: Muṣṭafā al-Bābī al-Ḥalabī, 1960.

Johansen, Baber, "Eigentum, Familie und Obrigkeit im hanafitischen Strafrecht: Das Verhältnis der privaten Rechte zu den Forderungen der Allgemeinheit in hanafitischen Rechtskommentare," in *Contingency in a sacred law: Legal and ethical norms in the Muslim fiqh*. Leiden: Brill, 1999 (Studies in Islamic Law and Society, 7): 349–420.

Juynboll, G.H.A., *Muslim tradition: Studies in chronology, provenance and authorship of early hadith*. Cambridge: Cambridge University Press, 1983.

Juynboll, G.H.A., "Some *isnâd* analytical methods illustrated on the basis of several woman-demeaning sayings from hadîth literature," *al-Qantara* 10 (1989): 343–84.

Juynboll, G.H.A., "Some notes on Islam's first fuqaha' distilled from the early hadit literature," *Arabica* 39 (1992): 287–314.

Juynboll, G.H.A., "Early Islamic society as reflected in its use of isnâds," *Le Muséon* 107 (1994): 151–94.

Mahdī, Muḥammad al-ʿAbbāsī al-, *al-Fatāwā al-Mahdiyya fī'l-Waqāʾiʿ al-Miṣriyya*. 7 vols. Cairo: al-Maṭbaʿa al-Azhariyya, 1301–3.

McKeating, Henry, "The development of the law of homicide in ancient Israel," *Vetus Testamentum* 25 (1975): 46–68.

Mitter, Ulrike, "Das frühislamische Patronat: Eine Untersuchung zur Rolle von fremden Elementen bei der Entwicklung des islamischen Rechts," Doctoral dissertation, Katholieke Universiteit Nijmegen, 1999.

Motzki, Harald, *Die Anfänge der islamischen Jurisprudenz: Ihre Entwicklung in Mekka bis zur Mitte des 2./8. Jahrhunderts*. Stuttgart: Franz Steiner Verlag, 1991 (Abhandlungen für die Kunde des Morgenlandes, Band L, 2).

Motzki, Harald, "Der Fiqh des -Zuhrī: Die Quellenproblematik," *Der Islam* 68 (1991): 1–45.

Motzki, Harald, "Quo vadis *Ḥadīth*-Forschung? Eine kritische Untersuchung von G.H.A. Juynboll: 'Nāfiʿ the *mawlā* of Ibn ʿUmar, and his position in Muslim *Ḥadīth* Literature'," *Der Islam* 73 (1996): 40–80, 193–231.

Motzki, Harald, "The Prophet and the Cat. On dating Mâlik's *Muwatta*ʾ and Legal Traditions," *Jerusalem Studies in Arabic and Islam* 22 (1998): 18–83.

Pedersen, J., *Der Eid bei den Semiten in seinem Verhaeltniss zu verwandten Erscheinungen sowie die Stellund des Eides im Islam*. Strassburg: Karl J. Truebner, 1914 (Studien zur Geschichte und Kultur des islamischen Orients, 3).

Powers, David S., *Studies in Qur'an and Hadith: The Formation of the Islamic Law of Inheritance*. Berkeley etc.: University of California Press, 1986.

Ṣanʿānī, ʿAbd al-Razzāq al-, *al-Muṣannaf*, ed. Ḥabīb al-Raḥmān al-Aʿẓamī. 11 vols. Simlak, Dabhel/Beirut, 1983.

Sarakhsī, Muḥammad b. Abī Sahl al-, *al-Mabsūṭ*. 30 vols. Cairo: Dār al-Maʿrifa, n.d.

Schacht, J., *The Origins of Muḥammadan Jurisprudence*. Oxford: Oxford University Press, 1950.

Shawkānī, Muḥammad b. ʿAlī al-, *Nayl al-awṭār*, 8 vols. Cairo: Dār al-Ḥadīth, n.d.

Wansharīsī, Aḥmad b. Yaḥyā al-, *al-Miʿyār al-muʿrib wa-'l-jāmiʿ al-mughrib ʿan fatāwā ʿulamāʾ Ifrīqiyya wa-'l-Maghrib*, ed. Muḥammad Ḥajjī, a.o. 13 vols. Beirut: Dār al-Gharb al-Islāmī, 1981.

Wāqidī, al-, *The Kitāb al-Maghāzī of al-Wāqidī*, ed. Marsden Jones. London: Oxford University Press, 1966.

Wellhausen, Julius, *Reste arabischen Heidentums*. 2. Aufl. Berlin, 1927.

Wensinck, A.J. a.o., *Concordance et indices de la tradition musulmane*. Leiden: E.J. Brill, 1936–1969. 7 vols.

CHAPTER 28

From Jurists' Law to Statute Law or What Happens When the Shariʿa is Codified

1 Introduction

Since the middle of the nineteenth century, the position of the Shariʿa in most Middle Eastern legal systems has changed drastically. In this essay, I want to explore this change and examine how the relationship between the state and the Shariʿa developed, focusing on the Ottoman Empire (including Egypt) and its successor states. Central to my analysis will be the question of who controls the production of Shariʿa norms, or, in other words, who has the authority to formulate the rules of the Shariʿa.

In the first part, I will discuss the position of the Shariʿa in the premodern period focusing on its religious character and its relationship with the state. Then I will move to the second half of the nineteenth century and go into the notion of codification and the changing role of the state. In the third part, I will analyse the present-day role of the Shariʿa. I will argue that the subject matter of the Shariʿa, codified or uncodified, has been politicized and has become very much a prominent issue in the public debate.

2 The Nature of the Shariʿa and *Fiqh* in the Pre-Modern Time

2.1 *The Shariʿa as Religious Law*

Unlike modern Western law, the Shariʿa is not regarded as an expression of the will of the state, but of God's will. The classical texts define the Shariʿa as: 'The rules given by God to His servants as set forth by one of the prophets (may God bless them and grant them salvation).'[1] A swift glance at the table of contents of the average legal textbook shows that they begin with purely religious topics like ritual prayer and fasting, before embarking on the discussion of the issues that are legal in the Western sense of the word, such as the contract of sale, legal capacity, succession and criminal law. The Shariʿa is, therefore, religious law, but this does not tell us very much. There are many different types of

1 Tahanawi, Muhammad Aʿla b. ʿAli (1984): *Kitab kashshaf istilahat*. Reprint of Calcutta, 1864 edn., 2 vols., i, Istanbul: Kahraman Yayınları, 759.

 | DOI:10.1163/9789004420625_029

religious law. We want to say something meaningful about the Shariʿa as religious law, and we must be more specific and define its religious character. This, I would argue, consists in two features: the fact that the basis of its validity is God's will and the fact that the Shariʿa also contains rules of a purely religious character.

In order to inform Mankind of his commands, God, according to Muslim belief, has sent down revelations to successive prophets, the last of whom was Muhammad. To him the Qur'an was revealed. After his death, the contents of the Qur'an were supplemented by his exemplary behaviour, the Sunna, as transmitted by later generations of Muslims and compiled in the hadith collections. These are the divine sources of the Shariʿa and, therefore, the foundation of its validity. This divine basis of the law may be compared with Kelsen's *Grundnorm*, the extra-legal norm explaining why laws are binding.[2]

A large part of the Shariʿa is law as understood in the West. The rules of this domain of the Shariʿa deal with the legal effects of certain acts or events and discuss the creation and extinction of rights and obligations between individuals and between the individual and the community. Here we find, for instance, the law of sale, of marriage, of tort, of procedure, laws that can be enforced by the *qadi* if the relevant facts can be established in court. However, the Shariʿa is also envisioned as a set of norms constituting the code of behaviour of a good Muslim, a guide to attain eternal bliss in Paradise. This representation of the Shariʿa emphasizes its religious character and focuses on the Hereafter, that is on whether, after one's death, one can expect to be rewarded or punished for certain acts. This is done by classifying them into five categories (obligatory, commendable, indifferent, reprehensible and forbidden) indicating their effects as far as reward and punishment are concerned. For instance, performing an obligatory act results in reward, whereas neglecting it will be punished. This applies not only to purely religious obligations, but also to legal ones, such as the obligation to pay one's debts. This part of the law falls outside the *qadi's* competence. It is the exclusive domain of the *mufti*, the legal expert whose guidance is sought by individual Muslims in matters of the Shariʿa, but whose opinions are not binding, unlike the sentences pronounced by *qadis*.

The following passage, taken from a seventeenth-century legal handbook that was popular in the Ottoman Empire may help elucidate the double-sided character of the Shariʿa:

2 Kelly, J.M. (1992): *A Short History of Western Legal Theory*, Oxford: Oxford University Press: 384–8.

> *It is not reprehensible to lease out a house in the countryside* (that is, in a village) *if it will subsequently be used as a Zoroastrian temple, a church or a monk's cell, or if wine will be sold in it* (at least according to the Imam [Abu Hanifa (d. 767)], because the lease confers the right to use the house and there is no sin in that. The sin is related to acts committed by the lessee of his own accord. That means that the relationship [between the landlord and the sin] is interrupted, just like in the case of the sale of a slave girl ... to a person who wants to have anal intercourse with her, or the sale of a young slave to a homosexual.... According to his companions [al-Shaybani (d. 805) and Abu Yusuf (d. 798)] *it is indeed reprehensible* (to lease a house for such a use, because it promotes sin. The other three imams are of the same opinion.... *There is agreement* [*among the imams*] *that such a lease is reprehensible in a village or a region inhabited mainly by Muslims.*[3]

Here the authors discuss an aspect of the law of lease. However, their concern in this passage is not whether or not under the given conditions such a contract is valid and binding, but whether a Muslim who concludes such a contract will be punished in the Hereafter because it is religiously reprehensible.

2.2 *The Shariʿa as Jurists' Law*

A second feature of the Shariʿa is that it is a jurists' law and that the jurists, and not the state, had the exclusive authority to formulate the rules of the Shariʿa. They did so in a scholarly, academic debate, in which conflicting and often contradictory views were opposed and discussed. Actually, we must use a more precise terminology and distinguish between the Shariʿa and the *fiqh*. If the Shariʿa is God's law, the *fiqh* is the scholarly discipline aimed at formulating the prescriptions of the Shariʿa on the basis of the revealed texts and using various hermeneutic devices. What we find in the *fiqh* texts is the jurists' approximation to the divine law. Because of differences in understanding the texts and in the use of the hermeneutical tools, the Shariʿa as laid down by the jurists is not uniform.

From the beginning, there were differences of opinion that resulted in the emergence of different schools of jurisprudence (*madhhab*, plur. *madhhahib*), that ascribed their doctrines to and derived their names from famous jurists from the eighth and ninth centuries. Controversies did not only exist between

3 Shaykhzade (d. 1667) and Ibrahim al-Halabi (d. 1549) (1884/1301H): *Majmaʿ al-anhur fi sharh Multaqa al-Abhur*, 2 vols., Istanbul, ii, 417. The passages in bold print are the translation of al-Halabi's elementary textbook; the remainder is Shaykhzade's commentary.

these schools, but also among the jurists of one single school, even on essential legal issues. The following passage, taken from the same Ottoman handbook, discusses the various opinions within the Hanafite school of jurisprudence on the question of whether a woman who is legally capable, may conclude her own marriage contract:

> *Marriage concluded by a free woman … of full legal capacity* (irrespective of whether or not she is a virgin) *is valid* (even if such a marriage is concluded without the consent and presence of a matrimonial guardian. This is the authoritative opinion of Abu Hanifa (d. 767) and Abu Yusuf (d. 798). This is so because she disposes of something to which she is exclusively entitled by being sound of mind and of age. For this reason she is entitled to dispose of her property and the principle here is that whoever may dispose of his property by his own right may conclude his own marriage and whoever may not [dispose of his property by his own right], may not [conclude his own marriage]…. According to the other *madhhabs* marriage cannot be concluded by a woman…. *However, the marriage guardian* (that is anyone of them as long as no one has given his consent) *is entitled to object* [*to such a marriage*] (that is he has the power to submit it to the judge for annulment. The annulment is only effective by a judgement of the court since it is a matter of appreciation. Until such a judgement is pronounced the marriage is valid and the spouses inherit from one another if one of them should die before the judgement.) *if the husband is not her coequal* (*kufʾ*) (This is to avert damage and disgrace. If one of the matrimonial guardians has approved of the marriage, those who stand in the same or in a more distant degree [to her] cannot object anymore. This right [of objection] continues until she gives birth. This rule can be found in most authoritative works. However, according to a less authoritative opinion this right of objection continues even after she has given birth to several children….) *Hasan ibn Ziyad* [*d. 819*] *has reported from the Imam* [*Abu Hanifa*] *that it is not valid* (that is that such a marriage is not valid if she marries herself without a matrimonial guardian to a man who is not her coequal. Many of our scholars have adopted this rule since many cases are not submitted to judges.) *and Qadikhan* [*d. 1196*] *has issued fatwas according to this opinion.* (This opinion is more correct and cautious and therefore preferable for fatwas in our days because not every matrimonial guardian is proficient in litigation and not every judge is just….) *According to Muhammad* [*al-Shaybani, d. 805*] *such a marriage is concluded conditionally* (that is, subject to approval by the matrimonial guardian) *even if the husband is her coequal.* (If a marriage

> is contracted conditionally this means that before approval sexual intercourse is not allowed, that a repudiation is void and that they do not inherit from one another....)[4]

Here we see that within the Hanafite school of jurisprudence there are three conflicting rules with regard to the marriages of a legally capable woman concluded on her own accord. According to one opinion, she is fully entitled to do so, except that in case of a misalliance, her agnatic male relatives may petition the *qadi* for an annulment. A second opinion holds that such a mis-alliance is *per se* invalid, whereas according to the third view, all marriages concluded by legally capable women need the ratification of their marriage guardians.

This passage, which could be replaced by many other ones, is typical of the books on Islamic jurisprudence. They juxtapose different opinions on the same issue and it would appear that the legitimacy of dissent is one of the essential characteristics of the *fiqh*. There are several classical works of comparative *fiqh* in which the controversies are discussed and explained in terms of different interpretations of Qur'anic texts of Prophetic sayings, or the application of different hermeneutical tools.

As illustrated by this passage, *fiqh* texts do not resemble law codes. They contain scholarly discussions, and are, therefore, open, discursive, and contradictory. This discussion is the monopoly of the religious scholars, the ulema. Because of their religious training they have the prerogative of formulating the law on the basis of the revealed texts. Although in the early history of Islam, this prerogative was contested by the rulers and state officials, the ulema ultimately emerged victorious.

The most important ideological device that they used to keep the state authorities at bay, was the idea of the closing of the gates of *ijtihad*. With the institutionalization of the schools of jurisprudence, the freedom of the jurists adhering to them was restricted. They regarded themselves as being under the obligation of following the views of the founders of the schools. Gradually, over the centuries, this idea developed into the notion that jurists had to abide by the *madhhab* doctrine in all its details and were not allowed to formulate new opinions. This is called the obligation of *taqlid*, the acceptance of a doctrine without questioning its bases. In the nineteenth century, both Muslim and Western scholars criticized this notion and blamed it for the stagnation and weakness of the Islamic world. However, recent research has shown that behind that façade of *taqlid*, the law did change under the impact of social

4 See Shaykhzade and Halabi, ibid.: i, 320–21.

and political developments.[5] Moreover, they failed to see its political and legal functionality. For one the obligation of *taqlid* could be used by the scholars to prevent state interference with the Shariʿa: if the jurists, who had been trained in jurisprudence and the related religious discipline were not allowed to interpret the sources of the law and formulate new views, this was *a fortiori* the case for state officials. Thus, the religious scholars could preserve their monopoly of formulating the Shariʿa. The obligation of *taqlid* also had practical advantages: it provided a certain amount of legal certainty and predictability, which would not exist if all judges and practical lawyers were entitled to formulate and apply their own interpretations of the revealed texts.

2.3 *Shariʿa and the State: Law Enforcement*

The Shariʿa, like Western legal systems, leaves the enforcement of the law to the state. But how could the legal doctrine, or the normative repertoire of the *fiqh*, in which on one topic often contradictory opinions were juxtaposed, function as positive law? This would require a transformation from legal doctrine to law of the land. In this transformation, both the head of the state and the judiciary played a role, but these roles could vary from · time to time and place to place. On the one hand, the head of state may content himself with creating a judiciary and leave the details of the application to the *qadis.* This means that the *qadi,* in adjudicating cases, has a great deal of discretion in selecting rules and even can use *ijtihad.* On the other hand, the head of state may limit the qadi's discretion by codification, thus instructing him to follow specific opinions from the doctrine. I will return to that later. For now, it suffices to say that the Ottoman Empire followed some sort of middle course: the Ottoman qadis were obliged to follow the most authoritative opinion of the Hanafite school.

In order to determine the most authoritative opinion, the founding fathers of the Hanafite school of jurisprudence were assigned a ranking: An opinion of Abu Hanifa would have the highest score and be more authoritative than the opinion of any other prominent Hanafi jurist. Next came Muhammad al-Shaybani, then Abu Yusuf, etc. With regard to certain topics, the sultan, for practical reasons, would reverse the order and impose another, not so authoritative Hanafi provision. The sultan was entitled to do so because he could give instructions to the *qadis* when appointing them and thus limit their jurisdiction. If a *qadi* would act against these instructions, the sentence pronounced by him would be null and void and not enforce-able. All this is strictly in agreement with the classical doctrine regarding the position of the judiciary: judges are not independent from the executive, but subordinated in the sense that the

5 See Johansen, Baber (1988): *The Islamic Law on Land Tax and Rent*, London: Croom Helm.

sultan would determine the limits of the *qadi's* jurisdiction. This he could do specifying the type of cases that the *qadi* could adjudicate, by imposing certain opinions within the doctrine that the qadi had to follow, or limiting the period during which claims could be brought to court. Through these instructions, a well-defined body of specifically Ottoman Hanafite law developed through which the sultan could control the *qadis'* adjudication.[6]

3 Codification of the Shariʿa

The notion of the Shariʿa as religious, divine law, monopolized by the ulema would *prima facie* seem to be contradictory to and incompatible with the existence of state enacted law. However, this was not the case, at least not in the Ottoman Empire. As from the fifteenth century, the sultans began to enact regulations (*qanun*) dealing with land law, fiscal and criminal law. They supplemented the Shariʿa where the Shariʿa was silent or did not give precise rules. This legislation, however, was regarded as part of the Islamic legal order and not as being in conflict with the Shariʿa. The enactment of these codes did not imply that the state had the monopoly of law-making, nor that state enacted law was of a higher order that other types of law.

Codification, however, is based on an altogether different concept, for codification presupposes that the state enacts legislation that completely regulates a certain domain of the law with the exclusion of other types of law (unless the codification itself confers force of law to such other types, like in the case of custom). Codification, therefore, implies that only the state determines what law is and that state law is the highest form of law. This notion of codification has its origins in the continental civil code tradition of the early nineteenth century.

In the Ottoman Empire, codification began in the second half of the nineteenth century. During the Tanzimat period (1839–76), the ideas on the relationship between the state and the law had begun to change. Tanzimat reform was very much administrative and legal reform and legislation became one of its most important instruments. The first reform decree, the Gülhane Rescript (1839), emphasizes the importance of legislation:

6 See Peters, Rudolph (2005): "What does it mean to be an official madhhab: Hanafism and the Ottoman Empire." In: *The Islamic School of Law: Evolution, Devolution, and Progress*. Ed. P. Bearman, R. Peters, F. Vogel. Cambridge MA: Harvard University Press, 2005, pp. 147–158.

> In order to better administer the Sublime Empire (*Devlet-i Aliyye*) and the Well-Protected Dominions (*Memalik-i Mahruse*), it is deemed necessary and important to enact some new laws. The most important provisions of these indispensable laws consist of more personal safety, of a better protection of honour, decency and property, of fixing the taxes and specifying the way of drafting the required soldiers and the period of their service.[7]

Legislation was not only an instrument of reform, but also of centralisation and legal unification. Under the influence of Western, continental, constitutional notions, the Ottoman ruling elite became convinced of the necessity of codification of all domains of the law, so as to emphasize that the state should determine what the law of the land is. As a consequence, codification was not only used to introduce Western law codes (for example, the Commercial Code of 1850, the Penal Code of 1858), but also to modernize existing law. Examples of the codification of traditional law are the Penal Codes of 1840 and 1851, the Land Law of 1858, the *Mecelle* which is the Ottoman Civil Code based on Hanafite *fiqh* enacted between 1868 and 1876, and, finally, the Code of Family Law (*Hukuk-i 'A'ile Kararnamesi*) of 1917. Behind this movement was the Western notion that traditional law, as found in the various, books of *fiqh*, in administrative practices and in custom was 'chaotic and inaccessible' and that 'codification is civilization' The need for codification was especially felt when new courts were established in which not all judges had a training in Islamic jurisprudence:

> Islamic jurisprudence, then, is an immense ocean and in order to find solutions for problems by bringing to its surface the pearls of the topics required [for solving the problems] needs an enormous skill and mastery. And especially for the Hanafite *madhhab*, there were, in subsequent generations, very many independent interpreters (*mujtahid*) and there emerged many controversies so that Hanafite jurisprudence, like Shafi'ite jurisprudence, has branched out and become diverse to the extent that it cannot anymore be examined carefully. Therefore it is tremendously difficult to distinguish the correct opinion among the various views and to apply it to the cases.... Therefore, if a book on legal transactions (*mu'amalat*) were to be composed that is easy to consult being free from

7 Text in *Düstur* (1865–66): 4 vols., Second Edition, Vol. 1, Istanbul: 2–3.

> controversies and containing only the preferred opinions, then everybody could read it easily and apply it to his transactions.[8]

During the same period, there emerged also semi-official codifications, that is, private compilations of the rules of the Shariʿa in a certain field, arranged in sections like law codes and presenting these rules in a conveniently arranged fashion so that they could be used as easy reference tools for legal practitioners. In Egypt, Muhammad Qadri Pasha, former minister of justice, published in the 1870s compilations on family law, law of property and contracts and *waqf* law.[9] These compilations had a semi-official status in those fields of law that continued to be governed by the Shariʿa after the reforms of 1883, when French civil, commercial, criminal and procedural law was adopted. In the Ottoman Empire, Ömer Hilmi, a former president of the Court of Cassation composed an authoritative compilation of the law of homicide and personal injury, a part of criminal law that was still enforced by the Shariʿa courts.[10]

If one compares the *fiqh* texts on a certain legal issue with the codified provisions, the differences are striking. As I said before, the *fiqh* doctrine is jurists' law and the *fiqh* texts are discursive and include various, often conflicting opinions on the: issue. They are open texts in the sense that they do not offer final solutions. Provisions of a law code, on the other hand, must be authoritative, clear and unequivocal. In a law code there is no room for contradictory opinions or argumentation and its provisions must be definitive and final. Therefore, choices have to be made when codifying the Shariʿa. This will become clear when we compare the codified provisions of the Hanafite doctrine regarding the marriage of a legally capable woman with the *fiqh* text on the same subject quoted above:

> Muhammad Qadri's compilation (ca.1875):
> If [a free and legally capable woman] concludes a marriage with someone who is socially her inferior (*ghayr kufʾ*) without her agnatic guardian's express consent before the marriage, then that marriage is *per se*

8 From the explanatory memorandum of the first book of the Mecelle (1868), see Kaşıkçı, Osman (1997): *Islâm ve Osmanlı hukukunda Mecelle: hazırlanışı, hükümlerinin tahlili, tadil ve tamamlama çalışmaları.* Istanbul: Osmanlı Araştırmaları Vakfı. 75–6.

9 See Qadri Pasha, Muhammad (1909a): *Al-Ahkam al-sharʿiyya fi al-ahwal al-shakhsiyya*, Second Edition, al-Qahira: al-Matbaʿa al-Ahliyya; Ibid. (1893): *Qanun al-ʿadl wa-l-insaf li-l-qadaʾ ʿala mushkilat al-awqaf*, Al-Qahira: Al-Matbaʿa al-Ahliyya; Ibid. (1909b): *Murshid al-hayran ila maʿrifat ahwal al-insan fi l-muʿamalat al-sharʿiyya*, Third Edition, Cairo: Al-Matbaʿa al-Amiriyya.

10 See Hilmi, Ömer (1881–82): *Miʿyar-i ʿAdalet*, Istanbul.

> invalid and the guardian's consent given after the conclusion of the marriage is of no avail. If she has no agnatic guardian and marries herself to a person who is socially her inferior or if her guardian has consented to her marriage with a socially inferior man, then the marriage is valid.[11]
>
> The Ottoman Code of Family Law (1917):
> If a woman of full age marries herself without informing her matrimonial guardian and without having obtained his consent, then the matter must be examined. If she has married herself to a person who is socially her equal, then the marriage is binding even if the bride price is less than her proper bride price. However, if she has married herself to someone who is socially her inferior, then the guardian can have recourse to the judge for rescission of the marriage.[12]

Both sections contain clear and unequivocal legal rules. The dissenting opinions that existed in the *fiqh* doctrine have been excised, in order to produce one authoritative, final statement of the law. But, if we read that sections carefully, it will be apparent that the authors of these texts have made different choices. Muhammad Qadri Pasha followed the more conservative view, attributed to Abu Hanifa by Hasan ibn Ziyad, which was the prevailing view in the Ottoman Empire. The Ottoman legislator of 1917 followed another authoritative Hanafite opinion, also ascribed to Abu Hanifa, that was more favourable to women. These two texts clearly illustrate the effects of codification: the transformation from a scholarly discourse in which different and opposing opinions are juxtaposed to an authoritative, definitive statement of the law, purged from all alternative views. But this is not the only effect. The adoption of the Western concept of law code also means the adoption of the Western: concept of law. As a result, the religious norms are also eliminated from the Shariʿa codes. Codified Shariʿa, then, is no more than a thinned out version of the rich *fiqh* doctrine.

When states during the second half of the nineteenth century took the power to define the Shariʿa, the role of the ulema did not end completely. Their co-operation was essential in order to legitimize the state-enacted Shariʿa codes. But more importantly, they were needed for their expertise. This explains the pivotal role of men like Ahmed Cevdet (1822–95) in legal reforms. Trained as religious scholars and having an open eye for reform, they staffed the committees that prepared the codification of the Shariʿa. The necessary

11 Qadri Pasha [1909a: Section 52].

12 *Huquq-i ʿA'ile Qararnamesi* [1917: Section 47].

participation of the ulema limited in practice the freedom of the state in codifying the Shariʿa. They had the power to refuse to participate if the state would enact laws that they would regard as repugnant to the Shariʿa. Such a step would greatly undermine the legitimacy of codifications of the Shariʿa.

4 Who Has the Authority to Define the Shariʿa Today?

In the course of the twentieth century, most legal systems in the Middle East were westernized, by the adoption of Western substantive and adjective laws and Western notions of law. However, in most national legal systems, the Shariʿa still had a role to play. This role varies and we can classify these legal systems in four types according to the position of the Shariʿa in it:

- The completely secularised legal systems, from which the Shariʿa has been removed. The Turkish system is the prototype of such a legal system. One has to bear in mind, however, that the Shariʿa, especially in rural areas, for a long time and even still today, is important at the unofficial level, for example, in the infrajudicial settlement of all kinds of conflicts.
- The legal systems that, are dominated by the Shariʿa, which means that the Shariʿa is the law of the land and that state legislation can only take place in areas where the Shariʿa is silent or not unequivocal. This is the case in Saudi Arabia[13] and Yemen. In the latter country, however, most of the Shariʿa based laws have by now been codified.
- The most common type of legal system, the one in which western law prevails, except in the field of personal status (family law, law of succession) and the law of *waqf*. However, nearly everywhere, the law in these fields has been codified. In its uncodified form, Shariʿa rules are enforced only in Egypt, where only parts of the family law and the law of succession have been enacted as state laws and uncodified Shariʿa is applied on all personal status issues for which there is no enacted law.[14] In some countries of this group, provisions have been introduced in the Constitution to the effect that the principles of the Shariʿa are the main source of legislation. This was done to take the wind out of the sails of the Islamist opposition. However,

13 On Saudi Arabia, see Vogel, Frank E. (2000): *Islamic Law and Legal System: Studies of Saudi Arabia*, Leiden: Brill.

14 For the modernization of the law of personal status, see Ebert, Hans-Georg (1996): *Das Personalstatut arabischer Länder: Problemfelder, Methoden, Perspektiven: Ein Beitrag zum Diskurs über Theorie*. Leipziger Beiträge für Orientforschung, 7, Frankfurt a.M.: Peter Lang; Beck-Peccoz, Roberta Aluffi (1990): *La modernizzazione del diritto di famiglia nei paesi arabi*, University. di Torino, Memorie dell'Istituto Giuridico, III, 35, Milano: Giuffre.

nowhere was the enforcement of this provisions more than cosmetic and did it result in noticeable changes in the law.
- Finally, there are those legal systems that have been re-Islamized. They developed out of the previous system, after Islamist regimes came to power. This re-Islamization was implemented by introducing Islamic law codes in many fields, noticeably in criminal law. This type exists in. Iran, Sudan, and, to some extent, in Libya. Outside the Middle East, we find it in Pakistan and many Northern, prevailingly Muslim, states of the Nigerian federation.[15]

It is striking that the Shariʿa, nowadays, is not applied by using the classical books of *fiqh*, but via legislation. The Shariʿa, interpreted in different ways, has become part of a great number of national legal systems. In the field of family law and the law of succession, codification was not only a means to ascertain state control over the law and to facilitate the finding of the law for judges, but also as an instrument of reform. In these fields, states have introduced changes in the law in order to eliminate some interpretations of the Shariʿa that were regarded: as socially undesirable. The legislators, however, went to great lengths to show that their newly enacted rules were still within the scope of the Shariʿa. Even in a country like Tunisia, where far-reaching reforms were introduced, such as the ban on polygamy and on extrajudicial divorce, an effort was made to show that these changes were in agreement with the Shariʿa.

It is even more striking that those Islamist regimes that re-Islamized legal systems (with the Taliban regime in Afghanistan as the one ephemeral exception) did so by introducing Islamic norms using modern Western legal forms. The explanation is that these states did not want to give up their control over the law and abandon it to the ulema. Only in Iran were attempts made at incorporating the notion of the authority of the Islamic jurisprudents (*velayat-i faqih*) into the constitution. But even here, the power to legislate is essentially vested in the parliament and the government.

As a result of the process of codification that has continued for nearly a century and a half, there are hardly any countries left where the Shariʿa is applied without codification. The only exceptions are Saudi Arabia, and, for a few topics of personal status law, Egypt. This means that nearly everywhere the state has assumed the power to determine what the Shariʿa norms are, at least in those fields that are enforced as parts of the national legal systems. This power has been withdrawn from the ulema, although they still do play some role in

15 For the Islamization of criminal law, see Peters, R. (1994): 'The Islamization of Criminal Law: A Comparative Analysis', *Welt des Islams*, 34/ii, pp. 246–74; and Peters, R. (2003): *Islamic criminal law in Nigeria*. Ibadan etc.: Spectrum Books.

preparing and legitimizing legislation. Defining the Shariʿa became a part of national politics, with the result that its codification varies from country to country. Of course, the doctrine of the *fiqh* regarding those topics that have been codified still exists. But only as an academic doctrine, a doctrine that by state legislation has been blocked from actual enforcement by the judiciary.

This led some, mainly Western, non-Muslim scholars to question whether this legislation can still be regarded as Shariʿa and as Islamic. Raising this question is, I believe, not very relevant and betrays a certain polemical point of view. By arguing that codified Shariʿa is not Shariʿa and not Islamic anymore, they want to demonstrate that the re-Islamization of the law that was introduced in some countries, was not a real re-introduction of the Shariʿa. In my opinion, outsiders are not competent to determine for Muslims what Islam and the Shariʿa is. The only correct answer would be that if Muslims hold that it is Islamic and a legitimate (albeit perhaps not the only) interpretation of the Shariʿa, which most Muslims do, there are no good arguments to view it differently.

As a result of the nationalisation of the Shariʿa, the ulema lost their time-honoured position as the exclusive, guardians of the law. This affected their status in society, which had already been impaired as their economic resources, especially employment opportunities, had declined. Traditionally, the ulema had the monopoly not only of religious functions connected with the mosques, but also of education and the administration of justice. Because of this monopoly, they enjoyed a high status in society.

However, all this began to change as from the end of the nineteenth century. Because of the creation of new types of schools for the training of military officers, civil servants, doctors and engineers, the ulema lost the monopoly of education. At the same time their intellectual authority was challenged by some of these new professionals and by those who had come into contact with the intellectual debates in the West. This decline of intellectual status went hand in hand with a gradual decline of the economic foundations of their livelihood. Whereas originally all judges and teachers were from the ulema class, now, after the introduction of new types of schools and the Westernization of the legal system, they had to compete with graduates of other schools. The ulema's intellectual leadership was not anymore unconditionally accepted. They were fiercely attacked by Islamist intellectuals, who did not unquestioningly accept the traditional interpretations of the revealed texts, propagated by the ulema. Although most Islamist intellectuals had not had a traditional religious education, they regarded themselves as competent in this field on the strength of their knowledge of the Qur'an and Hadith, which they often understood in new ways.

This has enormously affected the discourse on the Shariʿa, both the codified and the uncodified parts. For as we have seen, codified Shariʿa is only a section of the entire body of Shariʿa doctrine, Not subject to codification are the purely ritual, religious and ethical provisions of the Shariʿa, dealing, for example, with ritual prayer (*salat*), pilgrimage (*hajj*) and dietary prescriptions, and those rules that have a legal character but are not implemented, such as in most countries, Shariʿa private law (especially the provisions on interest), criminal and constitutional law. The rules of the Shariʿa that were not enforced by the judiciary, were traditionally the competence of the *muftis*, who belonged, to the ulema class and had a traditional religious training. They were the religious authorities who would counsel the believers on a specific question of the Shariʿa. Although there were controversies and disagreements among them, their authority was not fundamentally challenged. This however, has changed now. Many of the issues that used to belong exclusively to the domain of the muftis have now become subject to public debates, in which intellectuals without a traditional religious training also participate. During the twentieth century, intellectuals without a religious training have increasingly put their imprint on the religious debates and started to question accepted religious truths. Initially, these were intellectuals who, under the influence of western ideas, became critical of what they saw as backward religious views and practices that would block 'progress'. However, during the last decades other types of believers became more prominent in these debates. There is an increasing group of pious Muslims who argue that the traditional doctrine of the Shariʿa, as expounded by the ulema, has deviated from the pure teachings of Qur'an and Sunna and only want to take these pure teachings as guidelines for their daily lives.

These developments have resulted in a situation in which defining the Shariʿa is not anymore the exclusive competence of the ulema, but has become a public concern. As to codified Shariʿa, the debate is directly connected with national politics. Dependent on the extent to which a state has adopted democratic procedures of legislation, the Shariʿa codes are discussed in parliament and the media. Although the traditional ulema still may play a role in the preparation and the 'marketing' of these codes, the ultimate decision is with the politicians. Codification of the Shariʿa, as well as the question of which parts of the national legal system must be immediately based on the Shariʿa, therefore, have become prominent and important political issues.

Since the ulema have lost their intellectual monopoly, the legally unenforced sections of the Shariʿa are also publicly debated. Although this debate is less political than the discussions on the codified Shariʿa, it certainly has political aspects. Islamic symbols and doctrines are connected with political positions and are used to legitimize political points of view. Whether or not all existing views can be fully expressed depends, naturally, on the extent to which the media are free from government interference and censorship. There are many instances where certain religious views are not permitted to be expressed, because of the political associations of these views.

What does all this mean for the Shariʿa in contemporary Muslim society? The most important development has been that the authority of the ulema has been challenged and has declined. There are now also Muslims without a religious training who can have their say about Shariʿa issues. Those parts of the Shariʿa that have been codified and are part of the national legal systems are now brought under control of the state instead of being controlled by the ulema. This means that it has become political and if the structures of the state permit it, even democratized. Concerning the other aspects of the Shariʿa, here, too, the ulema have lost control, although not as drastically as in the purely legal domain. The issues of the Shariʿa that fall outside the scope of codified law, are now debated by all kinds of Muslim intellectuals, with and without a formal religious training. These debates have not only been politicized, as I have shown before, but also, at least potentially, democratized. However, to what extent this may lead to a real democratisation depends on whether these debates are free from political constraints that block freedom of expression.

CHAPTER 29

The Reintroduction of Shariʿa Criminal Law in Nigeria

New Challenges for the Muslims of the North

1 Introduction

The introduction of Shariʿa criminal law in most states of Northern Nigeria has been received with mixed feelings: jubilation and high expectations on the part of large sections of the Muslim population of the North and reserved feelings and even fears on the part of the Christian Nigerians. In addition, concerns have been expressed at the international level. An important cause of these fears was, and still is, the question of whether the newly introduced Shariʿa penal codes are consonant with the Nigerian constitutional order and, especially, whether they comply with the human rights standards of the Nigerian constitution and international conventions to which Nigeria is a signatory. In this article, I will precisely discuss this topic.

2 The Introduction of Shariʿa Criminal Law[1]

On 27 January 2000, Zamfara, one of the Northern states of the Nigerian federation, enacted the first Shariʿa Penal Code in Northern Nigeria, having first established Shariʿa courts to apply the code. Like in the United States, the states of the Federal Republic of Nigeria have the power to enact legislation in the domain of criminal law. The example of Zamfara was followed in May by Niger State, where the government, like that in Zamfara, fully supported the re-Islamisation of the legal system. Other Northern states, prompted by popular pressure, followed suit. In Katsina and Sokoto, Shariʿa criminal sentences were pronounced and executed (in one case a sentence of amputation of the right hand was carried out) even before a Shariʿa Penal Codes came into force, on the strength of Shariʿa Courts Laws stipulating that the Shariʿa courts must apply the provisions of the Koran and hadith and those found in the traditional authoritative Malikite works of law. By the beginning of 2004,

1 For a more detailed survey of the re-introduction of Shariʿa criminal law in Northern Nigeria, see Ruud Peters, *Islamic criminal law in Nigeria*, (Ibadan: Spectrum Books, 2003), viii, 87 pp.

 | DOI:10.1163/9789004420625_030

twelve Northern states have introduced Shariʿa criminal law by setting up Shariʿa courts with jurisdiction in criminal matters and promulgating Shariʿa Penal Codes.[2] These codes include the Malikite law of *hudud*, homicide and wounding, and under the heading of *taʿzir*, most offences mentioned in the 1959 Penal Code for Northern Nigeria that was in force until then and still effective for non-Muslims. All codes follow Malikite doctrine but there are some differences on points of detail. The Shar'ia Penal Codes apply only to Muslims (or to non-Muslims who desire to be tried under these codes and present a written document of consent to the court). Non-Muslim citizens are tried by Magistrate Courts under the 1959 Penal Code.

The swift success of the Islamisation movement in Northern Nigeria was due to powerful popular pressure. It is remarkable that Northern Nigeria is the only region where Islamic criminal law has been put into force by means of legislation passed by elected parliaments. Except in Zamfara and Niger State, the state governments were not enthusiastic about Islamisation of the legal system but were forced to enact it under popular pressure. The general clamour for Islamic criminal law was due to more factors than just religious zeal. The most prominent one was that many believed that Islamic criminal law would be the answer to widespread criminality and government corruption. Further, it was a protest against federal politics. Since the end of military dictatorship in 1997, the centre of gravity of Nigerian politics had moved to the mainly non-Muslim South. The Islamisation movement was a reaction against this: a challenge to federal politics and an attempt to reassert Muslim political power. There was also the idea that imposing Islamic norms on public life, by banning drinking and closing bars and by putting an end to prostitution, would secure God's help in making the Nigerian Muslims stronger. Finally, like in most other countries where Islamic criminal law has been introduced, it was a conscious reassertion of cultural roots against Western political and cultural dominance.

An important effect of the Islamisation of criminal law is that the codes are not regarded as exhaustive. Acts not mentioned in the codes may also be punishable offences, if they are so under classical Islamic criminal law. Most of the new codes contain the following provision:

2 Bauchi, Borno, Gombe, Jigawa, Kaduna, Kano, Katsina, Kebbi, Niger, Sokoto, and Yobe. The Shariʿa Penal Codes of most of these states follow the example of the Zamfara codes with minor changes. Whereas Kano State has enacted an independent Shariʿa Penal Code, Niger State has contented itself with adding a few amendments to the 1959 Penal Code for Northern Nigeria.

> Any act or omission which is not specifically mentioned in this Shari'ah Penal Code but is otherwise declared to be an offence under the Qur'an, Sunnah and *Ijtihad* of the Malikite School of Islamic thought shall be an offence under this code and such act or omission shall be punishable:
> (a) With imprisonment for a term which may extend to 5 years, or
> (b) With caning which may extend to 50 lashes, or
> (c) With fine which may extend to N5,000.00 or with any two of the above punishments.[3]

Some codes contain provisions about the applicability of the Islamic rules of evidence. That most codes are silent on this point, although it is an essential part of the laws of fixed penalties and retaliation, must be attributed to a conscious omission by the various legislators. They must have been aware of the fact that according to the federal constitution of Nigeria legislation in the field of evidence is a federal matter. By now it has become clear that the Shari'a courts follow the Malikite doctrine with regard to evidence. This means that unlawful intercourse may also be proven by extramarital pregnancy. Two women (Safiyyatu Hussaini in Sokoto State and Amina Lawal in Katsina State) were sentenced in 2002 by lower Shari'a courts to be stoned to death for unlawful sexual intercourse, on the strength of pregnancy without being married. Both sentences, however, were quashed on appeal. This was partly for technical reasons: they were charged of having had unlawful sexual relations at a time that the Shari'a Penal Code in their states had not yet been promulgated. But more importantly, both Shari'a Courts of Appeal ruled that pregnancy of an unmarried woman is, in and by itself, not sufficient evidence of unlawful sexual intercourse, in view of the Malikite doctrine that the maximum period of gestation is five years.[4]

In some codes certain offences are equated with theft and can also be punished by amputation. Most Penal Codes make the kidnapping of a child under seven (or before puberty in some codes) punishable by amputation. The Zamfara Penal Code (Art 259) has a clause imposing amputation as the penalty for forgery of documents if the value they represent is more than the *nisâb*. The Kano Penal Code has made embezzlement of public funds or of funds of a bank or company by officials and employees an offence punishable

3 Zamfara Shari'a Penal Code, Section 92. Other Penal Codes contain a similar section.

4 For a detailed discussion of the Safiyyatu Hussaini case, see Peters, R., "The re-Islamization of criminal law in Northern Nigeria and the judiciary: the Safiyyatu Hussaini case," in *Dispensing justice in Islam: Qadis and their courts*, ed. M.K. Masud, R. Peters, and D. Powers (Leiden: Brill, 2005), pp. 219–241.

by amputation (Art 134B). For these provisions there is some support of less authoritative Malikite opinions who regard amputation as lawful for these offences, but as a discretionary punishment. These provisions may result in more frequent enforcement of amputation, since, for these offences, the strict conditions for the application of the fixed penalty for theft, a critical constituent of this part of the law, do not seem to apply here.

The law of homicide and wounding follows closely the classical doctrine. Some codes specify that the killer can be sentenced to be executed in the same way as he killed his victim. As in Malikite law, assassination (*qatl ghila*, defined as "the act of luring a person to a secluded place and killing him" (Zamfara Shariʿa Penal Code Art 50; Kano Shariʿa Penal Code, 50) is a capital offence for which the position of the prosecutors is irrelevant. A striking omission in the Northern Nigerian Shariʿa Penal codes is that they are silent on the requirement of equivalence in value between victim and killer or attacker (See § 2.5.4.2). It is to be expected that on this points Malikite doctrine is applicable.

Several cases of judicial amputation have been reported. Appeals were not lodged, either because the convicts were put under pressure by their social environment with the argument that they would not be good Muslims if they would oppose the sentence, or because of their convictions that undergoing the punishment in this life would ease the sufferings in the Hereafter. In passing a sentence of retaliation for manslaughter, the qadi may order that the perpetrator is to be executed in the same way as he has killed his victim. At least one such sentence has been pronounced.[5] A few sentences of retaliation for wounding have been pronounced. On 26 May 2001 Ahmed Tijani was sentenced in Malunfashi, Katsina, to have his right eye removed after blinding a man in an assault. The victim was given the choice between demanding 'an eye for an eye' and 50 camels. In a bizarre case, a 45 year old man was sentenced in January 2003 by the Upper Shariʿa Court in Bauchi to have his right leg removed from the knee (without anaesthesia or painkillers, as the court directed) for having done the same to his wife, whom he had accused of overexposing herself to a doctor when she took an injection. I have no information on whether these sentences have actually been carried out.

The enforcement of the new Shariʿa Penal Codes is sometimes problematical due to the structure of the Nigerian federation. The police is a federal institution and police personnel often work outside the region of the origin, which means that in Muslim states there are also many non-Muslim policemen.

5 Zamfara Penal Code, Section 240. In November 2001, a Katsina Shariʿa Court sentenced Sani Yakubu Rodi to be stabbed to death in the same way as he had killed his victims. At this moment I do not know whether the sentenced has been carried out.

They are not overzealous in tracing specific Shariʿa offences. Indeed, there have been reports about police stations in the North that began to function as beer parlours after the prohibition of drinking alcohol was enforced. This lax attitude on the part of the police resulted in vigilantism: Muslims, discontent with the level of enforcement of Islamic criminal law, would form what they called *hisba* groups and start patrolling urban neighbourhoods, attacking places where they suspected that alcohol was served or prostitutes were plying their trade. To counter this phenomenon, some states established official *hisba* organisation that would operate in close co-operation with the police.

The reintroduction of Islamic criminal law in the North is surrounded by political and legal complications. It will remain a bone of contention between the Muslim North and the rest of Nigeria. One of the major legal problems is that the Shariʿa Penal Codes are on several scores at variance with the Nigerian federal constitution. The first controversy is on whether the introduction of these laws can be reconciled with the secular character of the Nigerian state. Article 10 of the Constitution reads: 'The Government of the Federation or of a State shall not adopt any religion as State religion.' The issue, however, is not as clear as it *prima facie* would seem to be, since the Shariʿa has for a long time been accepted as a part of the legal systems of the Northern states in the domain of family, private and commercial law. There is no doubt, however, about the unconstitutionality of the implicit introduction of the Malikite law of evidence: The Constitution stipulates that legislation on evidence is a prerogative of the federal legislature. Finally the Shariʿa Penal Codes are in conflict with several human rights guaranteed in the federal constitution. We will return to this issue in the following section, dealing with Islamic criminal law and human rights. So far no sentences awarding amputation of death by stoning under the Shariʿa Penal Codes, have been tested against the constitution by the Federal Supreme Court. Since it is expected that the court will find many of the provisions of these Shariʿa Penal Codes unconstitutional, there are widespread fears that such a decision might fuel the antagonism between the North and the South to the point of even endangering the existence of the federation.

3 Conflicts between the Shariʿa Penal Codes and the Constitution

Here we shall discuss the potential areas of conflict between the provisions of the Shariʿa penal codes and the constitutions. I want to stress, however, that the exact definition and purport of human rights provisions is in many cases subject to cultural interpretations. This means that their contents are not for 100% fixed and are, within limits, subject to negotiation. Defining them would be the task of the national judiciary, and, more specifically, the Supreme Federal Court.

3.1 *Torture or Cruel, Degrading or Inhuman Punishment*

Torture or cruel, degrading or inhuman punishment is outlawed by both the Constitution and the Convention against Torture and other Cruel, Degrading or Inhuman Punishment or Treatment, 1989 (CAT). They lay down that no person shall be subjected to torture or to inhuman or degrading punishments and that states shall take measures to prevent public servants from committing acts of torture or administer such punishment.[6]

Here we have one of the most conspicuous domains of conflict between the new Penal Codes and human rights principles. Few jurists would deny that amputation of limbs and retaliation for grievous hurt such as blinding or the pulling out of teeth are indeed a form of torture. The same is true in regard to death by stoning and crucifixion (at least if the latter punishment is taken to mean that the convict will be killed after having been crucified) and to the execution for manslaughter carried out in the same way as perpetrator killed his victim.[7]

3.2 *Violation of the Basic Rights of Children*

In classical Islamic law, majority begins with puberty. The criterion is a purely physical one: it is established by physical signs such as menstruation and the growth of breasts (women) and the appearance of hair under the armpits and ejaculation (men). The classical doctrine is adopted by the new Shariʿa penal codes. This means that children in their very early teens can be punished with mutilating *hadd* punishments, with retaliation for wounding and homicide,[8] which violates the Convention on the Rights of the Child (1989) (CRC). That this is not an academic question is shown by the sentence passed on 5 July 2001 of a fifteen year old boy to amputation for theft in Birnin Kebbi, the capital of Kebbi state.

Both the Zamfara and the Kano Penal Codes, following the 1959 Penal Code, explicitly recognise that parents, guardians, schoolmasters and masters are entitled to physically discipline their children, wards, pupils and servants, as long

6 Constitution, Section 34; CAT, Art. 1 (1) and 16 (1).

7 Zamfara Penal Code, Section 240. In November 2001, a Katsina Shariʿa Court sentenced Sani Yakubu Rodi to be stabbed to death in the same way as he had killed his victims. At this moment I do not know whether the sentenced has been carried out.

8 Zamfara Penal Code, Section 47, 63(1), 71; Kano Penal Code, Section 47, 62A.

as such castigation does not amount to grievous hurt and is not unreasonable in kind or degree.[9] This seems to justify quite severe physical injury, since the upper limit (grievous hurt) is defined as emasculation, permanent deprivation of one of the senses, deprivation or destruction of a member or joint, permanent disfigurement of the head and face, fracture or dislocation of a bone or tooth or injuries that endanger life or cause severe bodily pain or render the sufferer unable to pursue his ordinary pursuits (Kano Penal Code, Section 159; Zamfara Penal Code, Section 216).

3.3 *The Principle of Legality, i.e. That No Act Can Be Punished Unless It Has Been Made a Punishable Offence by Enacted Law*

Section 36 (12) of the Constitution stipulates that "a person shall not be convicted of a criminal offence unless that offence is defined and the penalty therefore is prescribed in a written law." In violation of the constitutional provision, all Shariʿa Penal Codes (with the exception of the Kano Penal Code) contain a section making punishable any act or omission that is an offence under the Shariʿa even if not mentioned in the Penal Code itself.[10]

3.4 *Equality Before the Law*

One of the most prominent principles in human rights discourse is that all persons are equal before the law and entitled to the same legal protection. This principle is embodied in Section 42 of the Constitution. The same principle is expressed in international human rights instruments.[11] Here we will examine whether the Shariʿa Penal Codes violate the principle of equality with regard to gender and religion.

In the new Penal Codes there are only a few provisions that discriminate on the basis of gender. As in the 1959 Penal Code,[12] the new Penal Codes allow the physical correction of a wife by her husband (Zamfara Penal Code, Section 76 (d)) and stipulate that, because of implied consent, a man is not capable of raping his wife in the sense of the law. The Niger Penal Code, Section 68 (A)(3)(b) is the only one stipulating that in the requirement for proving the offence of

9 Zamfara Penal Code, S.76; Kano Penal Code, Section 76.

10 Zamfara Penal Code, Section 92; Jigawa Penal Code, 92; Bauchi Penal Code, Section 95; Yobe Penal Code, Section 92; Kebbi Penal Code, Section 93.

11 Art. 14 and 26 International Convention for Civil and Political Rights (ICCPR): "All persons shall be equal before the courts and tribunals." "All persons are equal before the law and are entitled without any discrimination to the equal protection of the law."

12 Section 55 (1) (d), subject to the condition that such correction was lawful under customary law of the spouses.

zinâ, the testimony of men is of greater value than that of women. On the other hand, men are placed in a disadvantageous position in the Kano Penal Code (Section 125), where the punishment for *zinâ* committed by unmarried men is caning as well as imprisonment for one year, whereas unmarried women are only to be punished by caning. On the whole, there is little gender bias in the texts of the new Penal Codes. However, where the codes are silent, the courts apply classical Malikite doctrine, which at a number of issues is discriminatory. The most prominent form of gender discrimination is the application by Shariʿa courts, unwarranted by the Shariʿa Penal Codes, of the classical Malikite doctrine that extramarital pregnancy constitutes proof of unlawful intercourse. Now that two Shariʿa Courts of Appeal have reversed trial court sentences of stoning based of extramarital pregnancy, it seems that this is not anymore admitted as proof.[13] Another form of discrimination on the ground of gender, is the difference in the amount of bloodmoney for men and women in cases of homicide and hurt. The codes only specify the blood price of a Muslim male, implying that the lives of women and non-Muslims have a different monetary value.

With regard to religion, it is clear that Muslims and non-Muslims are treated differently. However, I have not found instances of discrimination against non-Muslims, since the Shariʿa Penal Codes apply only to Muslims. In fact, this also violates the principle of equality, but then to the advantage of non-Muslims. For example, the punishment for certain forms of theft, amputation for Muslims and imprisonment for Christians, is patently in conflict with this principle. However, since the 1959 Penal Code also distinguished between Muslims and Christians with regard to certain offences (e.g. drinking alcohol), it would seem that such distinctions are accepted and not regarded as an essential violation of the equality principle.

3.5 *Violations of the Freedom of Religion*

One of the most significant conflicts between the Shariʿa and internationally recognised human rights principles is the Shariʿa provision that Muslims cannot change their religion and that, if they do, they face a death sentence. Apostasy (*ridda*) also entails the loss of civil rights, such as the right to be married (the marriage of an apostate is dissolved immediately) and the right to hold property. However, none of the new Penal Codes has included apostasy as a punishable offence, no doubt because the conflict with Section 38 of the Constitution, which explicitly mentions the freedom to change one's religion,

13 See Peters, "The re-Islamization of criminal law in Northern Nigeria and the judiciary."

was too glaring. This does not necessarily mean that apostasy cannot be punished under these laws. The Zamfara Penal Code, as we have seen, stipulates in Section 92 that acts and omissions that are punishable offences under the Shari'a, may be punished even in the absence of a provision in the Penal Code. It is plausible that those who drafted the law had apostasy in mind. However, as yet no cases of prosecution for apostasy have been reported.

Since Christians are not governed by the new Shari'a Penal Codes, they cannot be said to suffer from religious oppression. However, the new codes contain some provisions which may affect the practice of traditional religions and magical practices. Section 406 (d) of the Zamfara Penal Code reads:

> Whoever presides at or is present at or takes part in the worship or invocation of any juju which has been declared unlawful under the provisions of Section 405 will be punished with death;

The previous Section 405, to which it refers, makes the worship or invocation of juju unlawful and explains that "juju" includes the worship or invocation of any subject or being other than Allah (S.W.T.). This forms part of Sections 405 to 409 (see Appendix Five), dealing with magical practices and witchcraft. The section in almost identical wording was included in the 1959 Penal Code, but with much lighter punishments. The explanation of Section 405, which extends the meaning of juju to the "worship or invocation of any subject or being other than Allah", and the fact that this has been made a capital offence render the provisions dangerous, since they could be used against all religious practices that are deemed un-Islamic. The exact purport of the section is not clear. Since the code only addresses Muslims, the provision seems to refer to persons who regard themselves as Muslims but nevertheless participate in the practices mentioned in these sections.

4 The Challenge

4.1 *Legislative Reform*

This tension between the Federation and the Muslim states of the North regarding the constitutionality of the Shari'a penal codes poses new challenges, especially to the Muslims of Nigeria. If the Northern states with their Muslim majorities want to stay in the Federation there must be compliance with the constitution, assuming that there is no majority to be found within the federation to drastically change it and to revoke the human rights conventions. The Northern states, then, must make clear that Shari'a criminal law does not necessarily constitute a problem in this respect. On the other hand, the South must realise that once Shariʿa law has been introduced, it is very difficult to abolish it. Any Muslim politician who would announce that he intends to do so, commits political suicide and loses his legitimacy. This means that the only option is reformulating Shariʿa codes. For a number of practical reasons, it is to be recommended that this be carried out as a common effort of all states that have introduced Shariʿa criminal law. Then, ultimately, there will be one Shariʿa Penal Code operative in all these states, as was the case with the Penal Code (1959) for Northern Nigeria.

Now, what are the options for reformulating the Shariʿa Penal Codes that are now in force? The first one is relatively simple: Drafting a Shariʿa penal code with the provision that the *hadd* penalties will not be applied until all citizens are free of want. This is not a totally novel notion with regard to the enforcement of *hadd* penalties. It was proposed for the first time, to the best of my knowledge, by the Egyptian Muslim Brothers in the 1940s and 1950.[14] Application of the *hadd* punishment for theft, they argued, can only be enforced after the state has taken care that all citizens are free from want by providing sufficient food, clothing and shelter. It is based essentially on the *hadith al-majaʿa* (famine), i.e. a report that the Caliph ʿUmar once, during a year of famine, suspended the enforcement of the *hadd* penalty for theft, because under such circumstances theft is excusable. The argument can be extended to the punishment for highway robbery (*hiraba, qatʿ al-tariq*) and even to illegal sexual intercourse (*zina*), in view of the material burdens that must be assumed in order to be able to conclude a marriage (residence, cost of wedding, bridal price, etc.).

Other options are a complete overhaul of the penal codes. Often such proposals are met with the reply that these codes contain God's law and that God's law cannot be changed. However, this argument does not cut ice. The Shariʿa Penal Codes that have been introduced so far are codifications of the Malikite school of jurisprudence complemented with a great many provisions take from the Penal Code of 1959 that was in force until then. This, however, cannot be regarded as the only legal doctrine of the Shariʿa, since as we all know, there are several schools of legal interpretation (*madhahib*). Therefore, these Shariʿa Penal Codes of the Northern States give an incorrect impression of what the Shariʿa really is, since they are based on a selection of several options offered by the various schools of jurisprudence.

14 See Mitchell, R.P., *The Society of the Muslim Brothers*, (London: Oxford University Press, 1969) 240–1, quoting Hasan al-Bannaʾ, Sayyid Qutb, and ʿAbd al-Qadir ʿAwda.

Moreover, the Shari'a is not a static body of rules, laid down once and for all by the jurists of the early centuries of Islam. Most authoritative Muslim scholars would nowadays agree that the obligation of *taqlid* (i.e. following the authoritative opinions of a School of Jurisprudence, without testing the arguments for such opinions) is now obsolete. However, *taqlid* of the Malikite opinions is exactly what those who drafted the Nigerian Shari'a Penal codes, have done. A view generally shared by a great number (and maybe a majority) of present-day Muslim scholars is that the Shari'a is a legal system suitable for all times and places. Some of its principles are fixed and unchangeable but the details can be adapted. Since society changes, this requires a continuous dialogue with the revealed sources of the Shari'a, i.e. the Koran and the Sunna, by means of ijtihad. This is a collective duty (*fard kifaya*) for the Muslim community.

If one regards this new *ijtihad* as too daring, it is possible to reformulate the codes by remaining within the orbit of the opinions accepted by the various schools of jurisprudence. This is the way in which in most Muslim countries nowadays family law and the law of succession have been reformed. The codes of personal status that have been enacted in the overwhelming majority of Muslim countries, have selected those opinions that were deemed to be most in consonance with the modern circumstances. Thus countries where the Hanafite doctrine was applied by the courts, the law codes have introduced parts of the Malikite law in order to expand the possibilities for wives to obtain a divorce, whereas some Malikite countries have adopted the Hanafite doctrine that legally capable women always must give their consent to marriage, even if they marry for the first time. In some cases these codes have introduced new interpretations based on *ijtihad*. Thus we find that in Egypt, since the year 2000, women can claim a divorce on the strength of *khul'*, even against their husbands' will. What this demonstrates is that it is regarded as perfectly acceptable in the world of Islam, to make creative use of the variety of opinions and even to use *ijtihad*, taking the notion of the common good (*maslaha*) as a guideline in order to reach socially desirable solutions.

Many codes of personal status that have been enacted in the Islamic world have introduced minimum ages for concluding a marriage, although this was not known in the classical doctrine. This reform was inspired by the idea of *maslaha*, since large parts of the population regarded child marriages as socially undesirable. A similar step could be taken in the Shari'a Penal Codes: restricting criminal responsibility for *hadd* offences and homicide and wounding to those older than eighteen years, which would then make these codes more in agreement with the International Convention on the Rights of the Child.

That enforcement of Shari'a penal law under the present circumstances does not just mean the slavish following of the texts of medieval Islamic jurists is gradually accepted even in countries where Shariʿa criminal has been codified, such as Iran and Pakistan. I will give a few examples to show that the scope for discussion is much larger that is usually thought.

One of the issues that have been widely discussed is the question of whether the penalty of stoning is really a *hadd* punishment. The problem is that it is not mentioned in the Koran. Koran 24:2 reads:

> (*Al-zaniya wa-l-zani fa-jlidu kulla wahidin minhuma miʾata jaldatin.*) Men and women who have unlawful intercourse, scourge ye each one of them (with) a hundred stripes. And let not pity for the twain withhold you from obedience to Allah, if ye believe in Allah and the Last Day. And let a party of believers witness their punishment. (K. 24:2)

When Libya introduced Shariʿa criminal codes in the early 1970s, unlawful sexual intercourse was not made punishable by stoning with the argument that stoning to death is not mentioned in the Koran. In the same vein, the Pakistani Federal Shariat Court ruled that the law imposing stoning as a punishment for unlawful intercourse was inoperative, as it was repugnant to the injunctions of Islam. The Pakistani Constitution lays down that laws are inoperative if they are repugnant to the injunctions of Islam. Unfortunately the decision was revoked when the President of the Republic interfered and replaced a number of judges in the court with more conservative ones. However, in spite of this, the punishment of stoning has never been enforced in Pakistan.

Even in Iran, which is regarded as one of the most conservative Islamic countries, such debates take place. Lately, a discussion about stoning was initiated and on 29 December 2002, the head of the judiciary ordered the courts not to pronounce sentences of stoning. This seems to have been the result of a campaign launched by a number of female MPs and fatwas pronounced by leading ayatollahs. Another issue that was discussed there was whether the differentiation in the blood price between men, women and non-Muslims is justified. As a result a draft bill has been introduced removing the difference in blood price between Muslims and Christians.

These examples show that even in countries that are regarded as conservative in applying the Shariʿa, debates take place on the assumption that the exact contents of the Shariʿa have to be determined according to the circumstances of time and place.

4.2 *The Role of the Judiciary*

One of the most serious problems that accompanied the introduction of the Shariʿa penal codes in Nigeria was the fact that the judiciary was not yet sufficiently equipped to enforce these laws. And this was the more serious because the new penal codes contained many gaps that had to be filled through case law. It is striking that in both the Safiyyatu Hussaini case and in the Amina Lawal case the sentences of the trial courts were quashed mainly on technical and procedural grounds. This, I am afraid, is indicative for the state of knowledge of Shari'a criminal law and procedure among the lower court *alkalis*. A number of elementary rules are expressed in the following hadith:

> A Muslim man came to the Prophet when he was in the mosque and shouted to him: "O Messenger of God, I have had illegal sexual relations." The Prophet then turned away from him. But the man moved in order to face him and said: "O Messenger of God, I have had illegal sexual relations." Again the Prophet turned away, until he had repeated it four times. After he had testified against himself four times, the Prophet called at him: Are you perhaps a bit insane? The man answered no. Then he asked: Have you ever been married. The man answered yes. Then the Prophet said: take him away and stone him.

From the sentences I have just mentioned, it appears that these lower court alkalis, did not even follow these basic rules stating that the court, before sentencing, must actively ascertain whether there are any legal defences and should not leave that to the defendant.

Legislative reform then cannot be successful unless the judges that must apply the laws have been better trained in the new codes and, even more importantly, in the spirit of Shari'a criminal law. There are so many hadiths expressing reluctance of the Prophet Mohammed and the Well Guided Caliphs in applying *hadd* penalties. The best known is the saying: "Ward off the fixed punishments on the strength of *shubha* as much as you can.' (*udru'u al-hudud bi-l-shubuhat ma istata'tum*).[15] In order to fully implement this principle, Northern Nigeria might follow the example of Pakistan. Here, sentences for *hadd* offences and sentences of retaliation must be confirmed by the Federal Shariat Court. Since this court very strictly applies the law of *hadd* and retaliation, no sentences of amputation, stoning, mutilation for wounding and crucifixion have ever been carried out. This is a very important step, since the Federal Court does not hear the case by way of appeal, conditional on whether the defendant has lodged an appeal, but as a legal obligation without which such sentences cannot be executed. A similar institution in Northern Nigeria

15 Ibn Hajr al-'Asqalani, *Bulugh al-maram min adillat al-ahkam* (Cairo: Dar al-Kitab al-'Arabi, n.d.), no. 1044.

would be beneficial. It could remedy the shortcomings of the lower courts and secure a more correct application of the law.

5 Conclusions

I will briefly summarise my findings with regard to the possible solutions for the conflicts between the present Shariʿa Penal Codes and the human rights guaranteed by the federal constitution. What I wanted to show is that the present stalemate can be overcome and that the claim of some Northern Muslims that the present Shariʿa Penal Codes are identical with Gods law and, therefore, cannot be changed is incorrect and can be refuted if we take a look at the Muslim world at large and especially at such countries as have recently reintroduced Shariʿa legislation.

My point of departure is, as many Islamic scholars have asserted, that the Shariʿa is a flexible and adaptable doctrine of law. It is a collective duty of Muslim scholars of every age to exercise *ijtihad* and search for new interpretations, taking into account the specific circumstances of their period and thus develop a viable legal system that can be applied in their time. This idea is contrary to what the legislators of the Northern states have done when they codified Shariʿa penal law. For they went back to the classical Malikite doctrine, which they thus slavishly adopted, without taking into account the requirements of this age and place, and, especially, the position of the Northern states in the Nigerian federation.

In trying to reformulate Shariʿa criminal law and achieve a greater compliance with human rights standards without abandoning the principle of application of the Shariʿa, three strategies might be followed:

1. Drafting a Shariʿa penal code with the provision that the *hadd* penalties will only be applied when all citizens re free of want
2. Drafting a penal code incorporating only the very few immutable and unambiguous source texts and further elaborated through ijtihad.
3. Drafting a Shariʿa penal code on the basis of the doctrines of the four (or five, if we include the Imami Shiites) schools of jurisprudence, selecting those provisions that are most in consonance with the modern times and in case of need, supplemented by provisions based on ijtihad.

But whichever of these strategies will be chosen, a prerequisite is a better training of the judges of the lower courts, who sometimes are overzealous in enforcing Shariʿa punishments but lack the knowledge required for adjudicating in matters of *hudud* and retaliation. In an Egyptian theft case tried in 1862, a lower qadi had sentenced two defendants to amputation of the right hand. The sentence was quashed by the High Court, which reprimanded the qadi and the mufti who confirmed the decision, saying that

> they ought to have been very cautious with regard to this kind of judgement and only have ventured to pronounce it after having reached complete certainty, for in this type of cases a sentence of amputation must not be pronounced like they did, by [only] dipping the fingertips in the sea of Abu Hanifa's jurisprudence.[16]

After nearly a century and a half, this warning has lost nothing of its aptness.

---

16 See R. Peters, "Islamic and secular criminal law in 19th century Egypt: the role and function of the qadi." *Islamic Law and Society*, 4 (1997), pp. 70–90.

CHAPTER 30

The Enforcement of God's Law

The Shariʿah in the Present World of Islam

1 Introduction

In the early nineteenth century, the *Shariʿah* was the law of the land in the larger part of the Muslim world. This changed as a result of a process of Westernisation that set in during the second half of that century and affected the extent to which the *Shariʿah* was applied by the courts and the way this was done. In this paper I want to examine to what extent the *Shariʿah* nowadays plays a role in the national legal systems in the Muslim world. In the following, I will focus on the phenomenon of codification of the *Shariʿah*. This is because this is a very recent phenomenon in Nigeria. Elsewhere, however, the first *Shariʿah* codes were already introduced more than 130 years ago.

2 The Westernisation of Legal Systems in the Muslim World

In this section I'll briefly sketch the process of legal Westernisation in the Islamic world. I'll start with a description of the principal characteristics of the *Shariʿah* and will then show how the process of Westernisation not only made parts of the *Shariʿah* inoperative, but also affected the *Shariʿah* itself as a result of codification.

2.1 *The Nature of the Shariʿa*

2.1.1 The *Shariʿah* as Religious Law

Muslims regard the *Shariʿah* as an expression of God's will. In this it is very different from modern Western law, which is seen as a purely human phenomenon, based either on conscious acts of the legislature or the judiciary, or on unconscious collective acts such as the gradual creation of customary law. The classical texts of Islamic jurisprudence define the *Shariʿah* as: "The rules given by God to His servants as set forth by one of the prophets (may God bless them and grant them salvation)."[1] A swift glance at the tables of contents of the standard legal text books shows that they begin with purely religious topics like ritual prayer and fasting, before embarking on the discussion of the issues that

1 Tahanawi, 1864, i, 759.

 | DOI:10.1163/9789004420625_031

are legal in the Western sense of the word, such as the contract of sale, legal capacity, succession, and criminal law. The *Shariʿah* is therefore religious law, but this does not tell us very much. There are many different types of religious law. If we want to say something meaningful about the *Shariʿah* as religious law, we must be more specific and define its religious character. This, I would argue, consists in two features: the fact that the basis of its validity is God's will, and the fact that the *Shariʿah* also contains rules of a purely religious character.

In order to inform mankind of His commands, God, according to Muslim doctrine, has sent down revelations to successive prophets, the last of whom was Muhammad. To him the Qur'an was revealed. The contents of the Qur'an were supplemented by the Prophet's exemplary behaviour, the Sunnah, which, after his decease, was transmitted by generations of Muslims and, ultimately, compiled in the *hadith* collections. These are the divine sources of the *Shariʿah* and, therefore, the foundation of its validity. This divine basis of the law may be compared with Kelsen's *Grundnorm*, the extra-legal norm explaining why laws are binding.[2]

A large part of the *Shariʿah* is law as understood in the West. The rules of this domain of the *Shariʿah* deal with the legal effects of certain acts or events and discuss the creation and extinction of rights and obligations between individuals and between the individual and the community. Here we find for instance the law of sale, of marriage, of tort, of procedure, laws that can be enforced by the qadi if the relevant facts can be established in court. However, the *Shariʿah* is also envisioned as a set of norms constituting the code of behaviour of a good Muslim, a guide to attain eternal bliss in Paradise. This representation of the *Shariʿah* emphasises its religious character and focuses on the Hereafter, i.e. on whether, after one's death, one can expect to be rewarded or punished for certain acts. This is done by classifying them into five categories (obligatory, commendable, indifferent, reprehensible and forbidden) indicating their effects as far as reward and punishment are concerned. Performing an obligatory act results in reward, whereas neglecting it will be punished. Committing a forbidden act will entail punishment in the hereafter, and avoiding it will be rewarded. This applies not only to purely religious obligations, such as praying, fasting or dietary prescriptions, but also to legal ones, such as the obligation to pay one's debts. This part of the *Shariʿah* falls outside the qadi's competence. It is the exclusive domain of the mufti, the legal expert whose guidance is sought by individual Muslims in matters of the *Shariʿah*, but whose opinions are not binding, unlike the sentences pronounced by qadis.

2 On Kelsen, see Kelly, 1992, 384–8.

The following passage, taken from a seventeenth-century legal handbook that was popular in the Ottoman Empire, may help elucidate the double-sided character of the *Shariʿah*:

> **It is not reprehensible to lease out a house in the countryside** (i.e. in a village) **if it will subsequently be used as a Zoroastrian temple, a church or a monk's cell, or if wine will be sold in it** ... (at least according to the Imam [Abu Hanifa (d. 767)], because the lease confers the right to use the house and there is no sin in that. The sin is related to acts committed by the lessee of his own accord. That means that the relationship [between the landlord and the sin] is interrupted, just like in the case of the sale of a slave girl ... to a person who wants to have anal intercourse with her, or the sale of a young slave to a homosexual ...). **According to his companions** [al-Shaybani (d. 805) and Abu Yusuf (d. 798)] **it is indeed reprehensible** (to lease a house for such a use, because it promotes sin. The other three imams are of the same opinion ...). **There is agreement [among the imams] that such a lease is reprehensible in a village or a region inhabited mainly by Muslims.**[3]

Here the authors discuss an aspect of the law of lease. However, their concern in this passage is not whether or not under the given conditions such a contract is valid and binding, but whether a Muslim who concludes such a contract will be punished in the Hereafter because it is religiously reprehensible.

2.1.2 The *Shariʿah* as Jurists' Law

A second feature of the *Shariʿah* is that it is a jurists' law and that the jurists and not the state had the exclusive authority to formulate the rules of the *Shariʿah*. They did so in a scholarly, academic debate, in which conflicting and often contradictory views were opposed and discussed. Actually, we must use a more precise terminology and distinguish between the *Shariʿah* and the *fiqh*. If the *Shariʿah* is God's law, the *fiqh* is the scholarly discipline aimed at formulating the prescriptions of the *Shariʿah*, on the basis of the revealed texts and using various hermeneutic devices. What we find in the *fiqh* texts is the jurists' approximation to the divine law. Because of differences in understanding the texts and in the use of the hermeneutic tools, the *Shariʿah* as laid down by the jurists in the *fiqh* is not uniform. From the beginning there were differences of

3 Shaykhzade (d. 1667) and Ibrahim al-Halabi (d. 1549), 1884 (1301 H), ii, 417. The passages in bold print are the translation of al-Halabi's elementary textbook; the remainder is Shaykhzade's commentary.

opinion that resulted in the emergence of different schools of jurisprudence (*madhhab*, plur. *madhahib*), that ascribed their doctrines to and derived their names from famous jurists from the eighth and ninth centuries. Controversies not only existed between these schools, but also among the jurists of single schools, even on essential legal issues. The following passage, taken from the same Ottoman handbook quoted above, discusses the various opinions within the Hanafite school of jurisprudence on the question of whether a woman who is legally capable, may conclude her own marriage contract:

> **Marriage concluded by a free woman … of full legal capacity** (irrespective of whether or not she is a virgin) **is valid** (even if such a marriage is concluded without the consent and presence of a matrimonial guardian. This is the authoritative opinion of Abu Hanifa [d. 767] and Abu Yusuf [d. 798]. This is so because she disposes of something to which she is exclusively entitled by being sound of mind and of age. For this reason she is entitled to dispose of her property and the principle here is that whoever may dispose of his property by his own right may conclude his own marriage and whoever may not [dispose of his property by his own right], may not [conclude his own marriage].... According to the other *madhhab*s marriage cannot be concluded by a woman …). **However, the marriage guardian** (that is anyone of them as long as no one has given his consent) **is entitled to object [to such a marriage]** (that is he has the power to submit it to the judge for annulment.... The annulment is only effective by a judgement of the court since it is a matter of appreciation. Until such a judgement is pronounced the marriage is valid and the spouses inherit from one another if one of them should die before the judgement.). **If the husband is not her coequal (*kuf'*)** (This is to avert damage and disgrace. If one of the matrimonial guardians has approved of the marriage, those who stand in the same or in a more distant degree [to her] cannot object anymore. This right [of objection] continues until she gives birth.... This rule can be found in most authoritative works. However, according to a less authoritative opinion this right of objection continues even after she has given birth to several children....) **Hasan ibn Ziyad [d. 819] has reported from the Imam [Abu Hanifa] that it is not valid** (that is that such a marriage is not valid if she marries herself without a matrimonial guardian to a man who is not her coequal. Many of our scholars have adopted this rule since many cases are not submitted to judges.) **and Qadikhan [d. 1196] has issued fatwas according to this opinion.** (This opinion is more correct and cautious and therefore preferable for fatwas in our days because not every matrimonial guardian

> is proficient in litigation and not every judge is just....) **According to Muhammad [al-Shaybani, d. 805] such a marriage is concluded conditionally** (i.e. subject to approval by the matrimonial guardian) **even if the husband is her coequal.** (If a marriage is contracted conditionally this means that before approval sexual intercourse is not allowed, that a repudiation is void and that they do not inherit from one another ...)[4]

Here we see that within the Hanafite school of jurisprudence there are three conflicting rules with regard to the marriage of a legally capable woman concluded on her own accord. According to one opinion she is fully entitled to do so, except that in case of a misalliance (*zawaj bi-ghayr kuf'*) her agnatic male relatives may petition the qadi for an annulment. A second opinion holds that such a misalliance is per se invalid, whereas according to the third view all marriages concluded by legally capable women need the ratification of their marriage guardians.

This passage, which could be replaced by many other ones to illustrate the same point, is typical of the books on Islamic jurisprudence. They juxtapose different opinions on the same issue and it would appear that the legitimacy of dissent is one of the essential characteristics of the *fiqh*. There are several classical works of comparative *fiqh* in which the controversies are discussed and explained in terms of different interpretations of Qur'anic texts or Prophetic sayings, or the application of different hermeneutic tools.

As illustrated by this passage, *fiqh* texts do not resemble law codes. They contain scholarly discussions, and are therefore open, discursive, and contradictory. This discussion is the monopoly of the religious scholars, the *ulama*. Because of their religious training they have the prerogative of formulating the law on the basis of the revealed texts. Although in the early history of Islam this prerogative was contested by the rulers and state officials, the *ulama* ultimately emerged victorious.

2.2 *Westernisation and Codification of the Law*

During the nineteenth century, the Western powers brought large parts of the Islamic world under their sway. In some regions this resulted in conquest and colonial rule; in others, Western influence was exerted through economic pressure (many states in the Middle East were heavily in debt to Western powers), unequal trade relations, and gunboat diplomacy. In either case, legal change took place: in the colonies it was imposed, in various forms, by the colonial powers; in the semi-independent countries it was introduced by their own

4 Ibid., i, 320–321.

governments under Western pressure. Only in those regions where Western impact was minimal, such as on the Arabian Peninsula, did the *Shariʿah* legal system persist without any restrictions. Northern Nigeria was a special case: there the form of indirect rule introduced by the British at the beginning of the twentieth century included the comprehensive preservation of Islamic justice, as long as it was not repugnant to British notions of natural justice, equity, and good conscience. This meant that the *Shariʿah* was applied within boundaries set by British administrators and courts.

Westernising legal reform was nearly everywhere based on a concept of law that, until then, was unknown in the Islamic world: the notion of law as the expression of the will of the state, in the form of enacted codes. With the exception of Great Britain,[5] the colonial powers introduced, in the colonies they ruled, law codes based on those of the metropolis. In Muslim lands, only the law of personal status continued to be governed by the *Shariʿah*, and even here the law courts applying the *Shariʿah* were controlled by the colonial powers. In the parts of the Islamic world that were not or not yet colonised, legal Westernisation was a part of the modernisation of the state. This process was most in evidence in the Ottoman Empire and its dependencies like Egypt and Tunis. In other parts of the Islamic world, such as Morocco and Iran, modernisation, including legal Westernisation, started much later. In the following I will focus on the Ottoman Empire, which can serve as an example for what happened in many other parts of the Islamic world.

The notion of the *Shariʿah* as religious, divine law, monopolised by the *ulama*, would *prima facie* seem to be contradictory to and incompatible with the existence of state-enacted law. However, this was not the case, at least not in the Ottoman Empire. As from the fifteenth century the sultans began to enact regulations (*qanun*) dealing with land law and fiscal and criminal law. These regulations did not replace the *Shariʿah* in the fields to which they applied; rather, they supplemented it where it was silent or did not give precise rules. This legislation was regarded as part of the Islamic legal order and not as being in conflict with the *Shariʿah*. The enactment of these codes did not imply that the state had the monopoly of law-making, nor that state-enacted law was of a higher order that other types of law.

5 The common law tradition of Great Britain, based on custom and case law, caused the British to proceed differently from other colonial powers in legal matters. They preferred not to legislate but to apply the local law (including the *Shariʿah*), but under the supervision of British administrators and courts that would regard as ineffective those laws that were repugnant to "natural justice, equity and good conscience". Only gradually did the British replace the local laws by enacted law.

Codification, on the other hand, is based on an altogether different concept, for codification presupposes that the state enacts legislation that completely regulates a certain domain of the law, "covering the field" to the exclusion of all other types of law previously applicable in that field (unless the codification itself confers force of law on such other types, as is sometimes done in the case of custom). Codification therefore implies that only the state determines what law is and that state-enacted law is the highest form of law. This notion of codification has its origins in the European civil code tradition of the early nineteenth century.

In the Ottoman Empire codification began in the second half of the nineteenth century. During the era of reform (Tanzimat period, 1839–1876) the ideas on the relationship between the state and the law had begun to change. Tanzimat reform was very much administrative and legal reform, and legislation became one of its most important instruments. The first reform decree, the Gülhane Rescript (1839) emphasises the importance of legislation:

> In order to better administer the Sublime Empire (*Devlet-i ʿAliyye*) and the Well-Protected Dominions (*Memalik-i Mahruse*), it is deemed necessary and important to enact some new laws. The most important provisions of these indispensable laws consist of more personal safety, of a better protection of honour, decency and property, of fixing the taxes and specifying the way of drafting the required soldiers and the period of their service.[6]

Codification was not only an instrument of reform, but also of centralisation and legal unification. Under the influence of Western, continental, constitutional notions, the Ottoman ruling elite became convinced of the necessity of codification of all domains of the law, so as to emphasise that the state should determine what the law of the land was. As a consequence, commercial (1850) and penal (1858) codes were introduced based on European models. Law cases in these fields were thenceforth heard by newly created courts and withdrawn from the competence of the *Shariʿah* courts. In Egypt, this happened three decades later when, in 1883, the whole legal system, with the exception of personal status, was Westernised by the introduction of a new court system and French-oriented law codes.

However, it was also deemed necessary to modernise existing law, i.e. the *Shariʿah* and customary law. Examples of the codification of traditional law are the Ottoman Penal Codes of 1840 and 1851 (abolished by the European type

6 Text in *Düstur*, 1865–66, i, 2–3.

Ottoman Penal Code of 1858), the Land Law of 1858, the *Mecelle*, the Ottoman Civil Code based on Hanafite *fiqh* enacted between 1868 and 1876, and, finally, the Code of Family Law (*Hukuk-i 'A'ile Kararnamesi*) of 1917. Behind this movement was the Western notion that traditional law, as found in the various books of *fiqh*, in administrative practices, and in custom, was "chaotic and inaccessible" and that "codification is civilisation". The need for codification was especially felt when new courts were established in which not all judges had a training in Islamic jurisprudence:

Islamic jurisprudence, then, is an immense

> ocean and in order to find solutions for problems by bringing to its surface the pearls of the topics required [for solving the problems] needs an enormous skill and mastery. And especially for the Hanafite *madhhab*, there were, in subsequent generations, very many independent interpreters (*mujtahid*) and there emerged many controversies so that Hanafite jurisprudence, like Shafi'ite jurisprudence, has branched out and become diverse to the extent that it cannot anymore be examined carefully. Therefore it is tremendously difficult to distinguish the correct opinion among the various views and to apply it to the cases.... Therefore, if a book on legal transactions (*mu'amalat*) were to be composed that is easy to consult being free from controversies and containing only the preferred opinions, then everybody could read it easily and apply it to his transactions.[7]

During the same period there emerged also semi-official codifications, i.e. private compilations of the rules of the *Shari'ah* in some fields, arranged in sections like law codes and presenting these rules in a conveniently arranged fashion so that they could be used as easy reference tools for legal practitioners. In Egypt Muhammad Qadri Pasha (d. 1889), former minister of justice, composed compilations on family law, the law of property, and contracts and waqf law, which were published between 1875 and 1890.[8] These compilations had a semi-official status in those fields of law that continued to be governed by the *Shari'ah* after the reforms of 1883, when French civil, commercial, criminal and procedural law was adopted. In the Ottoman Empire, 'Ömer Hilmi, a former president of the Court of Cassation, composed an authoritative compilation of the law of homicide and personal injury, a part of criminal law that

7 From the explanatory memorandum of the first book of the Mecelle (1868), quoted in Kaşıkçı, 1997, 75–6.

8 Qadri Pasha, 1909[a], 1893, and 1909[b].

was still enforced by the *Shari'ah* courts.[9] The French, ruling North Africa, commissioned Marcel Morand, a French specialist in Islamic law, to compile a code of the Malikite doctrine of personal status.[10]

If one compares the *fiqh* texts on a certain legal issue with the codified provisions, the differences are striking. As I said before, the *fiqh* doctrine is jurists' law and the *fiqh* texts are discursive and include various, often conflicting opinions on the issue. They are open texts in the sense that they do not offer final solutions. Provisions of a law code, on the other hand, must be authoritative, clear and unequivocal. In a law code there is no room for contradictory opinions or argumentation and its provisions must be definitive and final. Therefore, choices have to be made when codifying the *Shari'ah*. This will become clear when we compare the codified provisions of the Hanafite doctrine regarding the marriage of a legally capable woman with the *fiqh* text on the same subject quoted above.

> *Muhammad Qadri's Compilation* (*ca.1875*):
> If [a free and legally capable woman] concludes a marriage with someone who is socially her inferior (*ghayr kuf'*) without her agnatic guardian's express consent before the marriage, then that marriage is per se invalid and the guardian's consent given after the conclusion of the marriage is of no avail. If she has no agnatic guardian and marries herself to a person who is socially her inferior or if her guardian has consented to her marriage with a socially inferior man, then the marriage is valid.[11]
>
> *The Ottoman Code of Family Law* (*1917*):
> If a woman of full age marries herself without informing her matrimonial guardian and without having obtained his consent, then the matter must be examined. If she has married herself to a person who is socially her equal, then the marriage is binding even if the bride price is less than her proper bride price. However, if she has married herself to someone who is socially her inferior, then the guardian can have recourse to the judge for rescission of the marriage.[12]

Both these code sections contain clear and unequivocal legal rules. The dissenting opinions that existed in the *fiqh* text quoted previously have been

9 Hilmi, 1881–1882.
10 See Schacht, 1964, 98.
11 Qadri Pasha, 1909[a], Section 52.
12 *Huquq-i 'A'ile Qararnamesi* (1917), Section 47.

excised, in order to produce one authoritative, final statement of the law. But, if we read the two code sections carefully, it will be evident that the authors of these texts have made different choices. Muhammad Qadri Pasha followed the more conservative view, attributed to Abu Hanifa by Hasan ibn Ziyad, which was the prevailing view in the Ottoman Empire. The Ottoman legislator of 1917, however, followed another authoritative Hanafite opinion, also ascribed to Abu Hanifa, that was more favourable to women. These two texts clearly illustrate the effects of codification: the transformation from a scholarly discourse in which different and opposing opinions are juxtaposed, to an authoritative, definitive statement of the law, purged of all alternative views. But this is not the only effect. The adoption of the Western concept of the law code also means the adoption of the Western concept of law. As a result, the religious norms are also eliminated from the *Shari'ah* codes. Codified *Shari'ah*, then, is no more that an impoverished, reduced version of the rich *fiqh* doctrine.

When states during the second half of the nineteenth century assumed the power to define the *Shari'ah*, the role of the *ulama* did not end completely. Their co-operation was essential in order to legitimise the state-enacted *Shari'ah* codes. But more importantly, they were needed for their expertise. This explains the pivotal role of men like Ahmed Cevdet (1822–1895) in legal reforms. Trained as religious scholars and having an open eye for reform, they staffed the committees that prepared the codifications of the *Shari'ah*. The necessary participation of the *ulama* limited in practice the freedom of the state in codifying the *Shari'ah*. They had the power to refuse to participate if the state should enact laws that they would regard as repugnant to the *Shari'ah*. Such a step would greatly undermine the legitimacy of codifications of the *Shari'ah*.

3 The Present Situation

In the course of the twentieth century the Westernisation of the legal systems in the Islamic world continued, by the adoption of Western substantive and adjective laws and Western notions of law. However, in most national legal systems, the *Shari'ah* still has a role to play. These roles vary and we can classify these legal systems in four types according to the position of the *Shari'ah* in them.

- The completely secularised legal systems, from which the *Shari'ah* has been removed.
- The legal systems that are dominated by the *Shari'ah*, in the sense that the *Shari'ah* is the supreme law of the land and that state legislation can only take place in areas where the *Shari'ah* is silent or not unequivocal.

- The legal systems in which *Shariʿah* is applied in some domains, but within a Western constitutional and administrative framework. This is the most common type. Usually the domain left to the *Shariʿah* is the field of personal status (family law, law of succession) and the law of *waqf*, although in Northern Nigeria, other private transactions may also be governed by the *Shariʿah* at the election of the parties. However, nearly everywhere, the law in these fields has been codified.[13] In its uncodified form, *Shariʿah* rules are enforced only in Northern Nigeria and Egypt. In Nigeria there was, before 2000, no codification of the *Shariʿah* at all; in Egypt, family law and the law of succession have been only partially codified and uncodified *Shariʿah* is applied on all issues for which there is no enacted law.
- Finally there are those legal systems that have been re-Islamised. They developed out of systems of the previous type, after Islamist regimes came to power. This re-Islamisation was implemented by introducing Islamic law codes in many fields, noticeably in that of criminal law. This type of legal system exists in Iran, Sudan, and, to some extent, in Libya. Outside the Middle East we find it in Pakistan and in twelve Northern, predominantly Muslim states of the Nigerian federation.[14]

3.1 *The Completely Secularised Legal Systems*

The most prominent example of a completely secularised legal system exists in Turkey, as a result of the radical Westernisation policies of Atatürk, which resulted in drastic law reform in the 1920s. If *Shariʿah* still plays a role, it is at the informal level. For a long time, rural Turks would regulate their family life and inheritance according to the *Shariʿah* without recourse to the state law. Since Islamic marriages and births within those marriages were often not registered, this compelled the state, on several occasions, to issue regularisation laws.

3.2 *The Completely Islamic Legal Systems*

In those geographical regions that were not of interest to the West, or where the interest did not emerge until very late in the twentieth century, the *Shariʿah* remained the law of the land. This is the case in Yemen and in Saudi Arabia.[15] In Yemen most of the *Shariʿah*-based laws have by now been codified. This is not the case in Saudi Arabia, which has the purest form of a traditional Islamic

13 For the modernization of the law of personal status, see Ebert, 1996 and Beck-Peccoz, 1990.

14 For the Islamization of criminal law, see Peters, 1994; on Nigeria in particular see Peters, 2003.

15 On Saudi Arabia, see Vogel, 2000.

legal system in the world: the *Shari'ah* is applied by the courts by having recourse to the classical Hanbalite texts and no codification of *Shari'ah* law has been undertaken. Only in those fields where the *Shari'ah* is silent, such as with regard to company law or traffic law, has the state issued regulations, which, as a rule, are not enforced by the *Shari'ah* courts, but by special councils or commissions. The only *Shari'ah* rules that have been codified are the fiscal decrees on the zakat tax (Royal decree 17/2/28i/8634 of 29 Safar 1370 (7 April 1951).

3.3 Shari'ah *Application within the Framework of Westernised Legal Systems*

In the majority of Muslim countries, the legal systems have been Westernised by the introduction of Western type law codes, a Western type constitution and a Western type judiciary. The domain of personal status, however, continues to be governed by the *Shari'ah*, but within a Westernised legal order and usually in a codified form. In some countries, such as Egypt (since 1956), the *Shari'ah*, to the extent it is operative, is applied by the regular judiciary (the national courts). In other countries the *Shari'ah* is applied by special *Shari'ah* courts, in many cases functioning side by side with Christian ecclesiastical and Jewish courts in matters of personal status.

The most conspicuous change in this domain was the codification of the law of personal status (see Appendix 1). This was prompted by various motives:

- The wish to create greater legal security
- by removing ambiguities in the legal doctrine and thus facilitating the application of the *Shari'ah* by the courts, and
- by creating greater clarity about the civil status of persons (marriage, divorce, filiation), by introducing obligatory registration.
- The wish to introduce reforms of the substantive law (such as: minimum age for marriage, abolition of forced marriages, restriction of polygamy, introducing more grounds for obtaining divorce by women) with the aim of strengthening the rights of women.

In order to confer greater legitimacy on the reforms in the substantive law, the legislators took care to remain within the orbit of the *Shari'ah*. This was achieved by using the following expedients:

- Using adjective or penal law to realise a certain objective, without changing the substantive law of the *Shari'ah*. E.g. making child marriages punishable offences for the parents of the minor spouse and for the other spouse, if adult; or forbidding marriage registrars to register marriages in case one of the spouses has not reached a certain age and at the same time introducing the rule that marriages can only be proven by marriage documents issued by an official registrar. Another example is that in some countries polygamous marriages may only be registered after the court has been satisfied that the husband has a lawful reason for such a marriage and is financially able to support all wives.

- By selecting those opinions from the various schools of jurisprudence that are most conducive to the aims of the legislator. This was used in Hanafite countries when they introduced the Malikite grounds for divorce with the aim of extending the possibilities for women to end their marriages; and in Malikite countries, when they introduced the Hanafite rule that legally capable women always must give their consent to a marriage, and cannot be forced into a marriage by their fathers or grandfathers.
- By using *ijtihad*, i.e. a new interpretation of the relevant texts of the Qur'an and *hadith*. This was done, for example, when the Tunisian government, in 1956, abolished polygamy. The legislators argued that Q 4:3[16] in combination with 4:129[17] actually implied a ban on polygamy.

In some countries of this group the constitution stipulates that the principles of the *Shari'ah* are the main source of legislation. Such provisions were inserted into several constitutions by ruling elites to take the wind out of the sails of the Islamist opposition. So far little comparative research has been done on the effect of these provisions. In Egypt, which has one of them (Section 2 of the Egyptian constitution as amended in 1979), its effect is very limited. On the one hand, the Supreme Constitutional Court has interpreted Section 2 to mean that legislation enacted after 1979 which is in conflict with *Shari'ah* principles is unconstitutional. But in applying Section 2, the Court has measured challenged legislation only against those rare injunctions of the *Shari'ah* that are based on clear, unambiguous and unchangeable texts of the Qur'an and Sunnah that are not subject to interpretation. The result is that no legislation challenged under Section 2 has yet been overturned.

3.4 *Re-Islamised Legal Systems*

Since the 1970s the legal systems of a number of Islamic countries have been re-Islamised, by replacing Western type law codes by new ones based on the *Shari'ah*. (For a survey of the recent *Shari'ah* legislation, see Appendix 2.) This took place in various political contexts:

---

16 "And if ye fear that ye will not deal fairly by the orphans, marry of the women, who seem good to you, two or three or four; and if ye fear that ye cannot do justice (to so many) then one (only) or (the captives) that your right hands possess. Thus it is more likely that ye will not do injustice."

17 "Ye will not be able to deal equally between (your) wives, however much ye wish (to do so). But turn not altogether away (from one), leaving her as in suspense. If ye do good and keep from evil, lo! Allah is ever Forgiving, Merciful."

- after an Islamic revolution, such as in Iran (1979)
- after a coup d'état, for which Islam was used as a legitimisation (Pakistan, 1979)
- after a policy change of a sitting regime (Libya, 1972–3, Sudan, 1985)
- after popular pressure resulting in legislation passed by democratically elected legislative organs (twelve states of Northern Nigeria, from 2000 onwards)

When Islamist movements gained strength in the Muslim world, the prevailing Westernised legal systems came under attack. The Islamists wanted to establish an Islamic state and the main characteristic of an Islamic state was, for them, the enforcement of the *Sharīʿah* in all domains, including, of course, criminal law. In their view, full application of the *Sharīʿah* had come to an end when the Western colonial powers invaded the Muslim world and imposed Western laws. The introduction of the *Sharīʿah* became the rallying cry of many of the religiously inspired political movements. The idea of going back to the cultural roots and of imposing Islamic norms on society was appealing to large segments of the population that were opposed to the increasing Western political and cultural influence.

In 1972 Muʿammar al-Gaddafi surprised the world by announcing that he had re-introduced the *Sharīʿah* provisions on theft and robbery, making these offences punishable by amputation. Observers of the Arab and Muslim world were puzzled, since this return to Islamic criminal law did not fit in the prevailing modernisation theories that were based on the assumption of a continuous and unstoppable spread of secularisation. Most of these observers regarded Islamic criminal law as something of the past, enforced only in backward countries like Saudi Arabia, where, they believed, it would in due course disappear under the influence of modernity. Nobody expected that Gaddafi had inaugurated a trend and that from the 1970s more Muslim countries would adopt Islamic penal codes.

The re-introduction of Islamic criminal law is surrounded by a powerful ideological discourse, that was shaped by the propagandists of Islamism but has its roots in deeply felt religious convictions and emotions. The crucial element is that Muslims, in order to be good Muslims, must live in an Islamic state, a state which implements the *Sharīʿah*. It is not sufficient that such a state gives Muslims the choice whether or not they follow the *Sharīʿah*; it must actually impose the *Sharīʿah* on them, by implementing Islamic criminal law. Preaching and admonition do not suffice and a big stick is needed to change behaviour in an Islamic direction. Islamic criminal law is a tool to impose an Islamic moral order on society, by imposing rigorous rules, especially in the fields of sexual morality, the consumption of alcohol and drugs, and blasphemy and un-Islamic utterances.

The establishment of an Islamic state is presented as a religious duty for all Muslims and as an endeavour that may bring Paradise within their reach. And there is another felicitous prospect connected with it: that of a pious and virtuous community on earth that enjoys God's favour and is actively aided by Him to overcome poverty and humiliation. Such a community will be prosperous and strong. The re-introduction of Islamic criminal law is, in this perspective, a step towards salvation in the Hereafter as well as salvation in this life and, therefore, much more than merely a technical reform of penal law. The notions that are connected with it may make the project of enforcing Islamic criminal law attractive to both the ruling elite and to large parts of the Muslim population.

For the elite, the re-Islamisation of criminal law may have two sorts of advantages – ideological and practical. One ideological advantage is that it confers an Islamic legitimacy. Islamist regimes that have come to power as a result of a revolution or *coup d'état* need to demonstrate immediately that they make a start with the construction of a real Islamic state by implementing Islamic criminal law. Other regimes, that have already been in power for some time, have introduced Islamic criminal law merely as a political expedient to enhance their legitimacy and take the wind out of the sails of the Islamist opposition. Egypt is a case in point, although in the end Islamic criminal law was not implemented. Between 1976 and 1982 enormous efforts were made by various parliamentary committees set up to draft Islamic legislation, including an Islamic criminal code. This was done in order to demonstrate the Islamic character of the state as a reaction to the ideological attacks of the Islamist opposition. However, the fickle political nature of the process became clear a few years later. When in the early 1980s, after the assassination of President Sadat, the political climate changed and the government decided to take a firm stand against radical Islamist groups, these proposals were officially consigned to the dustbin.[18]

A second ideological motive for a regime to adopt Islamic criminal law is that, in doing so, it makes a clearly anti-Western statement. Islamic criminal law is one of those parts of the *Sharīʿah* that are most at variance with Western law and Western legal notions, much more so than e.g. the private or commercial law of the *Sharīʿah*. In implementing Islamic criminal law, there is a clear emphasis on the fixed punishments, because here the contradictions between

18 See Peters, 1988, 231–253.

Islamic criminal law and Western-type penal law are glaring. The fixed punishments, or *hudud*, which go directly back to the Qur'an and Sunnah, are very much at variance with the modern accepted system of legal punishment, both in the Islamic world and in the West. Islamic criminal law, then, and especially the law of *hudud*, has a highly symbolical value and its introduction is regarded by many Muslims as the litmus test for a real Islamisation of the legal system.

There are also two practical aspects that make the implementation of Islamic criminal law an attractive option for political elites in the Muslim world. The first one is that it provides an effective instrument of control and repression. The enactment of Islamic criminal legislation has been a pretext for the introduction, on a large scale, of corporal punishment, especially flogging, not only for *hadd* crimes, but also for offences that have nothing to do with Islamic criminal law *stricto sensu*. The Nimeiri regime in the Sudan, for instance, introduced flogging as a possible punishment for all offences mentioned in the Penal Code. Corporal punishment, especially when administered in public, is an effective instrument of repression. This is not only true with regard to those who are directly subjected to it, but even more so for society as a whole. The spectacle of public executions, amputations and floggings symbolises the supreme power of the regime and the futility of resistance against it.

The second reason why adopting Islamic criminal law might be attractive for a regime is that the way homicide is tried under Islamic criminal law is closer to the sense of justice of large parts of the population in the Islamic world. As we have seen, legal proceedings for homicide are based on private rather than state prosecution. The victim's heirs control the litigation in the sense that they are parties to the trial, the prosecution depends on their wills, and they can agree to an extrajudicial settlement. This is different from their position under the Western-inspired codes, where the victim's heirs are not admitted as parties to the trial and are, in the best case, relegated to the position of witnesses, without a say in the proceedings. The doctrine of Islamic criminal law is attractive in societies where private justice or revenge prevails, because it combines the idea of private prosecution with orderly judicial proceedings.

When Islamic criminal law was introduced in the various re-Islamising countries, it did not meet with much opposition among the Muslim population; on the contrary, in most countries it was supported by large groups in Muslim society. This is due to the powerful ideological discourse surrounding it, which holds promises for the "ordinary people". In the first place, there is the religious aspect, the idea that by implementing Islamic criminal law the community complies with God's wishes and will be rewarded. But on a practical level, Islamic criminal law also holds promises of eliminating crime and corruption as a result of its deterrence and its swift justice. Those who are apprehensive about rising crime rates and corruption, will welcome Islamic criminal law as a panacea for the cure of social evils and the restoration of a virtuous society. Its advocates argue that Islamic criminal law offers effective tools to fight crime because it allows the application of severe and painful punishments consisting in whipping, amputation and stoning to death. This is an often-used argument in favour of Islamic criminal law. The amputation of the hand of one thief, it is repeatedly asserted, will deter many others from violating the property of others. The advocates always contend that the crime rate in countries like Saudi Arabia, where fixed punishments are carried out, is much lower than elsewhere.

A further advantage mentioned in support of the introduction of Islamic criminal legislation is the fact that trials can be short and justice can be implemented quickly. Khomeini expressed this notion as follows:

> Islamic justice is based on simplicity and ease. It settles all criminal and civil complaints and in the most convenient, elementary, and expeditious way possible. All that is required is for an Islamic judge, with pen and inkwell and two or three enforcers, to go into a town, come to his verdict in any kind of case, and have it immediately carried out.[19]

These words show a desire not only for quick justice, but also for a simple and transparent procedure. With disapproval, attention is drawn to the slowness of justice under Western law, where trials can drag on for many years. Such statements express a longing among many groups in Muslim societies for a less complicated and orderly society, where good deeds are immediately rewarded and evil deeds punished right away. It has already been noticed that there are great similarities between the positive self-image of the Iranian clerics who administer justice, and the heroic sheriff that we know from Wild West pictures who single-handedly, with only his gun, restores law and order in a little town where crime is rife.[20]

A striking aspect of the way Islamic criminal law is implemented is that it is effectuated through state legislation. Islamic jurisprudence, the *fiqh*, is, as we have seen, essentially a legal doctrine formulated by scholars and not by the state. *Fiqh* is jurists' law. Judges applying the *fiqh* have to consult the scholarly works of jurisprudence and to select with regard to the case they must adjudicate, the most authoritative from several, often conflicting opinions with a bearing on the issue. The regimes that reintroduce Islamic criminal law in the

19 Quoted in Newman, 1982, 561.
20 Ibid.

form of penal codes claim that they are returning to the situation that prevailed before the West began to exert its influence in the Islamic world. This, of course, is illusory. Going back to the pre-colonial past would have meant introducing Islamic criminal law not by legislating it, but by referring the judges to the classical works on *fiqh*. Although this was done in two exceptional cases,[21] introducing Islamic criminal law by statute law has been the rule. This is a consequence of modern, Western ideas on the relationship between state and law that became current in the Islamic world, as we have seen in section 2.2. This means that, in spite of the ideology of returning to the *Shariʿah*, it is the state that determines which laws the courts must enforce. By instructing the courts to have recourse to state legislation and not to the classical body of *fiqh*, the *ulama* are relegated to the second level. The result of the reintroduction of Islamic criminal law, in most countries, is that something new is created, a hybrid form of criminal law consisting of Islamic substantive rules in a Western garb and embedded in a Western type adjective law, with Western type courts and Western institutions like the state prosecutor.

4 Conclusions

As a result of the codification of the *Shariʿah*, the *ulama* lost their time-honoured position as the exclusive guardians of the law. This affected their status in society, which had already been impaired as their economic resources, especially employment opportunities, had declined. Traditionally, the *ulama* had the monopoly not only of religious functions connected with the mosques, but also of education and the administration of justice. Because of this monopoly, they enjoyed a high status in society. However, all this began to change as from the end of the nineteenth century. Because of the creation of new types of schools for the training of military officers, civil servants, doctors, and engineers, the *ulama* lost the monopoly of education. At the same time, their intellectual authority was challenged by some of these new professionals and by those who had come into contact with the intellectual debates in the West. This erosion of their intellectual status went hand in hand with a gradual decline of the economic foundations of their livelihood. Whereas originally

21 In Afghanistan and the United Arab Emirates. When the Taliban came to power in Afghanistan they began to apply Islamic criminal law on the basis of the classical doctrine and did not codify Islamic criminal law. In the UAE, Islamic criminal law was introduced in 1987, when the Federal Penal Code laid down that *hadd* offences, homicide, and wounding, would henceforth be tried by the *Shariʿah* courts according to the *Shariʿah*. See al- Muhairi, 1996, 350–71.

all judges and teachers were from the *ulama* class, now, after the introduction of new types of schools and the Westernisation of the legal system, they had to compete for these employments with graduates of other schools. The *ulama*'s intellectual leadership was no longer unconditionally accepted. They were fiercely attacked by Islamist intellectuals, who did not unquestioningly accept the traditional interpretations of the revealed texts propagated by the *ulama*. Although most Islamist intellectuals had not had a traditional religious education, they regarded themselves as competent in this field on the strength of their knowledge of the Qur'an and *hadith*, which they often understood in new ways.

This has enormously affected the discourse on the *Shariʿah*, both the codified and the uncodified parts. For, as we have seen, codified *Shariʿah* is only a section of the entire body of *Shariʿah* doctrine. Not subject to codification are the purely ritual, religious and ethical provisions of the *Shariʿah*, dealing e.g. with ritual prayer (*salat*), pilgrimage (*hajj*) and dietary prescriptions, and those rules that have a legal character but are not implemented, such as, in most countries, *Shariʿah* private law (especially the provisions on interest), criminal, and constitutional law. The rules of the *Shariʿah* that were not enforced by the judiciary, were traditionally within the competence of the muftis, who belonged to the *ulama* class and had a traditional religious training. They were the religious authorities who would counsel believers on specific questions of the *Shariʿah*. Although there were controversies and disagreements among them, their authority was not fundamentally challenged. This, however, has changed now. Many of the issues that used to belong exclusively to the domain of the muftis have now become subject to public debates, in which intellectuals without a traditional religious training also participate. During the twentieth century, intellectuals without a religious training increasingly put their imprint on the religious debates and started to question accepted religious dogmas. Initially, these were intellectuals who, under the influence of Western ideas, became critical of what they saw as backward religious views and practices that would block "progress". However, during the last decades other types of believers have become more prominent in these debates. There is a growing group of pious Muslims who argue that the traditional doctrine of the *Shariʿah*, as expounded by the *ulama*, has deviated from the pure teachings of the Qur'an and Sunnah and who want to get back to these pure teachings as guidelines for their daily lives.

These developments have resulted in a situation in which defining the *Shariʿah* is not any more the exclusive competence of the *ulama*, but has become a public concern. As to codified *Shariʿah*, the debate is directly connected with national politics. Depending on the extent to which a state has adopted democratic procedures of legislation, the *Shariʿah* codes are discussed in parliament and the media. Although the traditional *ulama* still may play a role in the preparation and the "marketing" of these codes, the ultimate decision is with the politicians. Codification of the *Shariʿah*, as well as the question of which parts of the national legal system must be immediately based on the *Shariʿah*, have therefore become prominent and important political issues.

Since the *ulama* have lost their intellectual monopoly, the legally unenforced sections of the *Shariʿah* are also publicly debated. Although this debate is less political than the discussions on the codified *Shariʿah*, it certainly has political aspects. Islamic symbols and doctrines are connected with political positions and are used to legitimise political points of view. Whether or not all existing views can be fully expressed depends, naturally, on the extent to which the media are free from government interference and censorship. There are many instances where certain religious views are not permitted to be expressed, because of their political associations.

What does all this mean for the *Shariʿah* in contemporary Muslim society? The most important development has been that the authority of the *ulama* has been challenged and has declined. There are now also Muslims without a religious training who can have their say about *Shariʿah* issues. Those parts of the *Shariʿah* that have been codified and are part of the national legal systems are now brought under control of the state instead of being controlled by the *ulama*. This means that they have become political and, if the structures of the state permit it, even democratised. Concerning the other aspects of the *Shariʿah*, here, too, the *ulama* have lost control, although not as drastically as in the purely legal domain. The issues of the *Shariʿah* that fall outside the scope of codified law, are now debated by all kinds of Muslim intellectuals, with and without a formal religious training. These debates have not only been politicised, as I showed before, but also, at least potentially, democratised. However, to what extent this may lead to a real democratisation depends on whether these debates are free from political constraints that block freedom of expression.

Appendix 1: Codes and Legislation on Personal Status

1917 Ottoman Code of Family Law (*Huquq-i ʿAʾile Qararnamesi*)
1920–2000: series of Egyptian codes
1939 Dissolution of Muslims Marriages Act (India)
1951 Jordanian Code of Personal Status, replaced in 1976 by a new code

1953 Syrian Code of Personal Status, amended in 1975
1956 Tunisian Code of Personal Status, amended in 1993
1958 Moroccan Code of Personal Status, amended in 1993
1959 Iraqi Code of Personal Status
1961 Muslim Family Laws (Pakistan)
1967 Protection of the Family Law (Iran), amended in 1975; abolished in 1979 during the Iranian Islamic Revolution
1974 South-Yemeni Family Code (abolished in 1992 after the unification) 1975 Somalian Family Code (almost identical to the South-Yemeni one)
1977 Afghanistan Marriage Law
1982 Algerian Code of Personal Status
1984 Libyan Marriage Law
1984 Kuwaiti Code of Personal Status
1991 Sudan Code of Personal Status
1992 Yemeni Code of Personal Status

Appendix 2: Codes of Re-Islamization

Criminal Law

Libya

Law 148 of 11 October 1972 on theft and robbery, (Fr. tr.: Rycx, Jean-François (tr.), "Loi no 148 de l'année 1392 H correspondant à l'année 1972 C précisant les peines fixées par la Charia pour le vol et le brigandage," *Annuaire de l'Afrique du Nord* 11 (1972), pp. 763–768

Law 70 of 20 October 1973 on illegal sexual intercourse (amended by Law 10/1428). See YIMEL 5 (1998–9), 289

Law 52 of 16 September 1974 on unfounded accusation of fornication

Law 89 of 20 November 1974 on the drinking of alcoholic beverages

Law 6/1994 on homicide and wounding (Eng. tr. in YIMEL 1 (1994), pp. 543–4

Pakistan

Offences Against Property (Enforcement of Hudood) Ordinance, 1979

Offences of Zina (Enforcement of Hudood) Ordinance, 1979

Offences of Qazf (Enforcement of Hadd) Ordinance, 1979

Prohibition (Enforcement of Hadd) Ordinance, 1979

Execution of the Punishment of Whipping Ordinance, 1979

Texts in: Government of Pakistan, *New Islamic Laws: Enforcement of Hudood Ordinance 1979*. Lahore: Lahore Law Times Publications, n.d. 87 pp.

Qisas and Diyat Ordinance, 1990

Text in R. Mehdi, *The Islamization of the Law in Pakistan* (Richmond, UK, Curzon Press, 1990), pp. 298–320

Iran

Qânûn-i qisâs ve hudûd ve muqarrarât ân, 25 aug. 1982 *Rûznâma-yi Rasmi*, No. 10972, d.d. 26–10 1982

Persian text and English tr. in S. Naqvi (tr.), "Hudud and Qisas Act of Iran," *Islamic Studies*, 24 (1985), pp. 521–556, 25 (1986), pp. 107–50 (includes Persian text); English tr. in Government of Iran en Kia, Masouduzzafar Samimi (tr.), *Law of Hodoud and Qasas [Punishment and Retribution] and Provisions Thereof*. Tehran: Pars Associates, 1983. iv, 59 pp.

Qânûn-i diyât of 15–12 1982. *Rûznâma-yi Rasmî* No. 11.0–30, dd 8–1, 1983

Qânûn-i Ta'zîrât of 9–8 1983. *Rûznâma-yi Rasmî* No. 11.278, dd 14–11–83. This law was roughly identical with the pre-revolutionary penal code.

In 1991 the laws on qisas, *hudud*, diyat and the general provisions were incorporated into one penal code, to which, in 1996, a new chapter in ta'zîr was added. See Tellenbach (1996) and YIMEL 3 (1996), 342–351

German tr. Of all Iranian Criminal Codes by S. Tellenbach, *Strafgesetze der islamischen Republik Iran* (Berlin: W. de Gruyter, 1996)

Nigeria

Twelve northern states have introduced Islamic criminal legislation. See R. Peters, *Islamic Criminal law in Nigeria*, Ibadan: Spectrum Books, 2003

Sudan

Sudanese Criminal Code of 8 September 1983, replaced by the Criminal Code of 1991 (Law 8 of 1991)

Yemen

Yemeni Criminal Code of 1994 (Law 12 of 1994)

Tax Law

Libya

Law 89 of 1971 regarding the zakat

Pakistan

Ordinance XVIII of 1980 (Zakat and Ushr Ordinance)

Sudan

Zakat and Tax Law 1984 (Provisional order 3 of 1984); replaced by the Zakat Law of 1406 H (Law 72 of 1986); replaced by the Zakat law of 1990

Ban on Riba (Interest)

Pakistan

Banking and Financial Services Ordinance and Banking Tribunal Ordinance (1984). These ordinances banned interest-based transactions by banks, with the exception of transactions with parties abroad.

Iran

In Iran interest-based transactions have also been prohibited

References

al-Muhairi, B.S.B.A., "The Islamisation of Laws in the UAE: The Case of the Penal Code", *Arab Law Quarterly* 11/iv, 1996, 350–71.

Beck-Peccoz, Roberta Aluffi, *La modernizzazione del diritto di famiglia nei paesi arabi*, Università di Torino, Memorie dell'Istituto Giuridico, III, 35, Milano: Giuffrè, 1990.

Düstur, (official collection of Ottoman legislation enacted between 1839 and 1865), 2nd ed., 4 vols., Istanbul: Matbaʿa-yi Amira, 1865–1866.

Ebert, Hans-Georg, *Das Personalstatut arabischer Länder: Problemfelder, Methoden, Perspektiven: Ein Beitrag zum Diskurs über Theorie*, Leipziger Beiträge zur Orientforschung, 7, Frankfurt a.M. etc.: Peter Lang, 1996.

Government of Pakistan, *New Islamic Laws: Enforcement of Hudood Ordinance 1979*, Lahore: Lahore Law Times Publications, n.d.

Hilmi, Ömer, *Miʿyar-i ʿAdalet*, Istanbul: Bosnawi Haji Müharrem Matbaʿasi, 1881–1882.

Huquq-i ʿAʾile Qararnamesi, Istanbul: Kitabhane-yi Sudi, 1917.

Kaşıkçı, Osman, *Islam ve Osmanlı hukukunda Mecelle: hazırlanışı, hükümlerinin tahlili, tadil ve tamamlama çalışmalar*, Istanbul: Osmanlı Araştırmalı Vakfı, 1997.

Kelly, J.M., *A Short History of Western Legal Theory*, Oxford: Oxford University Press, 1992.

Mehdi, R., *The Islamization of the Law in Pakistan*, Richmond, UK: Curzon Press, 1990.

Newman, Graeme, "Khomeini and Criminal Justice: Notes on Crime and Culture", *Journal of Criminal Law and Criminology* 73, 1982, pp. 561–81.

Peters, Rudolph, "Divine Law or Man-Made Law? Egypt and the Application of the *Shariʿah*", *Arab Law Quarterly* 3, 1988, 231–253.

Peters, Rudolph, "The Islamization of Criminal Law: A Comparative Analysis", *Welt des Islams* 34/ii, 1994, 246–274.

Peters, Rudolph, *Islamic Criminal Law in Nigeria*, Ibadan: Spectrum Books Limited, 2003.

Qadri Pasha, Muhammad, *Qanun al-ʿadl wa-l-insaf li-l-qadaʾ ʿala mushkilat al-awqaf*, (repr.) Al-Qahira: Al-Matbaʿa al-Ahliyya, 1893.

Qadri Pasha, Muhammad, *Al-Ahkam al-sharʿiyya fi al-ahwal al-shakhsiyya*, 2nd ed., Cairo: Matbaʿat al-Saʿada, 1909[a].

Qadri Pasha, Muhammad, *Murshid al-hayran ila maʿrifat ahwal al-insan fi l-muʿamalat al-sharʿiyya*, 3rd ed., Cairo: Al-Matbaʿa al-Amiriyya, 1909[b].

Schacht, Joseph, *An Introduction to Islamic Law*, Oxford: Clarendon Press, 1964.

Shaykhzade and Ibrahim al-Halabi, *Majmaʿ al-anhur fi sharh Multaqa al-Abhur*, 2 vols., Istanbul: 1884 (1301 AH).

Tahanawi, Muhammad ʿAli b. ʿAli, *Kitab kashshaf istilahat al-funun*, repr. of Calcutta, 1864 ed., 2 vols., Istanbul: Kahraman Yayınları, 1984.

Tellenbach, S., *Strafgesetze der islamischen Republik Iran*, Berlin: W. de Gruyter, 1996.

Vogel, Frank E., *Islamic Law and Legal System: Studies of Saudi Arabia*, Studies in Islamic Law and Society, Leiden etc.: E.J. Brill, 2000.

CHAPTER 31

What Does It Mean to Be an Official Madhhab?

Hanafism and the Ottoman Empire

1 Introduction

In this chapter I will explore the special relationship between the Hanafi madhhab and the Ottoman Empire. I will do so by analyzing two aspects of this relationship. First I will discuss the question of how Hanafi doctrine, between the twelfth and sixteenth centuries, was molded into an unequivocal body of rulings ready to he applied by the qadis. Secondly I will examine how the relationship between the Hanafi and the other madhhabs was organized after the Ottoman conquest of non-Hanafi regions. My conclusion will be that the result of this combined activity was the emergence of a distinctive Ottoman Hanafism, one that accordingly was well suited to the requirements of the bureaucratic set-up of the Ottoman state.

If someone would like to know the ruling of the Shariʿa on some specific legal issue and consults the standard fiqh texts, he is likely to be bewildered by the multitude of opinions, even within one madhhab. One of the questions that has intrigued me for some time already is how such a fluid doctrine full of contradictions could be enforced by courts. Or in other words, how Islamic legal doctrine with its many conflicting views and rulings could be transformed into positive law. In theory, three institutions could play a role in this process: the madhhab, as a community of scholars and a doctrine, the State, and the qadi. Here I will focus on the madhhab and the State, since, in the Ottoman Empire, the role of the judge was relatively minor in this respect. The State and the Hanafi jurists developed a body of law that did not leave much room for judicial discretion on points of law. In this paper I will first pursue how this transformation from a scholarly, often contradictory doctrine into a more or less homogeneous body of law came about between roughly the twelfth and the seventeenth centuries.

The second aspect of the relationship between the Hanafi madhhab and the Ottoman State became practically relevant after the Ottoman conquests of the Arab Middle East, in the early sixteenth century. For then the Ottomans began to rule over large groups of Sunni Muslims following other madhhabs. I will show that the State, on the basis of existing Hanafi doctrine, elaborated a law of conflict that clearly regulated the position of the other madhhabs and their judges.

 | DOI:10.1163/9789004420625_032

2 Transforming the Doctrine into Positive Law

The process of transformation of the Shariʿa into positive law is an operation in which the jurists of a madhhab, the State, and the qadis have a role to play. These roles may vary. One may think of a model in which the State has a limited role in the process: it creates law courts and appoints qadis to whom the application of the doctrine is entrusted. These qadis then have extensive discretionary powers in applying the Shariʿa according to their independent reasoning (*ijtihād*). Since they are not bound by a clear and unequivocal body of rules, they can adjudicate cases on their own merits, using only the broad principles given by the Shariʿa doctrine. This type of justice would resemble closely what Max Weber called *Kadi-Justiz*. This is the situation in present-day Saudi Arabia, where the qadis are free to adjudicate according to any ruling within the Hanbali madhhab and even from other madhhabs, if their *ijtihād* leads them there.[1] This is also the way Lawrence Rosen describes the modus operandi of the Moroccan qadis.[2] At the other end of the spectrum we would have a state which considers itself the only source of the law to the exclusion of the legal scholars: Positive law then is what the State enacts and the qadis have to apply, without much room for discretionary decisions. This is the state of affairs that prevails in most of the Islamic world these days, now that nearly everywhere Islamic law, to the extent that it is applied, is enforced through state-enacted laws. The Ottoman type of justice that existed between the sixteenth and the nineteenth centuries stood somewhere between these two extremes. The Hanafi jurists and the State defined precisely what the prevailing Hanafi doctrine was, thus creating an unequivocal body of rules and restricting the qadis' freedom in choosing specific views from Hanafi doctrine.

That the State could thus interfere with the doctrine of the law was not self-evident. There is no agreement among the different madhhabs that this is allowed. If a qadi is appointed on the condition that he adjudicates according to one madhhab, all madhhabs, except the Hanafis, regard the appointment as void, or they hold that the appointment is valid, but the stipulation inoperative, at least if the qadi is a *mujtahid*.[3] If the head of state (*imām*) orders or forbids a qadi to follow a certain madhhab in specific cases, such an order

1 Vogel, Frank E. *Islamic law and legal system: Studies in Saudi Arabia, Studies in Islamic Law and Society*. Leiden: Brill, 2000.

2 Rosen, Lawrence. *The anthropology of justice: Law as culture in Islamic society, The Lewis Henry Morgan Lectures*. Cambridge etc.: Cambridge University Press, 1989.

3 Wizārat al-Awqāf wa–l-Shu'ūn al-Islāmiyya. *Al-Mawsūʿa al-fiqhiyya*. 34 vols. Kuwait: 1986: xxxiii, 300 (*Taqyīd al-qaḍāʾ bi-madhhab muʿayyan*).

or prohibition would also be void.[4] The only way for the State to influence the administration of justice, according to these madhhabs, is to prohibit the qadis from hearing certain types of cases.

For the Hanafis an appointment on the condition that the nominee exclusively applies one certain madhhab is valid, but only if he himself belongs to that madhhab. According to them, sentences pronounced by qadis according to the doctrine of another madhhab are invalid, since they cannot but be motivated by false and arbitrary personal views (*hawā bāṭil*). Later Hanafi jurists asserted that a qadi who is a *muqallid* may only adjudicate according to the correct opinion of the madhhab (*ṣaḥīḥ al-madhhab, ma ʿalayh al-ʿamal wal-fatwā*) and that, in addition, the sultan may oblige him to do so.[5] Their argument is that decisions based on other views are ultra vires, since the qadi has exceeded his competency, which is to give judgment according to the correct Hanafi opinions.

This process shows interesting similarities with the Roman *Lex citandi*, enacted in AD 426. This law had the same objectives, namely, imposing some order on the legal doctrine elaborated by the Roman jurists. It instructed judges to follow only the opinions included in the works of five specific jurists, regarded as eminently authoritative, and gave rules to select an opinion in case of difference of opinion among them.[6]

3 The Role of the Jurists

With regard to a specific point of law, the Hanafi madhhab usually gives several opinions, for often the three founding fathers, Abū Ḥanīfa, Abu Yūsuf and Muḥammad al-Shaybānī held different views. Sometimes there were even more views, since other opinions, ascribed to less important jurists from the formative period, such as Zufar or al-Ḥasan ibn Ziyād also found their way into the standard Hanafi works. In the older, more concise works, the various views would be juxtaposed. In more extensive works, such as *al-Mabsūṭ* by al-Sarakhsī (d. 483/1090) or in the collections of fatwas, the authors would argue why they would prefer certain opinions, for instance because they

4 The jurists liken this issue to the question of adding certain stipulations to nominate contracts. In this case it must be determined whether or not a given stipulation is valid, or whether or not it vitiates the contract to which it was added.

5 Ibn ʿĀbidīn, Muḥammad Amīn. *Radd al-Muḥtār*. 5 vols. Bulaq: Dār al-Ṭibāʿa al-Amīriyya, 1882 (1299 H). 5:464–465.

6 Lokin, J.H.A., and W.J. Zwalve. *Hoofdstukken uit de Europese codificatiegeschiedenis*. Groningen: Wolters-Noordhoff/Forsten, 1986:64–65.

considered the arguments in favor of them stronger, or because they regarded them as more fitting to changing social circumstances. Such preferred views could become generally accepted and then found their way into the standard textbooks.[7]

But in general, the different opinions were juxtaposed without an indication of what opinion was more correct. In the early centuries of the Hanafi madhhab this did not pose many problems. The selection of these views were always based on content. In the early centuries of the Hanafi madhhab this did not pose many problems. Lawyers, be they qadis of muftis, were supposed to be *mujtahid*s to some extent and capable of distinguishing between correct and incorrect views. However, gradually it was felt that the scholars were losing this ability. Nevertheless, they had to work with these standard texts of the Hanafi madhhab. In order to find the authoritative and correct views, they could not anymore rely on reasoning based on proofs (*adilla*) or on content. Instead, formal rules were needed for muftis and qadis to guide them in making the right selection of opinions.

During the late twelfth century jurists began to argue that there was a hierarchy of authority among the founders of the Hanafi madhhab and to formulate rules to determine whose opinion was most authoritative if there was a difference of opinion on a specific issue.[8] In the chronology of the early sixteenth-century Ottoman jurist Kamālpashazāde (d. 940/1534), this process coincided with the gradual extinction of the fifth class of jurists (out of seven, consisting of those capable of determining authoritative from non-authoritative opinions (*aṣḥāb al-tarjīḥ min al-muqallidīn*), such as al-Marghīnānī (d. 593/1197)[9]

The rules elaborated during the late twelfth century were not yet uniforms[10] nor undisputed. Some jurists, such as al-Ghazāwī (d. 593/1197), in his *al-Ḥāwī al-Qudsī*, continued to argue that it was better to examine the strength of the arguments for each opinion rather than to be led by formal criteria.[11] However, the doctrine that finally prevailed was the following: If confronted with conflicting opinions on an issue, the qadi or mufti must first follow the opinion of Abū Ḥanīfa, then that of Abū Yūsuf, then that of Muḥammad al-Shaybānī

7 *Al-mutūn al-arbaʿa: al-Mukhtār li-l-Fatwā* by al-Mawṣilī. (d. 593/1284); *Kanz al-daqāʾiq* by al-Nasafī (d. 710/1310); *al-Wiqāya* by Tāj al-Sharīʿa (8th/14th c.) and *Majmaʿ al-Baḥrayn* by Ibn al-Sāʿātī (d. 694/1285).

8 Later jurists usually quote al-Sajawandī (d. ca. 596/ 1200); the author of *al-Farāʾiḍ al-Sirājiyya*, as the auctor intellectualis of this hierarchy. See Ibn ʿĀbidīn 1882, 1:52.

9 Quoted in Ibn ʿĀbidīn 1882, 1:57.

10 See n. 12.

11 Ibn Nujaym, *Al-Baḥr al-Rāʾiq sharḥ Kanz al-Daqāʾiq li-l-Nasafī*. 8 vols. Beirut: Dār al-Kitāb al-Islāmī: i. n.d. 8:293.

and finally those of Zufar or al-Ḥasan b. Ziyād (without preference for either of them). Slightly different criteria were also proposed but did not prevail.[12] Even as late as the sixteenth century there were differences of opinion, e.g., about whether Zufar and al-Ḥasan b. Ziyād occupied the same rank or whether Zufar was more authoritative.[13] Later scholars added the rule that in questions related to the administration of justice Abū Yūsuf's opinion was to be preferred and in cases touching upon the cognate relationships (*dhawū l-arḥām*) Muhammad al-Shaybānī's view. If no opinion of any of the older jurists was known, then the opinion must be adopted of the majority of scholars from the following centuries, such as Abū Ḥafṣ al-Kabīr (d. 216/831), al-Ṭaḥāwī (d. 321/933), Abū Jaʿfar al-Hinduwānī (d. 362/973), or Abū l-Layth al-Samarqandī (d. ca. 390/1000). A final rule was that if on one issue there were two views, one based on analogy and the other on *istiḥsān*, the latter should be adopted.[14]

Through this process, Hanafi opinion by the sixteenth century became standardized, unequivocal and easy to apply.[15] Although the textbooks still mentioned the different opinions with regard to one issue, they clearly indicated which opinion was the prevailing one. The following passage from *Multaqā al-Abḥur* by Ibrāhīm al-Ḥalabī (d. 936/1594), one of the most popular textbooks in the Ottoman Empire,[16] makes this clear:

> Some people wanting to acquire more knowledge have asked me to compile a book containing the issues dealt with in [the *Compendium* by] al-Qudūrī [d. 428/1037], in *al-Mukhtār* [*li-l-Fatwā*, by al-Mawṣilī, d. 693/1284], in *Kanz* [*al-Daqāʾiq* by al-Nasafī, d. 710/1310] and the *Wiqāyat*

12 Some held that a mufti was free in following either opinion, if Abū Yūsuf and Muḥammad al-Shaybānī together had one opinion and Abū Ḥanīfa another. Ibn ʿĀbidīn 1882, 1:52. Other jurists held that if the three Hanafi founding fathers were divided, the majority opinion must he followed. Selle, F. *Prozessrecht des 16. Jahrhunderts im osmanischen Reich*. Wiesbaden, 1962. P.15 quoting Qāḍīkhān (d. 592/1196).

13 In the *Durr al-Mukhtār* al-Ḥaṣkafī (d. 1088/1677) mentions that ʿUmar b. Nujaym (d. 970/1563) held this last view. Ibn ʿĀbidīn, 1882: 4:419.

14 The most complete expose of these formal selection criteria can be found in Ibn ʿĀbidīn, Muḥammad Amīn. "Sharḥ al-manẓūma al-musammāh bi-ʿuqūd rasm al-muftī." In *Majmūʿat Rasāʾil Ibn ʿĀbidīn*. Istanbul: Muḥammad Hāshim al-Kutubī, 1907–1908 (1325 H). pp. 25 ff. See also Ibn ʿĀbidīn 1882, 1:51–52, and 4:419.

15 This seems to be a special Hanafi feature. An admittedly quick scanning of texts of other madhhabs revealed that only the Shafiʿis developed some formal criteria to determine the authoritative opinion in cases where there are conflicting views transmitted from al-Shafiʿi. See e.g. al-Ramlī (d. 1004/1595–6), *Nihāyat al-Muḥtāj ilā sharḥ al-Minhāj*. 8 vols. Beirut: Dār al-Fikr, 1984. 1:50–51.

16 Uzunçarşılı, Ismail Hakkı. *Osmanlı devletinin ilmiye teşkilâti*. Ankara: Türk Tarih Kurumu Basımevi, 1988: 115.

> [*al-Riwāya fī Masā'il al-Hidāya*, by Tāj al-Sharīʿa, d. 8th/14th c.] in an easy and accessible style. I responded to this request and added some indispensable issues dealt with in the *Majma*ʿ [*al-Baḥrayn wa-Multaqā al-Nayyirayn*, by Ibn Sāʿātī, d. 694/1285] and a small part from *al-Hidāya* [by al-Marghīnānī, d. 593/1197]. I clearly indicated the controversies among our Imams and [with regard to each issue] I have first mentioned the most preferable opinion (*al-arjaḥ*) among those held by them, and then the other opinions. However, in some places I have specifically connected them [the opinions not mentioned first] with words expressing preference (*al-tarjīḥ*) [ʿAbd al-Raḥmān Shaykhzāde: such as "the correct opinion, the preferable opinion, the opinion to be selected for giving fatwas"]. Regarding the controversies among the later scholars or among [the authors of] the books I just mentioned, all views that I introduced with the words "it has been said" (*qīla*) or "they have said" (*qālū*), even if they are linked to words like "the correct view" (*al-ṣaḥīḥ*) are less preferable than opinions not introduced in such a way.[17]

The final stage of this development was reached in the 19th century when texts on certain topics were written that only contained the authoritative opinions, leaving out the rejected views. Examples of these are the textbook on Islamic criminal law by ʿÖmer Ḥilmī[18] and the legal compilations by the Egyptian Qadrī Pasha.

4 The Role of the State

When the Ottoman State emerged, the Hanafi madhhab, brought by the Saljuqs from Central Asia, was already well established in Anatolia. Therefore it was the obvious choice for an official madhhab. The state appointed Hanafi qadis and instructed them to apply Hanafi doctrine. As we have seen, the Hanafi madhhab was the one that accepted such administrative practices without reservations. Moreover, this madhhab asserted that Hanafi qadis, especially if they were muqallids ought to pronounce their judgements according to the most authoritative opinion of the madhhab, and that their sentences otherwise would be void. To emphasize this point, a sultanic order was issued in 1537 to enjoin the qadis in Anatolia and the Balkans (Rūm) not to follow Shafiʿi

17 Shaykhzāde (d. 1667). *Majma*ʿ *al-anhur fī sharḥ Multaqā al-Abḥur* (*li-Ibrāhīm al-Ḥalabī, d. 1549*). 2 vols. Istanbul, 1883–1884 (1301 H): 1883, 1:7 (text of the *Multaqa*).

18 Ḥilmī, ʿUmar. *Miʿyār-i ʿadālet*. Istanbul: Bosnawī Ḥājjī Muḥarram Efendi, 1883–1884.

opinions for certain purposes.[19] Furthermore, the Ottoman sultans began to instruct qadis when they were appointed that they must adjudicate according to the most authoritative Hanafi views. The standard formula used in the letters of appointment was:

> (...) to adhere to enforcing the provisions of the laws of the Prophet [Mohammed] and to applying divine commands and interdictions, not to overstep the boundaries of the true Shariʿa, properly to follow in the questions that present itself the various opinions [transmitted] from Hanafi imams, to find their most correct opinions (*aṣaḥḥ-i aqwāl*) and to act accordingly.[20]

The sultan, however, could decide, for whatever reasons, to instruct the qadis with regard to certain cases not to follow the prevailing view, but another. In the sixteenth century, there were already thirty-two of such orders.[21] Many of these date from the period of office of the famous Ottoman state mufti (*shaykh al-Islām*) Abū al-Suʿūd (d. 1574).[22] Sometimes such an order would just corroborate an already existing preference of certain muftis for a specific opinion. Often, however, the sultan, prompted no doubt by leading jurists, would introduce a change in the legal system by enforcing a view that was regarded as weak and without authority. I will give two examples, one in which the sultan corroborated an existing preference and one in which the sultan abolished an authoritative opinion in favor of a weaker one.

In the *Multaqā al-Abḥur* the following statement is made regarding the marriage concluded by a legally capable woman without consent of her matrimonial guardian. The authoritative rule, ascribed to Abu Ḥanīfa, is that such a woman can validly contract her own marriage and that her marriage guardian

19 Akgündüz, Ahmet. *Osmanlı Kanunnameleri ve hukuki tahlilleri*. Istanbul: Fey Vakfi, 1990. 1. *Kitap*: 70. See also Horster, Paul. *Zur Anwendung des islamischen Rechts im 16. Jahrhundert: Die "juristische Darlegungen" (maʿruzat) des Schejch ul-Islam Ebu Suʿud (gest. 1574), Bonner Orientalistsiche Studien, 10*. Stuttgart: Kohlhammer, 1935: 30–31. The purpose of having recourse to a Shafiʿi qadi was to give a wife the right to demand a divorce on the ground that her husband was absent and had left her without means to support her. In Syria and Palestine, women would go in such cases to a Shafiʿi mufti to obtain such a divorce. See Tucker, Judith E. *In the House of the Law: Gender and Islamic law in Ottoman Syria and Palestine*. Berkeley etc.: Cambridge University Press, 1998.

20 Akgündüz, 1990:70.

21 Imber, Colin. *Ebu's-Suʿud: The Islamic legal tradition, Jurists: profiles in legal theory*. Edinburgh: Edinburgh University Press, 1997:169.

22 Imber, 1997:107–109, 168–169.

can demand rescission of the contract by the judge in the event she has married herself to a person who is not her coequal:

> Marriage concluded by a free woman of full legal capacity is valid. However, the marriage guardian is entitled to object [to such a marriage] if the husband is not her coequal (*kufʾ*). Al-Ḥasan ibn Ziyād [d. 204/819] has reported from the Imām [Abū Ḥanīfa] that it is not valid and Qāḍīkhān [d. 592/1196] has issued fatwas according to this opinion. According to Muḥammad [al-Shaybānī, d. 189/805] such a marriage is concluded conditionally even if the husband is her coequal.[23]

The commentator ʿAbd al-Raḥmān Shaykhzāde (d. 1667) observes regarding the opinion of Abū Ḥanīfa transmitted by al-Ḥasan ibn Ziyād:

> This opinion is more correct and cautious and therefore preferable for fatwas in our days because not every matrimonial guardian is proficient in litigation and not every judge is just. Therefore it is more appropriate to close this door, especially now that an order to that effect has been issued by the sultan and that he has instructed muftis to issue fatwas accordingly.[24]

This seems to be not entirely accurate. The text of the Abū al-Suʿūd's *Maʿrūżāt* mentions that the sultan has imposed an opinion of Muḥammad al-Shaybānī, according to which a legally capable woman may not conclude a valid marriage without her matrimonial guardian's consent, unless she does not have one. In that case, it is not required for her to obtain the qadis approval for concluding a valid marriage unlike persons who are legally incapable such as minors.[25] That the Sultan imposed al-Shaybānī's opinion rather than the one transmitted by al-Ḥasan b. Ziyād must have had practical reasons. According to the latter opinion it must first be examined whether the bridegroom is a coequal or not before the validity of the marriage can be established, whereas according to al-Shaybānī's no marriage is binding without the guardian's consent is inoperative. Although the sultan did not follow precisely the opinion that the jurists preferred for giving fatwas, he evidently followed a trend among the jurists aimed at imposing greater familial control over females.

23 Shaykhzāde, 1883–1884, 1:320–321.
24 Shaykhzāde, 1883–1884, 1:321.
25 Horster, 1935:28–29.

Another sultanic order dealt with the law of *qasāma* (extrajudiciary oath, repeated 50 times). When a body, with traces of violent death, is found on private property, the next of kin, after a special procedure consisting of accusing the owner or inhabitants of the property and having them swear a number of oaths, can demand the victim's blood price from them. In this connection, Abū Ḥanīfa and Muḥammad al-Shaybānī hold that the owner's solidarity group (*ʿāqila*) is liable, whereas according to Abu Yūsuf's view, the actual occupants (owners or tenants) and not their solidarity groups must pay it. The latter opinion was weaker, according to the formal rules, but socially more beneficial. For its enforcement would stimulate the vigilance of the residents and their diligence in keeping their neighborhood safe, since they themselves and not their solidarity groups were held liable. For that reason it was imposed by a sultanic order.[26] Other sultanic orders regarded the punishment of Muslims or Christians for insulting the Prophet Muhammad,[27] and the violation of price regulations for money lending (via *ḥīlas*).[28]

When Egypt became autonomous during the nineteenth century, the same procedure was used by the khedives in the field of Shariʿa justice. In 1858 the qadis were ordered to apply the opinion of Abu Yūsuf and Mūhammad al-Shaybānī in cases of manslaughter in order to determine whether the killing had been committed deliberately or not.[29] The prevailing view within the Hanafi madhhab, held by Abū Ḥanīfa, was that criminal intent is only assumed to exist if the killer used a sharp weapon or instrument that can sever parts of the body, or fire. According to Abū Yūsuf and Muḥammad al-Shaybānī, however, there is criminal intent if a weapon or implement is used that as a rule is lethal. Since in Egypt people were often killed by being beaten with the *nabbūt*, the long wooden stick Egyptian peasants usually carry with them, the khedive gave the less authoritative opinion force of law, so that killers using these sticks could be sentenced to death. A similar decree was issued in 1873, instructing qadis to follow Abū Yūsuf's non-authoritative view according to which a Muslim may be sentenced to death for killing a non-Muslim temporary resident (*mustaʾmin*).[30]

26 Horster, 1935:58–59; Imber 1997:108–109; Ebussuud Efendi, and Mehmet Ertuğrul Düzdağ (ed.). *Şeyhülislam Ebussuud Efendi Fetvaları ışığında 16. asır Türk hayatı*. 2 ed. Istanbul: Enderun Kitabevi, 1983: 156. no. 767.

27 Horster, 1935:32–36.

28 Horster, 1935:45.

29 Sāmī, Amīn. *Taqwīm al-Nīl*. 3 vols. Cairo: Maṭbaʿat al-Kutub al-Miṣriyya, 1928–1936: 3/1:294–297.

30 Egyptian National Archive (Dār al-Wathāʾiq al-Qawmiyya). Majlis al-Aḥkām. Maḥfaẓa 9, document 404/3, 3 Ṣafar 1290.

A special type of state interference with the application of Hanafi doctrine is the introduction of a statute of limitations of fifteen years, by forbidding the qadis to take cognizance of claims after this period unless the plaintiff had a legal excuse.[31] Here the sultan did not impose on the judiciary to follow a certain Hanafi opinion, but forbade the qadis to hear cases under certain conditions, unless the Sultan has issued a special order regarding the lawsuit.

5 From Hanafi Monopoly to Hanafi Hegemony

When in 1516–1517 the Ottomans conquered large parts of the Arab Middle East, they ruled for the first time over regions where the population followed non-Hanafi Sunni madhhabs. In these countries there was already a tradition of coexistence of qadis belonging to different madhhabs.[32] In Egypt and Syria the Ottomans preserved this system of madhhab plurality-, but placed it under Hanafi supremacy.[33] The qadis belonging to the other madhhabs were given the position of deputy (*nā'ib*) to the Hanafi qadi and were thus subordinated to him. Only the Hanafi qadis were paid by the State and rotated throughout the Empire as part of their career. The other qadis were locally recruited and usually appointed for life.[34] In this section I will analyze how, after these conquests. the Ottomans on the basis of Hanafi doctrine regulated the position of these other madhhabs and their qadis. I will show that they were able to use, with some specifications and modifications, the existing Hanafi doctrines on these issues. Thus they created and enforced a Hanafi inter-madhhab law of conflict. I will focus on two aspects of this law of conflict: the practical implications of

31 Selle 1962:59–61; Ibn ʿĀbidīn 1882, 4:475.

32 See e.g. Escovitz, Joseph H. "The establishment of the four chief judgeships in Cairo in Mamluk Egypt." *Bulletin of the School of Oriental and African Studies* 102 (1982): 529–531; Jackson, Sherman A. "The primacy of domestic politics: Ibn Bint al-Aʿazz and the establishment of the four chief judgeships in Mamluk Egypt." *Journal of the American Oriental Society* 115, no. 1 (1995): 52–65.

33 For the changes in the administration of justice in Egypt, immediately after the Ottoman conquest, see Behrens-Abouseif, D. *Egypt's Adjustment to Ottoman Rule: Institutions, Waqf and Architecture in Cairo (16th and 17th Centuries)*. Leiden, E.J. Brill, 1994:69–85.

34 Nahal, Galal H. El-. *The judicial administration of Ottoman Egypt in the seventeenth century*. Minneapolis etc.: Bibliotheca Islamica, 1979:14–17; Masters, Bruce. "Ottoman Policies towards Syria in the 17th and 18th Centuries." In *The Syrian Land in the 17th and 18th Centuries*, edited by Thomas Philipp. Stuttgart: Steiner Verlag, 1992:17; Gerber, Haim. *Islamic law and culture: 1600–1840*. Vol. 9, *Islamic law and society*. Leiden: Brill, 1999:69–70: Gibb, H.A.R., and Harold Bowen. *Islamic Society in the Eighteenth Century*. 2 vols, *Islamic Society and the West*, 1. London etc.: Oxford University Press, 1957: 2:123–124.

the coexistence of qadis following the different madhhabs and the status of their sentences.

Qadis had several functions. They not only decided legal disputes, but also registered important legal acts and contracts, such as the establishment of *waqf* (charitable trusts), the sale of real estate. commercial partnerships, and marriages. The availability of qadis following four different madhhabs enabled those who wanted to register their contracts and unilateral legal acts to select or exclude certain clauses or stipulations. For instance, if the founder of a *waqf* wanted to facilitate the replacement of the *waqf* property by other property (*istibdāl*), he would register the *waqf* with the Hanbali qadi, since this school allowed this. Or if the relatives of a minor girl whose father and grandfather had died, wanted to marry her off themselves rather than request the state authorities to act as marriage guardians, they would register the marriage with the Hanafi qadi, since this madhhab allowed all male agnatic relatives to act as marriage guardians for minor girls, whereas according to the other schools only the father or grandfather could do so. Litigation, too, was affected by the coexistence of qadis of different madhhabs. The party who was able to choose the forum could use this to his advantage. A woman who was irrevocably repudiated would prefer to sue her ex-husband for maintenance before a Hanafi qadi, since only according to the Hanafis is she entitled to full maintenance. And an abandoned wife, whose husband had left property for her maintenance, could only sue for a divorce before the Hanbali qadi.[35]

It is not clear how in the case of litigation the choice of forum was determined under Mamluk rule. After the Ottoman conquest, Hanafi doctrine was applied. The Hanafi jurists, however, held opposing views concerning the jurisdiction of the various qadis. Abū Yūsuf's position was that the plaintiff could choose the forum. His argument was that he is the one who claims something that is due him and wants to redress a wrong. Therefore, it is he who selects the court. Muḥammad al-Shaybānī, however, disagreed with Abū Yūsuf, at least in those cases where there are several qadis, each with his own territorial jurisdiction or his own jurisdiction regarding persons (such as a military qadi). In such a situation the choice of forum is the defendant's. This means that if there are two qadis, one with exclusive jurisdiction over neighborhood A and the other over neighborhood B, a defendant living in B cannot be forced to answer a claim before the court in A. Similarly, a civilian cannot be sued against his will before a military court. Muḥammad al-Shaybānī's argument here derives

35 For these and other practical issues related to the presence of four qadis, see al-Qalqashandī and Muḥammad Ḥusayn (ed.). *Ṣubḥ al-aʿshā fī ṣināʿat al-inshāʾ*. Beirut: Dar al-Fikr, 1987: ii: 197–202, quoting *al-Taʿrīf* by al-ʿUmarī (d. 749–1349).

from the definition of defendant as "the one who is forced to defend himself," whereas the plaintiff is the one who is free to sue or not to sue. Since the defendant can be forced to answer a claim, the qadi must have jurisdiction over him. This implies that only the qadi of the defendant's place of residence or the civilian qadi (if the defendant is not a soldier) is competent. Muḥammad al-Shaybānī's opinion has become the authoritative one among the Hanafis.

However, these rules did not apply to the situation in the large cities of the Arab Middle East. Although there were several qadis in one town, each belonging to a different madhhab, they all had full jurisdiction over the entire town (and its environments). In such a situation, Muḥammad al-Shaybānī's argument for giving the choice of forum to the defendant does not apply and the plaintiff may select any of these qadis, because they all have the required jurisdiction. Nevertheless, the sultan, as mentioned by Abū al-Suʿūd, forbade qadis to hear cases if the defendant had not agreed to the choice of forum. This was within his powers, for, as the jurists point out, if qadis acted against these instructions, they would exceed the terms of their appointment and their sentences would be void.[36] The fatwa in which the issue is dealt with is interesting and worth quoting:

> *Question*: If Zayd, who is a Hanafi, dies while being away [from his hometown], and his Shafiʿite creditors produce evidence of their claims [against the estate] in the absence of the heirs, and if the Shafiʿite qadi finds for them and the Hanafi qadi thereafter issues execution on the judgement, is this legally acceptable?
>
> *Answer*: No. The qadis in the Well-Protected Dominions have been forbidden to give judgement contrary to the defendant's madhhab and the Hanafi qadi's order of execution is therefore null and void. Abū al-Suʿūd. What we take into consideration is the defendant's qadi, according to Muḥammad [al-Muḥammad al-Shaybānī]. This is the ruling according to which fatwas must be issued. Qāḍīkhān and Majmaʿ al-Fatāwā.[37]

The fatwa probably points to the existence of a practice in the Arab regions of the Empire of applying Shafiʿi law whenever the defendant failed to appear in

36 Ibn ʿĀbidīn, 1882: 4:580–581; Ibn ʿĀbidīn 1882–1883: 1:218–219. In Egypt certain types of cases, such as those regarding long-term rentals of *waqf*, replacement of *waqf* property and rescission of marriage contracts, were first reviewed by the Hanafi qadi before being heard by a deputy belonging to another madhhab. Nahal, 1979:17.

37 Horster, 1935:48.

court. Under Hanafi law, the court in such cases cannot pronounce a sentence. It is clear that the Ottoman State wanted to uphold Hanafi law, even in cases where other madhhabs offered remedies for substantive and procedural legal problems. This, I believe, was motivated by a bureaucratic tendency to impose uniformity in the administration of justice based on Hanafi doctrine, at the expense of pragmatic flexibility.

This fatwa leads us to the other issue, namely, the status of the sentences pronounced by the non-Hanafi qadis. After the Ottoman conquest, the Hanafi qadi in the Arab regions was given precedence over the other qadis.[38] As appears from the fatwa quoted above, the non-Hanafi qadis heard cases and pronounced judgments only with the defendant's consent. However, for the enforcement of such a judgment, a warrant of execution was required, issued by the Hanafi qadi, who was higher in rank than the others. In principle, all sentences of other qadis would he endorsed. The basic rule here is that sentences based on *ijtihād* cannot be reversed by other qadis. Its rationale is to prevent endless litigation. Yet there were certain limits. Hanafi doctrine in this respect was very much like the modern law of conflict of many states with Western legal systems, according to which national courts, under certain conditions, may apply foreign law, but only if this does not violate the *ordre public* (public policy), i.e., essential values of the legal system. For the Hanafi jurists, these essential values consisted in unequivocal texts of the Quran and hadith or the *ijmāʿ*. The Hanafi qadi would issue warrants of execution for the sentences of the other qadis unless they violated such texts as interpreted by Hanafi doctrine.[39] Hanafi textbooks list a number of issues that are legal according to other madhhabs, but cannot be endorsed by Hanafi qadis. Among these issues we find the following:

1. Capital sentences based on the *qasāma* procedure, i.e., fifty oaths sworn by the victim's next of kin, a possibility recognized in Maliki law;
2. Sentences based on the testimony of one witness and an oath sworn by the plaintiff, recognized by all madhhabs except the Hanafis;
3. Sentences upholding the validity of a temporary marriage (*mutʿa*), recognized in Imami Shiite doctrine;
4. Capital sentences pronounced in spite of the fact that one of the victim's female heirs has waived her right to demand retribution, valid under Maliki law;

38 Nahal, 1979.

39 Ibn Nujaym, and al-Ḥamawī. *Ghamz ʿuyūn al-baṣāʾir sharḥ al-ashbāh wa-l-naẓāʾir li-Ibn Nujaym*. 2 vols. Istanbul: Dār al-Ṭibāʿa al-ʿāmira, 1873 (1290 H): 1:340–342.

5. Sentences regarding a triple repudiation pronounced in one session as a single one, based on an opinion espoused by some Hanbalis.[40]

The complete list of these cases merits separate study, because here we can find what the Hanafis would consider as the most essential part of their doctrine.

Through the application of this law of conflict, the Ottomans could both uphold Hanafi supremacy and meet the practical demands of the local population. However, we must not exaggerate the practical importance of this system. It functioned only in a few large cities. Elsewhere, the non-Hanafis would appeal to their muftis who would then act as arbitrators, thus enabling the population to live according to their own madhhab.[41]

At the moment I have no information about whether the Ottoman system of a plurality of jurisdictions under Hanafi hegemony continued to function in Syria into the nineteenth century. In Egypt it was abolished in 1802.[42] Later, in 1835–6 Egyptian muftis were forbidden to give fatwas according to other madhhabs[43] and Hanafi law was fully enforced.

6 Conclusions

In this paper I have argued that the application of Islamic law does not necessarily leave the qadi much room for discretion. In the particular case of the Ottoman Empire it can be shown that both Hanafi legal scholars and the State developed tools in order to restrict the qadis in their freedom to choose legal opinions for their decisions. Hanafi scholars developed formal criteria to determine which opinions were more authoritative or more correct and held that sentences pronounced in disregard of these rules were void. This was corroborated by the Ottoman State, which enjoined the qadis, when they were appointed, to follow the most authoritative opinions of the Hanafi madhhab.

40 Ibn Nujaym, n.d., 7:11–12; Ibn ʿĀbidīn, 1882: 4:451.

41 Gibb and Bowen, 1957: 2:127.

42 Jabartī, ʿAbd al-Raḥmān al-. *ʿAjāʾib al-āthār fī al-tarājim wa-l-akhbār*. 4 vols. Bulaq, 1879–1880: 4:248: "After the [political] had changed and the Turks and their qadis were in power again, they introduced several unwarranted innovations (*bidaʿ*), such as the abolition of the deputy judges (*nuwwāb*) and the three judges of the non-Hanafi law schools and [ordered] that all litigation must be conducted before him or his deputy." See also Gibb and Bowen, 1957:2:123 n. 5.

43 Tamīmī, Muhammad Efendi al-. *Tarjamat ḥayāt al-ʿallāma al-shaykh Aḥmad al-Tamīmī al-Dārī al-Khalīlī muftī Misr*: Ms.: Egyptian National Library, Tārīkh Taymūr 1096, n.d.: 4. See on the position of muftis in nineteenth-century Egypt: Peters, R. "Muhammad al-ʿAbbasi al-Mahdi (d. 1897), Grand Mufti of Egypt, and his al-Fawata al-Mahdiyya." *Islamic Law and Society*. 1, no. i (1994): 66–82.

In some cases, however, the qadis, for reasons of expediency, were instructed by the sultan to follow other opinions. In this way a typical Ottoman Hanafi doctrine came into existence, with legal textbooks that, although they contained the whole range of Hanafi opinions on a certain issue, could be read as clear legal codes. The result was a uniform legal doctrine and a predictable administration of the law.

When the Ottoman Empire, from the beginning of the sixteenth century, began to rule over regions with Muslim populations following other madhhabs, the Hanafi monopoly was limited to the Balkans and Anatolia. Here the qadis and muftis were explicitly forbidden to follow other madhhabs, which, it would seem, they sometimes did in order to circumvent certain difficulties within the Hanafi doctrine. In the newly conquered areas, however, the judges and muftis of other madhhabs were tolerated, but under the supremacy of the official, state-paid Hanafi qadi. On the strength of a sultanic decree, the competence of these qadis in regard to each lawsuit depended on the defendant's choice. The sentences of non-Hanafi qadis had to be approved and given a warrant of execution by the Hanafi court. Before doing so, the court would check whether the sentence violated, from the Hanafi perspective, texts of the Quran, the hadith, or the *ijmāʿ*. As we have lists of rulings that were regarded as unacceptable in this respect, we have an idea about what, according to Hanafi scholars, was seen as the inviolable core of Hanafi doctrine. This is comparable to the function of public policy in the law of conflicts in main or Western-inspired legal systems, which consists of the essential national legal principles that may not he violated when courts must apply foreign law.

Ottoman Hanafi doctrine developed and was elaborated by Hanafi jurists and the State, acting in close cooperation. As a result of this cooperation a legal doctrine and practice emerged that were both uniform and predictable. These qualities made the resulting legal system well suited to the bureaucratic character of the Ottoman State.

CHAPTER 32

The Re-Islamization of Criminal Law in Northern Nigeria and the Judiciary

The Safiyyatu Hussaini Case

1 Introduction*

Islamic penal law was introduced in twelve states of the Nigerian Federal Republic starting from 2000 and stoning sentences have been pronounced since that time. To date, however, none of these sentences have been carried out. The sentences against Safiyyatu Hussaini and Amina Lawal,[1] both quashed on appeal, have attracted a great deal of international attention, thanks to campaigns launched by international human rights and women's rights organizations. In this article I will analyze the proceedings against Safiyyatu Hussaini in an attempt to show how the Northern Nigerian judiciary is handling the re-Islamization of the penal law.

1.1 *The Re-Islamization of Islamic Criminal Law*[2]

As in the United States, the states of the Federal Republic of Nigeria have the power to enact their own laws. The re-Islamization of criminal law is, therefore, a choice of the separate states. On January 27, 2000, Zamfara State enacted the first Shariʿa Penal Code in Northern Nigeria, a few months after Shariʿa courts had been established.[3] In response to public pressure, eleven other Northern states followed suit and introduced Shariʿa courts and criminal legislation based on the Shariʿa.[4] The new Shariʿa penal codes are applicable only

* I would like to thank Dr. Delfina Serrano y Ruano of the Consejo Superior de Investigaciones Científicas, Madrid, for her comments on the first draft of this essay.

1 Amina Lawal was sentenced to death by stoning by the Shariʿa Court of Bakori, Katsina State on March 20, 2002. On August 19, 2002, this sentence was upheld on appeal by the Upper Shariʿa Court of Funtua. The Shariʿa Court of Appeal of Katsina State set this decision aside on September 25, 2003, and acquitted Lawal. Although I have not been able to see the appeal sentence, press reports indicate that the reasoning of the Court is very similar to that of the Shariʿa Court of Appeal of Sokoto State in the Safiyyatu Hussaini case.

2 As the Safiyyatu Hussaini case was tried in Sokoto State, I will refer here only to the Sokoto Shariʿa legislation, which follows closely the Zamfara Shariʿa laws.

3 Zamfara Shariʿa Courts Establishment. Law, 1999 (Law 5 of 1999).

4 Bauchi, Borno, Gombe, Jigawa, Kaduna, Kano, Katsina, Kebbi, Niger, Sokoto, and Yobe. Most of these states followed the example of the Zamfara codes with minor changes. Whereas

 | DOI:10.1163/9789004420625_033

to Muslims and to those non-Muslims who voluntarily and in writing submit to its jurisdiction. Non-Muslims continue to be governed by the 1959 Penal Code of Northern Nigeria.

The introduction of these new codes has restored the situation that existed before 1960. Until that date, Islamic law was the law applied to all Muslims in the North in civil, personal, and criminal matters. Criminal sentences pronounced under the Shariʿa were carried out by the British colonial administration. However, sentences of amputation or death by stoning were commuted into prison sentences, on the grounds that they are "repugnant to natural justice, equity, and good conscience." In 1960 a new Penal Code for the North put an end to the implementation of traditional, uncodified Islamic criminal law. The re-Islamization of criminal law has now restored the pre-1960 situation, but with two major changes: First, Islamic criminal justice is no longer subjected to direct state control, although it must, of course, be compatible with the provisions of the Constitution of the Federal Republic of Nigeria (CFRN).[5] Second, Islamic criminal law has now been codified, as required by Section 36(12) of the Constitution.[6]

The re-Islamization of the legal systems of the Northern states began with changes in the judiciary. Until the year 2000, there were two sets of courts in the Northern States:

- Magistrate Courts applying Common Law, with the State High Court as appellate court.
- Area Courts, in two or three levels, applying the Shariʿa in civil and personal, and the 1959 Penal Code in criminal cases. In matters of personal law, the State Shariʿa Court of Appeal was the appellate court; in other matters decisions of the area courts could be appealed to the State High Court.

Just before the promulgation of Shariʿa Penal Codes, the Northern states had set up Islamic courts as a first step towards Islamization. This was done by abolishing the Area Courts (traditionally known as *alkalis* courts, from the Arabic (*al-qāḍī*) and replacing them with Shariʿa Courts. In fact, only the name Area Courts was changed and the judges sitting in them kept their office. In

---

Kano State has enacted an independent Shariʿa Penal Code, Niger State has contented itself with adding a few amendments to the 1959 Penal Code for Northern Nigeria. See Ruud Peters. *Islamic Criminal Law in Nigeria*. Ibadan: Spectrum Books, 2003. pp. 81–2.

5 On the areas of conflict, see Peters (2003:31–43). The Supreme Federal Court has not yet ruled on any of these incompatibilities.

6 "Subject as otherwise provided by this Constitution, a person shall not be convicted of a criminal offense unless that offense is defined and the penalty therefor is prescribed in a written law, and in this subsection, a written law refers to an Act of the National Assembly or a Law of a State, any subsidiary legislation or instrument under the provisions of a law."

Sokoto two classes of these courts were established: Lower Shari'a Courts in which only one judge sits and Upper Shari'ah Courts[7] composed of a president and one member. (Section 3 Sokoto Shari'a Court Law, 2000; henceforth SSCL). These judges must be knowledgeable in Islamic Law as shown by diplomas or offices held previously, unless they were already serving on the area courts (Section 4 SSCL). The Shari'a courts have jurisdiction in civil and criminal cases and must adjudicate according to the Shari'a (Section 5(6), 5(7), 10 SSCL). Any law that is enacted will apply only insofar as it is not contrary to the principles of the Shari'a (Section 20 SSCL). This clause is in clear defiance of the Nigerian legal system, in which written, enacted law takes precedence over customary law and Islamic law. Further, the jurisdiction of the State Shari'ah Courts of appeal, which previously could hear appeals only in cases of personal law, was extended to all cases tried before the lower Shari'a courts (Section 5(1), 5(2) SSCL). The new Shari'a Courts are competent in all civil litigation, if both parties are Muslims, and in criminal proceedings, if the accused is a Muslim (Section 5(3), 5(4), 8 SSCL; Section 3 Shari'ah Criminal Procedure Code [henceforth SSCPC]).

The new courts are instructed to apply uncodified Maliki law, in both civil and criminal cases. Section 6 of the SSCL reads:

> The applicable laws in both civil and criminal proceedings before the Shari'a Court shall include: (a) The Holy Qur'an (b) Sunnah and Hadith (c) Ijma; (d) Qiyas; (e) Maslahat Marsala; (f) Istihsan; (g) Istishab; h) al-urf; Muzhabul-Sahabi [sic! *Madhhab al-Ṣaḥābī* RP]; and (j) Other subsidiary sources.

Section 7 of the SSCL lists sixteen Maliki *fiqh* texts that are authoritative in the Shari'a Courts.[8] Moreover, the law stipulates that practice, procedure, and

7 Sokoto State is not consistent in the spelling of the word "Shari'a". It appears without a final "h" in the SSCL and with the final "h" in the SSPC and SCPC.

8 In presenting the text of this Section, I have retained its spelling and have added the complete titles in square brackets.
(a) Al-Risālah [by Ibn Abī Zayd al-Qayrawānī (d. 996)]; (b) Muhtasar [by Khalīl b. Isḥāq (d. 1365]; (c) Tuhfah [*Tuḥfat al-ḥukkām* by Ibn ʿĀṣim (d. 1427)]; (d) Al-Adawi [Supercommentary by ʿAlī al-Ṣaʿīdī al-ʿAdawī (d. 1775) on a commentary by Abū al-Ḥasan al-Minūfī (d. 1532) on the *Risāla* of al-Qayrawānī]; (e) Al-Fawakih al-Dawani [*al-Fawākih al-Dawānī* by Aḥmad b. Ghunaym al-Nafrāwī, commentary on the *Risāla* by al-Qayrawānī]; (f) Ibn Ashir [not identified]; (g) Bidayat al-Mujtahid [by Ibn Rushd al-ḥafīd (d. 1198)]; (h) Al-Mudawanah [by Saḥnūn (d. 854); (i) Muwattah Malik; (j) Mayyara [Muḥammad b. Aḥmad Mayyāra (d. 1641–2), commentator of the *Tuḥfa* by Ibn ʿĀṣim]; (k) Bahjah [*Al-Bahja*, Commentary by al-Tasūlī (d. 1842) on the *Tuḥfa* of Ibn ʿĀṣim]; (l) Jawahir al-Iklil [Jawāhir al-Iklīl by Ṣāliḥ ʿAbd al-Samīʿ

evidence are to be regulated by Maliki doctrine (Section 10(1.a), 10(1.b) SCL). However, on January 31, 2001, a penal code and a code of criminal procedure replaced uncodified Shari'a when the Sokoto Shari'ah Penal Code (SSPC) and the Sokoto Shari'ah Criminal Procedure Code (SSCPC) came into force. They define the offenses and their punishments and stipulate that the investigation, inquiry, and procedure of Shari'ah offenses shall be governed by the SCPC. However, the introduction of the SSPC has not put an end to the direct enforcement of uncodified Islamic criminal law. Consider the following provision:

> Any act or omission which is not specifically mentioned in this Shari'ah Penal Code but is otherwise declared to be an offense under the Qur'an, Sunnah and *Ijtihad* of the Maliki School of Islamic thought shall be an offense under this code and such act or omission shall be punishable:
> a. With imprisonment for a term which may extend to 5 years, or
> b. With caning which may extend to 50 lashes, or
> c. With fine which may extend to Maim] 5,000.00 or with any two of the above punishments.[9]

The new codes do not contain provisions on a number of crucial issues, as, for example, evidence. This omission was probably deliberate. State legislation on points of evidence would violate the Federal Islamic Constitution, which stipulates that evidence is one of the fields in which the Federation has exclusive power to enact laws.[10] Since the law is silent, the Shari'a courts apply the Maliki doctrine of evidence in cases of homicide and *ḥadd* offenses.

The SSPC, like the other Shari'a Penal Codes enacted in Northern Nigeria, follows a model that was previously introduced in other countries.[11] Like these other Shari'a codes, the SSPC, under the heading *ta'zir*, contains the penal provisions taken from the previous penal codes (i.e., the 1959 Penal Code for

---

al-Ābī on the *Mukhtaṣar* of Khalīl b. Isḥaq]; (m) Dasuki [Supercommentary by Ibrāhīm al-Dasūqī (d. 1815) on the commentary by Aḥmad al-Dardīr (d. 1786) on the *Mukhtaṣar* of Khalīl b. Isḥaq]; (n) Al-Khirshi ['Abd Allāh al-Khirshī (d. 1689), author of two commentaries on the *Mukhtaṣar* by Khalīl b. Isḥāq]; (o) Bulgatil Salik [Bulghat al-Sālik, supercommentary by Aḥmad al-Ṣāwī (d. 1825) on the commentary on *Aqrab al-masālik li-madhhab al-Imām Mālik* of Aḥmad al-Dardīr]; (p) Mawahibul Hallaq [Abū Shitā' b. Ḥasan al-Ṣunhājl (d. 1946), *Mawāhib al-Khallāq 'alā sharḥ* al-Tāwudī (d. 1700) *li-Lāmiyat* Al-Zaqqāq (d. 1506).

9 Sokoto Shari'a Penal Code (SSCP), Section 94.

10 See the Federal Constitution of the Republic of Nigeria (FCRN), Section 4(2), (3 and the Exclusive Legislative List.

11 See Peters, R. "The Islamization of criminal law: a comparative analysis." *Welt des Islams* 34, no. ii (1994): 246–274.

Northern Nigeria in the case of the Northern Nigerian States) to which are added chapters defining the Qur'anic offenses (*ḥudūd*) and the Islamic law of homicide and hurt. In addition the SSPC increased the number of offenses punishable by corporal punishment (caning or flogging).

The chapter on general provisions, Section 95, lists the punishments and introduces the new Shari'a penalties, such as retaliation (for homicide and grievous hurt), amputation, caning and the payment of blood money (*diya*) as a compensation for homicide and hurt. The list, however, is not exhaustive. Death by stoning and crucifixion are not listed here, although they are mentioned in Section 129(h) SSPC, Section 231(c) and (d) SSCPC. On the other hand, punishments such as reprimand, public disclosure, boycott, and exhortation, which are mentioned in Section 95, do not occur elsewhere in the code.

1.2 *Unlawful Sexual Intercourse in Maliki Doctrine*

Under Islamic law sexual intercourse is allowed only within a marriage (or, in premodern times, between a slave woman and her owner). Extramarital intercourse is unlawful and may, under certain conditions, constitute a punishable offense, *zinā*, which is one of the *ḥadd* crimes, i.e. crimes mentioned in the Qur'an for which fixed punishments are specified. *Zinā* is to be punished with death by stoning if the offender is *muḥṣan*, i.e., adult, free, Muslim, and one who has previously experienced legitimate sexual relations within a marriage (regardless of whether the marriage still exists) with a person who is also *muḥṣan*. A person who is not *muḥṣan* is punished with 100 lashes, which is followed by banishment for one year. The offenders must have acted of their own free will: a woman who has been raped (*mustakraha*) cannot receive the *ḥadd* punishment. However, she must produce some form of evidence to substantiate her allegation of rape. *Zinā* may be established by a confession, the testimony of four eyewitnesses who are Muslim males of good reputation and, exclusive to the Maliki school, by the visible pregnancy of an unmarried woman. The witnesses must have seen the act in its most intimate details, i.e., the penetration ("like the kohl stick [entering] into the kohl container *mikḥala*," as the *fiqh* books put it). If the witnesses' testimonies do not satisfy the requirements, they can be sentenced to eighty lashes for an unfounded accusation of fornication (*qadhf*). However, even if the offense has been established, punishment can be averted in the event of *shubha* (uncertainty or doubt about the unlawfulness of the proven act) due to circumstances that cause it to appear as if it were legal, such as intercourse between two parties to a marriage which is null and void, between a master and his female slave of whom he is a co-owner or whom he has acquired on the strength of an invalid purchase, or between a blind man and a woman whom he mistook for his wife or female slave. An unmarried woman who is charged with zina on the strength of her pregnancy can plead in defense that the pregnancy resulted from intercourse with a man who penetrated her while she was sleeping and that she had no knowledge of it, or that the pregnancy resulted from intercourse between her thighs, without penetration. Her statement to this effect is regarded as sufficient grounds for *shubha*.[12] Rape, however, is difficult to establish. Such a plea must be substantiated by circumstantial evidence, for instance, the fact that the woman bled (if she was a virgin) or entered her village screaming for help. If she cannot produce such evidence, her defense is not accepted and, if she identified her attacker, she is also liable to prosecution for defamation (*qadhf*).

2 The Case

On 25 March 2002, the Shariʿa Court of Appeal of Sokoto State quashed the decision of the Upper Shariʿa Court of Gwadabawa that sentenced Safiyyatu Hussaini to be stoned to death for unlawful sexual intercourse. As a result she was acquitted. The Appeal Court found that on several grounds, the decision of the lower court could not stand: the lower court lacked jurisdiction, had not followed proper procedure and had erred in the application of the law. In the following I will discuss and analyse this decision, which is a clear illustration of how, after the re-introduction of Shariʿa penal law, Shariʿa courts deal with it. In the conclusion I will pay attention to the peculiarities of the Nigerian situation, as Northern Nigeria is the only region where Islamic criminal law is implemented within the framework of a non-Islamic and essentially secular constitution. Moreover I will point out the significance of this decision for future trials of similar cases.

The original decisions were written in Hausa and, to the best of my knowledge, not officially published. I have relied on two texts translated into English: one claiming to contain the full translation of the sentence[13] and one containing only a summary.[14] The English of the full translation is defective and

12 See e.g. Ṣāliḥ ʿAbd al-Samīʿ al-Ābī, *Jawāhir al-Iklīl sharḥ Mukhtaṣar Khalīl*. (Cairo: ʿĪsā al-Bābī al-Ḥalabī, n.d.) Vol. 2, p. 285; Al-Ṣāwī, *Ḥāshiyat al-Ṣāwī ʿalā al-Sharḥ al-Saghīr* (Cairo, Dār al-Maʿārif, n.d.), vol. 4, p. 455. Ch. Proving *zinā* (*Thubūt al-zinā*); Ibn Farḥūn, *Tabṣirat al-ḥukkām* (Cairo, 1986), vol. 2, p. 97 (Ch. 64 on giving judgement on *zinâ* on the strength of evidence of pregnancy).

13 *Safiyyatu's Case*. Tr. by Ibrahim Ladan. Enugu, Women's Aid Collective, 2003. 37 pp.

14 B. Babaji and Y. Dankofa, "Assessing the performance of the lower courts in the implementation of Shariʿa penal laws in Northern Nigeria." in J.N. Ezeilo, M.T. Ladan and A. Afolabi-Akiyode (eds), *Shafia implementation in Nigeria: Issues and challenges on*

sometimes almost incomprehensible. Moreover, its leaves out the Arabic texts of the quotations of the legal sources, that the original contained and only retains the references to them, although often in an almost unrecognisable form (e.g. "Bahjah fi – sharit – tufimam" for *al-Bahja fī sharḥ al-Tuḥfa*). At some points, therefore, my presentation of the case is founded on informed guess work, based on my familiarity with Islamic law and my access the pertinent Sokoto legislation and the quoted fiqh texts. The same is true regarding the quotations from the Arabic sources. In most cases I think that I succeeded in tracing them in spite of the fact that the references do not make mention of the editions that were used. Unless otherwise indicated, the footnotes list the sources of the quotations in the text of the sentence, although in most cases from different editions.

2.1 *The Trial Court and Its Sentence*

On October 9, 2001, the Upper Shariʿa Court of Gwadabawa (Sokoto State) pronounced a sentence of death by stoning for unlawful sexual intercourse against Safiyyatu Hussaini of the village of Tungkar Tudu. The execution of the sentence was stayed until the woman finished nursing her infant daughter. At the same time the court acquitted Yakubu Abubakar, who had been accused of the same offense and allegedly was the father of Safiyyatu Hussaini's child. The two had been charged with the offense of *zinā*, illegal sexual intercourse, which Section 128 and 129 SSPC make punishable with a caning of 100 lashes or death by stoning.[15] The charges against Safiyyatu Hussaini were based on the preliminary police investigation, during which Safiyyatu acknowledged that she had had intercourse with Yakubu Abubakar on four occasions, and, as a result, had become pregnant and given birth to a daughter who was now [i.e., during the trial session in July 2001) six-months old. During the police investigation Abubakar denied having had sexual relations with her. Subsequently, four prosecution witnesses testified to the truthfulness of Safiyyatu's acknowledgment and Yakubu's denial. Thereupon Yakubu was given the opportunity to challenge all the testimonies, whereas Safiyyatu was allowed to do so only

---

Women's rights and access to justice. Enugu: Women's Aid Collective, 2003, pp. 103–127. The summary of the sentence is found on pp. 123–125.

15 "Whoever, being a man or woman fully responsible, has sexual intercourse through the genital of a person over whom he has no sexual rights and in circumstances in which no doubt exists as to the illegality of the act, is guilty of the offense of zinā." (Section 128) "Whoever commits the offense of zinā shall be punished (a) with caning of one hundred lashes if unmarried and shall also be liable to imprisonment for a term of one year; or (b) if married, with stoning to death." (Section 129) It is to be noted that in the text of the code the technical term "*iḥṣān*" is incorrectly translated as "married." The court, apparently, construes "married" as *muḥṣan*.

with regard to two witnesses, both of them police officers. In response to the charges brought against her during the trial, she stuck to her previous statement and declared that to her knowledge it was Yakubu's semen ("water") that entered and made her pregnant, since after she left her husband's house she had three menstrual periods and she has cleansed herself before having sexual contact with Yakubu.

The court took note of Safiyyatu's statement in the presence of two male witnesses and it then formally charged the accused. When they told the court that they did not understand the charges, the court explained them as follows:

> What is meant by [the] charge[s] is that the court is suspecting you of *zinā*, [for] which if proved, your punishment will be death by stoning you to death, because you are all Muslims and both have been married before.

Before the judgement, the court asked the accused whether they had any defence that could prevent the court from sentencing them to death. Thereupon the court acquitted Yakubu for lack of proof and found Safiyyatu Hussaini guilty of the offence of *zinā* punishable by stoning to death as provided under Section 129(b) of SSPC[16] with the note that the sentences shall not be carried out until she has finished suckling her baby.

In support of the sentence the court quoted the *Risāla* (of Ibn Abī Zayd al-Qayrawānī, d. 996), one of the two leading sort textbooks of the Malikite school:

> A person who has had unlawful intercourse will not be punished with the *ḥadd* penalty unless there is a confession, a visible pregnancy (*ḥaml yaẓhar*) or the testimonies of four free adult men of good reputation (*ʿudūl*) who have seen [the male member in the vagina] like the kohl stick [entering] into the kohl container.[17]

In justification of the stay of execution, the court quoted a hadith listed in the *Muwaṭṭaʾ* of Mālik:

> On the authority of ʿAbd Allāh b. Abī Mulayka: A woman came to the Messenger of God and told him, while she was pregnant, that she had had unlawful sexual relations. The Messenger of God said to her: 'Go away until you have given birth.' After she had given birth she came back

16 The translation erroneously mentions Section 129(b) of the SSCPC.

17 Ṣāliḥ ʿAbd al-Samīʿ al-Ābī al-Azharī, *Al-Thamr Al-Dānī Sharḥ Risālat Ibn Abī Zayd Al-Qayrawānī*. Tunis: Maktabat al-Manār, n.d., p. 592.

and the Messenger of God said to her: 'Go away until you have finished suckling him.' After she had finished suckling him, she came back and he said: 'Go away and entrust him [to someone].' She then entrusted him to someone and came back. Thereupon he ordered her to be stoned.[18]

2.2 *The Appeal*

Safiyyatu Hussaini appealed against this sentence to the Sokoto Shariʿa Court of Appeal. She had availed herself of legal counsel, a team of no fewer that eleven lawyers. With the appeal she withdrew her confession made during the trial and asserted that the father of her child was her former husband and not Yakubu Abubakar. Her lawyers submitted that the decision of the Upper Shariʿa Court of Gwadabawa could not stand and had to be set aside. The Shariʿa Court of Appeal found substance in almost all of the grounds presented by the counsel for the appellant and quashed the decision of the trial court. The grounds for appeal related to three aspects of the trial: the trial court's lack of jurisdiction, errors in the procedure followed by that court, and errors in the application of the law. I will deal with the appeal and decision under these three headings, presenting the arguments of the counsel for the appellant (Safiyyatu Hussaini), the state counsel (representing the Attorney General of Sokoto State, who was the respondent) and, finally, the considerations of the Shariʿa Court of Appeal.

2.3 *Jurisdiction of the Trial Court*

The counsel for the appellant argued that the sentence of the lower court had to be set aside because that court lacked jurisdiction to try the case. The appellant was sentenced on the strength of s. 129(b) of the SSPC. This bill had been signed by the Governor of Sokoto State only on January 25, 2001, and was therefore not in force before that date. However, the appellant was arraigned before the trial court on the strength of a police report dated December 23, 2000. The offense of which she was accused must therefore have been committed before that date.[19] Now, neither under Islamic law, nor under the Constitution[20] can

18 Mālik b. Anas, *Muwaṭṭa'*, Ed. Muḥammad Fu'ād ʿAbd al-Bāqī. Cairo: Dār al-Shaʿb, n.d, p. 513. Section 253 (2) SSCPC contains the same rule.

19 Since Safiyyatu's infant daughter was six-months old in July 2001, she must have been born in late December 2000 or early January 2001. Although it is not expressly mentioned, it is likely that the police investigation began after Safiyyatu's delivery.

20 Section 4(9) CFRN stipulates, "Notwithstanding the foregoing provisions of this Section, the National Assembly or a House of Assembly shall not, in relation to any criminal offense whatsoever, have power to make any law which shall have retrospective effect." Section 36(12) CFRN reads: "Subject as otherwise provided by this Constitution, a person shall not be convicted of a criminal offense unless that offense is defined and the penalty therefor is prescribed in a written law, and in this subsection, a written law refers to an

a person be punished on the strength of a law that has not been enacted at the time when the offense was committed.

This argument was contested by the state counsel, who referred the court to the provisions of the Sokoto Shariʿa Courts Law, which had been promulgated in the year 2000. According to this law, the Shariʿa courts do have jurisdiction to take cognizance of criminal cases and apply Islamic law.[21] This jurisdiction in criminal cases, the state counsel asserted, is in agreement with Section 38(1)[22] of the Constitution which guarantees freedom of religion, and which includes the right to live under the Shariʿa. It is of no consequence that the SSPC, which in Sections 128 and 129 defines the offense of *zinā*, had not yet come into force at the time the offense took place, since the offense was already punishable under the SSCL. Starting from there, the state counsel asserted, the Upper Shariʿa Court was competent on the strength of s. 12(1)[23] of the SCPC that was in force at the time of the trial.

The court agreed with the counsel for the appellant and confirmed that the lower court did not have jurisdiction to try the case. It added that the official charge did riot mention the date on which the offense allegedly was committed or its location, but that, in any case, this must have been before the coming into force of the SSPC under which the appellant had been sentenced. In addition to the legal provisions cited by the counsel for the appellant in support of the principle that laws do not have retroactive effect, the court referred to Section 36(8) FCRN[24] and Section 7 SSPC.[25]

Act of the National Assembly or a Law of a State, any subsidiary legislation or instrument under the provisions of a law."

21 5(1): "A Shariʿah Court shall have jurisdiction ... and in criminal cases where the suspect(s) or accused person(s) is/are Muslims." Subsection (4) lists eighteen criminal offenses (among them *zinā*) that the Shariʿah courts are competent to try. Subsection (6) provides that the applicable law shall be Islamic law, whereas subsection (7) gives a list of Maliki authorities (see note 8).

22 "Every person shall be entitled to freedom of thought, conscience and religion, including freedom to change his religion or belief; arid freedom (either alone or in community with others, and in public or in private) to manifest and propagate his religion or belief in worship, teaching, practice and observance." Section 38(1) FCRN.

23 "Subject to the other provisions of this Shariʿah Criminal Procedure Code, the Upper Shariʿah Courts shall have jurisdiction to try any or all of the offenses listed in 'Appendix A' of this Code." This Appendix lists, among other offenses, *zinā* as an offense to be tried by the Upper Shariʿah Courts.

24 "No person shall he held to be guilty of a criminal offense on account of any act or omission that did not, at the time it took place, constitute such an offense, and no penalty shall be imposed for any criminal offense heavier than the penalty in force at the time the offense was committed."

25 "No act or omission committed by a person shall be an offense under the provisions of this law unless such act or omission was committed on or after the commencement date of this law."

2.4 *Proper Procedure*

2.4.1 The Investigation

The counsel for the appellant submitted that the police did not follow the proper procedure for investigating *zinā* cases and that the case was brought to the lower court in an unlawful manner. During the lifetime of the Prophet and the Rightly Guided Caliphs, it was the offenders themselves, in trials for *zinā*, who presented their cases to the authorities. In this case, however, people had pried into Safiyyatu's affairs and then brought her case to the attention of the authorities on the mere suspicion that she was pregnant out of wedlock. This is unlawful, for *zinā* cases can be brought to court only if there is a confession or four male Muslim eyewitnesses of good reputation.

The state counsel contested this principle, citing the Qur'an and the hadith. First he quoted Q. 16:90:[26]

> Lo! God enjoineth justice and kindness, and giving to kinsfolk, and forbiddeth lewdness and abomination and wickedness. He exhorteth you in order that ye may take heed.

Counsel inferred from this text that Muslims may take action if they are confronted with "lewdness, abomination, and wickedness." He then cited to two hadiths:

1. On the authority of Abu Saʿīd al-Khuḍarī, who said: "I heard the Messenger of Allah say: 'Whosoever of you sees an evil action, let him change it with his hand; and if he is not able to do so, then with his tongue; and if he is not able to do so, then with his heart; and that is the weakest of faith.'" (Muslim)[27]
2. On the authority of Abu Hurayra, who said: A Bedouin came to the Prophet and said: "O Messenger of God, I implore you by God to pass judgment on me in accordance with God's Book." And his adversary, who was better versed in jurisprudence than he, said: "Yes, pass judgment between us and allow me to speak." The Prophet said: "Talk." He said: "My son worked as a laborer for this man and then he fornicated with his wife. I was told that my son deserved to be stoned to death,

26 I have made use of the Qur'an translation of M.M. Pickthall, *The Meaning of the Glorious Qur'an*, except that I have replaced the word "Allah" with "God."

27 The State counsel refers to hadith No. 37 of the *Arbaʿūn Ḥadīth* of al-Nawawt, which makes no sense in this context, as this hadith deals with the consequences of *niyya* (intention) on the reward or punishment of human actions. He probably meant No. 34, which is the one I quote in the text.

> so I ransomed him for 100 sheep and a female slave. I then asked the people of knowledge and they informed me that my son deserved 100 lashes and banishment for one year and that the woman deserved to be stoned to death." The Prophet answered: "By the One Who holds my soul in His hand, I shall certainly pass judgment between you in accordance with God's Book. As for the slave girl and the sheep, they must be returned to you. Your son deserves 100 lashes and banishment for a year. Go, Unays, to this man's wife and if she confesses, stone her to death." Thereupon Unays went to the woman and she confessed. Then the Prophet ordered her to be stoned."[28]

The first hadith demonstrates that a Muslim may, indeed, he must take action if he is confronted with an evil deed. The second hadith, according to the state counsel, shows that the Prophet sent Unays to interrogate a woman who was suspected of having had unlawful sexual intercourse.

The court found substance in the submissions of the counsel for the appellant and went to great length to refute the arguments of the state counsel. The court's starting point was that it is forbidden, *ḥarām*, to pry into the affairs of others and to report cases of *zinā* merely on the basis of hearsay. This is based on Q. 49:12

> O ye who believe! Shun much suspicion; for lo! some suspicion is a crime. And spy not, neither backbite one another. Would one of you love to eat the flesh of his dead brother? Ye abhor that (so abhor the other)! And keep your duty (to God). Lo! God is Relenting, Merciful.

Further, the court mentioned (without quoting a source) that Imam al-Shafiʿi stated that a leader has no right to send someone to a person suspected of the offense of *zinā* in order to interrogate him. Finally, the court referred to texts quoted in *Kitab al-fiqh ʿalā al-madhāhib al-arbaʿa*.[29] The court concluded that the arrest of Safiyyatu on the mere suspicion of having committed *zinā* was unlawful.

---

28 The state counsel refers to the English translation of the *Ṣaḥīḥ* of al-Bukhārī: *The translation of the meanings of Sahih al-Bukhari* (Lahore: Kazi Publications, 1979) Vol. 8, p. 536. The translation I give here is based on the Arabic original found in Ibn Ḥajar al-ʿAsqalānī. *Bulūgh Al-Marām min adillat al-aḥkām*. (Cairo: Dār al-Kitāb al-ʿArabī, n.d.) No. 1031.

29 Jazīrī, ʿAbd al-Raḥmān al-, *Kitab al-fiqh ʿalā al-madhāhib al-arbaʿa* (Cairo: Dār al-Irshād, n.d.). Vol. 5, pp. 120–123 (the page number 233 mentioned in the translation is erroneous). Here a number of hadiths are quoted enjoining discretion (*satr*) with regard to the investigation of *zinā*.

The court dismissed the arguments submitted by the state counsel as inconclusive. The words "and forbiddeth lewdness and abomination and wickedness" in Q. 16:90, quoted by the state counsel, do not specifically refer to *zinā*, but rather, according to the *Jāmiʿ Aḥkām al-Qurʾān*, to all sins.[30] The verse, therefore, does not permit the arrest of anyone who is suspected of *zinā*. The same holds for the hadith about Unays quoted by the state counsel. The *Subul al-Salām sharḥ Bulūgh al-Marām* makes it clear that there is no conflict between the Prophet sending Unays to the woman with whom the Bedouin's son had had intercourse and the Prophet's instruction that fornication (*fāḥisha*) should be kept secret, both by the person who committed it and by others. Nor does this injunction contradict his prohibition of spying on others. The reason that the Prophet sent Unays to the woman was that she had been slandered (*qudhifat*). Therefore, she should either deny the allegation and demand the *ḥadd* punishment for false accusation of unlawful sexual intercourse (*qadhf*), or confess so that the accuser would not be punished. She confessed, thereby exposing herself to the *ḥadd* punishment.[31] This hadith, therefore, does not indicate that the authorities may investigate cases of *zinā* and report them to a court.

2.4.2 Explanation of the Charges to the Accused

A further procedural ground for appeal submitted by the counsel for the appellant was the fact that the charge frame did not sufficiently explain to the appellant the meaning of a *zinā* charge and its consequences. The counsel for the appellant argued that the trial court should have explained the meaning of the word zina, as is done in s. 128 SSPC, since the appellant is a Hausa village woman and not an Arab. He referred to the hadith of Māʿiz (without giving a source), according to which, after Māʿiz had confessed four times that he had committed *zinā*, the Prophet asked him whether he understood the meaning of the word and explained it to him.[32] Now, Māʿiz was an Arab whereas Safiyyatu

30 Al-Qurṭubī, *Jāmiʿ Aḥkām al-Qurʾān* (Beirut: Dār Iḥyāʾ al-Turāth al-ʿArabī, 1966) Vol. 10, p. 167.

31 Muḥammad al-Kaḥlānī, *Subul al-Salām sharḥ Bulūgh al-Marām li-Ibn Ḥajar al-ʿAsqalānī* (Cairo: Dār al-Fikr, n.d.) Vol. 4, p. 4.

32 The hadith, which is not quoted in the text, is as follows: On the authority of Abu Hurayra: "A Muslim man [n other sources identified as a certain Māʿiz came to the Prophet when he was in the mosque and called to him: 'O Messenger of God, I have had illegal sexual relations.' The Prophet then turned away from him. But the man moved in order to face him and said: 'O Messenger of God, I have had illegal sexual relations.' Again the Prophet turned away, until he had repeated it four times. After the man had testified against himself four times, the Prophet called to him: Are you perhaps a bit insane?' The man answered, 'No.' Then he asked: Have you ever been married? The man answered, 'Yes.'

does not speak or understand Arabic. Therefore the court should have made its meaning clear to her. Although the counsel for the respondent submitted that the trial court has sufficiently explained the nature of the offence with which the appellant was charged, the Shariʿa Court of Appeal agreed with the counsel for the appellant. In support the court referred to following text from ʿAbd al-Qādir ʿAwda, *al-Tashrīʿ al-Jināʾī al-Islāmī,* quoting from the *Subul al-Salām sharḥ Bulūgh al-Marām*:

> For a confession to be accepted it is required that it be detailed and clarify the actual action so that there is no more doubt as to the confession. This is important especially side the word *zinā* may be used for acts that do not entail the *ḥadd* penalty, such as intercourse without penetration. The requirement of detailed interrogation and the explicit clarification goes back to the *sunna* of the Messenger of God (May God bless him and grant him salvation), for when Māʿiz came to him to confess that he committed *zinā* and repeated his confession, the Prophet asked whether he was insane or whether he had drunk wine and ordered someone to smell his breath. Thereupon he questioned him about *zinā*, saying: "Have you perhaps just kissed her or touched her? In another version: "Did you lie down with her?" He said yes. Then [the Prophet] asked: "Did your body touch hers?" He answered yes. Then [the Prophet] asked: "Did you have intercourse with her (*a-jāmaʿtahā*)?" He said yes. In the hadith of Ibn ʿAbbās [the Prophet asked], calling a spade a spade (*lā yakunn*): "Did you f*** her?" (*a-niktahā*)?" He said yes. Then he asked: "Did that thing of yours enter that thing of hers?" He answered yes. He asked: "Like the kohl stick disappears in the kohl container and the bucket in the well?" He answered yes. Then he asked: "Do you know what *zinā* means?" He said: "Yes, I did with her unlawfully what a man does with his wife lawfully." Then the Prophet said: "What do you intend with these words?" He answered: "That you purify me." Then he ordered him to be stoned."[33]

Taking this hadith into consideration, the court is of the opinion that the nature of the charge has not sufficiently been explained to the accused. This is both repugnant to the principles of Islamic law and to s. 36(6) (a) of the

---

Then the Prophet said: 'Take him away and stone him.' Ibn Ḥajar al-ʿAsqalānī. (Cairo: Dār al-Kitāb al-ʿArabī, n.d.) no. 1033.

33 Abd al-Qādir ʿAwda, *al-Tashrīʿ al-Jināʾī al-Islāmī* (Cairo: Dār al-Turāth, n.d.) Vol. 2, pp. 433–4; As acknowledged in a footnote, ʿAwda cites this text from the *Subul al-Salām sharḥ Bulūgh al-Marām.* See Muḥammad al-Kaḥlānī, *Subul al-Salām sharḥ Bulūgh al-Marām li-l-ʿAsqalānī* (Cairo: Dār al-Fikr, n.d.) Vol. 4, 6–7.

Constitution.[34] Moreover, the charge did not specify when and where the offense took place, which is also contrary to Islamic law as illustrated by the hadith about Māʿiz) and in conflict with s. 170 of the SSCPC.[35]

2.4.3 Opportunity of Defense against Testimonies (*Iʿdhār*)

The counsel for the appellant further argued that the decision of the lower court had to be set aside because of another procedural error. Under Islamic law, the accused must be given the opportunity to defend himself or bring witnesses in his defense (Hausa *izari*, from Arabic *iʿdhār*). The trial court failed to accord Safiyyatu this opportunity with regard to the four witnesses who testified for the prosecution about the results of the police investigation. The counsel referred to the *Iḥkām al-aḥkām* and the *Bahja*.[36] This was contested by the counsel for the respondent who submitted that *iʿdhār* had taken place. The Court of Appeal, finally, considered that the complaint of the counsel for the appellant was not entirely valid. According to the trial record *iʿdhār* had taken place. However, the lower court did not offer it to the accused immediately before the final sentencing, as is mandatory.[37] Since the *iʿdhār* that took place during the trial was followed by further proceedings, it was nullified and the court had to initiate another one. This entails the nullification of the sentence, as stated in the *Bahja fī sharḥ al-Tuḥfa*.

2.4.4 Advising the Accused of His Right to Legal Counsel

The only issue on which the court disagreed with the counsel for the appellant was his submission that the trial court should have advised the accused of her

34 Section 36(6)(a) reads: "Every person who is charged with a criminal offence shall be entitled to be informed promptly in the language that he understands and in detail of the nature of the offence."

35 170(1) "Every charge under this Shariʿah Criminal Procedure Code shall have a statement of the offense complained of with elate and place.... (2) The charge shall also as much as possible define the offense so as to give the accused notice of the matter with which he is charged."

36 The text of the *Tuḥfa* by Ibn ʿĀṣim reads: "Before sentencing the *iʿdhār* must be established by two witnesses of good reputation, which is the preferred opinion." In the two commentaries of this poem to which the counsel refers, the authors lay down that a sentenced without *iʿdhār* is null and void and that *iʿdhār* must take place immediately before sentencing. If *iʿdhār* is followed by further proceedings, e.g. the testimonies of witnesses, the *qāḍī* must offer a new *iʿdhār*, for failure to do so entails the nullity of the judgement. See Muḥammad b. Yūsuf al-Kāfī (d. 1960), *Iḥkām al-Aḥkām sharḥ Tuḥfat al-Aḥkām li-Ibn ʿĀṣim*. Dār al-Bayḍāʾ: Dār al-Rashād al-Ḥadītha, 1991, pp. 21–22, and ʿAlī b. ʿAbd al-Salām al-Tasūlī. *Al-Bahja fī sharḥ al-Tuḥfa li-Muḥammad b. ʿĀṣim*. 3rd impr. Beirut: Dār al-Maʿrifa, 1977. Vol. 1, p. 64.

37 This is not clear from the translation of the decision of the trial court. RP.

right to legal counsel of her choice. This, the court of appeal held, is not a duty of the trial court.

2.5 *Errors in Applying the Law*

2.5.1 Withdrawal of Confession

The counsel for the appellant submitted that the trial court sentence must be set aside because the appellant had now withdrawn her confession, which, according to the *Al-Mukhtaṣar* of Khalil, is her right.[38] To this the state counsel responded that in *ḥadd* cases a confession may be withdrawn at any time, but that in this case such a withdrawal has no effect due to the pregnancy of the accused. In support of his assertion, he quoted the same passage from the *al-Thamr al-Dānī sharḥ Risalat al-Qayrawānī* as the trial court did (*vide supra*), and a text from Ibn Rushd's *Bidāyat al-mujtahid*:

> As to the controversy with regard to applying the *ḥadd* penalty [for *zinā*] on the strength of pregnancy in combination with the claim [of the woman] that she has been raped, there is a group that holds that in such a case the *ḥadd* penalty is mandatory on the strength of the hadith of 'Umar, mentioned by Malik in the *al-Muwaṭṭa'*.[39] This is the opinion of Malik. [She is to be stoned] unless he can produce circumstantial evidence (*amāra*) that she was raped.[40]

Counsel also submitted that Safiyyatu could withdraw her confession only in person.[41]

The court did not give an explicit ruling on the merits of this issue. Implicitly it accepted the submission of the counsel for the appellant, as shown from the fact that it discussed the appellant's claim that the child to which she had given birth was her husband's (*vide infra*).

38 "[*Zinā*] is proven by a confession made once, unless he [the defendant] retracts it." Khalīl b. Isḥāq, *Mukhtaṣar*. (Paris, Maṭba'at al-Dawla al-Jumhūriyya, 1900) P. 230. The counsel for the appellant further referred to the *Ṣaḥīḥ* al-Bukhārī, but I since he did not give the contents of the hadith, could not identify it.

39 The hadith, not quoted in the text reads: On the authority of Ibn 'Abbās: "I heard 'Umar ibn al-Khaṭṭāb say: 'Stoning is in God's Book, an obligation for men and women who have had unlawful sexual intercourse if they are *muḥṣan* and if there are witnesses, or pregnancy or a confession." Mālik, *Muwaṭṭa'*, p. 514.

40 Ibn Rushd (al-Ḥafīd), *Bidāyat al-Mujtahid wa-Nihāyat al-Muqtaṣid*. 3rd impr. (Cairo: Muṣṭafā al-Bābī al-Ḥalabī, 1960) Vol. 2, p. 440.

41 "... unless the person who has confessed having had unlawful sexual relations withdraws his confession, for in that case his withdrawal is accepted and he will not be punished with the *ḥadd* penalty." a al-Ābī, *Jawāhir al-Iklīl*. Vol. 2, pp. 284–5.

2.5.2 Pregnancy as Proof of *Zinā* and the Effect of Doubt (*Shubha*)

The counsel for the appellant argued that the trial court erred in law when it regarded the appellant's pregnancy out of wedlock as sufficient proof for the sentence of stoning, since, according to Maliki doctrine, a pregnancy may last for seven years. Therefore, conception may have occurred during her marriage. This constitutes doubt (*shubha*) that stands in the way of convicting a person of a *ḥadd* offense. In support, the counsel quoted the hadith about Māʿiz related on the authority of Abū Hurayra (*vide supra*) and a passage from *Fiqh al-sunna* by Sayyid Sābiq:

> The majority of scholars is of the opinion that pregnancy alone is not sufficient proof for [applying] the *ḥadd* penalty [for *zinā*] and that either a confession or full evidence by witnesses is required. It has been related on the authority of ʿAli – may God be pleased with him – that he said to a pregnant woman: Have you been raped?" She said: "No." Then he said: "Perhaps a man came to you in your sleep." And it has been related from ʿUmar that he accepted the statement of a woman who claimed that she was a heavy sleeper and that a man came to her at night, but that she still did not know who he was.[42]

Departing from the principle that pregnancy out of wedlock is in and of itself sufficient evidence of *zinā*, the counsel for the respondent contested the claim submitted by the counsel for the appellant that in this case doubt prevents the application of the *ḥadd* penalty. He asserted that unlike retaliation ((*qiṣāṣ*), the punishment for *zinā*, once it has been established by a confession, by four male witnesses or pregnancy out of wedlock, cannot be waived. Even if a woman claims that the pregnancy was a result of rape, she has to produce witnesses to this claim. In further support of his assertion, he quoted passages from *Al-Qawānīn al-Fiqhiyya*,[43] *al-Thamr sharḥ Risālat al-Qayrawānī*[44] and the *Bidāyat al-Mujtahid* by Ibn Rushd.[45] In this case the judgment was based on

42 Sayyid Sābiq. *Fiqh al-Sunna* (Beirut: Dār al-Kitāb al-ʿArabī, 1969) Vol. 2, p. 421.

43 "As to what establishes the *ḥadd* offense, that are three things: a confession, the testimonies of witnesses and the appearance of pregnancy." Ibn Juzayy, *Al-Qawānīn al-Fiqhiyya* (n.p., n.d.): 269.

44 "A person who has had unlawful intercourse will not be punished with the *ḥadd* penalty unless there is a confession, a visible pregnancy (*ḥaml yaẓhar*) or the testimonies of four free adult men of good reputation (*ʿudūl*) who have seen [the male member in the vagina] like the kohl stick [entering] into the kohl container." Al-Azharī, *Al-Thamr al-Dānī*, p. 592.

45 "As to the controversy with regard to applying the *ḥadd* penalty [for *zinā*] on the strength of pregnancy in combination with the claim [of the woman] that she has been raped, there is a group that holds that in such a case the *ḥadd* penalty is mandatory on the strength of the hadith of ʿUmar, mentioned by Mālik in the *Muwaṭṭaʾ*. This is the opinion

both confession (which, under Maliki law, does not need to be repeated four times) and pregnancy. In addition, he pointed out that the maximum duration of gestation according to the Maliki school is not seven but five years, as mentioned in the *Tuḥfat al-Ḥukkām*[46] and by *Ibn Juzayy* in his *Al-Qawānīn al-Fiqhiyya.*[47]

The court concurred with the counsel for the appellant. It held that it cannot ascertain the veracity of the appellant's claim that the child to whom she gave birth was fathered by her former husband from whom, according to her statement, she was divorced two years before the lower court trial, because the lower court did not investigate this issue. However, according to the *Tuḥfat al-Ḥukkām*, the minimum period of gestation is six months and the maximum period is five years.[48] Therefore, it is possible that the child was fathered by her former husband. This constitutes doubt (*shubha*), which prevents the application of the *ḥadd* penalty, on the basis of the maxim, mentioned in the *Mughnī* of Ibn Qudāma and transmitted on the authority of ʿAbd Allāh b. Masʿūd, Muʿādh b. Jabal and ʿUqba b. ʿĀmir: "If you are in doubt regarding [the enforcement of] a *ḥadd* penalty, avert it as much as you can.[49] If she persists in her claim, she can sue her previous husband before a proper court [for maintenance]. In addition, the court held that the counsel for the respondent apparently was ignorant of the difference between *ḥadd* punishments and retaliation for manslaughter (*qiṣāṣ*), as he seemed to confuse the principle that *shubha*, doubt, averts a *ḥadd* penalty with the principle that retaliation can be set aside by a pardon of one or more of the victim's heirs. No such waiver is possible with regard to a *ḥadd* penalty, which, once pronounced, must be carried out because it is God's judgment and the person who has notified the authorities of the offense cannot waive the punishment.[50]

of Mālik, unless she can produce circumstantial evidence (*amāra*) for her having been raped." Ibn Rushd (1960: 2: 440).

46 "Five years is the maximum in pregnancy and six months the minimum." al-Tasūlī. *Al-Bahja fī sharḥ al-Tuḥfa*, Vol. 1, pp. 391–2 ((*Bāb al-nafaqa wa-mā yataʿallaq bihā, Faṣl fīmā yajib ʿalā al-muṭallaqāt*), in the margin.

47 "The authoritative (*fī al-mashhūr*) opinion in the Malikite school is five years, but some scholars fixed it at four or seven years." Ibn Juzayy (n.d., 179) (Part 2, Book 2, Chapter 7: On *ʿidda* and *istibrāʾ* and related matters).

48 See note 46.

49 *Idhā ishtabaha ʿalayka al-ḥadd, fa-draʾ mā istaṭaʿta.* It is found in the compilation of al-Dāraquṭnī. See Ibn Qudāma, *al-Mughnī.* Beirut: *Dār Iḥyāʾ al-Turāth al-ʿArabī*, n.d., Vol. 8, p. 211.

50 Here the court refers to Abū Bakr b. Ḥasan al-Kishnāwī, *Ashal al-Madārik sharḥ Irshād al-Sālik fī fiqh Imām al-Aʾimma Mālik* (by ʿAbd al-Raḥmān b. Muḥammad Ibn ʿAskar (d. 1332)), vol. 3, p. 188. Unfortunately I have no access to this work.

2.5.3 Establishing *Iḥṣān*

The counsel for the appellant submitted that the trial court erred in complying with the law because it did not establish that the appellant is *muḥṣan*, i.e. an adult, free Muslim who has experienced sexual intercourse within a lawful marriage. This is evident from the following citation from the *Bidāya* of Ibn Rushd:

> There is a difference of opinion about the conditions of *iḥṣān*. According to Malik, they are: majority, being a Muslim, being free, and sexual intercourse on the basis of a valid contract during a period that intercourse is allowed. The type of intercourse that is forbidden (*maḥẓūr*), according to him, is intercourse during menstruation or during the fast. If someone has unlawful intercourse (*zinā*) after having had lawful intercourse as described above, and if he has the aforementioned characteristics, then, according to him, he must be stoned.[51]

The state counsel denied that *iḥṣān* had not been established and asserted that the lower court, on the strength of the accused's statement that she was divorced two years ago, did in fact ascertain that the appellant was *muḥṣana*.

The court, here too, concurred with the counsel for the appellant. It quoted the *Kitāb al-Fiqh ʿalā al-Madhāhib al-Arbaʿa* on the conditions of *iḥṣān*, for both men and women:

> (a) being free:, (b) being of age, (c) being sane, (d) being married or having been married) with a valid contract to a woman who is also a *muḥṣana*, (e) having had intercourse with her in a period during which this is allowed and when she also was a *muḥṣana*, (f) being a Muslim (according to the Malikis and the Hanafis.[52]

The trial court failed to investigate any of these conditions. The mere fact that Safiyyatu declared that she had been divorced two years ago is not sufficient proof of *iḥṣān*. For it is conceivable that she was married and that her marriage had been consummated, but that she nevertheless was not *muḥṣan* [because, for example, consummation and further intercourse took place during her menstruation or during Ramadan. RP]

---

51 Ibn Rushd (1960,2:435).

52 Jaziri (n.d., 5:50).

2.6 *State Counsel Introduces a New Claim: Prosecution for Qadhf*

Finally the state counsel submitted that if the sentence of stoning to death was not upheld, the accused must he sentenced under Section 141–3 SSPC[53] to caning for having defamed (*qadhf*) Abubakar. The court, however, did not agree with this submission, for such a sentence can be pronounced only at the request of the person who is defamed. This does not apply here, since Yakubu Abubakar did not appear in court to seek redress.[54]

3 Conclusions

The Safiyyatu Hussaini case has many interesting aspects. I will discuss two of them here. First, it illustrates the manner in which the judiciary applies codified Islamic criminal law. Second, it highlights the attitude of the courts towards the Qur'anic penalties.

Prior to the re-Islamization of the law, the area courts in the North would adjudicate civil matters according to uncodified Shari'a, referring to the classical works of Maliki doctrine. When the law was first Islamicized, the legislators, by giving the new Shari'a courts jurisdiction over criminal cases even before the Shari'a Penal Codes had been introduced, apparently envisioned that these courts would follow a similar procedure in criminal matters. This is stipulated in Sections 6 and 7 for the text, see above, §1.1) of the SSCL, enacted before the Sokoto Shari'a Penal Code. This direct application of uncodified Shari'a law in criminal cases, it seems, was accepted and even welcomed by the lower courts. As we have seen, the Upper Shari'a Court of Gwadabawa applied uncodified Shari'a criminal law in the case and found Safiyyatu Hussaini guilty. Similar sentences (some involving amputation) were pronounced in Sokoto

53 The text has Section 183 which is incorrect. The Sections of the SSPC dealing with *qadhf* are: Section 141: "Whoever by words either spoken or reproduced by mechanical means or intended to be read or by signs or by visible representations makes or publishes any false imputation of Zina or Sodomy concerning a chaste person (Muhsin), or contests the paternity of such person even where such person is dead, is said to commit the offence of qadhf, provided that person is deemed to be chaste (Muhsin) who has never been convicted of the offence of Zina or Sodomy. Section 142: Whoever commits the offence of qadhf shall be punished with eighty lashes of the cane; and his testimony shall not be accepted thereafter unless he repents before the court. Section 143: The offence of qadhf shall be remitted in any of the following cases: (A) where the complainant (maqzuf) pardons the accuser (qazif). (b) where the husband accuses his wife of zina and undertakes the process of mutual imprecation (lian). (c) where the complainant (maqzuf) is a descendant of the accuser (qazif."

54 The court here cites again from the *Ashal al-Madārik*. See note 50.

and other states.[55] However, since the Constitution requires that criminal offenses and their penalties he defined by a written law, the Northern states soon realized that they had to draft and enact Shariʿa Penal Codes and Shariʿa Codes of Criminal Procedure. This was done with great speed. However, important fields of criminal law, such as evidence, were not codified, probably because the legislators realized that the states do not have the power to do so. As a result, uncodified Shariʿa again began to play an important role in criminal proceedings. This is clear from the case discussed here. Although the Shariʿa Court of Appeal, which must adjudicate according to Islamic law, also refers to the Constitution, the main body of arguments and considerations derive from Maliki legal doctrine. In fact, on those points which the Shariʿa Court of Appeal set aside because the decision of the lower court violated constitutional provisions, the Court also argued that there was a conflict with the principles of Islamic law. This was the case, e.g., with regard to the principle that no act can be punished without a previous legal enactment, which, the Court asserted, was also a principle of Islamic. law. In general the Court cited a wide array of Maliki *fiqh* works. However, it is not clear why one authority rather than another was being referred to on certain points. In most cases the information that was required was found in several sources.

The second point of interest is that there is an obvious difference between the lower court and the court of appeal with regard to the enforcement of the more severe Qur'anic penalties. The Upper Shariʿa Court seemed to be quite willing to pronounce a sentence of death by stoning on the basis of what, even according to classical Islamic standards, are rather thin grounds, by superficially referring to some texts from Maliki compendia. This attitude is perhaps motivated by enthusiasm and zeal for Islamization and a desire to restore an Islamic moral order. The Shariʿa Court of Appeal seemed to adopt the opposite attitude, trying to prevent the application of the *ḥadd* punishment for unlawful intercourse insofar as possible. The court used all possible arguments and stretched the classical doctrine to the utmost in order to quash the trial court judgment on as many grounds as possible. Two motives may have played a role. First, as in classical Islam, there was always a reluctance to enforce the stoning penalty. Second, the Court may have been affected by political motives. If it upheld the trial court judgment (death by stoning), then the case would be submitted to the Supreme Federal Court, which might test the constitutionality of the Shariʿa Penal Codes. The constitutionality of the Code is, in fact, questionable on several counts, e.g., the prohibition of cruel, degrading or inhuman punishment, (Section 34 FCRN) and of discrimination on the basis of gender or

55 See Peters (2003:51–60).

religion (Section 42 FCRN). Thus, there was a chance that this Supreme Court would find that the new Shariʿa Codes are null and void on a number of important points. In order to prevent this, it is likely that the Shariʿa Court of Appeal set aside the decision of the lower court, lest the constitutionality of the Shariʿa legislation be put to the scrutiny of the Supreme Federal Court.

The decision of the Shariʿa Court of Appeal seriously restricts the enforcement of the penalty of death by stoning. The Maliki doctrine that admits as evidence for *zinā* the pregnancy of an unmarried woman has been seriously weakened, since the Shariʿa Court of Appeal has ruled that women may rebut such allegations of *zinā:* during the five years following the dissolution of her last marriage, her claim that the child with which she is pregnant was fathered by her former husband constitutes *shubha*, which averts the application of the *ḥadd* punishment, death by stoning. Moreover, the Court has emphasized that the investigation of *zinā* cases on the basis of mere suspicion (e.g., the pregnancy of an unmarried woman) is unlawful and, moreover, that, if a *zinā* case is tried in court, the court must explain to the accused the exact nature of the charge and question the accused in order to ascertain whether he/she might have a valid defense of which he/she was unaware. As mentioned at the beginning of this chapter, the Shariʿa Court of Appeal of Katsina has given a similar decision in the Amina Lawal case. It is to be hoped that this will deter lower Shariʿa courts from sentencing women to death by stoning solely on the evidence of extramarital pregnancy.

CHAPTER 33

Shari'a and 'Natural Justice'

The Implementation of Islamic Criminal Law in British India and Colonial Nigeria

1 Introduction[1]

Maintaining law and order is a central concern for any state. In colonies, however, where the danger of rebellion was always lurking and where drastic social and economic changes often resulted in higher crime rates, this was one of the foremost concerns of the administration. Criminal law was an essential tool for imposing and protecting colonial power relations and keeping the peace. Since colonial powers, as a rule, did not regard native penal laws as effective tools to these ends, they introduced almost everywhere penal codes from the metropolis adapted to the colonial situation. There are, however, two notable exceptions: In India and Northern Nigeria the British continued to enforce Islamic criminal law. In this paper I will try to explain why this was the case and describe how the colonial situation affected the application of Islamic criminal law.

Colonial law is an excellent window for studying the structures of colonialism.[2] It gives an insight into the major concerns of the colonial powers in administering their territories and the cultural assumptions that shaped colonial rule. Colonial administrators wanted to create new states with new power structures and new legal systems, directly subordinated to the state. This, of course, was a gradual process: the colonial state was not established the moment a colonial power, by conquest or otherwise, assumed control over certain territories. Essential for these colonial states were establishing bureaucratic forms of government and placing the law and its enforcement under state control and impersonal and were imposed. For the enforcement of criminal law this meant that prosecution was increasingly made the responsibility of state organs and that the scope for private prosecution and private settlements

1 The introduction is for a large part based on Lauren Benton, *Law and Colonial Cultures: Legal Regimes in World History, 1400–1900* (Cambridge 2002); Kristin Mann and Richard Roberts, 'Law in Colonial Africa', in Kristin Mann and Richard Roberts (eds), *Law in Colonial Africa* (Portsmouth NH 1991) 3–61; and W.J. Mommsen and J.A. de Moor (eds), *European Expansion and Law: The Encounters of European and Indigenous Laws in 19th C. Africa and Asia* (Oxford 1992).

2 Mann and Roberts, 'Law in Colonial Africa', 4.

 | DOI:10.1163/9789004420625_034

was restricted. Colonial administrators assumed that the indigenous forms of government and law enforcement were despotic, arbitrary and chaotic. In fact, colonial rule was often justified by the claim that it had brought justice and peace where previously these had been absent. Western civilization, it was argued, was of a higher order and, therefore, it was the "white man's burden" to spread his civilization to the rest of the world. These concerns and notions resulted in four distinctive traits of colonial legal systems.

The first one is that colonialism imposed new legal orders that were centralized, hierarchical and firmly anchored in the state apparatus. They replaced the pre-colonial local laws that were usually not written, based on informal ways of conflict settlement and not integrated in the power structure of the state. This does not mean that the colonial regimes introduced one unified substantive law – in fact legal pluralism was more often the rule than the exception –, but rather that a strict hierarchy of legal authority was introduced, that the jurisdictions of the various courts and laws were clearly delimited and that court procedures were formalized. Indigenous law, to the extent it was preserved, was usually reformed, if only by new, more formal ways of enforcement. Colonial authorities or high courts usually had the right to quash decisions of native courts if they regarded these as being repugnant to essential principle of civilization. In British colonies the terms "natural justice" or "justice, equity and good conscience" were used to refer to these principles of civilization.

Pre-colonial law was usually unwritten customary law or, in the case of the *Shari'a,* jurists' law to be found in scholarly works discussing a great variety of often contradictory legal opinions. If local laws and customs were allowed to be part of the new colonial legal order, the colonial powers needed to know them in order to have control over them. Therefore, the second characteristic of colonial legal systems is that local laws and customs were often put into writing and fixed. In many colonies projects were initiated to document and sometimes codify these local laws and to record court decisions. Codification was seen as a form of civilization as it brought clarity and order where previously, allegedly, disorder and confusion had reigned. However, recording and codifying native indigenous laws and recording decisions as precedents often changed these laws beyond recognition.

An assumption underlying all colonial rule was that the Europeans were more civilized than the indigenous population and that they should not mix. There was a sharp social divide between the small elite hailing from the metropolis and the indigenous population. This divide was given a legal basis and a third trait of colonial legal systems was that they conferred a separate legal status on the colonizers and a few privileged local notables and established special courts for them. This meant that if laws from the metropolis were introduced – in general based on equality before the law –, they had to be amended in order to reflect this divide. Often Europeans fell under the jurisdiction of a separate court system applying special laws.

Colonial law reform was as a rule a tool for the establishment of new, forms of government, the protection of colonial economic interests and the maintenance of law and order. However, it was sometimes also used as an end in itself, to impose "civilization". Although law reform to achieve this was in itself not instrumental in consolidating colonial power relations, there was an indirect relationship. One of the justifications of colonization, as I have mentioned before, was the spread of western civilization, or more specifically the imposition of justice and peace and the elimination of "barbaric" practices. If such practices were tolerated, the colonial enterprise would lose its credibility among public opinion in the homeland as well as, in the colonies themselves, among the Westernized local elites, among missionaries and the lower ranks of colonial administrators. Especially the latter groups, who were directly confronted with such practices, played an important role in attempts to abolish these customs and practices.[3]

After taking over power in the newly acquired territories the colonial administration had to decide in what domains western law had to be introduced and where indigenous law could be preserved. The outcome was usually contingent on practical, rather than on ideological considerations. Western law had the advantage that it was clear, familiar to the colonial administrators who had to enforce them and could easily be adapted to serve colonial interests. However, at the same time it was less suitable because it was alien to the local populations and based, essentially, on equality before the law, a notion that did not fit the colonial situation. In order to be practicable it had to be adapted, especially, to the existence of categories of persons with different legal statuses and distinct rights and obligations. Preserving indigenous law, on the other hand, was easier in the sense that the local population was accustomed to it and that local laws usually recognized differences in legal status. However, it had to be transformed to fit the colonial situation by redistributing and demarcating judicial authority, subordinating it under the all-embracing authority of the colonial state and by making its contents easily accessible by recording or codifying it. The choices made differed from colony to colony. In general, however, western law was introduced in those domains where the law had to

3 See J. Fisch, 'Law as a Means and as an End: Some Remarks on the Function of European and Non-European Law in the Colonies', in W.J. Mommsen and J.A. de Moor. *European Expansion and Law. The Encounters of European and Indigenous Laws in 19th C. Africa and Asia* (Oxford 1992) 15–38.

protect interests that were crucial to the colonizing powers. Commercial law – important for trade – and criminal law – essential for law and order – were in almost all colonies westernized. Land law was usually westernized only in those colonies where there were large groups of colonial settlers.

The ways colonizers dealt with the *Shariʿa* illustrate these observations. In general, the application of the *Shariʿa* was restricted to those parts of the law that regulated relations in the private domain and did not have an impact on colonial interests: the law of persons, family law and the law of succession. However, the colonial authorities kept some control over the law in these domains by creating a new hierarchical court system, sometimes with the possibility of appeal to western type courts, and by regulating the training of the judges. Where colonial interests were at stake such as, for instance, in the domain of trade and land ownership (in settler colonies) the *Shariʿa* was as a rule replaced by western laws. Since, as mentioned before, criminal law is central to the maintenance of law and order and the protection of colonial power relations, most colonial powers preferred to impose their own criminal laws on the colonies. That the British preserved the application of Islamic criminal law in two colonies is exceptional and in need of explanation.

2 Islamic Criminal Law

Islamic criminal law[4] is treated by the jurists under three headings:

1. *Jinayat*, or offences against a person (i.e. homicide and wounding)
2. *Hadd* crimes, i.e. offences mentioned in the Koran and entailing fixed penalties
3. *Taʿzir* and *siyasa*: discretionary punishment by the court or executive officials of sinful acts or acts endangering state security or public order.

The first group consists of homicide and bodily harm. These crimes can only be prosecuted by the victim or his heirs (in case of manslaughter) and they may pardon the defendant at any time. For intentional murder, the heirs may demand retaliation, i.e. the death penalty, whereas the penalty for intentional injury causing a loss of limbs or senses, is the infliction of the same injury on the perpetrator. If the death or injury are not caused intentionally or if the victim or his heirs are willing to waive their right to retaliation, it is then replaced by the payment of the blood price, the amount of which depends on gender and religion. The Malikis (but not the Hanafis) also require that the killer's

4 For a detailed survey of Islamic criminal law, see Rudolph Peters, *Crime and Punishment in Islamic Law: Theory and Practice from the 16th to the 21st Century* (Cambridge 2005) Ch. 2.

value (i.e. his blood price) be not higher that the victim's, except in the case of a man killing a woman.

The second category of offences consists of the crimes for which fixed penalties are provided in the *Shari'a*. They are the following:

1. Theft, to be punished with amputation of the right hand.
2. Robbery or disturbance of the peace. This is a complex crime and its punishment varies with the circumstances. If there is only disturbance of the peace (defined as frightening travellers in order to prevent them from continuing their journey), the punishment is exile, or, according to some, imprisonment; if the culprit has taken property, he is to be punished by alternate amputation, i.e. amputation of the right hand and the left foot; If a person has been killed, then the killer is to be put to death; finally, if the robber has both plundered and killed, his punishment is death and crucifixion. (Crucifixion entails that his body be exposed to the public after his execution.) If the culprit repents before he is caught, and reports himself to the authorities, the *hadd* punishment lapses.
3. Illegal sexual intercourse (*zina'*), i.e. all sexual relations out of wedlock or outside the relationship between master and female slave. This crime is punishable by death by stoning if the culprit, man or woman, is a *muhsan*, i.e. if he or she has previously enjoyed legitimate sexual relations, otherwise with one hundred lashes.
4. Unfounded accusation of fornication (*qadhf*), to be punished with eighty lashes.
5. Drinking alcoholic beverages, to be punished with forty, or according to others, eighty lashes.

Sentencing to death of to the severe *hadd* penalties was difficult since the doctrine set high standards for convictions. In the first place, there is the rule that uncertainty, *shubha*, prevents punishment. This means that a person who is mistaken or uncertain as to unlawfulness of his behaviour, resulting either from an error of fact or from an error of law, will not be punished with retaliation or a *hadd* penalty. There is not very much required to assume the existence of *shubha* in the sense of error of law. According to the Hanafites, the defendant's declaration that he believed that the act was allowed, suffices, even if this statement is made after the crime has been proven during the trial. In a number of cases there is a legal presumption that such an error exists regardless of the culprit's actual awareness of the rules. A person who kills a son or steals his property is assumed to act in the belief that he is entitled to it.

In the second place, application of retaliation and *hadd* punishments is complicated by rules of evidence that are stricter than in other domains of the law. In Islamic law, proof can be furnished by witnesses, admission, and oath.

For evidence by witnesses it is required that two Muslim male, or one male and two female, adult witnesses of good reputation give identical testimony in the presence of the qadi. Hearsay evidence is admitted. However, for a sentence a *hadd* punishment or to retaliation, the evidence of two Muslim male eyewitnesses of good reputation is required. Female witnesses are not accepted. And in order to prove fornication, four male eyewitnesses are necessary, who must have seen the act in its most intimate details. Moreover, if the defendant pleads guilty to a *hadd* crime, he can withdraw his statement at any moment, even after a sentence has been passed, and thus prevent the execution of the punishment.

In the third place, the application of *hadd* punishment is restricted by very precise definitions of the crimes and, sometimes, by procedural formalities. Theft, again, offers a clear illustration. According to the classical doctrine, theft in the legal sense exists, if a person who can speak and see, intentionally and surreptitiously takes away an object which is not liable to decay, with a certain minimal value, which is in another person's rightful possession, and which the thief takes out of a safe place suitable for the object in question. The snatching of a purse in the street falls outside the definition, since such an act is not surreptitious. Neither can a person be punished with amputation if he takes and sells another person's jewellery if the latter has left it on the table in his house, since they were not kept in a safe place suitable for jewellery.

The last category of offences (*taʿzir* or *siyasa*) is a residual one. Persons whose guilt is established but cannot be sentenced to retaliation or a *hadd* penalty for procedural reasons, may be punished under this heading. The same applies for habitual offenders, who, under this heading, may be sentenced to penalties that are more severe than the ones prescribed for their crimes.

3 India

3.1 *Introduction*

> On 22 August 1770, a murder case was tried by the judges of the Faujdari court of Bhaturia, attended by both Muslim and Hindu officers who examined witnesses in the presence of Rous [a young EIC official, appointed "supervisor"]. A pregnant woman, Noory by name, had been killed by Munsooran, Agni and Hooban. It was clearly proved that Hooban was employed by Munsooran and Agni and that the medicine administered by Hooban to cause abortion and the means she used to extract the foetus were the immediate causes of Noory's death. But the court hesitated

> to pronounce the death sentence; for according to the Mahomedan Law such a sentence required the attestation of a certain number of eye-witnesses of Muslim faith. Rous wrote to the Resident in Durbar to determine in consultation with Reza Khan whether it was permissible to set aside *these obstacles to the execution of penalty which was forbidden only by a religious bias, incompatible with equity and the natural laws*[5] *of society* (Italics mine, RP). But it was not in his powers to do more than making this recommendation.[6]

In 1770, when the case was tried, the British East India Company (EIC) had already acquired the right to collect taxes and to administer civil justice in Bengal (1765) but not yet the control of the military and the administration of criminal justice (1772). The EIC was no sovereign ruler but held Bengal as a grant from the Mughal emperor and constitutionally there prevailed a form of dual rule. The case shows the frustration of EIC officials with Islamic criminal law, which they regarded, as we will see, as unfit for keeping the peace. However, even after 1772, they could not abolish it because of their constitutional position with regard to the Mughal Empire. By the end of the eighteenth century they still lacked the conviction that their own legal system was superior and suited for all times and climes. They regarded the system prevailing in India as the best for the local population,[7] whereas officials of the EIC fell under special British jurisdiction. The imposition of English criminal law upon the local population would have been unpractical as it was not codified, consisting of common law and a great number of separate statutes. Since the British judges of the EIC lacked the intimate knowledge of Bengali society, culture and languages, is was deemed more convenient to leave the first stages of adjudication to local experts on the basis of the *Shariʿa* or Hindu laws. However, the case illustrates that from the very beginning there were frictions between the

5 The use of the words "*equity and the natural laws*" is interesting. It is the forerunner of the formula "justice, equity and good conscience," which played an important role in British colonies as a guideline for finding the law in situations where indigenous law is silent and for abolishing indigenous law if deemed to be repugnant to these principles. Derrett discusses the historical background and the legal uses of the formula but confines himself to its use as a guideline for finding the law and does not discuss its role in criminal law where it was used for abolishing local laws. J. Duncan M. Derrett, 'Justice, Equity and Good Conscience', in J.N.D. Anderson (ed.), *Changing Law in Developing Countries* (London 1963) 113–53.

6 Niharkana Majumdar, *Justice and Police in Bengal, 1765–1793: A Study of the Nizamat in Decline* (Calcutta 1960) 72–73.

7 Jörg Fisch, *Cheap Lives and Dear Limbs: The British Transformation of the Bengal Criminal Law 1769–1817* (Beiträge zur Südasienforschung 79, Wiesbaden 1983) 10.

local *Shariʿa* practice in criminal affairs and what the British regarded as just and effective for the maintenance of law and order.

As of 1790 the *Shariʿa* courts were subordinated under British judges. The *qadis* and muftis attached to the courts were relegated to the position of "law officers," i.e. scholars of Islamic law and Hindu law (the latter for civil cases between Hindus), who assisted the British judges in expounding the law in each case. The courts were "to pass sentence in the terms of the Futwa (*fatwa*), if it appears consonant to justice and conformable to the Muhamedan law."[8] The courts of first instance heard both criminal and civil cases. For purposes of appeal in criminal cases, the court of the Mughal governor of Calcutta was transformed into a high court (*Nizamat-i ʿAdalat*, or, according to the then current British orthography: *Nizamut Adaulut*). The criminal courts applied Hanafi law, which the British judges enforced on the basis of *fatwas* issued by law officers. In order to have some control over the pronouncements of the law officers, Hanafi works of Islamic law, such as the *Hidaya*[9] were translated into English. The theoretical primacy of the *Shariʿa* in criminal cases lasted until 1861 when the Indian Penal Code and the Code of Criminal Procedure were introduced. This was made possible by the demise of the Mughal Empire in 1858 and the transfer of India's sovereignty to the British Crown.

The way the British handled the *Shariʿa* has been dubbed "defective deference to Islamic norms,"[10] i.e. legal reform on English (or western) lines behind a façade of respect to the *Shariʿa*. This is especially true with regard to criminal law. For after the EIC had acquired the right to administer criminal justice it began to reform Islamic criminal law. They did so by legislation, without, however, formally replacing or modifying the *Shariʿa*. In general, the enacted regulations gave instructions to the law officers of the courts to issue their fatwas on the basis of legal fictions. For instance, in cases of homicide, the law officers were instructed to give their fatwas on the assumption that all the victim's heirs had demanded the death penalty, regardless of whether or not this was true. This possibly reflects the influence of English jurisprudence: In common law, fictions were frequently used in order to adapt the limited number of available writs to new circumstances. By allowing that fictitious details

8 Regulation 1793/9 § 47. James Edward Colebrooke, *Digest of the Regulations and Laws, Enacted by the Governor-General in Council for the Civil Government of the Territories under the Presidency of Bengal Arranged in Alphabetical Order* (Calcutta 1807) ii, 879.

9 ʿAli b. Abi Bakr al-Marghinani (d. 1196), *Al-Hidaya sharh al-Bidayat al-Mubtadi*', an authoritative work on Hanafi law, translated by Charles Hamilton (d. 1792) with the title: *The Hedaya, or Guide, Commentary on the Mussulman laws* (Calcutta, 1791).

10 Scott A. Kugle, 'Framed, Blamed and Renamed: The Recasting of Islamic Jurisprudence in Colonial South Asia', *Modern Asian Studies* 35 (2001), 257–313 and 266.

be added to the facts of the case, the working of a writ would be expanded, without formally changing the law.[11] British lawyers working in India at that time apparently compared the *Shariʿa* to common law, and had recourse to legal fictions in order to introduce reform. For the Muslim jurists this was not at all problematical: Muftis, according to Islamic legal theory, expound the law on the basis of the facts that are presented to them without examining their truth. Therefore, their fatwas are not binding. The British, however, erroneously thought they had force of law and regarded them as justifications for the harsher sentences desired by them.

The reforms of *Shariʿa* criminal law had three aims. First, to make its enforcement the exclusive duty of the state[12] and impersonal, without regard for individual characteristics; second, to forge it into an, in British eyes, effective instrument for keeping the peace; and third, to divest it of its "barbaric and cruel" elements. This was done through the following types of reforms:

1. Reforms to assert the right of the state to prosecute and to abolish the influence of the victims (or their heirs);
2. Reforms to introduce the notion of equality before the (criminal) law by eliminating personal circumstances unrelated to the offence that could influence the sentence, such as the *Shariʿa* rule that a father could not be sentenced to death for killing a child;
3. Reforms to eliminate "irrational" obstacles for sentencing such as the strict *Shariʿa* rules of evidence;
4. Reforms to abolish amputation of limbs and death by stoning as penalties;
5. Reforms to eliminate arbitrariness by defining *taʿzir* punishments and abolishing *siyasa* justice.

Between 1790 and 1817, the British totally and unrecognizably transformed Islamic criminal law. Although the law officers continued to function until 1832, the criminal law applied in the Indian courts by that time had entirely lost its Islamic character except in name. However, the criminal law thus created was only formally abolished by the introduction of the 1861 Indian Penal Code.

4 British Interference

4.1 *Establishing the Exclusive Right of the State to Prosecute Crime*

For the British, criminal law enforcement was essentially a matter for the state. It was part of public law, and not of private law. Therefore it was difficult for

11 Arthur R. Hogue, *Origins of the Common Law* (Indianapolis 1986) 11.

12 Although the EIC was a chartered trading company, I refer to it as "state" in view of the fact that it governed parts of India.

them to accept that under the *Shariʿa* the prosecution of homicide cases, as well as some other offences, was a private affair and depended on the wish of the victim or his heirs.[13] They could pardon the accused at any stage of the proceedings and make it conditional on a financial consideration. One of the first criminal regulations issued by the British instructed the law officers to give their fatwas in homicide cases on the assumption that the heirs demanded retaliation.[14] The British also wanted to put an end to the possibility of private settlements in criminal cases between victims and perpetrators. In order to underline the public interest in prosecuting and punishing crime, the British introduced the principle that criminal offences would be investigated and prosecuted by state organs, regardless of the wishes of the victim or his heirs.

Another aspect of the law of homicide that offended the British notions of public justice was the rule that unintentional homicide (i.e. culpable homicide or death by accident) was regarded as a tort entailing the payment of financial compensation to the victim's heirs. The British were appalled by the fact that the heirs were the recipients of the 'fine' as they called the blood price (*diya*). They interpreted this as a kind of monetary expiation and thus as an expression of the idea that human lives could be bought for money. In 1797 the British laid down that

> [n]o sentence of pecuniary compensation or damages, adjudged to or recoverable by individuals, shall be given on any criminal prosecution, nor any sentence of fine except to the use of Government.[15]

If the law officers would award *diya* in their *fatwas*, this should be commuted to imprisonment.[16] In 1801 the rule was formulated more precisely. Henceforth, the commutation of blood price into imprisonment was not applicable in cases of wilful homicide[17] (because then capital punishment would be in

13 In England the prosecution of crime was, until the first part of the nineteenth century, also the responsibility of private individuals. The difference, however, was that once they had brought an offender to justice, they could no longer influence the proceedings. During the first half of the nineteenth century, prosecution became a matter for the police until the office of the Director of Public Prosecution was created in 1879. A.H. Manchester, *Modern Legal History of England and Wales, 1750–1950* (London 1980) 226.

14 Tapas Kumar Banerjee, *Background to Indian Criminal Law* (Repr. ed, Calcutta 1990) 72–3. The instruction was repeated in a more detailed form in Regulation 1793/9, § 55, 76 and Regulation 1797/4, § 3, 4. See Colebrooke, *Digest of the Regulations and Laws*, i, 526, 34.

15 Regulation 1797/14 § 14, Colebrooke, *Digest of the Regulations and Laws* ii, 881.

16 Regulation 1797/14, § 3, Colebrooke, *Digest of the regulations and laws*, ii, 881.

17 Under the *shariʿa* wilful killing entails capital sentence. However, this depends on the wish of the victim's heirs, who may also demand a financial compensation. Moreover, certain circumstances (e.g. the fact that the victim was the child of the perpetrator) prevent

order), nor in cases of "homicides by real misadventure, in the prosecution of a lawful act, and without any malignant intention," even if the *fatwa* of the law officers awards blood price.[18] Under Islamic law, causing a person's death suffices for financial liability for the blood price and fault is not required. This is consistent with the *Shariʿa* rules of torts according to which the liability for damages is predicated on mere causation and not on fault. However, when the British brought this part of the law of homicide under the working of criminal law, where guilt is the determining principle for awarding punishment, a distinction had to be made between involuntary manslaughter entailing punishment and purely accidental killing. There are several decisions of the *Nizamat-i ʿAdalat* acquitting defendants who had accidentally killed persons while aiming at animals, although the *fatwa* of the law officers held them liable for blood price.[19]

4.2 *Removing "Irrational" Obstacles for Awarding Punishment*

Because the British felt bound to the provisions of strict *Shariʿa* criminal law and were loath to pronounce sentences on the strength of *siyasa*,[20] which offended their sense of rule of law, the possibilities of inflicting capital punishment and other severe punishments were limited by the many loopholes offered by the *Shariʿa*. Therefore they relaxed the standards of evidence set by the *Shariʿa* and abolished the pleas based on "uncertainty" (*shubha*) and personal circumstances not related to the crime.

As we saw in the report of the trial of the abortionist, the Islamic law of evidence offended British notions of justice. Under the strict rule of the *Shariʿa,* only testimonies given by Muslim eyewitnesses of good reputation could be admitted. In a country where the majority of the population were Hindus, the British regarded this rule as 'an odious distinction, the absurdity and injustice of which are too glaring to require comment.'[21] This 'absurdity' was remedied in 1793 when a regulation was enacted that stipulated that the law officers had to prepare their opinions assuming that the witnesses were Muslims of good

---

the death penalty. In such cases a *shariʿa* court would award the blood price to the heirs. See Peters, *Crime and Punishment in Islamic Law*, 38–53.

18 Regulation 1801/8, § 6, Colebrooke. *Digest of the Regulations and Laws*, ii, 882.

19 Fulwar Skipwith, *The Magistrate's Guide: Being an Abridgment of the Criminal Regulations and Acts of the Circular Orders and Constructions and of the Cases Decided and Reported by the Court of Nizamut Adawlut under the Presidency of Fort William in Bengal* (Calcutta 1843) 70.

20 *Siyasa* means administering discretionary punishment for acts threatening public security on the basis of summary trials. See Peters, *Crime and Punishment in Islamic Law*, 67–68.

21 Fisch, *Digest of the Regulations and Laws*, 47, quoting a British judge in the Nizamat-i ʿAdalat.

reputation (*'adl*).[22] In 1803 more restrictions of the Islamic law of evidence were removed: Legal deficiencies in the evidence were no longer to be taken into account:

> If no penalty shall be provided by a Regulation, but the legal penalty for the crime, by Muhamedan Law, would, on complete conviction have been Hud (*hadd*, RP) or Kissas (*qisas*, or retaliation, RP) and the Futwa shall adjudge discretionary punishment on the ground of some legal deficiency in the evidence, the law officer shall be required to state, in a second Futwa, what would have been the specific penalty, under the Muhamedan law, in case of legal conviction, and the Court shall sentence the prisoner accordingly.[23]

The same regulation laid down that convictions should be based on solid evidence, measured according to British standards, and not necessarily by the criteria of strict Islamic criminal law.[24]

Proving criminal intent has always been problematic for Muslim jurists. Since, under Islamic law, witnesses cannot testify to a person's mental state, the jurists held that criminal intent in cases of homicide could only be established by reference to the weapon or instrument of killing. Abu Hanifa's opinion, prevailing in the Hanafite school, was that only the use of sharp weapons or objects (capable of severing limbs), or fire would be indicative of intent. According to this opinion, killing with a stick or by administering poison could not be punished with death. For the British, this was, obviously, an irrational doctrine that stood in the way of adequately punishing murderers. Already in 1790 a regulation instructed the courts to follow a less authoritative Hanafite opinion to the effect that the use of any weapon, instrument or method which is as a rule fatal, is proof of criminal intent.[25] Three years later, in 1793, these restrictions for proving criminal intent were also removed and the courts were directed to "regulate the punishment by the intention of the criminal, not by the manner or instrument of perpetration, except as evidence of the intent."[26]

Under Islamic law there are many pleas that would prevent capital sentences even if the defendant had been convicted of wilful homicide. These

---

22 '(…) the law officer shall declare what would have been the Futwa if the witnesses had been Muhamedans (…)'. Regulation 1793/9 § 56, Colebrooke, *Digest of the Regulations and Laws*, i, 529.

23 Regulation 1803/53, § 2 C. 2, Colebrooke, *Digest of the Regulations and Laws*, i, 534.

24 Ibid. § 7.

25 Banerjee, *Background to Indian Criminal Law*, 72–73.

26 Regulation 1793/9, § 75, Colebrooke, *Digest of the Regulations and Laws*, i, 533.

included the circumstances not related to the seriousness of the crime, such as the fact that the victim was the perpetrator's descendant, one of the perpetrator's heirs, or the culprit's slave. Moreover, the fact that one of the accomplices in the killing was not liable for retaliation would prevent that the others were sentenced to death. In 1799 most defences against a charge of voluntary manslaughter were eliminated: Henceforth, there was no bar for capital punishment on "any ground of personal distinction."[27]

With regard to the *hadd* crimes a regulation issued in 1803 eliminated all special pleas, such as uncertainty as to the unlawfulness of the act with which the defendant is charged (*shubha*), and the strict rules of evidence. The pertinent section stipulated that if, in the absence of legislative provisions,

> the crime be liable to a specific penalty [i.e. *hadd* penalty, RP] by the Muhamedan law on full conviction, and the Futwa should award discretionary punishment in consequence of the conviction not being complete according to the Muhamedan law, the Court, if satisfied of the prisoner's guilt, shall require a second Futwa specifying the specific penalty on full conviction, and shall sentence the prisoner according to such second Futwa.

The same would apply "if the specific penalty of the Muhamedan law be barred by some special exception not affecting the criminality of the offence and repugnant to general justice."[28] This meant that if someone was accused of theft, for which there was evidence, but not sufficient for a sentence to a fixed penalty, or if the evidence was sufficient, but the accused had stolen from his child, he would nevertheless, in second instance, be sentenced to the fixed punishment for theft, which the British would commute to a long term of imprisonment. The same regulation specified this principle in detail with regard to armed robbery.

4.3 *Defining Taʿzir Offences in Order to Render Criminal Justice Less Arbitrary*

With regard to offences punishable with *taʿzir* the law officers would state in their fatwas the grounds for discretionary punishment, but leave the measure of it to the court. The upper limits of discretionary punishment were for the Courts of Circuit thirty-nine lashes ("stripes") or seven years imprisonment and for the *Nizamat-i ʿAdalat* any punishment but death. The latter court was

27 Regulation 1799/8, § 2–5, Colebrooke, *Digest of the Regulations and Laws*, i, 534.

28 Regulation 1803/53, § 2, C. 3–5, Colebrooke, *Digest of the Regulations and Laws*, ii, 884.

instructed 'to provide for the case in the future,' i.e. to enact legislation covering the offence.[29] The British were not comfortable with the notion of discretionary punishment. It offended their idea of the rule of law and they regarded it as arbitrariness.[30] Increasingly legislation was issued to regulate this field and to restrict the discretion of the courts. One of the first examples of such legislation can be found in the regulation of 1797, which made punishable by *taʿzir* the offence of perjury. The accused could be punished by public exposure, *tashhir*, or to corporal punishment, or to both. In particular cases, the culprit's forehead could be marked (branded).[31] *Taʿzir* made it possible to punish defendants for *hadd* crimes if the evidence was not sufficient for a conviction or if a convictions was impossible because of a plea not related to the seriousness of the offence. Most jurists, however, were of the opinion that in such a case the punishment should be less severe that the hadd penalty. In the aforementioned regulation of 1803 the distinction between *taʿzir* and *hadd* penalties for the same offence was removed: In such cases the law officers were requested to give a second fatwa specifying the *hadd* penalty on full conviction and the court would then pass sentence accordingly. After 1803 the British issued more penal regulations specifying offences and their punishments in order to limit the powers of the courts to mete out punishment on the strength of *taʿzir*.

4.4 *Cruel Punishments*

In the eighteenth and nineteenth centuries the English penal system was quite harsh. There were about two hundred capital offences and many others punishable by lifelong deportation or long terms of incarceration. Flogging was a common penalty. However, mutilation as a punishment was not accepted. There was a strange paradox in the British notions of penal law: Punishing by taking a life was considered to be normal, whereas taking a limb was regarded as cruel and barbaric. In his study of early British-Indian criminal law, Fisch refers to these sentiments in the title "Cheap Lives and Dear Limbs," and argues that the difference between English (and European) law and Islamic law in this respect are not related to ideas about penal law, but rather the result of different cultural notions. The British did not want to enforce punishments like amputation and the first substantive criminal regulation of 1793 confirmed the already existing practice of commuting sentences awarding mutilation into

29 Regulation 1803/53, § 2, C. 7, § 7, C. 1, 3, Colebrooke, *Digest of the Regulations and Laws*, i, 534 and ii, 462, 878.

30 Fisch, *Cheap Lives*, 20–21.

31 Regulation 1797/17, § 2, Colebrooke, *Digest of the Regulations and Laws*, ii, 882.

imprisonment and hard labour "of seven years for each limb."[32] Death sentences by stoning were also commuted into prison sentences, and not into another form of death penalty.

5 Northern Nigeria

5.1 *Introduction*

When, around 1900, the British occupied Northern Nigeria they intended to control the area through indirect rule. The main reason was financial: making use of the existing structures of authority and native government officials was much cheaper than setting up a special colonial administration, staffed with personnel from the motherland, as the British had done in large parts of India. They left the local emirs in their positions of power and exerted control through the existing administrative and judicial structures. The Native Courts Proclamation of 1900 was based on this principle: The British Resident (i.e. the provincial governor) could establish, with the consent of the emir (the local ruler), native courts with full jurisdiction in civil and criminal matters over the native population. The British used this power to confer official status to the courts of the emirs and the *alkali*s (Islamic judge, from Arabic *al-qadi*). The judges, who were to apply Maliki Islamic law, were appointed by the emirs, with the approval of the Residents. When in 1904 a Criminal Code based on English law was introduced in Northern Nigeria, *Shari'a* criminal law was not abolished. Section 4 of this code stipulated: 'No person shall be liable to be tried or punished in any court in Nigeria, other than a native tribunal, for an offence except under the express provisions of the Code or some other Ordinance or some law (…).' This section exempted the native courts from the principle that criminal sentences had to be founded on statute law and allowed them to try acts under Islamic law (*qua* native law), regardless of whether or not they were punishable under the Criminal Code. Therefore, they could sentence persons for illegal sexual intercourse (*zina*), which is an offence under Islamic law, but not under the 1904 Criminal Code.

5.2 *British Interference*

British interference in Northern Nigeria differed from the way the British dealt with Islamic criminal law in India. In Nigeria the colonial administration kept its distance from native criminal justice and did not attempt to change it

32 Regulation 1793/9, § 51, Colebrooke, *Digest of the Regulations and Laws*, ii, 879.

except with regard to the application of cruel punishments. Only in the 1940s did the British begin interfering with the *Shariʿa* law of homicide.

From the beginning the native courts had full jurisdiction in criminal cases. However, certain categories of penal sentences (among them capital sentences) had to be approved by the Governor-General after review by the Resident. The British Resident had extensive powers to supervise and control the courts: he could enter and inspect the courts, suspend, reduce and modify sentences or order a rehearing of the trial before another native court or a transfer to a provincial court (i.e. a court applying English common law). The courts of the emirs and alkalis could award any type of punishment. However, sentences awarding amputation or death by stoning or other punishments that were deemed repugnant to humanity and natural justice (later reformulated as natural justice, equity and good conscience) would not be carried out. In an address given in the Northern town of Sokoto in 1902, the British governor-general Lord Lugard described his policy as follows:

> The alkalis and emirs will hold the Law Courts as of old, but bribes are forbidden, and mutilation and confinement of men in inhuman prisons are not lawful. (…) Sentences of death will not be carried out without the consent of the Resident. (…) Every person has the right to appeal to the Resident who will, however, endeavour to uphold the power of the Native Courts to deal with native cases according to the law and the custom of the country.[33]

The application of Islamic law by the native courts in the North extended to the courts' practice and procedure. The British authorities gave these courts much latitude. In a 1930 decision the West African Court of Appeal, the highest appeal court for the British colonies in West Africa, recognized the Maliki *qasama* procedure, on the strength of which a suspect against whom there is some evidence, which is, however, not sufficient for a conviction, can be sentenced to death if the victim's male next of kin swear fifty oaths against him. The Emir of Katsina's court had found a certain Abdullah Kogi guilty of wilful homicide, although there was no admission nor any eyewitnesses, nor other legal evidence that could show that he had committed the offence. There was however circumstantial evidence (*lawth*) to support the conviction. The West African Court of Appeal did not uphold the sentence, but sent the case back and instructed the Emir's court to look for the victim's relatives to swear

33 A.G. Karibi-Whyte, *History and Sources of Nigerian Criminal Law* (Ibadan 1993) 177.

a *qasama* oath, in order to make the sentence lawful. The Court of Appeal explained its position as follows:

> There is no desire to interfere with decisions which are in accordance with native law, the principle has been that the verdict and sentence of a Native Court which is an integral part of our judicial system carried out in accordance with procedure enjoined by native law and not obviously inequitable will be accepted even though the procedure is widely different from the practice of English Criminal Courts.[34]

I have found only one decision in the field of criminal procedure in which a *Shari'a* provision was declared to be in conflict with natural justice. This was the rule that in the trial of *hadd* crimes, if the plaintiff produces full evidence, the defendant is not permitted to put forward a defence (except producing evidence to impugn the testimonies against him). In this case a native court found a man guilty of homicide while attempting to rob and therefore sentenced him to death. On appeal, the Federal Supreme Court annulled the judgement on the ground that the appellant was not allowed to defend himself. This is because according to the Islamic law of evidence, an accused is not allowed to give evidence on his behalf, while under English law, he can do so, but in a witness box. The court held that this rule of procedure and evidence of Islamic law was repugnant to natural justice, equity and good conscience.[35]

The main impact of British interference with Islamic criminal justice was the abolition of mutilating corporal punishments. Caning and flogging remained lawful punishments except for women, but sentences imposing these penalties had to be confirmed by the Emir or the District Officer.[36] Other forms of corporal punishment such as amputation were not outlawed. The same applied to death by stoning. If a native court would sentence a person under Islamic law to amputation or death by stoning, or impose the penalty of flogging against a woman, the British officials charged with the execution of sentences would routinely commute such sentences into imprisonment or a fine. As a result, the distinction between *hadd* offences and the corresponding non-*hadd* crimes to be punished by *ta'zir* had become obliterated since now they

34 Abdullahi Kogi & others vs Katsina Native Authority ((1930) 14 NLR 49 as quoted in Karibi-Whyte, *History and Sources of Nigerian Criminal Law*, pp. 162–4. See also Abdulmalik Bappa Mahmud, *A Brief History of Shari'ah in the Defunct Northern Nigeria*, [S.l. 1988) 18.

35 Guri vs Hadejia Native Authority (1959) 4 FSC 44. Discussed and criticized in Muhammad Tabi'u, 'The impact of the repugnancy test on the application of Islamic law in Nigeria', *Journal of Islamic and Comparative Law* (Zaria), 18 (1991), 53–76.

36 Native Court Ordinance 1933, § 16.

all entailed imprisonment as a punishment. With regard to illicit sex relations, there was not much difference in punishment for those who were *muhsan* and those who were not. The former would now be given a prison sentence (instead of death by stoning), whereas the latter would be sentenced to one hundred lashes and imprisonment if the accused was a man, and to imprisonment or a fine (in the place of the lashing) in the case of a woman.

The second area of interference was the law of homicide. It would seem that the British colonial judiciary wanted to impose the rules of English law with regard to the awarding of punishment in homicide cases. It is plausible that this was partly motivated by the symbolic value of capital justice as a sign of sovereignty. The interference had its origins in an amendment in the Criminal Code. In 1933 the words "other than a native tribunal" were deleted from article 4.[37] These words were understood as giving the native courts the jurisdiction to try under native law offences that were not included in the Criminal Code. Initially judicial practice did not change. The common interpretation of the phrase 'some other Ordinance' was that it referred to the Native Courts Ordinance, which expressly permitted the Native Courts to impose punishment under native law and custom, and thus under Islamic law.[38] However, in 1947 the West African Court of Appeal gave a different interpretation of the new wording of article 4. The court of the Emir of Gwandu had sentenced a man to death for having killed his wife's lover. The accused had pleaded that the homicide had been justified because of the affair between his wife and the victim. The court, however, had not accepted the defence, arguing that under Islamic law such a defence would only be admitted if his life had been threatened. On appeal the sentence was quashed. The Court of Appeal ruled, on the strength of the Criminal Code, that the accused had acted under provocation and that his act was therefore to be qualified not as murder, but as manslaughter, which under the Criminal Code is not a capital offence. Therefore a death sentence could not be passed, although under Islamic law it was justified.[39]

---

37 'No person shall be liable to be tried or punished in any court in Nigeria, *other than a native tribunal*, for an offence except under the express provisions of the Code or some other Ordinance or some law (…).'

38 Section 10 (2) of the Native Courts Ordinance of 1933 reads: 'Native courts (…) may impose a fine or imprisonment (…) or may inflict any punishment authorized by native law or custom provided it does not involve mutilation or torture, and is not repugnant to natural justice and humanity.'

39 Tsofo Gunna v. Gwandu Native Authority (1947) 12 W.A.C.A. 141, discussed in Mahmud, *A Brief History of Shariʿah in the Defunct Northern Nigeria*, 17–8, and Muhammad Tabi'u, 'Constraints in the Application of Islamic Law in Nigeria', in S. Khalid Rashid (ed.) *Islamic Law in Nigeria: Application and Teaching* (Lagos 1986) 75–85.

This decision gave rise to much confusion. A common interpretation of it was that the Native Courts in the North could apply Islamic criminal law only if there was no specific provision in the Criminal Code, and that otherwise the Native Courts had to pass sentence on the basis of the Criminal Code. In 1948, after Islamic judges had protested against what they regarded as an unwarranted intrusion upon their jurisdiction, the Native Courts Ordinance was also amended. The new text of the law stipulated that where the same act amounted to an offence under a written law and under a customary law, the maximum punishment that could be given in a trial by a native court was the one prescribed by the written law. The basic principle applied here was that for such offences guilt would be established under native law and that subsequently the court should turn to the Criminal Code for guidance on the sentence.

The application of the new principle led to complications with regard to the trial and punishment of homicide. The main problem was that under Islamic criminal law manslaughter (wilful killing) is a capital offence, whereas under the 1904 Nigerian Criminal Code homicide incurred the death penalty only if classified as murder, i.e. if the killing was not only wilful but also premeditated. Under the amended Ordinance, capital sentences for manslaughter without premeditation issued by an Emir's Court, could be quashed for being in conflict with the 1904 Criminal Code. A second complication was the idea of private prosecution and the notion that retaliation is only lawful if the victim's blood price is equal to or higher than the killer's. The pardon of the next of kin or the fact that the victim was a Christian would prevent the awarding of retaliation under Maliki law, even if the homicide had been committed with premeditation. In such cases the *Shari'a* Court could, under Maliki law, sentence the murderer only to one hundred lashes and one year imprisonment. According to the new text of the Native Courts' Ordinance, punishment would be awarded according to English law, after an Islamic court had established the facts of the case and the accused's guilt. This meant that in such cases death sentences could be pronounced.

The application of Islamic criminal law by Islamic courts came to an end in 1960 when the new Penal Code for the Northern Region 1959 came into force. Based on the 1861 Indian and the 1899 Sudanese Penal Code, this code was essentially an English code.

6 Conclusions

In the Introduction I said, referring to Mann and Roberts, that that colonial law is an excellent window for studying the structures of colonialism. Comparing the implementation and development if criminal law in India and Northern Nigeria in the colonial period is a case in point. It reveals not only the influence of local factors on colonial structures, but also the evolution in British colonialism between the turn of the nineteenth and the turn of the twentieth centuries.

British India and Northern Nigeria were, to the best of my knowledge, the only colonies where Islamic criminal law continued to be applied. The main reason that this was done in India was the constitutional position of the EIC, which, until 1858, ruled not as a sovereign but in name of the Mughal emperor. This meant that the British could not replace the legal system and had to maintain law and order through the enforcement of Islamic criminal law. It is, however, doubtful whether the British were prepared to introduce English penal law. By the end of the eighteenth century British colonialism was still in its infancy. Colonial administrators had no models that they could follow and tried to solve the problems with which they were confronted in pragmatic ways. As regards criminal law, they thought that Islamic law was most suited for the local population (officials of the EIC fell under a different jurisdiction). In addition, transplanting English penal law to India – had they wanted it – was complicated since there was no English penal code: English criminal law was a mixture of common law and a great number of statutes. The difficulties were compounded by the fact that criminal law usually was enforced by colonial administrators without a proper legal training.[40]

When, at the turn of the twentieth century, the British conquered Northern Nigeria, the situation was different. By that time British colonialism had developed and there were definite notions about how colonial rule ought to be exercised. One of these notions was that colonial domination could be based on existing pre-colonial power structures, by leaving local leaders in their position of authority, under British supervision. This model, it was argued, was cost efficient since only a handful of colonial administrators were needed to control an entire population. One of the advocates of this model, Lord Lugard (1858–1945), became the first High Commissioner of Northern Nigeria and

40 This was an important reason for the drafting and introduction of penal codes in other British colonies. See H.F. Morris, 'A History Of The Adoption Of Codes Of Criminal Law And Procedure In British Colonial Africa, 1876–1935', *Journal of African Law*, 3 (1973), 3.

could put his ideas into practice. Since the authority of the local leaders was partly founded on their judicial powers, these were preserved, but placed under British control. This meant that Islamic law, including Islamic criminal law, continued to be applied.

The way Islamic criminal law was applied was related to the different modes of domination. In India a semblance of Islamic legitimacy was upheld by the presence of the Muslim law officers in the courts, whose task it was to issue fatwas in each case in order to expound the law to the British judges. The latter would pass judgement accordingly, unless they regarded the applicable rule of Islamic law as repugnant to natural justice. Through statutes and the introduction of European legal principles, Islamic criminal law was gradually modified. In a period of 45 years, from 1772 till 1817, Indian criminal law lost its Islamic character, in the sense that most specific *Shari'a* traits were removed and that it became very similar to European criminal law. In Nigeria, in accordance with the model of indirect rule, Islamic, indigenous courts would hear criminal cases and pronounce sentence. The colonial authorities stood aloof, but exercised a certain amount of control because they had to approve certain sentences before these could be carried out. If they found such sentences repugnant to natural justice, they would commute them. Moreover, the sentences of the native courts could be appealed against to colonial courts of appeal. Although there was a marked difference between British Indian and Nigeria in the degree of interference with Islamic criminal law, there were also similarities. The most important one in this connection is the fact that Islamic courts were incorporated into a hierarchical court system with clearly defined jurisdictions and procedures and that the law was fixed by publishing the decisions of the higher courts and, in India but not in Nigeria, by statute law and translations of authoritative works of Islamic law.

In an official report published in India in 1813 Islamic criminal law was characterized not only as barbaric, cruel and savage, but also as inadequate, defective and absurd.[41] These judgements clearly illustrates British concerns and assumptions and explain the directions of British colonial legal policies in the field of criminal law.

The perceived inadequacy, defectiveness and absurdity of Islamic criminal law motivated most reforms of Indian criminal law during the first decades of colonial domination. The British were baffled by the inconsistencies of Islamic criminal law. On the one hand there were the strict rules regarding retaliation for homicide and wounding and the *hadd* crimes, according to which many defendants could not be adequately punished for reasons not related to the

41 Fisch, *Cheap Lives and Dear Limbs*, 87.

seriousness of the offences they had committed. But on the other hand there was *taʿzir* and *siyasa*, the extensive discretionary powers of the courts and executive officials to mete out severe punishment, including death, on the basis of summary proceedings.

The British found this absurd. Since *siyasa* and *taʿzir* offended against their notion of law, they did not want to impose punishment on the strength of *siyasa* and set out to define *taʿzir* offences and their punishment in order to close the door to arbitrary justice. However, left with the strict rules of retaliation and the *hadd* offences, they found that these were not adequate for maintaining law and order: It was difficult to get convictions because there were too many loopholes in the law. Moreover, in cases of homicide and bodily harm the government had no control over the prosecution of the perpetrator. Criminal law reform introduced in India during the first decades of colonial rule was aimed at transforming strict *Shariʿa* criminal law (i.e. the law of retaliation and *hadd*) into a type of European criminal law, based on public justice and equal treatment and eliminating the effect of accidental circumstances not related to the offence itself. In the process *Shariʿa* criminal law became much harsher as it became easier for the courts to pronounce death sentences. At the same time, statute law was introduced to define specific *taʿzir* offences and specify their penalties. This, of course, enhanced the control of the state over the implementation of criminal law and curbed arbitrariness of the courts, thus satisfying British ideas about the rule of law.

In Nigeria, no such legal policy was pursued. In conformity with the notion of indirect rule, keeping the peace through the implementation of criminal law was first and foremost the responsibility of the indigenous authorities and the colonial administration only interfered where Islamic criminal justice if it was regarded as violating "natural justice." Beyond the field of punishment itself, such interference hardly occurred. However, during the last decades of colonial rule, there were attempts, partly successful, to restrict or modify the Islamic law of homicide. As a result of new legislation and its interpretation by the colonial court of appeal, the role of Islamic law with regard to offences defined in the 1904 Criminal Code for Northern Nigeria was relegated to establishing the defendant's guilt, whereas the punishment was to be awarded according to the Criminal Code. In practice this had only consequences for the law of homicide and, more specifically, the pronouncing of capital sentences. It would seem that the colonial administration wanted to assert its sovereignty of which capital justice is one of the most powerful symbols. The result was a juristic monster that caused a great deal of confusion lasting until, in 1960, the new Penal Code for Northern Nigeria came into force that put an end to the implementation of Islamic criminal law.

It was a common and wide-spread assumption that Islamic criminal law was barbaric and cruel. Many of the reforms in India and Nigeria were intended to "civilize" Islamic criminal law by abolishing cruel penalties. As we have seen, cruel penalties were outlawed both in India and in Nigeria in the earliest stages of colonial rule. As I explained in the Introduction, this was not directly necessary for the preservation of colonial power relations. Nevertheless such reforms were of importance for colonial domination because they would create acceptance of colonial rule among the assimilated elites of the colonized peoples. In addition, since one of the justifications of colonialism was its civilizing mission, tolerating practices that were widely condemned as barbaric would have adverse effects for its support among the British themselves, both at home and in the colonies.

CHAPTER 34

Dutch Extremist Islamism

Van Gogh's Murderer and His Ideas

1 Introduction

Is there a special relationship between Islam and terrorism? Many would argue that there is, pointing at the many acts of terrorism committed in the name of Islam. But that only proves that Islamic doctrines, like those of other religions, can be interpreted to justify such acts of violence, not that there is an intrinsic relationship between both. In this chapter I will argue that those who want to invoke such justifications must actively construct them by choosing between different existing interpretations or by proposing new ones. My assumption is not that religion is unimportant in this context, but rather, as Jessica Stern (2003) also has demonstrated, that the primary motivation for contemplating the use of terror are feelings of alienation and humiliation. Such feelings can also be vicarious in the sense that the alienation or humiliation are not primarily perceived as connected with the person who justified violent action, but rather as connected with the group to which he belongs or with which he identifies. Religion plays a role in drawing the boundaries between 'us' and 'them' and thus defining the enemy. Moreover it can provide powerful incentives for entering violent struggles and convincing arguments to be used for recruitment.

In this chapter I will show how Mohammed Bouyeri, who killed the Dutch film maker and publicist Theo van Gogh on 2 November 2004 and is now serving a life sentence, gradually constructed an Islamic ideology that legitimized the use of violence in Dutch society.[1] By analysing the ideas of Mohammed Bouyeri I will show how he used and recombined existing interpretations and created a form of extremist Islamism containing all elements commonly associated with radicalism and extremism, regardless of whether these are formulated in religious or in secular terms. These elements are the rejection of the world order, since it is allegedly dominated by the forces of evil, the feeling that one's own group is under acute threat, the idea of a utopia that can be realized, against all odds, by a small and devoted vanguard prepared to use violence in

1 I was an expert witness in Mohammed Bouyeri's trial. This chapter is mainly based on my report, in which I analyzed the ca. sixty texts produced by Bouyeri. The report (in Dutch) is available at: http://www.sociosite.org/jihad/peters_rapport.pdf.

 | DOI:10.1163/9789004420625_035

order to defeat the forces of evil (Buys et al. 2003: 18–19). But before sketching Bouyeri's ideological development, I will give a brief general survey of the Islamic doctrines that are used by militants to justify their actions and those that enhance the fighting spirits.

2 Islamic Doctrines Associated with Violence

Islam, like other religions, has a Janus face: it contains many different and even contradictory sacred texts and interpretations and, in addition, doctrines that are not uniform and monolithic, but can, in concrete contexts, be used to deliver widely divergent messages. Among the Islamic texts and doctrines there are those that preach peace and tolerance, but also those that can justify violence and inculcate militants with a contempt for death and zeal for engaging in violent struggles. There are three doctrines or concepts that are associated with violent actions. The first, not surprisingly, is the doctrine of jihad, the second the concept of martyrdom and the last one, the apocalyptic notion that the End of Time is near. These notions can have very different meanings and impacts and they get their final and definitive content when used in a specific context.

Jihad (on the classical notion of jihad and its modern interpretations, see: Peters 2005) is a term occurring frequently in the Qur'an. Its basic meaning is effort, but in the Qur'an it is usually employed to denote the fighting against non-Muslims. Together with canonical stories about the Prophet Mohammed (*hadîth*), these Qur'anic verses are at the basis of the legal doctrine of warfare, that was elaborated in the first centuries of Islam. It contains two crucial notions: the obligation to expand the territory of Islam, i.e. the territory governed by an Islamic government and, secondly, the duty to defend that territory against outside aggression. The first obligation is a collective one, of which the whole community is discharged if a sufficient number of men carry it out. Its minimum, if the power relations do not allow conquest, is sending out an Islamic military patrol into enemy lands to keep the idea of jihad alive. The other duty is an individual one, incumbent on all able bodied men in the region under attack and, if necessary, the adjacent provinces and, ultimately, all Muslim territory. This in a nutshell the legal doctrine found in the classical works of Islamic jurisprudence. However, there are also other ways of conceptualizing jihad. Certain pious groups saw jihad primarily as a struggle against one's own evil inclinations, or pointed out that jihad was not necessarily waged by the sword, but could also be carried out by the pen and the mouth.

These doctrines were not mutually exclusive but could be used by the same person in the appropriate contexts.

By the end of the nineteenth century Islamic scholars in India and Egypt embarked on a project of reinterpretation of Islam. One of the objects of their endeavours was the legal doctrine of jihad. By redefining the relationship between the various Qur'anic verses and reading them in a different light, they came to the conclusion that the Qur'an does not enjoin warfare between Muslims and non-Muslims but, instead, peaceful coexistence, unless there is a serious *casus belli*, such as an attack on Muslim territory. This notion, i.e. jihad conceived as purely defensive warfare, has been adopted widely in the Islamic world, especially among the political and intellectual elites.

Thus, the word jihad refers to very different concepts. But even if we focus on the classical legal doctrine, we find that the ways the rules can be applied are not clearly defined. Take for instance the definition of the enemy: in principle, the non-Muslims who are no protected by the Islamic state. If certain groups define being a Muslim in a different way, the boundaries between Muslims and non-Muslims shift and include or exclude certain groups. Certain radical Islamists regard Muslim rulers who do not fully implement the Shari'a as unbelievers or rather apostates, since they have abandoned Islam. As a consequence, they are then seen as persons who have lost their right of protection and may lawfully be killed. This is called *takfîr*, declaring that someone who considers himself a Muslim is an unbeliever (*kâfir*). It is controversial whether this is allowed at all, but militant Islamists who follow a strict definition of being a Muslim, do apply *takfîr*.

Another example of the indefiniteness of the jihad doctrine is the legitimization of defensive warfare: what precisely constitutes aggression that makes jihad an individual duty? The fact that a government of alleged apostates rules part of the Muslim world? The assistance given by a non-Muslim army to one Muslim state in its warfare against another? Osama Bin Laden for instance regarded as an act of aggression the stationing of United States troops in Saudi Arabia in the First Gulf War, although the Saudi government had requested their presence. Militant interpretations of the jihad doctrine focus on defensive jihad presented as an individual religious obligation. Not taking part in it is then seen as a grave sin. These and similar applications of the jihad doctrine depend on the interpretation of the doctrine and on the appreciation of the facts to which the doctrine must be applied.

Once warfare or violence has been justified by a specific reading of the jihad doctrine, the notion of martyrdom (Todd Lawson 1995) can provide further incentives to participate in that struggle. It is a concept firmly rooted in the text of the Qur'an, where it is frequently referred to. According to widespread Islamic belief warriors killed in jihad are rendered free of sin and go directly to Paradise, where they will dwell close to God's throne. However, the doctrine of martyrdom also has its controversies. It is for instance disputed whether a person who actively seeks it can be regarded as a martyr. The debates on this issue, that date back to the early centuries of Islam, have acquired a new relevance in view of the phenomenon of suicide attacks.

A third concept that is germane to our topic is the idea that the End of Times is approaching. There exists a large body of Islamic eschatological writings, many of them going back to the first centuries of Islam. According to these accounts, the final stage of the apocalypse is marked by a deteriorating of the conditions in the world: injustice, oppression and famine will spread. This is followed by a cosmic struggle between the forces of evil and those of Islam in which the latter will be victorious. This victory will inaugurate a golden era lasting a specific but disputed number of years (forty, seventy, thousand) until the Hour comes. As in other religions, expectations about the coming of the millennium can have strong political consequences. Understanding and presenting a certain struggle as the apocalyptic battle is a powerful motivation for engaging in it. One cannot lose: the final victory is certain and if one is killed, the ultimate bliss of martyrdom will be his reward. It is also a strong argument that can be used for recruitment. On the other hand, apocalyptic expectations can be used to make people accept oppression and injustice by persuading them that these conditions are only temporary as they belong to a stage in the history of salvation, immediately preceding the millennium.

The bottom-line is that such doctrines and ideas are ambiguous and vague and need users to give them a specific meaning and content. What such users do is either selecting their ideas from a range of already existing interpretations and understandings, or creating new meanings. These may be combined to create a radical or extremist political-religious ideology.

3 Mohammed Bouyeri and the Hofstadgroep

When immediately after the assassination of Theo van Gogh Mohammed Bouyeri was arrested, the police found out that he belonged to a group of young Muslims who, for some time, had been under surveillance by the AIVD (the Dutch Intelligence and Security Service). Since they were first spotted in The Hague, the AIVD had dubbed them the 'Hofstadgroep', Hofstad (court city) being one of the epithets of The Hague (Chorus, Olgun 2005; Vermaat 2005; Benschop 2005; Wessels 2006). Later it became clear that most of its members, including Bouyeri, lived in Amsterdam. They were, with the exception of one or two converts to Islam, all of Moroccan descent and born or raised in the Netherlands. Some of them were old friends of Bouyeri's with whom he had grown up in his Amsterdam neighbourhood. Bouyeri, whom the AIVD first considered an insignificant follower of the group, later turned out to be its main ideologue. The group did not form a tight organization; its member used to visit on an irregular basis the same gatherings in Bouyeri's living room, where they discussed religion and exchanged digital documents with religious and radical Islamist contents. The police investigation did not reveal any direct organisational links with international Islamist terrorist groups. The Hofstadgroep, therefore, is an example of home-grown Islamic extremism. However, during the initial stages of the radicalisation period, a certain Abu Khaled Redouan el-Issa, a former Syrian army officer who had applied for political asylum in Germany, played a role. El-Issa spoke at informal living room meetings throughout the Netherlands and introduced groups of Muslims to the thought of the founding fathers of Islamic radicalism, such as Sayyid Qutb (1906–1966) and Abu al-Aʿlâ al-Mawdûdî (1903–1979). Among the groups he initiated into these ideas were Bouyeri and his friends.

At the time of the arrests of Bouyeri and other Hofstadgroep members the police seized their computers. The contents of the hard disks and other data carriers were copied into a special forensic program that allowed searching, book marking and copying without changes in the original. Within this enormous amount of data, I could identify about sixty texts produced by Bouyeri, either because they were signed with his sobriquets Abu Zubair or Sayf al-Dîn al-Muwahhid (The Sword of Religion, the monotheist), or because the document properties pointed to his computer. The type of texts varies. Some were Dutch translations of Islamist pamphlets or treatises, often preceded by a short introduction by Bouyeri. Other texts were entirely written by himself. With one exception the source texts of the translations were in English. It seems that Bouyeri's knowledge of Arabic was not sufficient for translating complicated religious treatises. The texts he produced were distributed among the other members of the group and some of them were published on the internet. Bouyeri was the ideological leader of the group and his texts were apparently used for ideological training. Apart from his texts the computers contained enormous libraries of religious written material, most of it in Arabic, as well as pictures and short video movies. Most of the latter were related to the oppression of Muslims in e.g. Palestine/Israel, Chechnya, Iraq and Afghanistan, and their armed struggles against oppression. The videos were probably used for recruitment, in order to convince potential members of the plight of Muslims all over the world and the need to do something about it.

An inventory of the documents found on his and other computers shows that he and the group were ideologically heavily indebted to the Egyptian Sayyid Qutb and the Indian/Pakistani Abu al-Aʿlâ al-Mawdûdî. Moreover large amounts of more recent Salafi material, especially from radical Saudi religious scholars and from authors who had fought in Afghanistan were found. However, many of these documents were in Arabic, and it is impossible to assess their real influence. Among Bouyeri's translations we find a few texts originally written by radical Saudi scholars and by Afghan jihad veterans. However, the impact of one figure stand out: Abu Hamza al-Misri (b. ca. 1957), the militant imam and preacher of the Finsbury Mosque in London. Born in Egypt, he emigrated to England in 1979. In early 1980s he fought with the mujahedin in Afghanistan where he lost his hands and an eye. Bouyeri translated quite a few of his writings, via English versions, into Dutch.

4 The Construction of a Dutch Extremist Islamist

On the basis of the document properties of Bouyeri's texts I could establish the chronological order in which they were produced. This enables us to follow the process of radicalisation which their author went through. Within this process we can distinguish four stages:
- Explicit rejection of Western values and norms (starting February 2003)
- Rejection of Western democracy and law (as of October 2003)
- Global call for jihad against democracy (March 2004)
- Justification of violent actions and the writing of threatening letters (summer 2004)

4.1 *'The Quest for the Truth'*

The beginnings of Bouyeri's radicalisation can be dated back to the year 2001. In the summer of that year he had served a prison sentence for assault and battery. Later he said that in prison he had started to read the Qur'an. His need for a new spiritual orientation was given a new impetus with the death of his mother in December of that year. In the testament drawn up by him shortly before he killed van Gogh, he mentioned that after his mother's death in December 2001 he set out on a 'quest for the truth'. That his ideas and behaviour changed during the following year is well documented by testimonies of friends and colleagues. He became more serious and religious. In his work – he had dropped out of college and found a part-time job as assistant-manager of a community centre in the neighbourhood where he lived – he began to take Islamic injunctions more seriously: he refused to order alcoholic drinks for receptions and parties and to organize activities where men and women would mingle.

Against the ensuing criticism he defended himself in a short article published in the centre's magazine in February 2003 and entitled 'Islam and integration'. This I consider as the first steps on the road that he was to follow until the end. Whereas the Dutch public debate at that time was dominated by the question of whether Islam is compatible with integration into Dutch society, Bouyeri turned the question on its head by positing that the only true integration was integration into Islam:

> The verb integrating means … becoming part of a larger whole. This includes for me the Islamic concept of submission (body and soul) to the Unique Power who is the Creator of the larger whole that we call universe and of which man is part.

This, he argues, imposes on him the duty of following Islamic prescriptions, even if these are in conflict with prevailing views in society. At that moment, however, it was not yet clear for him what Islam was. Among the document written by him in the spring and summer of 2003 we find texts showing that he was experimenting with character building through acts of piety and with numerological readings of the Qur'an. However, during that same spring fundamentalist notions become more prominent. This was the result of two events. The first one was that the authorities did not accept his proposal for a club for Moroccan youth. Assisted by the community centre where he was employed he had applied for government funding but his application was rejected. This must have adversely affected his trust in the Dutch political system and Dutch society in general.

The other event was that his contacts with the Syrian preacher Abu Khaled el-Issa intensified. Bouyeri and his friends had met him in one of the Amsterdam mosques in the previous fall, but El-Issa began to visit and teach them sometime during the spring of 2003. In the summer of that year documents were distributed among the members of the group consisting only of Qur'anic verses in Arabic with their Dutch translation and arranged around certain themes such as monotheism, unbelief, idolatry and jihad. Since most of these were stored in directories referring to Abu Khaled al-Issa, it is plausible that these were used for sessions with him. It seems that he thoroughly familiarized them with the ideas of Sayyid Qutb and Mawdûdî.

Although not all of their ideas are identical, their foundations are very similar. It is the notion that God has not only created the universe and humanity, but has also revealed rules for mankind to live by. God, in this perspective, is not only creator and the object of veneration but also lawgiver. Now, monotheism (*tawhîd*) implies that besides God no creator can be recognized and that nothing or no one may be worshipped apart from Him. The novel element is, however, that according to these ideas, no human being may legislate, because laying down the law is God's prerogative. States must not enact their own laws but implement the Shariʿa, God's law. Muslim rulers who refuse to do so commit acts of polytheism (*shirk*) and are, therefore, apostates who deserve the death penalty. A legal system based on man-made laws lacks legitimacy and cannot be recognized. Democracy must therefore be rejected, as, seen from this perspective, it implies slavery and oppression. For it is a political system of domination of men over other men, instead of the domination of God over men. Moreover it is founded on the idea that mankind may create its own laws instead of accepting God's law. Institutions and political and legal systems that violate the principles of monotheism, as well as persons of authority who rule by man-made laws and not according to the Shariʿa, are called *tâghût*, idols, because they arrogate privileges and positions that belong to God only. Obeying them is denying God His right to be obeyed. Accepting democracy and legal system based on man-mad laws is dubbed *shirk al-hâkimiyya*, i.e. polytheism by recognizing the sovereignty of humans and human institutions, thereby violating God's prerogatives. These ideas deriving from a strict interpretation of the concept of monotheism (*tawhîd*) are perfectly suitable for delegitimizing the political status quo and justify struggle to topple the government.

4.2 *'Rejecting the Tâghût' (October 2003)*

Abu Khaled's lessons were not lost on Bouyeri and he must have been an eager learner. By October 2003 he felt sufficiently confident to produce a text himself entitled *Democratie en islam* (Democracy and Islam) on the obligation to reject democracy. It is an introduction to the translation of two anonymous English texts that he downloaded from the internet and that argue that democracy is forbidden in Islam and that participating in it by voting or standing for elected bodies is an act of unbelief. In the introduction (written 13 October 2003), addressed to his brethren and sisters, he writes:

> The democratic system is bleeding to death, its putrid face becomes clearer by the day. We live in a world where the supporters of this system set themselves up as the masters of all other inhabitants of the earth. They claim the exclusive right to subject others. The foremost of all democratic countries is the pernicious America, the motherland and model of the democratic system. Although it becomes clearer by the day that

> democracy is only a smoke curtain to exploit other people as slaves, there are still those who cannot free themselves from the intellectual slavery [and think] that this system is indeed the best that has been created for humanity (better that the Shari'a).

In this passage we see that there is an identification of democracy with the West and especially with the United States. This we find in his other writings too. Democracy and 'the West' are often used interchangeably and criticism of Western or American international politics is also addressed to democracy as a political system.

It is evident that Abu Khaled's teachings had borne fruit by then. Bouyeri had been put on track and from the fall 2003 he continued to develop his ideas himself, aided by the internet. During the fall of 2003 and the spring of 2004 he translated documents gathered from the internet, all of them dealing with the rejection of democratic governments, with the view that resorting to tribunals not based on the Shari'a entails apostasy and with the urgency of establishing a political and legal order based on the Shari'a. A new element is a document on 'loyalty and distance' (Arabic: *al-walâ' wa-l-barâ'a*). This is the principle that Muslims must only consort with and give their loyalty to other Muslims and that they must keep their distance from non-Muslims. Since the definition of who is a Muslim used by this groups is rather narrow, this principle imposes sectarian isolation from mainstream Muslims.

In the introductions to his translations, Bouyeri repeatedly speaks of the struggle between the true Islam and its enemies:

> Since the turning point in our history, better known as 9/11, a struggle like the one between David and Goliath has broken out between the followers of Truth and those of Falsehood.... We see nowadays that every day the struggle comes closer to us. [Take for instance] the supervised sermons of imams preaching in the service of malicious tyrants. In doing so they give the truth a totally different meaning and show the followers of Truth in a bad light.

4.3 *'Join the Caravan of Martyrs'* (*March 2003*)

The logical consequence of seeing reality in terms of a struggle between the truth and falsehood was of course a call for participation in that struggle. The first summons to jihad dates from March 2003 and is found in a pamphlet entitled *To catch a wolf.* It is an emotional piece of about 3000 words written in great anger. Its style is slovenly and it contains passages that are not entirely intelligible. But although the wording is confused at times and the text lacks coherence, it is not the ranting and raving of a deranged person. Its overall message is plain.

The overall message of the text is that Islam is under attack by the West and that this attack must be resisted. The state of the Muslim community is described in almost apocalyptic terms:

> The earth is trembling, the sky is weeping and the wind is raging frenetically. So much injustice, so much misery, so much pain, so many tears, so much Muslim blood being shed daily. It is difficult not to be distressed and dejected when swamped by so many terrible images and reports about our brothers and sisters all over the world.

This is in the first place due to Western aggression, aiming at the total destruction of Islam:

> There are dark Satanic forces that have sown their seed of evil everywhere in the world. This seed has been sown in the Islamic world in the times of colonialism and has since then taken root. Since the fall of the Ottoman Empire and the Islamic caliphate the enemies of Islam have been active in gradually carrying out their plans aiming at the total destruction of Islam. The Islamic umma, once so powerful and proud, has become no more than a dead drunk and frustrated nation, begging at the doorsteps of the West for a piece of bread. Its honour has no more value than that of a barking mongrel on which passers-by take it out by spitting their gall at it.

The West is not only blamed for defeating the Muslim world but also for the injustice of the unequal distribution of wealth in the world. Addressing the Western leaders Bouyeri asks rhetorically:

> How did it happen that your bank vaults are full of gold although there are no goldmines in your countries? How did it happen that a rich continent like Africa is poverty-stricken? How did it happen that all those guns, landmines, tanks and other destructive weaponry produced in your democratic countries, have found their way to these poor victims?

The sorry state of the Muslims, however, is not only the doing of the West. Not only the West must be blamed. Part of the decay is the fault of Muslim leaders who have betrayed their community to its enemies:

> The Islamic umma seems to be visited by a cancerous growth that has disseminated all over the body. We are on the edge of an abyss and it seems that it is only a matter of time before we smash ourselves up. We are a frustrated nation betrayed by the so-called leaders of this umma, leaders who have sold themselves as cheap whores to the West and allow the spirits and souls of Muslim youth to be poisoned by the poison of *kufr* (unbelief).

The title of the document refers to an Inuit technique to catch wolves: they plant a sharp knife covered with layers of frozen blood in the snow. When a wolf passes he smells the blood, traces the knife and starts licking it, thereby cutting his tongue without noticing it. He then continues to lick his own warm blood and bleeds to death. This is related to a message concerning the nature of democracy: the democratic leaders ('the democratic vampires') try to reduce their subjects to a state of languor and inertia so as to better be able to exploit them. They do this by offering them goodies like coffee shops (where soft drugs are legally for sale in the Netherlands), discos, bars and gambling halls, where they become enslaved to their own lusts and desires and lose the will to resist. These goodies are likened to the bloody knife planted in the snow: enjoying them draws the strength from a person and is ultimately fatal.

Bouyeri then seems to suggest that there is a relationship between these goodies, intended to undermine the strength of the people, and the final downfall of the United States, although the passage is not fully clear. It can be read as a message of hope, like the Marxist prophecies of the final downfall of capitalism, but also as an argument for the strength of the elite, whose position is not affected by the ruin of society:

> If we take America, the Mother of all Democracies, as an example and compare the social statistics (crime, violence) with those of other countries then we must conclude that this country is sick to the core. It is only a matter of time before the social order becomes one big chaos. The laughing third parties in this big monopoly game are the democratic vampires. They fortify their bodies by injecting innocent blood into their veins because of their unquenchable thirst for it.

The last message is that a small group of responsible Muslims have emerged in the Netherlands, 'because Dutch politics stimulate its citizens (especially the migrants = Muslims) to participate in [discussions on] social questions and to take responsibility'. In these words we hear echoes of Bouyeri's former life, when he was active in social work in the community. This small group have assumed 'social responsibility, not only for the Netherlands but for the whole world and taken upon themselves the task of liberating the world from democratic slavery'. Its aim is to establish the domination of Islam and they call on other Muslims to join the jihad. In the last paragraph he addresses Muslim youths and shouts (witness the capitalization which is Bouyeri's):

> WAKE UP! LOOK AROUND! MUSLIMS ARE BEING SLAUGHTERED AND YOU CANNOT DO ANYTHING BECAUSE YOU ARE BLEEDING TO DEATH. Free yourself! Leave the coffee shop, leave the bar, leave that street corner. Answer the call of LA ILAHA ILLA ALLAH. Join the Caravan of Martyrs. Wake up from your stupor, rise and shake off the dust of humiliation. Rise and answer to the summons for jihad.

4.4 *'... Your Blood and Properties Have Become Halal'* (*Summer 2003*)

During the spring of 2004 members of the Hofstadgroep must have discussed what kind of actions they could carry out to help Islam. There must also have been suggestions for violent action in the Netherlands. However, on this point there existed an ideological problem that had to be resolved. The texts that Bouyeri downloaded from the internet and that inspired him related mainly to the situation in the Islamic world. Even Abu Hamza al-Misri, who was a British citizen and active in London, was hardly concerned with the situation in England, but rather with the Muslim world and could therefore rely on the theories formulated by Qutb and Mawdûdî. Their writings referred to the Muslim world and they argued that Muslim leaders had abandoned true Islam and become apostates. That was their principal justification for a revolutionary struggle against them. This doctrine, however, did not make sense in the Dutch context. Of course, the country was governed by non-Muslims, but not by apostates. And that made an enormous difference.

According to Shari'a principles generally accepted among pious Muslim migrants, the relationship of Muslims and the countries where they live, is governed by the notion of a treaty or contract. According to the classical doctrine of the Shari'a, non-Muslims living in the Dâr al-harb (the Abode of War, i.e. outside the boundaries of the Islamic state) and not in a country with which the Islamic state has concluded a treaty, are not protected by the Shari'a. They may be killed, enslaved or robbed with impunity. However, if they enter Muslim territory with a pledge of security (*amân*) granted by officials or by any adult male Muslim, their lives, property and freedom are protected by law, on the condition that they respect the laws of the land. Comparable rules apply if a Muslim enters the Dâr al-Harb with the express permission of the local non-Muslim authorities. If they grant him protection under the local laws, the

Shari'a obligates him to respect these laws. Contemporary Muslims equate visa and residence permits with such a permission and assert that Muslims legally residing in non-Muslim countries are bound by the local laws.

This doctrine posed problems to Bouyeri's ideas of calling for jihad in the Netherlands. We have no information on whether this was discussed in the group, but it is likely that it was. They were used to judge their behaviour by Islamic standards and discuss whether certain acts or ways of dressing were forbidden or permitted. There can be no doubt that lawfulness of the use of violence must have been debated. Two solutions were found, as we can ascertain from the documents produced during the summer of 2003. One was the use of violence against individuals, not within the framework of warfare and jihad, but by way of punishment for alleged crimes against Islam. The reasoning behind this must have been that in the absence of a really Islamic state and Shari'a courts, true Muslims were entitled or even obliged to punish individuals who committed serious offences. The other solution was to regard the 'treaty' of the Dutch state with Muslim residents as abolished on the ground that the Dutch government had violated it by supporting the U.S. and Israel in their warfare against Islam and by sending troops to Iraq.

There are three translated documents laying the groundwork for violence. They provided justifications and encouragement for violent actions. One text, incidentally the only one directly translated from the Arabic, probably with the help of others, is a fatwa by Ibn Taymiyya (d. 1328), stating that it is mandatory to execute persons insulting the Prophet Mohammed. For Ibn Taymiyya this meant that such persons were to be sentenced to death after a trial and a substantiation of the facts. Bouyeri, however, as we know from the ensuing events, misunderstood this and took it as an obligation for individual Muslims to take the law in their own hands. The other document is a fatwa issued in November 2002 by a certain Hâmid al-'Alî, a radical Muslim scholar from Kuwait, arguing that Yasser Arafat was an apostate because he was in favour of a secularist state in Palestine. The last document is a text listing the blessings of martyrdom and entitled *The battlefield: the safest place on earth*. Its author, Amîr Sulaymân, argues that he participated in jihad not because his faith is so strong, but rather because it is weak: death on the battlefield will save him from consequences of his sins and secures for him a privileged position in paradise.

During that summer Bouyeri produces seven open letters, most of which were published on the Internet. Three of them addressed groups of Muslims collectively: a letter to 'the mendacious "ulama" (religious scholars) and imams', summoning them to mend their ways and to convert to true Islam; one addressing Muslim youth and requesting them to set out on a quest for true Islam; and the third one depicting in lively terms the torture inflicted by

Americans on Iraqi Muslims – reports on the Abu Ghraib prison had been publicized earlier that year – and summoning the entire Muslims *Ummah* (global community of believers) to jihad against its enemies. Of the other four, three contained threats against Dutch individuals and one against the Dutch population collectively.

Of the open letters to individuals the most notorious is the one addressing Ayaan Hirsi Ali, at that time a Dutch MP of Somalian Muslim origin (Peters 2006). Bouyeri had skewered a copy of it to van Gogh's dead body after he had murdered him. Hirsi Ali had become one of the most vociferous critics of Islam in the public debate and had publicly announced that she was no Muslim anymore. The letter is somewhat confused. In the opening paragraphs Bouyeri blames Hirsi Ali not only for apostatizing but also for joining the ranks of the 'soldiers of evil'. On the other hand he alleges that she is an instrument in the hands of a clique of Jewish (and allegedly Jewish) politicians and quotes the Talmud 'proving' that non-Jews are not regarded as human and must be killed. These quotations come from an American anti-Semitic pamphlet downloaded by Bouyeri from a fundamentalist Islamic site, which had copied it from an anti-Semitic American site (Hoffman, Critchley, s.d.). The letter to Hirsi Ali has a curious end. It does not directly threaten her with death but challenges her to commit suicide. The reasoning behind this is the following: if she really does not believe anymore, she can show in that way that she is not afraid of all horrors that according to the Qur'an are awaiting the unbelievers in the hereafter. Since the letter was found on van Gogh's body it was understood as a death threat against her. On 29 August of that year (actually, after the letter had been written) a short documentary called 'Submission' produced by her and van Gogh had been shown on Dutch television. This movie was felt by many Dutch Muslims as an outrage against Islam.

Another letter was directed against Ahmed Aboutaleb, an Amsterdam alderman of Moroccan descent. He was criticized for being a 'secular Muslim (= KAFIR),' which immediately reminds us of the fatwa of Hâmid al-ʿAlî condemning Arafat for his secular political ideas. The letter concludes with the following warning: 'This letter has been drafted in order to warn you and the other minions of the unbelievers for the horrible consequences of their behaviour and to inform you about your status in Islam'. Since with 'status in Islam' Bouyeri meant that Aboutaleb was an apostate, the conclusion that this was a threatening letter is fully justified. The last letter to an individual was addressed to the MP Geert Wilders, who was known for his Islamophobic views. Since he used to dye his hair blond, Bouyeri and his group assumed that he was a homosexual and told him that he should be thrown from the Euro mast, a 185 meter high tower in Rotterdam, by way of Shariʿa punishment.

The last and most threatening letter was the open letter to the Dutch people. In it, Bouyeri expounds that a war is going on between the forces of evil, i.e. the coalition led by the United States, and Islam. In this war millions of Muslims have been brutally slaughtered and raped. The Dutch government, the letter goes on, dominated by Zionist Jews, supports Israel in its struggle against Islam and has joined the coalition forces. Since government policy is based on election, the non-Muslim Dutch have become lawful targets: their lives and properties have become *halâl*.

> The dark clouds of death assemble over your country. Prepare yourselves for that for which one cannot prepare oneself. The death and torture of our brothers and sisters must be redeemed with your own blood. You have become targets everywhere: in trams, the buses, in trains, in shopping malls etc. It won't take more than a fraction of a second and you'll be in the midst of dead persons. The unbearable stench of death will upset your stomach. You will taste the pain of loss and mutilation.... Life will become Hell for you and you will not find rest until our brothers and sisters have it.

Here ends the process of radicalisation of Mohammed Bouyeri. The next thing he did was put his ideas in practice by murdering van Gogh.

5 Conclusions

In the introduction I listed five more or less universal characteristics of extremist ideologies. They are:

- the rejection of the world order dominated by the fores of evil
- the feeling that one's own group is under acute threat
- the idea of a utopia that is within reach
- the notion of a small and devoted pure vanguard that is instrumental in bringing about the promised utopia
- by a violent struggle against the forces of evil.

Let us see to what extent the self-constructed Islam of Bouyeri includes these elements. The rejection of the global order is one of the most conspicuous traits in Bouyeri's text. The forces of evil are democracy (or the West), led by the U.S. who wage a cosmic struggle against the forces of the good, i.e. Islam. Moreover, democracy as a political system is unlawful according to Bouyeri's Islam, being based on the domination of man over man and not of God over man. The Dutch government and the Dutch people are part of the forces of evil. The government sent troops to Iraq and many politicians and journalists have started a media war against Islam. The Islamic camp, globally, is weakened because many of its political and religious leaders have abandoned the true religion and make common cause with the enemy. Although Bouyeri nowhere explicitly refers to the End of Time, the urgency of the struggle against the forces of darkness is repeatedly emphasised, often in terms that are almost apocalyptic. He claims that the struggle has now become different and that Muslims are attacked everywhere:

> The struggle against the Truth has been fought as long as humanity has existed, but in this time and age it has been fiercer and more massive than ever before. The army or the Satanic forces has its monsters everywhere ready to seize people who summon to the uncompromised truth and bury them alive in their brutal dungeons.[2]

However, the realization of the ideal, a state based on the Shari'a, is near:

> It is but a matter of time before the knights of Allah will march to the Binnenhof[3] in The Hague and raise the flag of TAWHID on the central square. They will (Insha' Allah) rename the parliament to Shari'a tribunal and the chairman's gavel will confirm Shari'a judgments. From the Prime Minister's turret[4] will sound the words LA ILAHA ILLA ALLAH and these words will be carried by the wind and be joined by other words of glory to God. The laudations will reach our Master on His Throne and the Islamic Umma will prostrate as if in one body before the Lord of the Worlds.[5]

Bouyeri does not give details about how this utopia can be established. However, it is clear that in his view it will be the working of a small group of true and devoted Muslims who have sought and found true Islam. They must wage jihad against the powers of Satan so that after their defeat the Shari'a state can be established. That true Islam will be victorious is certain for Bouyeri. But that requires violent action. However, those undertaking it cannot lose: if they

2 From Bouyeri's introduction to his translation of *Dit is de weg!* (March 2004).

3 The centre of both houses of parliament and the department of the PM.

4 A conspicuous turret attached to the PM's department, where his office is located. The text calls it 'Kok's turret' after Wim Kok, Prime Minister of the Netherlands from 1994–2002).

5 To catch a wolf.

are killed they will enter Paradise; if they live, they will see the utopia of the Shariʿa state.

References

Benschop, A., (2005) *Kroniek van een aangekondigde politieke moord: Jihad in Nederland*. Utrecht: Forum.

Buijs, F.J., F. Demant, and A. Hamdy, (2006) Islamitisch Radicalisme in Nederland, in *Hedendaags Radicalisme: Verklaringen & Aanpak*, edited by S. Harchaoui. Apeldoorn: Het Spinhuis.

Chorus, J., and A. Olgun, (2005) *In Godsnaam: Het Jaar van Theo van Gogh*. Amsterdam: Contact.

Hoffman, M.A., and A.R. Critchley, (n.d.) *The Truth about the Talmud: A Documented Expose of Jewish Supremacist Hate literature*. http://www.hoffman-info.com/talmudtruth.html.

Lawson, B. Todd, (1995) "Martyrdom" in: *The Oxford Encyclopedia of the Modern Islamic World*. Ed. J.L. Esposito. New York: University of Oxford Press, 54–59.

Peters, R., (2005) *Jihad in Classical and Modern Islam: A Reader*. 2nd rev. and exp. ed. Princeton, N.J.: Markus Wiener Publ.

Peters, R., (2006) *'A Dangerous Book': Dutch Public Intellectuals and the Koran*. San Domenico di Fiesole, Firenze: European University Institute, Robert Schuman Centre for Advanced Studies, EUI Working Papers; RSCAS, 2006/39. http://www.iue.it/RSCAS/WP-Texts/06_39.pdf.

Stern, Jessica, (2003) *Terror in the Name of God: Why Religious Militants Kill*. New York: Harper Collins.

Vermaat, E., (2005) *De Hofstadgroep: Portret van een Radicaal-Islamitisch Netwerk*. Soesterberg: Aspekt.

Wessels, W., (2006) *De Radicaal-Islamitische Ideologie van de Hofstadgroep: De Inhoud en de Bronnen*. Den Haag: Teldersstichting.

CHAPTER 35

(In)compatibility of Religion and Human Rights

The Case of Islam

1 Introduction

Religions, traditionally, make sharp distinction between believers and others. This distinction is not only a theological one, referring for instance to salvation after death, but also affects life in this world, by assigning to non-believers a social and, sometimes, political status different from the believers. In states where one religion is the religion of the state, following a religion often has legal consequences, as such states often have adopted religious law in certain domains as the law of the state. Before 1984, family law was governed in Italy by Roman Catholic canonical law. Israel, being a Jewish state, makes legal distinctions between Jews and non-Jews. Moreover, Israeli family law is the religious law of the spouses – Jewish, Islamic or Christian – and civil marriage is not recognized. Legislation connected with the establishment of a religion often entail violations of the principle of equality before the law or infringement on the freedom of the practice of other religions and expression of ideas critical to the state religion.

In the Muslim world most constitutions mention that Islam is the religion of the state and sometimes, in addition, that the principles of Islamic law (the Sharia) are the foundation of legislation. The legal effects of these clauses vary, but it is clear the Islam in such states occupies a privileged position. Now, with the growing secularism in the West, the political and legal position of Islam in the Muslim world has come under attack in the Western media. It is claimed in the West that Islam is essentially incompatible with human rights. *Prima facie*, this seems to be correct, witness the many documented human rights violations in the Muslim world. Nevertheless, many Muslims writers assert that Islam respects human rights and quote in support Islamic source texts such as the Koran and the Hadith (reports relating the Sunna, i.e. sayings and exemplary behavior of the Prophet Mohammed), without, however, expounding how these principles are to be transformed to enforceable law. Both claims are rather generalizing and informed by political and cultural assumptions. I think it is possible to formulate a more precise and better substantiated position.

Let's first look at what I understand by human rights. By this I mean the body of international and domestic law deriving from or inspired by the Universal Declaration of Human Rights (UDHR). Human rights must be more than just

 | DOI:10.1163/9789004420625_036

ideological declarations. Being law entails that these rights are enforceable, even if this enforcement is weak, such as is the case in the United Nations human rights covenants. They are vested by birth equally in every human being, are inalienable and universal. This universality precludes culturalist notions that assert that various civilizations have their own separate and distinct human rights systems. But on the other hand, the doctrine of "marginal appreciation" allows that there are different cultural interpretations of such rights, as long as they do not undermine the essence of these rights.

The definition of Islam is more complicated. Is Islam identical with the contents of the source texts? And if so, with what specific texts and what understandings and interpretations? Or may Islam be held identical with state legislation based on or inspired by the Sharia? Or by the practices of states in the Muslim world? In this paper I will not examine Islam theologically but confine myself to the legal aspects of Islam, i.e. the Sharia. Only here can we find legal rules that may be tested against human rights principles. I will first have a look at the classical doctrine of the Sharia and then at Sharia inspired present-day legislation of Muslim states and their policies regarding the international human rights covenants. Next I will address some prominent Muslim views on the relationship between Islam and human rights. Finally I will explore possibilities to enhance greater human rights compliance in the Islamic world.

2 Islam and Human Rights: the Law

Muslims regard the Sharia as an expression of God's will. This notion is very different from the idea of the origins of modern Western law, which is regarded as a purely human phenomenon, created by the state, that is the legislature or the judiciary. The classical texts of Islamic jurisprudence define the Sharia as: "The rules given by God to His servants as set forth by one of the prophets, may God bless them and grant them salvation." (Tahanawi 1984, i, 759) A swift glance at the tables of contents of the standard legal text books shows that they begin with purely religious topics like ritual prayer and fasting, before embarking on the discussion of the issues that are legal in the Western sense of the word, such as the contract of sale, legal capacity, succession, and criminal law. That the Sharia is religious law, consists in two features: the fact that the basis of its validity is God's will, and the fact that the Sharia also contains rules of a purely religious character.

In order to inform mankind of His commands, God, according to Islam, has sent down revelations to successive prophets, the last of whom was Muhammad, to whom the Koran was revealed. The contents of the Koran were supplemented by the Prophet's exemplary sayings and behavior, the Sunna, transmitted in the form of thousands of reports (*hadith*) by generations of Muslims and, ultimately, compiled in the *hadith* collections. These are the divine sources of the Sharia and, therefore, the foundation of its authority.

A large part of the Sharia is law as understood in the West. The rules of this domain of the Sharia deal with the legal effects of certain acts or events and discuss the creation and extinction of rights and obligations between individuals and between the individual and the community. Here we find for instance the rules of sale, of marriage, of tort, of procedure, of judicial punishment, rules that can be enforced by the qadi if the relevant facts can be established in court. However, the Sharia is also envisioned as a set of norms constituting the code of behavior for being a good Muslim, a guide to attain eternal bliss in Paradise. This aspect of the Sharia emphasizes its religious character and focuses on the Hereafter, i.e. on whether, after one's death, one can expect to be rewarded or punished for certain acts. Here we find the religious prescriptions such as those on rituals, on food, correct dress and gender relations.

A second feature of the Sharia is that it is a jurists' law and that the jurists and not the state or a religious organization had the exclusive authority to formulate the rules of the Sharia. They did so in scholarly debates, in which conflicting views were opposed and debated. Because of differences in the use of hermeneutic tools, the Sharia as laid down by the jurists is not uniform. From the beginning there were differences of opinion that resulted in the emergence of different schools of jurisprudence (*madhhab*, pl. *madhahib*), that ascribed their doctrines to and derived their names from famous jurists from the eighth and ninth centuries. Plurality seems to be a characteristic feature of Islamic jurisprudence. In the following I will present rules that are agreed upon by all legal schools, although there may be differences of opinion on some points.

Checking whether or not the Sharia complies with human rights standards is an anachronistic operation. Islamic jurisprudence was created and developed in pre-modern times, before the existence of a civil or human rights doctrine. Like other pre-modern legal systems, there are many rules conflicting modern human rights. If I examine whether and where the Sharia contradicts principles of human rights, this is not meant to be judgmental but rather regarded as a method that may help us find conflicts with human rights in modern Sharia inspired legislation.

The first question we have to answer is of whether the Sharia recognizes the notion of human rights, i.e. inalienable, enforceable rights endowed to all human beings.[1] This certainly seems to be the case. In the first place the Sharia

1 The view that the Sharia does not have the notion of human rights has been refuted by Baderin in his well-argued essay (Baderin 2001).

confers legal personality to all persons, including non-Muslims and slaves, although the contents of this personality may differ by category. Moreover, there exist some sort of proto-human rights, i.e. inalienable rights regarding human dignity. The Sharia stipulates that in legal relationships in which one of the parties has power over the other, the weaker person has certain rights that the other may not infringe. Thus, a husband may not subject his wife to acts that may impair her health, may not prevent her from performing religious duties, may not thwart her in owning and administering her property, and finally may not forbid her to have a minimum of lawful social relations, such as visiting her relatives and allowing her to have a companion at home in case there are no children or servants. Slaves have similar rights, with the exception of owning and administering property (because slave cannot legally own property) and the right to social intercourse. Thus the Sharia acknowledges to all persons the right to life and physical integrity and the right to practice one's religion. (Peters 1999, 10–13)

However, the Sharia being a pre-modern system of law, there are conflicts with human rights principles, the first of which is the absence of equality before the law. Article 1 of the Universal Declaration of Human Rights (UDHR) pronounces that "[a]ll human beings are born free and equal in dignity and rights," and article 7 states "[a]ll are equal before the law and are entitled without any discrimination to equal protection of the law." Under the Sharia, the legal status of human beings (i.e. the rights and obligations that they are assigned by law) varies according to sex and religion and, in addition, human beings may be commodities (slaves). The status of women is inferior to that of men. For instance, they are not entitled to hold certain offices (like being a judge), may not testify in court in many types of cases and inherit only one half of what a male person in the same position would take. In family law and the law of succession the differences between the rights and duties of men and women derive from the complementary roles of husband and wife. Women may not conclude a marriage themselves according to most legal schools but depend on their matrimonial guardians to represent them, men may be married up to four wives at the same time, whereas women can have only one husband. Moreover, men may terminate the marriage at will and without a judicial procedure whereas women need to go to court to get a divorce and must prove grounds. Finally, the law of succession lays down that women in general take half the share of men in the same relationship to the deceased. This is justified by the financial advantages women have in marriage: their husbands are obliged to pay them a bridal gift (*mahr*) and to provide maintenance. There is also a difference in the legal status of Muslim and non-Muslims. Non-Muslims lawfully residing on Islamic territory are regarded as protected minorities (*dhimmi*'s). They are generally protected by law, but have fewer rights and more obligations than

Muslims: they must pay special taxes, they may not hold public offices, cannot testify in court against Muslims, cannot inherit from Muslims, their men may not marry Muslim women and they must respect Islamic supremacy in their behavior. Non-Muslims living outside the Islamic territory, regarded as enemy aliens, have hardly any legal status: their lives and properties are not legally protected. Finally, there is conflict between the Sharia and articles 1 and 4 of the UDHR, which prohibit slavery. The Sharia recognizes slavery and regulates the status of slaves, that is human beings that are both a commodity that can be owned and a legal subject with a limited legal status.

The second area of conflict is freedom of religion. It is true that the Sharia allows the followers of recognized faiths (such as Christianity and Judaism) to practice their religions and protects their lives, properties and freedom (i.e. that they may not be enslaved). However, article 18 UDHR lays down that the freedom of religion also includes the freedom to change one's religion. Although under the Sharia non-Muslims may freely be converted to Islam, the reverse is not the case. Muslims who abandon their religion will lose their legal personality (which means that they cannot own property anymore and that their marriages are annulled) and will be sentenced to death.

The last issue is in the field of penal law. Art. 5 UDHR bans cruel, degrading and inhuman penalties. However, certain penalties under the Sharia, such as amputation of limbs, stoning to death and flogging must be qualified as such. (Peters 2005, 174–85)

So far it has been a rather anachronistic operation. But the analysis becomes relevant when we use it to find out human rights conflicts in present-day legal systems in the Muslim world. Most Muslim countries have now created modern legal systems by introducing Western inspired laws and some Islamic legal institutions have disappeared. This is the case with slavery, which has been outlawed by statute law in all countries of the Muslim world, and the inferior legal status of non-Muslims, which has been abolished by the constitution in most Muslim countries. However, the Sharia – usually codified now – still governs certain legal fields. In the following I will briefly outline in what fields the Sharia is applied nowadays and identify the conflicts with human rights standards.[2] Since I cannot present in details these conflicts in every Muslim country, I will illustrate these conflicts by reference to Egypt, whose legal system is fairly representative for most of those in the Muslim world.

Let us first look at family law and the law of succession. Here we find that in almost all Muslim countries, the field is governed by religious law. For Muslims

2 For a detailed and well documented survey of rights violations on the ground of Islamic norms, see Aldeeb Abu-Sahlieh 1994.

this is the Sharia, usually through legislation informed by the Sharia. Although many of these Sharia codes have improved the legal position of women, they did not achieve gender equality. Most constitutions in the Muslim world are consistent with this and lay down that family law is not subordinated to the principle that women and men are equal before the law.[3]

Freedom of religion is guaranteed in most constitutions in the Muslim world and as a rule these prohibit the discrimination on the basis of religion and stipulate that all citizens are entitled to practice their religion and that public offices are open to all regardless of their faiths.[4] Nevertheless there are sometimes some discriminatory legal practices. In Egypt (as well as some other Muslim countries), for instance, Christians, who constitute between 8 and 10% of the population, may not be the president of the republic. Although this is not explicitly stipulated in the constitution, this is inferred from the article stating that Islam is the religion of the state (article 2 of the Egyptian constitution of 1971). Moreover, Christians are confronted with limitations in obtaining permissions to build or restore churches, whereas such limitations do not exist with regard to the construction of mosques. Similar discrimination exists in many Muslim countries. However, the main human rights issue is the change of religion for Muslims, which, as we have seen, is unlawful under the Sharia and regarded as a capital crime. This still is the case in few countries where Sharia criminal law is applied. However, even there the authorities are extremely reluctant to have such sentences to be pronounced and executed. In most Muslim countries, apostasy of Muslims does not entail capital punishment, but there are other sanctions in family law by virtue of the Sharia codes. In general the effects of apostasy are not mentioned in the law, but will be applied by judges on the ground of articles that stipulate that the Sharia must be applied in cases the code is silent. As a result apostasy annuls a Muslim's marriage. Moreover, authorities do not recognize the change of religion, which

3 See e.g. the Egyptian constitution of 1971: "The State shall guarantee the proper coordination between the duties of woman towards the family and her work in the society, considering her equal status with man in the fields of political, social, cultural and economic life without violation of the rules of Islamic jurisprudence." (Article 11).
"All citizens are equal before the law. They have equal rights and duties without discrimination between them due to race, ethnic origin, language, religion or creed." (Article 40) Note that discrimination of gender is not mentioned.

4 See e.g. the Egyptian constitution of 1971: "The State shall guarantee the freedom of belief and the freedom of practice of religious rites." (Article 46) "All citizens are equal before the law. They have equal rights and duties without discrimination between them due to race, ethnic origin, language, religion or creed." (Article 40).

may involve administrative problems, such as obtaining correct identity cards and registration at the Registry Offices.[5]

As I mentioned before, a few countries do enforce Islamic criminal law. (Peters, 2005: 142–86) In these countries the law codes penalize certain offences with corporal punishments and modes of the death penalty (stoning to death), that must be qualified as violations of human rights for being cruel, degrading and inhuman.

The impact of the Sharia also extends to international law. Most Muslim states have become parties to the international human rights covenants, which, if ratified, are domestically binding. However, many of these states have made the reservation that the treaty would not be binding regarding provisions violating the Sharia.[6] In general the reservations are directed at the concept of the family, criminal punishments, freedom of religion and expression and certain rights of children. (Baderin 2001b: 271) However, most of these are related to gender equality.

TABLE 35.1 Adherence by Muslim states (57)[a] to human rights conventions[b]

	Signed and ratified	Reservations	Based on Sharia
ICCPR	40	20	4
CEDAW	41	18	12
CRC	55	24	17
CAT	38	8	1
CERD	48	13	1

a This is the number of the state members of the Organization of the Islamic Conferences.
b The abbreviations in this table refer to the following covenants: ICCPR: the International Covenant on Civil and Political Rights (1966); CEDAW: the Convention on the Elimination of All Forms of Discrimination Against Women (1979); CRC: the Convention on the Rights of the Child (1989); CAT: the Convention Against Torture and Other Cruel, Inhuman, or Degrading Treatment or Punishment (1984); CERD: the International Convention on the Elimination of Racial Discrimination (1966).

5 On the legal position of the apostate in Egypt, see Aldeeb 1979. 205–212; Berger 2005: 89–102; Pink 2003a; Pink 2003b.
6 For a detailed and well documented survey for the position of Muslim states regarding the U.N. human rights conventions, see Baderin (2001b) For a survey of adherence and reservations of the UN human rights conventions, see http://www.unhchumanrights.ch/tbs/doc.nsf/newhvstatbytreaty?OpenView&Start=1&Count=250&Expand=7.2#7.2.

Some of the signatories have submitted reservations that almost entirely erode the covenant. Egypt, for example, has made a reservation to the CEDAW concerning the equality of men and women in all matters relating to marriage and family relations during the marriage and upon its dissolution (art. 16) as well as to articles 1,2,4,6.2,9,16 and 29 regarding gender equality. Moreover, she has made a reservation to article 2 which stipulates that the signatories will abolish laws, customs, regulations and practices that are discriminatory against women, establish legal protection for equal right of men and women and, finally, that the principle of gender equality be embodied in the constitution or otherwise guaranteed by law. Egypt declares that it "is willing to comply with the content of this article, provided that such compliance does not run counter to the Islamic Sharia."

3 Islam and Human Rights: Alternative Views

Both in the West and in the Muslim world there are authors that hold that Islam is essentially incompatible to the principles of international human rights. They are of the opinion that the civilization of Islam and especially the Sharia are different from or even opposed to Western civilization. As cultures or civilizations are for them the decisive factor for their view, I will refer to them as culturalists. Western culturalists emphasize that the secular character of human rights derives from Western civilization and cannot be reconciled with the tenets of Islam. A prominent example of this view is the one presented by Samuel Huntington in his book *The Clash of Civilizations and the Remaking of World Order* (1996). Others in the West argue that the notion of human rights originated in the West and is therefore exclusively and inextricably bound to the Western civilization.[7] They point out that the idea is indebted either to the Protestant Reformation, whose followers espoused the idea of freedom of religion in its struggle against Roman Catholicism, or to Enlightenment whose political ideas of civil or fundamental rights were adopted in the American Declaration of Independence (1776) and the French Déclaration des droits de l'homme et du citoyen (1789). With regard to Islam, they claim that Muslim religion and culture resist the adoption of human rights and if Muslim states have become signatories to the U.N. human rights covenants, this is no more than window dressing or a tactical ploy in international relations, witness the reservations based on the Sharia. The Western monopoly of human rights, they assert, is a consequence of their Western origins. They seem to ignore that the

7 For a discussion of this view, see Bielefeldt (2001).

adoption of human rights was not a natural unfolding of "Western culture" but rather a struggle between classes, groups and institutions. The Roman Catholic Church was one of the powerful opponents to the idea of human right and did not accept before 1966 crucial human rights such as the freedom of religion and expression.

Some Muslims also espouse culturalist positions. They concur with the Western culturalists in the fact that the notion of human rights is essentially a Western invention and alien to Islam. However, they have a different perspective. Human rights policies of Western powers is seen as a threat to Islam, as a tool of the West used to weaken the Islamic civilization by depriving it from essential Islamic values. Islam, they claim, fully protects human rights. As a countermove, some Muslim authors and organizations have presented versions of Islamic human rights declarations. These have been made compatible to Islam by Islamizing the wording of the text and adapting it to the requirements of the Sharia.[8] Islamic human rights, these Muslims argue, are superior to the Western ones, since they are based on God's will, whereas the Western human rights are no more than work of man. Moreover, they are much, older as Islamic human rights have already been given by the Koran to mankind already 1400 years ago.

In the following I will present the idea of Islamic human rights, using as sources the influential fundamentalist thinker Mawdudi on the subject[9] and the Cairo Declaration of Islamic Human Rights (1981).[10] It is important to stress that the Cairo Declaration (like the other Islamic human rights declarations) is not binding.[11] It was adopted by the Organization of the Islamic Conference

8 For a critical assessment of Islamic human rights schemes, see Mayer (1995): ch. 9.

9 Abu al-Aʿla al-Mawdudi (1903–1979) was an Indian/Pakistani religious thinker. His works, written in Urdu, have been translated into many languages, among them Arabic, Turkish and English. His ideas have inspired many Muslim fundamentalists. Unfortunately, I could not consult Abu al-Aʿla Mawdudi, *Islam and human rights* (1976) and had to rely on a 29 pages English summary on the internet, http://www.witness-pioneer.org/vil/Books/M_humanrights/index.htm (accessed 7–11–2011). See ch.1. His ideas are not unique. Similar thoughts have been published for instance by Muhammad al-Ghazali (d. 1996). See Johnston (2007): 165–68. For detailed list of Muslim writings on Islamic human rights, see Brems (2004):19, note 3.

10 So far three of such declarations have been published: The Universal Islamic Declaration of Human Rights (1981), issued by the Islamic Council for Europe, the draft Islamic Constitution (al-Azhar University, 1979), Cairo Declaration on Human Rights in Islam (1990, adopted by the OIC). For a discussion of the contents, see Mayer (1995): *passim*; for an analysis of their background, see Brems (2004).

11 Text at http://www1.umn.edu/humanrts/instree/cairodeclaration.html (accessed 7-11-2011).

(OIC, in which 57 states participate) as "a general guidance for Member States in the field of human rights." The closing articles (arts. 24 and 25) show that the Declaration is subordinated to the Sharia: the text lays down that the rights and freedoms mentioned in it are subject to the Sharia and that the Sharia is the only reference for interpreting the text. Let's have a closer look at the areas of conflict with universal human rights. The first issue is equality before the law. As we have seen before, the Sharia does not stipulate such equality among all humanity and as, can be expected, neither Mawdudi nor the Cairo Declaration absolutely subscribes to this principle. Mawdudi states: "Islam not only recognizes absolute equality between men irrespective of any distinction of color, race or nationality, but makes it an important and significant principle, a reality." (Mawdudi, ch. 7) Here, gender and religion are not mentioned, implying that absolute equality does not exist between men and women and Muslims and followers of other religions. The same is true when the Declaration enounces the freedom to marry without "restrictions stemming from race, color or nationality," omitting religion. The Cairo declaration also fails to guarantee full legal equality of the sexes before the law, by restricting equality only to "equality in dignity and basic obligations and responsibilities."[12] This does not require absolute equality in the law, as shown by art. 6 laying down that men and women are equal in dignity but have different rights and obligations.[13] As to freedom of religion, both Mawdudi and the Cairo Declaration pronounce that non-Muslims are entitle to practice their religion and that nobody must use pressure to a person in order to try to change his religion. (Mawdudi, ch.8 and 9; Cairo Declaration, art. 10) The right for Muslims to change their religion is not mentioned and we must infer, in view of the prevailing opinion in Islamic jurisprudence, that Mawdudi nor the Declaration includes it in the freedom of religion. Finally, the use of cruel, degrading or inhuman punishment. Mawdudi nor the Declaration state that such punishment is unlawful. Mawdudi's text is silent and section 19.d of the Declaration implicitly admits as lawful all types of penalties mentioned in the Sharia, where it formulates the principle of legality with the words that "[t]here shall be no crime or punishment except as provided for in the Shariah." The following article (20) forbids to subject persons

12 Art. 1: All men are equal in terms of basic human dignity and basic obligations and responsibilities, without any discrimination on the basis of race, color, language, belief, sex, religion, political affiliation, social status or other considerations.

13 Art. 6.a: "Woman is equal to man in human dignity, and has her own rights to enjoy as well as duties to perform …" 6.b: The husband is responsible for the maintenance and welfare of the family.

"to physical or psychological torture or to any form of maltreatment, cruelty or indignity" and does not seem to apply to judicial punishment.

It is obvious that the ideas of the Islamic culturalists (represented by Mawdudi) and of the Islamic human rights declaration do have an "overlapping consensus" with the international human rights. However, the conflicts are serious, to the extent that Islamic human rights do not fully protect freedom of expression and of the practice of religion, and do not prohibit discrimination of adherents of different beliefs. In fact they are in conflict on the same issues as the classical Sharia was. It may be questioned whether these declarations would enhance greater human rights compliance. It is difficult to give an unequivocal answer. On the one hand, such declarations may help accept and spread the notion of human rights, possibly as a stage towards the acceptance of universal human rights, especially since there are also certainly overlapping rights and freedoms. However, making the step towards universal human rights may be hampered by the Islamic declarations, since conservatives could argue that the Muslim world already has achieved human rights. (Mayer (1995): 164–65)

Some Muslims hold that potentially the Sharia and universal rights are not incompatible. Since the 1970s human rights have become an important issue in the political discourse of most Muslim countries. As a result, Muslim thinkers have also discussed it from an Islamic point of view, trying to show that Islam respected international human rights principles. Such authors acknowledge the gap between traditional Sharia and its present-day enforcement on the one hand and universal human rights on the other, but argue that the Sharia may be subject to reinterpretation in order better to serve the interest of society and that compliance with human rights principles is necessary for a just society.

There are already a fair number of Muslim authors that have followed the same path. (See e.g. Bielefeldt (1995) and Johnston (2007)) Here I will focus on two Muslim authors who, I think, represent two schools of thought. One group seek answers directly from the source text without recourse to the established doctrines of the Sharia. As I do not want to go deeply into the juridical and theological details and controversies, I have selected only one, the Sudanese Abdullahi an-Naʿim, professor of law at Emory University in Atlanta, USA. An-Naʿim's approach represents the more radical current. He concentrates on adapting the Sharia to human rights standards suggesting "that it is Shariah which should be revised, from an Islamic point of view, to provide for these universal human rights." (An-Naʿim 1990: 171–72) In order to do so, he uses an original interpretative approach of the Koran, inspired by his religious mentor, Mahmud Muhammad Taha, who was sentenced to death and executed in Sudan in 1985 for apostasy. (An-Naʿim 1986) In this view, only the Koranic passages revealed[14] in Mecca contain the real message of Islam, whereas those revealed in Medina were transitional and often cancelled by Meccan texts (the real message) or later Medinan revelations (abrogating previous transitional norms). (See Taha 1987) This is at variance with the orthodox doctrine that awards all parts of the Koran the same authority, but accepts that later verses exceptionally may cancel previous ones. The hermeneutics of Taha and an-Naʿim gives more opportunities for radical reinterpretation.

The other scholar I want to discuss is the Nigerian Mashood Baderin (see Baderin 2003), professor of Islamic law at the London School of Oriental and African Studies. He represents those that do not ignore the classical body of the Sharia like an-Naʿim, but take Islamic jurisprudence as their basis and try to reform it. For both the aim is to show that the Sharia is not fundamentally opposed to the principles of universal human rights. However, for Baderin it is not a one-way process: he understands human rights not only according to exclusively Western views, but also by taking into account local cultures, having recourse to the doctrine of marginal appreciation, formulated by the European Court of Human Rights and laying down that states have discretion in enacting and following international human rights law, as long as these do not undermine the freedoms or rights. There must be a "overlapping of consensus" on the essential principles. According to Baderin, cultural adaptation is the only way to ensure a real mutual understanding and acceptance of human rights. Harmonizing human rights with the Sharia requires not only a new reading of the Sharia but also a certain adaptation to local cultures. (Baderin 2003: 28–29, 231–35)[15]

In the following I will discuss some of the opinions of an-Naʿim and Baderin on the issues of conflicts between human rights standards and traditional Sharia. The first point is the equality of the adherents of different religions before the law. An-Naʿim argues that the many Medinan Koranic verses like K.4:144 ("O ye who believe! Take not for friends unbelievers rather than believers.") must be regarded as transitional and should be abolished in favor of the Meccan verses preaching solidarity of all humanity. For the latter message is the eternal one. Reading the Koran in this way, an-Naʿim is able to adapt the

14 During the last 21 years of his life, Mohammed (ca. 570–632 CE), the Prophet of Islam, received revelations which eventually were collected in the Koran, the holy scripture of Islam. The texts revealed in Mecca, before Mohammed's Emigration to Medina (*Hijra*), were mainly theological and ethical, whereas those revealed in Medina, when he became the political leader of the community of Muslims, were often related to practical matters, such as law and warfare.

15 Brems (Brems 2004) fully agrees with Baderin, but approaches the issue chiefly from international law, whereas Baderin's focus is the Sharia.

Sharia to the principle of equality. Non-Muslims living in the Muslim states must be regarded as citizens and not as members of protected religious minorities (*dhimmis*). (Al-Naʿim 1990: 84–86, 144; an-Naʿim 2008: 128–36) Baderin also asserts that *dhimmis* under classical Sharia were citizens of the Islamic state. In the cases that Muslims violated the human rights of non-Muslims in history, these violations were committed against polytheists (i.e. not against the People of the Book, that is Christians and Jews) and in situations of warfare. (Baderin 2003: 167)

Al-Naʿim is emphatic that Islam acknowledges (or rather, should acknowledge) gender equality. The traditional view that women are subordinated to men, is based on the following Koranic passage: "Men are the protectors and maintainers of women, because God has given the one more (strength) than the other, and because they support them from their means. Therefore the righteous women are devoutly obedient (…)." (K.4:34) Contrary to the prevailing traditional opinion, an-Naʿim (as well some other contemporary Muslims) explains this text verse not as a proof of fundamental superiority of men, but rather as an expression of specific historical gender roles. He argues that the Koran justifies the subordination of women to men because in the time of the Prophet Mohammed they could not live independently and needed male protectors and maintainers. Since nowadays women can be independent from men, the control of men over women is not warranted anymore. (Al-Naʿim, 1990: 99–100) Similar ideas on gender equality have been expressed by several Muslim thinkers, but often with a different textual argumentation. (See e.g. Barlas 2002; Wadud 1999; Hassan 1996; Baderin 2003: 134–136)

One of the most well-known infringements of gender equality in the Sharia, is the lawfulness of polygyny. Men may be married up till four women at the same time, whereas women can have only one husband at the time. Both al-Naʿim and Baderin discuss the topic. Al-Naʿim understands the verse permitting polygyny (K. 4:3) within its historical context. He regards the permission of polygyny as a transitional rule. In the time of the Prophet Mohammed women were dependent on men for their security and maintenance. Therefore it was important that all women could marry, even if there was a shortage of men due for instance to warfare. Nowadays, women do not anymore need a husband for security and livelihood, which means that the grounds for the permission of polygyny have ceased and monogamy becomes the rule. (An-Naʿim 1990: 62–63) Baderin, to the contrary, is not in favor of prohibiting polygyny since it may be beneficial, for instance if a wife has turned out to be barren and the husband marries another woman to engender progeny. However, this must be with the consent of the first wife. Moreover, Baderin proposes that women when they marry, are informed that they are entitled to introduce a clause in the marriage contract to the effect that they may dissolve the marital bond if the husband takes a second wife. (Baderin 2003: 138–144) Although he does not say in this context it seems that here he wants to adapt gender equality to Islamic cultural norms and replace its for equivalence taking into account the complementary roles of man and woman.

Under the Sharia a Muslim woman may not be married to a non-Muslim man, whereas a Muslim man can lawfully marry a non-Muslim woman. This is justified by the idea of male superiority: a Muslim ought not to be controlled by a non-Muslim. The reverse is not problematic and, therefore, there are no objections for a Muslim man to marry a non-Muslim woman. However, if nowadays the Sharia accepts gender equality, the prohibition has lost its ground. (An-Naʿim 1990: 179–181; an-Naʿim 2008: 109–110, 128–137) This view, however, is highly controversial and it not shared by many Muslim authors. Baderin – as well as most Muslims – seem to be viscerally opposed to such a marriage and are not willing to accept such a union. Baderin's solution is to equalize the rights of men and women by reducing the rights of men. He does so on the authority of the well-known Egyptian scholar al-Qaradawi, who held that such a prohibition would be permitted by necessity in the situation that Muslim women could not find Muslim men because the latter preferred to marry non-Muslim women. (Baderin 2003: 144–146)

As regards freedom of religion, contemporary Muslim authors always quote the Koranic words: "There is no coercion in religion," (K. 2:256) as its foundation. Although most classical Koran scholars understand these words as a prohibition to force the People of the Book (i.e. the Christians and the Jews) to convert to Islam, present-day authors expand its meaning and regard this text as the basis of freedom of religion. However, only a few of these authors extend the reading of the text to allowing Muslims to abandon their religion, who, as we have seen, are still subjected to serious civil legal consequences and, may in some countries, be sentenced to death. Muslim scholars have discussed the issue of apostasy since the late nineteenth century. There are some sayings of the Prophet Mohammed that seem to impose capital punishments for apostasy. However, some scholars have argued that the apostates that, in the lifetime of the Prophet Muhammad, apparently were put to death for apostasy, were in fact punished for treason, for having left the community of Muslims and joined the enemy. So these contemporary scholars infer that capital punishment meant in those *Hadiths* was not a violation of the freedom of religion, but a criminal provision for preserve the security of the state. (Peters & de Vries 1976) Some contemporary authors also argue that apostasy in itself is not punishable, except if its manifestation threatens public safety, morals and the freedoms of others. They refer to article 18.3 ICCPR, allowing limitations to the freedom of religion necessary for the protection of public safety, order, health or morals, or the fundamental rights of morals and the freedom of others. (Baderin 2003: 123–125) An-Naʿim, however, presents a more radical doctrine of apostasy. He argues that neither capital punishment, nor the family law consequences are warranted in the religious sources. The textual basis for capital punishment are not the Koran, but, as said before, the *Hadith*. These reports, however, are either ambiguous or not solidly transmitted. Moreover, the punishment and the other legal effects of apostasy violate universal human rights standards and that means, in al-Naʿim's views, the Sharia must be modified according to this radical understanding of the Koran. (An-Naʿim 1986: 215–216; An-Naʿim 2008: 117–125)

An-Naʿim's position on cruel, degrading and in human punishment is somewhat complicated. Here he cannot abrogate the Medinan Koranic verses imposing severe corporal and mutilating penalties for certain crimes (*hudud* crimes), because the Meccan revelation does not include any principle to the contrary. In order to adapt the Sharia to human rights standards, he uses two general principles. The first is that the enforcement of the *hudud* punishment is religious and that therefore non-Muslims may not be subjected to it. However, treating non-Muslims in the enforcement of criminal law differently from Muslims, would create discrimination and violate the principle of equality before the law between adherents of different faiths. The tentative solution he comes up to is that such punishments may only be imposed voluntarily on those Muslims who felt religiously bound to be subjected to them.[16] In the end, however, his conclusion is that at this moment the enforcement of *hudud* penalties involves too much uncertainty and potential abuse and, in the current situation of the Sharia, ought therefore to be suspended to allow further discussion of the issue (Al-Naʿim 1990: 107–120). This in fact is similar to the moratorium to the enforcement of stoning for illegal sexual intercourse, proposed by the Swiss Muslim thinker Tariq Ramadan, who in fact was heavily criticized in the West because he did not outright distance himself from this penalty.[17] Other Muslim thinkers also aim at eliminating or restricting the application of *hudud* penalties, but use less radical arguments. One is that the severe punishments may not be administered by a state until society is really Islamic and social justice prevails. Since this is not (yet) the case, such penalties are not justified. Another argument is that if the strict rules of Sharia

16 There is a view in Islam that culprits, having been punished by *hudud* penalties, are granted dispensation for the punishment for these crimes in the Hereafter. (Peters 2005: 54).

17 For the text see http://www.tariqramadan.com/Appel-international-a-un-moratoire,258.html?lang=fr (accessed on 6 January 2012).

criminal procedure and evidence are enforced, it will be impossible in practice to sentencing culprits to the harsh punishments. (Baderin 2003: 84–85)[18]

How important are these and similar views? They are certainly not accepted by a majority of religious scholars. Yet, I think that they are crucial, because they demonstrate that the Sharia and human rights can be compatible and that the Sharia is sufficiently flexible to reform. The views I have just presented disprove the idea that human rights are an exclusively Western enterprise and help the inculturation of human rights in the Muslim world, that is that human rights are also part of Islamic cultures.

4 Perspectives of Greater Human Rights Compliance

Does the world of Islam need human rights? I pose this question, because human rights, as well as democracy or woman emancipation, cannot be imposed from the outside, but need to be accepted and struggled for by the peoples concerned or, at least, large segments of them. There are voices in the Muslim world saying that Islam is incompatible with human rights, that the Muslim world must resist international human rights and adhere to an Islamic version of them. However, as I argued before, the Islamic human rights schemes do not remedy the conflicts of Sharia legislation with international human rights. Compliance with international human rights needs more and there is evidence for the acceptance of universal human rights. Most Muslim states have constitutions that guarantee most human rights and freedoms, although in some countries, as we have seen, they have been restricted by clauses inspired by the Sharia. Moreover, it is encouraging that most Muslim states have acceded to the U.N. human rights covenants. Although certain Muslim states have been criticized because their adherence was merely a tactical move to improve relations with Western states, and although some of the Muslim states have not ratified these covenants or have made reservations, there is support for the notion of universal human rights. But what is most important is what is happening on the ground: there are many NGOs in the Muslim world fighting human rights violations and referring to international human rights instruments. And finally, the opinion polls in the Muslim world show that there is a vast majority of the population are in favor of democracy and human rights, although opposed to the politics of the Western powers. (Baderin 2003: 84–85)

18 See e.g. the multiple procedural grounds of the acquittal on appeal of the Nigerian woman Safiyatu Hussaini, who was first sentenced to be stoned to death by a trial court. (Peters 2006).

If there is substantial support for human rights, we must address question of how in the Muslim world the violations of the human rights norms found in the Sharia legislation can be remedied.

Let us first look at the obstacles. One complication derives from mistrust of Western human rights policies which can be criticized on two grounds: they are motivated by considerations of power politics rather than by a serious concern for human rights and, secondly, many Western countries themselves do not comply with human rights norms. Countries like the United States have subordinated their human rights policy to their foreign policy and they use sanctions allegedly to enforce respect of human rights as mere instruments to ensure their political and economic interests. Many Western states who profess that human rights are of paramount importance in fact have double standards: they only advocate punitive sanctions for human rights violations against states with which do not have good relations, whereas they will turn a blind eye to similar violations committed by friendly powers. This is not conducive to the acceptance of human rights principles by those states that are subjected to such sanctions. Many Muslims, if confronted with Western criticism of Sharia related violations, will be quick to point this out and stress the infringement on human rights principles by Western states. The United States, they assert, have lost its credibility on this score by torturing prisoners either directly or vicariously through rendition, and keeping hundreds of persons imprisoned in Guantanamo Bay while denying them their basic rights. And France, as many Muslims assert, violates the freedom of religion by banning headscarves in state schools. These objections, however justified they may be, do not depreciate the benefits of human rights compliant.

Another obstacle is culture. Many Muslim countries have cultures that have patriarchal traits. Cultures emphasize that women are inferior to men and should be subordinated to them. The prevailing interpretations of the Sharia legitimize these cultural norms and values. Patriarchal cultures are a main obstacle to the acceptance of interpretations of the Sharia based on gender equality. Culture changes and can be changed, but usually slowly. The introduction of legislation in family law and the law of succession may well take some time. However, in order to prevent that then whole Muslim world are excluded for the universality of the human rights community, they may appeal to the rule of progressive realization, (Brems 2004; 18) which means that states expression their intention to adapt legislation (or policies) to comply with human rights principles, but in the understanding that, in view of social or cultural obstacles, the full realization may take time.

However, the major problem is that we have a conflict between the Sharia and human rights. If there are secular laws contravening human rights principles, then it is a matter of politics, of the use of power and to try to have the legislature change the laws that infringe on human rights. But replacing Sharia law by secular law is a more complicated matter. Since it comes to religion, such changes will arouse deep emotions and will be strongly opposed by a large part of the Muslims. The Sharia is a body of norms and values that extend from ritual purity and funerals, to doing business or hiring workers. The combination of mundane with religious affairs makes the whole field of Sharia topics sacrosanct. Defending the prevailing traditional interpretations of the Sharia, including those that are violating human rights principles – think of the corporal penalties in Sharia criminal law – is promoted as resistance against the West. A government cancelling laws based on the Sharia will lose its legitimacy and probably commit political suicide. The worst scenario is that such a government will be regarded as apostates and that its members are regarded lawful targets for assassinations by radical Muslims on the ground of their alleged apostasy. But even in the best scenario there will be serious and widely supported religious objections that can easily be exploited by opposition groups. Although some would argue that secularism – in the sense of the separation of state and religion – is a condition for the acceptance of human rights standards, this does not seem to be a viable road to follow. The abolition of Sharia legislation is impossible. A greater compliance with human rights, therefore, cannot avoid dealing with the Sharia. This is something that the international human groups have failed to do. In general human rights organizations can address specific persons or groups of persons who are responsible for human rights violations: the perpetrators who commit the violence or are the legislators who have enacted laws that conflict human rights standards. However, with regard to Sharia based human rights violations, this is different because, in the perspective of believing Muslims, the Sharia has been created to God and not by man. Since international human rights organizations – like Amnesty International and Human Rights Watch – were averse to interfering with religion, their criticism of Sharia based human rights violations could not be directly addressed. Human rights activists are uncomfortable acknowledging the conflict between the Sharia and human rights standards. This has two reasons. On the one hand it was the concern for Muslim criticism of cultural imperialism. On the other hand it was the feeling that international human rights groups should not interfere with religion. As a result they did not try to become more familiar with the Sharia and to formulate a strategy to remedy the Sharia inspired human rights violations. (Modirzadeh 2006: 193) International human rights organizations would focus on trying to persuade Muslim states to change the law, without taking into consideration that this state law was based on the Sharia with its religious associations and implications. (Modirzadeh 2006: 218) Muslim states would retort that they were not in a position to change these laws because these were divine ordinances. Not familiar with the Sharia, human rights organizations would not be able to discuss this issue and attempt to refute such assertions.

As we have seen, plurality of views is a characteristic feature of Islamic jurisprudence. The Sharia, perhaps with the exception of the ritual part of the law, is not an unequivocal and authoritative law code, but rather a debate about the understanding of the source texts, in which different opinions are juxtaposed with their substantiations. The essence is a hermeneutical methodology, i.e. the ways of deriving sharia rules from the source texts, but even in this domain there are many controversies. The present-day drafters of the Sharia codes have made choices on each issue between several principally acceptable opinions and interpretations. This is a human activity and for a fair discussion about the Sharia and human rights, the process of selection must become more transparent, so that the drafters and supporters of the present codes cannot not counter any opposition against their codes with the argument that these codes embody God's law and that criticism of them is tantamount to heresy. These codes embody law that has been made by men, within the, or rather *a* framework of Sharia methodology. As we have seen before, it is possible to reformulate the codes in such a way that are more human rights compliant without going beyond the framework of the Sharia. However, this would require a two-pronged strategy.

On the one hand human rights organizations must act politically in order that states will support human rights compliant legislation. International organizations can certainly contribute to this if they are cautious not to be drawn into the cul-de-sac whose exit is blocked by the objections that Sharia informed law cannot be changed. International human rights organizations should have sufficient expertise to be able to argue that the Sharia based laws are partially in conflict with human rights principles, but that within the Sharia other options exist. In doing so, they should acknowledge that human rights are also flexible and dynamic and, may be interpreted within a cultural environment and therefore may differ from country to country. However, when it comes to proposing the concrete solutions of human rights compliant Sharia legislation, the international human rights organizations are not primarily participants in debating this. This would be a fundamental task of the local human rights organizations. They can address the Sharia inspired legislation and show the alternatives. However, these alternatives must gain religious authority and that requires challenging the prevalent views of the religious establishments, often backed by the state, through religious debates and alliances with religious scholars and religious organizations. That will a difficult task, but eventually not impossible.

References

Aldeeb, Sami A. (1979) "Non-Musulmans en Pays D'islam: Cas de L'égypte." Fribourg: Éditions universitaires Suisse.

Aldeeb, Sami A. (1994) *Les Musulmans Face Aux Droits De L'homme*, Bochum: Verl. Dr. Dieter Winkler.

An-Naʿim, Abdullahi A. (1986) "The Islamic Law of Apostasy and Its Modern Application: A Case from Sudan." *Religion* 16: 197–224.

An-Naʿim, Abdullahi A. (1990) *Towards an Islamic Reformation: Civil Liberties, Human Rights and International Law*, Syracuse, N.Y.: Syracuse University Press.

An-Naʿim, Abdullahi A. (2008) *Islam and the Secular State: Negotiating the Future of Shariʿa*, Cambridge Ma.: Harvard University Press.

Baderin, M.A. (2001a) "Establishing Areas of Common Ground between Islamic Law and International Human Rights." *The International Journal of Human Rights* 5, no. 2: 72–113.

Baderin, M.A. (2001b) "Macroscopic Analysis of the Practice of Muslim States Parties to International Human Rights Treaties: Conflict or Congruence." *Human Rights Law Review* 1, no. 2.

Baderin, M.A. (2003) *International Human Rights and Islamic Law*, Oxford/New York: Oxford Univ. Press.

Barlas, Amina (2002) *"Believing Women" in Islam: Unreading Patriarchal Interpretations of the Koran*, Austin: University of Texas Press.

Berger, Maurits S. (2005) "Sharia and Public Policy in Egyptian Family Law." PhD, Universiteit van Amsterdam.

Bielefeldt, H. (2000) "'Western' Versus 'Islamic' Human Rights Conceptions?: A Critique of Cultural Essentialism in the Discussion on Human Rights." *Political Theory* 28, no. 1: 90–121.

Brems, Eva (2004) "Reconciling Universality and Diversity in International Human Rights: A Theoretical and Methodological Framework and Its Application in the Context of Islam." *Human Rights Review*, no. April–June: 5–21.

Esposito, John L., and Dalia Mogahed (2007) *Who Speaks for Islam? What a Billion Muslims Really Think*, New York: Gallup Press.

Hassan, Riffat (1996) "Religious Human Rights and the Qur'an." *Emory International Law Review* 10: 85–96.

Johnston, David L. (2007) "Maqasid Al-Shariʿa: Epistemology and Hermeneutics of Muslim Theologies of Human Rights." *Die Welt des Islams* 27, no. 3: 149–88.

Mayer, A.E. (1995) *Islam and Human Rights: Traditions and Politics*. 2 ed, Boulder: Westview.

Modirzadeh, Naz K. (2006) "Taking Islamic Law Seriously: Ingos and the Battle for Muslim Hearts and Minds." *Harvard Human Rights Journal* 19: 191–233.

Peters, Rudolph, and G.J.J. de Vries (1976) "Apostasy in Islam." *Die Welt des Islams* 17: 1–26.

Peters, Rudolph (1999) "Islamic Law and Human Rights: A Contribution to an Ongoing Debate." *Islam and Christian-Muslim Relations* 10: 5–14.

Peters, Rudolph (2005) *Crime and Punishment in Islamic Law: Theory and Practice from the 16th to the 21st Century*, Cambridge: Cambridge University Press. (*Themes in Islamic Law, 2*).

Peters, Rudolph (2006) "The Re-Islamization of Criminal Law in Northern Nigeria: The Safiyyatu Hussaini Case." In *Dispensing Justice in Islamic Courts: Qadis, Procedures and Evidence*, edited by Muhammad Khalid Masud, Rudolph Peters and D.S. Powers, Leiden: Brill: 219–43.

Pink, Johanna (2003a) *Neue Religionsgemeinschaften in Ägypten: Minderheiten Im Spannungsfeld von Glaubensfreiheit, Öffentlicher Ordnung und Islam*, Würzburg: Ergon. (*Kultur, Recht und Politik in Muslimischen Gesellschaften, 2*).

Pink, Johanna (2003b) "A Post-Koranic Religion between Apostasy and Public Order: Egyptian Muftis and Courts on the Legal Status of the Baha'i Faith." *Islamic Law and Society* 10, no. 3: 409–34.

Taha, Mahmoud Mohamed (1987) *The Second Message of Islam*. Translated and introduced by Abdullahi Ahmed An- Naʿim, Syracuse N.Y.: Syracuse University Press.

Tahanawi, Muhammad ʿAli b. ʿAli al- (1984) *Kashshaf Istilahat Al-Funun*. 2 vols. 2e ed. Istanbul: Kahraman Yayinlari. (Repr. of first ed. 1864).

Wadud, Amina (1999) *Qur'an and Woman*, New York etc.: Oxford University Press.

Copyright Acknowledgments

The following articles by Rudolph Peters have been included in this volume. There were errors arising from characters not being recognised correctly when copying from old PDFs. Obvious mistakes (e.g. 1/0 (digits) and l/o (letters) mixed up) have been corrected. The Arabic diacritics were sometimes missing or wrong. Therefore, the transcription in many articles has been simplified. Other than that, the articles are unrevised.

Chapter	Titles
1	"Murder on the Nile: Homicide Trials in 19th Century Egyptian Shariʿa Courts" *Die Welt des Islams* 30 (1990), pp. 95–115.
2	"Muhammad al-ʿAbbâsî al- Mahdî (d. 1897), Grand Mufti of Egypt, and his al-Fatawa al-Mahdiyya" *Islamic Law and Society*, 1 (1994), pp. 66–82.
3	"Islamic and Secular Criminal Law in Nineteenth Century Egypt: The Role and Function of the Qadi" *Islamic Law and Society*, 4 (1997), pp. 70–90.
4	""For his Correction and as a Deterrent Example for Others": Meḥmed ʿAlī's First Criminal Legislation (1829–1830)" *Islamic Law and Society*, 6 (1999), pp. 164–193.
5	"Administrators and Magistrates: The Development of a Secular Judiciary in Egypt, 1842–1871" *Die Welt des Islams*, 39 (1999), pp. 378–397.
6	"Between Paris, Istanbul, and Cairo: The Origins of Criminal Legislation in Late Ottoman Egypt (1829–58)" In: A. Christmann and R. Gleave, *Studies in Islamic law: A Festschrift for Colin Imber.* Oxford, Oxford University Press, (2007) (*Journal of Semitic Studies*, supplement 23), pp. 211–232.
7	"The Significance of Nineteenth-Century Pre-Colonial Legal Reform in Egypt: The Codification of Criminal and Land Law" Revised and expanded paper presented at the workshop "New Approaches to Egyptian Legal History: Late Ottoman Period to the Present" (Cairo, AUC, 11–14 June, 2009).
8	"The Lions of Qasr al-Nil Bridge: The Islamic Prohibition of Images as an Issue in the ʿUrabi Revolt" In: *Islamic Legal Interpretation: Muftis and their Fatwas*, edited by M.K. Masud, B. Messick and D. Powers. Cambridge, Ma.: Harvard University Press, (1996), pp. 214–220.

 | DOI:10.1163/9789004420625_037

(cont.)

Chapter	Titles
9	"An Administrator's Nightmare: Feuding Families in Nineteenth Century Bahariya Oasis" In: *Legal Pluralism in the Arab World*, edited by B. Dupret, M. Berger e.a. Den Haag: Kluwer Law International, (1999), pp. 135–145.
10	"Petitions and Marginal Voices in Nineteenth Century Egypt: The Case of the Fisherman's Daughter" In: Robin Ostle (ed.), *Marginal Voices in Literature and Society*. Strasbourg: European Science Foundation, (2000). Pp. 119–133 (publ. in 2001).
11	"The Infatuated Greek: Social and Legal Boundaries in Nineteenth-Century Egypt" *Égypte/Monde arabe*, 34 (1998, publ. in 1999), pp. 53–65.
12	"The Violent Schoolmaster: The "Normalisation" of the Dossier of a Nineteenth Century Egyptian Legal Case" In: B. Dupret, B. Drieskens and A. Moors (eds.), *Narratives of Truth in Islamic Law.* London: Macmillan, (2008), pp. 69–85.
13	"Prisons and Marginalisation in Nineteenth Century Egypt" In: Eugene Rogan (ed.), *Outside In: On the Margins of the Modern Middle East.* London: I.B. Tauris, (2002), pp. 31–53.
14	"Egypt and the Age of the Triumphant Prison: Legal Punishment in Nineteenth Century Egypt" *Annales Islamologiques*, 36 (2002), pp. 253–285.
15	"Controlled Suffering: Mortality and Living Conditions in 19th-Century Egyptian Prisons" *International Journal of Middle Eastern Studies*, 36 (2004), pp. 387–407.
16	"New Sources for the History of the Dakhla Oasis in the Ottoman Period" In: *Proceedings of the International Conference on Egypt during the Ottoman Era, 26–30 November 2007, Cairo*, Istanbul: IRCICA/Supreme Council of Culture, Ministry of Culture, A.R.E., (2010), pp. 307–324.
17	"Sharecropping in the Dakhla Oasis: Shariʿa and Customary Law in Ottoman Egypt" In: P. Bearman, W. Heinrichs and B. Weiss (eds), *The Law Applied: Contextualizing the Islamic Shariʿa. A Volume in Honor of Frank Vogel.* London: I.B. Tauris, (2008), pp. 79–89.
18	"Body and Spirit of Islamic Law: *Madhhab* Diversity in Ottoman Documents from the Dakhla Oasis, Egypt" In: *Islamic Law in Theory: Studies on Jurisprudence in Honor of Bernard Weiss*, edited by A.K. Reinhardt and R. Gleave, Leiden: Brill, (2014), pp. 317–331.

(*cont.*)

Chapter	Titles
19	"The Battered Dervishes of Bab Zuwayla: A Religious Riot in Eighteenth-Century Cairo" In: *Eighteenth-Century Renewal and Reform in Islam*. Ed. by N. Levtzion and J.O. Voll. Syracuse: Syracuse University Press, (1987), pp. 93–116.
20	"Divine Law or Man-Made Law? Egypt and the Application of the Shariʿa" *Arab Law Quarterly* 3(1988), pp. 231–53.
21	"Apostasy in Islam" (with G.J.J. de Vries) *Die Welt des Islams* 17(1976), pp. 1–26.
22	"Dâr al-Harb, Dâr al-Islam und der Kolonialismus" In: XIX. *Deutscher Orientalistentag*. (Freiburg i.B., Sept.–Okt. 1975). Vorträge. Wiesbaden: 1977. ZDMG, Suppl. III, 1; pp. 579–88.
23	"*Idjtihad* and *Taqlid* in 18th and 19th Century Islam" *Die Welt des Islams* 20(1980), pp. 131–46 (Vortrag 10th Congress of the UEAI, Edinburgh, Sept. 1980).
24	"Islam and the Legitimation of Power: The Mahdi-Revolt in the Sudan" In: XXI. *Deutscher Orientalistentag* (Berlin, März 1980): Ausgewählte Vorträge. Hrsg. von F. Steppat. Wiesbaden: 1983; pp. 409–20. (ZDMG, Supplemente, V).
25	"Religious Attitudes towards Modernization in the Ottoman Empire: A Nineteenth Century Pious Text on Steamships, Factories, and the Telegraph" *Die Welt des Islams* 26 (1986), pp. 76–105.
26	"Islamic Law and Human Rights: A Contribution to an Ongoing Debate" *Islam and Christian-Muslim Relations* 10 (1999), pp. 5–14.
27	"Murder in Khaybar: Some Thoughts on the Origin of the *Qasāma* Procedure in Islamic Law" *Islamic Law and Society*, 9 (2002), 132–167.
28	"From Jurists' Law to Statute Law or What Happens When the Shariʿa is Codified" *Mediterranean Politics* 7(2002), 3, (special issue on Shaping the Current Islamic Reformation. Ed. by B.A. Roberson) pp. 82–95 (publ. in 2003).
29	"The Reintroduction of Shariʿa Criminal Law in Nigeria: New Challenges for the Muslims of the North" In: S. Tellenbach and Th. Hanstein. *Beiträge zum islamischen Recht*, IV. Frankfurt a.M.: Peter Lang, 2004 (Leipziger Beiträge zur Orientforschung, 15), pp. 9–23.

(*cont.*)

Chapter	Titles
30	"The Enforcement of God's Law: The *Shariʿah* in the Present World of Islam" In: *Comparative Perspectives on Shariʿah in Nigeria*. Ed. Ph. Ostien, Jamila M. Nasir and F. Kogelmann. Ibadan: Spectrum Books, (2005), pp. 207–134.
31	"What Does it Mean to be an Official Madhhab? Hanafism and the Ottoman Empire" In: *The Islamic School of Law: Evolution, Devolution, and Progress*. Ed. P. Bearman, R. Peters, F. Vogel. Cambridge MA: Harvard University Press, (2005), pp. 147–158.
32	"The Re-Islamization of Criminal Law in Northern Nigeria and the Judiciary: The Safiyyatu Hussaini Case" In: *Dispensing Justice in Islam: Qadis and their Judgements*, ed. M.K. Masud, R. Peters, and D. Powers, *Studies in Islamic Law and Society* Leiden: Brill, (2005), pp. 219–241.
33	"*Shariʿa* and 'Natural Justice': The Implementation of Islamic Criminal Law in British India and Colonial Nigeria" In: *Islamica: Studies in the memory of Holger Preißler (1943–2006)*. *Journal of Semitic Studies*, supplement 26. Oxford University Press, (2009), pp. 127–150.
34	"Dutch Extremist Islamism: Van Gogh's Murderer and his Ideas" In: Coolsaet, Rik, ed. *Jihadi Terrorism and the Radicalisation Challenge: European and American Challenges*. 2nd ed. Aldershot, UK: Ashgate, (2011), pp. 145–161.
35	"(In)compatibility of Religion and Human Rights: The Case of Islam" In: *Human Rights and the Impact of Religion*. J.A. v. d. Ven and H.-G. Ziebertz (eds). Leiden: Brill: (2013), pp. 75–96.

Index

9/11 653

'Abbadi, al-Hasan ibn Sa'd al- 449–451
'Abbas, Khedive 28, 118, 161, 193
'Abbasi al-Mahdi, Muhammad al- 7, 24–39, 135, 159–162, 166
Abbasids 443
'Abd Allāh b. Abī Mulayka 607
'Abd Allāh b. Numayr 510
'Abd Allāh b. Sahl 500
'Abd Allāh b. al-Zubayr 517
'Abd al-Mālik 500, 508, 510–511, 517, 607
'Abd al-Qadir ibn Muhiyy al-Din 424–426
'Abd al-Raḥmān b. Bujayd 509
'Abd al-Raḥmān b. Sahl 500, 511
'Abd al-Razzāq al-Ṣan'ānī 511
'Abduh, Muhammad 36, 369, 390
Abdulmecid, Sultan 406
abortion 50, 115–116, 627
Aboutaleb, Ahmed 658
Abū Bakr b. Muḥammad b. 'Amr b. Ḥazm 511
Abu Ghraib prison 658
Abū Ḥafṣ al-Kabīr 589
Abu Hamza al-Misri 650, 656
Abu Hanifa 11, 38n, 57, 123, 164, 327, 412, 419, 470, 521, 533–534, 536, 540, 560, 563–564, 570, 587–593, 633
Abu Hurayra 610, 612, 616
Abu Isma'il, Salah (*shaykh*) 369–370
Abū Ja'far al-Hinduwānī 589
Abu Khatir 323
Abū Laylā 505, 508–509
Abū l-Layth al-Samarqandī 589
Abu al-Majd 'Abd al-Rahman (*umda*) 211
Abū Qilāba 508, 513, 515, 517, 519
Abu Qir prison, *see* prisons
Abu Sa'īd al-Khuḍarī 610
Abū Salama b. 'Abd al-Raḥmān 512
Abu Shahba Fort 297
Abu Subul, Dasuqi 179, 183, 187–189
Abū al-Su'ūd 164, 336, 591–592, 596
Abu Talib, Dr Sufi 375
Abu 'Umar Yusuf b. 'Abd al-Barr 433, 438
Abū Yūsuf 11–12, 38, 327, 336, 401, 412, 419, 521, 533–536, 563–564, 587–589, 593, 595
Abu Zayd, 'Amr 37
Afghani, Jamal al-Din al- 36
Afghanistan 406, 542, 578, 581, 649–650
Africa 363, 636–640, 654
Aglanios, Fanîl 196
Aglanios, Mikhali 196–197
Ahmadiyyah 403, 406
Ahmad al-Khalifi 347, 349, 358
Ahmad Pasha 351
alcohol 58, 366, 369, 391, 451, 550, 553, 575, 626, 650
Alexandria 30, 32, 35, 43–44, 46–48, 68, 98–99, 104–105, 110, 117, 143, 161, 163, 184, 186, 196–199, 223, 229–230, 232–233, 248, 251, 255–256, 260, 272–273, 283–285, 287, 289–290, 294, 296–297, 300–301, 304, 384, 448
  arsenal 242, 252–256, 259, 261–264, 272, 282, 284–287, 291, 294–295, 299
Algeria 405, 410, 418–427
'Ali Agha 350
'Ali 'Atiyya 323
'Ali, Hamid al- 657–658
Allah 18, 25, 78, 397–399, 402–404, 407, 428–430, 432, 434–436, 438, 443, 471, 486, 554, 557, 610, 660
'amd (criminal intention) 11–12, 15, 245
America 274, 375–376, 492, 652, 655, 658
  Declaration of Independence 669
  Independence 300
  international politics 653
  revolution 485
amnesties 224–225, 229, 235–236, 251–252, 265, 273, 304
amputation 52–53, 56–57, 59–60, 64, 89, 142, 174, 221, 246, 267, 368, 388–389, 546, 548–551, 553, 558–560, 574, 576–577, 601, 604, 619, 626–627, 630, 635, 637–638, 666
'Amr b. Shu'ayb 510–512, 517n
Amsterdam 649–651, 658

Anatolia 334, 590, 599
Anṣār 499–501, 508–510, 512, 515, 519
Antiquities Organization, Egyptian 307, 320
apostasy (*ridda*) 35, 159n, 200, 244, 361, 392, 395–417, 435, 450, 553–554, 653, 667, 672, 675–676, 679
apostate (*murtadd*) 12, 195, 200, 392, 395–417, 452, 553, 647, 652, 656–658, 675, 679
Appellate Council, Court of Appeal (*majlis isti'naf*) 8n, 29n, 46, 56, 98–99, 103, 139, 406, 446, 548, 553, 601–602, 605, 608, 613, 620–621, 637–639, 643
'aqila 12, 16–18, 50, 498–499, 593
Arab 72, 74, 231, 275, 334, 337, 347, 356, 361, 374, 426, 461, 487, 502–504, 521, 574, 583, 585, 594, 596–597, 612
Arabian Peninsula 421, 502–504, 566
Arafat, Yasser 657–658
arbitrariness 43, 68, 70, 101–102, 108, 110, 129–130, 133, 143, 145, 147, 152, 222, 226, 246, 248, 278–280, 302, 587, 623, 630, 634–635, 643
arbitration 102, 177, 598
army 62, 71, 86, 92, 111, 117, 150–151, 189, 222, 224–225, 227, 236, 248, 251–253, 265, 270, 280, 350, 450, 469, 517, 647, 649
  see also military
arson 113n, 116, 245
assassination 366, 375, 549, 575, 648, 679
assault and battery 9, 21–22, 50–51, 116, 179, 356, 358, 379, 389, 650
Aswad, Mustafa al- 206, 210, 212–213
Aswan 257, 284
Asyut 60n, 96, 104–105, 169, 334
Atatürk 571
'Awda, 'Abd al-Qādir 404, 410, 613
Awqaf, Ministry of 454
'Awwam, Ahmad al- 448–450
'Azaban 349, 356–357
Azbakiyya, al-
  quarter 163, 165
  Square 30
  Mosque 163
Azhar 159–166, 347, 352–353, 358–359, 368, 374, 384–392, 404, 449, 452
  Committee of 384, 387
  Mosque 358
  scholar(s) 29, 161, 352, 360, 452
  Shaykh al- 27–30, 33, 47, 91–92, 160–162, 166, 352–353, 384, 386
  University 25, 160, 163, 372, 374, 377

Bab al-Khalq 223, 250
Bab al-Mitwalli 351
Bab Zuwayla 344–364
Badawi, Ahmad al- 96
Badrishayn 381
Baer, Gabriel 7n, 44, 109, 118–119
Bagdad 443
bagnes (hard-labour prisons) 239, 242, 285, 291–293
Baha'i 403–404, 406, 415
Bahariyya Oasis 168–177
Balkans 423, 590–591, 599
Balkh 402
Bani Suwayf 170–171, 283
banishment (*nafy*) 95, 97, 99, 121, 142, 203, 245, 248, 258, 260, 267, 271, 389–390, 392, 448n, 604, 611
bankruptcy 116, 197
Banna', Muhammad al- (Grand Mufti) 30
Banū Ḥāritha 500, 509
Baqli, 'Ali Efendi Mahmud al- 37
Barelvi, Sayyid Ahmad 422
Bauchi 549
Bawiti, al- (village) 168–177
Bayt al-Mal (Treasury) 33, 190, 232, 291, 297, 401, 495
Bayt al-Wālī, women's prison 260
Beccaria, Cesare 70
Bedouin 113n, 229–230, 253, 256, 503, 525, 610, 612
beggars, begging 62, 72, 86, 97, 110, 117
Bektaşiye 346, 355
Bengal 421, 628
Benha 179n, 183
Bentham, Jeremy 302
Bhaturia 627
bid'a 345n, 355, 363, 436–437, 461–462, 598n
Bin Laden, Osama 647
Birgewi, Muhammad al- (Mehmed Birgili) 345, 352, 355, 362, 461–462
Birgili, Mehmed, *see* Birgewi, Muhammad al-
Birnin Kebbi 551

Bizerta 405
blood money, blood price (*diya*) 10–18, 21, 23, 50, 53–54, 58, 60, 107, 112, 115, 174, 184, 186, 194, 207, 381, 489, 495, 497–528, 553, 557, 593, 604, 625, 631–632, 640
Bouyeri, Mohammed 645–661
Bowring, John 225, 255, 291, 294
bribery 115, 170, 189, 296, 351, 637
bride price, bride wealth (*mahr*) 51, 55, 312–315, 338, 402, 540, 569, 665
British, *see* Great Britain
Brown, Nathan 129–130, 151–153
Buḥayra Province 69, 105, 246
Bukhara 402
Bukhārī, al- 499
Bulaq 122, 198, 228, 256, 261, 282–283, 350
bureaucracy 24–25, 38, 46, 64, 93, 97, 99, 101–104, 109, 131, 143–146, 150–152, 191, 278, 300, 585, 597, 599, 622
Burullus 21
Bushayr b. Yasār 505–509, 527

Cairo 30–33, 40, 44–47, 58, 64, 85–86, 89–94, 96, 98–99, 104–105, 107, 117n, 123, 160–165, 175, 184, 196–197, 199, 202, 204, 223, 229, 231, 243, 246, 250, 252, 255, 257, 260, 283, 286, 288, 290–291, 296, 309, 311–315, 318, 333, 336, 343, 344–364, 369, 385–386
  Cairo Declaration of Islamic Human Rights (1981) 670–671
  Citadel 228, 231, 257, 283, 289
  Council 94, 98, 184, 193, 198–199, 201
  Police 32, 34, 39, 58, 98–99, 139, 196, 224, 231, 251, 257, 291
  Shariʿa Court 24, 26, 32–33, 35, 47, 160–161
  University 370
caning 14, 121–123, 142, 148, 201, 225, 242, 247, 250, 268, 548, 553, 603–604, 606, 619, 638
  see also corporal punishment, flogging, lashes
Canning, Stratford 406
capital punishment 8, 10–11, 21, 50–51, 59, 63, 65, 68, 71, 75, 90, 107, 110, 116, 119–121, 123–124, 141–142, 144, 149, 173, 175, 225, 238–240, 243–245, 258, 267, 269, 282, 295, 297, 389, 392, 395, 398, 405, 407, 414, 417, 516–517, 519–520, 631–632, 634, 667, 675–676
  see also crucifixion, death penalty, execution, impaling, stoning
capitalism 130, 363, 655
cassation, court of *see* Court(s) of Cassation
Catholicism *see* Roman Catholicism
Çavuş*an* 350, 356–357
Cemʿiyet-i Hakkaniye 64, 68, 90, 92–93, 101–102
  see also Jamʿiyya al-Haqqaniyya al-
Central Asia 590
Cevdet, Ahmed 540, 570
chaining 120–122, 232–233, 239, 257, 267, 283, 289–290, 295–296, 298–299
Chechnya 649
cholera epidemic (Egypt) 285
Christianity 200, 384, 391, 412, 414–415, 417, 484, 666
  Christians 12, 194–195, 201, 384, 406, 416, 490, 546, 553–554, 557, 572, 593, 640, 662, 667, 674–675
  conversion 197, 200–202, 384, 414, 417
  missionaries 406, 415–416
Circassian 29, 74, 162, 313, 315
civil administration 24, 43, 89, 92, 95
Civil Code 153, 365, 369, 373, 376–377, 537–538, 567–568
Civil Council 44, 65, 265
civil law 48, 53, 99–102, 134, 140, 152–153, 365–366, 395, 410, 414–415, 492
civil litigation 133, 205, 602
civil rights 70, 116, 120, 553
Clot Bey, A.-B. 237, 299
Code pénal 43–44, 63, 70, 115–116, 118, 124–125, 247, 299
codification 43, 70, 128, 134, 137, 151, 365, 385–387, 486, 531, 536–538, 540, 542, 544, 561, 565, 567, 570–572, 578–580, 623
colonialism 129, 418–427, 622–623, 641, 644, 654
  administration 129, 418, 421–422, 425–426, 601, 622–624, 636, 641, 643
  authorities 623, 625, 642
  colonial interests 624–625
  colonial law 622, 641

colonialism (*cont.*)
colonial powers 565–566, 574, 622–623, 625
colonial servants 278
colonization 624
courts 642
despotism 129
domination 642, 644
India 268
judiciary 639
legal order 623
legal policies 642
legal systems 623
power relations 622, 624–625, 644
pre-colonial laws 623
pre-colonial past 578
pre-colonial reform 151
reforms 129
rule 7, 410, 416, 565, 622–623, 641, 643–644
commercial law 61, 625
communism 403, 404, 409, 413
confession 9, 16, 19, 21, 94, 148–149, 197, 269, 388, 390, 499, 604, 607–608, 610, 613, 615–616
Constantinople 426, 451, 461, 480
constitutional law 61, 365, 367, 370, 377–381, 384, 414–416, 442, 448, 485, 492, 541–544, 546, 548, 550–554, 557, 559, 572–573, 579, 601, 603, 605, 608–609, 620–621, 662, 666–667, 677
Convention on the Elimination of Discrimination against Women (CEDAW) 668–669
conversion 197, 200–202, 384, 396, 399, 414, 419
Coptic Church 384
officials 72, 75, 95, 110
Copts 23, 72, 75, 82, 95, 367, 375, 383–384, 412
corporal punishment 64, 71, 73, 91, 95, 121–122, 128–129, 132, 139, 142, 147–149, 153–154, 221, 225, 238–243, 245–246, 248–249, 260, 266, 268–271, 278, 280–281, 293, 295, 301, 392, 576, 604, 635, 638, 668
see also amputation, caning, flogging, lashes
corruption 129, 449, 453, 461, 466–467, 473, 475, 477, 547, 576–577
corvée 113n, 148, 150–151, 179, 226, 236, 248, 268, 270
Council of Justice, *see* Jamʿiyyat al-Haqqaniyya
Council of Scholars 33, 160
Councils of First Instance 93–94, 98–99, 104, 139, 161, 184, 629
counterfeiting 43, 62, 82, 110, 116–117
Court(s) of Cassation 8, 35, 39, 161, 371, 379, 539, 568
crime rates 263, 383, 577, 622
Crimean War 454–455
criminal law 40–41, 53, 63, 65, 67–70, 101, 128, 131–132, 134, 136–137, 144, 151, 172, 200, 210, 238, 266, 378, 387, 406, 486, 531, 537, 539, 542, 546, 562, 566, 568, 571, 578, 622, 625, 628–629, 632, 641, 643, 663, 676
British 630, 635
Egyptian 59, 89, 120, 278
French 243
Islamic 59, 173, 547, 550, 574–578, 590, 600–601, 603, 605, 619, 622, 625, 628, 630, 633, 636, 640–642, 644, 668
Ottoman 247
shariʿa 546, 554, 558–559, 574, 619, 630, 632, 636, 643, 667, 679
see also penal law
Cromer, Lord 129, 147
Crone, Patricia 130n, 502–503, 523–526
crucifixion 56, 389, 551, 558, 604, 626
Curzon, Lord 415

Dakhla Oasis 307–319, 320–331, 332–343
Damascus 517
Damiens, Robert-François 239
Daqhaliyya 105, 204, 210
Dar al-harb 194, 356, 401, 412, 418–427, 488–489, 656
Dar al-Mahfuzat 41, 204, 321
Dar al-Watha'iq al-Qawmiyya (DWQ) 41, 61, 223, 241, 273–274, 279, 308, 321
see also Egypt, National Archives
Darb al-Jadîd 196
death penalty 49–50, 56, 59, 64, 66, 69, 72, 74–75, 114, 119, 122–124, 142, 147, 173, 184, 221, 242, 245, 267, 278, 398, 408, 414,

416, 525, 625, 629, 632, 636, 640, 643, 652, 668
see also capital punishment, stoning
debt, debtors 83–84, 112n, 113n, 197–199, 222, 229–231, 235–236, 252, 257, 263, 281, 283, 290, 300, 310–311, 321, 327, 333, 342, 377, 382, 386–387, 562, 565
decolonization 383
defamation (*qadhf*) 52, 141, 391, 409, 605, 619
defloration 51, 55, 59–60, 113n, 173–174, 198
democracy 383, 409, 484–485, 544–545, 580, 650, 652–656, 659, 677
Demür Kapu (Iron Gate) 346, 351
see also Bab Zuwayla
deportation 111, 114, 117, 121–122, 124, 147, 172, 184, 188, 198, 221, 225–226, 228, 237, 254, 256, 258–260, 262, 267, 271–272, 281–282, 285, 292, 635
dervishes 344–364
desertion 114n, 226–227, 264n
detention 64, 67, 74, 91, 95, 97, 99–100, 114, 116–117, 121–123, 139, 142, 147, 171, 201, 203, 225, 227–228, 233, 235, 243, 248–250, 255, 257, 263, 273, 281–284, 289, 293, 295, 298–299, 304, 493
see also habs, imprisonment, incarceration
deterrence 65–66, 70–71, 73, 75, 82, 123, 142, 147, 231, 239–242, 244, 254, 256, 263, 266, 271, 280–281, 283, 293, 302, 385, 409, 576–577
dhimmi 13, 196, 201, 419, 489, 665, 674
Dib, Muhammad al- 179, 183, 187–189
Dimas 204, 206, 210
district council(s) 19n, 100–101
Divan-i Hidivi, *see* Diwan Khediwi
Divine Law 347, 365–392, 467, 471, 474, 533, 537, 563, 566
see also shariʿa
divorce 36, 38, 310, 313, 331n, 340, 410n, 542, 556, 572–573, 591n, 595, 617–618, 665
diya, *see* blood money
Diwan al-Awqaf 8, 27n, 32
Diwan al-Katkhuda 95–96, 102, 139
Diwan al-Muʿawana al-Saniyya 98, 139, 181, 184
Diwan Khediwi (Divan-i Hidivi, Dīwān-i Hidīwī) 44, 47, 90–91, 93, 102, 108, 133, 138–139, 223, 241, 244
Dīwān-i Hidīwī, *see* Diwan Khediwi
Diwi, ʿAbduh al- 347, 358–360
Djabarti, ʿAbd al-Rahman al-, *see* Jabarti, ʿAbd al-Rahman al-
Djawziyya, Ibn Qayyim al- 362, 440
djihad, *see* jihad
doubt 8, 161, 175, 188, 616–617
see also shubha
dower, *see* bride price
drugs 55, 391, 575, 655
drunkenness 52, 95, 179, 189, 263, 380, 391, 399, 444
Dumyat 27n, 35n, 104–105, 161n, 184, 289n
Durbar 628
Dutch, *see* Netherlands, the
Dutch East Indies 402

East India Company (EIC) 421, 423, 627–630, 641
Edhem Bey 80, 86
Egypt *passim*
army 163, 450
codes 108–109, 120–121, 137, 193, 374, 580
courts 168–177, 412
criminal laws 303
economy 376
government 248, 411, 445
Governor of 44
Industry, Department of 224, 228, 251, 256, 282–283
judiciary 12, 335–336
law 27, 31, 38, 40, 42, 89, 120, 278, 410
legal system 115, 128–129, 132, 151–152, 154, 191–192, 204, 227, 342, 365, 373
National Archives 41, 61, 109, 221, 223, 241, 274, 279, 284, 298, 303, 321
see also Dar al-Wathāiq al- Qawmiyya
penal system 110, 150, 225, 238, 240, 270
politics 365–367
society 382–384, 386
State Railroad Company 404, 415
Upper Egypt 62, 69, 72, 74, 83, 96, 104, 110, 137, 139–140, 230, 253, 370
Elias, Norbert 239–240, 266
embezzlement 26, 43, 62, 67, 71, 74–75, 81–83, 110, 115, 117, 259–260, 271, 388, 548
England 30, 230, 237, 300, 452, 622–644, 656
English law 622–644

Enlightenment 144, 669
escapes from custody 223–225, 232–233, 251–252, 289, 294, 296–299
Ethiopia 142, 245, 258–259, 271
Europe 66, 68, 71, 92, 101, 145, 152–153, 223, 237, 239–240, 267, 269, 278, 287–288, 299, 383, 452, 567, 623–624
  European Court of Human Rights 673
  European expansion 363, 421
  influence 70, 165, 449
  law 124, 266–267, 383, 450, 567, 635, 642–643
  penal system 238
  Western Europe 70–71, 238–241, 244, 254, 265–266, 280, 300, 485, 492
execution, *see* capital punishment, death penalty, stoning
exile 10–11, 68, 72, 259, 350, 359n, 367, 448, 626
  see also banishment
existentialism 413
extortion 43, 67, 71–75, 81, 112n, 113n, 116, 151
extremism 385–386, 645–661

factories 62, 65, 71, 86, 110–111, 189, 198, 222, 228, 233, 236, 253–254, 256–257, 261–262, 282–283, 459–460, 464, 472
  see also forced labour
Fadil Pasha 293
Faḍl b. Dukayn, al- 510
Fahmy, Khaled 149n, 295, 301
family law 36, 107, 153, 195, 311, 411, 485–486, 490, 493, 538–542, 556, 568–569, 571, 625, 662, 665–667, 676, 678
famine 285, 386, 426, 555, 648
Farahat, Muhammad Nur 40–41
Farran, Muhammad al- 233
Faruh Katkhoda 346
Fatawa al-Mahdiyya fi'l-Waqaʾiʿ al-Misriyya, al- (FM) 7–10, 24–39
fatwas 7–10, 20, 24–39, 54, 134–136, 159–162, 166, 309, 321, 332–333, 336, 342, 359, 404, 430, 432, 497, 534, 557, 564, 587, 590, 592, 596, 598, 629, 631, 634, 642
Fayyum, al- 170, 172, 174, 257, 283
Fayzoghli (penal colony) 10–11, 111n, 114n, 117, 121, 172, 188, 259, 272
fellahin, *see* peasants
feuding 176–177, 226
fining 64, 100, 117–118, 137, 243, 638–639
Finsbury Mosque 650
Fiqarites 357
fiqh 13, 16, 41, 173, 332, 353, 365, 372, 388, 390, 442, 467, 485, 487–488, 490, 492–493, 495–496, 533, 535–536, 538–540, 542–543, 563, 565, 568–569, 577–578, 602, 604, 611, 620
  see also Islamic jurisprudence, Islamic law
Fisch, Jörg 635
Flemming, Barbara 344, 355–356
flogging 50–52, 54–60, 64–66, 68–69, 73–74, 95, 97, 110–112, 114, 117–118, 122, 139, 142–143, 147–150, 173–175, 225, 240, 242, 245–250, 267–270, 281–282, 289, 295, 388, 390–391, 576, 604, 635, 638, 666
  see also caning, corporal punishment, lashes
forced labour 45, 49–50, 56, 62–63, 65–68, 71–74, 93–97, 108–111, 114, 117–124, 147, 150, 172, 175, 184, 187–189, 198–199, 201, 223, 225, 227–228, 231–233, 237–238, 242–243, 251, 254–259, 258, 261–263, 267, 270–271, 281–283, 294, 296–297, 299, 636
  see also factories, labour camps
forgery 63, 116–117, 259, 548
forgiveness 324, 330, 464n, 473, 476–477, 483
fornication 51, 52, 55, 57–59, 119, 199–202, 385–386, 388–391, 452, 517, 535, 548, 553, 555, 557–558, 581, 604–607, 609–613, 615–616, 618–621, 626–627, 636, 639, 676
fortune tellers 87, 110
Foucault, Michel 71, 238–240, 265–267, 280–281
France 44, 48, 88–89, 100, 107, 116, 119, 133, 153, 165, 227, 229, 237, 239, 242, 255, 266–267, 280, 285, 291–292, 405, 423–426, 669, 678
  bagnes 242, 291–292
  French Code Pénal 43, 63, 70, 115–116, 118, 124–125, 299
  French law 7–8, 23, 35, 48, 89, 100, 107, 109, 124, 161, 172, 243, 247, 254, 261–262, 365, 379, 405, 411, 539, 567–568
  French revolution 485
fraud 75, 112n, 113n, 116

free persons 194–195, 315, 489–490
see also slavery
French, *see* France
Fulani 363
fundamentalism 344–345, 352–353, 356, 359, 362–364, 409–410, 414, 417, 423, 428–430, 434–435, 437, 439–440, 461–462, 651, 658, 670

Gaddafi, Muʿammar al- 574
gender 192, 195, 260, 311, 490–491, 552–553, 620, 625, 664, 671
equality 667–669, 674–675, 678
Germany 649
Gharbiyya 55, 96, 105, 248n
Ghazali, Muhammad al- 410, 413, 670n
Ghazāwī, al- 588
Ghazzi, Shakir al- 445n, 446
Ghitaz Bey 349
Ghunaym, ʿAli 204, 210
Girga 69, 334
Gogh, Theo van 645–661
Gordon, Major General C. G. 445n, 448n, 452
Gräf, E. 504
Grand Mufti 24–39, 47, 143n, 159–166, 248n, 347n
Grand Shariʿa Court 26, 32–33, 35, 160–161
Great Britain 29, 42, 124, 129, 137, 142, 152, 159, 162, 268, 278, 405–406, 415, 421–423, 425, 449–450, 453, 566, 622–623, 625, 628–639, 641–644, 656
British India 402–403, 423, 641
colonies 421, 601, 628
occupation of Egypt 147, 192, 221–222, 225, 238, 245, 278, 447–448, 452–453
troops 30, 162
greed 443, 471, 474, 482
Greek 163n, 196–199
Greek Orthodox 201
grievous bodily harm 50–51, 210, 551–552, 604
Grundnorm 532, 562
Guantanamo Bay 678
Gulf War 647
Gülhane Decree/Rescript (1839) 120, 537, 567
Gülşeniye 346, 354
Gwadabawa 605–606, 608, 619
Gwandu 639
gypsies 62, 64–65, 71–72, 85–86, 110

Habbâk, ʿÎsa al- 197–198
habs 95, 117, 121–122, 225, 227, 250, 257, 283, 289, 293, 295, 493
see also detention, imprisonment, incarceration
hadd, pl. *hudud* 9, 41, 51–52, 55–60, 89, 95, 173–174, 199, 202, 246–247, 366, 374, 380, 384–388, 390–392, 398, 547, 551, 555–559, 576, 578, 603–604, 607, 612–613, 615–617, 620–621, 625–627, 633–635, 638, 642–643, 676
Hadidi, Ahmad al- 179–180, 183, 187–189
Hadidi, Muhammad al- 179, 182–183, 188
Hadidi, Musa al- 179, 183, 189
Hadidi, Salim al- 180, 183, 187–189
Hadidi, Yusuf al- 179–182, 187–188
hadith 327–328, 337, 420, 426, 438, 485, 497–528, 543, 546, 558, 573, 610–616, 675–676
Hague, The 648, 660
hajj 424, 494, 496, 544, 579
Ḥajjāj b. Arṭa'a 512
Ḥalabī, Ibrāhīm al- 589
Hallam, Abu Zayd 168–177
Hallam, ʿAmmar Abu Zayd 168–177
Hallam, Yusuf 168–177
Hallaq, Muhammad b. Yusuf al- 345
Hallâq, Shîmî al- 196
Hanafi, Abū Ḥafṣ Sirāj al-Dīn ʿUmar al- 339
Hanafism 7–8, 16, 24–25, 27–28, 31–32, 36–39, 48, 93, 95, 123, 135, 159–160, 162, 164, 166, 195, 309–311, 322, 328, 330, 333–340, 343, 347, 359, 362, 397–401, 405, 415, 419–420, 443, 445, 490–491, 494, 502–503, 519–520, 525, 536–539, 556, 568–569, 573, 585–599, 618, 625, 626, 629
doctrine 36, 38–39, 337, 341, 443, 498, 502, 504, 519–521, 523–526, 585–586, 590, 594–595, 597, 599
opinions 16, 355, 402, 412, 414, 540, 570, 589, 633

Hanafism (*cont.*)
school 8, 24, 29, 37–38, 107, 112, 123, 131, 334–341, 399, 401–402, 411, 425, 534–536, 564–565, 633
Hanbalism 31, 327–328, 330, 337, 362, 433–434, 439, 572, 586, 595, 598
hanging 64–65, 71, 91, 142, 244, 267, 300
Hanifa, Abu, *see* Abu Hanīfa
harbi 194, 401, 488–489
see also Dar al-harb
hard labour, *see* forced labour
Hasan, ʿAbd al-Rahim 18
Ḥasan Agha 312–313
Hasan, Ahmad 297
Hasan ʿAli 18
Hasan, ʿAmr 297
Hasan al-Badr al-Hidjazi 360
Ḥasan al-Baṣrī, al- 519
Hasan b. Luqman 18
Ḥasan b. Makkī al-Jāwīsh 312–313
Hassan, ʿUmar 206, 210, 212
Ḥasan b. Ziyād, al- 534, 540, 564, 570, 587, 589, 592
hatk al-ʿird 51, 389
see also defloration, rape
Hausa 605, 612, 614
health service 279, 288, 290, 295, 299–302
highway robbery 43, 63, 389, 555
Hijaz, Hijazi 27, 85, 430n, 504, 513, 515–518, 520, 523–524
hijra 418–425
Hill, Enid 129
Hilmi Pasha, ʿAbd al-Qadir 445
Hilmi, Ömer 539, 568, 590
Hirsi Ali, Ayaan 658
Hittite laws 526
Hofstadgroep 648–650, 656
homicide 7–14, 16, 19, 23, 33, 38, 42, 48–49, 51, 54, 58–60, 62–63, 82, 95, 98, 100, 107, 110, 115–116, 119–123, 139, 173, 183–184, 208, 215, 225, 230, 234, 273, 304, 335, 388–389, 539, 547, 549, 551, 553, 556, 568, 576, 578, 581, 603–604, 625, 629, 631, 633, 637–640, 642–643
see also murder, qisas
homosexuality 195, 390, 452, 533, 563, 658
human rights 484–488, 492, 496, 546, 550–554, 559, 600, 662–670, 672–673, 676–678, 680
covenants 669
international 668–669, 672
Islamic 670, 672
organizations 680
universal 672–673
Huntington, Samuel 669
Hussaini, Safiyyatu 548, 558, 600–621, 677n

Ibn ʿAbbās 613, 615
Ibn ʿAbidin 164n, 166
Ibn ʿAshur, al-Tahir 405
Ibn Bujayd 509
Ibn Djamaʿah 443
Ibn Hanbal, Ahmad (imam) 439
Ibn Hazm 433, 436–437
Ibn Isḥāq 505, 509
Ibn Juzayy 617
Ibn Muʿammar, Hamd b. Nasir 430, 434, 437–439
Ibn al-Musayyib 512, 527
Ibn Nujaym 336
Ibn Qudāma 519, 617
Ibn Rushd 88, 499–501, 602, 615–618
Ibn Sāʿātī 590
Ibn Taymiyya 37, 362, 440, 462, 657
Ibrahim ʿAbd Allah Mustafa 324–325
Ibrahim Abu Shanab 349
Ibrahim Agha 14
Ibrahim Pasha 28, 30, 62, 71, 85, 159, 162–163, 166
Ibrahim, Musa 296
ʿId, Musa 179–180, 183, 187–188
ijtihad, idjtihad 337, 352–353, 365, 408, 428–430, 432–435, 439, 535–536, 556, 559, 573, 586, 597
ikhtilās, see embezzlement
ʿIllaysh, Muhammad 28–29, 162, 452
illicit sexual relations, *see* fornication
ʿImādī, Sayyidat al-Banāt bt. Abū al-ʿIzz al- 313
Imami Shiʿi doctrine 337
immorality 340, 442, 450
impaling 64–65, 142, 244, 267, 398
Imperial Penal Code 94–96, 119, 125, 137–138, 143, 147, 152, 173–175, 193, 201, 283
see also Qanun al-Sultani, al

imprisonment 50–51, 54, 56, 58, 60, 65–66, 68–69, 72–74, 81, 95, 97–99, 108, 110, 116, 137, 139, 142, 147, 149–150, 171, 173–174, 182, 184, 195, 200, 203, 212, 217, 221–222, 225–228, 230–231, 234, 236–240, 242–243, 246–247, 250, 253–254, 256–258, 260, 263–267, 270–271, 278, 280–281, 284–285, 301–302, 366, 381, 388–390, 408, 548, 553, 603, 606, 626, 631, 634, 636, 638–640
  see also detention, incarceration
Inbabi, Muhammad al- 29, 162–163
incarceration 45, 93, 116–118, 221, 262, 635
indecent assault 389
India 27, 268, 395, 402–403, 410, 421–427, 580, 622, 627–630, 636, 641–644, 647
infanticide 49, 123
inheritance 107, 131, 135, 154, 341, 365, 397, 401, 410, 412, 571
insolence 461, 470, 472, 475, 477, 479, 481
insurance 366, 372–374
international law 486, 668
Iran 542, 557, 566, 571, 574, 577, 581–583
Iraq 502–504, 510, 515–524, 526–527, 581, 649, 657–658, 660
Islamic jurisprudence 131, 173, 194, 201, 247, 322, 486, 497, 523, 527, 535, 538, 561, 565, 568, 577, 646, 663–664, 671, 673, 680
  see also fiqh, shariʿa
Islamic law 11, 16, 25, 31–32, 36, 48, 65, 73, 89, 130, 183–185, 187, 193–195, 199, 201, 230, 252, 322, 332, 378, 411, 416–417, 484–492, 496–497, 502, 526–527, 542, 551, 569, 571, 586, 598, 601–602, 604, 606, 608–609, 613–614, 620, 626, 629, 632–633, 635–639, 641–643, 662, 673
  see also fiqh, shariʿa
islamism 486, 541–543, 571, 573–575, 579, 645–661
Islamization 363, 542–543, 546–547, 571, 575–576, 581, 600–601, 619–620
Ismaʿil, Khedive 28, 48, 161, 165–166, 224, 251, 279, 288, 290, 300–301
Ismaʿil, Shaykh Salah Abu 369–370
isnād(s) 497–528
Israel 649, 657, 659, 662
Issa, Abu Khaled Redouan, el- 649, 651–653
Istanbul 119, 334, 336, 350, 355, 362, 405, 446–447, 453, 455, 461–462
Italy 662
ʿIzz al-Din b. ʿAbd al-Salam 433

jaʿala 310, 323–326, 328–329, 338, 341
  see also sharecropping
Jabal Dūl 259, 271
Jabal Qīsān 258–259, 271
Jabarti, ʿAbd al-Rahman al- (chronicler) 89, 245–246, 344, 360
Jad al-Haqq, Jad al-Haqq ʿAli 386
Jahili, Jahiliyya period 165, 407, 499–500, 502, 504, 513, 525–526
Jallad, Filib 40, 160
Jamʿiyya al-Haqqaniyya, al- 32, 45, 47, 64, 108, 120, 139, 145, 153, 259
  see also Cemʿiyet-i Hakkaniye
Janissaries 349–350, 356–357, 454
Jerusalem 350
Jews, Jewish 194, 327, 399, 436, 490, 500–501, 509–513, 515–516, 519, 524, 526, 572, 658–659, 662, 674–675
  law 502
  see also Judaism
jihad, djihad 363, 418, 426, 496, 646–647, 650–651, 653, 656–658, 660
jinayat 9, 16, 41, 625
Jirja 96, 104–105
jizya, djizyah 407n, 419, 489n, 666
Judaism 391, 414, 666
judicial councils 44, 64, 99–100, 102, 108, 120, 123–124, 136, 139–140, 146, 152–153, 160, 170, 173, 190, 228, 238, 241, 245, 278–279, 283
juju 554
Juynboll, Gautier 505, 511n, 513n

Kaʿban, Husayn Ahmad 168–177
Kaʿban, Kaʿban Ahmad 168–177
Kaʿban, Muwaymin Ahmad 168–177
Kamālpashazāde 588
Kano Penal Code 547–549, 551–553, 600
Kanun-i Cedid 118
Katsina 546–549, 600n, 621, 637
Kelsen, Hans 532, 562
Khadimi, Abu Saʿid Muhammad al- 458, 461–462

Khalifa, Muhammad 324–325
Khalīj Canal 314
Khalil Bey 301–302
Khalwatiyya order 354–355
Khan, Sayyid Ahmad 422
Kharga Oasis 308n, 334–335, 342
Khartoum 104, 228, 256, 296, 445–449
  Khartoum Province 121, 260, 271
Khaybar 327, 497–530
  murder hadith 497–530
Khedive 8, 10, 27–30, 32, 35, 45–46, 48, 92, 99, 102, 104, 107, 109, 113, 119, 122–124, 135, 140, 147, 149, 159, 161–162, 166, 181, 186, 191, 193, 209, 225, 235, 245, 269, 279, 297, 446, 448–450, 453, 593
  Khedival Council 33, 160, 184
Khomeini, Ayatollah 577
khulʿ 556
Kogi, Abdullah 637
Köprülü, Mehmed 355
Koran 22, 54, 91, 173, 204, 206, 210–211, 213–217, 329, 332, 337, 352–353, 365–366, 380, 382, 384, 387–389, 391, 397–398, 402, 404, 407–408, 413, 416, 428–430, 434–438, 449, 451, 461–462, 472–473, 482, 485–486, 515, 532, 543–544, 546, 548, 556–557, 562, 573, 576, 579, 597, 599, 602–604, 610, 625, 646–648, 650–651, 658, 662–663, 670, 672–675
Kufa, Kufan 510, 512, 515, 521
Kurani, Ibrahim al- 440
Kuwait 581, 657

labour camps 117, 259, 261, 265, 282
  see also forced labour
laicism 129
Laʾihat al-Mahakim al-Sharʿiyya 35, 47, 160, 378n
land law 128, 131, 134, 150–151, 537, 566
Lane, Edward William 56n, 64n, 405
lashes 49, 52, 57–58, 66–67, 72, 83–85, 108, 111–112, 118, 121–122, 171n, 246–247, 250, 388, 390–391, 548, 557, 603–604, 606, 611, 619n, 626, 634, 639–640
  see also corporal punishment, caning, flogging
law enforcement 89–90, 101–102, 242, 301, 623, 630
law of procedure 374, 499
law of succession 485, 541–542, 556, 571, 625, 665–666, 678
Lawal, Amina 548, 558, 600, 621
Leemhuis, Fred 307, 320
legal capacity 194–195, 200, 401, 489–491, 495, 531, 534, 562, 564, 592, 663
legal equality 490, 671
legal order 73, 236, 366, 537, 566, 572, 653
  colonial 129
legal personality 194, 489–491, 495, 665–666
legal pluralism 136, 168, 176, 623
Libya 308, 321, 542, 557, 571, 574, 581–582
London 650, 656
Lugard, Lord 637, 641
Luxor 308, 321

madhhab(s) 31, 33, 36–39, 160, 162, 310, 330, 332–343, 353–354, 365, 372, 395–397, 415, 428–434, 437–439, 445n, 484, 533–535, 538, 555, 564, 568, 585–599, 611, 618, 664
  see also Hanafism, Hanbalism, Malikism, Shafiʿism
magic, magicians 34, 72, 85, 87, 307, 320, 333, 398, 400, 444, 471, 554
Mahdi, Muhammad Amin al- 28, 159
Mahdi Revolt (Sudan) 441–453
Mahmud II, Sultan 454
Mahmud, ʿAbd al-Halim 374
mahr, see bride price
Maʿiyya al-Saniyya, al- 46, 97, 184
Māʿiz 612–614, 616
Majlis al-Ahkam 8, 10, 13, 32, 33, 37–39, 44–45, 47, 50, 93–98, 102–103, 108, 118, 120, 122–123, 125, 137–139, 141, 146–147, 172, 179, 184, 186–190, 192, 198, 201–202, 204, 207–210, 212–216, 224, 249, 251, 258–260, 265, 274, 278, 290, 293, 297, 299, 303
Majlis al-ʿIlmi, al- 46, 160
Majlis al-Khususi, al- 10, 27, 98–99, 166
Majlis Qumisyun Misr 37, 89, 134

Malik al-Mu'ayyad Shaykh al-Mahmudi, al- (sultan) 351
Malik b. Anas (imam) 500, 505, 508–511, 607, 615, 618
Malikism 27–29, 31, 36–37, 162, 165, 310, 312, 326–328, 330–331, 337–339, 341, 343, 347, 399, 405, 443, 451–452, 495, 498–499, 504, 524, 546–547, 549–550, 553, 556, 559, 573, 597, 602–604, 609, 617–618, 620, 625, 636–637
doctrine 340, 396, 499, 502–503, 525, 547–549, 553, 559, 569, 603–604, 616, 619–621, 640
school 27, 31, 162, 330, 398–399, 402, 548, 555, 604, 607, 617
Mallawani, Yusuf al- 344–346
Malunfashi 549
Mamluk 242, 334, 349–350, 357, 398n, 595
Mann, Kristin 641
manslaughter 65, 92–93, 102–103, 116, 139, 142–143, 171–172, 174–175, 187–189, 245, 248, 259–260, 271, 374, 504, 549, 551, 593, 617, 625, 632, 634, 639–640
see also homicide, murder
Mansura, al- 53, 204, 208, 211–213, 216
Marghīnānī, al- 588, 590
marginalisation 71–72, 74, 178–191, 221–237, 241
marriage 36, 38, 182, 194, 199–200, 202, 310–311, 313–317, 335, 337–338, 340, 390, 401–402, 404, 410–412, 415, 490, 492–495, 532, 534–535, 539–540, 553, 555–556, 562, 564–565, 569, 572–573, 581, 591–592, 595–597, 604, 616, 618, 621, 662, 664–665, 667, 669, 675
Marseilles 239
martyrdom 646–648, 656–657
Marxism 404, 655
Masiri, Muhammad Muhiy al-Din al- 409
Ma'tuq, Isma'il 'Ali (Ma'tuq bill) 370, 387–392
Maturidite doctrine 443
Maunoury, Jacques 44
Mawardi, Abu al-Hasan al- 492
Mawdudi, Abu al-A'la al- 486–487, 649–651, 656, 670–672
Mayer, Ann 488
Mecca 163, 165, 375n, 420, 423, 426–427, 430n, 436, 487, 673, 676
Mecelle 48, 365, 538, 568
Medina 27n, 440, 497–528, 673, 676
Mediterranean 110, 117, 242, 284
Meḥmed 'Alī 42, 44, 54, 61, 63–64, 66–71, 91–92, 101, 108, 110, 112, 114–115, 120, 133, 136, 138, 142–145, 148–149, 153, 159, 161, 163, 166, 192, 225, 231, 234, 242, 244–246, 248, 258–260, 264–270, 290, 301–302
see also Muḥammad 'Alī
Mevleviye 346, 355
Middle East 334, 526–527, 531, 541–542, 565, 571, 585, 594, 596
military 244, 254, 257, 284, 293, 314–315, 421, 423–424, 426, 523, 543, 547
administration 24, 42, 69, 89, 185, 240, 344, 357, 362, 451, 628
service (as punishment) 65, 72, 97, 110–111, 113–114, 148, 151, 189, 226–227, 236, 251, 263, 268, 281
tribunals 153, 336, 595
see also army
Minufiyya province, al- 105, 293
Minyat al-'Attar 180, 183, 189
Mirza Ghulam Ahmad 403
Mit Ghamr 204, 210, 380
modernization 128–130, 132–133, 146, 151–152, 154, 165, 392, 454, 541, 566, 574
Mongol 443
monotheism 363, 651–652, 660
morality 366, 370, 383, 575
see also immorality
Morand, Marcel 569
Morocco, Moroccan 406, 566, 581, 586, 649, 651, 658
mortality 150, 270, 276, 278–302, 316
Motzki, Harald 497, 505, 511, 527
Mu'ayyad Mosque, al- 345, 347, 349–351, 356
Mubārak, 'Alī 308
Mudīriyya Beni Suweif 257
Muhammad (Prophet) 33, 160, 163, 327, 329, 345, 347, 355, 360, 363, 382, 386, 397, 402, 407, 414, 428–429, 435, 439, 443–444, 447, 451, 468, 486, 499–503, 505, 508–510, 512–513, 515–516, 518–519,

Muhammad (Prophet) (*cont.*)
521, 527, 532, 558, 562, 591, 593, 610–613, 646, 657, 662, 664, 674–675
mujtahid, *mudjtahid* 353, 429–436, 439, 538, 568, 586
mufti 8–15, 24–39, 47, 53, 56–57, 95, 100, 134–135, 159–166, 173, 184, 195, 198, 207–213, 405, 423, 426–427, 446, 532, 544, 560, 562, 579, 588–592, 598–599, 629–630
Mughal Empire 628–629, 641
Muhaji, ʿAbd al-Latif Yusuf al- 324
Muhaji, Masʿud Muhammad al- 324
Muhaji, Muhammad Abu Khalifa al- 323
Muhaji, Muhammad Fayid al- 323–324
Muhammad Ahmad Ibn ʿAbd Allah 444–448, 451
Muḥammad ʿAlī 24, 28, 31, 250, 252–253
see also Meḥmed ʿAlī
Muḥammad b. Ibrāhīm 509
Muḥammad b. Isḥāq 509
Muhammad Bey 15
Muhassib Rida 323–324, 326
Muḥayyiṣa b. Maḥmūd 500
muqallids 432, 436, 587–588, 590
murder 8–9, 11–12, 17, 19, 21–22, 43–45, 49, 53, 90, 170–171, 176, 186, 188–189, 231, 244, 252, 297, 498, 502, 504, 511, 513, 518, 521, 525, 625, 627, 639–640
see also homicide, *qisas*
Murdjiʾite 442
murtadd, *see* apostate
Muskî 196, 200
Muslim Brothers 365–369, 386, 404, 555
Muṣṭafā Kāshif Kurd 246
Muṣṭafā b. Murtaḍā Agha 312–313
Mūṭ 307–308, 321
Mutafarriqa, regiment 312–313, 356
Muʿtazilite 347, 349, 359, 415
Muzani, Imam al- 438

Nador 406
Nafrawi, Ahmad al- 347, 349, 358
nafy, *see* banishment
Nahal, Galal H. El- 40–41
Najabin, al- 323
Nakhaʿī, Ibrāhīm al- 407, 408n, 518–519
naqib al-ashraf 33, 160
Nasser, Gamal Abdel 366–367
Native Courts Ordinance 639–640
naturalisation 405, 412
Navy 163, 251
arsenal 233, 294
Department of the Navy 228, 255, 282
Ministry of the Navy 258, 284
Nawawi, Yahya b. Sharaf Muhyi al-Din al- 433
negligence 12, 186, 188, 191, 226, 236, 279, 295, 297, 380, 466
Netherlands, the 645–661
law 8, 35, 161
New York 391
Niger State 546–547, 601
Nigeria 542, 546–560, 561, 566, 571, 574, 582, 600–621, 622, 636–644, 677n
Criminal Code 640
Nile 7, 54, 113, 155, 179–180, 183, 188–189, 244, 308, 321, 334, 405
Blue Nile 117, 259
White Nile 259, 272, 297
Nimeiri, Jaafar 576

Omdurman 448–449
Organization of the Islamic Conference 670
Oteifi, Gamal el- 370
Ottomans 7, 10, 13, 23, 25, 29, 31–32, 34, 40–42, 44, 46, 48, 61–62, 64, 76, 107–109, 111, 118–121, 123–124, 129, 131, 133–134, 137, 146, 148, 152–153, 159, 162, 184, 193, 196, 227, 234, 243, 245, 247, 254, 261, 279, 307, 309, 314, 321–322, 330, 332, 334–337, 339–340, 342, 346–347, 352, 354, 356–358, 361–362, 441, 446–450, 453–454, 457–462, 534, 537–538, 564, 567, 569, 580, 585–586, 588–591, 595, 597–599, 684
Code of Family Law 540
Criminal Code 42, 247
Empire 23, 42, 107, 118, 124, 131, 133, 148–149, 201–202, 264, 268–269, 281, 336, 355, 405, 413, 416, 449, 454–455, 459, 461, 531–532, 536–537, 539–540, 563, 566–568, 570, 585, 589, 598–599, 654

Padri Movement 363
Pakistan 403, 410, 542, 557–558, 571, 574, 581–583
Palestine 340n, 591n, 649, 657
Paris 165
peasants 9, 12, 43, 51, 69, 72–74, 111–113, 116–117, 121, 133, 137, 148–150, 171, 245, 253, 260, 268–271, 323, 593
Penal Code 96, 119–120, 198–199, 243, 370, 374, 380–381, 388, 390, 547, 576, 578, 601, 603, 643
  1810 115, 227
  1829 227, 246, 254, 272, 303
  1845 254, 257, 283, 299
  1849 43, 45, 47, 117, 120, 126, 245, 272, 303
  1850 184, 227, 254, 261
  1851 44, 109, 152
  1858 148, 268
  1937 383
  1949 117, 551
  1958 538
  1959 552–555, 601
  Egyptian 410
  French 261
  Indian 629–630
  Ottoman 120–121, 124, 184, 193, 245, 567
  shariʿa 546–556, 559, 600–601, 603, 619
  Sudanese 640
  Zamfara 548, 554
penal law 63, 70, 146, 234, 371, 380, 384, 511, 572, 575–576, 635, 666
  English 641
  Islamic 365–366, 368, 370, 375, 380, 386, 392, 450, 497, 600
  Ottoman 124
  shariʿa 556, 559, 605
  Western European 124
penal reform 70, 239, 241, 278–280
perjury 116, 635
Persian 397, 457
Peru 268
petitions 62, 90, 104, 110, 113, 146, 178–179, 190–191, 262, 264, 298, 340
poisoning 116, 633
political prisoners 222, 230, 236, 281n
polygamy 542, 572–573
polygyny 674
polytheism 346, 363, 436, 652, 674
poorhouses 117, 243
Porte 46, 118–119, 123, 147, 193, 330, 406
Porter, Roy 300
Powers, David 497, 527
prayer 22, 397, 399, 404, 452, 491, 496, 531, 544, 562, 579, 663
pregnancy 38, 57–58, 261, 400n
  extramarital 390, 548, 553, 604–607, 610, 615–617, 621, 627
prisons
  Abu Qir prison 68, 72, 74, 76, 81, 110, 117, 257, 284
  Dockyards Prison (Alexandria Arsenal) 49, 65, 72, 74, 81–84, 91, 109–110, 114, 116–117, 122, 187–189, 199, 224, 227–230, 233, 235, 242, 251, 254–255, 273, 284, 304
  Dutch prisons 285–286
  Egyptian prisons 221, 225, 252, 263, 278, 281–282, 285, 288
  European prisons 285
  French prisons 286
  see also bagnes, detention, imprisonment, incarceration
Privy Council 10, 27, 29, 32
property 11, 27, 52–53, 55–56, 60, 63, 66, 72–74, 81–83, 101, 110, 115, 120, 141, 172, 174, 194, 202, 312, 326, 342, 345, 385, 388–389, 400–401, 412, 447, 462, 489–490, 494–496, 509, 520, 534, 538–539, 553, 564, 567–568, 577, 595–596, 626, 656, 665–666
  government 234, 294
  private 62, 71, 120, 593
  rights 195, 326, 490
  state 62, 71–72
Prophet Muhammad, *see* Muhammad (Prophet)
prostitution 449, 451, 547, 550
Protestant 415
Protestant Reformation 669
provincial councils 8, 94
public executions 239, 266–267, 269, 576
public health 149, 269, 279, 301
punishment, *see* banishment, capital punishment, corporal punishment, detention, *hadd*, *taʿzir*

qadhf 52, 57, 202, 391, 604–605, 612, 619, 626
see also defamation
qāḍī xiv, 7–14, 16–18, 20–24, 31, 33, 35, 38–42, 46–60, 63–64, 68, 73, 82, 89–90, 92, 101–103, 107, 112–114, 116, 120–121, 123–124, 130, 133–134, 136- 139, 142, 160–161, 169–176, 182–186,192–193, 199, 204–214, 216, 223, 245, 247–248, 278, 308–312, 317, 322, 330–343, 346–350, 361, 419, 515, 517, 532, 535–537, 549, 559–560, 562, 565, 585–588, 591–599, 601, 627, 629, 636, 664
Qāḍīkhān 336, 534, 564, 592, 596
Qadizade Mehmed Efendi 355
Qadizadililer movement 355
Qadri Pasha, Muhammad 493n, 539–540, 568–570, 590
Qalʿa al-Saʿidiyya, al-, *see* Qanatir al-Khayriyya, al-
Qalyub 180
Qalyubiyya 105, 179, 181, 190
Qanatir al-Khayriyya, al- 94, 182, 223, 228–229, 232, 251, 255, 282
Qanāṭir al-Sibāʿ 311
Qanun al-Filaha (Code/Law of Agriculture) 43, 46, 52, 61–62, 65, 67, 110–111, 114, 117, 120, 125, 127, 227, 247, 283, 303
Qanun al-Humayuni, al- 119
see also Qanunname al-Sultani, al-
Qanun al-Muntakhab (QM, Code of Selected Enactments) 43, 111, 114–118, 120, 124–125, 127, 227, 234, 243, 245, 254–255, 259, 261–262, 283, 303
Qānūn al-Siyāsetnāme 63, 73, 134, 144
Qanun al-Sultani, al- 118–119, 121–122
Qanunname al-Sultani, al- (QS) 9, 19, 43–45, 48, 52–53, 119, 121–122, 124, 126–127, 173, 227, 234, 245, 247, 249, 251, 254, 257, 261–262, 273, 283, 303
see also Imperial Penal Code
Qaradawi, Yusuf al- 675
qasāma 16–18, 22, 337, 497–528, 593, 597, 637–638
Qasimites 357
Qasr, al- 307–316, 320–331, 332–343
Qasr al-Nil Bridge 30, 159–167
Qasr Dakhleh Project (QDP) 307, 320, 332
qatl khata' (killing by error) 12, 16
Qayrawānī, Ibn Abī Zayd al- 607
Qena 370
qisas 9, 11, 41, 50–51, 53, 91, 114, 116, 121, 184, 225, 245, 388, 498, 616–617, 633
see also homicide, murder
Qudūrī, al- 589
Quran, *see* Koran
Qurashī family 307, 311, 314, 320–321, 333
Qurashi, ʿAbd al-Ghafur Husayn al- 325
Qurashi, ʿĀyisha al- 312–315
Qurashī, Bayt al- 307, 333
Qurashi, Fāṭima al- 312–315
Qurashī, Muhammad al- 313, 315
Qurashi, Muhammad Salih al- 322–323
Qurashi, Ruqayya al- 312–315
Qurashī, Ṣāliḥ b. Ḥusayn al- 311–316
Qurashite 442, 446
Qūṣūn 312–313
Qutb, Sayyid 649–651, 656

Rabat 406
Rabbinical 503, 525
radicalism 352, 362, 367, 429, 434, 438, 575, 645–661, 672–673, 676, 679
see also extremism, fundamentalism, islamism
Rāfiʿ b. Khadīj 508, 512
Rahman, S.A. 414
railway 459–461, 465
Ramadan (month) 370, 403n, 494, 496, 618
Ramadan, ʿAli 168–177
Ramadan Musa 15
Ramadan, Tariq 676
rape 116, 179, 181, 189, 389, 552, 604–605, 615–616
Rashid Rida, Muhammad 404, 409, 413–414
Rashidi, Khalil al- 28, 159
Rasulzade, Qadi ʿAskar 361
rations, food 232, 291–293, 352
rebellion 29, 51, 71, 113, 162, 244, 406–407, 409–410, 413, 426, 442–444, 450–453, 622
reconciliation (*sulh*) 58–60, 90, 338, 341, 408
see also blood money
regional councils 10, 45, 94, 96–98, 100, 102, 139, 209, 249

rehabilitation 65–66, 182, 241–242, 254, 263, 270–271, 281
religion 163, 165, 195, 200–201, 344–346, 352, 354, 357–358, 361–362, 366, 383–384, 392, 395–399, 401–403, 407–409, 411, 413, 415–416, 420, 434, 442, 444–446, 448–449, 451–452, 466, 475, 482–483, 487, 491, 550, 552–553, 609, 621, 625, 645, 649, 660, 662, 665, 671–672, 679
  freedom of 383, 408, 413–415, 417, 487, 609, 666–669, 675, 678
religious law 531, 562, 662–663, 666
retribution 50–51, 53–54, 58–60, 65–66, 107, 114, 123, 173, 184–185, 193, 225, 231, 242, 245, 254, 263, 271, 281, 337, 489, 495, 513, 515, 517, 597
  see also qisas
revolution
  American 485
  French 485
Reza Khan 628
ridda, see apostasy
Rif'at, Muhammad 223, 250
robbery 8, 43, 62–63, 82, 110, 186, 230–231, 244–245, 253, 259, 366, 388–389, 526, 574, 581, 626, 634, 638
Roberts, Richard 641
Rochefort 285
Rodi, Sani Yakubu 549n, 551n
Roman Catholicism 415, 662, 669–670
Roman, law 485
Rosen, Lawrence 586
Rotterdam 658
Rous 627–628
rural crime 61, 125, 270
Russia 268

Sābiq, Sayyid 616
Sa'd b. Ḥizām 511
Sadat, Anwar 366, 375, 575
Sahl b. Abī Ḥathma 501, 505–512
Sahlul, Muhammad 179–180, 182, 186–189
Sa'īd b. 'Ubayd 505, 510
Sa'id, Khedive 28, 31, 33n, 46, 161, 224, 251
Sa'idi, 'Abd al-Muta'ali al- 407–408, 414
Sa'idi, Ahmad al- 233
salah, salat, see prayer
Salama, Hafiz 385
Salih Muhammad 324–325
Salim, Husayn 168–177
Salim, Khalaf Allah 168–177
Sālim, Laṭīfa 129
Salim, Muhammad 297–298
Salim, Sha'ban 168–177
Salim, Tantawi 168–177
Saljuqs 590
Sami, Amin 40
Sanusi, Muhammad b. 'Ali al- 431–440
Sarakhsī, Muḥammad b. Abī Sahl al- 587
Sassanids 443
Saudi Arabia 366, 405, 430–431, 541–542, 571, 574, 577, 586, 647, 650
Sayyad, Gimê'a al- 179, 183
Sayyad, Mitwalli al- 179–182, 186, 190
Sayyid Aḥmad, Fātima al- 312
Sayyid 'Ali, al- 37, 347, 349, 359
Schacht, Joseph 497, 524, 527
Schoelcher, Victor 65n, 237
secular law 9–10, 18, 23, 24, 34, 40–60, 89–106, 129, 184–185, 365, 411, 448, 459, 467, 482, 491, 541, 550, 570–571, 605, 669, 678–679
secularism, secularization 129, 365–367, 574, 645, 657–658, 662, 679
sentencing 99, 103, 139–141, 174, 218, 264–265, 558, 607, 614, 621, 630, 677
sexual intercourse, unlawful, *see* fornication
Sha'bī, al- 519, 521, 524, 527
shackles 249–250, 254, 298–299
  see also chaining
Shafi'ism 27–29, 31, 36, 58, 93, 95, 161–162, 309–310, 322, 327–331, 333–336, 338–343, 347, 358–359, 397–398, 401, 415, 419–420, 433–434, 442, 491, 538, 568, 590–591, 596
  school 27, 31, 58, 322, 328, 342
Shafi'i, al- (imam) 346, 516, 611
Shahâta, Sitêta 196–201
Shahâta, Sulaymân 196
Shahata, Umm 231–232
Shalabi, Ahmad al- 344, 347n, 349, 358n
Shaltut, Mahmud 404, 409, 414
Sha'rani, 'Abd al-Wahhab b. Ahmad al- 429
sharecropping 154, 309–310, 320–331, 333, 338, 341
  see also ja'ala

shariʿa *passim*
courts 7–8, 20, 26, 35, 41, 46–47, 107, 112, 122, 132–134, 139, 141–142, 147, 153, 160, 175, 209, 214–216, 238, 250, 260, 278, 283, 297, 308, 321–322, 343, 397, 411, 546, 548–549, 553, 567, 572, 578, 600–603, 605, 609, 619–621, 629, 640, 657
justice 7, 19, 24, 33, 40, 46, 48, 131, 152
see also criminal code, Islamic, *fiqh*, Islamic law, Islamic jurisprudence
Shawkani, Muhammad b. ʿAli al- 430, 434–436, 438–440
Shaybānī, Muḥammad al- 11, 38n, 164, 327, 336, 401, 412, 419, 521, 533–534, 536, 563, 565, 587–589, 592–593, 595–596
Shaykh al-Islam 34, 336, 345
Shaykhzāde(h), ʿAbd al-Rahman b. Muhammad 397, 590, 592
Shibin al-Qanatir 181
Shiʿite(s) 195, 337, 396, 399–401, 489n, 501n, 559, 597
shirk, *see* polytheism
shubha 21, 41, 51, 57, 89, 558, 604–605, 616–617, 621, 626, 632, 634
see also doubt
Shurayḥ 518–519
Sindi, Muhammad Hayah al- 440
Sivasi Efendi 355
siyāsa justice 41, 63, 89, 107, 119, 124, 131–133, 136, 138–139, 143–144, 147, 153–154, 201, 407, 450, 625, 627, 630, 632, 643
slander 123, 202, 612
see also defamation, *qadhf*
slavery 11, 13, 26, 54, 72, 85–86, 120, 169, 171–172, 194–195, 199, 207, 255, 290–291, 297, 312–313, 327, 363, 390, 396, 402, 442, 485, 489–496, 533, 563, 604, 611, 626, 634, 652–653, 656, 665–666
social exclusion 221–222, 236, 242, 258, 282
see also marginalisation
social justice 382, 385–386, 484, 676
socialism 366, 403
sodomy 390, 619n
see also homosexuality
Sokoto 546–548, 600, 602–603, 605–606, 608–609, 619, 637
solitary confinement 227, 232, 289–290, 399
Spain 242, 267, 399n, 426
Spierenburg, Pieter C. 239–240, 265–267
statute law 7, 51–52, 59, 107, 138, 145, 172, 175–176, 184, 216, 414, 578, 636, 642–643, 666
stealing, *see* theft
steam engine 465, 477n
steamships 459–461, 463
Stern, Jessica 645
stigmatisation 221–222, 236–237, 402
stoning 56, 60, 142, 174, 390, 406, 517, 548, 550–551, 553, 557–558, 577, 600–601, 604–608, 610–611, 613, 615–616, 618–621, 626, 630, 636–638, 666, 668, 676, 677n
see also capital punishment, death penalty
Sudan 10, 14, 27, 34, 85, 111n, 114n, 117, 121–122, 142, 150, 166, 172, 188, 226, 228, 237, 243, 245, 254, 256, 258–261, 263, 267, 270–271, 281–282, 285, 297, 387, 429, 441–453, 542, 571, 574, 576, 581–583, 640, 672
Suez 231, 291n, 381
Sufi, Sufism 34, 344–364, 454, 462
suicide 196, 297, 648, 658
Sulaymān Agha 313–314
Sulaymān b. Yasār 512, 515
Sulayman Majid 323
Sulaymân, Amîr 657
sulh 11, 16, 58–60, 338, 341–342
see also reconciliation
Sumatra 363
Sunnism, Sunnah 353, 355, 363, 384, 415, 428–430, 434–438, 441, 444, 449–451, 500, 532, 544, 548, 556, 562, 573, 576, 579, 585, 594, 602–603, 613, 662, 664
Suwayqat al-Lālā 312, 314
synallagmatic contracts 328–329, 495
Syria 350, 426, 581, 594, 598, 649, 651

Taʿayishi, ʿAbd Allah al- 448
taʾdib 12, 65n, 91, 241
taʿdil 22
Ṭaḥāwī, al- 589
Tahla 179–180
Tahta 96
Tahtawi, Rifʿat al- 92

takfir 647
Taliban 542, 578n
Tanta 96, 104, 181, 183, 187, 190–191, 244
Tantâwî, Sayyid 195
Tantawi, ʿUthman 168–177
Tanzimat 129, 537, 567
taqlid 37n, 353, 428–439, 535–536, 556
tattooing 299–300
Tawfiq, Khedive 29–30, 162, 166, 452n
taxation, tax collection 49–50, 62, 72, 75, 82–83, 110, 115, 129, 134, 148–149, 151, 154–155, 226, 248, 268, 270, 309, 321, 327, 333, 370, 382, 451, 572, 628, 666
see also zakah
Tayluni, Shaykh ʿAli al- 349
Tayyib Najjar, Muhammad al- 384
taʿzir 9, 15, 32, 35–36, 41–42, 50–52, 56, 58–60, 63, 73, 89, 118, 123, 159n, 173–174, 193, 199, 201–202, 247, 250, 374, 388, 390–391, 495, 547, 582, 603, 625, 627, 630, 634–635, 638, 643
tazkiya 22
tekke 346–347, 354–356, 359
telegraph 459, 461, 464, 470, 472
territorial liability 502–503, 515, 519–521, 523, 526
see also qasāma
terrorism 645–661
theft 9, 15, 40, 43–44, 52, 55–56, 58, 62–64, 66, 69, 71–73, 75, 81–87, 89–90, 92, 95–96, 107, 113–114, 116–117, 121, 139, 141–142, 169–172, 174–175, 223, 226, 245, 249–251, 259–263, 272, 366, 368, 380, 386, 388–389, 517, 526, 548, 551, 553, 555, 559, 574, 577, 581, 626–627, 634
Tijani, Ahmed 549
Tīmūrṭāshī, al- 336
Toledano, Ehud 9n, 40
torture 20, 94n, 128–129, 132, 143, 147–149, 153–154, 239–240, 248–249, 266, 268–269, 281, 551, 639n, 657, 659, 672, 678
transvestism 195
treason 44, 409–410, 675
tribal law 502–503, 525
Tungkar Tudu 606
Tunisia 264, 405, 426, 542, 566, 573, 581
Tura Prison 296
Turco-Egyptian government 441, 444, 446, 453
Turkey, Turks 9, 25, 27, 43, 61–62, 72, 74, 76, 89, 91, 109, 119, 129, 148, 151, 226, 231, 242, 256, 261, 268, 272, 315, 334, 344–345, 347, 351–352, 354–356, 358–359, 361–362, 364, 365, 416, 424–425, 444, 448–452, 455, 457–458, 460–461, 464, 468, 541, 571, 598

ʿUbayd ʿAbd al-Ghafur 323
ʿUbayd Allāh b. al-Aḥnas 512
ʿUbayd Allāh b. Mūsā al-Dīnārī 341
Ubayyid, al- 14
ʿUdjaymi, Abu l-Baqaʾ al-Hasan b. ʿAli al- 440
ʿulamaʾ (sg. *ʿālim*) 8n, 27, 29–33, 37, 41n, 46–47, 56, 73, 98, 100, 103n, 160–162, 166, 173–176, 202, 324, 330, 334, 341, 344, 347, 351–353, 358–362, 397, 405, 414, 445–448, 450, 453, 454, 461–462, 535, 537, 540–545, 565–566, 570, 578–580, 657
ʿUmar b. ʿAbd al-ʿAziz, Caliph 386, 499, 513, 515, 517, 519, 521, 524, 527, 555, 615–616
ʿUmar b. al-Khaṭṭāb 517, 520, 523
Umar Tal, al-Hajj 363
ʿumda (village head) 19–20, 169, 179–183, 186–191, 204, 208, 210–211, 214
Unays 611–612
unbelievers 165, 345–347, 361, 367, 395–417, 418–427, 444–453, 459, 461, 464–465, 468–483, 501, 647, 651–652, 655, 658, 673
see also apostasy, apostate
uncertainty, *see* doubt, *shubha*
United Arab Emirates 578n
United Nations (UN) 415, 663, 669, 677
United States 300, 375–376, 485, 492, 546, 600, 647, 652–653, 655, 657–659, 669, 678
Universal Declaration of Human Rights 413, 662, 665–666
unlawful intercourse, *see* fornication
ʿUqba/ʿAqaba 37
ʿUrabi, Ahmad 29–30, 162–163, 165–166
ʿUrabi, revolt 29, 35, 159–167, 448–449, 452n
usury 30, 164, 369, 380, 583

'Uthmān Aghā 246, 517
'Uthmān al-Batti 520
'Uthman, Muhammad 324
utopia 645, 659–661

vagrants 62, 64–65, 71–72, 110, 263
vendetta 176–177
village councils 100, 108
Voll, John 428, 440

Wahhab, Muhammad b. 'Abd al- 430–431, 440
Wahhabism 363, 421, 424, 427, 429–430, 432, 439
Wali Allah, Shah 422, 429, 432, 434, 437–440
waqf 7, 26n, 27n, 28, 30, 32, 34, 39, 107, 153, 161, 310, 330, 333, 351, 359, 462, 539, 541, 568, 571, 595–596
Wāqidī, al- 506, 511, 514
Weber, Max 130–131, 586
Weiss, Bernard 332
Well-Preserved Tablet (*al-Lawh al-Mahfuz*) 345, 347, 354, 360
West Africa 363, 637
West African Court of Appeal 637, 639
Western culture 484, 670
Western law 7, 410, 531, 538, 561, 575, 577, 624–625, 663
Western powers 405, 416, 449, 454, 565, 670, 677
Westernisation 129, 561, 565–566, 570–571, 579
Wilders, Geert 658
wine 386, 391, 451, 533, 563, 613
see also alcohol
witchcraft 554
see also magic

Yaḥyā b. Sa'īd b. Ḥayyān 512
Yaḥyā b. Sa'īd b. Qays 505, 508–512, 515, 524
Yakubu Abubakar 606–608, 619
Yemen, Yemeni 430, 541, 571, 581–582
Yoannis, Filippo 196–201
Yūsuf Efendi al-Ḥanafī, Jamāl al-Dīn 339

Zaghlul, Ahmat Fathi 40, 129
zakah 370, 382, 510, 572
see also taxation
Zamfara 546–549, 551–552, 554, 600
Zayd, Zaydism 336, 430, 441n, 498, 596
Zayni Salih, al- 323
zina, *see* fornication
Zionism 659
Zoroastrianism 478, 533, 563
Zufar 587, 589
Zuhrī, Ibn Shihāb al- 505–509, 512–516, 518–519, 524, 527

Printed in the United States
By Bookmasters